University Casebook Series

December, 1991

ACCOUNTING AND THE LAW, Fourth Edition (1978), with Problems Pamphlet (Successor to Dohr, Phillips, Thompson & Warren)

George C. Thompson, Professor, Columbia University Graduate School of Business.
Robert Whitman, Professor of Law, University of Connecticut.
Ellis L. Phillips, Jr., Member of the New York Bar.
William C. Warren, Professor of Law Emeritus, Columbia University.

ACCOUNTING FOR LAWYERS, MATERIALS ON (1980)

David R. Herwitz, Professor of Law, Harvard University.

ADMINISTRATIVE LAW, Eighth Edition (1987), with 1989 Case Supplement and 1983 Problems Supplement (Supplement edited in association with Paul R. Verkuil, Dean and Professor of Law, Tulane University)

Walter Gellhorn, University Professor Emeritus, Columbia University.
Clark Byse, Professor of Law, Harvard University.
Peter L. Strauss, Professor of Law, Columbia University.
Todd D. Rakoff, Professor of Law, Harvard University.
Roy A. Schotland, Professor of Law, Georgetown University.

ADMIRALTY, Third Edition (1987), with 1991 Statute and Rule Supplement

Jo Desha Lucas, Professor of Law, University of Chicago.

ADVOCACY, see also Lawyering Process

AGENCY, see also Enterprise Organization

AGENCY—PARTNERSHIPS, Fourth Edition (1987)

Abridgement from Conard, Knauss & Siegel's Enterprise Organization, Fourth Edition.

AGENCY AND PARTNERSHIPS (1987)

Melvin A. Eisenberg, Professor of Law, University of California, Berkeley.

ANTITRUST: FREE ENTERPRISE AND ECONOMIC ORGANIZATION, Sixth Edition (1983), with 1983 Problems in Antitrust Supplement and 1991 Case Supplement

Louis B. Schwartz, Professor of Law, University of Pennsylvania.
John J. Flynn, Professor of Law, University of Utah.
Harry First, Professor of Law, New York University.

BANKRUPTCY, Second Edition (1989), with 1991 Case Supplement

Robert L. Jordan, Professor of Law, University of California, Los Angeles.
William D. Warren, Professor of Law, University of California, Los Angeles.

BANKRUPTCY AND DEBTOR–CREDITOR LAW, Second Edition (1988)

Theodore Eisenberg, Professor of Law, Cornell University.

[i]

BUSINESS ASSOCIATIONS, AGENCY, PARTNERSHIPS, AND CORPORATIONS (1991)

William A. Klein, Professor of Law, University of California, Los Angeles.
Mark Ramseyer, Professor of Law, University of California, Los Angeles.

BUSINESS CRIME (1990), with 1991 Case Supplement

Harry First, Professor of Law, New York University.

BUSINESS ORGANIZATION, see also Enterprise Organization

BUSINESS PLANNING (1991)

Franklin Gevurtz, Professor of Law, McGeorge School of Law.

BUSINESS PLANNING, Temporary Second Edition (1984)

David R. Herwitz, Professor of Law, Harvard University.

BUSINESS TORTS (1972)

Milton Handler, Professor of Law Emeritus, Columbia University.

CHILDREN IN THE LEGAL SYSTEM (1983), with 1990 Supplement (Supplement edited in association with Elizabeth S. Scott, Professor of Law, University of Virginia)

Walter Wadlington, Professor of Law, University of Virginia.
Charles H. Whitebread, Professor of Law, University of Southern California.
Samuel Davis, Professor of Law, University of Georgia.

CIVIL PROCEDURE, see Procedure

CIVIL RIGHTS ACTIONS (1988), with 1991 Supplement

Peter W. Low, Professor of Law, University of Virginia.
John C. Jeffries, Jr., Professor of Law, University of Virginia.

CLINIC, see also Lawyering Process

COMMERCIAL AND DEBTOR–CREDITOR LAW: SELECTED STATUTES, 1991 EDITION

COMMERCIAL LAW, Second Edition (1987)

Robert L. Jordan, Professor of Law, University of California, Los Angeles.
William D. Warren, Professor of Law, University of California, Los Angeles.

COMMERCIAL LAW, Fourth Edition (1985), with 1991 Case Supplement

E. Allan Farnsworth, Professor of Law, Columbia University.
John Honnold, Professor of Law, University of Pennsylvania.

COMMERCIAL PAPER, Third Edition (1984), with 1991 Case Supplement

E. Allan Farnsworth, Professor of Law, Columbia University.

COMMERCIAL PAPER, Second Edition (1987) (Reprinted from COMMERCIAL LAW, Second Edition (1987))

Robert L. Jordan, Professor of Law, University of California, Los Angeles.
William D. Warren, Professor of Law, University of California, Los Angeles.

COMMERCIAL PAPER AND BANK DEPOSITS AND COLLECTIONS (1967), with Statutory Supplement

William D. Hawkland, Professor of Law, University of Illinois.

UNIVERSITY CASEBOOK SERIES—Continued

COMMERCIAL TRANSACTIONS—Principles and Policies, Second Edition (1991)

Alan Schwartz, Professor of Law, Yale University.
Robert E. Scott, Professor of Law, University of Virginia.

COMPARATIVE LAW, Fifth Edition (1988)

Rudolf B. Schlesinger, Professor of Law, Hastings College of the Law.
Hans W. Baade, Professor of Law, University of Texas.
Mirjan P. Damaska, Professor of Law, Yale Law School.
Peter E. Herzog, Professor of Law, Syracuse University.

COMPETITIVE PROCESS, LEGAL REGULATION OF THE, Revised Fourth Edition (1991), with 1991 Selected Statutes Supplement

Edmund W. Kitch, Professor of Law, University of Virginia.
Harvey S. Perlman, Dean of the Law School, University of Nebraska.

CONFLICT OF LAWS, Ninth Edition (1990)

Willis L. M. Reese, Professor of Law, Columbia University.
Maurice Rosenberg, Professor of Law, Columbia University.
Peter Hay, Professor of Law, University of Illinois.

CONSTITUTIONAL LAW, Eighth Edition (1989), with 1991 Case Supplement

Edward L. Barrett, Jr., Professor of Law, University of California, Davis.
William Cohen, Professor of Law, Stanford University.
Jonathan D. Varat, Professor of Law, University of California, Los Angeles.

CONSTITUTIONAL LAW, CIVIL LIBERTY AND INDIVIDUAL RIGHTS, Second Edition (1982), with 1991 Supplement

William Cohen, Professor of Law, Stanford University.
John Kaplan, Professor of Law, Stanford University.

CONSTITUTIONAL LAW, Twelfth Edition (1991), with 1991 Supplement (Supplement edited in association with Frederick F. Schauer, Professor, Harvard University)

Gerald Gunther, Professor of Law, Stanford University.

CONSTITUTIONAL LAW, INDIVIDUAL RIGHTS IN, Fifth Edition (1992), (Reprinted from CONSTITUTIONAL LAW, Twelfth Edition), with 1991 Supplement (Supplement edited in association with Frederick F. Schauer, Professor, Harvard University)

Gerald Gunther, Professor of Law, Stanford University.

CONSUMER TRANSACTIONS, Second Edition (1991), with Selected Statutes and Regulations Supplement

Michael M. Greenfield, Professor of Law, Washington University.

CONTRACT LAW AND ITS APPLICATION, Fourth Edition (1988)

Arthur Rosett, Professor of Law, University of California, Los Angeles.

CONTRACT LAW, STUDIES IN, Fourth Edition (1991)

Edward J. Murphy, Professor of Law, University of Notre Dame.
Richard E. Speidel, Professor of Law, Northwestern University.

CONTRACTS, Fifth Edition (1987)

John P. Dawson, late Professor of Law, Harvard University.
William Burnett Harvey, Professor of Law and Political Science, Boston University.
Stanley D. Henderson, Professor of Law, University of Virginia.

UNIVERSITY CASEBOOK SERIES—Continued

CONTRACTS, Fourth Edition (1988)

E. Allan Farnsworth, Professor of Law, Columbia University.
William F. Young, Professor of Law, Columbia University.

CONTRACTS, Selections on (statutory materials) (1988)

CONTRACTS, Second Edition (1978), with Statutory and Administrative Law Supplement (1978)

Ian R. Macneil, Professor of Law, Cornell University.

COPYRIGHT, PATENTS AND TRADEMARKS, see also Competitive Process; see also Selected Statutes and International Agreements

COPYRIGHT, PATENT, TRADEMARK AND RELATED STATE DOCTRINES, Third Edition (1990), with 1991 Selected Statutes Supplement and 1981 Problem Supplement

Paul Goldstein, Professor of Law, Stanford University.

COPYRIGHT, Unfair Competition, and Other Topics Bearing on the Protection of Literary, Musical, and Artistic Works, Fifth Edition (1990), with 1991 Statutory and Case Supplement

Ralph S. Brown, Jr., Professor of Law, Yale University.
Robert C. Denicola, Professor of Law, University of Nebraska.

CORPORATE ACQUISITIONS, The Law and Finance of (1986), with 1991 Supplement

Ronald J. Gilson, Professor of Law, Stanford University.

CORPORATE FINANCE, Third Edition (1987)

Victor Brudney, Professor of Law, Harvard University.
Marvin A. Chirelstein, Professor of Law, Columbia University.

CORPORATION LAW, BASIC, Third Edition (1989), with Documentary Supplement

Detlev F. Vagts, Professor of Law, Harvard University.

CORPORATIONS, see also Enterprise Organization and Business Organization

CORPORATIONS, Sixth Edition—Concise (1988), with 1991 Case Supplement and 1991 Statutory Supplement

William L. Cary, late Professor of Law, Columbia University.
Melvin Aron Eisenberg, Professor of Law, University of California, Berkeley.

CORPORATIONS, Sixth Edition—Unabridged (1988), with 1991 Case Supplement and 1991 Statutory Supplement

William L. Cary, late Professor of Law, Columbia University.
Melvin Aron Eisenberg, Professor of Law, University of California, Berkeley.

CORPORATIONS AND BUSINESS ASSOCIATIONS—STATUTES, RULES, AND FORMS (1991)

CORRECTIONS, SEE SENTENCING

CREDITORS' RIGHTS, see also Debtor-Creditor Law

CRIMINAL JUSTICE ADMINISTRATION, Fourth Edition (1991), with 1991 Supplement

Frank W. Miller, Professor of Law, Washington University.
Robert O. Dawson, Professor of Law, University of Texas.
George E. Dix, Professor of Law, University of Texas.
Raymond I. Parnas, Professor of Law, University of California, Davis.

CRIMINAL LAW, Fifth Edition (1992)

Andre A. Moenssens, Professor of Law, University of Richmond.
Fred E. Inbau, Professor of Law Emeritus, Northwestern University.
Ronald J. Bacigal, Professor of Law, University of Richmond.

CRIMINAL LAW AND APPROACHES TO THE STUDY OF LAW, Second Edition (1991)

John M. Brumbaugh, Professor of Law, University of Maryland.

CRIMINAL LAW, Second Edition (1986)

Peter W. Low, Professor of Law, University of Virginia.
John C. Jeffries, Jr., Professor of Law, University of Virginia.
Richard C. Bonnie, Professor of Law, University of Virginia.

CRIMINAL LAW, Fourth Edition (1986)

Lloyd L. Weinreb, Professor of Law, Harvard University.

CRIMINAL LAW AND PROCEDURE, Seventh Edition (1989)

Ronald N. Boyce, Professor of Law, University of Utah.
Rollin M. Perkins, Professor of Law Emeritus, University of California, Hastings College of the Law.

CRIMINAL PROCEDURE, Third Edition (1987), with 1991 Supplement

James B. Haddad, Professor of Law, Northwestern University.
James B. Zagel, Chief, Criminal Justice Division, Office of Attorney General of Illinois.
Gary L. Starkman, Assistant U. S. Attorney, Northern District of Illinois.
William J. Bauer, Chief Judge of the U.S. Court of Appeals, Seventh Circuit.

CRIMINAL PROCESS, Fourth Edition (1987), with 1991 Supplement

Lloyd L. Weinreb, Professor of Law, Harvard University.

DAMAGES, Second Edition (1952)

Charles T. McCormick, late Professor of Law, University of Texas.
William F. Fritz, late Professor of Law, University of Texas.

DECEDENTS' ESTATES AND TRUSTS, See also Family Property Law

DECEDENTS' ESTATES AND TRUSTS, Seventh Edition (1988)

John Ritchie, late Professor of Law, University of Virginia.
Neill H. Alford, Jr., Professor of Law, University of Virginia.
Richard W. Effland, late Professor of Law, Arizona State University.

DISPUTE RESOLUTION, Processes of (1989)

John S. Murray, President and Executive Director of The Conflict Clinic, Inc., George Mason University.
Alan Scott Rau, Professor of Law, University of Texas.
Edward F. Sherman, Professor of Law, University of Texas.

DOMESTIC RELATIONS, see also Family Law

DOMESTIC RELATIONS, Second Edition (1990), with 1992 Supplement

Walter Wadlington, Professor of Law, University of Virginia.

UNIVERSITY CASEBOOK SERIES—Continued

EMPLOYMENT DISCRIMINATION, Second Edition (1987), with 1990 Supplement

Joel W. Friedman, Professor of Law, Tulane University.
George M. Strickler, Professor of Law, Tulane University.

EMPLOYMENT LAW, Second Edition (1991), with Statutory Supplement and 1991 Case Supplement

Mark A. Rothstein, Professor of Law, University of Houston.
Andria S. Knapp, Visiting Professor of Law, Golden Gate University.
Lance Liebman, Professor of Law, Harvard University.

ENERGY LAW (1983), with 1991 Case Supplement

Donald N. Zillman, Professor of Law, University of Utah.
Laurence Lattman, Dean of Mines and Engineering, University of Utah.

ENTERPRISE ORGANIZATION, Fourth Edition (1987), with 1987 Corporation and Partnership Statutes, Rules and Forms Supplement

Alfred F. Conard, Professor of Law, University of Michigan.
Robert L. Knauss, Dean of the Law School, University of Houston.
Stanley Siegel, Professor of Law, University of California, Los Angeles.

ENVIRONMENTAL POLICY LAW, Second Edition (1991)

Thomas J. Schoenbaum, Professor of Law, University of Georgia.
Ronald H. Rosenberg, Professor of Law, College of William and Mary.

EQUITY, see also Remedies

EQUITY, RESTITUTION AND DAMAGES, Second Edition (1974)

Robert Childres, late Professor of Law, Northwestern University.
William F. Johnson, Jr., Professor of Law, New York University.

ESTATE PLANNING, Second Edition (1982), with 1985 Case, Text and Documentary Supplement

David Westfall, Professor of Law, Harvard University.

ETHICS, see Legal Ethics, Legal Profession, Professional Responsibility, and Social Responsibilities

ETHICS OF LAWYERING, THE LAW AND (1990)

Geoffrey C. Hazard, Jr., Professor of Law, Yale University.
Susan P. Koniak, Professor of Law, University of Pittsburgh.

ETHICS AND PROFESSIONAL RESPONSIBILITY (1981) (Reprinted from THE LAWYERING PROCESS)

Gary Bellow, Professor of Law, Harvard University.
Bea Moulton, Legal Services Corporation.

EVIDENCE, Seventh Edition (1992)

John Kaplan, Late Professor of Law, Stanford University.
Jon R. Waltz, Professor of Law, Northwestern University.
Roger C. Park, Professor of Law, University of Minnesota.

EVIDENCE, Eighth Edition (1988), with Rules, Statute and Case Supplement (1990)

Jack B. Weinstein, Chief Judge, United States District Court.
John H. Mansfield, Professor of Law, Harvard University.
Norman Abrams, Professor of Law, University of California, Los Angeles.
Margaret Berger, Professor of Law, Brooklyn Law School.

FAMILY LAW, see also Domestic Relations

UNIVERSITY CASEBOOK SERIES—Continued

FAMILY LAW Second Edition (1985), with 1991 Supplement

Judith C. Areen, Professor of Law, Georgetown University.

FAMILY LAW AND CHILDREN IN THE LEGAL SYSTEM, STATUTORY MATERIALS (1981)

Walter Wadlington, Professor of Law, University of Virginia.

FAMILY PROPERTY LAW, Cases and Materials on Wills, Trusts and Future Interests (1991)

Lawrence W. Waggoner, Professor of Law, University of Michigan.
Richard V. Wellman, Professor of Law, University of Georgia.
Gregory Alexander, Professor of Law, Cornell Law School.
Mary L. Fellows, Professor of Law, University of Minnesota.

FEDERAL COURTS, Eighth Edition (1988), with 1991 Supplement

Charles T. McCormick, late Professor of Law, University of Texas.
James H. Chadbourn, late Professor of Law, Harvard University.
Charles Alan Wright, Professor of Law, University of Texas, Austin.

FEDERAL COURTS AND THE FEDERAL SYSTEM, Hart and Wechsler's Third Edition (1988), with 1992 Case Supplement, and the Judicial Code and Rules of Procedure in the Federal Courts (1991)

Paul M. Bator, Professor of Law, University of Chicago.
Daniel J. Meltzer, Professor of Law, Harvard University.
Paul J. Mishkin, Professor of Law, University of California, Berkeley.
David L. Shapiro, Professor of Law, Harvard University.

FEDERAL COURTS AND THE LAW OF FEDERAL–STATE RELATIONS, Second Edition (1989), with 1991 Supplement

Peter W. Low, Professor of Law, University of Virginia.
John C. Jeffries, Jr., Professor of Law, University of Virginia.

FEDERAL PUBLIC LAND AND RESOURCES LAW, Second Edition (1987), with 1990 Case Supplement and 1990 Statutory Supplement

George C. Coggins, Professor of Law, University of Kansas.
Charles F. Wilkinson, Professor of Law, University of Oregon.

FEDERAL RULES OF CIVIL PROCEDURE and Selected Other Procedural Provisions, 1991 Edition

FEDERAL TAXATION, see Taxation

FIRST AMENDMENT (1991)

William W. Van Alstyne, Professor of Law, Duke University.

FOOD AND DRUG LAW, Second Edition (1991), with Statutory Supplement

Peter Barton Hutt, Esq.
Richard A. Merrill, Professor of Law, University of Virginia.

FUTURE INTERESTS (1970)

Howard R. Williams, Professor of Law, Stanford University.

FUTURE INTERESTS AND ESTATE PLANNING (1961), with 1962 Supplement

W. Barton Leach, late Professor of Law, Harvard University.
James K. Logan, formerly Dean of the Law School, University of Kansas.

GOVERNMENT CONTRACTS, FEDERAL, Successor Edition (1985), with 1989 Supplement

John W. Whelan, Professor of Law, Hastings College of the Law.

UNIVERSITY CASEBOOK SERIES—Continued

GOVERNMENT REGULATION: FREE ENTERPRISE AND ECONOMIC ORGANI-ZATION, Sixth Edition (1985)

Louis B. Schwartz, Professor of Law, Hastings College of the Law.
John J. Flynn, Professor of Law, University of Utah.
Harry First, Professor of Law, New York University.

HEALTH CARE LAW AND POLICY (1988)

Clark C. Havighurst, Professor of Law, Duke University.

HINCKLEY, JOHN W., JR., TRIAL OF: A Case Study of the Insanity Defense (1986)

Peter W. Low, Professor of Law, University of Virginia.
John C. Jeffries, Jr., Professor of Law, University of Virginia.
Richard C. Bonnie, Professor of Law, University of Virginia.

IMMIGRATION LAW AND POLICY (1992)

Stephen H. Legomsky, Professor of Law, Washington University.

INJUNCTIONS, Second Edition (1984)

Owen M. Fiss, Professor of Law, Yale University.
Doug Rendleman, Professor of Law, College of William and Mary.

INSTITUTIONAL INVESTORS (1978)

David L. Ratner, Professor of Law, Cornell University.

INSURANCE, Second Edition (1985)

William F. Young, Professor of Law, Columbia University.
Eric M. Holmes, Professor of Law, University of Georgia.

INSURANCE LAW AND REGULATION (1990)

Kenneth S. Abraham, University of Virginia.

INTERNATIONAL LAW, see also Transnational Legal Problems, Transnational Business Problems, and United Nations Law

INTERNATIONAL LAW IN CONTEMPORARY PERSPECTIVE (1981), with Essay Supplement

Myres S. McDougal, Professor of Law, Yale University.
W. Michael Reisman, Professor of Law, Yale University.

INTERNATIONAL LEGAL SYSTEM, Third Edition (1988), with Documentary Supplement

Joseph Modeste Sweeney, Professor of Law, University of California, Hastings.
Covey T. Oliver, Professor of Law, University of Pennsylvania.
Noyes E. Leech, Professor of Law Emeritus, University of Pennsylvania.

INTRODUCTION TO LAW, see also Legal Method, On Law in Courts, and Dynamics of American Law

INTRODUCTION TO THE STUDY OF LAW (1970)

E. Wayne Thode, late Professor of Law, University of Utah.
Leon Lebowitz, Professor of Law, University of Texas.
Lester J. Mazor, Professor of Law, University of Utah.

JUDICIAL CODE and Rules of Procedure in the Federal Courts, Students' Edition, 1991 Revision

Daniel J. Meltzer, Professor of Law, Harvard University.
David L. Shapiro, Professor of Law, Harvard University.

JURISPRUDENCE (Temporary Edition Hardbound) (1949)

Lon L. Fuller, late Professor of Law, Harvard University.

JUVENILE, see also Children

JUVENILE JUSTICE PROCESS, Third Edition (1985)

Frank W. Miller, Professor of Law, Washington University.
Robert O. Dawson, Professor of Law, University of Texas.
George E. Dix, Professor of Law, University of Texas.
Raymond I. Parnas, Professor of Law, University of California, Davis.

LABOR LAW, Eleventh Edition (1991), with 1991 Statutory Supplement

Archibald Cox, Professor of Law, Harvard University.
Derek C. Bok, President, Harvard University.
Robert A. Gorman, Professor of Law, University of Pennsylvania.
Matthew W. Finkin, Professor of Law, University of Illinois.

LABOR LAW, Second Edition (1982), with Statutory Supplement

Clyde W. Summers, Professor of Law, University of Pennsylvania.
Harry H. Wellington, Dean of the Law School, Yale University.
Alan Hyde, Professor of Law, Rutgers University.

LAND FINANCING, Third Edition (1985)

The late Norman Penney, Professor of Law, Cornell University.
Richard F. Broude, Member of the California Bar.
Roger Cunningham, Professor of Law, University of Michigan.

LAW AND MEDICINE (1980)

Walter Wadlington, Professor of Law and Professor of Legal Medicine, University of Virginia.
Jon R. Waltz, Professor of Law, Northwestern University.
Roger B. Dworkin, Professor of Law, Indiana University, and Professor of Biomedical History, University of Washington.

LAW, LANGUAGE AND ETHICS (1972)

William R. Bishin, Professor of Law, University of Southern California.
Christopher D. Stone, Professor of Law, University of Southern California.

LAW, SCIENCE AND MEDICINE (1984), with 1989 Supplement

Judith C. Areen, Professor of Law, Georgetown University.
Patricia A. King, Professor of Law, Georgetown University.
Steven P. Goldberg, Professor of Law, Georgetown University.
Alexander M. Capron, Professor of Law, University of Southern California.

LAWYERING PROCESS (1978), with Civil Problem Supplement and Criminal Problem Supplement

Gary Bellow, Professor of Law, Harvard University.
Bea Moulton, Professor of Law, Arizona State University.

LEGAL ETHICS (1992)

Deborah Rhode, Professor of Law, Stanford University.
David Luban, Professor of Law, University of Maryland.

LEGAL METHOD (1980)

Harry W. Jones, Professor of Law Emeritus, Columbia University.
John M. Kernochan, Professor of Law, Columbia University.
Arthur W. Murphy, Professor of Law, Columbia University.

UNIVERSITY CASEBOOK SERIES—Continued

LEGAL METHODS (1969)

Robert N. Covington, Professor of Law, Vanderbilt University.
E. Blythe Stason, late Professor of Law, Vanderbilt University.
John W. Wade, Professor of Law, Vanderbilt University.
Elliott E. Cheatham, late Professor of Law, Vanderbilt University.
Theodore A. Smedley, Professor of Law, Vanderbilt University.

LEGAL PROFESSION, THE, Responsibility and Regulation, Second Edition (1988)

Geoffrey C. Hazard, Jr., Professor of Law, Yale University.
Deborah L. Rhode, Professor of Law, Stanford University.

LEGISLATION, Fourth Edition (1982) (by Fordham)

Horace E. Read, late Vice President, Dalhousie University.
John W. MacDonald, Professor of Law Emeritus, Cornell Law School.
Jefferson B. Fordham, Professor of Law, University of Utah.
William J. Pierce, Professor of Law, University of Michigan.

LEGISLATIVE AND ADMINISTRATIVE PROCESSES, Second Edition (1981)

Hans A. Linde, Judge, Supreme Court of Oregon.
George Bunn, Professor of Law, University of Wisconsin.
Fredericka Paff, Professor of Law, University of Wisconsin.
W. Lawrence Church, Professor of Law, University of Wisconsin.

LOCAL GOVERNMENT LAW, Second Revised Edition (1986)

Jefferson B. Fordham, Professor of Law, University of Utah.

MASS MEDIA LAW, Fourth Edition (1990)

Marc A. Franklin, Professor of Law, Stanford University.
David A. Anderson, Professor of Law, University of Texas.

MUNICIPAL CORPORATIONS, see Local Government Law

NEGOTIABLE INSTRUMENTS, see Commercial Paper

NEGOTIATION (1981) (Reprinted from THE LAWYERING PROCESS)

Gary Bellow, Professor of Law, Harvard Law School.
Bea Moulton, Legal Services Corporation.

NEW YORK PRACTICE, Fourth Edition (1978)

Herbert Peterfreund, Professor of Law, New York University.
Joseph M. McLaughlin, Dean of the Law School, Fordham University.

OIL AND GAS, Fifth Edition (1987)

Howard R. Williams, Professor of Law, Stanford University.
Richard C. Maxwell, Professor of Law, University of California, Los Angeles.
Charles J. Meyers, late Dean of the Law School, Stanford University.
Stephen F. Williams, Judge of the United States Court of Appeals.

ON LAW IN COURTS (1965)

Paul J. Mishkin, Professor of Law, University of California, Berkeley.
Clarence Morris, Professor of Law Emeritus, University of Pennsylvania.

PENSION AND EMPLOYEE BENEFIT LAW (1990), with 1991 Supplement

John H. Langbein, Professor of Law, University of Chicago.
Bruce A. Wolk, Professor of Law, University of California, Davis.

PLEADING AND PROCEDURE, see Procedure, Civil

UNIVERSITY CASEBOOK SERIES—Continued

POLICE FUNCTION, Fifth Edition (1991), with 1991 Supplement

Reprint of Chapters 1–10 of Miller, Dawson, Dix and Parnas's CRIMINAL JUSTICE ADMINISTRATION, Fourth Edition.

PREPARING AND PRESENTING THE CASE (1981) (Reprinted from THE LAWYERING PROCESS)

Gary Bellow, Professor of Law, Harvard Law School.
Bea Moulton, Legal Services Corporation.

PROCEDURE (1988), with Procedure Supplement (1991)

Robert M. Cover, late Professor of Law, Yale Law School.
Owen M. Fiss, Professor of Law, Yale Law School.
Judith Resnik, Professor of Law, University of Southern California Law Center.

PROCEDURE—CIVIL PROCEDURE, Sixth Edition (1990), with 1991 Supplement

Richard H. Field, late Professor of Law, Harvard University.
Benjamin Kaplan, Professor of Law Emeritus, Harvard University.
Kevin M. Clermont, Professor of Law, Cornell University.

PROCEDURE—CIVIL PROCEDURE, Successor Edition (1992)

A. Leo Levin, Professor of Law Emeritus, University of Pennsylvania.
Philip Shuchman, Professor of Law, Rutgers University.
Charles M. Yablon, Professor of Law, Yeshiva University.

PROCEDURE—CIVIL PROCEDURE, Fifth Edition (1990), with 1991 Supplement

Maurice Rosenberg, Professor of Law, Columbia University.
Hans Smit, Professor of Law, Columbia University.
Rochelle C. Dreyfuss, Professor of Law, New York University.

PROCEDURE—PLEADING AND PROCEDURE: State and Federal, Sixth Edition (1989), with 1991 Case Supplement

David W. Louisell, late Professor of Law, University of California, Berkeley.
Geoffrey C. Hazard, Jr., Professor of Law, Yale University.
Colin C. Tait, Professor of Law, University of Connecticut.

PROCEDURE—FEDERAL RULES OF CIVIL PROCEDURE, 1991 Edition

PRODUCTS LIABILITY AND SAFETY, Second Edition (1989), with 1989 Statutory Supplement

W. Page Keeton, Professor of Law, University of Texas.
David G. Owen, Professor of Law, University of South Carolina.
John E. Montgomery, Professor of Law, University of South Carolina.
Michael D. Green, Professor of Law, University of Iowa

PROFESSIONAL RESPONSIBILITY, Fifth Edition (1991), with 1992 Selected Standards on Professional Responsibility Supplement

Thomas D. Morgan, Professor of Law, George Washington University.
Ronald D. Rotunda, Professor of Law, University of Illinois.

PROPERTY, Sixth Edition (1990)

John E. Cribbet, Professor of Law, University of Illinois.
Corwin W. Johnson, Professor of Law, University of Texas.
Roger W. Findley, Professor of Law, University of Illinois.
Ernest E. Smith, Professor of Law, University of Texas.

PROPERTY—PERSONAL (1953)

S. Kenneth Skolfield, late Professor of Law Emeritus, Boston University.

UNIVERSITY CASEBOOK SERIES—Continued

PROPERTY—PERSONAL, Third Edition (1954)

Everett Fraser, late Dean of the Law School Emeritus, University of Minnesota. Third Edition by Charles W. Taintor, late Professor of Law, University of Pittsburgh.

PROPERTY—INTRODUCTION, TO REAL PROPERTY, Third Edition (1954)

Everett Fraser, late Dean of the Law School Emeritus, University of Minnesota.

PROPERTY—FUNDAMENTALS OF MODERN REAL PROPERTY, Second Edition (1982), with 1985 Supplement

Edward H. Rabin, Professor of Law, University of California, Davis.

PROPERTY, REAL (1984), with 1988 Supplement

Paul Goldstein, Professor of Law, Stanford University.

PROSECUTION AND ADJUDICATION, Fourth Edition (1991), with 1991 Supplement

Reprint of Chapters 11–26 of Miller, Dawson, Dix and Parnas's CRIMINAL JUSTICE ADMINISTRATION, Fourth Edition.

PSYCHIATRY AND LAW, see Mental Health, see also Hinckley, Trial of

PUBLIC UTILITY LAW, see Free Enterprise, also Regulated Industries

REAL ESTATE PLANNING, Third Edition (1989), with Revised Problem and Statutory Supplement (1991)

Norton L. Steuben, Professor of Law, University of Colorado.

REAL ESTATE TRANSACTIONS, Revised Second Edition (1988), with Statute, Form and Problem Supplement (1988)

Paul Goldstein, Professor of Law, Stanford University.

RECEIVERSHIP AND CORPORATE REORGANIZATION, see Creditors' Rights

REGULATED INDUSTRIES, Second Edition (1976)

William K. Jones, Professor of Law, Columbia University.

REMEDIES, Third Edition (1992)

Edward D. Re, Professor of Law, St. John's University.
Stanton D. Krauss, Professor of Law, University of Bridgeport.

REMEDIES (1989)

Elaine W. Shoben, Professor of Law, University of Illinois.
Wm. Murray Tabb, Professor of Law, Baylor University.

SALES, Second Edition (1986)

Marion W. Benfield, Jr., Professor of Law, University of Illinois.
William D. Hawkland, Chancellor, Louisiana State Law Center.

SALES AND SALES FINANCING, Fifth Edition (1984)
John Honnold, Professor of Law, University of Pennsylvania.

SALES LAW AND THE CONTRACTING PROCESS, Second Edition (1991)
(Reprinted from Commercial Transactions, Second Edition (1991)

Alan Schwartz, Professor of Law, Yale University.
Robert E. Scott, Professor of Law, University of Virginia.

SECURED TRANSACTIONS IN PERSONAL PROPERTY, Second Edition (1987) (Reprinted from COMMERCIAL LAW, Second Edition (1987))

Robert L. Jordan, Professor of Law, University of California, Los Angeles.
William D. Warren, Professor of Law, University of California, Los Angeles.

SECURITIES REGULATION, Sixth Edition (1987), with 1991 Selected Statutes, Rules and Forms Supplement and 1991 Cases and Releases Supplement

Richard W. Jennings, Professor of Law, University of California, Berkeley.
Harold Marsh, Jr., Member of California Bar.

SECURITIES REGULATION, Second Edition (1988), with Statute, Rule and Form Supplement (1991)

Larry D. Soderquist, Professor of Law, Vanderbilt University.

SECURITY INTERESTS IN PERSONAL PROPERTY, Second Edition (1987)

Douglas G. Baird, Professor of Law, University of Chicago.
Thomas H. Jackson, Dean of the Law School, University of Virginia.

SECURITY INTERESTS IN PERSONAL PROPERTY (1985) (Reprinted from Sales and Sales Financing, Fifth Edition)

John Honnold, Professor of Law, University of Pennsylvania.

SELECTED STANDARDS ON PROFESSIONAL RESPONSIBILITY, 1992 Edition

SELECTED STATUTES AND INTERNATIONAL AGREEMENTS ON UNFAIR COMPETITION, TRADEMARK, COPYRIGHT AND PATENT, 1991 Edition

SELECTED STATUTES ON TRUSTS AND ESTATES, 1992 Edition

SOCIAL RESPONSIBILITIES OF LAWYERS, Case Studies (1988)

Philip B. Heymann, Professor of Law, Harvard University.
Lance Liebman, Professor of Law, Harvard University.

SOCIAL SCIENCE IN LAW, Second Edition (1990)

John Monahan, Professor of Law, University of Virginia.
Laurens Walker, Professor of Law, University of Virginia.

TAXATION, FEDERAL INCOME (1989)

Stephen B. Cohen, Professor of Law, Georgetown University

TAXATION, FEDERAL INCOME, Second Edition (1988), with 1991 Supplement (Supplement edited in association with Deborah H. Schenk, Professor of Law, New York University)

Michael J. Graetz, Professor of Law, Yale University.

TAXATION, FEDERAL INCOME, Seventh Edition (1991)

James J. Freeland, Professor of Law, University of Florida.
Stephen A. Lind, Professor of Law, University of Florida and University of California, Hastings.
Richard B. Stephens, late Professor of Law Emeritus, University of Florida.

TAXATION, FEDERAL INCOME, Successor Edition (1986), with 1991 Legislative Supplement

Stanley S. Surrey, late Professor of Law, Harvard University.
Paul R. McDaniel, Professor of Law, Boston College.
Hugh J. Ault, Professor of Law, Boston College.
Stanley A. Koppelman, Professor of Law, Boston University.

TAXATION, FEDERAL INCOME, OF BUSINESS ORGANIZATIONS (1991), with 1991 Supplement

Paul R. McDaniel, Professor of Law, Boston College.
Hugh J. Ault, Professor of Law, Boston College.
Martin J. McMahon, Jr., Professor of Law, University of Kentucky.
Daniel L. Simmons, Professor of Law, University of California, Davis.

TAXATION, FEDERAL INCOME, OF PARTNERSHIPS AND S CORPORATIONS (1991), with 1991 Supplement

Paul R. McDaniel, Professor of Law, Boston College.
Hugh J. Ault, Professor of Law, Boston College.
Martin J. McMahon, Jr., Professor of Law, University of Kentucky.
Daniel L. Simmons, Professor of Law, University of California, Davis.

TAXATION, FEDERAL INCOME, OIL AND GAS, NATURAL RESOURCES TRANSACTIONS (1990)

Peter C. Maxfield, Professor of Law, University of Wyoming.
James L. Houghton, CPA, Partner, Ernst and Young.
James R. Gaar, CPA, Partner, Ernst and Young.

TAXATION, FEDERAL WEALTH TRANSFER, Successor Edition (1987)

Stanley S. Surrey, late Professor of Law, Harvard University.
Paul R. McDaniel, Professor of Law, Boston College.
Harry L. Gutman, Professor of Law, University of Pennsylvania.

TAXATION, FUNDAMENTALS OF CORPORATE, Third Edition (1991)

Stephen A. Lind, Professor of Law, University of Florida and University of California, Hastings.
Stephen Schwarz, Professor of Law, University of California, Hastings.
Daniel J. Lathrope, Professor of Law, University of California, Hastings.
Joshua Rosenberg, Professor of Law, University of San Francisco.

TAXATION, FUNDAMENTALS OF PARTNERSHIP, Third Edition (1992)

Stephen A. Lind, Professor of Law, University of Florida and University of California, Hastings.
Stephen Schwarz, Professor of Law, University of California, Hastings.
Daniel J. Lathrope, Professor of Law, University of California, Hastings.
Joshua Rosenberg, Professor of Law, University of San Francisco.

TAXATION OF CORPORATIONS AND THEIR SHAREHOLDERS (1991)

David J. Shakow, Professor of Law, University of Pennsylvania.

TAXATION, PROBLEMS IN THE FEDERAL INCOME TAXATION OF PARTNER-SHIPS AND CORPORATIONS, Second Edition (1986)

Norton L. Steuben, Professor of Law, University of Colorado.
William J. Turnier, Professor of Law, University of North Carolina.

TAXATION, PROBLEMS IN THE FUNDAMENTALS OF FEDERAL INCOME, Second Edition (1985)

Norton L. Steuben, Professor of Law, University of Colorado.
William J. Turnier, Professor of Law, University of North Carolina.

TORT LAW AND ALTERNATIVES, Fourth Edition (1987)

Marc A. Franklin, Professor of Law, Stanford University.
Robert L. Rabin, Professor of Law, Stanford University.

TORTS, Eighth Edition (1988)

William L. Prosser, late Professor of Law, University of California, Hastings.
John W. Wade, Professor of Law, Vanderbilt University.
Victor E. Schwartz, Adjunct Professor of Law, Georgetown University.

UNIVERSITY CASEBOOK SERIES—Continued

TORTS, Third Edition (1976)

Harry Shulman, late Dean of the Law School, Yale University.
Fleming James, Jr., Professor of Law Emeritus, Yale University.
Oscar S. Gray, Professor of Law, University of Maryland.

TRADE REGULATION, Third Edition (1990)

Milton Handler, Professor of Law Emeritus, Columbia University.
Harlan M. Blake, Professor of Law, Columbia University.
Robert Pitofsky, Professor of Law, Georgetown University.
Harvey J. Goldschmid, Professor of Law, Columbia University.

TRADE REGULATION, see Antitrust

TRANSNATIONAL BUSINESS PROBLEMS (1986)

Detlev F. Vagts, Professor of Law, Harvard University.

TRANSNATIONAL LEGAL PROBLEMS, Third Edition (1986), with 1991 Revised Edition of Documentary Supplement

Henry J. Steiner, Professor of Law, Harvard University.
Detlev F. Vagts, Professor of Law, Harvard University.

TRIAL, see also Evidence, Making the Record, Lawyering Process and Preparing and Presenting the Case

TRUSTS, Sixth Edition (1991)

George G. Bogert, late Professor of Law Emeritus, University of Chicago.
Dallin H. Oaks, President, Brigham Young University.
H. Reese Hansen, Dean and Professor of Law, Brigham Young University.
Claralyn Martin Hill, J.D. Brigham Young University.

TRUSTS AND ESTATES, SELECTED STATUTES ON, 1992 Edition

TRUSTS AND WILLS, See also Decedents' Estates and Trusts, and Family Property Law

UNFAIR COMPETITION, see Competitive Process and Business Torts

WATER RESOURCE MANAGEMENT, Third Edition (1988), with 1992 Supplement

The late Charles J. Meyers, formerly Dean, Stanford University Law School.
A. Dan Tarlock, Professor of Law, IIT Chicago-Kent College of Law.
James N. Corbridge, Jr., Chancellor, University of Colorado at Boulder, and Professor of Law, University of Colorado.
David H. Getches, Professor of Law, University of Colorado.

WILLS AND ADMINISTRATION, Fifth Edition (1961)

Philip Mechem, late Professor of Law, University of Pennsylvania.
Thomas E. Atkinson, late Professor of Law, New York University.

WRITING AND ANALYSIS IN THE LAW, Second Edition (1991)

Helene S. Shapo, Professor of Law, Northwestern University.
Marilyn R. Walter, Professor of Law, Brooklyn Law School.
Elizabeth Fajans, Writing Specialist, Brooklyn Law School.

University Casebook Series

PROCESSES OF DISPUTE RESOLUTION:

THE ROLE OF LAWYERS

By

JOHN S. MURRAY

President and Executive Director
The Conflict Clinic, Inc.
George Mason University

ALAN SCOTT RAU

Thos. H. Law Centennial Professor of Law
University of Texas at Austin School of Law

EDWARD F. SHERMAN

Angus G. Wynne, Sr. Professor of Law
University of Texas at Austin School of Law

Westbury, New York
THE FOUNDATION PRESS, INC.
1989

Library of Congress Cataloging-in-Publication Data

Murray, John S., 1939–
    Processes of dispute resolution: the role of lawyers / by John S.
Murray, Alan Scott Rau, Edward F. Sherman.
        p.   cm.—(University casebook series)
    Includes index.
    ISBN 0–88277–688–6
    1. Dispute resolution (Law)—United States—Cases. 2. Lawyers—
United States—Cases. I. Rau, Alan Scott, 1942–   . II. Sherman,
Edward F., 1937–   . III. Title. IV. Series.
KF9084.A7M87   1989
347.73'9—dc19
[347.3079]   88–39106
                                                                          CIP

Copyright notices for certain material used with permission,
appear in the Acknowledgment section at p. xxiii.

M., R. & S. Proc. Dispute Res. UCB
1st Reprint—1992

PREFACE

Over the past two decades there has been a dramatic explosion of interest among academics, the bar, and (most importantly) users of legal services in ways that lawyers can help resolve disputes other than through litigation. Many law schools are now offering courses in the area of "alternatives," and innovative teaching materials have begun to appear. We have prepared this book as one "alternative" in filling the need for teachable materials that can be used in law school courses. The past decade has also seen a coming of age of the "ADR movement" as some of the initial zeal for alternatives has given way to a more balanced and temperate view. With greater awareness of the range of alternative processes has come the need for an objective assessment of their role in our dispute processing system, and for an objective look at the relationship of alternative processes to the formal public court system.

We have designed these materials to reflect this view of the subject. After a brief introduction to the nature of disputing in our society, we begin with the litigation process. Within the first months of law school—if not before—most law students are already likely to be socialized to believe that the lawyer's role in dispute processing finds its principal outlet in litigation before the courts. Because they will probably look at other processes in light of what they see as the "norm" of formal court adjudication, our first aim is to bring litigation into perspective—to bring students to see it as *a* system of dispute resolution, one with virtues and failings, but in any event *not the inevitable process* for resolving all disputes. We would like students to see that the various "alternative" processes of dispute resolution need not be treated as necessarily distinct from litigation, nor as mutually exclusive. The other processes can usefully be seen as complementary to litigation, and the contemporary lawyer needs to develop an ability to work with *all* available processes, separately, in series, or even simultaneously.

Following this introduction to litigation, we consider the other primary processes of dispute resolution in considerable detail. We begin with the negotiation process, which is so often closely tied to the lawyer's litigation role and then turn to other processes—mediation, arbitration, reality testing before third parties, and the administrative and legislative processes—considered in an order that reflects increasing third-party involvement and increasing structure and formality.

The title of this book indicates our focus on process. At times this is theoretical and policy-oriented. We think an understanding of the underlying philosophy, strengths, and weaknesses of each of the alternative dispute resolution techniques is necessary in order for a lawyer to appreciate how and when they can be used in a particular dispute. But we are also interested in their practical application. Thus we attempt to provide a comprehensive overview of the legal procedures and doctrines—whether from Civil Procedure, Remedies, Administrative Law, or Contracts—that a lawyer will need to know in order to use the techniques effectively. The legal aspects are sometimes highly technical—as in the legal aspects of a negotiated settlement, the technicalities of arbitration practice, and the formalities of court-administered alternative dispute resolution—and we believe these materials will equip the lawyer to handle them. We have included extensive citations to cases and other sources and believe that these materials will continue to be a helpful reference book for students once they are in practice.

These materials are specially suited for use in a general "dispute resolution" course for second- or third-year law students. Parts of the book can be selected for a two-hour survey course, but the materials are also extensive and detailed enough to support a longer course. We place particular stress on the role of "the law" in each type of dispute resolution process, on the role of the lawyer in choosing processes and implementing strategies, and on the skills needed to use the processes effectively. The skills component to the course can be substantial, since the materials are intended to provide insights into effective use of the various processes and the opportunity to use them in practical exercises. We hope the student will come to see that familiarity with the different processes is an integral part of the lawyer's bag of skills.

These goals could be served in other ways than through an upper-level "dispute resolution" course. For example, these materials might be assigned as a collective supplement to the materials used in the first-year courses, both to make students generally aware of the existence and consequences of the choice of process for dispute resolution, and to illustrate particular legal problems in their natural complexity (for example in Contracts, the concept of negotiation in good faith in the early stages of contract formation, the use of arbitration to fix contract terms, or the formation and enforceability of arbitration agreements; in Torts, the mini-trial as a method of structuring settlement of complex personal injury claims; in Civil Procedure, the blending of depositions and a motion for summary judgment with an attractive settlement option).

The materials might also be used as a supplement to more specialized courses. They would be suitable for use in a clinical course, where the choice of a dispute resolution process is critical to the student's ability to deal with the "real life" problems of the clinic's clients. They might also be used in a course which focuses primarily on a specific process like Arbitration, Mediation, or Negotiation, where the instructor wants to give students some general introduction to other adjacent processes as well as a thorough grounding in one. Finally, the book could be used as a supplement to a course or seminar in areas such as Trial Practice, Labor Law, or Family Law, where the existing text used by the instructor gives primary attention to substantive law and does not deal adequately with process issues or the use of alternatives to litigation.

PREFACE

A note on form: We have substantially edited most cases and selections to delete unnecessary material. Deletions of text due to our editing are indicated by spaced asterisks. Citations in the text, and footnotes from the text, have usually been omitted without indication. Where footnotes to selections do appear, however, we have retained the number they have in the original material.

We have benefited from the helpful comments of many colleagues and students who have used and reviewed these materials. We wish to express appreciation to Professors Robert Wood and James Viator of Texas Tech University School of Law, who used and critiqued early drafts in the course of teaching sections of a required first-year course, and to Helmut Wolff of the American Arbitration Association and Professor Nancy Rogers of Ohio State University College of Law, who provided extensive and insightful comments on portions of the materials when they were still in experimental form. The University of Texas Law School Foundation provided substantial financial support which helped make possible the completion of this project. We are grateful to our research assistant, Heather Steinle, for her help in all phases of the production of this book. We are also grateful to Karyn Lee, Barbara Hannon, Lu Quast, Dahlia Gutierrez, and Sylvia Sanders for their research and administrative assistance, and to our secretaries, Dawn Kalinosky, Teri Martin, and Norma Tanner, for their help, patience, and cheerfulness.

J.S.M.
A.S.R.
E.F.S.

November, 1988

*

ACKNOWLEDGMENTS

The following authors and publishers gave us permission to reprint excerpts from copyright material; we gratefully acknowledge their assistance.

CHAPTER I

Miller & Sarat, Grievances, Claims, and Disputes: Assessing the Adversary Culture, 15 Law & Soc'y Rev. 525, 526–27, 531–33, 536–46, 561–64 (1980–81). Reprinted by permission of the Law and Society Association.

Galanter, Reading the Landscape of Disputes: What We Know and Don't Know (And Think We Know) About Our Allegedly Contentious and Litigious Society, 31 U.C.L.A. L.Rev. 4, 13–14 (1983). Originally published in 31 U.C.L.A. L.Rev. 4, Copyright 1983, The Regents of the University of California. All rights reserved.

J. Auerbach, Justice Without Law? 10, 12–13 (1983). From Justice Without Law? by Jerold S. Auerbach. Copyright © 1983 by Oxford University Press, Inc. Reprinted by permission.

Trubek, Sarat, Felstiner, Kritzer & Grossman, The Costs of Ordinary Litigation, 31 U.C.L.A. L.Rev. 72, 89–90, 122 (1983). Originally Published in 31 U.C.L.A. L.Rev. 72, Copyright 1983, The Regents of the University of California. All rights reserved.

Newman, Rethinking Fairness: Perspectives on the Litigation Process, 94 Yale L.J. 1643, 1644–45 (1985).

Brazil, The Attorney as Victim: Towards More Candor About the Psychological Price Tag of Litigation Practice, 3 J. of the Legal Profession 107, 109–110, 114–17 (1978–79).

Fuller, The Forms and Limits of Adjudication, 92 Harv.L.Rev. 353, 364–71, 382–85, 393–400, 403 (1978). Copyright © 1978 by the Harvard Law Review Association.

The Role of Courts in American Society: Final Report of Council on the Role of Courts 102–114, 120–21 (J. Lieberman ed. 1984).

Chayes, The Role of the Judge in Public Law Litigation, 89 Harv.L. Rev. 1281, 1298–99 (1976). Copyright © 1976 by the Harvard Law Review Association.

Fiss, Against Settlement, 93 Yale L.J. 1073, 1075–78, 1082–90 (1984).

Edwards, Alternative Dispute Resolution: Panacea or Anathema, 99 Harv.L.Rev. 668, 678–79 (1986). Copyright © 1986 by the Harvard Law Review Association.

Galanter, The Day After the Litigation Explosion, 46 Maryland L.Rev. 3, 32–37 (1986).

Burger, *Isn't There a Better Way?*, March, 1982 *ABA Journal*, The Lawyer's Magazine, pp. 274–75.

ACKNOWLEDGMENTS

Cartoon, by Charles Schultz, reprinted by permission of U.F.S., Inc., Aug. 30, 1986.

CHAPTER II

E. Fink, A Lawyer's Landscape . . . the view from his office (1976), reprinted from 58 A.B.A. J. 311 (March, 1972), Poetry Corner by E. Fink.

G. Williams, Legal Negotiation and Settlement 24–25, 49, 115–17 (1983). Reprinted by permission of West Publishing Co.

Menkel-Meadow, Toward Another View of Legal Negotiation: The Structure of Problem Solving, 31 U.C.L.A. L.Rev. 754, 795, 798–801, 809–10 (1984). Originally published in 31 U.C.L.A. L.Rev. 754. Copyright 1983, The Regents of the University of California. All rights reserved.

R. Axelrod, The Evolution of Cooperation 8–9, 12, 14–15, 20–21 (1984). Copyright © 1984 by Robert Axelrod. Reprinted by permission of Basic Books, Inc., Publishers.

White, Essay Review: The Pros and Cons of Getting to Yes, with following Comment by Fisher, 34 J. of Legal Educ. 115–117, 119–22 (1984).

McCarthy, The Role of Power and Principle in Getting to Yes, 1 Negotiation J. 59, 64–65 (1985). Reprinted by permission of Plenum Publishing Corp.

Fisher, Beyond Yes, 1 Negotiation J. 67, 69 (1985). Reprinted by permission of Plenum Publishing Corp.

D. Harnett & L. Cummings, Bargaining Behavior 164–65 (1980). Reprinted by permission of Dame Publications, Inc.

R. Fisher & W. Ury, Getting to Yes 22–30 (1981). From Getting to Yes by Roger Fisher & William Ury. Copyright © 1981 by Roger Fisher and William Ury. Reprinted by permission of Houghton Mifflin Company.

M. Burley-Allen, Listening: The Forgotten Skill 101–02 (1982). Copyright © 1982. Reprinted by permission of John Wiley & Sons, Inc.

H. Edwards & J. White, The Lawyer As A Negotiator 113–16 (1977). Reprinted by permission of West Publishing Co.

H. Raiffa, The Art & Science of Negotiation 66–76, 118, 127–28 (1982). Copyright © 1982 by the President and Fellows of Harvard College. Reprinted by permission of Harvard University Press, Publisher.

Neely, Barter in the Court: The Hidden Cost of Divorce, The New Republic, Feb. 10, 1986, p. 13.

T. Schelling, The Strategy of Conflict 24, 27 (1960). Copyright © 1986 by The President and Fellows of Harvard College.

Mnookin & Kornhauser, Bargaining in the Shadow of the Law: The Case for Divorce, 88 Yale L.J. 950 (1979).

ACKNOWLEDGMENTS

Skywalk Settlements, 3 Alt. to the High Cost of Litigation 5–6 (Sept. 1985). Copyright © 1985 Center for Public Resources, Inc. Reprinted by permission.

W. Brazil, Settling Civil Disputes 44–46 (1985). Published by the American Bar Association.

Schuck, The Role of Judges in Settling Complex Cases: The Agent Orange Example, 53 U.Chi.L.Rev. 337, 344–48 (1986). Reprinted by permission of the University of Chicago Law Review.

Entman, Mary Carter Agreements: An Assessment of Attempted Solutions, 38 U. Fla. L. Rev. 521, 529–30 (1986). Reprinted with the permission of the University of Florida Law Review. Copyright 1986.

Coleman & Silver, Justice in Settlements, 4 Social Philosophy & Policy 102, 112–13 (1987).

White, Machiavelli and the Bar: Ethical Limitations on Lying in Negotiation, 1980 Am. B. Foundation Res. J. 926–30.

American Bar Association, Model Rules of Professional Conduct and Model Code of Professional Responsibility. Copyright by the ABA. All rights reserved. Reprinted with permission.

Rubin, A Causerie on Lawyers' Ethics in Negotiation, 35 La.L.Rev. 577, 589 (1975).

Lowenthal, A General Theory of Negotiation: Process, Strategy and Behavior, 31 Kansas L. Rev. 69, 107–08 (1982).

Lax & Sebenius, Three Ethical Issues in Negotiation, 2 Negotiation J. 363, 367 (1986). Reprinted by permission of Plenum Publishing Corp.

Rubin, "Negotiation: An Introduction to Some Issues and Themes," Am. Behavioral Scientist vol. 27, (Nov.–Dec. 1983), pp. 138–44. Copyright © 1983. Reprinted by permission of Sage Publications, Inc.

H. Cohen, You Can Negotiate Anything 32–37, 93–95 (1980). Reprinted by permission of Lyle Stuart, Inc.

Thomas W. Milburn & Kenneth H. Watman, On the Nature of Threat: A Social Psychological Analysis, (Praeger Publications, New York, 1981). pp. 17–18, 39, 43–45, 49, 103, 108–11 (1981). Copyright © 1981 by Praeger Publishers. Reprinted with permission.

J. Freund, Anatomy of a Merger: Strategies and Techniques For Negotiating Corporate Acquisitions 29–31 (1975). Reprinted with the permission of the publisher from Anatomy of a Merger: Strategies and Techniques For Negotiating Corporate Acquisitions by James C. Freund. Copyright 1975, Law Journal Seminars-Press, 111 Eighth Ave., N.Y., N.Y. 10011. All rights reserved.

Cartoon, by Ben Sargent, The Austin American Statesman, November 1985.

ACKNOWLEDGMENTS

CHAPTER III

Northrop, The Mediational Approval Theory of Law in American Legal Realism, 44 Va. L. Rev. 347, 349 (1958).

Danzig, Toward the Creation of a Complementary, Decentralized System of Criminal Justice, 26 Stan. L. Rev. 1, 42-3 (1973). Copyright 1973 by the Board of Trustees of the Leland Stanford Junior University. Article originally published in the Stanford Law Review.

Fuller, Mediation—Its Forms and Functions, 44 S. Cal. L. Rev. 305, 325-26 (1971), reprinted with the permission of the Southern California Law Review.

Odom, The Mediation Hearing: A Primer, in Palenski & Launer, Mediation: Contexts and Challenges 5-14 (1986). Reprinted with the permission of Charles C. Thomas, Publisher.

Silbey & Merry, Mediator Settlement Strategies, 8 Law & Policy 7, 12-19 (1986). Reprinted with permission from Basil Blackwell Limited.

Shaw, Divorce Mediation: Some Keys to the Process, 9 Mediation Q. 27 (1985). Reprinted with permission from Jossey-Bass, Inc.

Stulberg & Montgomery, Design Requirements for Mediator Development Programs, 15 Hofstra L. Rev. 499, 504 (1987).

C. Moore, The Mediation Process 281-82 (1987). Reprinted by permission of Jossey-Bass, Inc.

Bush, Using Process Observation to Teach Alternative Dispute Resolution: Alternative to Simulation, 37 J. Legal Educ. 46, 52 (1987).

Shonholtz, Neighborhood Justice Systems: Work, Structure, and Guiding Principles, 5 Mediation Q. 3, 13-16 (1984). Reprinted with the permission of Jossey-Bass, Inc.

Ericsson, How Dare You Sue One Another!, in Implications 3-4 (Christian Legal Society 1988).

N. Rogers & R. Salem, A Student's Guide to Mediation and the Law 19-20 (1987). Reprinted by permission of Matthew Bender.

McEwen & Maiman, Mediation in Small Claims Court: Achieving Compliance Through Consent, 18 Law & Soc'y Rev. 11, 40-47 (1984). Reprinted by permission of the Law and Society Association.

Vidmar, Assessing the Effects of Case Characteristics and Settlement Forum on Dispute Outcomes and Compliance, 21 Law & Soc'y Rev. 155, 162-63 (1987). Reprinted by permission of the Law and Society Association.

Winks, Divorce Mediation: A Nonadversary Procedure for the No-Fault Divorce, 19 J. of Fam. L. 615, 634-640 (1980-81).

Woods, Mediation: A Backlash to Women's Progress on Family Law Issues, 19 Clearinghouse Rev. 431, 435 (1985).

Mnookin & Kornhauser, Bargaining in the Shadow of the Law: The Case of Divorce, 88 Yale L. J. 950, 950-5, 968-69 (1979).

ACKNOWLEDGMENTS

Erlanger, Chambliss & Melli, Participation and Flexibility in Informal Processes: Cautions from the Divorce Context, 21 Law & Soc'y Rev. 585, 598–600 (1987). Reprinted by permission of the Law and Society Association.

Marlow, The Rule of Law in Divorce Mediation, 9 Mediation Q. 5, 10–13 (1985). Reprinted with permission from Jossey-Bass, Inc.

Murray, Improving Parent-Child Relationships Within the Divorced Family: A Call for Legal Reform, 19 U. Mich. J. Law Reform 563, 585–86 (1986).

Fineman, Dominant Discourse, Professional Language, and Legal Change in Child Custody Decisionmaking, 101 Harv. L. Rev. 727, 731–32, 756–57, 759–60 (1988). Copyright © 1988 by the Harvard Law Review Association.

Riskin, Mediation and Lawyers, 43 Ohio St. L.J. 29, 34–35, 37–41 (1982). Copyright © 1982 The Ohio State University.

D. Kolb, The Mediators 80–85 (1983), The MIT Press, Publisher.

E. Robins, A Guide for Labor Mediators 25–26 (1976). Reprinted by permission of the Industrial Relations Center of the University of Hawaii.

K. Feinberg, Avoiding Litigation Through Nonbinding Mediation, Alliance of American Insurers, 1987.

Chayes, The Role of the Judge in Public Law Litigation, 89 Harv. L. Rev. 1281, 1284, 1292, 1293–94, 1296 (1976). Copyright © 1976 by the Harvard Law Review Association.

McGovern, Toward a Functional Approach for Managing Complex Litigation, 53 U. Chi. L. Rev. 440, 456–66 (1986).

Sherman, Restructuring the Trial Process in the Age of Complex Litigation, 63 Tex. L. Rev. 721, 741–43 (1984). Published originally in 63 Texas Law Review 721, 741–42 (1984). Copyright 1984 by the Texas Law Review. Reprinted by permission.

D. Amy, The Politics of Environmental Mediation, 188–89 (1987). Copyright © 1987 Columbia University Press. Used by permission.

Freedman & Prigoff, Confidentiality in Mediation: The Need for Protection, 2 Ohio St. J. Dispute Res. 37, 39 (1986).

Green, A Heretical View of a Mediation Privilege, 2 Ohio St. J. on Dispute Resolution 1, 12, 29–30 (1986).

Kirkpatrick, Should Mediators Have a Confidentiality Privilege? 9 Mediation Q. 85, 94–6 (1985). Reprinted with permission from Jossey-Bass, Inc.

Protecting Confidentiality in Mediation, 98 Harv. L. Rev. 441, 452–53 (1984). Copyright © 1984 by the Harvard Law Review Association.

American Bar Association, Standards of Practice for Lawyer Mediators in Family Disputes (Adopted by the House of Delegates of the ABA, 1984). Copyright by the ABA. All rights reserved. Reprinted with permission.

CHAPTER IV

Landes & Posner, Adjudication as a Private Good, 8 J. Legal Stud. 235, 235–40, 245–47 (1979). The University of Chicago, Publisher.

Fuller, Collective Bargaining and the Arbitrator, 1963 Wisc. L. Rev. 3, 11–12, 17.

Galanter, Justice in Many Rooms: Courts, Private Order, and Indigenous Law, 19 J. Pluralism & Unofficial L. 1, 17–18, 25 (1981).

Mentschikoff, The Significance of Arbitration—A Preliminary Inquiry, 17 Law & Contemporary Problems 698, 709 (1952). Copyright 1952 Duke University School of Law.

Craver, The Judicial Enforcement of Public Sector Interest Arbitration, 21 B.C. L. Rev. 557, 558 n. 8 (1980).

Jones, Three Centuries of Commercial Arbitration in New York: A Brief Survey, 1956 Wash. U.L.Q. 193, 209–10, 218–19.

Mentschikoff, Commercial Arbitration, 61 Col. L. Rev. 846, 848–54 (1961). Copyright 1961 by the Directors of the Columbia Law Review Association Inc. All rights reserved. This article originally appeared at 61 Col. L. Rev. 848. Reprinted by permission.

W. Craig, W. Park & J. Paulsson, International Chamber of Commerce Arbitration § 355.02 at 3, § 13.03 at 39, § 3.02 at 30–31 (Oceana, 1984).

Tang, Arbitration—A Method Used by China to Settle Foreign Trade and Economic Disputes, 4 Pace L. Rev. 519, 533–34 (1984).

P. Hays, Labor Arbitration: A Dissenting View 112–13 (1966).

Getman, Labor Arbitration and Dispute Resolution, 88 Yale L.J. 916, 928–30 (1979).

Terry, The Technical and Conceptual Flaws of Medical Malpractice Arbitration, 30 St. Louis U. L.J. 571, 572–73, 586 (1986).

Henderson, Contractual Problems in the Enforcement of Agreements to Arbitrate Medical Malpractice, 58 Va. L. Rev. 947–994 (1972). Reprinted by permission of Fred B. Rothman & Co.

St. Antoine, Judicial Review of Labor Arbitration Awards: A Second Look at *Enterprise Wheel* and its Progeny, 75 Mich. L. Rev. 1137, 1140, 1142 (1977).

American Arbitration Association's Code of Ethics for Arbitrators in Commercial Disputes (1977).

Stein, The Selection of Arbitrators, N.Y.U. Eighth Annual Conference on Labor 291, 293 (1955).

Raffaele, Lawyers in Labor Arbitration, 37 Arb. J. No. 3 (Sept. 1982).

Roth, When to Ignore the Rules of Evidence in Arbitration, 9 Litigation 20 (Winter 1983). Copyright © 1983 American Bar Association. Reprinted with permission from Vol. 9, No. 2, Litigation. All rights reserved.

ACKNOWLEDGMENTS

The American Institute of Architects, Document A201, General Conditions of the Contract for Construction. Copyright © 1987 The American Institute of Architects. AIA copyrighted material has been reproduced with the permission of The American Institute of Architects. Further reproduction is prohibited.

Fuller, Collective Bargaining and the Arbitrator, Proceedings, Fifteenth Annual Meeting, National Academy of Arbitrators 8, 29–33, 37–48 (1962). Reprinted by permission of The Bureau of National Affairs, Inc.

Proceedings, 33rd Annual Meeting, National Academy of Arbitrators 232 (1981). Reprinted by permission of The Bureau of National Affairs, Inc.

J. Folberg & A. Taylor, Mediation 277–78 (1984). Reprinted by permission of Jossey-Bass, Inc.

Christensen, Private Justice: California's General Reference Procedure, 1982 American Bar Found. Research J. 79, 81–82, 103.

Note, The California Rent-A-Judge Experiment: Constitutional and Policy Considerations of Pay-As-You-Go Courts, 94 Harv. L. Rev. 1592, 1601–02, 1607–10 (1981). Copyright © 1981 by the Harvard Law Review Association.

Drawing by Dana Fradon; © 1987 The New Yorker Magazine, Inc.

CHAPTER V

Olson, An Alternative for Large Case Dispute Resolution, 6 Litigation 22 (Winter 1980). Copyright © 1987 American Bar Association. Reprinted with permission from Vol. 6, No. 2, Litigation. All rights reserved.

Green, Growth of the Mini-trial, 9 Litigation No. 1, 12, 17–20 (Fall 1982). Copyright © 1982 American Bar Association. Reprinted with permission from Vol. 9, No. 1, Litigation. All rights reserved.

Center for Public Resources, Model ADR Procedures: Rules for Loss Allocation in Toxic Tort Cases (1987).

R. Marcus & E. Sherman, "The Asbestos Claims Agreement" from Complex Litigation 834 (1985). Reprinted with permission of West Publishing Company.

Adler, Hensler, & Nelson, Simple Justice: How Litigants Fare in the Pittsburgh Court Arbitration Program vii–ix, 9–14, 87–94 (1983). Reprinted by permission of the Rand Corporation Institute for Civil Justice.

Lambros, Summary Jury Trial—An Alternative Method of Resolving Disputes, 69 Judicature 286, 286–290 (1986).

Brunet, Questioning the Quality of Alternative Dispute Resolution, 62 Tulane L. Rev. 1, 39–40 (1987).

Sherman, Reshaping the Lawyer's Skills for Court-Supervised ADR, 51 Tex. B.J. 47, 48–49 (1988). Copyright 1988 Texas Bar Journal.

ACKNOWLEDGMENTS

CHAPTER VI

Morrison, The Administrative Procedure Act: A Living and Responsive Law, 72 Va. L. Rev. 253 (1986). Reprinted by permission of Fred B. Rothman & Co., and the Virginia Law Review Association.

DeLong, New Wine for a New Bottle: Judicial Review in the Regulatory State, 72 Va.L.Rev. 399, 405–06, 411–13, 417–18 (1986). Reprinted by permission of Fred. B. Rothman & Co. and the Virginia Law Review Association.

DeMuth & Ginsburg, White House Review of Agency Rulemaking, 99 Harv. L. Rev. 1075, 1075–76 (1986). Copyright © 1986 by the Harvard Law Review Association.

Smith, Alternative Means of Dispute Resolution: Practices & Possibilities in the federal government, 1984 J. of Dispute Res. 9, 11–15.

Pou, Federal Agency Use of "ADR": The Experience to Date Sourcebook: Federal Agency Use of Alternative Means of Dispute Resolution 101, 102–14 (1987). Copyright © 1988 by the Center for Public Resources, 366 Madison Avenue, New York, New York 10176. Reprinted with permission of the Center for Public Resources from an article in *Containing Legal Costs: ADR Strategies for Corporations, Law Firms and Government* (CPR ed., Butterworth Legal Publishers 1988).

Moorman, The Superfund Steering Committee: A Primer, The Environmental Forum 13–14, 19–20 (Feb. 1986).

Linde, Due Process of Lawmaking, 55 Neb. L. Rev. 197, 220–23 (1976).

Stewart, Forward: Lawyers and the Legislative Process, 10 Harv. J. on Legislation 151, 152–58 (1973). Copied with permission. Copyright © 1973 by the Harvard Legislative Research Bureau.

Nelson & Heinz, Lawyers & the Structure of Influence in Washington, 22 Law & Soc'y Rev. 701, 756–58 (1988).

SUMMARY OF CONTENTS

SUMMARY OF CONTENTS

APPENDICES

TABLE OF CONTENTS

APPENDICES

TABLE OF CASES

Principal cases are in italic type. Non-principal cases are in roman type. References are to Pages.

*

PROCESSES OF
DISPUTE RESOLUTION:

THE ROLE OF LAWYERS

*

Chapter I

LAWYERS, LITIGATION, AND THE CHOICE OF PROCESS

A. INTRODUCTION

This book is about the processes by which lawyers help resolve the problems and disputes of their clients. Lawyers make choices about process in handling even the most routine cases: in writing a letter suggesting possible settlement options for a divorce case, filing a lawsuit for a personal injury claimant, requesting arbitration under the provisions of a supply contract, filing a request for a waiver of a local zoning restriction, asking a former school board member to mediate a dispute between a parent group and the elementary school principal, or preparing a draft revision of the state's securities laws for the State Bar Association's legislative lobbying effort. This book seeks to give lawyers greater awareness of the process choices they often make without reflection, and to expand their understanding of and ability to use a wide range of available dispute resolution processes.

Every legal case involves two major tasks—determining the substantive law applicable to the facts of the case, and choosing a dispute resolution process that will assure the client fair treatment and a just outcome. Most law school coursework concentrates on how to research, analyze, and apply the substantive law. Yet issues of process may be as important as substantive issues in determining whether the final result for a client is the best attainable. In addition, lawyers have been trained to accept litigation as the standard process for resolving client problems, perhaps including negotiation through the use of court procedures and lawyer contact incidental to litigation management. Several traditional courses, such as civil and criminal procedure and trial advocacy, focus on the litigation process, but they normally do not focus on the strengths and weaknesses of litigation as only one among many processes available to resolve disputes.

During the last few decades, however, increased concern has been expressed by both the professionals who are engaged in litigation and the public at large about our judicial system. Litigation has been criticized as too slow and costly and as failing ultimately to provide a resolution of disputes that is fair and that the parties will respect. Clients have begun to demand attention to process issues, and now expect their lawyers to know about the full range of alternative processes available for dispute resolution. And lawyers, trying to respond to this challenge, have begun to treat process as an important variable in the dispute resolution equation. A lawyer's decision on process is a subject capable of independent study and mastery, and these materials should help the student gain the knowledge necessary to use process effectively.

Our first step is to develop some background understanding of conflict and the lawyer's role in its resolution. The typical lawyer probably gives very little thought to the nature of conflict—for example, how a dispute arises, or how and why a person decides to come to an attorney for help with a particular dispute. The lawyer is likely to take the dispute as a "given," turning immediately to the processing of the dispute in order to arrive at a satisfactory resolution. Yet any human problem will have traversed a long route and gone through a complex transformation before arriving at the lawyer's office. Understanding the social context out of which a dispute has arisen will help the lawyer in the choice and application of the appropriate process. The following excerpt from an article by two social scientists suggests one starting point for this inquiry.

MILLER AND SARAT, GRIEVANCES, CLAIMS, AND DISPUTES: ASSESSING THE ADVERSARY CULTURE

15 Law & Soc'y Rev. 525, 526–27, 531–33, 536–46, 561–64 (1980–81).

One of the most important characteristics of dispute processing is the degree to which it emphasizes or requires adversariness. The comparison of mediation and other techniques is frequently structured as a comparison between conciliation and contention. Criticism is often directed against legal professionals and legal processes for unnecessarily intensifying hostility between disputants. * * * [T]his intensification occurs because lawyers treat disputes through the adversarial forms prescribed by the legal order and thus remove them from their natural context.

Many theoretical statements about dispute processing reflect this concern for its adversarial elements. Theories of dispute transformation examine techniques for "heating up" or "cooling down" disputes. Dispute processing researchers typically favor methods of resolution which minimize adversarial elements; informality and reconciliation are preferred over formality and coercion. Dispute processing research has thus acquired its own ideology, which, apart from its intrinsic merits, further obscures the social context of disputing. It denies, implicitly, that disputes and disputing are normal components of human association.

Disputes begin as *grievances*. A grievance is an individual's belief that he or she (or a group or organization) is entitled to a resource which someone else may grant or deny. People respond to such beliefs in various ways. They may, for example, choose to "lump it" so as to avoid potential conflict. They may redefine the problem and redirect blame elsewhere. They may register a *claim* to communicate their sense of entitlement to the most proximate source of redress, the party perceived to be responsible. As Nader and Todd suggest,

> The grievance or preconflict stage refers to a circumstance or condition which one person . . . perceives to be unjust, and the grounds for resentment or complaint. . . . The grievance situation . . . may erupt into conflict, or it may wane. The path it will take is usually up to the offended party. His grievance may be escalated by confrontation; or escalation may be avoided by curtailing further social interaction. . . .

Consumers, for example, make claims when they ask retailers to repair or replace defective goods. Claims can be rejected, accepted, or they can result in a compromise offer.

If the other party accepts the claim in full and actually delivers the resource in question in a routine manner ("Yes, we'll repair your new car; just bring it in"), there is no dispute. Outright rejection of a claim ("The car was not defective; it broke down because of your misuse") establishes an unambiguous dispute; there are now two (or more) parties with conflicting claims to the same resource. A compromise offer ("We'll supply the parts if you will pay for the labor") is a partial rejection of the claim, which initiates negotiation, however brief, and thus constitutes a dispute. * * * *A dispute exists when a claim based on a grievance is rejected either in whole or in part.* It becomes a civil legal dispute when it involves rights or resources which could be granted or denied by a court.

* * *

The manner and rate at which disputes are generated is sometimes taken as an indicator of societal "health." This view is most characteristic of the work of historians writing about World War II. They presented a picture of American society as a stable balance between conflict and calm, a society in which all disputes were resolved within a framework of consensus. Some may question the validity of that picture as a description of *any* period in American life, but the experience of the last two decades has certainly undermined both the social basis upon which the balance of conflict and calm may have existed and its viability as an ideology or a system of legitimizing beliefs. We increasingly hear the voices of those who perceive and fear the growth of an "adversary society", a society of assertive, aggressive, rights-conscious, litigious people ready and eager to challenge each other and those in authority. Images of our allegedly unprecedented assertiveness, or the ingenious ways which we have found to fight each other, flow through the popular culture, from *New Yorker* cartoons about children threatening to sue their parents for forcing them to drink their milk to palimony suits against celebrities.

There is, of course, another view of contemporary American society, a view which suggests that we are in fact, relatively uncontentious and even passive. Americans are said to be reluctant to admit that their lives are troubled and conditioned to accept circumstances and treatment which are far from ideal. Since our institutions respond slowly, inefficiently, and reluctantly, we learn not to complain, not to pursue our grievances or claim our rights. Even when we do, we find that appropriate institutions do not exist. As our society becomes ever more complex and expansive, it becomes easier to avoid conflict or to ignore it merely by moving on. People unable or unwilling to assert their rights or defend their interests may be easily victimized by self-interested organizations seeking to perpetuate a social and economic status quo. Proponents of this view typically question the adequacy of existing political, social, and economic arrangements to achieve justice.

It is ultimately both an empirical question and a matter of definition as to whether ours is a society of rights consciousness and conflict, or one of acquiescence and equilibrium. Arguments about the level and consequences of conflict in American society, to the extent that they are based on data at all, are often rooted in comparative analyses or cyclical interpretations of history. But there is another approach which might be employed to describe and assess levels of conflict in the United States. Lempert has suggested that the occurrence of particular types of conflict can be measured against a pre-established baseline. The baseline might be a measure of the number of transactions of a particular type, the number which result in injury, or the number which result in grievances and the making of claims. For example, the level of conflict about the quality of medical care might be measured by comparing the quantity of medical service—e.g., visits to doctors—to the amount of conflict generated by such services—e.g., the number of medical malpractice suits. Malpractice suits might also be compared to some measure of medical ineptitude such as rates of unnecessary or unsuccessful surgery. The baseline approach seeks to identify the realization of a social condition—e.g., conflict—against its potential.

* * *

DESCRIBING THE STRUCTURE OF CONFLICT: GRIEVING, CLAIMING, AND DISPUTING

Grieving

Disputes emerge out of grievances. Consequently we look first to the incidence of grievances to establish the baseline potential for disputes. There is, however, a conceptual problem. Grievances are composed of concrete events or circumstances which are relatively objective, but they are also composed of subjective perceptions, definitions, and beliefs that an event or circumstance is unwarranted or inappropriate. Individuals may react differently to the same experience. One buyer of a defective good may find it unacceptable and remediable; another may regard the bad purchase as "inevitable" and "lump it" or write it off to experience. According to our definition the first individual has a grievance; the second does not. Grievance rates reflect both the occurrence of certain events and a willingness by the participants to label those events in a particular way. * * *

Claiming

Given the perception that some event or circumstance is unacceptable and remediable, we can ask how assertive those who experience grievances are in seeking a remedy. Possible responses, as previously mentioned, range from avoidance, through repair without direct confrontation, registering a claim, to a demand for monetary compensation. Unless a claim is made, a dispute cannot occur. Other responses, such as avoidance, may be accompanied by feelings of bitterness or resentment which could lead to later conflict.

* * *

The Incidence of Disputes

When a claim is made, the allegedly offending party may accept responsibility and accede to the demand for redress. If this happens there is no dispute. Claims are made and promptly satisfied. But resistance may be engendered, responsibility denied. Even if responsibility is accepted, unacceptable levels of redress may be offered. Resistance to accepting responsibility or providing redress establishes adversarial interests.

* * *

The Role of Lawyers and Courts

The language of rights and remedies is preeminently the language of law. One might logically ask where, in all of this, the law and legal institutions play a role. There is relatively little empirical work on the role of lawyers and courts in disputing. An assessment of the role of law, legal institutions, and legal services in the development of, or response to, conflict requires us to confront the problem of baselines.

[The authors then analyze the results of a telephone survey of approximately 1000 randomly-selected households in each of five federal judicial districts. In this survey grievances involving less than $1000 were screened out.]

Examining [Figures 1A and 1B], we find that relatively few disputants use a lawyer's services at all. Lawyers were used by less than one-fourth of those engaged in the disputes we studied. There are, however, two significant exceptions to the pattern. The role of lawyers is much more pronounced in post-divorce and tort problems. In the former, the involvement of lawyers is a function of the fact that many of these problems, e.g., adjustment in visitation arrangements or in alimony, *require* court action. In the latter, the contingent fee system facilitates and encourages lawyer use.

Few disputants (11.2 percent) report taking their dispute to court. Excluding post-divorce disputes, where court action is often required, that number is approximately 9 percent. These findings do not mean that courts or lawyers play a trivial role in middle-range disputes. Claims are made, avoided, or processed at least in part according to each party's understanding of its own legal position and that of its opponent; that understanding reflects both the advice that lawyers provide and the rights and remedies which courts have in the past recognized or imposed.

Figure 1A. A Dispute Pyramid: The General Pattern
No. per 1000 Grievances

Court Filings	50
Lawyers	103
Disputes	449
Claims	718
Grievances	1000

Figure 1B. Dispute Pyramids: Three Deviant Patterns
No. per 1000 Grievances

	Tort	Discrimination	Post-Divorce
ourt Filings	38	8	451
wyers	116	29	588
sputes	201	216	765
aims	857	294	879
rievances	1000	1000	1000

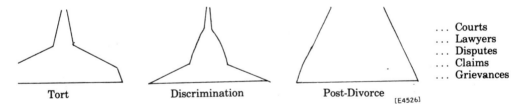

Tort   Discrimination   Post-Divorce

... Courts
... Lawyers
... Disputes
... Claims
... Grievances

[E4526]

Summary

We can visualize the process of dispute generation through the metaphor of a pyramid (see Figure 1A). At the base are grievances, and the width of the pyramid shows the proportions that make the successive transitions to claims, disputes, lawyer use, and litigation. Figure 1B presents three contrasting patterns—the disputing pyramids for torts, post-divorce, and discrimination grievances.

Torts show a clear pattern. Most of those with grievances make claims (85.7 percent), and most claims are not formally resisted (76.5 percent result in immediate agreement). As a result, disputes are relatively rare (23.5 percent of claims). Where they occur, however, lawyers are available, accessible, and are, in fact, often employed (57.9 percent). Moreover, the same can be said for the employment of courts (at least in comparison with other problems). The overall picture is of a remedy system that minimizes formal conflict but uses the courts when necessary in those relatively rare cases in which conflict is unavoidable.

The pattern for discrimination grievances is quite different. Seven of ten grievants make no claim for redress. Those who do are very likely to have their claim resisted, and most claimants receive nothing. Only a little more than one in ten disputants is aided by a lawyer, and only four in a hundred disputes lead to litigation. The impression is one of perceived rights which are rarely fully asserted. When they are, they are strongly resisted and pursued without much assistance from lawyers or courts. Of course, we do not know how many of these or any other grievances would be found meritorious in a court of law. Nonetheless, as perceived grievances, they are a source of underlying tension and potential social conflict.

Post-divorce problems engender high rates of grievances, claims, and disputes, and are characterized by frequent use of lawyers and courts. As a result, almost half of all grievances lead to court involvement. While the court's activity in many, possibly most, of these cases is more administrative than adjudicative, this is, at least formally, the most disputatious and litigious grievance type we have measured.

Dispute pyramids could be drawn for the other types of problems, but they would all be quite similar: high rates of claims (80 to 95 percent of grievances), high rates of disputes (75 to 85 percent of claims), fairly low proportions using a lawyer (10 to 20 percent of disputants), and low litigation rates (3 to 5 percent of disputants). Indeed, the most striking finding in these descriptive data is again the general uniformity of rates at each stage of the disputing process across very different types of middle-range grievances.

* * *

We have found that, when measured against a baseline of perceived injustices or grievances, disputing is fairly common. But we are in no position, absent historical or comparative data, to determine just how substantial or significant it is. Our own belief is that where there are grievances there ought to be claims, and that where there are claims conflict is not necessarily an undesirable or unhealthy result. Those who fear conflict or who advocate acquiescence in the face of grievances fear threats to the social status quo. They bear a substantial burden in showing how people benefit from lumping or enduring injurious experiences or the denial of rights or how the status quo is served in the longer run as frustrations increase and legitimacy decreases. Indeed, it may be that the most significant aspect of our data, at least to those interested in arguments about the adversary culture, is the relatively low grievance rate for most of the transactions or relationships which we studied. Either those transactions are routinely

efficient and satisfactory or people are reluctant to perceive or acknowledge trouble as it occurs. The incidence of social conflict ultimately
hinges both on the rates at which injurious experiences are inflicted
upon people and on what people define as acceptable performance of
obligations or tolerate as acceptable conditions of life. The fact that
almost 60 percent of our respondents report no recent middle-range
grievance indicates a relatively low level of "injury" and/or a relatively
high level of satisfaction or acquiescence.

Levels of "real" and perceived injuries, and the way people respond
to them, are not self-generating. Economic, social, and political forces
shape the context in which problems are perceived and conflicts generated, just as they affect the kind and amount of problems which occur.
Thus we found, for example, that grievance rates were affected not only
by the risk factors of particular transactions, statuses, and relationships, but also by educational levels and legal contacts. Particular
concerns and not others come to be seen as worthwhile; particular
responses and not others are legitimated; and those who declare
trouble or who participate in conflict are differentially rewarded or
stigmatized.

We wonder whether a survey of discrimination problems conducted
twenty or thirty years ago would have found, as we did, that female-
headed households reported a higher incidence of such problems or that
blacks with such grievances were more likely to make a claim for
redress. Not only have social and economic changes increased the
number of women at risk of discrimination in employment or housing,
but concomitant political and cultural changes have brought both
increased sensitivity to and legislative condemnation of such discrimination. We have no basis on which to speculate about changes, if any,
in blacks' "sensitivity" to racial discrimination, but social and political
developments clearly have both reflected and enhanced the willingness
and ability of blacks to resist such behavior.

Sex discrimination is a classic example of a movement from un-
perceived injurious experiences (unPIES) to perceived injurious experiences (PIES), which Felstiner *et al.* argue lies at the heart of the
process through which new grievances emerge and new types of disputes arise. With each newly recognized injurious experience comes a
strengthened or reinforced sense of harm and entitlement, both of
which prepare the way for higher rates of grievances and conflict.
Such cultural labeling is often matched by the use of official declarations, particularly the declaration of legal rights, as a device to regulate
grievance perception and the response to grievances. The political
forces that lead to declaration of legal rights may also result in the
establishment of specialized remedy systems. Such systems may arise
from other sources as well, such as an economic incentive to share
risks. In any case, it is possible that the balance of rights declared and
remedies provided is important in cueing responses to middle-range
problems.

Problems differ in terms of the availability and kind of *institutionalization of remedy systems*. By institutionalization of remedy systems we mean the extent to which there are well-known, regularized, readily available mechanisms, techniques, or procedures for dealing with a problem. Take, for example, automobile accident and discrimination problems. The remedy system for auto accidents is highly institutionalized. There are routinized, well-known, and widely available procedures for dealing with such problems. The problem itself is one which has been recognized and acknowledged in the society for a long time and the principles—at least, the legal principles—involved are relatively settled. The result is a high claim rate, a low dispute rate, and considerable success for claimants.

The same cannot be said for discrimination problems. Neither a clear and widely accepted definition of discriminatory behavior which creates an entitlement to redress nor notions about appropriate kinds of redress have yet evolved. Existing legislated definitions are not well understood by the public, and those definitions are themselves in flux. Furthermore, remedy systems are less well developed and certainly less accessible. One simply doesn't pick up the phone and call one's insurance agent about a discrimination problem, and the principles governing redress are both rather unsettled and highly controversial. Under these circumstances, it is not surprising that, while quite a few households report some discrimination grievance, only three in ten of these asked for any redress of their grievance.

[The authors had earlier suggested other possible explanations for the low level of "claiming" for discrimination grievances:

Perhaps a lack of assertiveness has more to do with the substance of the problem itself. In discrimination situations it seems easier for those who believe that they have been unfairly denied a job or home just to keep on looking. Securing a job or home is likely to be much more pressing and important than filing a claim for something which is made undesirable by the very act that generates the grievance. "I need a job, and who would want to work there anyway" would not be an inexplicable response. * * *

Furthermore, there may be some stigma attached to the grievance itself or to the act of assertion. Victims, for example, may blame themselves for the unfair treatment. In discrimination grievances, especially, victory may turn into defeat. Those who are assertive, even if vindicated, are branded as troublemakers. Furthermore, grievants may be uncertain about the fit between their own perceptions and definitions of grievances and those embodied in statutes or otherwise recognized in their community. Indeed, both the law and popular expectations in this area of relatively new rights appear unsettled. Many who experience discrimination problems are, as a result, uncertain whether their grievance constitutes a sustainable claim.]

The institutionalization of remedies affects grievance perception, claiming, and disputing in two ways: first, by legitimizing action, and second, by shaping the objective probabilities of success should action be taken. The institutionalization of remedies alone suggests that the frequency and importance of a problem, as well as the appropriateness of action taken in response to it, is recognized. Where remedies are institutionalized, the probability of successful action can be more accurately assessed and prospective action thereby more clearly shaped and considered. Higher levels of institutionalization, everything else being equal, would be associated with higher rates of grievance perception and claiming, lower rates of disputes, and higher rates of success in recovery for meritorious claims.

Disputing is minimized where remedies are most and least institutionalized. Conflict can be avoided where automatic remedies are provided for felt grievances or where the demand for redress is discouraged by making it uncertain and hard to obtain. It is easier, on the whole, for societies to declare rights than to provide remedies; indeed, the development of remedies almost inevitably lags substantially behind the recognition of rights. The inability to vindicate rights discourages their expression and thus helps avoid a precondition for overtly adversarial relations. At the same time, of course, the gap between rights and remedies contributes to feelings of frustration and alienation which breed adversity between individuals and institutions. It is this tension which drives the development of remedy systems. Where rights are not realized or realizable over a long period of time and among a substantial portion of the population, where raised expectations are disappointed, interpersonal conflict is discouraged at the price of social and political strain. The balance of rights recognized and remedies provided is, in our view, important to an understanding of the generation of disputes and adversarial behavior.

Notes and Questions

(1) Whether an individual even perceives that he has been "injured" may depend on his background and circumstances. A cancer victim previously exposed to asbestos may fail to perceive that he is ill; a consumer may fail to appreciate that a product is dangerous or not working as it is intended to. And among those experiences which *are* perceived as "injurious" "some may be seen as deserved punishment, some as the result of assumed risk or fickle fate"; only a limited number will be seen as a violation of some right or entitlement for which another person is responsible (that is, the subject of a "grievance"):

[C]haracterization of an event as a grievance will depend on the cognitive repertoire with which society supplies the injured person and his idiosyncratic adaptation of it. He may, for example, be liberally supplied with ideological lenses to focus blame or to diffuse it. * * *

The perception of grievances requires cognitive resources. Thus Best and Andreasen found that both higher income and white households perceive more problems with the goods they buy and complain more both to sellers and to third parties than do poor or black households. It seems unlikely that this reflects differences in the quality of goods purchased. Similarly, Curran reports that better educated respondents experience more problems of infringement of their constitutional rights.

Galanter, Reading the Landscape of Disputes: What we Know and Don't Know (And Think We Know) About Our Allegedly Contentious and Litigious Society, 31 U.C.L.A. L.Rev. 4, 13–14 (1983). See also Best & Andreasen, Consumer Response to Unsatisfactory Purchases: A Survey of Perceiving Defects, Voicing Complaints, and Obtaining Redress, 11 Law & Soc'y Rev. 701 (1977); Felstiner, Abel, & Sarat, The Emergence and Transformation of Disputes: Naming, Blaming, Claiming . . ., 15 Law & Soc'y Rev. 631 (1980–81).

Finally, even perceived grievances may not become the subject of complaints or claims. Despite much talk about our "litigious" society, many Americans seem reluctant to voice grievances. To do so, after all, may require them to acknowledge—both to themselves and to others—that they have been bettered by others or that they have allowed themselves to be victimized.

Should the legal profession play any role in this process by which grievances and claims are generated? How does the relationship between "sensitivity" to grievances and disputes affect a lawyer's practice? His relationship with the client?

(2) The Miller and Sarat data suggest that lawyers play a less significant role in processing disputes than is commonly thought. Only 10% of all grievances, or a little under 25% of all disputes, are brought to the lawyer's office. The lawyer does play a larger role in the more traditional areas of tort law and post-divorce conflict. But even in tort cases, over 42% of the injured persons do *not* hire lawyers. Why does this sizable minority choose not to seek legal help? Are lawyers not providing the kind of service that the disputants want or think they need? Do disputants have an effective alternative?

(3) Miller and Sarat specifically excluded the degree of injury and intensity of the dispute as variables for their study. Aren't these important to understanding the lawyer's role? Is it reasonable to suggest that the more intense the dispute and the greater the degree of injury, the more likely it is that an injured party will hire a lawyer to help resolve it?

(4) Miller and Sarat state: "Claims are made, avoided, or processed at least in part according to each party's understanding of its own legal position and that of its opponent; that understanding reflects both the advice that lawyers provide and the rights and remedies which courts have in the past recognized or imposed." The notion that dispute resolution may take place "in the shadow of the law" is central to the

lawyer's role and is the subject of a detailed discussion in Chapter II.
The authors imply, however, that the advice of lawyers may in some
way be different from the rights and remedies expressed by courts.
Why might this be true? It has been suggested that lawyers in
consumer disputes often see their major role to be that of "gatekeepers"
to the legal system: The individual client may be "cooled out"—
discouraged from pressing claims that the lawyer feels may not be in
the client's best interests to pursue, or that the lawyer *himself* for one
reason or another would rather not pursue. See Macaulay, Lawyers
and Consumer Protection Laws, 14 Law & Soc'y Rev. 115 (1979).

Problem: Sheridan v. Hopewell College [1]

You are practicing law in a large Houston firm. On several
occasions in the past you have handled some litigation on behalf of your
alma mater, Hopewell College. Hopewell is a small, well-regarded
liberal arts college located in the small, North Texas town of Mt.
Pleasant. The school was founded by the Lutheran Church in 1897 and
is now coeducational (women were admitted for the first time in 1959).

You have just received a copy of a complaint in a lawsuit filed
against the College by a former instructor in its Physical Education
Department, Mary Kate Sheridan. The complaint alleges discrimination on the basis of sex in violation of Title VII of the Civil Rights Act
of 1964, and names Hopewell, the College's President, and various other
school officials as defendants. Hopewell's "in house counsel" has very
little trial experience and has been used mostly for routine legal
problems. Your firm has therefore been asked to handle the defense of
this suit.

After reviewing the complaint, you discussed the matter briefly
with the College's counsel and have been able to obtain a certain
amount of background information about the case. You gather that
Sheridan was hired as an instructor in the Phys. Ed. Department eight
years ago; she taught Modern Dance and Tap Dance, and was apparently a popular teacher. In her fifth and sixth years the Department
put her name forward for promotion to Assistant Professor; despite
favorable recommendations by the Faculty Personnel Committee, the
President and the College Board of Trustees refused to promote her.
Again the following year the Department recommended her for both
promotion and tenure; again the FPC voted (unanimously) to approve
the recommendation, and again the President and the Board refused.
Last spring she was given a "terminal" contract for the current school
year. (An "up or out" decision is required after seven years of teaching
under the rules of both Hopewell and the American Association of

1. This problem draws on Lanoue &
Lee, Academics in Court: The Consequences of Faculty Discrimination Litigation (1987). See also Kunda v. Muhlenberg
College, 621 F.2d 532 (3d Cir.1980); McMillen, "The Residue from Academics' Lawsuits: Often Anguish for Everyone Involved," Chronicle of Higher Education,
April 1, 1987, p. 1; McMillen, "Colleges
Are Trying New Ways to Settle Campus
Grievances," Chronicle of Higher Education, May 6, 1987, p. 17.

University Professors.) Sheridan appealed to the elected "Faculty Board of Appeals," which unanimously voted that she be given tenure; this recommendation also was rejected. She filed suit against the College shortly after receiving a "right to sue" letter from the Equal Employment Opportunity Commission.

Ms. Sheridan received a Bachelors' Degree from the University of Texas 17 years ago, but has no higher degree. The Hopewell "faculty handbook" requires that before receiving tenure, a faculty member must hold a "terminal degree" (in Physical Education, this is a master's) or its "scholarly equivalent." At Hopewell this requirement has traditionally been honored in the breach (the head of the Phys. Ed. Department, a full professor, has only a bachelor's degree). However, the appointment six years ago of President Davies—who came to the job with a firm commitment to "upgrade the quality of the faculty"— has led to the degree requirement being rigorously enforced.

Sheridan's complaint asks for $450,000 in compensatory and punitive damages, attorneys' fees, and reinstatement to her job with the rank of Associate Professor with tenure.

President Davies is concerned. The College has no liability insurance that will cover this kind of discrimination claim. In addition, the negative publicity arising from a suit could be particularly damaging to a closely-knit school that depends heavily on private financial support. Davies assures you that this is the first such complaint that has ever been made against the College. However, he has heard disquieting stories about the impact of discrimination suits on other educational institutions—in terms of the burden of litigation on the time and energy of school officials, of the divisiveness and harm to institutional morale when one colleague is pitted against another, and of the difficulty thereafter in recruiting talented new faculty.

At the same time, of course, the financial, social, and career costs that such suits impose on plaintiffs can also be traumatic. You understand, by the way, that Sheridan would very much like to stay at Hopewell. She was born and raised in Mt. Pleasant, and her two young children are now in the local public schools. She continues to perform in her own physical fitness program that she developed some years ago and that is shown twice a week on the local television station. You believe that this show, along with sporadic employment as a substitute high-school teacher and manager of a health spa, have been her only sources of income following her divorce.

Davies has asked your firm for a memorandum on the legal issues raised by Sheridan's claim. He has also asked you for advice as to what process should be used to resolve the problem in the best interests of the college. What do you tell him?

Your first reaction is to focus on the *facts* relevant to the merits of the claim: You may want to ask, for example, whether Sheridan's failure to achieve promotion or tenure might be due to reasons other than discrimination—such as inadequate performance as an instructor.

The faculty "Board of Appeal" (FBA) did note that it had "uncovered no statement about Mary Kate's contribution to the College that was less than enthusiastic." Of course, adverse tenure decisions may frequently be based on any number of other considerations—including the College's future plans for the department, the number of tenured faculty already in the department, and the financial constraints both on the department and the College as a whole. (Last year the Phys. Ed Department at Hopewell was one of the biggest departments in the College, with 9 tenured and 3 untenured faculty members).

You would certainly also want to inquire into the College's practices with respect to promotion and tenure of *male* faculty. It appears that Davies has been adamant about uniformly requiring a "terminal" degree for tenure candidates, and that over the past five years no faculty member at Hopewell has been given tenure without such a degree. However, Sheridan claimed before the FBA that she had never been warned that any master's degree requirement would be insisted on in her case, although male candidates had been advised of the requirement and encouraged to make progress towards the higher degree. You also understand that two male instructors who did not have a master's were promoted to Assistant Professor without tenure four years ago, even though the faculty handbook states that a master's is "normally" required even for promotion to that rank.

At the same time you will need to refresh your memory concerning the relevant *law* invoked in the complaint: What elements does the plaintiff have to establish to make a prima facie case under Title VII? What standards apply in such a case to help determine whether the College is liable? Where are the burdens of proof and of producing evidence? What remedies do courts impose for violations of Title VII?

In addition to these fact and law issues, you are concerned with the *process* by which you will help Hopewell resolve this problem. You will probably think of the litigation process first—perhaps because you are more familiar with litigation than with any other process thanks to your law school training, and also, of course, because the opposing lawyer has already announced his intention to use the court system. But is litigation an inevitable process? Is it the best process for the College? What other processes might be useful? How do you evaluate and compare processes in terms of the best interests of the client? Do you have to accept the opposing lawyer's choice of litigation, or can you choose a different process that might be better suited to your client?

Litigation is far from being the only process available in a situation like this. The negotiation process is one obvious possibility. By filing a suit, Sheridan's lawyer has certainly gotten the College's attention: But he has not necessarily foreclosed the opportunity for immediate negotiation; even though the lawsuit has been filed, you will have many opportunities to negotiate a voluntary settlement without using the formal discovery procedures of the court or going to trial. Negotiation and litigation are complementary processes, and their interaction can help assure a desirable outcome. Although lawyers are expected to understand and use the negotiation process, they usually have very little formal instruction in this part of their work; there will be wide variations in the skill which different lawyers bring to bear in negotiation and the energy with which they pursue a negotiated settlement. Chapter II of this book provides a basic introduction to the negotiation process for the lawyer.

You might also recognize mediation or arbitration as other alternative processes that might be appropriate in the Sheridan case. Either of these processes might bring in third persons who have some special familiarity with the particular culture and problems of higher education, and either would insure some measure of privacy while the case was being resolved. However, you are not entirely clear how such suitable persons might be found, or what procedure they might use for the resolution of the dispute. And you have to recognize that both the College and Ms. Sheridan might want, or need, an authoritative judicial decision that they are in the "right." The materials in Chapters III and IV describe mediation and arbitration, and analyze the advantages and disadvantages and potential usefulness of these processes for lawyers. And this hardly exhausts the possibilities for resolving this dispute. There are many variants and "hybrid" processes as well, which would probably never be considered in this situation—not because they are necessarily inappropriate but because the typical lawyer is not trained to think about them.

What is clear, in any event, is that the choice of the process to use will have to be given sustained attention. As a starting point, consider this observation of Professor Auerbach:

> Whether disputants ignore their differences, negotiate, submit to mediation or arbitration, or retain lawyers to litigate is a matter of significant choice. How people dispute is, after all, a function of how (and whether) they relate. In relationships that are intimate, caring, and mutual, disputants will behave quite differently from their counterparts who are strangers or competitors. Selfishness and aggression are not merely functions of individual personality; they are socially sanctioned—or discouraged. So is the decision to define a disputant as an adversary, and to struggle until there is a clear winner and loser; or, alternatively, to resolve conflict in a way that will preserve, rather than destroy, a relationship. In some cultures, the patterns of interaction suggest that those who participate in litigation may be psychologically deviant. Among Scandinavian fishermen and the Zapotec of Mexico, in Bavarian villages and certain African tribes, among the Sinai Bedouin and in Israeli *kibbutzim* * * *, the importance of enduring relations has made peace, harmony, and mediation preferable to conflict, victory, and litigation. But in the United States, a nation of competitive individuals and strangers, litigation is encouraged; here, the bur-

den of psychological deviance falls upon those who find adversary relations to be a destructive form of human behavior.[2]

B. COURTS AND THE LITIGATION PROCESS

Lawyers and courts are closely linked in our society. For óne thing, the legal profession has a monopoly on advocacy within the judicial system; court procedures, evidentiary rules, and the demands of the substantive law are complex, requiring intensive training and licensing. Images and accounts in the press and the popular culture reflect and reinforce this close connection between lawyers and courts. And law schools contribute further to making this connection seem inevitable through a process of socialization beginning with the traditional first-year curriculum and continuing through many advanced courses and extracurricular programs. The dominance of the "casebook" and the hallowed "case method," while reflecting the importance of court decisions within the common law system, conveys the impression that a court is the inevitable forum for resolving disputes between individuals.

The monopoly the lawyer enjoys in the litigation process may, however, distort his understanding of the spectrum of processes available to resolve client problems. Most professionals are naturally inclined to use the process for which they hold exclusive control, regardless of foreseeable outcome or relative cost/benefit figures. To paraphrase psychologist Abraham Maslow, if the primary tool you have is a hammer, you tend to see every problem as a nail!

As a result, a "litigation standard" is created for the legal profession. A lawyer is likely to assume that because a client has brought a dispute or a problem to him, the client has selected litigation as the preferred dispute-resolving process. And a client is not surprised when a lawyer recommends litigation, because the client's decision to seek legal counsel was based at least in part on awareness of the intimate connection between the profession and the court system. Under the litigation standard, the lawyer's task is to mold the client's dispute to the procedural requirements and measures for relief accepted by the courts.

For the lawyer, therefore, the first place to start in the study of process is with litigation. Only after realizing the limitations as well as the advantages of taking a case to court can the lawyer begin to appreciate the roles that negotiation, mediation, arbitration, and the administrative and legislative processes play in a healthy law practice.

2. Auerbach, Justice Without Law? 7–
8 (1983).

1. The Dimensions of Litigation

AUERBACH, JUSTICE WITHOUT LAW?
10, 12–13 (1983).

Americans prefer to stand apart, separated from their ancestors, contemporaries, and descendents. Individualism means freedom— above all, the freedom to compete, acquire, possess, and bequeath. It is precisely this freedom that our legal system so carefully cultivates and protects. In a society where the dominant ethic is competitive individualism, regulated by the loose ground rules of the Darwinian struggle (with special protection reserved for crippled corporate giants), social cohesion is an enduring problem. Even as litigiousness expresses, and accentuates, the pursuit of individual advantage, the rule of law helps to hold such a fractured society together. At the least (usually it is also the most), people can agree upon how they will disagree. In a restless, mobile society of strangers, the staple scene of Western movies is perpetually reenacted: an American, at the first sign of danger, reaches for his (hired) gun and files a lawsuit. Yet contradictions abound. Our individualistic society encourages the assertion of legal rights as an entitlement of citizenship, but distributes them according to the ability to pay. Conflict is channeled into adversary proceedings with two combatants in every legal ring; but beyond the implicit assumption that every fight and any winner is good for society, the social good is ignored. Litigation is the all-purpose remedy that American society provides to its aggrieved members. But as rights are asserted, combat is encouraged; as the rule of law binds society, legal contentiousness increases social fragmentation.

* * *

The consuming American reverence for legal symbols and institutions slights the manifold ways in which law not only reinforces, but imposes, an atomistic, combative vision of reality. "Sue Thy Neighbor" is the appropriate modern American inversion of the Biblical admonition. So a newspaper photograph shows an angry woman, her face contorted with rage, who points menacingly at a cowering man, whose hands are raised in retreat and surrender. A judge looks on impassively, an American flag at his side. "If thy neighbor offend thee," the caption reads, "don't turn the other cheek. Slap him with a summons. And take him to Small Claims Court." It is only a blurb for a television special report, but the line between soap opera and reality is hopelessly blurred. Viewers are promised "a free course in self-defense," evidently a requirement for life among neighbors. (With neighbors like these, of course, enemies are superfluous.) Armed with the sword of litigation, Americans can wage ceaseless warfare against each other—and themselves.

Notes and Questions

(1) Does Auerbach's image of a rights-obsessed, combative, litigious American society ring true to you? Or does it strike you as something of a caricature? Does the picture he draws seem consistent with the data collected by Miller and Sarat on disputing patterns in America?

(2) The rhetoric of the preceding excerpt may obscure one crucial fact: Even where disputants do have recourse to the courts, "full-blown" adjudication remains extremely rare. In the early 1980s the Civil Litigation Research Project (CLRP), sponsored jointly by the U.S. Department of Justice and the University of Wisconsin, compiled data about civil litigation in five federal judicial districts. The following excerpt is based on data published in the Project's Final Report.

TRUBEK, SARAT, FELSTINER, KRITZER & GROSSMAN THE COSTS OF ORDINARY LITIGATION

31 U.C.L.A. L.Rev. 72, 89, 122 (1983).

What happens in ordinary litigation? There is a popular image that litigation involves extensive pretrial activity and protracted trials. Our data suggest the contrary. Trials are rare, pretrial activity modest, and most cases terminate through settlement negotiations.

Less than 8% of the cases in our sample went to trial. In another 22.5%, the judge dismissed the complaint or rendered judgment on the merits without a trial. The most frequent mode of termination is voluntary agreement between the parties, which occurred in over 50% of the cases. Our data suggest civil judges and juries provide final, authoritative third party dispute processing in less than a third of the cases. More often, the courts serve as the background for bargaining between the parties. Bargaining occurs "in the shadow of the law," but is conducted primarily, if not exclusively, by the parties and their lawyers.

* * *

One of the most striking aspects of our study of litigation was that bargaining and settlement are the prevalent and, for plaintiffs, perhaps the most cost-effective activity that occurs when cases are filed. This will come as no surprise to litigators, but it is remarkable how seldom this fact is taken into account in discussions of the litigation crisis, costs of litigation, and the need for "alternatives to litigation."

Much of the literature advocating alternatives to litigation naively assumes that what occurs in courts is adjudication, in the classical sense. Since "adjudication" by definition uses judicial time heavily, the literature deduces that increased litigation will increase court budgets dramatically. Since adjudication presents an imposed, rather than a bargained or mediated solution, many observers believe it to be ineffective for the resolution of certain kinds of disputes. Finally, if adjudication is expensive and intrusive, then what is needed, so it is argued, are cheaper, more flexible "alternatives." But if in the world of ordinary litigation judges rarely reach formal decisions on the merits, the parties negotiate, albeit "in the shadow of the law," judges actively intervene to encourage settlement, and settlement is the rule, not the exception, then perhaps the whole reform debate falls wide of the mark. Perhaps the right approach is not to reach for wholly new institutional alternatives to a hypothetical process of adjudication, but to understand the non-adjudicative dimensions of litigation, to see how and why they work, and to seek to make this dimension of the litigation process even more central and effective.

Notes and Questions

(1) The CLRP data also suggest that even where a lawsuit has been filed, the lawyers involved are likely to spend as much or more time in negotiation than in court-related activities. When asked how they allocated their time in the cases being studied, lawyers reported spending 15% of their time on "settlement discussions." In addition, we may assume that a substantial proportion of their time nominally devoted to other activities, such as conferring with the client (16%), investigating the facts (12.8%), and engaging in legal research (10.1%), must have been directly aimed at reaching a settlement.

This result underscores even further the complementary relationship between litigation and negotiation, and may suggest a need to revise our conceptual framework of litigation. Filing suit may be seen primarily as a rather pointed way of opening negotiations. It is one way to bring the other party to the bargaining table and one card to be played in the bargaining game. The CLRP study suggests that just as negotiation is an integral part of the dynamic of the litigation process, conversely, litigation may be just one stage—one strategic move—in the ongoing process of negotiation. Professor Marc Galanter has coined the term "litigotiation" to refer to this "single process of disputing in the vicinity of official tribunals"—"the strategic pursuit of a settlement through mobilizing the court process." Galanter, Worlds of Deals: Using Negotiation to Teach about Legal Process, 34 J.Legal Educ. 168 (1984).

(2) A careful study of the much-publicized "litigation explosion" acknowledges that there has been an increase over the last century in the per capita filings of civil cases in both state and federal courts. However, "there is no evidence to suggest an increase in the portion of cases that runs the whole course. ＊ ＊ ＊ [T]he percentage of cases reaching trial has diminished." On the other hand, for the small minority of cases that *do* run the full course, adjudication is likely to be "more protracted, more elaborate, more exhaustive, and more expensive." Galanter, Reading the Landscape of Disputes: What We Know and Don't Know (And Think We Know) About Our Allegedly Contentious and Litigious Society, 31 U.C.L.A. L.Rev. 4, 43–44 (1983). Perhaps of even greater interest is a comparison of American litigation rates

with rates in other countries. The evidence suggests that the rate at which Americans use the civil courts "is in the same range as England, Ontario, Australia, Denmark, [and] New Zealand," although far higher than in Japan, Spain, and Italy. Id. at 55. The inclusion of Spain and Italy—societies that are not usually considered models of harmony and lack of contentiousness—may suggest the danger of facile "cultural" generalizations about litigation patterns.

(3) A word about terminology: The words "adjudication" and "litigation" are often casually used as if they were interchangeable, and you may see examples of this confusion in material quoted throughout this book. "Adjudication" refers to the process by which final, authoritative decisions are rendered by a neutral third party who enters the controversy without previous knowledge of the dispute. The third party's solution may, if necessary, be enforced by recourse to governmental sanctions; he may (but need not) have the authority to resolve the dispute according to a set of objective norms and following an elaborate procedure for the presentation of arguments and proof. In this sense, arbitration—a private process that we will discuss in detail in Chapter IV—shares with the official court system some of the characteristics of dispute settlement through "adjudication." In "litigation," by contrast, the parties invoke the official court mechanism; as we have already seen, however, "litigation" need not lead to any final third-party decision. The dominance of negotiation and settlement has focused attention on what Trubek calls the "non-adjudicative dimensions of litigation." In addition, a number of mechanisms which aim at resolving disputes short of trial—such as the mini-trial, court-administered arbitration, or the summary jury trial—are closely connected to and may be considered part of the litigation process. These mechanisms are discussed in Chapter V.

2. The Limits of the Judicial Process

The high prestige and symbolic importance that Americans attach to the formal court system have never been incompatible with an intense awareness of the limitations and inadequacies of the litigation process. In 1850 Abraham Lincoln wrote in notes for a law lecture, "Discourage litigation. Persuade your neighbors to compromise whenever you can. Point out to them how the nominal winner is often a real loser—in fees, expenses, in waste of time."

Recent attention to the shortcomings of litigation also begins with complaints about the frequent delay and expense of legal proceedings, as does this excerpt from a speech by Judge Jon Newman of the Second Circuit:

Whether we have too many cases or too few, or even, miraculously, precisely the right number, there can be little doubt that the system is not working very well. Too many cases take too much time to be resolved and impose too much cost upon litigants and taxpayers alike. No one should have to wait five years for a case to come to trial, but many litigants in this country face this reality. Legal expenses should not exceed damage awards, yet in the asbestos litigation morass, for example, those expenses total $1.56 for every $1 provided to a victim. If long delays and high litigation costs were aberrational, systemic change could safely be avoided. But we know the problem is more serious. Even if the modern defenders of our current litigation level are right, systemwide averages should not obscure the long delays and high costs imposed upon hundreds or thousands who use or participate in the litigation process and the losses endured by those who are deterred from seeking redress in court.[3]

Moreover, the impact of delay and expense in litigation is not equally allocated. In a personal injury case, delay before trial will affect a plaintiff with mounting medical bills and without substantial resources far more than it will affect the defendant. And particularly where legal services are not available on a contingent fee basis, the costs of litigation may have made the courts inaccessible to large sections of the poor and middle class. As President Derek Bok of Harvard has commented, "There is far too much law for those who can afford it and far too little for those who cannot." [4] How are these factors of delay and expense likely to affect Mary Kate Sheridan and Hopewell College, respectively, in the dispute between them?

Notes and Questions

(1) Earlier we discussed the high rate of settlement in litigation. Is it reasonable to assume that the substantial commitment in time and money required for trial contributes to this settlement rate? Might this indicate that settlement is not always an unmitigated virtue?

(2) The CLRP study suggests that the typical lawsuit

is a "paying" proposition for the parties. The average plaintiff will recover some portion of the amount claimed, and the amount recovered will significantly exceed the money and the value of time spent on the case. Even the defendants can be said to have "gained" from the litigation, at least in the sense that their litigation expenditures are less than the amount by which plaintiff's claim was reduced during litigation.

However, while it may be true that litigation typically "pays" in the sense of yielding net monetary benefits, the study left open the question whether "these gains are wiped out by negative non-monetary

---

3. Newman, Rethinking Fairness: Perspectives on the Litigation Process, 94 Yale L.J. 1643, 1644–45 (1985).

Record of the Ass'n of the Bar of the City of New York 12, 13 (1983).

4. Bok, Law and its Discontents: A Critical Look At Our Legal System, 38

features of the litigation experience." Trubek et al., 31 U.C.L.A. L. Rev. at 84.

———

The delay and expense associated with litigation are largely a function of the limited resources that we are willing to allocate to the judiciary, and of our highly stylized and structured trial procedure. There are other shortcomings of the judicial process, however, which may be less contingent and more fundamental.

In resolving a dispute a court is likely to rely on the use of objective, abstract "rules." Not even the most conscientious fact-finder can come away from a trial with more than the most limited, partial view of any given situation; out of the complexity and messiness of a dispute, out of an infinite variety of elements, the court will select just what seems relevant to enable it to place the dispute into one of several pre-existing "categories" (for example, "this is an action based on anticipatory repudiation of an executory contract"). The appropriate rule to govern the category is then neatly applied. Courts will only rarely be willing to use more person-oriented norms of conduct. Only exceptionally, for example, will a court feel able to consider (at least openly) the personal characteristics of the disputants, the human texture of their relationship, what may be in their long-term interest, or what they themselves may perceive as critical to their own dispute. In this process, the disputants themselves participate only secondarily. The lawyers and judge are the principal actors; the parties themselves speak and act only within court-imposed restrictions.

One consequence is that the court's solution may not be particularly well-adapted to the parties' needs. It is certainly not likely to be as appropriate or efficient as something that the parties familiar with the situation might have worked out for themselves. A related point is that the range of remedies available to a court is traditionally limited. A court will reduce most claims to the payment of money or the transfer of goods; it necessarily avoids person- or relationship-oriented relief. It may not, for example, call for an apology, expression of regret, or acknowledgment of fault, although this might be the relief that would most satisfy a hurt or angry plaintiff. "Claims for personal injury are treated as if the issue is how to put a dollar price on pain and suffering, while claims essentially based on insult and psychic hurt are not dealt with well, if they are recognized at all."[5] Nor, in a commercial dispute, is a court in any position to try to "salvage" the deal by calling for the restructuring or renegotiation of the transaction for the future.

5. Wagatsuma & Rosett, The Implications of Apology: Law and Culture in Japan and the United States, 20 Law & Soc'y Rev. 461, 494 (1986); see also Note, Heal-ing Angry Wounds: The Role of Apology and Mediation in Disputes Between Physicians and Patients, 1987 J. of Dispute Res. 111.

In addition, a court's decision is "binary" in character:

[T]he "verdict of the court has an either/or character; the decision is based upon a single, definite conception of what has actually taken place and upon a single interpretation of the legal norms." This implies that adjudication operates largely in terms of black and white: This is the rule, that is not; this rule is superior to or more compelling than that one and therefore the latter is overridden; these facts are more probably correct, those are less probably, and therefore the latter are rejected; this disputant is in the right, the other is in the wrong.[6]

The result is not only to limit the court's creativity in the matter of remedies. Often, the "either/or" nature of adjudication may also polarize the parties and drive them still further apart. The dynamic of litigation brings with it a need for self-justification and for the strategic escalation of struggle; being caught up in the process is likely to be an intense, emotionally charged experience which can generate considerable antagonism. The parties may finally lose sight altogether of the problem that gave rise to the dispute in the first place. Nor is it only the behavior and attitude of the disputants that may be affected; as the following excerpt suggests, the process may affect their representatives as well.

BRAZIL, THE ATTORNEY AS VICTIM: TOWARDS MORE CANDOR ABOUT THE PSYCHOLOGICAL PRICE TAG OF LITIGATION PRACTICE

3 J. of the Legal Profession 107, 109–10, 114–117 (1978–79).

Some form of manipulation is a very real component of the professional lives of most litigators every day. The targets of the litigator's manipulatory efforts include people, data, documents, precedents, institutions—virtually everything that can be moved to serve some purpose. The potential human subjects of the litigator's manipulations are almost countless: clients, witnesses, opposing counsel, judges, clerks, jurors, expert consultants, court reporters, even colleagues. A few examples of lawyers manipulating other people will help flesh out this abstraction.

* * *

It is commonly believed by many litigators that to simply turn over all the relevant data to a consultant expert is to flirt with disaster: namely, the possibility that your expert will reach a negative conclusion about the role of your client. To reduce the chances of such an eventuality, many litigators carefully control the flow of information to their consultants. They first forward the data that would support a positive conclusion. Their hope is that the expert will form a positive opinion, will identify with the attorney's client, and will develop an ego

---

6. Gulliver, Disputes and Negotiations: A Cross–Cultural Perspective 13 (1979).

investment in the positive conclusion that the attorney wants reached. Thereafter, the attorney may feed the expert some negative data about the client's conduct in order to prepare the expert to withstand cross-examination. By the time the expert receives the bulk of the negative information (at least so goes the litigator's theory of manipulation), he has so heavily identified with the client's position and has invested so much of his own professional ego in his positive opinion that all his impulses are in the direction of defending rather than reevaluating that opinion. Thus the lawyer hopes to capitalize on the expert's relatively predictable reactions to cognitive dissonance.

* * *

I believe that "money" and "winning" are the primary motivations of a high percentage of the litigators who are most comfortable with their work and the current system of dispute resolution. The people who seem least disturbed by litigation and best adapted to its pressures are not people to whom justice and esthetics are the paramount values, but are people who thrive on competition and doing battle, who are thoroughly engaged by gamesmanship, who love the taste of victory, and to whom the power and status that accompany wealth in our culture are very important. * * *

I find some support for these generalizations in the ways many litigators measure their professional success. For too many attorneys, success is not primarily seen as a function of how close to a just result was achieved for their clients. Indeed, some attorneys have retreated so far back into mystical (and self-serving) veneration for the adversary process that they insist that justice is whatever result the system produces and that they would violate their role if they even tried to determine what a "fair" result would be. Instead of measuring success by fairness of result, the adversary system encourages its participants to estimate their achievements by determining how much more they got for their client than his just deserts, by how much better they did for their client than other attorneys might have done and than opposing counsel did for her client, and by how much money they made. The system, in short, is seen as rewarding competitors and winners, not humanists, esthetes or moralists. And the pressures the system imposes track the reward it offers. Since rewards go to the competitors and the winners, the pressures are to compete and to win. Woe to the peaceful. Woe to those to whom constant competition is not comfortable and to whom victory is less important than justice. They are the ones who will be most distorted and strained by a litigation practice.

Most of my suggestions about the psychic implications of the manipulative and exploitative behavior of litigators originate in my own experiences. As a litigator, I used or felt pressure to use most of the tactics described above. I also was the target of such tactics.

Every time I manipulated a person or a precedent, tried to exploit an opponent's weakness, or failed to disclose some clearly important information (case, argument, or evidence), I felt not only dishonest, but also in some measure distorted, alienated from the kind of human being our culture has taught me to respect and to strive to be. When I wanted to be open, candid, and cooperative I felt pressure to be closed, self-conscious, and contrived. I emerged from encounters with other lawyers where I had hidden some weakness in my own case or postured for some tactical advantage feeling lessened, cheapened, degraded, and shaken. Even when my tactics were completely "successful," I felt discomfort, dissatisfaction, and unhappiness. I did not like myself in this role and did not respect the product of my professional endeavors.

* * *

My manipulations and concealments not only eroded my self-respect, but also subtly discolored my feelings about others. The human subjects of my manipulatory tactics were converted in my eyes, by the process of manipulation itself, into something different from me, something less complex and sacred, something more like the inanimate objects in my environment that I move around more or less at will to satisfy myself. Manipulation, in short, bred objectification. If the people I manipulated were not fully reduced to inanimacy, they at least tended to become children in my clouded psychological vision—children in the old pejorative sense of only partial people, people not to be related to as equals. This kind of objectification of others probably leads to objectification of self and, thus, to the final closing of the circle of alienation. It must be very difficult to regularly view others as incomplete and manipulable without gradually coming to view oneself that way.

* * *

What assurance can an attorney who lives in a manipulation-oriented world for eight to ten hours a day have that she will be able to shift to another interpersonal gear in the evenings and on weekends? My experiences and my observations of other attorneys suggest that there is a very real danger that the modes of behavior that begin as adaptations to a special professional setting will gradually expand to fill virtually all of the lawyer's interpersonal space. Subtly, we may come to view all people as proper subjects for manipulation and become suspicious that all people will manipulate us if the opportunity and need arises. If manipulation and suspicion extend into our personal lives, they inevitably will bring with them their psychological baggage: a tendency to objectify and devalue others which invites a general cynicism and sense of alienation from the entire social fabric. The product of all this is hardly attractive: a person distorted and alone, unhappy with himself, suspicious of and separated from others.

———

Recent discussions of adjudication frequently sound other themes as well. One such theme suggests that there may be "functional" limits on the types of disputes that courts can appropriately handle— that is, that there are types of disputes that are inherently unsuited to resolution through the judicial process. What are these limits, and what effect might they have on a lawyer's choice of process for resolving a client's dispute? These questions are explored in the following excerpts.

FULLER, THE FORMS AND LIMITS OF ADJUDICATION
92 Harv.L.Rev. 353, 364–71, 393–400, 403 (1978).

* * * This whole analysis will derive from one simple proposition, namely, that the distinguishing characteristic of adjudication lies in the fact that it confers on the affected party a peculiar form of participation in the decision, that of presenting proofs and reasoned arguments for a decision in his favor. Whatever heightens the significance of this participation lifts adjudication toward its optimum expression. Whatever destroys the meaning of that participation destroys the integrity of adjudication itself.

* * *

When I am entering into a contract with another person I may present proofs and arguments to him, but there is generally no formal assurance that I will be given this opportunity or that he will listen to my arguments if I make them. (Perhaps the only exception to this generalization lies in the somewhat anomalous legal obligation to "bargain in good faith" in labor relations.) During an election I may actively campaign for one side and may present what I consider to be "reasoned arguments" to the electorate. If I am an effective campaigner this participation in the decision ultimately reached may greatly outweigh in importance the casting of my single vote. At the same time, it is only the latter form of participation that is the subject of an affirmative institutional guarantee. The protection accorded my right to present arguments to the electorate is almost entirely indirect and negative. The way will be clear for me, but I shall have to pave it myself. * * * The voter who goes to sleep before his television set is surely not subject to the same condemnation as the judge who sleeps through the arguments of counsel.

Adjudication is, then, a device which gives formal and institutional expression to the influence of reasoned argument in human affairs. As such it assumes a burden of rationality not borne by any other form of social ordering. A decision which is the product of reasoned argument must be prepared itself to meet the test of reason. We demand of an adjudicative decision a kind of rationality we do not expect of the results of contract or of voting. This higher responsibility toward rationality is at once the strength *and the weakness* of adjudication as a form of social ordering.

* * *

Now if we ask ourselves what kinds of questions are commonly decided by judges and arbitrators, the answer may well be, "Claims of right." Indeed, in the older literature * * * courts were often distinguished from administrative or executive agencies on the ground that it is the function of courts to "declare rights." If, then, we seek to define "the limits of adjudication," a tempting answer would be that the proper province of courts is limited to cases where rights are asserted.

* * *

Is this a significant way of describing "the limits of adjudication"? I do not think so. In fact, what purports here to be a distinct assertion is merely an implication of the fact that adjudication is a form of decision that defines the affected party's participation as that of offering proofs and reasoned arguments. It is not so much that adjudicators decide only issues presented by claims of right or accusations. The point is rather that *whatever* is submitted to them for decision, tends to be converted into a claim of right or an accusation of fault or guilt. This conversion is effected by the institutional framework within which both the litigant and the adjudicator function.

* * *

I have suggested that it is not a significant description of the limits of adjudication to say that its proper province lies where rights are asserted or accusations of fault are made, for such a statement involves a circle of reasoning. If, however, we regard a formal definition of rights and wrongs as a nearly inevitable product of the adjudicative process, we can arrive at what is perhaps the most significant of all limitations on the proper province of adjudication. Adjudication is not a proper form of social ordering in those areas where the effectiveness of human association would be destroyed if it were organized about formally defined "rights" and "wrongs." Courts have, for example, rather regularly refused to enforce agreements between husband and wife affecting the internal organization of family life. There are other and wider areas where the intrusion of "the machinery of the law" is equally inappropriate. An adjudicative board might well undertake to allocate one thousand tons of coal among three claimants; it could hardly conduct even the simplest coal-mining enterprise by the forms of adjudication. Wherever successful human association depends upon spontaneous and informal collaboration, shifting its forms with the task at hand, there adjudication is out of place except as it may declare certain ground rules applicable to a wide variety of activities.

* * * [T]he point I should like to stress is that the incapacity of a given area of human activity to endure a pervasive delimitation of rights and wrongs is also a measure of its incapacity to respond to a too exigent rationality, a rationality that demands an immediate and explicit reason for every step taken. Back of both of these incapacities lies the fundamental truth that certain kinds of human relations are not appropriate raw material for a process of decision that is institutionally committed to acting on the basis of reasoned argument.

THE LIMITS OF ADJUDICATION

Attention is now directed to the question, what kinds of tasks are inherently unsuited to adjudication? The test here will be that used throughout. If a given task is assigned to adjudicative treatment, will it be possible to preserve the meaning of the affected party's participation through proofs and arguments?

* * *

Some months ago a wealthy lady by the name of Timken died in New York leaving a valuable, but somewhat miscellaneous, collection of paintings to the Metropolitan Museum and the National Gallery "in equal shares," her will indicating no particular apportionment. When the will was probated the judge remarked something to the effect that the parties seemed to be confronted with a real problem. The attorney for one of the museums spoke up and said, "We are good friends. We will work it out somehow or other." What makes this problem of effecting an equal division of the paintings a polycentric task? It lies in the fact that the disposition of any single painting has implications for the proper disposition of every other painting. If it gets the Renoir, the Gallery may be less eager for the Cezanne but all the more eager for the Bellows, etc. If the proper apportionment were set for argument, there would be no clear issue to which either side could direct its proofs and contentions. Any judge assigned to hear such an argument would be tempted to assume the role of mediator or to adopt the classical solution: Let the older brother (here the Metropolitan) divide the estate into what he regards as equal shares, let the younger brother (the National Gallery) take his pick.

As a second illustration suppose in a socialist regime it were decided to have all wages and prices set by courts which would proceed after the usual forms of adjudication. It is, I assume, obvious that here is a task that could not successfully be undertaken by the adjudicative method. The point that comes first to mind is that courts move too slowly to keep up with a rapidly changing economic scene. The more fundamental point is that the forms of adjudication cannot encompass and take into account the complex repercussions that may result from any change in prices or wages. A rise in the price of aluminum may affect in varying degrees the demand for, and therefore the proper price of, thirty kinds of steel, twenty kinds of plastics, an infinitude of woods, other metals, etc. Each of these separate effects may have its own complex repercussions in the economy. In such a case it is simply impossible to afford each affected party a meaningful participation through proofs and arguments. * * *

We may visualize this kind of situation by thinking of a spider web. A pull on one strand will distribute tensions after a complicated pattern throughout the web as a whole. Doubling the original pull will, in all likelihood, not simply double each of the resulting tensions but will rather create a different complicated pattern of tensions. This would certainly occur, for example, if the doubled pull caused one or more of the weaker strands to snap. This is a "polycentric" situation because it is "many centered"—each crossing of strands is a distinct center for distributing tensions.

Suppose again, it were decided to assign players on a football team to their positions by a process of adjudication. I assume that we would agree that this is also an unwise application of adjudication. It is not merely a matter of eleven different men being possibly affected; each shift of any one player might have a different set of repercussions on the remaining players: putting Jones in as quarterback would have one set of carryover effects, putting him in as left end, another. Here, again, we are dealing with a situation of interacting points of influence and therefore with a polycentric problem beyond the proper limits of adjudication.

* * *

It should be carefully noted that multiplicity of affected persons is not an invariable characteristic of polycentric problems. This is sufficiently illustrated in the case of Mrs. Timken's will. * * * This insistence on a clear conception of polycentricity may seem to be laboring a point, but clarity of analysis is essential if confusion is to be avoided. For example, if a reward of $1000 is offered for the capture of a criminal and six claimants assert a right to the award, hearing the six-sided controversy may be an awkward affair. The problem does not, however, present any significant polycentric element as that term is here used.

Now, if it is important to see clearly what a polycentric problem is, it is equally important to realize that the distinction involved is often a matter of degree. There are polycentric elements in almost all problems submitted to adjudication. * * * It is not, then, a question of distinguishing black from white. It is a question of knowing when the polycentric elements have become so significant and predominant that the proper limits of adjudication have been reached.

THE ROLE OF COURTS IN AMERICAN SOCIETY: FINAL REPORT OF COUNCIL ON THE ROLE OF COURTS

102–114, 120–21 (J. Lieberman ed. 1984).

Which types of cases are and which are not fit for courts? We note at the outset that we can give no definitive answer to the question. Indeed, we believe that there is no single answer; rather, a number of criteria dictate various axes of inclusion and exclusion. What follows are meant as suggestions, not prescriptions. At best we can offer a series of observations that should help organize the inquiry.

* * *

These criteria can be grouped loosely in two categories; functional criteria and prudential criteria. Because no mathematical exactitude is possible, we state these criteria in the form of questions whose answers can be given only as a matter of degree.

FUNCTIONAL CRITERIA

By functional criteria we mean those factors that make a court peculiarly suited (or unsuited) to hear the matter in controversy. Here we are asking whether the court, as a particular type of governmental institution, is competent to hear and determine the dispute.

1. Objectivity

Does the dispute demand detached objectivity, in both reality and appearance? As we have seen, independence and impartiality are hallmarks of courts, and party participation in giving proof and making arguments are basic attributes of the judicial process that courts employ. In combination, the politics, psychology, and process are calculated to assure close, balanced, and open-minded scrutiny to contested claims. These in turn give integrity and respect to judicial decisions. When it is important for a decision to have the kind of integrity that the nature of the court and its process impart, the court is the proper forum. This criterion of objectivity surely applies in life-and-death cases, in constitutional claims, and in cases where liberty is at stake. It may or may not apply in cases turning on a dispute over a sum of money.

2. Necessity for Authoritative Standards

Can authoritative and ascertainable standards be applied to the facts of the dispute to produce a principled resolution? Courts are not as well suited as other institutions to adjudicate disputes in the absence of an ascertainable and authoritative standard. This inability is evident in disputes that present issues involving multiple criteria that cannot be weighed and ranked on an objective scale (e.g., selecting the position of players on a football team, picking the winner of a beauty contest).

To speak of authoritative and ascertainable standards is to speak in terms of degree, not mathematical precision. An authoritative standard can but need not be "black letter law." It may be a legal standard, as in a statute, or a private standard, as in a contract. It may be written, as in the commands of a constitution, or it may be found in the logic of common law decision or in the culture or traditions of a people. Likewise, to be ascertainable means to be capable of being discerned, possibly after some struggle. Of course an ascertainable standard may be one that is precisely spelled out, as in a statute of limitations that tells exactly after which date an action may no longer be pursued. But vague constitutional language like "due process of law" is, for all its frequent opaqueness, no less a standard that a court can apply. If some authoritative and ascertainable standard can be applied to a dispute to produce a principled resolution, the dispute likely belongs in court.

Nevertheless, not every "standard" capable of being applied by some person is proper for application in court. Thus courts are reluctant to intervene in questions of academic scholarship, not because professors do not use standards to evaluate student performance, but because the standards are not capable of easy or formulistic expression for application by an outsider. Compare, for example, a mathematics examination with an examination testing the student's knowledge of French literature. The math exam may call for answers that are ascertainable according to an authoritative standard; i.e., only one correct answer is possible for each question and any person knowledgeable in mathematics could state beforehand a precise formula for uncovering it. If a professor were to give a student a bad grade in the face of correct answers, a court could arguably intervene. But the French examination would pose an intractable difficulty: assuming that it did not call for such exact answers as a poet's birthdate, a court would have no standard to apply.

* * *

3. Determining Past vs. Future Events

Does resolution of the controversy primarily involve the reconstruction of past events or the determination of existing factual circumstances, as distinguished from efforts to forecast future events or design future courses of conduct? This criterion elicits considerable controversy, implicated as it is in the scope of a court's ability to declare law and to devise remedies in cases involving numerous persons and ongoing institutions and relationships.

Traditionalist critics insist that courts are better suited to determining historical facts—i.e., non-recurring facts about a past event—and attaching legal consequences to them than to shaping and directing a future course of action requiring continual fine-tuning and close monitoring (e.g., decrees in institutional reform cases). According to the traditionalist view, courts have no special capacity to evaluate the ramifications of general "social facts" (sometimes called "legislative facts")—i.e., probabilistic questions about recurrent patterns of behavior—that are relevant and important to informed law-declaring. "There is tension between two different judicial responsibilities: deciding the particular case and formulating a general policy. Two different kinds of fact-finding processes are required for these two different functions. The adversary system of presentation and rules of evidence were both developed for the former, and they leave much to be desired for the latter." One of the most forceful criticisms today of the work of appellate courts, including the United States Supreme Court, is the procedural irregularity by which these courts find social facts to make law in ways that ignore and undermine traditional adversary presentation and argument.

* * *

PRUDENTIAL CRITERIA

By prudential criteria, we mean those factors that make a court more or less suited than other institutions to hearing and resolving a dispute, given that on any view the court is competent to adjudicate the issue in controversy.

1. Costs

In a dispute over a monetary claim, is the cost of judicial resolution disproportionately large in relation to the amount at stake? When the dispute involves only money and the cost of determining the controversy is out of proportion to the amount at stake, some process of deciding that is less expensive and less time-consuming than adjudication should be sought * * *.

2. Particularized Consideration

Does the type of case typically present only repetitive kinds of factual or administrative questions not calling for particularized consideration of legal issues in each case? The deliberateness and individuated assessment associated with the judicial process may be of little use and may even be extraneous when courts are called upon to process en mass types of cases that pose only routine and repetitive issues. * * * In short, cases that do not require particularized consideration do not routinely call for courts. Examples are found in the administration of estates, in the determination and payment of various forms of public benefits, and in the routine disposition of traffic cases in lower courts.

3. Preference of the Parties

Would a sounder resolution of the controversy likely be achieved through a process giving effect to the parties' preferences rather than through the imposition of a third-party judgment? When the best solution is closely tied to giving effect to the parties' own preferences and utilities, bargaining rather than adjudication is desirable. A clear example is the case Fuller posed of the apportionment of paintings by a will * * *.

* * *

4. Vitality of Another Institution

Would judicial resolution of the matter at hand likely impair the vitality of an existing institution with means of dealing with the matter? When a decision would closely affect the continued vitality of another valued institution—a family, a school, a private political party—a court should supplant the traditional decision maker only in compelling cases. As one court put it in hearing a dispute over academic standards: "(I)n matters of scholarship, the school authorities are uniquely qualified by training and experience to judge the qualifications of a student, and efficiency of instruction depends in no small degree upon the school faculty's freedom from interference from other noneducational tribunals."

This seems also to be the reason that the courts ought to reject claims for monetary damages by a person whose date stood him up. It would be difficult to articulate a rule that would not, at the same time, materially interfere with a desirable fluidity in personal relationships (all spontaneity arguably would be destroyed if friendship were subject to suits for alleged slights and inconsiderate behavior).

This rule can be illuminated further by considering a few cases in which courts have been invited to intrude on that great bastion of private autonomy, the family. Traditionally, courts have refused to adjudicate disputes and grant legal relief between members of an intact family. Thus, in McGuire v. McGuire [157 Neb. 266, 59 N.W.2d 336 (1953)] the court refused to order a husband, financially able to do so, to provide more adequately for his elderly wife, who was compelled to live in meager circumstances in a rundown house without indoor plumbing. The court based its refusal to intervene on the observation that the couple were still living together as husband and wife. Although the wife's claim would have been cognizable had she been separated from her husband, her demand for support here was not properly resolvable in a judicial forum because it was "a matter of concern to the household." * * *

A few years ago, Justice Rehnquist issued a broad warning against adjudication of claims that "can only disrupt ongoing relations" because "the very crystalization of the parties' differences in the adversary process may threaten the future of the institutional relationship." Others, while acknowledging the importance of preserving the family, have advocated a more particularized analysis in each case. They would balance the likely harm that judicial intrusion into family matters would cause against the damage resulting from refusal to redress an individual family member's claim.

* * *

5. Immediate Resolution of a Specialized Problem

Is the controversy one that arises in a specialized area when an immediate, on-the-spot decision that must be final is necessary? Even though a dispute is justiciable and serious, courts are not the best forum when the decision calls for an expert, on-the-scene determination and when delaying matters to get a more careful and accurate judgment from the courts will destroy the values that immediate finality would assure. A clear example of this type of case is the athletic contest during which it is claimed that an official made an erroneous call.

6. Direct vs. Indirect Action

If a court is not the best institution to decide the case directly, can it nevertheless be helpful in hastening a resolution? Courts can act effectively to resolve disputes indirectly by spurring settlements, by deciding who may decide the issue, and by designing the process rules by which other, non-court agencies decide controversies. We examine these judicial abilities in the next section.

* * *

CASES IN WHICH COURTS SHOULD PLAY A BACKUP ROLE

1. Child Custody Cases

Courts now determine custody disputes. Does an analysis of the factors favoring and disfavoring judicial handling of the disputes support the conclusion that courts are the right place for these disputes to be resolved?

a. Factors Favoring Court Determination

(i) When parents disagree about the custody of a minor child, an institution enjoying high public confidence must resolve the disagreement.

(ii) Society has a deep interest in protecting children; it is essential to assure that injury to them is kept to a minimum. Courts can insist that the proceedings protect the child.

(iii) Some believe that the judicial process, with its emphasis on decency and dignity, may impart these qualities to the outcome.

b. Factors Opposing Court Determination

(i) In child custody disputes, "the actual determination of what is in fact in the child's best interest is ordinarily quite indeterminate." Because the standard of decision is so amorphous, courts are not able to apply it in a judicious way.

(ii) Determining the best interest of the child in part requires predicting future behavior patterns and interpersonal relationships, work in which courts do not excel.

(iii) Because the parties' own preferences and utilities are so crucial to the best possible outcome, the court's process is not especially useful. In these cases, consensual agreements may yield greater permanency than imposed arrangements.

(iv) Adversary adjudication intensifies frictions and exposes private affairs to no useful end in reaching the decision.

c. How the Courts May Be of Use

The foregoing list of pros and cons suggests that the court is not the proper institution to *make* the decision but is the proper forum to help *guide* the parties to reach their own decision. Obviously if the parents have reached no agreement, a dispute remains that urgently requires settlement. It seems far better to enlist the court than an administrative agency in the search for private agreement: The court process will ensure a modicum of decorum and decency along the way, and the court's imprimatur will be more convincing than a bureaucrat's. Courts thus have an important backup role to play in related-party cases, not "because judges can deftly resolve domestic controversies, but [because] . . . the very threat of their being called upon to do so can expedite negotiated settlement."

* * *

CASES NOT SUITABLE FOR COURTS

An ingenious enough lawyer can fashion any quarrel into the form of a legal dispute—or so it might seem. But few would argue that the courts should be open to hear any matter; problems that have not been shaped into disputes resting on a claim of legal entitlement ought not be aired in court. A matter may be of pressing moral concern, and proponents may make moral claims to remedial action by other institutions. Unless the moral claim is rooted in a legal entitlement, however, it is unsuited to judicial resolution. * * *

A second type of case that might be deemed unsuitable for the courts, no matter which view of courts' role is adopted, is that which raises issues that policy-makers would prefer to leave to the unfettered discretion of the individual. In fact, this category of cases—simple examples of which are claims based on breach of promise to marry or alienation of affection—is more properly seen as embracing matters that legislators on policy grounds would prefer not to see raised legally at all than as cases that jurisprudentially courts are unequipped to handle. Another example is the difference between fault and no-fault regimes in divorce law. If fault is an issue, then the question must be adjudicated—was the defendant guilty of adultery or abusive behavior or some other conduct that the law lays down as grounds for divorce? But cause is not a universal necessity: the legislature may decide, as many legislatures have decided, that a couple may divorce without assigning causes, leaving only disputes over the estate and custody of the children to be resolved in court. Diverting factual issues to other forums or denying the issues justiciability is one way of avoiding the difficulties that especially arise when adjudication must touch ongoing relations.

Notes and Questions

(1) The problem of Mrs. Timken's will and its unsuitability for adjudication were explored further in another article by Professor

Fuller, Collective Bargaining and the Arbitrator, Proceedings, 15th Annual Meeting, Nat. Academy of Arbitrators 8 (1962). Professor Fuller suggested that the typical cases falling neatly within the competence of the adjudicative process tend to be cases that call for a decision of "yes or no," or "more or less." By contrast, the available solutions in the Timken case "are scattered in an irregular pattern across a checkerboard of possibilities." To try to effect an "equal division" of the paintings within the framework of the adjudicative process would run into the difficulty that "meaningful participation by the litigants through proofs and arguments would become virtually impossible. There is no single solution, or simple set of solutions, towards which the parties meeting in open court could address themselves. If an optimum solution had to be reached through adjudicative procedures, the court would have had to set forth an almost endless series of possible divisions and direct the parties to deal with each in turn."

Professor Fuller also cautioned that he was not asserting

that an agency called a "court" should never under any circumstances undertake to solve a "polycentric" problem. Confronted by a dire emergency, or by a clear constitutional direction, a court may feel itself compelled to do the best it can with this sort of problem. All I am urging is that this sort of problem cannot be solved within the procedural restraints normally surrounding judicial office. Courts do in fact discharge functions that are not adjudicative in the usual sense of the word, as in supervising equity receiverships or in setting up procedures for admission to the bar. What I ask is clear thinking about the limits of the adjudicative process and about the value of those limits in the perspective of government as a whole. Thus, what I have said is relevant to the question whether courts should undertake to rewrite the boundaries of election districts to make them more representative of the distribution of population. It does not, however, pre-emptively decide that question.

Id. at 39–41.

(2) For Fuller, the essence of "court-ness" lies in the method by which affected parties participate in resolving the dispute. In adjudication, this involves presenting proofs and reasoned arguments to a neutral decision-maker, whose decision is expected to proceed from and respond to such proofs and arguments. It follows then that "rationality" must play a controlling part in adjudication, in apparent contrast to its more limited role in negotiation, mediation, and elections.

Do you agree that courts assume "a burden of rationality not borne by any other form of social ordering"? What appears to be meant here by "rationality"? Does the ordering principle of "rationality" in adjudication square with the attention paid by lawyers to the personality and values of individual judges, or with the intense public controversy that often surrounds judicial appointments? Is it consistent with the actions of juries? Does Professor Fuller's model of the essential features of the adjudicative process allow room for the jury at all?

(3) The concept of "polycentricity" is difficult to apply in the everyday administration of a judicial system. In which of the following situations is the problem to be solved by a court predominantly polycentric?

(a) A federal district court finds that a state's prison buildings and operations do not meet the constitutionally-mandated minimum standards for safety, health, and humane treatment, and orders the state corrections department to make certain improvements. The department must return to the court every three months to review the progress achieved.

(b) A district court judge grants a divorce, dividing the disputed property on a 40–60 basis between the husband and wife respectively, setting transitional alimony for wife at $500 per month for three years, giving her custody of the two children, setting child support at $400 per month per child until age 18 or graduation from high school, whichever is later, and restricting the husband's visitation to daytime every other Saturday.

(c) A federal district court judge finds that the present at-large election system for city council members discriminates against resident minorities and asks counsel for each party to submit a proposed ward system that would meet constitutional standards. The judge will choose the proposal that best satisfies the standards.

(4) One way that a court may handle polycentric problems is to encourage parties to negotiate a resolution acceptable to them. The degree of judicial involvement in negotiation will vary from judge to judge, as well as across different subject areas. See the further discussion of this subject in Chapters II and V. To a large extent, however, the litigation system relies on the negotiating ability and judgment of lawyers to provide fair, efficient, and durable solutions to disputes.

Consider, for example, the case of Mrs. Timken: The substantive law of wills, and the threat that a court may step in and itself resolve the dispute between the two museums, is likely to assure that negotiation and a satisfactory settlement take place. Compare also the discussion of the "backup" role of courts in child custody cases in the Report of the Council on the Role of Courts. This also seems to be the prevailing way in which ongoing remedies are worked out in the "public law" or "institutional reform" litigation which places so much strain on the Fuller model of adjudication. In these complex cases, which typically challenge the operation and organization of public schools, mental hospitals, or prisons, the litigation system provides a framework within which the parties can bargain:

> The court will ask the parties to agree on an order or it will ask one party to prepare a draft. * * * The draftsman understands that his proposed decree will be subject to comment and objection by the other side and that it must be approved by the court. He is

therefore likely to submit it to his opponents in advance to see whether differences cannot be resolved. Even if the court itself should prepare the initial draft of the order, some form of negotiation will almost inevitably ensue upon submission of the draft to the parties for comment.

The negotiating process ought to minimize the need for judicial resolution of remedial issues. Each party recognizes that it must make some response to the demands of the other party, for issues left unresolved will be submitted to the court, a recourse that is always chancy and may result in a solution less acceptable than might be reached by horse-trading. * * * Indeed, relief by way of order after a determination on the merits tends to converge with relief through a consent decree or voluntary settlement. And this in turn mitigates a major theoretical objection to affirmative relief—the danger of intruding on an elaborate and organic network of interparty relationships.

Chayes, The Role of the Judge in Public Law Litigation, 89 Harv.L.Rev. 1281, 1298–99 (1976).

(5) Does Professor Fuller's exclusive focus on "polycentricity" lessen the usefulness of his analysis in evaluating the appropriateness of adjudication? In what ways might the functional and prudential criteria suggested by the Report of the Council on the Role of Courts be more helpful? Does the choice of the members of a college golf team involve "polycentricity"? Is this choice any more suitable for adjudication than is the choice of the members of the football or baseball team? See Eisenberg, Participation, Responsiveness, and the Consultative Process: An Essay for Lon Fuller, 92 Harv.L.Rev. 410 (1978).

3. The Case for the Judicial Process

FISS, AGAINST SETTLEMENT
93 Yale L.J. 1073, 1075–78, 1082–90 (1984).

In a recent report to the Harvard Overseers, Derek Bok called for a new direction in legal education.[1] He decried "the familiar tilt in the law curriculum toward preparing students for legal combat," and asked instead that law schools train their students "for the gentler arts of reconciliation and accommodation." He sought to turn our attention from the courts to "new voluntary mechanisms" for resolving disputes. In doing so, Bok echoed themes that have long been associated with the Chief Justice,[4] and that have become a rallying point for the organized bar and the source of a new movement in the law. This movement is the subject of a new professional journal, a newly formed section of the

1. Bok, A Flawed System, Harv.Mag., May–June 1983, *reprinted in* N.Y.St.B.J., Oct. 1983, at 8, N.Y.St.B.J., Nov. 1983, at 31, *excerpted in* 33 J. Legal Educ. 570 (1983).

4. See, e.g., Burger, Isn't There a Better Way?, 68 A.B.A.J. 274 (1982); Burger, Agenda for 2000 A.D.—A Need for Systematic Anticipation, 70 F.R.D. 83, 93–96 (1976).

American Association of Law Schools, and several well-funded institutes. It has even-received its own acronym—ADR (Alternative Dispute Resolution).

The movement promises to reduce the amount of litigation initiated, and accordingly the bulk of its proposals are devoted to negotiation and mediation prior to suit. But the interest in the so-called "gentler arts" has not been so confined. It extends to ongoing litigation as well, and the advocates of ADR have sought new ways to facilitate and perhaps even pressure parties into settling pending cases.

[Professor Fiss discusses amendments to Rule 16 and Rule 68 of the Federal Rules of Civil Procedure intended to "sharpen the incentives for settlement." See Chapter II, infra pp. 158 and 167.]

The advocates of ADR are led to support such measures and to exalt the idea of settlement more generally because they view adjudication as a process to resolve disputes. They act as though courts arose to resolve quarrels between neighbors who had reached an impasse and turned to a stranger for help. Courts are seen as an institutionalization of the stranger and adjudication is viewed as the process by which the stranger exercises power. The very fact that the neighbors have turned to someone else to resolve their dispute signifies a breakdown in their social relations; the advocates of ADR acknowledge this, but nonetheless hope that the neighbors will be able to reach agreement before the stranger renders judgment. Settlement is that agreement. It is a truce more than a true reconciliation, but it seems preferable to judgment because it rests on the consent of both parties and avoids the cost of a lengthy trial.

* * *

In my view, however, this account of adjudication and the case for settlement rest on questionable premises. I do not believe that settlement as a generic practice is preferable to judgment or should be institutionalized on a wholesale and indiscriminate basis. It should be treated instead as a highly problematic technique for streamlining dockets. Settlement is for me the civil analogue of plea bargaining: Consent is often coerced; the bargain may be struck by someone without authority; the absence of a trial and judgment renders subsequent judicial involvement troublesome; and although dockets are trimmed, justice may not be done. Like plea bargaining, settlement is a capitulation to the conditions of mass society and should be neither encouraged nor praised.

By viewing the lawsuit as a quarrel between two neighbors, the dispute-resolution story that underlies ADR implicitly asks us to assume a rough equality between the contending parties. It treats settlement as the anticipation of the outcome of trial and assumes that the terms of settlement are simply a product of the parties' predictions of that outcome. In truth, however, settlement is also a function of the resources available to each party to finance the litigation, and those resources are frequently distributed unequally. Many lawsuits do not involve a property dispute between two neighbors, or between AT & T and the government (to update the story), but rather concern a struggle between a member of a racial minority and a municipal police department over alleged brutality, or a claim by a worker against a large corporation over work-related injuries. In these cases, the distribution of financial resources, or the ability of one party to pass along its costs, will invariably infect the bargaining process, and the settlement will be at odds with a conception of justice that seeks to make the wealth of the parties irrelevant.

The disparities in resources between the parties can influence the settlement in three ways. First, the poorer party may be less able to amass and analyze the information needed to predict the outcome of the litigation, and thus be disadvantaged in the bargaining process. Second, he may need the damages he seeks immediately and thus be induced to settle as a way of accelerating payment, even though he realizes he would get less now than he might if he awaited judgment. All plaintiffs want their damages immediately, but an indigent plaintiff may be exploited by a rich defendant because his need is so great that the defendant can force him to accept a sum that is less than the ordinary present value of the judgment. Third, the poorer party might be forced to settle because he does not have the resources to finance the litigation, to cover either his own projected expenses, such as his lawyer's time, or the expenses his opponent can impose through the manipulation of procedural mechanisms such as discovery. It might seem that settlement benefits the plaintiff by allowing him to avoid the costs of litigation, but this is not so. The defendant can anticipate the plaintiff's costs if the case were to be tried fully and decrease his offer by that amount. The indigent plaintiff is a victim of the costs of litigation even if he settles.

* * *

Of course, imbalances of power can distort judgment as well: Resources influence the quality of presentation, which in turn has an important bearing on who wins the terms of victory. We count, however, on the guiding presence of the judge, who can employ a number of measures to lessen the impact of distributional inequalities. He can, for example, supplement the parties' presentations by asking questions, calling his own witnesses, and inviting other persons and institutions to participate as amici. These measures are likely to make only a small contribution toward moderating the influence of distributional inequalities, but should not be ignored for that reason. Not even these small steps are possible with settlement. There is, moreover, a critical difference between a process like settlement, which is based on bargaining and accepts inequalities of wealth as an integral and legitimate component of the process, and a process like judgment, which knowingly struggles against those inequalities. Judgment aspires to an autonomy from distributional inequalities, and it gathers much of its appeal from this aspiration.

* * *

THE LACK OF A FOUNDATION FOR CONTINUING
JUDICIAL INVOLVEMENT

The dispute-resolution story trivializes the remedial dimensions of lawsuits and mistakenly assumes judgment to be the end of the process. It supposes that the judge's duty is to declare which neighbor is right and which wrong, and that this declaration will end the judge's involvement (save in that most exceptional situation where it is also necessary for him to issue a writ directing the sheriff to execute the declaration). Under these assumptions, settlement appears as an almost perfect substitute for judgment, for it too can declare the parties' rights. Often, however, judgment is not the end of a lawsuit but only the beginning. The involvement of the court may continue almost indefinitely. In these cases, settlement cannot provide an adequate basis for that necessary continuing involvement, and thus is no substitute for judgment.

The parties may sometimes be locked in combat with one another and view the lawsuit as only one phase in a long continuing struggle. The entry of judgment will then not end the struggle, but rather change its terms and the balance of power. One of the parties will invariably return to the court and again ask for its assistance, not so much because conditions have changed, but because the conditions that preceded the lawsuit have unfortunately not changed. This often occurs in domestic-relations cases, where the divorce decree represents only the opening salvo in an endless series of skirmishes over custody and support.

The structural reform cases that play such a prominent role on the federal docket provide another occasion for continuing judicial involvement. In these cases, courts seek to safeguard public values by restructuring large-scale bureaucratic organizations. The task is enormous, and our knowledge of how to restructure on-going bureaucratic organizations is limited. As a consequence, courts must oversee and manage the remedial process for a long time—maybe forever. This, I fear, is true of most school desegregation cases, some of which have been pending for twenty or thirty years. It is also true of antitrust cases that seek divestiture or reorganization of an industry.

The drive for settlement knows no bounds and can result in a consent decree even in the kinds of cases I have just mentioned, that is, even when a court finds itself embroiled in a continuing struggle between the parties or must reform a bureaucratic organization. The parties may be ignorant of the difficulties ahead or optimistic about the future, or they may simply believe that they can get more favorable terms through a bargained-for agreement. Soon, however, the inevitable happens: One party returns to court and asks the judge to modify the decree, either to make it more effective or less stringent. But the judge is at a loss: He has no basis for assessing the request. He cannot, to use Cardozo's somewhat melodramatic formula, easily decide whether the "dangers, once substantial, have become attenuated to a shadow," because, by definition he never knew the dangers.

* * *

Settlement also impedes vigorous enforcement, which sometimes requires use of the contempt power. As a formal matter, contempt is available to punish violations of a consent decree. But courts hesitate to use that power to enforce decrees that rest solely on consent, especially when enforcement is aimed at high public officials, as became evident in the Willowbrook deinstitutionalization case[33] and the recent Chicago desegregation case. Courts do not see a mere bargain between the parties as a sufficient foundation for the exercise of their coercive powers.

* * * Of course, a plaintiff is free to drop a lawsuit altogether (provided that the interests of certain other persons are not compromised), and a defendant can offer something in return, but that bargained-for arrangement more closely resembles a contract than an injunction. It raises a question which has already been answered whenever an injunction is issued, namely, whether the judicial power should be used to enforce it. Even assuming that the consent is freely given and authoritative, the bargain is at best contractual and does not contain the kind of enforcement commitment already embodied in a decree that is the product of a trial and the judgment of a court.

JUSTICE RATHER THAN PEACE

The dispute-resolution story makes settlement appear as a perfect substitute for judgment, as we just saw, by trivializing the remedial dimensions of a lawsuit, and also by reducing the social function of the lawsuit to one of resolving private disputes: In that story, settlement appears to achieve exactly the same purpose as judgment—peace between the parties—but at considerably less expense to society. The two quarreling neighbors turn to a court in order to resolve their dispute, and society makes courts available because it wants to aid in the achievement of their private ends or to secure the peace.

In my view, however, the purpose of adjudication should be understood in broader terms. Adjudication uses public resources, and employs not strangers chosen by the parties but public officials chosen by a process in which the public participates. These officials, like members of the legislative and executive branches, possess a power that has been defined and conferred by public law, not by private agreement. Their job is not to maximize the ends of private parties, nor simply to secure the peace, but to explicate and give force to the values embodied

33. New York State Ass'n for Retarded Children, Inc. v. Carey, 631 F.2d 162, 163–64 (2d Cir.1980) (court unwilling to hold governor in contempt of consent decree when legislature refused to provide funding for committee established by court to oversee implementation of decree). The First Circuit explicitly acknowledged limitations on the power of courts to enforce consent decrees in Brewster v. Dukakis, 687 F.2d 495, 501 (1st Cir.1982), and Massachusetts Ass'n for Retarded Citizens, Inc. v. King, 668 F.2d 602, 610 (1st Cir.1981).

in authoritative texts such as the Constitution and statutes: to interpret those values and to bring reality into accord with them. This duty is not discharged when the parties settle.

＊ ＊ ＊ To be against settlement is not to urge that parties be "forced" to litigate, since that would interfere with their autonomy and distort the adjudicative process; the parties will be inclined to make the court believe that their bargain is justice. To be against settlement is only to suggest that when the parties settle, society gets less than what appears, and for a price it does not know it is paying. Parties might settle while leaving justice undone. The settlement of a school suit might secure the peace, but not racial equality. Although the parties are prepared to live under the terms they bargained for, and although such peaceful coexistence may be a necessary precondition of justice,[35] and itself a state of affairs to be valued, it is not justice itself. To settle for something means to accept less than some ideal.

＊ ＊ ＊

THE REAL DIVIDE

To all this, one can readily imagine a simple response by way of confession and avoidance: We are not talking about those lawsuits. Advocates of ADR might insist that my account of adjudication, in contrast to the one implied by the dispute-resolution story, focuses on a rather narrow category of lawsuits. They could argue that while settlement may have only the most limited appeal with respect to those cases, I have not spoken to the "typical" case. My response is twofold.

First, even as a purely quantitative matter, I doubt that the number of cases I am referring to is trivial. My universe includes those cases in which there are significant distributional inequalities; those in which it is difficult to generate authoritative consent because organizations or social groups are parties or because the power to settle is vested in autonomous agents; those in which the court must continue to supervise the parties after judgment; and those in which justice needs to be done, or to put it more modestly, where there is a genuine social need for an authoritative interpretation of law. I imagine that the number of cases that satisfy one of these four criteria is considerable; in contrast to the kind of case portrayed in the dispute-resolution story, they probably dominate the docket of a modern court system.

Second, it demands a certain kind of myopia to be concerned only with the number of cases, as though all cases are equal simply because the clerk of the court assigns each a single docket number. All cases are not equal. The Los Angeles desegregation case, to take one exam-

---

35. Some observers have argued that compliance is more likely to result from a consent decree than from an adjudicated decree. See O. Fiss & D. Rendleman, Injunctions 1004 (2d ed. 1984). But increased compliance may well be due to the fact that a consent decree asks less of the defendant, rather than from its creating a more amicable relationship between the parties. See McEwen & Maiman, Mediation in Small Claims Court: Achieving Compliance Through Consent, 18 Law & Soc'y Rev. 11 (1984).

ple, is not equal to the allegedly more typical suit involving a property dispute or an automobile accident. The desegregation suit consumes more resources, affects more people, and provokes far greater challenges to the judicial power. The settlement movement must introduce a qualitative perspective; it must speak to these more "significant" cases, and demonstrate the propriety of settling them. Otherwise it will soon be seen as an irrelevance, dealing with trivia rather than responding to the very conditions that give the movement its greatest sway and saliency.

* * *

In fact, most ADR advocates make no effort to distinguish between different types of cases or to suggest that "the gentler arts of reconciliation and accommodation" might be particularly appropriate for one type of case but not for another. They lump all cases together. This suggests that what divides me from the partisans of ADR is not that we are concerned with different universes of cases, that Derek Bok, for example, focuses on boundary quarrels while I see only desegregation suits. I suspect instead that what divides us is much deeper and stems from our understanding of the purpose of the civil law suit and its place in society. It is a difference in outlook.

Someone like Bok sees adjudication in essentially private terms. The purpose of lawsuits and the civil courts is to resolve disputes, and the amount of litigation we encounter is evidence of the needlessly combative and quarrelsome character of Americans. Or as Bok put it, using a more diplomatic idiom: "At bottom, ours is a society built on individualism, competition, and success." I, on the other hand, see adjudication in more public terms: Civil litigation is an institutional arrangement for using state power to bring a recalcitrant reality closer to our chosen ideals. We turn to the courts because we need to, not because of some quirk in our personalities. We train our students in the tougher arts so that they may help secure all that the law promises, not because we want them to become gladiators or because we take a special pleasure in combat.

To conceive of the civil lawsuit in public terms as America does might be unique. I am willing to assume that no other country— including Japan, Bok's new paragon [43]—has a case like *Brown v. Board of Education* in which the judicial power is used to eradicate the caste structure. I am willing to assume that no other country conceives of law and uses law in quite the way we do. But this should be a source of pride rather than shame. What is unique is not the problem, that we

43. As to the validity of the comparisons and a more subtle explanation of the determinants of litigiousness, see Haley, The Myth of the Reluctant Litigant, 4 J. Japanese Stud. 359, 389 (1978) ("Few misconceptions about Japan have been more widespread or as pernicious as the myth of the special reluctance of the Japanese to litigate."); see also Galanter, Reading the Landscape of Disputes: What We Know and Don't Know (And Think We Know) About Our Allegedly Contentious and Litigious Society, 31 U.C.L.A.L.Rev. 4, 57–79 (1983) (paucity of lawyers in Japan due to restrictions on number of attorneys admitted to practice rather than to non-litigiousness).

live short of our ideals, but that we alone among the nations of the world seem willing to do something about it. Adjudication American-style is not a reflection of our combativeness but rather a tribute to our inventiveness and perhaps even more to our commitment.

Notes and Questions

(1) When, if at all, is it appropriate to rely on "private," non-official processes to resolve disputes in which "public" values are implicated? When should the diversion of such disputes from the court system be discouraged? Can we find techniques or approaches that might moderate any tension between the need to articulate and uphold societal values and the potential advantages of alternative processes? These are questions that recur constantly throughout these materials: You should not lose sight of them as you proceed to consider the variety of the available means of dispute resolution.

(2) Judge Harry Edwards tells the story of a seminar conducted by the Carter Center at Emory University, which brought together people on both sides of the tobacco controversy. As described by former First Lady Rosalynn Carter, "when those people got together, I won't say they hated each other, but they were enemies. But in the end, they were bringing up ideas about how they could work together." Judge Edwards comments:

> This result is praiseworthy—mutual understanding and good feeling among disputants obviously facilitates intelligent dispute resolution—but there are some disputes that cannot be resolved simply by mutual agreement and good faith. It is a fact of political life that many disputes reflect sharply contrasting views about fundamental public values that can never be eliminated by techniques that encourage disputants to "understand" each other. Indeed, many disputants understand their opponents all too well. Those who view tobacco as an unacceptable health risk, for example, can never fully reconcile their differences with the tobacco industry, and we should not assume otherwise. One essential function of law is to reflect the public resolution of such irreconcilable differences; lawmakers are forced to choose among these differing visions of the public good. A potential danger of ADR is that disputants who seek only understanding and reconciliation may treat as irrelevant the choices made by our lawmakers and may, as a result, ignore public values reflected in rules of law.

Edwards, Alternative Dispute Resolution: Panacea or Anathema, 99 Harv.L.Rev. 668, 678–79 (1986).

(3) Does it follow from the views expressed by Professor Fiss that all cases of power imbalance (such as consumer claims) and public values (such as discrimination) must reach court judgment? For example, does the critical importance of *Brown v. Board of Education* mandate that all discrimination disputes between parents and school boards need judicial attention? Once a body of law has become well-

developed and the applicable rules clearly defined, might not other processes be as good or better in resolving specific recurring problems?

(4) Where does the average plaintiff or defendant fit into a view of adjudication (such as that espoused by Professor Fiss) that rests so completely on the public interest? For example, what advice would Professor Fiss give a lawyer whose client wants to accept a negotiated (or mediated) settlement that the lawyer suspects does not conform to dominant "public values"? Should the community's need for the open development and enforcement of public values really "trump" in all cases the individual's choice of process? And will a party's willingness to settle an important and "public" dispute necessarily proceed, as Fiss suggests, solely from the willingness to accept "less than some ideal" in the interest of peace?

(5) The influence of the judicial process radiates far beyond the impact of litigation—actual or threatened—on the parties immediately involved. Beyond the effect on the individual disputants, one must consider what has been called the "general effects" of public adjudication which result from the communication to *others* of information about litigation. These effects are the subject of the following excerpt.

GALANTER, THE DAY AFTER THE LITIGATION EXPLOSION

46 Maryland L.Rev. 3, 32–37 (1986).

Special effects [arising from litigation] are changes in the behavior of the specific actors involved in a particular lawsuit—like the Princeton club [an all-male college eating club votes to admit women in response to the filing of a sex discrimination suit against the college] or the University of Georgia [dismissed English professor who refused to pass failing athletes receives $2.75 million verdict] or the plaintiffs who sued them. We can, in theory at least, isolate various kinds of effects on the subsequent activity of such actors. An actor may be deprived of resources for future violations. This is *incapacitation*. Or the result of litigation may be increased *surveillance* which renders future offending behavior less likely. The Georgia case dramatically illustrates this surveillance effect. Or the offending actor may be deterred by fear of being caught again. This is *special deterrence*. Or, the experience of being exposed to the law may change the actor's view that it is right to exclude women or pass failing athletes or whatever. This is *reformation*.

In addition to these special effects on the parties before the court, there may be effects on wider audiences that we may call general effects. Litigation against one actor may lead others to reassess the risks and advantages of similar activity. We see this displayed in our Cape Cod [bar owner, fearing law suits, teaches employees how to recognize intoxicated customers] and Madison Parks [city removes asphalt from children's play areas in parks because liability insurance settlements are high] examples. This is *general deterrence.* It neither presumes nor requires any change in the moral evaluation of the acts in question, nor does it involve any change in opportunities to commit them. It stipulates that behavior will be affected by acquisition of more information about the costs and benefits that are likely to attach to the act—information about the certainty, celerity, and severity of "punishment," for example. Thus the actor can hold to what Hart called the "external point of view," treating law as a fact to be taken into account rather than a normative framework that he is committed to uphold or be guided by. The information that induces the changed estimate of costs and benefits need not be accurate. What a court has done may be inaccurately perceived; indeed, the court may have inaccurately depicted what it has done.

On the other hand, communication of the existence of a law or its application by a court may change the moral evaluation by others of a specific item of conduct. To the extent that this involves not the calculation or the probability of being visited by certain costs and benefits, but a change in moral estimation, we may call this general effect *enculturation.* There is suggestive evidence to indicate that at least some segments of the population are subject to such effects. Less dramatically, perceiving the application of law may maintain or intensify existing evaluations of conduct, an effect that Gibbs calls *normative validation.*

In addition to these effects on the underlying behavior, litigation may produce effects on the level of disputing behavior. It may encourage or discourage the parties to a case from making (or resisting) other claims. And generally it may encourage claimants and lawyers to pursue claims of a given type. It may provide symbols for rallying a group, broadcasting awareness of grievance and dramatizing challenge to the status quo. On the other hand, grievances may lose legitimacy, claims may be discouraged, and organizational capacity dissipated. The effects may be labeled *mobilization* and *demobilization.*

While supposition about the effects of litigation is abundant, serious studies of these effects are relatively rare. During the 1960s political scientists (chiefly) accumulated a body of findings on the impact of decisions of the United States Supreme Court (mostly) and other appellate courts, exploring the extent to which these decisions elicited compliance from the lower courts, school boards, police and other agencies they were designed to regulate. A critical survey of this literature concluded that:

> [T]he decisions of the Court, far from producing uniform impact or automatic compliance, have varying effects—from instances in which no action follows upon them to wide degrees of compliance (usually underreported), resistance, and evasion. These varying effects include increases in the level of political activity and activity within the judicial system itself and changes in governmental structure. . . . Important social interests, both economic and

noneconomic, may be dislocated or legitimated, and the court's decisions also often perform an agenda-setting function for other political actors.

A new generation of "impact" research has widened its concerns from the United States Supreme Court to other courts, from public to private law, and from a focus on compliance with doctrinal pronouncements to ascertainment of a wider range of effects. Recent work includes studies tracing out the effects of specific tort cases. Thus Wiley found that a decision of the Supreme Court of Washington holding liable an ophthalmologist for failing to test a young patient for glaucoma did bring about an increase in the amount of testing for glaucoma in young patients. And Givelber, Bowers and Blitch found that a California decision [Tarasoff v. Regents of University of California, 17 Cal.3d 425, 131 Cal.Rptr. 14, 551 P.2d 334 (1976)], holding that therapists had a duty to exercise reasonable care to protect third parties from violence by their patients, had important effects nationwide. Eighteen months after its highly publicized original ruling that a therapist has a duty to warn the potential victim, the court, upon reconsideration, nullified its earlier opinion and modified the duty to one of exercising reasonable care to protect potential victims. The researchers found that the case was widely known by therapists throughout the nation, that observation of its ruling was felt to be obligatory by most even though technically it bound only those in California and "by and large the case appears to be misunderstood as involving and requiring the warning of potential victims" [i.e., in accordance with the withdrawn original opinion]—and to have influenced therapist responses to threatening behavior toward giving warnings, initiating involuntary hospitalizations and taking notes. The story is wonderfully complex. What happens is remote from a calculated intervention by the court designed to bring about these effects; and the therapists' response is more than a calculating re-estimation of costs and benefits.

In contrast to these studies focusing on the radiating effects of a single decision, other researchers have examined the way that an array of judicial decisions impinges on decision making by private actors. Thus a study of large manufacturers found that:

[E]xcept for firms subject to the maximally intrusive regulation of such agencies as the Food and Drug and the General Aviation administrations, product liability is the most significant influence on product safety efforts. Product liability, however, conveys an indistinct signal. The long lags between the design decision and the final judgment on product liability claims (frequently five or more years), the inconsistent behavior of juries, and the rapid change in judicial doctrine in the area, all tended to muffle the signal.

* * *

A study of small manufacturers of agricultural implements in California found that 22% had dropped product lines out of fear of product liability suits.

I am not claiming that these effects are optimal or that the benefits they produce outweigh all the costs or that existing litigation patterns represent the best way to achieve these benefits. But we should recognize that benefits are present and that any assessment of the social value of litigation must take account of them and must involve an attempt to estimate the *net* effects of present litigation patterns and the proposed or likely alternatives. These examples should also remind us that these effects are not ascertainable by supposition or by deduction.

Notes and Questions

(1) Professor Galanter suggests that when courts decide cases by authoritatively stating generally applicable "rules," they strongly influence the primary conduct of all actors in our society. The courts convey information and warnings that are intended to bring private conduct into compliance with norms of appropriate behavior. In addition, the communication by courts of rules of decision plays a part in the process by which disputes are managed. Information disseminated in the form of "legal precedents" is used every day by individuals and their lawyers in routine decisions concerning which claims they should assert, and under what circumstances they should settle those claims. The pattern of decided cases thus helps provide a "blueprint" for settlement, a background against which settlement negotiations can take place. We will discuss this function later when we consider in some detail the dynamics of settlement. See Chapter II, infra; see also Galanter, Justice in Many Rooms: Courts, Private Ordering, and Indigenous Law, 19 J.Legal Pluralism & Unofficial L. 1, 6–16 (1981).

(2) Is it possible that if too many suits are settled, and too many important cases taken out of the judicial system, this function of the courts in facilitating the settlement process might be impaired? What might be the ultimate effects of any resulting uncertainty? Might one consequence, paradoxically, be a decrease in the rate of settlement? See Posner, Economic Analysis of Law 421–22 (2d ed. 1977); cf. Coleman & Silver, Justice in Settlements, 4 Social Philosophy & Policy 102 (1986).

The "Alternative Dispute Resolution" Movement

The notion that use of the official court system is only one among an abundant variety of ways of solving disputes has flourished in recent years. There has been an outpouring of scholarly work, creative proposals, and practical experimentation. The "ADR movement" referred to by Fiss is one reflection of that idea—an idea that is, in fact, one impetus for this book.

Although Fiss speaks of the ADR "movement" as if it were unified and homogeneous, that is hardly the case. The proponents of alternatives to litigation are of diverse backgrounds—from "elite" lawyers like corporate counsel and luminaries such as President Bok of Harvard and former Chief Justice Burger, to the sponsors of neighborhood "community justice centers." Some innovations have been closely linked to the judicial system, while others have been designed to be separate from and independent of the courts.

Most important, each advocate of ADR is likely to have his own agenda. Encouragement of non-judicial means of dispute resolution may reflect differing goals and the desire to promote widely differing values. Thus one can identify in the ADR literature a "cool" theme—a theme that emphasizes "efficient institutional management: clearing dockets, reducing delay, eliminating expense, unburdening the courts."[1] And at the same time one can identify a "warm" theme, in which the search is for higher *quality* solutions than may be available in the courts. The stress here is often on replacing adversary conflict with "reconciliation" of the parties, and on finding processes which can restore mutual understanding and more satisfactory human relations.[2]

Take, for example, the "informality" that is often associated with processes like mediation and arbitration. "Informality" can hardly be an ultimate value in itself. "Informal" procedure may be valued by some who see in it merely a loosening of the rules, restrictions, and rituals of the judicial process. They praise it, then, for its potential for speedier and less expensive decisionmaking. But for others "informality" may be understood primarily to involve "a more relaxed flow of procedure, to make parties more comfortable and decrease enmity and disaffection costs."[3] Under this view it may be valued because of its beneficial effects on the relationship, and on the level of trust, respect, and understanding between the parties.

The goals that the various proponents of ADR seek to advance are not only diverse; in some cases they may actually be in conflict. Judge Harry Edwards has warned that

> Inexpensive, expeditious, and informal adjudication is not always synonymous with *fair* and *just* adjudication. The decisionmakers may not understand the values at stake and parties to disputes do

---

1. Galanter, The Emergence of the Judge as a Mediator in Civil Cases 2 (1985).

2. See, e.g., Smith, A Warmer Way of Disputing: Mediation and Conciliation, 26 Am.J.Comp.L. (Supp.) 205 (1978) ("Therapy and catharsis, rather than an attempt to arrive at some 'truth,' becomes the goal of dispute settlement"); McThenia & Shaffer, For Reconciliation, 94 Yale L.J. 1660 (1985) ("[T]he religious tradition seeks not *resolution* (which connotes the sort of doctrinal

integrity in the law that seems to us to be Fiss's highest priority) but *reconciliation* of brother to brother, sister to sister, sister to brother, child to parent, neighbor to neighbor, buyer to seller, defendant to plaintiff, *and judge to both.*").

3. See Bush, Dispute Resolution Alternatives and the Goals of Civil Justice: Jurisdictional Principles for Process Choice, 1984 Wisc.L.Rev. 893, 1006 fn. 251.

not always possess equal power and resources. Sometimes because of this inequality and sometimes because of deficiencies in informal processes lacking procedural protections, the use of alternative mechanisms will produce nothing more than inexpensive and ill-informed decisions. And these decisions may merely legitimate decisions made by the existing power structure within society.[4]

Consider, for example, the case for "alternatives" made by former Chief Justice Burger:

> One reason our courts have become overburdened is that Americans are increasingly turning to the courts for relief from a range of personal distresses and anxieties.
>
> Remedies for personal wrongs that once were considered the responsibility of institutions other than the courts are now boldly asserted as legal "entitlements." The courts have been expected to fill the void created by the decline of church, family, and neighborhood unity.
>
> Possibly the increased litigiousness that court dockets reflect simply mirrors what is happening worldwide. The press, television, and radio for hours every day tell us of events in Asia, Africa, Europe, and Latin America where there is seething political, social, and economic turmoil. It is not surprising that our anxieties are aggravated.[5]

What seems to be the underlying message that is being conveyed here? It has been suggested that in some cases, the recent discovery of alternatives to courts may be a reaction to an increased consciousness of legal rights and an explosion of claims to "entitlements" on the part of consumers, users of substandard housing, victims of sexual and racial discrimination or of domestic violence, and other disadvantaged groups. The encouragement of alternatives may not proceed entirely from the desire to ensure these groups broader access to inexpensive and meaningful dispute resolution—it may proceed instead from a desire to relieve the courts from the pressures and problems posed by these cases, enabling judges to deal more efficiently with more "traditional" types of judicial business. From this point of view ADR can indeed, as Professor Fiss suggests, be seen as subordinating legal rights and public values to accommodative bargaining, and justice to the single-minded objective of settling disputes.

In light of Chief Justice Burger's remarks, assess the claim that an enthusiastic support of non-judicial processes may be merely "another form of the deregulation movement, one that permits private actors

---

4. Edwards, Alternative Dispute Resolution: Panacea or Anathema, 99 Harv.L. Rev. 668, 679 (1986). See also Lazerson, In the Halls of Justice, the Only Justice is in the Halls, in 1 Abel (ed.), The Politics of Informal Justice 119 (1982) ("informalization" of New York City Housing Court— through introduction of hearing officers who encouraged "conciliation" in order to reduce court backlog—eroded the legal position of tenants in substandard housing).

5. Burger, Isn't There a Better Way?, 68 A.B.A.J. 274, 275 (1982).

with powerful economic interests to pursue self-interest free of community norms." [6]

4. Lawyers and the Choice of Process

As we have seen, the overwhelming majority of disputes, even where a lawsuit has been filed, terminate short of a trial. It may seem something of a paradox then to suggest that for the average member of the bar, awareness and acceptance of non-judicial processes of dispute resolution have been slow in coming. Nevertheless thinking about processes, and making conscious choices among them, have not as yet become habits that have penetrated very deeply into the everyday practice of law.

Some of the indifference to ADR on the part of the bar must be attributed simply to unfamiliarity with the potential for alternative processes and with the form they might take. This might be expected to change as a new generation of law students filters through the system. In addition, some lack of enthusiasm can be explained by the self-interest of lawyers. "Self-interest" here is partly a matter of simple economics. Lawyers, especially those paid by the hour, are able to extract substantial fees from prolonged conflict, and may have an incentive to shape disputes in such a way as to maximize their benefits from them. There is also a more fundamental point: Alternative processes often function in such a way as to transfer greater power and control over disputing to the parties themselves, or to other professionals (such as mediators) who may be involved in helping to resolve the dispute. To many lawyers, this may seem to threaten the attorney's exclusive control over dispute resolution, a feeling of dominance that only the judicial process can provide.

Perhaps an even more important explanation might be found in the education of lawyers. As lawyers, we have all gone through rigorous and stressful training, focusing almost exclusively on the virtues of "legal analysis" and argumentation—of "thinking like a lawyer." Carefully defining the issues, marshalling the arguments and counterarguments, manipulating the precedents—all in the interest of "zealous advocacy" in the assertion of one's legal "rights"—is made to seem the essence of the lawyer's craft. Having survived such a process, lawyers are likely to have an investment in the belief that this is the "natural" way for disputes in our society to be resolved. The role models and legendary cult figures held up to the admiration of law students are those who have proven themselves "toughest" as "hired guns" in the service of their clients' advantage. This process of socialization reinforces the thrust of the curriculum, with its emphasis on formal court adjudication. The result is that litigation and the

---

6. McThenia & Shaffer, For Reconciliation, 94 Yale L.J. 1660, 1665 fn. 33 (1985) (suggestion of Milner Ball).

adversary system tend to dominate the "mental landscape" of the lawyer and obscure other possibilities which may be in the background. "[T]he lawyer and client are apt to agree that adversary combat in a judicial arena is the normal, socially acceptable, and psychologically satisfying method of resolving disputes."[7]

It should not be surprising then that even when lawyers come into contact with non-judicial processes, they have a tendency to view them through the optic of litigation—to enter into these processes expecting them to mirror or mimic what happens in court. We will see later that this is particularly noticeable in the attitude of some lawyers to negotiation and arbitration. These processes may be approached as if they were merely variants or extensions of the judicial, adversarial model which to so many lawyers is the paradigm of disputing.

Cultural attitudes concerning the centrality of the adversary process may mold the assumptions of *clients* as well as lawyers. In such a case, the behavior of a lawyer may in fact often be a response to the desire or expectation of the client for a "valiant champion"[8]—or, perhaps, an attempt to live up to what the lawyer *assumes* the client expects. Is there any way to break out of this vicious circle?

Professor Lon Fuller, in the first excerpt below, presents the traditional justification for the adversary process in adjudication and for the role of the lawyer in that process. The assumptions behind the "adversary model" are tested, in a rather unique context, by the Supreme Court's decision in the *Walters* case, which follows.

FULLER, THE FORMS AND LIMITS OF ADJUDICATION
92 Harv.L.Rev. 353, 382–85 (1978).

The Lawyer's Role as Advocate in Open Court

In a very real sense it may be said that the integrity of the adjudicative process itself depends upon the participation of the advocate. This becomes apparent when we contemplate the nature of the task assumed by any arbiter who attempts to decide a dispute without the aid of partisan advocacy.

Such an arbiter must undertake, not only the role of judge, but that of representative for both of the litigants. Each of these roles must be played to the full without being muted by qualifications derived from the others. When he is developing for each side the most effective statement of its case, the arbiter must put aside his neutrality and permit himself to be moved by a sympathetic identification sufficiently intense to draw from his mind all that it is capable of giving,— in analysis, patience and creative power. When he resumes his neutral position, he must be able to view with distrust the fruits of this

7. Goldberg, Green & Sander, Dispute Resolution 487 (1985). See also Bush, Dispute Resolution Alternatives and the Goals of Civil Justice: Jurisdictional Principles for Process Choice, 1984 Wisc.L.Rev. 893, 995–1004.

8. Riskin, Mediation and Lawyers, 43 Ohio St.L.J. 29, 49 (1982).

identification and be ready to reject the products of his own best mental efforts. The difficulties of this undertaking are obvious. If it is true that a man in his time must play many parts, it is scarcely given to him to play them all at once.

It is small wonder, then, that failure generally attends the attempt to dispense with the distinct roles traditionally implied in adjudication. What generally occurs in practice is that at some early point a familiar pattern will seem to emerge from the evidence; an accustomed label is wanting for the case and, without awaiting further proofs, this label is promptly assigned to it. It is a mistake to suppose that this premature cataloguing must necessarily result from impatience, prejudice or mental sloth. Often it proceeds from a very understandable desire to bring the hearing into some order and coherence, for without some tentative theory of the case there is no standard of relevance by which testimony may be measured. But what starts as a preliminary diagnosis designed to direct the inquiry tends, quickly and imperceptibly, to become a fixed conclusion, as all that confirms the diagnosis makes a strong imprint on the mind, while all that runs counter to it is received with diverted attention.

An adversary presentation seems the only effective means for combatting this natural human tendency to judge too swiftly in terms of the familiar that which is not yet fully known. The arguments of counsel hold the case, as it were, in suspension between two opposing interpretations of it. While the proper classification of the case is thus kept unresolved, there is time to explore all of its peculiarities and nuances.

These are the contributions made by partisan advocacy during the public hearing of the cause. When we take into account the preparations that must precede the hearing, the essential quality of the advocate's contribution becomes even more apparent. Preceding the hearing, inquiries must be instituted to determine what facts can be proved or seem sufficiently established to warrant a formal test of their truth during the hearing. There must also be a preliminary analysis of the issues, so that the hearing may have form and direction. These preparatory measures are indispensable whether or not the parties involved in the controversy are represented by advocates.

* * *

These, then, are the reasons for believing that partisan advocacy plays a vital and essential role in one of the most fundamental procedures of a democratic society. But if we were to put all of these detailed considerations to one side, we should still be confronted by the fact that, in whatever form adjudication may appear, the experienced judge or arbitrator desires and actively seeks to obtain an adversary presentation of the issues. Only when he has had the benefit of intelligent and vigorous advocacy on both sides can he feel fully confident of his decision.

Viewed in this light, the role of the lawyer as a partisan advocate appears not as a regrettable necessity, but as an indispensable part of a larger ordering of affairs. The institution of advocacy is not a concession to the frailties of human nature, but an expression of human insight in the design of a social framework within which man's capacity for impartial judgment can attain its fullest realization.

———

WALTERS v. NATIONAL ASSOCIATION OF RADIATION SURVIVORS

Supreme Court of the United States, 1985.
473 U.S. 305, 105 S.Ct. 3180, 87 L.Ed.2d 220.

JUSTICE REHNQUIST delivered the opinion of the Court.

* * *

Congress has by statute established an administrative system for granting service connected death or disability benefits to veterans. The amount of the benefit award is not based upon need, but upon service connection—that is, whether the disability is causally related to an injury sustained in the service—and the degree of incapacity caused by the disability. A detailed system has been established by statute and Veterans Administration (VA) regulation for determining a veteran's entitlement, with final authority resting with an administrative body known as the Board of Veterans' Appeals (BVA). Judicial review of VA decisions is precluded by statute. The controversy in this case centers on the opportunity for a benefit applicant or recipient to obtain legal counsel to aid in the presentation of his claim to the VA. [38 U.S.C. § 3404(c) limits to $10 the fee that may be paid an attorney or agent who represents a veteran seeking benefits for service-connected death or disability, and § 3405 provides criminal penalties for anyone charging fees in excess of this $10 limitation.]

Appellees here are two veterans' organizations, three individual veterans, and a veteran's widow. The two veterans' organizations are the National Association of Radiation Survivors, an organization principally concerned with obtaining compensation for its members for injuries resulting from atomic bomb tests, and Swords to Plowshares Veterans Rights Organization, an organization particularly devoted to the concerns of Vietnam veterans. * * *

Appellees contended in the District Court that the fee limitation provision of § 3404 denied them any realistic opportunity to obtain legal representation in presenting their claims to the VA and hence violated their rights under the Due Process Clause of the Fifth Amendment and under the First Amendment. The District Court agreed with the appellees on both of these grounds, and entered a nationwide "preliminary injunction" barring appellants from enforcing the fee limitation. To understand fully the posture in which the case reaches us it is necessary to discuss the administrative scheme in some detail.

Congress began providing veterans pensions in early 1789, and after every conflict in which the Nation has been involved Congress has, in the words of Abraham Lincoln, "provided for him who has borne the battle, and his widow and his orphan." The VA was created by Congress in 1930, and since that time has been responsible for administering the congressional program for veterans benefits. In 1978, the year covered by the report of the Legal Services Corporation to Congress that was introduced into evidence in the District Court, approximately 800,000 claims for service-connected disability or death and pensions were decided by the 58 regional offices of the VA. Slightly more than half of these were claims for service-connected disability or death, and the remainder were pension claims. Of the 800,000 total claims in 1978, more than 400,000 were allowed, and some 379,000 were denied. Sixty-six thousand of these denials were contested at the regional level; about a quarter of these contests were dropped, 15% prevailed on reconsideration at the local level, and the remaining 36,000 were appealed to the BVA. At that level some 4,500, or 12%, prevailed, and another 13% won a remand for further proceedings. Although these figures are from 1978, the statistics in evidence indicate that the figures remain fairly constant from year to year.

As might be expected in a system which processes such a large number of claims each year, the process prescribed by Congress for obtaining disability benefits does not contemplate the adversary mode of dispute resolution utilized by courts in this country. It is commenced by the submission of a claim form to the local veterans agency, which form is provided by the VA either upon request or upon receipt of notice of the death of a veteran. Upon application a claim generally is first reviewed by a three-person "rating board" of the VA regional office—consisting of a medical specialist, a legal specialist, and an "occupational specialist." A claimant is "entitled to a hearing at any time on any issue involved in a claim. . . ." Proceedings in front of the rating board "are ex parte in nature"; no Government official appears in opposition. The principal issues are the extent of the claimant's disability and whether it is service-connected. The panel is required by regulation "to assist a claimant in developing the facts pertinent to his claim," and to consider any evidence offered by the claimant. In deciding the claim the panel generally will request the applicant's Armed Service and medical records, and will order a medical examination by a VA hospital. Moreover, the board is directed by regulation to resolve all reasonable doubts in favor of the claimant.

After reviewing the evidence the board renders a decision either denying the claim or assigning a disability "rating" pursuant to detailed regulations developed for assessing various disabilities. Money benefits are calculated based on the rating. The claimant is notified of the board's decision and its reasons, and the claimant may then initiate an appeal by filing a "notice of disagreement" with the local agency. If the local agency adheres to its original decision it must then provide the claimant with a "statement of the case"—a written description of the facts and applicable law upon which the panel based its determination—so that the claimant may adequately present his appeal to the BVA. Hearings in front of the BVA are subject to the same rules as local agency hearings—they are ex parte, there is no formal questioning or cross-examination, and no formal rules of evidence apply. The BVA's decision is not subject to judicial review.

The process is designed to function throughout with a high degree of informality and solicitude for the claimant. There is no statute of limitations, and a denial of benefits has no formal res judicata effect; a claimant may resubmit as long as he presents new facts not previously forwarded. Although there are time limits for submitting a notice of disagreement and although a claimant may prejudice his opportunity to challenge factual or legal decisions by failing to challenge them in that notice, the time limit is quite liberal—up to one year—and the VA boards are instructed to read any submission in the light most favorable to the claimant. Perhaps more importantly for present purposes, however, various veterans' organizations across the country make available trained service agents, free of charge, to assist claimants in developing and presenting their claims. These service representatives are contemplated by the VA statute, and they are recognized as an important part of the administrative scheme. Appellees' counsel agreed at argument that a representative is available for any claimant who requests one, regardless of the claimant's affiliation with any particular veterans' group.[4]

* * *

In reaching its conclusions the court relied heavily on the problems presented by what it described as "complex cases"—a class of cases also focused on in the depositions. Though never expressly defined by the District Court, these cases apparently include those in which a disability is slow-developing and therefore difficult to find service-connected, such as the claims associated with exposure to radiation or harmful chemicals, as well as other cases identified by the deponents as involving difficult matters of medical judgment. Nowhere in the opinion of the District Court is there any estimate of what percentage of the annual VA caseload of 800,000 these cases comprise, nor is there any more precise description of the class. There is no question but what the three named plaintiffs and the plaintiff veteran's widow asserted such claims, and in addition there are declarations in the record from 12 other claimants who were asserting such claims. The evidence contained in the record, however, suggests that the sum total of such claims is extremely small; in 1982, for example, roughly 2% of the BVA caseload consisted of "agent orange" or "radiation" claims, and what evidence there is suggests that the percentage of such claims in the regional offices was even less—perhaps as little as 3 in 1,000.

4. The VA statistics show that 86% of all claimants are represented by service representatives, 12% proceed pro se, and 2% are represented by lawyers. Counsel agreed at argument that the 12% who proceed pro se do so by their own choice.

With respect to the service representatives, the court again found the representation unsatisfactory. Although admitting that this was not due to any "lack of dedication," the court found that a heavy caseload and the lack of legal training combined to prevent service representatives from adequately researching a claim. Facts are not developed, and "it is standard practice for service organization representatives to submit merely a one to two page handwritten brief."

Based on the inability of the VA and service organizations to provide the full range of services that a retained attorney might, the court concluded that appellees had demonstrated a "high risk of erroneous deprivation" from the process as administered. The court then found that the Government had "failed to demonstrate that it would suffer any harm if the statutory fee limitation . . . were lifted." The only Government interest suggested was the "paternalistic" assertion that the fee limitation is necessary to ensure that claimants do not turn substantial portions of their benefits over to unscrupulous lawyers. The court suggested that there were "less drastic means" to confront this problem.

* * *

Appellees' first claim, accepted by the District Court, is that the statutory fee limitation, as it bears on the administrative scheme in operation, deprives a rejected claimant or recipient of "life, liberty or property, without due process of law," by depriving him of representation by expert legal counsel. Our decisions establish that "due process" is a flexible concept—that the processes required by the Clause with respect to the termination of a protected interest will vary depending upon the importance attached to the interest and the particular circumstances under which the deprivation may occur. See *Mathews* [v. *Eldridge*, 424 U.S. 319 (1976)] at 334. In defining the process necessary to ensure "fundamental fairness" we have recognized that the Clause does not require that "the procedures used to guard against an erroneous deprivation . . . be so comprehensive as to preclude any possibility of error," and in addition we have emphasized that the marginal gains from affording an additional procedural safeguard often may be outweighed by the societal cost of providing such a safeguard.

These general principles are reflected in the test set out in *Mathews,* which test the District Court purported to follow, and which requires a court to consider the private interest that will be affected by the official action, the risk of an erroneous deprivation of such interest through the procedures used, the probable value of additional or substitute procedural safeguards, and the government's interest in adhering to the existing system. In applying this test we must keep in mind, in addition to the deference owed to Congress, the fact that the very nature of the due process inquiry indicates that the fundamental fairness of a particular procedure does not turn on the result obtained in any individual case; rather, "procedural due process rules are shaped by the risk of error inherent in the truth-finding process as applied to the generality of cases, not the rare exceptions."

The government interest, which has been articulated in congressional debates since the fee limitation was first enacted in 1862 during the Civil War, has been this: that the system for administering benefits should be managed in a sufficiently informal way that there should be no need for the employment of an attorney to obtain benefits to which a claimant was entitled, so that the claimant would receive the entirety of the award without having to divide it with a lawyer. This purpose is reinforced by a similar absolute prohibition on compensation of any service organization representative. While Congress has recently considered proposals to modify the fee limitation in some respects, a Senate Committee Report in 1982 highlighted that body's concern that "any changes relating to attorneys' fees be made carefully so as not to induce unnecessary retention of attorneys by VA claimants and not to disrupt unnecessarily the very effective network of nonattorney resources that has evolved in the absence of significant attorney involvement in VA claims matters." Although this same Report professed the Senate's belief that the original stated interest in protecting veterans from unscrupulous lawyers was "no longer tenable," the Senate nevertheless concluded that the fee limitation should with a limited exception remain in effect, in order to "protect claimants' benefits" from being unnecessarily diverted to lawyers.

In the face of this congressional commitment to the fee limitation for more than a century, the District Court had only this to say with respect to the governmental interest:

> "The government has neither argued nor shown that lifting the fee limit would harm the government in any way, except as the paternalistic protector of claimants' supposed best interests. To the extent the paternalistic role is valid, there are less drastic means available to ensure that attorneys' fees do not deplete veterans' death or disability benefits."

It is not for the District Court or any other federal court to invalidate a federal statute by so cavalierly dismissing a long-asserted congressional purpose. If "paternalism" is an insignificant Government interest, then Congress first went astray in 1792, when by its Act of March 23 of that year it prohibited the "sale, transfer or mortgage . . . of the pension . . . [of a] soldier . . . before the same shall become due." Acts of Congress long on the books, such as the Fair Labor Standards Act, might similarly be described as "paternalistic" * * *.

There can be little doubt that invalidation of the fee limitation would seriously frustrate the oft-repeated congressional purpose for enacting it. Attorneys would be freely employable by claimants to veterans' benefits, and the claimant would as a result end up paying part of the award, or its equivalent, to an attorney. But this would not be the only consequence of striking down the fee limitation that would be deleterious to the congressional plan.

A necessary concomitant of Congress' desire that a veteran not need a representative to assist him in making his claim was that the system should be as informal and nonadversarial as possible. This is not to say that complicated factual inquiries may be rendered simple by the expedient of informality, but surely Congress desired that the proceedings be as informal and nonadversarial as possible.[11] The regular introduction of lawyers into the proceedings would be quite unlikely to further this goal. Describing the prospective impact of lawyers in probation revocation proceedings, we said in *Gagnon v. Scarpelli*, 411 U.S. 778, 787–788 (1973):

> "The introduction of counsel into a revocation proceeding will alter significantly the nature of the proceeding. If counsel is provided for the probationer or parolee, the State in turn will normally provide its own counsel; lawyers, by training and disposition, are advocates and bound by professional duty to present all available evidence and arguments in support of their clients positions and to contest with vigor all adverse evidence and views. The role of the hearing body itself . . . may become more akin to that of a judge at a trial, and less attuned to the rehabilitative needs of the individual. . . . Certainly, the decisionmaking process will be prolonged, and the financial cost to the State—for appointed counsel, . . . a longer record, and the possibility of judicial review—will not be insubstantial."

*   *   *

Knowledgeable and thoughtful observers have made the same point in other language:

> "To be sure, counsel can often perform useful functions even in welfare cases or other instances of mass justice; they may bring out facts ignored by or unknown to the authorities, or help to work out satisfactory compromises. But this is only one side of the coin. Under our adversary system the role of counsel is not to make sure the truth is ascertained but to advance his client's cause by any ethical means. Within the limits of professional propriety, causing delay and sowing confusion not only are his right but may be his duty. The appearance of counsel for the citizen is likely to lead the government to provide one—or at least to cause the government's representative to act like one. The result may be to turn what might have been a short conference leading to an amicable result into a protracted controversy.

11. The District Court stated in its opinion that "both claimants and attorneys familiar with the VA system view that system as adversarial. . . ." In reaching this conclusion, the District Court referred to statements by two attorneys and two claimants. One of the attorneys was admitted to practice in California in 1978, but does not take claims before the VA because of the fee limitation. His familiarity with VA procedures was acquired as a certified representative before the VA for appellee Swords to Ploughshares during his time as a law student. * * * Both stated that they regarded the VA procedures as "adversarial." Two claimants testified on the basis of their own experience, one that the VA had been "very adversarial" and the other that "the VA has opposed me at every turn. . . ."

*   *   *

. . .

"These problems concerning counsel and confrontation inevitably bring up the question whether we would not do better to abandon the adversary system in certain areas of mass justice. . . . While such an experiment would be a sharp break with our tradition of adversary process, that tradition . . . was not formulated for a situation in which many thousands of hearings must be provided each month." Friendly, "Some Kind of Hearing," 123 U.Pa.L.Rev. 1267, 1287–1290 (1975).

Thus, even apart from the frustration of Congress' principal goal of wanting the veteran to get the entirety of the award, the destruction of the fee limitation would bid fair to complicate a proceeding which Congress wished to keep as simple as possible. It is scarcely open to doubt that if claimants were permitted to retain compensated attorneys the day might come when it could be said that an attorney might indeed be necessary to present a claim properly in a system rendered more adversary and more complex by the very presence of lawyer representation. It is only a small step beyond that to the situation in which the claimant who has a factually simple and obviously deserving claim may nonetheless feel impelled to retain an attorney simply because so many other claimants retain attorneys. And this additional complexity will undoubtedly engender greater administrative costs, with the end result being that less Government money reaches its intended beneficiaries.

We accordingly conclude that under the *Mathews v. Eldridge* analysis great weight must be accorded to the Government interest at stake here. The flexibility of our approach in due process cases is intended in part to allow room for other forms of dispute resolution; with respect to the individual interests at stake here, legislatures are to be allowed considerable leeway to formulate such processes without being forced to conform to a rigid constitutional code of procedural necessities. It would take an extraordinarily strong showing of probability of error under the present system—and the probability that the presence of attorneys would sharply diminish that possibility—to warrant a holding that the fee limitation denies claimants due process of law. We have no hesitation in deciding that no such showing was made out on the record before the District Court.

* * * It is simply not possible to determine on this record whether any of the claims of the named plaintiffs * * * were wrongfully rejected at the regional level or by the BVA, nor is it possible to quantify the "erroneous deprivations" among the general class of rejected claimants. If one regards the decision of the BVA as the "correct" result in every case, it follows that the regional determination against the claimant is "wrong" in the 16% of the cases that are reversed by the Board.

Passing the problems with quantifying the likelihood of an erroneous deprivation, however, under *Mathews* we must also ask what value the proposed additional procedure may have in reducing such error. In this case we are fortunate to have statistics that bear directly on this question, which statistics were addressed by the District Court. These unchallenged statistics chronicle the success rates before the BVA depending on the type of representation of the claimant, and are summarized in the following figures taken from the record.

ULTIMATE SUCCESS RATES BEFORE THE BOARD OF VETERANS APPEALS BY MODE OF REPRESENTATION

American Legion	16.2%
American Red Cross	16.8%
Disabled American Veterans	16.6%
Veterans of Foreign Wars	16.7%
Other nonattorney	15.8%
No representation	15.2%
Attorney/Agent	18.3%

The District Court opined that these statistics were not helpful, because in its view lawyers were retained so infrequently that no body of lawyers with an expertise in VA practice had developed, and lawyers who represented veterans regularly might do better than lawyers who represented them only pro bono on a sporadic basis. * * *

We think the District Court's analysis of this issue totally unconvincing, and quite lacking in the deference which ought to be shown by any federal court in evaluating the constitutionality of an Act of Congress. We have the most serious doubt whether a competent lawyer taking a veteran's case on a pro bono basis would give less than his best effort, and we see no reason why experience in developing facts as to causation in the numerous other areas of the law where it is relevant would not be readily transferable to proceedings before the VA. * * *

The District Court also concluded, apparently independently of its ill-founded analysis of the claim statistics, (1) that the VA processes are procedurally, factually, and legally complex, and (2) that the VA system presently does not work as designed, particularly in terms of the representation afforded by VA personnel and service representatives, and that these representatives are "unable to perform all of the services which might be performed by a claimant's own paid attorney." Unfortunately the court's findings on "complexity" are based almost entirely on a description of the plan for administering benefits in the abstract, together with references to "complex" cases involving exposure to radiation or agent orange, or post-traumatic stress syndrome. The court did not attempt to state even approximately how often procedural or substantive complexities arise in the run-of-the-mill case, or even in the unusual case. * * *

The District Court's opinion is * * * short on definition or quantification of "complex" cases. If this term be understood to include all cases in which the claimant asserts injury from exposure to radiation or agent orange, only approximately 3 in 1,000 of the claims at the regional level and 2% of the appeals to the BVA involve such claims. Nor does it appear that all such claims would be complex by any fair definition of that term: at least 25% of all agent orange cases and 30% of the radiation cases, for example, are disposed of because the medical examination reveals no disability. What evidence does appear in the record indicates that the great majority of claims involve simple questions of fact, or medical questions relating to the degree of a claimant's disability; the record also indicates that only the rare case turns on a question of law. There are undoubtedly "complex" cases pending before the VA, and they are undoubtedly a tiny fraction of the total cases pending. Neither the District Court's opinion nor any matter in the record to which our attention has been directed tells us more than this.

The District Court's treatment of the likely usefulness of attorneys is on the same plane with its efforts to quantify the likelihood of error under the present system. The court states several times in its opinion that lawyers could provide more services than claimants presently receive—a fact which may freely be conceded—but does not suggest how the availability of these services would reduce the likelihood of error in the run-of-the-mill case. Simple factual questions are capable of resolution in a nonadversarial context, and it is less than crystal clear why *lawyers* must be available to identify possible errors in *medical* judgment. The availability of particular lawyers' services in so-called "complex" cases might be more of a factor in preventing error in such cases, but on this record we simply do not know how those cases should be defined or what percentage of all of the cases before the VA they make up. Even if the showing in the District Court had been much more favorable, appellees still would confront the constitutional hurdle posed by the principle enunciated in cases such as *Mathews* to the effect that a process must be judged by the generality of cases to which it applies, and therefore a process which is sufficient for the large majority of a group of claims is by constitutional definition sufficient for all of them. But here appellees have failed to make the very difficult factual showing necessary.

*   *   *

We have in previous cases, of course, held not only that the Constitution permits retention of an attorney, but also that on occasion it requires the Government to provide the services of an attorney. The Sixth Amendment affords representation by counsel in all criminal proceedings *   *   *.

In cases such as *Gagnon v. Scarpelli*, 411 U.S. 778 (1973), we observed that counsel can aid in identifying legal questions and presenting arguments, and that one charged with probation violation may have a right to counsel because of the liberty interest involved.
*   *   *

But where, as here, the only interest protected by the Due Process Clause is a property interest in the continued receipt of Government benefits, which interest is conferred and terminated in a nonadversary proceeding, these precedents are of only tangential relevance. Appellees rely on *Goldberg v. Kelly*, 397 U.S. 254 (1970), in which the Court held that a welfare recipient subject to possible termination of benefits was entitled to be represented by an attorney. The Court said that "counsel can help delineate the issues, present the factual contentions in an orderly manner, conduct cross-examination, and generally safeguard the interests of the recipient." But in defining the process required the Court also observed that "the crucial factor in this context . . . is that termination of aid pending resolution of a controversy over eligibility may deprive an *eligible* recipient of the very means by which to live while he waits. . . . His need to concentrate upon finding the means for daily subsistence, in turn, adversely affects his ability to seek redress from the welfare bureaucracy."

We think that the benefits at stake in VA proceedings, which are not granted on the basis of need, are more akin to the Social Security benefits involved in *Mathews* than they are to the welfare payments upon which the recipients in *Goldberg* depended for their daily subsistence. * * *

This case is further distinguishable from our prior decisions because the process here is not designed to operate adversarially. While counsel may well be needed to respond to opposing counsel or other forms of adversary in a trial-type proceeding, where as here no such adversary appears, and in addition a claimant or recipient is provided with substitute safeguards such as a competent representative, a decisionmaker whose duty it is to aid the claimant, and significant concessions with respect to the claimant's burden of proof, the need for counsel is considerably diminished. We have expressed similar concerns in other cases holding that counsel is not required in various proceedings that do not approximate trials, but instead are more informal and nonadversary. See *Parham v. J.R.*, 442 U.S., at 608–609; *Goss v. Lopez*, 419 U.S. 565, 583 (1975). *Wolff v. McDonnell*, 418 U.S., at 570.

* * *

JUSTICE O'CONNOR, with whom JUSTICE BLACKMUN joins, concurring.

I join the Court's opinion and its judgment because I agree that * * * the District Court abused its discretion in issuing a nationwide preliminary injunction against enforcement of the $10 fee limitation in 38 U.S.C. § 3404(c). I also agree that the record before us is insufficient to evaluate the claims of any individuals or identifiable groups. I write separately to note that such claims remain open on remand.

* * *

[I]t is my understanding that the Court, in reversing the lower court's preliminary injunction, does not determine the merits of the respondents' individual "as applied" claims. The complaint indicates that respondents challenged the fee limitation both on its face and as applied to them, and sought a ruling that they were entitled to a rehearing of claims processed without assistance of an attorney. Respondent Albert Maxwell, for example, alleges that his service representative retired and failed to notify him that he had dropped his case. Mr. Maxwell's records indicate that he suffers from the after effects of malaria contracted in the Bataan death march as well as from multiple myelomas allegedly a result of exposure to radiation when he was a prisoner of war detailed to remove atomic debris in Japan. Maxwell contends that his claims have failed because of lack of expert assistance in developing the medical and historical facts of his case. * * *

The merits of these claims are difficult to evaluate on the record of affidavits and depositions developed at the preliminary injunction stage. Though the Court concludes that denial of expert representation is not "per se unconstitutional," given the availability of service representatives to assist the veteran and the Veterans' Administration boards' emphasis on nonadversarial procedures, "[o]n remand, the District Court is free to and should consider any individual claims that [the procedures] did not meet the standards we have described in this opinion."

JUSTICE STEVENS, with whom JUSTICE BRENNAN and JUSTICE MARSHALL join, dissenting.

The Court does not appreciate the value of individual liberty. It may well be true that in the vast majority of cases a veteran does not need to employ a lawyer, and that the system of processing veterans benefit claims, by and large, functions fairly and effectively without the participation of retained counsel. Everyone agrees, however, that there are at least some complicated cases in which the services of a lawyer would be useful to the veteran and, indeed, would simplify the work of the agency by helping to organize the relevant facts and to identify the controlling issues. What is the reason for denying the veteran the right to counsel of his choice in such cases? The Court gives us two answers: First, the paternalistic interest in protecting the veteran from the consequences of his own improvidence; and second, the bureaucratic interest in minimizing the cost of administering the benefit program. I agree that both interests are legitimate, but neither provides an adequate justification for the restraint on liberty imposed by the $10–fee limitation.

* * *

The first fee limitation—$5 per claim—was enacted in 1862. That limitation was repealed two years later and replaced by the $10–fee limitation, which has survived ever since. The limitation was designed to protect the veteran from extortion or improvident bargains with unscrupulous lawyers. Obviously, it was believed that the number of scoundrels practicing law was large enough to justify a legislative prohibition against charging excessive fees.

At the time the $10–fee limitation was enacted, Congress presumably considered that fee reasonable. The legal work involved in preparing a veteran's claim consisted of little more than filling out an appropriate form, and, in terms of the average serviceman's base pay, a $10 fee then was roughly the equivalent of a $580 fee today. At its inception, therefore, the fee limitation had neither the purpose nor the effect of precluding the employment of reputable counsel by veterans. Indeed, the statute then, as now, expressly contemplated that claims for veterans' benefits could be processed by "agents or attorneys."

The fact that the statute was aimed at unscrupulous attorneys is confirmed by the provision for criminal penalties. Instead of just making an agreement to pay a greater fee unenforceable—as an anticipatory pledge of an interest in future pension benefits is unenforceable—the Act contains a flat prohibition against the direct or indirect collection of a greater fee, and provides that an attorney who charges more than $10 may be imprisoned for up to two years at hard labor. Thus, an unscrupulous moneylender or merchant who might try to take advantage of an improvident veteran might have difficulty collecting his bill, but the unscrupulous lawyer might go to jail.

The language in § 3405 * * * apparently would apply to consultations between a veteran and a lawyer concerning a claim that is ultimately allowed, as well as to an appearance before the agency itself. In today's market, the reasonable fee for even the briefest conference would surely exceed $10. Thus, the law that was enacted in 1864 to protect veterans from unscrupulous lawyers—those who charge excessive fees—effectively denies today's veteran access to all lawyers who charge reasonable fees for their services.

The Court's opinion blends its discussion of the paternalistic interest in protecting veterans from unscrupulous lawyers and the bureaucratic interest in minimizing the cost of administration in a way that implies that each interest reinforces the other. Actually the two interests are quite different and merit separate analysis.

In my opinion, the bureaucratic interest in minimizing the cost of administration is nothing but a red herring. Congress has not prohibited lawyers from participating in the processing of claims for benefits and there is no reason why it should. The complexity of the agency procedures can be regulated by limiting the number of hearings, the time for argument, the length of written submissions, and in other ways, but there is no reason to believe that the *agency's* cost of administration will be increased because a claimant is represented by counsel instead of appearing *pro se*. The informality that the Court emphasizes is desirable because it no doubt enables many veterans, or their lay representatives, to handle their claims without the assistance of counsel. But there is no reason to assume that lawyers would add confusion rather than clarity to the proceedings. As a profession, lawyers are skilled communicators dedicated to the service of their clients. Only if it is assumed that the average lawyer is incompetent or unscrupulous can one rationally conclude that the efficiency of the agency's work would be undermined by allowing counsel to participate whenever a veteran is willing to pay for his services. I categorically reject any such assumption.

*   *   *

The paternalistic interest in protecting the veteran from his own improvidence would unquestionably justify a rule that simply prevented lawyers from overcharging their clients. Most appropriately, such a rule might require agency approval, or perhaps judicial review, of counsel fees. It might also establish a reasonable ceiling, subject to exceptions for especially complicated cases. In fact, I assume that the $10–fee limitation was justified by this interest when it was first enacted in 1864. But time has brought changes in the value of the dollar, in the character of the legal profession, in agency procedures, and in the ability of the veteran to proceed without the assistance of counsel.

*   *   *

It is evident from what I have written that I regard the fee limitation as unwise and an insult to the legal profession. It does not follow, however, that it is unconstitutional. The Court correctly notes that the presumption of constitutionality that attaches to every Act of Congress requires the challenger to bear the burden of demonstrating its invalidity.

*   *   *

The Court recognizes that the Veterans' Administration's procedures must provide claimants with due process of law, but then concludes that the constitutional requirement is satisfied because the appellees have not proved that the "probability of error under the present system" is unacceptable. In short, if 80 or 90 percent of the cases are correctly decided, why worry about those individuals whose claims have been erroneously rejected and who might have prevailed if they had been represented by counsel?

The fundamental error in the Court's analysis is its assumption that the individual's right to employ counsel of his choice in a contest with his sovereign is a kind of second-class interest that can be assigned a material value and balanced on a utilitarian scale of costs and benefits. It is true that the veteran's right to benefits is a property right and that in fashioning the procedures for administering the benefit program, the Government may appropriately weigh the value of additional procedural safeguards against their pecuniary costs. It may, for example, properly decide not to provide free counsel to claimants. But we are not considering a procedural right that would involve any cost to the Government. We are concerned with the individual's right to spend his own money to obtain the advice and assistance of independent counsel in advancing his claim against the Government.

In all criminal proceedings, that right is expressly protected by the Sixth Amendment. As I have indicated, in civil disputes with the Government I believe that right is also protected by the Due Process

Clause of the Fifth Amendment and by the First Amendment. If the Government, in the guise of a paternalistic interest in protecting the citizen from his own improvidence, can deny him access to independent counsel of his choice, it can change the character of our free society. Even though a dispute with the sovereign may only involve property rights, or as in this case a statutory entitlement, the citizen's right of access to the independent, private bar is itself an aspect of liberty that is of critical importance in our democracy. Just as I disagree with the present Court's crabbed view of the concept of "liberty," so do I reject its apparent unawareness of the function of the independent lawyer as a guardian of our freedom.[24]

In my view, regardless of the nature of the dispute between the sovereign and the citizen—whether it be a criminal trial, a proceeding to terminate parental rights, a claim for social security benefits, a dispute over welfare benefits, or a pension claim asserted by the widow of a soldier who was killed on the battlefield—the citizen's right to consult an independent lawyer and to retain that lawyer to speak on his or her behalf is an aspect of liberty that is priceless. It should not be bargained away on the notion that a totalitarian appraisal of the mass of claims processed by the Veterans' Administration does not identify an especially high probability of error.

Notes and Questions

(1) Precisely what does Justice Rehnquist mean when he describes the VA's claim procedure as "nonadversarial"?

(2) Following the Supreme Court's decision, the *Walters* case returned to the district court so that the claims of the individual plaintiffs could be considered. In pretrial proceedings, the district court found that the VA had shown a "complete and reckless disregard of discovery obligations" by destroying thousands of documents relating to disability claims"; the court ordered the VA to pay the plaintiffs $105,000 in attorneys' fees and costs, plus a fine of $15,000. National Ass'n of Radiation Survivors v. Turnage, 115 F.R.D. 543 (N.D.Cal.1987). At the same time, discovery revealed that the VA had been rewarding employees on the basis of the number of disability claims they processed: In order to achieve high performance ratings, some employees had therefore been routinely denying claims without investigating or notifying claimants that documentation was required. See New York Times, January 15, 1987, p. A17; March 15, 1987, p. 22.

The VA's claims practices also came under sharp criticism in Congress. A House committee report concluded that "favoritism to

---

24. That function was, however, well understood by Jack Cade and his followers, characters who are often forgotten and whose most famous line is often misunderstood. Dick's statement ("The first thing we do, let's kill all the lawyers") was spoken by a rebel, not a friend of liberty. See W. Shakespeare, King Henry VI, pt. II, Act IV, scene 2, line 72. As a careful reading of that text will reveal, Shakespeare insightfully realized that disposing of lawyers is a step in the direction of a totalitarian form of government.

claimants who had the ear of certain influential Members of Congress," "undue emphasis on production quotas, and the failure to consider all medical evidence in some cases have hampered the Board of Veterans' Appeals from always operating in the best interests of veterans seeking reconsideration of claim denials." The report found that some members of the Board had been deciding cases at the rate of one every 8 minutes. It recommended raising the $10 limitation on attorneys' fees, and allowing judicial review in federal court of BVA denials of veterans' claims. "Investigation of Disability Compensation Programs of the Veterans' Administration," 58th Report by the Committee on Government Operations, H.R. 100–886, 100th Cong. 2d Sess. (1988).

(3) Does the *Walters* case suggest that there is a necessary trade-off between an "efficiency" interest in the mass processing of claims and an interest in the quality of decision in the individual case? Does it suggest that the efficiency interest is necessarily impaired by an "adversarial" procedure and the presence of lawyers? Do you agree with these propositions? Are the concerns expressed by Professor Fiss relevant in helping to draw a proper balance between the two interests?

(4) Consider the following student comment. Do you agree?

Justice Rehnquist's * * * argument, that the government has an interest in controlling administrative costs, is undermined by the existence of a congressional plan that permitted claimants to make use of attorneys. The fact that Congress has not banned the use of attorneys indicates that a concern with administrative costs did not motivate the fee cap.

Note, The Supreme Court—Leading Cases, 99 Harv.L.Rev. 120, 159 (1985).

C. THE WEALTH OF PROCESSES

With some understanding of the virtues—and the limits—of the judicial process, a lawyer should be able to develop a sense of whether litigation or some different process might be better suited for the resolution of a particular dispute. Throughout the rest of these materials we will be looking at the characteristics of other dispute resolution processes, and considering how they might be evaluated.

It is customary to identify six primary processes which lawyers use in helping their clients resolve problems: In addition to the *judicial process,* we will look at *negotiation, mediation, arbitration,* and the *administrative* and *legislative* processes.

Of course, lawyers seldom use just one process to try to resolve a single dispute. They may combine two or more and work them simultaneously, playing one against the other, or they may try them in succession. The dynamics of this interactive use of process is a substantial part of a lawyer's practice and therefore an important focus of these materials.

An equally important point is that these primary processes are ideal types; we use them primarily for purposes of organization. There are no sharp or clear distinctions between them, and the various techniques of dispute resolution represent points on a continuum rather than essentially distinct methods. There exist in fact any number of hybrid processes which reflect unique combinations of the primary forms. Only the limited creativity of the lawyers involved imposes any restrictions on the fashioning of new hybrid combinations. Moreover, our organization in terms of "primary processes" is not meant to imply that there is any fixed or rigid form which a particular process must inevitably take. The way a process works in practice will depend on the context and the personalities involved. Some "mediators" may be so active in devising solutions and so forceful in imposing them on the parties that it may in fact be hard to distinguish them from arbitrators.

The choice of a process will depend on a host of variables. Some of these factors relate to the nature of the processes themselves, and help to define and differentiate these processes. One obvious factor, for example, is the presence and authority of third parties.

By the time lawyers are involved, of course, the parties are no longer alone in the dispute. Yet lawyers represent the parties as advocates for their respective interests. Third parties may enter the dispute for other purposes—examples are a factfinder, ombudsman, mediator, arbitrator, administrative hearing officer, legislator, or judge. The presence or absence of a third party may give rise to still further considerations that distinguish various processes: For example, how is the third party chosen? At what point is she called in? What authority have the parties given her to help in the resolution of their problem? Is she expected merely to help facilitate the parties' own voluntary settlement by helping them bargain and communicate with each other? Or is she expected to render a "decision?" If the latter, is this decision intended to be binding or merely advisory? May the power of the state be harnassed to support this decision, and does the third party enjoy other sources of influence and authority? Is the third party expected to proceed by articulating and applying general "rules," or in a more ad hoc manner through compromise or persuasion?

Because of the importance of this process factor in choosing among dispute resolution mechanisms, the presence of a third party is used here as a natural organizing theme for these materials. After our brief look at litigation in this chapter, we will proceed to consider a variety of processes in which the participation of third parties becomes increasingly dominant and authoritative. There are, however, many other variables in the choice of process. Some of these variables are related to the context of the particular *dispute*. Particular case factors, for example, may make a dispute more or less suitable for resolution by a particular process.

One such variable involves the characteristics of the parties to the dispute. The number of parties, for example, may affect the choice of process. Some processes, especially negotiation, are more effective when numbers are small and parties homogeneous; the greater the number of participants, the harder it becomes to negotiate even the date and time of meetings much less the substance of the dispute. Also significant is whether the parties are individuals or organizations, and whether their representatives have important internal and external audiences. For example, labor union leadership usually looks to its own members as the critical audience, but it must also recognize the impact of a larger community audience. One mistake of the leadership of the air traffic controllers union in their 1981 fight with the Reagan Administration was a failure to recognize national public opinion as a decisive factor in determining the relative power of the parties and therefore the outcome of the dispute.

One of the most important case-related factors centers on the relationship between the disputing parties: Is the relationship an ongoing one, which looms large in the life of both parties? Is there an expectation of frequent or valuable interaction in the future? This may be true, for example, not only in family and neighborhood disputes, but in employment, collective bargaining, and many business disputes as well. In such cases, the value of the continuing relationship may furnish an incentive for both parties to participate in an alternative dispute resolution process even though it lacks the coercive effects of the court system. Stated in another way, the prospect of damage to an ongoing relationship may constitute one sanction for failing to participate in the process or to comply with the result reached.

That a dispute arises in the context of a continuing relationship may have implications for the choice of process. When the potential benefits from future contacts (and the costs from disruption or termination) are great, a process that seeks to restore and maintain satisfying patterns of personal interaction seems called for. Such a process might be structured in such a way as to help the parties to reduce the causes of future conflict by helping them to deal with and work at the "real," underlying problems in their relationship. Merely getting the parties to understand and to talk directly to each other in an "atmosphere of mutual recognition and empathy" [1] may go a long way in this respect. Adjudication, by contrast, seems ill-suited to the task, since it can easily sour future relations by escalating conflict and focusing on symptoms rather than on underlying causes. Indeed the very invocation of formal legal "rights" in the adversarial contest of litigation may be seen as a violation of the social norms governing a relationship. [2]

1. Bush, Dispute Resolution Alternatives and the Goals of Civil Justice: Jurisdictional Principles for Process Choice, 1984 Wisc.L.Rev. 893, 982.

2. This attitude seems fairly universal. See, e.g., Merry, Book Review, 100 Harv.L. Rev. 2057, 2061 (1987) (if murder occurred between two Nuer tribesmen and their kinsmen lived nearby and expected to see one another in the future, "they would mediate the dispute and pay bloodwealth in cattle"; however, if they lived further apart "they would refuse to pay damages and transform their relationship into a

The context of a particular dispute may thus lend support to the choice of one or another process. It may also determine what form the process takes. The same process may assume very different operating characteristics depending, for example, on the subject matter of the dispute. Although many of the same elements remain constant, mediation of a highly charged and emotional divorce or custody conflict will be substantially different from mediation of a complex public dispute or a labor crisis. The dimensions of the matter in controversy and whether the dispute is routine and regular, or unique and nonrecurring, may also affect the qualities of the process. The same is true for the general location in society in which the process and dispute are found. A jurisdictional continuum exists, from the most personal and intimate family level through the neighborhood, community, state, region, nation, and the international arena. Each level may develop unique structures and procedures to meet its particular needs, and each process may vary dramatically in operation depending on the jurisdictional level. For example, domestic and international commercial arbitration have many similarities in form, but the inevitable differences in operation are important to a lawyer's effective use of the process.

While the lawyer's search throughout is for the "appropriate" process to use in his particular case, the hope of being able to match particular processes of dispute resolution to particular types of disputes in any systematic way is probably illusory. Considerations are so diverse, and factual situations so fluid, that choice may ultimately have to made in a more intuitive fashion. In addition, as we have already noted, there may well be tensions in any given case between the different standards by which a particular process is to be judged. It will rarely be possible to satisfy in an optimum fashion *all* the criteria that we might expect a dispute resolution process to meet. We may wish, for example, that a dispute resolution process:

- *be efficient, both in terms of cost and of time* (the procedures required to process the dispute should be easily activated, require little wasted motion, and provide a result within an acceptably short period);

- *be fair* (protect the rights and recognize the interests of all the disputants, and respect due process notions such as neutrality and the opportunity to be heard);

- *reduce future conflict* by promoting more amicable relations and mutual respect among the disputants; and

feud."). See also Ellickson, "Why Ranchers Don't Use Lawyers," Stanford Lawyer (Spring, 1987), p. 7 (among the ranchers and farmers of Shasta County, California, "hiring a lawyer for help on a problem with a neighbor is virtually unthinkable. Only deviants—termed 'odd ducks' or 'bad apples'—would do such a weird thing"). Cf. Yngvesson, Re–Examining Continuing Relations and the Law, 1985 Wisc.L.Rev. 623 (courts and other official forums often resorted to in order to redefine and reshape terms of an ongoing relationship over the "long run").

> • *produce outcomes that are not only acceptable to the parties, but that over time are consistent with and promote conformity with existing community values.*

But the need for trade-offs between these (and other) goals is probably inevitable in any but an unattainable ideal world. The balance will have to be drawn differently in different cases, with attention to the nature of the dispute and the characteristics of the parties. And here too, as with the judicial process, there may be a basic ambiguity in the notion of "evaluating" processes. Are we to engage in this evaluation exclusively from the viewpoint of the social engineer, or philosopher-king? Or from that of the lawyer with a client sitting in front of him? In other words, is the choice of process to be entirely private? What role is there for public intervention and oversight of the decision on the basis of external social values? Should we aspire to replace our courthouses with "dispute resolution centers" where a "screening clerk" would "channel" parties to the process he considers "most appropriate" for the case?[3] Could this "screening" function more appropriately be performed in the lawyer's office? These are questions that you should be prepared to consider as we proceed through these materials.

3. Cf. Sander, Varieties of Dispute Processing, 70 F.R.D. 111, 131 (1976).

Chapter II

NEGOTIATION

Everyone who lives in a household and community is confronted with the need to negotiate many times each day. Lawyers have so much experience negotiating both professionally and personally—the process is so natural and familiar to them—that they may become insensitive both to the process and to the need to learn and improve the skills required to do it well. Unfortunately, experience alone does not translate directly into ability. The fact that I may play tennis every day does not make me a great tennis player. Negotiating is a skill, like playing tennis. A lawyer may have natural talent for it, but unless he studies the process and practices the correct methods, he will be unable to use his negotiating ability to the best effect.

A. NEGOTIATION THEORY AND STRATEGY

Many law students and lawyers are tempted to rely on intuitive knowledge and skill in negotiating situations. The effective negotiator, however, will be the one who resists this temptation, who instead develops an operating theory for his bargaining activities, and practices the strategies and styles that are consistent with that theoretical base.

There are two principal theories that attempt to explain the negotiation process: the competitive and the problem-solving. Both are integral to the process and contain elements essential to a full understanding of negotiation.[1] This section considers both theories individually, and then looks at game theory methodology to help identify and appreciate patterns of lawyer behavior. After a brief review of the concept of expected satisfaction, the section concludes with a detailed comparison and critique of the two primary approaches.

Theory should help the lawyer understand the nature of negotiating activities and select the strategies and styles that have the best chance of achieving his desired result. Some lawyers are attracted by a theory that mirrors their personalities or negotiating styles. But personality should not fully determine theory, strategy, and style: A good sense of theory is important in selecting the best strategies and style to complement the lawyer's personality.

Many lawyers confuse the terms theory, strategy, and style, often using them interchangeably. There are, however, important differences. *Theory* refers to a system of assumptions, accepted principles, and rules of procedure with which to analyze, predict, and understand the nature or behavior of a certain situation. It explains what is happening, but does not tell the negotiator how to respond to it. *Strategy,* on the other hand, directs the negotiator in his planning to carry out the project at hand. A negotiation strategy spells out the specific goals to be achieved and the pattern of conduct that should improve the chances of achieving these goals. *Style* is a more personalized behavioral pattern, directly flowing from individual traits, habits, and personality. It refers to the personal behavior the negotiator uses in carrying out the strategies he has chosen.

Negotiators use the terms "competitive", "problem-solving", "principled", or "cooperative" interchangeably, and sometimes confusingly, to describe specific theories, particular negotiation strategies, or special styles of personal behavior. It is true, as we shall see, that certain theories—certain pictures of the world—can sometimes seem to favor certain strategic behavior. But the correlation between the two is imperfect. There appear to be inconsistent patterns between theories, strategies, styles, and personalities. It is often assumed that someone who uses competitive strategies must use a style that is confrontational, hostile, and adversarial, but this is not necessarily true. A highly competitive negotiator can use a style that is friendly, relaxed, and pleasing, while still seizing every advantage to "win" for his client and "defeat" the opponent.

1. See Murray, Understanding Competing Theories of Negotiation, 2 Negotiation J. 179 (1986).

1. Competitive Theory

Negotiating

Is he bluffing
Does he sense my anxiety
Be firm but don't kill the deal
Balancing on the girders of Washington Bridge
Does his voice sound solicitous
Should have flown to take his blood pressure
Is he sweating as I am
No, we cannot pay a dollar more!
but we can
No, not a dollar more!
Okay, then, it looks like the deal is off!
what am I saying
Tumbling out of the plane, will the chute open,
I am sorry but THAT IS THE HIGHEST PRICE
did that sound convincing
All right, then, you'll let me know tomorrow
Goodby
What will he say tomorrow
What will my client say if he says no [2]

———

Most law students, lawyers, and members of the public view an effective lawyer-negotiator as one who is knowledgeable about the law and its effects within the community, has a zealous commitment to securing the maximum possible tangible outcome (usually in financial or other material terms) for his client, and understands power and is willing to use it without hesitation for the benefit of his client. In short, the paradigm for lawyer behavior is the competitive strategy. The ideal lawyer/negotiator is viewed as tough, principled, demanding, and effective in his effort to win—a survivor in the marketplace of the real world. Such a person is someone you would want as your advocate, but possibly not as your neighbor.

The primary assumption of competitive theory is that the community is governed by egocentric self-interest: In a negotiating situation each side (lawyer and client) desires to maximize its personal resources and satisfaction. One's personal needs, attitudes and positions form rigid guides for action to the exclusion of the other side's interests and tactics, which are relevant only as they can be used to maximize one's own return.

Competitive theory sees a world that has limited resources to be divided through competition in a succession of independent transactions—an antagonistic and adversarial world. The system for dividing

2. E. Fink, A Lawyer's Landscape . . . the view from his office (1976), reprinted from 58 A.B.A.J. 311 (March, 1972), Poetry Corner by E. Fink.

these limited resources is distributive: One side's gain is the other side's loss. And a deal made today will not materially affect the choices available tomorrow.

Competitive theory recognizes that some lawyers want their clients to receive only what is fair, act with forthrightness and good will, and trust other people to act ethically and cooperatively in response. But these noncompetitive lawyers are seen as failing to understand the self-interest that is the dominant force in human behavior. They are idealistic, trusting and naive participants in a game that is free-wheeling and jungle-like in its environment. Non-competitives may prosper in negotiations among themselves, but they and their clients are at the mercy of a more powerful reality when facing lawyers who understand the basic nature of the system. According to competitive theory, negotiating patterns are determined by self-interest that seeks to maximize one side's return at the expense of the other's. Given such a system, the strategies likely to succeed will be military-like maneuvers and deceptions that see victory as the only goal.

In the following excerpt, Professor Williams describes the behavioral patterns of the competitive lawyer. He headed a research team which questioned hundreds of practicing lawyers in the Denver and Phoenix areas. One objective was to describe lawyers on a competitive/cooperative scale and rate them as effective, average, or ineffective.

WILLIAMS, LEGAL NEGOTIATION AND SETTLEMENT
24–25, 49 (1983).

In contrast to the friendly, trustworthy approach of cooperative/effectives, effective/competitives are seen as dominating, competitive, forceful, tough, arrogant, and uncooperative. They make high opening demands, they use threats, they are willing to stretch the facts in favor of their clients' positions, they stick to their positions, and they are parsimonious with information about the case. They are concerned not only with maximizing the outcome for their client but they appear to take a gamesmanship approach to negotiation, having a principal objective of outdoing or outmaneuvering their opponent. Thus, rather than seeking an outcome that is "fair" to both sides, they want to outdo the other side; to score a clear victory.

Fees are obviously important to this type of negotiator. Obtaining a profitable fee is rated as the second highest priority on their agenda, a priority that can lead to conflicts. One attorney, describing an effective competitive opponent, said the case would have settled if the other attorney had approached the matter "from a realistic standpoint, i.e., the welfare of the children and future relationships of the parties (the divorcing parents) instead of being primarily interested in increasing his fee."

Competitive/effectives are careful about the timing and sequence of their actions which underscores the gamesmanship element of competitive negotiating behavior. This reflects a high level of interest in tactical or strategic considerations, suggesting that they orchestrate the case for best effect. One effective/competitive attorney laughed when his cooperative opponent said the objective of negotiation was to accomplish a just outcome. He said, "This is a poker game, and you do your best to put the best front on your case and you try to make the other fellow think that his weaknesses are bigger than he really ought to consider them."

* * *

* * * Videotapes of competitive lawyers engaged in negotiating do show a definite pattern of behavior of moving psychologically against the other (non-competitive) attorney. They make very high demands and few (if any) concessions. They use exaggeration, ridicule, threat, bluff, and accusation to create high levels of tension and pressure on the opponent.

What are the effects of these tactics? If used effectively, the tactics cause the opposing attorney to lose confidence in himself and his case, to reduce his expectations of what he will be able to obtain in the case, and to accept less than he otherwise would as a settlement outcome. As Simons observed, the combative approach is a manipulative approach, designed to intimidate the opponent into accepting the combative's demands.

Experimental studies of bargaining have shown that in many settings, use of toughness increases profits for the tough negotiator. Our Q–factor analysis showed that maximizing settlement value is the primary concern of tough negotiators. But they are not only after money. They take satisfaction in winning—in outdoing or outmaneuvering their opponents.

———

Under competitive theory, a primary objective for the lawyer is to control the process by which the dispute is negotiated. If egocentric self-interest dominates behavior, the lawyer who controls the timing and nature of that behavior determines the outcome. In a face-to-face confrontation between a lawyer who understands the competitive system and one who does not, the competitive has the advantage in determining the mode and pace of the negotiation. Hard bargaining drives out soft, so the competitive argument goes. The outcome is more difficult to predict when two effective competitive lawyers meet. After initial sparring, they will probably move rapidly either to a more cooperative strategy or to the most common alternative to settlement, a court. Competitive theory does not prejudge the choice of strategy or process. All strategies are equally usable, so long as they are consistent with the objective of winning with a maximum outcome for the client.

A lawyer accepts certain risks in adopting strategies favored by competitive theory. First, such strategies often have a strong bias toward confrontation, especially for lawyers who lack essential information about the dispute. Competitive theory assumes underlying antagonism in the negotiation. The less knowledge a lawyer has about the substance of the dispute or the process for resolution, the more internal pressure he feels to adopt defensive strategies. Confrontation, by encouraging rigidity and an unresponsiveness that prevent the lawyer from agreeing unwisely or too early, is an excellent defensive tool.

Second, competitive theory does not require a thorough analysis of the merits of the dispute or of the relevant criteria for resolving it. Tactics like a high and firm opening demand, control of the rate of concessions, use of ultimatums, threats, and arguments are the central concern. The focus is on manipulating the process for the client's advantage and not on studying the substance of the dispute to discover a mutually acceptable solution. A lawyer who stresses process manipulation over substance has more difficulty controlling the process or predicting the probable outcome, since his persuasive power rests primarily on uncontrollable factors such as tension, fear, threat, and the relative ability of the opposing lawyer.

Third, the lawyer under the competitive theory may not place a high priority on appreciating reality or satisfying the basic interests of the opposing side. Competitive theory does place a high value on guarding against openness and responsiveness to the opponent's message. This defensive one-sidedness blinds the lawyer to possible joint gains that could be achieved only through active listening and mutual understanding.

Fourth, a lawyer under the competitive theory creates tension and fear in the negotiation whenever it might be useful in producing a more advantageous outcome. These emotional pressures are hard on personal relationships, among clients as well as lawyers. Mistrust, anger, and frustration are frequent by-products. If the process ends with an agreement that is viewed as satisfactory by all the participants, this tension-filled experience may well be seen as an unfortunate ritual that is the price one has to pay for a good result. But if negotiations break down or the resulting agreement does not meet one side's standard of fairness or need for satisfaction, emotion-charged bargaining will likely be a negative experience not willingly repeated by either lawyer or client.

Fifth, as an outgrowth of a tension-filled competitive negotiation environment, communication is distorted in ways that significantly affect the probability of a fair result. Competitive theory favors strategies that protect against persuasive ideas from the other side, and therefore active listening is not a highly valued negotiating skill. Moreover, a highly-charged emotional level frustrates thoughtful understanding and response. Anger and fear are poor filters for effective information exchange. These distortions increase the chance for misinterpretation and misjudgment.

Finally, competitive theory favors strategies that encourage brinkmanship. The most-repeated statement of the competitive lawyer is: "This is my last offer. If you don't accept it, we should get a court date." The more often a lawyer threatens impasse during a negotiation, the greater the chances that an impasse will occur. Lawyers who adopt strategies that frequently risk breakdown as a method of securing agreement face impasse in their negotiations twice as often as those who adopt strategies that do not threaten impasse.[3] Impasse usually brings with it delay, more financial expense, and other less tangible costs. These added costs may not always be against a client's interests: The probable outcome at trial may be sufficiently large to justify the risk, and the client may be willing to accept the uncertainty and risk. In cases in which the alternative to agreement is not the court, impasse might only mean lost opportunities.

Professor Williams' data appear to substantiate the risks inherent in adopting strategies favored by the competitive theory. Twenty-four percent of the lawyers in his sample adopted competitive strategies, and of that twenty-four percent, only one-fourth (six percent of the total) were considered effective negotiators by their opponents. The remainder were deemed either average or ineffective. Cooperative (noncompetitive) attorneys had a much higher rate of effectiveness. Of the sixty-five percent of the sample that were considered cooperative, over one-half (or thirty-eight percent of the total sample) were considered effective. Despite these figures, the competitive theory and the strategies it favors hold a strong attraction for lawyers, fed by the adversarial model of justice, a basic desire to outperform opponents, and a fear of being professionally outmaneuvered and embarrassed.

The Williams data and conclusions raise many unanswered questions. What distortions are built into the personal preferences of lawyers who are asked to judge their opponents? What standards did the participants use to determine effectiveness, or any of the other qualities of personality or style which the questionnaire posited? Wouldn't the more cooperative lawyers in Williams' sample tend to rate their fellow cooperatives higher in effectiveness than the competitives? Did they confuse a competitive style of behavior with a competitive strategy or theory? Were cooperative lawyers effective only in negotiations against cooperatives? What was their contrasting level of effectiveness against competitives?

Under competitive theory, a negotiation takes on the elements of a game, with the goal being victory for one side and defeat for the opponent. A characteristic of lawyers who adopt this view is a personal desire to outdo the other lawyer. Commentators point frequently to the tale of Brer Rabbit and the Tar–Baby as an example of competitive bargaining at its most effective. In the following excerpt, Uncle Remus is relating the story to a young boy.

3. G. Williams, Legal Negotiation and Settlement 51 (1983).

THE TALE OF BRER RABBIT AND THE TAR BABY

[adapted from Harris, The Complete Tales of Uncle Remus, 12–14 (compiled by R. Chase 1955)]

*   *   *

When Brer Fox found Brer Rabbit mixed up with the Tar-Baby, he felt mighty good, and he rolled on the ground and laughed. By and by he up and said, "Well, I expect I got you this time, Brer Rabbit," he says; "maybe I ain't, but I expect I have. You've been running around here sassing after me a mighty long time, but I expect you've done come to the end of the row. You've been cutting up your capers and bouncing around in this neighborhood until you've come to believe yourself the boss of the whole gang. And then you're always somewhere where you've got no business," says Brer Fox. "Who asked you to come and strike up an acquaintance with this here Tar-Baby? And who stuck you up there where you are? Nobody in the round world. You just threw yourself on that Tar-Baby without waiting for any invitation," says Brer Fox, "and there you are, and there you'll stay until I fix up a brush-pile and fire her up, because I'm going to barbecue you this day for sure," says Brer Fox.

Then Brer Rabbit talked mighty humble.

"I don't care what you do with me, Brer Fox," he says, "so long as you don't fling me in that briar-patch. "Roast me, Brer Fox," he says, "but don't fling me in that briar patch."

"It's so much trouble to kindle a fire," says Brer Fox, "that I expect I'll have to hang you."

"Hang me just as high as you please, Brer Fox," says Brer Rabbit, "but for the Lord's sake don't fling me in that briar-patch."

"I ain't got no string," says Brer Fox, "and now I expect I'll have to drown you."

"Drown me just as deep as you please, Brer Fox," says Brer Rabbit, "but don't fling me in that briar-patch."

"There ain't no water near," says Brer Fox, "and now I expect I'll have to skin you."

"Skin me, Brer Fox," says Brer Rabbit, "snatch out my eyeballs, tear out my ears by the roots, and cut off my legs, but please, Brer Fox, don't fling me in the briar-patch," he says.

Of course Brer Fox wanted to hurt Brer Rabbit as bad as he could, so he caught him by the hind legs and flung him right in the middle of the briar-patch. There was a considerable flutter where Brer Rabbit struck the bushes, and Brer Fox sort of hung around to see what was going to happen. By and by he heard somebody call him, and way up the hill he saw Brer Rabbit sitting cross-legged on a log, combing the tar out of his hair with a chip of wood. Then Brer Fox knew that he had been fooled mighty bad. Brer Rabbit was happy to fling back some of his sass, and he hollered out,

"I was bred and born in a briar patch, Brer Fox—bred and born in a briar-patch!" And with that he skipped off, as lively as a cricket in the embers.

Notes and Questions

(1) The Brer Rabbit episode describes a game-like environment well-suited to the competitive lawyer. The pleasure this tale evokes is generated by the thrill of outmaneuvering an opponent and making him look ridiculous. Brer Rabbit adopts a strategy intended to change the perceptions of Brer Fox without any clear tie to what is either reasonable or true. Success comes because these new perceptions, when coupled with Brer Fox's principal objectives (to make Brer Rabbit suffer the most while doing as little work as possible himself), direct Brer Fox to do what Brer Rabbit wants—free him unharmed from the Tar–Baby. We frequently overlook the fact that Brer Fox also uses a competitive strategy. His mistake is in believing what Brer Rabbit says without independent verification. The lessons: (1) perceptions are one of the most important keys to persuasion, (2) you can change perceptions without any commitment to substantial logic or ethics, and (3) winning in a way that humiliates the opposing side is not only possible but also satisfying. Are these suitable guides for practicing lawyers?

(2) "Distributive" bargaining, which plays such an important role in competitive theory, refers to situations in which there are no joint gains for the parties through negotiation. Any proposed solution will result in an increase for one party and a decrease for the other. This is also referred to as "zero-sum" bargaining. The example often used to illustrate distributive bargaining is the seller who offers his home for $90,000 and the buyer who counters with an offer of $86,000. From the seller's perspective, for each dollar he concedes below $90,000, he is worse off and the buyer is that much better off. The buyer's perspective is exactly the reverse. There is only a fixed amount of gain (or loss) to be apportioned by the parties if they want a negotiated settlement (in this example, $4,000). Whatever is given to one party must be taken from the expected return of the other. Distributive bargaining is usually limited to situations which involve only one issue, typically the determination of a monetary amount or the division of an indivisible asset (*e.g.*, the life of Brer Rabbit).

2. Problem–Solving Theory

All participants in a negotiation have certain interests in common. If nothing else, they live in the same community environment and share a common problem along with the interest in discovering whether voluntary agreement is possible. Under problem-solving theory, a dispute is a mutual problem to be studied and resolved jointly by the parties. While competitive theory pictures two lawyers confronting each other face-to-face, each fighting to win an advantageous settlement for his side, problem-solving theory sees the two lawyers sitting side-by-side working together to resolve a shared problem to their mutual benefit.

In Getting to Yes: Negotiating Agreement Without Giving In, Professors Roger Fisher and William Ury define the prescriptive strategies they see as consistent with this problem-solving approach to negotiation.[4] Their five principles are:

(1) Separate the relationship problems from the merits of the dispute, and work on each independently. Do not mix the two by either conceding a substantive point or demanding a concession in return for a better relationship; the relationship is bound to suffer.

(2) Focus on the interests of the parties, not on their fixed positions. Focusing on positions hardens differences and makes compromise difficult. You can define and reshape interests in ways that bridge differences and emphasize common ground.

(3) Invent many options which can take advantage of potential joint gains. You should separate brainstorming from evaluation to generate creative solutions that meet the interests of all parties.

(4) Insist on using objective criteria to evaluate the options generated. "Objectivity" is based on external sources and not the whim of one of the parties.

(5) Know and develop your best alternative to a negotiated agreement (BATNA). The BATNA is the best measure with which to evaluate settlement offers. You should accept an offer only if it is better than your alternative to settlement.

These guidelines, known initially as "principled" negotiation, offer a method for analyzing and working jointly on a substantive problem. Recently Fisher, with Scott Brown, expanded the message of the first principle by outlining the strategies that should be used in building a good working relationship.[5] Fisher and Brown define a working relationship as the way people deal with their differences, and they suggest six guides for improving that relationship: act rationally while balancing your emotions, try to fully understand the other side's partisan perceptions, communicate effectively, behave reliably, use persuasion not coercion and be open to persuasion yourself, and accept the legitimacy of the other side. Your behavior should be "unconditionally constructive," that is, you should follow the six principles *regardless* of what strategy the other side follows.

Problem-solving theory makes several assumptions not entirely shared by competitive theory. First, problem-solving theory assumes that enlightened self-interest dominates human behavior. Enlightened self-interest, in contrast to the egocentric variety, is based on an

4. R. Fisher and W. Ury, Getting to Yes: Negotiating Agreement Without Giving In 10–14, 104 (1981).

5. R. Fisher and S. Brown, Getting Together: Building A Relationship That Gets to Yes 9–12 (1988).

understanding of interdependence and wholeness—a "we-are-all-in-this-together" attitude. Under this theory lawyers negotiate with each other as participants in a joint dispute-resolving environment, not as antagonists in a distributional game. There are limited resources to be divided, but the problem-solver recognizes an unlimited variation in individual preferences among those resources. Each side values the last dollar differently, so the distributional system is fundamentally integrative rather than distributive. The more egocentric elements of self-interest in human nature are seen as effectively contained by behavioral norms and the uncertainty concerning future interaction. Each side can make gains which are not necessarily at the expense of the other side—a concept known as "expanding the pie." In the language of game theory, more negotiations are "non-zero sum"—and more relationships are on-going—than we are usually led to believe, and therefore problem-solving behavior can serve self-interest well. See discussion of game theory, infra p. 89.

Second, problem-solving theory assumes that common interests exist between even the most antagonistic adversaries and that these interests provide natural pressures toward negotiated settlements. Parties can overcome the forces that pull them apart by approaching the task from shared perspectives rather than from a focus on differences.

Third, problem-solving goals are often defined in value-oriented terms, such as the desirability of arriving at an agreement that is wise, fair, efficient, and durable. This "fairness" goal is consistent with an enlightened self-interest that places long-term gains and relationship factors on a comparable footing with short-term monetary benefit. In contrast, goals under the competitive theory are defined in terms of direct benefits (usually monetary, almost always immediate, and frequently at the expense of the opponent's benefits).

Fourth, problem-solving theory recognizes the legitimacy of the values, interests, and positions of the other side. Not only are they substantively relevant to the process, but a lawyer should be open to persuasion concerning their impact on the negotiation.

Finally, problem-solving theory assumes that most negotiations involve more than one issue. The negotiating task is therefore one of integrating separate responses to the different issues into a single acceptable solution. Although some negotiations appear to focus on a single issue, a lawyer can usually break this issue into many dependent parts. For example, in a personal injury case the amount of money the insurance company will pay to compensate an accident victim appears to be a single and overriding issue. It is either $100,000 or $75,000, or some other figure. Yet, upon reflection this issue can be divided into many parts—the total amount of compensation, the amount of cash, the size and nature of annuity payments, the discount figure used for calculating the present value of future income, the timing of payments, the allocation of damages to pain and suffering, to name only a few.

The negotiators will usually have differing priorities for each separate part. The accident victim may prefer a high total compensation, either in a lump sum or with some present cash and a reasonable payout period for the remainder. The insurance company may prefer a lower total with little up-front cash, and an extended payment schedule. Negotiators discover mutual gains through a joint effort at balancing the differences in these individual value preferences.

Before examining the problem-solving approach more thoroughly, as the next excerpt does, we should define clearly what is meant by "integrative" bargaining. "Integrative" bargaining refers to a "non-zero sum" situation involving two or more parties who can each capture increased gains through negotiation. It is often called problem-solving negotiation, because the nature of the process to achieve these joint gains is usually more collaborative than combative. Normally, two or more different issues, decisions, or values are necessary for there to be joint gains available. Using a house sale example, the seller may include with his offer a proposed closing date two months away; the buyer may counter with a proposal to close within the month. There could be additional differences in financing plans, removable furnishings which might be left with the house, or size of the earnest money deposit. All these items are considered separate issues, with interdependent solutions possible. Each party can increase his gain by negotiating a settlement on all items together, using the differences in seller and buyer preferences on individual items as tools for maximizing each party's overall return.

The distributive/integrative distinction appears to describe two mutually exclusive states of the bargaining world—one where a fixed benefit is being divided among a certain number of parties, and the other where the benefit may be expanded to permit increased gains for some or all parties. Of course, every bargaining situation includes pieces of both states. The competitive/problem-solving distinction, on the other hand, appears to define two overlapping ways of reacting to or dealing with the bargaining world. Certain ways of dealing with the world (competitive, for instance) appear to be better suited to a particular state of that world (such as distributive), while other ways (problem solving) are more natural to the other state (integrative).

MENKEL–MEADOW, TOWARD ANOTHER VIEW OF LEGAL NEGOTIATION: THE STRUCTURE OF PROBLEM SOLVING

31 U.C.L.A. L.Rev. 754, 795, 798–801, 809–10 (1984).

Parties to a negotiation typically have underlying needs or objectives—what they hope to achieve, accomplish, and/or be compensated for as a result of the dispute or transaction. Although litigants typically ask for relief in the form of damages, this relief is actually a proxy for more basic needs or objectives. By attempting to uncover those underlying needs, the problem-solving model presents opportunities for discovering greater numbers of and better quality solutions. It offers the possibility of meeting a greater variety of needs both directly and by trading off different needs, rather than forcing a zero-sum battle over a single item.

The principle underlying such an approach is that unearthing a greater number of the actual needs of the parties will create more possible solutions because not all needs will be mutually exclusive. As a corollary, because not all individuals value the same things in the same way, the exploitation of differential or complementary needs will produce a wider variety of solutions which more closely meet the parties' needs.   *   *   *

To the extent that negotiators focus exclusively on "winning" the greatest amount of money, they focus on only one form of need. The only flexibility in tailoring an agreement may lie in the choice of ways to structure monetary solutions, including one shot payments, installments, and structured settlements. By looking, however, at what the parties desire money for, there may be a variety of solutions that will satisfy the parties more fully and directly. For example, when an injured plaintiff needs physical rehabilitation, if the defendant can provide the plaintiff directly with rehabilitation services, the defendant may save money and the plaintiff may gain the needed rehabilitation at lower cost. In addition, if the defendant can provide the plaintiff with a job that provides physical rehabilitation, the plaintiff may not only receive income which could be used to purchase more rehabilitation, but be further rehabilitated in the form of the psychological self-worth which accompanies such employment. Admittedly, none of these solutions may fully satisfy the injured plaintiff, but some or all may be equally beneficial to the plaintiff, and the latter two may be preferable to the defendant because they are less costly.

Understanding that the other party's needs are not necessary as assumed may present an opportunity for arriving at creative solutions. Traditionally, lawyers approaching negotiations from the adversarial model view the other side as an enemy to be defeated. By examining the underlying needs of the other side, the lawyer may instead see opportunities for solutions that would not have existed before based upon the recognition of different, but not conflicting, preferences.

An example from the psychological literature illustrates this point. Suppose that a husband and wife have two weeks in which to take their vacation. The husband prefers the mountains and the wife prefers the seaside. If vacation time is limited and thus a scarce resource, the couple may engage in adversarial negotiation about where they should go. The simple compromise situation, if they engage in distributive bargaining, would be to split the two weeks of vacation time spending one week in the mountains and one week at the ocean. This solution is not likely to be satisfying, however, because of the lost time and money in moving from place to place and in getting used to a new hotel room and locale. In addition to being happy only half of the time, each party to the negotiation has incurred transaction costs associated with this solution. Other "compromise" solutions might include alternating preferences on a year to year basis, taking separate vacations, or taking a longer vacation at a loss of pay. Assuming that husband and wife want to vacation together, all of these solutions may leave something to be desired by at least one of the parties.

By examining their underlying preferences, however, the parties might find additional solutions that could make both happy at less cost. Perhaps the husband prefers the mountains because he likes to hike and engage in stream fishing. Perhaps the wife enjoys swimming, sunbathing and seafood. By exploring these underlying preferences the couple might find vacation spots that permit all of these activities: a mountain resort on a large lake, or a seaside resort at the foot of mountains. By examining their underlying needs the parties can see solutions that satisfy many more of their preferences, and the "sum of the utilities" to the couple as a whole is greater than what they would have achieved by compromising.

In addition, by exploring whether they attach different values to their preferences they may be able to arrive at other solutions by trading items. The wife in our example might be willing to give up ocean fresh seafood if she can have fresh stream or lake trout, and so, with very little cost to her, the couple can choose another waterspot where the hikes might be better for the husband. By examining the weight or value given to certain preferences the parties may realize that some desires are easily attainable because they are not of equal importance to the other side. Thus, one party can increase its utilities without reducing the other's. This differs from a zero-sum conception of negotiation because of the recognition that preferences may be totally different and are, therefore, neither scarce nor in competition with each other. In addition, if a preference is not used to "force" a concession from the other party (which as the example shows is not necessary), there are none of the forced reciprocal concessions of adversarial negotiation.   *   *   *

Unlike the adversarial model which makes assumptions about the parties' desires to maximize individual gain, problem solving begins by attempting to determine the actual needs of particular clients. The problem-solving model seeks to avoid a lawyer who acts for a hypothetical, rather than a real, client by creating a "standardized person to whom he attributes standardized ends."

Ascertaining the client's needs will, of course, begin with the initial interview. This is not the place to review the extensive interview literature, but in thinking ahead to the negotiation which might occur, a lawyer might begin by asking the client such general questions as "how would you like to see this all turn out? " or "what would you like to accomplish here?" before channelling the client's objectives in directions the lawyer knows are legally possible. The client may be the best source of ideas that go beyond what the court or the legal system might commonly permit. Once the client's ideas are brought to the surface, the lawyer can explore the needs they are meant to satisfy, and the legal and nonlegal consequences of these and other solutions. * * *

Of course, the parties' needs will not be sufficiently complementary in all cases to permit direct solutions. Needs may conflict or there may be conflict over the material required to satisfy the needs. In addition to focusing on the parties' needs as a source of solutions, negotiators can attempt to expand the resources that the parties may eventually have to divide. In essence, this aspect of problem-solving negotiation seeks wherever possible to convert zero-sum games into non-zero-sum or positive-sum games. By expanding resources of the material available for division, more of the parties' total set of needs may be satisfied. Indeed, as the literature on legal transactions and the economic efficiency of such transactions makes clear, the parties come together to transact business precisely because their joint action is likely to increase the wealth available to both. To the extent that principles of wealth creation and resource expansion from transactional negotiation can be assimilated to dispute negotiation, the parties to a negotiation have the opportunity to help each other by looking for ways to expand what is available to them.

Various substantive strategies may increase the material available for distribution. Resources can be expanded by exploring what could be distributed, when it could be distributed, by whom it would be distributed, how it could be distributed and how much of it could be distributed.

————

As with competitive theory, there are some downside risks for the lawyer who adopts strategies that are favored by problem-solving theory. The problem-solver has a strong bias in favor of good relationships and common interests, creating internal pressures for cooperation, compromise, and accommodation. What does a problem-solver do, however, when the opposing negotiator clings inflexibly to competitive strategies? If he concedes on the issues, he admits the narrowness and vulnerability of the problem-solving approach. If he becomes stubborn and rigid himself, he confirms the superiority of competitive theory by adopting competitive strategies when conditions are tough.

Problem-solving theory also recognizes negotiation and other voluntary processes as the preferred means for resolving disputes. Impasse or stalemate in negotiation is a failure for the problem-solver. Its impact is softened only slightly by the suggestion that not all disputes can or should be settled by negotiation. A problem-solver will therefore tend to avoid confrontational strategies because of their likelihood of producing impasse. Under competitive theory, on the other hand, impasse in negotiations is a natural part of dispute resolution, serving only as a midpoint on the adversarial process continuum.

Furthermore, problem-solving theory favors strategies that require substantial knowledge and skill on a lawyer's part to work effectively. The skill of active listening demands continuing efforts over the full length of the negotiation to assure the lawyer of its benefits. Moreover, sensitivity to psychological movements within a negotiation and empathy for another's reality are also important skills for the problem-solver. Unfortunately, such skills may not come as naturally to the average lawyer as the more confrontational and argumentative behavior that competitive theory promotes.

To be effective, the problem-solving lawyer must have a high degree of confidence in his evaluation of his client's interests, in the accuracy of the information that he has discovered, and in his assessment of acceptable outcomes for the other side. When a lawyer bases his action on his own information, analyses, and skills, he takes a risk that his efforts and ability are inadequate in the circumstances. Without strong confidence in himself, the lawyer may be tempted to shift to the more protective strategies favored by competitive theory. Problem-solving theory is not defensive by nature: A lawyer/problem-solver is usually on the offensive, trying by positive action to achieve a fair and durable agreement. Following this strategy creates a potential vulnerability to the opponent who follows strategies that thrive on tension, misrepresentation, and manipulation.

Finally, the problem-solver places importance on shared interests and the legitimacy of the other side's position. Such sensitivity to another's perceptions increases his vulnerability to an able and deceptive opposing lawyer and creates a greater chance that the resulting settlement will be more favorable to the other side than fairness would warrant.

The data compiled by Professor Williams suggest that a majority of lawyers adopt cooperative negotiating strategies. Cooperative strategies and style as defined by Williams appear to meet many of the criteria favored by problem-solving theory. This apparent reliance on problem-solving theory by a majority of practicing lawyers runs counter to the myth of the competitive lawyer-negotiator. Perhaps the strategies that encourage tension and fear are more psychologically draining and not as satisfying personally as the more interactive and supportive environment promoted by strategies based on problem-solving theory. Professional interaction and bar association activity may also play a role in decreasing the reliance on intense competitive strategies. Without adequate empirical research, however, we can only speculate.

3. Other Useful Methodologies

a. Game Theory

The nature of a bargaining situation has intrigued researchers for many decades. Social scientists turned to the theory of games as a method of analysis that might be helpful in understanding the negotiation setting. Game theory provided a procedure for enacting and reenacting a specific bargaining situation so that the impact of a single variable, such as risk-proneness or gender, could be isolated and analyzed. Game theory is not a theory of negotiation, but a method of analysis to be used to determine the best strategy to achieve maximum results in a negotiating situation.

The typical game theory application is the "Prisoner's Dilemma." Assume two friends are arrested in connection with a single crime. The prisoners are placed in separate detention cells and questioned by police. Each must decide on his own whether to keep silent about the events (cooperate with his friend) or tell the story to the police (defect), but neither can learn what decision the other has made before making his own choice. The following matrix gives the choice possibilities and posits payoffs in terms of points for the prisoners' choices.

	Prisoner B	
	Cooperates	Defects
	"a"	"b"
Cooperates	A = 3	A = 0
	B = 3	B = 5
Prisoner A		
	"c"	"d"
Defects	A = 5	A = 1
	B = 0	B = 1

Figure II–1. The Prisoner's Dilemma

The payoff schedule has an important impact on the outcome of the game. The reward system places outmaneuvering the other prisoner (quadrant "c" if you are Prisoner A) at the highest value (5), joint cooperation ("a") next (3), joint defection ("d") next (1), and being outmaneuvered by the other prisoner ("b") at the lowest (0). With this fixed hierarchy, each player can increase his gains by interaction with the other player—either by cooperation or defection. Is this descending order of rewards consistent with those for the choices available to the typical lawyer? Over the short-term or the long-term?

In the following excerpt, a political scientist and game theorist uses the Prisoner's Dilemma to discover what is necessary for cooperation to emerge from situations in which the participants are pursuing their own self-interests.

ROBERT AXELROD, THE EVOLUTION OF COOPERATION *

8–9, 12, 14–15, 20–21 (1984).

What should you do in such a game? Suppose you are the row player [Prisoner A], and you think the column player [Prisoner B] will cooperate. This means that you will get one of the two outcomes in the first column. You have a choice. You can cooperate as well, getting the 3 points of the reward for mutual cooperation. Or you can defect, getting the 5 points of the temptation payoff. So it pays to defect if you think the other player will cooperate. But now suppose that you think the other player will defect. Now you are in the second column, and you have a choice between cooperating, which would make you a sucker and give you 0 points, and defecting, which would result in mutual punishment giving you 1 point. So it pays to defect if you think the other player will defect. This means that it is better to defect if you think the other player will cooperate, and it is better to defect if you think the other player will defect. So no matter what the other player does, it pays for you to defect.

So far, so good. But the same logic holds for the other player too. Therefore, the other player should defect no matter what you are expected to do. So you should both defect. But then you both get 1 point which is worse than the 3 points of the reward that you both could have gotten had you both cooperated. Individual rationality leads to a worse outcome for both than is possible. Hence the dilemma.

* * *

What makes it possible for cooperation to emerge is the fact that the players might meet again. This possibility means that the choices made today not only determine the outcome of this move, but can also influence the later choices of the players. The future can therefore cast a shadow back upon the present and thereby affect the current strategic situation.

But the future is less important than the present—for two reasons. The first is that players tend to value payoffs less as the time of their obtainment recedes into the future. The second is that there is always some chance that the players will not meet again. An ongoing relationship may end when one or the other player moves away, changes jobs, dies, or goes bankrupt.

For these reasons, the payoff of the next move always counts less than the payoff of the current move. * * *

The first question you are tempted to ask is, "What is the best strategy?" In other words, what strategy will yield a player the highest possible score? This is a good question, but as will be shown later, no best rule exists independently of the strategy being used by the other player. In this sense, the iterated Prisoner's Dilemma is completely different from a game like chess. A chess master can safely use the assumption that the other player will make the most feared move. This assumption provides a basis for planning in a game like chess, where the interests of the players are completely antagonistic. But the situations represented by the Prisoner's Dilemma game are quite different. The interests of the players are not in total conflict. Both players can do well by getting the reward, R, for mutual cooperation or both can do poorly getting the punishment, P, for mutual defection. Using the assumption that the other player will always make the move you fear most will lead you to expect that the other will never cooperate, which in turn will lead you to defect, causing unending punishment. So unlike chess, in the Prisoner's Dilemma it is not safe to assume that the other player is out to get you.

In fact, in the Prisoner's Dilemma, the strategy that works best depends directly on what strategy the other player is using and, in particular, on whether this strategy leaves room for the development of mutual cooperation. * * *

Here is the argument in a nutshell. The evolution of cooperation requires that individuals have a sufficiently large chance to meet again so that they have a stake in their future interaction. If this is true, cooperation can evolve in three stages.

1. The beginning of the story is that cooperation can get started even in a world of unconditional defection. The development *cannot* take place if it is tried only by scattered individuals who have virtually no chance to interact with each other. However, cooperation can evolve from small clusters of individuals who base their cooperation on reciprocity and have even a small proportion of their interactions with each other.

2. The middle of the story is that a strategy based on reciprocity can thrive in a world where many different kinds of strategies are being tried.

3. The end of the story is that cooperation, once established on the basis of reciprocity, can protect itself from invasion by less cooperative strategies. Thus, the gear wheels of social evolution have a ratchet.

Notes and Questions

(1) Professor Axelrod concludes that for those situations in which the "game" will continue for an indefinite period, a strategy of "Tit for Tat" is the best choice among all known strategies. Tit for Tat "is the policy of cooperating on the first move and then doing whatever the other player did on the previous move." The success of Tit for Tat is not that you will *ever* do better than the other person you are playing with in a particular game, but that you will do better *over the long term* than others playing your role in similar games. As a buyer, for instance, you are really competing with other buyers for the product, not with the seller with whom you are negotiating.

The reasons for the success of Tit for Tat are many: It avoids unnecessary conflict as long as the other person cooperates; it responds immediately and firmly to provocation so that one is not exploited; it gives the other person an incentive to cooperate after you retaliate because he knows you will cooperate in response; and it adopts a clear, long-term strategy that elicits an easily understood and stable responsive pattern.

Based on his computer simulations of the Prisoner's Dilemma, Axelrod makes some suggestions for successful behavior in bargaining: do not compare yourself with your opponent but with how someone else in your shoes would do; do not be the first to defect; reciprocate both cooperation and defection; and do not be too clever.

(2) Difficulties in applying this Tit for Tat strategy in real life are easily recognizable. In an ongoing relationship the parties are rarely without direct communication before decisions are made, especially after the first such "game." Communication between the players will substantially change the strategic issues, giving them many more options to cooperate and deceive. Furthermore, retaliating after an initial defection often leads to continued defection without any move to improve the relationship. Once a pattern of defection is established, mutual recrimination often takes over, making rational cooperation hard to reestablish. Tit for Tat places the responsibility on the other party for changing from defection to cooperation, an undependable way to determine the future of a bargaining relationship.

Roger Fisher and Scott Brown suggest that, whereas Tit for Tat may be an acceptable strategy for the substance of the dispute, it is "a mistake" and "can be dangerous" as a strategy for building a working relationship. Fisher and Brown, Getting Together: Building a Relationship That Gets to Yes 197–202 (1988). They assert that the entire Prisoner's Dilemma model—which says that you are worse off if you cooperate in the face of defection from the other side—is not applicable to relationship issues. With a bilateral relationship, for instance, if you are more reliable toward the other side, you are better off even if the other side is not reliable toward you. Do you agree? See also an earlier discussion of these arguments in Brown, The Superpower Dilemma: Can Game Theory Improve the U.S.–Soviet Negotiating Relationship? 2 Negotiation J. 371, 378–83 (1986).

(3) Axelrod's findings suggest that to be effective a lawyer must adjust his negotiating strategy to fit the situation he faces, and that he can also influence the situation he faces by the selection and adjustments he makes. These findings appear to support the fundamental assumptions of problem-solving theory. Yet, the payoff matrix for the Prisoner's Dilemma suggests a more competitive framework, precisely because the highest payoff is given for a win that outmaneuvers the opponent ("b" and "c" in Figure II–1). Are Axelrod's conclusions consistent with either the problem-solving or competitive approach?

Assume a change in the payoff matrix so that the least valued choice is when both players defect ("d"), and the next higher value is given for "you cooperate, other defects" ("b"). This game is known as "chicken"—for example, an escalated strike, a lengthy and expensive discovery process in a lawsuit, or a nuclear confrontation. How would this change affect your choices? Note that for the situation where you know the other side will defect, you receive a higher payoff if you cooperate even in the face of defection. The favored strategy, therefore, is to convince your opponent that you intend to defect regardless of his decision. His "rational" choice then is to cooperate. He receives the third-level payoff, while your defection garners the top payoff. See Goetz, Law and Economics 15–17 (1984). Again, however, this analysis runs into a reality problem when applied to the ongoing relationship. A "chicken" strategy cannot be used time after time without assuming irrational behavior from the other side. People do not routinely or regularly give others substantial profit based on obvious bluffing, misinformation, or other deceits. As long as existence is not at stake, as it may be in the nuclear confrontation example, a party will soon place as high a value on imposing a loss on the other side as on receiving a positive benefit.

Are there ways to alter the payoff matrix to reflect a more integrative process? What if quadrant "a" (both cooperate) were the highest value, or more realistically, yielded a dual possibility: a 70% probability that the pie would expand to accommodate a payoff higher than any fixed reward, and a 30% probability that you would receive a fixed reward that was only slightly lower than what you could achieve from "b"? Would this be an accurate reflection of reality, or at least as likely to be accurate as the payoff scheme in the original fact situation?

(4) The Prisoner's Dilemma raises interesting questions about human rationality and trust. Axelrod's primary prerequisite for cooperation is the possibility of continuing contact between the players. But assume a one-shot event, where the players know that they will never play a similar game with these opponents again. (This assumption is not improbable for the typical lawyer, especially for the larger urban areas or in many specialities, like antitrust, tax, or criminal law, in which the practice is statewide, regional, or national in scope.) If everyone is rational, each would analyze the problem in a similar manner, and all should come to the same conclusion: The best choice for any one player, not knowing what the other will do, is to defect. He must also recognize that the other players will analyze the problem as he has and choose to defect also. Understanding that, a more beneficial and therefore more rational choice would be to cooperate. Because all should make the same decision, all should then cooperate. See D. Hofstadler, Metamagical Themes: Questing for the Essence of the Mind and Patterns 739–54 (1985). Logic suggests, however, that a lawyer may still try for the maximum benefit (outmaneuvering the other side), relying on credible misrepresentation or deception to induce the other side to cooperate, while he defects. For the one-shot prisoners' dilem-

ma, then, the controlling force may be a fear of being found a naive sucker combined with the hope for asymmetry.

(5) Game theory was developed as a way to study and explain individual decision-making behavior in conflict situations, primarily in economic and business transactions. However, with its restrictive assumptions, is game theory useful to lawyer-negotiators, or does it simplify and quantify to the point of being an unusable distortion of reality?

b. Expected Satisfaction

Two parties to a dispute will presumptively not agree to settle their differences unless each is satisfied that entering into the agreement is better than having no agreement at all. Each agreement can be viewed as an exchange of satisfaction between the parties. From this perspective the exchange sets a market value for the bargained items in units of satisfaction.

In reality, parties accept many agreements which do not provide equal gains for both sides. Unequal bargaining power, the variable impact of deadlines, differences in knowledge and skill, personality clashes, and many other factors help one party achieve a higher than equitable gain. These gains are normally given in real terms, usually in money, time, or goods, not in units of satisfaction. In order to be motivated to sign an agreement, however, the two sides must theoretically agree on an acceptable rate of exchange or market value for the satisfaction that each expects to receive as a result of the agreement.

This exchange of satisfaction can vary among issues within a single negotiation and between similar negotiations because of different values that lawyers and their clients use to calculate satisfaction levels. No two lawyers will value the same result in the same way, nor will a lawyer rely on only the value structure of his client without some modification, usually made unconsciously, in light of his own values, attitudes, and personality. In addition, a client's or lawyer's satisfaction can come from avoidance as well as achievement. One side may receive as much satisfaction from avoiding a court battle as the other receives from negotiating $110,000 more than he expected. Moreover, the level of satisfaction achieved is usually calculated as a fraction or multiple of expected satisfaction and therefore may be subject to substantial analytical error by both parties. Inequality in the satisfaction exchanged would therefore not be unusual or surprising.

The fact that both parties can increase their satisfaction levels by coming to an agreement can be inferred from their willingness to negotiate. They both see potential gains to be achieved by negotiating, although not necessarily joint gains. Still, the ability of one lawyer and his client to achieve a level of satisfaction from reaching agreement equal to or greater than the satisfaction they might achieve from not reaching agreement depends entirely on their ability to allow the other lawyer and his client to achieve an equivalent level of satisfaction. This is the "expected satisfaction theory."

Two conclusions are apparent. First, there is a premium for discovering and understanding the other side's satisfaction range—its values, expectations, and goals. The lawyer will first make some assumptions about that range, and the negotiation may fairly be said to be a process of testing those assumptions. Second, the expected satisfaction range becomes a primary consideration and should be the focus of continuing dialogue between a lawyer and his client.[6]

The concept of expected satisfaction has not been accepted widely as a significant addition to the analysis of a negotiation. Why? There does not appear to be any conceptual difference between a bottom line and the minimum level of satisfaction needed to enter into an agreement. Is it helpful to the lawyer to translate real units of money, time, or goods into units of satisfaction? The expected satisfaction concept closely resembles the utility concept as used in economics. Economists do the same thing when they quantify utilities in order to state relationships and probabilities with more ease. In a particularly complex negotiation, such efforts might help the negotiator in sorting through the possible solutions, especially when his client as well as the other side is not one but many different organizations. The U.S.–Panama negotiations over the Panama Canal during the 1970's[7] and the Law of the Sea negotiation during the late 1970's and early 1980's[8] are two examples of such situations.

4. Comparison and Critique

Current literature is full of the attacks, responses, and counters among proponents of the two different theories of negotiation. As an example of this dialogue, we have chosen a critical review of the book Getting to Yes (see supra p. 83), with a response by co-author Fisher. The comparisons are explicit, the critiques beautifully expressed. Indeed, the character of the writings reflect in large part the qualities of the respective theories each author espouses.

By now you either have experienced several class simulations or can recall a number of personal negotiations that provide ample evidence of competing theories and strategies. As you read the following excerpts, ask yourself: What theory—what picture of the negotiating world—did I hold as I determined my strategies? What theory or theories were held by the other side? Did these theories and strategies, and the interaction among them, have an impact on the resulting outcome? What impact, and why?

6. See C. Karrass, The Negotiating Game 140–45 (1970).

7. See H. Raiffa, The Art & Science of Negotiation 166–83 (1982).

8. See J. Sebenius, Negotiating the Law of the Sea 113 (1984).

JAMES J. WHITE, ESSAY REVIEW: THE PROS AND CONS OF GETTING TO YES

with following Comment by Roger Fisher
34 J. of Legal Educ. 115–117, 119–22 (1984).

Getting to YES is a puzzling book. On the one hand it offers a forceful and persuasive criticism of much traditional negotiating behavior. It suggests a variety of negotiating techniques that are both clever and likely to facilitate effective negotiation. On the other hand, the authors seem to deny the existence of a significant part of the negotiation process, and to oversimplify or explain away many of the most troublesome problems inherent in the art and practice of negotiation. The book is frequently naive, occasionally self-righteous, but often helpful.

* * *

Unfortunately the book's emphasis upon mutually profitable adjustment, on the "problem solving" aspect of bargaining, is also the book's weakness. It is a weakness because emphasis of this aspect of bargaining is done to almost total exclusion of the other aspect of bargaining, "distributional bargaining," where one for me is minus one for you. Schelling, Karrass and other students of negotiation have long distinguished between that aspect of bargaining in which modification of the parties' positions can produce benefits for one without significant cost to the other, and on the other hand, cases where benefits to one come only at significant cost to the other. They have variously described the former as "exploring for mutual profitable adjustments," [2] "the efficiency aspect of bargaining," or "problem solving." The other has been characterized as "distributional bargaining" or "share bargaining." Thus some would describe a typical negotiation as one in which the parties initially begin by cooperative or efficiency bargaining in which each gains something with each new adjustment without the other losing any significant benefit. Eventually, however, one comes to bargaining in which added benefits to one impose corresponding significant costs on the other. * * *

One can concede the authors' thesis (that too many negotiators are incapable of engaging in problem solving or in finding adequate options for mutual gain), yet still maintain that the most demanding aspect of nearly every negotiation is the distributional one in which one seeks more at the expense of the other. My principal criticism of the book is that it seems to overlook the ultimate hard bargaining. Had the authors stated that they were dividing the negotiation process in two and were dealing with only part of it, that omission would be excusable. That is not what they have done. Rather they seem to assume that a clever negotiator can make any negotiation into problem solving and thus completely avoid the difficult distribution of which Karrass and

2. Schelling, [An Essay on Bargaining, 46 Am.Econ.Rev.] 281 (1956).

Schelling speak. To my mind this is naive. By so distorting reality, they detract from their powerful and central thesis.

Chapter 5, entitled "Insist on Objective Criteria," is a particularly naive misperception or rejection of the guts of distributive negotiation. Here, as elsewhere, the authors draw a stark distinction between a negotiator who simply takes a position without explanation and sticks to it as a matter of "will," and the negotiator who is reasonable and insists upon "objective criteria." Of course the world is hardly as simple as the authors suggest. Every party who takes a position will have some rationale for that position; every able negotiator rationalizes every position that he takes. Rarely will an effective negotiator simply assert "X" as his price and insist that the other party meet it.

The suggestion that one can find objective criteria (as opposed to persuasive rationalizations) seems quite inaccurate. As Eisenberg suggests, the distributive aspect of the negotiation often turns on the relative power of the parties. One who could sell his automobile to a particular person for $6,000 could not necessarily sell it for more than $5,000 to another person, not because of principle, but because of the need of the seller to sell and the differential need of the two buyers to buy. To say that there are objective criteria that call for a $5,000 or $6,000 price, or in the case of a personal injury suit for a million dollars or an $800,000 judgment, is to ignore the true dynamics of the situation and to exaggerate the power of objective criteria. Any lawyer who has been involved in a personal injury suit will marvel at the capacity of an effective plaintiff's lawyer to appear to do what the authors seem to think possible, namely to give the superficial appearance of certainty and objectivity to questions that are inherently imponderable. * * *

In short, the authors' suggestion * * * that one can avoid "contests of will" and thereby eliminate the exercise of raw power is at best naive and at worst misleading. Their suggestion that the parties look to objective criteria to strengthen their cases is a useful technique used by every able negotiator. Occasionally it may do what they suggest: give an obvious answer on which all can agree. Most of the time it will do no more than give the superficial appearance of reasonableness and honesty to one party's position.

* * *

Finally, because the book almost totally disregards distributive bargaining, it necessarily ignores a large number of factors that probably have a significant impact on the outcome of negotiations. For example, Karrass and Ross suggest that a party's aspiration level is an important factor in determining the outcome of a negotiation, other things being equal. There is evidence that the level of the first offer, and the pace and form of concessions all affect the outcome of negotiation, yet there is no consideration of those matters. Doubtless the authors can be forgiven for that. No book of 163 pages can be expected to deal with every aspect of negotiation. Yet this one suffers more than most, for implicitly if not explicitly, it seems to suggest that it is presenting the "true method."

COMMENT BY ROGER FISHER

* * *

Different purposes? To some extent, I believe, White is more concerned with the way the world is, and I am more concerned with what intelligent people ought to do. One task is to teach the truth—to tell students the unpleasant facts of life, including how people typically negotiate. But I want a student to negotiate better than his or her father. I see my task as to give the best possible prescriptive advice, taking into account the way other human beings are likely to behave as well as one's own emotions and psychological state.

Suppose a husband and wife come to an expert in negotiation asking advice on how best to negotiate the terms of a separation agreement that will involve children and jointly-held property. What is the best advice that such an expert could give to both about the process—about the manner of negotiating that would be most likely to produce a wise and fair outcome while maximizing their ability to deal with future problems and minimizing their costs in terms of time, resources, and emotional stress? If one of them alone asked for such advice, in what ways would wise recommendations differ? These are the questions I am interested in. * * *

Are distributional issues amenable to joint problem solving? The most fundamental difference between White's way of thinking and mine seems to concern the negotiation of distributional issues "where one for me is minus one for you." We agree on the importance of cooperation, imagination, and the search for creative options where the task is to reconcile substantive interests that are compatible. White, however, sees the joint problem-solving approach as limited to that area. In his view, the most demanding aspect of nearly every negotiation is the distributional one in which one seeks more at the expense of the other. Distributional matters, in his view, must be settled by the ultimate hard bargaining. He regards it as a distortion of reality to suggest that problem solving is relevant to distributional negotiation.

Here we differ. By focusing on the substantive issues (where the parties' interests may be directly opposed), White overlooks the shared interest that the parties continue to have in the process of resolving that substantive difference. How to resolve the substantive difference is a shared problem. Both parties have an interest in identifying quickly and amicably a result acceptable to each, if one is possible. How to do so is a problem. A good solution to that process-problem requires joint action.

The guts of the negotiation problem, in my view, is not who gets the last dollar, but what is the best process for resolving that issue. It is certainly a mistake to assume that the only process available for resolving distributional questions is hard bargaining over positions. In my judgment it is also a mistake to assume that such hard bargaining is the best process for resolving differences efficiently and in the long-term interest of either side. * * *

Objective criteria. It is precisely in deciding such distributional issues that objective criteria can play their most useful role. Here is a second area of significant disagreement. White finds it useful to deny the existence of objective standards. "The suggestion that one can find objective criteria opposed to persuasive rationalizations) seems quite inaccurate." To his way of thinking the only approach is for a negotiation first to adopt a position and later to develop rationalizations for it: ". . . every able negotiator rationalizes every position that he takes."

No one has suggested that in most negotiations there is a single objective criterion that both parties will quickly accept as determinative. The question is rather what should be treated as the essence of the negotiation, and what attitude should be taken toward arguments advanced in the discussion. White thinks it better to treat positions of the parties as the essence of the negotiation, and objective standards advanced by either party as mere rationalizations. That is one approach. A different approach is possible and, I believe, preferable. * * *

What we are suggesting is that in general a negotiator should seek to persuade by coming up with better arguments on the merits rather than by simply trying to convince the other side that he is the more stubborn. A good guideline is for the negotiator to advance arguments as though presenting them to an impartial arbitrator, to press favorable bases for decision, but none so extreme as to damage credibility. (On the receiving side a good guideline is for a negotiator to listen to arguments as though he were an impartial arbitrator, remaining open to persuasion despite self interest and preconceptions.) My experience suggests that this method is often more efficient and amicable than hard positional bargaining and more often leads to satisfactory results for both parties.

Notes and Questions

(1) Is the problem-solving theory always dependent on a situation where integrative bargaining is possible, as Professor White suggests? Does it ignore, rather than accept and explain, behavior in a distributive bargaining situation? What is the relationship between the distributive/integrative and the competitive/problem-solving distinctions?

(2) Critics accuse problem-solving theorists of overlooking—or finessing, depending on the point-of-view—the power implications of tough "distributional" bargaining by relying on interests, objective criteria, and the best alternative to a negotiated agreement—what Fisher and Ury call a BATNA. White calls this oversight "at best naive and at worst misleading." Lord McCarthy, a Fellow at Nuffield

College and an industrial relations adviser to the British government, writes:

> Yet in collective bargaining, it is often clear enough that one side or the other is in the stronger position, which is not the same as having the best of the argument. In circumstances of this kind, both sides realize that if agreement is to be reached a way must be found of coming to terms with this fact. Bargaining is seen as not just a matter of logic and argument. As it has been put to me, "The name of this game is poker, not chess." * * *
>
> The point here is that however long this process takes, the outlines of an acceptable settlement, in the end, will turn on the development of a shared view about the outcome of what can only be termed a "power struggle"—that is, the ability of one side to inflict more damage on the other than it receives in return. This struggle has its own logic and rationale, and the job of the good negotiator is to anticipate its outcome and secure the best deal possible when the power position of his or her own side is at its height. But this entails a willingness to recognize and respond to pressure, or the awareness of its existence, rather than an insistence on principle. It also has very little to do with objective standards, yet those who can do it best have the highest reputation among bargainers.

McCarthy, The Role of Power and Principle in Getting to Yes, 1 Negotiation Journal 59, 64–65 (1985).

> Professor Fisher responds:
>
> Negotiators, like other people, are influenced by more than risk of damage. Negotiators, like others, respond to logic, facts, friends, ideals, law, precedent, and persuasive rhetoric. It would be a mistake to assume that the final and decisive ingredient of negotiating power is either fear or a nice calculation of the relative costs of not reaching agreement.

Fisher, Beyond Yes, 1 Negotiation Journal 67, 69 (1985).

Is it fair to say that recognition of "raw power" is the main difference between the competitive and problem-solving theories? How would you explain the impact of power from the problem-solving perspective? Is power hidden in the concept of BATNA, as Lord McCarthy suggests in another section of his article? White and McCarthy seem to translate Fisher's reference to objective criteria into a commitment to rationality. Is rationality a condition precedent for success under problem solving?

(3) Are there really two mutually exclusive visions of the world, between which you as a negotiator must choose? Or can the two be seen merely as separate strategies that could be accommodated by one single unified "theory"?

B. ACQUIRING AND DISCLOSING INFORMATION

In this section we focus on information and communication—their interrelationship and the impact they have on negotiation process and outcome. The acquisition and disclosure of information, and the method of accomplishing both effectively, play a key role in negotiation. Information is considered the raw material for power ("knowledge is power", as they say), and communication is the medium of exchange. The lawyer should be skilled in acquiring and handling the one by the artful use of the other.

For our purposes, information refers to the *general* background that establishes the dispute environment and the *specific* facts that are relevant to the particular events, all relating to both the resolution *process* as well as the *merits* of the dispute. For example, in a contract case lawyers will focus on information relevant to the merits: when and where the contract was negotiated, objectives of the parties, details of the promised performance and breach, and characteristics of the parties. There are also equally important process facts that should not be overlooked: effective methods of communicating information in this situation (by telephone, letter or a personal office visit), the timing of release or acquisition for each set of information, psychological effects of certain conduct or statements, and the impact of different risk-preferences. Information about both substance and process are necessary prerequisites for negotiating an effective resolution.

The section begins with the concept of the parties' bottom line and the impact it has in the negotiation setting. We then look at important qualities of information, including the impact of its disclosure and the distortions caused by perception and assumption. Next, we look at active listening skills, plus the traditional legal rules of evidence and procedure, that the lawyer can use to acquire more—and more accurate—information to help shape an acceptable resolution. Finally, we analyze the importance of the opening offer and discuss its relationship to good faith bargaining and lawyer ethics.

1. Impact of the Bottom Line

Some commentators explain that the traditional lawyer's goals for acquiring and disclosing information are to discover the other side's bottom line while masking or distorting the perception of his own.[1] Before evaluating this approach to information exchange, we need to share a basic understanding of the "bottom line" and how it influences a negotiation. (Bottom line is also called "reservation price" by some

---

1. See White, Machiavelli and the Bar: Ethical Limitations on Lying in Negotiation, 1980 Am.B.Found.Res.J. 926, 927–29.

authors. Fisher and Ury use their concept of BATNA as a replacement for the bottom line.[2])

A bottom line is the minimum benefit a party must receive, or the maximum cost a party will incur, in order to agree voluntarily to a negotiated settlement. For example, a personal injury accident plaintiff may have a bottom line that would reimburse him for any out-of-pocket expenses caused by the accident, such as medical expenses, property damages, costs of inconvenience, and legal fees. The defendant's insurance company, on the other hand, may set the company's bottom line at the victim's estimated medical and property expenses, plus an extra sum for pain and suffering, discounted by possible comparative negligence or by a probability that a jury might find no liability. These two bottom lines, described in zero-sum terms, are shown graphically in Figure II–2.

Figure II–2. Bottom Lines of A (Plaintiff or Seller) and B (Defendant or Buyer), with Zone of Agreement, in Zero-Sum Negotiation.

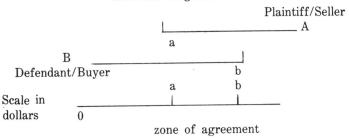

The plaintiff (A) is theoretically willing to accept a settlement offer of "a" or larger, and the insurance company (B) is willing to pay "b" or smaller. These negotiators should settle within a zone of agreement graphed as "ab" in Figure II–2. Agreement between the parties can result only if A's bottom line (where A is the seller) is less than B's (where B is the buyer).

The zero-sum situation described in Figure II–2 holds for such disparate negotiation examples as a New York Stock Exchange transaction, a tourist's purchase on the streets of Timbuctu, and an auction sale of an uncle's 1910 Morris chair. A lawyer, however, rarely handles a dispute with an exclusively zero-sum dimension. Any problem difficult enough for a client to seek legal help normally includes at least several issues with potentially differing value preferences. In the personal injury accident example, the parties may need to agree on the timing and method as well as the size of payment. The victim may want a lump sum amount payable next week, while the insurance company may want to structure payments over the victim's lifetime and purchase medical insurance for future health problems. Each party will have different priorities for the separate issues, and the

2. See R. Fisher and W. Ury, Getting to Yes 104–09 (1981).

resulting negotiation becomes non-zero sum. The impact of the bottom line in this case is more difficult to describe—and graph.

If you were to graph the non-zero-sum negotiation, it might look like Figure II–3. If A is considered the personal injury plaintiff and B the defendant, the vertical axis represents increasing utility (financial and other gain payable by the defendant) that A would receive in compensation for his injuries, and the horizontal axis represents increasing utility (decreasing amounts of damages payable to the plaintiff) for B. Perhaps an easier example to visualize is a business transaction, where A is the seller, B the buyer, the respective axis still represents increasing utility values for each, but B's utility could include more positive elements, such as a contract for future purchases at a favorable price or an introduction to new markets.

Figure II–3. Minimum Acceptable Utility Value (Bottom Line) for A (Plaintiff/Seller) and B (Defendant/Buyer), with Pareto Optimum and resulting Zone of Agreement, Non–Zero–Sum Negotiation.

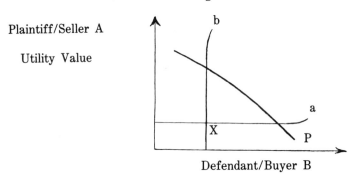

Plaintiff/Seller A

Utility Value

Defendant/Buyer B

Utility Value

The area from point X to line P represents the available bargaining range or zone of agreement for this negotiation. The limits of that zone are bounded by the respective bottom lines (a, b) and line P, which represents the locus of achievable points at which the parties' joint gains are at an optimum. In economic theory, the locus of these points is called the Pareto optimum.[3] Movement off line P from a point on that line toward the southwest or center means a loss in utility value for A, B, or both, and movement toward the northeast or away from the center yields a solution that is unachievable given the circumstances of the parties and their dispute. Some solutions are unachievable, for example, because the parties lack the resources to increase joint gains, or the transaction costs become so high that they offset other gains.

The respective bottom lines for A and B in Figure II–3 curve toward the northeast at the higher utility values for the other party. To this limited extent the parties' bottom lines are interdependent. As

3. See H. Raiffa, The Art & Science of Negotiation 139–40, 158–65 (1982).

A demands increasing value, at some point B will not be willing to settle voluntarily for an otherwise acceptable minimum amount because he will regard A's share as an unfairly high proportion of the total benefit available. In effect, B is jealous of A's outcome and will raise his bottom line amount to reflect this jealousy—a rather common psychological effect already seen in our review of game theory (see Axelrod, supra p. 91).

If the bottom lines of the two parties do not cross before reaching the efficient frontier, there is no zone of agreement. For example, a seller may be unwilling to sell his house for less than $90,000, while a buyer may have set $86,000 as the maximum he will pay. Resolution of the other issues, such as time and mode of payment, method of financing, date of closing, and property left with the house, may not change bottom line utility values enough to close the gap. Negotiation in this case is theoretically futile; in reality, however, the lack of a zone of agreement at the outset may not preclude a favorable settlement later. Each party's bottom line may change frequently and asymmetrically during negotiation as information is exchanged and understood, and its impact appreciated.

There may also be significant differences between real and apparent (perceived) bottom lines. From this perspective, the dynamics of a negotiation can make a fascinating intellectual exercise that is useful for improving a lawyer's negotiating skill. Again, let's discuss the zero-sum negotiation first. The lawyer's goal is to settle at a point that represents the minimum the other side will accept. Because only *apparent* bottom lines are visible, a negotiating lawyer would like to give the impression that his bottom line is higher than it really is, while bringing the apparent bottom line of the other side as close as possible to the real one. Logic suggests that the higher the apparent bottom line (or lower for the party required to pay—remember we are not dealing with utility values in the zero-sum case), the better the final settlement for that party. For example, lawyer A will decide to settle only if he thinks that the settlement is the best that lawyer B will let him have, and B will settle only if he thinks that it is the best A will let him have.

In Figure II–2, this settlement point would be at point *b* for A and *a* for B. If A can distort B's perception of *a* to correspond with *b*, he may be able to persuade B to settle at the higher figure. The more B can distort A's perception of B's bottom line (*b*) toward *a*, the better B's results. (This may go far to explain why the notion of "credibility" assumes such a large place in theoretical and practical discussions of negotiation.) A danger exists, however, if each is equally successful in persuading the other that his apparent bottom line is the real one. The result is no zone of agreement, and the parties will not settle even though each would benefit by settling anywhere between *a* and *b*. This risk of failure suggests that concentration on bottom lines and their distortion may frequently be unwise.

The non-zero-sum negotiation provides a closer approximation of a lawyer's reality. Using Figure II–4, if A and B discover their true bottom lines and decide to settle at the point of intersection (*X*), they leave substantial joint gains on the table. Both can increase their utility by finding mutually agreeable solutions closer to the efficient frontier. If A distorts B's perception of A's bottom line to line *a'*, the settling point for no joint gain will be at an increased utility for A, while remaining at B's true bottom line *b*. In Figure II–4, this point is R. Because B also wants to distort his bottom line while keeping an accurate reading of A's, the result from B's perspective is point S. What may occur is that A and B are both successful in distorting the other's perception, and the resulting settlement is the intersection of the perceived bottom lines (*a'*, *b'*) at point T. In the case of Figure II–4, this settlement remains within the zone of agreement, achieves most of the available joint gains, and is substantially improved over the result obtained if the parties only know their real bottom lines. At least in this one case, distortion *helps* the parties maximize joint gains. The danger, of course, is that T will wind up over line P and outside the zone of agreement, resulting in no settlement.

Figure II–4. Real and Apparent Minimum Acceptable Utility Value (Bottom Lines) for A (Plaintiff/Seller) and B (Defendant/Buyer), with Zones of Agreement, Non–Zero–Sum Negotiation.

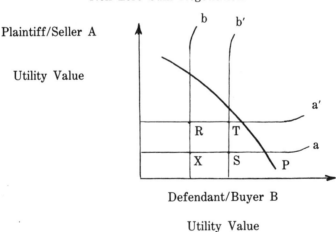

The more each party distorts his bottom line, the greater the possibility that the negotiators will find no zone of agreement. The risk of impasse will therefore be higher as the participants are more committed to distorting their bottom lines. This distortion objective is influenced by the lawyer's choice of negotiation strategy—the more competitive yielding the higher commitment to distortion. Data collected by Professor Williams in fact supports this, showing that lawyers who choose the competitive strategy have significantly higher impasse rates than those choosing a more cooperative strategy (see supra p. 80).

Let's return to the traditional competitive goals for information exchange mentioned at the beginning of this section—that the primary objective of legal negotiation is to mislead the other side about your bottom line while not being misled about the other side's. One effect is to place a priority on misinformation and the act of producing and identifying that misinformation, rather than on accurate information and the act of evaluating its accuracy and impact on possible outcomes. A second effect is to concentrate the negotiator's attention on bottom lines rather than on an aspiration level that corresponds to objective criteria. To use the house example, a competitive seller would focus on discovering the maximum a buyer would be willing to pay, while concealing the least he would accept, leaving the determination of reasonable market value for another day. This seller thereby accepts the risk that (1) this particular buyer's financial ability lies at the lower end of (or below) the range of market values, and (2) this buyer is experienced at deception as well. A third effect is to deemphasize the importance of the common interests of the parties, usually resulting in either a longer, more inefficient search before settlement is reached or a greater frequency of impasse.

Finally, significant problems with this method of information exchange surface when you consider what law practice would be like if all lawyers were committed to this objective. The most effective lawyer would be the most deceptive in disclosing information about his bottom line while having the greatest ability to see through the deceptive attempts by the other side. This high value on deception would increase the level of mistrust and tension in negotiation, lengthen the time needed to negotiate a case, and reduce the number of settlements. Most lawyers, knowing that the opposing lawyers are as committed to deception as they, would prefer to rely on court procedures rather than risk a poor result because of a particularly able (deceptive) opposing negotiator. The result would be frequent use of the full court process.

However, these results have not occurred, for a number of practical reasons. Use of deception on bottom lines is virtually universal, so it is a ritual dance lawyers go through without much conscious thought in most negotiations. Recognizing this, they focus on the factors which will signal when the other side is close to its bottom line. These factors may include standards that can be more objectively determined (the price paid for a similar business in the neighboring state), certain phrases that have become synonymous with "bottom line" among lawyers who negotiate together frequently ("I'm sorry . . ., but that's it!"), or psychological indicators (direct eye contact, movement to terminate a session). Lawyers often use the court's discovery process to test the veracity of the other side's information without committing the time to full use of the litigation process. Further, many clients themselves are demanding more timely and less costly resolution of their problems, and many are happy with a "fair" rather than a "maximum" result. Even if one side is successful in a deception, this fact is not often disclosed and the resulting settlement, despite being weighted in favor of one party, may still leave the other with a satisfactory result. Lastly, a total commitment to competitive deception would probably lead over time to a consistently tense and confrontational negotiating atmosphere, and most people would want to avoid such unpleasant working conditions.

2. Variable Qualities of Information

Developing a workable system for acquiring, evaluating, and disclosing accurate information is not only more efficient, but also aids in building a negotiating environment that will support good communication and trust. The tools that permit a lawyer to evaluate his information needs and help him develop a credible communication channel with the other side are valuable resources. A first step in acquiring these tools is to consider the impact of information in the negotiation setting, the role of perception, and the effect of assumptions.

a. The Impact of Information

Two business professors, one an economist and statistician, the other an organization and management expert, have conducted substantial research into the effect of information on the outcome of a negotiation. The following excerpt provides a summary of some of their findings.

HARNETT & CUMMINGS, BARGAINING BEHAVIOR
164–65 (1980).

One of the central themes throughout our research has been the significant role that information plays in the processes of negotiation and in determining the outcomes of bargaining. Early in our work we became interested in the strategic impact of ignorance; that is, in the impact that *not* knowing the needs and constraints of one's opponent has upon one's bargaining style and the results achieved. In addition, we were concerned with the role that knowledge by an opponent of his ignorance might have on bargaining. We found that, indeed, the information structure of the bargaining situation does exert an important impact. Specifically, our research has produced four important findings relating to this theme.

First, we have generally confirmed the Schelling hypothesis, namely, that information can be a disadvantage to a bargainer. This is particularly the case where unequal information exists between bargainers, where the informed party knows that the other party is uninformed and where norms of equity or equality seem to be operating. Most strikingly, we have found that informed bargainers will attempt to use an available communication system to provide information concerning the payoff structure of the bargaining context *to* the uninformed bargainer. Presumably, the motive operating in such a situation is to induce the uninformed bargainer to lower his/her aspiration level and to take equity or equality considerations seriously.

Second, we found that whether bargainers possess information about the payoff structure of the bargaining situation influences the predictability of the bargaining outcome. Specifically, measures of a bargainer's expectations and personality are more predictive of the amount earned in bargaining in the presence than in the absence of information. In addition, the predictability of individual predictions shifts when one contrasts bargaining under information versus no-information conditions. Information seems to operate as a reality input into the bargaining process, resulting in a greater covariance of personal aspiration, expectation, and personality on the one hand and actual bargaining achievements on the other.

Third, we have discovered that the amount of information available to a bargainer concerning payoffs influences the impact that the bargainer's risk-taking propensity has on his/her success (money earned). We have found in two separate studies that the impact of risk-taking propensity upon earnings is greater with less information. Our explanation of this is that, in general, the less structure available in the bargaining context, the greater the significance of the personal characteristics of the bargainer in influencing his/her behavior and the outcomes achieved.

Fourth, we have found strong evidence that the information available to a bargainer and the bargainer's aspiration level interact in influencing the bargaining process. Bargainers with relatively low aspiration levels prior to bargaining seem to gain bargaining strength when given information about their opponent's payoff structure while highly aspiring bargainers seem to lose strength with information. Our interpretation is that both types of bargainers adjust their aspiration levels (thus their behaviors) toward an intermediate ground when provided with the payoff structures of their opponents. Thus, information may serve to both raise and lower aspiration levels, depending on the initial discrepancy between a bargainer's *a priori* aspirations and the payoffs potentially available in the bargaining situation.

Notes and Questions

(1) The conclusions of Harnett and Cummings suggest that the negotiator with less information has several advantages over someone who is better informed. How can information be a disadvantage? What are the advantages of ignorance? Should the lawyer concentrate on disclosing as much information as possible in order to lower the other side's aspiration level, while trying to acquire as little information as possible to protect his own level? Are there countervailing incentives for a lawyer to learn as much information about the other side as possible?

(2) The impact of information depends in part on other factors, such as the lawyer's or client's propensity to take risks or their

aspiration levels. Are these separate factors measurable in a negotiation setting? How can a lawyer assess them in preparing for negotiation?

b. Perception

All participants in a specific dispute look at the same factual situation but perceive it in different ways. Each is selective about what he hears and reads, depending upon his own beliefs, assumptions, and choices. If the parties hope to come to a voluntary agreement, they will either have to arrive at a reasonably similar view of the underlying dispute, or to agree to disagree substantially on the facts so long as both perspectives point to a common solution.

A lawyer's personal perception of events can be significantly affected by acquiring more accurate information through diligent investigation and listening, and by assessing that information realistically. One way for the lawyer and his client to move their perceptions closer to reality is to place themselves psychologically in the other's shoes to determine how the other side views the situation.

Different perceptions are typically based on variances in the priorities people give to the same things. The existence of these variances is the raw material for argument and dispute, especially among people who do not think about, understand, or appreciate such variances. However, variances create opportunities for solutions that recognize and satisfy the top priorities of both sides.[4]

In order to produce a mutually agreeable solution by negotiation, clients and their lawyers try to reach a common perception of the problem. This general need for consensus appears on two levels. The parties need to bring into reasonable congruence their respective perceptions of the events creating the dispute. By assisting this process, the lawyer may provide his most useful service for the client. In addition, however, there is a necessary consensus on the right process for resolving the dispute. In order for negotiation to succeed, both parties must accept that process as an acceptable method of reaching the result. If one lawyer thinks that a court hearing is the only acceptable process for resolving the dispute, there is little hope for settlement. Varying perceptions also create different expectations of what can be done in a negotiation concerning such matters as whether a meeting can be scheduled, a concession made, a client's interest satisfied, a legitimate threat issued, an asset retained, or a favorable outcome achieved. Professor Schelling describes the convolutions of perception and expectation in bargaining: "[T]he best choice for either [negotiator] depends on what he expects the other to do, knowing that the other is similarly guided, so that each is aware that each must try to guess what the second guesses the first will guess the second to guess

4. See H. Raiffa, supra note 3, at 148–50.

and so on, in the familiar spiral of reciprocal expectations." [5] Recall the Prisoner's Dilemma, supra p. 90.

In the following selection, Professors Fisher and Ury discuss the impact of perception and the most useful responses to resulting distortions of reality.

FISHER & URY, GETTING TO YES
22–30 (1981).

Understanding the other side's thinking is not simply a useful activity that will help you solve your problem. Their thinking *is* the problem. Whether you are making a deal or settling a dispute, differences are defined by the difference between your thinking and theirs. When two people quarrel, they usually quarrel over an object—both may claim a watch—or over an event—each may contend that the other was at fault in causing an automobile accident. The same goes for nations. Morocco and Algeria quarrel over a section of the Western Sahara; India and Pakistan quarrel over each other's development of nuclear bombs. In such circumstances people tend to assume that what they need to know more about is the object or the event. They study the watch or they measure the skid marks at the scene of the accident. They study the Western Sahara or the detailed history of nuclear weapons development in India and Pakistan.

Ultimately, however, conflict lies not in objective reality, but in people's heads. Truth is simply one more argument—perhaps a good one, perhaps not—for dealing with the difference. The difference itself exists because it exists in their thinking. Fears, even if ill-founded, are real fears and need to be dealt with. Hopes, even if unrealistic, may cause a war. Facts, even if established, may do nothing to solve the problem. Both parties may agree that one lost the watch and the other found it, but still disagree over who should get it. It may finally be established that the auto accident was caused by the blowout of a tire which had been driven 31,402 miles, but the parties may dispute who should pay for the damage. The detailed history and geography of the Western Sahara, no matter how carefully studied and documented, is not the stuff with which one puts to rest that kind of territorial dispute. No study of who developed what nuclear devices when will put to rest the conflict between India and Pakistan.

As useful as looking for objective reality can be, it is ultimately the reality as each side sees it that constitutes the problem in a negotiation and opens the way to a solution.

Put yourself in their shoes. How you see the world depends on where you sit. People tend to see what they want to see. Out of a mass of detailed information, they tend to pick out and focus on those facts that confirm their prior perceptions and to disregard or misinter-

5. T. Schelling, The Strategy of Conflict
87 (1960, 1980).
M., R. & S. Proc. Dispute Res. UCB—6

pret those that call their perceptions into question. Each side in a negotiation may see only the merits of its case, and only the faults of the other side's.

The ability to see the situation as the other side sees it, as difficult as it may be, is one of the most important skills a negotiator can possess. It is not enough to know that they see things differently. If you want to influence them, you also need to understand empathetically the power of their point of view and to feel the emotional force with which they believe in it. It is not enough to study them like beetles under a microscope; you need to know what it feels like to be a beetle. To accomplish this task you should be prepared to withhold judgment for a while as you "try on" their views. They may well believe that their views are "right" as strongly as you believe yours are. You may see on the table a glass half full of cool water. Your spouse may see a dirty, half-empty glass about to cause a ring on the mahogany finish.

*   *   *

Understanding their point of view is not the same as agreeing with it. It is true that a better understanding of their thinking may lead you to revise your own views about the merits of a situation. But that is not a *cost* of understanding their point of view, it is a *benefit*. It allows you to reduce the area of conflict, and it also helps you advance your newly enlightened self-interest.

Don't deduce their intentions from your fears. People tend to assume that whatever they fear, the other side intends to do. Consider this story from the New York Times of December 25, 1980: "They met in a bar, where he offered her a ride home. He took her down unfamiliar streets. He said it was a shortcut. He got her home so fast she caught the 10 o'clock news." Why is the ending so surprising? We made an assumption based on our fears.

It is all too easy to fall into the habit of putting the worst interpretation on what the other side says or does. A suspicious interpretation often follows naturally from one's existing perceptions. Moreover, it seems the "safe" thing to do, and it shows spectators how bad the other side really is. But the cost of interpreting whatever they say or do in its most dismal light is that fresh ideas in the direction of agreement are spurned, and subtle changes of position are ignored or rejected.

*   *   *

Discuss each other's perceptions. One way to deal with different perceptions is to make them explicit and discuss them with the other side. As long as you do this in a frank, honest manner without either side blaming the other for the problem as each sees it, such a discussion may provide the understanding they need to take what you say seriously, or vice versa.

It is common in a negotiation to treat as "unimportant" those concerns of the other side perceived as not standing in the way of an agreement. To the contrary, communicating loudly and convincingly things you are willing to say that they would like to hear can be one of the best investments you as a negotiator can make.

* * *

Look for opportunities to act inconsistently with their perceptions. Perhaps the best way to change their perceptions is to send them a message different from what they expect. The visit of Egypt's President Sadat to Jerusalem in November 1977 provides an outstanding example of such an action. The Israelis saw Egypt and Sadat as their enemy, the man and country that launched a surprise attack on them four years before. To alter that perception, to help persuade the Israelis that he too desired peace, Sadat flew to the capitol of his enemies, a disputed capitol which not even the United States, Israel's best friend, had recognized. Instead of acting as an enemy, Sadat acted as a partner. Without this dramatic move, it is hard to imagine the signing of an Egyptian–Israeli peace treaty.

* * *

Face-saving: Make your proposals consistent with their values. In the English language, "face-saving" carries a derogatory flavor. People say, "We are doing that just to let them save face," implying that a little pretense has been created to allow someone to go along without feeling badly. The tone implies ridicule.

This is a grave misunderstanding of the role and importance of face-saving. Face-saving reflects a person's need to reconcile the stand he takes in a negotiation or an agreement with his principles and with his past words and deeds.

The judicial process concerns itself with the same subject. When a judge writes an opinion on a court ruling, he is saving face, not only for himself and for the judicial system, but for the parties. Instead of just telling one party, "You win," and telling the other, "You lose," he explains how his decision is consistent with principle, law, and precedent. He wants to appear not as arbitrary, but as behaving in a proper fashion. A negotiator is no different.

Often in a negotiation people will continue to hold out not because the proposal on the table is inherently unacceptable, but simply because they want to avoid the feeling or the appearance of backing down to the other side. If the substance can be phrased or conceptualized differently so that it seems a fair outcome, they will then accept it. Terms negotiated between a major city and its Hispanic community on municipal jobs were unacceptable to the mayor—until the agreement was withdrawn and the mayor was allowed to announce the same terms as his own decision, carrying out a campaign promise.

Face-saving involves reconciling an agreement with principle and with the self-image of the negotiators. Its importance should not be underestimated.

c. The Question of Assumptions

All lawyers make assumptions about the circumstances of the problem, their client's objectives, the objectives and resources of the other side, the nature of the process by which they will try to resolve the matter, and many other things. If these assumptions are consciously made and continually reassessed, they are a positive force in a negotiation. They allow the lawyer to categorize issues and focus on priorities. If the assumptions are unconscious, or if the lawyer holds on to them tenaciously although time and events make them inaccurate, they become chains that prevent the lawyer from recognizing, adjusting to, or capitalizing on the realities of the situation. But how does a negotiator recognize a valid or invalid assumption? Some examples may help.

(a) Plaintiff's lawyer practices in a small rural community. He represents Patient, a local resident, in a medical malpractice suit filed against Doctor and Hospital in an urban area at considerable distance from his county. Patient has permanent damage to his excretory and sexual functions resulting from what should have been routine urological surgery. During the initial discovery proceedings, the lawyers find that Doctor has had two prior malpractice complaints in the past five years. In this case Doctor failed to follow recognized surgical practices in three separate instances, each one causing additional damage to Patient. Defense lawyer, representing Doctor and his insurance company, welcomes settlement discussions. In evaluating the extent of his client's damages, plaintiff's lawyer uses his past experience in handling six medical malpractice cases in his home county, plus his knowledge of several other local jury awards in similar cases. He calculates a healthy damage figure of $120,000 and makes a demand for it. After ten days, defense lawyer reluctantly accepts the settlement offer with minor adjustments that bring the total to $118,600. On the recommendation of his lawyer, Patient accepts. Is there anything wrong?

Yes. Plaintiff lawyer's medical malpractice experience had been in a rural area of the state. His valuation of damages was based upon negotiations and awards with rural residents, defendants, and juries. He assumed that the amount of compensatory damages can be determined absolutely and that, once calculated accurately for a particular patient, it will not vary based on other factors, such as the geographical location of the court, local attitudes or prejudices, or the wealth or degree of culpability of the party at fault. In fact, defense lawyer and insurance company had valued this case for internal purposes at between $250,000 and $350,000. On average, urban juries award damages for medical malpractice up to three times higher than rural juries, independent of the degree of doctor's fault or the patient's place of residence.

(b) Wife tells Lawyer that she wants a divorce. She spells out her demands: at least 60% of the small amount of joint property the couple owns, custody of the minor daughter, $300 per month child support, and $500 per month alimony for the next three years to help her finish an accounting degree. Wife says that she has planned her needs carefully, with due (but not excessive) consideration for the constraints imposed by the salary Husband earns from his job. The demands sound reasonable to Lawyer, and he follows Wife's wishes in negotiating with the other side. The final settlement closely resembles Wife's initial package.

Four years later, Wife complains bitterly about the injustice of the divorce settlement and blames Lawyer for her plight. She graduated with her accounting degree, but since then has been unable to get an accounting job because of depressed economic conditions. She moved to a bigger city to take advantage of the greater job market, but the only result so far has been a higher cost-of-living. Alimony ceased a year ago, and Wife's living standards have decreased substantially. In the meantime, Husband changed jobs twice, moving up the management ladder each time, and is now earning two and one-half times the salary he was earning at the time of the divorce. Lawyer has been able to get increased child support based on Husband's new income, but it does not allow Wife to make ends meet. Why did the ideal settlement turn sour?

First, Wife and Lawyer assumed that Wife would be hired as an accountant at a reasonable salary upon graduation. If they thought about it at all, they probably assumed that her future salary would be at least at the average for new accountants. Although recessions and unemployment were known possibilities, Wife and Lawyer assumed that they either would not occur in the third year, or if they did, they would not affect Wife. Second, they assumed that Husband would continue in his then-current job after the divorce. Wife was probably unable to visualize better-than-average success for someone she was no longer interested in living with. Neither Wife nor Lawyer recognized the overconfidence with which people generally forecast their own prospects, the underestimation in viewing an opponent's future, and the wide variations in conditions that time can create.

———

We all have a tendency to assume that others see the world as we do. We are so obsessed with our own problems that we lose sight of the reality that other people may also have problems, constraints, assets, or needs which push them in an unexpected direction.

Three practices can help a lawyer identify assumptions made by the parties and lawyers in a dispute. First, solid preparation of the substance of the negotiation alerts the lawyer to potentially dangerous assumptions that she might make which could lead to unfavorable consequences for her client. More information, in this instance, would appear to support a more successful negotiation. Next, in preparing her case the lawyer should put herself in the shoes of the other side. She should practice arguing the case as if she were the opposing lawyer. This exercise can bring to light many assumptions that the other side may make for its benefit, enabling the lawyer to recognize these assumptions when raised in the heat of the negotiation and to respond to them appropriately and in timely fashion. Finally, the lawyer should be an active listener—empathetic and skeptical at the same time (see the next section on active listening skills). She cannot protect against unwarranted assumptions unless she is able to identify and understand them in context. Listening skills give her the tools to do this.

There will always be limits to the lawyer's ability to recognize and handle assumptions properly. This notion of limits is best expressed in the term "bounded rationality," which refers to the general constraints on one's ability to make decisions created by insufficient resources available (money, time, intelligence, patience) and a lack of total information.[6] Yet, the lawyer should always be working to push those "bounds of rationality" back as far as possible.

3. Skills and Structures for Acquiring Information

a. Active Listening

Thomas Schelling defined a bargaining situation as one "in which the ability of one participant to gain his ends is dependent to an important degree on the choices or decisions that the other participant will make."[7] In order to persuade the other lawyer to accept solutions which benefit his client, the first lawyer must focus on where that other participant is in his knowledge and analysis of the situation. For every option proposed, the first lawyer must evaluate the second's view of that option, the choices open to him, and his likely response. Of course, the second lawyer will be doing the same. Each sends information in an attempt to affect the other's evaluation and resulting decision, and each assesses the credibility of the information he receives. (This strategic interaction provides a ready application for systematic game theory analysis, supra p. 89.)

Active listening is a critically important tool in identifying and understanding the interests and aspiration level of the other side. Listening to what the other lawyer says about his client's situation and needs, gauging his reaction to what is said, and being sensitive to the changes in his attitude, demeanor, and physical position can provide essential information for determining credibility, interest in settlement, and bottom line. In terms of communication methods used, professional people spend about 50% of their time listening, 35% talking, 16% reading, and 9% writing. To gain information in usable form, the mind of the receiver must be open, nonjudgmental, and actively concentrated on the message the source is conveying. The listener must also be

---

6. See C. Karrass, The Negotiating Game 160–161 (1970).

7. T. Schelling, supra note 5, at 5.

aware of the distinction between what the source is trying to convey and what his actual message is. The two may be quite different.

The skill of listening properly is largely untaught in our educational system. Although trial advocacy and oral argument are important courses in law school, they focus on verbal skills—how to state the client's case in the most persuasive terms, defend a client's position when attacked, and object appropriately and effectively at trial. Law students also need to know when not to talk, and how to listen while not talking.

An effective method of listening to a persuasive speech or argument by the opposing lawyer is to organize the speaker's comments—preferably by using brief written notes—under five headings:

- What is he trying to get me to do? How does he want me to feel? Is his request explicit or implicit?

- Why does he want me to do or feel in that way? What facts or reasons is he presenting in support?

- What relevant facts has he failed to use in support of his request? Are there significant issues he has not raised?

- Why would he have omitted those facts or issues?

- What significant questions remain? Is he really talking about the right issues? [8]

The following excerpt gives some additional practical guides.

BURLEY–ALLEN, LISTENING: THE FORGOTTEN SKILL
101–02 (1982).

Guidelines for Empathetic Listening

1. Be attentive. Create a positive atmosphere through nonverbal behavior. When you are alert, attentive, nondistracted, and have eye contact, the other person feels important and more positive.

2. Be interested in the other's needs. Remember, you are to listen with understanding.

3. Listen from the "OK" listening mode.

    a. Be a sounding board; allow the sender to bounce ideas and feelings off you while assuming a nonjudgmental, non-criticizing manner.

    b. Don't ask a lot of questions. Remember, questions can come across as if the person is being "grilled."

    c. Act like a mirror: reflect back what you think the other is feeling and/or saying to you.

---

8. See M. Adler, How to Speak, How to Listen 109–10 (1983).

   d. Because they discount the person's feelings, don't use stock phrases such as:
   - Oh! It's not that bad.
   - You'll feel better tomorrow.
   - It will blow over; don't be so upset.
   - You shouldn't feel that way; it's only a small matter.
   - You're making a mountain out of a molehill.

4. Don't let the other person "hook you." This can happen when you get angry, hurt, or upset, allow yourself to become involved in an argument, jump to conclusions, or pass judgment on the other person.

5. Other ways to indicate you are listening:
   a. Encouraging, noncommital acknowledgement; brief expressions:

   "Hum." "Uh-huh." "I see." "Right." "Oh!" "Interesting."

   b. Nonverbal acknowledgements:

   Head-nodding.

   Facial expression (matching what the talker is saying).

   Body expression or movement that is relaxed and open.

   Eye contact.

   Touching.

   c. Door-openers. Invitations to say more, such as:

   "Tell me about it."

   "I'd like to hear what you're thinking."

   "Would you like to talk about it?"

   "Sounds like you've got some ideas or feelings about this."

   "I'd be interested in what you have to say."

6. Ground Rules
   a. Don't interrupt.
   b. Don't take the subject off in another direction.
   c. Don't rehearse in your own head.
   d. Don't interrogate.
   e. Don't teach.
   f. Don't give advice.
   g. Do: Reflect back to the sender what you observe and how you believe the speaker feels.

Notes and Questions

(1) The benefits that come from listening are increased substantially through more active intervention by the listener, thus eliciting

information by encouraging the other side to talk. Encouragement comes in many forms, as by setting a receptive psychological atmosphere and interjecting comments that draw the other person out, as well as by direct questioning. Questioning is an efficient method of acquiring useful information, but the lawyer must be sensitive to the complexities of its use. Questioning that is too focused and intense can destroy the environment for a good information exchange. Questioning that lacks direction and discipline may confuse more than enlighten, and allow the other side to answer in ways that will build its strengths and hide its weaknesses. Questions that are brief, clear, and unobtrusive, and are phrased in a non-threatening but direct way, are useful not only in acquiring information, but also in establishing an atmosphere conducive to active listening. See J. Folberg and A. Taylor, Mediation 109–12 (1984).

(2) Most law students begin by using questioning techniques modeled on the direct or cross-examination questioning used in litigation (and in many classrooms). The questions are pointed and direct, they are stated in a manner that demands an answer, and the questioner knows the answer to the question (or its general outline) before he asks it. The questioner and the person responding reflect different power positions, and the relationship is fixed: The questioner asks and the other person responds. The paradigm is the litigator or the law professor using the traditional "Socratic method." Is this style a helpful model for the negotiating lawyer? What are the qualities that make it useful, and those that make it non-productive or destructive?

(3) Silence is frequently overlooked as a questioning technique. Lawyers lose many opportunities to gain valuable information by too much talking—interjecting additional questions or comments just when an expectant silence would elicit more information (or even admissions or concessions). A lawyer's natural tendency to control conversation through speaking or arguing often destroys his ability to listen patiently. Edwards and White make the following comments on the use of silence as a negotiating tactic:

INSCRUTABILITY

The classic negotiator of Grade B movies is an oriental or middle eastern person who smiles in response to Peter Lorre's proposals. The same quality of being able to disguise one's reactions is recognized in the accolade "poker faced." The capacity of disguising one's reactions is one of the most important traits that a negotiator can have.

For most inscrutability equals silence, for to talk is to reveal one's true reactions and opinions. Of course, that is not always the case; some (though not many in our judgment) can talk a great deal during a negotiation and yet reveal little. We believe that such persons are exceptions to the rule, that a typical inexperienced negotiator has a compulsion to talk and that inevitably such a person reveals more about his position than he thinks he is revealing.

Needless to say, one who is naturally responsive and gregarious cannot be made closemouthed and inscrutable simply by wishing to be so. On the other hand all negotiators can exercise some control over their reactions and considerable control over the amount of talking they do. Again and again in the observation of student negotiating tapes we see opponents attempting to talk simultaneously. In that circumstance neither is convincing the other but more important, neither is learning what he can about the opponent's position by allowing the opponent to talk.

Every negotiator should consider how he can disguise his true reactions and true judgments when he wishes to do that. In most cases he should also restrain his natural desire to speak when a silence of any length in the negotiation occurs. One of the impediments that the Institute for Survey Research at Michigan has found to training interviewers is the interviewer's desire to talk. The Institute's experience reveals that silence in the presence of other people causes considerable and rising anxiety and that in response to that anxiety the inexperienced interviewer will not wait for an answer from the respondent but will offer the answer himself. The same anxiety will operate on the untrained negotiator and it must be resisted by conscious effort.

Edwards & White, The Lawyer As A Negotiator 114–15 (1977).

b. Rules of Evidence and Procedure

Choosing to focus on negotiation as the best process by which to resolve a dispute does not foreclose the simultaneous use of other processes, especially litigation. Rules of civil or criminal procedure and evidence can be positive forces in your efforts to acquire and disclose information necessary to arrive at a reasonable settlement. They establish deadlines which the other side (as well as you and your client) must meet, and they include important enforcement mechanisms. Lawyer and client affidavits and court-imposed sanctions can help increase confidence in the truthfulness of the resulting information. However, if you use these rules primarily to raise the other side's costs or to punish him for not compromising, they become counterproductive in most cases. The strategies of complementing the negotiation with effective use of litigation procedures are discussed more fully, infra p. 151.

The procedural rules governing discovery (Federal Rules of Civil Procedure 26–37; Federal Rules of Criminal Procedure 15, 16) are especially helpful in managing an exchange of information, even in cases that present little complexity or monetary reward. The major benefit lies in the structure that those rules bring, both to the lawyer's planning activities and to the process of information exchange. In addition, the rules of evidence (Federal Rules of Evidence 408, 409,

410—see Appendix C) can also affect the process of gaining information during negotiation, as well as its quality, and should be an important part of a lawyer's evaluation process (see the note on Rule 408, infra p. 181).

A lawsuit need not be filed for lawyers to agree to use these rules as informal guides for the acquisition and disclosure of information. Even when a client does not have a legal claim for which a court can give relief, rules of discovery and evidence can still guide the joint search for information.   Court rules provide legitimate and accepted procedural standards familiar to lawyers. If discovery rules would help in producing information more efficiently in a particular case, raising your confidence in the product of that search, you should ask the other lawyer to adopt the court rules, or a simpler version, as informal and flexible guidelines.

4. Opening Offers

When a lawyer makes an opening offer, he discloses important information to the other side. He communicates the high point of his bargaining range, the extent of his preparation and analysis, his expectations concerning the competitiveness of the negotiation, and the level of confidence he has in his own perception of the facts. For example, the $120,000 opening offer in the malpractice case, supra p. 114, could tell the insurance company's lawyer that plaintiff's lawyer does not know about higher awards from urban juries, that his aspirations are therefore low compared to what a court would award, and that he wants to conduct a cooperative negotiation. Any opening offer will usually foreclose settlement at a higher level, even if the other side had been expecting to settle at a higher amount. In other words, if you don't ask for it, you probably won't get it! In this way the offer itself can have a substantial impact on the final outcome. It can also affect the quality of the process. If a plaintiff's lawyer avoids the trap of making too low an offer by making an unreasonably high demand, he may generate an emotional stubbornness in the opposing lawyer or party that cannot be overcome by subsequent reasonableness. Moreover, the other side could conclude that it would take so much effort and time to educate the plaintiff and his lawyer about what is a reasonable settlement range that it would simply not be cost efficient to negotiate further. Similarly, an unreasonably high offer may adversely affect the future relationship between the parties, a typically important part of any ongoing business arrangement.

Considering these possible effects of the opening offer, is it any wonder that negotiators disagree over who should make it and when? Compare the views of Judge Edwards and Professor White with those of Professor Raiffa.

EDWARDS & WHITE, THE LAWYER AS A NEGOTIATOR
115–16 (1977).

FIRST OFFER, LARGE DEMAND

Almost without exception it is desirable to cause the opposing party in a negotiation to make the first realistic offer. If one has made a serious miscalculation about his position, the opponent's first offer may save a considerable sum. Assume for example that a new and totally inexperienced law school graduate is seeking a job in a middle-sized city. From his very limited perspective he believes that the yearly wage for beginning lawyers in that town is $10,000. He is pleasantly surprised therefore when his prospective employer offers him $17,000 to begin. If the employee had made the first offer, it would have cost him $7,000 and perhaps more. Thus, causing the opponent to make the first realistic offer is most helpful in circumstances in which one regards his opponent's case as stronger than the opponent regards it.

A standard defense to an opponent's demand for a first offer is to give him a large demand. Thus, if convention calls for one party to make the first move, he may choose to make that move by giving an outrageous demand simply to get the negotiation underway. Such an exchange is common place in the negotiation of personal injury cases in which the plaintiff's lawyer will often start with the demand far in excess of anything he thinks the defense will grant him. In fact such a demand is not a first offer at all but simply a way of instituting negotiation without having to set the level at the outset.

In contexts other than personal injury such as commercial litigation and the purchase or sale of goods or land, the large demand rule is not widely used. One who makes an outrageous demand in such circumstances may find that he has killed the deal entirely by signaling to the other party that he is not truly interested. For that reason it is more important in those situations that one concentrate on getting the first offer from the opponent.

The challenging question is not why one wants the first offer, but how he procures that offer from his opponent. In some situations one can rely upon the customary practice to require the other side to make the first offer. For example it is customary practice in the employment field for the employer to commence with an offer. Usually the employee is not expected to come up with an initial request of a specific dollar figure. There are similar customs in other areas.

Of course the simplest method of procuring the first offer in contexts in which there is no convention is simply to ask the opponent to state his price. An experienced negotiator is likely to reply that he is willing to offer, "Whatever you think it is worth," but the inexperienced negotiator may simply respond with a realistic first offer.

RAIFFA, THE ART & SCIENCE OF NEGOTIATION *
127–28 (1982).

Opening Gambits

Who should make the first concrete offer? Beware of opening so conservatively that your offer falls well within your adversaries' acceptance region. Beware of opening with so extreme a value that you hurt the ambience of negotiations; also, if you are too extreme you will have to make disproportionately large concessions. If you open first, and if your adversaries are ill prepared, you might influence their perception of their own reservation price by your opening offer: your opening offer anchors their thinking about the value of the venture to themselves. Be aware of this anchoring phenomenon if the situation is reversed.

Gauge your reaction to an extreme first offer. Don't get locked in by talking about your adversaries' extreme offer; don't let their offer be the vantage point for subsequent modifications. The best strategy in this case is to either break off negotiations until they modify their offer, or quickly counter with an offer of your own. When two offers are on the table, the midpoint is a natural focal point, so think about this when you make an initial counteroffer. Compare the midpoint of the two offers with your aspiration level.

Protect your integrity. Try to avoid disclosing information (such as your reservation price) as an alternative to giving false information. Use phrases like "This is what I would like to get" rather than "This is what I *must* get," when your "must" value is not really a must.

Notes and Questions

(1) Is there a conflict between the conclusions presented in these two excerpts? Who will make the opening offer in a negotiation between two lawyers who are committed to the Edwards and White approach? What is the result if the lawyers follow Raiffa?

(2) The best way to understand the importance and impact of the opening offer may be to experience directly the pressures in an actual negotiation. If you have not done a class exercise, you have undoubtedly negotiated recently with someone about something—your parents about money, a salesman about a new car or television, or the university financial aids office about a larger loan. Did the opening offer determine the outcome? If there were two offers on the table, did the outcome equal the midpoint? Why or why not?

(3) What advantages are gained by a lawyer who makes an appropriate opening offer? What are the disadvantages? One guide for opening offers might be: A lawyer should make an opening offer only if he has sufficient information to give him confidence that he knows the proper reference points (the bargaining range or payoff schedules) for

the negotiation, and when he makes the offer, he should state it with the confidence created by that information and preparation. Is this approach workable?

(4) Raiffa mentions the anchoring effect of an opening offer. When should a negotiator try to anchor the negotiation? What other methods perform an anchoring function without presenting the risks that an opening offer does? How would you protect your case from the anchoring effect of a very high offer by the other side? How would you protect your client from its psychological impact?

(5) In a non-zero-sum negotiation a lawyer may include false demands in his opening offer in order to build a bargaining structure that will accommodate later concessions that have little or no effect on the client's basic interests. A false demand is one that is not a part of the client's real request list, or at least not at the level of priority stated.

Richard Neely, West Virginia Supreme Court Judge and former trial lawyer, gives an example from his Family Law practice:

> I know how divorce laws' unpredictability can be used to terrorize women into bartering away their support because I've done it. I had a client, a railroad brakeman, who had fallen out of love with his wife and in love with motorcycles. Along the way he had picked up a new woman who was as taken with motorcycles as he. After about a year of competing with fast bikes and fast women, my client's wife filed for divorce. My client had two children at home—one about nine and the other about 12. Unfortunately for him, the judge in the county where his wife had filed for divorce was notorious for giving high alimony and child-support awards. The last thing that I wanted to do was go to trial. The wife had a strong case of adultery, and the best defense my client could manufacture was a lame countersuit for "cruel and inhuman treatment"—not exactly a showstopper in a rural domestic court 14 years ago.
>
> During the initial interview I asked my client about his children, and he told me that he got along with them well. Then I asked whether he wanted custody. He emphatically said no. Nonetheless, it occurred to me that if he told his wife that he would fight for custody all the way to the U.S. Supreme Court, we might settle the whole divorce fairly cheaply. That night he went home and began a guerilla campaign centering on the children. His likelihood of getting custody from the judge was negligible, but that did not discourage our blustering threats.
>
> As I had hoped, my client's wife was unwilling to take any chance of losing her children, and the divorce was settled exactly as I wanted. The wife got the children by agreement, but very modest alimony and child support. All we had needed to defeat her legitimate claims in the settlement process was a halfway credible threat of a protracted custody battle.

New Republic, Feb. 10, 1986, p. 13.

The danger of including a false demand is that it may be accepted, while other more valuable demands are lost. The wife of Judge Neely's client could have called her husband's bluff, either agreeing to his custody request and asking only for liberal visitation rights (she would obviously need to be far more risk-prone), or suggesting that they take the issue to court. Judge Neely does not tell us how the children regard their father now, having endured at least ten years of minority at "modest" support. Moreover, the use of this tactic, if discovered, could have a chilling effect on the negotiation and for any continuing relationships. Still, the possibility of a false issue is always present, and a lawyer must be able to identify and counter such tactics. A lawyer can best guard against it by carefully evaluating the accuracy of disclosed information and preparing thoroughly.

Problem: Opening to Close, or Boulware Beware

The management of the General Electric Company in the late 1940's developed a new collective bargaining strategy to demonstrate its interest in doing what was right for its employees and in becoming known as a good employer. The National Labor Relations Act (NLRA) had just been passed requiring companies and labor unions to bargain in good faith.[9] Under its new strategy G.E. management was to develop as much reliable information as possible on wage rates, economic conditions, market potential, and other factors relevant to the bargaining situation. It would share this information with the union and listen to any comments or criticism from union representatives. On the basis of all this data, management would then prepare a firm and fair offer that would include all practicable concessions. Once the offer was presented, it would not be changed by management unless the supporting information was shown to be erroneous or a material change in circumstances occurred. Management intended its first offer to be the final offer.

General Electric management used this strategy in 1960. After spending months gathering information, listening to employee needs and analyzing data, management decided on its offer in late August and discussed it briefly with union representatives the day before the offer was to be made public. Because they had some serious disagreements with the proposal, union leaders urgently requested that management reconsider going public right away. Nevertheless, management proceeded with the public announcement and on the next day, started a public relations campaign among the workers to convince them of the offer's fairness.

9. Section 8 of the National Relations Act requires both employees and unions "to meet at reasonable times and confer *in good faith* with respect to wages, hours, and other terms and conditions of employment ∗ ∗ ∗." 29 U.S.C. § 158(a) (5), (b)(3). (Emphasis added.)

The "bargaining" began after the offer was made. "On various occasions the Company indicated that it had not granted certain union demands because it had put such money as it had available into improvements which it had determined from its own research would best meet the employees' needs and desires. The Company summarily rejected all union suggestions for revision entailing added costs. . . ." [10] The union then asked for the estimated costs of the management offer so that it could determine how union members would prefer to allocate the money available. Although management had the cost estimates for the specific items in the offer, it "rejected, ignored or brushed aside union requests" for such cost and other information.[11] In mid-September, to demonstrate further commitment to the opening offer as its final position, management made the offer's provisions effective immediately for all non-union employees.

Union members went on strike in October, but ended the strike within three weeks, conceding to management on all important issues. At the same time, however, the union filed an unfair labor practice grievance with the National Labor Relations Board. After extensive hearings, the Board's Trial Examiner found that G.E. management had violated its good faith bargaining obligations under the NLRA. The Board affirmed this finding in 1964.[12] The Second Circuit Court of Appeals affirmed the Board's decision in 1969, and the U.S. Supreme Court denied certiorari in 1970.[13]

Notes and Questions

(1) This example of an opening offer as a take-it-or-leave-it position is so notorious that the bargaining tactic itself is called "Boulwarism" after the General Electric vice president responsible for developing it. The case is often cited as authority for the principle that such an opening offer at the bargaining table signals bad faith. Is there another way to interpret those facts?

(2) "Good faith" is a term that has a long history in labor negotiations, but past labor cases turning on the application of the good faith requirement contained in 29 U.S.C. § 158(b)(3) are singularly unhelpful in providing a predictive guideline. Each opinion stresses the subjective nature of good faith and limits the holding strictly to the specific facts in question. See, e.g., N.L.R.B. v. Katz, 369 U.S. 736 (1962); Olinkraft v. N.L.R.B., 666 F.2d 302 (5th Cir.1982); N.L.R.B. v. Reisman Bros., 401 F.2d 770 (2d Cir.1968).

What are the assumptions that this case makes about bargaining in good faith? If an opening offer cannot be a take-it-or-leave-it proposal without suggesting "bad faith," how should you develop an initial offer? Must concessions be made by both sides for there to be "good faith"

10. General Electric Co., 150 N.L.R.B. No. 36, at 230–31 (1964).

11. Id. at 231.

12. Id.

13. N.L.R.B. v. General Electric Co., 418 F.2d 736 (2d Cir.1969), cert. den. 397 U.S. 965 (1970).

bargaining? In collective bargaining under the NLRA, the federal law expressly provides that the duty to bargain in good faith "does not compel either party to agree to a proposal or require the making of a concession." 29 U.S.C. § 158(d). Does that resolve the problems posed by use of the Boulware strategy?

(3) Although some language in the *General Electric* decision suggests that making what is really a final offer as an opener is itself evidence of bad faith, a careful reading indicates that it must be a part of a larger pattern of bad faith activity. The judges found that G.E. management had developed a sophisticated campaign to sell its opening package to union employees, regardless of the employees' wishes or the offer's consequences. The "Boulware" tactic was only one element in a comprehensive program of isolating and eventually destroying the union. "Bad faith" would seem to apply, then, to those instances where one party's active objective is to eliminate the other side as a bargaining partner—an attempted hostile takeover, so to speak. Would a "final" opening offer, absent this destructive goal, be in good faith?

(4) Another form of Boulwarism is for one party to so commit himself publicly to the opening offer that he is unable realistically to accept anything less. Can you distinguish the G.E. case from the following examples given by Professor Schelling?

> When one wishes to persuade someone that he would not pay more than $16,000 for a house that is really worth $20,000 to him, what can he do to take advantage of the usually superior credibility of the truth over a false assertion? Answer: make it true. * * *

> [S]uppose the buyer could make an irrevocable and enforceable bet with some third party, duly recorded and certified, according to which he would pay for the house no more than $16,000, or forfeit $5,000. The seller has lost; the buyer need simply present the truth. Unless the seller is enraged and withholds the house in sheer spite, the situation has been rigged against him; the "objective" situation—the buyer's true incentive—has been voluntarily, conspicuously, and irreversibly changed. The seller can take it or leave it. This example demonstrates that if the buyer can accept an irrevocable *commitment,* in a way that is unambiguously visible to the seller, he can squeeze the range of indeterminacy down to the point most favorable to him. It also suggests, by its artificiality, that the tactic is one that may or may not be available; whether the buyer can find an effective device for committing himself may depend on who he is, who the seller is, where they live, and a number of legal and institutional arrangements (including, in our artificial example, whether bets are legally enforceable).

> * * *

> The foregoing discussion has tried to suggest both the plausibility and the logic of self-commitment. Some examples may suggest the relevance of the tactic, although an observer can seldom distinguish with confidence the consciously logical, the intuitive, or

the inadvertent, use of a visible tactic. First, it has not been uncommon for union officials to stir up excitement and determination on the part of the membership during or prior to a wage negotiation. If the union is going to insist on $2 and expects the management to counter with $1.60, an effort is made to persuade the membership not only that the management could pay $2 but even perhaps that the negotiators themselves are incompetent if they fail to obtain close to $2. The purpose—or, rather, a plausible purpose suggested by our analysis—is to make clear to the management that the negotiators could not accept less than $2 *even if they wished to* because they no longer control the members or because they would lose their own positions if they tried. In other words, the negotiators reduce the scope of their own authority, and confront the management with the threat of a strike that the union itself cannot avert, even though it was the union's own action that eliminated its power to prevent the strike.

Schelling, The Strategy of Conflict 24, 27 (1960).

(5) In the final analysis, how well did Boulwarism fulfill G.E. management's original, publicly-stated goal?

C. LAW AND LITIGATION

The last section discussed the role that information plays in a negotiating situation. In this section we focus on a different kind of information—knowledge of the law and the litigation process. A lawyer's understanding of the substantive law and of litigation procedures is a powerful negotiating tool that can be used effectively in achieving a settlement in the client's interests.

1. Law—The Blueprint for Agreement

The external norms of "the law" can provide a blueprint for building a negotiated settlement in much the same way that architectural drawings lay out the plan for a building. A lawyer researches the legal infrastructure of a dispute in order to construct the basic outline of an acceptable solution and then works with the client and the other side to construct a settlement of the dispute from that general blueprint of legal standards.

Carrying the analogy one step further, blueprint designs contain features on two different levels: those which are central to the basic structure of the building (such as load-bearing walls) and therefore cannot be changed without altering the entire design, and those which reflect the individual tastes of the owners (such as the placement of built-in kitchen cabinets) that can be modified to accommodate personal interests and conditions. Settlement agreements are shaped in similar ways, with basic public values contributing the load-bearing capacity and the general legal norms providing the framework for flexible change by parties and their lawyers.

The blueprint function in a particular case is normally served by a lawyer's evaluation of what a court would do if it were to act. Knowledge of relevant substantive law permits a lawyer to plot the relative rights, duties, claims, and defenses of the disputing parties, which in turn helps him analyze and prepare the case for negotiation. As an experienced trial lawyer stated, "What drives a lawyer to settle is his assessment of how he will do in court." Evaluation connects the law with the negotiation process (recall Miller and Sarat's reference to the lawyer's role in this relationship, supra p. 5).

To explain the law-negotiation relationship, many writers on dispute resolution talk about "bargaining in the shadow of the law." [1] Consistent with this metaphor, the lawyer shapes a final agreement by working with the bargaining endowments that legal standards create. And yet, parties in a negotiation are engaged in a form of private ordering that, while influenced by legal standards, is nonetheless free to deviate from what a court might decide. Professors Mnookin and Kornhauser use a divorce example to describe what is meant by "bargaining in the shadow of the law":

> Divorcing parents do not bargain over the division of family wealth and custodial prerogatives in a vacuum; they bargain in the shadow of the law. The legal rules governing alimony, child support, marital property, and custody give each parent certain claims based on what each would get if the case went to trial. In other words, the outcome that the law will impose if no agreement is reached gives each parent certain bargaining chips—an endowment of sorts.

> A simplified example may be illustrative. Assume that in disputed custody cases the law flatly provided that all mothers had the right to custody of minor children and that all fathers only had the right to visitation two weekends a month. Absent some contrary agreement acceptable to both parents, a court would order this arrangement. Assume further that the legal rules relating to marital property, alimony, and child support gave the mother some determinate share of the family's economic resources. In negotiations under this regime, neither spouse would ever consent to a division that left him or her worse off than if he or she insisted on going to court. The range of negotiated outcomes would be limited to those that leave both parents as well off as they would be in the absence of a bargain.

> If private ordering were allowed, we would not necessarily expect parents to split custody and money the way a judge would if they failed to agree. The father might well negotiate for more

1. Mnookin and Kornhauser, Bargaining in the Shadow of the Law: The Case for Divorce, 88 Yale L.J. 950 (1979).

child-time and the mother for less. This result might occur either because the father made the mother better off by giving her additional money to compensate her for accepting less child-time, or because the mother found custody burdensome and considered herself better off with less custody. Indeed, she might agree to accept less money, or even to pay the father, if he agreed to relieve her of some child-rearing responsibilities. In all events, because the parents' tastes with regard to the trade-offs between money and child-time may differ, it will often be possible for the parties to negotiate some outcome that makes both better off than they would be if they simply accepted the result a court would impose.[2]

Whether the appropriate metaphor is a blueprint or a shadow, the underlying theme is the same: Substantive law shapes the outcome of a negotiation, both in providing an assessment of the rights and remedies and in defining the bargaining chips possessed by the parties. The dominant role lawyers play in negotiating resolutions to serious disputes reflects this central role for the law. The relevance of legal standards thus makes a negotiation primarily legal, as contrasted with a commercial, educational, or interpersonal enterprise. Law may, however, be only one standard that serves the resolution of a dispute. Application of a client's personal sense of what is fair in the situation, or of a special custom of the trade, could produce a result that the parties might accept as more equitable than an outcome under the relevant legal rule. Lawyers must be prepared to negotiate solutions to disputes based on non-legal as well as legal standards.

The opposing lawyer's knowledge of the law is as important to the negotiating lawyer as his own knowledge. Both lawyers construct separate legal blueprints of the case using their own research and experience as a guide. An objective of the early phase of negotiation is to describe and contrast these competing blueprints and to try to agree on a joint design. Negotiations sometimes fail because a lawyer may commit himself to his own blueprint without recognizing legitimate criticisms by the other side. If both lawyers are well prepared on the substantive law and are willing to listen to each other, the negotiation process is likely to be efficient and professionally satisfying, with a result acceptable to the clients. If one lawyer is substantially more knowledgeable than the other, both may be uncomfortable, and the resulting negotiation may create problems for each. The unprepared lawyer may be defensive and competitive, forcing the negotiation into an early and unnecessary impasse. The prepared lawyer, on the other hand, may face a dilemma; whether to use ethically questionable tactics to take unfair advantage of the situation, or to provide the other side with information tending to compromise his client's case. An effective lawyer will be as sensitive to the opposing lawyer's knowledge of relevant law as he is to his own.

2. Id. at 968–69.

A lawyer cannot assume that the other lawyer knows the substantive law or appreciates its relevance; he must discover what the other knows during the introductory phase of the negotiation. If the other side does not understand or appreciate the relevant law, the lawyer's objective may not be to educate him. Each lawyer is accountable for his own competence and should be able to take opposing counsel as he finds him. Nevertheless, the lawyer's goal is an efficient resolution of the dispute in a way that is optimally favorable to his client. The law rarely dictates a particular result with great certainty, and a lawyer will usually place the most favorable "spin" on the law to bring his interpretation into accord with the client's interests. The lawyer's problem, then, is how to meet this goal in the face of inadequate preparation by the other side. Displays of legal knowledge and case analysis are usually intended to serve both as a ritualistic beginning to a competitive negotiation and a psychological tool to erode the other side's expectation level. Legal lectures may enhance credibility and convey some sense of the intensity with which one will hold to an opening position, but lecturing others often alienates rather than persuades. Other methods may be more effective in achieving a favorable outcome. Patience, good questioning techniques, and tactful volunteering of relevant statutes and cases may be preferable as a means of persuading the other side.

In those rare cases where the law does clearly dictate a result—and that result is unfavorable to the client—the best approach may be silence. Good judgment, however, may dictate that one should disclose the unfavorable authority and then work to establish other norms as more useful and appropriate to the particular case. A lawyer has a duty to disclose to a *tribunal* unfavorable authority in the controlling jurisdiction if the other side has not discovered it.[3] Ethical issues are discussed in more detail, infra p. 196. In addition, of course, the lawyer will want to avoid reaching a settlement that may be unenforceable in court for unconscionability, nondisclosure, or other legal grounds, or that in other ways creates an incentive for nonperformance by the other side.

The well-prepared lawyer who conveys an image of assured competence in the substantive law can have a powerful impact on the other side. An earned reputation for thorough preparation precedes the lawyer into a negotiation and affects the initial expectations of the other side. Of course, if talks break down, the lawyer is then expected to demonstrate competence as the case proceeds to the courtroom. Over time, it is difficult to bluff on issues of legal preparation and competence.

The effective lawyer will be alert to the manner in which the opposing lawyer is using legal knowledge. The credibility of the other side's perception of the probable court outcome, and how firmly they

---

3. See Model Code of Professional Responsibility, DR 7–106(B)(1).

believe it, affect the lawyer's own expectations. Negotiating style may hide or confuse the message sent and received. Threats and take-it-or-leave-it positions usually do not help one evaluate either credibility or intentions, nor for that matter do statements of authority made in a pleasing and cooperative manner. Style must be separated not only from strategy but also from substantive information. The focus here must be on legal knowledge and analysis as legitimate criteria to use in helping resolve the dispute.

2. Evaluating the Probable Court Outcome

A lawyer's initial work product will include an analysis of the probable court outcome. A lawyer should evaluate the litigation alternative by determining the likely rewards that the parties would receive and costs they would incur from a successful trial of the case. Such an assessment not only prepares the lawyer and his client for the realities of trial, but also provides an excellent measure to use in deciding whether to accept any offer of settlement.[4] Moreover, this assessment can show the lawyer how to improve both the client's potential result at trial and the probability of receiving that result, thereby increasing his bargaining power.[5] A good analysis will also permit the lawyer to evaluate efficiently information given by the other side and to seek added information that can be helpful if the case goes to trial.

Unfortunately, too many lawyers fail to analyze the potential court result with the degree of thoroughness and objectivity necessary to arrive at a realistic assessment. The following excerpt provides some insight into the rigors of this task.

RAIFFA, THE ART & SCIENCE OF NEGOTIATION
66–76 (1982).

The Sorensen Chevrolet File

Mrs. Anderson, a young housewife of nineteen, picked up her automobile from the repair shop of Sorensen Chevrolet not realizing that her left front headlight was inoperative, perhaps through the negligence of Sorensen Chevrolet. On a misty, rainy evening with poor visibility, driving alone in a no-pass zone she "peeked out"—or more than "peeked out"—from behind a truck and had a frightful head-on collision. She was left permanently disfigured, disabled, and blind. Allegedly, she had been traveling at 70 miles per hour in a 50–mile-per–hour zone.

The accident occurred in October 1968, and two years later (not an unreasonable length of time) her lawyer, Mr. Miller, brought suit

---

4. See R. Fisher and W. Ury, Getting to Yes 104 (1981).

5. See Murray, A Negotiator's View of the Court Alternative, 2 Ohio St. Dispute Resolution J. 223, 239 (1987); Fisher, Negotiating Power: Getting and Using Influence, 27 Am. Behavioral Scientist 149, 156–57 (Nov.–Dec. 1983).

against Sorensen Chevrolet for $1,633,000. Sorensen Chevrolet was insured with a company we shall call Universal General Insurance (UGI), under a policy that included protection of up to $500,000 per person for bodily injury caused by faulty repairs.

The case extended over more than four years and comprised more than seven hundred pages in UGI's files. The successive steps involved in the suit illustrate what I call "the negotiation dance." In this case it's not a pas de deux, but a pas de trois with principals: the lawyer for the plaintiff, the representative of UGI, and, in a lesser role, the lawyer for Sorensen Chevrolet. * * *

According to the case study, "UGI policy required a claims supervisor within thirty days after initial notification to estimate the amount for which the case would be settled, the so-called reserve. This amount was treated as the amount of loss for accounting purposes until modified or until the claim was actually settled. Regulatory authorities required that a part of UGI's assets be earmarked for settling the case. If additional information substantially altered the estimated settlement amount, reserves were to be modified accordingly. The reserve first set in the Sorensen Chevrolet case when the suit was brought was $10,000." That reserve was set aside in November 1970. On March 12, 1972, Mr. Miller, the lawyer-negotiator for the plaintiff, wrote to Mr. Bidder, the lawyer-negotiator for UGI, saying: "I am aware of the fact that the Defendant, Sorensen Chevrolet, Inc., has liability coverage with the Universal General Insurance Company in the amount of only $500,000. While I think the settlement value of this case is above that $500,000 figure, I will at this time on behalf of the Plaintiff offer to settle this case for the insurance limits available (that is, $500,000), reserving the right to withdraw this offer at any time." Indeed, Miller argued in the same letter that it was "very probable that the jury would return a verdict in the approximate amount of $1,000,000 to $1,200,000."

As one might expect, Sorensen was extremely afraid that the case would go to court and that the jury would award the plaintiff an amount greater than Sorensen's insurance would cover. Sorensen urged UGI to settle at $500,000. Moreover, they hired counsel to pressure UGI to settle out of court, threatening to sue UGI for bargaining in bad faith if the jury awarded an amount in excess of their insurance coverage. UGI was not impressed.

Let's imagine that it's now the eve of the trial and that one round of negotiations remains. What type of analyses might help each of the protagonists?

First of all, it appears that Sorensen can't do much except reiterate the position that UGI should settle out of court for an amount less than $500,000 or else be sued for bad faith. Surprisingly, at the last moment before the scheduled trial, Sorensen actually offered to pay a modest amount ($25,000 for openers) of the out-of-court settlement figure. Thus, if UGI agreed with the plaintiff to settle for $350,000, UGI's actual cost would be $350,000 minus x, where x would be Sorensen's contribution. From Sorensen's perspective the higher the value of x, the higher the probability that UGI would agree to settle out of court. Their decision analysis would thus center on the question of how high an x Sorensen could afford. That maximum value would be Sorensen's reservation price in bargaining with UGI.

In a formal analysis, Sorensen must assess: (1) the chance of a settlement out of court without a Sorensen contribution; (2) the chance of a settlement out of court with a Sorensen contribution of x; (3) if there were no settlement out of court, the chance that the plaintiff might win a jury trial; (4) if the plaintiff were to win, the chance that the jury award might be above $500,000; and (5) if the jury award were above $500,000, the chance of winning a bargaining-in-bad-faith case against UGI and the chance of settling that case out of court for various amounts as a function of the jury award to Mrs. Anderson. * * *

Such formal analyses were not done by Sorensen. Indeed, UGI rejected out of hand any contribution by Sorensen because it would adversely affect UGI's business image; from their vantage point, there was a linkage between this problem and other business affairs.

UGI's Analysis

From UGI's perspective, ignoring all costs to date, what should their reservation price be in the last stage of pretrial negotiations? In a formal analysis, UGI would need to assess: (1) the chance that the plaintiff might win the court case; (2) if the plaintiff were to win, the probability distribution of the award; and (3) if the award were above $500,000, the uncertainties surrounding a secondary negotiation with Sorensen.

Suppose that Mr. Reilly, vice-president of UGI, assesses a .8 chance that the jury will decide in favor of the plaintiff. * * * The judgmental probability that an award will be given is .8, and, if one is given, the probability that it will be above $500,000 is .3. The mean (expected value) of Reilly's judgmental distribution is about $360,000, which includes a .2 chance of no payment at all.

Figure 14 depicts UGI's decision tree for the last stage of pretrial negotiations. If they do not settle out of court and if they lose, the continuum of possible awards is approximated for convenience by five equally likely awards: $200,000, $300,000, $400,000, $500,000, and $850,000. We shall assume that UGI is concerned with three components: an insurance cost (award to plaintiff), a transaction cost (lawyer's fees), and a penalty for linkages to other problems. Note that if UGI fights the case and wins, this linkage penalty is negative. (Some might want to quibble with these assessments. But let's suppose that UGI has reasons for these numbers. In a more sophisticated analysis it is customary to run sensitivity studies, letting the more controversial numbers roam over plausible ranges; for brevity's sake, we're not going to do this.)

If UGI goes down the do-not-settle path, they assess a .8 chance of losing the court trial. If they lose and if the jury grants an award of $850,000, UGI will have Sorensen to contend with. This might prove messy, requiring transaction costs, and it would be a bad precedent for a UGI policy holder to sue them: sympathy would be on the side of the little guy. All things considered, UGI would rather settle out of court with Sorensen if the jury were to award the plaintiff over $500,000. In the decision diagram, UGI assigns a value of $780,000 to the node following an $850,000 award to the plaintiff.

If they choose not to settle and if they lose, they encounter a five-pronged chance node giving equal probabilities to payoffs of $210,000, $310,000, $410,000, $520,000, and $780,000. The expected value average of these payoffs is $446,000, and that's the value that would be assigned to the UGI node. Finally, the chance node immediately following the do-not-settle branch can be assigned a value of $357,000—or, rounded off, $360,000. Hence, UGI from this analysis should want to settle out of court for any value less than $360,000, taking into account future transaction and linkage costs. This analysis uses expected values and makes no allowances for risk aversion—as is roughly appropriate for an insurance company.

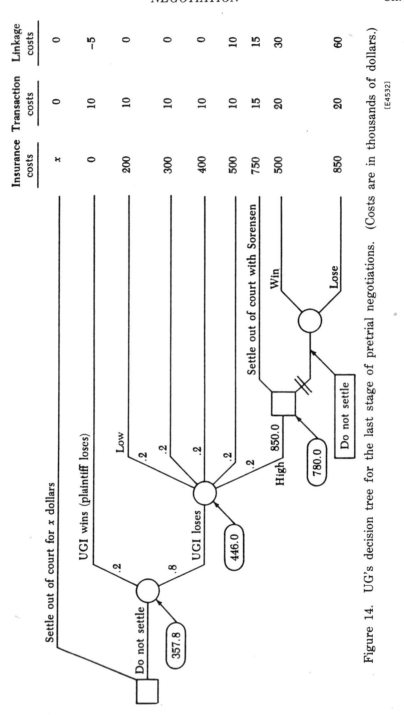

Figure 14. UG's decision tree for the last stage of pretrial negotiations. (Costs are in thousands of dollars.)

[E4532]

The Plaintiff's Analysis

What should Mrs. Anderson's reservation price be in the last stage of pretrial negotiations? Let's suppose that she has agreed to pay her lawyer-negotiator 30 percent of what she is awarded.

The plaintiff's decision tree is depicted in Figure 15. The consequences are described in terms of the payoff to the plaintiff—she gets 70 percent of the award—and a transaction (anxiety) cost; let's assume that the cost of going to court would be an even $10,000. If the plaintiff were risk-neutral (which she is not), then an expected monetary value analysis would lead to a reservation price of about $350,000, using Reilly's probability assessments.

So we see that if both sides use the same probability assessments, and if both sides are risk-neutral, then there is a small zone of agreement: the plaintiff wants $350,000 or more, whereas the insurance company is willing to pay $360,000 or less. With the assumptions we have made (identical probabilities), it is the transaction and linkage costs on one side and the anxiety costs on the other side that create this small zone of agreement. But it would be surprising if both sides were to agree on the probability assessments.

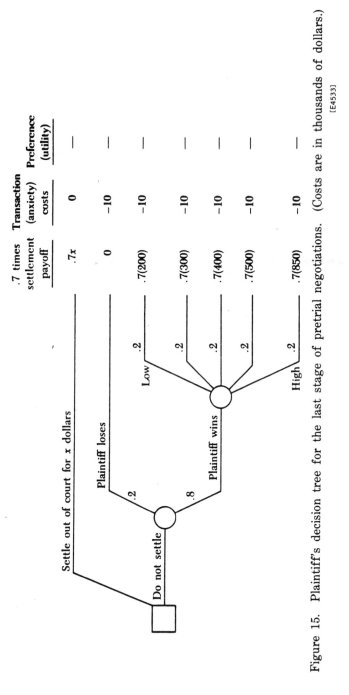

Figure 15. Plaintiff's decision tree for the last stage of pretrial negotiations. (Costs are in thousands of dollars.)

* * * It has been noted in other contexts as well that subjects bias their probability assessments according to the roles they play. Furthermore, in this case the displacement was in the direction of

decreasing, or even of eliminating, the zone of agreement when calculations were based on expected values. Even so, many civil liability cases are settled out of court. I suspect that the reasons for this are primarily risk-aversion and decision-regret, and secondarily the desire to avoid paying lawyer's fees.

Mrs. Anderson and her lawyer, Mr. Miller, probably don't realize it, but they too have an inherent conflict of interest, although the lawyer's incentive structure is designed to motivate him to get as much as possible for his client. Suppose that Mrs. Anderson has a choice between $275,000 for certain, or taking her chances with a jury. Most plaintiffs in Mrs. Anderson's position are probably far more risk-averse than their lawyers. * * * Mrs. Anderson might ruminate, "How would I feel if I decided to take my chances and lost? I would be plagued with the thought that I had made a terrible error. I would feel such regret that I had been greedy and that I had turned down a certainty of $275,000. I would feel far worse in such a situation than I would if no compensation were ever possible. It would be far better to follow the path of certainty now and not risk embarrassing myself." This is the avoidance of anticipated decision-regret.

Risk-aversion and avoidance of decision-regret will also affect the plaintiff's lawyer—but to a considerably lesser degree. One might speculate that the reservation prices of plaintiffs in civil liability suits would tend to be lower than their lawyers', once they fully share their probabilistic beliefs of courtroom uncertainties. If we were to push back the time frame of our analysis from just before the trial to a much earlier stage in the negotiations, the discrepancy in attitudes between the plaintiff and her lawyer would be even deeper: she doubtless would suffer more continuing anxiety than would her lawyer, and she would probably have a greater need for money at an earlier rather than at a later date. This would tend to make her reservation price lower than her lawyer's. The lawyer, for his part, would have to consider the great deal of time involved in handling a court case; but this might be offset by the possible advantages to his career and reputation. Of course, all these concerns to the lawyer are irrelevant for his client, and herein lies a possible conflict.

The insurance company, on the other hand, is far less risk-averse; * * * the choice of a definite, certain negative amount is less appealing than a gamble with the same expected value. But one shouldn't make too much of this from the insurance company's point of view. They should think in terms of expected value—but allowances should be made for transaction and linkage costs. * * * What, incidentally, happened in the real case? On January 10, 1975, Mr. Miller made a last offer—a "rock-bottom" figure of $325,000. Sorensen frantically urged UGI to accept, and made an offer for a contributory payment. But UGI was adamant and prepared for trial. Although Miller claimed to have made a binding commitment that he "could not back down from," UGI learned—literally on the steps of the courthouse—that Miller had been replaced by another counsel who (undoubtedly with

Miller's coaching) offered UGI a last-last offer: a rock-rock-bottom price
of $300,000.

It had become a game of chicken. Who would back down at the
very last second? Would they collide by going to court? UGI gracious-
ly agreed to $300,000.

Notes and Questions

(1) Professor Raiffa uses decision-tree analysis to evaluate what the
Sorensen Chevrolet case would bring in court. Note that although the
probability is .8 that a jury will find in favor of the plaintiff on the
liability issue, the probability of the plaintiff winning an award of
$400,000 or more in damages is only .48 (.8 × .6).

This analysis is simplified in order to demonstrate the analytical
method. A decision tree may be greatly expanded by adding the
probabilities for winning (or losing) important pre-trial motions, for
collecting an award once received, and for discounting the result due to
delay in pre- and post-trial activity. Thorough analysis using a decision
tree can be complex and time-consuming, without a significantly high
predictive quality.

(2) Sensitivity analysis is a more thorough extension of decision
theory (see the reference by Raiffa, supra p. 134) and may be useful to
lawyers with computer or calculus skills for complex cases with high
stakes. Professor Nagel defines sensitivity analysis (sometimes called
policies/goals or "PG" analysis) as referring "to how the bottom-line
conclusion of going to trial, accepting a settlement, or choosing another
alternative is affected by changes in the inputs, which mainly relate to
such matters or criteria as (1) the predicted damages, (2) the probability
of receiving them, (3) the settlement offered, (4) the litigation costs, and
(5) the settlement costs." Nagel, Microcomputers, Risk Analysis, and
Litigation Strategy, 19 Akron L.Rev. 35, 36 (1985). Sensitivity analysis
tests for the best option by locating the margins and describing the net
gain or loss as inputs vary.

Let's use the Sorenson figures to explain the difference in the two
methods. The plaintiff may believe the case has an "excellent chance"
for a jury verdict of $500,000, and the insurance company is only
offering $160,000 in settlement. The settlement offer is certain and
immediate, once accepted. Using the decision-tree method, however,
we must adjust the probable award for the risk of receiving an award
different than the predicted $500,000, including a finding of no liability.
The Sorenson table would therefore change the lawyer's "ballpark"
figure to $360,000. Further adjustment would need to be made for time
lost because the trial would probably not be scheduled for one year or
more, depending on the jurisdiction. Assuming a one-year delay and
an 8% interest rate, the present value would be roughly $347,000.
Because the client's costs are higher for trial than settlement, the net
values are closer together. Assuming contingent fees are 25% for
settlement and 35% after trial begins, and other expenses are $10,000

and $20,000 respectively, the expected value to the client would be $110,000 in settlement and $201,000 after trial. You also need to build in the risk of an appeal from the trial verdict, including value lost from the added delay—for our purposes, an adjustment of, say, $20,000, leaving an expected value to plaintiff after trial of $181,000. Given these figures, the best option for the plaintiff is trial.

The analysis so far has been based on the decision-tree method. The product is a fixed amount showing the lawyer's choice given a certain set of probabilities. But reality always presents a set of uncertain factors, and the lawyer's prediction is usually in the form of a specific event—for example, a jury award of $500,000. Sensitivity analysis assumes a specific result rather than a group of differing results, each with a different probability of occurring. It then builds an equation based on the factors important in determining that result. Using the Sorenson example, for instance, sensitivity analysis would show, for every $1,000 increase in the cost of the trial option (witness fees, court filings, delay expense, lawyer fees), how much the plaintiff's expected value would be reduced—in mathematical terms, the first derivative of the equation. It answers the question how large an increase there must be in defendant's settlement offer, or in estimated costs, or in a revised trial outcome prediction, before plaintiff's best option is to settle. This information also provides the lawyer with an insensitivity range—the range within which the plaintiff has no incentive to change in response to single or successive increases in the defendant's offer. For instance, if the plaintiff's offer is already at his bottom line, additional concessions by the defendant below that bottom line will not provide an incentive for the plaintiff to make further concessions. The second derivative of the equation would show the rate of change in the gap between the expected values for settlement and for trial as each input (costs, offer, recovery) increases by one unit, say $1,000. For example, as the expenses and delay increase by each successive unit of $1,000, the expected value gained from trial might decrease at an increasing rate—suggesting that substantial added delay or expense over the original estimates may alter the initial rejection of a fixed settlement offer.

Sensitivity analysis raises questions that might not otherwise be asked, permits a greater number of options, an almost unlimited gradation in net benefit valuation, and more useful guidance for the changing conditions of a negotiation. On the other hand, it requires a thorough understanding of computers and calculus, and tends to build user confidence in explicit mathematical relationships that are only fuzzy approximations at best.

(3) Lawyers often use published reports of past jury awards as a realistic way to predict trial results in a current case. Some examples from Personal Injury Valuation Handbooks (Jury Verdict Research, Inc., 1986) include:

Cervical Strain (1984): Midpoint $7,700; Probability Range [middle 50% of verdicts] $3,345–18,750; Verdict Range $253–100,000; Average $14,614.

Knee Injury (1984): Midpoint $58,500; Probability Range $15,000–150,000; Verdict Range $500–655,000; Average $114,006.

This report also provides general descriptions of selected cases to give the lawyer a clearer picture whether the verdict in the particular case can be used as a guide. An example:

Specials: $3,804   Verdict: $15,000

A 34–year old secretary fell down the stairs of a building owned by the defendants. The plaintiff contended that the stairway was maintained in violation of applicable building codes and that those violations were the proximate cause of the accident and her resulting back strains and contusions. (Knych et al. v. Tenoke Associates et al., Memphis, Tenn., No. 53818, June 1981).

These descriptions and averages, however, are not able to convey a good feel for the differences in lawyer abilities, varying medical characteristics, relative credibility of witnesses, or special dynamics peculiar to certain juries, just to name a few of the important variables. Still, they provide one more analytical tool for the lawyer. See also Harley & Magee, What's It Worth?: A Guide to Current Personal Injury Awards and Settlements (1985).

(4) Professor Williams outlines other methods of evaluating the fair settlement value of a case—methods that are less elaborate than decision-tree analysis or even past jury awards. They may be useful for cases which are small in financial value or more routine, or for lawyers who have had extensive experience in specific subject and geographic areas.

In evaluating routine personal injury cases, attorneys and insurance claims adjusters have developed formulas or rules of thumb that produce a value based on some multiple of "special damages" or actual medical and other costs of the injury. They decide upon an arbitrary multiplier that may be as low as two or three or as high as ten. For example, the formula of "three times special damages" has been described as allocating "one third to the lawyer, one third to the physician, and one third to the claimant." In cases involving more complex damages such as continued pain and suffering, evaluators often propose an arbitrary fixed dollar amount per week for general pain and suffering; i.e., $200 per week for the period of total disability and $100 per week for the period of partial disability. These formulas provide "ballpark" figures, but they obviously ignore individual differences between cases and severely simplify issues of actual harm done.

* * *

One widely recognized formula, developed by Robert L. Simmons, invites the attorney to subdivide the case into six categories and estimate a value for each. They include:

PAV — The probable average verdict.
PPV — The probability of a plaintiff's verdict.
UV — The uncollectible portion of the verdict.
PC — The plaintiff's cost in obtaining verdict.
DC — The defendant's estimated cost of defense.
I — The value of the intangible factors.
FSV — The fair settlement value.

Expressed algebraically, the formula looks like this:

$$(PAV \times PPV) - UV - PC + DC + I = FSV$$

This formula uses some time value concepts and seeks to arrive at a net valuation figure for the client. This and similar methods are all useful to the extent that they help the attorney arrive at an objective valuation and be aware of the components of that valuation.

G. Williams, Legal Negotiation and Settlement 115–17 (1982).

(5) Risk preference is present in every negotiation. A party is *risk neutral* if he ranks options in the order of their expected values, without adjustment for subjective preferences favoring one more than another. The Sorenson tables, for example, are based on the parties being risk neutral. A party is *risk averse* if he prefers an option with a lower expected value because of the higher risk (stakes or uncertainty) involved with the other choices. Sorenson Chevrolet was more risk-averse than UGI, wanting to settle at a higher figure because of a fear that trial might lead to a judgment in excess of its insurance policy limits. (Of course, an insured defendant is generally completely risk-averse to litigating when a settlement can be achieved within his policy limits, since only the insurance company would thereby have to pay. For a discussion of an insurance carrier's duty to settle within policy limits, see infra p. 180, note (4).) A party is *risk-prone* if he prefers those options that include more risk. UGI was willing to accept the greater uncertainty of a trial which could result in a judgment at UGI's policy limits ($500,000), than to settle for an amount that yielded a lower expected value ($325,000).

To use a simple example, suppose a plaintiff files a $10,000 lawsuit against defendant for injuries suffered in an automobile accident. Assume no transaction costs, a 75% probability of winning the full amount at trial, and a 25% chance of winning nothing. A risk-neutral plaintiff will be indifferent to the choice between accepting a settlement offer of $7,500 or going to trial with the 75% probability of receiving $10,000. If the plaintiff is risk-averse, he will prefer an offer of $7,500 or even lower to the chance of receiving the full $10,000 at trial (he will usually concentrate on the 25% probability of receiving nothing). If the plaintiff is risk-prone, he may turn down an offer of $7,500 or even more in favor of the opportunity to win $10,000 at trial.

(6) What drives a lawyer to settle may be his assessment of the probable court outcome—the better the outcome, the more likely a lawyer will be to negotiate a more favorable settlement. Instead of using the probable court outcome as a crude threat or an easy escape, however, a lawyer should adopt a more flexible process perspective. In theory, a plaintiff should agree to a settlement if the net benefit of accepting a specific offer equals or outweighs the estimated benefit to be gained by using any other process, including litigation, to resolve the dispute. A defendant should settle if the estimated burden of continuing with other processes, including litigation, outweighs the cost of accepting a specific settlement offer now. Note, however, that the benefits and burdens to be balanced may include (1) specific outcomes that can be achieved only by negotiation and not in court (such as an apology for past vindictiveness, see Wagatsuma & Rossett, The Implications of Apology: Law and Culture in Japan and the United States, 20 Law & Soc'y Rev. 461 (1986), a guarantee of future business, a new joint venture, a favorable price on related terms, a joint custody arrangement, or a high alimony figure for special tax benefits), or (2) outcomes achievable in court but probably not by negotiation (treble damages, a legal precedent, or an enforceable injunction). Lawyers for both sides can use their separate predictions of the probable court outcome as the standard for deciding whether to recommend settlement to their respective clients.

The probable court outcome may be the dominant standard, but a lawyer's concentration should remain fixed on building the most favorable outcome possible for the client. If the court becomes the lawyer's psychological focus, the negotiation period will be a succession of court pleadings, motions, hearings, depositions, interrogatives, document production, and adversarial posturing. Such a focus turns the court into the lawyer's only process. The chances for a favorable settlement are maximized when the lawyer tackles the problem with the least restrictive outcome—a negotiated agreement—as the primary goal.

3. Present Value, Future Income, and Structured Settlements

Because a trial and any subsequent judgment are future events and a settlement offer normally provides for immediate payment, the lawyer must translate any estimated probable court outcome to present value for proper comparison. Present value will depend on several variables: the length of time before receipt, the effective interest rate, and the period over which the interest is compounded. Thus, the expected receipt of a $100,000 judgment two years from now, assuming an 8% interest rate compounded annually, is worth only $85,730 in current dollars. Present value tables make these calculations easier, but those who are mathematically inclined may prefer to use the appropriate formula:

$$\text{PV (present value)} = \text{FV} \left(\frac{1}{1+i} \right)^n$$

where "FV" is future value, "i" is the interest rate per period, and "n" the number of periods of compounding.[6]

An often difficult calculation in many personal injury cases is lost future income, which can be a sizable amount in cases of permanent disability or wrongful death. The U.S. Supreme Court discussed an appropriate method of measuring damages in a compensation case for a longshoreman injured in the course of employment.

JONES & LAUGHLIN STEEL CORP. v. PFEIFFER

Supreme Court of the United States, 1983.
462 U.S. 523, 532–47, 103 S.Ct. 2541, 76 L.Ed.2d 768.

[The U.S. District Court held that the plaintiff was permanently disabled due to the defendant's negligence, was unable to return to the same or similar work, and was entitled to a separate damage recovery for lost future income under the Longshoremen's and Harbor Workers' Compensation Act. In calculating damages the district court did not apply either an inflation factor, reflecting estimated price increases in the future, or a discount factor, reflecting the impact of interest rate earnings on a lump sum award; it assumed that these two factors would offset each other. The Third Circuit Court of Appeals affirmed, presenting a conflict between circuits on the question of acceptable methods of measuring lost future income. A unanimous Supreme Court, in an opinion by Justice Stevens, reversed and remanded the case for recalculation in accordance with the Court's description of acceptable methods.]

The District Court found that respondent was permanently disabled as a result of petitioner's negligence. He therefore was entitled to an award of damages to compensate him for his probable pecuniary loss over the duration of his career, reduced to its present value. It is useful at the outset to review the way in which damages should be measured in a hypothetical inflation-free economy. We shall then consider how price inflation alters the analysis. * * *

I.

In calculating damages, it is assumed that if the injured party had not been disabled, he would have continued to work, and to receive wages at periodic intervals until retirement, disability, or death. An award for impaired earning capacity is intended to compensate the worker for the diminution in that stream of income. The award could in theory take the form of periodic payments, but in this country it has traditionally taken the form of a lump sum, paid at the conclusion of the litigation. The appropriate lump sum cannot be computed without first examining the stream of income it purports to replace.

---

6. For a brief explanation of this computation, see G. Williams, Legal Negotiation and Settlement 120–21 (1983). Calculation of future values can be avoided by using an annuity table or the following formula: $FV = PV (1+i)^n$.

The lost stream's length cannot be known with certainty; the worker could have been disabled or even killed in a different, non-work-related accident at any time. The probability that he would still be working at a given date is constantly diminishing. Given the complexity of trying to make an exact calculation, litigants frequently follow the relatively simple course of assuming that the worker would have continued to work up until a specific date certain. In this case, for example, both parties agreed that the petitioner would have continued to work until age 65 (12 + more years) if he had not been injured.

Each annual installment in the lost stream comprises several elements. The most significant is, of course, the actual wage. In addition, the worker may have enjoyed certain fringe benefits, which should be included in an ideal evaluation of the worker's loss but are frequently excluded for simplicity's sake. On the other hand, the injured worker's lost wages would have been diminished by state and federal income taxes. Since the damages award is tax-free, the relevant stream is ideally of after-tax wages and benefits. Moreover, workers often incur unreimbursed costs, such as transportation to work and uniforms, that the injured worker will not incur. These costs should also be deducted in estimating the lost stream.

In this case the parties appear to have agreed to simplify the litigation, and to presume that in each installment all the elements in the stream would offset each other, except for gross wages. However, in attempting to estimate even such a stylized stream of annual installments of gross wages, a trier of fact faces a complex task. The most obvious and most appropriate place to begin is with the worker's annual wage at the time of injury. Yet the "estimate of the loss from lessened earnings capacity in the future need not be based solely upon the wages which the plaintiff was earning at the time of his injury." Even in an inflation-free economy—that is to say one in which the prices of consumer goods remain stable—a worker's wages tend to "inflate." This "real" wage inflation reflects a number of facts, some linked to the specific individual and some linked to broader societal forces. * * *

To summarize, the first stage in calculating an appropriate award for lost earnings involves an estimate of what the lost stream of income would have been. The stream may be approximated as a series of after-tax payments, one in each year of the worker's expected remaining career. In estimating what those payments would have been in an inflation-free economy, the trier of fact may begin with the worker's annual wage at the time of injury. If sufficient proof is offered, the trier of fact may increase that figure to reflect the appropriate influence of individualized factors (such as foreseeable promotions) and societal factors (such as foreseeable productivity growth within the worker's industry).

Of course, even in an inflation-free economy the award of damages to replace the lost stream of income cannot be computed simply by totaling up the sum of the periodic payments. For the damages award is paid in a lump sum at the conclusion of the litigation, and when it— or even a part of it—is invested, it will earn additional money. * * *

The discount rate should be based on the rate of interest that would be earned on "the best and safest investments." Once it is assumed that the injured worker would definitely have worked for a specific term of years, he is entitled to a risk-free stream of future income to replace his lost wages; therefore, the discount rate should not reflect the market's premium for investors who are willing to accept some risk of default. Moreover, since * * * the lost stream of income should be estimated in after-tax terms, the discount rate should also represent the after-tax rate of return to the injured worker.

Thus, although the notion of a damages award representing the present value of a lost stream of earnings in an inflation-free economy rests on some fairly sophisticated economic concepts, the two elements that determine its calculation can be stated fairly easily. They are: (1) the amount that the employee would have earned during each year that he could have been expected to work after the injury; and (2) the appropriate discount rate, reflecting the safest available investment. The trier of fact should apply the discount rate to each of the estimated installments in the lost stream of income, and then add up the discounted installments to determine the total award.

II.

Unfortunately for triers of fact, ours is not an inflation-free economy. Inflation has been a permanent fixture in our economy for many decades, and there can be no doubt that it ideally should affect both stages of the calculation described in the previous section. * * *

The first stage of the calculation required an estimate of the shape of the lost stream of future income. For many workers, including respondent, a contractual "cost-of-living adjustment" automatically increases wages each year by the percentage change during the previous year in the consumer price index calculated by the Bureau of Labor Statistics. Such a contract provides a basis for taking into account an additional societal factor—price inflation—in estimating the worker's lost future earnings.

The second stage of the calculation requires the selection of an appropriate discount rate. Price inflation—or more precisely, anticipated price inflation—certainly affects market rates of return. If a lender knows that his loan is to be repaid a year later with dollars that are less valuable than those he has advanced, he will charge an interest rate that is high enough both to compensate him for the temporary use of the loan proceeds and also to make up for their shrinkage in value. * * *

In this country, some courts have * * * endorsed the economic theory suggesting that market interest rates include two components— an estimate of anticipated inflation, and a desired "real" rate of return on investment—and that the latter component is essentially constant over time. They have concluded that the inflationary increase in the estimated lost stream of future earnings will therefore be perfectly "offset" by all but the "real" component of the market interest rate.

Still other courts have preferred to continue relying on market interest rates. To avoid undercompensation, they have shown at least tentative willingness to permit evidence of what future price inflation will be in estimating the lost stream of future income. * * *

Within the past year, two Federal Courts of Appeals have decided to allow litigants a choice of methods. Sitting en banc, the Court of Appeals for the Fifth Circuit has * * * held it acceptable either to exclude evidence of future price inflation and discount by a "real" interest rate, or to attempt to predict the effects of future price inflation on future wages and then discount by the market interest rate. A panel of the Court of Appeals for the Seventh Circuit has taken a substantially similar position.

Finally, some courts have applied a number of techniques that have loosely been termed "total offset" methods. What these methods have in common is that they presume that the ideal discount rate—the after-tax market interest rate on a safe investment—is (to a legally tolerable degree of precision) completely offset by certain elements in the ideal computation of the estimated lost stream of future income. They all assume that the effects of future price inflation on wages are part of what offsets the market interest rate. The methods differ, however, in their assumptions regarding which if any other elements in the first stage of the damages calculation contribute to the offset. * * *

* * * The Pennsylvania Supreme Court [taking a third approach concluded] that the plaintiff could introduce all manner of evidence bearing on likely sources—both individual and societal—of future wage growth, except for predictions of price inflation. However, it rejected those courts' conclusion that the resulting estimated lost stream of future income should be discounted by a "real interest rate." Rather, it deemed the market interest rate to be offset by future price inflation. * * *

The litigants and the amici in this case urge us to select one of the many rules that have been proposed and establish it for all time as the exclusive method in all federal trials for calculating an award for lost earnings in an inflationary economy. We are not persuaded, however, that such an approach is warranted. For our review of the foregoing cases leads us to draw three conclusions. First, by its very nature the calculation of an award for lost earnings must be a rough approximation. Because the lost stream can never be predicted with complete confidence, any lump sum represents only a "rough and ready" effort to put the plaintiff in the position he would have been in had he not been injured. Second, sustained price inflation can make the award substantially less precise. Inflation's current magnitude and unpredictability create a substantial risk that the damages award will prove to have little relation to the lost wages it purports to replace. Third, the question of lost earnings can arise in many different contexts. In some sectors of the economy, it is far easier to assemble evidence of an individual's most likely career path than in others.

Notes and Questions

(1) Can you outline the Court-approved methods for estimating lost future income?

(2) Was Justice Stevens suggesting, with his remark about "rough and ready" efforts, that lawyers need not be rigorous in their economic analysis of lost future income? If not, what was he saying?

(3) Time can be put to work in the settlement agreement itself: You can voluntarily "structure" payments over a period of years rather than receiving a lump sum at closing. See Danninger, Johnson & Lesti, Negotiating a Structured Settlement, 70 A.B.A.J. 67 (May 1984). (Federal courts and some state courts even have statutory authority in certain cases to award structured payments without voluntary acceptance by the parties.) For example, assume facts similar to Sorenson Chevrolet, with the plaintiff requesting over $360,000 and the defendant wanting to pay less than $280,000. If the $360,000 were structured, with $60,000 paid immediately and the remainder in ten annual installments of $30,000, the present value of the settlement, assuming an 8% discount rate compounded annually, would be roughly $261,300.

The advantages of a structured settlement can be significant. In the example, the plaintiff receives over time what he sees as the value of his claim, and the defendant insurance company has to pay less than it sees as its liability. And a settlement, which otherwise would be outside of reach, looks doable. The defendant resolves an outstanding liability at a substantially lower cost—the company would probably pay present value for an annuity, which is almost $100,000 (28%) below the agreed value of the claim, and in some cases the cost could be below present value because of possible waiver of commissions in the purchase of the annuity, cost savings in intercompany transfers, and other variables available to an insurance company.

Although in theory the plaintiff should be indifferent between an immediate payment of $261,300 and a structured payment of $360,000, certain tax and financial advantages may increase the expected value of the structured settlement considerably above present value. Each year's payment is fully non-taxable to the recipient, thus providing tax shelter benefits for the period of the annuity. If the plaintiff received the present value in a lump sum payment and invested it, the income would, of course, be taxable. See Winslow, The Seven Most Common Questions About Structured Settlements, 1986 Trial Lawyer's Guide 14; Rev.Rule 79–220, 1979–2, C.B. 74. Moreover, the structured settlement assures the party of the agreed-upon amount each year, regardless of fluctuations in market interest rates or the stock market. This financial stability may be especially desirable when investment returns are fluctuating widely. Finally, depending on individual circumstances, *not* receiving a large lump sum payment can be personally advantageous—the recipient avoids both the risk of receiving bad financial advice from well-intentioned family members or friends, and the risk of giving in to the temptation to purchase unnecessary luxuries because the amount received *seems* so inexhaustible.

The structured settlement, however, may not be appropriate for an injured plaintiff whose health is unpredictable or whose needs are highly variable. In addition, annuity payments are normally fixed amounts which do not reflect future inflation; the purchasing power of the tenth $30,000 payment in 1998 may be considerably lower than the first $30,000 payment in 1989. Furthermore, the plaintiff's lawyer faces a difficult fee calculation, assuming she has the standard contingent fee arrangement (25–35% of the settlement paid). How do you value the settlement? Usually the computation is based either on the settlement "cost" or its present value; courts usually approve either method if explicitly agreed to by the lawyer and client. The favored method in federal tort claims cases is to use present value, defined as settlement cost. Wyatt v. U.S., 783 F.2d 45 (6th Cir.1986). The lawyer negotiating the structured settlement may be able to structure her fee over some or all of the payment period, thereby avoiding the tax consequences of a large increase in income in any one year. (A lawyer trying to postpone income in this way, however, must be careful to avoid "constructive receipt" treatment.)

(4) Negotiating lawyers sometimes demand substantial and largely arbitrary amounts for punitive damages. The probability and size of punitive damages are difficult to assess for both plaintiff and defendant, but analysis can bring greater accuracy in prediction. Recent studies suggest that punitive damages are most frequent in cases of personal violence, fraud, false arrest and insurance bad faith. Even in these areas, however, the probability of award is typically less than 20 per cent of those cases that go to trial, and the median award is less than $25,000. Despite these statistics, the risk of a high punitive damage award, combined with the uncertainty of winning at court, may add significantly to the fair settlement value of a case.

Treble damage claims under the antitrust laws, the Racketeer Influenced and Corrupt Organizations Act (RICO), and state deceptive trade practices acts (DTPA) raise similar issues for negotiating lawyers. The bargaining power that these claims represent is directly proportional to their legitimacy under the facts of the case. Rule 11 sanctions (see infra p. 153) may become a useful response to the automatic inclusion of such treble damage claims by an over-zealous plaintiff's lawyer.

(5) Legal fees can also have a significant impact on the lawyer's choice of negotiating strategy and the level of his interest in negotiating. We have already referred to fee estimates in working with

decision-tree analysis. Fee arrangements also affect the analysis of client interests, the generation of creative options for resolution, and the pace of the negotiation. Take the Sorenson Chevrolet example: the plaintiff's attorney is being paid by contingent fee; the defendant's, by hourly rate. Mrs. Anderson may be willing to take a new car as part of the settlement, and Sorenson (and maybe UGI) would benefit by giving something that has a higher monetary value to her than the cost to it. But how does Mrs. Anderson's lawyer take his share of the car? Mrs. Anderson will probably have little problem paying the lawyer's fee portion of the car value out of the additional money the defendants are paying in that case, but what if the car were the only item exchanged? Professor Kritzer, in studying data collected during the Civil Litigation Research Project at the University of Wisconsin, concludes:

> The [data] shows clearly the overriding importance of money in the demands of the contingent fee lawyer: only 3% of the contingent fee lawyers reported asking demands that contained no monetary element (and one must wonder how those lawyers expected to be paid) compared to 19% for the hourly fee lawyers' demands and offers; 77% of the contingent fee lawyers' demands were entirely monetary compared to 51% for the hourly fee lawyer.

Kritzer, The Lawyer as Negotiator: Working in the Shadows 18–19 (Wisc. Disputes Processing Research Project, Working Series 7–4, Jan. 1986).

Are there ways to collect fees that would make non-monetary settlements more desirable to the lawyers? Does the escalating contingent fee itself (at 25–30% if settled, 35–40% if it goes to trial, and 45–50% if appealed) encourage the lawyer to be risk-prone—to err on the side of litigation rather than negotiation—while serving as an incentive for the client to be risk-averse? For the ordinary case (under $10,000 demanded) do economic realities for the lawyer promote early settlement even though it might not be the best solution for the client? See Johnson, Lawyer's Choice: A Theoretical Appraisal of Litigation Investment Decisions, 15 Law & Soc'y Rev. 567 (1981).

These issues raise serious ethical questions, particularly the lawyer's obligation to represent a client zealously within the bounds of the law. See Model Code of Professional Responsibility, Canon 7.

4. Litigation Processes Affecting Negotiation and Settlement

Data from actual practice show that the majority of cases are settled, with only a small percentage ending in trial.[7] One conclusion you can reach is that the paradigm is working: By concentrating on the

7. See, e.g., H.L. Ross, Settled Out of Court 3–5 (2d ed. 1980); S. Nagel and M. Neef, The Legal Process: Modeling the System 149 (1977).

court process, lawyers are effectively doing what is necessary to settle those cases that should settle.

But there are reasons for seeking more study before accepting such a conclusion. Over the past decade many regular users of legal services (such as corporate counsel and business officials) have been highly critical of the expense of the pro-litigation focus and the lack of consideration given to the client's ongoing relationships. Moreover, few studies have evaluated the quality of the settlements measured against what could possibly have been worked out by trained and experienced lawyer-negotiators. A more responsible conclusion might be that the use of litigation procedures is helpful in legal negotiation and that lawyers are settling cases *in spite of* (rather than because of) their inattention to negotiation process and skills.

Some have tried to reflect this complementary relationship between litigation and negotiation by using new terminology. "Litigotiation," coined by Professor Galanter, represents one view of the linkage of the two processes (see supra pp. 18–20), but it also suggests that negotiation is subsumed under general litigation practice. This focus does increase the attention given to nonjudicial elements in litigation, but leaves litigation as the dominant theme. Our purpose, by contrast, is to stress that negotiation is the primary resolution process (as the statistics demonstrate), with litigation serving, first, as a useful support for negotiation and, second, as a viable alternative if reasonable settlement is not possible. Thus, litigation becomes primarily a tool to assist the lawyer during the negotiation process.

There are a number of ways in which a lawyer can use litigation procedures to help develop negotiating conditions favorable for settlement. The most obvious procedure is the filing of the complaint itself. Starting the court process can have a sobering effect on the other side, or it can simply make him angry; it can demonstrate that you intend to press your claim in the normal course of business, or that you are irrational and ill-tempered; it can encourage immediate and serious negotiations, or incite hostile treatment in which no constructive dialogue is possible. Timing and the manner of filing make the difference.

One thing, however, is clear: Filing in court tolls the statute of limitations on your client's claim, something that negotiation cannot do by itself. The risk of ignoring the statute of limitations lies largely with the attorney, not the client; many malpractice complaints arise because lawyers fail to file an action before the statute of limitations deadline. In rare instances the existence of negotiations may toll the statute, but only if the lawyer can show deceptive or fraudulent negotiating behavior by the other side.[8]

Once the case is filed, discovery procedures are useful in acquiring information to help negotiate properly and in assessing your client's case for possible settlement. "Depositions are the most important of the pre-trial discovery tools. In evaluating the strength of a case for

---

8. See generally 39 A.L.R.3d 127 (1971).

settlement purposes, litigators accord great weight to the performance in depositions of both their own and their opponents witnesses." [9] Depositions, interrogatories, motions for the production of books and records, and other court-enforced activities can have a powerful psychological impact on negotiating parties. Like a bulldozer moving slowly forward, the litigation process forces the other lawyer and his client to face the realities of the dispute with greater objectivity. The lawyer's job is to bring this incentive for objectivity and reality to bear at the earliest moment warranted by the circumstances. The court process provides a recognized succession of deadlines for lawyer action.

The probability of a negotiated settlement depends on at least four separate decision-makers: the lawyer, his client, the other side's lawyer, and the other client. It takes only one person to sabotage an otherwise satisfactory deal; therefore, an effective lawyer must be able to influence the choices and decisions of the other three. A lawyer's own client may be a likely source of rejection. Results from Professor Williams' study suggest that of cases not settled, over 50 percent reached impasse because the lawyer could not convince his client of the acceptability of the proposed settlement.[10] The inexorable movement of litigation may be as important a motivating tool for the lawyer's client as it is for the opposing client and his lawyer.

a. Sanctions for Improper Litigation Conduct

Parties and their attorneys are not entirely free to pursue any course of litigation conduct. Although it was once thought that an attorney could use any valid procedural device which he found to be in his client's interests—even if it meant delay or a multiplying of litigation costs—this is no longer the case. Significant limitations have been placed on litigation conduct and are enforced by sanctions applicable to both parties and attorneys. The risk of these sanctions now constitutes a check on unduly adversary behavior and should significantly affect negotiation and settlement strategy.

Judicial sanctions are available in a federal court under 28 U.S.C. § 1927, which permits sanctions for "multipl[ying] the proceedings in any case unreasonably and vexatiously." The discovery rules were amended in 1980 to provide for sanctions for failure to make or cooperate in discovery. Fed.R.Civ.Pro. 37(b)(2). In 1983, Rule 11 (see Appendix A) was amended to provide broad new sanctions for a variety of litigation conduct. Under Rule 11 the lawyer's signature on a pleading or motion creates a duty of "reasonable inquiry" that the statements made are: 1) well-grounded in fact and warranted by law and 2) not interposed for an improper purpose, such as to harass, cause undue delay, or increase costs needlessly. Upon motion or their own initiative, courts may impose appropriate sanctions for violations, in-

9. Suplee, Depositions: Objectives, Strategies, Tactics, Mechanics and Problems, 2 Rev. Litigation 255, 257 (1982).

10. See G. Williams, supra note 6, at 59.

cluding payment of the opposing party's expenses caused by the violation. "Sanctions have been awarded in response to several types of
violation, including the filing of a claim after the statute of limitations
had expired, or without subject matter jurisdiction, and frivolous motions to disqualify defendant's attorney, for summary judgment, or for a
change of venue." [11]

NATIONAL ASSOCIATION OF GOVERNMENT EMPLOYEES
v. NATIONAL FEDERATION OF FEDERAL EMPLOYEES
844 F.2d 216 (5th Cir.1988).

Before RUBIN, KING, and WILLIAMS, CIRCUIT JUDGES.

ALVIN B. RUBIN, CIRCUIT JUDGE:

"[Labor] representation campaigns are frequently characterized by
bitter and extreme charges, countercharges, unfounded rumors, vitu-
perations, personal accusations, misrepresentations and distortions."
Linn v. United Plant Guard Workers of America, Local 114, 383 U.S.
53, 58, 86 S.Ct. 657, 661, 15 L.Ed.2d 582 (1966). The certification
contest between two unions from which this libel action arose was
comparatively mild. The union seeking to supersede the incumbent
bargaining agent did, however, publish a pamphlet stating in one
paragraph that the incumbent union had refused to help an employee
because she was not a union member and perhaps implying that the
employee was consequently forced to return to her job while pregnant
and later died as a result.

The incumbent union thereupon brought a defamation action
against the challenger and two persons who had participated in con-
fecting the statement. The jury ruled for the defendants because the
plaintiff union had not proven its case by "clear and convincing
evidence." The district court then imposed sanctions on the plaintiff
for having brought the lawsuit, even though the court had earlier
suggested both sides were at fault and should settle their dispute.

* * *

[W]e review the district court's imposition of sanctions under Federal Rule of Civil Procedure 11. That rule provides in relevant part:

The signature of an attorney or party constitutes a certificate by
the signer that the signer has read the pleading, motion, or other
paper; that to the best of the signer's knowledge, information, and
belief formed after reasonable inquiry it is well grounded in fact
and is warranted by existing law or a good faith argument for the
extension, modification, or reversal of existing law, and that it is
not interposed for any improper purpose, such as to harass or to
cause unnecessary delay or needless increase in the cost of litigation. . . . If a pleading, motion, or other paper is signed in
violation of this rule, the court, upon motion or upon its own

11. Kassin, An Empirical Study of Rule
11 Sanctions 6 (Fed.Judicial Center 1985).

initiative, shall impose upon the person who signed it, a represented party, or both, an appropriate sanction.

Our recent en banc decision in Thomas v. Capital Security Services, Inc., 836 F.2d 866 (5th Cir.1988) (en banc), an opinion not available to the district court at the time of trial, requires that we review the court's imposition of sanctions only for abuse of discretion.

The district court did not suggest that the Association or its counsel had signed any paper without complying with Rule 11 or had failed to investigate prior to filing the complaint. Instead, the court referred to the Association's conduct in bringing and prosecuting a meritless lawsuit. As we pointed out in *Thomas*, however, Rule 11 focuses on an attorney's obligation "at the time a 'pleading, motion, or other paper' is signed," and sanctions "should not amount to an 'accumulation of all perceived misconduct, from filing through trial,' resulting in a 'single post-judgment retribution in the form of a massive sanctions award.' " Rule 11, therefore does not permit the imposition of sanctions simply for bringing a meritless lawsuit, without any finding that a party or his lawyer signed a paper in violation of the Rule.

The district court [relied] upon 28 U.S.C. § 1927, which authorizes the imposition of sanctions on any person who "multiplies the proceedings in any case unreasonably and vexatiously." In *Thomas*, we noted that this section prohibits "the persistent prosecution of a meritless claim." In this regard, the district court stated that the Association's suit lacked true merit and could have succeeded only with good fortune and "extensive extrapolation and bootstrapping" by the jury. The court, however, acted on the basis of the perceived lack of merit in the litigation despite the fact that it had thrice urged the defendants to pay something to settle it. If the litigation were frivolous, the court should certainly have known it by the time the Association had adduced all of its evidence and rested. There is patent anomaly then in its imposition of sanctions for filing a suit that it considered worthy of compromise.

The court, in addition, denied directed verdicts both at the conclusion of the Association's evidence and at the end of the case. While this may have been a prudent precaution against possible later reversal on appeal, the court did not merely reserve judgment or grant the motion after receiving the jury's verdict. Instead it entered judgment on the verdict. As Judge William Schwarzer has stated: "One might well wonder how a case could be so frivolous as to warrant sanctions if it has sufficient merit to get to trial." William W. Schwarzer, Rule 11 Revisited, 101 Harv.L.Rev. 1013, 1019 & n. 7 (1988).

Moreover, in denying the Federation's motion for a directed verdict at the close of the Association's case, the court observed that the Federation "should have some responsibility in this," because it had not checked the statement, and should "apologize for its distribution for negligence." The court, therefore, found some merit, if not the requisite clear and convincing showing, in the Association's allegation that the Federation had acted recklessly. Such negligence would constitute evidence of "actual malice." In addition, the court proposed a sweeping remedy for the Federation's carelessness—that it be barred from Fort Bliss for five years and apologize for distributing the statement—yet when the trial had ended, the court placed all the blame on the Association for the parties' failure to settle before trial.

As we have pointed out, the Association indeed produced evidence of malice although it failed to establish that element with convincing clarity. The Association, therefore, did not proceed so "unreasonably and vexatiously" as to warrant sanctions under 28 U.S.C. § 1927.

As a second ground for sanctions, the court noted that the Association had not accepted the settlements the court had suggested at the pretrial conference or at the close of its case. Failure to compromise a case, however, even pursuant to terms suggested by the court, does not constitute grounds for imposing sanctions—especially when, as in this case, both parties make colorable arguments but the burden of sanctions falls entirely upon one.

As a third reason for its action, the court concluded that the Association had brought suit "not because [it] had a cause of action that truly had merit, but . . . more for the purpose of harassing the Defendant and to serve as a campaign tactic." In these remarks, the court did not find either that the suit was totally lacking in merit or that it was brought solely to harass and gain a campaign advantage; it found that these were the major motives.

We do not condone litigation instituted for ulterior purposes rather than to secure judgment on a well-grounded complaint in which the plaintiff sincerely believes. Yet the Rule 11 injunction against harassment does not exact of those who file pleadings an undiluted desire for just deserts. In Zaldivar v. City of Los Angeles, 780 F.2d 823 (9th Cir. 1986), the Ninth Circuit held that the filing of a complaint that complies with the "well grounded in fact and warranted by existing law" prong of Rule 11 cannot, as a matter of law, "harass" the defendant as Rule 11 forbids, regardless of the plaintiff's subjective intent. In a footnote in Robinson v. National Cash Register Co., 808 F.2d 1119, 1130 n. 20 (5th Cir.1987), a decision that was in another respect overruled by *Thomas,* a panel of this circuit agreed with *Zaldivar* that if an initial complaint passes the test of non-frivolousness, its filing does not constitute harassment for the purposes of Rule 11.

The *Zaldivar* rule comports with the text and spirit of amended Rule 11. The history of the Rule, as traced by the *Zaldivar* court, indicates that "subjective bad faith" is no longer an element in Rule 11 inquiries. Instead, the court must focus on objectively ascertainable circumstances that support an inference that a filing harassed the defendant or caused unnecessary delay. As Judge Schwarzer has stated: "If a reasonably clear legal justification can be shown for the filing of the paper in question, no improper purpose can be found and sanctions are inappropriate." Schwarzer, 104 F.R.D. at 195. Amended

Rule 11 mandates the court to focus on objective circumstances in determining whether an attorney has conducted "reasonable inquiry" and a paper is "well grounded" in fact and law, and purely subjective elements should not be reintroduced into the determination concerning "improper purpose."

Like the *Zaldivar* court, we do not hold that the filing of a paper for an improper purpose is immunized from Rule 11 sanctions simply because it is well grounded in fact and law. The case can be made, for example, as *Zaldivar* noted, that the filing of excessive motions, even if each is "well grounded," may under some circumstances constitute "harassment" sanctionable under the Rule. A plaintiff must file a complaint, however, in order to vindicate his rights in court. We find no indication that the filing here was unnecessary, for the Federation had refused to retract the statement. Under the circumstances, the Association had a proper interest in suing to attempt to vindicate its reputation.

The court based its decision to impose sanctions on three district court cases.   *   *   *

Each of these cases involved repetitious or excessive filings. The filing of an original complaint, as we noted above, presents no such redundancy and, therefore, when the allegations of the complaint are well grounded, cannot generally serve as a basis for imposing sanctions.

We conclude, therefore, that the district court abused its discretion in imposing sanctions on the Association.

Notes and Questions

(1) How should the possibility of sanctions affect negotiations between parties? Should a party who believes his opponent's case is based on a frivolous claim or defense (i.e., one "not well grounded in fact" or "warranted by existing law or a good faith argument" for its extension) raise the possibility of sanctions as a means of getting a more favorable settlement? Would a party's willingness to talk settlement indicate that the opponent's case really isn't frivolous? Would an actual offer of settlement so indicate?

(2) When the judge becomes involved in settlement discussions and urges the defendant to give up something, does *National Association* indicate that sanctions can never be imposed on the basis of frivolousness? Note that in *National Association* the judge had denied defendant's motions for summary judgment and directed verdict. Can sanctions ever be imposed for frivolousness when these motions are denied?

(3) If the determination of frivolousness must be made as of the time the complaint is filed, can sanctions for filing a frivolous suit ever be assessed against a party who reasonably believed his suit was justified when he filed it but who thereafter should reasonably have realized that he had no case? The Fifth Circuit in *Thomas* (which was relied on in *National Association*) stated that there is no continuing

duty to review and reevaluate one's case in light of developments to insure that it is not frivolous. 839 F.2d at 874. But could sanctions be based on some future filing of a motion or paper necessary for the continuation of the case? Alternatively, could the other prong of Rule 11—imposing sanctions for filing a paper "for any improper purpose"— justify sanctions in such a case?

(4) Rule 11 has been interpreted as imposing an objective standard for frivolousness. Does that mean that any party who loses a suit is a likely candidate for imposition of sanctions? Does this discourage parties from seeking redress when the present law seems to be against them or where the potential witnesses are biased in favor of their opponent? Does the possibility that sanctions will be imposed after judgment prevent closure of litigated disputes and further poison the parties' feelings about each other?

(5) Is there a way to factor in a value for the possibility of Rule 11 sanctions in determining the settlement value of a case? What considerations would go into determining the size of that discount?

(6) The federal rules were also amended in 1983 to encourage use of sanctions for violation of the discovery rules. One of the reasons was a feeling that lawyers would not seek, and judges would not award, sanctions. A federal district judge commented: "A lawyer who wants the option to abuse discovery when it is to his client's advantage will hesitate to seek sanctions when his client is the victim of such practices—especially if the sanctions are imposed on the attorney instead of, or in addition to, the client. As a result, a kind of gentlemen's agreement is reached, with the tacit approval of the bench, which is extremely convenient for the attorneys who avoid the just imposition of sanction and extremely unfair to the litigants who pay more and wait longer for the vindication of their rights than they should." Renfrew, Discovery Sanctions: A Judicial Perspective, 67 Cal.L.Rev. 264, 272 (1979). Today, however, requests for sanctions for misuse of discovery requests, responses, and objections are legion, and sanctions are frequently imposed against attorneys, the parties, or both. Have the beefed-up sanction rules gone too far the other way, encouraging further disputes involving great personal acrimony over collateral matters like discovery and whether the claim or defense should have been raised in the first place?

b. Rule 68 Offer of Settlement

Rule 68 of the Federal Rules of Civil Procedure (see Appendix A) is an important tool encouraging serious negotiation efforts by parties in some lawsuits. Twenty-nine states and the District of Columbia have rules similar in language and effect to Federal Rule 68.[12] The proce-

---

12. Jurisdictions include Ala., Alaska, Ariz., Cal., Colo., Conn., Del., D.C., Fla., Hawaii, Ind., Ky., Maine, Minn., Miss., Mo., Neb., Nev., N.J., N.M., N.C., N.D., N.Y., Ohio, Ore., R.I., Vt., W.Va., Wis., and Wyo. See Woods, For Every Weapon, A Counterweapon: the Revival of Rule 68, 14 Fordham Urban L.J. 283, 286–87 n. 19

dure works like this: Any party defending a claim may make a settlement offer to the plaintiff pursuant to Rule 68. That offer must provide a specific amount for the claim and costs, or an offer of non-monetary relief, or both, and must be made more than ten days prior to trial. Costs include court charges for filings and hearings, deposition expenses, witness and jury fees—but attorney fees only in certain statutory fee cases. If the plaintiff rejects the Rule 68 offer and does not receive a more favorable court judgment at trial, he must pay the defendant's court costs and fees incurred after the date of the offer. If the plaintiff recovers more than the offer—or nothing—at trial, or if the defendant's offer was not realistic or in good faith, the cost-shifting sanctions of Rule 68 do not apply.[13]

Lawyers have not used Rule 68 frequently, but when they have, they have used it in a wide variety of cases, including airplane crash, wrongful death, contract, admiralty, class action, maritime salvage, and of course automobile accident cases. The rule shifts the burden and increases the stakes in the negotiation. A defendant benefits from a realistic offer—avoiding trial expense and uncertainty if the offer is accepted, and, if it is rejected and not later surpassed at trial, being reimbursed the post-offer court costs. A plaintiff benefits by having the defendant motivated to make a realistic offer before the final preparation for trial.

A special application of Rule 68 has drawn particular attention and controversy. In the federal civil rights area defendants may offer to settle the suit for a specific sum, _including_ attorney fees, even though the plaintiff's lawyer may be entitled to fees charged as costs under the Civil Rights Attorney Fees Act of 1976, 42 U.S.C. § 1988. In Marek v. Chesny, 473 U.S. 1 (1985), defendant police officers made a timely Rule 68 offer of $100,000, including costs and attorney fees. The plaintiff refused the offer, and at the subsequent trial recovered $57,000 on two substantive claims, $3,000 punitive damages, plus costs and attorney fees. The amount of the fees and costs incurred prior to the Rule 68 offer was $32,000, bringing the total plaintiff recovery after trial for Rule 68 purposes to $92,000—less than the defendant's offer. The U.S. Supreme Court held that when attorney fees are explicitly charged as costs, as under § 1988, they come within the sweep of Rule 68, and therefore the defendants in this case were not liable for the court costs and attorney fees incurred after the Rule 68 offer was made (an additional $140,000).

The dilemma of the plaintiff's lawyer in such a situation can be intense: Any statutory attorney fees he might recover must be a negotiable item on the table, and his client, who has no liability for those statutory fee amounts if not awarded, has discretion to accept or reject the settlement offer. Lawyers, especially in civil rights cases, have relied on statutory fees to permit adequate compensation in cases

(1986) (the federal rule, enacted in 1938, was based on rules already in operation in Minnesota, Montana, and New York).

13. See Delta Air Lines, Inc. v. August, 450 U.S. 346, 350–53 (1981).

that otherwise would not warrant the amount of legal service required
to prosecute the claim. The Court intensified this dilemma in Evans v.
Jeff D., 475 U.S. 717 (1986). In that case, a § 1983 class action suit, the
parties arrived at a settlement which included the plaintiff's lawyer
waiving his statutory fees. His (reluctant) agreement to the settlement
was conditioned on the court's specific approval of the waiver along
with the settlement, both of which the district court provided. On
appeal, the Sixth Circuit reversed, holding such agreements, barring
unusual circumstances, unfair per se because of inherent conflicts the
negotiation tactic generates between the plaintiff and his lawyer. The
Supreme Court reversed, holding that a settlement offer may link the
merits with a waiver of statutory attorney fees, confirming "the possibility of a trade off between merits relief and attorney's fees." [14]

While the Court's interpretation increases the negotiating options
available to the parties, it does give some clients in pro bono and civil
rights areas the authority to waive attorney fees for which they have no
personal liability. This negotiating practice may lead to settlements in
some existing cases, but in the long run it may restrict future access to
legal services by other plaintiffs similarly situated. Lawyers may no
longer be willing or able to take cases in reliance only on statutory
sources for adequate fees. Several bar associations have responded by
adopting ethics opinions holding that a defense lawyer violates the code
of ethics by making a settlement offer contingent on the plaintiff's
lawyer waiving or limiting his rights to a statutory fee.[15]

Notes and Questions

(1) One observer concludes generally that the primary effect of
Rule 68 "is not to encourage settlement but to benefit defendants and
harm plaintiffs by shifting downward the relevant settlement range."
Miller, An Economic Analysis of Rule 68, 15 J. Legal Studies 93 (1986).
The argument goes like this: A defendant will make a lower settlement
offer under Rule 68 than he would otherwise, knowing the effect that
the added impact of cost-shifting will have on the plaintiff's decision.
Plaintiff, for his part, will accept something less than he otherwise
would, knowing the increased cost of not surpassing the offer at trial.
Thus, the entire settlement range is shifted downward. The effect is
even more pronounced if the plaintiff is risk-averse (as many are) and
the defendant is risk-prone (as is customary before trial begins).

(2) Deficiencies in Rule 68 led to a proposal by the Judicial Conference of the United States in 1983 to amend the rule. The drafting
committee noted that the original purpose "to encourage settlements
and avoid protracted litigation" had not been achieved because the rule
"has rarely been invoked and has been considered largely ineffective as

14. Evans v. Jeff D., 475 U.S. 717 (1986).

15. See, e.g., D.C. Bar Ethics Opinion 147 (Jan. 22, 1985); N.Y. City Bar Comm. on Prof. and Judicial Ethics, Opinion 80–94; Maine Bar Grievance Comm'n, Advising Opinion No. 17 (1983).

a means of achieving its goals." Preliminary Draft of Proposed Amendments to the Federal Rules of Civil Procedure, 98 F.R.D. 337, 363–67 (1983). The reasons given for its disuse were that it was a "one-way street," available only to defendants, and that the "costs" that were recoverable did not generally include attorneys fees.

The amendments, which have not been adopted, proposed: (1) making the rule available to both parties, (2) allowing an offer to be made up to 30 days before trial (the old provision for up to 10 days before trial was considered too short to enable offerees to act upon the offer) and requiring that it remain open for 30 days, (3) requiring a party who refused an offer, if the judgment is not more favorable to him, to pay costs and expenses, including reasonable attorney fees, incurred by the offeror after making of the offer, plus interest from the date of the offer on the amount that a claimant offered to accept to the extent it was not included in the judgment, (4) allowing expenses and interest to be reduced to the extent found by the court to be excessive or unjustified, and (5) prohibiting the award of costs, expenses, and interest on amounts not to be awarded if the court found the offer was made in bad faith. Is this a better rule? Does it still present problems?

c. Award of Prejudgment Interest

The award of prejudgment interest to a prevailing party who receives a money judgment is a consideration of some importance in the negotiation of a settlement. Prejudgment interest is thought to have a particular impact on the willingness of defendants to make an early settlement because without it, the defendant has the use of the money interest-free while the case is pending. The value of delay is of considerable value to insurance companies.

The availability of prejudgment interest has had a checkered history and varies considerably from jurisdiction to jurisdiction.[16] It was first allowed in cases involving specific performance of contracts that expressly provided for payment of interest on a fixed amount in the event of breach.[17] This "fixed sum-fixed time" requirement was enlarged in many jurisdictions to allow a prejudgment award if the precise value of the claim could be calculated.[18] Courts began extending prejudgment interest to noncontract cases early in this century, but often restricted it to those elements of damages that could be objectively quantified. Professor McCormick's analysis, adopted by a number of jurisdictions, distinguished between pecuniary and nonpecu-

---

16. See C. McCormick, Handbook on the Law of Damages §§ 54–57 (1935); Note, A Device for Faster Dispute Resolution and More Complete Compensation: The Pretrial Settlement Offer System, 3 Rev. of Lit. 459, 461–64 (1983).

17. See Robinson v. Bland, 97 Eng.Rep. 717 (1760); 1 Sedgwick, Treatise on Measure of Damages § 285 (9th ed. 1912).

18. See Board of Comm'rs v. United States, 308 U.S. 343 (1939); Robert C. Herd & Co. v. Krawill Machinery Corp., 256 F.2d 946 (4th Cir.1958); General Facilities, Inc. v. National Marine Service, Inc., 664 F.2d 672 (8th Cir.1981).

niary elements so that, for example, loss of wages and medical expenses would be eligible, but mental anguish would not.[19] Most courts today still do not allow prejudgment interest for nonpecuniary elements of damages.[20]

Notes and Questions

(1) How should the availability of prejudgment interest affect negotiations for settlement? Unlike Rule 11 sanctions, prejudgment interest can be determined with some exactitude in advance. Thus it can be calculated as an additional award to the plaintiff in a jurisdiction with prejudgment interest or as a benefit to the defendant in one without it (or with severe limitations on it). But should it be viewed simply in dollar terms? There are surely other intangible costs to a defendant from delaying a settlement which might off-set the interest-free value of retaining the settlement money longer. Likewise, although a plaintiff might be encouraged to hold out for a higher settlement where he can get prejudgment interest, the attractiveness of getting an early payment, both for the client and the attorney (particularly if on a contingent fee), often dilutes that incentive.

(2) Consider the Texas prejudgment statute, passed in 1987, and ask yourself what incentives it is trying to create:

Article 5069–1.05, Vernon's Tex.Civ.Stat.:

> Sec. 6(a) Judgments in wrongful death, personal injury, and property damage cases must include prejudgment interest. Except as provided by Subsections (b), (c), and (d) of this section, prejudgment interest accrues on the amount of the judgment during the period beginning on the 180th day after the date the defendant receives written notice of a claim or on the day the suit is filed, whichever occurs first, and ending on the day preceding the date judgment is rendered.

> (b) If judgment for a claimant is less than the amount of a settlement offer by the defendant, prejudgment interest does not accrue on the amount of the judgment for the period during which the offer may be accepted.

> (c) If judgment for a claimant is more than the amount of the settlement offer by the defendant, prejudgment interest does not include prejudgment interest on the amount of the settlement offer for the period during which the offer may be accepted.

Could subsection (c) be abused by defendants by routinely making a low offer and keeping it open throughout the suit in order to prevent prejudgment interest from running on the amount of that offer? What incentives does this provision attempt to create?

19. C. McCormick, Handbook on the Law of Damages §§ 56–57 (1935); Mass. Gen. Laws Ann. ch. 231, § 6B (West Supp. 1982–83); cf. In re Air Crash Disaster Near Chicago, 480 F.Supp. 1280 (N.D.Ill.1979), 644 F.2d 633 (7th Cir.1981).

20. Note, A Device for Faster Dispute Resolution, supra note 16, at 463.

(3) State law governs the award of prejudgment interest in federal court diversity cases, but, in federal question cases, its award "is a question of fairness within the District Court's sound discretion." Wolf v. Frank, 477 F.2d 467, 479 (5th Cir.1973); cf. Osterneck v. E.T. Barwick Industries, 825 F.2d 1521 (11th Cir.1988). A discretionary award of prejudgment interest must not be punitive and should be "tempered by an assessment of the equities." Norte & Co. v. Huffines, 416 F.2d 1189, 1191–92 (2d Cir.1969).

d. Settlement Devices in Mass Tort Cases

In recent years lawyers have built challenging and lucrative practices in the area of mass tort litigation.[21] An airplane crash, the release of toxic gas from a chemical plant, the longterm effects of toxic waste dumps, asbestos, and Agent Orange, and the harm caused by dangerous drugs or other products have created thousands of injured plaintiffs and a growing group of defendants forced to consider Chapter 11 bankruptcy. Courts have set up several procedures to handle these situations: the class action suit (Federal Rule of Civil Procedure 23), consolidation of tort actions for purposes of trial (Federal Rule of Civil Procedure 42(a)), and coordinated pretrial proceedings (28 USC § 1407). The effectiveness of these procedures often depends on the creativity of the lawyers and on an active and courageous judge who will not hesitate to use litigation deadlines and his own prestige to encourage the lawyers to develop satisfactory options for settlement.

Serious problems plague society in resolving these cases. The main objective is often lost in the complex procedure and adversarial culture surrounding this litigation. The goal is to compensate a victim who has suffered injury at the hands of modern industrialized society; yet, this victim frequently goes uncompensated for years while lawyers and judges discover, argue, and rule on pre-trial motions. In the end the victim generally receives only a fraction of the total spent to resolve the problem. For example, statistics on asbestosis litigation suggest that of the total invested per case, the victims receive only 35 percent. The remainder is divided between plaintiff lawyer fees (30 percent) and defense lawyer fees and costs (35 percent). It is an on-going challenge to devise a system for resolving mass tort cases that would allocate a higher proportion of the committed dollars to compensating the victims.

SKYWALK SETTLEMENTS
3 Alt. to the High Cost of Litigation 5–6 (Sept. 1985).

[The lobby of the Hyatt Regency Hotel, located in the prestigious Crown Center development in Kansas City, was crowded with up to 1500 people on July 17, 1981. The event was a popular city-wide tea

---

21. See Note, Mass Exposure Torts: An Efficient Solution to a Complex Problem, 54 U.Cin.L.Rev. 467 (1985).

dance. Party-goers packed the hotel skywalks which were suspended at
three levels over the lobby floor. As the crowd danced rhythmically
with the music, two of the skywalks collapsed under the stress: 114
people were killed and 239 were injured seriously enough to be hospital-
ized.]

The "extremely intense" litigation that ensued was under continuous scrutiny by the media: 187 separate cases were filed in the state
courts, and 18 in the federal courts, against a total of about 25
defendants. "We had over a million documents in a document deposito-
ry," said Sisk, "plus a warehouse full of debris from the fallen
skywalks." [Robert J. Sisk was counsel for defendant Crown Center
Redevelopment, a subsidiary of Hallmark Cards.] A mandatory class
was certified by the federal court, then decertified by the Eighth Circuit
because it interfered with settlements in the state court.

How was this complex litigation settled in 18 months—"record
time" for a major construction failure?

"We were given very tight schedules and trial dates by both the
federal and the state courts. Operating under this pressure from the
courts and the media, we began to think about how to avoid what were
bound to be highly emotional jury trials, likely to run 4 to 6 months or
longer.

"The claims totalled approximately $3 billion, at least two thirds of
which was for punitive damages. We estimated that we could settle the
cases for $100 to $150 million. There was more than enough insurance
to cover those amounts. Most of the insurance was that of Hallmark,
Crown Center, and the hotel operator, the Hyatt Corporation.

"We had tried to settle the cases earlier during the pendency of the
mandatory class and had reached a tentative agreement with respect to
the punitive damage claims, but could not get our co-defendants to go
along. Meanwhile, the insurance money of those co-defendants (primarily construction defendants—architects, engineers, contractors, inspec-
tors, etc.)—was gradually being eroded by their counsel fees.

"We finally accomplished the settlement shortly before the scheduled date of the federal trial. The main vehicle for settlement—a basic
class action—was not unique. The key was that we created a class in
the state court and settled in that court simultaneously with the
creation of the class. The class was coextensive with the 23(b)(3) opt-
out class which the federal judge established after his mandatory class
was thrown out. So we had two competing classes—a settled class of
all claimants in the state court identical to an unsettled class of all
claimants in the federal court.

"Although the class aspect of the settlement was not unusual, the
four techniques we used to make it work were. The first and most
unusual was the 'Syndicated Settlement.' To my knowledge, this had
never been done before, and I have not heard of anybody doing it since.
Hallmark and Crown Center undertook to be the sole underwriters and
pay all compensatory damages that anyone might obtain in a compen-

satory damage trial or by means of settlement. We also agreed to create a bonus pool to dispose of punitive damage claims. In exchange, Hallmark and Crown Center were released by plaintiffs in the state court and—this is the unusual part—were given the right to 'sell' participation in the settlement to our co-defendants on Hallmark and Crown Center's terms. Eventually we sold participation in the settlement to every one of them, bringing into the settlement pool the entire $25 million of their remaining insurance funds and terminating the erosion of those funds by legal fees. We didn't wait for, and didn't have to get agreement from our twenty-odd co-defendants to do this. We just did it. We had one month to go before the federal trial and, if we hadn't created this syndicated settlement, we would have been on trial in federal court."

The second unusual aspect to the settlement was an agreement to create a "Floating Fund," or bonus pool, of up to $20 million. Sisk explained, "Conceptually, this was similar to, but not denominated as, a punitive damage fund. It was to be created after all settlements and all trials for compensatory damages were concluded.

"Under the settlement agreement, nobody could try a case for punitive damages. One could try a case for compensatory damages, or one could settle. The floating fund created a pool to pay a bonus to those who didn't want to settle equivalent to that negotiated by those who did settle. However, we didn't want to create a big carrot that would encourage people to go to trial to get a piece of the $20 million rather than settle. Instead, we wanted a disappearing fund that would encourage settlement as quickly as possible. Our insurance carriers negotiated with the claimants to determine not only how much specific injuries were worth, but also how much on top of the "normal" compensation was needed to settle these extraordinary claims.

"How would these settlements affect the $20 million? We created an equation to take them into account in determining how much would be left of the fund. (The equation was

$$\frac{x}{c+x} = \frac{a-x}{b}$$

a equals the initial fund, b the total settlement, c the total amount of the verdicts, and x the final sum. In simplest terms, if there were, for example, $40 million in settlements and $10 million in trial verdicts for compensatory damages, there would be a $50 million total of compensatory payments. Of the $20 million fund, approximately $5 million would be left to divide among those who tried their cases. After all the litigation was over, we in fact had $90 million in settlements and roughly $20 million in trial verdicts, meaning that approximately $7 million will be paid out of the floating fund.)"

The third unique aspect of the settlement was the "Bystander Buy-Off." "There were 900 to 1500 people who weren't injured, but were in the lobby during the collapse and could have claimed they suffered emotional trauma. Missouri case law at the time allowed recovery for emotional trauma only if impact could be proved. The Missouri Supreme Court later overruled that decision, enabling people to recover for emotional trauma without proof of impact. Even though we did not anticipate that reversal, we wanted to find a way to handle the 900 to 1500 people who were in the lobby. We therefore provided that anybody who could prove he was in the lobby at the time of the collapse would be entitled to $1,000. In exchange for $1,000, the recipient had to give us a release that in effect opted him out of the federal class. In three weeks before Christmas and just before the federal trial was to begin, 1000 people were removed in this way from the federal class, leaving only 24 in it.

"The fourth unique device involved 'Charitable Contributions' as a way to dispose of the federal case. We were left with only 24 claimants in the federal court. Their damages were mostly minor—scratches, sprained ankles, contusions. The jury was to be impaneled on a Monday, and during the weekend before trial we worked out our final class action settlement.

"We felt we had to preserve parity between settlements for state court plaintiffs and those for federal court plaintiffs. We would not treat the federal claimants better, particularly since they did not have serious injuries. But this would have produced a relatively small settlement in terms of dollars, against a background of media hype and greater expectations. Our solution was to devise a charitable contribution formula. We created a fund of $3 million (comparable to the floating fund) from which the federal claimants could obtain the equivalent of punitive damages. In addition, we set aside an extra half million in case that $3 million was not enough. Plaintiffs' lawyers' fees and punitive damages were to come out of that $3.5 million. Hallmark then agreed to make a charitable contribution of $6.5 million, to be spread over four years. Just as the jury was being impaneled, the federal judge was able to announce that there was a '$10 million settlement' of the case."

Sisk drew three principal lessons from the skywalks settlements. First, intense, dedicated trial preparation is essential. "We could never have worked out the settlements if the federal and state plaintiffs had not been fully aware that we [Hallmark and Crown Center] were prepared to go to trial, that it was going to be a long trial, and that we had a very good chance of proving there was no liability on the part of the owner."

Second, it is important to work with insurance carriers and maintain good communications with them. "Although we still are in litigation with some of our carriers, we were able to cooperate with our major carriers to work out the basis for this unique settlement."

Third, defense counsel should be creative in the use of the class device. "Class actions, to those of us who primarily represent defendants, are frequently undesirable because they give plaintiff's counsel tremendous leverage. But there are times, from the defense point of view, when class actions can be used to dispose of massive, multiple claims. You have to work with the plaintiff's lawyers and find a way to do it. In the emotional arena in which the skywalks litigation took place, this was the best route to follow. Our client was pleased, and the litigation ended in a record time."

Notes and Questions

(1) What was it about the "Syndicated Settlement" scheme that led to a settlement in the Skywalk cases? Was it that Hallmark and Crown Center took the risk of paying all compensatory damages? Their apparent liability and the existence of enough insurance to cover all the claims undoubtedly contributed to their willingness to do that. Their success in selling participation rights to the co-defendants indicates a high degree of cooperation and trust among the defendants. Could this have been achieved if a court had tried to impose it on the parties?

2. The most ambitious form of structured negotiation and settlement to date is the Asbestos Claims Facility, created in 1984 by representatives of insurance companies and manufacturers of asbestos products in an attempt to resolve the tens of thousands of asbestos cases pending (and still to be filed) in state and federal courts around the country. The Facility, governed by a Board of Directors with equal representation from manufacturers and insurers, provides adjustors who make offers of compensation to asbestos victims who submit claims to it. If the claimant rejects the offer, he may pursue relief in court. The Facility also provides ADR procedures for claims by producers against insurers. See description in R. Marcus & E. Sherman, Complex Litigation 835–36 (1985) and infra p. 626. The Facility has had a modest success in resolving claims, but some asbestos manufacturers and insurers and many plaintiffs have chosen to stay out. Why would claimants spurn such a non-binding settlement process?

e. Judicial Promotion of Settlement

A lawyer's efforts to use litigation procedures to help assure a more successful negotiation can be made more effective if a judge assumes responsibility for managing the litigation with a goal of resolving the dispute voluntarily, fairly, and efficiently. Judicial administrators at both the federal and state levels currently emphasize the judge's role in promoting settlement.[22]

Rule 16 of the Federal Rules of Civil Procedure (see Appendix A) is the source for judicial activism in managing litigation and promoting settlement. Many states have similar language in their rules. It gives the federal district judge authority to hold "a conference or conferences" for such purposes as expediting disposition, establishing early and continuing control so that the case will not be protracted because of

22. See Miller, The August 1983 Amendments to the Federal Rules of Civil Procedure: Promoting Effective Case Management and Lawyer Responsibility 11–34 (Fed.Judicial Center 1984).

lack of management, discouraging wasteful practices, improving the quality of trial through preparation, and facilitating settlement (Rule 16(a)). Among the subjects appropriate for consideration in pretrial conferences are "the possibility of settlement or the use of extrajudicial procedures to resolve the dispute" (Rule 16(c)(7)). Failure to obey a pretrial order, being "substantially unprepared to participate in the conference," or failure "to participate in good faith" may subject a party or its attorney to sanctions upon the motion of a party or on the judge's own initiative (Rule 16(f)). The judge *shall* require the party or attorney or both to pay "the reasonable expenses incurred because of any noncompliance," including attorney fees, unless noncompliance is found to be "substantially justified or that other circumstances make an award of expenses unjust" (Rule 16(f)).

A judge's Rule 16 powers to encourage settlement are broad. In Lockhart v. Patel, 115 F.R.D. 44 (E.D.Ky.1987), a judge held several settlement conferences following a non-binding summary jury trial (see infra p. 652 for discussion of this device) that had recommended an award to the plaintiff of $200,000 for a lost eye in a medical malpractice case. The plaintiff agreed to settle for $175,000, but the attorney for the doctor's insurer told the judge he was authorized to offer $125,000 and no more and not to negotiate any further. The judge then called a settlement conference, directing the defense attorney to bring the representative of the insurance company from the home office who had issued these instructions and one with equal authority. He said: "Tell them not to send some flunky who has no authority to negotiate. I want someone who can enter into a settlement in this range without having to call anyone else."

The defense attorney only brought an adjuster from the local office who advised the court that her instructions from the home office were to reiterate the previous offer "and not to bother to call them back if it were not accepted." The judge then made findings that the insurer "had deliberately refused to obey the order of the court." He struck the pleadings of the defendant, declared him in default, and ordered a show cause hearing why the insurer should not be punished for criminal contempt. Later that day, the insurer settled for $175,000. At the contempt hearing, the judge accepted the assurances of the insurer that "it had all been a misunderstanding" and permitted it to purge itself with a letter of apology from its Chief Executive Officer. The judge then wrote an opinion "to discuss the authority of the court to hold meaningful settlement conferences and the propriety of the civil sanction imposed."

The opinion found that the sanction power in Rule 16(f) applied to a party's liability insurer as well as to a party and that striking pleadings is an appropriate sanction under Rule 37. It noted that "the exigencies of modern dockets demand the adoption of novel and imaginative means lest the courts, inundated by a tidal wave of cases, fail in their duty to provide a just and speedy disposition of every case. These means may take the form of compulsory arbitration, summary jury trials, imposing reasonable limits on trial time, or, as here, the relatively innocuous device of requiring a settlement conference attended by the clients as well as the attorneys." It concluded that "the court cannot require any party to settle a case, whether the court thinks that party's position is reasonable or not, but it can require it to make reasonable efforts, including attending a settlement conference with an open mind."

Other courts have upheld similar sanctions for misdeeds involving settlement conferences. For example, in Barsoumian v. Szozda, 108 F.R.D. 426 (S.D.N.Y.1985), a plaintiff's attorney failed to appear at the pre-trial conference because he did not note the scheduled date on his calendar, and the court imposed a sanction of $300 attorney fees and $200 court costs. In In re McDowell, 33 Bankr. 323 (Bankr.D.Ohio 1983), a bankruptcy court awarded a default judgment against the defendant as the sanction for the lawyer not appearing at the scheduled pre-trial conference. In Flaherty v. Dayton Elec. Mfg. Co., 109 F.R.D. 617 (D.Mass.1986), a district court approved sanctions against a plaintiff's attorney who was "substantially unprepared" to participate in a pre-trial conference. She apparently did not know her client's injuries, medical expenses, lost earnings, or whether any worker's compensation payments were received. The sanction imposed was payment of the fees and costs of defense counsel's preparation for and attendance at the conference.

A recent ABA-sponsored study of lawyers in four federal districts concluded that "85 percent of the responding attorneys from the entire four-district sample agree that involvement by federal judges in settlement discussions is likely to improve significantly the prospects of achieving settlement." [23] The data, summarized in the following selection, provide interesting insight into the relationships of lawyers and judges in the negotiation area.

W. BRAZIL, SETTLING CIVIL DISPUTES
44–46 (1985).

Our question remains: Why do lawyers say that judicial involvement can significantly improve prospects for achieving settlement? Our data do not provide a definitive answer, but they offer clues and suggest hypotheses. Even though a large percentage of cases ultimately settle, the process through which the parties eventually reach agreement often is difficult to launch, then can be awkward, expensive, time-consuming, and stressful. The route to resolution can be tortuously indirect and travel over it can be obstructed by emotion, posturing, and interpersonal friction. Counsel and clients can be distracted by irrelevancies and resources can be consumed by feints or maneuvers designed primarily to save face with opponents or to retain credibility

23. W. Brazil, Settling Civil Suits 39 (1985).

with the people paying the bills. Parties and lawyers can be slow to feel confidence in the wisdom or fairness of proposals developed through such an awkward, adversarial process, a process in which people assume that their opponents are not disclosing significant information and are offering only self-serving assessments of the implications of evidence and the relative strengths of competing positions.

Since at least some of these problems burden private settlement negotiations in many cases, lawyers well might feel that federal judges can make significant contributions to the settlement process by reducing frictions and removing obstacles that otherwise would impede it. As we will demonstrate, the pattern of lawyer responses to our questions suggests an important unifying hypothesis; judicial involvement is likely to improve prospects for achieving settlement because judges are professional decision makers.

Litigators, by contrast, are professional advocates. The skills that are central to the litigator's professional self-image and role revolve around marshalling evidence and arguments for one side, selecting and packaging information to make it as persuasive as possible. Lawyers are trained to uncover evidence, then to arrange its display to others; the others have ultimate responsibility to decide what the evidence means. Thus the litigator's job is to present persuasively, not to judge dispassionately.

Judges, on the other hand, are paid to make decisions, and to do so rationally and impartially. Good judges know that their central responsibility is to resolve disputes fairly, to terminate conflicts by making neutral decisions. Judges also know that the data on which they must make decisions will be presented to them by advocating litigators seeking persuasive advantages. To achieve their objective of making rational decisions in this environment, good judges become skillful at cutting through verbal and emotional camouflage to identify pivotal issues, at ferreting out key evidence, assessing credibility and analyzing strengths and weaknesses of arguments. The pursuit of fair solutions teaches judges to probe, to ask about matters not presented. The responsibility to make decisions puts a premium on efficiency. The responsibility to decide rationally sharpens the judge's analytical edge.

A judge who enters the settlement dynamic with these instincts and skills is in a position to make unique and valuable contributions. The presence of a judicial officer can create an expectation of decision making and can help overcome lawyers' and litigants' natural resistance to realistically assessing their positions. The judge can initiate settlement discussions earlier than counsel otherwise would and can relieve lawyers of the onus of being the first to suggest discussion of settlement. Some lawyers are reluctant to initiate settlement talks because they are afraid that raising the issue of settlement will be perceived by their opponents as a sign of weakness. That fear might help explain why so many of our respondents think settlement conferences should be mandatory in most actions in federal court and that judges should take steps to encourage settlement even when no one has asked them to do so.

Our data indicate, however, that lawyers believe that initiating dialogue about settlement is by no means the principal contribution judges can make to the process. What judges have to contribute to settlement that lawyers value most is skill in judging. Lawyers value penetrating, analytical exposition and thoughtful, objective, knowledgeable assessment. They want the judges' opinions. They want the judges' suggestions. They want the perspective of the experienced neutral. Data we discuss in a subsequent section shows that a judge's opinion that a settlement offer is reasonable is likely to have a great effect on a recalcitrant client, especially if that client is not often involved in litigation.

There also are many ways judges can contribute to the quality of the settlement dialogue itself: they can defuse emotions, set a constructive and analytical tone, help parties focus on the pertinent matters, and ask questions that expose underdeveloped areas. Judges can help keep litigants talking when they otherwise might retreat into noncommunication. In these and other ways, a judicial officer can improve the civility, efficiency, and efficacy of the negotiation process.

Thus, we infer that when lawyers say judicial involvement is likely to improve significantly prospects for achieving settlement, they mean that the right kind of judicial activism can initiate the process earlier, expedite it, and lead to earlier agreement by improving litigant and lawyer confidence in the fairness or wisdom of specific settlement proposals.

Notes and Questions

(1) The survey data showed that a majority of litigators (90% in one judicial district) preferred that judges in settlement conferences "actively offer suggestions and observations" for the settlement of the case. Opinions were sharply divided, however, as to whether the "settlement judge" should be the same judge who would ultimately try the case. What reasons might litigators have for wanting a different judge at trial than at the settlement conference?

(2) Two sitting judges, speaking to an audience of other judges, used the following language to describe the judge's role in settlement negotiations:

> One of the fundamental principles of judicial administration is that, in most cases, the absolute result of a trial is not as high a quality of justice as is the freely negotiated, give-a-little, take-a-little settlement. * * * Therefore, it is essential as part of your procedures to provide some techniques that will maximize the possibility of freely negotiated settlements in cases for which you are responsible. * * *

There's no point in talking about settlement at a time when the parties are not well enough informed to rationally discuss the elements in the case, and so that they can tell you enough about it so you can make an intelligent contribution to an evaluation of the case. * * *

If you get to that point, then you are faced with the question as to what your role should be. I always say, "Do you want me to participate in your discussions, or do you want to go off and have them by yourselves?" This is because * * * the use of judge time in settlement negotiations is valuable only if desired. * * *

We are catalysts in settlement. Our role is not that of a traditional judge. Our role at that stage is that of a mediator.

———

Panel Discussion, Comments by Judge Hubert L. Will, The Role of the Judge in the Settlement Process (Fed.Judicial Center 1983).

———

I thought it might be well for us to examine our own experiences as practicing lawyers, and think a little bit about why cases settle, because I think that helps us best to analyze the judge's role in the settlement process. * * *

[T]here appear to be two primary factors that lead to settlement. One is anxiety, and the other is the necessity for doing something. Now, none of us like anxiety. * * * It's not a desirable human emotion. * * * [A]nd lawyers, sharing with their clients the desire to eliminate anxiety, want to get rid of it. We eliminate anxiety, of course, by replacing uncertainty with certainty.

But that alone of itself won't settle anything because we are capable of tolerating anxiety for long periods. So, the second thing that seems to me to be an important component of the settlement process is the need to do something by a certain time. All settlement procedures are more efficient if there is a more or less inexorable trial date.

Panel Discussion, Comments by Judge Alvin B. Rubin, The Role of the Judge in the Settlement Process (Fed.Judicial Center 1983).

(3) A Colorado state district court issued an administrative order that parties in civil cases who settle after the case has been scheduled for trial shall be assessed a fine of no less than $550 for failure to resolve the case in a timely manner. Do you see any problems, either in terms of policy or due process, with this rule? See Raymond Lloyd Co. v. District Court for the Twentieth Judicial District, 732 P.2d 612 (Colo.1987).

Problem: Agent Orange

In 1967 the United States military forces faced serious obstacles in their efforts to support the Government of South Vietnam. The war, which had begun (for the U.S.) in the early 1960's and had been escalating rapidly since 1965, included an estimated 500,000 American military personnel and showed few signs of completion. A major problem was the infiltration of North Vietnamese guerillas throughout South Vietnam under cover of heavy forestation and undergrowth. The obvious solution, recognizable immediately to the military mind, was to create and apply a chemical that would eliminate the foliage, thereby exposing the enemy to rifle fire. Several American chemical firms prepared the defoliant, named Agent Orange, and the U.S. military used it to spray enormous forested areas in rural South Vietnam. The results were not only disappointing in terms of military strategy, but disastrous (at least allegedly) for the health of those required to live and work in an Agent Orange environment.

In 1978, three years after the last Americans left Vietnam, many veterans and their families filed individual and class action lawsuits in federal court against the chemical companies responsible for manufacturing and distributing Agent Orange. The plaintiffs complained of multiple diseases caused by exposure to the defoliant. By the conclusion of the district court case in 1985, it involved a plaintiff class of over 2.4 million veterans and family members, seven defendant corporations, the U.S. Government as a potential indemnitor, a docket sheet containing 375 pages and roughly 6,000 entries, and one entire room full of filed documents.

The lawyers settled this complex case on Monday, May 7, 1984, the date set for trial to begin, after intense nonstop settlement discussions led by Judge Jack B. Weinstein throughout the weekend. In the following selection, Professor Schuck describes the final three months:

SCHUCK, THE ROLE OF JUDGES IN SETTLING COMPLEX CASES: THE AGENT ORANGE EXAMPLE

53 U.Chi.L.Rev. 337, 344–48 (1986).

In February 1984, Weinstein requested and obtained permission to retain, at the defendants' expense, an unnamed consultant to develop a settlement strategy and plan. That consultant was later revealed to be Ken Feinberg, a lawyer whom Weinstein knew and trusted. Feinberg was not only knowledgeable about toxic tort litigation, but also had a reputation as an effective mover, shaker, and conciliator. By mid-March, he had prepared a settlement plan. It stated no dollar amount but contained three sections: an analysis of the elements for determining the aggregate settlement amount, especially the various sources of uncertainty and the likely number and nature of claims; a discussion of alternative criteria for allocating any liability among the chemical companies; and a discussion of alternative criteria for distributing any settlement fund to claimants. This document, which the judge made available to the lawyers, occasioned considerable disagreement but succeeded in setting the terms for the negotiations that followed.

On April 10, less than three weeks before trial, Weinstein appointed three special masters for settlement. Feinberg and David I. Shapiro, a prominent class action expert and skillful negotiator, would work with the lawyers. Leonard Garment, a Washington political insider, would explore what resources the government might contribute to a settlement. Feinberg and Shapiro immediately identified three major obstacles to settlement: the parties were more than *a quarter of a billion dollars* apart; each side was deeply divided internally over whether and on what terms to settle (and in defendants' case, how to allocate liability); and the government was manifestly unwilling to contribute toward a settlement fund or even to participate in settlement negotiations.

The judge and special masters decided to convene an around-the-clock negotiating marathon at the courthouse during the weekend before the trial. The lawyers were ordered to appear on Saturday morning, May 5, with their "toothbrushes and full negotiating authority." On that morning, while preliminary jury selection work was proceeding in another room, Weinstein met with the lawyers and gave them a "pep talk" about settlement. Then the special masters undertook a grueling two-day course of shuttle diplomacy, holding separate meetings with each side interspersed with private conferences with Judge Weinstein. On several occasions, the judge met privately with each side.

Several features of the discussion were particularly salient in generating the settlement agreement. First, the court did not permit the two sides to meet face-to-face until the very end, after the terms of the deal had been defined. This strategy preserved the court's control over the negotiations and prevented them from fragmenting. In particular, it stymied the plaintiffs' lawyers in their last-ditch effort to improve on the deal by settling with five of the defendants and isolating Monsanto and Diamond Shamrock, the two companies they thought most vulnerable to liability and punitive damages.

Second, the masters attempted to break log-jams in the negotiations by helping the lawyers to predict the consequences of the various approaches under consideration, and by proposing alternative solutions. For example, when the chemical companies' lawyers expressed the fear that a settlement would be rendered worthless if a large number of veterans decided to opt out of the class and sue on their own, Shapiro devised a "walk-away" provision that would minimize those concerns. The tax implications of a settlement were also questions that the masters helped to clarify.

Third, when especially difficult issues arose that threatened to derail the settlement, the parties agreed to be bound by the judge's decision. The most important example of the judge acting as arbitrator involved perhaps the most difficult question facing the defendants— how to allocate liability among themselves. Another example involved the question of one of the defendants' "ability to pay" its share.

Fourth, the judge and his special masters, while being careful not to be duplicitous, did emphasize different things to each side. In their discussions with plaintiffs' lawyers, they stressed the weakness of the evidence on causation, the novelty of many questions of law in the case, the consequent risk of reversal on appeal of a favorable verdict, the prospect that they might lose everything if they rejected settlement, and the enormous costs of continued litigation. To the defendants' lawyers, they stressed the presumed pro-plaintiff sympathies of Brooklyn juries, the reputational damage that protracted litigation and unfavorable publicity would cause their clients, and the high costs of the trial and of the inevitable appeals.

Fifth, a common theme in all discussions was the pervasive *uncertainty* that surrounded the law, the facts, the duration and ultimate outcome of the litigation, and the damages likely to be awarded. By almost all accounts, it was this uncertainty that proved to be the decisive inducement to settlement. On one count, however, Judge Weinstein left little doubt in the lawyers' minds: the court, having crafted and taken responsibility for the settlement, was in a position to make it stick.

Sixth, the imminence and ineluctability of trial "concentrated the minds" of the lawyers as nothing else could have done. This deadline imparted to their deliberations an urgency and a seriousness that swept aside objections that might have undermined negotiations in less compelling circumstances. The lawyers' growing physical and mental exhaustion during that weekend of feverish intensity abetted the conciliatory effect. As one plaintiff's lawyer later complained in his challenge to the validity of the settlement, "the Judge wore us all down with that tactic."

Seventh, the judge and special masters displayed a degree of skill, sophistication, imagination, and artistry in fashioning the settlement that almost all the participants viewed as highly unusual. But even this would not have availed had Judge Weinstein not inspired an extraordinary measure of respect, even awe, in the lawyers, and had the special masters not been viewed as enjoying the authority to speak and make commitments for him.

Eighth, the settlement was negotiated without any agreement (or even any serious discussion) of how the settlement fund would be distributed among the claimants, and without reliable information as to the number of claims that would be filed. The first, of course, was of great interest to the plaintiffs and a matter of indifference to the defendants. The second, however, was significant to both sides. It is not at all certain that settlement could have been reached had the parties been required to resolve these issues in advance. The problem was not simply that preparation of a distribution plan required an immense amount of analysis. A protracted process of political compromise and education was also needed to gain support for the plan, a process whose results even now remain doubtful and perhaps legally vulnerable.

Ninth, the lawyers on the PMC at the time of the settlement possessed very different personalities, ideologies, and incentives than those of the group of lawyers that had launched the case and carried it through its first five years. These differences likely affected the lawyers' disposition to settle. The veterans' passionate desire for vindication at trial, quite apart from their wish for compensation, had strongly driven their chosen lawyer, Victor Yannacone, during the earlier stages of the litigation. Yet the PMC's deliberations concerning the settlement were strongly influenced by lawyers who had only the most attenuated relationship to the veterans. And under the terms of an internal fee-sharing agreement, these lawyers would be secured financially by even a "low" settlement.

Finally, the court was prepared to allocate substantial resources to the quest for a settlement. Judge Weinstein devoted a great deal of his own time to thinking through and implementing a settlement strategy. His three special masters for settlement commanded high compensation and worked long hours. Their billings to the court totaled hundreds of thousands of dollars, even excluding the massive amount of work they later invested in connection with the distribution plan.

According to virtually all of the lawyers who participated in the negotiation of the Agent Orange settlement, Judge Weinstein's distinctive intervention was essential to the settlement. It is possible, of course, that the lawyers are wrong, and that a pretrial settlement would have been reached even without Weinstein's intervention—or, at the very least, that a settlement would have been reached after some witnesses had testified and "blood" had been drawn. But the court's settlement activity was regarded as crucial by those in the best position to know.

The Agent Orange settlement cannot be used as a guide for lawyers in the typical lawsuit since the case was anything but typical. Still, several lessons are important:

- the settlement process often needs a manager—if a lawyer does not serve in that role (in addition to his role as advocate), the judge or a master may.
- creativeness and flexibility are frequently indispensible to settlement.
- a judge has many available and appropriate resources which can improve the climate for settlement.
- the judge can easily assume the role of a "mediator with muscle," giving rise to charges of possible overreaching and coercion (see infra p. 257).
- the trial deadline is perhaps the single most effective tool promoting settlement, a fact that may achieve its formidable effect prima-

rily from the impact of human psychology in the bargaining situation.

5. Law Governing Settlement Negotiations and Agreements

a. Law Governing Negotiations

In our review of *General Electric Co.* and the Boulware tactic (see supra p. 125), we noted that the National Labor Relations Act requires the parties to bargain in "good faith." This statutory requirement is not generally reflected in the law of private contracts; lawyers still assume, often with good reason, that they are completely free during negotiations to change direction or walk away at any time. In some cases, however, this freedom may give rise to abuse of the bargaining process, and courts have begun to respond to such abuses. Consider the following two cases.

The Case of The Ice Cream Donut

Plaintiffs had conceived the idea of a circular ice cream product with a hole in the middle, which they referred to as an "ice cream donut." Realizing that mass production would be necessary for any real success, they looked around for a company which had the proper manufacturing equipment and national distribution network. They approached the Eskimo Pie Corporation and after receiving samples of the product and full details on how it was made, the company indicated a definite interest in manufacturing and marketing it. For the next two years Eskimo Pie Corporation continued to express enthusiasm for the project, but it put plaintiffs off with an elaborate variety of excuses: its executives were out of the office or on "extended trips;" "preliminary engineering work" had to be done; and "major reorganization activities" were occurring within the company. Often the plaintiffs' urgent calls and telegrams were not returned. Meanwhile, Eskimo Pie had been doing a test run of its own "Eskimo Do-nuts," and eventually it launched this product nationwide. Plaintiffs were left without an agreement—and no product. The court found that Eskimo Pie had "followed a steadied course of seeming deception":

> Defendant's action was deliberately calculated to keep plaintiffs expecting that they would be able to do business with defendant, while at the same time defendant went forward with its own plans to introduce its own product independently of any arrangement with the plaintiffs. * * * [D]efendant was deliberately stalling for time so as to keep plaintiff from soliciting the assistance of others or from proceeding on its own behalf, while the

defendant went forward with its own plans for marketing its own Eskimo Do-nut.[24]

Nevertheless, the court concluded that on the facts plaintiffs had not made a case for relief.

The Case of The Red Owl Store

A second case may raise a more difficult and subtle form of abuse of the negotiation process. Plaintiff operated a bakery and wanted to set up a grocery store. He contacted Red Owl Stores, which expressed interest in the venture. Plaintiff stated that $18,000 was all the capital he had available and the Red Owl negotiations repeatedly assured him that this amount would be sufficient for him to set up business as a Red Owl Store. On the advice of Red Owl management, plaintiff bought the inventory and fixtures of a small grocery store to give him some experience; before the summer tourist season he was told that he had to sell this store if he wanted a bigger one. Plaintiff was then told, "Everything is ready to go, we are set," and he was told to sell his bakery business—that this was the only "hitch" in the entire plan. Time dragged on. At later meetings, the company raised the amount of capital required of plaintiff to $24,000, then to $26,000, and then to $34,000. Finally, the plaintiff had had enough and broke off negotiations. His suit against Red Owl was met with the defense that the parties had not yet agreed on all the details of the franchise, such as the design and layout of the store building and the terms of the lease. The Wisconsin Supreme Court nevertheless held Red Owl liable to the prospective franchisee even in the absence of such an agreement, applying the doctrine of promissory estoppel incorporated in § 90 of the Restatement of Contracts:

> The record here discloses a number of promises and assurances given to Hoffman by Lukowitz in behalf of Red Owl upon which plaintiffs relied and acted upon to their detriment.
>
> * * *
>
> We determine that there was ample evidence to sustain the answers of the jury to the questions of the verdict with respect to the promissory representations made by Red Owl, Hoffman's reliance thereon in the exercise of ordinary care, and his fulfillment of the conditions required of him by the terms of the negotiations had with Red Owl.
>
> There remains for consideration the question of law raised by defendants that agreement was never reached on essential factors necessary to establish a contract between Hoffman and Red Owl. Among these were the size, cost, design, and layout of the store building; and the terms of the lease with respect to rent, maintenance, renewal and purchase options. This poses the question of whether the promise necessary to sustain a cause of action for

24. See Gray v. Eskimo Pie Corp., 244 F.Supp. 785 (D.Del.1965).

promissory estoppel must embrace all essential details of a proposed transaction between promisor and promisee so as to be the equivalent of an offer that would result in a binding contract between the parties if the promisee were to accept the same.

Originally the doctrine of promissory estoppel was invoked as a substitute for consideration rendering a gratuitous promise enforceable as a contract. In other words, the acts of reliance by the promisee to his detriment provided a substitute for consideration. If promissory estoppel were to be limited to only those situations where the promise giving rise to the cause of action must be so definite with respect to all details that a contract would result were the promise supported by consideration, then the defendants' instant promises to Hoffman would not meet this test. However, Sec. 90 of Restatement, 1 Contracts, does not impose the requirement that the promise giving rise to the cause of action must be so comprehensive in scope as to meet the requirements of an offer that would ripen into a contract if accepted by the promisee. Rather the conditions imposed are:

(1) Was the promise one which the promisor should reasonably expect to induce action or forbearance of a definite and substantial character on the part of the promisee?

(2) Did the promise induce such action or forbearance?

(3) Can injustice be avoided only by enforcement of the promise?

* * *

We conclude that injustice would result here if plaintiffs were not granted some relief because of the failure of defendants to keep their promises which induced plaintiffs to act to their detriment.[25]

Notes and Questions

(1) What does good faith mean in the context of these two cases? The company in *Red Owl* appeared to be using the escalation game as a negotiating technique. The Red Owl negotiator encouraged Hoffman to increase his investment in successive increments, and, as Hoffman's sunk costs increased, so did the price of the franchise. To view it in the best light for Red Owl, its negotiator may not have fully appreciated the strategy he was following, or understood its impact, until late in the process. Is an unknowing use of escalation tactics a form of bad faith bargaining? Is the conscious use of such tactics bad faith per se? Perhaps the only mistake Red Owl made was in refusing to conclude a deal of some sort with Hoffman. Is an escalation strategy ethical if an agreement results, regardless of any inequities that might exist? Are

---

25. Hoffman v. Red Owl Stores, Inc., 26 Wis.2d 683, 696–99, 133 N.W.2d 267, 274–75 (1965).

there differences between the promissory estoppel and good faith standards? "Good faith" does not have to be subjective. See UCC § 2–103(1)(b): " 'Good faith' in the case of a merchant means honesty in fact and the observance of reasonable commercial standards of fair dealing in the trade." See generally Knapp, Enforcing the Contract to Bargain, 44 N.Y.U.L.Rev. 673 (1976).

(2) What if the changes by Red Owl were not part of an escalation game, but were based on changing conditions in the local market or in the company, or a changing assessment of needed commitments from franchisees by company officials at successively higher levels of the Red Owl corporate heirarchy? What could Red Owl negotiators do to protect the company in future negotiations with prospective franchisees to prevent the kind of result reached by the court?

(3) Can the use of other negotiating techniques be bad faith bargaining independent of the user's motivation? Boulwarism refers to the tactic of making a reasonable first offer with an acknowledged no-concession rule. See Problem: Opening to Close, or Boulware Beware, supra p. 125. The other side must either accept the offer, demonstrate how it is based on incorrect facts (in which case regular negotiating will begin), or choose not to agree. Does the refusal to concede from what is objectively determined a reasonable first offer constitute bad faith bargaining? Under what conditions should it be considered bad faith? In *General Electric Co.*, Boulwarism was found to constitute bad faith bargaining because the surrounding facts suggested an improper motivation. Is such a subjective standard helpful to the negotiating lawyer? How do you recognize elements of bad faith bargaining in the typical legal negotiation?

(4) As a further twist on the *Red Owl* theme, special rules may apply when certain parties fail to agree after substantial negotiation. If an insurance company representing its insured in a personal injury accident case rejects a bona fide settlement offer which is both reasonable and within the insured's policy limits, the company assumes the risk that a later trial judgment will result in a judgment in excess of the insured's coverage. See, e.g., Slater v. Motorists Mutual Ins. Co., 174 Ohio St. 148, 187 N.E.2d 45 (1962); G.A. Stowers Furniture Co. v. American Indemnity Co., 15 S.W.2d 544 (Tex.Com.App.1929). In other words, if the defense attorney fails to use good faith and reasonable care in looking after the interests of the insured, the insurance company may lose the protection of its policy limits and be forced to pay even the insured's share of the judgment. For discussion of the duty of an insurance liability carrier to settle within policy limits, see Koenan, Bad Faith and Negligence Approaches to Insurer Excess Liability for Failing to Settle Third–Party Claims: Problems and Suggestions, 54 Def.Counsel J. 179 (1987); Alleman, The Reasonable Thing to Do: The Insurer's Duty to Settle Claims Against Its Insured, 50 U.M.K.C.L.Rev. 251 (1982).

The possibility of holding the insurance company liable for a judgment in excess of the offer to settle is especially useful for the plaintiff's lawyer where the policy limits are within mid-range of a reasonable recovery. Note the plaintiff's first offer in the Sorensen Chevolet File, supra p. 133. Similar strategies may attach to the use of Rule 68 offers of judgment, supra p. 158. The defense lawyer in this situation faces a particularly sensitive dilemma: his two clients (insured and insurance company) now have conflicting interests, with possible substantial unfavorable consequences for one or the other, depending on the lawyer's decision. Information or directions received from one client may be adverse to the interests of the other, presenting the lawyer with a difficult ethical problem. For example, an insurance agent may disclose to the defense lawyer information which would tend to show the company's lack of good faith in refusing to accept a settlement within contract limits—information which would help the insured avoid liability over that limit at a later trial.

Rule 408, Federal Rules of Evidence

Confidentiality of information disclosed and of statements made during negotiations is a matter of considerable importance to lawyers and clients. You do not want to say anything during the settlement process that tends to admit liability on your part, only to have that evidence introduced by the opposing party at trial after settlement negotiations break down. Federal Rule of Evidence 408 (see Appendix C) excludes from a later trial any evidence of statements, conduct, or offers or acceptance of offers made in settlement negotiations if introduced for the purpose of proving liability for or invalidity of the claim or its amount. Most states closely follow this federal language.

Rule 408 is an expanded version of the protection that was available at common law to offers to compromise. Originally, at common law, the only policy that underlay such protection was the belief that an offer to compromise was not reliable evidence of the value of the offeror's claim; there was no general policy of support for negotiated settlements. Unfortunately for the unguarded speaker, any "independent" admission of liability was unprotected. The means for determining what was an independent admission were unreliable and the outcomes unpredictable, leaving the protection of little practical value. The Federal Rule eliminates this distinction by protecting both the offer and "evidence of conduct or statements made in compromise negotiations".[26]

Some exceptions to this general protection exist—primarily for information, statements, or conduct used for the purpose of impeach-

---

26. See Bottaro v. Hatton Assoc., 96 F.R.D. 158 (E.D.N.Y.1982), infra p. 347 (where remaining co-defendants sought discovery of a settling defendant's compromise agreement, the court held that defendants were not entitled to disclosure absent showing of likelihood that it would generate admissible evidence).

ment, negativing a contention of undue delay, or proving obstruction in criminal investigation or prosecution. The lawyer must therefore be careful not to disclose information in areas in which he suspects it could be used within these exceptions. Still, he should be able to rely on Rule 408 protection for his actions and statements in the typical negotiation.

This protection, however, does not eliminate the lawyer's need to be careful what information to disclose during settlement. What you say or do can lead the other side to focus its discovery in areas it might have overlooked. Moreover, material or communications revealed during negotiations which are otherwise discoverable cannot be immunized from discovery or admission at trial by introduction into a settlement conference. These issues, and others relating generally to confidentiality, are often raised in the mediation setting. See infra p. 341.

THOMAS v. RESORT HEALTH RELATED FACILITY

United States District Court, Eastern District of New York, 1982.
539 F.Supp. 630.

NEAHER, DISTRICT JUDGE.

Plaintiff, a black male originally from Granada, West Indies, brought this action to redress alleged discrimination in employment, pursuant to the Civil Rights Act of 1866 and 1871, 42 U.S.C. § 1981, and Title VII of the Civil Rights Act of 1964, as amended, 42 U.S.C. § 2000e et seq. (1976). * * * The complaint alleged that plaintiff's employer, Resort Health Related Facility ("Resort"), and the individual defendants Kornegay, Brown, and Tenanbaum, supervisory and administrative personnel employed by Resort, discriminated against plaintiff during his employment at Resort because of his race, color, national origin and sex.

[After nearly 5 years of employment, plaintiff was suspended for refusal to submit to a psychiatric examination to be performed by a doctor chosen by the employer.] His complaint seeks injunctive and declaratory relief, reinstatement, back pay, and $200,000 in money damages for mental anguish, humiliation, and loss of self-respect.

The action is now before the court upon several motions by defendants, [among them a motion] for a partial summary judgment limiting the period of plaintiff's potential back pay recovery to the date when plaintiff rejected defendants' unconditional offer of reinstatement.

The defendants' next requests for relief all relate to their attempt to limit plaintiff's back pay recovery to the period between the February 1980 suspension and the date they made, and plaintiff rejected, an offer of unconditional reinstatement without prejudice to his claim for back pay. In Title VII, Congress specifically provided that "[i]nterim earnings or amounts earnable with reasonable diligence by the person . . . discriminated against shall operate to reduce the back pay otherwise allowable." The measure of damages for the back pay claim under § 1981 is identical.

Accordingly, defendants have moved to terminate plaintiff's claim for back pay as of February 24, 1981 or March 2, 1981, dates on which they claim to have offered to reinstate plaintiff to his former position, unconditionally without prejudice to his present attempt to secure back pay for any prior period, and so limit a liability that could otherwise run until trial. Alternatively, defendants have moved for an order disqualifying present counsel for both parties on the ground that they ought to testify about the alleged offers and plaintiff's refusal. In addition, defendants have sought an order severing trial of the liability issues from those relating to damages, on the ground that defendants will be prejudiced before the jury, since the evidence they intend to introduce to reduce or mitigate plaintiff's back pay claim unavoidably will expose the parties' unsuccessful settlement negotiations.

Neither side disputes that on February 24, 1981, the parties and their present attorneys met to discuss settlement of this lawsuit. There is also no question that at this meeting the defendants, through present counsel, offered to reinstate plaintiff to the terms and conditions of his former position, or that on March 2, 1981, defendants' counsel wrote to plaintiff's counsel purporting to summarize the February 24 discussions and "reiterate that the offer of reinstatement of Mr. Thomas to his former terms and conditions of employment was without conditions and did not require him to waive his claims for back pay." Furthermore, neither plaintiff nor his counsel has denied that the initial offer was rejected solely because it did not compensate plaintiff for pay and other benefits (holiday and sick days) he lost during his suspension. There is considerable question, however, whether the offer "reiterated" by defendants' counsel's March 2 letter was ever communicated to the plaintiff himself.

The circumstances under which the February 24 offer was made also are in dispute but, as will become clear, this fact issue is not material. Plaintiff's counsel clearly considered that all the discussions between the parties that day were being held "without prejudice." Defendants' counsel now claims that the offer was made to plaintiff independent of that day's settlement discussions, which assertedly had reached an impasse. Disputing this latter contention, plaintiff's counsel also contends that the "without prejudice" understanding of the parties prevents the reinstatement offer from being used to limit his client's back pay award.

The foregoing facts raise two main questions which must be resolved before defendants' motions can be decided. First, does Rule 408, F.R. Evid., preclude defendants from submitting evidence as to the reinstatement offers on the motion for summary judgment? If evidence of the offers is excluded, defendants' various motions relating to the offers must be denied. But if evidence of the offers is admissible, the legal effect upon plaintiff's back pay claim must then be addressed, the second issue.

[The opinion quotes the text of Rule 408, which is located in Appendix C.] Evidence of the reinstatement offers and of plaintiff's rejection is admissible for the following reasons. First, there is no genuine issue that the reinstatement offers were not made to compromise the claim for back pay, which puts the proffered evidence outside the scope of the first sentence of the Rule. Although defendants made their initial offer at the same meeting at which they discussed settlement of the entire case with plaintiff and his attorney, the offer could not reasonably be viewed as one to settle the back pay claim, since plaintiff's acceptance of its terms was without prejudice to his demand for back pay. Thus, the fact issue whether or not settlement negotiations had reached an impasse is not material.

For this same reason, evidence as to the offer and its rejection falls within the admissible scope of Rule 408's third sentence, and does not suffer the exclusionary effect of the Rule's second sentence. Regardless of when the offer was made, there is no question that legally it was unrelated to the discussions about settling the lawsuit including the back pay claim, although plaintiff's counsel may not have realized it.

Plaintiff's counsel urges that all the discussions on February 24 were "without prejudice." But to deny legal effect to an unconditional offer of reinstatement and preclude a defendant-employer from attempting to reduce a potential back pay award by an amount "earnable with reasonable diligence" from itself, because counsel for the offeree plaintiff insisted that all the discussions were "without prejudice," would grant the plaintiff too much control over the litigation, and subject employers to unnecessarily burdensome claims for back pay. In providing that a Title VII back pay award "shall be reduced by amounts earnable with reasonable diligence," Congress undoubtedly sought to achieve two desirable economic goals, to prevent a "double recovery" by a discriminatee of both back pay and income from employment the plaintiff would otherwise not have obtained, and with respect to discriminatees who did not seek other jobs, to discourage unjustified idleness and thus minimize the consequent detriment to the defendant and the economy. Significantly, Congress did not expressly exclude the alleged discriminating employer from the class of persons from whom a plaintiff might reasonably be required to seek employment.

Even if the evidence as to the offers and rejection could be considered within Rule 408, it would be admissible under the Rule's last sentence because "offered for another purpose" than the one proscribed by Rule 408. Defendant is not seeking to use its offer and plaintiff's rejection of it as an admission by either party as to the "invalidity" of the back pay claim, or its "amount," which is the chief evidentiary purpose on which Rule 408 focuses. Defendants' purpose is to show that back pay otherwise recoverable after the date of its offer should not be allowed because the loss of back pay during that period is not attributable to defendants' discrimination. Accordingly, the evidence as to the reinstatement offers is ruled admissible and not barred by Rule 408.

* * *

With the foregoing discussion in mind, we turn to the issues in this case. Plaintiff's attorney declared at plaintiff's deposition that he had rejected defendants' offer of reinstatement because it did not compensate plaintiff for the time lost during his suspension, including holiday and sick pay. Defendants offered to reinstate plaintiff to his former terms and conditions of employment without prejudice to his back pay claim. Under the principle reached in this decision, however, defendant was not required to compensate plaintiff for his past economic losses, liability for which was in dispute, in order to end its liability for back pay by an offer that in all other respects put all claims of discrimination to rest. Accordingly, plaintiff's claim for back pay is limited under both Title VII and § 1981 to amounts accruing between the date of his suspension and the date he rejected defendants' offer.

Notes and Questions

(1) Is *Thomas* correctly decided? Why wasn't the defendants' offer of unconditional reinstatement considered to fall under Rule 408's second sentence as a "statement" made in compromise negotiations? Was that offer really "unrelated to the discussions about settling the lawsuit," as the court says? Why wouldn't such an offer be an aid in settling the suit? Must Rule 408 be so strictly construed as not to protect statements made during compromise negotiations unless they are part of the *quid pro quo* for settlement? Wasn't the offer of reinstatement a direct attempt by defendants to mitigate damages that is related to settlement?

(2) Is *Thomas* correct that in any event the defendant was not seeking to introduce the offer of reinstatement to prove "liability for or invalidity of the claim or its amount"? Why isn't the introduction of the offer for the purpose of mitigating damages considered to go to the validity of the "amount" of the claim?

(3) The exclusion of settlement offers has been invoked in the criminal context as well. See Stamicarbon, N.V. v. American Cyanamid Co., 506 F.2d 532 (2d Cir.1974). Federal Rule of Criminal Procedure 11(e)(7) protects offers to compromise in negotiations and plea bargains.

(4) Lawyers should also be aware of Federal Rule of Evidence 409, which prohibits the use of evidence at a subsequent trial relating to payment of plaintiff's medical, hospital, or similar expenses submitted for the purpose of proving liability (see Appendix C). This rule encourages early payment of medical expenses by defendant insurance companies even before liability has been admitted or damages fully agreed upon. It is an attempt—perhaps ineffective in the absence of clear liability and an insurance company committed to consumer service—to

give injured persons lacking substantial financial resources some reasonable bargaining power.

b. Validity and Effect of Settlement Agreements

The law governing the enforcement and effect of settlement agreements is for the most part ordinary contract law—with which, by this point, you are certainly likely to be familiar. A signed settlement agreement will normally be a complete bar to any subsequent action by one of the parties on the underlying claim. The requirements of the doctrine of consideration will be easily met for the settlement agreement by the avoidance of the uncertainty, extra expense, and delay of enforcing the disputed claim in court. Even if the disputed claim was in fact clearly invalid, a compromise settlement will be upheld if the party surrendering the claim has merely an honest belief that it *may* be valid. (Restatement of Contracts, Second, § 74). However, settlement agreements are vulnerable to the same attacks as other contracts—attacks based, for example, on fraud, unconscionability, mistake, or impossibility.

These contract doctrines may call for careful attention on the part of the negotiating lawyer. For example, in arriving at a settlement agreement both parties may have been mistaken as to a "basic assumption," whether of fact or of law. In such cases the party who is adversely affected by this mistake may avoid the agreement "unless he bears the risk of the mistake." (Restatement of Contracts, Second, § 152). Even where the agreement does not allocate the risk of mistake to one of the parties, a court may find that he should bear that risk if "it is reasonable in the circumstances," or if that party was aware when the contract was made "that he has only limited knowledge with respect to the facts to which the mistake relates but treats his limited knowledge as sufficient." (§ 154). Some courts show on occasion a rather extreme willingness to relieve a party from the consequences of his own mistaken beliefs. Consider Taylor v. Chesapeake & Ohio Railway Co., 518 F.2d 536 (4th Cir.1975), in which an employee sued under the Federal Employers' Liability Act for injuries sustained at work. The employee had earlier signed a written release in exchange for a settlement of $2000; the settlement provided that the parties "acknowledge that the injuries * * * may be permanent and progressive; that recovery may be uncertain and indefinite and that injuries * * * may not now be fully known and may be more numerous and more serious than now believed." The court held that the validity of the release was an issue to be resolved by a jury: "Neither party to the release, it would seem, understood at the time that the plaintiff had sustained a ruptured disc," but both proceeded "on the basis" that the injury "was merely a temporary, though painful strain." [27]

27. See also Wooten v. Skibs A/S Samuel Bakke, 431 F.2d 821 (4th Cir.1969).

The doctrine of mistake may have obvious implications for the quality of drafting and the amount of discovery for which a party is responsible. It may also have implications for the amount of disclosure that is due to the *other* party: For even if only one party is mistaken as to a "basic assumption" of the contract, the agreement is voidable if "the other party had reason to know of the mistake" or if the effect of the mistake is such that enforcement would be unconscionable. (Restatement of Contracts, Second, § 153). In addition, contract-law notions of unconscionability and "bargaining in good faith," see supra p. 177, help to shape the lawyer's ethical responsibilities during a negotiation, as do contract and tort-law restrictions on deception and misrepresentation. See infra p. 198. See also the discussion of the enforceability of agreements reached in mediation, at infra p. 372. These obligations may form an outside limit beyond which the lawyer acts at his own professional peril.

Cases with multiple defendants raise opportunities for plaintiffs' lawyers to negotiate settlements before trial with one or two—but not all—defendants. Some plaintiffs secure an agreement from one defendant that guarantees payment of a certain sum in settlement, leaving the plaintiff free to pursue the non-settling defendant in subsequent court action; any recovery in excess of an amount fixed in the agreement with the settling defendant will lower the amount owed by the settling defendant. These agreements are known as Mary Carter agreements after the name of a prominent Florida case, Booth v. Mary Carter Paint Co.[28] This practice has a complicated and controversial impact on all parties, in both the negotiation and court processes.

ENTMAN, MARY CARTER AGREEMENTS: AN ASSESSMENT OF ATTEMPTED SOLUTIONS *

38 U. Fla.L.Rev. 521, 529–30 (1986).

* * * [T]here are various benefits of a Mary Carter agreement for the agreeing parties. The plaintiff is guaranteed a minimum recovery regardless of the outcome of trial or settlement negotiations. The plaintiff also may realize a recovery far in excess of the guaranteed amount if there is a large enough verdict against the nonsettling defendant. In addition, the likelihood of such a verdict is enhanced by the cooperation at trial between the plaintiff and the settling defendant.

The benefit of the agreement to the settling defendant is that his liability to the plaintiff is set at a maximum amount, which may be reduced to zero if a sufficiently large verdict against the nonsettling defendant is recovered. In a jurisdiction that does not provide for contribution among tortfeasors, the settling defendant's total liability is established by the Mary Carter agreement. Even in a jurisdiction that

28. 202 So.2d 8 (Fla.App.1967).

provides for contribution, the settling defendant may be able to avoid liability above the amount guaranteed in the agreement. If, through the agreeing parties' cooperation at trial, there is a verdict in favor of the settling defendant, he then is not liable for contribution. Even if there is a verdict against both defendants, the settling defendant is able to avoid contribution if * * * the court construes the Mary Carter agreement to be the type of settlement that bars contribution against the settling defendant.

There are two distinct problems caused by Mary Carter agreements. The most easily recognized problem is the presence at trial of a defendant who has an identity of interest with the plaintiff. * * * [T]he opportunity for collusion between the plaintiff and a codefendant may lead not only to a substantial verdict for the plaintiff, but also to exoneration for the settling defendant. Thus, as the result of an unfair trial, the nonsettling defendant loses both the case brought by the plaintiff and the possibility of contribution from the settling tortfeasor.

The second problem is the effect a Mary Carter agreement has on the apportionment of responsibility among joint tortfeasors. For instance, [suppose that George's car is struck by a car driven by Martha, who entered the intersection without stopping at the stop sign. She first says that she did not see the stop sign, but later claims that she was unable to stop because of the negligence of Shade Tree Mechanics in failing to repair her brakes properly. George sues both, and enters a Mary Carter agreement with Martha by which Martha, while remaining a defendant in the suit, would pay George $50,000 to be released from liability; however, the agreement provides that if George should obtain a settlement or judgment against Shade Tree for *more* than $50,000, Martha would not have to pay George anything (and if *less* than $50,000, Martha would pay George only the difference between the judgment against Shade Tree and $50,000). If the jury] found Martha and Shade Tree jointly and severally liable for George's injuries, Shade Tree [nonsettling] would be entitled in most jurisdictions to seek contribution from Martha [settling]. Martha may then contend that she had settled with George and, therefore, is not liable for contribution. Under the Uniform Contribution Among Tortfeasors Act, Martha's success in resisting contribution depends upon whether the court finds that the settlement between George and Martha was in good faith. Thus, Martha may be able to escape contribution, either because she was exonerated at trial of liability to George or because she has settled with George. If she is not liable for contribution, and if there is no reduction in George's judgment against Shade Tree because of the settlement with Martha, the result is that the entire burden of compensating the plaintiff falls upon one of two jointly liable tortfeasors.

Judicial responses to Mary Carter agreements vary widely. Some courts have taken steps to eliminate the use of Mary Carter agreements, either because of their distortion of the adversary process or because of their effect on the allocation of liability among defendants. The steps taken include outright prohibition of these agreements, refusal to enforce the agreement between the parties, and frustrating the agreement's purpose by either reducing the plaintiff's judgment on the basis of the agreement or refusing to permit the agreement to bar the nonsettling defendant's right to contribution.

Other courts have rejected both the notion that Mary Carter agreements are hopelessly irreconcilable with fair trials and that the liability shifting caused by a Mary Carter agreement should be prevented. These courts permit the use of Mary Carter agreements, but acknowledge that the agreements may adversely affect the fairness of a trial against the nonsettling defendant. Even courts that allow Mary Carter agreements, therefore, do not permit the agreement to be kept secret and often allow the nonsettling defendant to inform the trier of fact of the parties' true positions.

Notes and Questions

(1) Professor Entman concludes her analysis by calling for the outright prohibition of Mary Carter agreements (as several jurisdictions already do). How would this ban alter the power balance between multiple defendants during negotiations with the plaintiff? If one defendant is more risk-averse than the other, which one would prefer the Mary Carter approach? If one uses more competitive negotiation strategies than the other? A ban would seem to favor the co-defendant who uses more stubborn and recalcitrant tactics. Is this the negotiation environment we want to encourage?

(2) If the basic injustice of a Mary Carter agreement is in encouraging collusion between settling defendant and plaintiff at the trial, are there options to solve this short of an outright ban on the agreement? If collusion can be shown, would setting aside the judgment return the parties to their appropriate pre-trial status? Can the jury ever determine fairly the nonsettling defendant's liability, absent active participation at trial by the settling defendant? Is disclosure of the agreement sufficient to insure truthful testimony by the settling defendant—or at least a reasonable chance for the trier of fact to evaluate that truthfulness? For discussion of further effects of Mary Carter agreements, see Note, Admission Into Evidence of a Mary Carter Agreement from a Prior Trial is Harmful Error, 18 Tex.Tech L.Rev. 997 (1987).

(3) One problem caused by Mary Carter agreements, according to Entman, is their effect on the allocation of liability among joint tortfeasors. If the court finds joint and several liability among the co-defendants, should the nonsettling defendant be able to demand contribution from the settling defendant, assuming good faith in negotiating the settlement and fairness at trial? Should parties be limited in how their voluntary settlements respond to different possible future events?

(4) Multiple defendants can avoid arguments among themselves by negotiating a "joint defense agreement" prior to trial. This agreement spells out the percentage of joint loss allocation among defendants in case of settlement or adverse judgment. The joint defense agreement is

especially suitable to toxic tort cases, where the number of defendants, the stakes, and the technical uncertainties are high. Parties can build into these agreements ADR methods for resolving questions concerning contribution amounts should a dispute occur after trial. See Special Supplement: Dauer and Nyhart, An ADR Procedure for Loss Allocation in a Joint Defense Agreement, 2 Alternatives to the High Cost of Litigation 14 (Dec.1984) (co-defendants agree not to cross-claim against one another, nor to use separate attorneys, deferring their rights against each other to later negotiation or ADR proceedings). Does this represent an undesirable form of collusion among co-defendants?

(5) California courts have interpreted state statutes as allowing enforcement of "sliding scale recovery agreements," the California equivalent of Mary Carter Agreements, only if in "good faith," that is, that the amount of the settlement is within the reasonable range of the settling tortfeasor's proportional share of the comparative liability for the plaintiff's injuries. See Tech–Bilt Inc. v. Woodward–Clyde & Assoc., 38 Cal.3d 488, 213 Cal.Rptr. 256, 698 P.2d 159 (1985).

c. Judicial Approval of Settlement Agreements

Within the boundaries of the ordinary rules of contract law, courts usually do not evaluate the merits of a voluntary settlement; court involvement is terminated merely by a dismissal filed by the plaintiff, with or without prejudice. In special circumstances, however, courts may require a finding that a proposed settlement is "fair." A divorce action is a good example. The court may not consider the parties to be arm's-length negotiators, and therefore any proposed settlement may be the result of an imbalance of power or a one-sided psychological dependency within the marriage. Moreover, there may be children or other dependents whose interests are not represented by counsel, but whose rights are affected by the proposed agreement. Therefore, states uniformly require divorce settlement agreements to be approved by the court before they are binding on the parties. The standards for this approval are typically what the court deems just and right in the situation, or what is in the best interests of the children.

Another example of a situation where court approval is required is when one party is a fiduciary, has a representational relationship, or has special need for protection. Courts must approve settlements by guardians for the benefit of minors or other wards, and for parties in class action and shareholder derivative suits. Judge Hill in Cotton v. Hinton, 559 F.2d 1326, 1329–30 (5th Cir.1977), summarizes the judicial standards applicable to settlement agreements by parties in class action litigation:

> From the growing body of decisional law, a number of principles have emerged for the guidance of district judges in making the determination to give or withhold approval of a proposed settlement. * * * In determining that a compromise is fair, adequate and reasonable and therefore should be approved, the trial judge is

essentially called upon to do a balancing task. The application of the principles to which we refer, as well as others, will be dependent upon the facts of each case.

In determining whether to approve a proposed settlement, the cardinal rule is that the District Court must find that the settlement is fair, adequate and reasonable and is not the product of collusion between the parties. * * *

A threshold requirement is that the trial judge undertake an analysis of the facts and the law relevant to the proposed compromise. A "mere-boiler-plate approval phrased in appropriate language but unsupported by evaluation of the facts or analysis of the law" will not suffice.

In addition to undertaking such an analysis, it is essential that the trial judge support his conclusions by memorandum opinion or otherwise in the record. An appellate court, in the event of an appeal, must have a basis for judging the exercise of the trial judge's discretion. * * *

In determining the fairness, adequacy and reasonableness of the proposed compromise, the inquiry should focus upon the terms of the settlement. The settlement terms should be compared with the likely rewards the class would have received following a successful trial of the case. * * *

Yet, in evaluating the terms of the compromise in relation to the likely benefits of a successful trial, the trial judge ought not try the case in the settlement hearings. * * *

Neither should it be forgotten that compromise is the essence of a settlement. The trial court should not make a proponent of a proposed settlement "justify each term of settlement against a hypothetical or speculative measure of what concessions might have been gained: inherent in compromise is a yielding of absolutes and an abandoning of highest hopes."

These judicial standards also include numerous practical considerations, such as the amount of time that further litigation would involve, additional expense, the effect of such time and expense on both parties, and the judgment of experienced counsel in the case.

Courts also require approval of all criminal plea-bargains before they are implemented. Federal Rule of Criminal Procedure 11(e) is an example of the special standards and detailed review necessary for court approval of plea bargains. See Appendix B. An interesting extension of this court review is in cases where a potential defendant negotiates the dismissal of charges in return for a waiver of his right to sue under § 1983. The U.S. Supreme Court has upheld this negotiating tactic, one which has become a standard tool for many prosecuting attorneys.[29]

29. See Town of Newton v. Rumery, 480 U.S. 386 (1987).

As the last example suggests, a settlement agreement may also be called into question in subsequent litigation, especially where the public interest may be compromised. For example, parties to a trademark dispute may agree to a settlement in which one agrees not to use the mark or is permitted to use the mark in certain ways or areas. In later litigation where a plaintiff sues to enjoin this use and the defendant relies on the settlement agreement, the court may investigate the public interest. An agreement permitting use by more than one party may raise the possibility of public confusion as to the source; an agreement prohibiting use of what would be considered a descriptive or generic term would invade the general vocabulary available to the public. Courts will weigh the interests of contract enforcement against the public interest involved.[30]

Notes and Questions

(1) Courts take special interest in voluntary settlements in areas such as divorce, class actions, trademark, antitrust, or criminal cases. Do these areas reflect a particular societal interest in the conflict?

(2) Settlements, of course, may not always be desirable, especially where the public interest would be ill-served. Recall Professor Fiss' comments to this effect at supra p. 43. Professor Fiss has questioned in particular the public interest in settlement of class litigation, suggesting that in such litigation, involving "nebulous social entities" like racial minorities, residents of institutions for the mentally retarded, and consumers, the process for generating "authoritative consent" from members of the group may be seriously flawed. See Fiss, Against Settlement, 93 Yale L.J. 1073, 1078–82 (1984). Coleman and Silver, Justice in Settlements, 4 Soc. Philosophy & Policy 102, 112–113 (1987), observe:

> In fairness, it must be said that judges can refuse to permit settlements that violate public policy, and they can invalidate existing settlements for the same reason. Nonetheless, many objectionable agreements may go unnoticed. First, judges cannot expect parties to call attention to questionable aspects of settlements. Once parties form an agreement, their interest is to get a judge to approve it, not to invite an inspection of its terms. After a settlement is approved, the parties to it will raise the issue of its acceptability only if one of them thinks it is worthwhile to begin the trial of the dispute anew. Even in this event, however, it may be difficult for a judge to decide whether a settlement is contrary to public policy because the issues presented by the underlying dispute will not have been aired. Second, institutional pressures discourage judges from acting *sua sponte* to invalidate settlements. As the amount of civil litigation grows, judges must process cases more quickly. Consequently, they have less time to familiarize

---

30. See, e.g., T & T Manufacturing Co. v. A.T. Cross Co., 587 F.2d 533 (1st Cir. 1978); Beer Nuts, Inc. v. King Nut Co., 477 F.2d 326 (6th Cir.1973).

themselves with the facts and issues cases present and must rely more heavily on counsel's opinions and recommendations. As a result, judges are more likely to miss objectionable elements of settlements. Third, parties can sometimes appeal a judge's decision to refuse to dismiss a case, which means that a judge who interferes with settlements sometimes risks being reversed by a superior court. Thus, although judges can take steps to insure that settlements accord with public policy, there is no cause for optimism that they will do so as often as needed nor reason to think that the efforts they make will succeed.

(3) Court standards for approval of settlements in special areas can help a lawyer even in cases where court approval is not required. They represent guidelines by which society evaluates fairness, adequacy, and reasonableness in a negotiated settlement. Other standards, of course, may be relevant and can be used, but societal standards often provide acceptable common ground for both sides. They constitute what Roger Fisher and William Ury call objective criteria (see supra p. 83) and can be used effectively to measure settlement offers during the negotiation process.

Problem: Pennzoil v. Texaco

The owners of Getty Oil disagreed on the future of the company. The majority wanted to accept a takeover bid from some other oil company. During the first week of January 1984, Getty management and owners agreed in principle with Pennzoil for the latter's purchase of 43 percent of Getty shares at $112.50 per share. Four days later Getty owners accepted a Texaco bid for all shares at $125 per share, or $9.89 billion.[31] The fallout from these events has been catastrophic. They imposed substantial lost earnings and opportunities on both Pennzoil and Texaco, sent chills through the Wall Street merger community, and created a boom economy for lawyers in Houston and New York. Pennzoil filed suit immediately in Delaware to force Getty to honor the initial agreement in principle. Getty countered that there had been no binding agreement—and, in fact, there had been no written agreement with Pennzoil, only a memorandum of agreement and a press release announcing Pennzoil's option on Getty shares.[32] Texaco pressed ahead with its merger, ignoring Pennzoil's claims and requests.

Meanwhile, Pennzoil had also filed an action in a Texas state court for damages caused by Texaco's interference with the merger agreement between Pennzoil and Getty. On November 19, 1985, a Houston jury stunned Texaco, the stock exchanges, and the nation's business community by holding Texaco liable for negligent interference with a contract and awarding Pennzoil $11.12 billion in compensatory and punitive damages. That verdict triggered months of court actions

31. See Wall St.J., Jan. 9, 1984, p. 1, col. 6.

32. See Wall St.J., Jan. 12, 1984, p. 14, col. 3.

questioning, first, the impartiality of the judge appointed to replace the original judge who fell sick; attacking the legality of the original trial verdict; and finally, in a New York federal district court, challenging the Texas appeal-bond requirements.

After the adverse Texas decision, and simultaneously with taking all possible litigation steps to reverse or mitigate that decision, Texaco made some clumsy attempts to discuss settlement. Its main proposal was to buy Pennzoil for what it (Texaco) considered a fair price, but a premature information leak, some dispute as to what was fair, and an already soured personal relationship between the two corporate presidents made these early efforts unproductive.

By spring 1986, Texaco was facing conflicting pressures from many litigation battles. It had received a favorable decision from the federal district court in New York lowering the Texas appeal bond from $11 billion to $1 billion. The Second Circuit had affirmed this decision, and Pennzoil had appealed to the U.S. Supreme Court. In Texas, briefs were filed in the appeal of the original $11 billion verdict. In addition, many Texaco shareholders had filed suit against the Texaco management seeking compensation for the harm caused by the Getty takeover bid. To make matters more complicated, an original owner of Getty stock filed suit against Texaco for damages caused by Texaco's alleged repudiation of the letter and spirit of an indemnity agreement for claims arising out of the transaction.

In late March 1986, the presidents of Pennzoil and Texaco met again—briefly—and opened the way for more serious settlement talks. But the litigation process continued to hamper these attempts to resolve the dispute. A three-month standstill agreement signed by the two companies expired on that same March day, and Pennzoil lawyers wanted to extend the agreement in order to prevent Texaco from mortgaging any Getty assets. The over 50 percent decrease in crude oil prices from December 1985 to March 1986 had substantially reduced the value of Texaco properties—a worry to Pennzoil, too—and placed heavy cash-flow demands on both companies.[33]

Those in control of both Texaco and Pennzoil had other worries too: a personal animosity between the two presidents, multiple shareholder demands (seven lawsuits had already been filed against Texaco, and Pennzoil shareholders were calling for payment of the full judgment), and continued stress and disruption created by this case for other business relationships. Nevertheless, these costs seemed to pale in the face of the billions of dollars at stake.[34]

By fall 1986, litigation was continuing with all deliberate speed, with nothing new on the negotiation front. Only three settlement offers had been exchanged: a Texaco bid to purchase Pennzoil for between $90 and $100 per share, and two separate proposals, one from

33. See Wall St.J., Mar. 26, 1986, p. 14, col. 3; Mar. 25, 1986, p. 7E, col. 1.

34. Sherman, Inside the Texaco-Pennzoil Poker Game, Fortune, Feb. 3, 1986, p. 90, 94.

each company, to have Pennzoil acquire certain former Getty assets. The parties were nearly $3 billion apart in their offers. Other options being discussed included cash, first mortgage bonds, debentures, some form of royalties in producing properties, or an exchange in oil industry services. The appeal of the Texas trial court decision was the next court hurdle, and both parties waited expectantly for confirmation of their respective positions.

In early 1987, Texaco received a double blow from the courts. On February 12, the Texas Court of Appeals affirmed the original verdict with a remittitur of only $2 billion in punitive damages, leaving a $10 billion plus judgment (including interest) against Texaco. On April 6, the U.S. Supreme Court reversed the Second Circuit's decision approving a reduction in the appeal bond required under Texas law. The $11 billion dollar figure was reinstated.

On April 13, Texaco filed for bankruptcy protection, thus avoiding a requirement to post a $10 billion appeal bond, foiling Pennzoil's attempts to seize Texaco assets, and shifting attention to the operating procedures under Chapter 11 of the Federal Bankruptcy Code. The move into bankruptcy appeared at first to be a masterful tactic for the Texaco defense, but the rigorous procedures limiting business activity and permitting creditors (including Pennzoil) to control certain operations quickly evened the score. Meanwhile, the appeal process continued, and on November 2, the Texas Supreme Court upheld the Pennzoil verdict, stating that the lower courts had made no reversible errors. Texaco served notice that it would appeal the case to the U.S. Supreme Court—a potential two-year process if the Court agreed to hear it, eight to ten months if it did not. And the parties were still far apart—at least in public—in their ideas of a fair settlement. Pennzoil offered to limit Texaco's ultimate liability to $5 billion in return for an immediate nonrefundable $1.5 billion cash payment. Texaco rejected the proposal as being "clearly unreasonable."

Any settlement had to be a part of a creditor's plan to bring Texaco out of bankruptcy; in fact, this last Pennzoil proposal had been made in response to a request by the chairman of the general creditors committee. The bankruptcy judge had set January 11, 1988, as the deadline for presenting a settlement formula, asking the creditors to offer a plan if the parties could not. Time pressure was increasing and the appeal process was running out on Texaco. In late December 1987, the two companies agreed on a settlement of $3 billion in cash, and the process of securing agreement from Texaco creditors and shareholders and the bankruptcy judge began.

On March 23, 1988, the federal bankruptcy judge ruled that the $3 billion cash settlement was "fair and equitable," ending over four years of intense, expensive legal fighting. The residue of this legal war remained, however, as the *Washington Post* headline on March 24 heralded: "Bitterness Lingers Even as Pennzoil, Texaco Settle Suit."

Notes and Questions

(1) Probably no one at either Texaco or Pennzoil fully analyzed, at an early stage of the dispute, the costs and benefits of continued litigation. Even if they had, few would have predicted the size of the Texas jury's verdict. Can lawyers and parties rely on such analysis for negotiation and settlement strategy?

(2) What can you do to persuade an angry and adamant client to consider objectively the costs of continuing litigation? Might a structured process such as a mini-trial or mediation (see Chapter III) be more successful in these circumstances than the arguments of outside counsel?

(3) Was the general creditors committee instrumental in bringing about the settlement? Could the court have established early in the case a less intrusive form of mediation which might have avoided the costs and uncertainty of bankruptcy?

(4) Risk is a function of the size of the stakes and the degree of uncertainty in the outcome. The Pennzoil–Texaco problem highlights the variable effects of the balance in risk-averse and risk-prone behavior by corporate leaders and their lawyers. It is difficult to imagine higher stakes than $10.1 billion, plus interest growing at $3 million per day. The "high-low contract" was the method proposed to control risk during the final negotiations during November 1987. This contract is a clever way to permit the uncertainty to continue while lowering or managing the stakes involved. The proposal in this case was for Texaco to pay $1.5 billion to Pennzoil immediately, for Pennzoil to cap Texaco's liability at $5 billion, and then for both to play their litigation and bankruptcy hands within those limits.

If the parties had agreed to this proposal, Pennzoil would obviously have avoided the risk of a "no liability" ruling by the U.S. Supreme Court, and Texaco would have secured a ceiling on its liability well below what an affirming Court opinion would allow. But in the end the lawyers and clients chose to settle the dispute without receiving a final court decision, rather than merely limiting their risk during the wait. Settlement may have looked more desirable because of the difficulty in getting agreement on specific figures that would lower the risk for both parties equitably. Where stakes are lower, the "high-low contract" may be a useful tool. See Finz, The Hi/Low Contract: A Trial By Chance, N.Y. State Bar J. 186 (April 1976) (application in tort litigation, especially areas of medical malpractice and products liability).

D. ETHICAL DILEMMAS FOR THE NEGOTIATOR

Lawyers are often of two minds about legal ethics: They want to live up to the high ideals of a profession that zealously advocates justice, yet they are committed to the individual realities of social and commercial life in the community—a life that is often uniformly self-interested, with more concern about ends than about the morality of the means used to achieve those ends. This dilemma exists in all areas of lawyer activity, but is even more pronounced in the negotiating environment. This section tries both to organize our thinking about this rather intangible and elusive subject and to ask the right questions.

Lawyer behavior is officially governed by the code of ethics adopted by the highest court in the jurisdiction in which the lawyer practices. For our purposes, we will refer to the *Model Code of Professional Responsibility*, adopted by the American Bar Association in 1969 and, with only minor changes, in most states during the early 1970's, and to the *Model Rules of Professional Conduct*, adopted by the ABA in 1983 as an updated revision of the Model Code and, so far, by a limited number of states.[1]

Several provisions warrant printing in full:

DR 1–102(A)   A Lawyer shall not ∗   ∗   ∗

> (4) Engage in conduct involving dishonesty, fraud, deceit, or misrepresentation.

[The same language is found in Model Rule 8.4(c).]

DR 7–102(A)   In his representation of a client, a lawyer shall not:
∗   ∗   ∗

> (2) Knowingly advance a claim or defense that is unwarranted under existing law, except that he may advance such claim or defense if it can be supported by good faith argument for an extension, modification, or reversal of existing law.

> (3) Conceal or knowingly fail to disclose that which he is required by law to reveal.

> (4) Knowingly use perjured testimony or false evidence.

> (5) Knowingly make a false statement of law or fact.

[Similar language is contained in Model Rules 3.3, 4.1, and 4.4.]

DR 7–105(A) A lawyer shall not present, participate in presenting, or threaten to present criminal charges solely to obtain an advantage in a civil matter.

[No similar language is found in the Model Rules.]

The consideration of lawyer ethics in negotiating is complex in its subtlety and far-reaching in its implications. "Honesty" and "fairness" seem to take on different dimensions in the negotiation setting than when used in the abstract. As we have seen, lawyers often convey misimpressions of attitude, situation, or bottom line as an expected part of the negotiation "dance." Moreover, the negotiating lawyer faces

---

1. The following provisions are particularly relevant to negotiation: *Model Code*: Disciplinary Rules (DR) 1–102(A); 4– 101(B), (C); 6–101(A); 7–102(A), (B); 7–105(A); 9–101(C). *Model Rules*: Rules 1.1; 1.2(a); 1.6; 3.3; 4.1; 4.4; 8.4.

ethical dilemmas in many areas besides misrepresentation or dishonesty, from the lawyer's relationship with his client (who is to control the decision to settle for a certain amount or go to trial?) to the lawyer's work in areas heavily regulated by governmental agencies (must the lawyer disclose untruthful statements made by the client in a filing with the Securities and Exchange Commission?).

And in the final analysis, the primary constraints on lawyer behavior are probably matters of prudence rather than ethical codes enforced by external authority. After all, given the importance of credibility and trust in the negotiating environment, a lawyer's reputation for honesty and fairness will certainly play a major role in his effectiveness as a negotiator over time.

1. Misrepresentation and Other Tactical Behavior

The language of DR 1–102(A)(4) is very clear: do not misrepresent. Yet, most lawyers know that it is accepted practice to obscure—even to misrepresent—the bottom line in a negotiation (see the discussion of apparent bottom lines, supra p. 105). Therefore, the Model Code or Model Rules probably do not mean misrepresentation per se. But if the ethical terms ("dishonesty", "deceit", "misrepresentation") do not have their ordinary meanings, what do they mean? Do they mean only what societal norms would dictate in any event? A body of contract and tort law does exist relating to misrepresentations, omissions, and mistakes made by private parties in the course of their transactions:[2] Such existing law may be the best guide to acceptable negotiation practice. But do applicable ethical restraints on lawyers impose still higher standards? If so, does this mean that clients are put at a disadvantage when they are represented in negotiations by lawyers rather than by someone else?

Several distinctions are important to the way "misrepresentation" should apply to lawyers in negotiation situations. Should a lawyer be able to misrepresent "opinions" or "aspirations," but not "facts"? Is it proper to inflate what you think the property is worth, but not what the appraisal report said? In the law of sales and of advertising, allowance is often made for something called "puffing." As Judge Learned Hand remarked, "Neither party usually believes what the seller says about his opinions, and each knows it. Such statements, like the claims of campaign managers before elections, are rather designed to allay the suspicion that would attend their absence than to be understood as having any relationship to objective truth."[3] Are greater restrictions imposed on statements of "intrinsic" facts (such as

---

2. See Restatement, Second, Contracts §§ 152 (mutual mistake), 154 (bearing the risk of mistake), 159 (misrepresentation), 161 (nondisclosure); Restatement, Second, Torts § 551 (liability for nondisclosure).

3. Vulcan Metals Co. v. Simmons Mfg. Co, 248 Fed. 853 (2d Cir.1918).

the book value or existing profit/loss statement for a company being sold) than on "extrinsic" facts (such as the seller's personal reasons for selling or the time the profit/loss statement was received from the auditors)? Is the intrinsic-extrinsic distinction just another way to differentiate what is relevant and material to the outcome of the negotiation from what is not?

Does misrepresentation occur if the lawyer does not *knowingly intend* to misrepresent? If the other side misunderstands a factually true statement made by the lawyer, must the lawyer correct the misinterpretation once he discovers the other side's error? Does the answer to that question depend on whether the statement is misinterpreted in a way that is relevant or material to the outcome of the negotiation, that is, whether it would make a difference in the other side's negotiating position?

In this connection, the Comment to Model Rule 4.1 provides some clarification.

Misrepresentation

A lawyer is required to be truthful when dealing with others on a client's behalf, but generally has no affirmative duty to inform an opposing party of relevant facts. A misrepresentation can occur if the lawyer incorporates or affirms a statement of another person that the lawyer knows is false. Misrepresentations can also occur by failure to act.

Statements of Fact

This Rule refers to statements of fact. Whether a particular statement should be regarded as one of fact can depend on the circumstances. Under generally accepted conventions in negotiation, certain types of statements ordinarily are not taken as statements of material fact. Estimates of price or value placed on the subject of a transaction and a party's intentions as to an acceptable settlement of a claim are in this category, and so is the existence of an undisclosed principal except where nondisclosure of the principal would constitute fraud.

The following excerpt by Professor White touches on these and other ethical issues. (The draft provision to which he refers was deleted before adoption of the final version of the Model Rules in August 1983.[4])

4. Rule 4.2 of the January 1980 Discussion Draft, Model Rules of Professional Conduct, read in part:

4.2 Fairness to Other Participants

(a) In conducting negotiations a lawyer shall be fair in dealing with other participants.

(b) A lawyer shall not make a knowing misrepresentation of fact or law, or fail to disclose a material fact known to the

lawyer, even if adverse, when disclosure is:

(1) Required by law or the rules of professional conduct; or

(2) Necessary to correct a manifest misapprehension of fact or law resulting from a previous representation made by the lawyer or known by the lawyer to have been made by the client, except that counsel for an

WHITE, MACHIAVELLI AND THE BAR: ETHICAL LIMITATIONS ON LYING IN NEGOTIATION

1980 American Bar Foundation Research J. 926–30.

* * *

The difficulty of proposing acceptable rules concerning truthfulness in negotiation is presented by several circumstances. First, negotiation is nonpublic behavior. If one negotiator lies to another, only by happenstance will the other discover the lie. If the settlement is concluded by negotiation, there will be no trial, no public testimony by conflicting witnesses, and thus no opportunity to examine the truthfulness of assertions made during the negotiation. Consequently, in negotiation, more than in other contexts, ethical norms can probably be violated with greater confidence that there will be no discovery and punishment. Whether one is likely to be caught for violating an ethical standard says nothing about the merit of the standard. However, if the low probability of punishment means that many lawyers will violate the standard, the standard becomes even more difficult for the honest lawyer to follow, for by doing so he may be forfeiting a significant advantage for his client to others who do not follow the rules.

The drafters [of the Model Rules] appreciated, but perhaps not fully, a second difficulty in drafting ethical norms for negotiators. That is the almost galactic scope of disputes that are subject to resolution by negotiation. One who conceives of negotiation as an alternative to a lawsuit has only scratched the surface. Negotiation is also the process by which one deals with the opposing side in war, with terrorists, with labor or management in a labor agreement, with buyers and sellers of goods, services, and real estate, with lessors, with governmental agencies, and with one's clients, acquaintances, and family. By limiting his consideration to negotiations in which a lawyer is involved in his professional role, one eliminates some of the most difficult cases but is left with a rather large and irregular universe of disputes. Surely society would tolerate and indeed expect different forms of behavior on the one hand from one assigned to negotiate with terrorists and on the other from one who is negotiating with the citizens on behalf of a governmental agency. The difference between those two cases illustrates the less drastic distinctions that may be called for by differences between other negotiating situations. Performance that is standard in one negotiating arena may be gauche, conceivably unethical, in another. More than almost any other form of lawyer behavior, the process of negotiation is varied; it differs from place to place and

accused in a criminal case is not required to make such a correction when it would require disclosing a misrepresentation made by the accused.

(c) A lawyer shall not:

(1) Engage in the pretense of negotiating with no substantial purpose other than to delay or burden another party;

(2) Illegally obstruct another party's rightful access to information relevant to the matter in negotiation;

* * *

from subject matter to subject matter. It calls, therefore, either for quite different rules in different contexts or for rules stated only at a very high level of generality.

A final complication in drafting rules about truthfulness arises out of the paradoxical nature of the negotiator's responsibility. On the one hand the negotiator must be fair and truthful; on the other he must mislead his opponent. Like the poker player, a negotiator hopes that his opponent will overestimate the value of his hand. Like the poker player, in a variety of ways he must facilitate his opponent's inaccurate assessment. The critical difference between those who are successful negotiators and those who are not lies in this capacity both to mislead and not to be misled.

Some experienced negotiators will deny the accuracy of this assertion, but they will be wrong. I submit that a careful examination of the behavior of even the most forthright, honest, and trustworthy negotiators will show them actively engaged in misleading their opponents about their true positions. That is true of both the plaintiff and the defendant in a lawsuit. It is true of both labor and management in a collective bargaining agreement. It is true as well of both the buyer and the seller in a wide variety of sales transactions. To conceal one's true position, to mislead an opponent about one's true settling point, is the essence of negotiation.

Of course there are limits on acceptable deceptive behavior in negotiation, but there is the paradox. How can one be "fair" but also mislead? Can we ask the negotiator to mislead, but fairly, like the soldier who must kill, but humanely?

* * *

Pious and generalized assertions that the negotiator must be "honest" or that the lawyer must use "candor" are not helpful. They are at too high a level of generality, and they fail to appreciate the fact that truth and truthful behavior at one time in one set of circumstances with one set of negotiators may be untruthful in another circumstance with other negotiators. There is no general principle waiting somewhere to be discovered as Judge Alvin B. Rubin seems to suggest in his article on lawyer's ethics.[10] Rather, mostly we are doing what he says we are not doing, namely hunting for the rules of the game as the game is played in that particular circumstance.

The definition of truth is in part a function of the substance of the negotiation. Because of the policies that lie behind the securities and exchange laws and the demands that Congress has made that informa-

10. Rubin states his position as follows:

The lawyer must act honestly and in good faith. Another lawyer, or a layman who deals with a lawyer should not need to exercise the same degree of caution that he would if trading for reputedly antique copper jugs in an oriental bazaar. It is inherent in the concept of an ethic, as a principle of good conduct, that it is morally binding on the conscience of the professional, and not merely a rule of the game adopted because other players observe (or fail to adopt) the same rule. Alvin B. Rubin, A Causerie on Lawyers' Ethics in Negotiation, 35 La.L.Rev. 577, 589 (1975).

tion be provided to those who buy and sell, one suspects that lawyers engaged in SEC work have a higher standard of truthfulness than do those whose agreements and negotiations will not affect public buying and selling of assets. Conversely, where the thing to be bought and sold is in fact a lawsuit in which two professional traders conclude the deal, truth means something else. Here truth and candor call for a smaller amount of disclosure, permit greater distortion, and allow the other professional to suffer from his own ignorance and sloth in a way that would not be acceptable in the SEC case. In his article Rubin recognizes that there are such different perceptions among members of the bar engaged in different kinds of practice, and he suggests that there should not be such differences.[12] Why not? Why is it so clear that one's responsibility for truth ought not be a function of the policy, the consequences, and the skill and expectations of the opponent?

Apart from the kinds of differences in truthfulness and candor which arise from the subject matter of the negotiation, one suspects that there are other differences attributable to regional and ethnic differences among negotiators. Although I have only anecdotal data to support this idea, it seems plausible that one's expectation concerning truth and candor might be different in a small, homogeneous community from what it would be in a large, heterogeneous community of lawyers. For one thing, all of the lawyers in the small and homogeneous community will share a common ethnic and environmental background. Each will have been subjected to the same kind of training about what kinds of lies are appropriate and what are not appropriate.

Moreover, the costs of conformity to ethical norms are less in a small community. Because the community is small, it will be easy to know those who do not conform to the standards and to protect oneself against that small number. Conversely, in the large and heterogeneous community, one will not have confidence either about the norms that have been learned by the opposing negotiator or about his conformance to those norms.

Notes and Questions

(1) Is it true, as White states, that the truth of assertions can only be examined by trial or by public testimony by conflicting witnesses?

(2) The legal profession appears to distinguish between "lying," which is considered unacceptable behavior, and certain other forms of deception, which are often considered skillful negotiation practices.

---

12. Rubin writes:

The esteem of a lawyer for his own profession must be scant if he can rationalize the subclassifications this distinction implies. * * *

Lawyers from Wall Street firms say that they and their counterparts observe scrupulous standards, but they attribute less morality to the personal injury lawyer, and he, in turn, will frequently point out the inferiority of the standards of those who spend much time in criminal litigation. The gradation of the ethics of the profession by the area of law becomes curiouser and curiouser the more it is examined, if one may purloin the words of another venturer in wonderland. Rubin, supra note 10, at 583–84.

See Peters, The Use of Lies in Negotiation, 48 Ohio State L.J. 1, 9–15 (1987). Examples of such other deceptions include the use of silence to give a false impression, a verbal diversion to draw attention away from a particularly weak fact or argument, and feigned intense interest in certain items on the agenda to increase their trading value when giving them up later (recall Judge Neely's anecdote, supra p. 124). Professor Peters argues that even if lying is generally more offensive than the other deceits, this distinction is not useful when judged by the criterion of efficiency in negotiations. The goal of a negotiation, according to Peters, is an efficient or optimal allocation of value. "The inefficiencies would be largely eliminated if we negotiated using a convention that forbade all deception. Stated positively, the convention would require a party to disclose all facts known to that party and known to be important to the other party." Id. at 50.

But applying White's analysis, would this uniform requirement for truthfulness really be desirable? Can we expect to change the universal practice of misrepresenting one's bottom line ("I'm sorry, I just can't take less than $95,000 for this house."), or authority ("My client was most adamant—I can't offer more than $86,000.")? Efficiency may be a valuable goal, but other considerations may be equally important, including support for the human relationships involved. Ethical conventions that apply to negotiations should be consistent with the natural inclinations of most negotiators (see role and cultural factors, infra pp. 228 and 233).

(3) Professor Lowenthal describes some additional ethical problems which arise out of relationships among lawyer-negotiators themselves.

> Continuing professional relationships between lawyer-negotiators may cause the most serious ethical problems associated with bargaining, since an individual client's interests may be sacrificed for those of other clients or for the lawyer's desire to get along with other members of the bar. For example, counsel for a party in a civil action may be less inclined to file a series of pretrial motions and written interrogatories for the purpose of gaining leverage in settlement negotiations if the law firm representing the adverse party is in a position to reciprocate with similar tactics in other cases. The public defender, who tempers plea bargaining arguments to preserve credibility and fails to push cases to the brink of trial to extract better deals, also illustrates this problem. Collaborative strategies may be chosen over competitive alternatives to enhance a lawyer's long range negotiation effectiveness, rather than the gain of the client in the instant case.

> Although neither the Model Code of Professional Responsibility or the Model Rules of Professional Conduct address this issue specifically in the context of negotiation, both take the position that a lawyer should *never* compromise the legitimate interest of a client for either the lawyer's own personal interest or the interests of any other clients. Instead, lawyers are expected to decline

employment that may result in conflicting client interests, withdraw from representing clients whose interests conflict with those of other clients, or obtain the informed consent of all affected clients. The underlying premise of these rules is that "[l]oyalty is an essential element in the lawyer's relationship to the client. The lawyer must be free of other responsibilities that would significantly inhibit giving advice or assistance to the client."

Such laudatory principles are unassailable in the abstract, but impractical in many contexts. Can a public defender fight tooth and nail for every competitive bargaining advantage for *every* client, repeatedly using threats and statements of inflexible commitment, while still maintaining credibility? Moreover, withdrawal may not be a realistic alternative when the conflict of interest is an inherent tension affecting every client represented by a negotiator with a high volume, specialized practice. Informed consent also can be unrealistic, since not many clients are likely to agree to counsel's failure to use applicable competitive tactics in order to maintain other—unnamed—clients. In the end, lawyers must—and inevitably do—balance individual client interests in seeking competitive advantage in negotiations.

There is, unfortunately, no easily formulated rule to draw the line between individual client loyalty and overall effectiveness in representing all clients in negotiation. When a lawyer represents multiple clients in the same case or transaction and must negotiate competitively on behalf of each client individually, the tension between competing client interests is greatest. Thus, a criminal defense lawyer jointly representing codefendants rarely can negotiate on behalf of either client effectively without impairing the interests of the remaining client, and multiple representation should be explicitly prohibited in such situations. On the other hand, it is more difficult to devize and implement a rational ethical rule to prohibit the criminal defense lawyer's tempering of competitive negotiation tactics on behalf of a particular client when there are no codefendants in the case but instead the lawyer is concerned with maintaining credibility in future negotiations.

Lowenthal, A General Theory of Negotiation: Process, Strategy and Behavior, 31 Kansas L.Rev. 69, 107–08 (1982).

(4) In a class negotiation exercise or a recent personal negotiation, did you experience any peer-group pressure? Was it counterproductive to the client's or your own interests? What are some guidelines that might help insulate a negotiation's outcome from the personal interests and pressures of the lawyer?

(5) Is a rule like that advocated by Judge Rubin (discussed in White's article, supra p. 201 n. 10)—that the lawyer must act honestly and in good faith—practical in negotiation? In a case like "Sorenson," is it honest to give the opposing side the impression that your client (the plaintiff) will not settle for under $360,000, when in fact she told

you she would gladly accept $300,000 as payment in full? Is it good faith not to return phone calls to the other lawyer because you want to increase his anxiety level and perhaps reduce his demands. Is it honest, in a land purchase deal, to state that your client wants the land for a personal residence, when he told you that he is planning a residential facility for the mentally retarded? Is it good faith to negotiate the sale of a business based on last month's balance sheet when this month's, which is substantially less favorable, is available on the day before the agreement is to be signed? What if the opposing lawyer does not ask for the updated balance sheet?

(6) What does "honestly" or "in good faith" mean when negotiations do not end in an agreement (recall the *Hoffman* case, supra p. 178). What relief would you provide to the aggrieved party? How would you calculate damages? One criticism is that the Rubin/Peters proposals create a new "cause of action" that would just generate more litigation rather than improve the quality of legal negotiation as currently practiced by the bar.

Problem: The Plea Bargain

The following simulated dialogue between a county prosecutor and a local defense lawyer concerns a defendant arrested the previous week for burglary, assault, and attempted rape. The italicized part represents what each lawyer is thinking at the time he or she makes the statement.

Prosecutor:

Fred, thanks for stopping by. We really do have the goods on your client Baker. Our witnesses saw him enter the apartment, and they heard the arguments, the threats, and the noise of the struggle. In addition, the victim, Mrs. Owen, will make a most convincing witness, as you know. You might as well have Baker plead to the charges. *Maybe if I open tough, Fred will think that we have a better case than we do and give in. He has shown a less than aggressive attitude towards trial in past cases—I think I'll play him a bit on this one. Frankly, I'll be lucky to get the two witnesses into court sober; I hope that no one will pick up on how drunk they were that night. And Mrs. Owen was really unsure of her identification. She's so flighty anyway, and under the trauma of a surprise attack in her own living room. . . .*

Defense Counsel:

But Sue, you know as well as I that the search of Baker's apartment was without justification. You surely don't intend to rely on any evidence that the police found there, do you? *That testimony from Owen and the witnesses could be devastating. I'd better interview them in the next two weeks and get the bad news early. To counter that, I'll make her think we see the physical evidence as more damaging. Actually I don't think the clothes they picked up at Baker's apartment will yield anything substantial against Baker, but a feint in that direction can't hurt.*

Prosecutor:

Well, I don't see it that way at all. I. . . .

He is spending his time on the physical evidence, which must mean he thinks it's important. That's fine with me. Those clothes haven't given us anything; I probably won't even use them at trial. Still, I don't want to give any indication of weakness. . . . Boy, am I glad he interrupted me!

Defense Counsel:

Let's face it, Sue. The identification of my client isn't all that solid. Two hours after the attack on Owen, the cops broke in on Baker—they probably just wanted to bust him for something else and thought this was as good an excuse as any. I'll admit, he isn't the world's most dependable citizen, but from the facts I know, you are really scratching to dig up a case here.

When I interviewed Baker in jail yesterday, he denied everything, but don't they all! Sue appears to have a good case . . . perhaps if I keep attacking at every point I can, she will back down a little to give me something to go to Baker with.

Prosecutor:

Maybe, maybe not. Anyway, I've given you our offer. I'll work with you only on the recommended sentence, not on any lesser-included offense plea. Baker has too long a history with us; the public needs to know that we are being tough on crime.

There's plenty of time before trial, and both Fred and his client need a good scare. Once they become realistic, I'm sure we'll be able to plead this out for something that will look good in the newspapers when I kick off my reelection campaign in two months.

Defense Counsel:

I'll tell you right now, the answer's no. Baker has no priors, for God's sake! I'll file that motion to suppress later this week, and we'll see what the judge says. By the way, if you are going to the county Bar meeting tomorrow night, I'll see you there. Should be an interesting talk by Judge Finn. Take care.

There's lots of time before trial. No sense in giving ground this early, and maybe if I keep the pressure on Sue, something might give. She's certainly being hard on this one; Baker is going to be lucky to get probation.

Notes and Questions

(1) What did this exchange reveal about the preparation each lawyer made for this session? Adequate preparation for negotiation has an important impact on the lawyer's ethical behavior, from the initial client interview through the implementation of any agreement.

In fact, adequate preparation is an ethical requirement for the lawyer. Model Code, DR 6–101(A) states in part: "A lawyer shall not * * * (2) Handle a legal matter without preparation adequate in the circumstances." Although settlement negotiations would seem to be covered by this provision, the implications of applying it to any particular case may be obscure. As with many things, it is easier to identify after the fact a case in which a lawyer was inadequately prepared than to outline beforehand the boundary between adequate and inadequate preparation. A lawyer also has a duty to advocate his client's interests zealously throughout the representation (Model Code, Canon 7), and adequate preparation is basic to that effort.

(2) The quality of negotiating conduct depends frequently on the level of preparation achieved. Unethical acts (for example, false statements of law or fact) may be unplanned, instinctive, or protective reactions by a lawyer who feels trapped in a negotiating position unfavorable to his client. Adequate preparation serves to reduce the chances that the lawyer will be so trapped and thereby eliminates an incentive to resort to ethically questionable methods. Would it be helpful—or even possible—for a lawyer to evaluate the opposing negotiator's level of preparation in order to predict the likelihood of unethical conduct? Is there a possibility that a lawyer, faced with an unprepared opponent, will be tempted to misrepresent the law or the facts?

The Model Code and Model Rules limit their description of most unethical conduct to "knowing" or "willful" acts. Would less preparation help the lawyer avoid unethical conduct by reducing his knowledge and understanding, making any misstatements accidental rather than knowing? What if a lawyer fails to correct a misrepresentation after discovering information that proves the statement false? Does the answer depend on whether or not the negotiation has been concluded?

(3) A public prosecutor must comply with special ethical duties during plea-bargaining activities. Model Code Ethical Consideration 7–13 states in part: "The responsibility of a public prosecutor differs from that of the usual advocate; his duty is to seek justice, not merely to convict." DR 7–103(B) requires the prosecutor to "make timely disclosure to counsel for the defendant * * * of the existence of evidence, known to the prosecutor * * *, that tends to negate the guilt of the accused, mitigate the degree of the offense, or reduce the punishment." (Model Rule 3.8(d) contains similar language.) Did Sue comply with these requirements? Should she have to? Did Fred expect her to? Are expectations of opposing lawyers good standards by which to evaluate ethical conduct? Would Sue have had to comply if Fred had asked her directly for that information? If so, what good is the specific affirmative duty to disclose; why not rely on the general prohibition against false statements or misrepresentation?

(4) Lawyers have special responsibilities to their clients when settlement proposals are made during a negotiation. Model Code EC 7–7 states:

In certain areas of legal representation not affecting the merits of the cause or substantially prejudicing the rights of a client, a lawyer is entitled to make decisions on his own. But otherwise the authority to make decisions is exclusively that of the client and, if made within the framework of the law, such decisions are binding on his lawyer. As typical examples in civil cases, it is for the client to decide whether he will accept a settlement offer or whether he will waive his right to plead an affirmative defense. A defense lawyer in a criminal case has the duty to advise his client fully on whether a particular plea to a charge appears to be desirable and as to the prospects of success on appeal, but it is for the client to decide what plea should be entered and whether an appeal should be taken.

Model Rule 1.2(a) states in part that a "lawyer shall abide by a client's decision whether to accept an offer of settlement of a matter."

A lawyer can prepare for immediate response to offers by working through settlement possibilities beforehand with his client. The ethical issue becomes more difficult to resolve as the proposed offer varies increasingly from what the lawyer has already discussed with his client. At some point the lawyer is ethically required to check with his client before saying "No" to an offer of settlement. Because the answer to this duty to inform varies with each negotiation, such a requirement may truly be unenforceable. Is there any way to hold lawyers accountable for omissions, like not informing clients of proposed offers? What could Baker do if Fred does not inform him of Sue's plea-bargain proposal? What might the damages be if this were a legal rather than an ethical responsibility?

2. Fairness in Outcome

In the United States lawyers often argue that as long as the process by which the decision is made is fair, the outcome will be justifiable and proper. But are we really that indifferent to the fairness of the result?

LAX AND SEBENIUS, THREE ETHICAL ISSUES IN NEGOTIATION

2 Negotiation J. 363, 367 (1986).

One reason that a tactical choice can be uncomfortable is its potential effect on the distribution of value created by agreement. If a "shrewd" move allows a large firm to squeeze a small merchant unmercifully or an experienced negotiator to walk away with all the profit in dealings with a novice, something may seem wrong. Even when the nature of the tactics is not in question, the "fairness" of the outcome may be.

This difficulty is inherent in negotiation: Since there is a bargaining set of many potential agreements that are better for each person than his or her respective alternatives to agreement, the value created by agreement must necessarily be apportioned. Ultimately, when all joint gains have been discovered and common value created, more value for one party means less for another. But just where should the value split be? This, of course, is the age-old problem of "distributive justice," of what a just distribution of rewards and risks in a society should be. In the same way that this is a thorny, unresolved problem at the social level, so it is for individual negotiators—even when less well-recognized. And this is why the problem is so hard, and does not admit easy answers.

A classic problem among game theorists involves trying to develop fair criteria to arbitrate the division of $200 between two people. An obvious norm involves an even split, $100 for each. But what if one is rich and the other poor? More for the poor man, right? "Not at all!" protests the rich woman, "you must look at *after-tax* revenue, even if you want a little more to end up going to the poor man. Moreover, you should really try to equalize the amount of good done for each of us—in which case $20 to him will improve his life much more than $180 will mine. Or look at it the other way: Ask who can better afford to *lose* what amounts—and he can afford to lose $5 about as much as I can $195. Besides, he is a wino and completely on his own. I will sign this pledge to give the money to Mother Teresa, who will use it to help dozens of poor people in India. After all, that poor man *was* rich just two weeks ago, when he was convicted of fraud and had all his money confiscated to pay back his victims."

Who "should" get what in a negotiated agreement? The preceding tongue-in-cheek discussion should not obscure the importance of distributional questions; certainly negotiators argue for this solution or that on the basis of "fairness" all the time. But the rich woman's objections should underscore how fragile and divisive conceptions of equity may be. One person's fairness may be another's outrage.

And fairness not only applies to the process of bargaining but also to its underlying structure. Think of the wage "bargaining" between an illegal alien and her work supervisor who can have her deported at a moment's notice. Is such a situation so loaded against one of the participants that the results are virtually certain to be "unfairly" distributed?

Notes and Questions

(1) Judge Rubin's second rule—that a lawyer must not accept a result that is unconscionably unfair to the other party (see the White excerpt and notes following, supra p. 201)—appears to be an attempt to build an ethical standard to support a "fair result" principle in legal negotiations. But is there any requirement that settlement terms be fair? If there is or should be, would lawyer-negotiators have a duty to achieve fairness not shared by non-lawyers?

(2) Does the requirement of court review of settlements in special situations—such as class actions, divorces, fiduciary activities, and criminal cases—support Judge Rubin's rule that lawyers have a duty to assure that a settlement is not unconscionably unfair to the other party? Or, to the contrary, does it indicate that there is no such general rule and special situations can be taken care of by judicial oversight?

3. The Public Interest

Legal ethics and fairness in negotiation raises the issue of the public interest. Recall Professor Fiss' message in Chapter I (supra p. 39) that private non-official processes of dispute resolution are inappropriate for, indeed damaging to, the handling of issues involving important public values. As Professors Lax and Sebenius said, "It is often easy to solve the negotiation problem for those in the room at the expense of those who are not."[5]

Who represents the public interest in private negotiations? Lawyers and their clients consider themselves free privately to work out settlement provisions which might not be accepted by a court, or the legislature or executive. If the parties in an ongoing relationship decide to act in ways that are not consistent with established national policy, should the public be able to overturn their action? If the dispute involves matters of substantial public policy (for example, race discrimination, toxic waste control, or antitrust violations), should the courts be required to give full review to any settlement worked out privately among the parties and their lawyers?

Let's take an example. An American car dealership agrees to handle cars produced by a Japanese manufacturer. The negotiated agreement calls for the dealership to sell a certain number of cars each year for a period of years. Prosperity gives way to economic downturn, and the dealership asks to renegotiate the number of cars it is required to sell under the contract. Assume the contract terms are probably in violation of the U.S. antitrust laws. Should the parties and their lawyers be able to settle the antitrust claim privately and reconfirm the offending terms in a new contract? We seem to have little trouble defending the result: If the "public" is sufficiently interested, it will intervene through action by the U.S. Department of Justice. Otherwise, the parties and their lawyers are free to handle their own affairs privately.

If the parties can't resolve their differences voluntarily, should we come to a different result? Taking the same example, assume the parties have the same differences, but they can't agree on new terms. The dealership then sues the Japanese firm in federal district court,

---

5. Lax and Sebenius, Three Ethical Issues in Negotiation, 2 Negotiation J. 363, 368 (1986).

charging certain antitrust violations, and the Japanese firm seeks to have the dispute settled by arbitration in Japan, in accordance with an arbitration clause in the agreement. The dealership opposes private arbitration in Japan, pointing to the overriding public interest in enforcing a uniform antitrust policy in the United States; it argues that parties should not be allowed to set up beforehand dispute resolution methods that are not "public"—and that might therefore arrive at solutions which could be inconsistent with established public values. In *Mitsubishi v. Soler Chrysler–Plymouth,* the U.S. Supreme Court rejected this argument. It held the parties to their privately-made obligation to arbitrate any dispute under the contract, even though the dispute involved an issue of national antitrust policy. The Court's opinion in *Mitsubishi* is reprinted infra p. 501.

The problem of upholding the "public interest" arises even where one would least expect it—in actions of public agencies. For instance, the Environmental Protection Agency had known for some time that several major oil companies were releasing too high a level of toxic chemicals from their plants in Oklahoma. After several years of delay, and then more years of investigation, the EPA and the oil companies negotiated an agreement to stop the violations, including payment of substantial fines. The appropriate congressional committee staff investigated these negotiations and released its conclusions two years later: The EPA had mishandled the situation from the beginning, and had "given in" to the demands of corporate violators when the "public interest" required them to uphold the law to its fullest extent. Who really does speak for the public interest—public agency heads and their lawyers, or congressional representatives and their staffs? Or only judges within the court system?

When a lawsuit has been filed and the negotiated agreement falls within that narrow category of cases that must receive court approval before taking effect, the lawyer should be able to rely on the court to represent the public interest. (But remember how cursory the court review process may be, supra p. 192.) In other situations, however, the lawyer has a dilemma: to act solely as an advocate for his client without concern for fairness to unrepresented parties or to the public, or to modify his "zealous advocacy" to accommodate in some way the interests not represented at the table. If the public interest does not conflict with the client's interest, the lawyer faces no dilemma; in fact, he can be counted on to present forcefully the public's case in support of his own client's position. But when the public interest conflicts with the interests of the parties at the table, or when the parties can't agree on what the public interest is, lawyers are faced with having to decide whether, and to what extent, they should consider the public interest.

Clearly, under the current codes of ethics, the lawyer has a duty to provide all relevant information to the client, especially information on the "public interest." But the client has the final decision on whether action taken on his behalf will be consistent with that interpretation of the public interest. Should lawyers have a greater responsibility to see that the "public interest" is adequately represented? How could this responsibility be exercised without creating conflicting loyalties? The structure of dispute resolution processes in society should provide adequate protection for the public interest. But given the role of private negotiation, does it?

E. POWER, PSYCHOLOGY, THREATS, AND NEGOTIATING STRATEGIES

1. Bargaining Power

Power holds special meaning for lawyers, whose dreams often include the dramatic and timely production of the crucial document, direct authority, convincing expert, reluctant eye-witness, or insightful question that wins an otherwise hopeless case for an adoring client, typically in front of a respectful judge.

But what is power in the negotiation setting? Many lawyers are tempted to evade the question by saying, "I may not be able to define power, but know it when I see it!" Avoiding the issue in this way, however, may be especially damaging. Business negotiator Chester Karrass gives a typical definition of bargaining power: "The ability of a negotiator to influence the behavior of an opponent." [1] This definition focuses on the qualities or actions of the actor, but in a larger sense power can only be given by the other party—the target. If the defendant does not acquiesce in the plaintiff's attempts at influence, has the plaintiff shown any power? Not in the usual sense of the word. The actor's power is therefore dependent on the target's perception and response. Professors Milburn and Watman have explained this characteristic as it pertains to threats: "Power is a relational matter; it is a function of the resources controlled by the source of the threat and the needs or other vulnerability of the target." [2]

We begin the study of power with several theoretical perspectives that focus on the analysis of power inherent in a specific situation. Next, we consider the impact of this theory for the practical lawyer or negotiator. How can a lawyer optimize for his client's benefit the power resources that are available in a particular case? In the following sections, we look at personality traits and social psychological variables to understand the other lawyer's likely responses to our negotiating style and strategies. Because threats dominate traditional legal communication, we then analyze the nature of threats and how to use and respond appropriately to them. Finally, we translate these power elements, psychological forces, and threat guidelines into useful negotiating techniques. Negotiating tactics can create, exploit, or increase certain perceived power advantages in a bargaining situation, and practical anecdotes are helpful reminders for the active negotiator.

1. C. Karrass, The Negotiating Game 56 (1970).

2. T. Milburn and K. Watman, On the Nature of Threat 29 (1981).

a. A Theoretical Base

At any one time each negotiation exhibits an inherent and initially-fixed balance of power. The client may be a profitable corporation with many alternate suppliers, or an individual debtor needing cash; the legal blueprint may be favorable or unfavorable to the client; time may be precious or of no consequence; the client may be risk-prone, risk-neutral, or risk-averse; the traditional process for resolving the client's dispute may be highly structured or only loosely organized; the client may control the selection of dispute resolution process, or he may have to accept the process decisions of the other side. Each element suggests a different relative power relationship between disputants.

A lawyer would do well to analyze the anatomy of power and relate it to the negotiation setting. In his book, *The Anatomy of Power,* John Kenneth Galbraith provides a unique analysis of power, describing the "three sources of power—the attributes or institutions that differentiate those who wield power from those who submit to it" and the "three instruments for wielding or enforcing it." [3] The Galbraith elements are:

Instruments	Sources
compensatory	property
condign	personality
conditioned	organization

The first two instruments and sources are widely known and understood, although perhaps not by the terms Galbraith uses. Compensatory power is "the giving of something of value" to the person who is the target of the power—buying his compliance by some positive reward. The natural, although not the only, source for this instrument is property or wealth. Condign power is the ability to harm the object or target of the power—to threaten to so change unfavorably the environment of the target that he will submit to the actor's conditions rather than face such unpleasant consequences. The source of condign power is often personality, which includes the qualities of appearance, speech, mental ability, moral character, and other personal traits. Personality can also serve as the source for compensatory power; the thing of value is a friendly relationship or another product of the personal character of the actor.

The most unique categories of Galbraith's "anatomy" are conditioned power as an instrument and organization as a source. These categories are often linked, but need not be. Conditioned power is the state of mind or belief that causes the target to submit to the will of the actor—"[p]ersuasion, education, or the social commitment to what seems natural, proper, or right." Conditioned power is most closely associated with organization as a source. Organization is an important source of power in the modern world, not only shaping the beliefs or states of mind we share (conditioned power), but also controlling mas-

---

3. J.K. Galbraith, The Anatomy of Power 4–5 (1983).

sive resources of money, professional advancement, and status (compensatory and condign power).

Galbraith's theory helps us analyze events more systematically. In the Texaco–Pennzoil case, supra p. 193, Texaco initially misjudged the power relationship by placing unbounded faith in three elements: (a) that Texaco was in control of Getty's corporate assets, which were the subject of the dispute (property), (b) that the Getty officers sided with Texaco, agreeing that it had not interfered in Pennzoil's bid to buy Getty (organization), and (c) that a lawsuit was a time-consuming and expensive obstacle for Pennzoil (property). Texaco failed to evaluate properly the degree of personal commitment the President of Pennzoil had to this fight (personality), the organizational resources that Pennzoil was willing to allocate to this dispute (property), or the effect of a court decision in Pennzoil's favor on the issue of willful harm to an existing Getty–Pennzoil contractual relationship (organization). The 1985 Texas state court decision gave Pennzoil an ever-increasing instrument of power (condign) to use on Texaco.

On the other hand, by invoking the bankruptcy process in 1987, Texaco successfully used an organizational power source (the structured bankruptcy court procedure) both to force Pennzoil to recognize the legitimate interests of other Texaco creditors (conditioned power) and to raise the costs of implementing any final court decree (condign power). Structuring an analysis of power in this way directs us toward a more thorough understanding of the forces at work in a case, requires us to ask different and perhaps more insightful questions about the power balance, and suggests possibilities for settlement earlier in the disputing process.

The Galbraith model is only one of several available for evaluating the balance of power in a dispute. Chester Karrass, a businessman who recognized early the importance of approaching negotiations systematically, developed another model based on eight general principles. (It may be more than mere chance that the primary models of power analysis are from an economist and a businessman, and not a lawyer.)

The principles are:

- power "is always relative."
- power changes over time.
- power is always limited.
- power is either real or apparent.
- power "exists to the extent that it is accepted."
- power may be exercised without action.
- the exercise of power incurs costs and risks.
- the means and the ends of power cannot be separated.[4]

4. See C. Karrass, The Negotiating Game 56–57 (1970).

From these principles Karrass draws an elaborate design of nine power sources. Four sources are more or less inherent in the negotiating environment and outside the direct control of the lawyer: the balances of rewards, of punishments, of legitimacy, and of competition. At any one time, the lawyer usually must accept resources available to the client, the opportunities to punish or withhold benefits from the other side, the level of support the legal norms give to his client's cause, and the competitive opportunities available outside of settlement.

The remaining five sources are more personal and variable, depending on the relative abilities and personalities of the lawyers themselves: the balances of personal knowledge and bargaining skill, of courage, of willingness to exert time and effort, of willingness to tolerate uncertainty, and of ability to make a commitment.[5] The lawyer has the personal capacity to alter these elements as they relate to a case at any particular time.

Three examples demonstrate how these principles are useful in analyzing negotiating situations. "Brinkmanship" is a term often associated with international diplomacy, and refers to a strategy made famous by Secretary of State John Foster Dulles during the 1950's. As the word implies, the power resides in coming as close to the "brink" of invoking the alternative to settlement (nuclear war under Dulles, or going to trial for most lawyers) and relying on a favorable balance of personal knowledge and skill, courage, and willingness to tolerate uncertainty to "force" the other side to settle on acceptable terms. Of course, a key to countering brinkmanship is the ability to recognize that the exercise of power incurs costs and risks for the source as well as the target, and that by calculating those costs a target can often determine whether the threat is real or only a bluff.[6]

There is also power in "focal points," that is, in natural or common sense answers to the problem.[7] If you must divide two cars between husband and wife upon divorce, the normal solution is to award each the car he or she is driving currently, even though it may not be the best answer for the children or for future work patterns. If the client's medical costs, other expenses, and lost wages add up to $5,500, and the defendant's insurance limit is $10,000 (per injured person), you may settle for $10,000, even though the only reason supporting that figure is that it is the insured's insurance limit. Mathematical precision also has this "focal point" power—if you are to divide $100,000 among four children, $25,000 to each will be the typical choice, even if the children have very different incomes, lifestyles, ages, needs, etc. This power rests primarily on the balance of power sources inherent in the negotiating environment, especially the balance of legitimacy.

Finally, there is a power in "irrationality." An unreasonable, arbitrary, and emotional lawyer is using this power of irrationality to persuade the other side to settle on the lawyer's terms. "Irrationality

5. Id. at 59–64.   7. Id. at 69–71.

6. Id. at 68–69.

may be an appropriate tactic if the negotiator can 1) be sure that his opponent understands what he can gain by reaching an agreement, and 2) can convince the opponent that he is emotionally committed to the reasonableness of his 'irrational' position."[8] Irrationality uses the balance of punishment to generate its power and relies on adversely affecting the other side's willingness to tolerate uncertainty. One difficulty with using this strategy, of course, is that the means and ends of power cannot be separated—that to rely on irrational or illogical means will over the long term be reflected in an unpredictable and illogical set of solutions.

Notes and Questions

(1) Galbraith places great importance on organization as a power source and on conditioned power as an instrument. Is this a reflection of his background and expertise as an economist, or do they also play a significant role in legal negotiations? What are some examples of organization and conditioned power in the criminal practice? In the civil practice?

(2) Lawyers talk more often about condign and compensatory power instruments as keys to successful negotiation. Is this the result of greater visibility, or do punishment and material reward carry more weight with lawyers than a conditioned value or belief system? What elements of the adversary system have the most impact on a personal injury accident negotiation? The low cost of filing suit? The ease of securing continuances? The right to depose all witnesses before trial? We take these procedures for granted, but their exercise frequently favors one side to the detriment of the other. How does a lawyer protect a client from the exercise of such conditioned power?

(3) Karrass stresses the power implications of uncertainty and risk within a negotiation. For example, the powers of brinkmanship and irrationality depend on a high level of uncertainty along with a good chance that an unfavorable option will be chosen. We have already seen the impact of uncertainty on the lawyer's interest in settling, supra p. 139 (Sorenson Chevrolet) and p. 175 (Agent Orange). Karrass points to courage as being a power source. "The person who is willing to accept a greater burden of uncertainty with respect to reward or punishment enhances his power. * * * Courage plays a part in the decision to make a concession, to hold one's ground or to force a deadlock." C. Karrass, The Negotiating Game 62–63 (1970). Is Karrass suggesting that a party's power increases as his behavior becomes more risk-prone?

b. Practical Use of Power Variables

The lawyer's goal should be to maximize the power balance over time in favor of his client. In this section our focus shifts from a

---

8. Id. at 71–72.

theoretical understanding of the elements of power to an operational awareness of how to use available power resources.

Professor Fisher has translated his theoretical model of negotiation (supra p. 83) into a checklist for analyzing the balance of power in a dispute. The list is meant to be prescriptive rather than descriptive, providing the vehicle for determining the preferred strategies in a negotiation. Fisher's power formula: [9]

1. The Power of Skill and Knowledge—your bargaining power increases as you achieve a better understanding of the merits of the problem with which you are working, coupled with improving your skill in handling the negotiation process. Clever, shrewd or deceptive moves don't enhance power; as Benjamin Franklin's Poor Richard said in 1751, "Cunning proceeds from a lack of capacity."

2. The Power of a Good Relationship—your power increases with effective, articulate and timely communication that is easily understood by the other side. Respect and a reputation for honesty translate into trust, and when the other side trusts you, you improve your power.

3. The Power of a Good Alternative to Agreement—an attractive alternative to settling with the other side reduces your need and desire to come to agreement. It may also increase your attractiveness to the other side.

4. The Power of Good Options for Agreement—it is difficult for the other side to turn down a proposal which satisfies his basic interests. If you consistently generate options that are attractive both to you and the other side, you create many more agreement opportunities.

5. The Power of Legitimacy—legitimacy means having the support of an independent standard that is not derived solely from the personal whim of one side. It is difficult to ignore or attack options which have this legitimate quality. Recognition by the other side as a serious and equal bargaining partner (role legitimacy) will also improve your power.

6. The Power of Commitment—every offer to settle contains both an affirmative commitment to agree if the conditions of the offer are accepted, and a negative commitment (often implicit) not to agree if conditions vary from those specified. Explicit negative commitments (threats) are often used outside the context of a specific offer, especially when a lawyer becomes frustrated in his attempt to control the other side's response and wants to stress the harmful or bad consequences that will befall the other side if no agreement results.

Fisher implies in these six principles that there are differences between apparent and actual bargaining power, and suggests that the negotiator's goal should be to close the gap between the two. The

---

9. Fisher, Negotiating Power: Getting and using Influence, 27 Am. Behavioral Scientist 149 (Nov.–Dec. 1983).

lawyer is able to pull the real from the apparent through applying the six principles: In applying those principles, the lawyer should identify the power sources important to each case, seek ways to expand or improve that power, and use those sources in an internally consistent pattern within the negotiation. For instance, although negative commitment or threat may be a necessary part of a negotiation, its use should be blended well in context so as not to reduce or destroy the other power sources. Immediate and frequent references to how you will bury the other side in court may eliminate any influence you may have arising from a good relationship. On the other hand, concentrating on being a good friend may be inconsistent with maximizing other power variables, such as improving a good alternative to a negotiated agreement (BATNA), brainstorming independent standards for evaluating options, and establishing credible commitments.

The lawyer should also handle these power sources consistently with his own personality. An aggressive, businesslike person could create suspicion by trying to develop a warm, nurturing relationship with the other side; a good relationship comes in many forms and colors, but sincerity and reliability appear to be prerequisites.[10]

Fisher suggests that the power not to agree, to harm, or to cause bad consequences is typically not the power to persuade the other side to accept a settlement on your terms. "To make a negative commitment either as to what we will not do or to impose harsh consequences unless the other side reaches agreement with us, without having previously made a firm and clear offer, substantially lessens our ability to exert influence."[11]

Notes and Questions

(1) Before accepting the Fisher analysis, you should apply it to several negotiation examples to see if the perspective it generates increases your understanding in a way that improves your ability or success in a negotiation setting. Describe the following situations in Fisher's terms:

(a) *The bank loan.* The average consumer, farmer, business person, or organization who borrows from a community bank is not usually in a position to renegotiate the loan requirements (amount, interest rate, due date, repayment schedule) when financial troubles make it difficult to meet the loan terms. The bank requests payment, threatening foreclosure on the collateral if the response is unsatisfactory. Yet, if the Chrysler Corporation, or Brazil or Mexico, has trouble repaying a loan of $3 billion, the banks initiate renegotiation. Why? During a recent Midwest farm crisis, local banks reworked interest rates and

10. See R. Fisher and S. Brown, Getting Together: Building A Relationship That Gets to Yes (1988), in which the authors discuss six elements of the working relationship: balancing rationality and emotion, understanding, effective communication, reliability, persuasion not coercion, and mutual acceptance.

11. Fisher, supra note 9, at 160.

repayment schedules with many financially troubled farmers to avoid foreclosure of the farms. Why?

(b) *The lawyer.* An ordinary consumer frequently receives a hasty and not too gentle brush-off when he approaches a store owner, realtor, car dealer, or landlord with a legitimate grievance. The consumer's next step may be to hire a lawyer to contact the same business person to discuss the same claim. Whether calling or writing a letter, the lawyer typically receives a more polite reception, with due regard for the merits and seriousness of the claim. What has changed?

(c) *An appealing settlement.* A case goes to trial, with both lawyers presenting what each client thinks are convincing arguments for a judgment favoring his side. The judge rules for the plaintiff, with the monetary award well within the defendant's insurance limits. The attorney representing the insurance company files a notice of appeal, and notifies plaintiff that he is willing to settle at 80% of judgment. Plaintiff accepts, and the appeal is dismissed. Where is the power?

(d) *An inside job.* You recently accepted a position as an associate in a 20–lawyer firm and received word yesterday that you passed the state bar exam. You have been working closely with two young partners in a rather specialized area of bankruptcy law and have relied on a relatively new set of books available only at the law school library located in the city. You think you could work more efficiently if the firm had the set in its own library, but it costs $1875.00. You mention it to the senior partner one evening as the two of you wait for the elevator, and upon hearing the cost, he gives an emphatic "No." The next week at a conference on one of the cases, you ask the partners with whom you work for authority to order the set, giving them details of expected hours saved over the next six months. They approve your request and ask the supply clerk to order the set. What power was used the second time that was absent the first?

(2) The use of power is a subject of consuming interest to commentators in all fields. Politics is a universally recognized arena for power. In his classic work on presidential power, Richard Neustadt referred to the "essence of a President's persuasive task" as "to induce them [congressmen and the public] to believe that what he wants of them is what their own appraisal of their own responsibilities requires of them to do in their interest, not his." R. Neustadt, Presidential Power 46, (1960). Common threads exist in Neustadt and Fisher: the importance of a good relationship, the concepts of status and authority (Fisher would say legitimacy), the skill and knowledge of the bargainer, and the impact of presenting the option so that the other person will accept it as being in his own interest (Fisher calls it the power of good options). However, Neustadt stresses the controlling role of personal choice in developing and expending power, an understandable emphasis when focusing on the power of the President of the United States. Does Fisher ignore this factor, or is it included in his skill and knowledge

category? Does Fisher's analysis give personal choice the weight it deserves?

(3) The possession of power can sometimes have undesirable side effects. Power has a mesmerizing influence on the user. If a lawyer knows his client has superior resources, or no time pressures, or the ability to inflict costly damage on the other side, he will often use that power regardless of need. The other side may be close to signing an acceptable agreement, but if the power is there, chances are high that the lawyer will want to use it. As Norman Cousins states regarding the impact of power in American foreign affairs: "Power has a way of victimizing its users. It tends to create a dark and subterranean world in which decisions affecting the life of a nation can be taken without reference to their moral implications or the obligations to inform the people truthfully about issues of transcendent importance to their well-being and indeed survival." N. Cousins, The Pathology of Power 50 (1987). Cousins is speaking here about President Truman's public justification for his decision to drop the atomic bomb in August 1945, a public position which conflicted with some confidential military assessments of the day. For the practicing lawyer, the existence and use (or misuse) of court procedures, threats, or other resources can be equally as alluring, even in the face of a similar lack of necessity. The opposite situation may also present a problem for some lawyers: the client may demand the untrammeled use of power by the lawyer regardless of need or good sense, for purposes of principle, vindication, or vengence. Clients often want a "tough" lawyer—a role expectation that may be difficult to live up to.

2. Psychological and Interpersonal Variables

To blend an evaluation of existing power balances into negotiating strategies requires an understanding of the psychological environment in which we act. Psychological and interpersonal variables are important in legal negotiation. Without a workable bridge between the law and psychology, a lawyer is handicapped in his efforts to optimize the client's interests. Our objective in this section is to lay the foundation for that bridge. Our inquiry begins with an overview of some personality variables that influence the negotiation setting. We then examine the social psychological variables of role, gender, culture, and structure to understand their impact on negotiating lawyers. This material is not intended to be a substitute for either a course in social psychology or a thorough review of psychological literature. We provide cites to additional reference books and articles on psychology in the Further References section, infra p. 729, for the student who may want to do more thorough research on special topics of personal interest.

a. Personality Variables

Personality plays a role in every negotiation. The more important variables for our purposes are self-esteem, the drive to achieve, personal leadership qualities, risk-taking propensity, the need to control, aggressiveness, ethical flexibility, the level of mistrust of others, tolerance for ambiguity, disorder and confrontation, and the need for close rapport and support from colleagues. People vary across each one of these dimensions—and over time. Each lawyer therefore has a unique combination of these variables at any one time which, when mixed with that of the opposing lawyer, establishes a psychological environment that strongly influences the negotiation outcome.

Therefore, each negotiation is different. An agreement by one set of negotiators may be substantially different from that of another set. Moreover, the fewer the negotiators in a dispute and the more informal the interaction, the greater the likely effect of individual personalities on the negotiation outcome. A simulated negotiation experiment conducted by Professor Williams among experienced trial lawyers in Des Moines, Iowa, graphically supports that conclusion. Out of eleven sets of lawyers, all negotiating with the same personal injury accident facts, no two results were the same, and the settlements ranged from $15,000 to $95,000.[12] Although other variables may have contributed to this wide variation in outcomes, including imbalances of skill and knowledge and differing assumptions about client interests, the interaction of personality traits had to be a significant contributing factor.

To be effective a lawyer should be able to recognize personality variables, whether in himself or the opposing lawyer, and appreciate their significance for a favorable outcome. Professor Rubin describes several that have an important impact on legal negotiations.

RUBIN, NEGOTIATION: AN INTRODUCTION TO SOME ISSUES AND THEMES

27 Am. Behavioral Scientist 135, 138–44 (Nov.–Dec. 1983).

THE NEED TO IMPRESS OTHERS

Each of us, in our own way, craves the approval of others. As a result we are inclined to say or do those things that we believe will generate this approval. If such concerns are with us in all aspects of our daily lives, they are particularly poignant in negotiation. Here, after all, we perform on a stage of sorts, where our toughness and mettle are the objects of considerable interest to our adversary, and various constituencies, as well as ourselves.

Brown has demonstrated experimentally the considerable lengths to which negotiators will go in an effort to maintain an appearance of strength. In one of these studies, participants negotiated against an

---

12. G. Williams, Legal Negotiation and Settlement 6–7 (1983).

adversary who was in league with the experimenter and who was instructed to behave in ways that resulted in the systematic exploitation of the participant. During the second half of the negotiation session, the participant was given an opportunity to retaliate. Retaliation involved levying a monetary fine against the adversary at increasing monetary cost to self. Brown's negotiators were so eager to restore face once it had been lost or damaged that they went out of their way to punish their adversary as strenuously as the negotiation context allowed—even though such punishment required that they absorb more of a financial beating themselves than they could impose on the other.

* * *

INTERPERSONAL SENSITIVITY

We all know the virtues of being tuned to the behavior of another, and these same virtues obtain in negotiation as well. Such sensitivity promotes effective negotiation in several ways. Negotiators are able to do a better job of anticipating and evaluating how the other person is likely to respond to the offers that are made. Similarly, attentiveness and sensitivity enable negotiators to read the difference between what the other person says and what the other really means. Again, in negotiation one does not get to see the other's cards but only what the other says these cards are. An effective negotiator must therefore be able to decipher the language of an opponent's offers and demands, translating what is said into what is really meant. The more sensitive one is to the other's behavior, the easier this is.

Psychological research indicates that interpersonal sensitivity may help increase negotiating effectiveness but only up to a point. To be unduly sensitive to the other's behavior is to risk two kinds of problems. First, negotiators may end up being inappropriately and excessively reactive to everything the other says and does. Given conciliatory gestures by the adversary, they are likely to be cooperative and conciliatory in return; but given the slightest hint of intransigence or exploitiveness on the part of the other, these inordinately sensitive negotiators are likely to react quite viciously and with considerable vengeance. If it is counterproductive to ignore everything another negotiator says and does, then it is also just as problematic to develop a "knee-jerk" response to each jowl jiggle that inevitably occurs during the transaction.

The second and more important problem with undue interpersonal sensitivity is that it may lead negotiators to forge an agreement that is less than optimal. * * *

AFFECTING THE OTHER'S SENSE OF COMPETENCE

As indicated in the section on impressing others, negotiators are reluctant to make concessions when they believe these moves imply loss of face. Negotiators want to believe that their concessions will be construed not as weakness but as a sign of their willingness to deal from a position of strength. I have made a conciliatory move not because you forced me to do so but because my competence as a negotiator has led to the development of a mutually satisfactory quid pro quo. If this line of reasoning is correct, then, paradoxically, the key to inducing conciliatory behavior is not coercion and intimidation but a set of moves that encourage the other negotiator to feel competent and effective.

Psychological research on the various strategies for inducing cooperation in an adversary lends general support to the importance of perceived competence. * * *

Negotiators want to believe that they are capable of influencing their adversary's behavior. If you negotiate with someone who appears to ignore your fiercest threats or kindest conciliatory gestures, and instead persists in a course of consistent cooperation or competition, you are likely to conclude that you have been pitted against a saint, a devil, or a fool—in any event, surely an adversary who has not the slightest interest in, let alone respect for, your negotiating skill. In contrast, an adversary whose behavior is contingent upon your own is letting you know that you have the skill and competence necessary to shape his or her behavior. The bottom line, then, is that negotiators are more likely to make concessions when they feel competent. So if ways can be found to let the other negotiators know that they are regarded as tough and worthy negotiators—perhaps by coordinating a few concessions on relatively minor issues with some of your adversary's moves—then it may be possible to induce even greater concessions on those issues that really count.

AVOIDING COMMITMENTS TO INTRANSIGENCE

Negotiators often find it tempting, particularly when discussions bog down and things appear not to be going the way they would like, to commit themselves to tough negotiating positions from which they swear they will never retreat. Like the players in the proverbial game of "chicken", each negotiator threatens not to turn aside (to concede) until the other does so first. There are several problems with such bold, seemingly irrevocable commitments. First, if they work—that is, if they succeed in eliciting some long-sought concession—the adversary is likely to think twice before sitting down to negotiate again. Why deliberately elect to walk into a buzz saw if one can help it? On the other hand, should the negotiation commitment fail to work—that is, should the adversary refuse to knuckle under—then the perpetrator is likely to be confronted with a nasty choice: To go back on one's stated commitment is to run the risk of losing credibility in the eyes of the adversary, while opening the way to subsequent exploitation by the other; on the other hand, to carry through a commitment to intransigence, in light of the adversary's determination to resist concession, is in turn to run the risk of engineering unnecessary havoc for both sides.

* * *

CONFLICT INTENSITY

Many of the moves, gestures, and gambits that work quite well when conflict is relatively low in intensity may prove ineffective or may even backfire in conflict-intensified circumstances. Consider a few research-documented examples of this generalization.

In the spirit of being sensitive (but not overly sensitive) negotiators, it seemingly makes good sense for people to place themselves in their adversary's shoes as best they can in an effort to see the world as the adversary sees it. Research has indicated that this technique of role reversal is likely to work well, so long as the dispute in question is based on illusory rather than real differences. In the midst of a genuinely tough issue, however, the kind in which face-saving concerns are likely to crop up, role reversal is likely to produce a most unwanted effect: As a result of efforts to see the world as the other sees it, each negotiator is likely to be reminded of precisely how very different this world looks. If negotiators are far apart on every issue that confronts them, then efforts to take the other's part are likely to serve only as a painful reminder of the shared hopelessness of their situation.

Similarly, standard armchair psychologese dictates that we should never let the sun set on our anger. If we have some gripe, we should let the other person know about it, venting our spleen in the service of giving all feelings an open airing. The problem with this advice is that it is only half right. Negotiators in the midst of relatively small-scale conflicts do fine when encouraged to talk with each other about how they're feeling; communication is used to identify points of overlapping interest, of which there are many, and the chances of agreement are thereby increased. Research has indicated, however, that things go rather differently under conditions of intense conflict.

[After describing a set of experiments with pairs of negotiators in which some were required to communicate under conditions of intense conflict, Rubin continues:] In fact, the requirement of communication led negotiators to heap abuse on each other, hurling insults, threats and lies. Rather than facilitating the reduction of intense conflict, compulsory communication only made things worse.

In general, then, the intensity of conflict must be taken into careful account as negotiators plot their moves and countermoves. It is particularly important not to assume automatically that the techniques that prove effective under conditions of low conflict intensity will continue to work well when conflict is protracted or exacerbated. In the throes of a conflict that appears to be deteriorating into rancor, it may make sense to adhere to a general "rule of change." If the negotiators have been talking a blue streak, perhaps they should consider taking a breather for a while; if they've gone through a period of stony silence, perhaps they need some vehicle for getting communication going again. Negotiators stuck in hostility may need to shake things loose by experimenting with different arrangements: where they sit, what they talk about, whether they talk at all, whose turf they negotiate on, and so forth—anything that may help break the negative momentum the disputants have generated.

Notes and Questions

(1) Rubin's suggestion that a negotiator wants to affect the other's sense of competence may explain the success of Axelrod's Tit for Tat strategy, supra p. 92. It signals to the other side that you regard her as an intelligent and rational negotiator, and that what she does next will affect your behavior toward her. Regardless of what she has done in the past, she can reestablish cooperation—and induce you to cooperate—by cooperating herself.

(2) Rubin suggests that conflict intensity varies over time within the dispute. Can you define points of high and low intensity during a recent negotiation exercise or real-life dispute? How would you improve your responsiveness to the different levels of intensity?

––––––

Lawyers, like all humans, develop complex systems of assumptions which mask and distort realities that are either not understood or too painful to admit consciously.[13] Our propensity for self-deception—the development of defense mechanisms—influences significantly the course and outcome of the negotiation. Self-deception is based in part on certain personality and background factors, such as self-esteem, a generalized level of mistrust, leadership qualities, ethical flexibility, intelligence, and parental and educational influence. However, a lack of sensitivity, knowledge or interest in the subject under negotiation may also play a big role.

Self-deception is a two-edged sword. Its positive effect is often the basis for self-confidence and assertiveness in the face of high risk. "The mind often represses the recognition of fear, anxiety, and other painful thoughts, screening them from awareness so that a person can continue to think and act as if little risk or danger were present. Negative pressure usually inhibits human achievement. An ironworker or window-washer is trained not to think about the risk of falling from the high perch."[14] But when self-confidence induced by self-deception is founded upon false assumptions or incorrect interpretations, there can be a negative impact on a lawyer's performance. For example, a lawyer may have walked into a negotiating session without having looked at the case file; nevertheless, the client on the other side may be unusually risk-averse and the other lawyer may not be well prepared, and for whatever reason the lawyer may walk out with a favorable settlement. From this experience she may be able to persuade herself for the future that her lack of preparation allowed her to think imaginatively and respond with flexibility—or she may even be

---

13. See D. Goleman, Vital Lies, Simple Truths 61–83 (1985).

14. Murray, Considering a Negotiator's View of the Court Process, 2 Ohio St. J. on Dispute Res. 223, 226 (1987).

able to persuade herself that her pre-negotiation activity actually did include significant intellectual analysis.

In another situation, a lawyer may settle "too quickly" because of the intimidating personality of the other negotiator and the high stress of the negotiation. To avoid suspicion that she caved in out of fear or discomfort, she may persuade herself that she could not have done better either with more thorough preparation, more negotiating time, or at trial. These lawyers seldom analyze reality in an objective way because their view of reality remains controlled by a pre-existing frame of reference.

Social psychological research has confirmed that people bias their search for information based on their own need for a positive self-image.[15] People pursue information more vigorously if they expect what they will find will support their favorable self-evaluation. A lawyer is particularly prone to this bias. She is professionally dedicated to her client's case and will commit most of her resources toward proving her client right, or at least pulling together as much supportive argument as precedent allows. The result: lawyers as a group tend to predict the outcome of their trials more favorably for their clients than what a disinterested or objective lawyer might do. The danger in this distortion lies in the inherent bias it permits against negotiated settlement and in favor of trial (see the discussion on bottom lines, supra p. 105).

The struggle for the psychologist and the lawyer is to find the key to avoiding destructive self-deception. One way to recognize self-deception is to identify and analyze the assumptions that are woven in the fabric of a dispute (revisit the discussion of assumptions, supra p. 114). Another method is to develop a habit of adequate and early preparation of your case, with special care to discover the support the other side may have for its claims. A third method relies on role-playing the opposing lawyer, either by the lawyer or his partners. The desired result is, of course, an objective assessment of the probable court outcome and the realistic chances of negotiating a settlement.

To negotiate well, a lawyer first needs to understand her own personality variables and the resulting psychological strengths and weaknesses they may create in the negotiation setting. For example, the lawyer may be an habitual gambler with a client's resources in negotiation, but reluctant to move into a courtroom on the same issues because his own competence will be "on trial." While this combination of risk-prone behavior for representational roles and risk-averse for personal obligations is probably natural and not uncommon among lawyer-negotiators, it may distort case results unfavorably for the client (see the risk preference discussions, supra pp. 143 and 216). A lawyer's confidence in her personal ability in the courtroom has a substantial

---

15. Pyszczynski, Greenberg and LaPrelle, Social Comparison After Success and Failure: Biased Search for Information Consistent with a Self–Serving Conclusion, 21 J. Experimental Social Psychology 195 (1985).

impact on the psychological environment of the negotiation. The lawyer should be as risk-neutral where her own resources are being tested as she is where her client's are involved. Some lawyers who do not like trial practice or have little confidence in their ability in court, routinely refer cases that fail to settle to experienced trial lawyers, and in this way establish a risk-neutral confidence in their BATNA.

Another example is the initial level of mistrust or trust a lawyer brings into a negotiation. Some harbor an irrational mistrust of large business organizations, or of lawyers in big urban firms, wealthy criminal defendants, or state judges in rural areas. This mistrust influences the way a lawyer prepares for a negotiation and may distort the communication messages sent back and forth. At another extreme, a lawyer may have an unquestioning trust of lawyers from a particular firm, or of a bank president, a neighbor, or a relative. The effect of this trusting attitude, without adequate independent justification, can be even more disastrous than too much mistrust.

Two authors suggest the following traits as being successful in a negotiating setting: (1) The negotiator should view others "as objects to be manipulated rather than as individuals with whom one has empathy. The greater the emotional involvement with others, the greater is the likelihood of identifying with their point of view." (2) The negotiator should "have an utilitarian rather than a moral view of [his] interactions with others." (3) The negotiator should take "an instrumentalist or rational view of others", avoiding distortions caused by emotional needs.[16] Do you agree?

Besides knowing herself in order to avoid the perils of self-deception, a lawyer should be aware of the other side's psychological framework for making decisions. The same elements relevant to a personal psychological assessment are important to the proper evaluation of the other side. To repeat Schelling's important definition, a bargaining situation is one "in which the ability of one of the participants to gain his ends depends to an important degree on the choices or decisions that the other participant will make."[17] Understanding the opposing lawyer's psychological and interpersonal variables is a necessary step toward influencing his decisions. After conducting a business-like redistributive-bargaining experiment, a research psychologist concluded:

> [T]he results indicate that negotiators with significantly different personality profiles and situational expectations are likely to employ very different behavioral bargaining strategies. Each distinct bargaining style is activated by a decidedly different set of motivational elements. Furthermore, the empirical findings show that these motivations are not always obvious or self-evident. Needs for achievement, dominance, aggression, defense, and counteraction against harsh demands were not significant predictors of

16. R. Christie and F. Geis, Studies in Machiavellianism 3–4 (1970).

17. T. Schelling, The Strategy of Conflict 5 (1960, 1980).

strategy choice. Instead, several nonobvious motivational structures were found to activate the use of four basic behavioral patterns:

(1) Highly cooperative bargainers who agreed to *share their payoff* were motivated by self-oriented needs for social approval and emotional support rather than outgoing needs for cooperation and friendship.

(2) Altruistic bargainers who *transferred payoff* that could have been theirs to the opposing side were motivated by defeatist and harm-approaching needs.

(3) Bargainers who *bluffed and deceived* were motivated by needs for play, seduction, cleverness, and exhibitionism.

(4) Hostile bargainers who employed elements of *coercion* were motivated by the mirror-image hostility of their opponents.[18]

Clearly, personality variables and the interaction of the two negotiating personalities have a substantial impact on negotiation behavior and motivation—and consequently on the choice of strategy.

b. Social Psychological Variables

Social psychological variables, such as role, gender, culture, and structure, influence lawyer behavior within a negotiating context. Expectations that surround these variables shape a lawyer's negotiating ability and the possibilities for success.

(1) *Role.* The legal profession defines a lawyer's role as combining the function of zealous advocate and thoughtful adviser within the framework of the adversarial system of justice. A lawyer will try to act in accordance with the proper role expectations to justify the best professional reputation she can achieve, and reputation is a powerful tool in shaping common expectations.[19] This craving for approval, as Professor Rubin would say, strengthens existing role expectations. Because these role expectations are continually reinforced by the actions of practicing lawyers, they are stable and self-sustaining behavorial guides in the negotiation setting.

Role expectations are frequently linked with either saving or losing face in a negotiation. The more experience a lawyer has and the more developed her reputation as a negotiator, the more sensitive she becomes to implications of image loss connected with certain tactics and concessions. Experienced lawyers do not want to look weak or foolish to either their negotiating colleagues or their clients. This concern for appearing weak may cause a lawyer to become rigid when she should be flexible, refusing to consider settlement options that are objectively

18. Spector, Negotiation as a Psychological Process, in I. Zartman, The Negotiation Process 65 (1978).

19. See Roth and Schoumaker, Expectations and Reputation in Bargaining: An Experimental Study, 73 Am.Econ.Rev. 362, 371 (June 1983).

in her client's interest or failing to reevaluate the probable court outcome after discovering new information during the negotiation.[20]

These considerations are especially applicable when the negotiating lawyers are from different status levels. Some examples of different status levels might be a partner from a large prestigious law firm versus a sole practitioner, general counsel of a large corporation or government agency versus a new associate in a public interest law firm, or a prominent urban defense attorney, experienced in high-profile murder cases, versus a newly elected county attorney in a rural area. A high status lawyer may be more willing to negotiate and compromise with a low status opponent if the opponent affirms the lawyer's effectiveness by positive feedback and validates her negotiating position. Any rejection may be interpreted by a high status lawyer as an attack on her personal competence. If that happens, the low status lawyer can mitigate the damage of this rejection by simultaneously reinforcing a favorable image of the other lawyer's ability.[21]

The lawyer is a representative for her client. This representational role brings other factors to light. One will tend to bargain more competitively or aggressively as a representative than if she were bargaining for herself. One reason may be the difference in risk: As a representative you have less at stake than as a principal, so you can afford to be more risk-prone. In addition, a client may pressure the lawyer to be more aggressive and adversarial, reflecting perhaps the general expectation the client has of a proper role for a lawyer. It is important that lawyers recognize the difference between client demands for quality legal service and those for a particular personal behavioral style. The former is a justifiable expectation of all lawyers; the latter should be the lawyer's own choice. One commentator described the lawyer-client relationship:

> Lawyers often must try to convert a client's desire for vindication and revenge into a willingness to accept what the lawyer sees as the only reasonable settlement that can be obtained with the effort the lawyer is willing to invest in the case.[22]

Accountability may also vary within the lawyer-client relationship. If a client demands a high degree of accountability, the lawyer will likely be more aggressive or competitive in face-to-face negotiations with the other side.[23] If the client is demanding daily briefings and approval, the lawyer will frequently use threats, positional commitments, arguments to get the other side to concede, efforts to dominate, and other pressure tactics. In contrast, the more trust and confidence

---

20. See D. Pruitt, Negotiation Behavior 29 (1981).

21. See Tjosvold and Huston, Social Face and Resistance to Compromise in Bargaining, 104 J. Social Psychology 57, 66 (1978).

22. Macauley, Lawyers and Consumer Protection Laws: An Empirical Study 4 (1979).

23. See Carnevale, Pruitt and Seilheimer, Looking and Competing: Accountability and Visual Access in Integrative Bargaining, 40 J. Personality and Social Psychology 111, 118–A (1981).

there is between client and lawyer, the less strict the accountability and the more flexible the lawyer may be during the negotiation.

(2) *Gender.* Studies suggest that stereotypes of male and female negotiators are generally exaggerated and untrue; yet, many lawyers continue to accept them as descriptions of reality. The stereotypic man is more competitive and distributional in negotiating style, apparently due to a youthful experience in athletics. The stereotypic woman is more concerned for others, open about her emotions and sensitive to human relationships, apparently due again to early socialization.[24]

One reason why these stereotypes persist may be the joint effects of role expectations and self-deception. If lawyers believe that the stereotypes exist, they will consciously notice information that supports the stereotype and repress other data that refutes it. Furthermore, a lawyer's responses to interpersonal contact will tend to confirm the perceived expectations of the other negotiator. For example, a female lawyer's response to a male opponent will likely confirm whatever behavioral stereotypes the man has, because she will try to match the expectations that he expresses through his words and behavior in order to improve her chances of succeeding in the negotiation.

In empirical tests, men and women behave similarly in most negotiation settings. Nevertheless, women have more often been found to be less comfortable with a competitive bargaining role. Female negotiators speak less, show more self-doubt, make fewer explicit threats and derogatory putdowns, use fewer positional commitments, are less willing to form coalitions in three-or-more-party negotiations, and exhibit more persuadable and conforming behavior. In other words, women use less standardized competitive tactics compared with men. Psychologists attribute these behavioral characteristics to a woman's greater concern for maintaining harmonious interpersonal relationships. On the other hand, the same empirical study suggests that women consider themselves as competitive as the men.[25] The following is a clear statement of the differences:

> In the mid–1970s, Rubin and Brown,[26] reviewing laboratory studies of bargaining behavior, encountered a large number of contradictory and apparently irreconcilable findings. In Prisoners' Dilemma-type games in particular, they found a pattern of relationships between gender and bargaining. In some studies, males were more cooperative than females, while in other studies males were more competitive. Closer examination revealed that the studies were not strictly comparable. In some studies subjects

24. J. Nierenberg and I. Ross, Women and the Art of Negotiating 102, 153–56 (1985); see also Skrypnek and Snyder, On the Self–Perpetuating Nature of Stereotypes About Women and Men, 18 J. Experimental Social Psychology 277 (1982).

25. Kimmel, Pruitt, Magenau, Kon Goldband, and Carnevale, Effects of Trust, Aspiration and Gender on Negotiating Tactics, 38 J. Personality and Social Psychology 9, 21–22 (1980).

26. J. Rubin and B. Brown, The Social Psychology of Bargaining and Negotiation 172–75 (1975).

played against a fixed strategy that gave the greatest reward to consistently competitive behavior, while in others subjects played against an adversary whose behavior was contingent on the subject's own—games that gave the greatest reward to consistently cooperative behavior. This distinction helped to make sense of the disparate findings about gender and bargaining. In the games that rewarded consistent cooperation, males tended to be more cooperative than females. In the games that rewarded consistent competition, males tended to be more competitive than females. Males, then, appeared to be more oriented toward the impersonal task of maximizing their own earnings. Females, in contrast, seemed more sensitive and reactive to the interpersonal aspects of their relationship. Males and females do not differ in their propensity to bargain cooperatively, Rubin and Brown concluded; they tend to differ in *interpersonal orientation.*[27]

In the final analysis, the gender impact may be described in terms of bell-shaped curves, where the curve for men may be skewed slightly toward a competitive drive to achieve the specific goal, and the one for women, toward a more problem-solving approach that places importance on interpersonal relationships, but the areas of overlap seem to be substantial.

A negotiation study using MBA students at Dartmouth College produced data with implications for women who are learning negotiating skills:

> Differences in socialization are one of many factors that give rise to personality differences among negotiators. There is no one best way to negotiate that is suitable for all personalities; rather, each person must develop an approach that capitalizes on unique strengths and compensates for weaknesses. Given this premise, the development of individuals' negotiating approaches must be a highly individualized process that begins with personality assessment. * * *

> Tailoring the learning experience to the unique needs of individuals provides the opportunity specifically to address the special needs of women preparing for professional careers in organizations. For instance, the tendency for women to think of interpersonal interactions in the context of a continuous time perspective can be a considerable asset in some bargaining situations and a clear liability in others. It is an asset when the relationship-oriented, cooperative, and empathic behavior it spawns elicits similar behavior from the other party and leads to constructive mutual accommodation and the preservation and enhancement of an interdependent relationship. The liability of this time perspective is that it can make the negotiator vulnerable to exploitation by an opponent who seeks only short-term gain.

27. World Politics, vol. 39, no. 1, pp. 97–98.

The need to adapt to different approaches of the other party requires women to develop flexibility in their negotiating approaches. In practice this means that we encourage women to begin with a positive approach but to have ready an approach that raises the cost of the other party's behaving exploitatively. Specifically, we would hope to develop the woman's skill at expressing her commitment to a longer-term relationship and to persuade the other party of the advantages of this predisposition. If this "olive-branch" approach does not work, the woman needs the deterrent capability of a more hard-line approach to counter the tactics of an episodic-oriented opponent, an approach that involves teaching women to mobilize the several bases of power at their disposal but to use such power wisely.

The woman negotiator may also need to address process issues, particularly the implicit rules by which the interaction is proceeding. In particular, when two parties' interests are partly in conflict, men have a tendency to conceptualize interactions with others in terms of a sports metaphor. An important element of their childhood socialization experience, preoccupation with zero-sum, episodic, competitive situations may be dysfunctional in negotiations. Thus the woman may need to induce a male counterpart to adopt the rules of cordial relationships rather than the rules within which contests are won.

Another example of the ways in which women can constructively adapt their developmental differences to negotiation situations is to capitalize on their natural tendency to be empathic. Empathic tendencies give rise to empathic inquiries, which can elicit a wealth of information about the other party. An empathic appeal is one of the most effective tactics that can be used to exert influence in a negotiation: it involves simply pointing out how settlements that are of benefit to oneself meet the other party's needs. Information gained through empathic inquiries could be used exploitatively but could also be used in a way that ensures mutual accommodation and maximizes goodwill. Women's tendency to approach interactions from a continuous time perspective makes the latter the more likely outcome.[28]

Combining the pressure of saving face with gender differences produces an interesting result. Stalemates are more likely in mixed gender negotiations where the woman lawyer is representing a male-dominated client (such as corporate management) and the male lawyer is representing a female-dominated client (such as a union of women workers).[29] Expectation pressures on each lawyer flow from both the

28. Gilkey and Greenhalgh, Developing Effective Negotiating Approaches Among Professional Women in Organizations, Paper Submitted to Third Annual Conference on Women and Organizations, Simmons College, August 1984.

29. See Wall, The Intergroup Bargaining of Mixed–Sex Groups, 62 J. Applied Psychology 208, 212 (April 1977).

client and the other negotiator. In the mixed-gender case, however, both lawyers tend to exhibit competitive behavior in order not to lose face before either their clients or the opposing lawyer.

(3) *Culture.* There are many cross-cultural contacts within the law practice. The most obvious is in international business and diplomacy. For example, negotiators from different nations may approach and handle the same negotiation problem in varying ways based on their separate experiences and expectations. One study suggests that organizational decision-making will typically be a slow consensus-building process for the Japanese; for the Mexicans, a sensitive yet centralized process dependent on certain key personalities who have leverage; for the French, a process that emphasizes long-range objectives and principles over short-term gain; and for Americans, an open, often impatient process, dependent on the authority of certain positions, with short-term results as the chief aim.[30]

Practical experiences demonstrate the effect that these cultural differences may have on the lawyer's results:

> I was on a plane en route to Tokyo for the fourteen-day negotiation. I'd taken along all these books on the Japanese mentality, their psychology. I kept telling myself, "I'm really going to do well."
>
> When the plane landed in Tokyo, I was the first passenger to trot down the ramp, raring to go. At the bottom of the ramp two Japanese gentlemen awaited me, bowing politely. I liked that.
>
> The two Japanese helped me through customs, then escorted me to a large limousine. I reclined comfortably on the plush seat at the rear of the limousine, and they sat stiffly on the two fold-up stools. I said expansively, "Why don't you people join me? There's plenty of room back here."
>
> They replied, "Oh, no—you're an important person. You obviously need your rest." I liked that, too.
>
> As the limousine rolled along, one of my hosts asked, "By the way, do you know the language?"
>
> I replied, "You mean Japanese?"
>
> He said, "Right—that's what we speak in Japan."
>
> I said, "Well, no, but I hope to learn a few expressions. I've brought a dictionary with me."
>
> His companion asked, "Are you concerned about getting back to your plane on time?" (Up to that moment I had not been concerned.) "We can schedule this limousine to transport you back to the airport."
>
> I thought to myself, "How considerate."

30. See G. Fisher, International Negotiation: A Cross–Cultural Perspective 28–34 (1980); Unterman, Negotiation and Cross–Cultural Communications, in International Negotiation: Art and Sciences 69, 74 (Center for the Study of Foreign Affairs 1984).

Reaching into my pocket, I handed them my return flight ticket, so the limousine would know when to get me. I didn't realize it then, but they knew my deadline, whereas I didn't know theirs.

Instead of beginning negotiations right away, they first had me experience Japanese hospitality and culture. For more than a week I toured the country from the Imperial Palace to the shrines of Kyoto. They even enrolled me in an English-language course in Zen to study their religion.

Every evening for four and a half hours, they had me sit on a cushion on a hardwood floor for a traditional dinner and entertainment. Can you imagine what it's like sitting on a hardwood floor for all those hours? If I didn't get hemorrhoids as a result, I'll probably never get them. Whenever I inquired about the start of negotiations, they'd murmur, "Plenty of time! Plenty of time!"

At last, on the twelfth day, we began the negotiations, finishing early so we could play golf. On the thirteenth day, we began again, and ended early because of the farewell dinner. Finally, on the morning of the fourteenth day, we resumed our negotiating in earnest. Just as we were getting to the crux of things, the limousine pulled up to take me to the airport. We all piled in and continued hashing out the terms. Just as the limousine's brakes were applied at the terminal, we consummated the deal.

How well do you think I did in that negotiation? For many years my superiors referred to it as "The first great Japanese victory since Pearl Harbor." [31]

Language reflects culture, and translation without cultural nuance can be the essence of misunderstanding and dispute. To take another Japanese example, the trade differences between the United States and Japan have been going on for decades. Twenty years ago, amid a flurry of publicity over Japanese textile imports, President Nixon demanded of the visiting Japanese Prime Minister that Japan "exercise restraint in exports." Prime Minister Eisaku Sato responded, "Zensho Shimasu," literally translated as "I will do my best"—which Nixon accepted as a promise—whereas to most Japanese the response meant "No way!" [32] Is it any wonder that negotiations between the two nations are difficult, frustrating, and often less than successful?

This cultural impact may also exist among different ethnic subgroups within the heterogeneous American community. The degree to which a lawyer will reflect ethnic role expectations may depend on how long his family has lived in America, how much his local community reflects "the old country," and whether his client reflects the ethnic culture. At any one time, American lawyers with strong ethnic ties to Ireland, Italy, Eastern Europe, China, and Mexico may be negotiating together.

31. H. Cohen, You Can Negotiate Anything 93–95 (1980).

32. N.Y. Times, Mar. 27, 1988, p. 3.

Another example of cross-cultural contact lies in variations among different professional disciplines, variations that could also be described in terms of differences in role expectations. A banker, lawyer, realtor, professor, accountant, or physician, even though they are all Americans, may view the same problem from different perspectives, as reflected in separate professional language and education. A lawyer confronts this cross-cultural element frequently during direct and cross examination at deposition or trial, but the importance is similar during negotiation. As experienced international businessmen suggest, "Successful intercultural negotiators are aware that people indeed think, feel, and behave differently and are at the same time, equally logical and rational." [33]

(4) *Structure.* Institutional pressures frequently influence a negotiation outcome. The judicial system, for example, is an institution that generates its own set of expectations governing the people and procedures operating within it; the lawyer's customary role responds to such expectations. Position and procedure serve to allocate status within an organization, and status can have controlling impact on the structure and outcome of intra-organizational decision-making. Corporations, government agencies, large law firms, and many other organizations develop their own accepted methods and limits for negotiation.[34]

Within institutional structures a lawyer who is in a more central position with regard to information tends to be more influential than one on the periphery—the more centrally-placed being viewed by other participants as more competent and having greater power.[35] Galbraith's concept of conditioned power would seem to apply equally within as without the organization (see supra p. 213). Structure can encourage or obstruct agreement, and a lawyer should harness its effect in support of his client's interests.

3. Threats and Other Highly Competitive Behavior

We have placed the special consideration of threats in this section because of the impact threats have on apparent balance of power, a negotiator's personality (especially self-esteem), his need to control, and the psychological environment of the negotiation. The following excerpt is a comprehensive psychological view of threats which a lawyer will find useful in the negotiation setting:

33. P. Casse and S. Deol, Managing Intercultural Negotiations xvi (1985).

34. See Negotiating in Organizations (M. Bazerman and R. Lewicke, eds. 1983).

35. Stolte, Power Structure and Personal Competence, 106 J. Social Psychology 83, 87, 90 (1978).

MILBURN AND WATMAN, ON THE NATURE OF THREAT: A SOCIAL PSYCHOLOGICAL ANALYSIS
17–18, 39, 43–45, 49, 103, 108–11 (1981).

Threats operate by reducing the control of the target. A successful threat causes him to do something he does not want to do. An unsuccessful threat subjects him to a sanction which he cannot avoid or ameliorate. It follows that when a target assesses a threat, he does more than estimate the benefits of performing the proscribed act versus the costs of the sanction. He must include, among the costs, the cost of a loss of control to himself. We have seen that this, typically, is very high. Therefore, for the threat to succeed, the threatener must present the target with a very large sanction, certainly much in excess of the value of the proscribed behavior. Often this is impossible and the threat fails. The amount of excess will rise with the worth of the proscribed behavior to the target and the scope of the threat. * * * Lest we believe threats have no redeeming value, consider the converse of the above argument. Just as a loss of control is aversive, an increase of control is enjoyable. Though it may be true that threats are inefficient because the costs to the target of giving in are apt to be well in excess of the value of the proscribed behavior to him, it is also true that the benefits to the threatener of successfully threatening are often well in excess of the value of preventing the proscribed behavior. This is because a successful threat not only accomplishes the threatener's specific objective, but also demonstrates vividly his mastery. In a word, using threats can be quite satisfying. If nothing else, a threat, ultimately successful or not, usually generates an immediate response from which the threatener derives a sense of initiative and influence.

* * *

Credibility

Credibility refers to the perception by the target that the threatener intends to carry out the sanction if the terms of the threat are not met. Thus, credibility has two facets: the credibility of the threatener and the credibility of the threat. The credibility of the threatener usually depends upon his reputation for truthfulness, for not bluffing, and, to some extent, his past willingness to carry out threats. In addition, certain personality traits can enhance credibility, depending upon the situation. Being known as a pragmatist would increase the credibility of one's threats in favorable situations and decrease it in unfavorable ones. The threats of a gentle romantic might carry much weight in situations where a damsel is in distress. The threat of a strict moralist might have little impact in Machiavellian contexts, yet be quite credible when someone has strayed from the fold. Schelling (1960) has discussed the effect of a reputation for maniacal or erratic behavior upon credibility. In situations where a threatener's credibility would otherwise be low, such a reputation can increase a target's uncertainty. In situations where a threatener's credibility is already high, a history of maniacal behavior would diminish that credibility.

Presumably, the traits of toughness or implacability would be a general aid to credibility.

The target analyzes the credibility of the threat to discover whether it is the kind of threat that will be carried out. Generally, this calculation involves the weighing of the cost of compliance, the demand, the cost of the sanction to the target, the cost of the sanction to the threatener, the value of compliance to the threatener, and the number of alternative courses open to the threatener. If the threatened sanction is greatly out of proportion to the demand, the threat loses credibility; or if the threatened sanction would cost the threatener more to inflict than it would the target to receive, the threat loses credibility. Conversely, the credibility of a threat increases when it is clear that the threatener had several alternative courses and consciously chose to threaten. It is self-evident that a threat which the threatener is not capable of carrying out lacks credibility. In theory, if the target deduced that the threatener lacked all personal credibility, the analysis need not go further. The same is true if the target calculated that the threat lacked all credibility. This is almost never the case, however. Usually, uncertainty exists for both calculations, and the target must make his final determination by combining the two. The relationship between the two areas of credibility seems to be multiplicative. When either is zero, the net credibility is zero. A threat's low credibility may be increased if it is issued by a threatener who has never bluffed. An irrational threat gains credibility when issued by a maniac. Likewise, a well-known liar may be adjudged to be highly credible when his threat is rationally designed and thought through.

* * *

LEGITIMACY AS A FACTOR IN THREAT

* * *

We define legitimacy in terms of status, norms, and situation. By status, we mean membership in one or more social equivalence classes.

* * *

For example, imagine a neighborhood street, late at night, down which a group is walking while engaged in noisy conversation. Out of one of the houses bursts a woman who tells the group, with intensity, that her child is sick and asleep, that the group's noise will disturb him, and that she will call the police if the group does not quiet down. Such a threat is likely to be effective not so much because of the reference to the police, but because of the legitimate reliance on the norms connected with motherhood and proper behavior around helpless children. Contrast this with the identical situation, but this time the woman simply threatens to call the police if the group does not get quiet. She does not identify her status to the targets of the threat. This threat should be much less effective even though the sanction in each version of the example is identical. In the second version, the status of the threatener has not been made clear and, therefore, her normative armament is also unclear to the group. From their point of view, she may only have the status accruing to any member of the equivalence class of all American women. With that status, the norms she has recourse to (e.g., one should not make noise on residential streets at certain hours) are apt to be weak, vague, or simply not honored by the targets. It follows that the force of the threat now comes solely from the relationship between the explicit sanction (the police) and the strength of the desire of the group to persist in making noise. Since the police are not likely to arrive very quickly, it is safe to predict that the group will not be greatly impressed by the threat.

* * *

Keep in mind the relevance of status and norms to threats. We believe that legitimate threats are most frequently encountered in everyday living and are the most effective type of threat. Legitimacy comes about when the occupant of a particular status position uses a threat whose demand and sanction are permitted by the norms of the position and situation. * * *

REACTIONS AND RESPONSES TO THREATS

* * *

What are effective ways of dealing with threats? First, it must be recognized that threats are all subjective probabilities, beliefs in the degree of truth of certain statements. A person may believe that danger is more likely or less likely than actuarial studies would suggest. It is interesting that some objects and experiences arouse fear and anxiety much more readily than do others. People tend to fear snakes and spiders even—some would say especially—if they have never or rarely encountered them. * * * Thus, we must recognize that some persons are far more susceptible to threats than are others: Their thresholds for perceiving threats or criticism that is threatening to their self-esteem is much lower than for others. They readily and often move over the fear threshold. In crises and disasters, it is notable how few persons suffer pathological impairment because of fear, and how many, in critical roles, are extremely effective.

So, what reduces susceptibility to threats? Several factors seem important: Past experience at dealing with them helps, even if such experience was not such as to permit a person to demonstrate his effectiveness, but only to reduce his perception of danger. * * *

For some situations, trust in oneself as an expert will reduce the sense of danger; in others, it is trust in the other expert or authority who has primary responsibility for handling the situation; in still others, it is trust in the expertness and dependability of a set of peers.

The feeling that one does indeed know how to deal tactfully, yet effectively, with waiters, garage mechanics, plumbers, electricians, politicians, the mentally ill, policemen, and physicians, among others, helps. It may suggest a repertoire of generally useful social skills, and a quietly assertive manner that may readily communicate their existence nonverbally to those who might otherwise readily use threats at one level or another. Different social skills may be necessary in dealing with subordinates, bosses, strangers, and intimates. By contrast, the person who is readily flustered in social interaction tempts those who derive a sense of power from threatening others. Disorganized or confused individuals and organizations are ready targets of influence efforts by those with needs to exercise power coercively. Those with less confidence in their own social skills or with inordinate power needs are more likely to employ coercion, however disguised.

*   *   *

One is more likely to submit to a threat if the situation is perceived to be a once-only affair rather than a habit: "We may not mind giving you your way this time, but we shall object strenuously if you attempt to make a habit of it."

The rational, cool, and collected individual faced with threats has several alternative ways of attempting to deal with them. Each alternative can be regarded as having a different set of advantages and its own set of costs. The target of a threat can feel tempted to eliminate the danger posed by the threat (we may look for flyswatters when we hear the buzz of mosquitoes), unless the threat is associated with a demand that he do what he wants to do anyway. If a boy's parent threatens to give no allowance this week unless he washes the family car (when he already wants to wash it so that it will look nice for his date, when he borrows the car), he can cheerfully submit. His parent can have a sense of power for having used a threat to induce compliance, and the lad can have managed to give an impression of docility and obedience to his parent. Sometimes, no acquiescence to demands, if made under penalty of threat, has more of a long-term payoff. When one of us was in the eighth grade, he was occasionally afflicted with a bully, a bully given to making threats as well as engaging in tormenting. All of this stopped after an incident in which the bully was faced with a violent response, and also with laughter as a response to his blows. Future threats from the bully were trivialized, and the cost of carrying them out increased.

Notes and Questions

(1) Threats and other competitive behavior may become the norm for a lawyer concerned about control. The lawyer who is the target of these threats will want to respond in kind, but his goal should be to respond in a way that will improve the chances for a favorable outcome for his client. Milburn and Watman argue persuasively for thorough preparation for legal negotiation when they state, "Disorganized or confused individuals and organizations are ready targets of influence efforts by those with needs to exercise power coercively." Even for such a disorganized lawyer, however, the knowledge that he is being threatened may be so menacing to his sense of self-esteem that he may in reaction dig in his heels deeper, making settlement more difficult.

(2) How might the authors' conclusions apply to a lawyer's professional situation?   The authors suggest that "[m]ost of us deny the existence of, or fail to heed, some dangers, and controlled dangers are fun, not scary."   Would a lawyer view a trial as a "controlled danger"? If so, what effect should a threat to go to trial have on a competent opposing lawyer?   For example, an opposing lawyer may routinely threaten to cut off negotiations and take the case to court unless you agree to his proposed settlement.   The credibility of that threat depends in part on your evaluation of the probable court outcome. Because you and the opposing lawyer undoubtedly differ in your estimates of court outcome, a threat that he may consider real may be perceived by you as only raising an opportunity for you to win in court without being blamed by your client for the extra time and expense of trial.

4. Negotiating Strategies and Tactics

One's negotiating strategies and tactics are derived from many sources and influences.   Personal experience and anecdotes based on the experience of others are important tools for learning about power and psychology.   They personalize concepts that otherwise might remain abstract and little-used.   For example, a lawyer may forget that time, deadlines, and cultural differences can affect the negotiation outcome, but she will certainly remember the lessons of the Tokyo business trip (supra p. 233).   There is, however, one significant problem with experiential learning—there is too much of it to put to use consciously without some organization.   To organize this experience, the lawyer needs theory in the form of general categories and analysis.

For the law student, anecdotes containing specific tactics breathe life into the general principles and analysis described earlier in this section.   For instance, a lawyer can draw a number of lessons from applying the theory of power to the use of anger as described by Edwards and White:

> A display of anger, real or feigned, is a standard negotiating technique.   Most have read of the use of the technique particularly in diplomatic and labor negotiations where one party stages an angry departure from the negotiating table.   Depending upon the circumstances and the experience of the opposing negotiator, a convincing display of anger is likely to cause a strong emotional and perhaps intellectual response.   The one using the technique may be using it to signal the seriousness of his position or merely to make the opponent believe that he is serious.   In some cases a negotiator may use anger for the public relations effect upon other members of his negotiating committee or constituency.

> A convincing expression of anger by an opponent is likely to raise doubts in an inexperienced negotiator's mind about the reasonableness of his position.   Moreover, in some circumstances it

may intimidate the opponent at least if he is unaccustomed to such displays. Of course there is always the possibility, as there is with almost every effective technique, that the expression of anger will only stimulate an equal or stronger angry response from an opponent and will strengthen his desire to resist.[36]

Applying Fisher's analysis to the use of anger as a negotiating technique might include the following lessons:

(1) Anger's effectiveness depends on the perception of, and response by, the receiving lawyer. With knowledge of this technique, the other lawyer can reduce its impact to what the merits of the issue warrant. Furthermore, the use of such negative personal behavior may place the outcome in the control of certain unpredictable personality traits of the other side, such as a risk-prone attitude and courage in the face of uncertainty and hostility. Finally, anger suggests irrationality, which has inherent power characteristics by itself.

(2) Anger confirms the existence of a poor relationship and creates an imposing obstacle to a better one.

(3) Before using anger, a lawyer should carefully evaluate the alternative to a negotiated settlement. Anger may signal a willingness to accept an alternative rather than continue the present negotiation pattern, and a hostile response from the other side may trigger an impasse.

(4) Anger often contains an implicit threat (negative commitment) that expresses a definite message about the lawyer's bottom line.

(5) By increasing tension and ill will, anger reduces the attention lawyers will give to creating new settlement options that might satisfy the interests of both sides.

(6) Anger may indicate that an element of legitimacy has been overlooked. Justifiable anger may follow a direct attack on a position or interest that a lawyer considers legitimately fair and just.

Some interesting strategies come from experiences in other cultures. The notion of the yin and yang pervades much of Oriental thought—the idea that each force carries within it a countervailing force. Each strength includes a weakness; each weakness, a strength. A negotiation strategy flowing naturally from this philosophical outlook is based on jujitsu, the Japanese art of using the strength of the opposing attack as part of the counterattack.[37] For example, in a buyer-seller negotiation, the buyer may say, "I'm concerned about your meeting the delivery deadline." Wanting to be cooperative, the seller may reply: "Don't worry. We have more than enough in stock to meet your needs for the next six months." This response, of course, gives the buyer information about the condition of the seller's inventories which he might use to negotiate a lower price or more favorable terms. A

36. H. Edwards and J. White, The Lawyer as a Negotiator 113–14 (1977).

37. See R. Fisher and W. Ury, Getting to Yes: Negotiating Agreement Without Giving In 112–14 (1981).

better response for the seller: "Why are you concerned? Do you have some marketing problems that we should know about?" With this quite natural response, the seller deflects the buyer's query into a request for more information from the buyer himself.

The following excerpts provide a sampling of some traditional strategies used by lawyers.

FREUND, ANATOMY OF A MERGER: STRATEGIES AND TECHNIQUES FOR NEGOTIATING CORPORATE ACQUISITIONS
29–31 (1975).

Timing—of the Essence

As with most aspects of life, proper timing can be critical in a negotiation. The precise point in the discussions at which a certain subject is brought up may be just as important as its substantive content. The game of chess, where the sequence of moves is so crucial, provides an apt analogue: at one stage of the match a particular pawn thrust may be innocuous, whereas several moves later it can be devastating.

Take a simple example. Assume that the seller is positively paranoid on the subject of an escrow of part of the purchase price. No holdback for him; he wants to get paid every cent at the closing. This man is well-advised to make his point, take his stand and get the matter resolved before issues surface that reveal his fear of making certain representations. If the order is reversed, and the seller's uneasiness becomes known at the outset—there he is, asking for a "basket," trying to get a key representation stated "to the best of his knowledge," introducing "materiality" concepts by the score—then by the time the escrow issue arises, the purchaser will probably decide that he needs a holdback to protect himself. But if the purchaser has already yielded on the escrow point, it will be difficult for him to take it back. So, a certain amount of planning is advisable to ensure the optimum timing, notwithstanding the ordinary chronology of events.

Similarly, when you are making a series of points, the order of presentation should not necessarily follow the order in which the points appear in the agreement, but should rather be designed for maximum impact. For instance, assume that the seller has objected to provisions in paragraphs 2, 3, 6 and 7. Paragraph 2 deals with an issue that seriously concerns you, as purchaser's counsel; but the points raised with respect to paragraph 3, 6 and 7 are not significant and can be yielded. In that situation, you might very well approach opposing counsel as follows (although obviously not so briskly):

"With respect to the point in 3, I'll give you that one. . . . Now on the issue in 6, I'm not inclined to argue about that. . . . With respect to the point in 7, I still think the provision is fair but if it really bothers you we can change it as you suggested. . . . Now, about that question in number 2. . . ."

If you handle the matter in this fashion, there may be an understandable predisposition on the part of your adversary to be cooperative on paragraph 2, especially if you can drum up some reasonable support for your position. On the other hand, if you had kicked off the negotiating session by saying, "Now, on number 2, I have a lot of trouble . . .," the other lawyer doesn't know whether you are going to have the same sort of problems on every one of his points, and he will probably be less inclined to go along with you.

Another thought on timing for which I have no objective evidence—purely a visceral reaction—is that when you are winning points in the negotiation, when you have the momentum, you should not stop to analyze the mechanics or draft the language to implement those points. It is much better to solve the issue in principle now and draft later, recognizing that there might have to be further discussion down the road and that perhaps you don't have everything wrapped up in a neat package at this juncture. For all you know, you may have caught your adversary on the day that his boy got into Princeton; it would be a shame to bog down and waste the opportunity.

To Swap, Perchance to Cede

Remember that seller of a few paragraphs back who timed his discussion of the escrow so exquisitely? Well, it all went for naught. Unfortunately, even though the purchaser was inclined to yield and eliminate the escrow when the subject arose early in the game, he reacted in this fashion to the seller's arguments: "Okay, I understand what you're saying. We'll come back later and decide whether there will be an escrow, after I hear all your other points." Aside from the obvious desirability of becoming educated about the seller's problems prior to the ultimate decision on an escrow, there is another principle at work here: namely, that many negotiators, faced with an issue which they are willing to cede, avoid immediate concession so as to retain bartering material for future use. The issue can always be passed with a line such as, "Well, that's a tough one; why don't we come back to it?" or "I'm inclined to be negative but let me think about it" or "I've got to go back to my clients on that." Even if your opponent knows exactly what you are up to, it is rare for him to insist upon a decision on the spot; at worst, he will also save some trading bait for later.

On the other hand, there may be times when you will want to concede points gracefully, without deferral, especially when they are particularly obvious and no advantage is to be gained by holding them back. Occasionally, it is good bargaining to make a concession that has not even been requested, the idea being to impart to the proceedings a certain bonhomie that might stand you in good stead at a later time.

To be effective, though, this has to be accomplished with no visible strings.

———

COHEN, YOU CAN NEGOTIATE ANYTHING
32–37 (1980).

Satisfying needs

You have other options, and they pivot on the satisfaction of your needs, real or fictionalized. In a fundamental sense, *every* negotiation is for the satisfaction of needs. Sears presents you with a $489.95 asking price [for a refrigerator] that meets *its* needs . . . but what about yours? After all, you're the other party in the transaction. Ideally, both parties should win, or come out ahead, when a transaction is consummated.

There are several ways you can snap the Sears salesman into a keen awareness of your needs. You can ask, "What colors does this model come in?" If the salesman replies, "Thirty-two," you say, "What are they?" When he finishes telling you, you exclaim, "That's *it*? Those are the *only* colors you have?"

When he says, "Yes. Just what are you looking for?" you explain, "We have a psychedelic kitchen. These colors are much too square. They'd clash! I hope you'll make some adjustment in the price."

A second way to express your needs is to discuss the refrigerator's icemaker. You comment, "I notice this model comes with a built-in icemaker."

The salesman replies, "Yes, it does. It'll make cubes for you twenty-four hours a day, for only two cents an hour!" (Note that he's made a totally unwarranted assumption about your needs.)

You counter this false assumption by saying, "That presents a difficult problem. One of my kids has a chronic sore throat. The doctor says: 'Never any ice! Never!' Could you possibly remove the icemaker?"

He retorts, "But the icemaker's the whole door!"

You say, "I know . . . but what if I promise not to use it? Shouldn't that affect the price?"

A third way to express your needs—and your dissatisfaction with the refrigerator's features—is to discuss its door. You can say, "This model swings open from the left. My family's right-handed." Comments like this indicate to the salesman that your needs aren't being met fully. Therefore, *his* needs shouldn't be totally satisfied.

* * *

What if . . .?

Another extremely effective option at your disposal is the use of the words "What if?" "What if?" is a magic phrase in negotiations. For example: What if I buy four refrigerators? Will that affect the price? What if I take it home in a pick-up truck, instead of having *you* deliver it? Will that affect the price? What if I buy a washer-dryer and a waffle iron at the same time? Will that affect the price? What if over the next six months, our neighborhood syndicate buys one refrigerator a month? Will that affect the price?

You may not always get precisely what you want when asking "What if . . .?" but nine out of ten times, the person you're dealing with will make a counter-offer in your favor.

Don't forget that although the posted $489.95 price was arbitrarily arrived at, many things are buried in that figure, including installation, delivery charges, service contract, and warranty, all of which cost Sears money. If you can save Sears any or all these expenses, the store should kick the savings back to you. For example, if you ask the salesman, "Does that price include an installation charge?" and he replied, "Yes, it does," you then comment, "Good . . . I have a set of tools at home. I can make any necessary connections and adjustment myself."

The ultimatum

Supposing your time is limited and you don't feel like negotiating. You approach the first salesman you see and say, "Look . . . you want to sell this refrigerator, and I want to buy it. I'll give you $450.00 right now, take it or leave it."

When you turn on your heel and walk away, will the salesman follow you out to the street? Nope, I don't think so. Why? Because he has nothing whatsoever invested in a relationship with you or in the overall transaction. Furthermore, he resents your curt approach. The key to making an ultimatum prevail is always the extent to which the other side makes an investment of time and energy.

Keeping this principle in mind, let's try another way. You casually walk into the Large Appliances Department at two o'clock on a Monday afternoon when floor activity is at a minimum. You say to the salesman, "I'm interested in seeing your entire line of refrigerators!" From two to four have him show you every model on the floor, explaining all the benefits.

Finally you remark, "Before I make up my mind, I'll have to come back tomorrow with my spouse."

The salesman has now wasted two hours of his time on you.

On Tuesday, again at two o'clock, you arrive with your spouse. You seek out the same salesman. You repeat the process of examining every model on the floor. Finally, you say to him, "Before we make up our minds, we'd like to come back with a refrigerator engineering specialist: my mother-in-law. She knows a lot about these things. See you tomorrow afternoon!"

The salesman now has four hours invested in you.

On Wednesday, at the appointed hour, you walk into the department with your spouse and mother-in-law. You induce the salesman to repeat his demonstrations till four, at which time you mumble, "Hmmm . . . know what? I can't quite make up my mind!"

The salesman now has six hours of his life invested in you.

On Thursday afternoon, as expected, you walk in alone and say, "Hi there—remember me? I'm interested in buying a refrigerator."

The salesman will make a wry face and say, "I should hope so!"

You continue, "Look . . . I only have this $450.00 plus a book of matches, a fountain pen, and eight cents in change. I just love this model. Please . . . maybe we can make a deal." Then if he doesn't respond immediately, you shrug, pivot, and slowly start for the exit.

Will the salesman follow you? Yes. He has an investment in the situation, and he wants some return on the effort he has expended. He'll probably mutter, "Okay, okay! Enough is enough. It's a deal."

Why does he take your "Take it or leave it" offer (though you didn't use those words)? Because you've set up your ultimatum in such a way that its acceptance is virtually guaranteed. You've made the ultimatum palatable and have forced the salesman to spend an inordinate amount of time with you.

Notes and Questions

(1) Analyze these examples of successful strategies and tactics in the same way we analyzed the technique of anger. A lawyer may never find himself in a similar situation to those cited, but he can certainly use the same power tactics if comparable situations arise. No matter how skillful he is, a lawyer's bargaining power will depend in large part on the specific case. Clever strategies and tactics will never allow a lawyer to "win" with an unmeritorious case, nor will they give the lawyer advantages over an equally able opponent. The lawyer who relies on power tactics alone is counting, perhaps unconsciously, on the other lawyer's lack of skill, knowledge, or preparation. Knowledge of bargaining strategies and tactics is important in developing the necessary skill to negotiate effectively, but once in a negotiation with an able opposing lawyer, a focus on tactics may only decrease the bargaining power already inherent in the situation.

(2) Consider Professor Menkel–Meadow's comments:

> The literature is replete with advice to overpower and take advantage of the other side. But as one of the popular guides to negotiation has so wisely stated, "a tactic perceived is no tactic." If two competitive negotiators read the same literature, it is difficult to see how these strategies will be employed to maximize individual gain. Who will win when both sides know all the same tricks? [38]

---

38. Menkel–Meadow, Toward Another View of Legal Negotiation: The Structure of Problem Solving, 31 U.C.L.A. L.Rev. 754, 779–80 (1983).

Chapter III

MEDIATION

A. THE PROCESS

When parties are unable to resolve their dispute through discussion and negotiation, a logical next step is to seek the assistance of a third party to facilitate communication and the search for a solution. "Mediation" is the broad term used to describe the intervention of third parties in the dispute resolution process. The term "conciliation" is sometimes used to describe the same process of involving third parties, often in the context of labor relations when neutral intervention is used to break a stalemate.

Mediation probably predates the formal creation and enforcement of law, for humans in the social state seem to have a natural instinct to seek the approval and guidance of others in settling differences between individuals. Indeed, formal legal structures may have developed out of informal attempts by family members, neighbors, and friends to mediate between disputing individuals. The Classical Chinese viewed the use of mediation as superior to recourse to law for settlement of disputes. F.S.C. Northrop has described the view of the Confucian Chinese that "litigation" was a "second best" solution to disputes:

> The "first best" and socially proper way to settle disputes, used by the "superior man," was by the method of mediation, following the ethics of the "middle way." This consisted in bringing the disputants to something they both approved as a settlement of the dispute, by means of an intermediary. This middle man served largely as a messenger. Proper behavior prescribed that he refuse even to arbitrate the differences at the request of the disputants. "Good" dispute settling consisted in conveying the respective claims of the disputants back and forth between them until the disputants themselves arrived at a solution which was approved by both.[1]

In many societies, mediation through a third party has been a favored alternative to formal legal processes. The mediator may be chosen because of special qualities, for example, the "prestige-mediators" among the Singapore Chinese, the "big man" among the Ifugao tribe, or the Iranian bazaar mediators.[2] On the other hand, the mediator may simply be a friend or a disinterested person. The "Book

---

1. Northrop, The Mediational Approval Theory of Law in American Legal Realism, 44 Va.L.Rev. 347, 349 (1958). See also Luban, Some Greek Trials: Order and Justice in Homer, Hesiod, Aeschylus and Plato, 54 Tenn.L.Rev. 280 (1987), describing Greek approaches to the conflicting objectives of "justice" and "reconciliation."

2. P.H. Gulliver, Disputes and Negotiations: A Cross–Cultural Perspective 214 (1979).

of Discipline" of the Society of Friends stated that when differences arise between persons, their friends shall "forthwith speak to and tenderly advise, the persons between whom the difference is, to make a speedy end thereof; and if that friend or those friends do not comply with their advice, that then they take to them one or two friends more, and again exhort them to end their difference." [3]

Mediation has often existed alongside formal legal structures, offering a community-based, consensual alternative to legal remedies. In African societies, tribal "moots" were an informal mediation process which continued after the imposition of colonial law:

> A court system, established by the British, was primarily adjudicative, while a tribal "moot" performed an integrative, conciliatory function. Whereas the court was characterized by social distance between judge and litigants, rules of procedure which narrowed the issues under discussion, and a resolution which ascribed guilt or innocence to a defendant, the moot emphasized the bonds between the convenor and the disputants, it encouraged the widening of discussion so that all tensions and viewpoints psychologically—if not legally—relevant to the issue were expressed, and it resolved disputes by consensus about future conduct, rather than by assessing blame retrospectively.[4]

At the heart of the modern mediation process is the notion that any agreement should be voluntarily arrived at by the parties. The belief is that the parties will be more satisfied, and thus more likely to abide by the agreement, if it is of their own creation. The mediator should not desire, nor have the authority, to impose a particular settlement. In this classical form of mediation, the mediator strives to be only a facilitator and not to interject his views, values, or solutions into the process or the agreement. It is recognized, however, that the mediator may have an influence on the mediation by his role in helping to define the problem and to consider options for its solution.

Another theme of modern mediation is that it permits the parties to achieve their own resolution of a dispute without being bound to a formal, and possibly inflexible, legal solution. Professor Lon Fuller noted this quality of mediation:

> [M]ediation is commonly directed, not toward achieving conformity to norms, but toward the creation of the relevant norms themselves. This is true, for example, in the very common case where the mediator assists the parties in working out the terms of a contract defining their rights and duties toward one another. In

3. Rules of Discipline of the Yearly Meeting 3 (New Bedford 1809). The Rules go on to provide, if mediation is not successful, for "arbitration" by a group composed of persons selected by each party and third persons selected by the parties' arbitrators. Id. at 7.

4. Danzig, Toward the Creation of a Complementary, Decentralized System of Criminal Justice, 26 Stan.L.Rev. 1, 42–3 (1973). See also Galanter, Justice in Many Rooms: Courts, Private Ordering, and Indigenous Law, 19 J. of Legal Pluralism & Unofficial Law 1 (1981); Nader, Styles of Court Procedure: To Make the Balance, in L. Nader (ed.), Law in Culture and Society (1969).

such a case there is no pre-existing structure that can guide mediation; it is the mediational process that produces the structure.

* * *

This quality of mediation becomes most visible when the proper function of the mediator turns out to be, not that of inducing the parties to accept formal rules for the governance of their future relations, but that of helping them to free themselves from the encumbrance of rules and of accepting, instead, a relationship of mutual respect, trust and understanding that will enable them to meet shared contingencies without the aid of formal prescriptions laid down in advance. Such a mediational effort might well come into play in any of the various forms of mediation between husband and wife associated with "family counseling" and "marriage therapy." In the task of reestablishing the marriage as a going concern the mediator might find it essential to break up formalized conceptions of "duty" and to substitute a more fluid sense of mutual trust and shared responsibility. In effect, instead of working toward achieving a rule-oriented relationship he might devote his efforts, to some degree at least, in exactly the opposite direction.[5]

Some contemporary proponents of mediation have viewed it as an "empowering" process by which the parties can fashion their own norms. The degree, however, to which the norms of the parties should govern in contrast to those imposed by the law is a subject of some controversy which will be considered in a later section. Some proponents of mediation have also claimed that by virtue of its voluntariness, it empowers the less powerful party to confront the opposing party with shared and community standards and thus to achieve fairness that might not be possible in a formal legal proceeding. Others, however, see the "empowerment" issue in a more critical light, viewing mediation in some contexts as a surrendering of legal rights by the less powerful through participation in a process in which they are at a competive disadvantage. Thus some have termed mediation as simply a ratification of existing power imbalances. These issues will also be explored in a later section.

Today there are many forms of mediation. Some hew closely to the ideal of voluntariness, both as to the parties' participation and as to the way in which an agreement is reached. Some, however, view mediation as a process of carefully-managed imposition of social pressures to resolve disputes. Thus, in some situations, the parties' participation in mediation is encouraged, or even coerced, as by the courts or governmental agencies. Likewise, some mediation processes embrace much greater mediator activism in the belief that to be a good facilitator, the mediator must use a variety of techniques actively to encourage and shape a settlement. Under this view, the mediator plays a creative role

5. Fuller, Mediation—Its Forms and Functions, 44 S.Cal.L.Rev. 305, 308, 325–26 (1971).

in the process, not only structuring the dialogue between the parties in a manner suited to getting agreement, but also in suggesting, or even promoting, particular solutions. The differences in approach reveal significant differences in philosophy. They also raise questions as to the amenability of different approaches depending on the nature of the legal dispute and the parties involved.

The following description of the mediation process in a Community Mediation Center is fairly typical of the classical model of mediation:

ERNIE ODOM,
THE MEDIATION HEARING: A PRIMER
in Palenski & Launer, Mediation: Contexts and Challenges 5–14 (1986).

[The author is Executive Director of Training of the Community Mediation Center, Coram, New York.]

BEFORE THE SESSION BEGINS

The Community Mediation Center is set up to handle a large volume of cases. For this reason, each person at the Center has specific and diverse responsibilities. The Intake staff schedules the mediations and handles all case records. Others are responsible for training, public relations, community relations and office management.

The volunteer mediator is not involved with the problems arising in the course of scheduling a mediation. The mediator's responsibility is to arrive at the Center on time and be prepared to deal with the case at hand. The mediator's role in the case ends when the mediation session concludes. Any breach of agreement or follow-up action is taken by the Intake staff.

Each mediation session is conducted by a panel consisting of two mediators. The mediators are selected by the Intake staff and are not a permanent team. In certain instances, two mediators may be paired fairly frequently because they complement each other well. It is not the policy of the Mediation Center to encourage fixed mediation teams. Mediators should be prepared to work with a wide variety of personalities.

On rare occasions, a situation may arise where a mediator knows a disputant, or is in some way associated with a disputant's family. When this happens, the mediator will notify the Intake staff and ask to be disqualified. Impartiality is the cornerstone of a mediation session, and great care must be taken to ensure that there is not the slightest hint of any impropriety in any facet of the proceedings.

Upon arriving at the Community Mediation Center or one of its satellite offices, the two mediators assigned to a case will be given only the sketchiest of information about the case to be heard. This is done to ensure the impartiality of the proceedings. The Center's experience indicates that prior information adds nothing to the mediators' ability to mediate a dispute. If anything, an abundance of information can cause problems. The only information the Center provides is the complainant's and respondent's names, the charge(s) and the referral source (court, district attorney or voluntary). All other information comes from the disputing parties.

Before the mediation session begins, the mediators meet informally. Since they may not have worked together previously, it is desirable for them to chat and get to know each other. The team concept is important, and it is much easier to work as a team if both mediators have some familiarity with each other's style and background. For example, some mediators are more assertive than others; some are listeners while others take the initiative. All these factors need consideration before mediators can work together effectively.

After they have chatted informally, the mediators make some basic decisions. First, they consider seating arrangements. If the parties are hostile, the mediators will most likely decide to seat them physically as far apart as possible. If witnesses are to appear, the mediators must ascertain that there is adequate seating. Considerable care may be required in planning seating for cases with a large number of participants.

When witnesses are expected at a hearing, the mediators will explore several possible scenarios. They need to consider whether it is advisable to meet with the parties before calling any witnesses. The reason is that it may become apparent that witnesses are not necessary. Their testimony may not be relevant and may serve no other purpose than to aggravate and inflame matters. It may well be that the witnesses will deliberately try to confuse and prolong the proceedings. Similarly, if a scheduled witness fails to appear, thought must be given to the weight of the witness' contribution. If the testimony is to be a crucial part of the session, the mediators may decide to postpone the session until the absentee can be located. Conversely, if postponement might jeopardize resolution of the dispute, the mediators must decide whether or not to proceed with the hearing.

Before the disputants are shown in, the mediators consider how to present the introduction to the session. Care must be taken to ensure impartiality. In their introduction, the mediators may want to mention certain facts they feel will be helpful in starting the session off on the right foot. The disputants may be in a very agitated state. A single seemingly innocent statement may be misconstrued by an upset disputant, causing the atmosphere of the session to be more highly emotionally charged than otherwise. A good rule is to keep the introduction as short as possible so as not to open any additional avenues for disagreement or conflict.

BEGINNING THE SESSION: THE INTRODUCTION

The opening remarks made by the mediators set the tone for the hearing. At the Community Mediation Center, both mediators share the introductory remarks to demonstrate their co-equal status. It is not desirable to allow disputants to feel that one mediator is the spokesperson or chief mediator. By sharing the introduction, both mediators have an opportunity to establish the rapport so essential to the mediation process.

The mediators always cover several points in their opening remarks. They present these points in a natural way and may elaborate on a particular point or points, depending on the nature of the case. They try to avoid making their presentation sound like a canned speech, which would cast doubt on their sincerity and make it more difficult to gain the parties' confidence.

Introductory remarks at the Community Mediation Center always cover the following points:

1. Words of welcome.
   Care is taken to set a casual yet professional atmosphere.

2. Description of the Center's operation.
   The mediators explain the process of mediation and outline what the parties can expect from the session.

3. Description of the mediators' role in the proceedings.
   The mediators are there to help the parties themselves come to an agreement.

4. Confidentiality.
   The only records kept are of the outcome of the session, and the mediators have taken an Oath of Confidentiality.

5. Note taking.
   The parties must be told that the mediators will be taking some notes for their own information and that these notes will be destroyed at the end of the session.

6. Description of the use of separate caucusing.
   The parties need to know that the mediators will meet with each disputant individually one or more times during the session in order to explore all aspects of the dispute as fully as possible. The disputants receive assurances that these meetings will not result in an advantage to either party and that the mediators will not repeat anything said in confidence.

7. Ground rules.
   First, each party must allow the other party to finish speaking before adding to or refuting any statement. This is essential because tempers are short and emotions run high at the outset of a session. If order is not maintained, it is difficult to get to the root of the problem. Second, the mediators stress to the parties that they must remain seated at all times. This rule works; the Community Mediation Center has never had an incident involving physical contact between the disputing parties.

PUBLIC POSITION

The term "public position" refers to those parts of a mediation session in which the disputants meet together with the mediators to discuss their conflict. * * *

Since mediation is a process where the parties themselves come to a solution to their dispute, the mediators do not feel obligated to lead or control the conversation. They allow the parties to speak their minds. They let the disputants stray from the central issue if there is an indication that the information shared may be of value to the proceedings. In this manner, the mediators are often able to bring out underlying issues causing the present conflict.

At times, it may be necessary for the mediators to allow the parties to raise their voices—perhaps even shout—if they believe this may relieve the tension. This is a procedure known as "venting." Experienced mediators are careful when allowing parties to vent; a very real danger exists that the mediators may lose control of the session. At no time should the venting continue for an extended period; very little constructive progress can be expected when voices are at a high decibel level. The mediators will use their powers of persuasion to calm the parties so that the session can continue in a professional and rational manner.

PRIVATE POSITION

During a mediation session, the mediators will meet separately with each disputant, the "private position." Since parties new to mediation often feel uncomfortable about meeting privately, the mediators offer assurances that anything said will be held in confidence unless they are otherwise instructed by the disputant. They also explain that the private position helps them to explore settlement possibilities with each disputant.

The primary purpose of meeting privately with a disputant is for the mediators to try to obtain some movement from the disputant's public position towards settling the conflict. After reiterating that the discussion is confidential, the mediators stress how far the parties have progressed, discuss the consequences of failure to reach an agreement—going to court—and explore alternatives with the disputant. They frame their questions not as suggestions or advice, but in a hypothetical "what if" manner: "What if she did this . . . would you do that?"

When the mediators become aware that a disputant is willing to compromise on a point, they ask if they can reveal the new position to the other disputant. Ordinarily, the mediators do not simply tell the other disputant. He or she may interpret the offer as a sign of weakness, reject it and demand further concessions as settlement terms. Instead, the mediators will communicate the offer to compromise as a hypothetical possibility not yet explored, thus minimizing the risk of rejection. If the hypothetical possibility is rejected, the effect of rejection is minimal. The offering disputant's position has not been weakened, because no offer has been made. The "possibility" was just a thought, nothing else.

TECHNIQUES USEFUL FOR GATHERING INFORMATION

Mediators use several techniques to elicit information from the disputants. These techniques are readily used by people in all walks of life, but are particularly well suited to mediation. A description of several techniques follows:

1. Mediators ask questions that cannot be answered by a simple "yes" or "no." Many times mediators sense that there is more to the case than the disputants are willing to tell. In such instances, mediators may want to elicit additional facts by encouraging the parties to speak at greater length. If a party is responding rather than contributing to the discussion, it will be difficult to evoke more than the information already given. Also, it may seem to the disputants that the mediators, not the parties, are controlling the discussion. This may give the disputants the feeling that the mediators are resolving the dispute, not the disputants themselves.

The mediators use questions requiring a descriptive answer: "Why do you say that?" "What do you mean by that?" "What happened?" "How do you feel about this?" The basic idea is to call on the disputant to explain how or why, to describe something.

2. Mediators preface Key Words with "what about" or "how about." This is another technique mediators use to encourage a reluctant disputant to contribute additional information. By using these opening phrases, they try to move the discussion in a particular direction. Once the disputant starts talking, the mediators can key in on specific areas deemed important.

For example, in a dispute between neighbors, a mediator may lead with, "What about your relationship with your other neighbors?" This question requires the disputant to consider information not yet discussed. Once the party is encouraged to reflect on new factors, pertinent information may come to light that may never have surfaced if the conversation had been more tightly controlled.

3. Mediators repeat back Key Words. A third technique found effective in drawing out information is to repeat certain key phrases the party used in his or her previous answer. The purpose of this technique is to keep the dialogue going and gather as much information as possible by leading the disputant from one thought to the next.

4. Mediators summarize back. The advantage of repeating key words has been discussed. Sometimes mediators may feel an even greater elaboration may be necessary. They may find it helpful to summarize their understanding of the point the person is trying to make. In some instances, this is necessary to clarify the positions.

For example, a mediator may say, "Am I to understand you feel that . . .?" Great care must be taken to assure that the summarization comes out sounding as impartial as possible; the mediator runs the serious risk of further confusing the issue by either misconstruing the person's thoughts or phrasing remarks in such a way that the opposing party is led to believe the mediator is taking sides or offering unfair advantage to the other party.

THE AGREEMENT

Once the parties resolve their dispute, the mediators put the terms of the agreement in written form for both disputants to sign. The mediators take care to ensure the agreement is written in a straightforward manner. It cannot be ambiguous and should accurately reflect the points the parties want included in the agreement.

An important reason for written agreements is that once a person commits himself or herself on paper, that commitment cannot be easily ignored. The psychological effect of a written agreement is one of the main reasons why mediation works. The parties cannot "forget" what they have agreed to, and have a permanent reminder which tends to hold them responsible to their word.

On occasions, the Community Mediation Center handles cases in which monetary restitution is part of the agreement. In such instances, checks are made payable to the other disputant and are sent or delivered to the Center, which forwards the checks. This procedure prevents people from using "the check is in the mail" ploy. To avoid potential misunderstandings, mediators will include a specific date when monies are due.

A disputant may wish to consult an attorney before signing the agreement. This presents the mediators with a predicament; they are anxious to attain an agreement but must be sensitive to the fact that both sides must be comfortable with the agreement if it is to be honored. The mediators at the Community Mediation Center simply add a clause to the agreement, stating that the terms of the contract will go into effect five business days after signing unless the attorney for either party notifies the Center in writing of objections to the contract. This affords disputants ample time to obtain the necessary legal advice.

On rare occasions, it is advisable not to push for an agreement at the end of the session. Additional information or witnesses may be needed in order to come to a just resolution. If the parties are amenable to a second session, the mediators make the necessary arrangements with the Center's Intake staff for a second session. They ascertain that the parties understand why a second session is necessary and discuss with the disputants the information or witnesses required for the next session.

Regardless of the outcome of the session, the mediators thank the parties for coming and stress once again the rule of confidentiality. If the case involves a formal complaint, they remind the defendant of the obligation to keep his or her next court date, regardless of the outcome of the mediation session. This is very important because failure to appear in court can result in an arrest warrant. If a successfully mediated case involves an information complaint—charges have not entered the legal system—the mediators advise the parties that the Center will notify the referral source as to the disposition of the case. If the mediation has been unsuccessful, the mediators advise the complainant that he or she is free to pursue the matter through the criminal justice system.

Notes and Questions

(1) What Odom refers to as "the private position" is often called a "caucus." It is a private meeting held by the mediator with individual parties. What is said in a caucus is usually held in confidence, but the mediator may set the ground rules by informing the party at the beginning of the caucus that, for example, anything that is said will not be kept from the other party or that he will convey certain kinds of information about the caucus to the other party. What are the advantages and disadvantages of having a caucus confidential? If the ground rules are that the caucus is confidential, how should the mediator deal with a situation in which one party reveals information in the caucus that is not known to the other party and that the mediator deems to be important to the decision-making process?

The caucus allows the mediator to work with parties "to improve their attitudes and perceptions of the other, design procedures to test the accuracy of perceptions, or plan activities that will change negative attitudes." Moore, The Caucus: Private Meetings That Promote Settlement, 16 Mediation Q. 87, 89 (1987). A caucus may permit the mediator to talk frankly with one party, even discussing weak points in that party's case; doing this in the presence of the other party, on the other hand, might give the impression that the mediator favors the other party's side. A caucus may also allow the mediator to test the willingness of the party to accept certain positions or solutions.

A caucus may be initiated by either of the parties or the mediator. Care must be given to the way the mediator introduces the caucus. Generally the parties are told in the opening remarks that a caucus with either of them may be held and that its purpose is to clarify certain matters and not to make a private deal without the other. One commentator suggests: "Once the mediator initiates the caucus, he or she should take (1) steps to join psychologically with the party and build rapport, trust, and confidence in the mediator and the process, and (2) actions to assist the party in overcoming the specific barriers to settlement. . . . Statements such as 'I can see why it has been so tough to negotiate' or 'Looks like it's been pretty hard on you in the session' may indicate to the parties an interest in and empathy for how they are feeling." Moore, supra, at 93. Is there a danger that establishment of too much empathy may affect the mediator's neutral role or imply that the mediator is taking sides? By its very nature the caucus divides the parties. When the mediator is with one, he cannot be with the other; as he builds rapport with one he may be losing credibility with the other. Odom assumes that the mediator "will meet separately with each disputant." Is this wise in every case?

Does the caucus provide too great an opportunity for manipulation by the mediator? "If the intervenor has more information about the parties' sources of power, acceptable settlement ranges, psychological states, and so forth, and controls all communication between them, there is an increased potential for the mediator to shape or actually dictate the terms of settlement." Moore, supra, at 100. The issue of mediator manipulation will be considered further at infra pp. 257–70.

(2) The role of an attorney to a party in a mediation varies greatly. The classical model envisions the parties mediating without attorneys present. The parties may or may not have consulted attorneys, but any such legal advice should have taken place before the mediation. On the other hand, there are mediation models in which attorneys may sit through the mediation with their client but not take an active role (perhaps like attorneys representing a testifying witness in a congressional hearing) or in which the attorneys will take an active part. The role of the attorney will be explored later, infra pp. 300–302, 376–86.

B. THE ROLE OF THE MEDIATOR

The role of the mediator is directly relevant to the concern that mediation should be consensual. The ideal of consensual mediation may be offended not only by coerced participation, but also by an unduly manipulative mediator. Nothing could be more destructive of a process of self-determination between parties than a mediator who determines the outcome through authoritarian behavior or undue influence, or who attempts to dictate the outcome.

The classical model of mediation views the mediator as a facilitator who should not impose upon the parties her view of the dispute or her solution to settlement. But even under the classical nondirective model, the mediator may take a more active role in order to facilitate an agreement. She may use a variety of devices such as focusing the parties on the issues that will achieve a resolution, clearing up the facts and any misconceptions, encouraging understanding of the other party's position, and avoiding unfairness in the mediation process. Whether the mediator should also take an active role in shaping the quality of the agreement, as in achieving what she considers to be substantively "fair," is a more difficult question.

The following materials consider the question of the proper role of the mediator.

SUSAN S. SILBEY & SALLY E. MERRY,
MEDIATOR SETTLEMENT STRATEGIES
8 Law & Policy 7, 12–19 (1986).

[The authors are, respectively, professors of sociology and anthropology at Wellesley College. They spent three years studying a court-related mediation program which handled primarily criminal cases arising out of neighborhood, marital, family, and interpersonal disputes, and a community-based mediation program located in a social service agency which received both interpersonal and small claims case referrals.]

Mediators nudge parties toward settlement by the way in which they describe themselves and their role as mediators. They claim authority based upon either expert knowledge or legal authority. Claims to authority, and by implication deference, are made as the mediators present themselves in their introductions and intermittently throughout the mediation session when they may offer advice, give information about alternatives and factual matters, or brandish language and symbols associated with the law or helping professions.

First, mediators emphasize their expertise as dispute settlers; they describe and present themselves as people who are trained, in the same sense as other experts, and command a store of experience and knowledge that they can bring to the present case. Second, they claim additional sources of authority. In the court-related program, mediators stress their linkage to the court by emphasizing that the court has administered an oath of confidentiality to them; occasionally mediators will claim that they are actually working for the court. In the community-based program, they stress that they are trained to help people reach an understanding of one another. This explanation makes claims to the expert authority associated with helping professionals who employ a communication/therapy frame of reference. In the family program, mediators also present themselves as trained to work with families. Despite the ideology of the mediation movement and orientations of each program, mediators rarely stress their commonality with the disputants or their shared values and norms. Thus they eschew a claim to authority based upon traditional sources of legitimacy.

When parties resist settling, mediators often make statements about the parties' alternatives. Since most cases were referred by the court, it is the logical alternative to a mediation settlement. Mediators in the court-based program stress that going to court is time-consuming and expensive, and that outcomes may be serious. They emphasize the loss of control and possible arbitrariness of the court so that "one just can't predict what may happen." The characterization of the "anarchic" court is offered at the same time that the mediators seek to legitimize themselves and the outcomes of mediation through association with the court. Mediators do not stress that the court process is inherently bad, but that access to its better services is difficult. In contrast, mediators in the community-based program emphasize that the court process is adversarial, perfunctory, and inappropriate to the disputants' problem. They stress that the adjudicative process itself is unhelpful. They are also much less likely to make statements about what a court outcome would look like. Mediators in both programs describe mediation as an alternative to court but an alternative in very different senses. In the first program, they present themselves as people who know the court better than the parties and as agents of the court, and in the second, as people who know how to manage relationships and therefore know what is best for the parties.

Discussion of alternatives is not a series of threats, although mediators suggest that things will go badly in court, and that the disputant is bound to lose and may even go to jail. The allusions to the awful things that could happen in court are neither threats nor coercion in the sense used in the analytic literature because the mediators do not control the outcomes they are describing; the mediators cannot in fact make the situation worse for the participants if they choose not to settle in mediation. Nor are these statements about alternatives a form of persuasion. Although mediators attempt to change the parties' attitude toward the court alternative by emphasizing the inappropriateness of the process, the loss of control, the dichotomous win/lose outcomes, the costs in time and expense, and the unfairness and perhaps even corruptness of the court, it is a covert process. Because the argumentation about alternatives is subtle and implicit, because the mediators do not state outright their intent to the parties, and because it is not a free exchange of communication and argument, it cannot be persuasion in the technical sense of the term, but rather constitutes a form of manipulation.

* * *

Mediators work towards settlement of cases by controlling interaction and communication in the mediation session. This is an important function for mediators in general and a critical aspect of their ability to settle cases. Because mediators help direct the parties toward settlement by focusing discussion, procedurally and substantively, toward a settlement, their actions constitute a form of manipulation. Mediators control the speakers, the audience, the topic, and the length of the discussion. Management of the shape of the discussion is interconnected with manipulating the substance of discussion so that disputants attend to what can be agreed upon and ignore or give up on issues where there is not consensus.

Mediators control the communication flow between the parties by determining the extent to which they speak directly to each other rather than through the mediators. They can control who speaks, allow or disallow interruptions, and encourage and regulate the amount of participation by all parties. The mediators can interrupt and cut off discussion in order to focus it on grounds of settlement. The control of the communication flow is most direct and powerful when mediators caucus frequently. Quite simply, mediators determine when public and private sessions begin and end, the types of information to be exchanged, and the point at which it will be cut off. With more extensive caucusing, the parties speak most often to the mediators, much of the time without the other party present. Thus control over the flow of information creates extended control over the substance of communication as well since the mediators decide what information to pass between the parties.

When the agreement is written without the presence of the parties, it limits further communication and interchange about the exact wording of clauses. In the caucusing model, mediators control almost completely the information that is passed between the parties and thus gently move the parties closer together by slight changes in wording and phrasing, and more forcefully by simply not telling all that was said. At the point of writing an agreement, the mediators pull together the threads of ideas and suggestions made by the parties, rephrase them into more euphemistic, morally neutral terms, often associated with legalistic language, and present the parties with a written document which is designed not to offend. For example, in one dispute in which a family accused a neighbor of throwing eggs at their house and the neighbor denied doing so, after two hours they produced an agreement which read, "X, while not admitting responsibility for the egging, regrets that it occurred and will avoid such actions in the future." As Mather and Yngvesson's (1980–1981) model of dispute transformation suggests, the process of rephrasing a dispute is an important part of the power exercised by a third party. * * * In essence, the rephrasing process "presents a formulation which disputants and others might accept, and at the same time satisfies the interests of a third party." Control of the substantive issues seems to involve four distinct steps: broadening, selecting, concretizing, and finally, postponing issues.

1. *Broadening the Dispute*

In general, mediators regulate the account that is being developed by interpretation and reinterpretation of disputants' statements, determinations of relevance and irrelevance of statements, and styles of discourse. Mediators usually begin by asking questions that will elicit discussion and explanation of what has occurred to bring the parties to mediation. They are looking for a starting narrative and will ask disputants to expand upon simple statements such as "he struck me" to the circumstances and history of the blow. They will then broaden the discussion to encompass other events and circumstances, seeking areas of agreement, shared values, and shared experiences that could be emphasized and built upon for a settlement. "Tell me about how things were before all this started" is a common way of beginning this search. Although there is no single set of questions that can guarantee discovering commonalities, the broadening and searching process is indicated by such statements as: "Did you ever like each other?"; "Do you belong to the same church?"; "Do the children play together?"; "Had anything like this ever happened before the new neighbors moved in?"; and "Was there a time when you were friends or had good relations in the past?"

2. *Selecting Issues*

Through this process mediators uncover a broad range of problems to discuss and acknowledge. From this range of issues, mediators select the ones most likely to be settled. In one case, for example, in which lovers quarreled about the damage the man caused to the woman's apartment in a fit of jealousy, the mediators explored at some length the history of the relationship, their interest in continuing to see each other and the prospects for a future together. Unable to achieve consensus on these issues, the mediators returned to and focused upon the particular damages and losses sustained in the quarrel.

Mediators also establish an appropriate discourse by eliminating issues or people from the discussion. For example, some parties arrive with an extensive apparatus of legalistic "evidence" of past offenses such as logs of harassing phone calls, pictures of offensively parked cars, and bills and receipts from transactions. When this evidence points to fundamental conflicts or irresolvable issues of fact, the mediators define this legalistic, evidentiary mode of discourse as irrelevant and shift the discussion to feelings, morality, and an examination of how future relations should be ordered. Most of the discussion then deals with moral justifications of behavior, of character, and of being reasonable. There is very little explicit discussion of norms. Parties and mediators clearly assume that they share the same "paradigm of argument", and therefore leave norms unstated and implicit.

On the other hand, mediators will seek to narrow disputes, not by defining and eschewing legalistic discourse as irrelevant, but by turning directly to the law and legal charges as means of eliminating other unmanageable issues. They will frequently say that they cannot deal with all the issues presented at this time, but are here to deal with a specific criminal complaint. Thus the legal mode of discourse, which previously may have been irrelevant, is pulled back into the discussion as a means of eliminating other troublesome issues, some of which the mediators may have dredged up themselves.

In addition to eliminating issues, mediators will attempt to eliminate parties from the dispute. Parties will be told that the agreement deals only with the person who signed the original complaint and the person accused, so that the interests and concerns of others present at the session or involved in the dispute are eliminated.

3. *Concretizing Issues*

Once the dispute has been broadened and issues amenable for settlement or more appropriate for discussion have been selected, the next step is to concretize the issues. Mediators will often push for agreements by asking directly, "What is it you are looking for in an agreement?", thereby casting aside all issues but those that constitute a "bottom line." Mediators reshape general complaints and demands into specific behavioral requests. They will make concrete demands for respect between neighbors, more care between spouses, and better service by business people, focusing on a few specific points rather than general attitudinal orientations. For example, a man furious at the loud music next door might be urged to accept a promise that the music will be turned down at 10:00 p.m. every weekday night and 12:00 p.m. on the weekends. Parents quarreling with children about their friends, their social life, and their lack of respect may end up agreeing to have the child phone in nightly at 11:00 p.m. At first glance, this may seem to be a major redefinition of the family problem; however, it is possible to regard this agreement as a behavioral acknowledgement of parental authority and self-control on the part of the child, which was a substantial part of the original disagreement.

Insofar as possible, issues of insult and injury are transformed into property demands. The conversion of interpersonal injuries into property exchanges is the essence of tort law and has a long history in small-scale societies; the same approach is pursued here. For example, a man who was continually harassed by a neighbor's teenage son, which included a barrage of chocolate donuts at his door, reluctantly accepted the price of a gallon of paint to repaint the door as a settlement. Similarly, mediators will rephrase demands and accounts in order to eliminate emotionally loaded language which might connote moral blame or liability.

4. *Postponing Issues*

Finally, when problems seem too difficult to resolve in one session, or simply unresolvable, mediators postpone them. They suggest a future mediation session or a limited time to a present agreement; although only 6 per cent of the cases in the court-affiliated program and 13 per cent of the cases in the community program were postponed, 44 per cent of the agreements in the family program called for a second session. Typically, such agreements read, "X agrees not to drink for three weeks and to pay his wife $80 a week until the next mediation session, scheduled in three weeks." Or, they might read, "X agrees to talk to Mrs. Jones about the placement of the fence while Y agrees to talk to his tenant about his working hours. They will return to mediation in two weeks to discuss the results of their inquiries."

Sometimes, issues which are not easily resolved are sent to counseling, thus suggesting that they belong in a therapeutic arena and not in a process designed to settle "disputes" of legitimate differences. Alcoholics, spouse-abusers, parents who cannot control their children, and husbands and wives who continually fight are routinely sent to counseling. The family mediation program increased the use of social services for almost half the families.

* * *

From [our observations of mediation sessions in a two-year study of mediation programs] we constructed two ideal types of mediation styles: the bargaining and the therapeutic.

These mediation styles are modal/ideal types constructed by synthesizing and typifying the characteristics of over forty mediators. They do not categorize mediators, but describe instead regular patterns of dealing with problems. A single mediator usually uses both styles to some extent, and a single mediation session has some elements of each style. Any particular mediator may adopt one or another strategy, depending upon the particular problem or case, and strategies may change within the duration of any mediation session. Neither the relationship of the parties, nor the type of case (small claims, spouse abuse, neighborhood dispute), nor the sex of the mediator seems to determine which style eventually predominates. Mediation strategies develop through interaction with the parties who come to mediation with sets of expectations, wants and skills with which they endeavor to impose their view of things upon the situation. Thus the degree to which a mediation session is a bargaining or therapeutic event is constructed by implicit negotiation between the parties. Nevertheless, where the parties are known to have longstanding relations, or the issues are emotional ones, mediators often begin with the therapeutic approach. Mediators who are known to adopt one style more than the other may be assigned to cases on this basis. Moreover, mediator strategies seem to become more pronounced and stylized toward one or the other mode with increased experience.

In the bargaining mode, mediators claim authority as professionals with expertise in process, law, and the court system, which is described as costly, slow and inaccessible. The purpose of mediation is to reach settlement. The bargaining style tends toward more structured process, and toward more overt control of the proceedings. In the bargaining style, mediators use more private caucuses with disputants, direct discussion more, and encourage less direct disputant communication than in the therapeutic style. Moreover, in the bargaining style the mediators tend to write agreements without the parties present, summarizing and synthesizing what they have heard from the parties. The job of the mediator is to look for bottom lines, to narrow the issues, to promote exchanges, and to sidestep intractable differences of interest. Typically disputants will be asked directly "What do you want?", ignoring emotional demands and concentrating on demands that can be traded off. Following this bargaining mode, mediators seem to assume that conflict is caused by differences of interest and that the parties can reach settlement by exchanging benefits. When parties resist, the role of the mediator is to become an "agent of reality" and to point to the inadequacy of the alternatives, the difficulty of the present situation and the benefits of a settlement of any kind.

By contrast, the therapeutic style of mediation is a form of communication in which the parties are encouraged to engage in a full expression of their feelings and attitudes. Here, mediators claim authority based on expertise in managing personal relationships and describe the purpose of mediation as an effort to help people reach mutual understanding through collective agreements. Like the bargaining style, the therapeutic mode also takes a negative view of the legal system; but, instead of emphasizing institutional values and inadequacies, the therapeutic style emphasizes emotional concerns, faulting the legal system for worsening personal relationships. In this mode, agreement writing becomes a collective activity, with mediators generally maximizing direct contact between the parties wherever it may lead. Following the therapeutic style, mediators will typically ask, "How did this situation start?", or, "What was your relationship beforehand?" They rely more heavily upon expanding the discussion, exploring past relations, and going into issues not raised by the immediate situation, complaint or charge. There is less discussion of legal norms than within the bargaining mode, and statements about alternatives tend to focus upon appropriateness of process rather than particular outcomes. In addition, the therapeutic mode tends to emphasize the mutuality, reciprocity, and self-enforcement of the agreement in contrast to court or program monitoring.

* * *

The communication approach assumes that misunderstandings or failures of communication, rather than fundamental differences of interest, are the source of conflict, and that with sufficient "sharing" of feelings and history the empathy required for consensus and harmony will be achieved. It assumes that the expression of conflict will help resolve it and that the recognition of shared norms and underlying shared interests will lead to the maintenance of good relationships. Questions typical of the therapeutic approach are generally open, yet probing: "Tell me how you feel about that," or "Are there other things you want to talk about?" It is assumed that parties do not always know what they want and that the job of mediation is to help them define their real wants by exploring their lives and values. Mediators who are more typically therapeutic are often stymied in a way that mediators who are typically bargaining are not, when direct conflicts of interest emerge. Moreover, because of the length of sessions in the therapeutic mode (often four hours or more) there is a sense of wearing the parties down. The mandate for the mediator is clear: to facilitate conversation, not to bargain. Bargaining mediation takes a pragmatic view that parties should settle because they must and because they need to live together, while therapeutic mediation emphasizes the value of handling conflict through rational discourse.

Two cases can serve as examples of mediation style. The first is a case in which the dominant mediator style was bargaining; the second is a case in which the mediator style was essentially therapeutic.

The first case concerns a dispute between a married couple and their teenage daughter over her defiance, overuse of the family's telephone, unwillingness to help with chores, and her spending patterns. The parents filed an application for a complaint against their daughter in juvenile court. In the mediation session, the two mediators begin by asking the family (mother, father, daughter) to describe the situation. After a half-hour discussion, the mediators meet privately, decide that the phone is the major issue and begin to talk about what an agreement might look like. In a private caucus with the child, they ask her to discuss further what is bothering her and whether she thinks it is getting worse. They soon begin asking for suggestions: "What would be a reasonable arrangement for the phone?"; "Is your sister old enough to clean up after herself, and would she be willing to help?"; "If we were going to work out some rules for everyone in the house, what could we work out that might work?" After forty minutes of exploring specific options, the mediators again hold a private discussion, then invite the mother in by herself.

In the private session with the mother, they ask her who does the chores, how the children are punished for failure to do them, and if there is a curfew. They ask the mother what she sees as the problem with the phone, chores, and friends and what she would like to see changed in the family. The mediators then summarize the three major issues: the phone, going out, and how the members of the family deal with one another. They ask the mother to be specific about the chores her daughter is expected to do and when she is to do them. Together, they hammer out a list of rules for chores, phone use, and curfews.

One hour later, the father is called in for a brief (20–minute) session with the mother and the mediators. The mediators again stress that they are working out an arrangement in which the daughter knows what she has to do. In a final private discussion with the daughter, the mediators ask her if she had any other thoughts or concerns. They present the specific proposals and ask if she agrees to them. Their proposals include a promise that her father will talk to her calmly instead of yelling at her. These provisions are incorporated into a formal written document which parents and daughter sign, with the mediators serving as witnesses. The session lasts three hours and fifteen minutes, and the family members seem satisfied.

In this session, the mediators structured the discussion around specific issues through questions which narrowed rather than expanded the dispute. The extensive use of caucusing enabled them to control the exchange of information and to develop and transfer acceptable arrangements. They took an active role in working out the details, rather than encouraging the parties to talk directly to one another or to formulate arrangements entirely on their own. They typically asked clarifying or informational questions or ones which invited the parties to narrow the problem. As this example shows, the extensive use of private sessions with individual parties maximizes the control of the mediators. The parents, searching for guidance and help, did not seem unhappy with this level of intervention by the mediators.

A therapeutic mediation session is a contrast in many ways. One example also concerns a family conflict, but the style of the mediator (there was only one in the session) was quite different. Instead of closing down the emotional issues, the mediator constantly sought to open them up and to expand the frame of the discussion.

The dispute concerns debts which a young man, in his late 20s, had acquired during his marriage. The couple are now living separately and in the process of filing for a divorce. He wants his ex-wife to help him bear the burden of these consumer debts, while she claims that he spent money irresponsibly and she is not liable. He sued her for $750 in small claims court, and the mediation program invited the couple to try mediation. The couple has a hearing in probate court about their divorce in two months, where they expect to settle financial issues and the contested custody of their 10–year–old child. This couple married interracially but found the racial barriers increasingly difficult to handle. The man drank and was violent to his wife, which persuaded her to leave him. He blames the stress of the interracial marriage and her lack of support for his behavior. She wants the divorce and he is resisting it strongly.

The mediator begins this session by allowing the parties to inspect the bills and argue over the amount of the debt and the degree of liability of each. After 35 minutes of mutual accusations about money and past poor behavior, the mediator caucuses with the woman and asks her about the bills and how much she is willing to pay. He then inquires what, besides the bills, she would like to see in an agreement. She replies that she would like the agreement to be final so that he would not come back and go over the incidents between them over and over again. At this point, the mediator asks her to tell him about the incidents and anything else that is bothering her, promising not to convey this to her husband. She responds that, if it is helpful, she will give her version of the incidents, but she is not sure that it is relevant. One hour and ten minutes later, she has thoroughly reviewed the reasons for the breakup of the marriage, her feelings about the divorce, and the nature of the divorce settlement.

In the next caucus, with the man, the mediator spends one hour hearing the husband's version of the conflict and his feelings about the divorce. The mediator then brings them back together and asks the man what he would like from the woman. They renew discussion of the unpaid bills and again try to decide who is responsible for each bill; this is the point at which they began two-and-one-quarter hours earlier. They cannot agree upon responsibility, but finally settle on a plan in which the wife would make a regular, monthly small contribution for one year, at which time the agreement would be renegotiated. Although unwilling to acknowledge responsibility for the bills, the wife is willing to agree to this payment schedule because she expects that the upcoming divorce decision will eventually change this agreement, as well as their relationship. The final discussion of a payment schedule lasts forty-five minutes, and the entire mediation session takes three-and-one-half hours. The woman leaves feeling angry that she has made a concession she does not like, while the man is pleased. Both say they want another session, although they do not come again, nor does the woman make all the payments she promised.

In this session, the mediator began with a narrow financial problem, expanded it into far broader and more emotional areas, even when the parties resisted slightly, then returned at the end to the narrower problem of negotiating the money. Behind his strategy was the theory that the expression of feelings is a necessary precondition to reaching a resolution. As a result, he pursued a strategy we have labeled therapeutic. He constantly invited them to expand the arena of discussion and to move into other facets of their conflict. It is impossible to say if a mediator could have produced the same or a better settlement through focused bargaining, but it is clear that this approach differs a great deal from the bargaining approach. This mediation was unusual for a therapeutic session in its use of private sessions for the bulk of the mediation process, but not unusual in the scope of issues considered and the role of the mediator in probing into feelings.

Comments from mediators about the techniques they use to settle cases further illustrate the differences between the two mediation styles. As these statements suggest, mediator strategies grow out of assumptions about the nature of conflict, conflict resolution, and their own particular capacities and skills. When asked how they settle cases, for example, several mediators expressed a view of their work which leads them to adopt a bargaining mode:

(a) I get people talking, then focus on some issues to get to agreement points. You can't just keep talking.

(b) I take a ball of broad issues and expand it by breaking it down into concrete ones. I see what issues really matter to them and I work on those.

(c) As a mediator, your job is to convince one or the other party to give up something; to negotiate together. The essence of the process is negotiation. You don't accept blame from others of each other, and you also don't accept their version of the facts. I am firm with a loudmouth. In small claims cases, I say that when a person won't settle, I will give it back to the judge and the judge will give him only 30 days to pay.

Here, mediators express a view which leads them to adopt the more therapeutic approach:

(a) My strategy is to try to get the recalcitrant person to see the other's view. If the other person doesn't do it, I do it in caucus myself. It usually works to point out how the other person sees things—that usually produces an agreement.

(b) I look for people's concerns, the reasons why this issue is important to each of them, and try to create an environment where they feel safe enough to articulate that concern. I do this by being open and non-judgmental and by listening to their feelings.

(c) I try just to get people talking, to get them to explain their side fully so that the other side really understands them. The problem is that people don't understand each other's thinking. I try to help them look for solutions.

Notes and Questions

(1) Are any of the techniques described by Silbey and Merry for nudging parties toward settlement inconsistent with the consensual nature of mediation?

(2) Beginning the mediation by asking the parties to state the problem as they see it is designed to allow them to frame the issues and set the agenda. When is it appropriate for the mediator to rephase or refocus the issues? Consider the following analysis of a mediation over a complaint that Spruce's barking dog is interfering with his neighbor Smith's ability to study, from Shaw, Divorce Mediation: Some Keys to the Process, 9 Mediation Q. 27 (1985):

> Suppose the mediator, having heard this statement of the problem by Smith and Spruce, said, "Let's talk about the issue of the howling dog." Consider the course of the discussion that is likely to ensue: "My dog does not howl." "Your dog has barked endlessly day and night for weeks." "None of the other neighbors have complained." "If you don't shoot that dog, I will." "Why don't you find some other place to live if you don't like it."

> Characterizing the issue as "the howling dog" presents two major problems. The first is that the mediator has adopted the issue as framed by one of the parties. The issue so framed assumes a judgment that the dog howls. This leads clearly and inevitably to an offensive-defensive debate between Smith and Spruce.

> A mediator who simply accepts the statement of the problem in the terms used by one or the other of the parties is locked into that person's perceptions of the dispute, perceptions that are a large part of the reason the parties have reached a stalemate and sought outside help. A principle opportunity afforded by mediation is the mediator's ability to perceive the dispute in a different way from the parties and thereby to help them discuss and resolve the dispute effectively.

> The second major problem with framing the issue as "the howling dog" (or indeed even as "the dog") is a more subtle one. Even if the characterization of the dog as howling is eliminated, the discussion that ensues will focus on the dog's behavior. How often has the dog barked in the past? During what hours? How loud? Have other neighbors been bothered?

> Mediation is not a search for the truth. While the truth or falsity of the facts the parties bring may be relevant to a court proceeding, they are not what the issues are all about in mediation.

What if Smith is right that the dog is loud, noisy, beyond Spruce's control, and disturbing to the neighborhood? Perhaps the solution is indeed for Spruce to get rid of the dog. If it is established that the dog's barking is in fact not constant and that none of the other neighbors have complained, then Spruce's position that Smith should "put up or shut up" becomes more persuasive.

Consider the difference in the discussion that would ensue with respect to both the matters in dispute and the possible range of solutions if the mediator characterized the issues as "Smith's study time" and "Spruce's protection." The process would unfold very differently. Is Smith's need for quiet time greatest at night? Would Spruce be willing to take her dog to obedience school in exchange for Smith's studying in the library several nights a week for a defined period?

Is Shaw correct in stating that "[m]ediation is not a search for the truth"? What obligation does a mediator have towards insuring that the truth, at least as to the facts, is presented?

(3) Is the mediator who adopts a theraputic approach more likely to impose his values on the bargaining process? Should there be a distinction between imposing her values and seeking to serve valid mediation objectives such as a consensual agreement? Is the notion of mending the relationship and achieving reconciliation, if possible, a proper objective? See supra pp. 82–89, concerning this objective in negotiating. Is the bargaining approach likely to overlook an opportunity for the mediator to move the parties toward reconciliation?

(4) Is a mediator constrained to work within the structure of rights and obligations established by the law? Consider the following comments in Stulberg & Montgomery, Design Requirements for Mediator Development Programs, 15 Hofstra L.Rev. 499, 504 (1987):

> What distinguishes the mediator's frame of reference from that of other intervenors is that a mediator cajoles parties to agree to settlement terms that are legally permissible even if not legally required. For instance, a mediator might prod a landlord to consider letting a tenant remain in his apartment and accept a schedule of periodic payments for rent in arrears even though the application of the pertinent legal rules in that jurisdiction would incontrovertibly result in a favorable judgment for the landlord. Similarly, a mediator might try to persuade a tenant to consider paying for a necessary improvement to the apartment, even though it is arguably an expense that the landlord should absorb, if the tenant's so acting might induce the landlord to renew the lease for a stated term. * * * What gives mediated negotiations their flexibility is that the mediator is not simply a compliance officer who blindly demands obedience to one set of rules.

The issue of the role of law in mediation is explored more fully in connection with family law mediation, infra p. 294.

(5) Should a mediator be expected to inform herself of the applicable law? Is it realistic to expect that of a non-lawyer mediator? Should a mediator also be expected to inform the parties of the law? Or should that be their own responsibility? Parties engaged in a negotiation surely understand that although they bargain against the backdrop of the law, they choose, by entering a negotiated agreement, to make their own arrangement and to forego the legal procedures available to them, such as discovery from the opponent and examination of witnesses. Is the same true of parties to a mediation? Unlike negotiation where there is no one comparable to a mediator to preside, parties to a mediation have reasonable expectations that the mediator will insure that fair procedures are followed. Are they also entitled to expect the mediator to insure that they are adequately apprised of their legal rights? Should they at least be warned that they may be giving up certain legal rights? When the mediation is conducted under an institutional auspices, as in a court-mandated Conciliation Court, shouldn't they expect a process that gives them more protection than the rough-and-tumble of a negotiation? Would the same be true of a mediation to which they were coerced to attend by a court's or prosecutor's letter?

Dealing With Power Imbalances

Power imbalances, or at least potential power imbalances, arise in every mediation. They can arise out of personality features: one party may be more forceful, articulate, smarter, tougher, have been dominant in the prior relationship between the parties, or be more willing to take the risk of going to court. They can arise out of strategic considerations: one party may have superior information, better access to legal advice, or a better ability to find favorable witnesses or evidence. They can arise out of the inherent strength of one's case: one party may have a more sympathetic position or a stronger legal position. See supra p. 212, for an analysis of power variables in a negotiation setting.

One of the most challenging tasks for a mediator is how to deal with power imbalances. Not all power imbalances are real. The sources of the parties' power may be different and, because the comparative strengths are difficult to assess, one party may not fully appreciate that it has countervailing powers of its own. Mediators often deal with such situations by trying to enhance the perception of equal power. Techniques include encouraging each party to list its bases of power and then identifying the costs and benefits to each from exercising that power.[1] Another method is to shift the focus from power relationships to interests by calling attention to the process of how the parties' needs can be satisfied.[2] The openness of the mediation process is seen as enabling the mediator to remind the parties that they have

1. See Bellows & Moulton, Assessment: Framing the Choices, in The Lawyering Process 998–1017 (1978).

2. See C. Moore, The Mediation Process 280 (1987).

agreed to certain process values such as respect for the other party and a commitment not to intimidate.[3]

Situations in which there is unequal power may arise from one or both parties having a misperception of their strengths or weaknesses or from a genuine "asymmetrical relationship" in which one party is actually in a weaker position and both parties are aware of it. Consider the following discussion by Moore[4] of mediator tactics in such situations:

> Mediators work with both weaker and stronger parties to minimize the negative effects of unequal power. When a mediator encounters a situation in which the balance of power is unequal, the weaker party bluffs about his or her power, and the stronger party accepts the bluff, the mediator should usually meet with the bluffing party to educate him or her about the potential costs of being found out or called on to carry out the bluff. The other party's discovery of the deception can lead to a deterioration in relationships and may lead to retaliation if the victim of the bluff is the stronger party.

> If the intervenor is successful in convincing the party that the costs of bluffing are too high, the mediator and the party should jointly search for a way to retreat from the bluff or minimize the importance of power dynamics in the context of the negotiations. Retreating from a bluff or minimizing the effects of bluff can often be achieved by ceasing to make threatening statements or false promises and obscuring the explicitness of statements describing the consequences of disagreement.

> In power situations in which parties appear to have an asymmetrical relationship and the bases of power are different, the mediator may attempt to obscure the strength of influence of both parties. Mediators can pursue this strategy to create doubt about the actual power of the parties by questioning the accuracy of data, the credibility of experts, the capability of mobilizing coercive power, or the degree of support from authority figures. These techniques will prevent the parties from ascertaining the balance of power. If a party cannot determine absolutely that he or she has more power than another, he or she usually does not feel free to manipulate or exploit an opponent without restraint.

> By far the most difficult problem mediators face regarding power relationships is the instance in which the discrepancy between the strength of means of influence is extremely great. The mediator, because of his or her commitment to neutrality and impartiality, is ethically barred from direct advocacy for the weak-

---

3. Davis & Salem, Dealing with Power Imbalances in the Mediation of Interpersonal Disputes, 6 Mediation Q. 17, 21 (1984).

4. C. Moore, The Mediation Process 281–82 (1987).

er party, yet is also ethically obligated to assist the parties in reaching an acceptable agreement.

* * *

[T]he mediator should initiate moves to assist the weaker party in mobilizing the power he or she possesses. The mediator should not, however, directly act as an organizer to mobilize or develop new power for the weaker disputant unless the mediator has gained the stronger party's approval. To act as a secret advocate puts the mediator's impartiality and effectiveness as a process intervenor at risk.

Empowering moves may include assisting the weaker party in obtaining, organizing, and analyzing data and identifying and mobilizing his or her means of influence; assisting and educating the party in planning an effective negotiation strategy; aiding the party to develop financial resources so that the party can continue to participate in negotiations; referring a party to a lawyer or other resource person; and encouraging the party to make realistic concessions.

Fairness of the Settlement

Related to the question of power imbalances is that of the mediator's role in assuring fairness. There is general agreement that a mediator should insure fairness in process, but whether she should also take steps to insure that the final agreement is fair is a more controversial issue. A continuing debate in mediation literature is that of mediator neutrality versus accountability.[5] The classical position is that the mediator should avoid taking responsibility for the fairness of the settlement.[6] If the parties, acting with consent after an open discussion that is fair in process terms, decide on a solution, it is said that the mediator should not impose her view of what the result should have been. This view gains support from the reality that there is no easily-agreed upon objective standard as to what is fair in the particular case. This resolution, however, continues to be troubling to some:

> One student, however, in observing a divorce mediation, saw that the mediator very clearly assessed whether a certain financial settlement would be fair and adequate for the wife, and that when he found it would not be, encouraged the wife to refuse it and pressured the husband to make a more generous offer. Troubled by the role conflicts inherent in adopting this kind of judgmental posture as mediator, the student grasped much more powerfully the conflict between the neutrality and accountability arguments in mediation theory. He also saw that the orthodox theory may simply not apply when mediators face the practical test of sitting

---

5. Compare Susskind, Environmental Mediation and the Accountability Problem, 6 Vt.L.Rev. 1 (1981) with McCrory, Environmental Mediation—Another Piece of the Puzzle, 6 Vt.L.Rev. 49 (1981).

6. Stulberg, The Theory and Practice of Mediation: A Reply to Professor Susskind, 6 Vt.L.Rev. 85, 86–87 (1981).

passively by and watching a disadvantaged party willingly accept a grossly unfair settlement.[7]

C. SOME FREQUENT USES OF MEDIATION

1. Community Disputes

Although labor-management relations was the first significant area in which mediation was used in the United States, community dispute mediation has, in the last twenty years, become the most pervasive use of the technique.   Neighborhood Justice Centers sprang up in the 1960's under the impetus of federal government grants under the poverty and other Great Society programs.   They were sometimes adjuncts of the Legal Services offices established to provide legal assistance to the poor.   At the same time there was increased interest at the local level in establishing alternatives to courts, and community mediation centers began to develop with sponsorship from such sources as local governments, churches and charities, and community organizations.   Specialized forms of mediation were sometimes developed by particular institutions and government agencies to attempt to resolve misunderstandings in such areas as community-police relations, race relations, hospital and health care services, environmental protection, and divorce and family law problems.

The common purpose of neighborhood and community mediation centers was to provide free, or low-cost, services to the public to resolve disputes.   Originally conceived of as a source of resolving "minor disputes," the community mediation movement has come to embrace a broad range of local and interpersonal problems.   There has often been an emphasis on encouraging participation by residents of the particular community to be served both as board members and mediators.   Certain vague social and political ideals underlay this movement.   These included the desirability of having individuals voluntarily resolve their own disputes; a distrust of governmental agencies as tending to impose "bureaucratic" and "outside" solutions on the community; a conviction that courts are unresponsive to the needs and interests of disadvantaged persons and communities and that legal rules are often inflexible and unpragmatic; an assurance that personal relationships within a community are more important than juridical relationships; and a belief that lawyers are often elitist, expensive, and coopted by the system.   Neighborhood centers varied considerably in the extent to which these attitudes were motivating forces in the operation of mediation services, but they are clearly part of the historical and ideological baggage of the community mediation movement.

Community mediation services also shared a common methodological approach to dispute resolution.   Although the exact form of mediation varied from center to center, a standard methodology gradually

---

7. Bush, Using Process Observation to Teach Alternative Dispute Resolution: Alternative to Simulation, 37 J. Legal Educ. 46, 52 (1987).

became accepted. This methodology was spread by mediator trainers and training handbooks. The methodology has some affinities to the social ideals of community dispute resolution already discussed. If people should be encouraged to resolve their own disputes, the mediator should use a non-directive style that encourages the parties to communicate but minimizes his role. If voluntariness is important, the mediation should be initiated by the parties who should not be coerced into engaging in it. If parties are more likely to abide by agreements that they have worked out between themselves, the mediator should only be a facilitator for discussion and problem solving and should not attempt to influence the parties in favor of or against particular solutions. And if the legal system is distrusted, both because of its procedures and the inflexibility of the law, mediation should encourage parties to resolve disputes without concern for how the legal system would resolve them if the case went to trial.

The degree of acceptance of these ideals varies from community to community and from mediator to mediator. But there is probably still more similarity between mediation philosophy and styles than difference among community mediators.

RAYMOND SHONHOLTZ, NEIGHBORHOOD JUSTICE SYSTEMS: WORK, STRUCTURE, AND GUIDING PRINCIPLES

5 Mediation Q. 3, 13–16 (1984).

[The author is the president of the Community Boards Program of San Francisco, California, the nation's first program, begun in 1976, for providing "neighborhood justice" services such as dispute resolution, crime prevention, and community education and outreach.]

Conceptually, the community board model advances a community-based normative justice system. The model is premised on a community perspective, and it is based on four rationales: First, the diversity and complexity of societal life directly encourage the strengthening of nonstate social entities. This rationale urges the commitment of social resources within the community and the revival of community responsibility to articulate and project social mores. Second, suppression of conflict, whether individual or community, is destructive to the safety and vitality of individual and community life. Community justice forums provide a ready vehicle for the early expression and potential resolution of conflict. Third, community justice forums correspond to resident needs to organize local conflict resolution mechanisms and recognize that conflicts provide important contextual material for individuals and communities. Fourth, the development and maintenance of community justice forums is a democratic right and responsibility of citizens.

Organizationally, the community board model emphasizes community and individual referral of cases to neighborhood panels composed of three to five local residents trained in value building, communication, and conciliation skills. Panel sessions are open and generally held in community or church facilities. The program stresses the importance and values of conflict expression. In the training programs, hearing sessions, and community meetings, the program seeks community expression of shared (normative) values. Specifically, through the case hearing experience, the program addresses normative values within the neighborhood and panel community.

Four basic assumptions underlie the community board approach. First, conflict is seen as having positive value. Conflict has important contextual meaning, and it is conducive to improvement and change. In sharp contrast, the justice and medical models view conflict as acting out—a manifestation of individual deviance or social illness. From these negative models, the justice system has developed a practice and procedure for conflict avoidance, suppression, and manipulation that is destructive to individual change and community awareness.

Second, peaceful expression of conflict within the community is also seen as having positive value. This is because the expression of hostilities and differences within the community serves to inform and educate, which creates a base for greater understanding and mutual work between disputants. The greater the degree of conflict expression, the greater the likelihood for reduced tensions and the greater the potential for common accords. The justice system practice of having the conflict expressed by the disputants' representatives robs the disputants not only of the expression of the conflict but of the conflict itself.

Third, the community board approach emphasizes that the individual and the neighborhood should exercise responsibility for a conflict. This emphasis is based on the view that nonstate social entities are weakened in society in large part by the state's assumption that they are incompetent and by transfer of the problem to a state agency. By promoting professional attention to conflicts and by controlling the scope, procedures, and remedies allowed by means of state licensing and school accreditation requirements, the state deskills individuals and nonstate social entities and makes them dependent on external state-funded or state-licensed entities. In contrast, by placing the conflict within the skill and competence of trained community people, many of whom are former disputants, the forum is able to place responsibility for the expression and resolution of conflict on the disputants themselves. Moreover, the forum is the community's statement of its capacity and confidence to accept responsibility for handling conflicts at the neighborhood level. The assumption of individual and community responsibility is a positive value that serves to enhance the vitality and stability of the neighborhood.

Fourth, the voluntary resolution of conflict between disputants is held to have positive value, because coerced resolutions have inherent limitations: of parties, of enforcement, of attitude, of future relations, of understanding, and of future conflict resolution modeling. Voluntary resolutions are first and foremost a positive statement between the disputants about themselves, each other, and the situation. If there are limitations, disputants recognize what they are. If other parties participate in the dispute, disputants recognize their contribution. If additional social resources are needed, disputants make the determination. If future problems arise, disputants have a process to model, or they can invoke the forum anew. Voluntary resolutions made in the interests of disputants do not need coercion to be maintained. Nor are power differentials (for example, between landlord and tenant) minimized by the introduction of coercive forms. The broad community endorsement of the forum and the respect for its process are the boundary lines of its authority and force.

By building a system of community justice forums, community boards demonstrate that neighborhoods have important civil functions to perform. Certainly, local residents perform civic functions when they are directly engaged in the resolution of conflicts. This civic activity is an attempt by neighborhoods to manage themselves and their own conflicts. The civic function is not prescribed by statute; rather, it is an aspect of the right and responsibility of citizens in a democratic society to prevent violence and assert social harmony. Community justice forums are embryonic democratic activity and institutions in the urban neighborhood. Since this democratic responsibility and assertion of neighborhood self-governance is not based on state authority, it cannot be imposed. To be effective, community justice forums must be relevant to all segments of the community. It is important to recognize that the widest possible representation of the community's diversity is more important for the effectiveness of the community justice forum than the speed with which the service system is established or with the volume of cases handled.

Notes and Questions

(1) What is the community from which the norms invoked in the "community-based normative justice system" described by Shonholtz are derived? Does the mere fact that parties live in the same neighborhood or city insure that they recognize a common set of values? Can you identify any generally-shared societal and community values that would be useful in settling disputes? Is it appropriate to infuse individual disputes with a community-value overlay? Does this approach improperly impose an overlay of abstract ideals on problem-solving?

(2) Should mediation sessions be open to the public, as Shonholtz says is done under the San Francisco program? Do parties really want to resolve their disputes in public? What is the public interest that justifies this? Most community mediation centers do not follow this practice and conduct mediations in private.

(3) Mediation sponsored by religious organizations for their members obviously can invoke a broader set of shared norms. Consider the

following account of a mediation by the executive director of the Christian Legal Society:

> [W]e must never forget that the goal behind each step of the process, as outlined in Matthew 18:15–20, is to achieve reconciliation. The goal is never "to come out on top." This is the chief difference between the secular approach and the Christian approach to settling disputes. The world says, "Win the marbles!" The Lord says, "Reconcile the parties!" The issue, as far as the Lord is concerned, is not who wins the marbles, because they're all His to begin with. We would do well to remember that we are merely the Lord's stewards, and that from time to time He shifts trusteeship among us. Of much more concern to the Lord is the restoration of broken relationships.

> A couple of years ago the church I attend was involved in the construction of a new facility—a 2.3 million dollar project. The church had a fixed-price contract, which means that the contractor is expected to cover any unforeseen contingencies. To lock in the price the church had to pay a little extra up front.

> Well, half way through the project, there was a $180,000 cost overrun. The contractor maintained that the county had required him to shift the location of the building, among other things, resulting in the cost overrun. The church said, "We're sorry about that, but that's your problem, not ours. You should have known." So a dispute arose. Finally, it got to the point where the pastor announced to the congregation that the board of trustees would be meeting with the contractor. "If we don't settle this thing then," the pastor said, "we may have to go to court."

> Afterward, I went to the chairman of the trustees and said, "It was my impression that the contractor is a Christian."

> "Well, Sam, that's what he tells us. But Christians should not act this way."

> I then asked the chairman for permission to attend the meeting as an observer, and permission was granted. At the meeting, I listened for an hour and a half as the two parties discussed the $180,000 overrun. It was fairly obvious that both parties had acted in good faith. There was no intentional wrongdoer here, but there was still the problem of the $180,000. Both sides had good legal grounds. What should they do?

> I gradually got into the discussion and talked about 1 Corinthians 6:1–11, "How dare you sue one another?" Within another hour and a half the two parties had reached a settlement. The church agreed to pay an additional $70,000, and the contractor was willing to absorb $110,000. My law school professors would have been proud. Only one and a half hours to settle a dispute of this nature without the necessity of a lawsuit.

Ericsson, How Dare You Sue One Another!, in Implications (Christian Legal Society 1988).

What were the shared norms relied on in this mediation? Is it an aversion to suits derived from the Biblical passage from Matthew, a greater willingness to compromise derived from the religious principle that we are merely stewards of worldly goods, or something else? Biblical passages can sometimes be found to support conflicting sentiments or courses of action. Should "Christian mediators" set out the relevant passages by which the parties agree to be governed? Can the Bible, or other religious tenets, replace legal standards as the proper standards for the mediation?

(4) Community dispute resolution centers (DRC's) usually operate with volunteer mediators. The type of person willing to devote time and energy to such volunteer work varies considerably. There are community centers in low income areas where mediators come from the community, but many mediation centers draw heavily from middle and upper-middle class persons and disproportionately from professionals in law, social work, government, or education. Their motivations are varied and complex, probably including a desire to help others and the community, to broaden their experiences, to learn new skills, to find a community of like souls, and to further their career advancement or a change of occupation. There is increasing pressure for state licensing or certification of mediators with requirements of mandatory training. See SPIDR Commission on Qualifications, Draft Issues and Preliminary Principles (Oct. 1988); Comment, The Dilemma of Regulating Mediation, 22 Hous.L.Rev. 841 (1985); R. Coulson, Professional Mediation of Civil Disputes 20–22 (1984).

(5) Relying on volunteers reduces the cost of operation, but a source of funding is still needed for a professional staff, rent, and operating expenses. Methods of financing community mediation include grants by governmental bodies from general tax revenues, budgetary support as an integral part of a government agency, gifts from religious, charitable, or nonprofit organizations, and payments for services based on user fees or contracts. In Texas, a statute gives county commissioners the authority to add up to $10 to the filing fee to fund alternative dispute resolution. The county may use the fund to pay a county agency or a not-for-profit entity under contract to operate a DRC. Tex.Rev.Civ.Stat.Ann. art. 2732aa. Is it fair to make plaintiffs fund ADR? Could it be unconstitutional? See LeCroy v. Hanlon, 713 S.W.2d 335 (Tex.1986) (a statute, unrelated to ADR, that increased filing fees to benefit general revenues was found to violate a Texas constitutional provision guaranteeing "open courts.") DRC's, however, have a direct relationship to the judicial function, and arguably increasing the filing fee to support an ADR fund is different from simply aiding the general revenues. No legal challenge has been made to the Texas ADR statute.

(6) Community DRC's get their cases from a variety of sources, including "walk-ins" and "call-ins," but referrals from government

entities, prosecutors and police, and courts are often a principal source. Such referrals raise questions as to the voluntariness of participation, since they sometimes carry the suggestion, for example, that the prosecutor, court, or agency will go harder on the parties unless they go through mediation. The manner of referral also raises questions as to the independence of the DRC from the government, a concern that may affect its ability to win the confidence of persons having disputes with the government.

(7) Persons with problems arising out of disputes often do not know where to go for assistance in solving them. During the 1975 National Conference on the Causes of Popular Dissatisfaction with the Administration of Justice, Professor Frank Sander proposed the "multi-door courthouse" concept, a coordinated system at the county or city level for referring citizens to the most appropriate dispute resolution process to solve their particular problem. See Sander, The Multidoor Courthouse, 63 National Forum: The Phi Kappa Phi Journal (Fall 1983). It has been implemented in a number of cities, including Houston, Tulsa, and Washington, D.C.

Under a multi-door program, an information and referral network links the various trial courts (justice of the peace, small claims, and basic trial courts); prosecutors' offices; governmental and private service agencies (including mental health); and alternative dispute resolution centers. Complaints and requests, in person or by telephone, are sent to an intake specialist who refers the individual to the most appropriate office. "After clarifying the issues and analyzing 'case type' characteristics, the intake specialist attempts to match the dispute with 'process' characteristics of the referral agency, such as financial eligibility requirement; immediate availability of services; likelihood of sanctions or financial compensation; protection of rights; necessity of evidence or witnesses; and the degree of 'agency' or 'citizen' control maintained by the referred service." Wolff & Ostermeyer, Dispute Resolution Centers: Citizen Access to Justice, 51 Tex.Bar J. 51, 52 (1988).

Can we really expect personalized attention from an intake office of this kind? What criteria would the specialist use to determine whether a complaint about criminal conduct should go to a prosecutor or a mediation center? Should the choice of process be made by the complainant, or should it be encouraged or required by the intake office? If the complainant is represented by an attorney, should he be forced to go through this process? Can we assume that attorneys take the same time and attention in advising a client of the varied remedies available? Should more time be spent in training attorneys in the possibilities of dispute resolution process choices?

The Significance of Consent in Mediation

A recurring theme in mediation literature is that mediation works because the parties have consented to participate and because any agreement must be mutually acceptable. "By definition," Professors Folberg and Taylor have written, "a consensual agreement, whether reached through mediation or direct negotiation, reflects the participants' own preferences and will be more acceptable in the long run than one imposed by a court. In the process of mediation, participants formulate their own agreement and make an emotional investment in its success. They are more likely to support its terms than those of an agreement negotiated or imposed by others." [1]

Like many processes, mediation does not always live up to its advance billing, and the touted element of consent is a prime example. If mediation were strictly limited to situations in which the parties' participation is entirely consensual, many of its contemporary uses would be foreclosed. As appreciation of the utility of mediation has grown, so too have mediation devices in which the parties are encouraged or pressured in a variety of ways into participation.

The most obvious form of coerced participation is in a dispute that has been the subject of a criminal complaint. Professor Nancy Rogers and mediator Richard Salem provide the following example:

> Mediation workers in New York City interview complainants in minor assault, cohabitant violence, criminal trespass and related cases at the Municipal Court in Manhattan. If the intake worker deems the case appropriate for mediation, the respondent will be "served" by the complainant or by mail, with a form, headed "Criminal Court of the City of New York," listing the allegations and requesting the party to appear at the mediation center "at which time an inquiry will be made of the said allegation." If the respondent fails to appear, the form warns, "a criminal action against you may be commenced without your having an opportunity to be heard." [2]

Similar kinds of pressure arise when government agencies require parties to go through mediation as a prerequisite, for example, to being allowed to continue to rent an apartment in a low income housing project, to receive welfare or other assistance, to avoid expulsion of a child from school, or to obtain enforcement of zoning, land use, or other governmental regulations. Pressure may also arise in the private sector, for instance, when an employer requires an employee to mediate with a disputing co-employee or with an outsider, like a merchant, over an ongoing dispute.

Mediation mandated by law is the ultimate form of coercion. This includes requirements of mediation in cases involving child custody or visitation,[3] labor disputes,[4] and employment discrimination.[5]

1. J. Folberg & A. Taylor, Mediation: A Comprehensive Guide to Resolving Conflicts Without Litigation 10 (1984).

2. N. Rogers & R. Salem, A Student's Guide to Mediation and the Law 19–20 (1987).

3. See Cal.Civ.Code § 4607; Me.Rev. Stat.Ann. title 19, § 752(4).

4. See Ohio Rev.Code Ann. § 4117.14; 44 Ind.Code Ann. §§ 20–7.5–1–12, 20–7.5–1–13.

5. See 42 U.S.C. § 2000e–4(g).

Even where participation in mediation is not coerced, parties often agree to participate in it because of pressure. Pressure that a party cannot resist can come from a judge or prosecutor who "encourages" mediation, a counsellor or member of the clergy, members of the family or friends, or even the opposing party. Thus in some mediations, at least one party is a reluctant participant. This does not mean, of course, that a resulting mediation is not voluntary, but it signifies that the degree of cooperativeness may vary considerably from party to party and that the mediator must be aware of this possibility. It should also be remembered that coerced participation is not coerced agreement; no party to mediation can be forced to enter an agreement.

The consensual nature of mediation is often claimed to promote compliance by the parties with the result. If the parties have been free to formulate their own agreement, the conventional wisdom goes, they are more willing to abide by it. But parties come away from mediation with varying attitudes, just as do parties from litigation. It is human nature to relive the mediation, rehashing what one would have liked to have said or liked to have presented. Parties to a mediation sometimes feel surprised or unfairly treated as do litigants. Like the audience at an auction, mediating parties are sometimes capable of being swept up in the flow of the proceeding, resulting in later regrets. An objective of a mediator, of course, is to prevent the mediation from having this effect and to insure that any settlement is acceptable to both sides. But the success of mediation in terms of individual satisfaction and compliance is still a matter of some dispute.

The following materials consider the significance of consent on achieving agreement and compliance in mediation.

CRAIG A. McEWEN & RICHARD M. MAIMAN, MEDIATION IN SMALL CLAIMS COURT: ACHIEVING COMPLIANCE THROUGH CONSENT

18 Law & Soc'y Rev. 11, 40–47 (1984).

[The authors, respectively professors of sociology/anthropology at Bowdoin College and of political science at University of Southern Maine, studied small claims disputes in Maine in the late 1970's, concluding that mediation is more likely to produce greater compliance by the parties than litigation.]

Participatory, consensual settlements of conflict differ substantially from adjudicated outcomes in both their character and underpinnings. The form of adjudication constrains both the information presented in court and the range of available solutions. Even without such constraints, people not only have reasons for acting that third parties cannot perceive and so cannot take into account, but the actors themselves may not appreciate their motives and the balance between them unless the decision-making process encourages self-realization. The adjudicator must reach closure on the basis of information presented in court and can do so because solutions can be imposed.

For consensual agreements the key to closure is litigant satisfaction. Even where satisfaction is contextually dependent in the sense that an outcome is satisfactory because it is "least undesirable," feelings of satisfaction are likely to respond to a range of considerations that will have little or no influence when solutions are imposed. These include values and norms embedded in non-legal institutions, tastes for risk, and the idiosyncratic ways in which time, money, and aggravation can be relatively weighted. While settlements are no doubt shaped by the parties' shared expectations of what going to court means, the fact that so many variables may come into play creates substantial pressure to break the mold of traditional adjudicative outcomes. Thus, it is not surprising that mediation and negotiation produced six of the seven outcomes we observed in which the defendant was obliged to do something other than pay money to the plaintiff, and twelve of the fourteen in which the plaintiff undertook some obligation to the defendant.

Facilitating the free consideration of multiple variables is the fact that consensual settlements do not have to be explicitly justified. The legitimacy of a judge's decision depends on an explicit, reasoned connection between the result and a general rule, but an individual or group can explain a decision to settle on vague and general grounds—"it's fair" or "it's the best I could expect".[18] When rationales do not have to be well articulated, decisions can more easily reflect idiosyncratic value preferences, feelings that are not easily identified, and inconsistencies that are hard to reconcile. By contrast, when a judge articulates a reason for a decision, he or she provides a clear target for dissatisfaction and criticism. This may happen even where it is possible to advance reasons that the disadvantaged party would accept, since the judge may not know which of the possible justifications for his or her decision are acceptable. The failure to articulate reasons provides no escape so long as the parties expect a decision accompanied by reasons.[19]

The consensual settlement process has an important interpersonal component as well, although this aspect of the process may vary substantially depending on the type and extent of participation allowed the parties to the dispute. In particular, interaction in mediation or negotiation often has a strong normative character. Bargainers use norms as levers to persuade other parties to accept particular settlements (e.g., "Don't you think it's fair that you pay me something for using my property?"). Bargainers also remind one another of the

18. For this reason, groups in conflict may find it more difficult to achieve consent than individuals in conflict. The representatives of a group must articulate reasons for accepting or rejecting a proposed outcome in order to convince the group to endorse a position. This process requires articulation of criteria by which an outcome can be judged and thus moves the decision process closer to adjudication.

19. When a jury renders a verdict and in certain forms of arbitration, such as baseball salary arbitration, there is no expectation that the verdict will be accompanied by supporting reasons.

practical consequences of their decisions (e.g., "You can save time and aggravation."). Mediators similarly highlight relevant norms, mutual obligations, and the practical implications of choices, but they do it from the vantage point of a formally disinterested third party. They also provide a third party's view of the relative merits of the conflicting cases. This allows each party to make what may be a more realistic prediction of the likely results of adjudication and so may help induce a settlement. Conversely, by highlighting the merits of opponents' positions, mediators may lead both parties to exaggerate their risks of loss in adjudication. Where a pair of predictions is unrealistic in this way, the chance of settlement is high.

While the sense that an agreement is fair is one inducement to settle, it is by no means necessary. Participants in consensual processes are only slightly more likely than recipients of court judgments to assess outcomes as fair. The multiplicity of rationalizations that consensual processes allow neatly absorbs the wide range of inducements for settlement that affect the disputants in the interaction, and the fact that rationales do not have to be articulated helps avoid the impasse that could be created by the need to save face. The multidimensionality of consent is illustrated by a sampling of the reasons given by litigants for agreeing to mediated settlements that they later characterized as unfair:

> "I felt we still were going nowhere—the mediator, actually, I felt the mediator leaned toward them and the judge would have done the same." (plaintiff)

> "By then I was worn down; I was tired of it. I wanted to finish and get out of there, to get away from them." (plaintiff)

> "I felt I'd accomplished my goal. I'd let her know that she couldn't get away with it." (plaintiff)

> "Because it was proved I was partially wrong. I was happy to get it off my back." (defendant)

> "Best agreement we could expect to get." (defendant)

> "Time. I had to catch a plane. I knew that the judge might have hit me with the whole bill. I think the judge would've had a fit if we brought it to court for just a few dollars difference." (defendant)

The internal and interactional dynamics of consensual settlement processes combine to create pressures toward compliance that are largely lacking in adjudication. In the interactive process, opportunities exist for reciprocal obligations that provide powerful incentives for performing in accordance with the agreement. Such reciprocation is clearest in cases where the plaintiff assumes an obligation to the defendant in return for payment. The establishment of payment schedules and the arrangement of immediate payment are less obvious examples of such concessions. In the former case, the defendant typically concedes a larger proportion of the debt in return for the opportunity to pay it off in relatively small amounts over a long period of time. Thus, we find that the consensual settlements as proportions of claims are higher, on the average, in cases where payment schedules are laid out than in cases where they are not (69 percent compared to 43 percent). It may be that there is on both sides a substantial amount of face-saving in such arrangements, for both parties may anticipate that only some of the scheduled payments will be made.

On the other hand, immediate payment of a debt is a substantial concession by the defendant and is purchased by the plaintiff through reduction of the claim. Consensual settlements are, on the average, only 39 percent of claims when immediate payment is arranged and 54 percent when it is not.[20] Overall, the pattern of compliance suggests strongly that we see the norm of reciprocity at work.

Even when reciprocity is slight, the very act of choosing to accept a settlement that might have been rejected may generate pressures that favor compliance. Agreement may, in effect, reinstitutionalize legal norms at the personal level, adding guarantees of personal honor to the formal guarantees of law. Also, pressures toward cognitive consistency, as suggested by a variety of social-psychological theories, may lead one to structure later behavior in accordance with prior commitments, as may the possibility of embarrassment. These overlapping pressures presumably work independently of formal controls emanating from the courts.[21]

Compliance, of course, is not guaranteed either by commitments arrived at through consent or by obligations imposed by a legitimate authority. Considerations of self-interest may override the internal controls activated by consent or command. People motivated by self-interest have a substantial capacity to forget or reinterpret obligations. The less clearly defined the behavior required for compliance and the

20. In part because they are aware of this calculus, judges make similar trade-offs when they issue judgments involving either immediate payment or payments over time. In adjudication cases the amount of the judgment is a lower proportion of the claim (50%) when immediate payments are arranged than when they are not (63%) and a higher proportion of the claim (77%) when time payments are arranged than when they are not (58%). Although we have little direct evidence to demonstrate it, we suspect that the same combinations of settlement level and payment arrangements have different meanings if they are imposed than if they are arrived at through the give-and-take of bargaining. In particular, the imposition of such a "compromise" judgment carries with it none of the pressures for compliance generated by reciprocal concessions. Thus, the relationship between settlement size as a proportion of the claim and compliance is weaker for adjudicated cases than for those resolved consensually. There is a non-compliance rate of 6% in cases settled by consent for 45% or less of the claim as compared to 24% among comparable adjudicated cases.

21. The legitimacy that individuals may accord agreements ratified by a court can also contribute to compliance with settlements. Legitimacy, among other things, reflects the beliefs of individuals in the rightness and/or inevitability of institutionalized authority. People comply with commands in part because such behavior is consistent with belief in that authority. Obedience may occur because disobedience is difficult to contemplate or because it helps one maintain a consistent self-image as a good and loyal citizen. There is, however, no clear distinction between court-ratified settlements and judgments with respect to this source of legitimacy.

longer the obligation remains unfulfilled, the easier it becomes to justify non-compliance.[22]

Indeed, one might well ask why any small claims defendants meet their obligations at all. The power of the small claims court to enforce compliance is extremely limited. Self-interest seems to invite defiance, and defiance does occur, although considerably more often in adjudicated than in mediated or negotiated cases. But complete defiance, even in adjudication, is the exception rather than the rule. This suggests that losing litigants extend legitimacy to judicial judgments and/or that they exaggerate the likelihood of punishment should they fail to comply. When a judgment confirms a consensual settlement, these pressures toward compliance may be reinforced and are complemented by others we have identified.

Consent, unlike command, brings with it an assumption of responsibility for the settlement and for its implementation. This sense of responsibility, along with general normative pressures to live up to commitments, can weigh heavily on disputants, even those who may regret having given consent in the heat of negotiation or mediation. The more explicit these pressures, the more effective they are. Our data suggest that the personal and immediate commitments generated by consensual processes bind people more strongly to compliance than the relatively distant, impersonal obligations imposed by authorities.

* * *

Our data on small claims mediation and adjudication provide strong evidence that consent is a powerful adjunct to command in securing compliance with behavioral standards. Consent enlists a sense of personal obligation and honor in support of compliance, and consensual processes are more open than command to the establishment of reciprocal obligations and of detailed plans for carrying out the terms of an agreement. Consent may also be more likely than command to leave both parties—not just the winner—with the feeling that the outcome was fair or just. These characteristics of consent mean that consensual solutions are more likely to be complied with than those imposed by adjudication, at least when they are ratified by a court or backed up by the threat of adjudication.

Notes and Questions

(1) Following the McEwen and Maiman study of Maine small claims disputes, Neil Vidmar conducted a study of small claims disputes

---

22. Thus, the simpler, the more immediate, and the less ambiguous the commitment or judgment, the greater the likelihood of compliance. For example, a commitment to pay $100 within two weeks is clear and simple as compared with a promise never again to insult one's neighbor. In the latter case, one can justify a violation of the promise because the behavior constituting an insult is not clear (e.g., "I didn't really insult him; he just thinks I did."). In addition, when an agreement extends over time, one can often find in the other party's behavior a subjectively acceptable rationale for breaking an agreement. One may also develop substantial motives for doing so if changed conditions mean that compliance over time is more onerous than one anticipated.

in Ontario. Vidmar, The Small Claims Court: A Reconceptualization
of Disputes and an Empirical Investigation, 18 Law & Soc'y Rev. 515
(1984); Vidmar, An Assessment of Mediation in a Small Claims Court,
41 J. Social Issues 127 (1985). He concluded that a case characteristic,
namely whether the defendant admits partial liability, is more important than effects produced by the type of procedural forum. McEwen
and Maiman, looking at his data, disagreed. McEwen & Maiman, The
Relative Significance of Disputing Forum and Dispute Characteristics
for Outcome and Compliance, 20 Law & Soc'y Rev. 439 (1986). Regarding their conclusion that there is greater compliance with consensual,
than with authoritative, decisions, Vidmar commented [Vidmar, Assessing the Effects of Case Characteristics and Settlement Forum on
Dispute Outcomes and Compliance, 21 Law & Soc'y Rev. 155, 162–63
(1987)]:

> In systematic observations of 204 mediated hearings I and the
> members of my research team uncovered the fact that defendants
> owing money were given subtle and not-so-subtle hints about the
> need for compliance and the possible sanctions if compliance was
> not forthcoming. This occurred even when specific payment ar-
> rangements were not made by the referee. Interestingly, these
> kinds of pressures were more likely to be exerted in Partial
> Liability cases than in No Liability cases. In contrast, observations
> of 73 trials yielded not a single instance of discussions of payment;
> judges dealt only with liability and damage assessment. Thus
> while I cannot rule out the possibility that defendants owing money
> derived a sense of obligation through consensual processes, there is
> evidence suggesting that in mediation obligations were emphasized
> in an authoritative, coercive way while in adjudication payment
> obligations were completely ignored.

> This raises the third matter, namely what one wants to consid-
> er as "consensual" processes. McEwen and Maiman (1986) argue
> that if disputing processes differ and produce differing effects on
> compliance, this finding tells us only how these processes differ, not
> that process is unimportant. I submit that if the mediation process
> that results in compliance is authoritative and coercive we should
> not ascribe consensual characteristics to it. The methodological
> lesson is that we need to examine each mediation (or adjudication)
> session to determine what occurred; only then can we assess the
> relative contributions of coercive versus consensual processes.

* * *

McEwen and Maiman and I agree, I think, that both forum
type and case characteristics play their part in contributing to
dispute outcomes and compliance, so the real issue for future
research should be how and when these factors combine with one
another. The methodological message of my reply to the reanal-
ysis by McEwen and Maiman is that just because a procedure is
labeled as mediation or adjudication that does not necessarily make
it so. We must examine the process of resolution and do so on a

case-by-case basis. A satisfactory resolution of the issues raised in our debate will require some new data sets.

(2) If McEwen and Maiman's study correctly indicates that mediation is better able than adjudication to create a sense of obligation to make payments, what theory would account for that? Is it that the consensual nature or the interpersonal contact of mediation create a greater sense of personal obligation? But isn't this largely dependent on the individual parties' perceptions of the process and the result? Is it that mediation just leaves the participants with a better feeling than litigation? If so, how do we explain that, as McEwen and Maiman point out, the satisfaction level is only slightly higher? Is deterrence a key ingredient in parties' willingness to make payments under each system? What will happen to a party who violates a court order to make payments as opposed to one who violates a mediation agreement? See infra p. 372, for discussion of the enforceability of mediation agreements. Recall Fiss' suggestion that the mediation compliance rate is better in certain kinds of cases because the defendants succeed in getting a more favorable agreement that requires less of them. See supra p. 43 n.35.

2. Family Law Disputes

Divorce and related family law disputes (such as separation, child custody, property settlement, and post-divorce modification of decrees) are often said to be a paradigm for the useful application of mediation. Mediation is thought to work best when there is a prospect of a future relationship between the parties. That is always the case in a divorce with minor children, and often the case even in the absence of minor children because of continuing relations by both parties with family and friends. But divorce also presents problems for effective mediation. It is one of the most emotion-charged and potentially vitriolic of disputes. Furthermore, habits and roles derived from the marriage relationship can undermine the ability of parties to act with independence, and equality of bargaining power can be seriously compromised by the parties' particular economic and psychological circumstances.

The attractiveness of mediation as an alternative to an adversary divorce trial was recognized early in the modern mediation movement. By the 1930's, divorce courts had begun to recommend mediation or "conciliation" as it was often called. In 1939, California created the Conciliation Court, with parties allowed to go through that process, usually in an uncontested divorce, as an alternative to the normal adversary divorce process. The rapid spread of no-fault divorce in the last several decades has further spurred the movement towards replacing an adversary divorce trial with a mediated settlement. In the last decade, California has mandated conciliation for issues of child custody or visitation as a prerequisite to a divorce trial, and judges in some other states have imposed this requirement through court rule.

Mandatory mediations, of course, violate the principle that participation in mediation should be voluntary.

The demand for divorce mediation has led to a specialized group of family mediators around the country with training and experience in that process. Family mediators have been in the forefront of the movement to require training and other requirements for mediators and to devise rules of professional conduct for mediators. Mental health and counselling professionals have tended to dominate the family mediation field, but lawyers have increasingly become involved as mediators, raising questions as to conflicts with their legal professional responsibilities.

One model of divorce mediation is to use two mediators, one with training in psychology or a related field and one with training in law. It is sometimes urged that they be of different sexes. This "luxury" model of divorce mediation, however, cannot be afforded in many divorce situations. The "stripped-down" model of mediation has to rely on volunteer mediators from a community dispute resolution center, religious organization, or social service agency, or, at times, simply on a local family lawyer. Sometimes, community mediation services refuse to mediate divorces when child custody or division of property is at issue, in recognition that specialized training and legal knowledge is needed.

Family law mediators have generally embraced the principle that mediation should be a non-directive process, with the mediator acting as facilitator, rather than creator, of the dialogue and agreement. But there are many approaches, and the complexity of issues that must be resolved concerning child custody, property division, and future relationships, plus the confusion and distraction caused by family miscommunication, are often cited as warranting a more activist mediator role. In addition, face-to-face mediation is not always viewed as desirable in divorce mediation, and "shuttle mediation," with only limited face-to-face meeting between the parties, has attracted support in certain divorce situations.

PATRICIA L. WINKS, DIVORCE MEDIATION: A NONADVERSARY PROCEDURE FOR THE NO–FAULT DIVORCE

19 J.Fam.L. 615, 635–40 (1980–81).

Communication with both parties may begin even before the first interview. When a client calls for an appointment, one mediator asks that the other spouse call to confirm. Because mediation is so uncommon, couples often have little notion of what is involved. The two telephone conversations serve to emphasize the procedure's mutuality.

The constraints of the mediation process are carefully explained at the initial interview. The couple are made aware of the necessity for full consent and disclosure, the attorney's inability to represent either party in litigation and confidentiality of all attorney-client communications. Failure to warn leaves the attorney open to the charge of legal malpractice. The parties are told that they may consult outside attorneys at any time. Both sign a consent form which explains their rights and responsibilities. They are reminded that the mediator "is not acting as attorney for either party nor as attorney for both parties." Clients are alerted to their differing interests. A letter from Henry Elson to his clients includes the following admonition:

> [I]t is important to recall that I advised each of you that you have adverse legal interests. This means that a particular resolution of any of the outstanding issues, such as spousal support or property division, or even the date of separation, may be relatively advantageous or detrimental to either of you, depending on how the issue is decided.

As one adversary lawyer put it: "Clients come to me saying they want an uncontested divorce, but they soon learn there are plenty of things to contest." In mediation, "things to contest" are fully disclosed to both parties so that they become things to negotiate and to compromise.

The initial interview is of special importance. The joint visit to the attorney is the couple's first formal admission that the marriage has failed. Although the parties may have already agreed in general on the course of action, the actual decision to divorce is nearly always initiated by one party alone. Since the other must "catch up" emotionally, the two do not arrive at the lawyer's office in the same state of readiness. At first clients may feel constrained to be on their best behavior and to try to impress the mediator with their mature cooperation. Or they may welcome the audience as a chance to catalogue the wrongs no-fault prevents them from parading in the courtroom.

The attorney proceeds with special care at the initial interview. Neutral, open-ended questions elicit responses that enable the interviewer to observe the dynamics of the marital relationship. Traditional legal skills of definition, clarification and summarization come into play. By summarizing what each party has said, the lawyer enables them to hear themselves more clearly and to identify problems with some detachment.

After the initial interview, the lawyer may see each client separately, then together again. This procedure, similar to the technique used by family therapists, has been adopted by Ann Diamond, who estimates that the average mediated case requires four to six sessions. Some spouses may unburden themselves more freely in a separate interview. The mediator learns which areas each considers important, and where concessions can be made. Then when the parties are together, negotiations can proceed more swiftly.

Henry Elson prefers to see clients together, to avoid the "paranoia" of the spouse who thinks he or she might be missing out on something. George Norton has clients come to the office together, but may speak with them individually during the session. Sometimes an agreement is worked out in the course of a marathon session rather than over an extended period.

Attorney Harriet Lee, accompanied by a male attorney, meets clients together so that mediation becomes a four-way process. Male and female lawyers who work with husband and wife deflect the transference and countertransference which commonly occurs in therapeutic relationships. A client may perceive the attorney of the other sex as prejudiced, the attorney of the same sex as an ally. The attorney may become identified with one of the partners. Co-lawyers can check each other's perceptions, guard against bias and blunt the problem of taking sides. A possible disadvantage is the creation of a deadlock, two against two.

A single attorney must avoid being co-opted by one party, and needs to monitor his or her own reactions in order to maintain strict impartiality. This does not mean that the mediator does not take sides. In the give and take of negotiation the skilled mediator will know when and how to alter the balance. When a stalemate occurs the mediator may shift the topic of negotiation, then reopen the issue when it provides an area for compromise.

If there are children, most lawyers deal with child support, custody and visitation first.[99] Resolution of these issues shows the couple that cooperation will be possible in other areas as well. Custodial arrangements necessarily involve financial planning. The parties must balance their own financial and economic needs with those of the children to arrive at an agreement that will not make one spouse the sacrificial victim, a role ultimately damaging to both parent and child. Shared responsibility for the resolution of the custodial issue makes resolution of other issues easier.

In helping the couple draft an agreement, the lawyer uses the therapeutic tool of having each clarify goals and objectives. Do both parties expect their children to go to college? How will this expense be taken care of? Do both expect to be self-supporting? Will one spouse need or want vocational training? These decisions have legal and financial consequences for both parties, who can be guided to consider what will be spent rather than merely who will spend what.

The mediator does not naively assume that parties will willingly disclose financial or other secrets. Self-protection is both inevitable and desirable. The motivation for full and fair disclosure is realistic awareness that if the parties cannot agree, the courts will make the agreement for them. They are dependent on each other's cooperation and must bargain in good faith.

Just as the personal injury lawyer "cools the client out," or prepares the client to accept less than the anticipated windfall, so the family lawyer prepares both spouses to accept a realistic division of assets. Each party must adjust expectations. They cannot merely

99. The Family Mediation Association recommends that the couple focus on financial planning before resolving custodial arrangements.

discard the detritus (the inconveniently present spouse and sometimes the community debts) and hold on to the fruits of the marriage. The client who dreams of "winning big" may need to be reminded that even in adversary proceedings no one wins big any more. Additionally, it does little good to be awarded a whopping settlement if the other spouse, understandably resentful and antagonistic, will not abide by the provisions. The statistics on alimony, child support and visitation are a sad indicator of the minimal enforcement of settlement provisions. An agreement that reflects realistic expectations may well prevent future litigation.

Sometimes the clients prepare an agreement that the attorney revises, but usually the attorney drafts it. The couple's names appear on the petition in propria persona, or they may obtain separate attorneys of record. Although some states permit both parties to appear on record as petitioners, and California law does not specifically prohibit such a practice, the author has not heard of its being done.

The mediator may accompany the clients to court and appear as a friend of the court, or stay away entirely. One attorney pointed out that his presence is not needed, and his absence saves the clients money. The parties' appearance in court on their own behalf serves to underscore their autonomy and responsibility for the agreement.

Notes and Questions

(1) The mediation process described by Winks involves a lawyer as the mediator. Lawyer mediators are used more frequently in family law disputes than in community disputes because of the complexity of legal issues involved in divorce law and in custody, visitation, and property settlements. However, non-lawyer mediators and interdisciplinary mediator teams are also common. Issues regarding lawyers as mediators are discussed infra pp. 376–86.

(2) Since 1981, California has required conciliation for issues of child custody or visitation as a prerequisite to judicial resolution. Cal. Civ.Code § 4607 (West Supp.1980). The Family Conciliation Courts provide conciliation counselors who will mediate between the parties. Under local court rules, the counselors may make a recommendation to the court, and the courts are said to rely heavily on their reports. The availability of court-annexed conciliators under local rules in the San Francisco Bay area resulted in the virtual elimination of child custody hearings there. Winks, supra, at 638 n. 101 (1980–81). Does this suggest that the counselors are more than mere facilitators because their reports, even without an agreement between the parties, are likely to be adopted by judges? Does that affect the counsellors' ability to serve as a mediator? We will consider this question again in the context of "med-arb," infra p. 594.

(3) The California compulsory mediation approach to child custody and visitation issues is much debated. There is concern that the parents will be less likely to mediate in good faith, see Schepard,

Philbrick & Rabino, Ground Rules for Custody Mediation and Modification, 48 Albany L.Rev. 616 (1984), or that they will refuse to cooperate, leaving custody decisions to be decided by the courts, see Evarts & Goodwin, The Mediation and Adjudication of Divorce and Custody from Contrasting Premises to Complementary Processes, 19 Idaho L.Rev. 277 (1984). However, the Denver Custody Mediation Project study, in which mediation services were offered but not required, indicates that while only about 50% of parents chose to mediate when given the choice, one of them was usually eager to mediate. Pearson et al., The Decision to Mediate: Profiles of Individuals Who Accept and Reject the Opportunity to Mediate Contested Child Custody and Visitation Issues, 6 J. of Divorce 17 (1982). This suggests that compulsory mediation may only be compulsory for one of the parties in most cases. The same study reports that 80% of those exposed to the mediation process reached agreement, and that 90% of parties who mediated were satisfied with the process (compared with a 50% satisfaction rate with the courts). Pearson & Thoennes, Mediating and Litigating Custody Disputes: A Longitudinal Evaluation, 17 Fam.L.Q. 497, 504, 514 (1984). Does the high agreement and satisfaction rates for mediation demonstrate the success of the process or simply reflect that those who chose to use it were a self-selected group more predisposed to satisfactory settlements?

(4) Power imbalances are a recurring spectre in divorce mediation. There may be a long history of dominance of one spouse by another, often a wife by a husband. One spouse may also be in a superior economic position, again often a husband who has greater earning power and social mobility. There may also be imbalances of knowledge, experience, sophistication with business and property matters, and negotiating ability, that are, in particular cases, gender-specific. See supra p. 212, concerning various kinds of power affecting the ability to bargain.

As we have seen, there are techniques for dealing with power imbalances. See supra pp. 270–72. These may have to be applied in the divorce context with an awareness of gender relationships in our society. See Folger & Bernard, Divorce Mediation: When Mediators Challenge the Divorcing Parties, 10 Mediation Q. 5, 20 (1985) (studies indicate that female mediators intervene more often than males on behalf of either spouse). It is also argued that divorce mediations should not take place without the presence of attorneys to provide support and information. But some critics of mediation believe that no techniques can ever really empower a seriously-dominated spouse in a divorce mediation. There is a prominent feminist critique that maintains that mediation is inappropriate in family law disputes because it reinforces the gender-advantage of the husband and removes the protection of the legal process. Consider the following analysis in Woods, Mediation: A Backlash to Women's Progress on Family Law Issues, 19 Clearinghouse Rev. 431, 435 (1985):

Mediation can be effective if and only if (1) the issue is capable of resolution through modification of perceptions, attitudes and/or behavior; (2) relative parity of power exists between the parties; (3) there is no need for punishment, deterrence or redress; and (4) the parties are capable of entering into and carrying out an agreement. These criteria are not met in divorce or family law mediation.

* * *

Mediation trivializes family law issues by relegating them to a lesser forum. It diminishes the public perception of the relative importance of laws addressing women's and children's rights in the family by placing these rights outside society's key institutional system of dispute resolution—the legal system—while continuing to allow corporate and other "important" matters to have unfettered access to that system. Loss of one's children and protection of one's physical safety should be considered too important to entrust to any other but the legal system.

(5) The possibility that one spouse will not disclose the true state of affairs as to which he or she has superior knowledge (such as finances or access to the children) is also a concern in divorce mediation. Woods, supra at 435, argues: "In divorce or family law mediation there is no process by which the dependent spouse can verify the extent of the assets or attempt to discover hidden assets of the propertied spouse." But, as seen in Chapter II, supra p. 121, resort to ADR procedures like mediation need not foreclose the availability of legal devices like discovery, which can be used in conjunction with mediation to insure full disclosure of the facts. In addition, the mediation agreement can explicitly confer discovery powers on the mediator. Cornblatt, Matrimonial Mediation, 23 J.Fam.L. 99, 107 (1984–85), suggests guidelines requiring that the mediator have the ability and authority to examine all earning, asset and liability records and if necessary, to engage experts to examine property and records and report their findings, and, if custody or visitation issues are involved, that mediators have the ability to interview children and to obtain independent psychological or psychiatric input. Does this undermine the nondirectional model of mediation?

(6) Not all family law disputes arise out of divorce. Marital disputes not related to separation or divorce may not lead to litigation, and mediation may be appropriate for those disputes which the courts will not hear. In Kilgrow v. Kilgrow, 268 Ala. 475, 107 So.2d 885 (1958), the Alabama Supreme Court held that judicial intervention to resolve a dispute over what school a child was to attend (the father wanted to send her to a Catholic school, the mother to a public school) was inappropriate when the parents were living together. See also McGuire v. McGuire, 157 Neb. 226, 59 N.W.2d 336 (1953) (refusing judicial enforcement of a wife's right to support within an intact family). It is questionable whether such judicial reluctance would be followed in all courts, but mediation offers an alternative which does not raise the concern expressed by the Kilgrow court that suit would

"open wide the gates for settlement in equity of all sorts and varieties of intimate family disputes concerning the upbringing of children."

(7) In 1984, the Center for Dispute Settlement, a District of Columbia mediation center, received a grant from the U.S. Department of Health and Human Services to explore the use of mediation in resolving problems between parents and adolescents. The program has since been extended by grants to other centers throughout the country. The purpose is to resolve family conflicts underlying such adolescent behavior as truancy, curfew violations, hanging out with undesirable friends, and runaway. Referrals are encouraged from schools, police, social service agencies, court programs, and parents and adolescents themselves.

The mediation begins with a joint opening session, but then moves to individual sessions. See Center for Dispute Settlement, Parent/Adolescent Training Manual (Nov. 1987). This is seen as a way to offset some of the inequity in power by treating the teen as an equal. While "[m]ediators must be careful never to make the parents feel that their authority is questioned or their values not accepted," "[t]he mediator must help parents and teens understand each other's point of view." Id. at 11. The private session with the teen is seen as "critical to getting the teen to 'buy in' to mediation and become an active participant in the process" and as providing an "opportunity for the mediator to develop trust with the teen, convince her/him that mediation is different and that s/he has a chance to determine the outcome if s/he participates." Id. at 28. Does this process involve the mediator too much in manipulating the parties.

The Role of Legal Rules in Mediation

The very essence of mediation is that the parties are free to reach their own resolution of the dispute. Much like negotiation, mediation is a form of private ordering by which the parties may choose a settlement quite different from the rights and obligations set out in the law. This raises questions, however, as to what role legal rules should play in the mediation process.

The question as to the appropriate role of legal rules is especially relevant to family law mediation because rights and obligations in this area are generally set out in formal legal standards. Divorce and related family law cases require resolution of important individual rights and responsibilities, often with implications far into the future, as to property, alimony, child custody, and visitation and support. Furthermore, because changing the legal status of a marriage requires a court order, family law mediation is generally conducted in anticipation of, or as an adjunct to, litigation.

As we saw in the chapter on negotiation, Professors Mnookin and Kornhauser have suggested that "divorcing parents do not bargain over the division of family wealth and custodial prerogatives in a vacuum; they bargain in the shadow of the law." See supra p. 129. Mnookin and Kornhauser thus viewed the law as imposing restraints on, or providing touch-stones for, private ordering by providing expectations or entitlements on which the parties bargain and a process for review of any agreement reached. If parties do indeed negotiate against a backdrop of the law, then it seems likely that there is a similar effect in mediation. Indeed, the law may play an even more central role in mediation due to the presence of the mediator who has responsibilities to insure adequate exchange of information and fairness. Thus an analysis of the "shadow of the law" thesis should be useful for answering what role the law plays in mediation.

The following materials explore the phenomenon of private ordering in relation to legal standards and consider the impact of law on mediation conduct.

ROBERT H. MNOOKIN & LEWIS KORNHAUSER, BARGAINING IN THE SHADOW OF THE LAW: THE CASE OF DIVORCE
88 Yale L.J. 950, 950–55, 968–69 (1979).

We see the primary function of contemporary divorce law not as imposing order from above, but rather as providing a framework within which divorcing couples can themselves determine their postdissolution rights and responsibilities. This process by which parties to a marriage are empowered to create their own legally enforceable commitments is a form of "private ordering."

Available evidence concerning how divorce proceedings actually work suggests that a reexamination from the perspective of private ordering is timely. "Typically, the parties do not go to court at all, until they have worked matters out and are ready for the rubber stamp." Both in the United States and in England, the overwhelming majority of divorcing couples resolve distributional questions concerning marital property, alimony, child support, and custody without bringing any contested issue to court for adjudication.

This new perspective and the use of the term "private ordering" are not meant to suggest an absence of important social interests in how the process works or in the fairness of its outcomes. The implicit policy questions are ones of emphasis and degree: to what extent should the law permit and encourage divorcing couples to work out their own arrangements? Within what limits should parties be empowered to make their own law by private agreement? What procedural or substantive safeguards are necessary to protect various social interests?

* * *

A legal system might allow varying degrees of private ordering upon dissolution of the marriage. Until recently, divorce law attempted to restrict private ordering severely. Divorce was granted only after an official inquiry by a judge, who had to determine whether "appropriate grounds"—very narrowly defined in terms of marital offenses—existed. When a divorce was granted, the state asserted broad authority to structure the economic relationship of the spouses and to maintain regulatory jurisdiction over the children and their relationship to the parents. Doctrines such as collusion, connivance, and condonation were meant to curtail the degree to which parties themselves could bring about a divorce through agreement; the procedural requirements reflected the view that everyone was "a suspicious character." Obviously, the marital-offense regime could not, even at its most restrictive, eliminate collusion entirely. Some divorcing spouses worked things out for themselves and then (with their lawyers' help) staged a carefully rehearsed and jointly produced play for the court. Nevertheless, the legal system was structured to minimize private ordering.

Dramatic changes in divorce law during the past decade now permit a substantial degree of private ordering. The "no-fault revolution" has made divorce largely a matter of private concern. Parties to a marriage can now explicitly create circumstances that will allow divorce. Indeed, agreement between spouses is not necessary in most states; either spouse can unilaterally create the grounds for dissolution simply by separation for a sufficient period of time.

The parties' power to determine the consequences of divorce depends on the presence of children. When the divorcing couple has no children, the law generally recognizes the power of the parties upon separation or divorce to make their own arrangements concerning marital property and alimony. A spousal agreement may be subject to some sort of judicial proceeding—or, in England, submission to a Registrar—but on both sides of the Atlantic the official review appears to be largely perfunctory. In some American states a couple may make its agreement binding and final—i.e., not subject to later modification by a court.

In families with minor children, existing law imposes substantial doctrinal constraints. For those allocational decisions that directly affect children—that is, child support, custody, and visitation—parents lack the formal power to make their own law. Judges, exercising the state's *parens patriae* power, are said to have responsibility to determine who should have custody and on what conditions. Private agreements concerning these matters are possible and common, but agreements cannot bind the court, which, as a matter of official dogma, is said to have an independent responsibility for determining what arrangement best serves the child's welfare. Thus, the court has the power to reject a parental agreement and order some other level of child support or some other custodial arrangement it believes to be more desirable. Moreover, even if the parties' initial agreement is accepted by the court, it lacks finality. A court may at any time during the child's minority reopen and modify the initial decree in light of any subsequent change in circumstances. The parties entirely lack the power to deprive the court of this jurisdiction.

On the other hand, available evidence on how the legal system processes undisputed divorce cases involving minor children suggests that parents actually have broad powers to make their own deals. Typically, separation agreements are rubber stamped even in cases involving children.

———

HOWARD S. ERLANGER, ELIZABETH CHAMBLISS, & MARYGOLD S. MELLI, PARTICIPATION AND FLEXIBILITY IN INFORMAL PROCESSES: CAUTIONS FROM THE DIVORCE CONTEXT
21 Law & Soc'y Rev. 585, 598–600 (1987).

[The authors conducted open-ended interviews with the parties and lawyers in twenty-five divorce cases in Dane County (Madison), Wisconsin that had been informally settled in the summer of 1982.]

In divorce, the problems of the informal process are theoretically counteracted by the requirement of judicial review. The "shadow of the law" argument implies that while flexibility and cooperation may not occur in every case, at least all cases will be subject to legal constraints, first, because parties will negotiate with legal expectations in mind, and second, because of the review process itself, when judges will presumably refuse to ratify one-sided or unworkable arrangements.

* * *

Yet there are some problems with this argument, as to both the efficacy of review and the existence of endowments that review requirements are said to create. First, as Mnookin and Kornhauser acknowledge, the existing review process is widely considered to be a "rubber stamp," with harried judges eager to finalize any arrangements made by the parties. In our interviews, the need for court ratification was typically dismissed as an insignificant concern, as one client commented: "I'd heard that if things are settled when you go to the judge, then it's a relatively pro forma appearance. And that's exactly what it turned out to be". Thus, the general view is that as long as issues are settled, the judge will accept whatever decisions the parties present. As one of the judges remarked: "If they know what they're doing, even if it's out of line, then it's not my job to change their decision. . . . I don't know if I have ever changed an amount [for support] set by a couple".

The hypothesis that endowments will structure the bargaining process because parties will bargain with judicial review in mind is also problematic. First, it assumes parties have access to legal information, or at least to information about their judge's expectations regarding child support and property division. The parties we interviewed received most of their legal information from their attorneys. Thus, to the extent that formal endowments exist, they are subject to attorneys' interpretations, which potentially alters the entitlements created by the law. At the very least, then, we would argue that the shadow of the law is being cast by the lawyers, who declare their expectations of judicial behavior. * * *

Perhaps more fundamentally, the existence of consistent formal criteria for decision making is itself debatable. Several of the lawyers we interviewed report that they have difficulty discerning court standards and that they cannot predict the outcomes of court processes. Some lawyers also indicate they feel uncomfortable trying to advise clients about what is fair or what to aim for in a given divorce case. One lawyer remarks: "So much of it is judgmental. . . . [Clients] ask questions like 'Is it fair?' and I just want to say—forgive my language—'Well, shit, I don't know, I'm just guessing like you' ".

Even the lawyers in our sample who do think there are set standards and who do say they can predict outcomes differ in their opinion of the content of those court standards; obviously, they cannot all be correct. Some lawyers attempt to "divide hardship," that is, to make each parent absorb equal deficiencies of income. Others measure the adequacy of support by looking at the custodial parent's budget, trying to make sure the custodian can make ends meet, or by looking at the supporting parent's ability to pay. Still others focus on a flat amount of support per child. Many lawyers also stress that their settlement strategy in any given case depends heavily on who is representing the other spouse. Thus, it is doubtful that parties receive consistent legal information and advice.

Over 90% of divorce cases, according to most estimates, are settled through stipulation, and it is the rare case that is completely litigated. This fact opens the possibility that the shadow of the law, which presumably constrains negotiating parties, is instead cast by them. In other words, in litigation, judges may be following the patterns they see in informal settlements rather than the other way around; thus, instead of "bargaining in the shadow of the law," one should refer to "litigating in the shadow of informal settlement." Even one who accepts the logic of this argument might still defend the endowments assumption. One could say that what matters is not some abstract analysis about who sets the patterns but rather the participants' *perceptions* of that process. Parties who feel constrained will act as if they are, whether or not they in fact are.

To our respondents, however, legal constraints are decidedly less important than the other pressures we have discussed; many parties even disregarded the advice of their attorneys. For instance, in some cases in which the client was impatient to settle, the lawyer's dissatisfaction with the terms was ignored:

> My lawyer . . . wanted to wait until fall to make sure, to try to get a better handle on if [my husband's] business was successful. He thought my name should remain on it as part-owner. . . . I really wanted to get out of it, and didn't want to just mess around. I mean [he may have been] right—[but] I didn't care who was right

at that point, and I still don't. It was more important to get out of the marriage.

While lawyers are often accused of stirring up trouble in divorce cases, it is clear that in some cases, they are unable to do so even when they think it is necessary to protect their client's interests. Against custody threats and other tactics, a lawyer's reassurances and support may be insufficient to keep clients from folding, as one lawyer explains:

> Her husband was using the threat of a custody issue to keep his payments down and she was insisting that I follow that approach. In other words, I take it very easy on him and as I recall, even from the beginning, no support [was] ordered. . . . She wanted me to forget about the father's responsibility to the children as far as money goes. . . . She was such a basket case. . . . He had just frightened her to death.

Thus, even if the "shadow of the law" is a factor in informal settlement decisions, it is not the only factor, and its impact should not be overestimated.

LENARD MARLOW, THE RULE OF LAW IN DIVORCE MEDIATION
9 Mediation Q. 5, 10–13 (1985).

[The author is a fellow of the American Academy of Matrimonial Lawyers and Director of legal services of Divorce Mediation Professionals in New York.]

Divorce mediation rejects the idea that legal rules should be used as weapons to improve one party's position at the expense of the other. Similarly, it rejects the idea that these legal rules and principles embody any necessary wisdom or logic. In fact, it views them as being arbitrary principles, having little to do with the realities of a couple's life and not superior to the judgments that the couple could make on their own. What relevance do these rules and principles have in mediation then, and why is it necessary to know them?

Whether laws are fair or unfair, parties believe them to be significant and this shapes their expectations. This is just a fact. If the law says that when title to a couple's home is in the husband's name alone, and that the wife will not have an interest in it, then the husband does not expect to have to give her any portion of it—this is so whether the wife feels this to be fair or unfair. This is a reality with which a mediator must deal. However, unlike a lawyer in an adversarial setting, he is not bound by it. He does not believe that these rules embody any necessary logic, let alone guarantee any necessary justice. They may be limiting factors, but they are not absolutes. In fact, from his standpoint, the problem is that the expectations created by these rules and principles will produce an agreement between the parties that is not fair. In this instance, therefore, the law is an obstacle to a fair agreement. The mediator's job is to effect a fairer agreement than the law would provide, despite the expectations that the husband (in this case) has based on the law.

In other instances, the mediator will treat the law not as an obstacle to overcome but will use it as a protective shield. For instance, a lack of agreement between the parties is occasioned by the fact that they disagree as to whether it is fair that the wife should have an interest in her husband's business. As arbitrary as the law may be in its determination (at one time it may have said no, at another time it may have said yes), the mediator can, nevertheless, invoke it as a means of resolving the disagreement when all else fails. When the husband refuses to concede that his wife should have any interest in his business, the mediator intervenes and says, "But that is the law." In this instance, he invokes the law not for the purpose of resolving the disagreement but to end it. The law is a reality, and although it may go against the husband's intentions, he cannot deny it.

The mediator is trying to effect change, in this case, a change from a lack of agreement to an agreement. Moreover, the mediator does not view these legal rules and principles as embodying either wisdom or justice, and does not believe that they represent a necessary yardstick by which to judge the agreement that has been concluded. Rather, these legal rules and principles are simply realities that can either limit or aid the mediation process.

How does this view of the law affect the way a mediator would treat legal rules and principles? To begin with, if a mediator suggested to a couple that they seek legal counsel, it would [sic] be so that they could each determine what their rights and obligations were and to thereby assure that their agreement accurately mirrored those rights and obligations. It would be difficult to find out exactly what their rights were (that is, the parties could not find out, save by going to court, what a court would decide in their particular case). Nor would the parties' agreement necessarily be better if it exactly resembled the one that the law would give them—assuming they could find out what such an agreement would be without going to court.

If the mediator suggested that the couple consult with attorneys, it would be for very different reasons. The first reason would be to avoid concluding an agreement that one or the other of the parties would later feel was unfair. Perhaps it would be extremely unfair in a particular instance for one of the parties to share in the other's pension (for instance, if the husband does not have a pension but his parents are extremely wealthy and he will be well provided for in his old age and the wife, on the other hand, will need every penny of her own pension to support herself when she retires.) Before the husband waives his interests in her pension, however, it would be better that he knows that legally he has an interest in it. The disposition that the law would make in this case would not necessarily be fairer. (Since the court could not take cognizance of the husband's future inheritance, or therefore consider it, it might be far less fair.) It is that the mediator does not want to jeopardize the efficacy of the agreement as one that both of the parties can live with. This might occur if the husband concluded an agreement without being aware that he could legally make claims on his wife's pension and later might feel that he had been taken advantage of.

Another instance in which the mediator might recommend that the parties consult with an attorney would be as a strategy to break an impasse, for example if the couple disagreed as to whether it was fair that the wife should share in her husband's pension. It is not the purpose of mediation to have endless philosophical debates as to what is ultimately fair or unfair; there will be as many opinions on that issue as there are people who are asked. If the couple does not start out with a common view of what is fair or unfair, and if the mediator is unable to produce a common view, then there must be a way to break the impasse. In this case, referring the couple for legal counsel (to find out what the law says) may serve to do that, since the couple will feel obligated to accept what the law says. (Since this is the only reason why the mediator is referring the couple for legal counsel, it is not necessary (as would be the case if legal rules and principles were viewed as rights) that they consult with separate attorneys. The only question at issue is whether the law in the particular jurisdiction would give the wife an interest in her husband's pension. In fact, one lawyer is preferable, since the mediator wants an answer, not a range of legal opinions.

Since legal rules and principles are therefore simply a means to an end and are used by a mediator as an intervention of strategy to achieve a desired result, the mediator does not consider himself slavishly bound to them. Rather, he is free to deal with them in a far less constricted manner. Suppose, for example, that there is a dispute between a husband and a wife as to how long she will have the right to live in their marital residence with their children. The husband asks the mediator (who happens to be a lawyer), "How long do I have to let her live in the home?" What he is of course asking is how long the law will allow her to live there. The husband is now attempting to use the law as a strategy, not because he feels that the legal answer makes sense or is right, but simply because he believes that the law will support his opinion. The mediator, of course, does not believe that there are or should be legal answers to personal questions. More important, the mediator's job is to impress this fact on the husband. Instead of answering the question, therefore, the mediator asks the husband, "Tell me, how are your children taking your separation? If they were required to leave their home and be uprooted from their community at this time, do you think that this would make it more difficult for them? And what about your son who is in the tenth grade? Do you think it would be a good idea to disrupt the continuity of his high school experience by being required to relocate to a new school district before he graduates?" In short, what the mediator is doing is forcing the husband to deal with the resolution of this issue on the basis of the same kinds of practical considerations that the couple used during their marriage (for instance they bought their home because they felt it would be a good place to raise their children and because they wanted them to have the benefit of the good schools in the area), rather than on the basis of what would be the result if they applied arbitrary legal rules and principles that have little to do with their lives.

Notes and Questions

(1) If, as Mnookin and Kornhauser indicate, courts tend to rubber-stamp even parental agreements that involve custody of children, can we really say that legal rules have much influence on divorce negotiations and mediations? Of course, the parties' initial positions and expectations may still derive largely from their understanding of their rights and obligations under the law. But if, as Erlanger, Chambliss, and Melli argue, parties do not really have access to adequate legal information, then is the "shadow of the law" simply a myth? Is this due primarily to the failing of lawyers, and, if so, how could the practice of divorce law be changed to remedy it?

(2) Where do mediating parties get their information about the law? Remember that in many mediations (particularly community mediations) the parties may not have consulted lawyers and the mediator is not a lawyer. Should a lawyer mediator be required in divorce mediations because of the significance of legal issues? Should prior consultation with a lawyer normally be required? Note that there are a number of models in divorce mediation, utilizing varying roles for lawyers: lawyers may provide advice before, and review of any agreement after, the mediation but not actually attend; or may attend as either a silent advisor or an active participant. These roles will be considered more fully infra, p. 376.

(3) Do you agree with Marlow's observations that there is no need to have the parties to a divorce mediation consult with separate attorneys, "as would be the case if legal rules and principles were viewed as rights?" Surely legal rules and principles *are* rights, even if the parties choose not to follow them exactly in their mediation agreement. Are you satisfied with his conclusion that "one lawyer is preferable, since the mediator wants an answer, not a range of legal opinions?" Are the parties' interests adequately represented by sending them to the same lawyer so the mediator can get "an answer"?

(4) What happens in a mediation when the values of the parties—deriving from either community or personal standards—are in conflict with the law? Is it the duty of the mediator to at least point out the conflict?

(5) Mnookin and Kornhauser note that the advent of no-fault divorce made divorce "a largely private concern." Similarly a trend towards joint custody of children and use of mediation has further reduced the role of the law and increased the role of private ordering.

Consider the following arguments supporting a proposal to extend this development by making parental rights and duties regarding children *after* divorce entirely a matter of private agreement and by eliminating a court determination of legal custody:

First, adjustments in parental responsibility would not be an issue for court determination upon divorce or thereafter. Parents in divorce would continue to share general parental rights and duties as co-equals under the law the same as during the ongoing marriage. Parental control patterns would change because of the divorce, but this change would take place through consensual processes, for the most part, rather than by court dictate. Courts would no longer determine legal custody, exclusive, joint, or otherwise.

Two significant issues for postdivorce parent-child relationships would remain: determining when the children would be physically present with each parent, and determining the financial need of the children and allocating that need between the parents. These issues are more amenable than the issue of legal custody to resolution by consensual problem-solving methods such as negotiation and mediation. If the parties are unable to reach agreement voluntarily, these issues are suitable for mandatory arbitration that is more informal, efficient, and flexible than court proceedings. Although the arbitration would be mandatory, the procedures and standards applied could be shaped by agreement of the participants. Court adjudication would be unnecessary.

Second, the best interests of the child standard would require modification. At present, it is an evaluation tool comparing a child's possible life in the mother's sole custody with one in the father's, and with one in joint custody for those states having that option, so that the court can choose among the alternatives. If this proposal were adopted, the family would not divide along parental responsibility lines. Each parent would remain fully and jointly responsible for his or her children. The choices are more limited in scope and relate only to the time of a child's physical presence within each parent's household and the allocation of financial support. The optimum result for these issues is a schedule and allocation supporting the best parent-child relationships possible within the divorced family as a unit. Therefore, the appropriate standard shifts from a comparative "best interests of the child" to the supportive "best interests of the divorced family." The parties, not the court, would apply this standard through negotiation and mediation, or at the extreme, an arbitrator would use it to set schedules and allocation levels. It would not be a tool for a win-lose court decision.

Third, courts would be unavailable to divorced parents, just as they are to parents with intact families, as decisionmakers of last resort in disputes over childrearing issues. Courts would remain available for complaints involving alleged abuse, neglect, delinquency, or other gross failure of parental care regardless of the marital status of the parent, and a termination of parental rights action would continue to be an avenue of last resort.

Intact and divorced family structures do not always differ significantly. In the divorced family, parents live in separate residences. The kind of routine daily contact that builds important psychological family bonds is absent. Yet these structural realities may not translate into stereotypical antagonism or psychological distance. Many divorced parents enjoy substantial family cooperation and active participation in their children's activities. For its part, the perceived unity in the intact family may often be a misperception. An "intact" family may harbor a mixture of parental separation, violent disagreement, and parent-child confusion. Any general descriptions of parental interaction within the two structures may be so fraught with exceptions and special cases that they become inappropriate, or worse, counterproductive as guides for community response.

*   *   *

This proposal would create a very different environment for divorcing families. Financial, psychological, and structural pressures of the divorce process, including the personal preferences and biases of local lawyers, judges, and jury members, currently determine the allocation of parental responsibilities within the divorced family. Under the proposal the allocation of specific duties within the divorced family setting would be the shared task of the mother, father, and children alone, the same as it is within the ongoing marriage. The allocation may be considerably different in divorce than it was during marriage, but it will continue to be a function of the personalities, attitudes, lifestyles, and relationships of the two parents and their children. Divorced parents may openly negotiate how they would divide the duties and decisions of parenthood, or consciously decide to share these obligations under a more flexible and unstated set of guidelines, or develop a relationship pattern more or less unconsciously as their personalities and the needs demand. The possible permutations are unlimited in recognition of the uniqueness of each family.

If the divorced family is treated more like the intact family, the two parents would be expected to develop patterns of behavior as their interests, activities, locations, and the physical presence of the children might require. The legal fact of divorce would have little impact on the resulting parent-child relationships, which would be primarily determined by the practical realities involved in physically separating the lives of the parents. The legal structure would be neutral. It would accommodate the variety of human behavior.

Murray, Improving Parent–Child Relationships Within the Divorced Family: A Call for Legal Reform, 19 U.Mich.J.Law Reform 563, 585–86 (1986).

Are post-divorce parent-child relationships an appropriate subject for replacing judicial oversight with mediation or private ordering? For a very different viewpoint, consider the excerpt in the next note.

(6) The movement towards private ordering in divorce disputes has been subjected to severe criticism by others. Consider the following account of the trend towards joint custody and mandatory mediation under the particular influence of the helping professions, from Fineman, Dominant Discourse, Professional Language, and Legal Change in Child Custody Decisionmaking, 101 Harv.L.Rev. 727, 731–32, 756–57, 759–60 (1988):

> Traditional divorce policy envisioned the termination of the spouses' relationship as its goal, establishing different legal relationships with differing legal consequences for the custodial and noncustodial parents. In this way, the law recognized the status of sole custodian as an institution or legal category and presumed that the law should designate, recognize, and protect the relationship between custodial parent and child. At the same time, the law acknowledged the noncustodial parent's relationship with the child through the imposition of visitation rights.
>
> Helping professionals and other proponents of joint custody asserted that the win/lose philosophy of naming a sole custodian was inappropriate, because parents had equal rights and responsibilities in relation to their children during marriage. In addition, they found the notion of "visiting" one's child ideologically and emotionally offensive. By contrast, the symbolic ideal of parental equality was compelling. Desirable custody policy, therefore, was post-divorce shared parenting. It was this notion of a legally mandated and constructed continuing relationship between divorced parents, so central to joint custody, that was so foreign to traditional family law policy. In essence, the social workers' ideal of shared parenting was a rejection of the desirability of a legally acknowledged sole custodian.
>
> As this view has become accepted, it has altered the way we articulate and conceive of custody issues. The dominant rhetoric no longer describes divorce as a process that terminates the relationship between spouses, establishing one as the custodial parent with clear responsibilities. Rather, divorce is now described as a process that, through mediation, restructures and reformulates the spouses' relationship, conferring equal or shared parental rights on both parents although one, in practice, usually assumes the primary responsibility for care of the children. This is an important substantive shift.

* * *

The helping professions' ideal process "avoids" or "reduces" conflict and is typified by mediation. Helping professionals believe that mediation, employing a therapeutic process, is within their exclusive domain because lawyers, unlike social workers, ignore the underlying causes of divorce and give little regard to the "real reason" for the split-up. Therapeutic skills can facilitate acceptance of the divorce and foster a positive approach to the crisis.

Lawyers' skills are downgraded and social workers' and mediators' skills are mystified and reified.

* * *

The rhetoric of mediators also intersects with and complements the concerns of members of the legal profession. This convergence is probably one of the most significant factors in the success of the helping professions' reforms. Mediators have been empowered by judges and court administrators who dislike custody decisionmaking under the best interest test, or who believe that such cases clog up the system. The substantive implications may be lost and the discussion focused merely on the transfer of troublesome custody issues to an "alternative" system. This is particularly true when the alternative system is characterized as "more humane and caring" and appears to resolve everyone's problems.

Further, family law attorneys who are uncomfortable in courtroom settings or bored with their profession may find it attractive to envision themselves as mediators, employing a whole new set of mechanisms that will enhance their prestige, their self-worth, and the quality of what they do on a day-to-day basis. There is a mystique about mediation that many find compelling. Mediators do not choose sides but are counsel for the situation. Mediators are disinterested advisors whose only role is to assist the family in making nonadversarial decisions. Family lawyers have a bad image in the press, in the eyes of the public, and in their own eyes; mediation may be a way of rehabilitating that image.

Legislatures also have found the reallocation of decisionmaking power attractive. The reallocation can be accomplished by using existing court-associated personnel—the social workers who previously performed custody investigations can now try their hand at mediation. Further, it has symbolic appeal. Because the goal of shared parenting leads to equal division or joint custody, it is consistent with the recent trend in all of family law toward mathematical formulas for decisionmaking.

To those uncertain about or upset with the function of the present family law system, the mediators' vision presents a more coherent and more encompassing ideal referencing deeply held beliefs and assumptions. In the procedural context, it offers a process free of conflict. In the substantive context, it appeals to ideals of equality, sharing, and caring. The mediators' view is also one that seems distinctly utopian. Its underlying premise is that one can seek personal happiness and fulfillment by terminating a marriage relationship, yet not lose any of the benefits that marriage provides. The hidden message is that divorce can be painless. One can retain one's children, even one's "family," although the family structure may be slightly altered. It is a grand dream: everybody wins, nobody loses.

(7) Concerning the relative benefits and risks of an "alegal" mediation process, consider the following comments from Riskin, Mediation and Lawyers, 43 Ohio St.L.J. 29, 34–5 (1982):

> [M]ediation is less hemmed-in by rules of procedure or substantive law and certain assumptions that dominate the adversary process. There are, of course, assumptions that affect the procedure and results achieved in mediations—assumptions about mutuality, cooperation, and fairness, and general principles that ought to govern; in some systems, rules that approximate applicable law even serve as starting points. But in mediation—as distinguished from adjudication and, usually, arbitration—the ultimate authority resides with the disputants. The conflict is seen as unique and therefore less subject to solution by application of some general principle. The case is neither to be governed by a precedent nor to set one. Thus, all sorts of facts, needs, and interests that would be excluded from consideration in an adversary, rule-oriented proceeding could become relevant in a mediation. Indeed, whatever a party deems relevant is relevant. In a divorce mediation, for instance, a spouse's continuing need for emotional support could become important, as could the other party's willingness and ability to give it. In most mediations, the emphasis is not on determining rights or interests, or who is right and who is wrong, or who wins and who loses because of which rule; these would control the typical adjudicatory proceeding. The focus, instead, is upon establishing a degree of harmony through a resolution that will work for these disputants.

> A danger inheres in this alegal character: individuals who are not aware of their legal position are not encouraged by the process to develop a rights-consciousness or to establish legal rights. Thus, the risk of dominance by the stronger or more knowledgeable party is great. Accordingly, for society to maximize the benefits of mediation while controlling its dangers, it must carefully adjust the role of lawyers in the mediation process.

> Though mediation agreements typically neither set nor follow legal precedent, they often have important legal consequences. Frequently, the mere making of an agreement defers legal action by one of the disputants or the government. The agreement itself may establish or avoid legally enforceable rights. To reduce the danger that less powerful persons unwittingly will give up legal rights that would be important to them, they must be afforded a way of knowing about the nature of the adversary process and the

result it would likely produce. But the very presentation of the rules that would probably govern a decision if the matter were litigated may impel parties toward adopting the predicted results, rather than regarding the law as simply one factor—to be blended with a variety of economic, personal, and social considerations—in reaching a decision. At the same time, if such information is not readily available to them, they are not necessarily free from influence by the law; they may be basing their decisions to mediate and their judgments during mediation upon inaccurate assumptions about what result would follow from adversary processing.

3. Labor Disputes

Labor disputes were the first significant area in which mediation was routinely used in this country. Attempts at mediating labor disputes were made in the 19th century both in England and the United States. Government-sponsored mediation dates from 1913 when the Department of Labor appointed "commissioners of conciliation" to be made available to the parties in labor disputes. They were reconstituted in 1947 as the Federal Mediation and Conciliation Service, which continues to function today in providing arbitrators and mediators for labor disputes. The Labor–Management Relations Act of 1947 provides that "[t]he Service may proffer its services in any labor dispute in any industry affecting commerce * * * whenever in its judgment such dispute threatens to cause a substantial interruption of commerce." [1] The FMCS has some 300 full-time mediators located in seventy field offices around the country, with regional offices and a headquarters in Washington. It participates in some 25,000 mediations annually. There are similar state mediation services in a number of states.

Apart from the formal mediation role of the FMCS and similar state agencies, mediation is increasingly performed today under procedures agreed upon by the parties in collective bargaining or other labor-management agreements. Mediations may concern a wide variety of bargaining, grievance, or dispute issues. Arbitration, of course, is the principal device adopted in collective bargaining agreements for settlement of disputes (see infra p. 421). However, mediation can play a critical role in the bargaining process leading up to an agreement and—either informally or formally if provided in the agreement—in the resolution of grievances and disputes arising under the collective bargaining agreement.

The term "conciliation" has long been used in the labor context. It has been described as the process for "the bringing of disputing parties together, under circumstances and in an atmosphere most conducive to the discussion of the problem in an objective way for the purpose of

1. 29 U.S.C. § 171(a)(b).

seeking a solution to the issue or issues involved." [2] Mediation is generally considered to involve a more active role for the mediator than conciliation, with the mediator acting not merely as a facilitator but "interject[ing] himself into the discussions and mak[ing] affirmative suggestions and recommendations for developing areas of possible agreement." [3] Today the two terms are often used interchangeably.

One unique feature of labor mediation is that the participants are chosen from the complex organizational structures of labor and management. The mediator is therefore dealing with experienced and well-prepared adversaries and generally starts at a higher level of understanding and structuring of positions than in community and family dispute mediation. The challenge here is not only to facilitate communication and understanding between the participants but also to recognize the large constituencies behind them that will have to be persuaded of the merits of any agreement. Labor mediation thus requires the mediator to be sensitive not only to the agreement that can be achieved between the company and union but also to the need for approval by the union bureaucracy and rank-and-file, on the one hand, and the different management teams on the other.

Labor disputes subject to mediation are of two kinds—"grievance" disputes over the application of the collective bargaining agreement or individual rights and responsibilities under the workforce rules, and "collective bargaining" concerning interests in the terms of a new agreement (compare the discussion of "rights" and "interest" arbitration, infra p. 403). Collective bargaining generally involves large and complex groupings of negotiators on each side. The issues are at times amorphous, and the agenda generally flexible and open-ended. The role of the mediator is often expansive and active. Grievance mediation, on the other hand, is generally performed by a single or a small number of representatives on each side. The issues here are limited to those that have arisen in the individual case. Even here, however, the resolution of grievances in the labor context may have important precedential effect on the institutional parties that may far outweigh the interest of the individual. Thus, in distinction to community disputes, there is a potential policy overlay in even the simplest individual grievance dispute. This may affect the mediator's role, causing him to be more activist than his counterpart in other forms of mediation.

The following materials will focus on collective bargaining mediation.

2. W. Maggiolo, Techniques of Mediation in Labor Disputes 10 (1971). **3.** Id.

DEBORAH M. KOLB, THE MEDIATORS *
80–85 (1983).

[The author observed sixteen labor mediations by the Federal Mediation and Conciliation Service and a state labor mediation agency in the late 1970's.]

Bard Manufacturing: A Narrowing Strategy in a Federal Case

The union committee, five members of the unit and a representative from the International arrived first at the FMCS office. The mediator assigned them a front room and, at the request of the representative, allowed them time to caucus. When the management committee arrived, Bard's director of industrial relations, four technical support staff and their attorney, the mediator informed them that the union was in caucus. In the mediator's office, the management attorney told Baker, the mediator, that the case looked as if it would settle, the central issue being health insurance. The union rep announced that the union was ready.

A joint meeting was convened. The mediator asked the union to present first: "Okay, Charlie [union rep], why don't you give me a summary of where you are. Then Bill [management attorney] can tell me. We need to agree on where to disagree. The number one item as I understand it is the health and welfare."

The union presented its proposal on health and welfare (H & W). The discussion that ensued on this issue was cut short by the mediator: "Obviously, we have to talk more about H & W. Next item, COLA (cost-of-living adjustment)." On each of the issues, the mediator had the union present its position and followed with some clarifying questions: "Your proposal on COLA, is it to continue as now constituted? You're both talking a two-year contract? How is the pension formula figured? Any sick leave now? How many holidays do you have now? What kind of bonus was it? A Christmas deal?" After the union finished its presentation, the mediator turned to the management attorney: "Bill, I'd like the benefit of your comments." Management presented its proposal along with its justification for certain of its positions. The mediator checked to see whether there were other issues and announced his intention to meet with the union first.

Baker began his meeting with the union by describing the posture of FMCS vis-à-vis the voluntary wage/price guidelines that had just been issued: "We are not enforcers. We are neutral. All we do is provide you with the necessary information. Because Bard has government contracts, I have to warn you that you run a risk with wages that exceed it. But remember the fringes are folded into the base. So it isn't just 7 percent of the standard average hourly rate. My function is to assist you to reach agreement."

After some calculations and discussion on the precise dollar-amount increase that would fall within the wage/price guidelines, Baker instructed the union to caucus: "You need to run down all the issues. You need a caucus, with or without the guidelines. No way you'll get the 10 percent and with 1 percent (from COLA), that's 11 percent. No way. That can't be firm. Charlie, what you have to do is go over each item individually and frame up a counter. Include your proposal on H & W, include just what you want. You want to keep COLA, put it in. You have to give them [management] a complete proposal so they can respond."

While the union caucused, the mediator gave me his diagnoses of the case:

> The union needs to get its act together, shape up their position on H & W and cut the wages down. Then this thing can come into focus. If they're asking 10 percent and COLA, that's 11 percent. They have as much chance of getting that as flying. Other things will have to come off—sick leave—there's no chance. They don't have it in manufacturing, it's covered in the weekly Sickness and Accident (S & A). There are a few more items they can cut. But the next move is for the union to cut down their proposal. At a point, we'll recess to give the union time to get its act together.

A joint meeting was held. There the union presented its proposal, noteworthy for a complete H & W plan and a 1 percent reduction in the wage demand. The session adjourned because the mediator had another case in progress.

At the start of the second session, the management attorney drifted back into the mediator's office for some informal talk. The mediator suggested that management respond to the union's proposal, particularly the H & W plan, so that the union could caucus again. The attorney left and Baker commented on the union's H & W plan that called for full company participation: "Charlie knows the company won't buy it, but he had to pursue it. He took this case over from another rep so he couldn't just come in and pull the whole proposal down in one session. He had to show his committee he tried. That's why nothing happened in the first session, he needed time. Today, we'll get Bill's answer that full participation is out. That will show the committee Charlie tried, but management said no. Then I'll spend some time with the union committee to get them to make a counterproposal."

The joint meeting was convened. Baker asked the management attorney for the response to the union's proposal. After it was given, the mediator remained with the union: "At this juncture you see that bringing in all employees is out. You showed the cost savings and they still say no. Now in light of that you should look at your proposal and prepare a response." The union rep requested that the mediator obtain the cost of the company's fringe benefits in order to prepare a response within the guidelines. The mediator agreed and further instructed the union committee: "Charlie, your job is to work to bring this into focus."

En route to management's room, Baker commented that it helped the union rep to have no said directly across the table on the H & W participation.

Baker met with management and requested the cost figures. It gave him total cost, but he pressed for itemized costs, which it needed time to get.

The mediator returned to his office and was joined by the union rep, who did want the itemized costs. However, his purpose in meeting with the mediator was to request that the next mediation session be deferred until after the upcoming holiday because ratification meetings were hard to schedule at that time. The rep went on to report that his relationship with his committee was much improved, that they were listening to him. The mediator asked the management attorney to join them in his office to discuss deferring the next session. The attorney agreed to this and after some reluctance also agreed to provide the itemized fringe costs. They planned that the mediator would meet with the union and give it the total cost, the rep would ask for cost breakdowns, and they would arrange for the union to meet in the interim to prepare a proposal based on these costs. While the attorney checked dates with his committee, the mediator suggested that the union rep return to his also: "Incidentally, does your committee know you're in here? Maybe you should go back and tell them I called you in."

After the rep left, the mediator discussed the meeting between the spokesmen:

> This is unusual. You can't do it with everybody. I know these guys. People think this kind of thing happens in the majority of cases. It doesn't, but it would be nice if it did. But here the principals are both "pros." They've been in the business a long time. There are no emotions. But you have to remember that they are negotiating with each other and with me too. They represent their constituencies very well. If you think they're here for you to make a deal, you're wrong. Charlie gets what is best for his committee.

After the management attorney set a date for the transmittal of the cost data, the mediator met with the union to report: "We're finished with the logistics part. I pointed out to Bill that it was essential to get the breakdowns. Charlie, the plant manager will give them to you and then you can get in touch with your guys to work out a counterproposal. During that time, you can meet at our offices if you want."

Baker adjourned the session and explained his final meeting with the union committee:

When you do a lot of one on one, you have to update the committee and let them know what you are doing. The bottom line in this thing is ratification of the contract. And you can't get to that unless you have a recommendation from the full committee. If you don't keep them up to date, they will balk. So when you short-circuit, you have to inform the committee. You never short-circuit their participation in the process because they have to recommend it. In the ideal situation, you try to get the last move from the union with their recommendation. Then you are asking people to ratify their position, not the company's.

The third session started with a union caucus. Although it had met in the interim, the union rep said he needed more time. Shortly after the start of the session, the rep asked the mediator to meet with his committee to talk about its proposal, which was written on the blackboard.

Mediator: You haven't changed anything since last time. You're still at 9 percent and you've gone backward on the pensions.

Union Rep: We're prepared to do more.

Mediator: When? Do you want to be here all night? In terms of bringing this into focus, this is nothing. The people in the other room may look at this and say, that's it—take it or leave it. Now you guys know me. It would be easy for me to sit here silent. But I have to give you my reaction. My reaction is that you are going backwards. Now I don't have to tell you, Charlie. You know the game better than I do. We're looking at the same stuff as two weeks ago. They'll think, what encouragement do they have to change their position? You are doing yourself an injustice with this kind of proposal. Now before you caucus, let me say that this is your version. It's your proposal, but you asked for my opinion. It's easy for me to sit silent. So take a few minutes to kick this thing around.

Baker left the union to caucus, and back in his office discussed what had transpired in the union meeting: "Charlie was having trouble with his committee, so I helped. Yes, I used a bullet in there. You see you let them go to the extent that they can drop things by themselves. You have to massage, but you don't use your ammunition too soon."

Later the union rep came into Baker's office and complimented him. "You really do fine work. We changed the figures. I was playing straight for them, giving you the numbers. Then you came in and said it was crazy. I love FMCS."

The mediator met with the union, reviewed its proposal, and called a joint meeting for its presentation. Management stated that it had already done the best it could, but agreed to take another look. The rep indicated the union's willingness to modify further, but it too was not far from where it hoped to settle.

The mediator met briefly with management to clarify some questions it seemed to have on the new proposal: "Just to keep the dialogue going, look at what your premiums are now and what they are proposing. I'm just trying to clarify this."

While management caucused, the union rep drifted into the mediator's office to chat about old friends, but at the mediator's suggestion returned to his committee. "Procedurally, I think it's a good idea to stay with your troops because I may be calling you out later."

The management attorney told Baker that his committee had made some improvements on their proposals, but that little was left after that. Baker suggested that it present its proposal in joint session and then get the union rep out to decide what to do next. The joint meeting was held, and the mediator instructed the union to caucus and call him when it was ready.

At this juncture, the mediator considered a strike unlikely because most of the major issues had been addressed by management. When the union rep came into Baker's office to use the phone, he and Baker discussed the procedure. Said Baker, "I think it might be helpful for you and me and Bill to sit down. Unless Bill is playing poker with me, I don't think there's much more. What are you going to do in your counter? It looks to me like you'll get the bonus and something on the pension, and that's the ball game, but it's a good ball game."

After some discussion the mediator suggested that the rep return to his committee. The rep replied, "I'll go back and tell them I have been on the phone."

A joint meeting was held, and the union presented its proposal. Again the rep needed to use the phone to ask some questions about benefits, and this provided the occasion for a three way off-the-record meeting. Baker began it with the comment that "the time has come to talk. Put yourself on dial-a-prayer, Charlie."

The spokesmen discussed certain aspects of the H & W plan, employee contributions, and the changing costs. Baker participated only to ask questions about things he did not understand. The union rep introduced the remaining issues that had yet to be resolved:

> Attorney: You want me to tell you. I will if you make a commitment. I'll tell you the most we'll give if you promise you won't chisel for any more. Earlier, you said that when I give you my bottom line, you can always come up with more. That hurt. I won't tell you if you are still talking about some of these other issues. If that's the case, there's no point.
>
> Union Rep: I know I can't bleed a stone.
>
> Mediator: What's the best way to get this on the table?
>
> Union Rep: Didn't you get the last proposal?
>
> Mediator: This either has to be the final-final, or Charlie, maybe you can get your troops to do it.

Attorney: [To Baker] You can give it without commitment.

Mediator: I have no compunction about telling them that this is it, that you don't have it yet but are willing to do the work for it.

Attorney: That's what I like about mediator recommendations. It's not a new plateau.

The mediator wrote down his understanding of management's proposal and checked it with both spokesmen. He rechecked the proposal and reviewed how he would present it. The union rep claimed it was going to be difficult to sell it to his committee. Both spokesmen left, and the mediator explained why he thought his actions were likely to succeed: "This is why the process of narrowing down is so important. The wage offer is the union's. The complete H & W is theirs. They got the bonus and COLA they asked for. When you get them to narrow down a lot, the issues are theirs."

Before going into the union meeting, the mediator checked the proposal again with the management attorney. He then met with the union:

To get to the bottom of this, while Charlie was on the phone I called Bill into my office. He was firm about the last proposal. I told him there were still some areas he should address—the pension and the bonus. He justified his position. To make a long story short, I told him to keep talking. The way he tells it, he'll give the pension and bonus, your proposal on H & W and S & A. I called Charlie in and he made an impassioned plea for the vacation and personal leave. No way. Bill doesn't even have this, but he said he'll work for it. I don't have it either. He told me with Charlie there that if this represents an agreement, he would try to get it. But only up to this point. His people said no more.

The mediator reiterated the monetary benefits the union would receive, how hard Charlie had tried for the other issues, and that these concessions were based on the union's proposals: "In my humble opinion, this is the best chance to get the three big things. But if that doesn't do it, I'll tell him not to waste our time. As I told you, Charlie, I can't guarantee it. He has [to] sell it."

The mediator left the union to caucus. Some time later the union spokesman came out to call the mediator in. Vacations were still a sticking point. The mediator argued that it couldn't get them. If it did, the demand would represent 1 percent of the total package, which would affect only fifteen members of the unit. Further, if it struck over it, the last formal position, without the bonus and pension, would hold, and it was not assured of recouping them after a strike. With further discussion along these lines, the union agreed to recommend the package unanimously. The proposal was presented at a joint meeting. Management caucused and accepted.

Two weeks later the union membership ratified the contract.

Notes and Questions

(1) What was the narrowing strategy used by the mediator in the Bard mediation? Was the series of formal exchanges of proposals part of this strategy? How were the sides encouraged to refine their proposals?

(2) Does the Bard mediation reflect the following comment by Professor Julius Getman on the peculiar role of the union mediator?

> The internal bargaining process of a union is often the most difficult and emotional aspect of the bargaining process. If not properly dealt with, it might lead to an intransigent union position. The most serious charge against union negotiators is "selling out the members," a vague term which generally refers to improperly trading off the claims of one of the constituencies. Thus, union membership is often under heavy pressure not to accept compromises. Mediators can play a key role in combatting this pressure either because they persuade the union leadership that compromise is necessary or because they can legitimately articulate and argue for a sensible compromise which would be politically impossible for anyone within the union to champion or otherwise accept.

(3) Clearly the role of the mediator in the Bard mediation was far more activist than under the classical mediation model. Did he risk losing neutrality by any of the pressuring he did? What about his *ex parte* conversations and meetings with one side or the other?

(4) Bard was an example of a mediation by a federal (FMCS) mediator. Kolb notes some differences in approach by state agency mediators. Federal mediators tended to be "orchestrators" while state mediators tended to be "dealmakers." Kolb, The Mediators at 23–45. Federal mediators sought to narrow the differences until agreement emerged, while state mediators sought to discern what the parties needed or wanted and to build a proposal that satisfied those criteria. Kolb suggested as a reason for the different approach that federal mediators were generally more professional and the employees generally had a right to strike, thus facilitating negotiations. The state mediators worked with public sector disputes where there was no right to strike, and they may have felt they had to try to equalize the balance. Id. at 134–49.

(5) The union bargaining structure is often complex, but so too can be that of management. Consider Robins, A Guide for Labor Mediators 24–26 (1976):

> It is enormously valuable for the mediator to know who is present and in what capacity, who is influential and whether the influential person is the principal negotiator. The final employer decision on any issue in the private sector may be made by the president or a committee of officers of the company or representatives of the industry. They do not participate in negotiations, first,

because they do not generally possess the skills of a labor negotiator and, second, because it is considered desirable to protect them from direct questions and the need for direct answers. But they may be available to the mediator, with or without the blessing of the negotiator, and in any case should be recognized as the decision-makers. For the unions, the decision-makers are at the bargaining table, subject in most cases to the membership's ratification of the contract.

In the public sector it is not so easy to determine or have access to the employer decision-makers. In some cities, the mayors or comptrollers or budget officers determine what will be agreed to, but they frequently do not participate in the negotiations. Very often it is impossible until the last minute to identify who is "calling the shots," and tentative agreements reached by negotiators may be subject not only to union membership ratification, but also to employer acceptance at several levels. Frequently, neither the mediator nor the union negotiator knows whether an employer offer has been cleared with the executive of the jurisdiction (whether mayor, governor, county executive) or with the budget office, school board, the jurisdiction's lawyers, the comptroller, or other officials. In school district negotiations, a further complication may be the involvement of the state's education office in the decision-making. The need for legislative action to implement a settlement represents another possible breakdown in the negotiations. It is imperative that the mediator understand the authority of those who purport to represent the public employers in bargaining. Without clear understanding, grievous errors can be made, particularly in public sector disputes. If the mediator is to convey offers from one side to another, it is helpful to know if the offer is firm.

(6) Labor mediation, particularly involving collective bargaining, probably involves a greater range of specialists among the participants than other forms of mediation. Full time negotiators may be employed by both management and the union. Mediation often involves repeat players. Kolb, The Mediators, at 115–25, notes that mediators recognize certain negotiators as "pros":

> Pros work for either a law firm, union, or corporation in positions that give them primary responsibility for conducting contract negotiations in concert with the local client or unit. Because his job is negotiations, the pro knows mediation; he has been in it often and frequently knows the mediator personally.
>
> *   *   *
>
> The federal mediators expect the pros to move their committees. Since they have extensive exposure to labor negotiations, pros are assumed by the federal mediators to know as much as the mediator about settlement patterns and to be capable of identifying the level of wages and benefits that would comprise a "good"

settlement. Therefore, the pros and the mediator could coolly and rationally develop the substance of a reasonable package, but the de facto existence of such a package, as equitable and reasonable as it might be, in no way ensures that it will become an acceptable settlement. Acceptance of the package rests first with the committees, who must be so invested, committed, and "sold" on the package, so that they can enthusiastically and actively endorse its ratification to their constituencies. Only then is there a settlement. Narrowing is the process by which the priority issues are defined and commitment built. The chief engineer of this process is the pro working with his committee.

(7) Grievance mediation is increasingly being used as an alternative to arbitration. It was first used in the bituminous coal industry in a 1980 experiment funded by the Department of Labor. 89% of the 153 grievances mediated were resolved without need for arbitration. This lead to the establishment of the Mediation Research & Education Project, Inc., a not-for-profit Illinois corporation that operates a mediation scheduling service and provides mediation training for company and union personnel in a number of industries. The average cost of mediation is $300, less than 25% of the average arbitrator's fee. The lower cost results from the absence of a written transcript, briefs, written opinions, and attorneys. "Grievance Mediation Seen as New Alternative to Labor Arbitration," 1 BNA ADR Rptr. 93 (1987).

Professor Stephen Goldberg maintains that "mediation offers substantial promise of resolving grievances more quickly, inexpensively, and informally than arbitration," is more satisfactory to employees because of its "cathartic value," and improves "the parties' problem-solving ability and their relationship in a way that arbitration cannot." Goldberg, The Mediation of Grievances Under a Collective Bargaining Contract: An Alternative to Arbitration, 77 Nw.L.Rev. 270, 314 (1982). He describes the informal nature of the process: "The mediation process is entirely informal. The facts are brought out in narrative fashion rather than through examination and cross-examination. The rules of evidence do not apply, and no record of the proceeding is made. All persons involved in the events giving rise to the grievance are encouraged to participate fully in the proceedings, both by stating their views and by asking questions of the other participants in the hearing." 1 BNA ADR Rptr. 93 (1987). Are there any disadvantages to such full participation at the mediation session when the dispute may go on to arbitration if an agreement is not reached? See discussion of "med-arb," infra, p. 594.

4. Commercial Disputes

Commercial disputes have long been recognized as being especially suited to methods of resolution short of trial. By the mid–20th century, arbitration pursuant to an advance contractual provision had emerged as the favored vehicle for resolution in many commercial areas (see infra pp. 410, 435). But because many disputes are not covered by arbitration agreements, and because complaints about arbitration costs and delay persist, less structured processes like mediation have increasingly gained favor. The attraction of mediation is enhanced by the fact that the parties in commercial disputes would often like to have future dealings and thus have a strong incentive to find a workable solution without imposing the bitterness or burden on the business relationship frequently entailed by any adversary process.

There is less uniformity of procedures and process in commercial mediation than in most other areas of mediation. Community, family, and labor mediation each have a history of shared values and philosophical attitudes. This is less true of commercial mediation, where the history has been more eclectic, using whatever is believed will work without much concern for philosophical purity. Commercial mediation has certainly not escaped the influences of the mediation movement at large, but it is distinctive in its essentially utilitarian approach to process. In addition, commercial mediators, usually being drawn from business people and lawyers, are less likely to have contacts with the general mediation community apart from the narrow focus of commercial mediation.

In recent years, a number of attempts to formulate a comprehensive process for commercial mediation have been undertaken by not-for-profit organizations, trade groups, mediators, and corporations and other business entities. A certain number of common themes emerge. Considerable emphasis is put on the background, expertise, and personality of the mediator. Because commercial disputants can usually pay for a mediator, they want someone respected in the business community with recognized interpersonal skills. They want the mediator to be unquestionably impartial, but they recognize that the kind of person they are looking for often has ties with one or another segment of the business community and therefore they are not necessarily unwilling to accept one whose relationships might pose a conflict in the abstract so long as both parties are aware of that history. The role of the mediator varies dramatically depending on such considerations as the type of dispute, the nature of the parties, and the personality of the mediator. Some commercial mediators impose considerable formality of process, resulting in a proceeding not unlike arbitration or administrative hearings. Others will operate informally, some, in fact, with little face-to-face contact between the parties. One effective method is a form of "shuttle diplomacy," with the mediator as the key to all communications with full power to disclose, or not, what the parties have communicated to her. Finally, the preferred form for recording the agreement in a commercial setting is usually formal, pursuant to a detailed contract with which business people are familiar.

The following are rules drawn up by a New York attorney who served as mediator in the Agent Orange Litigation (see supra p. 172):

KENNETH R. FEINBERG,
AVOIDING LITIGATION THROUGH NONBINDING
MEDIATION

(Alliance of American Insurers, 1987).

PHASE I: Retaining a Mediator to Resolve the Dispute

Any party involved in the dispute may unilaterally initiate the mediation process by contacting the other parties and suggesting the use of a neutral third party mediator to hear the dispute, recommend settlement terms and, if necessary, attempt to facilitate a settlement. A meeting with the mediator and all parties may then be held to discuss the proposed rules governing the mediation. The following key points should be emphasized at such a meeting:

(1) Although one party may have initiated the process by recommending a person to be retained as the mediator, any person selected must be mutually acceptable to all parties to the dispute. Once retained the mediator will be strictly neutral and scrupulously fair to all sides; unless all parties otherwise agree, neither the initiating party nor any other party will unilaterally communicate with the mediator, except as specifically provided for pursuant to the procedures outlined herein.

(2) In the interest of moving the process forward, the party initiating the process, and recommending a particular mediator, may agree to pay the mediator's initial fees and expenses associated with Phase II of the mediation process without requesting contribution from the other parties. Only if all sides consent to proceed with Phase III (and, if necessary, Phase IV) will the costs of the mediator be borne in a manner determined and agreed to by the parties. The mediator's per diem or hourly charge shall be established at the time of his or her appointment.

(3) The initial meeting is explanatory and gives all parties an opportunity to size up the mediator and learn about the various phases of the mediation process. The mediator explains the ground rules— the private, voluntary, nonbinding nature of the process, his absolute neutrality (notwithstanding the role of the initiating party in recommending his appointment), the cost-sharing arrangement, and the procedures governing the mediator's efforts to settle the dispute. (Phase II, Phase III, and Phase IV.) The mediator emphasizes that at any phase of the process, even at the very end of the mediation, any party may withdraw and pursue more traditional remedies.

(4) The mediator explains that the entire mediation process is a compromise negotiation. Accordingly, all offers, promises, conduct, and statements, whether oral or written, made in the course of the mediation process by any of the parties or their representatives, are confidential. Such information is inadmissible and not discov-

erable for any purpose in litigation among the parties. By agreement of the parties, the mediator is disqualified as a litigation witness for any party and his or her oral and written opinions are deemed inadmissible for all purposes. All written submissions presented to the mediator, and all discussions had between the mediator and a particular party, will not be transmitted to any other party unless designated by the mediator as worthy of transmission and only if the permission of the party providing the information is obtained in advance.

(5) If the dispute giving rise to mediation is already the subject of litigation pending between the parties, the mediator may ask the consent of all parties to notify the Court of his or her retention. (The parties may also decide to present a joint motion to the Court requesting a stay of all proceedings pending conclusion of the mediation process.) Unless the consent of all parties is given, however, no such notification shall be made. The mediator may renew his request at any time, again, however, requiring the consent of all parties.

(6) A proposed schedule is discussed and agreed to for the completion of the mediation, including (if necessary) a "mini-discovery" process for obtaining documents and/or certain testimony.

PHASE II: Familiarizing the Mediator With the Facts of the Dispute

The mediator having been selected with the consent of all parties to the dispute, the mediation process commences:

(1) The mediator asks each party to provide, pursuant to an agreed upon schedule, such materials as each party deems necessary for the purpose of familiarizing the mediator with the facts and issues in dispute. This submission may consist, for example, of a written summary accompanied by already available court documents, a letter, a formal memorandum, a legal brief, etc. Upon studying the documents and reviewing the facts, the mediator may contact any party separately requesting further clarification and additional information. The parties shall comply promptly with all reasonable requests by the mediator for further information relevant to the dispute. Written materials submitted to the mediator are confidential and may not be disseminated to anyone without the consent of the submitting party.

(2) An initial group meeting is held with the mediator presiding and all sides being present. Each party may be represented by whomever it wishes—outside counsel, in-house counsel, a corporate official or a combination of persons. *Experience proves, however, that an in-house representative is more likely to move the mediation process forward in an efficient, effective manner.*

(3) In the event of a complex, multi-party dispute, a series of public mediation sessions may be necessary, e.g., a session involving

plaintiffs and defendant, a second session involving the insurance carriers, or a third session involving the subcontractors (in a construction defect dispute).

(4) Each representative of the parties shall have appropriate authority to negotiate a settlement on behalf of the party he or she represents.

(5) The mediator first asks if, in fact, each party really desires that the dispute be settled. If not, e.g., the parties wish to litigate the case, the mediator declines to go forward and the process terminates at this point.

(6) The mediator explains that this initial meeting will likely be the only time that the parties will meet together unless the case is particularly complex or unless a group meeting is deemed necessary by the mediator near the end of Phase IV of the process. Remaining meetings will be held separately between the mediator and each party; communications between the various parties concerning settlement terms will be made only by the mediator.

(7) The public session consists of a statement made by each party in the presence of the mediator and the other parties—in effect a summation. This statement of between 30 and 45 minutes (it can be waived but such a tactic is deemed inadvisable) gives all other parties (especially the principals) and the mediator an opportunity to hear a first-hand account of the strengths of each party's position. At the conclusion of the public session the mediator meets privately and in confidence with each party in order to: (a) gather additional facts not brought out during the public session, and (b) elicit such further confidential information as is thought necessary in light of the written submissions and public statements.

(8) The mediator may also raise legal arguments and questions of law with any party during the private, confidential meetings, in an effort to evaluate that party's ultimate likelihood of success if the dispute were to be resolved by litigation. (Legal uncertainty has proven to be a critical variable promoting settlement through mediation prior to full-blown litigation and trial.)

(9) If necessary, time may be set aside during the public session(s) in order to permit the parties to engage in "mini-discovery," for example, by permitting examination of witnesses or authorizing the exchange of certain documents. Such a mini-discovery procedure must be agreed to in advance, including limitation on the time to be expended in such discovery. In addition, the mediator presides over the process and makes sure that the parties adhere to the agreed upon schedule.

After receiving all relevant materials, reviewing all of the facts, analyzing all of the various key legal issues, and permitting each party an opportunity to present its best case, the mediator announces that he has sufficiently familiarized himself with the facts and legal issues in issue. Phase II of the process has been completed and the mediator is now prepared, with the consent of all parties, to present proposed settlement terms for separate consideration by each party. (This usually takes place between four to six weeks after the public session.) The mediator explains that only if the parties consent to proceed to Phase III will the process go forward.

PHASE III: The Mediator's Presentation of Settlement Terms and the Initial Reaction of the Parties

Phase III begins with the mediator separately explaining to each party the proposed settlement terms and the reasons underlying his proposal. There are two key features underlying the mediator's Phase III presentation:

(1) The presentation is based on a good faith effort by the mediator to offer the fairest settlement terms at the very outset of Phase III, i.e., the mediator is not engaging in an opening negotiation gambit or offering terms which he or she anticipates will lead to further negotiation. The latter may indeed occur as part of Phase IV *but the purpose of the mediator's Phase III proposal is to give all parties the immediate opportunity to accept what the mediator has concluded is the fairest resolution of the dispute without the necessity of further Phase IV negotiation.* It is the mediator's goal to settle the dispute promptly by offering optimum settlement terms at the outset of Phase III, terms which will prove immediately acceptable to all sides.

(2) The separate, private reaction of each party to the mediator's proposed terms is sealed and is not communicated to the other parties (unless, of course, all parties agree to the proposed terms, thereby settling the dispute). Accordingly, each side does not know of the reaction of the other parties to the mediator's proposed terms, nor does each side know of any counterproposal offered by the other side to the mediator as part of Phase IV. The mediator— and the mediator alone—communicates with the other parties. For example, if the mediator proposes a settlement figure in the range of $400,000–$500,000, and one party counteroffers with a demand for $600,000, this latter figure, as well as the reasons offered to justify it, are not conveyed to the other parties. Instead, the mediator, with the consent of all parties, begins Phase IV shuttle diplomacy.

PHASE IV: Shuttle Diplomacy

Phase IV is the final phase of the mediation process and commences only if the mediator's Phase III presentation of "best" settlement terms proves unacceptable to any party.

There are two critical aspects to this final phase:

(1) The mediator first meets separately with each party and then shuttles back and forth among the various parties (by telephone and, if necessary, in face-to-face meetings) in an effort to bridge differences and reach an accommodation. *Until and unless the mediator sees an advantage to a group meeting of the parties, no such meeting occurs. Instead, the mediator attempts to fashion a settlement through separate meetings and communications with the other parties.*

(2) As already indicated, the substantive conversations had with each party are confidential and are not conveyed to the other parties. Instead, the mediator listens to each party's settlement terms and transmits only such information to the other parties as is agreed upon and which the mediator believes will foster settlement of the dispute.

Shuttle diplomacy may take place over a concentrated period, as the mediator communicates separately with each party in an effort to hammer-out final settlement terms. The mediator uses his Phase III "best" settlement proposal as a starting point, and attempts to convince, cajole, and implore the parties to minimize their differences with respect to the Phase III proposal.

If the parties remain unable to agree upon settlement terms, the mediator may eventually suggest that "the heat be turned up" in an effort to secure a settlement. For example:

(1) If a formal litigation is already pending, the mediator may again suggest that the Court be notified of the mediation process and its assistance solicited;

(2) The mediator may call for an "around-the-clock" group meeting to resolve remaining disagreements face-to-face;

(3) The mediator may request that senior corporate officials be brought into the negotiations, in order to get the remaining issues resolved;

(4) As a last resort, the mediator may suggest that the parties agree to accept, as final and binding, new settlement terms proposed by the mediator.

As already indicated, no such Phase IV mediation options may be imposed unilaterally by the mediator, but, rather, require the consent of *all* parties. At any time during the process, a party may withdraw and pursue more traditional remedies.

At the conclusion of Phase IV, if settlement is reached, one of the parties (or the mediator) is designated to draft a written settlement document reflecting all settlement terms. This document is circulated among the parties, edited to reflect their exact understanding, and formally executed. If a formal litigation is pending, and the Court has not yet been made aware of the mediation process, it is notified in order that the case may be dismissed.

Notes and Questions

(1) The use in Feinberg's procedures regarding shuttle diplomacy and separate meetings at the discretion of the mediator is in marked contrast to the classical model of the mediator. The mediator "transmits only such information to the other parties as is agreed upon and which the mediator believes will foster settlement of the dispute." The mediation begins "with the mediator separately explaining to each party" his proposed settlement terms so as to "give all parties the immediate opportunity to accept what the mediator has concluded is the fairest resolution of the dispute." Obviously this is a very activist mediator model. There is no reason that all commercial mediation must accord the mediator such a dominant role, and there are a variety of other commercial mediation models.

(2) In conjunction with his procedures, Feinberg recommends that companies adopt a screening process for referring disputes to mediation and have "a visible high-level commitment" to "the concept of mediation." The decision to institutionalize mediation techniques should be publicized "by notifying the world at large that, as part of its decision-making process, the company automatically considers use of mediation in all cases, regardless of the size of the case or the strength of its legal position." It should further "include in all its commercial contracts and dealings with outside parties" a provision that mediation, arbitration or other form of dispute resolution "shall automatically be considered in the event of a dispute." All members of its general counsel's staff, as well as outside counsel, should be familiar with mediation techniques.

Feinberg recommends a system for screening disputes whereby any recommendation of litigation should be referred to "a centralized decision-making authority" that would include the general counsel (or a high-level staff member) and non-lawyer business officials with expertise in the area and familiarity with the ongoing business relationships at stake in the dispute. If the matter is rejected for mediation, periodic monitoring should continue at regular intervals—for example, every six months. Before the company commits additional resources to a particular case (for example, filing a major motion or engaging in expensive discovery), it should reevaluate the potential for mediation.

Do these procedures reflect a distrust of lawyers and a desire to temper the legal judgment with a "business perspective."? Is this necessary, and is the solution realistic?

(3) In recent years, the mediation movement in business and industry has taken on a zeal reminiscent of an anti-drinking crusade. The Center for Public Resources (CPR), founded in 1979, is a non-profit organization with members from major corporations, law firms, and law schools that seeks to develop private alternatives to litigation. Members are asked to sign a pledge that "[i]n the event of a business dispute between our company and another company which has made or will

then make a similar statement, we are prepared to explore with that other party resolution of the dispute through negotiation or ADR techniques before pursuing full-scale litigation." Corporate Policy Statement: Alternative Dispute Resolution, Center for Public Resources. Are such pledges effective?

(4) The CPR has also issued a Model Procedure for Mediation of Business Disputes. See 4 Alternatives to the High Cost of Litigation 113 (1986). It encourages counsel drafting commercial agreements to incorporate the following clause:

The parties will attempt in good faith to resolve any controversy or claim arising out of or relating to this agreement by mediation in accordance with the CPR Model Procedure for Mediation of a Business Dispute.

The CPR procedure puts considerable emphasis on the selection of the mediator who may play a very activist role in attempting to achieve agreement. The desired qualities suggest nothing short of a philosopher king: "He must be absolutely impartial and fair and so perceived"; inspire trust and motivate people to confide in him; be able to size up people, understand their motivations, relate easily to them; set a tone of civility and consideration in his dealings with others; be a good listener; be capable of understanding thoroughly the law and facts of a dispute, including surrounding circumstances; and be creative, imaginative and ingenious in developing proposals that will "fly" and know when to make such proposals. Contrary to community mediation, a mediator who has a reputation may be more desirable: "It can be helpful for the mediator to have prestige and a personal stature that command respect." Special expertise is usually required: "When legal issues are critical, there are significant advantages to selecting a lawyer or legal academic as the mediator. When the subject matter of the dispute is technical, it may well be desirable to select a person who has an understanding of the technology." A single mediator is to be used in most cases, but in complex cases two mediators may be selected to represent different disciplines relevant to the dispute, e.g., science and law.

Under the CPR model, the mediator is the mover and shaker of the mediation process. He may conclude that it is better to keep the parties apart at a given stage, and parties only communicate through him. "At separate meetings a party can share information with the mediator which it is not then willing to share with the other party. Such a meeting also provides an opportunity for the mediator and the party to consider the party's underlying interests and to informally explore settlement options."

Is it not curious that the parties in business mediation, who are generally more sophisticated in the art of negotiation than are parties in community mediation, should be willing to cede such powers to a mediator? Would this work better than a passive-mediator model?

(5) What kinds of business disputes are likely candidates for mediation? Feinberg offers the following considerations: (a) where the parties are unsure of the likelihood of success in litigation, or there is a potential for great exposure (or minimal recovery), (b) where protracted litigation indicates inefficiencies in terms of costs and diversion of lawyer and company official time (including a plaintiff's contingent fee case where the attorney sees advantages to prompt settlement without the need to "bankroll" the litigation), (c) where there are mixed questions of fact and law involving application of settled law to complex factual issues, (d) in a high stakes case, after extensive discovery has taken place and the imminence of trial exerts pressure for settlement, (e) where a settlement may set parameters for future conduct enforceable as contractual obligations or incorporated in a consent decree, (f) where negotiating positions are far apart, suggesting that at least one of the parties is taking an unrealistic view of the case, (g) where parties find it necessary to retain technical, economic or other experts and a neutral expert may instead be looked to.

(6) Use of mediation in international and trans-national business disputes has been slow in coming, an indication in part of the dominant role of arbitration in that area. The United Nations Commission on International Trade Law (UNCITRAL), established by the UN General Assembly in 1966, chose international commercial arbitration as one of three priority topics at its opening session in 1968. It issued in 1976 the UNCITRAL Rules for International Arbitration, which are widely used in ad hoc arbitrations or in arbitrations administered by institutions like the AAA (see infra pp. 413–16). It was not until 1978 that UNCITRAL included mediation/conciliation in its work program.

The UNCITRAL Conciliation Rules, finalized in 1980, has thus far attracted only limited interest and usage (although serving as a model for other rules). Dore, Arbitration and Conciliation Under the UNCITRAL Rules 213 (1986). The other principal sources of regulation of international commercial mediation are the Rules of Conciliation and Arbitration of the International Chamber of Commerce and the Rules of the International Center for the Settlement of Investment Disputes (ICSID) (see infra p. 418). Various countries have also set up arbitration centers that address mediation/conciliation (such as the Canadian Arbitration, Conciliation and Amicable Composition Center and the Arbitral Centre of the Federal Economic Chamber in Vienna). In some non-Western legal cultures, the line between "arbitration" and "mediation" in international commercial disputes may be difficult to draw (see infra p. 418, note (3)).

(7) One of the most innovative uses of commercial dispute mediation arose out of the farm recession of the 1980's. With large numbers of farmers facing foreclosure, some eleven states, mostly in the midwest, passed farm debt mediation laws. Some, like Iowa, Minnesota, and South Dakota, make mediation mandatory, forbidding creditors from instituting foreclosure or forfeiture proceedings until mediation is offered to the farmer-debtor and either rejected or completed. The

South Dakota law applies to creditors owed more than $50,000 by an individual farmer; once a mediation notice is sent to the farmer, it must be completed in 42 days unless either side requests an extension. "South Dakota Requires Mediation Before Foreclosure of Farm Debts," 2 BNA ADR Rptr. 158 (1988). Other states, like Kansas, Wyoming, Oklahoma, and Wisconsin, make mediation voluntary.

The mediation programs are funded in a number of ways. Minnesota's funding ($2.8 million for two years) comes primarily from the state. Iowa's funding ($900,000 for two years) comes from a combination of client fees and state allocations. The Farm Credit Act of 1987 provides matching funds from the federal government for complying programs. Mediators are paid in Kansas and Iowa; in the other programs they are volunteers.

Consider the following description of the programs by Micheal Thompson, administrator of the Iowa program, and Judy Corder, mediation consultant:

Iowa has kept a record of the number of farmers who have refused to mediate. The turndown rate the first year was 42 percent, and 30% the second year. Other states do not keep track of turn-down rates, although it is obviously difficult to get all parties to the table, even when mediation is mandatory. One of the major differences between mandatory and voluntary programs is the number of cases processed each year. Iowa handled 6,000 cases the first year and 2,400 the second; Minnesota 7,000 cases the first year and 5,000 the second. The voluntary programs handle many fewer cases (Mississippi had 45 to 50 cases in one year, Oklahoma 25 cases in the first six months, Wisconsin 36 cases in two years, and Kansas 15 cases).

Resolution rates of cases mediated or conciliated also vary. Iowa's resolution rate the first year was 67% and the second year between 80 and 87%; Minnesota's was 60% the first year and 70% the second; Mississippi's was between 67% and 80%; Wisconsin's was 75%. In the voluntary programs, the single biggest obstacle is getting creditors to agree to mediate. Many creditors believe they are already mediating; most are actually negotiating, not mediating.

The mediated agreements reached in farm-credit cases range from agreements that specifically detail how a debt will be restructured, to temporary agreements until information can be gathered and provided at a subsequent session, to those that include very detailed behaviors regarding how people will deal with each other in the future. In some states, these agreements, like those reached in other kinds of mediation programs, are considered legal contracts. Especially when agreements are made contingent on review by experts, the agreement may provide for the parties to come back to mediation if they have difficulty finalizing the agreement.

There are differences between farm-credit mediations and other kinds of mediation. Farm-credit mediations often involve substantial sums of money (the range is from $5,000 to $15 million). These mediations are much more likely to include attorneys, perhaps in as many as 50% of the cases. Another difference is the potential psychological dysfunction of the involved parties. The farmers are often depressed and may even be suicidal. Very often there are marital and family difficulties. To the extent that the families of the farmer and creditor(s) know each other, the conflict may affect the whole community, particularly in small rural communities where everyone knows everyone else. The intensity of the emotions tends to create an additional dynamic for mediators that can be difficult to deal with constructively. Farm-credit mediations often involve many parties. Usually the farmer's side includes the entire farm family, and there may be multiple creditors involved. This increases the likelihood of complex mediations, because often there is conflict within as well as between the two sides.

5. Public Law Disputes

Public law disputes encompass a vast variety of issues concerning such matters as land use, the environment, civil rights and liberties, allocation of resources and services, voting rights, consumer concerns, employment claims, and political controversies. They frequently involve governmental entities as parties (in part a consequence of the "state action" requirement of the Fourteenth Amendment), but may also embrace disputes between private parties. They draw, for their substantive basis, on constitutional provisions, both federal and state, as well as on statutes, common law, and private contracts.

In 1976, Professor Abram Chayes attached the term "public law litigation" to the phenomenon that had been developing since the New Deal, and had gained momentum in the previous decade of expanded constitutional and substantive remedies and new procedural mechanisms like the class action. He saw the public law litigation model as structurally different from the traditional private dispute model:

> The party structure is sprawling and amorphous, subject to change over the course of the litigation. The traditional adversary relationship is suffused and intermixed with negotiating and mediating processes at every point. The judge is the dominant figure in organizing and guiding the case, and he draws for support not only on the parties and their counsel, but on a wide range of outsiders—masters, experts, and oversight personnel. * * *
>
> The class suit is a reflection of our growing awareness that a host of important public and private interactions—perhaps the most important in defining the conditions and opportunities of life for most people—are conducted on a routine or bureaucratized basis

and can no longer be visualized as bilateral transactions between private individuals. From another angle, the class action responds to the proliferation of more or less well-organized groups in our society and the tendency to perceive interests as group interests, at least in very important aspects. * * *

The form of relief does not flow ineluctably from the liability determination, but is fashioned ad hoc. * * * And relief is not a terminal, compensatory transfer, but an effort to devise a program to contain future consequences in a way that accommodates the range of interests involved. * * * In the remedial phases of public law litigation, factfinding is even more clearly prospective. * * * The elaboration of a decree is largely a discretionary process within which the trial judge is called upon to assess and appraise the consequences of alternative programs that might correct the substantive fault.[1]

It is interesting to note how many of the principles and themes identified by Chayes as central to public law litigation also underlie the alternative dispute resolution movement. The concern for consideration of all interests, flexibility of process, cooperative mechanisms, and creative solutions found in ADR sound similarly responsive chords in the Chayes description of public law litigation. With such similarity of values and process objectives, ADR should have something to contribute to resolving public law disputes. The public law litigation model described by Chayes actually contemplates an informal form of mediation in which the judge and surrogate court personnel offer third-party intervention in working out a solution by less formal means than the ultimate trial will provide. But formal mediation may also be useful in such disputes, either as an integral part of the litigation process (see Chapter V), or as an alternative to the litigation itself. On the other hand, not all advocates of the public law model would see mediation as consistent with preserving rights in the public law arena.

Public law mediation is perhaps the most complex of the various mediation processes. No single model, as in community dispute mediation, can serve as the procedural structure for most public law mediations. Public law disputes involve so many differing features that their resolution is necessarily *ad hoc.* Like the judicial personnel involved in public law litigation, the mediator must develop a structure that is workable and devise procedures as she goes along. Special talents, skills, and knowledge are usually required of mediators, and the support of other experts or staff may be necessary. The ultimate resolution may require a good deal more than a simple written agreement and, like the equity decree that is central to public law litigation, may require ongoing monitoring and relationships between the parties.

1. Chayes, The Role of the Judge in Public Law Litigation, 89 Harv.L.Rev. 1281, 1284, 1291, 1293–1294, 1296 (1976).

Consider the following description of a public law mediation in an environmental case.

FRANCIS McGOVERN, TOWARD A FUNCTIONAL APPROACH FOR MANAGING COMPLEX LITIGATION
53 U.Chi.L.Rev. 440, 456–466 (1986).

[The author, a law professor at the University of Alabama, was appointed by U.S. District Court Judge Enslen to serve as special master to assist in pre-trial preparation and exploration of settlement in *United States v. Michigan,* a suit involving rights to tribal treaty waters of the Great Lakes.]

A. Problem

In 1979 Judge Fox of the Eastern District of Michigan ruled that the Treaty of 1836 between the United States and the Ottawa and Chippewa peoples reserved to the tribes the right to fish in the treaty waters of the Great Lakes unfettered by regulation by the State of Michigan. The U.S. Department of the Interior subsequently ceased regulating Great Lakes fishing, leaving two independent sovereigns to govern a common natural resource. The tribal commercial fishers and other Michigan commercial and sport fishers competed for fish in most of the Michigan waters of Lakes Superior, Huron, and Michigan.

This competition triggered significant resource depletion and violence among the competitors. In an attempt to save the basic stocks of fish, the tribes, the state, and the United States agreed to close the fishery each year as soon as a certain amount of fish had been caught. As the competition increased, closure occurred earlier and earlier each year, and the tribes took a smaller and smaller percentage of the catch. The tribes could not compete technologically with the state commercial fishers, nor were they numerous enough to compete with the burgeoning state sport fishers.

As a result of the reduced catch and threats of violence, the tribes moved Judge Fox's successor, Judge Enslen, to allocate the treaty waters between the tribes and the state. A literal reading of Judge Fox's original opinion supported the tribes' view that they had a primary right to the resource and thus should be able to take whatever fish were necessary to maintain reasonable tribal living standards. Given the tribes' depressed economic state, they might obtain a virtual monopoly on Great Lakes fish stocks. The State of Michigan countered that any allocation should be made on equitable grounds, taking into account not only the tribes' subsistence needs but also how best to maximize the fishery's potential economic benefits to all Michigan citizens. Because sports fishing generated far more direct and indirect income than tribal fishing, an economic analysis would tilt the scales toward control of the fishery by Michigan sports fishers. The United

States argued for a 50–50 split between the tribes and the state. The treaty itself contained little guidance for resolving the allocation issue.

Given the paucity of precedent for any allocation scheme, the parties' wildly differing approaches, the extreme volatility of the situation, the complexity of any allocation process, and institutional weaknesses associated with continuing judicial management, Judge Enslen decided that if allocation was appropriate, the parties preferably should do it. He also believed that an expeditious decision was necessary to minimize the potential for violence in the uncertain situation. Judge Enslen appointed a special master to prepare the case for trial within eight months and explore the possibilities for settlement. The master's duties did not include ruling on substantive issues, and all his decisions were subject to de novo review by the judge.

B. Diagnosis

United States v. Michigan was relatively complex litigation; the five named parties represented virtually all Michigan citizens. The issues and information involved every conceivable problem associated with managing the largest lakes in the world. From one perspective the case was a generic conflict—a distributional dispute to divide a common pool among competing users. Large numbers of equally situated parties, the fishers, had similar incentives to use a common asset, the Great Lakes, as much as possible. Without intervention, the cumulative use would destroy the resource through massive overfishing. The essential problem was to determine what kind of intervention would help to resolve the dispute.

Under this view of the lawsuit, its big issues were polycentric, not susceptible to the yes-or-no answers or mutually exclusive inquiries typical of special interrogatories posed to juries. The solution to any given question concerning resource division was dependent upon the solutions reached on the other questions: no issues were independent. This complex interrelationship of issues created difficulties which were compounded by the lack of any—much less clear—legal standards. The court was being asked to make extremely complex management decisions by using policy differences unreflected in the substantive law— "reasonable living standards," "subsistence," "maximizing value," and "equal distribution." Because of the continuing relationship among the parties, any court-imposed solution would probably generate future conflict. Even under optimal conditions, changes in the resource itself would breed future controversies.

Judge Enslen concluded that these characteristics begged for an allocation plan developed by the parties themselves. It was a classic case for integrative bargaining. The parties could identify their respective interests, share information concerning how they valued those interests, and reach for a combination of trade-offs that would maximize each side's use of the resource. Under an economic analysis of integrative bargains, they could seek superior allocations, reduce conflicts of interest, and possibly achieve an optimal solution. Given constraints on a court's ability to gather and evaluate this type of information, the parties would be in a superior position to locate an optimal allocation plan. A party-developed plan would also eliminate any dislocation that could accompany a court-ordered resolution.

However, this diagnosis posed two major problems. First, the parties asserted that the case involved fundamental political values not subject to compromise. Leaders on both sides had invested substantial political capital in their incompatible positions and had constructed arguments slicing to the core of the relationship between two sovereigns in the United States. Second, these political leaders had attempted to achieve a negotiated resolution on numerous occasions over the years. Thus major behavioral impediments had arisen from personal animosities and low expectations of reaching satisfactory agreement. The tribal leaders, in particular, had witnessed a long history of negotiation that had not brought prosperity to their peoples. If the behavioral and value-laden components of the lawsuit predominated, judicial resolution was almost inevitable.

C. Prescription

1. *Parties.* The plaintiffs consisted of three Indian tribes and the United States; the defendant was the State of Michigan. The tribes had extremely varying interests: one tribe desired to perpetuate the traditional cultural values of Indian fishing, another desired to maximize the tribes' overall economic benefit, and the third valued accommodation consistent with limited tribal fishing in one area of Lake Michigan. The United States represented the tribal interests and the concerns of the Fish and Wildlife Service in restoring the Great Lakes to their earlier economic prosperity—goals that were not always consistent.

The State of Michigan also represented competing interests: those of state commercial fishers, the developing sports fishing and tourist industry, Indian citizens of Michigan living outside the reservations, and the public peace. The state's prime mover was its Department of Natural Resources, but the organized commercial and sports fishers were independent, politically powerful constituents. Judge Enslen decided, therefore, to bring these groups of state fishers into the litigation, but without full party status. He named them litigating amici: they had a participatory role in discovery and at trial, but could not veto a potential settlement. This innovative organization of parties ensured that all the key decisionmakers were present in the litigation.

The court then assigned the special master to mediate among the named parties and the litigating amici. Because the case would eventually be tried to the judge, his ability to facilitate negotiation was limited by his strong ethical constraints against prejudging the outcome of the case. Therefore, the master performed this role while insulating the judge from the details of any bargaining. As a part of the mediation role, the master also kept the parties' critical decisionmakers aware of the progress of the litigation and the negotiations. He met with the leaders and sometimes virtually all the members of the tribes, officials of the U.S. Department of the Interior, and Michigan's Governor, Attorney General, and the Director of its Department of Natural Resources.

2. *Issues.* The issues were both simplified and expanded. The resource allocation was narrowed to involve five major variables: species of fish, quantity of fish, fishing gear, geography, and time. Even with this gross simplification, a virtually infinite number of combinations of variables and numerous measuring criteria still remained. The parties were asked to narrow these issues further by proposing management plans that they would support at trial. Timing became important in setting the deadlines for identifying plans, because a party might lock itself into a given negotiating posture by solidifying behind a single management plan.

While the parties were narrowing issues, an intensive educational effort was undertaken to broaden the horizons to include additional issues suitable for negotiation. All the parties were questioned in great detail concerning their interests—some totally unrelated to the case—to see if they might be interested in placing them on the bargaining table.

3. *Information.* Normal discovery had been expedited somewhat by the parties' agreement to pool data concerning Great Lakes fishing. A tripartite group of biologists from the tribes, the state, and the United States had cooperated in developing consensus recommendations based upon shared information. In addition, the tribes turned over all of their fish catch reports to the state so that the data could be computerized and made available to everyone.

Early in the lawsuit it had appeared that disagreements among the biologists would constitute a major portion of the evidence during trial. Some thought was given to appointing an expert to assist in resolving scientific issues. Because the biologists were cooperating in some areas, however, they were asked if they could develop a joint computer model of the five critical variables. If this could be done, computer runs could be made for each suggested management plan to determine the effects of that plan on these variables. A neutral expert in modeling was asked to assist the biologists and the special master in creating the computer model.

This process has been called computer-assisted negotiation. Experts attempt to create a consensus model of a complex phenomenon that will, in effect, constitute a negotiated dispute resolution or enable the policymakers to negotiate a result. The created model then scrutinizes hypothetical solutions to verify that any chosen solution can meet parties' expectations.

* * *

In conjunction with the Program on Negotiation at Harvard, the master attempted to develop a scorable game that would mimic the actual dispute. The task involved identifying each party's interests, selecting all feasible elements to any allocation plan, stating the parties' priorities, and determining the variety of systems that could be used to organize those interests and elements. Each priority was then quantified in regard to each issue. The negotiation theory applied to the game was so-called differences orientation. For example, each party might value the same portion of Lake Michigan differently. The tribes living in the northern Michigan peninsula would probably prefer unlimited access to waters close to their homes. In contrast, the sports fishers generally lived in southern Michigan and would value the southern waters more highly. Differences orientation was particularly valuable here because of the economic and cultural disparities among the parties: what appeared in the litigation context to be a major problem of fundamental value differences was actually an asset in developing a mutually acceptable allocation plan. Once relative differences had been identified, they were entered into a computer.

A program was run to determine if any scenario would satisfy each party's minimum priorities. When the game was limited to the case's legal issues, no negotiated outcome seemed possible. If, however, the issues were expanded to include other items that might be subject to negotiation, some solutions might satisfy the hypothetical minimum interests of the parties. A court, for example, was limited to interpreting the treaty in perpetuity; an agreement by the parties could be for a term of years. A negotiated disposition, unlike a typical court decision, could also include provisions for plantings of fish, monetary payments, and market development. When these and other issues were added to the computer, there emerged combinations of components which indicated different possible solutions where agreement was feasible.

As originally designed, the scorable game had another, more important function. Its primary purpose was as an educational tool, not just to provide specific answers, but to teach the parties how to negotiate. If all of the key decisionmakers could play the game, typically separately, they might better appreciate their own and their adversaries' positions. Moreover, they might develop more confidence in their own abilities and power as negotiators. The negotiation prong thus became an educational and behavioral task, aimed at educating the parties concerning the potential for maximizing their own interests, developing their strategic negotiating capacity, expanding the roster of issues subject to bargaining, and softening communication and behavioral barriers to face-to-face negotiation.

*   *   *

In this situation the computer-assisted negotiation was enormously successful, but for a different reason. Negotiations over the model soon revealed that the biologists were generally in agreement, except in areas of massive uncertainty or where basic policy choices were involved. Thus the major by-product of developing this model was to resolve most of the case's biological issues.

Finally, information was added to the lawsuit concerning parallel litigation over Indian salmon fishing rights in the Pacific Northwest. In *United States v. Washington,* various tribes won a share of the Washington salmon catch. The parties had declined to negotiate a solution to their allocation dilemma, and years of intense litigation ensued. Representatives of several parties to that case were invited to speak to the participants in *United States v. Michigan* concerning the court's management of their resource. They reported in detail how the court made decisions—even on a fish-by-fish basis—and how fishery managers and fishers coped with these decisions. They also recounted some of the spillovers to tribal relations that had developed out of the case. They generally recommended that a negotiated management plan—if feasible—was preferable to a litigated one.

D. Results

After three days of negotiations the parties reached a settlement on March 28, four weeks before the scheduled trial. The settlement agreement closely paralleled one of the scorable game solutions that indicated possible areas of compromise. The court approved the settlement, but one of the tribes overruled its leaders on a subsequent 31–29 vote and decided to proceed with the litigation. All the other parties ratified the negotiated agreement. The judge severed the two alternative management plans for trial, conducted a trial, and ruled on the merits in favor of the negotiated plan.

Notes and Questions

(1) Despite the complexity of the issues in public law disputes, their settlement often turns on some of the same basic principles that characterize other forms of mediation—creating trust between the parties, getting out the real facts, ventilating emotions and past misunderstandings, and searching for workable solutions. But it can be difficult to get down to such basics in a process that involves large numbers of parties and representatives and many meetings and proceedings. Are game playing and computerized models, as used in the "treaty waters" case described by McGovern, effective? What other techniques might be useful?

(2) Fuller believed that mediation is generally feasible when there are only two parties. See Fuller, Mediation—Its Forms and Functions, 44 S.Cal.L.Rev. 305, 313 (1971) (arguing that with three parties (A, B, & C), if the mediator X "asks A's acquiescence in a proposed solution, A may reply that he will give his assent if X will undertake to persuade B to withdraw a concession B made in favor of C" and thus the mediator may become "the manipulated tool of those he sought to guide"). Does McGovern's account of the successful "treaty waters" mediation indicate that this is too narrow a view of mediation? Note that the use of

computerized data and game playing is just one of the techniques used by McGovern that may not have been thought of in Fuller's earlier analysis.

(3) Is a special master, the role performed by McGovern, in a better position than an ordinary mediator to resolve a dispute? Does he carry greater authority because of his official position and his relationship to the judge who may preside over the trial? Could this feature work the other way by undermining his neutrality?

(4) The use of mandatory "settlement conferences" pursuant to Fed.R.Civ.Pro. 16 may involve a federal judge, magistrate, or special master in a role not unlike that of a mediator in attempting to assist (or some would say persuade) the parties to reach a settlement. See supra p. 167. Judge William Schwarzer of the U.S. District Court for the Northern District of California urges active judicial involvement in settlement but cautions that "the judge must take care not to become so committed to achieving a settlement that he sacrifices his objectivity or becomes coercive." W. Schwarzer, Managing Antitrust and Other Complex Litigation: A Handbook for Lawyers and Judges 199 (1982). Will a federal judge who will ultimately preside over the case if it is not settled inevitably exert coercive power over the attorneys and parties in a settlement conference? As we have seen in Chapter II, supra p. 171, some trial attorneys feel strongly that a judge who conducts the settlement conference should not preside over the trial.

Consider the following account of Judge Schwarzer's recommendations concerning the conduct of settlement conferences in Sherman, Restructuring the Trial Process in the Age of Complex Litigation, 63 Tex.L.Rev. 721, 741–42 (1984):

> [T]he judge [should] raise the subject of settlement with the parties and open communication between them, but go no further without their invitation and without offering them an opportunity for settlement conferences before another judge. When the parties request his participation, the judge can act as a catalyst by drawing attention to the weaknesses in each side's case, by indicating probable jury reactions to evidence and helping the parties evaluate the case more realistically by suggesting alternative approaches, compromises, and face-saving arrangements, and by lending support to a lawyer faced with a recalcitrant or unrealistic client. Schwarzer also recommends that the clients be present or on call during settlement conferences and that house counsel attend the conference if his company requires him to approve any settlement.

(5) Environmental disputes are an obvious subject for use of mediation, but there is controversy over whether mediation simply reinforces power imbalances that already exist between the parties. In environmental disputes, large companies, landholders, or even the government may be arrayed against adjoining landowners, citizens groups, or public interest organizations. At other times, a governmental body may be

expected to uphold the public interest against powerful private interests.

Professor Susskind has commented that elected officials may be ignorant of the concerns that citizens have about environmental threats and fail adequately to represent their interests. Susskind, Resolving Development Disputes Through Ad–Hocracy, Environmental Consensus 3–5 (Summer 1980). Government bureaucrats may have even less rapport and identity of interests with affected groups and individuals. Thus negotiation or mediation, without assurance that all interested parties are involved, introduces risks of "sweetheart" deals. It is argued that "[t]his was the case, for instance, in the Love Canal controversy where the new Reagan administration quickly reached an agreement with the Hooker Chemical Company—an agreement that local citizens protested, claiming it would not guarantee a clean-up or protect their health and safety." D. Amy, The Politics of Environmental Mediation 137 (1987). "When environmental groups feel outmanned and out-gunned in the conventional political institutions, they may be forced to turn to mediation as a last resort—even though they know they will be bargaining from a position of weakness. They may know that they will be forced to give up a lot and are likely to receive only a few token concessions, but they may decide that even those few concessions are better than losing totally." *Id.* at 147. Jane Mansbridge puts the argument starkly: "The claim that people have common interests can be a way of misleading the less powerful into collaborating with the more powerful in schemes that mainly benefit the latter." J. Mansbridge, Beyond Adversarial Democracy 5 (1983).

Are coopting and power-plays inevitable in environmental mediation? Did that happen in the "treaty waters" mediation? Was it significant that the mediation there was under court sponsorship with ongoing court supervision? What kinds of checks could be built into environmental mediation to avoid these concerns? See Talbot, Environmental Mediation: Three Case Studies (The Institute for Environmental Mediation 1981).

(6) The ADR movement has been criticized, as we have seen (see supra pp. 38, 45), for elevating the settlement of disputes above the protection of legal rights and public interests. Mediation, it is suggested, can be dangerous in public law litigation because it encourages accommodation when certain rights and public interests should simply not be compromised. Proponents of mediation, however, maintain that it may be better able to insure direct participation of all interested parties and to assure a better understanding of the technical and policy issues involved. See Susskind & Ozawa, "Mediated Negotiation in the Public Sector: Objectives, Procedures and the Difficulties of Measuring Success" (Harvard Law School Negotiation Project 1984); Susskind, Environmental Mediation and the Accountability Problem, 6 Vt.L.Rev. 1 (1981). They also point out that a trained public law mediator is well aware of the problems of power imbalances and impropriety of compromising certain principles. Consider the following comments on this

issue from D. Amy, The Politics of Environmental Mediation 188–89 (1987):

Many proponents of mediation scoff at allegations that the process distorts the nature of environmental conflict, or distracts participants from more appropriate approaches. They readily admit that some environmental conflicts involve nonnegotiable matters of principle, and that mediation would bring an inappropriate perspective to these issues—but they do not see that as a problem. They argue that no reputable mediator would try to mediate such basic disputes in the first place. Most mediators, it is suggested, would quickly identify which disputes are principled and which are not, and would simply avoid attempting to mediate the former. It would be a waste of time to try to mediate those disputes, they argue, because the disputants would be unlikely to compromise. Thus, Gerald Cormick has specifically advised mediators not to attempt to mediate controversies such as those involving nuclear power plants. Recognizing that many environmentalists are philosophically opposed to nuclear power per se, he points out that "there is no possible area of accommodation and no scope for good-faith negotiation and mediation."

But this suggestion that the problem of distortion can be eliminated by mediators simply avoiding principled disputes may not be as simple and workable as proponents seem to think it is. It assumes, for instance, that one can easily differentiate principled disputes from less basic ones—but this is not always the case. The boundary lines separating different kinds of disputes are obscure, and there is often a large grey area between them. Disputes do not come prepackaged with labels identifying them as "Value Conflicts" or "Misunderstandings." Even the disputants may be unclear as to the exact nature of the controversy. In such uncertain cases, the mediator plays a key role in defining the nature of the conflict; and there is an understandable inclination to define conflicts in ways which make mediation appropriate. Mediators have an obvious self-interest in expanding the market for their services, and so, as one scholar has concluded, they "face incentives to apply their techniques inappropriately." Thus, there is always the temptation for mediators to take on cases that involve matters of principle, and then attempt to convince participants to compromise.

An example of a mediator who has yielded to this temptation is Dr. Irving Goldaber of the Center for the Practice of Conflict Management. He sees no problem at all with trying to mediate disputes over nuclear power plants. He holds seminars for utility company executives to teach them his "win-win" approach to nuclear plant controversies. In one such seminar, a simulated negotiation resulted in "utility executives" and "environmentalists" arriving at a mutually satisfactory agreement. The agreement stipulated that the two sides would (a) cosponsor a public hearing on general nuclear issues, (b) form a joint consumer advisory committee, and (c) allow a peaceful demonstration outside the secured area of the plant. One participant reported that Goldaber, quite happy with the agreement, declared, "You see? There *is* a win-win solution, ladies and gentlemen, even in your situation, which at times seems so hopeless." When asked if he really believed that people in the antinuclear movement would believe they had won if the plant remained under construction, Goldaber responded that "they made some concessions, of course; but look what they're getting away with."

(7) The Community Relations Service was established in the 1960's to provide mediation services regarding community conflict, especially involving racial incidents and law enforcement. It was premised on the belief that independent mediators would be accorded greater credibility in such situations and could aid in diffusing violent and hostile confrontations. As a division of the Department of Justice, it has offices in a number of cities around the country.

(8) When Congress enacted the Civil Rights Act of 1964, 42 U.S.C. § 2000e et seq. (Title VII), it created the Equal Employment Opportunity Commission (EEOC) as an administrative agency to which complaints should be brought before a suit alleging employment discrimination could be filed. The EEOC was viewed as an inexpensive forum for employees to air their complaints and for using education and non-coercive persuasion on employers to resolve employment discrimination claims. It provides services in investigating the claim and conciliation services through a nonadversary proceeding in which Commission personnel act in an ombudsman style to attempt to resolve the complaint. To encourage local involvement in insuring compliance with the federal law, the Act also required exhaustion of administrative remedies provided under state antidiscrimination laws.

"The state-EEOC double-exhaustion requirement potentially established a labyrinthine process in which complaints were likely not to be cured by exhaustion but to die from it." C. Abernathy, Civil Rights: Cases and Materials 518 (1980). However, the EEOC generally deemphasized technicalities and, despite severe case backlogs, it has processed a large number of complaints. If the complaint is not resolved within 180 days of filing, a complainant may file suit. The conciliation services have not enjoyed marked success, as in a large percentage of the cases the employer has rejected findings that it has discriminated and the employee has exercised his "right to sue."

(9) In 1978, the Department of Health, Education, and Welfare (now Department of Health and Human Services) adopted procedures for mediation of complaints filed with federal agencies under the Age Discrimination Act, 47 C.F.R. 57850, 57855 (Dec. 28, 1982). Mediation services were provided in half of the federal regions by the FMCS and in the others by community conciliators. A report found that although few complaints were mediated and the agreement rate fell from 43% in

1979 to 26% in 1983, "where the mediation process has been successful, it has resolved complaints quickly." It urged that "more thought be given both to the role of legal standards in the mediation of civil rights complaints and to the role of mediators and the specific processes that should be used in mediating disputes between individuals and institutions." Singer & Schechter (Center for Community Justice), Mediating Civil Rights: The Age Discrimination Act, 4 NIDR Reports 20 (1986).

(10) Mediation has often been used in international affairs. American Presidents from Theodore Roosevelt to Jimmy Carter have served as intermediaries between states. See, e.g., J. Carter, Keeping Faith: Memoirs of a President (1982), in which former President Carter provides a day-by-day diary account of the 1978 Israeli–Egyptian Accord. In the difficult area of the "law of the sea," the United Nations served as the convenor of a convention which brought together most of the states of the world and, after a decade of work, resulted in a significant international treaty. The Red Cross has for years served a similar function regarding international conventions on the "law of war." For discussion of the possibilities of international mediation, see Fisher & Ury, International Mediation: A Working Guide (Harvard Negotiation Project Publication 1978).

D. CONFIDENTIALITY IN MEDIATION

In the usual case, what was said in a mediation will be of no further legal relevance after the mediation is over. But there are occasions on which someone will attempt to discover what was said in a mediation or to use it as testimony in a future proceeding. This is more likely to occur when no agreement was reached in the mediation and the dispute later goes to trial (or to some other form of resolution, such as arbitration). Even when an agreement was reached in the mediation, there may be a future attempt to discover what was said or to use it in testimony. This can occur when there is a disagreement between the parties as to what the mediated agreement was or when one party seeks to enforce the agreement and the other claims that it was obtained improperly. A later proceeding for which mediation testimony is sought may be based directly on the dispute that was the basis of the mediation (for example, a suit between partners who had tried to mediate their differences) or on a matter separate from that dispute (for example, a suit by a creditor, against one of the partners, as to which something said in the mediation is relevant).

Many proponents of mediation claim that confidentiality is critical to the success of the process. They maintain that parties will not speak freely if confidentiality is not guaranteed and that the ability to get to the heart of the dispute will be jeopardized. They also argue that the independence of the mediator would be undermined if she could be required to testify about the mediation at some future time. Consider the following discussion of the need for confidentiality:

LAWRENCE R. FREEDMAN & MICHAEL L. PRIGOFF, CONFIDENTIALITY IN MEDIATION: THE NEED FOR PROTECTION

2 Ohio St.J. Dispute Res. 37, 39 (1986).

[The authors are, respectively, staff attorney for the ABA Standing Committee on Dispute Resolution and a practicing attorney in a New Jersey firm.]

Effective mediation requires candor. A mediator, not having coercive power, helps parties reach agreements by identifying issues, exploring possible bases for agreement, encouraging parties to accomodate each others' interests, and uncovering the underlying causes of conflict. Mediators must be able to draw out baseline positions and interests which would be impossible if the parties were constantly looking over their shoulders. Mediation often reveals deep-seated feelings on sensitive issues. Compromise negotiations often require the admission of facts which disputants would never otherwise concede. Confidentiality insures that parties will voluntarily enter the process and further enables them to participate effectively and successfully.

Fairness to the disputants requires confidentiality. The safeguards present in legal proceedings, qualified counsel and specific rules of evidence and procedure, for example, are absent in mediation. In mediation, unlike the traditional justice system, parties often make communications without the expectation that they will later be bound by them. Subsequent use of information generated at these proceedings could therefore be unfairly prejudicial, particularly if one party is more sophisticated than the other. Mediation thus could be used as a discovery device against legally naive persons if the mediation communications were not inadmissible in subsequent judicial actions. This is particularly important where a mediation program is affiliated with an entity of the legal system, such as a prosecutor's office.

The mediator must remain neutral in fact and in perception. The potential of the mediator to be an adversary in a subsequent legal proceeding would curtail the disputants' freedom to confide during the mediation. Court testimony by a mediator, no matter how carefully presented, will inevitably be characterized so as to favor one side or the other. This would destroy a mediator's efficacy as an impartial broker.

Privacy is an incentive for many to choose mediation. Whether it be protection of trade secrets or simply a disinclination to "air one's dirty laundry" in the neighborhood, the option presented by the mediator to settle disputes quietly and informally is often a primary motivator for parties choosing this process.

Mediators, and mediation programs, need protection against distraction and harassment. Fledgling community programs need all of their limited resources for the "business at hand." Frequent subpoenas can encumber staff time, and dissuade volunteers from participating as mediators. Proper evaluation of programs requires adequate record keeping. Many programs, uncertain as to whether records would be protected absent statutory protection, routinely destroy them as a confidentiality device.

———

In opposition to a broad claim for mediation confidentiality is our tradition that all relevant evidence should be available in judicial proceedings. The right to "every man's evidence" is a basic procedural principle only outweighed in the case of certain limited privileges.

Professor Eric D. Green points out that there are a number of considerations bearing on the degree of confidentiality that should be accorded.[1] These include *what* should be confidential (i.e., the fact of settlement, its terms, statements by parties, documents and evidence disclosed by parties, statements by or notes of the mediator, or the mediator's impressions, opinions, or recommendations); *who* should be able to enforce confidentiality (i.e., parties, non-party participants such as witnesses, the mediator, interested non-participants, or the courts and public agencies); and *against whom* confidentiality can be enforced (parties, the mediator, non-party participants, private third parties, or public third parties). It is apparent that the justification for confidentiality may be more or less compelling, depending on the combination of these factors (Green provides five charts for this purpose).

Green sees the paradigm case for confidentiality as one in which (a) one party to a mediation, (b) to advance its own interests, tries to (c) introduce either the (d) statements of another party or the impressions, notes, or opinions of the mediator (e) in subsequent litigation over the same event (f) between the same parties (g) when the interests of third parties and the public are not involved. Do you agree that these factors make the strongest case for confidentiality? What factors would weaken the case?

Our inquiry in this section will be focused on the scope of the present legal protections for confidentiality in mediation, and whether they are adequate. Those protections will be discussed under the categories of (1) evidentiary exclusion for compromise discussions, (2) discovery limitations, (3) mediation privileges, and (4) contractual agreements of confidentiality.

1. Evidentiary Exclusion for Compromise Discussions

As has been discussed in connection with settlement negotiations, Federal Rule of Evidence 408 (and a large number of state rules based on it) expands the common law privilege by excluding from evidence both offers to compromise and "evidence of conduct or statements made

———

1. Green, A Heretical View of a Mediation Privilege, 2 Ohio St.J. Dispute Res. 1, 32 (1986).

in compromise negotiations," if introduced "to prove liability for or invalidity of the claim or its amount."

Can a mediation be analogized to a settlement negotiation for purposes of Rule 408? The policy behind the rule, to promote "the out-of-court settlement of disputes,"[1] should apply to any form of settlement discussion, whether it be an informal negotiation between counsel or parties, a structured settlement conference, or a mediation. There has been little occasion for courts to rule on the application of Rule 408 to mediation. But unless a mediation is so limited as to exclude any discussion of settlement of a dispute, it would seem to apply. The judge in one case, in which evidence arising in an EEOC conciliation was sought to be introduced, stated that "it probably is inadmissible under Fed.R.Evid. 408."[2]

Colorado has settled any uncertainty as to whether the rule protecting settlement discussions applies to mediation by passing a statute that "[m]ediation processes shall be regarded as settlement negotiations." It provides that "no admission, representation, or statement made in mediation not otherwise discoverable or obtainable shall be admissible as evidence or subject to process requiring the disclosure of any matter discussed during mediation proceedings."[3] See infra, p. 363, concerning other statutory approaches to mediation confidentiality.

Rule 408 applies to unsuccessful as well as successful compromise discussions and thus should accord protection regardless of the outcome of the mediation. It also specifically provides that it "does not require the exclusion of any evidence otherwise discoverable merely because it is presented in the course of compromise negotiations." This is intended to prevent a participant from immunizing otherwise available evidence simply by presenting it during mediation. "If, for example, evidence of child abuse already existed, it does not become inadmissible because it is additionally blurted out during custody mediation."[4]

Rule 408 has a number of limitations that severely restrict the scope of its protections regarding mediations. First, it only applies to subsequent litigation and is inapplicable, for example, in subsequent administrative or legislative hearings. It also provides no protection against public disclosure of information revealed in mediation. Second, it only protects parties to a subsequent litigation, and thus mediation participants who are not parties to the litigation (including the mediator) cannot invoke its protections. Third, although it protects not only offers to compromise but also "evidence of conduct or statements made in compromise negotiations," some narrow court interpretations have

---

1. J. Weinstein, 2 Weinstein's Evidence 408–3 (1986).

2. U.S. Equal Employment Opportunity Comm'n v. Air Line Pilots Ass'n Intern., 489 F.Supp. 1003, 1008 n. 4 (D.Mn.1980), rev'd on other grounds, 661 F.2d 90 (8th Cir.1981).

3. Colo.Rev.Stats. § 13–22–307 (Supp. 1985).

4. J. Folberg & A. Taylor, Mediation: A Comprehensive Guide to Resolving Conflicts Without Litigation 271 (1984).

found that not everything said in a negotiation has a sufficient relationship to discussions of settlement to come under the rule (see the *Thomas* case, supra p. 182).

Finally, Rule 408 is limited to the situation in which a party in a subsequent litigation seeks to introduce mediation evidence to prove liability or the amount of damages. Further, it does not apply if the evidence is introduced for another purpose such as bias, negating undue delay, and obstruction (which, although specifically cited, are only examples of other purposes).[5]

Notes and Questions

(1) What if suit is brought to enforce a mediation agreement and the plaintiff seeks to introduce testimony as to what was said in order to prove what the agreement was? Is this a purpose *other* than proving liability for the claim or its amount, so that the testimony would not be protected under Rule 408? Is this a situation in which confidentiality would undermine the effectiveness of mediation by making it more difficult to enforce the agreement?

(2) What if testimony as to what was said or agreed upon in the mediation is introduced only for the purpose of impeaching a party or witness? Is it outside the protection of Rule 408? See Brocklesby v. United States, 767 F.2d 1288, 1293 (9th Cir.1985) (indemnity agreement could be introduced to attack credibility of witnesses); John McShain, Inc. v. Cessna Aircraft Co., 563 F.2d 632, 635 (3d Cir.1977) (release could be introduced to show consultant was released in return for testimony); Reichenbach v. Smith, 528 F.2d 1072, 1075 (5th Cir.1976) ("Rule 408 codified a trend in case law that permits cross-examination concerning a settlement for the purpose of impeachment").

(3) Consider the following hypothetical suggested by Green, supra note 1, at 12, in reference to the applicability of Rule 408 (and again in relation to the other bases for confidentiality discussed in subsections 2 through 4 that follow this subsection):

Jane and Frank Smith have decided to divorce. They have been married twelve years and have two children, Mary, 7 and Peter, 5.

The Smiths engage Patrick Brave, an experienced divorce mediator, to help them work out a separation agreement covering custody and property issues. During mediation, Jane admits to Patrick during a private session that she does not really want custody of the children, but is only using the custody issue as a device to get a better property settlement. In addition, Jane tells

---

5. See Belton v. Fibreboard Corp., 724 F.2d 500, 505 (5th Cir.1984) (fact of settlement by co-defendants was admissible to explain why they were not in court); Central Soya Co., Inc. v. Epstein Fisheries, Inc., 676 F.2d 939, 944 (7th Cir.1982) (evidence of settlement admissible to show partial forgiveness of debt in guaranty case); Breuer Electric Manufacturing Co. v. Toronado Systems of America, Inc., 687 F.2d 182, 185 (7th Cir.1982) (evidence of settlement negotiations admissible in hearing to set aside default to show defendant's awareness of claim).

Patrick that the children might be better off with Frank because she doesn't seem to be able to control herself with the children very well; she has lost her temper with them on a number of occasions and found herself hitting them in the face. She gave Mary a black eye last week.

Later, at a joint session, Jane admits that she is using the custody issue as leverage for a larger property settlement. Upon hearing this, Frank gets mad and breaks off the mediation.

Frank's lawyer schedules Patrick's deposition. At Patrick's deposition, the lawyer asks Patrick to repeat what Jane has told him about her interest in custody of the children and about her feelings with regard to the best interest of the children. Frank's lawyer also asks Patrick if he has any information or opinions about what would be in the best interest of the children. At trial, Patrick is called as a witness by Frank's lawyer and asked the same questions.

Jane obtains custody of Mary and Peter. Six months later, at the request of Mary's second grade teacher, the Department of Social Services conducts an investigation into Jane's treatment of the children. The DSS social worker asks Patrick what he knows about Jane's care and treatment of the children.

2. Discovery Limitations

The limitations imposed on discovery in the Federal Rules accord a degree of protection that could apply in certain mediation situations. Rule 26(b) allows discovery "regarding any matter, not privileged, which is relevant to the subject matter involved in the pending action." It further states that "[i]t is not ground for objection that the information sought will be inadmissible at the trial if the information sought appears reasonably calculated to lead to the discovery of admissible evidence." Therefore discovery is not limited to information that would be admissible into evidence.

Even the broad scope of discovery under the rules, however, contains limitations which may provide some protection for mediations. First, discovery may not be made as to any privileged matter. Mediations may fall in this category if a privilege has been accorded in the particular jurisdiction (as will be discussed in the next subsection). Second, information sought to be discovered must be relevant and must at least be reasonably calculated to lead to admissible evidence. Consider the following case:

BOTTARO v. HATTON ASSOCIATES

United States District Court, Eastern District of New York, 1982.
96 F.R.D. 158.

NEAHER, DISTRICT JUDGE.

This action was commenced by plaintiffs to remedy a variety of alleged federal and State securities law violations. During the parties' pre-trial maneuvering, one defendant, Alexander Grant and Company, entered into a settlement agreement with plaintiffs and was dismissed from the lawsuit. The settling parties agreed in their stipulation of settlement not to divulge the terms of their agreement. Unable to obtain voluntary discovery, two of the remaining defendants have moved to compel disclosure of their former co-defendant's compromise agreement, pursuant to Rule 37, F.R.Civ.P. For the reasons stated below, this motion is denied.

The Federal Rules of Civil Procedure provide for a very liberal range of discovery. Rule 26(b), which applies to all forms of discovery, provides generally that the parties "may obtain discovery regarding any matter not privileged, which is relevant to the subject matter involved in the pending action." Relevance in this context is broader than that required for admissibility at trial. Moore's Federal Practice ¶ 26.56[1] at 26–116 (2d ed. 1982). The Rule itself states: "It is not ground for objection that the information sought will be inadmissible at the trial if the information sought appears reasonably calculated to lead to the discovery of admissible evidence." F.R.Civ.P. 26(b). Thus, while admissibility and discoverability are not equivalent, it is clear that the object of the inquiry must have some evidentiary value before an order to compel disclosure of otherwise inadmissible material will issue.

In this case, defendants contend that although the settling parties' agreement is inadmissible under Rule 408, Fed.R.Evid., "to prove liability for or invalidity of the claim or its amount," an inquiry into the terms of a codefendant's settlement agreement is permissible because it may produce admissible evidence on the question of damages. In support of this argument, defendants rely upon the district court opinion in *Broadway & Ninety–Sixth St. Realty Co. v. Loew's, Inc.,* 21 F.R.D. 347 (S.D.N.Y.1958), the only reported decision allowing such a request.

In allowing discovery, the court in *Loew's* reasoned that discovery into the terms of the agreement could produce factual admissions on the issue of damages, which would be admissible under the traditional caveat to the evidentiary immunity of settlement agreements and negotiations. This common-law exception, however, was expressly overruled by Congress when it enacted Rule 408 of the Federal Rules of Evidence in 1975.

The exception relied upon in *Loew's* was contained in the House version of Rule 408. This bill was rejected by the Senate Committee on the Judiciary as "constitut[ing] an unjustifiable restraint upon efforts to negotiate settlements—the encouragement of which is the purpose of the rule." S.Rep. No. 1277, 93d Cong. 2d Sess. 10 (1974). The Senate bill, which was subsequently adopted as Rule 408, id., made it clear that only admissions of liability or the extent of liability "otherwise discoverable" would be exempt from Rule 408's evidentiary exclusion.

Thus, Rule 408 would not immunize documents or factual admissions merely because they were exchanged in the course of negotiating a settlement, see Grumman Aerospace Corp. v. Titanium Metals Corp., 91 F.R.D. 84, 90 (E.D.N.Y.1982), if they are independently admissible either as pre-existing documents or "provable by evidence other than conduct or statements that make up compromise negotiations." Fed.R. Evid. 408 advisory committee note.

Clearly, discovery into negotiations can be based on the reasonable belief that it may produce information on the question of damages that can be brought into evidence independent of the settlement context. The question in this case, however, is whether an inquisitor should get discovery into the terms of the agreement itself based solely on the hope that it will somehow lead to admissible evidence on the question of damages. Given the strong public policy of favoring settlements and the congressional intent to further that policy by insulating the bargaining table from unnecessary intrusions, we think the better rule is to require some particularized showing of a likelihood that admissible evidence will be generated by the dissemination of the terms of a settlement agreement. Since the terms of settlement do not appear to be reasonably calculated to lead to discovery of admissible evidence and the defendants have not made any showing to the contrary, this justification for a Rule 37 order must fail.

The final argument advanced by defendants in support of their discovery request is that the amount of the settlement is relevant to determining whether Alexander Grant and Company may be liable to defendants for contribution despite its settlement with plaintiff. While it is true that a settling defendant's liability for contribution depends on whether he paid his share of any damage award, this determination cannot be made until a final judgment has been rendered. Only at that juncture will the full liability of all defendants be known, and the pro rata share owed by the settling party ascertained. Even then, the settlement would not be evidence relevant to any issue in this case other than the ministerial apportionment of damages, a mathematical computation which the Court rather than the jury will perform. Hence, the amount of the settlement is not relevant to any issue in this case at this time.

Notes and Questions

(1) Why wouldn't the request of the remaining defendants in *Bottaro* to discover the nature of the plaintiff's settlement agreement with the settling defendant be deemed to reasonably lead to admissible

evidence? Defendants argued that it might lead to admissible evidence on the question of damages. Might the fact that the settling defendant paid the plaintiff a large sum lead to admissible evidence? It might indicate that plaintiff had a stronger case than the defendants thought (or if the settlement was small, that he had a weaker case). Could defendants argue that knowing the amount of the settlement might reveal something that the plaintiff and settling defendant knew that they didn't and thus lead them to admissible evidence as to damages?

(2) Rule 408 clearly prohibits introduction of the fact or amount of a settlement for the purpose of proving liability or the amount of damages due. But it may be introduced for "another purpose, such as proving bias or prejudice or interest of a witness or a party." Could the defendants have succeeded on a theory that they wanted to use the settlement information to impeach the settling defendant if he testified? When there is a "Mary Carter agreement" (see supra p. 187) between plaintiff and a settling defendant (an agreement by which the settling defendant retains a financial interest in the plaintiff's recovery against non-settling defendants), evidence of the agreement may be introduced for the purpose of impeaching the settling defendant. See General Motors Corp. v. Simmons, 558 S.W.2d 855, 858 (Tex.1977). Should the same be true when there is no "Mary Carter agreement," but the defendant desires to show that the settling defendant was "paid off" in return for testimony favorable to the plaintiff?

(3) Why wasn't the amount of the settlement in *Bottaro* relevant to the claim that the remaining defendants had against the settling defendant for contribution? Would it be relevant in a state in which the negligence of a settling defendant must be compared by the jury to the negligence of the remaining defendants (and of the plaintiff if contributory negligence is alleged), and thus the contribution claim would be determined in the same suit? See Tex.Civ.Prac. & Rem.Code Ann. § 33.003 et seq. (Vernon 1987).

(4) The settlement in *Bottaro* resulted from a negotiation, but a similar agreement not to disclose the amount of settlement could arise out of a mediation. Would the decision as to confidentiality have come out the same way after a mediation? Do the possibilities suggested in notes (1) through (3) that settlement information might be discoverable and admissible indicate that the discovery rules are insufficient to protect mediation confidentiality?

(5) The discovery rules also offer the possibility of protection of confidentiality through a court protective order, as in incorporating a mediation agreement of confidentiality or in sealing a mediation record. Rule 26(c) provides that a court may "for good cause shown . . . make any order which justice requires to protect a party or person from annoyance, embarrassment, oppression, or undue burden or expense." Rule 26(c)(7) specifically provides for a protective order that "a trade secret or other confidential research, development, or commercial information not be disclosed or be disclosed only in a designated way."

Information disclosed in a mediation would seem to be appropriate for protection under Rule 26 if "good cause" is shown by demonstrating a particular need for protection. See Cipollone v. Liggett Group, Inc., 785 F.2d 1108, 1121 (3d Cir.1986). Such protection might be provided even if a formal mediation privilege were not available. Moore comments that "[t]here is no true privilege against discovery of trade secrets or other 'confidential' business information, but the courts nevertheless will exercise their discretion to avoid unnecessary disclosure of such information." 4 Moore's Federal Practice (2d ed.) 2519–2520. In Adler v. Adams, No. 675–73C (W.D.Wash., May 3, 1979), a court used a balancing test in granting a motion to quash a subpoena to a mediator in an environmental case. It used an analogy to Hickman v. Taylor, 329 U.S. 495, 508 (1947), deeming the mediator's communications to be protected "work product. See discussion in Green, Heretical View of Mediation Privilege, supra, at 25–29.

(6) Note that offers to compromise are also protected in the criminal context. See Fed.R.Crim.Proc. 11(e)(6), in Appendix B, infra p. 740.

3. Mediation Privilege

Some jurisdictions recognize a mediation privilege. Such a privilege may be created by court or by statute. At common law, a sizable number of privileges were recognized, reaching such status situations as attorney-client, clergyman-penitent, physician-patient, and husband-wife. The modern trend is to narrow the number of privileges. The Federal Rules of Evidence provide that privilege will be governed by "the principles of the common law in the light of reason and experience," [1] and the federal courts have severely cut back on the range of privileges. The Supreme Court, in rejecting a constitutionally-based reporter's privilege, has indicated that claims of privilege should be carefully scrutinized in light of their denial of the right to evidence and that courts should ordinarily defer to the legislative branch for the creation of privileges.[2]

a. Judicially–Created Privilege

Wigmore provided the classic statement of conditions which should be met in creating a privilege, which has been followed by many courts:

(1) The communications must originate in a confidence that they will not be disclosed;

(2) This element of confidentiality must be essential to the full and satisfactory maintenance of the relationship between the parties;

1. Federal Rules of Evidence, Rule 401.

2. Branzburg v. Hayes, 408 U.S. 665 (1972).

(3) The relationship must be one which in the opinion of the community ought to be sedulously fostered; and

(4) The injury that would inure to the relationship by the disclosure of the communications must be greater than the benefit thereby gained for the correct disposal of the litigation.[3]

The first condition would normally be satisfied in the mediation setting. Mediators usually tell parties that the mediation is confidential, thus creating an expectation that it will be held in confidence. The expectation, however, must be reasonable in terms of the courts' willingness to recognize it. Thus the means by which mediators inform clients of confidentiality could be important. A written statement, signed by the mediator and parties, would be best, but sometimes, as in initial telephone conversations, this is not possible. In such situations, the expectation of confidence may be insufficient and, if it is to be protected, a statutory privilege would be needed.

The second condition—that confidentiality be essential to the full and satisfactory maintenance of the relationship—is not easily proven. How does one, for example, demonstrate that confidentiality is essential to the relationship between physician-client or husband-wife? Professor Green points out that mediation has flourished without a privilege and argues that on occasions when confidentiality is essential, a limited, rather than absolute privilege, is sufficient.[4] Consider the following comments by Kirkpatrick in favor of a privilege: [5]

> [S]uppose I came to you as a mediator for assistance with my spouse and had embarrassing things to tell. I will want you to understand me and my situation, since I can expect that you will be able to help me only if you have an opportunity to know all of the relevant data. Otherwise, you are making guesses about the situation, and creating alternatives that cannot help because they apply to other circumstances. If you, as the mediator, pledge confidentiality, I will be more likely to feel comfortable and speak more openly than if I am unsure about your discretion.

> People may not avoid the mediator altogether if confidentiality does not extend to the judicial setting, but they must feel secure that their secrets will not be passed along to friends, family, the press, and foes. The revelation of secrets in court is only one of many fears.

> * * *

> It [may be] contended that the belief that mediators would become personae non grata is also insufficiently substantiated. Would marriages cease, lawyers be without work, doctors without patients if the principals were required to testify? Probably not.

---

3. Wigmore on Evidence § 2285 (McNaughton ed. 1961).

4. Green, A Heretical View of the Mediation Privilege, 2 Ohio St.J. on Dispute Res. 1, 32 (1986).

5. Kirkpatrick, Should Mediators Have a Confidentiality Privilege?, 9 Mediation Q. 85, 94–6 (1985).

The mediator-client relationship probably would not cease either, although this relationship is more fragile than those between attorneys and clients, husbands and wives, doctors and patients, all of which are more established and recognized. But the validity of the contention that mediators would be spurned if their testimony was admissible is not necessary for the privilege to be desirable. Rather, it is sufficient that the confidentiality privilege would help the mediator-client relationship. This could perhaps be best established through polling potential clients to determine if they would continue using mediators if they could be subpoenaed, and by research that would make experimental determinations of the effect of subpoenability.

[The assertion may be] made that prohibiting testimony might make the proceeding less rather than more attractive to potential litigants, especially those who bargain or otherwise attempt to settle in good faith before seeking judicial review. There is no doubt that this could be the case. However, in mediation, participation is voluntary. Therefore, one can allow those who decide that their time in mediation is not likely to be productive to choose other avenues of redress. In those instances where the parties choose mediation, they can still do so while retaining the confidentiality of the process.

It [may be said] that the privilege could prevent finding the guilty party. This is a broad attack against any privilege, and on the face of it is undeniable. However, several considerations bring this legitimate concern into focus. First, forcing the mediator to testify does not mean that the truth will come out. The mediator can lie; this means that the innocent will sometimes lose their case. Also, as was mentioned earlier in this section, if the clients are aware that the mediator can be subpoenaed, they have a motive for lying to the mediator. The mediator may then unwillingly (or otherwise) transmit the lies uttered during the mediation. Once again, the innocent may suffer. The mediator's testimony may not be excluded as hearsay evidence, especially if the trial is without jury. The mediator could testify about what he remembers without having to testify to the truth of what he heard and could affirm or deny previous testimony of the clients.

The mediator usually views the problem as a conflict to be solved, not as a situation in which someone is to be blamed and punished. Therefore, the mediator may not make a good witness in the adversarial setting, which is designed to discover who or what is right, because his orientation will probably lead him away from making that judgment.

The contention that secrecy and privilege serve the guilty must be considered along with the belief that the unabridged access to private lives leaves the innocent subject to the unjust examination of life's details. The rights associated with privacy are, of course, subject to abuse by criminals and sociopaths, who use the shield of privacy to rob, murder, and abuse others. For example, the need to obtain a search warrant may delay police officers looking for a drug dealer while the accomplice meanwhile destroys evidence. Or an abusive spouse may relentlessly pursue the victim after very brief stays in jail. But the criminal justice system hopes to secure the rights of those who may be unjustly accused by their enemies or by the misinformed and assumes innocence until guilt is proven. Similarly, privileged relationships may be misused but they can nonetheless be justified.

Thus, while acknowledging that privileged communication does have its drawbacks, there are benefits as well. It seems that the benefits could prevail in some circumstances because the need for privacy is legitimate and basic and must be respected because of the practical benefits that accrue from recognizing the confidentiality privilege.

Wigmore's last two conditions—that the relationship be one that the community strongly believes should be fostered and that the injury from disclosure outweigh the benefit to be gained—are also subject to debate. Green argues that "there is a substantial and respectable body of opinion that holds that mediation and other informal methods of dispute resolution ought not be encouraged,"[6] and that "given the unwillingness of courts to strike the balance between injury to the relationship and benefit to the justice system in favor of executive privilege and reporter's privilege, it is doubtful that courts will conclude that the balancing of interests" will come out in favor of a mediation privilege.[7]

Several courts have wrestled with the issue of a common law privilege and, under certain circumstances, have found it appropriate. Consider the following cases:

N.L.R.B. v. JOSEPH MACALUSO, INC.
United States Court of Appeals, Ninth Circuit, 1980.
618 F.2d 51.

Before DUNIWAY and WALLACE, CIRCUIT JUDGES, and JAMESON, DISTRICT JUDGE.

WALLACE, CIRCUIT JUDGE:

The single issue presented in this National Labor Relations Board (NLRB) enforcement proceeding is whether the NLRB erred in disallowing the testimony of a Federal Mediation and Conciliation Service (FMCS) mediator as to a crucial fact occurring in his presence. The decision and order of the Board are reported at 231 N.L.R.B. 91. We enforce the order.

6. Green, supra note 4, at 33.   7. Id. at 34.

I.

In early 1976 Retail Store Employees Union Local 1001 (Union) waged a successful campaign to organize the employees of Joseph Macaluso, Inc. (Company) at its four retail stores in Tacoma and Seattle, Washington. The Union was elected the collective bargaining representative of the Company's employees, was certified as such by the NLRB, and the Company and Union commenced negotiating a collective bargaining agreement. Several months of bargaining between Company and Union negotiators failed to produce an agreement, and the parties decided to enlist the assistance of a mediator from the FMCS. Mediator Douglas Hammond consequently attended the three meetings between the Company and Union from which arises the issue before us. To frame that issue, it is necessary first to describe the history of this litigation.

During the spring and summer of 1976 the Company engaged in conduct which led the NLRB to charge it with unfair labor practices. Proceedings were held and the NLRB ruled that the Company had violated section 8(a)(1) of the National Labor Relations Act (NLRA) by threatening pro-union employees, and section 8(a)(3) of the NLRA by discharging an employee for union activity. At this unfair labor practice proceeding the NLRB also found that the Company and Union had finalized a collective bargaining agreement at the three meetings with Hammond, and that the Company had violated NLRA sections 8(a) (5) and (1) by failing to execute the written contract incorporating the final agreement negotiated with the Union. The NLRB ordered the Company to execute the contract and pay back-compensation with interest, and seeks enforcement of that order in this court. In response, the Company contends that the parties have never reached agreement, and certainly did not do so at the meetings with Hammond.

The testimony of the Union before the NLRB directly contradicted that of the Company. The two Union negotiators testified that during the first meeting with Hammond the parties succeeded in reducing to six the number of disputed issues, and that the second meeting began with Company acceptance of a Union proposal resolving five of those six remaining issues. The Union negotiators further testified that the sixth issue was resolved with the close of the second meeting, and that in response to a Union negotiator's statement "Well, I think that wraps it up," the Company president said, "Yes, I guess it does." The third meeting with Hammond, according to the Union, was held only hours before the Company's employees ratified the agreement, was called solely for the purpose of explaining the agreement to the Company accountant who had not attended the first two meetings, and was an amicable discussion involving no negotiation.

The Company testimony did not dispute that the first meeting reduced the number of unsettled issues to six, but its version of the last two meetings contrasts sharply with the Union's account. The Company representatives testified that the second meeting closed without the parties having reached any semblance of an agreement, and that the third meeting was not only inconclusive but stridently divisive. While the Union representatives testified that the third meeting was an amicable explanatory discussion, the Company negotiators both asserted that their refusal to give in to Union demands caused the Union negotiators to burst into anger, threaten lawsuits, and leave the room at the suggestion of Hammond. According to the Company, Hammond was thereafter unable to bring the parties together and the Union negotiators left the third meeting in anger.

In an effort to support its version of the facts, the Company requested that the administrative law judge (ALJ) subpoena Hammond and obtain his testimonial description of the last two bargaining sessions. The subpoena was granted, but was later revoked upon motion of the FMCS. Absent Hammond's tie-breaking testimony, the ALJ decided that the Union witnesses were more credible and ruled that an agreement had been reached. The Company's sole contention in response to this request for enforcement of the resulting order to execute the contract is that the ALJ and NLRB erred in revoking the subpoena of Hammond, the one person whose testimony could have resolved the factual dispute.

II.

Revocation of the subpoena was based upon a long-standing policy that mediators, if they are to maintain the appearance of neutrality essential to successful performance of their task, may not testify about the bargaining sessions they attend. Both the NLRB and the FMCS (as amicus curiae) defend that policy before us. We are thus presented with a question of first impression before our court: can the NLRB revoke the subpoena of a mediator capable of providing information crucial to resolution of a factual dispute solely for the purpose of preserving mediator effectiveness?

Statutory authority for NLRB subpoena revocation is found in NLRA section 11(1), 29 U.S.C. § 161(1):

> Within five days after the service of a subpoena on any person requiring the production of any evidence in his possession or under his control, such person may petition the [NLRB] to revoke, and the [NLRB] shall revoke, such subpoena if in its opinion the evidence whose production is required does not relate to any matter under investigation, or any matter in question in such proceedings, or if in its opinion such subpoena does not describe with sufficient particularity the evidence whose production is required.

We have interpreted this provision broadly, stating:

> The statute in question does not state that petitions to revoke subpoenas can only be made on the two grounds therein stated, or that the [ALJ] or [NLRB] may revoke only on those grounds. It does provide that a person served with such a subpoena may

petition for revocation of the subpoena and the [NLRB] *shall* revoke it if one of the two specified circumstances exist [sic]. Insofar as the statute is concerned, the [NLRB] may also revoke a subpoena on any other ground which is consonant with the overall powers and duties of the [NLRB] under the [NLRA] considered as a whole.

General Engineering, Inc. v. NLRB, 341 F.2d 367, 372–73 (9th Cir.1965) (emphasis in original). We must determine, therefore, whether preservation of mediator effectiveness by protection of mediator neutrality is a ground for revocation consistent with the power and duties of the NLRB under the NLRA. Stated differently, we must determine whether the reason for revocation is legally sufficient to justify the loss of Hammond's testimony. The NLRB's own regulation authorizing revocation states:

> The administrative law judge or the [NLRB] as the case may be, shall revoke the subpoena if in its opinion the evidence whose production is required does not relate to any matter under investigation or in question in the proceedings or the subpoena does not describe with sufficient particularity the evidence whose production is required, *or if for any other reason sufficient in law the subpoena is otherwise invalid.*

29 C.F.R. § 102.31(b) (1979) (emphasis added).

The NLRB's revocation of Hammond's subpoena conflicts with the fundamental principle of Anglo–American law that the public is entitled to every person's evidence. Branzburg v. Hayes, 408 U.S. 665, 688, 92 S.Ct. 2646, 2660, 33 L.Ed.2d 626 (1972); United States v. Bryan, 339 U.S. 323, 331, 70 S.Ct. 724, 730, 94 L.Ed. 884 (1950); 8 Wigmore, Evidence § 2192, at 70 (McNaughton Rev. 1961). According to Dean Wigmore this maxim has existed in civil cases for more than three centuries, and the Sixth Amendment guarantee of compulsory process was created "merely to cure the defect of the common law by giving to parties defendant in criminal cases the common right which was already . . . possessed . . . by parties in civil cases . . . ." Id. at § 2191, at 68.

The facts before us present a classic illustration of the need for every person's evidence: the trier of fact is faced with directly conflicting testimony from two adverse sources, and a third objective source is capable of presenting evidence that would, in all probability, resolve the dispute by revealing the truth. Under such circumstances, the NLRB's revocation of Hammond's subpoena can be permitted only if denial of his testimony "has a public good transcending the normally predominant principle of utilizing all rational means for ascertaining truth." Elkins v. United States, 364 U.S. 206, 234, 80 S.Ct. 1437, 1454, 4 L.Ed.2d 1669 (1960) (Frankfurter, J., dissenting), quoted in United States v. Nixon, 418 U.S. 683, 710 n. 18, 94 S.Ct. 3090, 3108, 41 L.Ed.2d 1039 (1974). The public interest protected by revocation must be substantial if it is to cause us to "concede that the evidence in question has all the probative value that can be required, and yet exclude it because its admission would injure some other cause more than it would help the cause of truth, and because the avoidance of that injury is considered of more consequence than the possible harm to the cause of truth." 1 Wigmore, Evidence § 11, at 296 (1940). We thus are required to balance two important interests, both critical in their own setting.

We conclude that the public interest in maintaining the perceived and actual impartiality of federal mediators does outweigh the benefits derivable from Hammond's testimony. This public interest was clearly stated by Congress when it created the FMCS:

> It is the policy of the United States that—
>
> (a) sound and stable industrial peace and the advancement of the general welfare, health, and safety of the Nation and of the best interests of employers and employees can most satisfactorily be secured by the settlement of issues between employers and employees through the processes of conference and collective bargaining between employers and the representatives of their employees;
>
> (b) the settlement of issues between employers and employees through collective bargaining may be advanced by making available full and adequate governmental facilities for conciliation, mediation, and voluntary arbitration to aid and encourage employers and the representatives of their employees to reach and maintain agreements concerning rates of pay, hours, and working conditions, and to make all reasonable efforts to settle their differences by mutual agreement reached through conferences and collective bargaining or by such methods as may be provided for in any applicable agreement for the settlement of disputes . . . .

29 U.S.C. § 171(a)(b). Since Congress made this declaration, federal mediation has become a substantial contributor to industrial peace in the United States. The FMCS, as amicus curiae, has informed us that it participated in mediation of 23,450 labor disputes in fiscal year 1977, with approximately 325 federal mediators stationed in 80 field offices around the country. Any activity that would significantly decrease the effectiveness of this mediation service could threaten the industrial stability of the nation. The importance of Hammond's testimony in this case is not so great as to justify such a threat. Moreover, the loss of that testimony did not cripple the fact-finding process. The ALJ resolved the dispute by making a credibility determination, a function routinely entrusted to triers of fact throughout our judicial system.

The FMCS has promulgated regulations which explain why the very appearance of impartiality is essential to the effectiveness of labor mediation.

> Public policy and the successful effectuation of the Federal Mediation and Conciliation Service's mission require that commissioners and employees maintain a reputation for impartiality and integrity. Labor and management or other interested parties

participating in mediation efforts must have the assurance and confidence that information disclosed to commissioners and other employees of the Service will not subsequently be divulged, voluntarily or because of compulsion, unless authorized by the Director of the Service.

* * *

No officer, employee, or other person officially connected in any capacity with the Service, currently or formerly shall, in response to a subpoena, subpoena duces tecum, or other judicial or administrative order, produce any material contained in the files of the Service, disclose any information acquired as part of the performance of his official duties or because of his official status, or testify on behalf of any party to any matter pending in any judicial, arbitral or administrative proceeding, without the prior approval of the Director.

29 C.F.R. § 1401.2(a), (b) (1979). This need for the appearance of impartiality, and the potential for loss of that appearance through any degree of mediator testimony, was well expressed by the NLRB in the decision relied upon by the ALJ when revoking Hammond's subpoena:

> However useful the testimony of a conciliator might be to the [NLRB] in any given case, we can appreciate the strong considerations of public policy underlying the regulation [denying conciliator testimony] and the refusal to make exceptions to it, because of the unique position which the conciliators occupy. To execute successfully their function of assisting in the settlement of labor disputes, the conciliators must maintain a reputation for impartiality, and the parties to conciliation conferences must feel free to talk without any fear that the conciliator may subsequently make disclosures as a witness in some other proceeding, to the possible disadvantage of a party to the conference. If conciliators were permitted or required to testify about their activities, or if the production of notes or reports of their activities could be required, not even the strictest adherence to purely factual matters would prevent the evidence from favoring or seeming to favor one side or the other. The inevitable result would be that the usefulness of the [FMCS] in the settlement of future disputes would be seriously impaired, if not destroyed. The resultant injury to the public interest would clearly outweigh the benefit to be derived from making their testimony available in particular cases.

Tomlinson of High Point, Inc., 74 N.L.R.B. 681, 688 (1947). We agree.

During oral argument the suggestion was made that we permit the mediator to testify, but limit his testimony to "objective facts" as suggested by International Association of Machinists and Aerospace Workers v. National Mediation Board, 425 F.2d 527, 540 (D.C.Cir.1970). We do not believe, however, that such a limitation would dispel the perception of partiality created by mediator testimony. In addition to the line-drawing problem of attempting to define what is and is not an "objective fact," a recitation of even the most objective type of facts would impair perceived neutrality, "for the party standing condemned by the thrust of such a statement would or at least might conclude that the [FMCS] was being unfair." Id. at 539. "[N]ot even the strictest adherence to purely factual matters would prevent the evidence from favoring or seeming to favor one side or the other." Tomlinson of High Point, Inc., supra, 74 N.L.R.B. at 688.

We conclude, therefore, that the complete exclusion of mediator testimony is necessary to the preservation of an effective system of labor mediation, and that labor mediation is essential to continued industrial stability, a public interest sufficiently great to outweigh the interest in obtaining every person's evidence.[2] No party is required to use the FMCS; once having voluntarily agreed to do so, however, that party must be charged with acceptance of the restriction on the subsequent testimonial use of the mediator. We thus answer the question presented by this case in the affirmative: the NLRB can revoke the subpoena of a mediator capable of providing information crucial to resolution of a factual dispute solely for the purpose of preserving mediator effectiveness.[3] Such revocation is consonant with the overall powers and duties of the NLRB, a body created to implement the NLRA goals of "promot[ing] the flow of commerce by removing certain recognized sources of industrial strife and unrest" and "encouraging practices fundamental to the friendly adjustment of industrial disputes . . . ." 29 U.S.C. § 151.

FENTON v. HOWARD
Arizona Supreme Court, 1978.
118 Ariz. 119, 575 P.2d 318.

HAYS, JUSTICE

Guillermo Martinez, real party in interest, sustained severe facial scarring as a result of an automobile accident involving Bruce Parsil, the other real party in interest. As a result of the facial scarring, Martinez claimed his marriage began to deteriorate. About a year later, he filed for dissolution of his marriage. He and his wife participated in counseling through the Court of Conciliation. Later Martinez brought an action against Parsil for personal injuries. Some of the damages alleged in the personal injury action were for emotional stress resulting from the scarring of Martinez's face. Martinez subpoenaed Don Crawford, the assistant director of the Court of Conciliation of

2. We need not reach the question whether a different result would occur if the FMCS Director granted authority for the mediator to testify pursuant to 29 C.F.R. § 1401.2(b) (1979).

3. The Company argued that revocation of Hammond's subpoena was improper because communications made to him during the course of the bargaining sessions were necessarily made in the presence of the opposing party and were not, therefore, confidential. Such a contention misapprehends the purpose of excluding mediator testimony which is to avoid a breach of impartiality, not a breach of confidentiality.

Pima County, for the purpose of taking his deposition. The subpoena required Crawford to bring to the deposition "any and all documents, records, reports, and/or notes concerning counseling services rendered to the above-named Plaintiff."

Pima County Superior Court Judge Norman S. Fenton indicated in a minute entry that at the request of Crawford, the court on its own motion quashed the subpoena. Martinez moved to set aside the order quashing the subpoena. Citing A.R.S. § 25–381.16,[1] Judge Fenton refused to set aside the order on the basis that the confidential nature of the counseling at the Conciliation Court was the very heart of the Conciliation Court's effectiveness in rendering proper service to the persons it served. Although Martinez and his wife had signed forms authorizing Crawford to release information relevant to Martinez's emotional problems, the court stated that the "form" authorization was inadequate to cover the unique situation where more than communications by the plaintiff was involved, and the "form" did not cover the confidentiality of such things as the counselor's notes and observations.

Martinez then brought a Special Action in the Court of Appeals alleging that the lower court had abused its discretion. * * * The Court of Appeals granted the relief requested by Martinez and ordered Judge Fenton to vacate the order quashing the subpoena.

* * *

[W]e believe that the subpoena as presently written is overbroad. A.R.S. § 25–381.16 gives a privilege to the *communications of the parties* to persons acting for the Conciliation Court and to reports of outside resource agencies. This does not mean that other matters coming to the attention of the Conciliation Court during the counseling of the parties must be freely and easily disclosed. Every court has inherent power to do those things which are necessary for the efficient exercise of its jurisdiction. See State v. Superior Court, 39 Ariz. 242, 5 P.2d 192 (1931). The jurisdiction of the Conciliation Court is set forth in A.R.S. § 25–381.08 which provides:

> "Whenever any controversy exists between spouses which may, unless a reconciliation is achieved, result in the legal separation, dissolution or annulment of the marriage or in the disruption of the household, and there is any minor child of the spouses or either of them whose welfare might be affected thereby, the conciliation court shall have jurisdiction over the controversy, and over the parties thereto and all persons having any relation to the controversy, as further provided in this article. Added Laws 1962, Ch. 119, § 1. As amended Laws 1973, Ch. 139, § 3."

The Conciliation Court's jurisdiction is further defined by A.R.S. § 25–381.01 which states:

1. [ed.] "Hearings or conferences . . . shall be held in private. . . . All communications, verbal or written, from the parties to the judge, commissioner or counselor in a proceeding under this article shall be deemed confidential communications, and shall not be disclosed without the consent of the party making such communication."

"The purposes of this article are to promote the public welfare by preserving, promoting and protecting family life and the institution of matrimony, to protect the rights of children, and to provide means for the reconciliation of spouses and the amicable settlement of domestic and family controversies. Added Laws 1962, Ch. 119, § 1."

Under these statutes and State v. Superior Court, supra, the Conciliation Court may refuse to disclose matters not made privileged by A.R.S. § 25–381.16, if disclosure will hamper the Conciliation Court in carrying out its purposes.

However, the court's right to protect its ability to function effectively by prohibiting disclosure must be balanced by the need of a litigant for the information sought. When, as in this case, a person claims that information in the custody of the Conciliation Court will be necessary, or very helpful, to him in another proceeding, an in-camera hearing must be held to determine the need for disclosure and the harm to the Conciliation Court if the desired disclosure is allowed. The judge should order disclosure of that material shown to be appropriate by a just balancing of the needs of the individual for the information and the need of the Conciliation Court for confidentiality.

CAMERON, C.J., STRUCKMEYER, V.C.J., and GORDON, J., concur.

HOLOHAN, JUSTICE, specially concurring.

* * *

I part company with the majority on the resolution of this case as one involving the "inherent powers" of the judiciary. The majority leave the impression that the Conciliation Court system may be disrupted by requiring one of the conciliation counselors to testify at a deposition, and of course a judge has inherent power to prevent this. There is no suggestion or inference in the statute that the counselors of the Conciliation Court are entitled to any special treatment or have a personal privilege protecting their so-called work product.

The only privilege of confidentiality belongs to the parties appearing in the Conciliation Court. A.R.S. § 25–381.16(D). If there is a waiver of that privilege I find nothing implied in the statute which gives the counselors or director any basis to object to giving testimony on the matters conducted by them.

The form of consent to disclosure submitted by the parties to conciliation was inadequate to cover the situation. The consent form was the usual release of information form used in personal injury litigation. It authorized release of information to the signer's attorney. Since the deposition would involve disclosure to others not covered by the form, the waiver was not broad enough to waive the statutory privilege created by A.R.S. § 25–318.16(D). The Judge of the Conciliation Court was, therefore, justified in quashing the subpoena.

Notes and Questions

(1) Do you think the court in *Macaluso* would have reached the conclusion that "the complete exclusion of mediator testimony is neces-

sary to the preservation of an effective system of labor mediation" without the provisions in the NLRA and FMCS statutes and regulations suggesting limitations on the subpoena power and the desirability that mediators not be required to testify? Is the privilege recognized in *Macaluso* limited to the labor mediation situation or to the FMCS? See Drukker Communications, Inc. v. N.L.R.B., 700 F.2d 727, 731–34 (D.C. Cir.1983) (NLRB testimony accorded qualified privilege). Is the need for privilege really any greater in labor relations than other mediation situations?

(2) Is the privilege recognized in *Macaluso* restricted by the fact that the parties agreed to the mediation process, including the FMCS regulation prohibiting mediator testimony? See N. Rogers & R. Salem, A Students' Guide to Mediation and the Law 92–3 (1987).

(3) How did the *Macaluso* court conclude that the public interest in confidentiality outweighs "the interest in obtaining every person's evidence?" Should the balancing of the potential injury from disclosure against the harm resulting from denial of the testimony be made on the basis of the facts in the particular case or on the general policies of availability of evidence versus mediation confidentiality? In this case it appears that the only alternative sources for the mediator's testimony was the conflicting testimony of the parties. Shouldn't the uniqueness of his testimony cut against finding a privilege? If one party is lying about what happened in the mediation, why isn't it critical to the success of mediation *as a process* that the mediator be able to set the record straight?

(4) Why does the *Macaluso* court reject a limited privilege that would only allow the mediator to testify about "objective facts"? Would parties really be less willing to engage in mediation if they knew the mediator would be allowed to testify about "objective facts"? Why wouldn't this provide a workable standard to allow testimony as to what actually happened and what was said, but not as to more subjective matters?

(5) McCormick observes, regarding evidentiary privileges, that "the right to object does not attach to the opposing party as such, but to the person vested with the outside interest or relationship fostered by the particular privilege." C. McCormick, Handbook of the Law of Evidence 152 (1954). Whose interest is protected by the privilege in *Macaluso* and *Fenton*? If the purpose of the privilege is to encourage the *parties* to speak freely during mediation, what is the need for it when, as in *Macaluso,* the parties already chose to testify about what happened in the mediation and, as in *Fenton,* the plaintiff and his wife both signed forms authorizing the mediator to release the information? Does the privilege then run to the *mediator*? If so, what purpose is served by such a privilege? Is it to protect the mediator's interest in preserving his neutrality? How valid is that interest? It has been said that a mediator's neutrality is not compromised by testimony under subpoena and with consent of both parties and that "what's really at stake is

careerism and professional self-interest." 2 BNA ADR Rptr. No. 8 (1988) (reporting on speech by Professor Eric Green). Do you agree? Is there more justification for protecting mediator neutrality in the case of an institutional mediator (as in *Macaluso* where the mediator was under the FMCS)?

(6) Is the privilege in *Macaluso* and *Fenton* limited to court testimony, or would it apply to any attempt outside of court to obtain testimony from the mediator, as in an administrative proceeding? Could it be used to prevent the mediator voluntarily from disclosing what went on in the mediation, as to the press? Note that although "communication privileges often cover licensed professionals who are under an ethical duty not to disclose such information without a waiver from the client," most mediators are not licensed or certified and therefore are subject to discipline only from their employers. N. Rogers & R. Salem, supra, at 88–9. Tort or contract remedies may be available to a wronged party for violation of confidentiality, and one statute creates criminal penalties for mediator disclosure of information obtained in confidence (see 42 U.S.C. § 2000g–2).

(7) The Arizona confidentiality statute, as noted in the concurring opinion in *Fenton,* provides a privilege only to the parties since it allows disclosure only with their consent. How did the court in *Fenton* reach the position that the mediator may assert a privilege? Is this a common law or statutory privilege?

b. Statutory Privilege

A number of states have extended a statutory privilege to mediation. They range from short, broadly-stated provisions to long, narrowly-drawn statutes. The passage of a statute rarely resolves all issues as to mediation confidentiality. Often there are difficult problems of interpretation and application. There may be situations which the drafters did not foresee. Grants of confidentiality sometimes have not taken into account hard cases in which the policy favoring confidentiality is less compelling and the need for disclosure is greater. The variety of statutory approaches indicates that there is not yet a totally satisfactory solution to confidentiality questions. Consider the following comments on statutes that accord a sweeping privilege:

PROTECTING CONFIDENTIALITY IN MEDIATION
98 Harv.L.Rev. 441, 452–453 (1984).

Recent legislative enactments in several states have provided near-absolute protection for communications made in mediation, whether among the parties or with the mediator.[79] Though this approach creates a straightforward rule suitable to an informal process, it is an overreaction to the shortcomings of evidentiary rules and contractual

79. See e.g., Fla.Stat.Ann. 749.01(3) (West Supp.1984); N.Y.Jud.Law 849–b(6) (McKinney Supp.1983–1984); Okla.Stat. tit. 12, § 1805 (Supp.1983).

arrangements. Any protection of mediation must recognize the limits imposed on confidentiality by the nature of a negotiation process itself, and must also articulate conditions for compelling mediator testimony that adequately protect the mediator's neutrality.

* * *

Although broad statutory protection is important to the success of mediation, the recent statutes have generally failed to retain two important exceptions provided in the rules of evidence, exceptions that are crucial to the integrity of mediation. The first exception recognizes that confidentiality must yield to a demonstrable need for parol evidence when one of the parties to a mediation agreement sues to enforce or rescind that agreement. The second exception guards against abuse of the mediation process by allowing confidentiality to be pierced when a party brings suit alleging the breach of a duty owed by another party or the mediator in the course of mediation, such as an obligation to bargain in good faith.

The failure to provide for the use of parol evidence when necessary to a suit to rescind or enforce an agreement reached in mediation is the greatest defect in the new statutes. By treating mediated contracts differently from other settlement agreements, the statutes undermine parties' legitimate interests both in realizing the fruits of mediation and in protecting themselves from fraud, duress, and mistake. As a result, the new statutes may detract from the very climate of truthfulness that confidentiality should foster. Although confidentiality is crucial to preserving the position of parties that have failed to reach an agreement, parties that have reached agreement should not be forced to purchase free discussion at the cost of waiving traditional contract law protection against unfairness.

Moreover, all parties to mediation, successful and unsuccessful, have an interest in seeing that any legal duties owed them in the course of mediation are honored. In many areas of relatively informal mediation—such as small claims mediation—these "duties" may not reach much beyond not assaulting one's adversary. In a more structured field such as labor mediation, however, such duties are more extensive. Obligations to bargain in good faith or to reduce an agreement to writing do not evaporate when parties enter mediation, and enforcing these obligations may require use of evidence from mediation sessions. Moreover, even in the course of mediation unconstrained by a legal bargaining structure, the mediator may owe the parties a minimal duty of care,[87] the enforcement of which may require a waiver of confidentiality.[88]

---

87. See Colo.Rev.Stat. 13–22–306(2) (Supp.1983) (providing that a mediator is liable for "willful or wanton misconduct"); Okla.Stat. tit. 12, § 1805(E) (Supp.1983) (requiring "gross negligence with malicious purpose" in order to render a mediator liable for civil damages).

88. See, Okla.Stat. tit. 12, § 1805(F) (Supp.1983).

The following three statutes take rather different approaches to the protection of mediation confidentiality:

COLO.REV.STAT. § 13–22–307 (Supp.1986).

Confidentiality. Dispute resolution meetings may be closed at the discretion of the mediator. Mediation processes shall be regarded as settlement negotiations, and no admission, representation, or statement made in mediation not otherwise discoverable or obtainable shall be admissible as evidence or subject to process requiring the disclosure of any matter discussed during mediation proceedings.

MASS.ANN.LAWS ch. 233, § 23C.

All memoranda, and work product prepared by a mediator and a mediator's case files, shall be confidential and not subject to disclosure in any judicial or administrative proceeding involving any of the parties to any mediation. And any communication made in the course of and relating to the subject matter of any mediation and which is made in the presence of such mediator by any participant, mediator or other person shall be a confidential communication and not subject to disclosure in any such judicial or administrative proceeding; provided, however, that the provisions of this section shall not apply to the mediation of labor disputes.

For the purposes of this section a mediator shall mean a person not a party to a dispute who enters into a written agreement with the parties to assist them in resolving their disputes and has completed at least thirty hours of training in mediation and who either has four years of professional experience as a mediator or is accountable to a dispute resolution organization which has been in existence for at least three years or one who has been appointed to mediate by a judicial or governmental body.

TEXAS CIVIL PRACTICE AND REMEDIES CODE
tit. 7, ch. 154.

AN ACT relating to alternative dispute resolution procedures.

Sec. 154.002. POLICY. It is the policy of this state to encourage the peaceable resolution of disputes, with special consideration given to disputes involving the parent-child relationship, including the mediation of issues involving conservatorship, possession, and the support of children, and the early settlement of pending litigation through voluntary settlement procedures.

* * *

Sec. 154.023. MEDIATION. (a) Mediation is a forum in which an impartial person, the mediator, facilitates communication between parties to promote reconciliation, settlement, or understanding among them. (b) A mediator may not impose his own judgment on the issues for that of the parties.

* * *

Sec. 154.073. CONFIDENTIALITY OF COMMUNICATIONS IN DISPUTE RESOLUTION PROCEDURES. (a) Except as provided by Subsections (c) and (d), a communication relating to the subject matter of any civil or criminal dispute made by a participant in an alternative dispute resolution procedure, whether before or after the institution of formal judicial proceedings, is confidential, is not subject to disclosure, and may not be used as evidence against the participant in any judicial or administrative proceeding.

(b) Any record made at an alternative dispute resolution procedure is confidential, and the participants or the third party facilitating the procedure may not be required to testify in any proceedings relating to or arising out of the matter in dispute or be subject to process requiring disclosure of confidential information or data relating to or arising out of the matter in dispute.

(c) An oral communication or written material used in or made a part of an alternative dispute resolution procedure is admissible or discoverable if it is admissible or discoverable independent of the procedure.

(d) If this section conflicts with other legal requirements for disclosure of communications or materials, the issue of confidentiality may be presented to the court having jurisdiction of the proceedings to determine, *in camera*, whether the facts, circumstances, and the context of the communications or materials sought to be disclosed warrant a protective order of the court or whether the communications or materials are subject to disclosure.

Notes and Questions

(1) How would you describe the difference in approach in these three statutes? How would you rank them in terms of the absoluteness of their protection for mediation confidentiality?

(2) Does the Colorado statute fully protect against discovery, disclosure, and admissibility into evidence? Are there any limits on what kinds of mediation information it protects? Are there any limits on the persons it applies to or the persons who can invoke it? What problems do you see with this statute?

(3) Consider the following criticisms of the Massachusetts statute by Professor Green, supra, at 29–30:

> The primary problem with the Massachusetts statute, as with all statutes of this sort that I have seen, is that it is both over-inclusive and under-inclusive. The act is over-inclusive because, unlike the attorney-client privilege, the husband-wife privilege, and the evidentiary exclusionary rule, it contains no exception for bad faith, illegal conduct, fraud, or any other abuse of the mediation

process, nor any exception when other important values are at stake. Thus, the mediation related statements in the *Smith* hypothetical [supra p. 345] would be secreted under the terms of the Massachusetts statute, notwithstanding the strong countervailing public interests. Exceptions to prevent such results arguably could be inferred by a court, but there is not a textual hook in the statute on which to peg such judicial legislation. Moreover, if exceptions are to be inferred on an ad hoc basis, what is the advantage of a statute that appears absolute but which, in fact, is subject to case-by-case determination? Would it not be better simply to leave matters to courts to apply a public policy approach to mediation results and fruits?

The statute is under-inclusive in that it applies only to judicial or administrative proceedings involving former parties to the mediation. By implication, an attempt to discover or use mediation results or fruits in other circumstances is not privileged, even though protection may be appropriate. The statute is under-inclusive for the further reason that it applies only to mediation conducted by a "mediator" as the term is defined in the second paragraph of the statute. To qualify, a mediator must have certain training and experience and must act pursuant to a written agreement with the parties. Again, the negative implication is that mediation conducted by anyone else or without a written agreement is to be totally discoverable and admissible. Many mediators, such as internal ombudsmen in corporations, educational institutions, and governmental agencies constantly conduct mediation without any opportunity to enter into a written agreement with the parties. Confidentiality is probably more important and appropriate for such mediation than other mediation covered by the statute, yet the existence of the statute invites judicial interpretation that is not covered, and hence not confidential.

Finally, by tying coverage of the statute to a restrictive definition of a mediator, the act attempts to set standards of practice and define who is qualified to be a mediator and who is not. Many commentators do not believe the field of mediation is ready for restrictive standards and licensure. And if standards of training and experience are going to be set, it should be done as a part of an explicit standard setting process, not through the back door as a definition in a privilege statute.

(4) What kinds of mediation information are protected by the Texas statute under the term "communication relating to the subject matter of any civil or criminal dispute made by a participant in an alternative dispute resolution procedure, whether before or after the institution of formal judicial proceedings"? Would the specifics of a settlement be a "communication"? Who may invoke the statute's protections?

(5) The Texas statute forbids use of communications "as evidence against the participant in any judicial or administrative proceeding." Would this forbid use for purposes other than to prove the truth of the assertion (as for impeachment purposes)?

(6) Oklahoma's Dispute Resolution Act creates a mediator privilege and makes the proceedings non-public, thereby not subject to open-records acts. Okla.Stat. tit. 12 § 1805 (Supp.1987). The Oklahoma Rules, Regulations and Guidelines for the Act, however, provide for disclosure to proper authorities of any information the mediator learns about child abuse or neglect during the mediation. Rule VIII(B)(5)(a)(3).

4. Contractual Agreements of Confidentiality

A contractual agreement by which the parties and mediator agree not to disclose information arising in the mediation can, if properly executed, provide protection of confidentiality. Many mediation programs routinely require such an agreement at the beginning of the mediation. The ABA Standards of Practice for Lawyer Mediators in Family Disputes, sec. II.A., provide:

> At the outset of the mediation, the participants should agree in writing not to require the mediator to disclose to any third party any statements made in the course of mediation. The mediator shall inform the participants that the mediator will not voluntarily disclose to any third party any of the information obtained through the mediation process, unless such disclosure is required by law, without the prior consent of the participants. The mediator shall inform the participants of the limitations of confidentiality such as statutory or judicially mandated reporting.

Like any contract, such an agreement must satisfy the requirements for a valid contract, and thus must be written with sufficient clarity and specificity to constitute a proper manifestation of mutual consent. Coercion, mistake, or fraud or misrepresentation may constitute a defense. Enforceability of such an agreement is a potential problem (see further discussion infra p. 374). However, "agreements not to disclose have been ruled valid against disclosure outside litigation. Thus, for example, a professional [psychiatrist] has been held liable for promising confidentiality and then writing an article about conversations with the client [Doe v. Roe, 93 Misc.2d 201, 400 N.Y.S.2d 668, 674–75 (N.Y.Sup.Ct.1977)]." N. Rogers & R. Salem, supra at 98.

SIMRIN v. SIMRIN
California District Court of Appeals, 1965.
233 Cal.App.2d 90, 43 Cal.Rptr. 376.

STONE, JUSTICE.

Appellant, the mother of four minor children, seeks their custody by modification of the final decree of divorce which awarded custody to the father. The interlocutory decree and custody order was entered March 29, 1962, and became final April 14, 1963. This motion to modify the custody provisions of the decree was filed three months later. Appellant also moved for attorney fees and costs.

Respondent husband countered with an improperly noticed motion to modify the child custody provisions of the final decree by reducing from each weekend to one weekend a month, the mother's right to have the children visit with her.

The trial court denied appellant's motion for change of custody, denied her attorney fees, and granted the husband's motion to reduce the mother's visitation rights to one weekend a month.

Since the welfare of the children was the paramount issue and only one year and four months had elapsed between the original custody order and the mother's motion to modify it, the court allowed evidence to be introduced concerning the conduct of the mother and father prior to the divorce as well as during the interval between the final decree and the hearing on the motion to modify.

The evidence leaves no doubt as to the wisdom of the trial court in awarding custody of the children to the father in the first place, and the case narrows to whether the mother proved rehabilitation during the interval between the original custody award and the hearing on the motion. In these circumstances we are guided by Sanchez v. Sanchez, 55 Cal.2d 118, at page 121, 10 Cal.Rptr. 261, at page 535, 358 P.2d 533, at page 263:

> "The rule is, of course, that 'In a divorce proceeding involving the custody of a minor, primary consideration must be given to the welfare of the child. The court is given a wide discretion in such matters, and its determination will not be disturbed upon appeal in the absence of a manifest showing of abuse. "Every presumption supports the reasonableness of the decree." ' "

Following the rule of Sanchez, we find no abuse of discretion in the order denying the wife's petition for modification, and limiting the mother's right to have the children visit with her to one weekend each month.

From the printed page, without the advantage of observing the witnesses and the children, the trial judge's decision is within the bounds of his discretion. The most favorable testimony adduced by the mother was that of her psychiatrist. But his testimony left room for doubt that sufficient time had elapsed for a determination of whether appellant had become rehabilitated. Clearly, there is no room for conjecture when the welfare of children is involved, and in accordance with the well settled principles enunciated in the Sanchez case, the trial court resolved conjecture in the best interests of the children; "every presumption supports the reasonableness of the decree."

We turn from the sufficiency of the evidence to alleged errors in the trial.

* * *

A more intricate question arises from the court's ruling that a rabbi who acted as a marriage counselor for the parties need not reveal conversations with them. The wife called as a witness a rabbi, who declined to testify, not on the ground of privilege, but that he undertook marriage counseling with the husband and wife only after an express agreement that their communications to him would be confidential and that neither would call him as a witness in the event of a divorce action. He imposed the condition so they would feel free to communicate with him. After lengthy voir dire examination of the rabbi, the husband, and the wife, the court ruled that the rabbi need not relate the confidential communications.

The husband asserted the communications were privileged under Code of Civil Procedure section 1881, subdivision (3); the wife, on the other hand, waived any privilege that might exist. The question of waiver of joint husband-and-wife privilege was argued, but we think the question academic for under the statute there is no privilege here in the first place. Section 1881, subdivision (3), is limited to confessions in the course of discipline enjoined by the church. It would wrench the language of the statute to hold that it applies to communications made to a religious or spiritual advisor acting as a marriage counselor. We think this result regrettable for reasons of public policy expressed below in our discussion of the agreement, but the wording of the statute leaves us no choice.

As to the agreement, appellant argues that to hold her to her bargain with the rabbi and with her husband is to sanction a contract to suppress evidence contrary to public policy. However, public policy also strongly favors procedures designed to preserve marriages, and counseling has become a promising means to that end. The two policies are here in conflict and we resolve the conflict by holding the parties to their agreement. If a husband or wife must speak guardedly for fear of making an admission that might be used in court, the purpose of counseling is frustrated. One should not be permitted, under cover of suppression of evidence, to repudiate an agreement so deeply affecting the marriage relationship. For the unwary spouse who speaks freely, repudiation would prove a trap; for the wily, a vehicle for making self-serving declarations.

It is true, as appellant points out and as respondent concedes, there is no California case in point. But two analogies are close aboard. Since appellant stresses the trial or evidentiary aspects of the agreement, we note, first, the analogy to statements that are made in offer of compromise and to avoid or settle litigation, which are not admissible in evidence. Likewise, statements made to a counselor in an effort to save a marriage, as here, should not be admissible since they, too, are made for the purpose of settling a dispute, to save a marriage and to prevent litigation. The other analogy is to proceedings in the conciliation court. Of them Mr. Witkin says in his work, California Evidence, section 477(b), page 533:

"*Proceedings of Conciliation Court.* The superior court sitting as a conciliation court conducts its proceedings in private . . ., and communications from parties to the judge, commissioner or counselor are deemed made 'in official confidence' under C.C.P.1881 (5), supra, § 438. (C.C.P.1747.)"

We do not equate a confidential communication made to a churchman acting as a marriage counselor, with a communication made in a judicial proceeding. The analogy holds nonetheless, since the purpose of making such communications confidential in each instance is to encourage the husband and wife to speak freely and to preserve the marriage.

Notes and Questions

(1) The court in *Simrin* notes that a contract to suppress evidence is contrary to public policy. Wigmore said that "no pledge of privacy * * * can avail against demand for the truth in a court of justice." 8 J. Wigmore, Evidence in Trials at Common Law § 2286, at 528 (1964). Here the court found that the testimony of the psychiatrist introduced by the mother "left room for doubt that sufficient time had elapsed" to determine that she had become rehabilitated. Thus the rabbi's testimony appears to have been of critical importance. Why then did the need for confidentiality override the mother's need for the evidence? Did the court engage in a balancing of the two policies, or simply rule that confidentiality agreements must be enforced? Would there have been any protection of confidentiality without the agreement?

(2) In *Simrin* the rabbi acted as a marriage counselor rather than a formal mediator. Does the court's reliance on the policy favoring confidentiality in California Conciliation Court proceedings suggest that similar confidentiality agreements would be upheld in all forms of mediation?

(3) Despite the protection that California courts have accorded to mediation confidentiality, due process concerns may undermine that protection. In McLaughlin v. Superior Court for San Mateo County, 140 Cal.App.3d 473, 189 Cal.Rptr. 479 (1983), it was held that both parties are entitled to call as a witness or cross-examine a Conciliation Court counselor who renders a report to the judge. The notion is that the parties must be able to examine the counselor to insure that her recommendation has a basis in the facts and law and is not influenced by bias. What does this do to mediation confidentiality? J. Folberg & A. Taylor, Mediation 280 (1984), observe that "allowing the mediator to make a recommendation and testify creates an untenable Hobson's choice for divorcing parents: either refrain from being candid in mediation discussions or reveal relevant confidences knowing that they can be used later against your individual interests. This challenge has been countered with the argument that parties to a court-compelled mediation are unlikely to reveal confidences that would threaten their

desired custody resolution, whether or not those confidences would be revealed in court."

(4) If a contractual agreement does not contain any exceptions, would it be upheld when a statute imposes a duty to report certain information or events, for example, reports of felonies, child neglect or abuse, or gunshot wounds? Even if there is no such express statute, should a court weigh the policy favoring such disclosure against that favoring confidentiality under the agreement?

E. ENFORCEABILITY OF MEDIATION AGREEMENTS

Mediation agreements, like contracts and court judgments, are not always complied with. When that happens the question arises as to what remedies are available to invoke the coercive power of the courts to enforce the agreement.

Enforceability of mediation agreements may be critical to obtaining an agreement. The parties may want to know that the agreement is final and effective. This is especially true in such areas as labor, commercial, and public law dispute mediation. There the usual expectation is that any agreement reached will be a legally enforceable contract, and it is usually drawn up by lawyers.

Some advocates of community dispute mediation do not view legal enforceability as central to its objectives. Particularly where the parties have an ongoing relationship, as in a family or church, it is said that the nature of the relationship is critical and that failure of compliance calls for a return to mediation or renegotiation rather than court action.[1] Since empirical evidence suggests that mediated agreements have a higher compliance rate than court judgments,[2] it is argued that judicial enforcement does not enhance the mediation process. It is further argued that focusing on legal enforceability during mediation can undermine the process of trust and reconciliation and may require the parties to consult legal counsel, undercutting the desire to avoid legalism.

Whatever the attractiveness of such arguments in certain contexts such as church mediations, the desire for closure of the dispute is generally viewed as requiring some expectation of enforcement. Most mediation centers retain the agreement in their files and offer their services in helping to assure compliance. Centers often hold in escrow sums of money to be paid by one party until the other party complies with its part of the agreement. Sometimes they oversee and assist in exchanges of property and other tangible forms of compliance. If the center's assistance fails to accomplish compliance, the only recourse

1. See Note, The Dilemma of Regulating Mediation, 22 Hous.L.Rev. 841, 864–65 (1985).

2. See Note, Enforceability of Mediated Agreements, 1 Ohio St.J. Dispute Res. 385,

385 n. 5 (1986) (citing McEwen & Maiman, see supra p. 281).

may be to seek enforcement by a court. Mediation centers are not comfortable with that turn of events; court proceedings may threaten mediation confidentiality and seems to signal failure of the process. But increasingly parties are told both in advance of mediation and upon signing an agreement that it may be legally enforceable, and mediators find such expectations necessary for closure.

To be legally enforceable, settlement agreements must of course satisfy the requisites of contract law; however, a general policy favoring enforcement, and specific policies underlying certain particular causes of action, may enhance enforceability.[3] "The power of a trial court to enter a judgment enforcing a settlement agreement has its basis in the policy favoring the settlement of disputes and the avoidance of costly and time-consuming litigation."[4] An agreement to settle a federal suit need not be in writing to be enforceable.[5] However, in some states, settlement agreements must be in writing.[6] In some states, also, an attorney who signs a settlement agreement must have actual, rather than apparent, authority in order to bind the client unless the client ratifies it or accepts partial satisfaction.[7] Of course, the entry of a settlement agreement as a judgment of the court gives it the effect of a judgment, with the attendant rights to judicial enforcement remedies.

A mediation agreement that is intended by the parties to be a contract is enforceable under the rules of contract law. Some contracts, however, are not enforceable for public policy reasons. This may include contracts that interfere with highly personal matters relating to family life and social mores (recall supra p. 293, note (6)). Since mediation agreements sometimes involve this sort of agreement, not all mediation agreements are enforceable. There is also sometimes a question as to whether the parties actually intended an agreement to be legally enforceable. A Minnesota statute provides that the effect of a mediated settlement agreement is to be "determined under principles of law applicable to contract"; however, under the statute such an agreement is *not* binding unless it contains "a provision stating that it is binding," as well as provisions stating that the parties were advised in writing

> that (a) the mediator has no duty to protect their interests or provide them with information about their legal rights; (b) signing a mediated settlement agreement may adversely affect their legal

---

3. See Fulgence v. J. Ray McDermott & Co., 662 F.2d 1207, 1209 (5th Cir.1981) (Title VII includes a congressionally mandated policy of encouraging settlement); Strange v. Gulf & South American Steamship Co., 495 F.2d 1235, 1237 (5th Cir.1974) (agreement challenged on grounds of mutual mistake).

4. Kukla v. National Distillers Products Co., 483 F.2d 619, 621 (6th Cir.1973).

5. Bergstrom v. Sears, Roebuck and Co., 532 F.Supp. 923, 932 (D.Minn.1982).

6. N.Y.Civ.Prac.R. 2104.7 (McKinney 1976 & Supp.1987); Moore v. Gunning, 328 So.2d 462 (Fla.App.1976) (applying Fla.R. Civ.P. 1.030).

7. See citations in N. Rogers & R. Salem, A Student's Guide to Mediation and the Law 157 (1987).

rights; and (c) they should consult an attorney before signing a mediated settlement agreement if they are uncertain of their rights * * *.[8]

Assuming that the nature of a mediation agreement would admit of judicial enforcement, enforceability is determined by reference to contract law. There must be a manifestation of mutual assent and consideration. Consideration is rarely a problem since a mediation agreement will generally involve a bargained-for exchange, whether of tangible goods, promises, forbearance, or the creation, modification or destruction of a legal relation.[9] The most likely defenses to the manifestation of mutual consent are duress, mistake, or fraud or misrepresentation.

The question of duress may arise when a party comes to a mediation under pressure, as when a prosecutor or court orders him to mediate or suffer certain consequences. Under certain Neighborhood Justice Center programs, for example, a party may receive a letter from an intake official informing him of the complaint and the time and place of the hearing and containing the notation that "failure to appear may result in this complaint being referred to an appropriate criminal or civil law enforcement agency for possible charges in accordance with the law." [10] "If a party's manifestation of assent is induced by an improper threat by the other party that leaves the victim no reasonable alternative, the contract is voidable by the victim." [11] A threat is improper if it threatens criminal prosecution, but not if it threatens the use of the civil process unless made in bad faith.[12] It might be argued that the threat in the letter quoted above was not to induce a manifestation of intent to enter the contract but merely to talk about the dispute in mediation. If it were made clear at the outset of the mediation that the agreement was entirely voluntary, duress would seem difficult to establish in that case.

A defense based on mistake may be more likely in a mediation agreement than other forms of contract. The process seeks to assure the parties that by settling the dispute themselves without intermediaries, they rely on the actual facts of which they have the best knowledge. But since the proceeding is not adversary, there is greater likelihood of a mistake as to an essential element of the agreement which, if it satisfies the legal criteria for mistake, will prevent enforceability.[13]

Fraud or misrepresentation may also occur in a mediation. To establish the defense of misrepresentation, there must be an assertion or omission that is not in accord with the facts, that is either fraudulent

8. Minn.Stat. § 572.35 (West 1986).

9. Restatement of Contracts, § 75 (1932).

10. Note, The Dilemma of Regulating Mediation, supra note 1, at 4845 n. 34.

11. Restatement, Second, Contracts § 175.

12. Restatement, Second, Contracts § 179.

13. Restatement, Second, Contracts § 152.

or material, and that is justifiably relied on by the recipient in manifesting his assent.[14] It is possible that one party may misrepresent a material fact and that the best efforts of the mediator will not succeed in bringing out the true state of the facts. In such a case, the defense of misrepresentation would prevent enforcement.

Unconscionability provides another possible defense to the enforcement of a mediation agreement. At times, the mediation process of preventing serious power imbalances fails, and an agreement is markedly unfair to one party. Sometimes the extent of the unfairness may not be fully appreciated until a later time. Under the unconscionability clause of the Uniform Commercial Code [15] and those jurisdictions that recognize unconscionability as a defense,[16] a court may refuse to enforce the contract or any provision thereof.

Enforcement remedies create special problems in the context of mediation agreements. When, as in community dispute mediation, the mediator is often not a lawyer, the agreement may be written in layman terms or inartful legal jargon. That may be perfectly satisfactory to enable a court to enforce it if the terms are clear and unambiguous. But if the terms are vague, ambiguous, or contradictory, problems arise. For specific performance, a higher degree of specificity is generally required, and the terms must be certain in all particulars essential to enforcement.[17] Inartful drafting is not necessarily fatal to the enforcement of contracts. Courts have held that even though the draftmanship leaves something to be desired and could have been more clearly stated, the contract should be specifically enforced if its intent can be determined.[18]

Courts should give some consideration to the nature of the mediation process in striving to determine the intent of the agreement. They should be apprised of the fact that the parties voluntarily engaged in a process involving mutual discussion in an attempt to resolve the dispute and achieve reconciliation. In such a process, drafting requirements should be liberal if the intent can be devined. Furthermore, it might be argued "that the harm suffered from denial of the specific performance order would be more than just that of the parties involved, but would also include the harm to the program of public knowledge that settlements are not enforced on their terms." [19] There are, however, occasions when mediation contracts simply lack the specificity necessary for specific enforcement.

In addition, specific performance will not be enforced if "the character and magnitude of performance would impose on the court burdens in enforcement or supervision disproportionate to the advan-

---

14. A. Farnsworth, Contracts 232 (1982); Restatement, Contracts §§ 162–64.

15. Uniform Commercial Code § 2–302.

16. See Restatement, Contracts § 208.

17. Manss–Owens Co. v. H.S. Owens & Son, 129 Va. 183, 105 S.E. 543, 547 (1921).

18. Wilkinson v. Vaughn, 419 S.W.2d 1, 6 (Mo.1967).

19. Freedman, Are Mediation Agreements Enforceable? 9 (ABA Spec.Comm. on Alt. Means of Dis. Res.).

tages gained from enforcement and the harm suffered from denial." [20]
An agreement, for example, that calls for a party "to stay away" from
the other might fail under that standard.

Damages, in lieu of specific performance, seems an inappropriate
remedy for mediation, at least in agreements dealing with relationships
and other intangibles. The goal of mediation is to allow the parties to
structure their own resolution of the dispute, and damages would seem
contrary to that objective. In such cases, the inadequacy of damages,
as required for specific performance, should generally be easily demonstrated: damages fail to carry out the parties' resolution and could be
difficult to prove for breach of an agreement that seeks to define
interpersonal relations and nontangible benefits. It has been suggested
that "if a damage award is made, it should be made on the original
dispute, and not on the agreement reached in settlement of the original
dispute." [21] On the other hand, in such areas as labor, commercial,
public law, and even certain family law (as with property settlements),
disputes, damages may provide an adequate substitute for the loss of
compliance with the mediation agreement.

F. LAWYERS AND MEDIATION

A lawyer may be involved in mediation in a variety of ways. For
one thing, he may give advice to a client on the subject of engaging in
mediation, or be told by the client that she desires to mediate. Professor Riskin has analyzed the reluctance of some lawyers to allow their
clients to mediate, a reluctance sometimes based on misperceptions of
the process and sometimes on an unwillingness or inability to appreciate the advantages of a non-adversary proceeding.[1] If the client does go
to mediation, the lawyer is confronted with determining just what his
role will be. He could advise the client before and/or after the
mediation, but not attend it himself; he could attend but not actively
participate; or he could attend and actively participate. These are
distinct roles, requiring different skills and a sophisticated understanding of the mediation dynamic.

Especially troubling to a lawyer is just how his legal advice to the
client fits into a process in which the parties are encouraged to establish
their own norms. The interplay of legal rules and private ordering has
been discussed extensively (supra pp. 294–308), and provides a continuing
challenge for the lawyer. What advice, for example, does a lawyer give
to a client before the mediation? Presumably he should inform the
client fully of her legal rights so that she can mediate with an appreciation of what the legal outcome might be if an agreement is not reached.
But there are ways for a sensitive lawyer both to provide full advice as to
the state of the law and to support and complement the mediation
process. How does the lawyer review and give advice concerning a

20. Restatement, Second, Contracts § 366.

21. Freedman, supra, at 7.

1. Riskin, Mediation and Lawyers, 43 Ohio St.L.J. 29, 43–51 (1982).

mediation agreement that does not follow the result that is most likely in a legal proceeding? Again the lawyer has clear duties to inform the client of the legal standards, but if he is too rigid in holding to such standards, he may undermine a satisfactory solution.

The second context in which the lawyer may confront mediation is as a mediator himself. If he acts as a formal mediator in a dispute not involving present or past clients, there are few professional problems. He is required to clearly differentiate his role as a lawyer from that of a mediator.[2] As a mediator, for example, he is not to give legal advice. But so long as the roles are kept separate, a lawyer may act as a mediator, and many do in such areas as divorce and family law, commercial matters, and community disputes.

A more difficult question arises when a lawyer seeks to mediate, either formally or informally, in a dispute involving one of his clients. The paradigm situation in which this arises is a divorce. We will consider in some detail the kinds of ethical problems raised by this form of lawyer mediation.

The 1969 American Bar Association Code of Professional Responsibility specifically addressed the issue of the lawyer as mediator:

> A lawyer is often asked to serve as an impartial arbitrator or mediator in matters which involve present or former clients. He may serve in either capacity if he first discloses such present or former relationships. After a lawyer has undertaken to act as an impartial arbitrator or mediator, he should not thereafter represent in the dispute any of the parties involved.[3]

A 1981 opinion of the New York City Bar Association Committee on Professional and Judicial Ethics stated that the Code "does not impose a per se bar to lawyers participating in divorce mediation activities."[4] But it warned that "[t]he lawyer may not participate in the divorce mediation process where it appears that the issues between the parties are of such complexity or difficulty that the parties cannot prudently reach a resolution without the advice of separate and independent legal counsel."[5]

The new Model Rules of Professional Conduct, Rule 2.2, provides specific guidelines for lawyer mediation, allowing him to act as intermediary between clients if:

    (1) the lawyer explains the advantages and risks associated with common representation and obtains each client's consent to the common representation;

    (2) the lawyer reasonably believes that the matter can be resolved on terms compatible with the clients' best interests, that each

---

2. See Comment, The Attorney As Mediator—Inherent Conflict of Interest?, 32 UCLA L.Rev. 986 (1985); Pirie, The Lawyer As Mediator: Professional Responsibility Problems or Profession Problems?, 63 Canadian Bar Rev. 378 (1985).

3. Code of Professional Responsibility, 1969, EC 5–20.

4. N.Y. City Bar Assoc. Comm. on Professional and Judicial Ethics, Op. No. 80–23 (1981), 7 Fam.L.Rep. 3097.

5. Id. at 3099.

client will be able to make adequately informed decisions in the matter and that there is little risk of material prejudice to interests of any of the clients if the contemplated resolution is unsuccessful; and

(3) the lawyer reasonably believes that the common representation can be undertaken impartially and without improper effect on other responsibilities the lawyer has to any of the clients.[6]

The comment goes on to warn:

In considering whether to act as intermediary between clients, a lawyer should be mindful that if the intermediation fails the result can be additional cost, embarrassment and recrimination. In some situations the risk of failure is so great the intermediation is plainly impossible. For example, a lawyer cannot undertake common representation of clients between whom litigation is imminent or who contemplate contentious negotiations. More generally, if the relationship between the parties has already assumed definite antagonism, the possibility that the clients' interests can be adjusted by intermediation ordinarily is not very good.[7]

In 1983, the Family Law Section of the American Bar Association adopted six standards for practice for family mediators, that were approved by the ABA in 1984:

STANDARDS OF PRACTICE FOR LAWYER MEDIATORS IN FAMILY DISPUTES
(Adopted by the House of Delegates of the ABA, 1984).

Preamble

For the purposes of these standards, family mediation is defined as a process in which a lawyer helps family members resolve their disputes in an informative and consensual manner. This process requires that the mediator be qualified by training, experience and temperament; that the mediator be impartial; that the participants reach decisions voluntarily; that their decisions be based on sufficient factual data; and that each participant understands the information upon which decisions are reached. While family mediation may be viewed as an alternative means of conflict resolution, it is not a substitute for the benefit of independent legal advice.

I. The Mediator Has a Duty to Define and Describe the Process of Mediation and Its Cost Before the Parties Reach an Agreement to Mediate.

Specific Considerations

Before the actual mediation sessions begin, the mediator shall conduct an orientation session to give an overview of the process and to

6. ABA Model Rules of Professional Conduct, Rule 2.2 (1983).　　**7.** Id.

assess the appropriateness of mediation for the participants. Among the topics covered, the mediator shall discuss the following:

(A) The mediator shall define the process in context so that the participants understand the differences between mediation and other means of conflict resolution available to them. In defining the process, the mediator shall also distinguish it from therapy or marriage counselling.

(B) The mediator shall obtain sufficient information from the participants so they can mutually define the issues to be resolved in mediation.

(C) It should be emphasized that the mediator may make suggestions for the participants to consider, such as alternative ways of resolving problems, and may draft proposals for the participants' consideration, but that all decisions are to be made voluntarily by the participants themselves, and the mediator's views are to be given no independent weight or credence.

(D) The duties and responsibilities that the mediator and the participants accept in the mediation process shall be agreed upon. The mediator shall instruct the participants that either of them or the mediator has the right to suspend or terminate the process at any time.

(E) The mediator shall assess the ability and willingness of the participants to mediate. The mediator has a continuing duty to assess his or her own ability and willingness to undertake mediation with the particular participants and the issues to be mediated. The mediator shall not continue and shall terminate the process, if in his or her judgment, one of the parties is not able or willing to participate in good faith.

(F) The mediator shall explain the fees for mediation. It is inappropriate for a mediator to charge a contingency fee or to base the fee on the outcome of the mediation process.

(G) The mediator shall inform the participants of the need to employ independent legal counsel for advice throughout the mediation process. The mediator shall inform the participants that the mediator cannot represent either or both of them in a marital dissolution or in any legal action.

(H) The mediator shall discuss the issue of separate sessions. The mediator shall reach an understanding with the participants as to whether and under what circumstances the mediator may meet alone with either of them or with any third party. Commentary: The mediator cannot act as lawyer for either party or for them jointly and should make that clear to both parties.

(I) It should be brought to the participants' attention that emotions play a part in the decision-making process. The mediator shall attempt to elicit from each of the participants a confirmation that each understands the connection between one's own emotions and the bargaining process.

II. The Mediator Shall Not Voluntarily Disclose Information Obtained Through the Mediation Process Without the Prior Consent of Both Participants.

Specific Considerations

(A) At the outset of mediation, the parties should agree in writing not to require the mediator to disclose to any party any statements made in the course of mediation. The mediator shall inform the participants that the mediator will not voluntarily disclose to any third party any of the information obtained through the mediation process, unless such disclosure is required by law, without the prior consent of the participants. The mediator also shall inform the parties of the limitations of confidentiality such as statutory or judicially mandated reporting.

(B) If subpoenaed or otherwise noticed to testify, the mediator shall inform the participants immediately so as to afford them an opportunity to quash the process.

(C) The mediator shall inform the participants of the mediator's inability to bind third parties to an agreement not to disclose information furnished during the mediation in the absence of any absolute privilege.

III. The Mediator Has a Duty to Be Impartial.

Specific Considerations

(A) The mediator shall not represent either party during or after the mediation process in any legal matters. In the event the mediator has represented one of the parties beforehand, the mediator shall not undertake the mediation.

(B) The mediator shall disclose to the participants any biases or strong views relating to the issues to be mediated, both in the orientation session, and also before these issues are discussed in mediation.

(C) The mediator must be impartial as between the mediation participants. The mediator's task is to facilitate the ability of the participants to negotiate their own agreement, while raising questions as to the fairness, equity and feasibility of proposed options for settlement.

(D) The mediator has a duty to ensure that the participants consider fully the best interests of the children, that they understand the consequences of any decision they reach concerning the children. The mediator also has a duty to assist parents to examine the separate and individual needs of their children and to consider those needs apart from their own desires for any particular parenting formula. If the mediator believes that any proposed agreement of the parents does not protect the best interests of the children, the mediator has a duty to inform them of this belief and its basis.

(E) The mediator shall not communicate with either party alone or with any third party to discuss mediation issues without the prior consent of the mediation participants. The mediator shall obtain an agreement from the participants during the orientation session as to whether and under what circumstances the mediator may speak directly and separately with each of their lawyers during the mediation process.

IV. The Mediator Has a Duty to Assure That the Mediation Participants Make Decisions Based Upon Sufficient Information and Knowledge.

Specific Considerations

(A) The mediator shall assure that there is full financial disclosure, evaluation and development of relevant factual information in the mediation process, such as each would reasonably receive in the discovery process, or that the parties have sufficient information to intelligently waive the right to such disclosure.

(B) In addition to requiring this disclosure, evaluation and development of information, the mediator shall promote the equal understanding of such information before any agreement is reached. This consideration may require the mediator to recommend that either or both obtain expert consultation in the event that it appears that additional knowledge or understanding is necessary for balanced negotiations.

(C) The mediator may define the legal issues, but shall not direct the decision of the mediation participants based upon the mediator's interpretation of the law as applied to the facts of the situation. The mediator shall endeavor to assure that the participants have a sufficient understanding of appropriate statutory and case law as well as local judicial tradition, before reaching an agreement by recommending to the participants that they obtain independent legal representation during the process.

V. The Mediator Has a Duty to Suspend or Terminate Mediation Whenever Continuation of the Process Would Harm One or More of the Participants.

Specific Considerations

(A) If the mediator believes that the participants are unable or unwilling to meaningfully participate in the process or that reasonable agreement is unlikely, the mediator may suspend or terminate mediation and should encourage the parties to seek appropriate professional help. The mediator shall recognize that the decisions are to be made by the parties on the basis of adequate information. The mediator shall not, however, participate in a process that the mediator believes will result in harm to a participant.

(B) The mediator shall assure that each person has had the opportunity to understand fully the implications and ramifications of all options available.

(C) The mediator has a duty to assure a balanced dialogue and must attempt to diffuse any manipulative or intimidating negotiation techniques utilized by either of the participants.

(D) If the mediator has suspended or terminated the process, the mediator should suggest that the participants obtain additional professional services as may be appropriate.

VI. The Mediator Has a Continuing Duty to Advise Each of the Mediation Participants to Obtain Legal Review Prior to Reaching Any Agreement.

Specific Considerations

(A) Each of the mediation participants should have independent legal counsel before reaching final agreement. At the beginning of the mediation process, the mediator should inform the participants that each should employ independent legal counsel for advice at the beginning of the process and that the independent legal counsel should be utilized throughout the process and before the participants have reached any accord to which they have made an emotional commitment. In order to promote the integrity of the process, the mediator shall not refer either of the participants to any particular lawyers. When an attorney referral is requested, the parties should be referred to a Bar Association list if available. In the absence of such a list, the mediator may only provide a list of qualified family law attorneys in the community.

(B) The mediator shall inform the participants that the mediator cannot represent either or both of them in a marital dissolution.

(C) The mediator shall obtain an agreement from the husband and wife that each lawyer, upon request, shall be entitled to review all the factual documentation provided by the participants in the mediation process.

(D) Any memo of understanding or proposed agreement which is prepared in the mediation process should be separately reviewed by independent counsel for each participant before it is signed. While a mediator cannot insist that each participant have separate counsel, they should be discouraged from signing any agreement which has not been so reviewed. If the participants, or either of them, choose to proceed without independent counsel, the mediator shall warn them of any risk involved in not being represented, including where appropriate, the possibility that the agreement they submit to a court may be rejected as unreasonable in light of both parties' legal rights or may not be binding on them.

———

LEONARD RISKIN, MEDIATION AND LAWYERS
43 Ohio St.L.J. 29, 37–41 (1982).

A lawyer may function explicitly as a divorce mediator, * * * by representing one of the spouses, leaving the other unrepresented; both of the spouses; or neither of the spouses.

Each of these models has strengths and weaknesses.

[Representing One of the Spouses]

Parties who have independent counsel can benefit from an adversarial look at their position. A prediction of the likely results of adversary processing is necessary for an informed, fully voluntary decision about a mediated solution. Sometimes lawyers also aid the mediation process by urging their clients to accept a reasonable compromise. There is a concomitant likelihood, however, that a lawyer's advice will work to undermine a mediation. Of course, this occasionally will be in the client's best interest. But some lawyers may tend to deliver advice in a way that exaggerates the importance of the adversary perspective and the accuracy of their predictions. When this occurs, the client may be drawn away inappropriately from a mediated resolution. But the risk of inappropriate disruption by outside lawyers also is directly related to the level of the parties' commitment to nonadversarial processing. A person who truly wanted to resolve his problem in a nonadversarial, personal fashion—if he is satisfied with the results of mediation—would not be inclined to give high value to the possible advantages proferred by the adversary lawyer.

[Representing Both of the Spouses]

One way to lessen the likelihood of a lawyer's undermining a mediation is to employ an impartial attorney to advise both parties, but this raises a number of worries. There are, as examples, mild possibilities of charges of aiding in the unauthorized practice of law (a violation of DR 3–101(A)) or practicing law in association with or otherwise sharing fees with a layman (a violation of DR 3–102(A)). The most substantial concern, however, is the enormous difficulty of giving impartial or neutral legal advice if the parties have conflicting interests. This raises the spectre of breaching the requirement of Canon 5 that a lawyer exercise independent professional judgment on behalf of a client. A recent opinion imposed, *inter alia,* the conditions that "the issues not be of such complexity that the parties cannot prudently reach resolution of the controversy without the advice of separate and independent legal counsel," and that the lawyer advise the parties of the limitations and risks of his role and of the advantages of independent legal counsel, obtain their informed consent, give legal advice only in the presence of both, and refrain from representing either in a subsequent proceeding concerning divorce. If one lawyer advises the couple, each partner is deprived of the benefit of an adversarial look at his or her situation.

The interdisciplinary approach seems to offer enormous promise. It can attend at once to legal, emotional, value, and relational needs. Each of the professionals can learn from the other and broaden his own view of the situation. The problems, though, seem just as great as those presented to the lawyer-mediator alone. Here again, the *Code of Professional Responsibility* may present obstacles: the Canon 5 injunction to exercise independent professional judgment; the Canon 3 mandate to assist in preventing the unauthorized practice of law; and the DR 3–102(A) prohibition of practicing law or sharing fees with a layman. But practical difficulties seem even weightier. Anyone who has tried it knows that interdisciplinary work is difficult. Lawyers and therapists look at the world differently. In addition, the team approach presents problems of control, responsibility, and jurisdiction that will severely tax the talents and personalities of those who try it. The lawyer-therapist/mediator team can work very well, but only rarely will an adequate match-up of professionals occur.

When a lawyer functions explicitly as a mediator while representing both of the parties, or just one of the parties while leaving the other unrepresented, the principal professional responsibility concern is again the Canon 5 requirement that a lawyer exercise independent professional judgment on behalf of a client. Bar associations have traditionally prohibited dual representation in matrimonial cases, but have recently shown some signs of liberalization. The Ohio state bar ethics committee recently permitted a lawyer to draft a separation agreement for a couple so long as he was representing one of the parties and the other was protected by giving a knowing consent. The Arizona committee also has permitted dual representation, as has a California appellate court in limited circumstances, including full disclosure of risks.

The *Model Code of Professional Responsibility*, EC 5—20, permits a lawyer to mediate in a matter that involves "present or former clients . . . if he first discloses such . . . relationships . . . and [does not] thereafter represent in the dispute any of the parties involved." The Wisconsin bar ethics committee has ruled that a lawyer who educated the parties about their legal rights and responsibilities, mediated disputes during the negotiations, drafted documents, and appeared in court would find himself beyond the protection of EC 5–20, even though each party would receive independent legal review of the agreement and the lawyer would not represent either party subsequently. And, of course, there are significant risks of a malpractice action.

The principal danger of dual representation is that one of the parties will take unfair advantage of the other, knowingly or not. With this in mind, Rule 2.2 of the proposed final draft of the American Bar Association *Model Rules of Professional Conduct,* which would apply where a lawyer represents both parties.

This model offers significant potential advantages to clients who wish to save time and money and avoid an adversarial confrontation.

Yet when assets or interests that the parties consider significant are involved, they will usually want the benefit of a partisan look at their case.

[*Representing Neither of the Spouses*]

The most recent development—the lawyer serving as divorce mediator but not representing either party—has earned the qualified approval of the Boston and Oregon bar ethics committees. The Oregon opinion imposed the conditions that the attorney

1. . . . must clearly inform the parties he represents neither of them and they both must consent to this arrangement;

2. . . . may give legal advice only to both parties in the presence of each other;

3. . . . may draft the proposed agreement but he must advise, and encourage, the parties to seek independent legal counsel before execution of the agreement; and

4. . . . must not represent either or both of the parties in the subsequent legal proceedings.

This model seems to offer the best possibilities for the appropriate use of law and lawyers in mediation of some matters that normally pass through the adversary process. The attorney-mediator can attempt to provide impartial legal information while making clear the risks to the clients in his doing so. The outside consultations with lawyers can defend against the possibility of bias (deliberate or not) in the lawyer-mediator's work and reduce the chances that one party will inappropriately exercise power over the other.

Another advantage is that information about what a court would do can be integrated into the mediation process in a way that suits the needs of the parties. Because he is an expert on law, the lawyer-mediator can help the parties free themselves, when appropriate, from the influence of legal norms so that they can reach for a solution that is appropriate to them. In addition, the experienced lawyer who functions as a mediator can offer a variety of business arrangements to accomplish the objectives of the parties. These options can become part and parcel of the decision process, and the law-trained mediator who is present at all the sessions and thoroughly familiar with the various needs of the parties can propose alternatives finely tuned to such needs. Moreover, the lawyer-mediator can, better than the lay mediator, identify a myriad of legal issues that must be addressed in the final agreement, and press the disputants to reach decisions. He can incorporate the results in a draft final agreement, which—because of the lawyer-mediator's skill in identifying issues and preparing documents— would be less vulnerable to upending by the outside lawyers than would one drafted by a nonlawyer.

Notes and Questions

(1) Suppose a lawyer regularly represents a businesswoman in all of her affairs. The lawyer has also handled some of her personal affairs with her husband, such as a will and retirement plan. Can the lawyer agree to mediate between the husband and wife in a divorce that involves child custody? Does the prior relationship with the wife give the lawyer confidential information that would have to be disclosed to the husband? Or, does it create implicit bias toward the wife? Would your answer change if the husband was not a sophisticated businessman? How would your answer change if the parties had worked out all of the details of the divorce and they simply wanted you to draft a contract?

(2) Does a lawyer who purports to draft partnership agreements in a whole series of similar transactions with one promoter and different investors limit her liability by stating that "the lawyer is not obligated to disclose any information, whether positive or negative, about similar deals involving this promoter"? Is this sufficient to protect the lawyer if she finds out that several investors have sued this promoter for fraud? Or does the lawyer have a duty to tell the clients about this fact?

(3) Suppose a real estate lawyer who normally represents landlords in drafting leases agrees to mediate disputes between landlords and tenants. Should the lawyer disclose to the tenants who agree to submit to mediation, that he normally represents landlords? Does the tenant have a right to see a record of prior mediations?

(4) Professor Riskin indicates that a "lawyer may function explicitly as a divorce mediator" while representing one or both of the spouses. How would a lawyer accomplish this consistent with his responsibility of "zealous" representation? Does the agreement of the parties to this mixed role resolve any such problems? Is it any wonder that some lawyers are uncomfortable in playing such a mixed role?

"Then it's agreed. Watson, Smith, Teller, and Wilson go to Heaven; Jones, Paducci, and Horner go to Hell; and Fenton and Miller go to arbitration."
Drawing by Dana Fradon; © 1987 The New Yorker Magazine, Inc.

Chapter IV

ARBITRATION

A. THE PROCESS OF PRIVATE ADJUDICATION

1. Introduction

LANDES & POSNER, ADJUDICATION AS A PRIVATE GOOD

8 J. Legal Stud. 235, 235–40 (1979).

Adjudication is normally regarded as a governmental function and judges as public officials. Even economists who assign a highly limited role to government consider the provision of judicial services as indisputably apt function of government; this was, for example, Adam Smith's view. Few economists (and few lawyers) realize that the provision of judicial services precedes the formation of the state; that many formally public courts long had important characteristics of private institutions (for example, until 1825 English judges were paid out of litigants' fees as well as general tax revenues); and that even today much adjudication is private (commercial arbitration being an important example).

* * *

1. *Introduction.* A court system (public or private) produces two types of service. One is dispute resolution—determining whether a rule has been violated. The other is rule formulation—creating rules of law as a by-product of the dispute-settlement process. When a court resolves a dispute, its resolution, especially if embodied in a written opinion, provides information regarding the likely outcome of similar disputes in the future. This is the system of precedent, which is so important in the Anglo–American legal system.

* * *

The two judicial services are in principle severable and in practice often are severed. Jury verdicts resolve disputes but do not create precedents. Legislatures create rules of law but do not resolve disputes. In the Anglo–American legal system rule formation is a function shared by legislatures and (especially appellate) courts; elsewhere judicial law making tends to be less important.

2. *Dispute Resolution.* Imagine a purely private market in judicial services. People would offer their services as judges, and disputants would select the judge whom they mutually found most acceptable. The most popular judges would charge the highest fees, and competition among judges would yield the optimum amount and quality of judicial services at minimum social cost. This competitive process would produce judges who were not only competent but also impartial—would thus fulfill the ideals of procedural justice—because a judge who was not regarded as impartial could not get disputes submitted to him for resolution: one party would always refuse.

A voluntary system of dispute resolution does not presuppose that the dispute has arisen from a consensual relationship (landlord-tenant, employer-employee, seller-buyer, etc.) in which the method of dispute resolution is agreed on before the dispute arose. All that is necessary is that when a dispute does arise the parties to it choose a judge to resolve it. Even if they are complete strangers, as in the typical accident case, the parties can still choose a judge to determine liability.

Although dispute resolution could thus be provided (for criminal as well as civil cases) in a market that would operate free from any obvious elements of monopoly, externality, or other sources of "market failure," it may not be efficient to banish public intervention entirely. Public intervention may be required (1) to ensure compliance with the (private) judge's decision and (2) to compel submission of the dispute to adjudication in the first place. The first of these public functions is straightforward, and no more compromises the private nature of the adjudication system described above than the law of trespass compromises the private property rights system. The second function, compelling submission of the dispute to judge, is more complex. If A accuses B of breach of contract, the next step in a system of private adjudication is for the parties to select a judge. But suppose B, knowing that any impartial judge would convict him, drags his feet in agreeing to select a judge who will hear the case, rejecting name after name submitted by A for his consideration. Although a sanction for this kind of foot-dragging (a sanction analogous to the remedies that the National Labor Relations Board provides for refusals to bargain collectively in good faith) is conceivable, there may be serious difficulty in determining when the bargaining over the choice of the judge is in bad faith—it is not bad faith, for example, to reject a series of unreasonable suggestions by the other side.

Two ways of overcoming the submission problem come immediately to mind. The first is for the parties to agree on the judge (or on the method of selecting him) before the dispute arises, as is done in contracts with arbitration clauses. This solution is available, however, only where the dispute arises from a preexisting voluntary relationship between the parties; the typical tort or crime does not. * * *

Another type of private solution to the problem of enforcement and the selection of a private judge is available when both parties to the dispute are members of the same (private) group or association. The group can expel any member who unreasonably refuses to submit to an impartial adjudication (perhaps by a judge selected by the group) or to abide by the judge's decision. To the extent that membership in the group confers a value over and above alternative opportunities, members will have incentives to bargain in good faith over the selection of the judge and to abide by his decision. In these circumstances dispute resolution can operate effectively without public intervention.

* * *

3. *Rule Production.* Private production of rules or precedents involves two problems. First, because of the difficulty of establishing property rights in a precedent, private judges may have little incentive to produce precedents. They will strive for a fair result between the parties in order to preserve a reputation for impartiality, but why should they make any effort to explain the result in a way that would provide guidance for future parties? To do so would be to confer an external, an uncompensated, benefit not only on future parties but also on competing judges. If anything, judges might deliberately avoid explaining their results because the demand for their services would be reduced by rules that, by clarifying the meaning of the law, reduced the incidence of disputes. Yet, despite all this, private judges just might produce precedents. We said earlier that competitive private judges would strive for a reputation for competence and impartiality. One method of obtaining such a reputation is to give reasons for a decision that convince the disputants and the public that the judge is competent and impartial. Competition could lead private judges to issue formal or informal "opinions" declaring their interpretation of the law, and these opinions—though intended simply as advertising—would function as precedents, as under a public judicial system. * * *

The second problem with a free market in precedent production is that of inconsistent precedents which could destroy the value of a precedent system in guiding behavior. If there are many judges, there is likely to be a bewildering profusion of precedents and no obvious method of harmonizing them. An individual contemplating some activity will have difficulty discovering its legal consequences because they will depend on who decides any dispute arising out of the activity.

*   *   *

[A] system of voluntary adjudication is strongly biased against the creation of precise rules of any sort. Any rule that clearly indicates how a judge is likely to decide a case will assure that no disputes subject to the rule are submitted to that judge since one party will know that it will lose. Judges will tend to promulgate vague standards which give each party to a dispute a fighting chance.

2. Arbitration and Dispute Resolution

The traditional model of arbitration is precisely that of the "private tribunal"—private individuals, chosen voluntarily by the parties to a dispute in preference to the "official" courts, and given power to hear and "judge" their "case." The materials that follow explore the ramifications of this model, which is still the prevalent one. "Arbitration," however, cannot be so easily pigeon-holed, and in recent years the term has come to serve for a broad spectrum of dispute resolution processes. We will see later in this section how other models of arbitration have altered our conventional view of the process. Arbitration, for example, is sometimes imposed as a *mandatory,* non-consensual form of dispute resolution (See infra p. 583), and it has been used to resolve kinds of disputes different from the traditional sort of "cases" which might otherwise have found their way into the judicial system.

There are many reasons why parties may choose arbitration as a more "efficient" means of dispute settlement than adjudication. There is likely to be less wait before a hearing takes place than is commonly imposed by crowded court dockets. Arbitration procedure, as we will see, is relatively informal; pre-trial procedures, elaborate pleading, motion practice, and discovery are substantially streamlined or in many cases completely eliminated. It seems likely therefore that a dispute processed through arbitration will be disposed of more quickly than if the parties had made their way through the court system to a final judgment. (In construction industry arbitrations administered by the American Arbitration Association in 1986, an average of 192 days elapsed between the date a case was filed and the arbitration award.) In addition, the arbitrator's decision is likely to be final: There is no delay imposed by any appeal process, and as we will see, court review is highly restricted. These savings in time and in related pre- and post-trial work are likely to be reflected in savings in expense—for example, in lawyers' fees—although there can be no assurance that this will always be the case.

There may be other benefits as well. Taking a dispute out of the courtroom and into the relative informality of arbitration may reduce the enmity and heightened contentiousness which so often accompany litigation, and which work against a future cooperative relationship. The privacy of the process may also contribute to a lessening of hostility and confrontation. An arbitration hearing (unlike a trial) is not open to the public, and unless the result later becomes the subject of a court proceeding it is not a matter of public record.

Finally, the parties themselves are able to choose their "judges." They are free, therefore, to avail themselves of decision-makers with expert knowledge of the subject matter in dispute. The arbitrator may have a similar background to the parties, or be engaged in the same business; he is likely, then, to be familiar with the presuppositions and understandings of the trade. The usefulness of such expertise is particularly apparent when a contract dispute hinges on interpretation of the agreement—which in turn may depend on the content of trade custom and usage—or when the dispute is over whether goods sold meet the necessary technical standards. In such cases arbitration avoids the task (which may in some cases be insuperable) of educating judge or jury as to the content of these industry norms. In short, "the evidence from arbitration is that a single qualified lay judge is superior to six or twelve randomly selected laymen—on reflection, a not implausible suggestion." [1]

FULLER, COLLECTIVE BARGAINING AND THE ARBITRATOR
1963 Wisc.L.Rev. 3, 11–12, 17.

Labor relations have today become a highly complicated and technical field. This field involves complex procedures that vary from industry to industry, from plant to plant, from department to department. It has developed its own vocabulary. Though the terms of this vocabulary often seem simple and familiar, their true meaning can be understood only when they are seen as parts of a larger system of practice, just as the umpire's "You're out!" can only be fully understood by one who knows the objectives, the rules and the practices of baseball. I might add that many questions of industrial relations are on a level at least equal to that of the infield fly rule. They are not suitable material for light dinner conversation.

In the nature of things few judges can have had any very extensive experience in the field of industrial relations. Arbitrators, on the other hand, are compelled to acquire a knowledge of industrial processes, modes of compensation, complex incentive plans, job classification, shift arrangements, and procedures for layoff and recall.

1. Landes & Posner, Adjudication as a Private Good, 8 J. Legal Stud. 235, 252 (1979).

Naturally not all arbitrators stand on a parity with respect to this knowledge. But there are open to the arbitrator, even the novice, quick methods of education not available to courts. An arbitrator will frequently interrupt the examination of witnesses with a request that the parties educate him to the point where he can understand the testimony being received. This education can proceed informally, with frequent interruptions by the arbitrator, and by informed persons on either side, when a point needs clarification. Sometimes there will be arguments across the table, occasionally even within each of the separate camps. The end result will usually be a clarification that will enable everyone to proceed more intelligently with the case. There is in this informal procedure no infringement whatever of arbitrational due process. On the contrary, the party's chance to have his case understood by the arbitrator is seriously impaired if his representative has to talk into a vacuum, if he addresses his words to uncomprehending ears.

The education that an arbitrator can thus get, say, in a half an hour, might take days if it had to proceed by qualifying experts and subjecting them to direct and cross examination. The courts have themselves recognized the serious obstacle presented by traditional methods of proof in dealing with cases involving a complex technical background.

* * *

Courts have in fact had difficulty with complicated commercial litigation. The problems here are not unlike those encountered in dealing with labor agreements. There are really few outstanding commercial judges in the history of the common law. The greatest of these, Lord Mansfield, used to sit with special juries selected from among experienced merchants and traders. To further his education in commercial practice he used to arrange dinners with his jurors. In Greek mythology it is reported that Minos prepared himself for a posthumous career as judge of shades by first exposing himself to every possible experience of life. It is not only in labor relations that the impracticability of such a program manifests itself.

Notes and Questions

(1) Consider the possible use of arbitration in the following circumstances, and weigh its advantages and disadvantages from the perspective of dispute settlement:

In 1986, the Hunt brothers of Dallas filed two lawsuits in federal court seeking a total of $13.8 billion against some of the country's biggest banks. The banks were accused of fraud, breach of contract, and banking and antitrust law violations after they refused to restructure about $1.5 billion in debts owed by certain Hunt companies, including Placid Oil Company. In December 1986 the Hunts hired a Houston attorney, Stephen Susman, to take charge of the two lawsuits. Placid Oil was then involved in Chapter 11 bankruptcy proceedings. In a court filing seeking the bankruptcy judge's approval to represent Placid, Susman proposed to charge $600 per hour for his time:

> If the Susman firm is terminated by the Hunts for any reason other than malpractice—or the Hunts drop their lawsuits—the firm can pocket the entire retainer [of $1 million]. A malpractice or fee dispute would be arbitrated by the dean of the University of Texas School of Law, Mr. Susman's alma mater. A decision by the dean is final, the fee agreement says.

The Wall Street Journal, December 30, 1986, p. 4.

(2) Lawyers are quick to perceive the advantages which inhere in the expeditious, "businesslike," expert settlement of a controversy provided by arbitration. They are largely advantages of "efficiency." Nevertheless, the arbitration mechanism is similar enough to the context of adjudication to be comfortably familiar to most lawyers. After all, does not arbitration—like the judicial process—entail the settlement of a dispute by the binding decision of a neutral third party, after an adversary presentation of evidence and argument? Can one assume, then, that when lawyers look at arbitration, they may tend to see a "courtroom"? This deceptive familiarity may account for some of the ambivalence of lawyers in relation to arbitration, explaining much of their benevolence towards it as a dispute settlement mechanism as well as much of their criticism of the process.

Lawyers, for example, often agree to serve as arbitrators. What would be more natural than for such a lawyer to begin to think of himself as a "judge"? It is a role for which every lawyer thinks himself admirably suited, and a subject of the fantasies of most. The pervasive influence of the judicial model is also reflected in frequent criticism by attorneys of the conduct of the arbitrators themselves. It appears, for example, in the common complaint that arbitration often results in compromise decisions ("splitting the difference") as opposed to the all-or-nothing results (a "winner's" claim is enforced; a "loser's" claim is rejected) which tend to characterize the judicial process. (See infra p. 427.)

Such attitudes surface occasionally in judicial opinions as well. One federal court observed that "[t]he present day penchant for arbitration may obscure for many parties who do not have the benefit of hindsight that the arbitration system is an inferior system of justice, structured without due process, rules of evidence, accountability of judgment and rules of law. * * * No one ever deemed arbitration successful in labor conflicts because of its superior brand of justice." Stroh Container Company v. Delphi Industries, Inc., 783 F.2d 743, 751 n. 12 (8th Cir.1986). However, comments of this sort are likely to miss the point. Despite a superficial similarity of form or of function, arbitration is not merely another (perhaps cheaper and "inferior") kind of "trial." It seems misleading to approach arbitration simply as a variation on a common theme—another adjudicatory forum of the same sort that law students are accustomed to study in casebooks and lawyers to deal with throughout their professional lives. This chapter is intended instead to assess the arbitration mechanism on its own terms; our goal is to highlight the peculiar characteristics of arbitration which make it a unique process of dispute settlement.

———

As we will see, arbitration has been used in a number of diverse contexts, to resolve many different types of disputes. However, it has flourished most in situations where parties to a contract have or aspire to have a continuing future relationship in which they will regularly deal with each other. The paradigm is the relationship between management and union in the administration of a collective bargaining agreement, or, perhaps, the relationship between a buyer and a seller of fabric in the textile industry. In both cases there is a history and a likelihood of continued mutual dependence by which both parties may profit; there also exist non-legal sanctions allowing either party to withdraw from (or seek to adjust) the relationship, or at least to withhold vital future cooperation. All this makes it easier to settle in advance on arbitration as a less disruptive method than litigation for resolving any future disputes. It also tends to induce the parties to comply with arbitration decisions once they are handed down (as does the feeling, in a long-term relation, that "awards are likely to be equalized over the long run and that erroneous awards can be dealt with through negotiation"[2]). In both cases there is an understandable reluctance to assert officially-defined legal "rights," or to rely on formal, technical arguments or on accusations of misconduct or impropriety—all of which may seem inappropriate in the context of a "family row" and which may hurt the prospects of future collaboration. And in both cases the parties may be more willing in advance to entrust to arbitrators the task of working out the details of their arrangement in accordance with the common values, the "shared norms," of the trade or of the "shop."

LANDES & POSNER, ADJUDICATION AS A PRIVATE GOOD
8 J. Legal Stud. 235, 245–47 (1979).

[I]f one party to a dispute expects that an impartial arbitrator would rule against him, he has an incentive to drag his feet in agreeing to the appointment of an arbitrator. Consistently with this point, writers on arbitration agree that the problem of selection makes arbitration a virtually unusable method of dispute resolution where there is no preexisting contractual or other relationship between the disputants. This suggests a clue to the superior ability of primitive compared to advanced societies to function without public institutions

___

2. Getman, Labor Arbitration and Dispute Resolution, 88 Yale L.J. 916, 922–23 (1979).

of adjudication. Primitive communities tend to be quite small and their members bound together by a variety of mutually advantageous relationships and interactions. Expulsion, outlawry, ostracism, and other forms of boycott or collective refusal to deal are highly effective sanctions in these circumstances. Another way of putting this point is that reputation, a factor recognized in the literature as deterring people from breaking contracts even in the absence of effective legal sanctions, is a more effective deterrent in a small community, where news travels rapidly throughout the entire circle of an individual's business and social acquaintances, than in large, modern, impersonal societies.

Yet even in modern society, certain trade, religious, and other associations correspond, to a degree, to the close-knit, primitive community. For example, securities or commodities exchanges whose members derive substantial benefits from membership can use the threat of expulsion as an effective sanction to induce members to submit to arbitration. So can a religious association in which excommunication is regarded by members as a substantial cost[30]; so can a university. Exchanges, religious associations, and (private) universities are in fact important examples of modern "communities" in which private adjudication (whether called arbitration or something else) is extensively utilized in preference to public adjudication.

IN THE MATTER OF THE ARBITRATION BETWEEN MIKEL AND SCHARF

Supreme Court, Special Term, Kings County New York, 1980.
105 Misc.2d 548, 432 N.Y.S.2d 602.

ARTHUR S. HIRSCH, J.

This is a motion to confirm an arbitration award rendered by a rabbinical court.

[Respondents are the shareholders of a corporation that operates a nursing home. In 1973, the corporation agreed to lease premises from a partnership. Negotiations on behalf of the partnership were conducted primarily by Barad, one of the partners, and the agreed monthly rental was $25,208.

[In 1977 respondents contacted Barad and told him that because of business reverses, they would have to vacate the premises unless there were a substantial reduction in rent. After negotiations, an oral agreement was reached to reduce the monthly rental by $8000, and a writing to this effect was signed by respondents on behalf of the corporation and by Barad on behalf of the landlord.]

---

30. The threat of excommunication was, for example, the ultimate sanction for refusal to submit to, or obey the decision of, the medieval English ecclesiastical courts, which had an immense jurisdiction covering matrimonial disputes, perjury, and a variety of other matters as well as strictly religious disputes.

During the negotiations, respondents had met with other partners besides Barad, but at no time had they come in contact with petitioner or with his father, who acted as his son's surrogate in the arbitration proceedings and from whom petitioner had received the 6% interest in the partnership. * * *

In November, 1977, respondents received notice from the Union of Orthodox Rabbis to appear before a rabbinical court for a *"Din Torah"* or arbitration of a claim brought against them by petitioner. Respondents testified they refused to appear at first on grounds that they had no knowledge of petitioner, but did appear after receiving written notice that refusal would result in the court's invoking a "sirov."

The first meeting of the rabbinical court, presided over by the requisite three rabbis, took place on Sunday, May 14, 1978. The respondents appeared with their attorney, who was present as their legal representative and to testify as witness to all meetings between [landlord] and [tenant], at which the attorney was present.

Respondents are persistent in their claim that theirs was a special appearance before the rabbinical tribunal to establish that there was never a business nor contractual relationship between the claimant and themselves, and therefore, a *Din Torah,* or arbitration, would be improper and invalid. Their participation thereafter was to obtain a determination on this limited issue, i.e., whether a Din Torah should be convened and not for a determination as to the merits of the claim.

The respondents were required by the court to sign a Hebrew Document entitled a "Mediation Note" which, in effect, is an agreement to voluntarily arbitrate "the dispute existing" between the parties. Respondent Asher Scharf, who has a complete understanding of the Hebrew language, contends that much discussion ensued until it was unequivocally established that the "dispute" referred to in the "Mediation Note" was the question of the propriety of having a *Din Torah* and that he overcame his conceded reluctance to sign the document when he was assured by the court of the limited scope of the dispute. Respondents were summoned and attended two additional meetings. At the insistence of the rabbinical court, respondents' attorney did not attend any meeting after the first. On December 31, 1978, a written judgment of the rabbinical court was rendered, in which respondents were directed, among other things, to pay to petitioner a lump sum of $9,000 and to make monthly payments of 6% of $23,000, representing petitioner's share of the rental due and owing to the [landlord].

Petitioner has moved for an order confirming the award, with respondents opposing and moving to vacate the award on numerous grounds.

Rabbinical Court–Din Torah

As earlier indicated, the customary arbitration proceeding was not utilized by the parties. An accepted, but more unusual forum was selected, that of arbitration by a tribunal of rabbis conducting a *Din Torah.*

The beginnings of Jewish arbitral institutions are traceable to the middle of the second century. Throughout the centuries, thereafter, in every country in which Jews have been domiciled, Jewish judicial authority has existed, via the institute of arbitration conducted by special rabbinical courts. Orthodox Jews, prompted by their religious, national feelings, accepted Jewish judicial authority, by resorting to the arbitration procedure of their own free will. This method of arbitration has the imprimatur of our own judicial system, as a useful means of relieving the burdens of the inundated courts dealing with civil matters. Through Talmudic sages, it is learned that special rules or procedures have been provided under which the rabbinical courts function as a *Din Torah* (literally translated as torah judgment), with Judaic or torah law as its basis. As examples, it was required that a deed or note of arbitration be drawn confirming the consent of the parties to submit to arbitration; a decision on a matter not included in the issues submitted renders the determination by the rabbinical court void pro tanto; if an award was made without giving both parties opportunity to be fully heard, or if the judges acted otherwise improperly, the decision is voidable.

In addition to the procedural rules established by Judaic Law, there are state, civil, procedural rules for arbitration (CPLR, Article 75) to which the rabbinical court, as an arbitration forum, must also adhere.

*   *   *

Respondents [challenge] the rabbinical court's award, claiming first, the arbitration agreement was entered involuntarily, under duress and is consequently void, [and] second charging the arbitrators with misconduct * * *.

Involuntary Agreement–Duress

Both parties are members of the orthodox Jewish community. Respondent's denial of the existence of any disputable issue between themselves and petitioner convinced them to refuse to appear for a *Din Torah* and they would not have done so had they not received the threat of a "sirov." Rabbis testifying for respondents stated that a sirov, literally translated as contempt of court, is a prohibitionary decree that subjects the recipient to shame, scorn, ridicule and ostracism by his coreligionists, fellow members of his community. Ostensibly, he is ostracized and scorned. Other Jews refuse to eat or speak with him. He is discredited and dishonored. The respondents maintain that the draconian measures of a sirov are sufficiently threatening so as to compel their compliance with the demand to appear. They claim they would have become outcasts among their friends and coreligionists. However, from other testimony, it appears that the sirov, while most assuredly ominous in its potential power, is honored in its breach. The court cannot, of course, know the actual state of mind of respondents and it may be that their fear of a sirov decree was real. However, it seems more plausible that if respondents believed the consequences so fearful, they would not, at this point be willing to defy the rabbinical court by refusing to accept the arbitrator's determination. Undoubtedly, pressure was brought to bear to have them participate in the *Din Torah*, but pressure is not duress. Their decision to acquiesce to the rabbinical court's urgings was made without the coercion that would be necessary for the agreement to be void.

Misconduct

CPLR 7511 (subd [b], par 1, cl [i]) allows for the vacation of an award if the rights of a party are prejudiced by corruption, fraud or misconduct. Courts have used the term misconduct to denote actions of fundamental unfairness, whether intentional or unintentional.

Respondents charge misconduct by the rabbinical tribunal in their refusal to permit respondents to have legal representation and, further, to hear testimony or accept material documents offered by respondents' attorney, as witness to the lease negotiations. This, they contend, violated their due process rights. Respondents appeared at the first meeting with their attorney, Abraham Bernstein. From the beginning, it became apparent the tribunal would not tolerate the presence of an attorney at a *Din Torah*. Petitioner's father strenuously objected, claiming he had no attorney to represent petitioner. At first, attorney Bernstein was not permitted to speak, but later was allowed to make a short statement in which he attempted to establish the fact that a lease was executed between the corporation tenant and the landlord partnership without personal involvement of the parties and when he offered to submit the lease and other documents for the perusal of the court, the papers were returned to him. Thereafter, he interjected himself wherever possible to explain respondents' position regarding the lack of legal connection between the parties. For the most part, the court refused to acknowledge him, quelling his attempts to speak or take part in the proceedings. He was not permitted to ask questions of petitioner or his father, who at all times acted as representative and voice of petitioner.

* * *

Biblical law requires that parties appear before a magistrate in person and not by proxy (*Deuteronomy* 19:17). For many years, this supported a Jewish judicial prejudice against proxies, including attorneys and even interpretors, it being determined essential that argument be heard directly from the mouths of litigants or witnesses. There was a tradition, however, that the high priest, when sued in court, could appoint an attorney to represent him (*Talmud Yerushalmi*, Sanhedrin 2:1, 19d). It may be this tradition that precipitated the admittance of defense attorneys into rabbinical courts. Where the parties were present to give testimony, thus permitting Judges to perceive their demeanor and evaluate their credibility, legal counsel was no longer considered to be anathema. The rabbinical court in the instant matter obviously did not abide by this accepted legal concept.

The tribunal's proclivity for conducting their court under outdated concepts resulted in inadvertent violations. Respondents were denied due process. The right of counsel, which is a constitutional right, is further enunciated in Article 75 of the CPLR, and is an unwaivable right. Consequently, respondent's participation without counsel, after receiving the court's warning to appear alone, did not have a negative effect on their inherent right to legal representation, the deprivation of which is sufficient to vitiate the award.

Respondent Asher Scharf's unrebutted testimony indicated that at a session he attended, one of the three rabbi arbitrators called him out to talk with him privately. The rabbi argued for a cash settlement, to be paid by respondent on the grounds that petitioner was a poor student. Scharf testified the rabbi asked, "Well, what does a few thousand dollars mean to you?"

Under Judaic law (*Deuteronomy* 1:17), a Judge must judge impartially in favoring the rich or the poor. In an interpretation of this portion of the Torah, the foremost authority, Rashi, in *Commentary Rashi*, states that the version should be understood as follows: A judge "should not say: 'This is a poor man and his fellow (opponent) is rich and he will consequently obtain some support in a respectable fashion.'"

To ensure fairness, it is axiomatic and imperative that an arbitrator's impartiality be above suspicion. The rabbinical court was obviously prejudiced against respondents because of their affluence and considered the financial status of the parties above the issues. Such conduct, forbidden by the Torah, the law under which the rabbinical court has jurisdiction, constitutes another instance in which the tribunal deviated from its own *Din Torah* precepts.

The procedural format of the sessions was haphazard; no prescribed order was followed. A rabbinical court normally operates in a set manner, with presentation of claims, counterclaims, testimony of witnesses and cross-examinations conducted in a fairly orderly manner. This is not to say that any formal hearings are required. However, it appears that no semblance of administrative court proceeding, formal or informal, was followed by this rabbinical court. Witnesses were not called, real evidence was not accepted and no recognizable and required *Din Torah* procedure was followed. Under these highly unusual and chaotic conditions, a fair award could not be given.

* * *

Despite the established and well-grounded precedent that courts rarely set aside an arbitration award, in this instance the court finds it obligatory to vacate the award of the rabbinical court for the reasons enunciated above. A new arbitration proceeding will not be scheduled, as the court is convinced that no legal dispute exists between these particular parties.

Notes and Questions

(1) Closely-knit Jewish communities throughout the Western world developed—out of necessity—a long-standing proscription against submitting intragroup disputes to hostile or uncomprehending secular courts. See Congregation B'nai Sholom v. Martin, 382 Mich. 659, 173 N.W.2d 504 (1969). At the same time such communities developed their own systems of dispute resolution. With assimilation into the wider society, the role of these autonomous tribunals has naturally declined; even today, however, a practice of rabbinical "arbitration" still persists in Jewish communities. The majority of cases heard in this country by Jewish courts seem to concern divorce matters. See, e.g., Avitzur v. Avitzur, 58 N.Y.2d 108, 459 N.Y.S.2d 572, 446 N.E.2d 136 (1983). For the modern history of Jewish tribunals, see Note, Rabbinical Courts: Modern Day Solomons, 6 Col.J.Law & Soc. Prob. 48 (1970); I. Goldstein, Jewish Justice and Conciliation (1981); J. Yaffe, So Sue Me! The Story of a Community Court (1972).

(2) In a business or employment dispute, it is usually understood by the parties that a Jewish rabbinical tribunal "may seek to compromise the parties' claims, and is not bound to decide strictly in accordance with the governing rules of Jewish law, but may more carefully weigh the equities of the situation." See Kingsbridge Center of Israel v. Turk, 98 A.D.2d 664, 469 N.Y.S.2d 732, 734 (1983). Is that what the tribunal attempted to do in the principal case?

(3) Professor Marc Galanter has written that "[j]ust as health is not found primarily in hospitals or knowledge in schools, so justice is not primarily to be found in official justice-dispensing institutions. People experience justice (and injustice) not only (or usually) in forums sponsored by the state but at the primary institutional locations of their activity—home, neighborhood, workplace, business deal and so on * * *." This social ordering, found in a variety of institutional settings (such as universities, sports leagues, housing developments, and hospitals) he refers to as "indigenous law." He notes that although

> indigenous law may have the virtues of being familiar, understandable and independent of professionals, it is not always the expression of harmonious egalitarianism. It often reflects narrow and parochial concerns; it is often based on relations of domination; its coerciveness may be harsh and indiscriminate; protections that are available in public forums may be absent.

Galanter, Justice in Many Rooms: Courts, Private Ordering, and Indigenous Law, 19 J. Pluralism & Unofficial L. 1, 17–18, 25 (1981).

(4) For further discussion of court review of "arbitration" awards, see infra p. 480. For discussion of arbitration procedure, see infra p. 540.

3. Arbitration and the Application of "Rules"

The Landes and Posner excerpt at the beginning of this chapter introduces another recurrent theme in these materials. Many writers suggest that arbitration, as a voluntary and private process, may not proceed by formulating, applying, and communicating general principles of decision, or "rules." A number of related points form an essential backdrop for this discussion.

First of all—particularly outside the field of labor arbitration—arbitrators (unlike judges) commonly do not write reasoned opinions attempting to explain and justify their decisions. In fact the American Arbitration Association, which administers much commercial arbitration, actively discourages arbitrators from doing so. In addition, we do not in any event expect that an arbitrator will decide a case the way a judge does. We do not expect that he will necessarily "follow the law"—or indeed apply or develop any body of general rules as a guide to his decision. An arbitrator, it is said, "may do justice as he sees it, applying his own sense of law and equity to the facts as he finds them to be and making an award reflecting the spirit rather than the letter of the agreement." [1] An arbitrator's decision under an installment sales contract may, for example, award damages to the seller for breach but relieve the buyer of any further performance. This may be somewhat difficult to rationalize in terms of the doctrines of contract law—although it may nevertheless make some rough sense in terms of the business situation and equities of the parties. Furthermore, a decision by any particular arbitrator will not necessarily control the result of later cases involving other parties—or, indeed, have any precedential value at all for later arbitrators. And finally, an arbitrator's decision is not subject to later review and correction by a court to insure that general rules of law have been complied with. The highly restricted role courts play in passing on arbitration awards is discussed in detail beginning at p. 480 infra.

Obviously, these points are connected. The failure of arbitrators to write opinions can certainly be attributed to a desire to insulate decisions from later judicial scrutiny, quite as much as to any desire to avoid the delay or added expense that written opinions would entail. As we will see, the tactic of insuring the finality of arbitration by harnessing Delphic decisions to a hard-to-rebut presumption of validity has been extremely effective.

What are some of the implications of a system of private justice in which cases are "decided," but without the use or communication of consistent rules of decision? When cases are diverted into a private forum, operating without a formal system of precedent, any judicial function of shaping future activity may be neglected. In addition, it may be more difficult for private parties to predict the future results of

1. In the Matter of the Arbitration between Silverman v. Benmor Coats, Inc., 61   N.Y.2d 299, 308, 473 N.Y.S.2d 774, 779, 461 N.E.2d 1261, 1266 (1984).

cases heard in these private tribunals. Information disseminated by courts in the form of precedents is used every day by private actors in routine decisions concerning which claims they should assert, and under what circumstances they should settle those claims. See the discussion in Chapter I, supra p. 46, and Chapter II, supra p. 128. With no certainty as to the rule a particular arbitrator would apply—and with no consistent application of rules across the entire community of "competing" arbitrators, purporting independently to decide particular cases without reference to each other or to generally accepted rules—any firm basis on which to build future conduct is undermined:

> You cannot say today that a check need not contain an unconditional promise or order to pay to be negotiable and tomorrow that it must. You cannot say today that F.O.B. means free on board and tomorrow that it means only that the seller must get the goods as far as his shipping room. And so on. Mankind needs an irreducible minimum of certainty in order to operate efficiently. That irreducible minimum would seem to be better handled by the courts than by arbitration even though in the particular case the result would have been better decided in arbitration.[2]

However, unless the parties to an arbitration are "repeat players"—with a stake in the rules applied that extends beyond the result in the particular case—creating and promulgating "rules" of decision could from their point of view serve only to confer a benefit on *other* people, at the cost of increasing the duration and the expense of their own proceedings.

Of course, much of the above discussion has to be qualified. Any dichotomy between an ad hoc, particularistic system of private arbitration and a rule- and precedent-bound judiciary can easily be overstated. All first-year law students know that such a characterization can grotesquely exaggerate the predictability of court decisions and the meaningfulness of rules of decision in predicting or explaining the results of litigation. And even in the absence of a formal system of precedent, criteria of decision can be agreed on, developed, and communicated in other ways: by private associations, through past practice and the evolution of trade custom, and particularly through the pre-existing contractual relations of the parties. Lawyers who are experienced in arbitration tend to feel that they are able to predict the results of arbitration with some certainty, at least in part because these sources supply rules of decision likely to be consistently applied. It is, of course, a separate question whether the rules so applied will be consonant with officially-declared public values, or whether the arbitration process may implicate important public policy concerns which should be reserved to the official court system. This is a subject which is explored further in later sections.

---

2. Mentschikoff, The Significance of Arbitration—A Preliminary Inquiry, 17 Law & Contemporary Problems 698, 709 (1952).

In addition, the arbitration of disputes arising under collective bargaining agreements has come to evolve certain unique characteristics, distinguishing it from other forms of private dispute resolution. It does appear to be the general practice for *labor* arbitrators to write explanations and justifications—sometimes elaborate ones—for their decisions; these decisions are often publicly reported, cited to later arbitrators, and relied on in later cases. "An extensive survey of labor arbitration disclosed that 77 percent of the 238 responding arbitrators believed that precedents, even under *other* contracts, should be given 'some weight.' " [3] As we will see, there has developed a "common-law" of labor arbitration. In addition, the growth of labor arbitration over the last 40 years to a central place in the settlement of labor disputes has been accompanied by the development of the profession of "labor arbitrator." In the commercial area it may be unusual for an arbitrator to decide more than one or two cases a year, but for many labor arbitrators arbitration constitutes a primary source of their livelihood. One may suspect that Landes and Posner's point concerning the advertising value of reasoned opinions may have particular relevance here.

4. "Rights" Arbitration and "Interest" Arbitration

"Interest" arbitration is distinguished from the more familiar grievance or "rights" arbitration by the fact that in the former situation the designated neutral is employed to determine the actual contract terms which will bind the parties during the life of their new agreement, while in the latter situation the arbitrator is only empowered to decide disputes concerning the interpretation and application of the terms of an already existing contract. The grievance arbiter is generally precluded from adding to or modifying the terms of the contract in dispute.[4]

The distinction between "rights" and "interest" arbitration is a familiar one. You will often see reference to it, particularly in relation to the arbitration of labor-management disputes. The paradigm of a "rights" arbitration is a hearing on the grievance of an employee alleging that he has been discharged "without just cause." The paradigm of an "interest" arbitration is a hearing held at the expiration of a collective bargaining agreement, after negotiations over a union's demand for higher wage rates in a "new" contract have failed. While "interest" arbitration remains an unusual and infrequent device in comparison to other forms of arbitration, it is quite commonly resorted to in resolving disputes over the terms of employment of public employees. Public employees, such as police or school teachers, are usually forbidden to engage in strikes; economic pressure, and the usual tests

3. F. Elkouri & E. Elkouri, How Arbitration Works (4th ed. 1985) 418.

4. Craver, The Judicial Enforcement of Public Sector Interest Arbitration, 21 B.C.L.Rev. 557, 558 n. 8 (1980).

of economic strength used in the private sector to determine contract terms after a bargaining impasse, are therefore limited in the public interest. "Interest" arbitration to determine the terms of a new contract when bargaining fails provides a common alternative mechanism. In many cases, in fact, state statutes impose this as a *mandatory* means of settlement. See infra p. 587. Such legislation in effect gives to public employee unions the "right" to resort to the arbitration mechanism to determine the future terms of employment.

Now compare the following three cases. Are these examples of "rights" or of "interest" arbitration? What precisely are the differences, if any, between them?

(a) A law firm entered into a lease of space in an office building. The term of the lease was ten years. At the firm's request, a clause was added to the lease by which it would have the option to renew the lease for an additional ten years; it provided that "rental for the renewal term shall be in such amount as shall be agreed upon by the parties based on the comparative rental values of similar properties as of the date of the renewal and on comparative business conditions of the two periods." The lease contained a general arbitration clause providing that "all disputes relating to" the lease shall be settled by arbitration. The parties fail to agree on a rental for the renewal term.

(b) A coal supply agreement provided that for a period of ten years a coal company would tender and a power company would purchase specified quantities of coal. There was a base price per ton, and a provision for the calculation of adjustments in base price upon changes in certain labor costs and in "governmental impositions." The agreement also provided:

> Any gross proven inequity that may result in unusual economic conditions not contemplated by the parties at the time of the execution of this Agreement may be corrected by mutual consent. Each party shall in the case of a claim of gross inequity furnish the other with whatever documentary evidence may be necessary to assist in effecting a settlement.

Another clause called for "any unresolved controversy between the parties arising under this Agreement" to be submitted to arbitration. Four years later, after a rapid escalation in the price of coal, the open market price of coal of the same quality was more than three times the current adjusted base price under the agreement. The coal company requested an adjustment in the contract price which the power company adamantly rejected.[5]

(c) An agreement between a newspaper and its employees was to last for three years, with a provision that "this contract shall remain in effect until all terms and conditions of employment for a succeeding contract term are resolved either through negotiation or through arbitration." After a bargaining deadlock, the union moved for arbitration.

---

5. See Georgia Power Co. v. Cimarron Coal Corp., 526 F.2d 101 (6th Cir.1975).

The employer presented to the arbitrator a number of items which it wanted included in the agreement for the new term, including the right to make layoffs on account of automation or the introduction of new processes. The Union also presented a number of issues to the arbitrator, including "wages; mailers brought up to mechanical department [wage] scale; proof room brought up to composing room scale; pension; sick leave; vacations; increased mileage; grievance procedure; jurisdiction of jobs—need for job descriptions; holidays; jury and witness duty; overtime after thirty hours during holiday weeks; night differential; life insurance; option under Blue Cross for eyeglasses; option under Dental Plan for payment for dentures; paid uniforms for pressmen; addition of grandparent and guardian to funeral leave."

As these examples illustrate, it may sometimes be difficult satisfactorily to distinguish an "interest" dispute from one concerning "rights." Moreover, from a broader perspective, even in what are assumed to be "rights" disputes (such as employee grievances) the process of interpretation must necessarily involve considerable flexibility. In complex and long-term relationships there will inevitably be some uncertainty concerning matters inadvertently (or purposely) left open when the contract was entered into, or where past solutions are no longer neatly adapted to changed needs. When the parties participate in this procedure, they are in a very real sense taking part in a process which "involves not only the settlement of the particular dispute but also interstitial rule-making" [6]—a process aimed at creating, refining, and elaborating for the future the rules which will govern their relationship.

The supposed distinction between "rights" and "interest" arbitration may then be—as are most distinctions in the law—a mere question of degree or emphasis. However, this is not to say that it is without analytic utility or practical importance. Parties to a contract who are considering arbitration as a device to handle future disputes must ask themselves a number of questions. The distinction between "rights" and "interest" arbitration forces them to ask some important ones. To what extent is arbitration suitable for establishing the basic structure, the essential parameters of the relationship? What important differences are there between doing this, and asking the arbitrator merely to spell out the implications of a bargain they have hammered out for themselves? Are there reasons to hesitate before confiding this task to arbitrators as a substitute for their own bargaining? A few of the relevant considerations are suggested in the paragraphs that follow.

Assume that the parties know from the outset—either because of a mandatory statutory procedure, or a contractual agreement—that they will later be able to turn to arbitration to determine their future rights.

6. See Feller, A General Theory of the Collective Bargaining Agreement, 61 Calif. L.Rev. 663, 744–45 (1973).

How might this affect the dynamics of the bargaining process? Is it likely that one or the other of them may assume more extreme positions at the bargaining stage, trusting that an arbitrator will later seek out a middle ground? Is there a danger that the parties may use the possibility of arbitration as a crutch, and resort to it too readily rather than face the hard issues themselves? Is it likely that negotiators will resort to the arbitration mechanism to insulate themselves from the dissatisfaction of their own constituencies—union members, or taxpayers—who might personally hold them accountable for inevitable concessions made in negotiation?

If the contract confides to arbitrators the ultimate responsibility for determining the essential rights of the parties in the future, what standards are the arbitrators to use? The possible value choices are far more diverse, the possible criteria of decision far more nebulous, than in cases where an arbitrator acts more "judicially" in deciding whether particular goods are defective or whether certain employee conduct merited discharge.

In Twin City Rapid Transit Co., 7 Lab. Arb. 845 (1947), a collective bargaining agreement between a privately-owned company and an employee union provided that "if at the end of any contract year the parties are unable to agree upon the terms of a renewal contract, the matter shall be submitted to arbitration." In his decision, the arbitrator wrote:

> Arbitration of contract terms * * * calls for a determination, upon considerations of policy, fairness, and expediency, of what the contract rights ought to be. In submitting this case to arbitration, the parties have merely extended their negotiations—they have left it to this board to determine what they should, by negotiation, have agreed upon. We take it that the fundamental inquiry, as to each issue, is: what should the parties themselves, as reasonable men, have voluntarily agreed to?

> In answering that question, we think that prime consideration should be given to agreements voluntarily reached in comparable properties in the general area. For example, wages and conditions in Milwaukee, the city of comparable size nearest geographically to Minneapolis and St. Paul, whose transit company is neither bankrupt, municipally owned, nor municipally supported, might reasonably have had greater weight in the negotiations between the parties than Cleveland or Detroit, both municipally owned and farther distant, or Omaha and Council Bluffs, more distant in miles and smaller in population. Smaller and larger cities, however, and cities in other geographical areas should have secondary consideration, for they disclose trends and, by indicating what other negotiators, under different circumstances, have found reasonable, furnish a guide to what these parties, in view of the differing circumstances, might have found reasonable. * * * To repeat, our endeavor will be to decide the issues as, upon the evidence, we

think reasonable negotiators, regardless of their social or economic theories might have decided them in the give and take process of bargaining. We agree with the company that the interests of stockholders and public must be considered, and consideration of their interests will enter into our considerations as to what the parties should reasonably have agreed on.

Notes and Questions

(1) Does the inquiry in *Twin City Rapid Transit* ("what should the parties themselves, as reasonable men, have voluntarily agreed to?") seem meaningful to you in light of the discussion of the negotiation process in Chapter II supra? Should the arbitrator try to reconstruct the murky totality of the bargaining process, including the various dimensions of bargaining power, when the parties' own negotiations have failed? Can he do so? Or is he necessarily reduced to acting as a "legislator" and mandating what he thinks the "fair" result would be? Presented with all the outstanding bargaining issues with which the arbitrator was faced in case (c) above, how does he go about distinguishing between issues as to which the parties have reached a serious impasse and "throwaway" issues placed on the table for bargaining advantage? Is it feasible to impose criteria in advance on the arbitrator, by statute or contract? Or to structure the process so as to limit the scope of his discretion? (See infra p. 591 [Final–Offer Arbitration]).

(2) Of course, *courts* daily adjudicate grievances and disputes concerning "rights." Do they *also* handle types of disputes which might be characterized as "interest" disputes? In contracts cases, as you remember, the traditional wisdom is that courts "interpret" agreements, but they will not "make a contract for the parties" or enforce arrangements where the parties have merely "agreed to agree." The received learning has it that

> "[b]efore the power of law can be invoked to enforce a promise, it must be sufficiently certain and specific so that what was promised can be ascertained. Otherwise, a court, in intervening, would be imposing its own conception of what the parties should or might have undertaken, rather than confining itself to the implementation of a bargain to which they have mutually committed themselves. * * * [A] mere agreement to agree, in which a material term is left for future negotiations, is unenforceable." Joseph Martin, Jr. Delicatessen, Inc. v. Schumacher, 52 N.Y.2d 105, 436 N.Y.S.2d 247, 417 N.E.2d 541 (1981).

Is that distinction in contract law the equivalent of the "rights"/ "interest" dichotomy?

An economist would say that when courts insist on a certain level of clarity and completeness in the terms of a contract, they are attempting to insure that the deal is "allocatively efficient"—roughly, that it serves to reallocate resources to higher-valued uses—and that they do so by assuring that the deal has been bargained out by the parties themselves, in terms of their own assessments of their own interests. They may also be trying to prevent parties from taking a "free ride" on the public court system by shifting onto the courts the burden of determining contract terms. Do any of the same objections apply to "interest" arbitration?

The reluctance of courts to help in fashioning bargains left incomplete by the parties may be changing. Compare Sun Printing & Publishing Ass'n v. Remington Paper & Power Co., 235 N.Y. 338, 139 N.E. 470 (1923)—a wooden mainstay of the Contracts curriculum—with David Nassif Associates v. United States, 557 F.2d 249 (Fed.Cir.1977), 644 F.2d 4 (Ct.Cl.1981). See also Uniform Commercial Code §§ 2–204(3), 2–305. Or is it fair to say that courts, like arbitrators, have been doing much the same thing all along, under the guise of "interpretation"—but without admitting it?

(3) Recall Lon Fuller's suggestion that the adjudicative process may not be well-suited to resolve what he calls "polycentric" disputes. See Chapter I, supra p. 26. Are any of the "interest" disputes we are looking at here "polycentric"? Do Fuller's objections apply to arbitration as well as to the judicial process? How might an "interest" arbitrator proceed so as to minimize the problems that Fuller raises?

(4) The arbitrator in an "interest" arbitration may be asked to determine the wages to be paid to employees in a "new" or renewal contract. How relevant in such a determination is the employer's claim of financial hardship or inability to pay? Is the answer in any way dependent on whether the arbitrator suspects the employer's "hardship" is due to managerial inefficiency, or to general conditions in a declining industry?

In one case an arbitrator, granting a union's requested wage increase, rejected the employer's claim by writing that

> The *price of labor* must be viewed like any other commodity which needs to be purchased. If a new truck is needed, the City does not plead poverty and ask to buy the truck for 25% of its established price. It can shop various dealers and makes of truck to get the best possible buy. But in the end the City either pays the asked price or gets along without a new truck.

In re City of Quincy, Illinois and International Association of Machinists, 81 Lab.Arb. 352, 356 (1982).

(5) Where the employer is a private company, the employees themselves may have a long-term stake in the financial health of the employer. Is it appropriate for the arbitrator to consider that in such cases the vindication of high wage demands might be a "pyrrhic victory"—and, conversely, that moderation of wage demands may ultimately work to conserve jobs? See In re League of Voluntary Hospitals and District 1199, Hospital and Health Care Employees, 67 Lab.Arb. 293, 303 (1976). Or is this a consideration that the union has presumably already weighed in deciding how best to advance the interests of the employees whom it represents?

In the case of a *public* employer, can the arbitrator weigh the claims of employees against other claims to public funds? Should the arbitrator take into account the employer's ability to pass on any increase in wages to others—to taxpayers or to the customers of a public utility? This may of course entail the exercise of some delicate judgment on matters of social and economic policy. In addition, the arbitrator is a creature of contract, hired and paid by employer and union: Is it appropriate for him in the course of making his decision to weigh the interests of those who are *not* parties to the agreement? See In re Nodak Rural Elect. Coop. and Int'l Bro. of Elect. Workers, 78 Lab. Arb. 1119 (1982) (rural North Dakota electrical cooperative; "This arbitrator grew up on an Iowa farm in the 1930's so he understands the meaning of a depressed farm economy and is sympathetic to the farmer's current conditions. * * * It is not likely that it would be wise for either the company or the union to ignore the condition of the farm economy. After all, the farmers and Nodak employees are dependent on each other. The farmers must be able to pay their bills in order for Nodak employees to retain their jobs and get paid.").

B. SOME FREQUENT USES OF ARBITRATION

1. Commercial Arbitration

JONES, THREE CENTURIES OF COMMERCIAL ARBITRATION IN NEW YORK: A BRIEF SURVEY

1956 Wash.U.L.Q. 193, 209–10, 218–19.

[I]t is commonplace among those who write about arbitration that it has been in use for centuries.

* * *

[E]nough material on arbitration has been uncovered to show fairly conclusively that arbitration was in constant and widespread use throughout the colonial period in New York. * * * Seemingly, arbitration was used primarily in situations where the decision would not be entirely for one side or the other, but where there was, rather, considerable area for negotiation. The settlement of an account resulting from a long course of dealing between two merchants is an example. Land boundaries and the distribution of the proceeds from a privateering expedition are others. Evidently, from the way in which individuals felt it worthwhile to advertise in the newspapers their willingness to arbitrate, there was some social pressure to arbitrate a dispute before taking it to court, and even to submit it to arbitration after the suit was begun. This tends to substantiate a feeling that one function of arbitration was to supply a final stage in the negotiation process between two disputants and that a willingness to negotiate was highly esteemed in the community.

* * *

[T]he existence of the practice of extensive arbitration over so long a period of time in the mercantile community tends to show that, as used by merchants, arbitration is not really a substitute for court adjudication as something that is cheaper or faster or whatever,[112] but is rather a means of dispute settling quite as ancient—for all practical purposes anyway—as court adjudication, and that it has, traditionally, fulfilled quite a different function. The primary function of arbitration is to provide the merchants fora where mercantile disputes will be settled by merchants. This, in turn, suggests that merchants wish to form, and have for a long time succeeded in forming, a separate, and, to some extent, self-governing community, independent of the larger unit. For law this means that courts may perform, in the commercial field at least, a different function from that which we usually assign to them. In many cases, they may not be the primary fora for adjudication. If this is true, when they are called upon to decide a commercial case in one of these areas, it will be either after another adjudicatory agency has acted or because the other system cannot, or will not, cope with the case. In some areas, courts may almost never get a case. * * * Insofar as this area, in which arbitration is and—most importantly— has always been the primary dispute-settling agency, is an important one (and an area which includes stockbrokers, produce brokers, coffee merchants, etc., seems to be such an area), it cannot really be said that one has studied commercial law, in the sense of the rules that actually guide the settlement of disputes involving commercial matters, if he has studied only the reports of appellate courts and legislation. We cannot even understand the significance of the "law" contained in the reports and statutes until we have studied arbitration decisions. * * *

Having gone so far with hypothesis, one may be forgiven for going a little farther and suggesting that the existence of a sufficient sense of community identity or separateness on the part of merchants to cause them to have a separate adjudicatory system tends to show that there is a mercantile community which is, to a considerable degree, self-governing. This community has existed in this form for centuries. Its existence suggests that there may be others—religious and educational communities come to mind.

MENTSCHIKOFF, COMMERCIAL ARBITRATION
61 Col. L.Rev. 846, 848–54 (1961).

The first thing to be noted is that although commonly thought of as a single type phenomenon, both the structure and the process of commercial arbitration are determined by the different institutional contexts in which it arises. There are three major institutional settings in which commercial arbitration appears as a mechanism for the settlement of disputes.

---

112. Though, interestingly enough, arbitration was presented as such an alternative in the eighteenth century in almost the same language as is used today.

The simplest is when two persons in a contract delineating a business relationship agree to settle any disputes that may arise under the contract by resort to arbitration before named arbitrators or persons to be named at the time of the dispute. In this, which can be called individuated arbitration, the making of all arrangements, including the procedures for arbitration, rests entirely with the parties concerned. Although we do not know, we believe that the chief moving factors here are: (1) a desire for privacy as, for example, in certain crude oil situations where such arrangements exist; (2) the availability of expert deciders; (3) the avoidance of possible legal difficulties with the nature of the transaction itself; and (4) the random acceptance by many businessmen of the idea that arbitration is faster and less expensive than court action.

A second type of arbitration arises within the context of a particular trade association or exchange. The group establishes its own arbitration machinery for the settlement of disputes among its members, either on a voluntary or compulsory basis, and sometimes makes it available to non-members doing business in the particular trade. A particular association may also have specialist committees, which are investigatory in character, with the arbitration machinery handling only the private disputes involving nonspecialist categories of cases.

* * *

The third setting for commercial arbitration is found in administrative groups, such as the American Arbitration Association, the International Chamber of Commerce, and various local chambers of commerce, which provide rules, facilities, and arbitrators for any persons desiring to settle disputes by arbitration. Many trade associations with insufficient business to warrant separate organizations make special arrangements with one of these groups to process disputes that arise among their members.

* * *

Factors Determining the Need for Arbitration

At this point it is useful to distinguish between those factors that can be said to produce a need for arbitration machinery in commercial groups and those factors that merely make it desirable. The reasons commonly given for arbitration—speed, lower expense, more expert decision, greater privacy—are appealing to all businessmen, and yet not all utilize arbitration. It seems reasonably clear, therefore, that for some trades these factors are of greater importance than for others, and that for some trades there must be countervailing values in not resorting to arbitration. We postulated three factors as being theoretically important in determining whether or not a particular trade needed institutionalized use of arbitration, and incorporated questions relating to these factors in our trade association questionnaire.

The first factor was the nature of the economic function being performed in relation to the movement of the goods by the members of the association. We postulated that persons primarily buying for resale, that is merchants in the original sense of the term, were much more likely to be interested in speed of adjudication, and that since price allowance would be a central remedy for defects in quality or, indeed, for nondelivery, the speed and low cost characteristics of arbitration would be particularly attractive to them, thus leading to the creation of institutionalized machinery. The trade associations in which such merchants constitute all or part of the membership reported as follows: 48 percent use institutionalized machinery, 34 percent make individual arrangements for arbitration, and only 18 percent never arbitrate. These figures are to be contrasted with the reports from those trade associations that stated that their memberships did not include any merchants. In those groups 23 percent reported the existence of institutionalized arbitration, 44 percent reported individual arrangements, and 33 percent reported no arbitration whatever.

The second major factor that we thought would be important in determining the need for arbitration was the participation of the members of the association in foreign trade. Apart from the enhanced possibility of delay inherent in transnational law suits, when the parties to a transaction are governed by different substantive rules of law, resort to the formal legal system poses uncertainty and relative unpredictability of result for at least one of the parties. This uncertainty and unpredictability is increased by the fact that the very rules governing the choice of the applicable law are themselves relatively uncertain and are not uniform among the nations of the world. Faced with such an uncertain formal legal situation, any affected trade group is apt to develop its own set of substantive rules or standards of behavior as the controlling rules for its members. Obviously, when a trade group develops its own rules of law, it requires as deciders of its disputes persons who are acquainted with the standards it has developed. Since this knowledgeability does not reside in the judges of any formal legal system, the drive toward institutionalized private machinery is reinforced.

*   *   *

The third factor that we thought would bear on the need for arbitration machinery relates to the kind of goods dealt with by the members of the association. One of the major areas of dispute among businessmen centers on the quality of the goods involved.[4] If, therefore, the goods are such as not to be readily susceptible of quality determination by third persons, arbitration or, indeed, inspection, is an unlikely method of settling disputes. If goods are divided into raws, softs, and hards, the differences in their suitability for third party adjudication becomes relatively clear. On the whole, raws are a fungible commodity, one bushel of # 1 wheat being very much like another bushel of # 1 wheat. On the other hand, hards, which consist of items like refrigerators and automobiles, are not viewed by their producers as

---

4. At the American Arbitration Association, for example, quality disputes ac-   counted for approximately 40% of the sales cases.

essentially fungible, however they may appear to the layman. We did not believe that Ford would like to have General Motors sitting on disputes involving the quality of Ford cars, or vice versa. Moreover, quality differentials in raws can normally be reflected by price differentials, but defects in hard goods frequently affect their usefulness and therefore price differential compensation is not feasible. Thus, the normal sales remedy for raws has come to be price allowance, whereas the normal sales remedy for hard goods has come to be repair or replacement. Raws, involving fungibility and ease of finding an appropriate remedy, are therefore highly susceptible to third party adjudication, whereas hard goods tend to move away from such adjudication. Soft goods, which are an intermediate category and range from textiles to small hardware, we thought would constitute a neutral category.

In our survey of exchanges dealing in grain and livestock, 100 percent of those responding reported the use of institutionalized arbitration. There are, of course, other reasons for such a unanimous response by the exchanges, but the nature of the goods involved is a very important one. The trade association survey showed that of all the reporting associations, dealings in raws, 46 percent had machinery, 29 percent made individual arrangements, and only 25 percent never arbitrated. On the other hand, only 4 percent of those reporting hards as their basic goods had machinery, 46 percent made individual arrangements, and 50 per cent never arbitrated. * * *

To the extent that the factors leading to institutionalized machinery reinforce each other, as, for example, in the case of an association reporting that its members have an import relationship to foreign trade, deal in raws, and consist of merchants, the existence of arbitration machinery rises to approximately 100 percent. When the contrary report is made, that is, that the membership consists of manufacturers of hard goods engaged only in domestic business, the percentage drops off to about 8 percent.

We can thus say that the presence of institutionalized arbitration is a strong index of the existence of a generally self-contained trade association having its own self-regulation machinery and that the forces leading to institutionalized arbitration also, therefore, tend to lead to the creation of self-contained, self-governing trade groups.

The American Arbitration Association

The AAA is a private non-profit organization founded in 1926 "to foster the study of arbitration, to perfect its techniques and procedures under arbitration law, and to advance generally the science of arbitration." It works actively to publicize and promote arbitration. Of far greater importance, however, is its central role in the administration of much of the arbitration that takes place in this country. The parties to a contract will frequently stipulate that disputes which later arise are to be arbitrated under the auspices of the AAA. This means, for one thing, that the proceedings will automatically be governed by AAA rules. In a commercial case, the AAA's "Commercial Arbitration Rules" will resolve questions concerning the method of choosing arbitrators, their powers, time limits for various steps in the proceedings, and the conduct of the hearing. There are also alternative sets of rules available for adoption in particular trades. In the construction industry for example, use of the AAA's Construction Industry Arbitration Rules (recommended by such trade groups as the American Institute of Architects and the American Society of Civil Engineers) has become standard. The AAA also administers a large number of labor arbitrations under its Voluntary Labor Arbitration Rules, and uninsured motorist accident arbitrations under its Accident Claims Arbitration Rules. In all these cases, using contracts that incorporate pre-existing bodies of rules saves the parties the burden, costs, and delay of having to negotiate and spell out an entire code for the conduct of the arbitration.

Over 53,000 cases were filed with the AAA in 1987. (Of these, more than 12,000 were commercial cases and more than 19,000, labor cases). The Association maintains a panel of more than fifty thousand arbitrators willing to serve in commercial cases; the parties select their arbitrators from a number of names suggested by AAA administrators, who furnish information concerning the background and experience of the candidates. The AAA itself will appoint the arbitrator to hear the case if the parties cannot agree on a name. In addition, during the course of the proceeding the AAA staff will furnish a variety of administrative services, concerning, for example, notice to the parties, pre-hearing conferences, and the scheduling, location, and conduct of the hearing—all intended to insure that the process runs smoothly and that the chances of a successful later challenge to the award are minimized. Selection of arbitrators and arbitration procedure are discussed in some detail in Section D, infra p. 540.

Notes and Questions

A survey of textile disputes arbitrated through the AAA found that much textile arbitration was handled by a relatively small group of lawyers: Only five lawyers were counsel to 43 of the 182 parties who submitted to arbitration in one of the years studied. "When asked to compare the predictability of an arbitrator's decision to that of a judge or the verdict of a jury, each of the five lawyers replied without hesitation that the decision of an arbitrator was by far the 'most predictable,' that a judge's decision was 'predictable at some but not all times,' and a jury's decision was 'virtually one of pure chance.'" Bonn, The Predictability of Nonlegalistic Adjudication, 6 Law & Soc'y Rev. 563 (1972). However, the author attributed this predictability largely to the fact that sellers would carefully "screen" or "preselect" cases they took to arbitration. Sellers would pursue arbitration primarily against "buyers who are marginal firms or who have weak or specious claims"; where a buyer had "a strong case, say one based on a legitimate quality claim," and was a good future business prospect, sellers would choose instead to settle the dispute informally.

In another survey of textile arbitration cases the same author found that out of 78 cases, "business relations were resumed" following the arbitration in only 14. Bonn, Arbitration: An Alternative System for Handling Contract Related Disputes, 17 Admin.Sci.Q. 254, 262 (1972). Is this clearly an indication that arbitration may be as "lethal to continuing relations" as litigation? Cf. Galanter, Reading the Landscape of Disputes: What We Know and Don't Know (And Think We Know) About Our Allegedly Contentious and Litigious Society, 31 U.C. L.A.L.Rev. 4, 25 n. 117 (1983).

2. International Commercial Arbitration

Many of the same factors inducing parties to choose arbitration as a dispute settlement technique in domestic commercial transactions are likely to be present when the transaction expands across national boundaries. Indeed, as Professor Mentschikoff points out, the involvement of more than one body of law and more than one court system is likely to provide even further impetus to nonjudicial dispute resolution. The time, expense, and procedural complexities of litigating in another country's courts are likely to be considerable. There may not even be any effective protection against parallel litigation proceeding simultaneously in the courts of the United States and of a foreign country. There is likely to be far greater uncertainty with respect to the rules of decision that will govern the dispute in a foreign tribunal, and thus as to the outcome; the rules of "conflict of laws" will not always give a bankable answer even to the question of *which* nation's law will apply to the transaction. In addition, the "foreign" party to the litigation will not only feel disadvantaged by his relative unfamiliarity with the "rules of the game," but may also doubt how fairly and even-handedly he will be treated in comparison to his "local" opponent.

Another troubling cause of unpredictability in international litigation stems from uncertainty when and to what extent a judgment obtained in one country will be enforceable in another. A favorable decision against a French supplier in a New York court, for example, may be of little value if the courts of France will not recognize the New York judgment. However, "[c]ompared with ordinary court decisions, arbitration is far ahead as far as enforcement in other countries is concerned." [1] In many countries, enforcement of a foreign arbitral award is simpler and more assured than is enforcement of a foreign judgment—a difference in outcome perhaps explained by the common tendency to regard an arbitral award as "the outcome of contractual relationships, rather than of the exercise of state powers." [2] This

1. Sanders, International Commercial Arbitration—How to Improve its Functioning?, [1980] Arbitration 9.

2. Gardner, Economic and Political Implications of International Commercial Ar-

favorable treatment of foreign arbitral awards has been reinforced by international treaty. See infra p. 500.

It is therefore not surprising that in international commercial contracts, arbitration clauses "not only predominate but are nowadays almost universal" and are "virtually taken for granted." [3] The Supreme Court has on a number of occasions recognized the unique value of international arbitration in promoting "the orderliness and predictability essential to any international business transaction," and has drawn from it a strong policy favoring international commercial arbitration. See Scherk v. Alberto–Culver Co., 417 U.S. 506, 516 (1974); Mitsubishi v. Soler, infra p. 501. It has been suggested that international arbitrators have been moving towards a "common law of international arbitration"—that they have been developing a "supranational law based on international customs," [4] which stresses general norms of conduct suited to international business practices independent of the rules of particular bodies of national law. This is particularly marked in arbitration decisions dealing with such thorny recurring problems in international trade as the effect on contracts of "impossibility" (*force majeure*) or currency fluctuations.

Parties to international transactions often prefer to proceed with arbitration outside of any institutional framework, and to administer the arbitration themselves on an "ad hoc" basis. However, dispensing with the administrative support of organizations like the AAA is not likely to be successful in cases where the level of cooperation and trust between the parties is low and one of them may be dragging his feet in resolving the problem. In addition, where a recognized institution has supervised the arbitration, the institution's reputation may lend credibility to the award should a national court ever come to review the arbitration. There exist a large number of other organizations besides the AAA which compete in the administration of international commercial arbitrations; by far the most important of these is the International Chamber of Commerce (ICC), based in Paris.

It is inevitable that international arbitration will often turn out to be considerably more protracted and expensive than its domestic counterpart. The ICC in particular is often criticized on this account. In ICC proceedings the administrative charges paid to the ICC for its services, and the fees paid to the arbitrators themselves, are calculated on the basis of the amount in dispute between the parties. In a $10 million case these may range from a bare—and unlikely—minimum of $51,950 to a maximum, if three arbitrators are used, of $264,500. The most articulate apologists for ICC arbitration respond to criticisms of excessive expense with a plea that

bitration, in Domke (ed.), International Trade Arbitration 20–21 (1958).

3. Kerr, International Arbitration v. Litigation, [1980] J. Business Law 164, 165, 171.

4. W.L. Craig, W. Park, & J. Paulsson, International Chamber of Commerce Arbitration § 35.02 at 3 (Oceana 1984). See also R. David, Arbitration in International Trade §§ 16 ("Search for an autonomous commercial law"), 17 (1985).

the cost must be evaluated in relation to the alternatives. Certainly ICC arbitration seems cheaper than abandoning one's rights altogether. Litigation, even in one's own home courts, is not necessarily a less expensive alternative, given the possibility of one or more appeals. More importantly, it simply is not always reasonable to expect that one's home forum will be acceptable to a foreign contracting party. ICC arbitration is too often compared—unrealistically and unfairly—with a perfect world in which there are no administrative difficulties, no judicial prejudice against foreign parties, no language problems, no uncooperative parties, and where the just always prevail at no cost to themselves.[5]

Notes and Questions

(1) In many countries the government assumes a far more active role in economic transactions—particularly those involving capital investment and the exploitation and development of national resources—than it does in the United States. The foreign state or one of its instrumentalities will often be a party to such contracts, which are likely to have political and economic implications and symbolic importance far greater than in the case of domestic transactions. This can be a factor which complicates the question of dispute resolution. A foreign state will understandably be reluctant to submit to the jurisdiction of the courts of another sovereign (as, of course, the foreign investor will be reluctant to submit to the courts of the host country.) However, developing countries in particular have long been sensitive to the implications of submitting to *any* forum where the location or the decision-maker is foreign, and such reluctance has been extended to foreign arbitrations as well.

This unwillingness to submit to foreign arbitration is probably most marked in Latin American countries, where historical memory of one-sided international "arbitrations" dominated by European or North American partners is still vivid. A Brazilian writer has recently argued that:

> Functioning as an active element to denationalize (or internationalize) the contract, arbitration by removing a dispute from resolution by local courts applying local law, takes it to a plane where the rules are made by the great international commercial interests, a process from which Third World countries normally are excluded.

Quoted in Nattier, International Commercial Arbitration in Latin America: Enforcement of Arbitral Agreements and Awards, 21 Tex. Int'l L.J. 397, 407 (1986). See also Norberg, General Introduction to Inter–American Commercial Arbitration, in 3 Yrbk. of Commercial Arbitration 1, 14 (1978). In many Latin American countries the validity even of private agreements to submit disputes to foreign

5. W.L. Craig, W. Park, & J. Paulsson, International Chamber of Commerce Arbitration § 3.02 at 30–31 (Oceana 1984).

arbitral tribunals remains uncertain. See Samtleben, Arbitration in Brazil, 18 U.Miami Inter–Am.L.Rev. 1 (1986).

(2) In December 1985, Walt Disney Productions and the French Government signed a letter of intent for the construction of a new Disneyland, to be located near Paris. France and Spain had both competed vigorously for this project, which French officials estimated would involve long-term American investment of as much as $6.7 billion and the creation of more than 30,000 jobs. The French Government had made commitments to build rail and highway networks linking the site to Paris and to develop an infrastructure, including roads and telephone trunk lines, for the area.

The contract negotiations, however, proved extremely difficult. Political opposition to the project—French Communists denounced it as "the encroachment of an alien civilization next to the city of enlightenment"—figured in the parliamentary elections held throughout France in March 1986. Another major snag was Disney's demand that any disputes which might later arise out of the French Government's undertakings be resolved by arbitration through the International Center for the Settlement of Investment Disputes (ICSID).

ICSID was established by treaty in 1966 to provide a neutral forum for the resolution of disputes between states and foreign investors, and to reduce "the fear of political risks" that might act as a "deterrent to the flow of private foreign capital to developing countries." Amerasinghe, The International Centre for Settlement of Investment Disputes and Development through the Multinational Corporation, 9 Vand.J.Trans.L. 793, 795 (1976). ICSID functions under the auspices of the World Bank and is a "public" body, administered by representatives of the various participating governments. By the end of 1986 only 20 cases had been referred to the Center; most of these cases had involved disputes arising out of mining, construction, or joint venture agreements with states in Africa or Asia.

Fear was expressed in France that acceding to Disney's demand would create a "precedent" by which all new foreign investments might have to go to arbitration. And one French official was said to have commented that "Disney's request for ICSID was shocking and a bit dumb. France is not a banana republic." International Herald Tribune, March 15, 1986, pp. 1, 15; see also Washington Post, August 21, 1986, p. C8; "The Real Estate Coup at Euro Disneyland," Fortune, April 28, 1986, p. 172.

The agreement between Disney and the French Government was finally signed in March 1987. It did contain a provision for dispute settlement by arbitration—but through the ICC, to take place in France.

(3) In concluding commercial contracts with foreign businesses, negotiators from the People's Republic of China usually try to obtain an agreement that any future disputes will be arbitrated in China by the Foreign Economic and Trade Arbitration Commission (FETAC).

FETAC arbitrators are all of course Chinese nationals. Some insight into the nature of an "arbitration" conducted under FETAC auspices can be gleaned from this account by a leading official of the organization:

> A foreign buyer ordered 500 cases of goods from a Chinese seller. According to the contract, the goods were to be shipped from a Chinese port to Hong Kong and then transshipped from Hong Kong to the port of destination. Upon arrival at the port of destination, part of the goods were found damaged. The buyer claimed against the seller for compensation of the losses incurred * * * on the grounds that the packing was defective. The seller argued that the packing was not defective because it was the normal packing he used for exporting the goods and no extra or special requirements for packing were specified in the contract. * * * The buyer then applied to the FETAC for arbitration. With the consent of both parties, the arbitration tribunal decided the case according to principles of conciliation. It was the opinion of the arbitration tribunal that although no extra or special requirements for packing were specified in the contract, the seller knew that the goods were to be transshipped at Hong Kong, which was different from shipment directly from a Chinese port to the port of destination. The packing should be suitable for that specific transportation. However, the nails and the wood used for the packing were not appropriate for the purpose. The arbitration tribunal proposed an appropriate compensation to the buyer for his losses. The seller accepted the arbitration tribunal's proposal but pointed out that the amount claimed by the buyer was too large and asked for a reduction. The arbitration tribunal consulted the buyer and eventually the buyer agreed to reduce his claim by seventy percent. Both parties came to a compromise agreement from which the arbitration tribunal delivered a Conciliatory Statement and closed the case.

Tang, Arbitration—A Method Used by China to Settle Foreign Trade and Economic Disputes, 4 Pace L.Rev. 519, 533–34 (1984).

FETAC acts under the supervision of a Chinese state institution (CCPIT) whose mission is to promote foreign trade and investment. Its arbitrators may understandably be reluctant to finally adjudicate the merits of a dispute between a Western trading company and a domestic state unit; such a decision might well affect the future business relations between the parties. Cf. Chew, A Procedural and Substantive Analysis of the Fairness of Chinese and Soviet Foreign Trade Arbitrations, 21 Tex.Int'l L.J. 291, 330–34 (1986). In addition, a general aversion to formal third-party adjudication and a predilection for conciliation and compromise have long marked Chinese legal culture. See, e.g., Schwartz, On Attitudes Toward Law in China, in Katz (ed.), Government Under Law and the Individual 27–39 (1957). In any event, as this excerpt illustrates, FETAC will proceed to "decide" a dispute only in those (rare) cases where its efforts to induce a voluntary agreement through conciliation have failed. To what extent does this model correspond to the American understanding of the arbitration process?

(4) Fujitsu (Japan's largest computer company) developed and marketed IBM-compatible operating system software, which IBM claimed was in violation of its copyrights. The companies agreed to submit the dispute to two arbitrators (a law professor and a retired computer executive) under AAA auspices. The arbitrators were determined from the outset "to avoid becoming engulfed in an extensive adjudicatory fact-finding process with respect to hundreds of programs previously released by [Fujitsu]." "While this might determine in particular instances whether IBM's intellectual property rights had been violated, it would not directly address and resolve the parties' dispute with respect to [Fujitsu's] ongoing use of IBM programming material in its software development process."

Through their mediation efforts, the parties came instead to agree on the concept of a "coerced license" that was to be administered by these arbitrators into the future. The arbitrators' award allowed the Japanese company to examine IBM programs in a "secured facility" for a period of five to ten years and, "subject to strict and elaborate safeguards," to use such information in its software development; this would provide Fujitsu with a "reasonable opportunity to independently develop and maintain IBM-compatible operating system software." Fujitsu was to "fully and adequately compensate" IBM for such access in amounts to be determined by the arbitrators. In effect the arbitrators' award and subsequent decisions "will constitute the applicable intellectual property law until the end of the Contract Period, notwithstanding copyright decisions of U.S. or Japanese courts * * *." One of the arbitrators later commented that their decisions "will be considerably more detailed than existing copyright law, because there haven't been all that many cases and they haven't got into as many areas as we've gotten into." Wall St.J., July 1, 1988, p. 4. The text of the arbitration award appears at 4 J. Int'l Arb. 153 (1987).

(5) As we have seen, the practice in domestic commercial arbitration is to dispense with reasoned opinions. In contrast, parties in international cases do usually expect arbitrators to provide a written opinion which sets out the reasons for their award. The ICC requires its arbitrators to give reasoned awards; under the ICSID treaty, an award may be "annulled" by an ad hoc appellate committee if "the award has failed to state the reasons on which it is based." This expectation of a reasoned opinion in international arbitration reflects in part the pervasive influence of Continental legal systems, where unreasoned awards are often considered contrary to public policy and thus unenforceable. See R. David, Arbitration in International Trade 319–328 (1985); W.L. Craig, W. Park & J. Paulsson, International Chamber of Commerce Arbitration § 19.04 (1984).

3. Labor Arbitration

A collective bargaining agreement between an employer and the union that represents the firm's employees is likely to be a complex document. It will deal with a large number of subjects, among many other things setting wages and other terms of employment, imposing limits on the employer's right to discharge or discipline employees, and providing for seniority for purposes of layoffs, promotion, and job assignments. It will constitute, in short, an overall framework for employer-employee relations.

Most agreements also spell out a process by which the inevitable questions of interpretation and application arising during the life of the contract will be settled. There are typically a number of steps in this process: At the beginning, for example, there may be informal attempts to adjust a grievance on the shop floor by consultations between the employee's immediate supervisor and the union shop steward; if the dispute is not settled at this stage it will move to successively higher levels. The agreement is likely to make it clear that at all stages work is not to be interrupted because of the dispute but is to continue pending a final settlement, and is likely also to impose strict time limits to insure that a grievance is heard and processed speedily. The final stage in the grievance process, to handle those "cases that are not winnowed out by the process of day-to-day negotiation," [6] is likely to be binding arbitration. The Department of Labor estimates that more than 96% of all collective bargaining agreements—covering a total of almost 6½ million workers—provide for arbitration of grievance disputes.[7]

Section 301 of the Labor Management Relations Act of 1947 (the Taft–Hartley Act) granted jurisdiction to federal district courts to hear suits for violation of collective bargaining agreements "in an industry affecting commerce." In Textile Workers Union v. Lincoln Mills, 353 U.S. 448 (1957), the Supreme Court held that § 301 was "more than jurisdictional," and that it "authorizes federal courts to fashion a body of federal law for the enforcement of these collective bargaining agreements." "Plainly the agreement to arbitrate grievance disputes is the *quid pro quo* for an agreement not to strike." Federal policy therefore was that promises to arbitrate grievances under collective bargaining agreements should be specifically enforced, and that "industrial peace can be best obtained only in that way."

Federal courts have for the past thirty years engaged in "fashioning" a federal common law dealing with the enforcement of arbitration agreements—to such an extent that it is not an exaggeration to say that the field of "labor law" is now to a large degree the law of labor arbitration. In 1960, in what is still the Supreme Court's most signifi-

---

6. Getman, Labor Arbitration and Dispute Resolution, 88 Yale L.J. 916, 919 (1979).

7. U.S. Dept. of Labor, Characteristics of Major Collective Bargaining Agreements 112 (1981).

cant pronouncement on the subject, Justice Douglas undertook an evaluation of the purpose and function of labor arbitration and of the central place it occupies in our system of workplace bargaining. Some extracts from his discussion follow.

UNITED STEELWORKERS OF AMERICA v. WARRIOR & GULF NAVIGATION CO.

United States Supreme Court, 1960.
363 U.S. 574, 80 S.Ct. 1347, 4 L.Ed.2d 1409.

Opinion of the Court by MR. JUSTICE DOUGLAS.

* * *

The present federal policy is to promote industrial stabilization through the collective bargaining agreement. A major factor in achieving industrial peace is the inclusion of a provision for arbitration of grievances in the collective bargaining agreement.

Thus the run of arbitration cases * * * becomes irrelevant to our problem. There the choice is between the adjudication of cases or controversies in courts with established procedures or even special statutory safeguards on the one hand and the settlement of them in the more informal arbitration tribunal on the other. In the commercial case, arbitration is the substitute for litigation. Here arbitration is the substitute for industrial strife. Since arbitration of labor disputes has quite different functions from arbitration under an ordinary commercial agreement, the hostility evinced by courts toward arbitration of commercial agreements has no place here. For arbitration of labor disputes under collective bargaining agreements is part and parcel of the collective bargaining process itself.

* * *

A collective bargaining agreement is an effort to erect a system of industrial self-government. When most parties enter into [a] contractual relationship they do so voluntarily, in the sense that there is no real compulsion to deal with one another, as opposed to dealing with other parties. This is not true of the labor agreement. The choice is generally not between entering or refusing to enter into a relationship, for that in all probability preexists the negotiations. Rather it is between having that relationship governed by an agreed-upon rule of law or leaving each and every matter subject to a temporary resolution dependent solely upon the relative strength, at any given moment, of the contending forces. The mature labor agreement may attempt to regulate all aspects of the complicated relationship, from the most crucial to the most minute over an extended period of time. Because of the compulsion to reach agreement and the breadth of the matters covered, as well as the need for a fairly concise and readable instrument, the product of negotiations (the written document) is, in the words of the late Dean Shulman, "a compilation of diverse provisions: some provide objective criteria almost automatically applicable; some provide more or less specific standards which require reason and judgment in their application; and some do little more than leave problems to future consideration with an expression of hope and good faith." Gaps may be left to be filled in by reference to the practices of the particular industry and of the various shops covered by the agreement. Many of the specific practices which underlie the agreement may be unknown, except in hazy form, even to the negotiators. Courts and arbitration in the context of most commercial contracts are resorted to because there has been a breakdown in the working relationship of the parties; such resort is the unwanted exception. But the grievance machinery under a collective bargaining agreement is at the very heart of the system of industrial self-government. Arbitration is the means of solving the unforeseeable by molding a system of private law for all the problems which may arise and to provide for their solution in a way which will generally accord with the variant needs and desires of the parties. The processing of disputes through the grievance machinery is actually a vehicle by which meaning and content are given to the collective bargaining agreement.

Apart from matters that the parties specifically exclude, all of the questions on which the parties disagree must therefore come within the scope of the grievance and arbitration provisions of the collective agreement. The grievance procedure is, in other words, a part of the continuous collective bargaining process. It, rather than a strike, is the terminal point of a disagreement.

* * *

The labor arbitrator's source of law is not confined to the express provisions of the contract, as the industrial common law—the practices of the industry and the shop—is equally a part of the collective bargaining agreement although not expressed in it. The labor arbitrator is usually chosen because of the parties' confidence in his knowledge of the common law of the shop and their trust in his personal judgment to bring to bear considerations which are not expressed in the contract as criteria for judgment. The parties expect that his judgment of a particular grievance will reflect not only what the contract says but, insofar as the collective bargaining agreement permits, such factors as the effect upon productivity of a particular result, its consequence to the morale of the shop, his judgment whether tensions will be heightened or diminished. For the parties' objective in using the arbitration process is primarily to further their common goal of uninterrupted production under the agreement, to make the agreement serve their specialized needs. The ablest judge cannot be expected to bring the same experience and competence to bear upon the determination of a grievance, because he cannot be similarly informed.

———

Arbitration of labor disputes serves, then, to give "meaning and content" over time to the vague or ambiguous terms of the collective bargaining agreement. In addition, the very existence of this dispute resolution mechanism itself may affect the dynamic of the parties' relationship. Through the processing of a grievance dispute, for example, useful information may be communicated about the needs and attitudes of one party to the agreement, and about potential trouble spots in the relationship. Another function of labor arbitration was highlighted by Justice Douglas in a formulation which has now attained something of the status of a cliche: In a companion case to *Warrior & Gulf,* Justice Douglas noted that "[t]he processing of even frivolous claims may have therapeutic values of which those who are not a part of the plant environment may be quite unaware." [8]

Any particular "grievance" under a collective bargaining agreement is likely to be that of the individual *employee,* who may have been dismissed or whose job classification may have been changed. However, the parties to the agreement are the employer and the *union;* the union, as the exclusive representative of all the employees in the bargaining unit, is in exclusive control of the administration of the contract and controls access to the grievance procedure at every stage. In these circumstances, pursuing even a hopeless claim to arbitration has at least the virtue of giving the employee the assurance that his case has been heard and that he has been taken seriously. Grievance arbitration may thus serve as a "safety valve for troublesome complaints." [9] There may be other advantages for the union as well. It is often more politic for union representatives to "pass the buck" to the arbitrator, who they know will reject the grievance, than to be obliged *themselves* to convince their constituent that he is wrong and that the claim should be dropped. In addition, a union that is found to have "arbitrarily" refused to pursue an employee's grievance to arbitration, or to have "process[ed] it in a perfunctory fashion," may well be open to a suit by the employee for "unfair representation". [10]

Nevertheless, the overwhelming proportion of employee grievances are screened or settled without resort to arbitration just as the overwhelming proportion of lawsuits are settled before trial. It has been estimated that a grievance rate of 10 to 20 per 100 employees per year is "typical" in this country [11]. If any substantial proportion of those cases were to go to arbitration the entire grievance system would collapse.

Awards handed down by labor arbitrators generally reveal considerable sensitivity to those considerations mentioned by Justice Douglas in his paean to labor arbitration in *Warrior & Gulf*—the need to reduce tensions and to foster a good working relationship within the plant setting, the need to pay attention to the "common law of the shop" and to the "customs and practices which the parties have come to consider

8. United Steelworkers of America v. American Mfg. Co., 363 U.S. 564, 568 (1960).

9. Cox, Current Problems in the Law of Grievance Arbitration, 30 Rocky Mt. L. Rev. 247, 261 (1958).

10. Vaca v. Sipes, 386 U.S. 171 (1967); see also Bowen v. U.S. Postal Service, 459 U.S. 212 (1983).

11. See Feller, A General Theory of the Collective Bargaining Agreement, 61 Cal. L.Rev. 663, 755 (1973).

as settled patterns of conduct." [12]   Some selections from recent arbitral awards give a good flavor of how labor arbitrators purport, at least, to see their role in the process.   Would you expect to find opinions like these written by "judges"?

(a) The employee was discharged for having used "foul language" which her supervisor claimed was "threatening" and "intimidating" towards her and "harmful to productivity."   The employee had a history of similar episodes in the past, for which she had been disciplined.   The arbitrator held that the discharge was unwarranted and wrote:

> Although grievant and supervisor affirm that there are no personal problems, they are manifest to this observer through the testimony of witnesses.   If grievant were allowed to return to the work site she would be rewarded as her coworkers and the immediate superiors would be implicitly punished.   The poor social relations would, I believe, deteriorate and explode.   This is unacceptable both for the justice of the case and the requirements of the productivity of the unit.
>
> The grievant should be reinstated but not in her old position nor in her old work area.   The grievant is banished from that area.
>
> The period between formal severance and this order shall serve as a large and severe suspension.   She shall be returned to a comparable position or if one is not available a lesser one with a lower grade and lesser pay and no back [pay] or rights for this suspension period.   *   *   *
>
> Her future capacity for work and promotion is in her hands.   The burden of proof is with her.   If she is abusive or violates other rules, the progressivity of discipline should continue to the next step, severance.

In re Social Security Administration and American Federation of Government Employees, 84 Lab.Arb. 1100 (1985).

(b) A collective bargaining agreement provided that the employer, a grocery chain, would remain closed on January 1 "contingent upon similar limitations being contractually required of other organized food stores and/or being generally observed by major unorganized food competitors in the cities in which the Employer operated."   The arbitrator found that the employer violated this agreement by opening on January 1.   He then turned to the question of the proper remedy to be granted the Union.   The arbitrator denied the Union's request for punitive damages, since he was "of the view that they are bad medicine when administered to a participant in an ongoing, union-management relationship."   Although the employer's violation was "clear and unmistakable," "it is always hard to say that a beleaguered competitor, as Kroger undoubtedly considered itself, acted subjectively in bad faith.   Moreover, it seems to me that a healing process is what is most needed in the

---

12. See In re Standard Bag Corp. and Paper Bag, Novelty, Mounting, Finishing   and Display Workers Union, 45 Lab.Arb. 1149 (1965).

relations between this Company and the Union, and I question whether punitive damages will contribute to that end." Nor, he held, was there any basis for awarding damages to the employees: "I do not mean that it would be impossible to attach a dollar value to a January 1 with family and friends, perhaps in front of the TV set watching a bowl game * * * but I do not find that such a showing was made here."

However, to prevent "unjust enrichment," the arbitrator did award to the union "restitution of any profits that may be attributable to the Company's operations on January 1." In re The Kroger Company and United Food and Commercial Workers, 85 Lab.Arb. 1198 (1985).

(c) The employee had worked for the employer for eight years and had never been disciplined. He was discharged for being disrespectful to the Company President ("If you don't like the way I'm doing the work, do it yourself") in the presence of a number of the company's other employees. The arbitrator held that the employer did not have "proper cause" to discharge the employee and that he should be reinstated, although without recovering back pay or accruing seniority or vacation benefits for the seven months he was off work:

> Since discharge is in essence "capital punishment" in the work place, it is necessary to examine with extreme care all of the evidence before determining whether it is appropriate or not. This would include the facts and circumstances leading to the discharge, the grievant's length of service, the degree of aggravation involved in the offense, whether the conduct was intended or rather an accidental outburst, the grievant's past record and finally whether the events are likely to recur were the grievant to be reinstated.
>
> * * *
>
> Management's main argument was that it would be difficult for [the President] to run his operation with employees knowing that they could talk back to the President of the Company and get away with it. However, with this employee having been off work for over seven months without pay, I doubt that any employee will seriously think that he "got away with" very much. Upholding the discharge would be the most severe form of industrial penalty, but giving the grievant his job back without the seven months of back pay is still a very significant penalty. In salary alone that amounts to approximately $6,000.00 of gross earnings. (The grievant did not collect unemployment compensation and has not worked.) * * *
>
> On the day he returns to work, but as a condition precedent to returning to work, the grievant will apologize to [the President] either privately or in front of the employees of Stylemaster. (The presence or lack thereof of other employees to be at the discretion of the Company.)

In re Stylemaster, Inc. and Production Workers Union of Chicago, 79 Lab.Arb. 76 (1982).

Compromise Decisions

POSNER: The arbitration literature says—something that is very difficult to find out independently—that arbitrators are not supposed to compromise. Arbitrators are supposed to decide a dispute as if they were judges.

LEFF: The literature says that for the same reason that signs in subways say, "Don't Smoke," because there is a very strong tendency to smoke and therefore you have to say it over and over again. That reflects the fact that arbitrators compromise a great deal * * *.[13]

Observers often note that arbitrators have a propensity to tailor their decisions so as to make them acceptable to both parties. Such a criticism is heard most vociferously perhaps with respect to labor arbitrators, although it is by no means confined to the labor area. It is often supposed that this is done to insure the future "acceptability" of the arbitrator *himself.* Labor arbitrators are paid, often quite handsomely, for their work; what would be more natural than for this to create an incentive to try to assure themselves of repeat business? This incentive may often result in compromise decisions, "splitting the difference" so as not to appear unduly to favor either of the two parties whose future goodwill must be retained. A similar dynamic might be reflected in a *course* of decisions by the same arbitrator which over time, taken together, appears to show a rough balance between awards favorable to labor and those favorable to management.

As might be expected, this tendency to engage in compromise decisions appears particularly marked in "interest" arbitrations. In such cases the arbitrator is likely to be aware that the stakes riding on his decision are high, that the impact of his decision may be great and felt in all sorts of ways that he cannot be sure of in advance, and that intense dissatisfaction with a "mistaken" award may adversely affect the working relationship of the parties for some time to come. Do you expect that judges are often impelled to take such considerations into account in deciding cases?

Compare the following two excerpts, whose authors appear to take sharply differing views of the propriety of this behavior and of its function within the context of labor-management relations:

A proportion of arbitration awards, no one knows how large a proportion, is decided not on the basis of the evidence or of the contract or other proper considerations, but in a way calculated to encourage the arbitrator's being hired for other arbitration cases. It makes no difference whether or not a large majority of cases is decided in this way. A system of adjudication in which the judge depends for his livelihood, or for a substantial part of his livelihood or even for substantial supplements to his regular income, on

13. Discussion by Seminar Participants, 8 J. Legal Stud. 323, 345 (1979).

pleasing those who hire him to judge is per se a thoroughly undesirable system. In no proper system of justice should a judge be submitted to such pressures. On the contrary, a judge should be carefully insulated from any pressure of this type.

P. Hays, Labor Arbitration: A Dissenting View 112–13 (1966).

———

Compare Getman, Labor Arbitration and Dispute Resolution, 88 Yale L.J. 916, 928–930 (1979):

In none of the literature is it suggested that an arbitrator's desire to promote acceptability might affect the process in a way that is basically desirable. However, if, as I contend, economic efficiency is promoted by arbitration partly because through it the parties conclude their negotiations, then it is likely that the desire to maintain acceptability plays a useful role in helping to achieve the resolution that the parties would have achieved had they had the opportunity to negotiate with respect to the issues in dispute. Such a resolution would by definition further the goal of efficiency.

The negotiating process reflects both the relative economic strength and the differing priorities of the parties. * * * Economic strength is necessarily a factor in arbitration because it shapes the language of the collective-bargaining agreement, which is always the starting point, and sometimes the sole basis, for the arbitrator's decision. The parties' priorities are more difficult to ascertain. The arbitrator must pay careful attention to the clues that the parties give concerning how strongly they feel about a particular case. My judgment is that the need to maintain acceptability makes arbitrators more attentive to such clues than judges and more likely than judges would be to utilize them in their decision. Arbitrators whose decisions over time accurately reflect the priorities of the parties are likely to maintain and enhance their acceptability more than arbitrators who take either a more narrowly judicial role or a personally activist role. Thus, the process of selection will tend to produce arbitrators and a body of arbitral precedent that facilitate and extend the process of negotiation. * * *

The careful selection process also motivates arbitrators to try to please both sides, if possible, with their decision. Thus, the split award and the decision in which it is difficult to tell which side has won are frequent in labor relations. Although the parties constantly insist it is contrary to their wishes, this system of giving a little bit to each side permits the process to achieve the results of successful negotiation.

Notes and Questions

(1) As Getman suggests, it is almost inevitable that in the course of a hearing an arbitrator will receive some intimation from the parties or

their attorneys as to what an "acceptable" settlement will look like, and that he will be influenced by such hints or suggestions. In an extreme case this may even take the form of what is called a "rigged award." The union representative and the management may actually *agree* between themselves as to how a case should be resolved; this understanding is conveyed to the arbitrator, who incorporates it in the final award as "his" decision without openly revealing that it is in fact the result of the parties' compromise. The hearing itself then becomes a mere charade. The practice of the "rigged award" has been often and scathingly condemned as "the crassest infringement of adjudicative integrity," "the most severe criticism which could be made of arbitration," "vicious" and "a shocking distortion of the administration of justice." See Fuller, Collective Bargaining and the Arbitrator, 1963 Wisc.L.Rev. 3, 20 (1963); Eaton, Labor Arbitration in the San Francisco Bay Area, 48 Lab.Arb. 1381, 1389 (1967); P. Hays, Labor Arbitration: A Dissenting View 113, 65 (1966).

Why might the parties want the arbitrator to proceed in this way, when they could simply "settle" the case and withdraw it from the purview of the arbitrator? And just *why* is the arbitrator not entitled to do this? What is wrong with the "rigged award"? Might there be a difference if this practice is used in "interest" arbitration rather than with respect to a "rights" dispute? Finally, if the arbitrator is unwilling merely to rubber-stamp the parties' understanding, how should he proceed? What as a practical matter is he able to do?

(2) Some writers have suggested that the "procedures for arbitration that have been developed in the context of labor relations make the technique particularly adaptable to prison problems." To resolve disputes arising out of grievances by prison inmates, "third-party neutrals who have particular expertise in corrections may be chosen by both prisoners and the officials. Furthermore, the parties could stipulate in advance the rules to be followed and the issues to be settled." Goldfarb & Singer, Redressing Prisoners' Grievances, 39 Geo.Wash.L. Rev. 175, 316 (1970); see also Keating, Arbitration of Inmate Grievances, 30 Arb.J. 177 (1975). Do you agree?

4. Medical Malpractice Arbitration

A dramatic increase in the number and size of medical malpractice claims and awards first entered the public consciousness during the 1970's, under the banner of the "malpractice crisis." The threatened effects of this "crisis" on the health and insurance industries spawned a large variety of legislative responses. These have ranged from tinkering with the formal legal standard of negligence [14] or the statute of limitations in malpractice cases, to more dramatic reforms such as

---

14. See, e.g., Fla.Stat. § 768.45(4) (no "inference or presumption" of negligence from medical injury).

abolishing the collateral source rule or imposing ceilings on recoverable damages or on attorney's contingent fees.[15]   Among these legislative "reforms" there inevitably appeared changes in the *process* by which malpractice claims could be asserted, and attempts to divert such claims entirely from the time-honored system of tort litigation.

(a) Some states have imposed preliminary hurdles on malpractice litigation by *requiring* that claims first be submitted to a "medical review" or "professional liability review" panel. (These may sometimes be called "arbitration boards.")   Under some statutes, this required panel must consist of three physicians.[16]   Another common pattern is for the panel to consist of a physician, an attorney, and a member of the "general public"[17]; still other states simply provide for a "tripartite board" (with one member named by each party and a chairman selected by the other two members or by the court) without specifying the profession or background of the arbitrators.   Under the various statutes the fees and expenses of the arbitrators may be shared equally by the parties, may be assessed by the arbitrators as an element of costs, or may in some cases come directly from state funds.[18]

If either party is dissatisfied with the arbitration award, he has the right to demand a trial de novo to be held in the regular state courts. In consequence it is often said that the review panels serve not so much to "decide" disputes, as to provide "an expert opinion" based on evidence submitted to them—that they act "in the nature of a pretrial settlement conference," or that, by giving the parties a preliminary, disinterested evaluation of the merits of a claim they serve an "advisory" function and help to "promote an early disposition of many cases by a voluntary settlement."[19]   For further discussion of this and similar dispute resolution mechanisms, see Chapter V infra.

(2) Somewhat less common are statutes which expressly authorize *voluntary* agreements to arbitrate malpractice claims between a patient and a medical defendant. (In many jurisdictions, however, such voluntary agreements may also be enforceable under the state's general arbitration statute.   See the discussion of such statutes infra p. 435.) As in the case of traditional arbitration, such an agreement can be entered into either prior to treatment or as the submission of an existing dispute; where such an agreement is made, the arbitrator's decision will be final and binding on both parties.

---

15. See P. Huber, Liability: The Legal Revolution and Its Consequences (1988).

16. See, e.g., Neb.Rev.Stat. § 44–2841 (each party selects one physician and the two thus chosen select a third; panel also includes attorney who acts in "advisory capacity" and has no vote).

17. See, e.g., Md.Code §§ 3–2A–03, 3–2A–04 (state "Health Claims Arbitration Office" circulates lists of arbitrators in each category to the parties, who may strike unacceptable names); 18 Del.Code § 6805 (panel consists of two "health care providers," one attorney, and two "lay persons" chosen from a "list of 100 objective and judicious persons of appropriate education and experience" maintained by Commissioner of Insurance.)

18. The Louisiana statute is unique in mandating that the costs of the panel are to be paid by the party *in whose favor* the panel decided. La.Rev.Stat. § 40:1299.-47(I).

19. Prendergast v. Nelson, 199 Neb. 97, 256 N.W.2d 657, 666–67 (1977).

Even in the case of voluntary agreements, it is not unusual to find detailed legislative regulation of the conduct of medical malpractice arbitration. A Michigan statute mandates that where the parties agree to arbitrate medical malpractice claims, the case *must* be heard by a panel of three arbitrators, including one attorney and one physician— the latter "preferably" from the defendant's medical specialty. (Where a claim is against a hospital only, a hospital administrator may be substituted for a physician.) By statute, also, the claimant is to bear none of the costs of malpractice arbitration charged by the institution (such as the AAA) which administers it.[20] Another common provision in statutes regulating medical malpractice arbitration is a "cooling off period": The Michigan statute, for example, allows the patient to "revoke" his agreement to arbitrate within 60 days after "execution" (in the case of a hospital, within 60 days "after discharge").[21]

Notes and Questions

(1) Is the requirement of a physician on the arbitration panel troubling? Does every physician's interest in minimizing the costs of malpractice insurance give rise to an inference that this arbitrator will be disposed to rule against the claimant? The Michigan statute was upheld against a challenge on these grounds in Morris v. Metriyakool, 418 Mich. 423, 344 N.W.2d 736 (1984), where the state supreme court held that it did not deprive patients of "constitutional rights to an impartial decisionmaker." Cf. Graham v. Scissor Tail, infra p. 463.

Should such questions of arbitrator impartiality be decided on an a priori basis? One alternative is to approach the question as a matter of contract formation in each individual case. See, for example, Moore v. Fragatos, 116 Mich.App. 179, 321 N.W.2d 781 (1982), discussed at infra p. 466.

(2) In most states the decision of a mandatory malpractice "screening" panel is confined to the question of liability; determination of damages is excluded. Why?

(3) What is the point of a statutory "cooling off" period? Is it that a patient may *retroactively* withdraw his consent to arbitrate disputes over treatment already received? The Louisiana statute, however, is explicit that while an arbitration agreement is "voidable" within 30 days after execution, it is nevertheless "binding" as to acts of malpractice committed "prior to the revocation date." La.Rev.Stat. § 9:4233. On this point, how would you interpret the California statute, which reads:

20. Mich.Comp.Laws § 600.5044(1), (2). But cf. § 600.5053(2) ("cost of each arbitrator's fees and expenses, together with any administrative fee, may be assessed against any party in the award.")

M., R. & S. Proc. Dispute Res. UCB—16

21. Mich.Comp.Laws § 600.5041(3); § 600.5042(3).

Once signed, such a contract governs all subsequent open-book account transactions for medical services for which the contract was signed until or unless rescinded by written notice within 30 days of signature.

Cal.Code Civ.Pro. § 1295(c); cf. Ramirez v. Superior Court, 103 Cal.App. 3d 746, 163 Cal.Rptr. 223, 229 (1980).

5. Arbitration of Consumer Disputes

Another area where there has been recent experimentation with use of the arbitration process has been in disputes between consumers and manufacturers. General Motors and some other automobile manufacturers, for example, have agreed to submit disputes over new-car warranties to the "Autoline" program administered by the Better Business Bureau. In this program the consumer's complaint is heard by volunteer arbitrators—"professionals, educators, retirees, lawyers, housewives, and others"—who have gone through a short training program but who have no necessary background in either the law or in automobile mechanics. The arbitrators will hear any claims under an automobile warranty, although they will not consider claims for consequential damages such as for personal injury or lost wages. While the manufacturer generally agrees in advance to accept the award, the consumer is not bound by the arbitrator's decision and is free to reject it and pursue any claim in court. The program is funded by the manufacturer, operates at no cost to the consumer, and is designed to resolve any complaint within 40 days after filing. See Better Business Bureau, Autoline: A National Program of Mediation/Arbitration for Automotive Disputes (1984).

Other manufacturers, like Ford and Chrysler, have chosen instead to set up their own internal dispute resolution processes. Procedure in these in-house programs appears to be somewhat more perfunctory than with the BBB. There are no oral hearings, and decisions are made on the basis of written submissions by the consumer and the manufacturer. The "arbitrators" are selected by the manufacturer; having seen neither the consumer nor the vehicle in question, they will rarely overturn the manufacturer's recommendation.

As part of the expansion of consumer protection legislation over the last two decades, most states have enacted so-called "lemon laws" aimed at insuring that automobile manufacturers conform the vehicle to any express warranty. These statutes require the manufacturer to refund the purchase price or provide the consumer a new replacement vehicle if it cannot correct any defect after a "reasonable number of attempts." These statutes also commonly provide that where the manufacturer has set up a "third party dispute resolution process" to hear warranty claims, complying with regulations of the Federal Trade Commission, the consumer must first assert any "lemon law" claims through this mechanism. In some states (such as New York) consumers have the option of electing the AAA as an "alternative" mechanism instead of the process that the manufacturer sets up or sponsors. In such a case the consumer must pay a filing fee of $200 and will be bound by the result in the same way as the manufacturer.[21] In other states (such as Texas), "lemon law" complaints are first heard by "official" state agencies like the Motor Vehicle Commission.[22]

Notes and Questions

(1) In this and the preceding section, you have been introduced to a use of "arbitration" quite different from the models presented in the labor and commercial areas. You can see that the term "arbitration" is commonly applied to describe any number of different processes, developing along different lines and responding to different needs. Indeed, the long-standing acceptability and respectability of "arbitration" make it a useful term to be coopted by innovators in the dispute resolution field.

Some of the attributes traditionally claimed for arbitration may be present here as well. In consumer arbitration, an arbitrator is typically asked to apply fairly straightforward rules of decision to limited and tractable fact questions; in addition, the stakes are likely to be small and the procedure extremely informal. In such circumstances there are likely to be advantages, at least to the plaintiff, of reduced delay and costs—similar to the advantages often claimed for small claims courts. Studies indicate also that arbitration, at least where it is voluntary in inception and binding in result, may bring similar benefits to medical malpractice claimants in the form of increased speed and reduced expense. See, e.g., Note, Medical Malpractice Arbitration: A Patient's Perspective, 61 Wash.U.L.Q. 123, 153–155 (1983).

However, there are also some significant differences. The usefulness of arbitration may be diluted where the parties do not (as they may in labor and commercial disputes) "have an interest in the pie of continued collaboration." See H. Hart & A. Sacks, The Legal Process 341 (1958). Especially where the parties' autonomy in the choice of the process or in the selection of arbitrators is reduced, the decision-makers are no longer "their" arbitrators, spelling out the meaning of "their" agreement in terms of their probable preferences or past practice. It then becomes more appropriate to view arbitration not as part of the world of "private ordering" but simply as a form of economic regulation. Particularly in the field of medical malpractice such regulation is often responsive to a not-very-well-hidden agenda, as the following excerpt indicates:

> The push for the arbitration of malpractice claims * * * must not be seen as linked to the general interest in alternative dispute resolution mechanisms exhibited over the past two decades.

---

21. See N.Y.Gen.Bus.Law § 198–a(k), (m).

22. See Chrysler Corp. v. Texas Motor Vehicle Com'n, 755 F.2d 1192 (5th Cir. 1985).

This examination of alternative mechanisms has had as its primary goal the identification of fora and procedures suitable for the resolution of meritorious claims that, for essentially economic reasons, had been excluded from the litigation system. In direct contrast, malpractice claims have always been guaranteed judicial resolution because of the contingency fee system. * * *

There are two primary goals set forth by those propounding the arbitration of malpractice claims: first, to chill attorney interest in what are labelled *vel non* as frivolous or unmeritorious claims; and second, to reduce the size of damage awards in meritorious claims. Neither goal is related to providing a resolution for otherwise unresolvable claims. Both are intimately linked, however, to the widely held belief that the judiciary is unwilling or unable to exercise effective control over juries in civil trials.
* * *

Arbitration and pretrial review of medical malpractice claims serve different legislative goals. At the most general level, both are designed to freeze or slow the acceleration of the size of malpractice insurance premiums. The effect of pretrial review, however, is to chill plaintiff interest in pursuing marginal claims, both practically and psychologically, and to encourage settlement by forcing additional plaintiff expenditure without providing for concomitant recovery. Arbitration, on the other hand, is viewed primarily as a constitutionally safe method of avoiding jury determinations of liability and quantum of damages.

Terry, The Technical and Conceptual Flaws of Medical Malpractice Arbitration, 30 St. Louis U.L.J. 571, 572–73, 586 (1986).

(2) The Federal Trade Commission brought proceedings against Volkswagen of America, alleging that Volkswagen knew of an "abnormally high" number of engine problems related to excessive oil consumption but failed to tell consumers; the FTC estimated that many owners had incurred repair costs ranging from $125 to $2000 for engine damage caused by insufficient lubrication. The FTC later entered into a consent order with Volkswagen, in which Volkswagen agreed to make arbitration of the claims available without charge to consumers under Better Business Bureau auspices. Volkswagen also agreed to provide owners with "background statements" describing the oil consumption problem to help them prepare their cases in arbitration. The arbitrator's award was to be binding on Volkswagen but not on the consumer. See 54 Antitrust & Trade Reg.Rep. 786 (BNA 1988). A similar consent order had been entered into by the FTC with General Motors in 1983; it was severely criticized by consumer groups and by a group of 29 state attorneys general, who complained that "similarly situated consumers could get a whole loaf, a half a loaf or no loaf at all. Arbitrary arbitrations are not the answer to resolving this case." In the Matter of General Motors, 102 F.T.C. 1741, 1743 (1983) (statement of Commissioner Pertschuk).

(3) Do you expect that resolution of consumer and medical claims that is "private" (that is, which uses non-"official" decision makers, does not establish precedent or communicate its decisions in reasoned opinions, and is otherwise withdrawn from public scrutiny) is likely to have the deterrent or accident-reduction effects of tort litigation?

C. ARBITRATION AND THE COURTS

1. Introduction

The traditional attitude of judges towards arbitration has been one of considerable hostility, "explained," if at all, by ritual invocation of the phrase that agreements to submit disputes to arbitration "oust the jurisdiction of the courts." Perhaps this rhetorical flourish masked some concern over the diversion from the court system of cases implicating public values, or fear that private tribunals might ignore or undermine the enforcement of "legal" rules. Somewhat more cynically, one might also suppose that it originated in considerations of competition for business, at a time when judge's salaries still depended on fees paid by litigants.

At common law, if the parties did voluntarily submit a dispute to arbitration *and* the arbitrator proceeded to render an award, the award would be considered binding. Barring some exceptional defense such as arbitrator misconduct, the award could be enforced in a separate court action brought by the successful plaintiff. However, purely *executory* agreements to arbitrate had little force. A party could refuse to honor such an agreement and could revoke it at any time; a court would not specifically enforce an agreement to arbitrate existing or future disputes. While damages could in theory be awarded for breach of this contract, how could they possibly be calculated?[1] So a potential "defendant" could deprive the arbitration agreement of any effect simply by giving notice of his objection and refusing to participate in the process. A potential "plaintiff" could, after revocation, simply bring his own lawsuit, and the court would hear the case without regard to the agreement to arbitrate. A readable summary of the situation at common law can be found in Judge Frank's opinion in Kulukundis Shipping Co. S/A v. Amtorg Trading Corp., 126 F.2d 978 (2d Cir.1942).

Beginning with New York in 1920, most states have now passed statutes completely reversing the common law position on arbitration. The Uniform Arbitration Act, on which many modern state statutes have been modeled, was adopted by the National Conference of the Commissioners on Uniform State Laws in 1955. The Federal Arbitration Act (FAA) was enacted in 1925. All of these statutes are quite

---

1. See Munson v. Straits of Dover S.S. Co., 102 Fed. 926 (2d Cir.1900) (plaintiff sought damages, in the form of lawyer's fees and costs incurred in defending a lawsuit, for breach of agreement to arbitrate; held, plaintiff entitled to nominal damages only; judicial process is "theoretically at least, the safest and best devised by the wisdom and experience of mankind.").

similar in their broad outlines, although there is considerable variation in detail. The Federal Act, because of its overwhelming importance, is set out in Appendix E, infra p. 750. Read the text of the Act carefully; it is deceptively simple for a statute which has grown to assume such pervasive importance. What does the Act do to change the common law attitude towards arbitration? How does it assure the enforceability of agreements to arbitrate?

Similar statutes are in force in most states. (But not everywhere: In a small number of states, courts will now specifically enforce agreements to submit *existing* disputes to arbitration, but not clauses in contracts concerning *future* disputes.) See generally M. Domke, Commercial Arbitration § 3.02 (rev. ed.).

The situation is further complicated by the fact that even in states with "modern" statutes modeled on the New York or Uniform Act, the statute is usually not interpreted to be exclusive. As a consequence, "common law arbitration" still survives. Thus, in cases where consent to arbitrate has not been revoked and the parties proceed to an award, the arbitrator's decision will have the same binding force it would have at common law, even where the statute has not been complied with— for example, where there has been no written agreement to arbitrate or where the subject matter of the dispute has been specifically excluded from the coverage of the arbitration statute. See, e.g., L.H. Lacy Co. v. City of Lubbock, 559 S.W.2d 348 (Tex.1977) (construction contract); see generally Sturges and Reckson, Common–Law and Statutory Arbitration: Problems Arising From Their Coexistence, 46 Minn. L.Rev. 819 (1962).

Nor have state arbitration statutes frozen the independent *development* of the common law. On the contrary, in a number of places they seem to have aided in its growth. Increasingly, decisions can be found where courts will rely on the "pro-arbitration" policy of the state statute to enforce an arbitration agreement *outside* the statute's substantive scope, and *despite* one party's prior attempt to "revoke." See Olshan Demolishing Co. v. Angleton Independent School District, 684 S.W.2d 179 (Tex.App.1984) (agreement to arbitrate lacked statutory notice; "[e]ncouraging arbitration will reduce some of the backlog in our trial courts"); Kodak Mining Co. v. Carrs Fork Corp., 669 S.W.2d 917 (Ky.1984) (statute then in force applied only to submission of existing disputes to arbitration).

2. The Federal Arbitration Act and State Law

The FAA was enacted before *Erie v. Tompkins* (in 1938) called for a fundamental rethinking of the relationships between state and federal courts. Over the last 50 years, problems of federalism in the enforcement of arbitration agreements have surfaced on a number of occasions. Only recently have some fundamental issues been more or less settled.

Bernhardt v. Polygraphic Co. of America, Inc., 350 U.S. 198 (1956), was a diversity case in federal court. The contract provided that any future disputes would be settled by arbitration; the transaction was assumed *not* to "involve" interstate commerce. At that time, Vermont law made an agreement to arbitrate revocable at any time before an award was actually handed down. In such circumstances, could the federal court enforce the arbitration agreement? The Supreme Court said "no": In the absence of a "transaction involving commerce," *state* law on arbitration was to be applied in federal courts in diversity cases. Arbitration was therefore "substantive" for *Erie* purposes: "The change from a court of law to an arbitration panel may make a radical difference in ultimate result." Furthermore, the Court said, the "procedures" for enforcing arbitration agreements in section 3 of the Federal Act were limited by section 2; applying the FAA, therefore, even in a federal court, is dependent on the existence of "a transaction involving commerce."

It later became settled that the FAA had been enacted as an exercise of Congress' commerce and admiralty powers. The Act thus laid down substantive rules of decision, binding on federal courts even in diversity cases as long as interstate or foreign commerce or maritime matters were involved. In this respect, though, the FAA remains something of an anomaly among federal statutes: Although enacted under Congress' commerce power, of itself it confers no federal question *jurisdiction.* Therefore, an action to enforce an arbitration agreement under the Act does not "arise under" federal law but requires an *independent* source of federal jurisdiction, such as diversity or some other federal statute.

This line of cases raised still further questions: In cases that *do* involve foreign or interstate commerce, does the body of law fashioned by federal courts bind *state* courts as well? For example, would a Vermont court, in such a case, still be free to hold an arbitration agreement revocable, or is Vermont law to that effect preempted by the FAA?

SOUTHLAND CORPORATION v. KEATING

Supreme Court of the United States, 1984.
465 U.S. 1, 104 S.Ct. 852, 79 L.Ed.2d 1.

CHIEF JUSTICE BURGER delivered the opinion of the Court.

This case presents the questions (a) whether the California Franchise Investment Law, which invalidates certain arbitration agreements covered by the Federal Arbitration Act, violates the Supremacy Clause and (b) whether arbitration under the federal Act is impaired when a class-action structure is imposed on the process by the state courts.

I

Appellant Southland Corp. is the owner and franchisor of 7–Eleven convenience stores. Southland's standard franchise agreement provides each franchisee with a license to use certain registered trademarks, a lease or sublease of a convenience store owned or leased by Southland, inventory financing, and assistance in advertising and merchandising. The franchisees operate the stores, supply bookkeeping data, and pay Southland a fixed percentage of gross profits. The franchise agreement also contains the following provision requiring arbitration:

> "Any controversy or claim arising out of or relating to this Agreement or the breach hereof shall be settled by arbitration in accordance with the Rules of the American Arbitration Association . . . and judgment upon any award rendered by the arbitrator may be entered in any court having jurisdiction thereof."

Appellees are 7–Eleven franchisees. Between September 1975 and January 1977, several appellees filed individual actions against Southland in California Superior Court alleging, among other things, fraud, oral misrepresentation, breach of contract, breach of fiduciary duty, and violation of the disclosure requirements of the California Franchise Investment Law, Cal.Corp.Code § 31000 et seq. Southland's answer, in all but one of the individual actions, included the affirmative defense of failure to arbitrate.

In May 1977, appellee Keating filed a class action against Southland on behalf of a class that assertedly includes approximately 800 California franchisees. Keating's principal claims were substantially the same as those asserted by the other franchisees. After the various actions were consolidated, Southland petitioned to compel arbitration of the claims in all cases, and appellees moved for class certification.

The Superior Court granted Southland's motion to compel arbitration of all claims except those claims based on the Franchise Investment Law. The court did not pass on appellees' request for class certification. Southland appealed from the order insofar as it excluded from arbitration the claims based on the California statute. Appellees filed a petition for a writ of mandamus or prohibition in the California Court of Appeal arguing that the arbitration should proceed as a class action.

The California Court of Appeal reversed the trial court's refusal to compel arbitration of appellees' claims under the Franchise Investment Law. That court interpreted the arbitration clause to require arbitration of all claims asserted under the Franchise Investment Law, and construed the Franchise Investment Law not to invalidate such agreements to arbitrate. Alternatively, the court concluded that if the Franchise Investment Law rendered arbitration agreements involving commerce unenforceable, it would conflict with § 2 of the Federal Arbitration Act and therefore be invalid under the Supremacy Clause.

The Court of Appeal also determined that there was no "insurmountable obstacle" to conducting an arbitration on a classwide basis, and issued a writ of mandate directing the trial court to conduct class-certification proceedings.

The California Supreme Court, by a vote of 4–2, reversed the ruling that claims asserted under the Franchise Investment Law are arbitrable. The California Supreme Court interpreted the Franchise Investment Law to require judicial consideration of claims brought under that statute and concluded that the California statute did not contravene the federal Act.

* * *

The California Franchise Investment Law provides:

> "Any condition, stipulation or provision purporting to bind any person acquiring any franchise to waive compliance with any provision of this law or any rule or order hereunder is void." Cal. Corp.Code Ann. § 31512.

The California Supreme Court interpreted this statute to require judicial consideration of claims brought under the state statute and accordingly refused to enforce the parties' contract to arbitrate such claims. So interpreted the California Franchise Investment Law directly conflicts with § 2 of the Federal Arbitration Act and violates the Supremacy Clause.

In enacting § 2 of the federal Act, Congress declared a national policy favoring arbitration and withdrew the power of the states to require a judicial forum for the resolution of claims which the contracting parties agreed to resolve by arbitration. * * *

We discern only two limitations on the enforceability of arbitration provisions governed by the Federal Arbitration Act: they must be part of a written maritime contract or a contract "evidencing a transaction involving commerce" and such clauses may be revoked upon "grounds as exist at law or in equity for the revocation of any contract." We see nothing in the Act indicating that the broad principle of enforceability is subject to any additional limitations under state law.

The Federal Arbitration Act rests on the authority of Congress to enact substantive rules under the Commerce Clause. In Prima Paint Corp. v. Flood & Conklin Mfg. Co., 388 US 395 (1967) [infra p. 455], the Court examined the legislative history of the Act and concluded that the statute "is based upon . . . the incontestable federal foundations of 'control over interstate commerce and over admiralty.' " The contract in *Prima Paint,* as here, contained an arbitration clause. One party in that case alleged that the other had committed fraud in the inducement of the contract, although not of the arbitration clause in particular, and sought to have the claim of fraud adjudicated in federal court. The Court held that, notwithstanding a contrary state rule, consideration of a claim of fraud in the inducement of a contract "is for the arbitrators and not for the courts." The Court relied for this holding on Congress' broad power to fashion substantive rules under the Commerce Clause.

At least since 1824 Congress' authority under the Commerce Clause has been held plenary. Gibbons v. Ogden, 9 Wheat 1, 196 (1824). In the words of Chief Justice Marshall, the authority of Congress is "the power to regulate; that is, to prescribe the rule by which commerce is to be governed." The statements of the Court in *Prima Paint* that the Arbitration Act was an exercise of the Commerce Clause power clearly implied that the substantive rules of the Act were to apply in state as well as federal courts.

* * *

Although the legislative history is not without ambiguities, there are strong indications that Congress had in mind something more than making arbitration agreements enforceable only in the federal courts. The House Report plainly suggests the more comprehensive objectives:

> "The purpose of this bill is to make valid and enforceable agreements for arbitration contained *in contracts involving interstate commerce* or within the jurisdiction or admiralty, *or* which may be the subject of litigation in the Federal courts." HR Rep No. 96, 68th Cong, 1st Sess, 1 (1924). (emphasis added).

This broader purpose can also be inferred from the reality that Congress would be less likely to address a problem whose impact was confined to federal courts than a problem of large significance in the field of commerce. The Arbitration Act sought to "overcome the rule of equity, that equity will not specifically enforce an[y] arbitration agreement." The House Report accompanying the bill stated:

> The need for the law arises from . . . . the jealousy of the English courts for their own jurisdiction. . . . This jealousy survived for so lon[g] a period that the principle became firmly embedded in the English common law and was adopted with it by the American courts. The courts have felt that the precedent was too strongly fixed to be overturned without legislative enactment . . .

Surely this makes clear that the House Report contemplated a broad reach of the Act, unencumbered by state-law constraints.

* * *

Justice O'Connor argues that Congress viewed the Arbitration Act "as a procedural statute, applicable only in federal courts." If it is correct that Congress sought only to create a procedural remedy in the federal courts, there can be no explanation for the express limitation in the Arbitration Act to contracts "involving commerce." For example, when Congress has authorized this Court to prescribe the rules of procedure in the federal Courts of Appeals, District Courts, and bankruptcy courts, it has not limited the power of the Court to prescribe rules applicable only to causes of action involving commerce. We would expect that if Congress, in enacting the Arbitration Act, was creating what it thought to be a procedural rule applicable only in federal courts, it would not so limit the Act to transactions involving commerce. On the other hand, Congress would need to call on the Commerce Clause if it intended the Act to apply in state courts. Yet at the same time, its reach would be limited to transactions involving interstate commerce. We therefore view the "involving commerce" requirement in § 2, not as an inexplicable limitation on the power of the federal courts, but as a necessary qualification on a statute intended to apply in state and federal courts.

Under the interpretation of the Arbitration Act urged by Justice O'Connor, claims brought under the California Franchise Investment Law are not arbitrable when they are raised in state court. Yet it is clear beyond question that if this suit had been brought as a diversity action in a federal district court, the arbitration clause would have been enforceable. The interpretation given to the Arbitration Act by the California Supreme Court would therefore encourage and reward forum shopping. We are unwilling to attribute to Congress the intent, in drawing on the comprehensive powers of the Commerce Clause, to create a right to enforce an arbitration contract and yet make the right dependent for its enforcement on the particular forum in which it is asserted. And since the overwhelming proportion of all civil litigation in this country is in the state courts, we cannot believe Congress intended to limit the Arbitration Act to disputes subject only to *federal-court jurisdiction.*[9] Such an interpretation would frustrate congressional intent to place "[a]n arbitration agreement . . . upon the same footing as other contracts, where it belongs." HR Rep No. 96, 68th Cong, 1st Sess, 1 (1924).

In creating a substantive rule applicable in state as well as federal courts,[10] Congress intended to foreclose state legislative attempts to undercut the enforceability of arbitration agreements.[11] We hold that

9. While the Federal Arbitration Act creates federal substantive law requiring the parties to honor arbitration agreements, it does not create any independent federal question jurisdiction under 28 USC § 1331 or otherwise. This seems implicit in the provisions in § 3 for a stay by a "court in which such suit is pending" and in § 4 that enforcement may be ordered by "any United States district court which, save for such agreement, would have jurisdiction under title 28, in a civil action or in admiralty of the subject matter of a suit arising out of the controversy between the parties."

10. The contention is made that the Court's interpretation of § 2 of the Act renders §§ 3 and 4 "largely superfluous." This misreads our holding and the Act. In holding that the Arbitration Act preempts a state law that withdraws the power to enforce arbitration agreements, we do not hold that §§ 3 and 4 of the Arbitration Act apply to proceedings in state courts. Sec-

tion 4, for example, provides that the Federal Rules of Civil Procedure apply in proceedings to compel arbitration. The Federal Rules do not apply in such state-court proceedings.

11. * * * Justice Stevens dissents in part on the ground that § 2 of the Arbitration Act permits a party to nullify an agreement to arbitrate on "such grounds as exist at law or in equity for the revocation of any contract." We agree, of course, that a party may assert general contract defenses such as fraud to avoid enforcement of an arbitration agreement. We conclude, however, that the defense to arbitration found in the California Franchise Investment Law is not a ground that exists at law or in equity "for the revocation of *any* contract" but merely a ground that exists for the revocation of arbitration provisions in contracts subject to the California Franchise Investment Law. Moreover, under this dissenting view, "a state policy of providing special protection for franchis-

31512 of the California Franchise Investment Law violates the Supremacy Clause.

The judgment of the California Supreme Court denying enforcement of the arbitration agreement is reversed; as to the question whether the Federal Arbitration Act precludes a class-action arbitration and any other issues not raised in the California courts, no decision by this Court would be appropriate at this time. As to the latter issues, the case is remanded for further proceedings not inconsistent with this opinion.

JUSTICE STEVENS, concurring in part and dissenting in part.

The Court holds that an arbitration clause that is enforceable in an action in a federal court is equally enforceable if the action is brought in a state court. I agree with that conclusion. Although Justice O'Connor's review of the legislative history of the Federal Arbitration Act demonstrates that the 1925 Congress that enacted the statute viewed the statute as essentially procedural in nature, I am persuaded that the intervening developments in the law compel the conclusion that the Court has reached. I am nevertheless troubled by one aspect of the case that seems to trouble none of my colleagues.

For me it is not "clear beyond question that if this suit had been brought as a diversity action in a federal district court, the arbitration clause would have been enforceable." The general rule prescribed by § 2 of the Federal Arbitration Act is that arbitration clauses in contracts involving interstate transactions are enforceable as a matter of federal law. That general rule, however, is subject to an exception based on "such grounds as exist at law or in equity for the revocation of any contract." I believe that exception leaves room for the implementation of certain substantive state policies that would be undermined by enforcing certain categories of arbitration clauses.

The exercise of state authority in a field traditionally occupied by state law will not be deemed preempted by a federal statute unless that was the clear and manifest purpose of Congress. Moreover, even where a federal statute does displace state authority, it "rarely occupies a legal field completely, totally excluding all participation by the legal systems of the states . . . . Federal legislation, on the whole, has been conceived and drafted on an ad hoc basis to accomplish limited objectives. It builds upon legal relationships established by the states, altering or supplanting them only so far as necessary for the special purpose." P. Bator, P. Mishkin, D. Shapiro, & H. Wechsler, Hart and Wechsler's The Federal Courts and the Federal System 470–471 (2d ed. 1973).

ees . . . can be recognized without impairing the basic purposes of the federal statute." If we accepted this analysis, states could wholly eviscerate Congressional intent to place arbitration agreements "upon the same footing as other contracts" simply by passing statutes such as the Franchise Investment Law. We have rejected this analysis because it is in conflict with the Arbitration Act and would permit states to override the declared policy requiring enforcement of arbitration agreements.

The limited objective of the Federal Arbitration Act was to abrogate the general common-law rule against specific enforcement of arbitration agreements, and a state statute which merely codified the general common-law rule—either directly by employing the prior doctrine of revocability or indirectly by declaring all such agreements void—would be pre-empted by Act. However, beyond this conclusion, which seems compelled by the language of § 2 and case law concerning the Act, it is by no means clear that Congress intended entirely to displace state authority in this field. Indeed, while it is an understatement to say that "the legislative history of the . . . Act . . . reveals little awareness on the part of Congress that state law might be affected," it must surely be true that given the lack of a "clear mandate from Congress as to the extent to which state statutes and decisions are to be superseded, we must be cautious in construing the act lest we excessively encroach on the powers which Congressional policy, if not the Constitution, would reserve to the states."

The textual basis in the Act for avoiding such encroachment is the clause of § 2 which provides that arbitration agreements are subject to revocation on such grounds as exist at law or in equity for the revocation of any contract. The Act, however, does not define what grounds for revocation may be permissible, and hence it would appear that the judiciary must fashion the limitations as a matter of federal common law. In doing so, we must first recognize that as the " 'saving clause' in § 2 indicates, the purpose of Congress in 1925 was to make arbitration agreements as enforceable as other contracts, but not more so." The existence of a federal statute enunciating a substantive federal policy does not necessarily require the inexorable application of a uniform federal rule of decision notwithstanding the differing conditions which may exist in the several States and regardless of the decisions of the States to exert police powers as they deem best for the welfare of their citizens. Indeed the lower courts generally look to state law regarding questions of formation of the arbitration agreement under § 2, which is entirely appropriate so long as the state rule does not conflict with the policy of § 2.

A contract which is deemed void is surely revocable at law or in equity, and the California Legislature has declared all conditions purporting to waive compliance with the protections of the Franchise Investment Laws, including but not limited to arbitration provisions, void as a matter of public policy. Given the importance to the State of franchise relationships, the relative disparity in the bargaining positions between the franchisor and the franchisee, and the remedial purposes of the California Act, I believe this declaration of state policy is entitled to respect.

* * *

[A] state policy of providing special protection for franchisees, such as that expressed in California's Franchise Investment Law, can be recognized without impairing the basic purposes of the federal statute. Like the majority of the California Supreme Court, I am not persuaded that Congress intended the pre-emptive effect of this statute to be "so unyielding as to require enforcement of an agreement to arbitrate a dispute over the application of a regulatory statute which a state legislature, in conformity with analogous federal policy, has decided should be left to judicial enforcement."

Thus * * * I respectfully dissent from [the Court's] conclusion concerning the enforceability of the arbitration agreement. On that issue, I would affirm the judgment of the California Supreme Court.

JUSTICE O'CONNOR, with whom JUSTICE REHNQUIST joins, dissenting.

* * *

The majority opinion decides three issues. First, it holds that § 2 creates federal substantive rights that must be enforced by the state courts. Second, though the issue is not raised in this case, the Court states that § 2 substantive rights may not be the basis for invoking federal-court jurisdiction under 28 U.S.C. § 1331. Third, the Court reads § 2 to require state courts to enforce § 2 rights using procedures that mimic those specified for federal courts by FAA §§ 3 and 4. The first of these conclusions is unquestionably wrong as a matter of statutory construction; the second appears to be an attempt to limit the damage done by the first; the third is unnecessary and unwise.

One rarely finds a legislative history as unambiguous as the FAA's. That history establishes conclusively that the 1925 Congress viewed the FAA as a procedural statute, applicable only in federal courts, derived, Congress believed, largely from the federal power to control the jurisdiction of the federal courts.

In 1925 Congress emphatically believed arbitration to be a matter of "procedure." At hearings on the Act congressional Subcommittees were told: "The theory on which you do this is that you have the right to tell the Federal courts how to proceed."

* * *

Since Bernhardt, a right to arbitration has been characterized as "substantive," and that holding is not challenged here. But Congress in 1925 did not characterize the FAA as this Court did in 1956. Congress believed that the FAA established nothing more than a rule of procedure, a rule therefore applicable only in the federal courts.

* * *

Yet another indication that Congress did not intend the FAA to govern state-court proceedings is found in the powers Congress relied on in passing the Act. The FAA might have been grounded on Congress' powers to regulate interstate and maritime affairs, since the Act extends only to contracts in those areas. There are, indeed, references in the legislative history to the corresponding federal powers. More numerous, however, are the references to Congress' pre-Erie power to prescribe "general law" applicable in all federal courts. At the congressional hearings, for example: "Congress rests solely upon its power to prescribe the jurisdiction and duties of the Federal courts." * * * Plainly, a power derived from Congress' Art III control over federal-court jurisdiction would not by any flight of fancy permit Congress to control proceedings in state courts.

* * *

Section 2, like the rest of the FAA, should have no application whatsoever in state courts. Assuming, to the contrary, that § 2 *does* create a federal right that the state courts must enforce, state courts should nonetheless be allowed, at least in the first instance, to fashion their own procedures for enforcing the right. Unfortunately, the Court seems to direct that the arbitration clause at issue here must be *specifically* enforced; apparently no other means of enforcement is permissible.[20]

It is settled that a state court must honor federally created rights and that it may not unreasonably undermine them by invoking contrary local procedure. " '[T]he assertion of federal rights, when plainly and reasonably made, is not to be defeated under the name of local practice.' " Brown v. Western R. Co. of Alabama, 338 U.S. 294, 299 (1949). But absent specific direction from Congress the state courts have always been permitted to apply their own reasonable procedures when enforcing federal rights. Before we undertake to read a set of complex and mandatory procedures into § 2's brief and general language, we should at a minimum allow state courts and legislatures a chance to develop their own methods for enforcing the new federal rights. Some might choose to award compensatory or punitive damages for the violation of an arbitration agreement; some might award litigation costs to the party who remained willing to arbitrate; some might affirm the "validity and enforceability" of arbitration agreements in other ways. Any of these approaches would vindicate § 2 rights in a manner fully consonant with the language and background of that provision.

The unelaborated terms of § 2 certainly invite flexible enforcement. At common law many jurisdictions were hostile to arbitration agreements. That hostility was reflected in two different doctrines: "revocability," which allowed parties to repudiate arbitration agreements at any time before the arbitrator's award was made, and "invalidity" or "unenforceability," equivalent rules that flatly denied any remedy for the failure to honor an arbitration agreement. In contrast, common-law jurisdictions that enforced arbitration agreements did so in at least three different ways—through actions for damages, actions for specific enforcement, or by enforcing sanctions imposed by trade and commercial associations on members who violated arbitration

20. If my understanding of the Court's opinion is correct, the Court has made § 3 of the FAA binding on the state courts. But * * * § 3 by its own terms governs only *federal-court* proceedings. Moreover, if § 2, standing alone, creates a federal right to specific enforcement of arbitration agreements §§ 3 and 4 are, of course, largely superfluous. And if § 2 implicitly incorporates §§ 3 and 4 procedures for making arbitration agreements enforceable before arbitration begins, why not also § 9 procedures concerning venue, personal jurisdiction, and notice for enforcing an arbitrator's award after arbitration ends? One set of procedures is of little use without the other.

agreements. In 1925 a forum allowing any one of these remedies would have been thought to recognize the "validity" and "enforceability" of arbitration clauses.

This Court has previously rejected the view that state courts can adequately protect federal rights only if "such courts in enforcing the Federal right are to be treated as Federal courts and subjected pro hac vice to [federal] limitations. . . ." Minneapolis & St. Louis R. Co. v. Bombolis, 241 U.S. 211 (1916). As explained by Professor Hart:

> "The general rule, bottomed deeply in belief in the importance of state control of state judicial procedure, is that federal law takes the state courts as it finds them. . . . Some differences in remedy and procedure are inescapable if the different governments are to retain a measure of independence in deciding how justice should be administered. If the differences become so conspicuous as to affect advance calculations of outcome, and so to induce an undesirable shopping between forums, the remedy does not lie in the sacrifice of the independence of either government. It lies rather in provision by the federal government, confident of the justice of its own procedure, of a federal forum equally accessible to both litigants."

In summary, even were I to accept the majority's reading of § 2, I would disagree with the Court's disposition of this case. After articulating the nature and scope of the federal right it discerns in § 2, the Court should remand to the state court, which has acted, heretofore, under a misapprehension of federal law. The state court should determine, at least in the first instance, what procedures it will follow to vindicate the newly articulated federal rights.

The Court rejects the idea of requiring the FAA to be applied only in federal courts partly out of concern with the problem of forum shopping. The concern is unfounded. Because the FAA makes the federal courts equally accessible to both parties to a dispute, no forum shopping would be possible even if we gave the FAA a construction faithful to the congressional intent. In controversies involving incomplete diversity of citizenship there is simply no access to federal court and therefore no possibility of forum shopping. In controversies *with* complete diversity of citizenship the FAA grants federal-court access equally to both parties; no party can gain any advantage by forum shopping. Even when the party resisting arbitration initiates an action in state court, the opposing party can invoke FAA § 4 and promptly secure a federal court order to compel arbitration. See, e.g., Moses H. Cone Memorial Hospital v. Mercury Construction Corp., 460 U.S. 1 (1983).

Ironically, the FAA was passed specifically to rectify forum-shopping problems created by this Court's decision in Swift v. Tyson, 16 Pet. 1, 10 L.Ed. 865 (1842). By 1925 several major commercial States had passed state arbitration laws, but the federal courts refused to enforce those laws in diversity cases. The drafters of the FAA might have anticipated Bernhardt by legislation and required federal diversity courts to adopt the arbitration law of the State in which they sat. But they deliberately chose a different approach. As was pointed out at congressional hearings, an additional goal of the Act was to make arbitration agreements enforceable even in federal courts located in States that had no arbitration law. The drafters' plan for maintaining reasonable harmony between state and federal practices was not to bludgeon States into compliance, but rather to adopt a uniform federal law, patterned after New York's path-breaking state statute, and simultaneously to press for passage of coordinated state legislation. The key language of the Uniform Act for Commercial Arbitration was, accordingly, identical to that in § 2 of the FAA.

In summary, forum-shopping concerns in connection with the FAA are a distraction that do not withstand scrutiny. The Court ignores the drafters' carefully devised plan for dealing with those problems.

Today's decision adds yet another chapter to the FAA's already colorful history. In 1842 this Court's ruling in Swift v. Tyson set up a major obstacle to the enforcement of state arbitration laws in federal diversity courts. In 1925 Congress sought to rectify the problem by enacting the FAA; the intent was to create uniform law binding only in the federal courts. In Erie R. Co. v. Tompkins, 304 U.S. 65 (1938), and then in Bernhardt Polygraphic Co., 350 U.S. 198 (1956), this Court significantly curtailed federal power. In 1967 our decision in Prima Paint upheld the application of the FAA in a *federal-court* proceeding as a valid exercise of Congress' Commerce Clause and admiralty powers. Today the Court discovers a federal right in FAA § 2 that the state courts must enforce. Apparently confident that state courts are not competent to devise their own procedures for protecting the newly discovered federal right, the Court summarily prescribes a specific procedure, found nowhere in § 2 or its common-law origins, that the state courts are to follow.

Today's decision is unfaithful to congressional intent, unnecessary, and, in light of the FAA's antecedents and the intervening contraction of federal power, inexplicable. Although arbitration is a worthy alternative to litigation, today's exercise in judicial revisionism goes too far. I respectfully dissent.

Notes and Questions

(1) The California Labor Code regulates in an elaborate way the payment of employee wages. (For example, § 201.5 requires that discharged employees in the motion picture business must be given their earned and unpaid wages within "24 hours after discharge excluding Saturdays, Sundays, and holidays."). Section 229 provides:

> Actions to enforce the provisions of this article for the collection of due and unpaid wages claimed by an individual may be maintained without regard to the existence of any private agreement to arbitrate.

In 1973 the Supreme Court sustained a challenge to this statute, commenting sympathetically that it "was due, apparently, to the legislature's desire to protect the worker from the exploitative employer who would demand that a prospective employee sign away in advance his right to resort to the judicial system for redress of an employment grievance. * * * It may be, too, that the legislature felt that arbitration was a less than adequate protection against awarding the wage earner something short of what was due compensation." Merrill Lynch, Pierce, Fenner & Smith, Inc. v. Ware, 414 U.S. 117, 131 (1973). More recently, however, the California statute has been struck down as in conflict with the FAA. Perry v. Thomas, 107 S.Ct. 2520 (1987).

(2) Now that § 2 of the FAA makes arbitration agreements enforceable in state courts (at least in cases involving foreign or interstate commerce), does the enforcement mechanism provided by the *rest* of the Act accompany it? To what extent are state courts required to supply remedies equivalent to those in § 3 (stay of court proceedings) and § 4 (order to compel arbitration)? Compare footnote 10 of the majority opinion in *Southland* with footnote 20 of Justice O'Connor's dissent. What about Justice O'Connor's suggestion that specific performance of arbitration agreements is not necessary to vindicate the federal right because damages might be an acceptable alternative?

The same question can be raised in relation to other FAA provisions. Might § 9 (time limit for confirmation of award by the court) apply to the states? What about § 10 (limited grounds for overturning award) or § 11 (grounds for modifying or correcting award)? See Note, State Enforcement of Federally Created Rights, 73 Harv.L.Rev. 1551 (1960).

(3) Toyota terminated one of its dealers in Pennsylvania for "weak sales/penetration performance." State law prohibits the termination of a dealer's franchise "unfairly, without due regard to the equities of said dealer and without just provocation." The dealer filed a complaint with the State Board of Vehicle Manufacturers claiming that his termination was unlawful. Toyota moved to dismiss on the basis of the franchise agreement, which provided that "arbitration shall be the exclusive method for determining whether the termination is proper under the terms of this Agreement." The contract also provided that it was to be governed by Maryland law but that

> If any provision herein contravenes the laws of any state or other jurisdiction wherein this Agreement is to be performed, such provision shall be deemed to be modified to conform to such laws
> * * *.

The Board held that it had jurisdiction over the dispute, and the court affirmed. *Southland* did not govern:

> [I]n this case, it is not a provision of state law which purports to invalidate the arbitration clause, but the parties' *own* agreement which expresses their intention to consider the laws of the states in which the Agreement is performed as controlling. We believe it is

more than just a policy favoring arbitration which is at issue here. It is a policy which favors enforcing an *agreement* between parties. Thus, if the agreement of the parties is to limit the scope of arbitration, then that is the agreement which should be enforced. We think that is clearly the case here.

The court also found that the policy of *Southland* extended "only to *judicial* as opposed to *administrative* forums." It noted a "long-standing public policy of hesitancy to interfere with administrative proceedings before all administrative remedies have been exhausted," and observed that since the state had set up a special administrative tribunal to deal with such claims, the Supreme Court's concern about forum shopping was "wholly inapplicable." Mid–Atlantic Toyota Distributors, Inc. v. Charles A. Bott, Inc., 101 Pa.Cmwlth. 46, 515 A.2d 633 (1986).

Is there anything to either of these points?

(4) Oddly enough, it does not appear settled whether the FAA applies to collective bargaining agreements. Note the proviso in § 1 of the Act. But see Miller Brewing Co. v. Brewery Workers Local Union No. 9, 739 F.2d 1159, 1162 (7th Cir.1984) (§ 1 exclusion "limited to workers employed in the transportation industries"); United Electrical, Radio and Machine Workers of America v. Litton Microwave Cooking Products, 704 F.2d 393, 395 n. 2 (8th Cir.1983) (reviewing conflicting authorities). There has been little pressure to apply the Act in such circumstances, given the well-developed body of law enforcing arbitration clauses in collective bargaining agreements under § 301 of the Labor Management Relations Act.

3. The Agreement to Arbitrate

a. Arbitration Clauses and Contract Formation

Under the modern federal and state statutes we have just been introduced to, the first requisite, of course, is an *enforceable agreement* providing for arbitration between the parties to the dispute. Where an arbitration clause calls for arbitration of any *future* dispute that may arise out of a contractual relationship, the clause may well be a small, little-noticed part of a much more complex document. Parties are likely to plan primarily for their performance, and only desultorily for what may happen should trouble arise from non-performance. And where firms exchange forms printed in advance, without separately agreeing (or even paying particularly careful attention) to everything that these forms contain, the challenge to the legal system to make some sense out of the transaction is at its most intense. The stage is then set for what lawyers and law students are trained to call "the battle of the forms."

Whether an arbitration clause has become part of a valid and enforceable contract is at least in the first instance a question of ordinary contract law. You may recall in fact the rather tortured attempt of the Uniform Commercial Code to provide some solution to the "battle of the forms" problem. UCC § 2–207 provides that

> (1) A definite and seasonable expression of acceptance or a written confirmation which is sent within a reasonable time operates as an acceptance even though it states terms additional to or different from those offered or agreed upon, unless acceptance is expressly made conditional on assent to the additional or different terms.

> (2) The additional terms are to be construed as proposals for addition to the contract. Between merchants such terms become part of the contract unless:

>> (a) the offer expressly limits acceptance to the terms of the offer;

>> (b) they materially alter it; or

>> (c) notification of objection to them has already been given or is given within a reasonable time after notice of them is received.

Assume that an exchange of forms creates a contract under UCC 2–207(1) but that only the *second* form contains a clause providing for the arbitration of future disputes. Does this clause become part of the contract?

The New York Court of Appeals considered this question in In the Matter of the Arbitration between Marlene Industries Corp. v. Carnac Textiles, Inc., 45 N.Y.2d 327, 408 N.Y.S.2d 410, 380 N.E.2d 239 (1978). This case involved conflicting forms sent in confirmation of an *oral order* placed by the buyer; the seller's "acknowledgment" form, sent last, alone provided for arbitration but was not made "expressly conditional" on the buyer's assent to that or any other term. The Court of Appeals held that

> the inclusion of an arbitration agreement materially alters a contract for the sale of goods, and thus, pursuant to section 2–207(2)(b) it will not become a part of such a contract unless both parties explicitly agree to it.

> It has long been the rule in this State that the parties to a commercial transaction "will not be held to have chosen arbitration as the forum for the resolution of their disputes in the absence of an express, unequivocal agreement to that effect; absent such an explicit commitment neither party may be compelled to arbitrate." The reason for this requirement, quite simply, is that by agreeing to arbitrate a party waives in large part many of his normal rights under the procedural and substantive law of the State, and it would be unfair to infer such a significant waiver on the basis of anything less than a clear indication of intent.

> Since an arbitration agreement in the context of a commercial transaction "must be clear and direct, and must not depend upon implication, inveiglement or subtlety . . . [its] existence . . .

should not depend solely upon the conflicting fine print of commercial forms which cross one another but never meet." Thus, at least under this so-called "New York Rule", it is clear that an arbitration clause is a material addition which can become part of a contract only if it is expressly assented to by both parties. Applying these principles to this case, we conclude that the contract between Marlene and Carnac does not contain an arbitration clause; hence, the motion to permanently stay arbitration should have been granted.

In New York, therefore, an arbitration clause has been said to be a "per se material alteration" of any agreement. Fairfield–Noble Corp. v. Pressman–Gutman Co., 475 F.Supp. 899 (S.D.N.Y.1979). Cf. Jack Greenberg, Inc. v. Velleman Corp. (E.D.Pa.1985) (Lexis) (clause provided for arbitration under AAA rules "as supplemented or modified by the Meat Importers Council of America, Inc.'s Arbitration Rules"; held, "[e]ven assuming that it was not a per se material alteration, I would conclude that the clause here was material in that it would deprive Greenberg of its right to come into court to enforce the contract, without first bringing its claim before the Meat Importers Council of America.").

Notes and Questions

(1) The UCC does not define the term "materially alter." However Comment 4 to UCC § 2–207, in giving some examples, refers to clauses that would "result in surprise or hardship if incorporated without express awareness by the other party." The idea seems to be that a clause which is sufficiently important and unusual that a party would expect to have his attention specifically directed to it, should not come into the contract by way of a form that is by hypothesis commonly unread. Examples in Comment 5 of clauses which by contrast "involve no element of unreasonable surprise" are couched in terms of what is "within the range of trade practice" or "customary trade tolerances."

In many industries, of course, arbitration is a routinely-invoked, standard method of dispute resolution. Courts have even been willing to take "judicial notice" of the "common practice" of arbitration in the textile business. See Helen Whiting, Inc. v. Trojan Textile Corp., 307 N.Y. 360, 367, 121 N.E.2d 367, 370 (1954). Given the widespread acceptance of arbitration in these industries, could it be argued that an arbitration clause would not in light of the policies behind UCC § 2–207 be a "material alteration"? See Schulze and Burch Biscuit Co. v. Tree Top, Inc., 831 F.2d 709 (7th Cir.1987) (given the prior course of dealing between the parties, the buyer "had ample notice" that the seller's confirmation might include an arbitration clause; the clause was therefore not a material alteration to the contract). Cf. N & D Fashions, Inc. v. DHJ Industries, Inc., 548 F.2d 722 (8th Cir.1976) (since commercial arbitration is commonly used as a means of resolving disputes in the garment industry, "it may be inferred that the buyers should not have been surprised or subjected to unnatural hardship upon finding the clause in the contract"; *held,* however, that the district court did not err in finding the arbitration provision to be a material alteration).

(2) Might the practice of dispute resolution through arbitration be so widespread in a given trade, or so well-established in the prior dealings of the parties, that under ordinary contract principles arbitration might be an implied term of the bargain *from the very beginning*? If so, then the arbitration term would not even be an "addition" to or an "alteration" of the contract *at all.* See UCC §§ 1–201(3), 1–205(3). In Schubtex, Inc. v. Allen Snyder, Inc., 49 N.Y.2d 1, 424 N.Y.S.2d 133, 399 N.E.2d 1154 (1979), a seller had confirmed a buyer's oral order by sending a form with an arbitration clause, and the buyer (as he had done several times in the past) retained the form without objection. The Court of Appeals conceded that "a determination that [the] oral agreement included a provision for arbitration could in a proper case be implied from a course of past conduct or the custom and practice in the industry," but concluded that such evidence was lacking in that case. Three judges, including the author of the *Marlene* opinion, concurred in the result but "strongly disagree[d]" with such a suggestion:

> It is true, of course, that evidence of a trade usage or of a prior course of dealings may normally be utilized to supplement the express terms of a contract for the sale of goods. General rules of contract law, however, are not always applicable to arbitration clauses because of overriding policy considerations. * * * "[T]he threshold for clarity of agreement to arbitrate is greater than with respect to other contractual terms." * * * Where there exists good reason to require an explicit agreement, * * * it would seem most imprudent to allow a presumption of intent to supplant the need for such an agreement.

(3) Sometimes the writings exchanged by the parties will *not* create a contract under UCC § 2–207(1). Nevertheless, the parties may recognize the existence of a contract by their conduct—for example, by shipping, accepting, and paying for the goods before any dispute arises. In such a case, § 2–207(3) provides that the terms of the contract consist of "those terms on which the writings of the parties agree, together with any supplementary terms incorporated under any other provisions of this Act." May an agreement to arbitrate be brought into the contract in such circumstances as a "supplementary term" implied from custom and usage?

Recall that the FAA provides for the enforceability of "*a written provision*" in a contract to submit future disputes to arbitration. Section 1 of the Uniform Arbitration Act makes enforceable "*a provision in a written contract*" to arbitrate future disputes. Do either or both of these statutes require the arbitration clause to be an *express* part of a valid written agreement—preventing an arbitration provision from being incorporated into a contract solely on the basis of custom, trade usage, or past dealing? See C. Itoh & Co. (America) Inc. v. Jordan

Intern. Co., 552 F.2d 1228 (7th Cir.1977); Compare Collins, Arbitration and the Uniform Commercial Code, 41 N.Y.U.L.Rev. 736, 738–42 (1966) with Bernstein, The Impact of the Uniform Commercial Code upon Arbitration: Revolutionary Overthrow or Peaceful Coexistence?, 42 N.Y.U.L.Rev. 8, 9–17 (1967).

(4) A number of state statutes impose special requirements on the formation of arbitration agreements—presumably to guard against "surprise" and to insure that consent to arbitration has been knowing and informed. The Missouri arbitration statute requires a statement in ten point capital letters adjacent to or above the signature line, reading "THIS CONTRACT CONTAINS A BINDING ARBITRATION PROVISION WHICH MAY BE ENFORCED BY THE PARTIES." V.A.M.S. § 435.460. Similar disclosure requirements commonly appear in statutes governing the arbitration of medical malpractice claims. For example, Cal.Civ.Pro.Code § 1295(b) mandates that the following notice must appear in "at least ten-point bold red type" in every contract for medical services containing an arbitration clause:

"NOTICE: BY SIGNING THIS CONTRACT YOU ARE AGREEING TO HAVE ANY ISSUE OF MEDICAL MALPRACTICE DECIDED BY NEUTRAL ARBITRATION AND YOU ARE GIVING UP YOUR RIGHT TO A JURY OR COURT TRIAL. SEE ARTICLE 1 OF THIS CONTRACT."

Another model singles out certain types of arbitration agreements and conditions their validity on the parties' having first received independent legal advice. The Texas statute requires that any agreement for arbitration in a contract where an individual acquires real or personal property, services, or money or credit, for an amount of $50,000 or less, must be signed by the attorneys of both parties. The same requirement applies to agreements to arbitrate any personal injury claim. Tex.Civ.Stat. art. 224(b), (c).

Finally, an arbitration agreement may run afoul of disclosure requirements applied generally to wide classes of contracts. New York, for example, imposes precise legibility requirements (not less than "eight points in depth or five and one-half points in depth for upper case") for printed contracts in all "consumer transactions." An arbitration clause in a customer's agreement with a stockbroker was invalidated for failure to meet this requirement in Hacker v. Smith Barney, Harris Upham & Co., Inc., 131 Misc.2d 757, 501 N.Y.S.2d 977 (Special Term 1986).

(5) Would the special disclosure requirements discussed in note (4) survive challenges based on federal preemption? Even before *Southland v. Keating* a court refused to apply an earlier Texas statute—which then required that *all* arbitration clauses be signed by the parties' attorneys—to a contract within the coverage of the FAA. Collins Radio Company v. Ex–Cell–O Corp., 467 F.2d 995 (8th Cir.1972) (FAA "plainly voids all doctrines of invalidity, unenforceability and revocability which apply only to arbitration agreements.") More re-

cently, Missouri's statutory notice requirement was held inapplicable on the same grounds to an interstate commercial contract. Bunge Corp. v. Perryville Feed & Produce, Inc., 685 S.W.2d 837 (Mo. banc 1985).

The court in *Hacker v. Smith Barney,* supra note (4), perfunctorily dismissed a preemption argument based on *Southland v. Keating.* But *Hacker* is rather easily distinguishable from *Collins* and *Bunge,* isn't it?

(6) What about the "New York Rule" on contract formation exemplified by the *Marlene* case, supra? Is it likely that the FAA has any preemptive effect on this rule? The Fourth Circuit, rejecting this idea, pointed out that UCC § 2–207 is "a general rule of contract formation. * * * [It] does not apply only to arbitration clauses. Many sorts of clauses, including those disclaiming an otherwise applicable warranty of merchantability or fitness and those requiring a complaint to be made within an uncustomarily short time, are also considered material alterations under § 2–207." Supak & Sons Manufacturing Co., Inc. v. Pervel Industries, Inc., 593 F.2d 135 (4th Cir.1979). For the contrary view, arguing that the "New York Rule" is now "unacceptable" in light of *Southland v. Keating,* see Hirshman, The Second Arbitration Trilogy: The Federalization of Arbitration Law, 71 Va. L.Rev. 1305, 1358–60 (1985).

(7) A defendant refuses to participate in arbitration, asserting that he never agreed to arbitrate the dispute. Should the plaintiff first seek an order under § 4 of the FAA to "compel" arbitration? Or should he simply proceed without the defendant? The AAA Commercial Arbitration Rules permit arbitrators to proceed despite the absence of one party, although the award may not be made solely by default and the party who is present must submit evidence supporting his claim. (Rule 30).

If the defendant fails to appear and the arbitration does proceed without him, may the defendant later resist judicial enforcement of the resulting award? As in the case of default in litigation, the defendant has lost the ability to defend the claim on the merits. May he also be found to have "waived" the right to assert any defense of lack of agreement? The commentators assume that a defendant who remains out of the proceeding may still at a later time challenge the existence of an agreement to arbitrate. See M. Domke, Commercial Arbitration § 18:04 at 266 (rev. ed.). This seems also to be the sense of the Uniform Arbitration Act, which allows a court to vacate an arbitration award where "[t]here was no arbitration agreement and the issue was not adversely determined [by a court on a motion to compel or stay arbitration] and the party did not participate in the arbitration hearing without raising the objection." § 12(a)(5).

However, see Comprehensive Accounting Corp. v. Rudell, 760 F.2d 138 (7th Cir.1985). The defendants in this case refused to participate in an arbitration, and later opposed confirmation of the award on the ground that they did not actually know about the arbitration clause when they signed the agreement. The court commented that this was "irrelevant," even if the defendants could make out a claim of fraud in the inducement. "[A]fter an award has been entered, § 4 [of the FAA] is no longer in play." It was "too late" for the defendants to "sit back and allow the arbitration to go forward, and only after it was all done * * * say: oh by the way, we never agreed to the arbitration clause. That is a tactic that the law of arbitration, with its commitment to speed, will not tolerate." See also Ramonas v. Kerelis, 102 Ill.App.2d 262, 243 N.E.2d 711 (1968) ("in refusing to appear," defendant "acted at [his] own peril," and his "defense that he did not sign the contract nor was a party to the contract was lost due to a situation of his own creation"). What, then, should the defendants have done when they were notified of the arbitration?

b. The "Separability" of the Arbitration Clause

PRIMA PAINT CORP. v. FLOOD & CONKLIN MFG. CO.

Supreme Court of the United States, 1967.
388 U.S. 395, 87 S.Ct. 1801, 18 L.Ed.2d 1270.

MR. JUSTICE FORTAS delivered the opinion of the Court.

This case presents the question whether the federal court or an arbitrator is to resolve a claim of "fraud in the inducement," under a contract governed by the United States Arbitration Act of 1925, where there is no evidence that the contracting parties intended to withhold that issue from arbitration.

The question arises from the following set of facts. On October 7, 1964, respondent, Flood & Conklin Manufacturing Company, a New Jersey corporation, entered into what was styled a "Consulting Agreement," with petitioner, Prima Paint Corporation, a Maryland corporation. This agreement followed by less than three weeks the execution of a contract pursuant to which Prima Paint purchased F & C's paint business. The consulting agreement provided that for a six-year period F & C was to furnish advice and consultation "in connection with the formulae, manufacturing operations, sales and servicing of Prima Trade Sales account." These services were to be performed personally by F & C's chairman, Jerome K. Jelin, "except in the event of his death or disability." F & C bound itself for the duration of the contractual period to make no "Trade Sales" of paint or paint products in its existing sales territory or to current customers. To the consulting agreement were appended lists of F & C customers, whose patronage was to be taken over by Prima Paint. In return for these lists, the covenant not to compete, and the services of Mr. Jelin, Prima Paint agreed to pay F & C certain percentages of its receipts from the listed customers and from all others, such payments not to exceed $25,000 over the life of the agreement. The agreement took into account the possibility that Prima Paint might encounter financial difficulties, including bankruptcy, but no corresponding reference was made to possible financial problems which might be encountered by F & C. The agreement states that it "embodies the entire understanding of the parties on the subject matter." Finally, the parties agreed to a broad arbitration clause, which read in part:

"Any controversy or claim arising out of or relating to this Agreement, or the breach thereof, shall be settled by arbitration in the City of New York, in accordance with the rules then obtaining of the American Arbitration Association. . . ."

The first payment by Prima Paint to F & C under the consulting agreement was due on September 1, 1965. None was made on that date. Seventeen days later, Prima Paint did pay the appropriate amount, but into escrow. It notified attorneys for F & C that in various enumerated respects their client had broken both the consulting agreement and the earlier purchase agreement. Prima Paint's principal contention, so far as presently relevant, was that F & C had fraudulently represented that it was solvent and able to perform its contractual obligations, whereas it was in fact insolvent and intended to file a petition under Chapter XI of the Bankruptcy Act shortly after execution of the consulting agreement. Prima Paint noted that such a petition was filed by F & C on October 14, 1964, one week after the contract had been signed. F & C's response, on October 25, was to serve a "notice of intention to arbitrate." On November 12, three days before expiration of its time to answer this "notice," Prima Paint filed suit in the United States District Court for the Southern District of New York, seeking rescission of the consulting agreement on the basis of the alleged fraudulent inducement. The complaint asserted that the federal court had diversity jurisdiction.

Contemporaneously with the filing of its complaint, Prima Paint petitioned the District Court for an order enjoining F & C from proceeding with the arbitration. F & C cross-moved to stay the court action pending arbitration. F & C contended that the issue presented— whether there was fraud in the inducement of the consulting agreement—was a question for the arbitrators and not for the District Court.
* * *

The District Court granted F & C's motion to stay the action pending arbitration, holding that a charge of fraud in the inducement of a contract containing an arbitration clause as broad as this one was a question for the arbitrators and not for the court. * * * The Court of Appeals for the Second Circuit dismissed Prima Paint's appeal.
* * *

[The Court first determined that "[t]here could not be a clearer case of a contract evidencing a transaction in interstate commerce."]

Having determined that the contract in question is within the coverage of the Arbitration Act, we turn to the central issue in this case: whether a claim of fraud in the inducement of the entire contract is to be resolved by the federal court, or whether the matter is to be referred to the arbitrators. The courts of appeals have differed in their approach to this question. The view of the Court of Appeals for the Second Circuit, as expressed in this case and in others, is that—except where the parties otherwise intend—arbitration clauses as a matter of federal law are "separable" from the contract in which they are embedded, and that where no claim is made that fraud was directed to the arbitration clause itself, a broad arbitration clause will be held to encompass arbitration of the claim that the contract itself was induced by fraud.[9] The Court of Appeals for the First Circuit, on the other hand, has taken the view that the question of "severability" is one of state law, and that where a State regards such a clause as inseparable a claim of fraud in inducement must be decided by the court.

With respect to cases brought in federal court involving maritime contracts or those evidencing transactions in "commerce," we think that Congress has provided an explicit answer. That answer is to be found in § 4 of the Act, which provides a remedy to a party seeking to compel compliance with an arbitration agreement. Under § 4, with respect to a matter within the jurisdiction of the federal courts save for the existence of an arbitration clause, the federal court is instructed to order arbitration to proceed once it is satisfied that "the making of the agreement for arbitration or the failure to comply [with the arbitration agreement] is not in issue." Accordingly, if the claim is fraud in the inducement of the arbitration clause itself—an issue which goes to the "making" of the agreement to arbitrate—the federal court may proceed to adjudicate it. But the statutory language does not permit the federal court to consider claims of fraud in the inducement of the contract generally. Section 4 does not expressly relate to situations like the present in which a stay is sought of a federal action in order that arbitration may proceed. But it is inconceivable that Congress intended the rule to differ depending upon which party to the arbitration agreement first invokes the assistance of a federal court. We hold, therefore, that in passing upon a § 3 application for a stay while the parties arbitrate, a federal court may consider only issues relating to the making and performance of the agreement to arbitrate. In so concluding, we not only honor the plain meaning of the statute but also the unmistakably clear congressional purpose that the arbitration procedure, when selected by the parties to a contract, be speedy and not subject to delay and obstruction in the courts.

* * *

In the present case no claim has been advanced by Prima Paint that F & C fraudulently induced it to enter into the agreement to arbitrate "[a]ny controversy or claim arising out of or relating to this Agreement, or the breach thereof." This contractual language is easily broad enough to encompass Prima Paint's claim that both execution

---

9. The Court of Appeals has been careful to honor evidence that the parties intended to withhold such issues from the arbitrators and to reserve them for judicial resolution. We note that categories of con- tracts otherwise within the Arbitration Act but in which one of the parties characteristically has little bargaining power are expressly excluded from the reach of the Act. See § 1.

and acceleration of the consulting agreement itself were procured by fraud. Indeed, no claim is made that Prima Paint ever intended that "legal" issues relating to the contract be excluded from arbitration, or that it was not entirely free so to contract. Federal courts are bound to apply rules enacted by Congress with respect to matters—here, a contract involving commerce—over which it has legislative power. The question which Prima Paint requested the District Court to adjudicate preliminarily to allowing arbitration to proceed is one not intended by Congress to delay the granting of a § 3 stay. Accordingly, the decision below dismissing Prima Paint's appeal is

Affirmed.

MR. JUSTICE BLACK, with whom MR. JUSTICE DOUGLAS and MR. JUSTICE STEWART join, dissenting.

The Court here holds that the United States Arbitration Act, as a matter of federal substantive law, compels a party to a contract containing a written arbitration provision to carry out his "arbitration agreement" even though a court might, after a fair trial, hold the entire contract—including the arbitration agreement—void because of fraud in the inducement. The Court holds, what is to me fantastic, that the legal issue of a contract's voidness because of fraud is to be decided by persons designated to arbitrate factual controversies arising out of a valid contract between the parties. And the arbitrators who the Court holds are to adjudicate the legal validity of the contract need not even be lawyers, and in all probability will be nonlawyers, wholly unqualified to decide legal issues, and even if qualified to apply the law, not bound to do so. I am by no means sure that thus forcing a person to forgo his opportunity to try his legal issues in the courts where, unlike the situation in arbitration, he may have a jury trial and right to appeal, is not a denial of due process of law. I am satisfied, however, that Congress did not impose any such procedures in the Arbitration Act. And I am fully satisfied that a reasonable and fair reading of that Act's language and history shows that both Congress and the framers of the Act were at great pains to emphasize that nonlawyers designated to adjust and arbitrate factual controversies arising out of valid contracts would not trespass upon the courts' prerogative to decide the legal question of whether any legal contract exists upon which to base an arbitration.

* * *

Let us look briefly at the language of the Arbitration Act itself as Congress passed it. Section 2, the key provision of the Act, provides that "[a] written provision in . . . a contract . . . involving commerce to settle by arbitration a controversy thereafter arising out of such contract . . . shall be valid, irrevocable, and enforceable, *save upon such grounds as exist at law or in equity for the revocation of any contract.*" (Emphasis added.) Section 3 provides that "[i]f any suit . . . be brought . . . *upon any issue referable to arbitration* under an agreement in writing for such arbitration, the court . . . *upon being* *satisfied that the issue involved in such suit . . . is referable to arbitration under such an agreement,* shall . . . stay the trial of the action until such arbitration has been had . . ." (Emphasis added.) The language of these sections could not, I think, raise doubts about their meaning except to someone anxious to find doubts. They simply mean this: an arbitration agreement is to be enforced by a federal court unless the court, not the arbitrator, finds grounds "at law or in equity for the revocation of any contract." Fraud, of course, is one of the most common grounds for revoking a contract. If the contract was procured by fraud, then, unless the defrauded party elects to affirm it, there is absolutely no contract, nothing to be arbitrated. Sections 2 and 3 of the Act assume the existence of a valid contract. They merely provide for enforcement where such a valid contract exists. These provisions were plainly designed to protect a person against whom arbitration is sought to be enforced from having to submit his legal issues as to validity of the contract to the arbitrator. * * *

Finally, it is clear to me from the bill's sponsors' understanding of the function of arbitration that they never intended that the issue of fraud in the inducement be resolved by arbitration. They recognized two special values of arbitration: (1) the expertise of an arbitrator to decide factual questions in regard to the day-to-day performance of contractual obligations,[13] and (2) the speed with which arbitration, as contrasted to litigation, could resolve disputes over performance of contracts and thus mitigate the damages and allow the parties to continue performance under the contracts. Arbitration serves neither of these functions where a contract is sought to be rescinded on the ground of fraud. On the one hand, courts have far more expertise in resolving legal issues which go to the validity of a contract than do arbitrators.[15] On the other hand, where a party seeks to rescind a contract and his allegation of fraud in the inducement is true, an arbitrator's speedy remedy of this wrong should never result in resumption of performance under the contract. And if the contract were not procured by fraud, the court, under the summary trial procedures provided by the Act, may determine with little delay that arbitration must proceed. The only advantage of submitting the issue of fraud to arbitration is for the arbitrators. Their compensation corresponds to the volume of arbitration they perform. If they determine that a contract is void because of fraud, there is nothing further for them to

---

13. "Not all questions arising out of contracts ought to be arbitrated. It is a remedy peculiarly suited to the disposition of the ordinary disputes between merchants as to questions of fact—quantity, quality, time of delivery, compliance with terms of payment, excuses for non-performance, and the like. It has a place also in the determination of the simpler questions of law—the questions of law which arise out of these daily relations between merchants as to the passage of title, the existence of warranties, or the questions of law which are complementary to the questions of fact which we have just mentioned." Cohen & Dayton, The New Federal Arbitration Law, 12 Va.L.Rev. 265, 281 (1926).

15. "It [arbitration] is not a proper remedy for . . . questions with which the arbitrators have no particular experience and which are better left to the determination of skilled judges with a background of legal experience and established systems of law." Cohen & Dayton, supra, at 281.

arbitrate. I think it raises serious questions of due process to submit to an arbitrator an issue which will determine his compensation.

* * *

The avowed purpose of the Act was to place arbitration agreements "upon the same footing as other contracts." The separability rule which the Court applies to an arbitration clause does not result in equality between it and other clauses in the contract. I had always thought that a person who attacks a contract on the ground of fraud and seeks to rescind it has to seek rescission of the whole, not tidbits, and is not given the option of denying the existence of some clauses and affirming the existence of others. Here F & C agreed both to perform consulting services for Prima and not to compete with Prima. Would any court hold that those two agreements were separable, even though Prima in agreeing to pay F & C not to compete did not directly rely on F & C's representations of being solvent? The simple fact is that Prima would not have agreed to the covenant not to compete or to the arbitration clause but for F & C's fraudulent promise that it would be financially able to perform consulting services.

* * *

Prima here challenged in the courts the validity of its alleged contract with F & C as a whole, not in fragments. If there has never been any valid contract, then there is not now and never has been anything to arbitrate. If Prima's allegations are true, the sum total of what the Court does here is to force Prima to arbitrate a contract which is void and unenforceable before arbitrators who are given the power to make final legal determinations of their own jurisdiction, not even subject to effective review by the highest court in the land. That is not what Congress said Prima must do. It seems to be what the Court thinks would promote the policy of arbitration. I am completely unable to agree to this new version of the Arbitration Act * * *.

Notes and Questions

(1) There is a good review of recent authority in Ericksen, Arbuthnot, McCarthy, Kearney & Walsh, Inc. v. 100 Oak Street, 35 Cal.3d 312, 197 Cal.Rptr. 581, 673 P.2d 251 (1983). A law firm, complaining that the air conditioning in its offices was defective, brought suit against its landlord for breach of contract, of the covenant of quiet enjoyment, and of the warranty of habitability. The lease provided for arbitration "in the event of any dispute * * * with respect to the provisions of this Lease exclusive of those provisions relating to payment of rent." The lessor filed a motion to compel arbitration; the lessee responded that "[g]rounds exist for revocation of the agreement to arbitrate the alleged controversy in that [lessee] was falsely and fraudulently induced to enter into the lease agreement." The Supreme Court of California noted that "[t]he high courts of our sister states with cognate arbitration acts have followed the rule in *Prima Paint* with near unanimity" and held that the lessor's motion should have been granted:

> [T]he issue of fraud which is asserted here "seems inextricably
> enmeshed in the other factual issues of the case." Indeed, the
> claim of substantive breach—that the air conditioning did not
> perform properly—is totally embraced within the claim of fraud—
> that the lessor knew, at the time of the lease, that the air condi-
> tioning would not perform. Thus, if the trial court were to proceed
> to determine the fraud claim it would almost certainly have to
> decide the claim of substantive breach as well, and the original
> expectations of the parties—that such questions would be deter-
> mined through arbitration—would be totally defeated. However
> the fraud claim were determined, there would be virtually nothing
> left for the arbitrator to decide.

Two dissenting judges found the majority's result "Incredible!" and
commented that "[t]his is resupination: logic and procedure turned
upside down."

(2) The contract in *Ericksen* may not have been within the coverage of the FAA. When dealing with a contract *within* the scope of the
Federal Act, would a state court be free in any event to ignore the rule
of separability established by *Prima Paint?* For the (rather idiosyncratic) view that it would, see Atwood, Issues in Federal–State Relations
Under the Federal Arbitration Act, 37 U.Fla.L.Rev. 61, 91–93 (1985).

(3) Employee was hired as Employer's Vice–President in charge of
sales; under the agreement, his employment was to continue until he
"voluntarily leaves the employ of [Employer] or dies." The agreement
also provided for "any dispute arising out of or in connection with this
agreement" to be settled by arbitration. Employee worked for four
years before a dispute arose. The employer opposed arbitration on the
ground that since the employee had the right to quit at any time, the
employment contract was "lacking in mutuality" and therefore unenforceable; the court held that a stay of arbitration should be denied:

> In our view, the question whether the contract lacked mutuality of
> obligation, depending as it does primarily on a reading and con-
> struction of the agreement, and involving, as is obvious from the
> disagreement amongst the judges of this court and the courts
> below, substantial difficulties of interpretation, is to be determined
> by the arbitrators, not the court.

Therefore, this "contract"—which the court assumed might very possibly be invalid—nevertheless gave to the arbitrators the power to decide
the very question of validity. The court made no mention at all of the
notion of "separability." Matter of Exercycle Corp. v. Maratta, 9
N.Y.2d 329, 214 N.Y.S.2d 353, 174 N.E.2d 463 (1961).

Applying the analysis of *Prima Paint* to the facts of *Exercycle*, what
result? Compare 6A A. Corbin, Contracts § 1444, n. 40.5 (1962):

> No arbitrator has power to invent rules of law that will validate
> the contract by which his power as an arbitrator is created * * *.
> If the agreement was void for "lack of mutuality," the arbitration
> clause fell with the rest. The fact is, however, that it was not void.

Maratta had the privilege of quitting his job "at will"; but he reserved no such privilege with respect to arbitration. His promise to serve may have been "illusory" when it was made; but it was not illegal. Accompanied as it was by his promise to arbitrate differences, there was a sufficient consideration for the corporation's return promise.

(4) Contrast *Exercycle* with Hull v. Norcom, Inc., 750 F.2d 1547 (11th Cir.1985). When the employee in this case was discharged after working for almost three years, he brought suit seeking damages; the employer filed a motion to compel arbitration in accordance with the employment agreement. The contract contained a broad arbitration clause providing for arbitration of "any controversy or claim arising out of or relating to this Agreement, or the breach thereof." However, it also contained another clause granting the employer *alone* the right to bring proceedings "in any court of competent jurisdiction * * * to obtain damages for any breach of this Agreement, or to enforce the specific performance thereof by [Employee.]" As construed by the majority, this meant that the Company's obligation to arbitrate was "illusory" and that there was no "mutual obligation to arbitrate." Under New York law, said the court, arbitration agreements are not enforceable unless "mutually binding"; "the consideration exchanged for one party's promise to arbitrate must be the other party's promise to arbitrate at least some specified class of claims. Mere presence of an arbitration clause is insufficient to enforce the arbitration agreement." It therefore followed that the arbitration clause was invalid for lack of consideration.

The court rejected the proposition that *Southland v. Keating* had any bearing on the case: "[A]pplicability of the general provisions of state contract law to the determination of 'the making of an arbitration agreement' does not contravene the Federal Arbitration Act or its underlying policy."

Note that the *overall* employment contract in *Hull* was not challenged on the ground of lack of "mutuality" or "consideration." See 1 A. Corbin, Contracts §§ 125 ("One Consideration Exchanged for Several Promises"), 164 (1963). This is "separability" with a vengeance, isn't it?

Even if the Eleventh Circuit was correct in its reading of New York law in *Hull*, do you agree that the application of state law in such circumstances does not implicate federal policy?

(5) The question of "separability" is posed also by challenges on a number of other grounds to the validity of the overall agreement. See, e.g., Amicizia Societa Navegazione v. Chilean Nitrate & Iodine Sales Corp., 274 F.2d 805 (2d Cir.1960) (contract allegedly void "for want of a meeting of the minds"; arbitration award confirmed; "there is no contention of lack of a meeting of the minds in respect to the arbitration clause"). Cf. El Hoss Engineering & Transport Co. v. American Independent Oil Co., 289 F.2d 346 (2d Cir.1961) (party's acceptance of

bid subject to condition; held, error to direct arbitration); Cancanon v. Smith Barney, Harris, Upham & Co., 805 F.2d 998 (11th Cir.1986) (defendant misrepresented the nature of brokerage agreement to plaintiffs, who could not read English; held, "where the allegation is one of fraud in the factum, i.e., ineffective assent to the contract," the issue is for the court). Further dimensions of this problem are explored in the sections that follow.

c. Contracts of Adhesion and Unconscionability

Leon Russell, a recording artist and leader of a musical group, signed a contract with a promoter for the production of a series of concerts. The contract was on a standard form prepared by Russell's union, the American Federation of Musicians. It provided that Russell would be paid a stipulated percentage of the "gross receipts" of the concerts "after bona fide, receipted, sanctioned expenses," and also provided that any disputes would be submitted to the International Executive Board of the Federation for final determination. One of the concerts resulted in a net loss. A dispute then arose between Russell and the promoter over who was to bear that loss, and in particular whether the loss could be offset against the profits of the other concerts. The union president named a "referee" to hear the dispute; the referee, a former executive officer of the union, recommended that most of Russell's claim be upheld. The union's International Executive Board made its award in accordance with this recommendation, and a California trial court confirmed the award.

The California Supreme Court found the agreement to be a "contract of adhesion": "a standardized contract, which, imposed and drafted by the party of superior bargaining strength, relegates to the subscribing party only the opportunity to adhere to the contract or reject it." "All concert artists and groups of any significance or prominence" are members of the A.F. of M., and the promoter "was required by the realities of his business" to sign A.F. of M. form contracts with any concert artist with whom he wished to deal. That alone, however, did not render the contract invalid, given that adhesion contracts are widely used and are "an inevitable fact of life for all citizens." However, the court went on to find the agreement "unconscionable and unenforceable" because "it designates an arbitrator who, by reason of its status and identity, is presumptively biased in favor of one party":

> [W]e do not believe—and the Arbitration Act does not require— that the parties are or should be strictly precluded from designating as arbitrator a person or entity who, by reason of relationship to a party or some similar factor, can be expected to adopt something other than a "neutral" stance in determining disputes. At the same time we must note that when as here the contract designating such an arbitrator is the product of circumstances suggestive of adhesion, the possibility of overreaching by the domi-

nant party looms large; contracts concluded in such circumstances, then, must be scrutinized with particular care to insure that the party of lesser bargaining power, in agreeing thereto, is not left in a position depriving him of any realistic and fair opportunity to prevail in a dispute under its terms.

* * * [T]he Legislature has determined that the parties shall have considerable leeway in structuring the dispute settlement arrangements by which they are bound; while recognizing that the leeway may permit the establishment of arrangements which vary to some extent from the dead-center of "neutrality," we at the same time must insist—most especially in circumstances smacking of adhesion—that certain "minimum levels of integrity" be achieved if the arrangement in question is to pass judicial muster.

It is for the courts of course to determine—largely on a case by case basis—what these "minimum levels of integrity" shall be. In doing so it must not be lost sight of that the "contractual machinery" of the parties is intended by them to serve as a substitute for—although of course not a duplicate of—formal judicial proceedings. What is contemplated, then, is a tribunal—i.e., an entity or body which "hears and decides" disputes. (See Webster's New Internat. Dict. (2d ed. 1941) p. 2707.) * * * [A]n entity or body which by its nature is incapable of "deciding" on the basis of what it has "heard" * * * does not qualify. "Unless we close our eyes to realities, the agreement here becomes, not a contract to arbitrate, but an engagement to capitulate."

* * *

[A] contract which purports to designate one of the parties as the arbitrator of all disputes arising thereunder is to this extent illusory—the reason being that the party so designated will have an interest in the outcome which, in view of the law, will render fair and reasoned decision, based on the evidence presented, a virtual impossibility. Because, as we have explained, arbitration (as a contractually structured substitute for formal judicial proceedings) contemplates just such a decision, a contractual party may not act in the capacity of arbitrator—and a contractual provision which designates him to serve in that capacity is to be denied enforcement on grounds of unconscionability. We have also indicated that the same result would follow, and for the same reasons, when the designated arbitrator is not the party himself but one whose interests are so allied with those of the party that, for all practical purposes, he is subject to the same disabilities which prevent the party himself from serving.

Graham v. Scissor–Tail, Inc., 28 Cal.3d 807, 171 Cal.Rptr. 604, 623 P.2d 165 (1981).

Notes and Questions

(1) Further discussion of the selection of arbitrators and of arbitrator impartiality appears in Section D.1, infra p. 541.

(2) Absent such elements of potential bias on the part of the arbitrators that the court found in *Graham*, under what circumstances is an arbitration clause likely to be considered "unconscionable"?

Courts are quick to strike down as "unconscionable" arbitration clauses in adhesion contracts when they suspect that one party was not aware of the clause or that adequate efforts were not made to bring it to his attention. One such case is Wheeler v. St. Joseph Hospital, 63 Cal.App.3d 345, 133 Cal.Rptr. 775 (1976). Wheeler was admitted to the hospital one evening "for an angiogram and catheterization studies in connection with a coronary insufficiency." On admission he signed a form entitled "CONDITIONS OF ADMISSION" which included a paragraph entitled "ARBITRATION OPTION." There was a blank space which the patient could initial to indicate his refusal of arbitration, but Wheeler did not do so. After the tests were performed, Wheeler suffered a brainstem infarction rendering him a total quadriplegic. The court held that he was not required to submit his malpractice claim to arbitration. According to his wife he had signed the admission form without reading it, and neither of them was aware that it contained an arbitration clause; "it was hurriedly signed under the stressful atmosphere of a hospital admitting room without any procedures calculated to alert the patient to the existence of the 'ARBITRATION OPTION.' Nor was the patient given a copy of the agreement to permit him to study its terms under less anxious circumstances":

> Although an express waiver of jury trial is not required, by agreeing to arbitration, the patient does forfeit a valuable right. The law ought not to decree a forfeiture of such a valuable right where the patient has not been made aware of the existence of an arbitration provision or its implications. Absent notification and at least some explanation, the patient cannot be said to have exercised a "real choice" in selecting arbitration over litigation. We conclude that in order to be binding, an arbitration clause incorporated in a hospital's "CONDITIONS OF ADMISSION" form should be called to the patient's attention and he should be given a reasonable explanation of its meaning and effect, including an explanation of any options available to the patient. These procedural requirements will not impose an unreasonable burden on the hospital. The hospital's admission clerk need only direct the patient's attention to the arbitration provision, request him to read it, and give him a simple explanation of its purpose and effect, including the available options. Compliance will not require the presence of the hospital's house counsel in the admission office.

(3) A California statute requiring certain disclosures in contracts for the arbitration of medical malpractice claims was enacted in 1975,

after the events that give rise to the litigation in *Wheeler*. See supra p. 453. The court in *Wheeler* left open the question whether compliance with the prescribed statutory format of disclosure would satisfy "the requirements of awareness and understanding" laid down by the case. Would it? The California legislation does say that a contract complying with statutory formalities "is not a contract of adhesion, nor unconscionable nor otherwise improper." Cal.Civ.Pro.Code § 1295(e). Nevertheless, it has been held that even where the contract satisfies the statutory requirements, a patient may avoid arbitration if he can prove that he "did not read the many waiver notices provided and did not realize that the agreement was an agreement to arbitrate." A legislative presumption to the contrary, it was said, would impair the constitutional right to a jury trial. Ramirez v. Superior Court, Santa Clara County, 103 Cal.App.3d 746, 163 Cal.Rptr. 223 (1980).

(4) A patient was admitted to the hospital for surgery. The hospital's "standard procedure" was to have the admitting clerk explain to patients that they were signing an arbitration agreement "to settle all grievances that they have against the hospital outside of court before an arbitration panel." The trial court found the arbitration agreement binding and dismissed the patient's malpractice action; *held*, reversed. The patient's waiver of his right to a jury trial was not "knowing," since there was insufficient evidence that he had read the agreement or was even aware that it contained an arbitration clause: "Surely, in a criminal proceeding, the prosecution could not withstand a *Miranda* challenge merely by presenting a police officer's testimony that it was his 'usual practice' to inform suspects of their rights before attempting to obtain confessions." Nor was the waiver "intelligent," since the agreement did not disclose the composition of the arbitration panel. Under Michigan law, one member of the panel was required to be a doctor or hospital administrator. The court found a "substantial likelihood that a health care provider's decisions will be swayed by *unconscious subliminal bias*, impossible to detect"; it therefore held that the patient must be fully informed in advance not only of the composition of the arbitration panel but also that doctors and hospital administrators on such panels may have "an incentive to minimize the number and size of malpractice awards, because their malpractice insurance rates are directly affected by those awards." Finally, the waiver was not "voluntary," in part because on signing the agreement upon admission to the hospital, the patient was in "considerable pain." Moore v. Fragatos, 116 Mich.App. 179, 321 N.W.2d 781 (1982).

(5) If the patients in any of the preceding cases had had the opportunity to consult you in advance of treatment, would you have advised them that it was in their best interests to sign the arbitration agreement? Is it likely that the "disclosures" required in cases like *Moore* will have the same effect?

(6) Investors entered into a margin account agreement with a stock brokerage firm. The firm later sold securities worth $3 million that were held in the account as collateral for the repayment of loans it had

made to the investors. The investors brought suit claiming that this sale violated the agreement; the firm moved to compel arbitration in accordance with an arbitration clause. The investors asserted that they had been "fraudulently induced" to enter into the arbitration agreement by the firm's "failure to disclose the effect of the arbitration clause." The court held that the investors were not entitled to a jury trial of this issue:

> We know of no case holding that parties dealing at arm's length have a duty to explain to each other the terms of a written contract. We decline to impose such an obligation where the language of the contract clearly and explicitly provides for arbitration of disputes arising out of the contractual relationship. This is not a criminal case; the [plaintiffs'] argument that there was no "showing of intelligent and knowing waiver of the substantive rights at issue" is simply beside the point. * * * We see no unfairness in expecting parties to read contracts before they sign them.

Cohen v. Wedbush, Noble, Cooke, Inc., 841 F.2d 282 (9th Cir.1988). Is this consistent with the cases in the preceding notes?

(7) In addition to one party's lack of awareness of the arbitration clause, what other defects might there be in an arbitration agreement which could give rise to an argument of unconscionability? See Henderson, Contractual Problems in the Enforcement of Agreements to Arbitrate Medical Malpractice, 58 Va. L.Rev. 947, 994 (1972):

> Assuming the conventional expectations test is applied widely to medical arbitration clauses, it is essential to underscore the point that the primary reason for application of such a test is that the disadvantaged bargaining party is harmed or unfairly overreached. The factor of harm or prejudice measures the range of reasonable expectation induced by a standardized contract. * * * So unless it can be said that a medical arbitration term operates in a coercive or oppressive manner, it is difficult to see that the courts will regard it as exceeding the expectations of the average patient who accepts it.

One possible illustration of an arbitration clause that "operates in a coercive or oppressive manner" is found in Player v. Geo. M. Brewster & Son, Inc., 18 Cal.App.3d 526, 96 Cal.Rptr. 149 (1971). This was a dispute between two businesses: Brewster was a New Jersey company that had entered into a prime contract with the Army Corps of Engineers to build a dam in California; the subcontract for concrete was given to Player, a local company. The contract was "a 'house attorney' prepared form intended by Brewster to be submitted to all of its subcontractors on a take-it-or-leave-it basis," and contained a clause providing for arbitration to take place in New Jersey. The court refused to order arbitration; it noted that to enforce the contract "would be to furnish Brewster with quite a weapon," and suggested that the agreement was drafted not "for the purpose of expeditious disposition of controversies with its subcontractors," but to "discourage subcontractors with possibly legitimate claims from urging such claims because of the expense involved."

(8) The Iowa arbitration statute provides that agreements to submit future disputes to arbitration are not enforceable at all if part of a "contract of adhesion." This has been interpreted to mean that an *insured* cannot seek arbitration of a policy dispute against the objections of the insurance company! See Mutual Service Casualty Insurance Co. v. Iowa District Court, 372 N.W.2d 261 (Iowa 1985).

(9) Are general state contract-law principles of unconscionability applicable to a contract within the coverage of the FAA? See Hope v. Dean Witter Reynolds Organization, Inc., 181 Cal.App.3d 446, 226 Cal. Rptr. 439 (1986), holding that the "saving clause" in § 2 of the FAA refers to *state* law: "[U]nconscionability is a general defense to *any* contract"; "Congress did not intend to displace state contract principles of general applicability." But see Tonetti v. Shirley, 173 Cal.App.3d 1144, 219 Cal.Rptr. 616 (1985) ("California adhesion contract principles are inapplicable to the enforcement of an arbitration clause in a contract governed by the Act").

d. Arbitrability

Even if a valid agreement to arbitrate exists, that does not end the matter. The question may still arise whether the particular dispute falls within the ambit of the agreement—that is, whether the parties have agreed to submit *this* matter in controversy to decision by arbitration. This is the inquiry whether the dispute is "arbitrable"—in effect, an inquiry into the "subject matter jurisdiction" of the arbitrator to hear the case.

A T & T TECHNOLOGIES, INC. v. COMMUNICATIONS WORKERS OF AMERICA

Supreme Court of the United States, 1986.
475 U.S. 643, 106 S.Ct. 1415, 89 L.Ed.2d 648.

JUSTICE WHITE delivered the opinion of the Court.

The issue presented in this case is whether a court asked to order arbitration of a grievance filed under a collective-bargaining agreement must first determine that the parties intended to arbitrate the dispute, or whether that determination is properly left to the arbitrator.

I

AT & T Technologies, Inc. (AT & T or the Company) and the Communications Workers of America (the Union) are parties to a collective-bargaining agreement which covers telephone equipment installation workers. Article 8 of this agreement establishes that "differences arising with respect to the interpretation of this contract or the performance of any obligation hereunder" must be referred to a mutually agreeable arbitrator upon the written demand of either party. This Article expressly does not cover disputes "excluded from arbitration by other provisions of this contract."[1] Article 9 provides that, "subject to the limitations contained in the provisions of this contract, but otherwise not subject to the provisions of the arbitration clause," AT & T is free to exercise certain management functions, including the hiring and placement of employees and the termination of employment.[2] "When lack of work necessitates Layoff," Article 20 prescribes the order in which employees are to be laid off.[3]

On September 17, 1981, the Union filed a grievance challenging AT & T's decision to lay off 79 installers from its Chicago base location. The Union claimed that, because there was no lack of work at the Chicago location, the planned layoffs would violate Article 20 of the agreement. Eight days later, however, AT & T laid off all 79 workers, and soon thereafter, the Company transferred approximately the same number of installers from base locations in Indiana and Wisconsin to the Chicago base. AT & T refused to submit the grievance to arbitration on the ground that under Article 9, the Company's decision to lay off workers when it determines that a lack of work exists in a facility is not arbitrable.

The Union then sought to compel arbitration by filing suit in federal court pursuant to § 301(a) of the Labor Management Relations Act, 29 U.S.C. § 185(a). Ruling on cross-motions for summary judgment, the District Court reviewed the provisions of Articles 8, 9, and 20 and set forth the parties' arguments as follows:

> "Plaintiffs interpret Article 20 to require that there be an actual lack of work prior to employee layoffs and argue that there was no such lack of work in this case. Under plaintiffs' interpretation, Article 20 would allow the union to take to arbitration the threshold issue of whether the layoffs were justified by a lack of work. Defendant interprets Article 20 as merely providing a sequence for

1. Article 8 provides, in pertinent part, as follows:

If the National and the Company fail to settle by negotiation any differences arising with respect to the interpretation of this contract or the performance of any obligation hereunder, such differences shall (provided that such dispute is not excluded from arbitration by other provisions of this contract, and provided that the grievance procedures as to such dispute have been exhausted) be referred upon written demand of either party to an impartial arbitrator mutually agreeable to both parties.

2. Article 9 states:

The Union recognizes the right of the Company (subject to the limitations contained in the provisions of this contract, but otherwise not subject to the provisions of the arbitration clause) to exercise the functions of managing the business which involve, among other things, the hiring and placement of Employees, the termination of employment, the assignment of work, the determination of methods and equipment to be used, and the control of the conduct of work.

3. Article 20 provides, in pertinent part, "[w]hen lack of work necessitates Layoff, Employees shall be Laid–Off in accordance with Term of Employment and by Layoff groups as set forth in the following [subparagraphs stating the order of layoff]." Article 1.11 defines the term "Layoff" to mean "a termination of employment arising out of a reduction in the force due to lack of work."

any layoffs which management, in its exclusive judgment, determines are necessary. Under defendant's interpretation, Article 20 would not allow for an arbitrator to decide whether the layoffs were warranted by a lack of work but only whether the company followed the proper order in laying off the employees."

Finding that "the union's interpretation of Article 20 was at least 'arguable,'" the court held that it was "for the arbitrator, not the court to decide whether the union's interpretation has merit," and accordingly, ordered the Company to arbitrate.

The Court of Appeals for the Seventh Circuit affirmed. The Court of Appeals understood the District Court to have ordered arbitration of the threshold issue of arbitrability. The court acknowledged the "general rule" that the issue of arbitrability is for the courts to decide unless the parties stipulate otherwise, but noted that this Court's decisions in *Steelworkers v. Warrior & Gulf Navigation Co.*, 363 U.S. 574 (1960), and *Steelworkers v. American Mfg. Co.*, 363 U.S. 54 (1960), caution courts to avoid becoming entangled in the merits of a labor dispute under the guise of deciding arbitrability. From this observation, the court announced an "exception" to the general rule, under which "a court should compel arbitration of the arbitrability issue where the collective bargaining agreement contains a standard arbitration clause, the parties have not clearly excluded the arbitrability issue from arbitration, and deciding the issue would entangle the court in interpretation of substantive provisions of the collective bargaining agreement and thereby involve consideration of the merits of the dispute."

All of these factors were present in this case. Article 8 was a "standard arbitration clause," and there was "no clear, unambiguous exclusion from arbitration of terminations predicated by a lack of work determination." Moreover, although there were "colorable arguments" on both sides of the exclusion issue, if the court were to decide this question it would have to interpret not only Article 8, but Articles 9 and 20 as well, both of which are "substantive provisions of the Agreement." The court thus "decline[d] the invitation to decide arbitrability," and ordered AT & T "to arbitrate the arbitrability issue."

* * *

We granted certiorari and now vacate the Seventh Circuit's decision and remand for a determination of whether the Company is required to arbitrate the Union's grievance.

II

The principles necessary to decide this case are not new. They were set out by this Court over 25 years ago in a series of cases known as the *Steelworkers Trilogy: Steelworkers v. American Mfg. Co.; Steelworkers v. Warrior & Gulf Navigation Co.;* and *Steelworkers v. Enterprise Wheel & Car Corp.*, 363 U.S. 593 (1960). These precepts have served the industrial relations community well, and have led to continued reliance on arbitration, rather than strikes or lockouts, as the preferred method of resolving disputes arising during the term of a collective-bargaining agreement. We see no reason either to question their continuing validity, or to eviscerate their meaning by creating an exception to their general applicability.

The first principle gleaned from the *Trilogy* is that "arbitration is a matter of contract and a party cannot be required to submit to arbitration any dispute which he has not agreed so to submit." This axiom recognizes the fact that arbitrators derive their authority to resolve disputes only because the parties have agreed in advance to submit such grievances to arbitration.

The second rule, which follows inexorably from the first, is that the question of arbitrability—whether a collective-bargaining agreement creates a duty for the parties to arbitrate the particular grievance—is undeniably an issue for judicial determination. Unless the parties clearly and unmistakably provide otherwise, the question of whether the parties agreed to arbitrate is to be decided by the court, not the arbitrator.

The Court expressly reaffirmed this principle in *John Wiley & Sons, Inc. v. Livingston*, 376 U.S. 543 (1964). The "threshold question" there was whether the court or an arbitrator should decide if arbitration provisions in a collective-bargaining contract survived a corporate merger so as to bind the surviving corporation. The Court answered that there was "no doubt" that this question was for the courts. " 'Under our decisions, whether or not the company was bound to arbitrate, as well as what issues it must arbitrate, is a matter to be determined by the Court on the basis of the contract entered into by the parties.' . . . The duty to arbitrate being of contractual origin, a compulsory submission to arbitration cannot precede judicial determination that the collective bargaining agreement does in fact create such a duty."

The third principle derived from our prior cases is that, in deciding whether the parties have agreed to submit a particular grievance to arbitration, a court is not to rule on the potential merits of the underlying claims. Whether "arguable" or not, indeed even if it appears to the court to be frivolous, the union's claim that the employer has violated the collective-bargaining agreement is to be decided, not by the court asked to order arbitration, but as the parties have agreed, by the arbitrator. "The courts, therefore, have no business weighing the merits of the grievance, considering whether there is equity in a particular claim, or determining whether there is particular language in the written instrument which will support the claim. The agreement is to submit all grievances to arbitration, not merely those which the court will deem meritorious."

Finally, where it has been established that where the contract contains an arbitration clause, there is a presumption of arbitrability in the sense that "[a]n order to arbitrate the particular grievance should not be denied unless it may be said with positive assurance that the arbitration clause is not susceptible of an interpretation that covers the asserted dispute. Doubts should be resolved in favor of coverage." *Warrior & Gulf*, 363 U.S. at 582–583. Such a presumption is particularly applicable where the clause is as broad as the one employed in this case, which provides for arbitration of "any differences arising with respect to the interpretation of this contract or the performance of any obligation hereunder . . . ." In such cases, "[i]n the absence of any express provision excluding a particular grievance from arbitration, we think only the most forceful evidence of a purpose to exclude the claim from arbitration can prevail." *Warrior & Gulf*, 363 U.S., at 584–585.

This presumption of arbitrability for labor disputes recognizes the greater institutional competence of arbitrators in interpreting collective bargaining agreements, "furthers the national labor policy of peaceful resolution of labor disputes and thus best accords with the parties' presumed objectives in pursuing collective bargaining." The willingness of parties to enter into agreements that provide for arbitration of specified disputes would be "drastically reduced," however, if a labor arbitrator had the "power to determine his own jurisdiction. . . ." Cox, Reflections Upon Labor Arbitration, 72 Harv.L.Rev. 1482, 1509 (1959). Were this the applicable rule, an arbitrator would not be constrained to resolve only those disputes that the parties have agreed in advance to settle by arbitration, but instead, would be empowered "to impose obligations outside the contract limited only by his understanding and conscience." This result undercuts the longstanding federal policy of promoting industrial harmony through the use of collective-bargaining agreements, and is antithetical to the function of a collective-bargaining agreement as setting out the rights and duties of the parties.

With these principles in mind, it is evident that the Seventh Circuit erred in ordering the parties to arbitrate the arbitrability question. It is the court's duty to interpret the agreement and to determine whether the parties intended to arbitrate grievances concerning layoffs predicated on a "lack of work" determination by the Company. If the court determines that the agreement so provides, then it is for the arbitrator to determine the relative merits of the parties' substantive interpretations of the agreement. It was for the court, not the arbitrator, to decide in the first instance whether the dispute was to be resolved through arbitration.

The Union does not contest the application of these principles to the present case. Instead, it urges the Court to examine the specific provisions of the agreement for itself and to affirm the Court of Appeals on the ground that the parties had agreed to arbitrate the dispute over the layoffs at issue here. But it is usually not our function in the first instance to construe collective-bargaining contracts and arbitration clauses, or to consider any other evidence that might unmistakably demonstrate that a particular grievance was not to be subject to arbitration. The issue in the case is whether, because of express exclusion or other forceful evidence, the dispute over the interpretation of Article 20 of the contract, the layoff provision, is not subject to the arbitration clause. That issue should have been decided by the District Court and reviewed by the Court of Appeals; it should not have been referred to the arbitrator.

The judgment of the Court of Appeals is vacated, and the case is remanded for proceedings in conformity with this opinion.

JUSTICE BRENNAN, with whom THE CHIEF JUSTICE and JUSTICE MARSHALL join, concurring.

I join the Court's opinion and write separately only to supplement what has been said in order to avoid any misunderstanding on remand and in future cases.

The Seventh Circuit's erroneous conclusion that the arbitrator should decide whether this dispute is arbitrable resulted from that court's confusion respecting the "arbitrability" determination that we have held must be judicially made. Despite recognizing that Article 8 of the collective-bargaining agreement "is a standard arbitration clause, providing for arbitration of 'any differences arising with respect to the interpretation of this contract or the performance of any obligation hereunder,'" and that "there is no clear, unambiguous exclusion [of this dispute] from arbitration," the Court of Appeals thought that "there [were] colorable arguments both for and against exclusion." The "colorable arguments" referred to by the Court of Appeals were the parties' claims concerning the meaning of Articles 9 and 20 of the collective-bargaining agreement: the Court of Appeals thought that if the Union's interpretation of Article 20 was correct and management could not order lay-offs for reasons other than lack of work, the dispute was arbitrable; but if AT & T's interpretation of Article 20 was correct and management was free to order lay-offs for other reasons, the dispute was not arbitrable under Article 9. Because these were the very issues that would be presented to the arbitrator if the dispute was held to be arbitrable, the court reasoned that "determining arbitrability would enmesh a court in the merits of th[e] dispute," and concluded that the arbitrability issue should be submitted to the arbitrator.

The Court of Appeals was mistaken insofar as it thought that determining arbitrability required resolution of the parties' dispute with respect to the meaning of Articles 9 and 20 of the collective-bargaining agreement. This is clear from our opinion in *Steelworkers v. Warrior & Gulf Navigation Co.* In *Warrior & Gulf*, the Union challenged management's contracting out of labor that had previously been performed by Company employees. The parties failed to resolve the dispute through grievance procedures, and the Union requested arbitration; the Company refused, and the Union sued to compel arbitration under § 301 of the Labor Management Relations Act, 29 U.S.C. § 185. The collective-bargaining agreement contained a standard arbitration clause similar to Article 8 of the AT & T/CSA contract, i.e., providing for arbitration of all differences with respect to

474 ARBITRATION Ch. 4

the meaning or application of the contract. We held that, in light of the congressional policy making arbitration the favored method of dispute resolution, such a provision requires arbitration "unless it may be said with positive assurance that the arbitration clause is not susceptible of an interpretation that covers the asserted dispute. Doubts should be resolved in favor of coverage."

The Company in *Warrior & Gulf* relied for its argument that the dispute was not arbitrable on a "Management Functions" clause which, like Article 9 of the AT & T/CWA agreement, excluded "matters which are strictly a function of management" from the arbitration provision. We recognized that such a clause "might be thought to refer to any practice of management in which, under particular circumstances prescribed by the agreement, it is permitted to indulge." However, we also recognized that to read the clause this way would make arbitrability in every case depend upon whether management could take the action challenged by the Union; the arbitrability of every dispute would turn upon a resolution of the merits, and "the arbitration clause would be swallowed up by the exception." Therefore, we held that, where a collective-bargaining agreement contains a standard arbitration clause and the "exception" found in the Management Functions clause is general, "judicial inquiry . . . should be limited to the search for an explicit provision which brings the grievance under the cover of the [Management Functions] clause. . . ." "In the absence of any express provision excluding a particular grievance from arbitration, . . . only the most forceful evidence of a purpose to exclude the claim from arbitration can prevail. . . ."

The Seventh Circuit misunderstood these rules of contract construction and did precisely what we disapproved of in *Warrior & Gulf*— it read Article 9, a general Management Functions clause, to make arbitrability depend upon the merits of the parties' dispute. As *Warrior & Gulf* makes clear, the judicial inquiry required to determine arbitrability is much simpler. The parties' dispute concerns whether Article 20 of the collective-bargaining agreement limits management's authority to order lay-offs for reasons other than lack of work. The question for the court is "strictly confined" to whether the parties agreed to submit disputes over the meaning of Article 20 to arbitration. Because the collective-bargaining agreement contains a standard arbitration clause, the answer must be affirmative unless the contract contains explicit language stating that disputes respecting Article 20 are not subject to arbitration, or unless the party opposing arbitration—here AT & T—adduces "the most forceful evidence" to this effect from the bargaining history. Under *Warrior & Gulf*, determining arbitrability does not require the court even to consider which party is correct with respect to the meaning of Article 20.

* * *

Notes and Questions

(1) The presumption of arbitrability established by the *Steelworkers* "Trilogy" rested in large part on the unique value that arbitration was thought to have, as a "substitute for industrial strife," in the context of the administration of a collective bargaining agreement. See the excerpts from Justice Douglas' opinion in the *Warrior and Gulf* case, supra p. 422. Is there any reason to apply a similar presumption in other areas? See Schneider Moving & Storage Co. v. Robbins, 466 U.S. 364 (1984) (*Steelworkers* presumption of arbitrability "is not a proper rule of construction" in a case brought against employers by the trustees of certain multi-employer trust funds).

In cases within the coverage of the FAA, the statute's "liberal federal policy favoring arbitration agreements" has led to a similar presumption that "any doubts concerning the scope of arbitrable issues should be resolved in favor of arbitration." Moses H. Cone Memorial Hospital v. Mercury Construction Co., 460 U.S. 1, 24–25 (1983); see also Mitsubishi Motors Corp. v. Soler Chrysler–Plymouth, infra p. 501. Courts applying the FAA will tend even in commercial arbitration cases to cite routinely and to rely indiscriminately on the labor precedents. See, e.g., In the Matter of the Arbitration between the Singer Co. v. Tappan Co., 403 F.Supp. 322, 330 (D.N.J.1975), aff'd, 544 F.2d 513 (3d Cir.1976) (if the policy of judicial non-interference in labor cases is grounded on the belief that "a labor arbitrator is better able to decide complex labor issues than a judge, then it can likewise be said here that the accounting complexities which led to disagreement between well known and highly regarded accounting firms should likewise be best left for arbitration").

(2) The *Steelworkers* "Trilogy" also established that the question of "arbitrability" is not affected by the fact that the claim asserted may clearly be without any substantive merit. "Issues do not lose their quality of arbitrability because they can be correctly decided only one way." New Bedford Defense Prods. Div. v. Local No. 1113, 160 F.Supp. 103, 112 (D.Mass.1958). Is the same proposition true, as a general matter, of the "subject matter jurisdiction" of a court?

In an influential article relied on by Justice Douglas in the "Trilogy," Professor Cox argued that a dispute can rarely be confidently labeled as "frivolous" until "its industrial context," "the parties' way of life and general industrial practice," have all been brought to light: "Since the true nature of a grievance often cannot be determined until there is a full hearing upon the facts, the reasonable course is to send all doubtful cases to arbitration * * *." Cox, Reflections Upon Labor Arbitration, 72 Harv. L.Rev. 1482, 1515, 1517 (1959). And in addition, the Supreme Court was convinced that in the collective bargaining context the airing even of claims that *are* clearly "frivolous" might have a "therapeutic" or "cathartic" value, "as a safety valve for troublesome complaints." See supra p. 424. Is this likely to be true of disputes outside of the collective bargaining area?

(3) Any "presumption" in favor of arbitration remains, at least in theory, only a rule of construction. The ultimate goal is to effectuate the parties' intent, and the presumption can be overcome by language or other evidence indicating an intent to *exclude* certain items or claims from the arbitrator's consideration. See, e.g., Instructional Television Corp. v. National Broadcasting Co., 45 A.D.2d 1004, 357 N.Y.S.2d 915 (1974) (clause provided that "[a]ny unresolved questions of fact, as distinguished from questions of law, shall at the behest of either party be submitted to arbitration").

Conversely, it is at least conceivable that the parties could go so far as to entrust to the arbitrator *alone* the authority to determine the scope of his own jurisdiction. After all, is not a dispute about "arbitrability" a dispute (in the language of the arbitration clause involved in *Warrior & Gulf* "as to the meaning and application of [one of] the provisions of [the] Agreement"? However, is it likely that the parties will have wanted to do this? Are arbitrators likely to be entirely objective in deciding whether or not they have the authority to hear the merits of a case? "Once they have bitten into the enticing fruit of controversy, they are not apt to stay the satisfying of their appetite after one bite." Trafalgar Shipping Co. v. International Milling Co., 401 F.2d 568, 573–74 (2d Cir.1968) (Lumbard, C.J., dissenting). The Supreme Court has warned in collective bargaining cases that the party who asserts that the arbitrator is empowered to decide questions of arbitrability "must bear the burden of a clear demonstration of that purpose." *United Steelworkers of America v. Warrior & Gulf Navigation Company,* 363 U.S. at 583 n. 7.

(4) The "separability" principle of *Prima Paint* is also nominally a rule of construction. A court will frequently compel arbitration only after indulging in mock deference to the parties' presumed "intention" to entrust to the arbitrator the question whether the overall agreement had been induced by fraud. See, e.g., Weinrott v. Carp, 32 N.Y.2d 190, 344 N.Y.S.2d 848, 298 N.E.2d 42 (1973) (proceeding to confirm arbitration award; "technical argument about separability or nonseparability has often obscured the main goal of the court's inquiry which is to discern the parties' intent"). It need hardly be pointed out that this is little more than a fiction. It will be rare indeed that parties resisting arbitration will be able to present sufficient evidence to satisfy "their heavy burden of proving an intent not to arbitrate" the issue of fraudulent inducement. See Stateside Machinery Co., Ltd. v. Alperin, 591 F.2d 234 (3d Cir.1979).

Nevertheless, judicial reliance on rules of construction may occasionally entail some curious consequences in terms of party planning and drafting. For example, in 1961 (prior to *Prima Paint*) the Second Circuit considered an arbitration clause calling for arbitration of "any dispute or difference [that] should arise under" the agreement. It was held that this was not broad enough to cover a dispute over the fraudulent inducement of the contract. In re Kinoshita & Co., Ltd., 287 F.2d 951 (2d Cir.1961). In 1984 the same court was presented with a clause requiring arbitration of "any question or dispute [that] shall arise or occur under" the agreement. This time—despite another claim of fraudulent inducement—the court held that arbitration should be compelled. The earlier case could be "confin[ed] to its precise facts":

> We are confident that parties who have actually relied on *Kinoshita* in an attempt to formulate a narrow arbitration provision, have adopted the exact language of the arbitration provision involved in *Kinoshita.* * * * Thus, to ensure that an arbitration clause is narrowly interpreted contracting parties must use the foregoing phrase or its equivalent, although the better course, obviously, would be to specify exactly which claims are and are not arbitrable.

S.A. Mineracao Da Trindade–Samitri v. Utah International, Inc., 745 F.2d 190, 194 (2d Cir.1984).

What does "or its equivalent" mean? Does the result in *Utah International* strike you as a sensible one? Can you think of a case which is less likely to inspire confidence in the judicial process?

(5) The AAA recommends the following standard arbitration clause for use in all commercial contracts:

> Any controversy or claim arising out of or relating to this contract, or the breach thereof, shall be settled by arbitration in accordance with the Commercial Arbitration Rules of the American Arbitration Association, and judgment upon the award rendered by the Arbitrator(s) may be entered in any Court having jurisdiction thereof.

One of the advantages of arbitration is that this grant of jurisdiction can be limited or tailored to meet the particular needs and circumstances of the parties. However, more detailed clauses are likely to invite litigation over arbitrability, and may invite courts to speculate as to just what the parties were aiming at. And the departure from hallowed formulas may leave the door open to idiosyncratic judicial rulings.

For example, in Beckham v. William Bayley Co., 655 F.Supp. 288 (N.D.Tex.1987) the parties had provided for arbitration of "any disagreement * * * as to the intent of this contract." The plaintiff, a general contractor, complained that the casements and doors delivered by the defendant were warped and otherwise defective. The court held that this complaint concerning the defendant's *performance* under the contract was not covered by the arbitration clause. The court did not suggest *why* the parties might have wanted to distinguish between disputes over "intent" and disputes over "performance." (And aren't issues of "performance" precisely the kind of factual questions for which arbitration may be most suited?) Another example is Higgins v. United States Postal Service, 655 F.Supp. 739 (D.Me.1987), where the contract provided that the arbitration award was to be "final and binding." The court held that it lacked the power to confirm the award, since the contract did not stipulate that "judgment of the court shall be entered upon the award." See the FAA, § 9.

(6) Should the attitude of a court be different if the case to be decided by an arbitrator falls towards the "interest" side of the dispute spectrum? In such cases should a court begin with a different presumption as to arbitrability?

Consider Bowmer v. Bowmer, 50 N.Y.2d 288, 428 N.Y.S.2d 902, 406 N.E.2d 760 (1980). Husband and wife entered into a 37-page separation agreement providing for payment of alimony and child support according to a complex formula. Certain matters such as adjustments to the formula in the event of changes in the tax laws or in the Government's cost of living index were expressly made arbitrable. The agreement also provided that:

> Any claim, dispute or misunderstanding arising out of or in connection with this Agreement, or any breach hereof, or any default in payment by the Husband, or any matter herein made the subject matter of arbitration, shall be arbitrated.

Five years later the husband gave notice that because of changed circumstances he would be reducing his support payments, and sought to compel arbitration of this issue. The court held that the husband's claim was not arbitrable since the arbitration clause "was not intended to encompass the dispute here":

> Arbitration clauses are by now familiar provisos in separation agreements. Indeed, aside from expressing the parties' preference for a means of dispute resolution more informal, more expedient and possibly less costly than litigation, an arbitration provision may well have been intended to furnish insulation from the potential for notoriety and other stresses that so often accompanies the airing of marital disputes in court. Moreover, resort to the arbitral forum may afford the spouses an opportunity to have their grievances heard by someone who they think may be especially well qualified in matrimonial matters.
>
> But as with such provisions in the commercial context generally, the rule is clear that unless the agreement to arbitrate expressly and unequivocally encompasses the subject matter of the particular dispute, a party cannot be compelled to forego the right to seek judicial relief and instead submit to arbitration.
>
> * * *
>
> [What the husband] seeks, in essence, is to have the arbitrator rewrite the terms of the agreement because he now views them as onerous. This cannot be considered merely a claim arising from the contract. Instead, it requires the making of a new contract, not by the parties, but by the arbitrator. Obviously, the parties never agreed to such a procedure for it would mean that, once the agreement made provision for arbitration, the arbitrator would be

completely unfettered by the terms of the contract in resolving disputes.

Compare Egol v. Egol, 118 A.D.2d 76, 503 N.Y.S.2d 726 (1986), where a husband and wife in a pre-divorce agreement expressly provided for arbitration of any claims for reduction in the husband's maintenance and support obligations should he "suffer a substantial, adverse and involuntary change in his financial circumstances, making his support obligations under this Agreement inequitable or a substantial hardship for him."

(7) Agreements between brokerage firms and their employees commonly provide for arbitration of disputes "arising out of employment or the termination of employment." A former account executive brought suit against his employer for prima facie tort and slander, alleging that his superiors had (1) made defamatory statements to former customers and falsely informed others that his broker's license had been suspended, (2) attempted to "scrounge up" complaints from former customers concerning the handling of their investments, and (3) told fellow office workers that the plaintiff had stolen things from their desks at night. The court held that the first two claims were arbitrable, because they "involved significant aspects of the employment relationship," but that the third was not: "No customers or securities agencies are implicated, and no significant issue of [plaintiff's] job performance *qua* broker is implicated." Morgan v. Smith Barney, Harris Upham & Co., 729 F.2d 1163 (8th Cir.1984). Cf. Coudert v. Paine Webber Jackson & Curtis, 705 F.2d 78 (2d Cir.1983) (plaintiff claimed that she had voluntarily resigned but that her employer later falsely told customers and regulatory agencies she had been discharged for cause; defamation claim held not arbitrable). See also Dean Witter Reynolds, Inc. v. Ness, 677 F.Supp. 866 (D.S.C.1988) (brokerage firm caused former employee to be arrested for trespass when he repeatedly visited the office; employee's suit for false arrest, imprisonment, and intentional infliction of emotional distress held not arbitrable).

(8) A particular dispute may be conceded to be within the scope of the contract's arbitration clause. However, one of the parties may resist on the ground that the other has lost the right to arbitration through his delay in asserting it. The defense may be phrased indiscriminately in terms of "waiver" or "laches" or may be based on the other party's failure to comply with time limits or procedures specified in the contract for seeking arbitration. Is this a matter for the court or the arbitrator to decide?

The cases frequently distinguish between "substantive" and "procedural arbitrability" and hold that the latter is a question for the arbitrator: "Once it is determined * * * that the parties are obligated to submit the subject matter of a dispute to arbitration, 'procedural' questions which grow out of the dispute and bear on its final disposition should be left to the arbitrator." John Wiley & Sons, Inc. v. Livingston, 376 U.S. 543, 557 (1964). In *Wiley* the employer argued that the union had failed to follow the various grievance steps required in the collective bargaining agreement as prerequisites to arbitration; the Supreme Court held that this question was itself arbitrable. The Court noted that "procedural" questions will often be intertwined with the merits of the dispute, and that reserving "procedural" issues for the court "would thus not only create the difficult task of separating related issues, but would also produce frequent duplication of effort" and delay in a final decision. See also Trafalgar Shipping Co. v. International Milling Co., 401 F.2d 568 (2d Cir.1968) (laches) ("in the often esoteric field of commercial dealings," severity of prejudice suffered through delay should be submitted to "expertise of the arbitrators"). Compare, however, the fact pattern presented by General Drivers, Warehousemen & Helpers, Local Union 89 v. Moog Louisville Warehouse, 852 F.2d 871 (6th Cir.1988). In this case a collective bargaining agreement expressly provided that if the union failed to request arbitration within 15 days after the company answered an employee grievance, "then the Union shall be conclusively presumed to have accepted the Company's answer * * * and said grievance shall not thereafter be arbitrable." The court held that the employer could not be compelled to arbitrate a grievance that was untimely under this clause.

Frequently a party wishing to arbitrate a dispute will have earlier taken an active part in litigation concerning the same dispute. Perhaps he will have filed a counterclaim or engaged in discovery. He may then be met with the assertion that he has "waived" his right to arbitration. In such cases courts will often pass on the "waiver" issue, sometimes without expressly addressing the appropriateness of their doing so. It has in fact been suggested that a claim of waiver "predicated solely upon participation in the lawsuit by the party seeking arbitration" should be decided by a court, while the issue of waiver "by other conduct" should be for the arbitrator. See The Brothers Jurewicz, Inc. v. Atari, Inc., 296 N.W.2d 422 (Minn.1980). Why should this be true? See also Sherrill v. Grayco Builders, Inc., 64 N.Y.2d 261, 486 N.Y.S.2d 159, 475 N.E.2d 772 (1985) (appropriate for court to determine that party's "courthouse conduct" constituted "election" to litigate).

Does the final proviso of § 3 of the FAA have any bearing at all on the questions raised in this note?

The danger of a finding of "waiver" is discussed further in connection with the procedural aspects of arbitration; see infra p. 565.

4. Judicial Supervision and Review

For arbitration to function as an efficient process of private dispute resolution—to realize the benefits of expert decision-making with reduced cost and delay—litigation challenging the process, or aimed at upsetting the resulting award, must be minimized. One danger is exemplified by a tongue-in-cheek comment of a lawyer from Latin

America, a region where arbitration is neither familiar nor generally accepted:

> "We lawyers like arbitration. It assures us three litigations: one before, one during and one after the arbitration." [1]

In addition, arbitrators faced with heightened judicial scrutiny might ultimately come to focus less on the merits of the particular dispute, or the relationship between the parties, and more on the task of producing opinions or building a record that would enable their awards to survive later challenge.

There is thus a need to prevent a "judicialization" of the arbitral process. But at the same time, some sort of "public" supervision and control may be necessary to protect wider social interests that may be ignored or jeopardized by "private" arbitrators. The inevitable tension between these two values is a theme that figures in much of these materials.

a. Judicial Review of Arbitral Awards

By far the greatest number of the many awards rendered by arbitrators are voluntarily complied with. This seems especially true in collective bargaining cases: Elkouri hazards the rough estimate that only between 1% and 1.5% of labor arbitration awards in the private sector are ever challenged in court.[2] However, where one party is recalcitrant, official sanctions to enforce the award may be needed. Modern arbitration statutes make available the assistance of courts in enforcing arbitration awards; see, for example, §§ 9 and 13 of the FAA. How closely will a court scrutinize an arbitration award? Under what circumstances will it decline to give the award legal effect?

The conventional wisdom is that successful challenges to arbitration awards are extremely rare. "In the overwhelming majority of that miniscule portion which are appealed, only an infinitesimal few have ever been vacated." [3]

Modern arbitration statutes provide only limited grounds on the basis of which a court may refuse to enforce an award. See §§ 10 and 11 of the FAA. What does it mean to say (as in § 10(d)) that an award can be overturned if the arbitrators have "exceeded their powers"? Among other things, this can often be a peg on which to hang a challenge—even after an award is rendered—to the "arbitrability" of the dispute, at least if the point has been preserved by a proper objection before the arbitrator. The question then becomes whether the arbitrator has in fact determined an issue which the parties in their agreement have empowered him to decide. See also § 11(b).

---

1. Quoted in Nattier, International Commercial Arbitration in Latin America: Enforcement of Arbitral Agreements and Awards, 21 Tex. Int'l L.J. 397, 408 (1986).

2. F. Elkouri & E. Elkouri, How Arbitration Works 23–24 n. 5 (4th ed. 1985).

3. Jones, Evidentiary Concepts in Labor Arbitration: Some Modern Variations on Ancient Legal Themes, 13 U.C.L.A. L.Rev. 1241, 1296 (1966).

Does § 10 of the FAA have a bearing on *other* challenges to arbitration awards besides assertions that under the agreement the underlying dispute was not "arbitrable"? And are the grounds specified in the federal statute *exclusive*? Or are there other grounds on which a court can rely in refusing to enforce an award? In the materials that follow you will come across a number of variant formulations, sometimes in terms borrowed from labor arbitration cases. Do these constitute alternative grounds to vacate an award? Or do they instead amount to nothing more than dressing up the same idea in different semantic garb?

UNITED PAPERWORKERS INTERNATIONAL UNION v. MISCO, INC.

Supreme Court of the United States, 1987.
__ U.S. __, 108 S.Ct. 364, 98 L.Ed.2d 286.

JUSTICE WHITE delivered the opinion of the Court.

The issue for decision involves several aspects of when a federal court may refuse to enforce an arbitration award rendered under a collective-bargaining agreement.

I

Misco, Inc. operates a paper converting plant in Monroe, Louisiana. The Company is a party to a collective-bargaining agreement with the United Paperworkers International Union, AFL–CIO, and its union local; the agreement covers the production and maintenance employees at the plant. Under the agreement, the Company or the Union may submit to arbitration any grievance that arises from the interpretation or application of its terms, and the arbitrator's decision is final and binding upon the parties. The arbitrator's authority is limited to interpretation and application of the terms contained in the agreement itself. The agreement reserves to management the right to establish, amend, and enforce "rules and regulations regulating the discipline or discharge of employees" and the procedures for imposing discipline. Such rules were to be posted and were to be in effect "until ruled on by grievance and arbitration procedures as to fairness and necessity." For about a decade, the Company's rules had listed as causes for discharge the bringing of intoxicants, narcotics, or controlled substances on to plant property or consuming any of them there, as well as reporting for work under the influence of such substances.[2] At the time of the events involved in this case, the Company was very concerned about the use of drugs at the plant, especially among employees on the night shift.

2. Rule II.1 lists the following as causes for discharge:

"Bringing intoxicants, narcotics, or controlled substances into, or consuming intoxicants, narcotics or controlled sub-

stances in the plant, or on plant premises. Reporting for duty under the influence of intoxicants, narcotics, or controlled substances."

Isiah Cooper, who worked on the night shift for Misco, was one of the employees covered by the collective-bargaining agreement. He operated a slitter-rewinder machine, which uses sharp blades to cut rolling coils of paper. The arbitrator found that this machine is hazardous and had caused numerous injuries in recent years. Cooper had been reprimanded twice in a few months for deficient performance. On January 21, 1983, one day after the second reprimand, the police searched Cooper's house pursuant to a warrant, and a substantial amount of marijuana was found. Contemporaneously, a police officer was detailed to keep Cooper's car under observation at the Company's parking lot. At about 6:30 p.m., Cooper was seen walking in the parking lot during work hours with two other men. The three men entered Cooper's car momentarily, then walked to another car, a white Cutlass, and entered it. After the other two men later returned to the plant, Cooper was apprehended by police in the backseat of this car with marijuana smoke in the air and a lighted marijuana cigarette in the front-seat ashtray. The police also searched Cooper's car and found a plastic scales case and marijuana gleanings. Cooper was arrested and charged with marijuana possession.[3]

On January 24, Cooper told the Company that he had been arrested for possession of marijuana at his home; the Company did not learn of the marijuana cigarette in the white Cutlass until January 27. It then investigated and on February 7 discharged Cooper, asserting that in the circumstances, his presence in the Cutlass violated the rule against having drugs on the plant premises.[4] Cooper filed a grievance protesting his discharge the same day, and the matter proceeded to arbitration. The Company was not aware until September 21, five days before the hearing before the arbitrator was scheduled, that marijuana had been found in Cooper's car. That fact did not become known to the Union until the hearing began. At the hearing it was stipulated that the issue was whether the Company had "just cause to discharge the Grievant under Rule II.1" and, "[i]f not, what if any should be the remedy."

The arbitrator upheld the grievance and ordered the Company to reinstate Cooper with backpay and full seniority. The arbitrator based his finding that there was not just cause for the discharge on his consideration of seven criteria.[5] In particular, the arbitrator found that the Company failed to prove that the employee had possessed or used marijuana on company property: finding Cooper in the backseat

3. Cooper later pleaded guilty to that charge, which was not related to his being in a car with a lighted marijuana cigarette in it. The authorities chose not to prosecute for the latter incident.

4. The Company asserted that being in a car with a lit marijuana cigarette was a direct violation of the company rule against having an illegal substance on company property.

5. These considerations were the reasonableness of the employer's position, the notice given to the employee, the timing of the investigation undertaken, the fairness of the investigation, the evidence against the employee, the possibility of discrimination, and the relation of the degree of discipline to the nature of the offense and the employee's past record.

of a car and a burning cigarette in the front-seat ashtray was insufficient proof that Cooper was using or possessed marijuana on company property. The arbitrator refused to accept into evidence the fact that marijuana had been found in Cooper's car on company premises because the Company did not know of this fact when Cooper was discharged and therefore did not rely on it as a basis for the discharge.[6]

The Company filed suit in District Court, seeking to vacate the arbitration award on several grounds, one of which was that ordering reinstatement of Cooper, who had allegedly possessed marijuana on the plant premises, was contrary to public policy. The District Court agreed that the award must be set aside as contrary to public policy because it ran counter to general safety concerns that arise from the operation of dangerous machinery while under the influence of drugs, as well as to state criminal laws against drug possession. The Court of Appeals affirmed, with one judge dissenting. The court ruled that reinstatement would violate the public policy "against the operation of dangerous machinery by persons under the influence of drugs or alcohol." The arbitrator had found that Cooper was apprehended on company premises in an atmosphere of marijuana smoke in another's car and that marijuana was found in his own car on the company lot. These facts established that Cooper had violated the Company's rules and gave the company just cause to discharge him. The arbitrator did not reach this conclusion because of a "narrow focus on Cooper's procedural rights" that led him to ignore what he "knew was in fact true: that Cooper *did* bring marijuana onto his employer's premises." [The Court of Appeals also suggested that the arbitrator's "baffling view of evidence that would with ease have sustained a civil verdict and probably a criminal conviction" might in part be explained by his formal training "as an engineer and not as a lawyer." 768 F.2d 739, 741 n. 2.] * * *

Because the Courts of Appeals are divided on the question of when courts may set aside arbitration awards as contravening public policy, we granted the Union's petition for a writ of certiorari, and now reverse the judgment of the Court of Appeals.

II

The Union asserts that an arbitral award may not be set aside on public policy grounds unless the award orders conduct that violates the positive law, which is not the case here. But in the alternative, it submits that even if it is wrong in this regard, the Court of Appeals otherwise exceeded the limited authority that it had to review an arbitrator's award entered pursuant to a collective-bargaining agreement. Respondent, on the other hand, defends the public policy decision of the Court of Appeals but alternatively argues that the judgment

---

6. The arbitrator stated: "One of the rules in arbitration is that the Company must have its proof in hand before it takes disciplinary action against an employee. The Company does not take the disciplinary action and then spend eight months digging up supporting evidence to justify its actions. * * *"

below should be affirmed because of erroneous findings by the arbitrator. We deal first with the opposing alternative arguments.

A

Collective-bargaining agreements commonly provide grievance procedures to settle disputes between union and employer with respect to the interpretation and application of the agreement and require binding arbitration for unsettled grievances. In such cases, and this is such a case, the Court made clear almost 30 years ago that the courts play only a limited role when asked to review the decision of an arbitrator. The courts are not authorized to reconsider the merits of an award even though the parties may allege that the award rests on errors of fact or on misinterpretation of the contract. "The refusal of courts to review the merits of an arbitration award is the proper approach to arbitration under collective bargaining agreements. The federal policy of settling labor disputes by arbitration would be undermined if courts had the final say on the merits of the awards." *Steelworkers v. Enterprise Wheel & Car Corp.*, 363 U.S. 593, 596 (1960). As long as the arbitrator's award "draws its essence from the collective bargaining agreement," and is not merely "his own brand of industrial justice," the award is legitimate.

> "The function of the court is very limited when the parties have agreed to submit all questions of contract interpretation to the arbitrator. It is confined to ascertaining whether the party seeking arbitration is making a claim which on its face is governed by the contract. Whether the moving party is right or wrong is a question of contract interpretation for the arbitrator. In these circumstances the moving party should not be deprived of the arbitrator's judgment, when it was his judgment and all that it connotes that was bargained for." *   *   * *Steelworkers v. American Mfg. Co.*, 363 U.S. 564, 567–568 (1960).

The reasons for insulating arbitral decisions from judicial review are grounded in the federal statutes regulating labor-management relations. These statutes reflect a decided preference for private settlement of labor disputes without the intervention of government. *   *   * Because the parties have contracted to have disputes settled by an arbitrator chosen by them rather then by a judge, it is the arbitrator's view of the facts and of the meaning of the contract that they have agreed to accept. Courts thus do not sit to hear claims of factual or legal error by an arbitrator as an appellate court does in reviewing decisions of lower courts. To resolve disputes about the application of a collective-bargaining agreement, an arbitrator must find facts and a court may not reject those findings simply because it disagrees with them. The same is true of the arbitrator's interpretation of the contract. The arbitrator may not ignore the plain language of the contract; but the parties having authorized the arbitrator to give meaning to the language of the agreement, a court should not reject an award on the ground that the arbitrator misread the contract. So, too, where it is contemplated that the arbitrator will determine remedies for contract violations that he finds, courts have no authority to disagree with his honest judgment in that respect. If the courts were free to intervene on these grounds, the speedy resolution of grievances by private mechanisms would be greatly undermined. Furthermore, it must be remembered that grievance and arbitration procedures are part and parcel of the ongoing process of collective bargaining. It is through these processes that the supplementary rules of the plant are established. * * * [A]s long as the arbitrator is even arguably construing or applying the contract and acting within the scope of his authority, that a court is convinced he committed serious error does not suffice to overturn his decision. Of course, decisions procured by the parties through fraud or through the arbitrator's dishonesty need not be enforced. But there is nothing of that sort involved in this case.

B

The Company's position, simply put, is that the arbitrator committed grievous error in finding that the evidence was insufficient to prove that Cooper had possessed or used marijuana on company property. But the Court of Appeals, although it took a distinctly jaundiced view of the arbitrator's decision in this regard, was not free to refuse enforcement because it considered Cooper's presence in the white Cutlass, in the circumstances, to be ample proof that Rule II.1 was violated. No dishonesty is alleged; only improvident, even silly, factfinding is claimed. This is hardly sufficient basis for disregarding what the agent appointed by the parties determined to be the historical facts.

Nor was it open to the Court of Appeals to refuse to enforce the award because the arbitrator, in deciding whether there was just cause to discharge, refused to consider evidence unknown to the Company at the time Cooper was fired. The parties bargained for arbitration to settle disputes and were free to set the procedural rules for arbitrators to follow if they chose. Section VI of the agreement, entitled "Arbitration Procedure," did set some ground rules for the arbitration process. It forbade the arbitrator to consider hearsay evidence, for example, but evidentiary matters were otherwise left to the arbitrator. Here the arbitrator ruled that in determining whether Cooper had violated Rule II.1, he should not consider evidence not relied on by the employer in ordering the discharge, particularly in a case like this where there was no notice to the employee or the Union prior to the hearing that the Company would attempt to rely on after-discovered evidence. This, in effect, was a construction of what the contract required when deciding discharge cases: an arbitrator was to look only at the evidence before the employer at the time of discharge. As the arbitrator noted, this approach was consistent with the practice followed by other arbitrators.[8] And it was consistent with our observation in *John Wiley &*

---

8. Labor arbitrators have stated that the correctness of a discharge "must stand or fall upon the reason given at the time of discharge," see, e.g., West Va. Pulp & Pa-

Sons, Inc. v. Livingston, 376 U.S. 543, 557 (1964), that when the subject matter of a dispute is arbitrable, "procedural" questions which grow out of the dispute and bear on its final disposition are to be left to the arbitrator.

Under the Arbitration Act, the federal courts are empowered to set aside arbitration awards on such grounds only when "the arbitrators were guilty of misconduct . . . in refusing to hear evidence pertinent and material to the controversy." [9] If we apply that same standard here and assume that the arbitrator erred in refusing to consider the disputed evidence, his error was not in bad faith or so gross as to amount to affirmative misconduct.[10] Finally, it is worth noting that putting aside the evidence about the marijuana found in Cooper's car during this arbitration did not forever foreclose the Company from using that evidence as the basis for a discharge.

Even if it were open to the Court of Appeals to have found a violation of Rule II.1 because of the marijuana found in Cooper's car, the question remains whether the court could properly set aside the award because in its view discharge was the correct remedy. Normally, an arbitrator is authorized to disagree with the sanction imposed for employee misconduct. In *Enterprise Wheel,* for example, the arbitrator reduced the discipline from discharge to a 10-day suspension. The Court of Appeals refused to enforce the award, but we reversed, explaining that though the arbitrator's decision must draw its essence from the agreement, he "is to bring his informed judgment to bear in order to reach a fair solution of a problem. *This is especially true when it comes to formulating remedies.*" The parties, of course, may limit the discretion of the arbitrator in this respect; and it may be, as the Company argues, that under the contract involved here, it was within the unreviewable discretion of management to discharge an employee once a violation of Rule II.1 was found. But the parties stipulated that the issue before the arbitrator was whether there was "just" cause for the discharge, and the arbitrator, in the course of his opinion, cryptically observed that Rule II.1 merely listed causes for discharge and did not expressly provide for immediate discharge. Before disposing of the case

per Co., 10 Lab.Arb. 117, 118 (1947), and arbitrators often, but not always, confine their considerations to the facts known to the employer at the time of the discharge.

9. The Arbitration Act does not apply to "contracts of employment of . . . workers engaged in foreign or interstate commerce," but the federal courts have often looked to the Act for guidance in labor arbitration cases, especially in the wake of the holding that § 301 of the Labor Management Relations Act of 1947 empowers the federal courts to fashion rules of federal common law to govern "[s]uits for violation of contracts between an employer and a labor organization" under the federal labor laws.

10. Even in the very rare instances when an arbitrator's procedural aberrations rise to the level of affirmative misconduct, as a rule the court must not foreclose further proceedings by settling the merits according to its own judgment of the appropriate result, since this step would improperly substitute a judicial determination for the arbitrator's decision that the parties bargained for in the collective-bargaining agreement. Instead, the court should simply vacate the award, thus leaving open the possibility of further proceedings if they are permitted under the terms of the agreement. The court also has the authority to remand for further proceedings when this step seems appropriate. See [FAA] § 10(e).

on the ground that Rule II.1 had been violated and discharge was therefore proper, the proper course would have been remand to the arbitrator for a definitive construction of the contract in this respect.

C

The Court of Appeals did not purport to take this course in any event. Rather, it held that the evidence of marijuana in Cooper's car required that the award be set aside because to reinstate a person who had brought drugs onto the property was contrary to the public policy "against the operation of dangerous machinery by persons under the influence of drugs or alcohol." We cannot affirm that judgment.

A court's refusal to enforce an arbitrator's award under a collective-bargaining agreement because it is contrary to public policy is a specific application of the more general doctrine, rooted in the common law, that a court may refuse to enforce contracts that violate law or public policy. *W. R. Grace & Co. v. Rubber Workers*, 461 U.S. 757, 766 (1983). That doctrine derives from the basic notion that no court will lend its aid to one who founds a cause of action upon an immoral or illegal act, and is further justified by the observation that the public's interests in confining the scope of private agreements to which it is not a party will go unrepresented unless the judiciary takes account of those interests when it considers whether to enforce such agreements. In the common law of contracts, this doctrine has served as the foundation for occasional exercises of judicial power to abrogate private agreements.

In *W.R. Grace*, we recognized that "a court may not enforce a collective-bargaining agreement that is contrary to public policy," and stated that "the question of public policy is ultimately one for resolution by the courts." We cautioned, however, that a court's refusal to enforce an arbitrator's interpretation of such contracts is limited to situations where the contract as interpreted would violate "some explicit public policy" that is "well defined and dominant, and is to be ascertained 'by reference to the laws and legal precedents and not from general considerations of supposed public interests.' " In *W.R. Grace*, we identified two important public policies that were potentially jeopardized by the arbitrator's interpretation of the contract: obedience to judicial orders and voluntary compliance with Title VII. We went on to hold that enforcement of the arbitration award in that case did not compromise either of the two public policies allegedly threatened by the award. Two points follow from our decision in *W.R. Grace*. First, a court may refuse to enforce a collective-bargaining agreement when the specific terms contained in that agreement violate public policy. Second, it is apparent that our decision in that case does not otherwise sanction a broad judicial power to set aside arbitration awards as against public policy. Although we discussed the effect of that award on two broad areas of public policy, our decision turned on our examination of whether the award created any explicit conflict with other "laws and legal precedents" rather than an assessment of "general considerations of supposed public interests." At the very least, an alleged public policy must be properly framed under the approach set out in *W.R. Grace*, and the violation of such a policy must be clearly shown if an award is not to be enforced.

As we see it, the formulation of public policy set out by the Court of Appeals did not comply with the statement that such a policy must be "ascertained 'by reference to the laws and legal precedents and not from general considerations of supposed public interests.' " The Court of Appeals made no attempt to review existing laws and legal precedents in order to demonstrate that they establish a "well defined and dominant" policy against the operation of dangerous machinery while under the influence of drugs. Although certainly such a judgment is firmly rooted in common sense, we explicitly held in *W.R. Grace* that a formulation of public policy based only on "general considerations of supposed public interests" is not the sort that permits a court to set aside an arbitration award that was entered in accordance with a valid collective-bargaining agreement.

Even if the Court of Appeals' formulation of public policy is to be accepted, no violation of that policy was clearly shown in this case. In pursuing its public policy inquiry, the Court of Appeals quite properly considered the established fact that traces of marijuana had been found in Cooper's car. Yet the assumed connection between the marijuana gleanings found in Cooper's car and Cooper's actual use of drugs in the workplace is tenuous at best and provides an insufficient basis for holding that his reinstatement would actually violate the public policy identified by the Court of Appeals "against the operation of dangerous machinery by persons under the influence of drugs or alcohol." A refusal to enforce an award must rest on more than speculation or assumption.

In any event, it was inappropriate for the Court of Appeals itself to draw the necessary inference. To conclude from the fact that marijuana had been found in Cooper's car that Cooper had ever been or would be under the influence of marijuana while he was on the job and operating dangerous machinery is an exercise in factfinding about Cooper's use of drugs and his amenability to discipline, a task that exceeds the authority of a court asked to overturn an arbitration award. The parties did not bargain for the facts to be found by a court, but by an arbitrator chosen by them who had more opportunity to observe Cooper and to be familiar with the plant and its problems. Nor does the fact that it is inquiring into a possible violation of public policy excuse a court for doing the arbitrator's task. If additional facts were to be found, the arbitrator should find them in the course of any further effort the Company might have made to discharge Cooper for having had marijuana in his car on company premises. Had the arbitrator found that Cooper had possessed drugs on the property, yet imposed discipline short of discharge because he found as a factual matter that Cooper could be trusted not to use them on the job, the

Court of Appeals could not upset the award because of its own view that public policy about plant safety was threatened. In this connection it should also be noted that the award ordered Cooper to be reinstated in his old job or in an equivalent one for which he was qualified. It is by no means clear from the record that Cooper would pose a serious threat to the asserted public policy in every job for which he was qualified.[12]

The judgment of the Court of Appeals is reversed.

So ordered.

JUSTICE BLACKMUN, with whom JUSTICE BRENNAN joins, concurring.

I join the Court's opinion, but write separately to underscore the narrow grounds on which its decision rests and to emphasize what it is *not* holding today. In particular, the Court does not reach the issue upon which certiorari was granted: whether a court may refuse to enforce an arbitration award rendered under a collective-bargaining agreement on public policy grounds only when the award itself violates positive law or requires unlawful conduct by the employer. The opinion takes no position on this issue. See n. 12. Nor do I understand the Court to decide, more generally, in what way, if any, a court's authority to set aside an arbitration award on public policy grounds differs from its authority, outside the collective-bargaining context, to refuse to enforce a contract on public policy grounds. Those issues are left for another day.

I agree with the Court that the judgment of the Court of Appeals must be reversed and I summarize what I understand to be the three alternative rationales for the Court's decision:

1. The Court of Appeals exceeded its authority in concluding that the company's discharge of Cooper was proper under the collective-bargaining agreement. The Court of Appeals erred in considering evidence that the arbitrator legitimately had excluded from the grievance process, in second-guessing the arbitrator's factual finding that Cooper had not violated Rule II.1, and in assessing the appropriate sanction under the agreement. Absent its overreaching, the Court of Appeals lacked any basis for disagreeing with the arbitrator's conclusion that there was not "just cause" for discharging Cooper.

2. Even if the Court of Appeals properly considered evidence of marijuana found in Cooper's car and legitimately found a Rule II.1 violation, the public policy advanced by the Court of Appeals does not support its decision to set aside the award. The reinstatement of Cooper would not contravene the alleged public policy "against the operation of dangerous machinery by persons under the influence of drugs or alcohol." The fact that an employee's car contains marijuana gleanings does not indicate that the employee uses marijuana on the job or that he operates his machine while under the influence of drugs,

---

12. We need not address the Union's position that a court may refuse to enforce an award on public policy grounds only when the award itself violates a statute, regulation, or other manifestation of positive law, or compels conduct by the employer that would violate such a law.

let alone that he will report to work in an impaired state in the future. Moreover, nothing in the record suggests that the arbitrator's award, which gives the company the option of placing Cooper in a job equivalent to his old one, would require Cooper to operate hazardous machinery.

3.   The public policy formulated by the Court of Appeals may not properly support a court's refusal to enforce an otherwise valid arbitration award.   In *W.R. Grace & Co. v. Rubber Workers*, 461 U.S. 757 (1983), we stated that the public policy must be founded on "laws and legal precedents."   The Court of Appeals identified no law or legal precedent that demonstrated an "explicit public policy" against the operation of dangerous machinery by persons under the influence of drugs.   Far from being "well defined and dominant," as *W.R. Grace* prescribed, the Court of Appeals' public policy was ascertained merely "from general considerations of supposed public interests."   I do not understand the Court, by criticizing the company's public policy formulation, to suggest that proper framing of an alleged public policy under the approach set out in *W.R. Grace* would be sufficient to justify a court's refusal to enforce an arbitration award on public policy grounds. Rather, I understand the Court to hold that such compliance is merely a necessary step if an award is not to be enforced.

It is on this understanding that I join the opinion of the Court.

Notes and Questions

(1) In Hill v. Norfolk and Western Ry. Co., 814 F.2d 1192, 1194–95 (7th Cir.1987), Judge Posner wrote that

> As we have said too many times to want to repeat again, the question for decision by a federal court asked to set aside an arbitration award—whether the award is made under the Railway Labor Act, the Taft–Hartley Act, or the United States Arbitration Act—is not whether the arbitrator or arbitrators erred in interpreting the contract; it is not whether they clearly erred in interpreting the contract; it is not whether they grossly erred in interpreting the contract; it is whether they interpreted the contract.
> * * * A party can complain if the arbitrators don't interpret the contract—that is, if they disregard the contract and implement their own notions of what is reasonable and fair. * * * But a party will not be heard to complain merely because the arbitrators' interpretation is a misinterpretation.   Granted, the grosser the apparent misinterpretation, the likelier it is that the arbitrators weren't interpreting the contract at all.   But once the court is satisfied that they were interpreting the contract, judicial review is at an end, provided there is no fraud or corruption and the arbitrators haven't ordered anyone to do an illegal act.

In *Hill,* the district court had refused to disturb an award against a discharged employee.   Finding that the employee's appeal was "based largely on frivolous grounds," the Seventh Circuit on its own initiative imposed sanctions on his attorney. Judge Posner remarked that "[t]his court has been plagued by groundless lawsuits seeking to overturn arbitration awards * * *. [W]e have said repeatedly that we would punish such tactics, and we mean it." Cf. Miller Brewing Co. v. Brewery Workers Local Union No. 9, 739 F.2d 1159 (7th Cir.1984) ("because there are so few grounds for attacking arbitration awards, it is easy to pronounce most such attacks utterly groundless").

(2) Collective bargaining agreements commonly contain a clause providing that arbitrators have "no power" to "add to" or "modify any provision of the agreement." What (if anything) does this mean? What sort of contingencies is it designed to guard against? Recall Justice Douglas' observation in the *Warrior & Gulf* case that the labor arbitrator must not be confined to the express provisions of the contract, "as the industrial common law—the practices of the industry and the shop—is equally a part of the collective bargaining agreement although not expressed in it." See supra p. 423.

(3) Different arbitrators may on different occasions come to hear cases arising under the same collective bargaining agreement, and they may, on identical facts, give opposite or conflicting interpretations of the same contractual provision. In such circumstances a court may well conclude that *neither* award should be vacated, since *each* "draws its essence" from the agreement. E.g., Graphic Arts Intern. Union Local 97B v. Haddon Craftsmen, Inc., 489 F.Supp. 1088 (M.D.Pa.1979). Cf. Connecticut Light & Power Co. v. Local 420, Intern. Brotherhood of Elec. Workers, 718 F.2d 14 (2d Cir.1983) (first arbitrator had issued cease and desist order for the future; where both awards could not be implemented, the court must "select that interpretation which most nearly conforms to the intent of the parties").

———

Arbitral Decision–Making and Legal "Rules"

Some years ago a survey of commercial arbitrators found that 80 per cent of the studied arbitrators "thought that they ought to reach their decisions within the context of the principles of substantive rules of law, but almost 90 per cent believed that they were free to ignore these rules whenever they thought that more just decisions would be reached by so doing." [1] The readiness of arbitrators to depart from legal "rules" varies, of course. It will depend in part on the presumed willingness of the parties to allow them to do so, as well as on the presence or absence of attorneys and the arbitrator's own profession and degree of expertness. For example, in the highly informal "Autoline" program administered by the Better Business Bureau, volunteer arbitrators are expressly enjoined not to try to interpret a state's "lemon law" or even the language of the automobile manufacturer's warranty. Rather than basing a decision on the fact that a car

---

1. Mentschikoff, Commercial Arbitration, 61 Col.L.Rev. 846, 861 (1961).

may be "out of warranty," for example, they are told instead to be more "flexible" and to decide only on the basis of the "facts."

At the other end of the spectrum, international commercial contracts regularly contain provisions that stipulate which substantive law the arbitrator is to apply. In international transactions the choice of law is likely to affect any number of questions, from warranty obligations to prejudgment interest, as to which the various national legal systems involved may give radically different answers. Where the parties are of different nationalities they may think it fairer to insure that the transaction is governed by the law of a *third* country, unrelated to either. Another possibility is exemplified by a contract between a German and an English company, where the arbitrators were instructed to apply German law if the English company was the claimant, and English law if the German company was the claimant![2] However, there does exist a familiar alternative in international arbitration. The parties may sometimes expressly provide that the arbitrators shall decide "according to natural justice and equity" or "ex aequo et bono." (The comparable French phrase, rooted in civil law tradition, is that the arbitrators shall act as *"amiables compositeurs."*) The rules of international arbitral institutions such as the ICC and ICSID make this device available to parties who choose to give the arbitrator such authority.[3] In what sorts of cases might the parties prefer that their arbitrators proceed on the basis of general "equitable" standards of fairness? In what sorts of cases might they prefer instead that their arbitrators apply a particular body of national law?

The extent to which arbitrators are expected to follow external legal "rules" has given rise to considerable controversy in labor relations cases. The classic statement of the dilemma usually goes like this: Assume that an industrial plant begins Sunday operations; when work crews cannot be filled with volunteers, the employer selects workers for Sunday work on a rotating basis. An employee refuses to work on Sunday for religious reasons; he is discharged and a grievance is filed which proceeds to arbitration. The collective bargaining agreement forbids discharge without "just cause." Title VII of the 1964 Civil Rights Act makes it unlawful for an employer to discriminate on the basis of religion unless he can demonstrate "that he is unable to reasonably accommodate" the employee's religious practices "without undue hardship" on the conduct of his business. How should the arbitrator proceed?

The "orthodox" position among labor arbitrators seems to be that the arbitrators should adhere to the agreement and "ignore the law." The arbitrator, on this view, is merely

2. See Kerr, International Arbitration v. Litigation, [1980] J.Bus.Law 164, 172.

3. See W.L. Craig, W. Park, & J. Paulsson, International Chamber of Commerce Arbitration §§ 7.04, 18.01–18.03 (1984);

Branson & Wallace, Choosing the Substantive Law to Apply in International Commercial Arbitration, 27 Va.J.Int'l L. 39 (1986).

the parties' officially designated "reader" of the contract. He (or she) is their joint *alter ego* for the purpose of striking whatever supplementary bargain is necessary to handle the anticipated unanticipated omissions of the initial agreement * * * [T]he arbitrator's mandate is plain: tell the parties (and the courts) what the contract means and let them worry about the legal consequences.[4]

Finding "the law" and interpreting statutes and cases are tasks likely to be beyond the special competence of most arbitrators, whether legally trained or not—beyond, that is, the reasons for which they were chosen by the parties, and beyond the reasons supporting the presumption of arbitrability and the practice of deference to arbitral awards. So the conventional view is that whether an agreement is in accord with the external "law" is a question best "postponed" for later determination by the courts.[5] The fear is frequently expressed that by presuming to decide such questions themselves, arbitrators might actually be inviting closer judicial scrutiny and thus more active judicial intervention in the arbitral process—for professional arbitrators, one of the most menacing of nightmares.

There exist in the literature all sorts of nuanced variations on this "orthodox" view. An exception is usually made for situations where the parties themselves seem to "invite" the arbitrator to decide according to the law—for example, by expressly tracking the language of a statute in their agreement. It may be, though, that the entire subject is of more academic than practical interest. The paradigm case— where both law and agreement are clear and irreconcilably in conflict— will not often arise. There is usually plenty of room to reinterpret the agreement in light of the arbitrator's understanding of the requirements of the external law, and most arbitrators can be expected to deploy adequate resourcefulness to avoid any contradiction.

It is clear from the *Misco* case that *after* an award has been rendered, the arbitrator will not be treated as a sort of "lower court": A court will not decline enforcement of an award merely because the arbitrator has decided the case differently from the way a trial judge would. The books have long been full of reminders to this effect:

> If an arbitrator makes a mistake either as to law or fact, it is the misfortune of the party, and there is no help for it. There is no right of appeal, and the court has no power to revise the decisions of "judges who are of the parties' own choosing."[6]

Of course, in thinking about judicial review on matters of "law" we should distinguish between mere rules of construction, which come into play in the absence of a contrary agreement, and mandatory rules. After all, most "rules" of contract or commercial law are nothing more

4. St. Antoine, Judicial Review of Labor Arbitration Awards: A Second Look at *Enterprise Wheel* and its Progeny, 75 Mich. L. Rev. 1137, 1140, 1142 (1977).

5. Meltzer, Ruminations about Ideology, Law and Labor Arbitration, Proceedings, 20th Annual Meeting, Nat. Academy of Arbitrators 1, 17 n. 40 (1967).

6. Patton v. Garrett, 116 N.C. 847, 21 S.E. 679, 682–83 (1895).

than "gap-fillers." They supply a term where the parties have not expressly supplied one themselves; modern commercial law looks in particular to industry custom and course of dealing to furnish the "framework of common understanding controlling any general rules of law which hold only when there is no such understanding." [7] But where the parties have bargained for dispute resolution through arbitration, the method *they* have chosen to fill any gaps in the agreement is the arbitrator's interpretation. His interpretation *is* their bargain. In contrast, legal "rules" in other areas may reflect stronger and overriding governmental or societal interests. In such cases, obviously, some greater degree of arbitral deference should be expected.

In addition, the whole subject of assuring compliance with legal "rules" can often take on an air of unreality. This is particularly true in the commercial area. The obvious lesson of innumerable commercial arbitration cases is that lack of a reasoned opinion will help to insulate an award from judicial scrutiny. Consider, for example, Stroh Container Co. v. Delphi Industries, Inc., 783 F.2d 743 (8th Cir.1986). In confirming an award in this contract dispute, the court first considered whether §§ 10 and 11 of the FAA were the exclusive grounds on the basis of which an award could be vacated or modified:

> Some courts * * * have suggested that an award may be set aside if it is in "manifest disregard of the law," is completely irrational in that it fails to draw its "essence" from the agreement, or contravenes a deeply rooted public policy. These exceptions to the facial restraints on judicial review set forth in the Act are generally derived from language in United Steelworkers of America v. Enterprise Wheel & Car Corp., 363 U.S. 593 (1960), establishing the scope of judicial review in labor arbitration cases, and from dictum in Wilko v. Swan, 346 U.S. 427, 436 (1953), recognizing "manifest disregard" as a possible ground for vacating an award. * * *
>
> We need not decide, however, whether to adopt any of these exceptions since, under any one of them, the award must nevertheless be affirmed. * * * [N]either the award itself nor the record before us suggests that the arbitrators in any way manifestly disregarded the law in reaching their decision. In *Wilko,* the Court carefully distinguished an arbitrator's interpretation of the law, which is insulated from review, from an arbitrator's disregard of the law, which may open the door for judicial scrutiny. Further, such disregard must "be made clearly to appear," and may be found "when arbitrators understand and correctly state the law, but proceed to disregard the same." In the case before us, the arbitrators' decision does not clearly delineate the law applied, nor expound the reasoning and analysis used. Rather, the award presents, as the district court stated, "only a cursory discussion of

---

7. UCC § 1–205 comment 4; see also §§ 1–102(3), (4).

what the arbitrators considered to be the key points underlying the award." It therefore cannot be said that it clearly appears that the arbitrators identified applicable law and proceeded to reach a contrary position in spite of it. Nor does the absence of express reasoning by the arbitrators support the conclusion that they disregarded the law. Arbitrators are not required to elaborate their reasoning supporting an award, and to allow a court to conclude that it may substitute its own judgment for the arbitrator's whenever the arbitrator chooses not to explain the award would improperly subvert the proper functioning of the arbitral process.

Notes and Questions

(1) One California judge has advised commercial arbitrators that in the event "they feel impelled by some uncontrollable urge, literary fluency, good conscience, or mere garrulousness to express themselves about a case they have tried, the opinion should be a separate document and not part of the award itself." Loew's, Inc. v. Krug (Cal.Super.1953); *quoted in* Sherman, Analysis of Pennsylvania's Arbitration Act of 1980, 43 U.Pitts.L.Rev. 363, 397 n. 94 (1982). Or, as the AAA's Guide for Commercial Arbitrators (1985) puts it, "The obligations to the parties are better fulfilled when the award leaves no room for attack."

(2) A collective bargaining agreement provided that the contract was to continue from year to year, unless 60 days notice of termination was given by either party. An arbitrator found that the agreement had been automatically renewed in accordance with this provision: He held that the employer's letter that purported to terminate the agreement was ineffective because the employer, in violation of the National Labor Relations Act, had refused to bargain with any of the unions claiming to represent the company's employees. On a motion to vacate the award, what result? See Roadmaster Corp. v. Production & Maintenance Employees' Local 504, 851 F.2d 886 (7th Cir.1988).

(3) Under a construction contract, the contractor was entitled to a maximum of $30,000 per month for overhead costs resulting from delays in the work beyond his control. The defendants asserted that this provision would limit the contractor to $317,420; however, the contractor, in addition to other claims, demanded $647,420 for overhead. The arbitrators awarded the contractor a lump sum of $4.9 million "for all claims presented." Defendants argued that the sheer size of the total award indicated that the contractor had received the higher overhead figure. The court confirmed the award. It noted that the contractor "received only half of the damages it sought," and went on to say that "[d]efendants' position is pure speculation. The panel has not itemized its award, and there is no way to tell which portion of it is attributable to overhead. A panel is not required to itemize its award." Benjamin F. Shaw Co. v. Cincinnati Gas & Electric, 633 F.Supp. 841 (S.D.Ohio 1986). See also Craig v. Barber, 524 So.2d 974

(Miss.1988) (by agreeing to arbitration, parties contracted for an award without a reasoned opinion, and thus "waived any right to an explanation or clarification").

(4) Section 9 of the Uniform Arbitration Act permits a reviewing court to resubmit a case to the arbitrators "for the purpose of clarifying the award." Such power is occasionally used to determine the effect or scope of an award—to determine just what it was that the arbitrator had in fact decided—but rarely to compel the arbitrator to explain his reasoning process. Courts proceeding under the FAA have asserted a similar power to demand "clarification" of an award. See, e.g., Diapulse Corp. of America v. Carba, Ltd., 626 F.2d 1108 (2d Cir.1980) (arbitrator's injunction against sale of competing "similar devices" was not adequately specific as to definition of devices nor as to geographical scope or duration of injunction). A broader and more unusual exercise of judicial power is illustrated by Sargent v. Paine Webber, Jackson & Curtis, Inc., 674 F.Supp. 920 (D.D.C.1987). In this case the arbitrators, without any explanation, had awarded the customers of a brokerage firm a fraction of the amount they were claiming from the firm. The court vacated the award and remanded to the arbitrators "for a full explanation of the manner in which damages were computed": "For this Court to engage in meaningful judicial review of plaintiff's award the basis for the calculations underlying the award must be made known."

(5) A sales contract provided that the buyer would have no right to consequential damages in the event the goods proved defective, and limited damages to the difference in value between the goods as promised and those actually delivered. The total purchase price for the goods was only $984. However, the buyer claimed $7000 and the arbitrator awarded it $3780. The plaintiff defended the award by suggesting that the arbitrator must have found the contractual limitation of damages "unconscionable" "in light of trade and industry practice." The trial court, however, vacated the award on the ground that the arbitrator had "exceeded his powers." On appeal, what result? See Granite Worsted Mills, Inc. v. Aaronson Cowen, Ltd., 25 N.Y.2d 451, 306 N.Y.S.2d 934, 255 N.E.2d 168 (1969).

(6) Imagine that you have agreed to act as arbitrator in one of the cases discussed in the previous notes. Will the process by which you reach a decision be different depending on whether you are obligated to write an opinion which explains and justifies the reasons for your result? In what ways?

(7) Except in the most complex or technical cases, it is not common practice to make a record or transcript of the proceedings in commercial arbitration. See Domke, Commercial Arbitration § 24:07 (rev. ed.). This of course reinforces the absence of a reasoned opinion in making the work of a reviewing court that much more problematical. See House Grain Co. v. Obst, 659 S.W.2d 903 (Tex.App.1983) (in absence of transcript, there was insufficient evidence to support trial court's

finding that arbitration award was the result of "such gross mistake as would imply bad faith and failure to exercise honest judgment").

(8) A common rationale for deference to arbitration is that the parties have bargained for the judgment of an arbitrator rather than a court to resolve their disputes and that this bargain, once made, should be respected. Might it follow that the scope of judicial review should be broader in arbitrations arising out of "adhesion" contracts? Consider, for example, the arbitration of uninsured motorist claims under standard automobile insurance policies. Is judicial deference due to an arbitrator's award of $500 (one-sixth of funeral expenses) to the widow of a 23-year old man with two children? See In the Matter of the Arbitration of Torano v. Motor Vehicle Accident Indemnification Corp., 19 A.D.2d 356, 243 N.Y.S.2d 434 (1963) ("The award here need not be justified."). Cf. A. Widiss, Uninsured and Underinsured Motorist Insurance § 26.4 (2d ed. 1985) ("increasing number of appellate opinions" indicate that courts are more carefully scrutinizing arbitration awards in uninsured motorist cases).

Judicial Review of Awards and "Public Policy"

At the end of his shift a worker suffered a nervous breakdown; he "flew into a rage," attacked other employees, and damaged company property. He was discharged and later spent 30 days in a hospital psychiatric ward. The arbitrator found that the likelihood of a recurrence was "remote" and that he was "not at fault for his outburst"; the company was ordered to reinstate him. The district court vacated the award, noting "public policy concerns regarding the safety of the workplace." The Court of Appeals reversed, E.I. DuPont de Nemours & Co. v. Grasselli Employees Ind. Ass. of East Chicago, Inc., 790 F.2d 611 (7th Cir.1986). In his concurring opinion, Judge Easterbrook wrote:

> Suppose DuPont's contract expressly excused a single psychotic tantrum, provided the problem was unlikely to recur, or suppose a contract excused a single episode of larceny from the employer. If the firm, honestly implementing its contract with the employees, reinstated the berserker or the thief (or never discharged him), no public policy would stand in the way. If the person's immediate supervisor fired him, and someone higher in the line of command reversed that decision as a result of a grievance, there would be no greater reason for review. A contract of arbitration transfers the power of this manager to the arbitrator. If the arbitrator carries out the contract, the decision should be treated the same as the management's own. Firms may place decisionmaking authority where they please, and the Arbitration Act restricts the court to ascertaining that the arbitrator was a faithful agent of the contracting parties.

The FAA, wrote Judge Easterbrook, eliminates "any equitable power courts formerly enjoyed to decide which awards to enforce"; it is only when the contract (as construed by the arbitrator) "violates a rule of law" that the outcome may be set aside.

Notes and Questions

(1) An employee in a nuclear power plant, in order to leave early for lunch, removed a fuse that controlled a secured interlock door. He was fired for flouting safety regulations. However, an arbitrator found this "too severe" and not justified "under the total circumstances of the case," and ordered that he be reinstated. The court held that this violated "the public policy of this nation concerning strict compliance with safety regulations at nuclear facilities." *Misco* was distinguished on the ground that the safety rules were put in place pursuant to a federal regulatory scheme "to protect not only employees but also the general public." Iowa Elec. Light & Power Co. v. Local Union 204, 834 F.2d 1424 (8th Cir.1987). See also Stead Motors of Walnut Creek v. Automotive Machinists Lodge No. 1173, 843 F.2d 357, (9th Cir.1988), where an automobile mechanic was fired for recklessness in failing to tighten lug bolts on the front wheels of an automobile. This arbitrator also found discharge "too severe," since "discipline is aimed at rehabilitation," and decided instead on suspension for 120 days. The court vacated the award, holding that the arbitrator had showed a "manifest disregard" for state law: It noted that there exists in California a "well defined and dominant public policy" regarding automobile safety and maintenance.

A letter carrier was fired after being found with more than 3500 undelivered pieces of mail in his automobile. His sentence for unlawful delay of the mail was suspended, pending his completion of a rehabilitation program for compulsive gamblers. An arbitrator ordered that he be reinstated. The district court vacated the award on the ground that the policy of deference to arbitral awards had to give way to one which "gives best assurance of an efficient and reliable postal service": "The mails are simply too important to the country to make them dependent upon the vicissitudes of rehabilitation of a single letter carrier." The Court of Appeals reversed. U.S. Postal Service v. National Assoc. of Letter Carriers, 810 F.2d 1239 (D.C.Cir.1987).

Is it likely that in these cases the process of labor arbitration—so oriented towards "industrial due process" and the maintenance of good working relations between employer and union—will adequately protect the interests of society generally? Are these cases governed by *Misco*? How would Judge Easterbrook have voted to decide these cases?

(2) In an effort to promote the sale of its fighter aircraft to Saudi Arabia, Northrop entered into a "marketing agreement" with Triad. In exchange for commissions on sales, Triad was to act as Northrop's exclusive agent in soliciting contracts for aircraft for the Saudi Air Force. Some of the sales were to be made through the United States Government as a result of contracts between Northrop and the Defense

Department. The agreement was to be governed by California law and contained an arbitration clause.

Several years later the Saudi Arabian government issued a decree prohibiting the payment of commissions in connection with armaments contracts, and requiring that existing obligations for the payment of commissions be suspended. Northrop ceased paying commissions and the dispute was submitted to arbitrators, who awarded Triad over $31 million. The district court held that the arbitrator's award was "contrary to law and public policy." California's Civil Code provides that "performance of an obligation" is "excused" when it is "prevented * * * by the operation of law." The court interpreted the Saudi decree as applying to and indeed "formulated specifically with the Northrop–Triad agency relationship in mind." In addition, it noted that the Defense Department "wished to conform its policy precisely to that announced by Saudi Arabia" and was now requiring that arms suppliers under contract to the Department certify that their price included no costs for agent's commissions not approved by the purchasing country.

On appeal, what result? See Northrop Corp. v. Triad International Marketing S.A., 811 F.2d 1265 (9th Cir.1987).

(3) The United Nations Convention on the Recognition and Enforcement of Foreign Arbitral Awards (the "New York Convention") has been ratified by most important commercial nations, including the United States. This Convention requires participating states to enforce commercial arbitration awards, rendered in another state, with the same effect as if they were domestic awards (Art. III). There are a number of exceptions to the mandate of Art. III. Two of the most important are cases where

> "The award has * * * been set aside or suspended by a competent authority of the country [where the award took place]" (Art. V(1)(e)); and where

> "The recognition or enforcement of the award would be contrary to the public policy [of the country where enforcement is sought]" (Art. V(2)(b)).

American cases have narrowly confined the latter defense to the exceptional situation "where enforcement would violate the forum country's most basic notions of morality and justice." Parsons & Whittemore Overseas Co., Inc. v. Societe Generale De L'Industrie Du Papier (Rakta), 508 F.2d 969, 974 (2d Cir.1974). See also Brandeis Intsel Ltd. v. Calabrian Chemicals Corp., 656 F.Supp. 160 (S.D.N.Y. 1987) (defense of "manifest disregard of the law" does not rise to the level of a "public policy" violation within the meaning of Art. V).

(4) A defendant in an arbitration asserts that if the dispute had been litigated, the state's statute of limitations would have barred the underlying claim. The arbitrator finds that questions relating to the statute of limitations are within the scope of the arbitration clause, and rules in favor of the claimant. On a motion to vacate the award, what

result? See Har–Mar, Inc. v. Thorsen & Thorshov, Inc., 300 Minn. 149, 218 N.W.2d 751 (1974) (statute of limitations applies only to "judicial proceedings" and does not bar arbitration); Hanes Corp. v. Millard, 531 F.2d 585 (D.C.Cir.1976) ("the arbitrator may be forced to decide at what point any breach might have occurred and when the [plaintiffs] did or should have acquired knowledge of the alleged breach. Such an inquiry will require considerable factual probing"). A New York statute permits a party, by application to the court, to assert the statute of limitations "as a bar to arbitration"; "the failure to assert such bar by such application shall not preclude its assertion before the arbitrators, who may, in their sole discretion, apply or not apply the bar." N.Y.C.P. L.R. § 7502(b).

b. "Public Policy" and Arbitrability

MITSUBISHI MOTORS CORP. v. SOLER CHRYSLER– PLYMOUTH, INC.

Supreme Court of the United States, 1985.
473 U.S. 614, 105 S.Ct. 3346, 87 L.Ed.2d 444.

JUSTICE BLACKMUN delivered the opinion of the Court.

The principal question presented by these cases is the arbitrability, pursuant to the federal Arbitration Act and the Convention on the Recognition and Enforcement of Foreign Arbitral Awards (Convention), of claims arising under the Sherman Act, 15 U.S.C. § 1 et seq., and encompassed within a valid arbitration clause in an agreement embodying an international commercial transaction.

I

Petitioner-cross-respondent Mitsubishi Motors Corporation (Mitsubishi) is a Japanese corporation which manufactures automobiles and has its principal place of business in Tokyo, Japan. Mitsubishi is the product of a joint venture between, on the one hand, Chrysler International, S.A. ("CISA"), a Swiss corporation registered in Geneva and wholly owned by Chrysler Corporation, and, on the other, Mitsubishi Heavy Industries, Inc., a Japanese corporation. The aim of the joint venture was the distribution through Chrysler dealers outside the continental United States of vehicles manufactured by Mitsubishi and bearing Chrysler and Mitsubishi trademarks. Respondent-cross-respondent Soler Chrysler–Plymouth, Inc. (Soler), is a Puerto Rico corporation with its principal place of business in Pueblo Viejo, Guaynabo, Puerto Rico.

On October 31, 1979, Soler entered into a Distributor Agreement with CISA which provided for the sale by Soler of Mitsubishi-manufactured vehicles within a designated area, including metropolitan San Juan. On the same date, CISA, Soler, and Mitsubishi entered into a Sales Procedure Agreement (Sales Agreement) which, referring to the

Distributor Agreement, provided for the direct sale of Mitsubishi products to Soler and governed the terms and conditions of such sales. Paragraph VI of the Sales Agreement, labeled "Arbitration of Certain Matters," provides:

> "All disputes, controversies or differences which may arise between [Mitsubishi] and [Soler] out of or in relation to Articles I–B through V of this Agreement or for the breach thereof, shall be finally settled by arbitration in Japan in accordance with the rules and regulations of the Japan Commercial Arbitration Association."

Initially, Soler did a brisk business in Mitsubishi-manufactured vehicles. As a result of its strong performance, its minimum sales volume, specified by Mitsubishi and CISA, and agreed to by Soler, for the 1981 model year was substantially increased. In early 1981, however, the new-car market slackened. Soler ran into serious difficulties in meeting the expected sales volume, and by the spring of 1981 it felt itself compelled to request that Mitsubishi delay or cancel shipment of several orders. About the same time, Soler attempted to arrange for the transshipment of a quantity of its vehicles for sale in the continental United States and Latin America. Mitsubishi and CISA, however, refused permission for any such diversion, citing a variety of reasons, and no vehicles were transshipped. Attempts to work out these difficulties failed. Mitsubishi eventually withheld shipment of 966 vehicles, apparently representing orders placed for May, June, and July 1981 production, responsibility for which Soler disclaimed in February 1982.

The following month, Mitsubishi brought an action against Soler in the United States District Court for the District of Puerto Rico under the federal Arbitration Act and the Convention.[2] Mitsubishi sought an order to compel arbitration in accord with ¶ VI of the Sales Agreement. Shortly after filing the complaint, Mitsubishi filed a request for arbitration before the Japan Commercial Arbitration Association.

Soler denied the allegations and counterclaimed against both Mitsubishi and CISA. It alleged numerous breaches by Mitsubishi of the Sales Agreement, raised a pair of defamation claims, and asserted causes of action under the Sherman Act; the federal Automobile Dealers' Day in Court Act; the Puerto Rico competition statute; and the Puerto Rico Dealers' Contracts Act. In the counterclaim premised on the Sherman Act, Soler alleged that Mitsubishi and CISA had conspired to divide markets in restraint of trade. To effectuate the plan, according to Soler, Mitsubishi had refused to permit Soler to resell to buyers in North, Central, or South America vehicles it had obligated itself to purchase from Mitsubishi; had refused to ship

2. The complaint alleged that Soler had failed to pay for 966 ordered vehicles; that it had failed to pay contractual "distress unit penalties," intended to reimburse Mitsubishi for storage costs and interest charges incurred because of Soler's failure to take shipment of ordered vehicles; that Soler's failure to fulfill warranty obligations threatened Mitsubishi's reputation and good will; * * * and that the Distributor and Sales Agreements had expired by their terms or, alternatively, that Soler had surrendered its rights under the Sales Agreement.

ordered vehicles or the parts, such as heaters and defoggers, that would be necessary to permit Soler to make its vehicles suitable for resale outside Puerto Rico; and had coercively attempted to replace Soler and its other Puerto Rico distributors with a wholly owned subsidiary which would serve as the exclusive Mitsubishi distributor in Puerto Rico.

After a hearing, the District Court ordered Mitsubishi and Soler to arbitrate each of the issues raised in the complaint and in all the counterclaims save two and a portion of a third. [The Court of Appeals agreed that the arbitration clause "encompass[ed] virtually all the claims arising under the various statutes, including all those arising under the Sherman Act." [9] It held, however, that arbitration of Soler's antitrust claims could not be compelled.]

* * *

II

At the outset, we address the contention raised in Soler's cross-petition that the arbitration clause at issue may not be read to encompass the statutory counterclaims stated in its answer to the complaint. In making this argument, Soler does not question the Court of Appeals' application of ¶ VI of the Sales Agreement to the disputes involved here as a matter of standard contract interpretation. Instead, it argues that as a matter of law a court may not construe an arbitration agreement to encompass claims arising out of statutes designed to protect a class to which the party resisting arbitration belongs "unless [that party] has expressly agreed" to arbitrate those claims, by which Soler presumably means that the arbitration clause must specifically mention the statute giving rise to the claims that a party to the clause seeks to arbitrate. Soler reasons that, because it falls within the class for whose benefit the federal and local antitrust laws and dealers' acts were passed, but the arbitration clause at issue does not mention these statutes or statutes in general, the clause cannot be read to contemplate arbitration of these statutory claims.

We do not agree, for we find no warrant in the Arbitration Act for implying in every contract within its ken a presumption against arbitration of statutory claims. * * *

9. As the Court of Appeals saw it, "[t]he question . . . is not whether the arbitration clause mentions antitrust or any other particular cause of action, but whether the factual allegations underlying Soler's counterclaims—and Mitsubishi's bona fide defenses to those counterclaims—are within the scope of the arbitration clause, whatever the legal labels attached to those allegations." * * *

The court read the Sherman Act counterclaim to raise issues of wrongful termination of Soler's distributorship, wrongful failure to ship ordered parts and vehicles, and wrongful refusal to permit transship-

ment of stock to the United States and Latin America. Because the existence of just cause for termination turned on Mitsubishi's allegations that Soler had breached the Sales Agreement by, for example, failing to pay for ordered vehicles, the wrongful termination claim implicated [several] provisions within the arbitration clause [including]: Article I–D(1), which rendered a dealer's orders "firm" * * * and Article I–F, specifying payment obligations and procedures. The court therefore held the arbitration clause to cover this dispute.

* * *

[T]he first task of a court asked to compel arbitration of a dispute is to determine whether the parties agreed to arbitrate that dispute. The court is to make this determination by applying the "federal substantive law of arbitrability, applicable to any arbitration agreement within the coverage of the Act." And that body of law counsels "that * * * any doubts concerning the scope of arbitrable issues should be resolved in favor of arbitration * * *." Thus, as with any other contract, the parties' intentions control, but those intentions are generously construed as to issues of arbitrability.

There is no reason to depart from these guidelines where a party bound by an arbitration agreement raises claims founded on statutory rights. * * * Of course, courts should remain attuned to well-supported claims that the agreement to arbitrate resulted from the sort of fraud or overwhelming economic power that would provide grounds "for the revocation of any contract." [FAA, § 2]. But, absent such compelling considerations, the Act itself provides no basis for disfavoring agreements to arbitrate statutory claims by skewing the otherwise hospitable inquiry into arbitrability.

That is not to say that all controversies implicating statutory rights are suitable for arbitration. There is no reason to distort the process of contract interpretation, however, in order to ferret out the inappropriate. Just as it is the congressional policy manifested in the federal Arbitration Act that requires courts liberally to construe the scope of arbitration agreements covered by that Act, it is the congressional intention expressed in some other statute on which the courts must rely to identify any category of claims as to which agreements to arbitrate will be held unenforceable. For that reason, Soler's concern for statutorily protected classes provides no reason to color the lens through which the arbitration clause is read. By agreeing to arbitrate a statutory claim, a party does not forego the substantive rights afforded by the statute; it only submits to their resolution in an arbitral, rather than a judicial, forum. It trades the procedures and opportunity for review of the courtroom for the simplicity, informality, and expedition of arbitration. We must assume that if Congress intended the substantive protection afforded by a given statute to include protection against waiver of the right to a judicial forum, that intention will be deducible from text or legislative history. Having made the bargain to arbitrate, the party should be held to it unless Congress itself has evinced an intention to preclude a waiver of judicial remedies for the statutory rights at issue. Nothing, in the meantime, prevents a party from excluding statutory claims from the scope of an agreement to arbitrate.

In sum, the Court of Appeals correctly conducted a two-step inquiry, first determining whether the parties' agreement to arbitrate reached the statutory issues, and then, upon finding it did, considering whether legal constraints external to the parties' agreement foreclosed the arbitration of those claims. We endorse its rejection of Soler's proposed rule of arbitration-clause construction.

III

We now turn to consider whether Soler's antitrust claims are nonarbitrable even though it has agreed to arbitrate them. In holding that they are not, the Court of Appeals followed the decision of the Second Circuit in *American Safety Equipment Corp. v. J.P. McGuire & Co.*, 391 F.2d 821 (1968). Notwithstanding the absence of any explicit support for such an exception in either the Sherman Act or the federal Arbitration Act, the Second Circuit there reasoned that "the pervasive public interest in enforcement of the antitrust laws, and the nature of the claims that arise in such cases, combine to make . . . antitrust claims . . . inappropriate for arbitration." We find it unnecessary to assess the legitimacy of the *American Safety* doctrine as applied to agreements to arbitrate arising from domestic transactions. As in *Scherk v. Alberto–Culver Co.*, 417 U.S. 506 (1974), we conclude that concerns of international comity, respect for the capacities of foreign and transnational tribunals, and sensitivity to the need of the international commercial system for predictability in the resolution of disputes require that we enforce the parties' agreement, even assuming that a contrary result would be forthcoming in a domestic context.

* * *

[The Court in *Scherk*] categorized "[a]n agreement to arbitrate before a specified tribunal [as], in effect, a specialized kind of forum-selection clause that posits not only the situs of suit but also the procedure to be used in resolving the dispute." * * * [T]he Court emphasized:

> "A contractual provision specifying in advance the forum in which disputes shall be litigated and the law to be applied is . . . an almost indispensable precondition to achievement of the orderliness and predictability essential to any international business transaction. . . .

> "A parochial refusal by the courts of one country to enforce an international arbitration agreement would not only frustrate these purposes, but would invite unseemly and mutually destructive jockeying by the parties to secure tactical litigation advantages. . . . [It would] damage the fabric of international commerce and trade, and imperil the willingness and ability of businessmen to enter into international commercial agreements."

* * *

Thus, we must weigh the concerns of *American Safety* against a strong belief in the efficacy of arbitral procedures for the resolution of international commercial disputes and an equal commitment to the enforcement of freely negotiated choice-of-forum clauses.

At the outset, we confess to some skepticism of certain aspects of the *American Safety* doctrine. As distilled by the First Circuit, the doctrine comprises four ingredients. First, private parties play a pivotal role in aiding governmental enforcement of the antitrust laws by means of the private action for treble damages. Second, "the strong possibility that contracts which generate antitrust disputes may be contracts of adhesion militates against automatic forum determination by contract." Third, antitrust issues, prone to complication, require sophisticated legal and economic analysis, and thus are "ill-adapted to strengths of the arbitral process, i.e., expedition, minimal requirements of written rationale, simplicity, resort to basic concepts of common sense and simple equity." Finally, just as "issues of war and peace are too important to be vested in the generals, . . . decisions as to antitrust regulation of business are too important to be lodged in arbitrators chosen from the business community—particularly those from a foreign community that has had no experience with or exposure to our law and values."

Initially, we find the second concern unjustified. The mere appearance of an antitrust dispute does not alone warrant invalidation of the selected forum on the undemonstrated assumption that the arbitration clause is tainted. A party resisting arbitration of course may attack directly the validity of the agreement to arbitrate. See *Prima Paint Corp.* [supra p. 455]. Moreover, the party may attempt to make a showing that would warrant setting aside the forum-selection clause— that the agreement was "[a]ffected by fraud, undue influence, or over-weening bargaining power"; that "enforcement would be unreasonable and unjust"; or that proceedings "in the contractual forum will be so gravely difficult and inconvenient that [the resisting party] will for all practical purposes be deprived of his day in court." But absent such a showing—and none was attempted here—there is no basis for assuming the forum inadequate or its selection unfair.

Next, potential complexity should not suffice to ward off arbitration. We might well have some doubt that even the courts following *American Safety* subscribe fully to the view that antitrust matters are inherently insusceptible to resolution by arbitration, as these same courts have agreed that an undertaking to arbitrate antitrust claims entered into after the dispute arises is acceptable. And the vertical restraints which most frequently give birth to antitrust claims covered by an arbitration agreement will not often occasion the monstrous proceedings that have given antitrust litigation an image of intractability. In any event, adaptability and access to expertise are hallmarks of arbitration. The anticipated subject matter of the dispute may be taken into account when the arbitrators are appointed, and arbitral rules typically provide for the participation of experts either employed by the parties or appointed by the tribunal. Moreover, it is often a judgment that streamlined proceedings and expeditious results will best serve their needs that cause parties to agree to arbitrate their disputes; it is typically a desire to keep the effort and expense required to resolve a dispute within manageable bounds that prompts them mutually to forgo access to judicial remedies. In sum, the factor of potential complexity alone does not persuade us that an arbitral tribunal could not properly handle an antitrust matter.

For similar reasons, we also reject the proposition that an arbitration panel will pose too great a danger of innate hostility to the constraints on business conduct that antitrust law imposes. International arbitrators frequently are drawn from the legal as well as the business community; where the dispute has an important legal component, the parties and the arbitral body with whose assistance they have agreed to settle their dispute can be expected to select arbitrators accordingly.[18] We decline to indulge the presumption that the parties and arbitral body conducting a proceeding will be unable or unwilling to retain competent, conscientious, and impartial arbitrators.

We are left, then, with the core of the *American Safety* doctrine— the fundamental importance to American democratic capitalism of the regime of the antitrust laws. Without doubt, the private cause of action plays a central role in enforcing this regime. As the Court of Appeals pointed out:

> "A claim under the antitrust laws is not merely a private matter. The Sherman Act is designed to promote the national interest in a competitive economy; thus, the plaintiff asserting his rights under the Act has been likened to a private attorney-general who protects the public's interest."

The treble-damages provision wielded by the private litigant is a chief tool in the antitrust enforcement scheme, posing a crucial deterrent to potential violators.

The importance of the private damages remedy, however, does not compel the conclusion that it may not be sought outside an American court. Notwithstanding its important incidental policing function, the treble-damages cause of action conferred on private parties by § 4 of the Clayton Act, and pursued by Soler here by way of its third counterclaim, seeks primarily to enable an injured competitor to gain compensation for that injury.

> "Section 4 . . . is in essence a remedial provision. It provides treble damages to '[a]ny person who shall be injured in his business or property by reason of anything forbidden in the antitrust laws. . . .' Of course, treble damages also play an important role in penalizing wrongdoers and deterring wrongdoing, as we also have frequently observed. . . . It nevertheless is true that the treble-damages provision, which makes awards available only to injured parties, and measures the awards by a multiple of the injury actually proved, is designed primarily as a remedy." *Bruns-*

---

18. * * * [T]he arbitration panel selected to hear the parties' claims here is composed of three Japanese lawyers, one a former law school dean, another a former judge, and the third a practicing attorney with American legal training who has written on Japanese antitrust law.

The Court of Appeals was concerned that international arbitrators would lack "experience with or exposure to our law and values." The obstacles confronted by the arbitration panel in this case, however, should be no greater than those confronted by any judicial or arbitral tribunal required to determine foreign law. See, e.g., Fed.Rule Civ.Proc. 44.1. Moreover, while our attachment to the antitrust laws may be stronger than most, many other countries, including Japan, have similar bodies of competition law.

wick Corp. v. Pueblo Bowl–O–Mat, Inc., 429 U.S. 477, 485–486 (1977).

* * *

There is no reason to assume at the outset of the dispute that international arbitration will not provide an adequate mechanism. To be sure, the international arbitral tribunal owes no prior allegiance to the legal norms of particular states; hence, it has no direct obligation to vindicate their statutory dictates. The tribunal, however, is bound to effectuate the intentions of the parties. Where the parties have agreed that the arbitral body is to decide a defined set of claims which includes, as in these cases, those arising from the application of American antitrust law, the tribunal therefore should be bound to decide that dispute in accord with the national law giving rise to the claim.[19] And so long as the prospective litigant effectively may vindicate its statutory cause of action in the arbitral forum, the statute will continue to serve both its remedial and deterrent function.

Having permitted the arbitration to go forward, the national courts of the United States will have the opportunity at the award enforcement stage to ensure that the legitimate interest in the enforcement of the antitrust laws has been addressed. The Convention reserves to each signatory country the right to refuse enforcement of an award where the "recognition or enforcement of the award would be contrary to the public policy of that country." Art. V(2)(b). While the efficacy of the arbital process requires that substantive review at the award-enforcement stage remains minimal, it would not require intrusive inquiry to ascertain that the tribunal took cognizance of the antitrust claims and actually decided them.[20]

19. In addition to the clause providing for arbitration before the Japan Commercial Arbitration Association, the Sales Agreement includes a choice-of-law clause which reads: "This Agreement is made in, and will be governed by and construed in all respects according to the laws of the Swiss Confederation as if entirely performed therein." The United States raises the possibility that the arbitral panel will read this provision not simply to govern interpretation of the contract terms, but wholly to displace American law even where it otherwise would apply. Brief for United States as *Amicus Curiae* 20. The International Chamber of Commerce opines that it is "[c]onceivabl[e], although we believe it unlikely, [that] the arbitrators could consider Soler's affirmative claim of anti-competitive conduct by CISA and Mitsubishi to fall within the purview of this choice-of-law provision, with the result that it would be decided under Swiss law rather than U.S. Sherman Act." Brief for International Chamber of Commerce as *Amicus Curiae* 25. At oral argument, however, counsel for Mitsubishi conceded that

American law applied to the antitrust claims and represented that the claims had been submitted to the arbitration panel in Japan on that basis. The record confirms that before the decision of the Court of Appeals the arbitral panel had taken these claims under submission.

We therefore have no occasion to speculate on this matter at this stage in the proceedings, when Mitsubishi seeks to enforce the agreement to arbitrate, not to enforce an award. Nor need we consider now the effect of an arbitral tribunal's failure to take cognizance of the statutory cause of action on the claimant's capacity to reinitiate suit in federal court. We merely note that in the event the choice-of-forum and choice-of-law clauses operated in tandem as a prospective waiver of a party's right to pursue statutory remedies for antitrust violations, we would have little hesitation in condemning the agreement as against public policy.

20. See n. 19, supra. We note, for example, that the rules of the Japan Commercial Arbitration Association provide for

As international trade has expanded in recent decades, so too has the use of international arbitration to resolve disputes arising in the course of that trade. The controversies that international arbitral institutions are called upon to resolve have increased in diversity as well as in complexity. Yet the potential of these tribunals for efficient disposition of legal disagreements arising from commercial relations has not yet been tested. If they are to take a central place in the international legal order, national courts will need to "shake off the old judicial hostility to arbitration," and also their customary and understandable unwillingness to cede jurisdiction of a claim arising under domestic law to a foreign or transnational tribunal. To this extent, at least, it will be necessary for national courts to subordinate domestic notions of arbitrability to the international policy favoring commercial arbitration.

Accordingly, we "require this representative of the American business community to honor its bargain," by holding this agreement to arbitrate "enforce[able] . . . in accord with the explicit provisions of the Arbitration Act."

The judgment of the Court of Appeals is affirmed in part and reversed in part, and the cases are remanded for further proceedings consistent with this opinion.

JUSTICE STEVENS, with whom JUSTICE BRENNAN joins, and with whom JUSTICE MARSHALL joins except as to Part II, dissenting.

One element of this rather complex litigation is a claim asserted by an American dealer in Plymouth automobiles that two major automobile companies are parties to an international cartel that has restrained competition in the American market. Pursuant to an agreement that is alleged to have violated § 1 of the Sherman Act, those companies allegedly prevented the dealer from transshipping some 966 surplus vehicles from Puerto Rico to other dealers in the American market.

The petitioner denies the truth of the dealer's allegations and takes the position that the validity of the antitrust claim must be resolved by an arbitration tribunal in Tokyo, Japan. Largely because the auto manufacturers' defense to the antitrust allegation is based on provisions in the dealer's franchise agreement, the Court of Appeals concluded that the arbitration clause in that agreement encompassed the antitrust claim. * * *

This Court agrees with the Court of Appeals' interpretation of the scope of the arbitration clause, but disagrees with its conclusion that the clause is unenforceable insofar as it purports to cover an antitrust claim against a Japanese company. * * * Because I am convinced that the Court of Appeals' construction of the arbitration clause is erroneous, and because I strongly disagree with this Court's interpretation of the relevant federal statutes, I respectfully dissent. In my

the taking of a "summary record" of each hearing, for the stenographic recording of the proceedings where the tribunal so orders or a party requests one, and for a statement of reasons for the award unless the parties agree otherwise. * * *

opinion, (1) a fair construction of the language in the arbitration clause in the parties' contract does not encompass a claim that auto manufacturers entered into a conspiracy in violation of the antitrust laws; (2) an arbitration clause should not normally be construed to cover a statutory remedy that it does not expressly identify; (3) Congress did not intend § 2 of the Federal Arbitration Act to apply to antitrust claims; and (4) Congress did not intend the Convention on the Recognition and Enforcement of Foreign Arbitral Awards to apply to disputes that are not covered by the Federal Arbitration Act.

* * *

II

The plain language of [§ 2 of the FAA] encompasses Soler's claims that arise out of its contract with Mitsubishi, but does not encompass a claim arising under federal law, or indeed one that arises under its distributor agreement with Chrysler. Nothing in the text of the 1925 Act, nor its legislative history, suggests that Congress intended to authorize the arbitration of any statutory claims.

Until today all of our cases enforcing agreements to arbitrate under the Arbitration Act have involved contract claims. * * * [T]his is the first time the Court has considered the question whether a standard arbitration clause referring to claims arising out of or relating to a contract should be construed to cover statutory claims that have only an indirect relationship to the contract. In my opinion, neither the Congress that enacted the Arbitration Act in 1925, nor the many parties who have agreed to such standard clauses, could have anticipated the Court's answer to that question.

On several occasions we have drawn a distinction between statutory rights and contractual rights and refused to hold that an arbitration barred the assertion of a statutory right. Thus, in *Alexander v. Gardner–Denver Co.*, 415 U.S. 36 (1974), we held that the arbitration of a claim of employment discrimination would not bar an employee's statutory right to damages under Title VII of the Civil Rights Act of 1964, notwithstanding the strong federal policy favoring the arbitration of labor disputes. [See p. 536 infra.]

* * *

In *Barrentine v. Arkansas–Best Freight System, Inc.*, 450 U.S. 728 (1981), we reached a similar conclusion with respect to the arbitrability of an employee's claim based on the Fair Labor Standards Act. We again noted that an arbitrator, unlike a federal judge, has no institutional obligation to enforce federal legislative policy:

"Because the arbitrator is required to effectuate the intent of the parties, rather than to enforce the statute, he may issue a ruling that is inimical to the public policies underlying the FLSA, thus depriving an employee of protected statutory rights."

* * *

In view of the Court's repeated recognition of the distinction between federal statutory rights and contractual rights, together with the undisputed historical fact that arbitration has functioned almost entirely in either the area of labor disputes or in "ordinary disputes between merchants as to questions of fact," it is reasonable to assume that most lawyers and executives would not expect the language in the standard arbitration clause to cover federal statutory claims. Thus, in my opinion, both a fair respect for the importance of the interests that Congress has identified as worthy of federal statutory protection, and a fair appraisal of the most likely understanding of the parties who sign agreements containing standard arbitration clauses, support a presumption that such clauses do not apply to federal statutory claims.

*   *   *

It was Chief Justice Hughes who characterized the Sherman Anti-Trust Act as "a charter of freedom" that may fairly be compared to a constitutional provision. * * * More recently, the Court described the weighty public interests underlying the basic philosophy of the statute:

> "Antitrust laws in general, and the Sherman Act in particular, are the Magna Carta of free enterprise. They are important to the preservation of economic freedom and our free-enterprise system as the Bill of Rights is to the protection of our fundamental personal freedoms. And the freedoms guaranteed each and every business, no matter how small, is the freedom to compete—to assert with vigor, imagination, devotion, and ingenuity whatever economic muscle it can muster." * * * *United States v. Topco Associates, Inc.*, 405 U.S. 596, 610 (1972).

The Sherman and Clayton Acts reflect Congress' appraisal of the value of economic freedom; they guarantee the vitality of the entrepreneurial spirit. Questions arising under these Acts are among the most important in public law.

The unique public interest in the enforcement of the antitrust laws is repeatedly reflected in the special remedial scheme enacted by Congress. Since its enactment in 1890, the Sherman Act has provided for public enforcement through criminal as well as civil sanctions.

*   *   *

The provision for mandatory treble damages—unique in federal law when the statute was enacted—provides a special incentive to the private enforcement of the statute, as well as an especially powerful deterrent to violators. What we have described as "the public interest in vigilant enforcement of antitrust laws through the instrumentality of the private treble damage action" is buttressed by the statutory mandate that the injured party also recover costs, "including a reasonable attorney's fee." The interest in wide and effective enforcement has thus, for almost a century, been vindicated by enlisting the assistance of "private Attorneys General"; we have always attached special importance to their role because "[e]very violation of the antitrust laws is a blow to the free-enterprise system envisaged by Congress."

There are, in addition, several unusual features of the antitrust enforcement scheme that unequivocally require rejection of any thought that Congress would tolerate private arbitration of antitrust claims in lieu of the statutory remedies that it fashioned. * * * [A]n antitrust treble damage case "can only be brought in a District Court of the United States." The determination that these cases are "too important to be decided otherwise than by competent tribunals" surely cannot allow private arbitrators to assume a jurisdiction that is denied to courts of the sovereign States.

* * *

Arbitration awards are only reviewable for manifest disregard of the law, and the rudimentary procedures which make arbitration so desirable in the context of a private dispute often mean that the record is so inadequate that the arbitrator's decision is virtually unreviewable.[31] Despotic decision making of this kind is fine for parties who are willing to agree in advance to settle for a best approximation of the correct result in order to resolve quickly and inexpensively any contractual dispute that may arise in an ongoing commercial relationship. Such informality, however, is simply unacceptable when every error may have devastating consequences for important businesses in our national economy and may undermine their ability to compete in world markets.[32] Instead of "muffling a grievance in the cloakroom of arbitration," the public interest in free competitive markets would be better served by having the issues resolved "in the light of impartial public court adjudication."

* * *

The Court's repeated incantation of the high ideals of "international arbitration" creates the impression that this case involves the fate of an institution designed to implement a formula for world peace. But just as it is improper to subordinate the public interest in enforcement of antitrust policy to the private interest in resolving commercial disputes, so is it equally unwise to allow a vision of world unity to distort the importance of the selection of the proper forum for resolving this dispute. Like any other mechanism for resolving controversies, international arbitration will only succeed if it is realistically limited to tasks it is capable of performing well—the prompt and inexpensive

---

31. The arbitration procedure in this case does not provide any right to evidentiary discovery or a written decision, and requires that all proceedings be closed to the public. Moreover, Japanese arbitrators do not have the power of compulsory process to secure witnesses and documents, nor do witnesses who are available testify under oath. Cf. 9 U.S.C. § 7 (arbitrators may summon witnesses to attend proceedings and seek enforcement in a district court).

32. The greatest risk, of course, is that the arbitrator will condemn business practices under the antitrust laws that are efficient in a free competitive market. In the absence of a reviewable record, a reviewing district court would not be able to undo the damage wrought. Even a Government suit or an action by a private party might not be available to set aside the award.

resolution of essentially contractual disputes between commercial partners. As for matters involving the political passions and the fundamental interests of nations, even the multilateral convention adopted
under the auspices of the United Nations recognizes that private
international arbitration is incapable of achieving satisfactory results.

In my opinion, the elected representatives of the American people
would not have us dispatch an American citizen to a foreign land in
search of an uncertain remedy for the violation of a public right that is
protected by the Sherman Act. This is especially so when there has
been no genuine bargaining over the terms of the submission, and the
arbitration remedy provided has not even the most elementary guarantees of fair process. Consideration of a fully developed record by a jury,
instructed in the law by a federal judge, and subject to appellate
review, is a surer guide to the competitive character of a commercial
practice than the practically unreviewable judgment of a private arbitrator.

Unlike the Congress that enacted the Sherman Act in 1890, the
Court today does not seem to appreciate the value of economic freedom.
I respectfully dissent.

Notes and Questions

(1) Consider carefully footnote 19 to the Court's opinion in *Mitsubishi.* The ICC's concession that it was "unlikely" the arbitrators would
apply Swiss law in deciding Soler's antitrust claims "came as a bad
surprise to many long time users of ICC arbitration," according to one
commentator: One of "the very basics" of arbitration is that it functions within the limits fixed by the agreement of the parties, and "what
is indeed very unlikely, to say the least, is that arbitrators would accept
to apply U.S. antitrust law to claims to be ruled, according to [the]
parties' clear will, by Swiss law!" Werner, A Swiss Comment on
Mitsubishi, 3 J. of Int'l Arb. 81, 83 (1986). Cf. Lowenfeld, The *Mitsubishi* Case: Another View, 2 Arb. Int'l 178, 186 (1986) ("antitrust law is
'mandatory law,' on the same level as export controls, criminal law, or
tax law, i.e., law that cannot ordinarily be avoided by party choice of
law in the same way that, for instance, otherwise applicable statutes of
limitations, or law governing the extent of implied warranties, or the
measure of damages for breach of contract, can be avoided by the
parties through a choice of law clause."). The opposing views are
canvassed thoroughly in Mayer, Mandatory Rules of Law in International Arbitration, 2 Arb. Int'l 274 (1986).

(2) How convincing is the court's assurance that the arbitral
award, once rendered, can be effectively reviewed at the enforcement
stage to "ensure that the legitimate interest in the enforcement of the
antitrust laws has been addressed"? In light of the highly restricted
scope of judicial review of the merits of awards, is this a realistic
prospect? Will it be enough if a reviewing court is satisfied that the
Japanese arbitrators merely "took cognizance of the antitrust claims

and actually decided them"? Or will *Mitsubishi* encourage courts to engage in a more extensive review of the substantive issues? Does *Mitsubishi* envisage a special standard for antitrust cases of exceptionally close review?

(3) Separation agreements usually contain detailed provisions relating to the children of the marriage. Where children are involved, the unravelling of the family can never be complete, and so there will be a need to lay down ground rules for all sorts of matters: custody and visitation rights, child support, and various other continuing incidents of the family relationship (such as the choice of a school or summer camp, religious training, medical treatment, or trips and vacations). With increasing frequency, agreements provide that the inevitable disputes over such matters will be settled by arbitration. Some courts deny on grounds of "public policy" that such disputes are arbitrable. Other cases permit arbitration, but with the caveat that "a special review" of the resulting award is necessary: "The courts should conduct a de novo review unless it is clear on the face of the award that the award could not adversely affect the substantial best interests of the child." Faherty v. Faherty, 97 N.J. 99, 477 A.2d 1257 (1984); see also Sheets v. Sheets, 22 A.D.2d 176, 254 N.Y.S.2d 320 (1964)("Once the court's paternal jurisdiction is invoked, it would examine into the matter, *de novo*, and in doing so could utilize the proof adduced before the arbitration tribunal, could call for new proof, or could employ a combination of both.").

What is the justification for permitting arbitration of domestic disputes, but at the same time treating the process as something of a rehearsal for a separate judicial inquiry? Are there aspects of arbitration which make it particularly attractive as a device for settling domestic disputes over child support and custody? Cf. Agur v. Agur, 32 A.D.2d 16, 298 N.Y.S.2d 772 (1969) (separation agreement provided that custody disputes would be decided by three arbitrators, including an Orthodox rabbi, versed in "Jewish religious law"; court refused to order arbitration). One court has observed that "the process of arbitration, useful when the mundane matter of the amount of support is in issue, is less so when the delicate balancing of the factors comprising the best interests of a child is the issue. The judicial process is more broadly gauged and better suited in protecting these interests." Nestel v. Nestel, 38 A.D.2d 942, 331 N.Y.S.2d 241 (1972). What precisely do you think this means? Do you agree?

See generally Spencer and Zammit, Mediation–Arbitration: A Proposal for Private Resolution of Disputes Between Divorced or Separated Parents, 1976 Duke L.J. 911; Murray, Improving Parent–Child Relationships Within the Divorced Family: A Call for Legal Reform, 19 U.Mich.J.L. Reform 563 (1986).

(4) Recall the concerns about ADR expressed by commentators such as Professor Fiss; see Chapter I, supra p. 38. Are concerns of this

kind relevant to the Court's decision in *Mitsubishi?* Do any of the other cases in this section raise similar issues?

(5) Plaintiff and defendant entered into a transaction in the form of a sale of stock. Plaintiff, however, claimed that this was merely a disguise for what was in fact a usurious loan and sought a declaratory judgment to that effect. The defendant moved to compel arbitration pursuant to an arbitration clause in the agreement. The motion was denied "pending a trial of the issues whether the written agreements are usurious and invalid." "If usurious agreements could be made enforceable by the simple device of employing arbitration clauses the courts would be surrendering their control over public policy * * *. [A]nyone desiring to make a usurious agreement impenetrable need only require the necessitous borrower to consent to arbitration and also to arbitrators by name or occupation associated with the lending industry." Durst v. Abrash, 22 A.D.2d 39, 253 N.Y.S.2d 351 (1964), aff'd, 17 N.Y.2d 445, 266 N.Y.S.2d 806, 213 N.E.2d 887 (1965). Cf. Rosenblum v. Steiner, 43 N.Y.2d 896, 403 N.Y.S.2d 716, 374 N.E.2d 610 (1978) (*borrower* sought to compel arbitration; held, borrower's planned defense of usury was arbitrable).

Compare supra p. 455 ("The 'Separability' of the Arbitration Clause"). In what way is *Durst* different from cases like *Prima Paint?* See also Lawrence v. Comprehensive Business Services Co., 833 F.2d 1159 (5th Cir.1987) (claim that license of trade name for use in accounting practice violated Texas law must be submitted to arbitrators; plaintiffs "do not challenge the legality of the arbitration provision itself, but the legality of the entire contract").

(6) A train controlled by Conrail failed to heed a series of signals and collided with a high-speed passenger train operated by Amtrak. There were 16 deaths, several hundred injuries, and millions of dollars in property damage; a number of lawsuits were filed against both Conrail and Amtrak. Conrail and Amtrak were parties to a contract in which Amtrak agreed to indemnify Conrail for "any and all liability for injuries to or death of any Amtrak Passenger," "irrespective of any negligence or fault of Conrail or Conrail Employees." On the basis of that provision Conrail sought indemnification from Amtrak for all the injuries arising from the accident. Amtrak, however, claimed that it was not obligated to reimburse Conrail because Conrail's conduct causing the accident was "reckless, wanton, willful, or grossly negligent."

The agreement also contained an arbitration clause. Conrail's motion to compel arbitration was denied "because the Court finds that the merits of this case are inextricably linked to public policy determinations and arbitration is an improper mechanism for such a decision."

> Whether an arbitration panel refuses to consider public policy or erroneously decides the issue, this Court will inevitably be requested to review the decision. Both the petitioner and the respondent have represented that they will not settle cases with passenger victims of the Chase, Maryland disaster until liability apportion-

ment is clear. Given the public interest in expeditiously compensating those aggrieved parties and of lessening the burden of the federal judiciary, the Court is reluctant to submit to arbitration a case which cannot be finally decided by arbitrators. Referral would beget only delay and, accordingly, the Court refuses to require arbitration.

In the Matter of the Arbitration Between Consolidated Rail Corp. v. National Railroad Passenger Corp., 657 F.Supp. 405 (D.D.C.1987).

What is the nature of the "public policy" that the court saw as implicated in *Consolidated Rail*? Does it follow from the court's opinion that no aspect of the dispute between the parties, including any issues of contract interpretation, may be submitted to the arbitrators?

Assume that the original agreement had not contained an arbitration clause. After the accident, could the parties have entered into a settlement agreement by which Amtrak promised to indemnify Conrail for some portion of the injuries to passengers? Could they at that time have stipulated instead that Conrail's claim for indemnification should be submitted to arbitration?

(7) An important tenet of American patent law is that the validity of patents must be freely challengeable, so as not to impede free competition in the exploitation of the "public domain." Invalid patents are "vicious Zombis." Aero Spark Plug Co. v. B.G. Corp., 130 F.2d 290, 299 (2d Cir.1942) (Frank, J. concurring). Patent licensees, therefore, are free to attack the patents of their licensors. Lear, Inc. v. Adkins, 395 U.S. 653 (1969). And once a patent has been successfully challenged in court, its invalidity is established not only between the litigants but as to the world generally; the owner of the patent will be estopped from claiming infringement in a later suit against a third party. Blonder–Tongue Labs., Inc. v. University of Illinois Found., 402 U.S. 313 (1971).

Until 1982, courts held that given the public interest in challenging invalid patents, patent infringement disputes were not arbitrable. In that year Congress expressly authorized the arbitration of "any dispute relating to patent validity or infringement." 35 U.S.C. § 294. The statute provides that the arbitration award is to be "final and binding between the parties to the arbitration," but that it "shall have no force or effect on any other person." What does this mean? See Goldstein, Arbitration of Disputes Relating to Patent Validity or Infringement, 72 Ill.Bar J. 350, 351 (1984) ("phrase is intended to remove the defense of collateral estoppel and permit the patentee to enforce a patent against others").

SHEARSON/AMERICAN EXPRESS, INC. v. McMAHON

Supreme Court of the United States, 1987.
___ U.S. ___, 107 S.Ct. 2332, 96 L.Ed.2d 185.

[Plaintiffs opened an account with a brokerage firm. The agreement provided that "any controversy arising out of or relating to" their account would be settled by arbitration under the rules either of the National Association of Securities Dealers or of the New York or American Stock Exchanges. They later brought a lawsuit claiming that the firm had violated § 10(b) of the Securities Exchange Act of 1934 and Rule 10b–5 promulgated under that Act by the Securities and Exchange Commission. The claimed violations involved "churning" the plaintiffs' accounts (making numerous trades in order to increase commissions), "making false statements and omitting material facts from the advice given" them. Plaintiffs also asserted state law claims for fraud and for breach of fiduciary duties in the management of their account, and claims under the Racketeer Influenced and Corrupt Organizations Act ("RICO"), 18 U.S.C. § 1962(c). Plaintiffs claimed that by the time they closed their account, they had suffered trading losses of $350,000 and incurred brokerage fees of $216,000.

[Rule 10b–5 prohibits the making of false statements or the failure to disclose material facts in connection with the sale of securities; it also makes it unlawful to engage "in any act, practice, or course of business which operates or would operate as a fraud or deceit upon any person." Provisions of this Rule have been used to attack a wide variety of securities practices such as "insider trading," and a private cause of action for those injured by violations has long been implied.

[Defendant moved for an order compelling the plaintiffs to arbitrate all their claims. The district court granted the motion as to all except the RICO claim; the Court of Appeals, however, held that arbitration of both the federal securities claims *and* the RICO claims should be denied. It relied on *Wilko v. Swan,* 346 U.S. 427 (1953), which held that a customer of a brokerage firm could litigate a misrepresentation claim against the firm under the Securities Act of 1933. The *Wilko* Court held that the statute should be read as preventing a "waiver of judicial trial and review," and therefore that any agreement to arbitrate was "void."

[The Supreme Court reversed. In her opinion for the Court, Justice O'Connor first noted the "federal policy favoring arbitration": "The burden is on the party opposing arbitration * * * to show that Congress intended to preclude a waiver of judicial remedies for the statutory rights at issue."]

* * *

When Congress enacted the Exchange Act in 1934, it did not specifically address the question of the arbitrability of § 10(b) claims. The McMahons contend, however, that congressional intent to require a judicial forum for the resolution of 10(b) claims can be deduced from

§ 29(a) of the Exchange Act, which declares void "[a]ny condition, stipulation, or provision binding any person to waive compliance with any provision of [the Act]."

First, we reject the McMahons' argument that § 29(a) forbids waiver of § 27 of the Exchange Act. Section 27 provides in relevant part:

> "The district courts of the United States . . . shall have exclusive jurisdiction of violations of this title or the rules and regulations thereunder, and of all suits in equity and actions at law brought to enforce any liability or duty created by this title or the rules and regulations thereunder."

The McMahons contend that an agreement to waive this jurisdictional provision is unenforceable because § 29(a) voids the waiver of "any provision" of the Exchange Act. The language of § 29(a), however, does not reach so far. What the antiwaiver provision of § 29(a) forbids is enforcement of agreements to waive "compliance" with the provisions of the statute. But § 27 itself does not impose any duty with which persons trading in securities must "comply." By its terms, § 29(a) only prohibits waiver of the substantive obligations imposed by the Exchange Act. Because § 27 does not impose any statutory duties, its waiver does not constitute a waiver of "compliance with any provision" of the Exchange Act under § 29(a).

* * *

The second argument offered by the McMahons is that the arbitration agreement effects an impermissible waiver of the substantive protections of the Exchange Act. Ordinarily, "[b]y agreeing to arbitrate a statutory claim, a party does not forego the substantive rights afforded by the statute; it only submits to their resolution in an arbitral, rather than a judicial, forum." The McMahons argue, however, that § 29(a) compels a different conclusion. Initially, they contend that predispute agreements are void under § 29(a) because they tend to result from broker overreaching. They reason, as do some commentators, that *Wilko* [*v. Swan*] is premised on the belief "that arbitration clauses in securities sales agreements generally are not freely negotiated." According to this view, *Wilko* barred enforcement of predispute agreements because of this frequent inequality of bargaining power, reasoning that Congress intended [the Act] to ensure that sellers did not "maneuver buyers into a position that might weaken their ability to recover under the Securities Act." The McMahons urge that we should interpret § 29(a) in the same fashion.

We decline to * * * adopt such an unlikely interpretation of § 29(a). The concern that § 29(a) is directed against is evident from the statute's plain language: it is a concern with whether an agreement "waive[s] compliance with [a] provision" of the Exchange Act. The voluntariness of the agreement is irrelevant to this inquiry: if a stipulation waives compliance with a statutory duty, it is void under § 29(a), whether voluntary or not. Thus, a customer cannot negotiate a reduction in commissions in exchange for a waiver of compliance with the requirements of the Exchange Act, even if the customer knowingly and voluntarily agreed to the bargain. Section 29(a) is concerned, not with whether brokers "maneuver[ed customers] into" an agreement, but with whether the agreement "weaken[s] their ability to recover under the [Exchange] Act." The former is grounds for revoking the contract under ordinary principles of contract law; the latter is grounds for voiding the agreement under § 29(a).

The other reason advanced by the McMahons for finding a waiver of their § 10(b) rights is that arbitration does "weaken their ability to recover under the [Exchange] Act." That is the heart of the Court's decision in *Wilko,* and respondents urge that we should follow its reasoning. *Wilko* listed several grounds why, in the Court's view, the "effectiveness [of the Act's provisions] in application is lessened in arbitration." First, the *Wilko* Court believed that arbitration proceedings were not suited to cases requiring "subjective findings on the purpose and knowledge of an alleged violator." *Wilko* also was concerned that arbitrators must make legal determinations "without judicial instruction on the law," and that an arbitration award "may be made without explanation of [the arbitrator's] reasons and without a complete record of their proceedings." Finally, *Wilko* noted that the "[p]ower to vacate an award is limited," and that "interpretations of the law by the arbitrators in contrast to manifest disregard are not subject, in the federal courts, to judicial review for error in interpretation." *Wilko* concluded that in view of these drawbacks to arbitration, [Securities Act] claims "require[d] the exercise of judicial direction to fairly assure their effectiveness."

As Justice Frankfurter noted in his dissent in *Wilko,* the Court's opinion did not rest on any evidence, either "in the record . . . [or] in the facts of which [it could] take judicial notice," that "the arbitral system . . . would not afford the plaintiff the rights to which he is entitled." Instead, the reasons given in *Wilko* reflect a general suspicion of the desirability of arbitration and the competence of arbitral tribunals—most apply with no greater force to the arbitration of securities disputes than to the arbitration of legal disputes generally. It is difficult to reconcile *Wilko*'s mistrust of the arbitral process with this Court's subsequent decisions involving the Arbitration Act. See, e.g., *Mitsubishi Motors Corp. v. Soler–Chrysler–Plymouth Inc.* [supra p. 501]; *Dean Witter Reynolds Inc. v. Byrd* [infra p. 527]; *Southland Corp. v. Keating* [supra p. 437].

Indeed, most of the reasons given in *Wilko* have been rejected subsequently by the Court as a basis for holding claims to be nonarbitrable. In *Mitsubishi,* for example, we recognized that arbitral tribunals are readily capable of handling the factual and legal complexities of antitrust claims, notwithstanding the absence of judicial instruction and supervision. Likewise, we have concluded that the streamlined procedures of arbitration do not entail any consequential restriction on substantive rights. Finally, we have indicated that there is no reason to assume at the outset that arbitrators will not follow the law; although judicial scrutiny of arbitration awards necessarily is limited, such review is sufficient to ensure that arbitrators comply with the requirements of the statute. See [*Mitsubishi*] n. 19.

* * *

Thus, the mistrust of arbitration that formed the basis for the *Wilko* opinion in 1953 is difficult to square with the assessment of arbitration that has prevailed since that time. This is especially so in light of the intervening changes in the regulatory structure of the securities laws. Even if *Wilko*'s assumptions regarding arbitration were valid at the time *Wilko* was decided, most certainly they do not hold true today for arbitration procedures subject to the SEC's oversight authority.

In 1953, when *Wilko* was decided, the Commission had only limited authority over the rules governing self-regulatory organizations (SROs)—the national securities exchanges and registered securities associations—and this authority appears not to have included any authority at all over their arbitration rules. Since the 1975 amendments to § 19 of the Exchange Act, however, the Commission has had expansive power to ensure the adequacy of the arbitration procedures employed by the SROs. No proposed rule change may take effect unless the SEC finds that the proposed rule is consistent with the requirements of the Exchange Act, and the Commission has the power, on its own initiative, to "abrogate, add to, and delete from" any SRO rule if it finds such changes necessary or appropriate to further the objectives of the Act. In short, the Commission has broad authority to oversee and to regulate the rules adopted by the SROs relating to customer disputes, including the power to mandate the adoption of any rules it deems necessary to ensure that arbitration procedures adequately protect statutory rights.

In the exercise of its regulatory authority, the SEC has specifically approved the arbitration procedures of the New York Stock Exchange, the American Stock Exchange, and the National Association of Securities Dealers, the organizations mentioned in the arbitration agreement at issue in this case. We conclude that where, as in this case, the prescribed procedures are subject to the Commission's § 19 authority, an arbitration agreement does not effect a waiver of the protections of the Act. While *stare decisis* concerns may counsel against upsetting *Wilko*'s contrary conclusion under the Securities Act, we refuse to extend *Wilko*'s reasoning to the Exchange Act in light of these intervening regulatory developments. The McMahons' agreement to submit to arbitration therefore is not tantamount to an impermissible waiver of the McMahons' rights under § 10(b), and the agreement is not void on that basis under § 29(a).

* * *

Accordingly, we hold the McMahons' agreements to arbitrate Exchange Act claims "enforce[able] . . . in accord with the explicit provisions of the Arbitration Act."

Unlike the Exchange Act, there is nothing in the text of the RICO statute that even arguably evinces congressional intent to exclude civil RICO claims from the dictates of the Arbitration Act. This silence in the text is matched by silence in the statute's legislative history.

* * *

Because RICO's text and legislative history fail to reveal any intent to override the provisions of the Arbitration Act, the McMahons must argue that there is an irreconcilable conflict between arbitration and RICO's underlying purposes. Our decision in *Mitsubishi Motors Corp. v. Soler Chrysler–Plymouth Inc.*, however, already has addressed many of the grounds given by the McMahons to support this claim. In *Mitsubishi*, we held that nothing in the nature of the federal antitrust laws prohibits parties from agreeing to arbitrate antitrust claims arising out of international commercial transactions. Although the holding in *Mitsubishi* was limited to the international context, much of its reasoning is equally applicable here. Thus, for example, the McMahons have argued that RICO claims are too complex to be subject to arbitration. We determined in *Mitsubishi*, however, that "potential complexity should not suffice to ward off arbitration." * * *

Likewise, the McMahons contend that the "overlap" between RICO's civil and criminal provisions renders § 1964(c) claims nonarbitrable. Yet § 1964(c) is no different in this respect from the federal antitrust laws. * * * *Mitsubishi* recognized that treble-damages suits for claims arising under § 1 of the Sherman Act may be subject to arbitration, even though such conduct may also give rise to claims of criminal liability. We similarly find that the criminal provisions of RICO do not preclude arbitration of bona fide civil actions brought under § 1964(c).

* * *

Not only does *Mitsubishi* support the arbitrability of RICO claims, but there is even more reason to suppose that arbitration will adequately serve the purposes of RICO than that it will adequately protect private enforcement of the antitrust laws. Antitrust violations generally have a widespread impact on national markets as a whole, and the antitrust treble-damages provision gives private parties an incentive to bring civil suits that serve to advance the national interest in a competitive economy. RICO's drafters likewise sought to provide vigorous incentives for plaintiffs to pursue RICO claims that would advance society's fight against organized crime. See *Sedima, S.P.R.L. v. Imrex Co.* [473 U.S. 479 (1985)]. But in fact RICO actions are seldom asserted "against the archetypal, intimidating mobster." Id., at 499; see also id., at 506 (MARSHALL, J., dissenting) ("only 9% of all civil RICO cases have involved allegations of criminal activity normally associated with professional criminals"). The special incentives necessary to encourage civil enforcement actions against organized crime do not support nonarbitrability of run-of-the-mill civil RICO claims brought against legitimate enterprises. The private attorney general role for the typical RICO plaintiff is simply less plausible than it is for the typical antitrust plaintiff, and does not support a finding that there is an irreconcilable conflict between arbitration and enforcement of the RICO statute.

In sum, we find no basis for concluding that Congress intended to prevent enforcement of agreements to arbitrate RICO claims. The McMahons may effectively vindicate their RICO claim in an arbitral forum, and therefore, there is no inherent conflict between arbitration and the purposes underlying § 1964(c). * * * Accordingly, the McMahons, "having made the bargain to arbitrate," will be held to their bargain. Their RICO claim is arbitrable under the terms of the Arbitration Act.

* * *

JUSTICE BLACKMUN, with whom JUSTICE BRENNAN and JUSTICE MARSHALL join, concurring in part and dissenting in part.

I concur in the Court's decision to enforce the arbitration agreement with respect to respondents' RICO claims * * *. I disagree, however, with the Court's conclusion that respondents' § 10(b) claims also are subject to arbitration.

Both the Securities Act of 1933 and the Securities Exchange Act of 1934 were enacted to protect investors from predatory behavior of securities industry personnel. In *Wilko v. Swan,* the Court recognized this basic purpose when it declined to enforce a predispute agreement to compel arbitration of claims under the Securities Act. Following that decision, lower courts extended *Wilko*'s reasoning to claims brought under § 10(b) of the Exchange Act, and Congress approved of this extension. In today's decision, however, the Court effectively overrules *Wilko* by accepting the Securities and Exchange Commission's newly adopted position that arbitration procedures in the securities industry and the Commission's oversight of the self-regulatory organizations (SROs) have improved greatly since *Wilko* was decided. The Court thus approves the abandonment of the judiciary's role in the resolution of claims under the Exchange Act and leaves such claims to the arbitral forum of the securities industry at a time when the industry's abuses towards investors are more apparent than ever.

* * *

Even if I were to accept the Court's narrow reading of *Wilko,* as a case dealing only with the inadequacies of arbitration in 1953,[14] I do not think that this case should be resolved differently today so long as the policy of investor protection is given proper consideration in the analysis. Despite improvements in the process of arbitration and changes in the judicial attitude towards it, several aspects of arbitration that were seen by the *Wilko* court to be inimical to the policy of investor protection still remain.

---

14. This argument, in essence, is a functional one. It suggests that, although Congress *intended* to protect investors through the provision of a judicial forum for the enforcement of their rights under the securities acts, this intention will not be contravened by sending these claims to arbitration because arbitration is now the "functional equivalent" of the courts.

* * *

It is true that arbitration procedures in the securities industry have improved since *Wilko's* day. Of particular importance has been the development of a code of arbitration by the Commission with the assistance of representatives of the securities industry and the public.

Even those who favor the arbitration of securities claims do not contend, however, that arbitration has changed so significantly as to eliminate the essential characteristics noted by the *Wilko* Court. Indeed, proponents of arbitration would not see these characteristics as "problems," because, in their view, the characteristics permit the unique "streamlined" nature of the arbitral process. As at the time of *Wilko,* preparation of a record of arbitration proceedings is not invariably required today.[17] Moreover, arbitrators are not bound by precedent and are actually discouraged by their associations from giving reasons for a decision. Judicial review is still substantially limited to the four grounds listed in § 10 of the Arbitration Act and to the concept of "manifest disregard" of the law.[18]

The Court's "mistrust" of arbitration may have given way recently to an acceptance of this process, not only because of the improvements in arbitration, but also because of the Court's present assumption that the distinctive features of arbitration, its more quick and economical resolution of claims, do not render it inherently inadequate for the resolution of statutory claims. Such reasoning, however, should prevail only in the absence of the congressional policy that places the statutory claimant in a special position with respect to possible violators of his statutory rights. As even the most ardent supporter of arbitration would recognize, the arbitral process *at best* places the investor on an equal footing with the securities-industry personnel against whom the claims are brought.

Furthermore, there remains the danger that, *at worst,* compelling an investor to arbitrate securities claims puts him in a forum controlled by the securities industry. This directly contradicts the goal of both securities acts to free the investor from the control of the market professional. The Uniform Code provides some safeguards [19] but de-

---

17. Under the Uniform Code of Arbitration,

"Unless requested by the arbitrators or a party or parties to a dispute, no record of an arbitration proceeding shall be kept. * * * If a party or parties to a dispute elect to have the record transcribed, the cost of such transcription shall be borne by the party or parties making the request."

18. The Uniform Code of Arbitration and the SRO codes modeled upon it do provide for limited discovery, and the ability to subpoena witnesses. Yet, by arbitrating their disputes, investors lose the wide choice of venue and the extensive discovery provided by the courts.

19. The Uniform Code mandates that a majority of an arbitration panel, usually composed of between three to five arbitrators, be drawn from outside the industry. Each arbitrator, moreover, is directed to disclose "any circumstances which might preclude such arbitrator from rendering an objective and impartial determination." In addition, the parties are informed of the business associations of the arbitrators, and each party has the right to one peremptory challenge and to unlimited challenges for cause. The arbitrators are usually individuals familiar with the federal securities laws.

spite them, and indeed because of the background of the arbitrators, the investor has the impression, frequently justified, that his claims are being judged by a forum composed of individuals sympathetic to the securities industry and not drawn from the public. It is generally recognized that the codes do not define who falls into the category "not from the securities industry." Accordingly, it is often possible for the "public" arbitrators to be attorneys or consultants whose clients have been exchange members or SROs. See Panel of Arbitrators 1987–1988, CCH American Stock Exchange Guide (53 out of 70 "public" arbitrators are lawyers). The uniform opposition of investors to compelled arbitration and the overwhelming support of the securities industry for the process suggest that there must be *some* truth to the investors' belief that the securities industry has an advantage in a forum under its own control. See N.Y. Times, Mar. 29, 1987, section 3, p. 8, col. 1 (statement of Sheldon H. Elsen, Chairman, American Bar Association Task Force on Securities Arbitration: "The houses basically like the present system because they own the stacked deck").[20]

* * *

[T]he Court's complacent acceptance of the Commission's oversight is alarming when almost every day brings another example of illegality on Wall Street. Many of the abuses recently brought to light, it is true, do not deal with the question of the adequacy of SRO arbitration. They, however, do suggest that the industry's self-regulation, of which the SRO arbitration is a part, is not functioning acceptably. Moreover, these abuses have highlighted the difficulty experienced by the Commission, at a time of growth in the securities market and a decrease in the Commission's staff, to carry out its oversight task. Such inadequacies on the part of the Commission strike at the very heart of the reasoning of the Court, which is content to accept the soothing assurances of the Commission without examining the reality behind them. Indeed, while the *amici* cite the number of arbitrations of securities disputes as a sign of the success of this process in the industry, see Brief for Securities Industry Association, Inc., these statistics have a more portentous meaning. In this era of deregulation, the growth in complaints about the securities industry, many of which find their way to arbitration, parallels the increase in securities violations and suggests a market not adequately controlled by the SROs. In such a time, one would expect more, not less, judicial involvement in resolution of securities disputes.

There is, fortunately, a remedy for investors. In part as a result of the Commission's position in this case, Congress has begun to look into the adequacy of the self-regulatory arbitration and the Commission's oversight of the SROs. [The Chairman of the House Subcommittee on

---

20. * * * The *amici* in support of petitioners and some commentators argue that the statistics concerning the results of arbitration show that the process is not weighted in favor of the securities industry. Such statistics, however, do not indicate the damages received by customers in relation to the damages to which they believed they were entitled. It is possible for an investor to "prevail" in arbitration while recovering a sum considerably less than the damages he actually incurred.

Oversight and Investigations has informed the SEC that the Subcommittee is] "particularly concerned about increasing numbers of complaints in connection with churning and violations of suitability requirements, as well as complaints that arbitration procedures are rife with conflicts of interest (since the arbitrators are peers of the brokerage firm being sued) and are inadequate to enforce the statutory rights of customers against broker-dealers." * * * Thus, there is hope that Congress will give investors the relief that the Court denies them today.

In the meantime, the Court leaves lower courts with some authority, albeit limited, to protect investors before Congress acts. Courts should take seriously their duty to review the results of arbitration to the extent possible under the Arbitration Act. As we explained in *Mitsubishi Motors Corp. v. Soler Chrysler–Plymouth, Inc.,* "courts should remain attuned to well-supported claims that the agreement to arbitrate resulted from the sort of fraud or overwhelming economic power that would provide grounds 'for the revocation of any contract.'" Indeed, in light of today's decision compelling the enforcement of predispute arbitration agreements, it is likely that investors will be inclined, more than ever, to bring complaints to federal courts that arbitrators were partial or acted in "manifest disregard" of the securities laws. It is thus ironic that the Court's decision, no doubt animated by its desire to rid the federal courts of these suits, actually may *increase* litigation about arbitration.

[Justice Stevens also dissented from the Court's holding on the Exchange Act claim, in an opinion which is omitted.]

Notes and Questions

(1) Broker-customer contracts commonly provide for arbitration under the auspices of an industry organization such as the New York Stock Exchange. As Justice Blackmun's opinion notes, there has been much criticism with respect to the impartiality of exchange-appointed arbitration panels. See, e.g., "When Investors Bring Claims Against Brokers," New York Times, March 29, 1987, Sec. 3, pp. 1, 8 (lawyer who represents investors says, "I would rather defend a capitalist before the comrades' court than a client before an arbitration panel of the New York Stock Exchange"). See generally Katsoris, The Arbitration of a Public Securities Dispute, 53 Fordham L.Rev. 279 (1984); Lipton, Arbitration in the Securities Industry: Too Much of a Good Thing?, 1985 J. of Dispute Res. 151. Professor Lipton collected information with respect to a small sample of securities arbitrations. Of 41 cases studied, there was a monetary award to the plaintiff in 22. In only five, however, was the award for more than 60% of the amount claimed; in 55% of the cases in which there *was* a monetary award, "the award was close (within ten percent) to being half of the amount claimed."

Under the uniform "Code of Arbitration" developed by the securities industry with the approval of the SEC, arbitrations are administered by the exchange; the exchange itself, not the parties, names the arbitrators who will hear particular cases. A majority of the panel must be "public" arbitrators, "not from the securities industry." See notes 17–19 to Justice Blackmun's opinion. An SEC staff report issued after the *McMahon* case called for changes in the Code to meet some of the concerns expressed. For example, the SEC proposal would define more clearly and restrictively who could serve as a "public" arbitrator; anyone with "significant professional ties" to the industry—including retired industry employees and lawyers who regularly represent brokerage firms—would be barred. See Wall St. J., September 11, 1987, p. 23; see also "NYSE Implements Revised Guidelines for Classifying 'Public' Arbitrators," 20 Sec.Reg. & L.Rptr. 325 (BNA 1988).

(2) Arbitration of disputes between members of a trade and "outsiders" often brings to the surface a tension between two widely-accepted values underlying the arbitration process. On the one hand there are the often-cited advantages of expert knowledge and experience on the part of decision-makers familiar with industry practice. The task, for example, of educating a jury or even the average judge in the conventions of securities or commodities trading may be a daunting one. On the other hand, there is a need to preserve the fairness of the process by avoiding onesidedness. Even decision-makers who think of themselves as scrupulously neutral are often hard put to avoid the predispositions and preconceptions that seem to accompany technical "expertise." This is particularly true where one of the parties claims to have observed "trade standards," and the dispute seems likely to call into question long-standing practices and patterns of behavior widespread throughout an entire industry. The arbitration of broker-customer disputes illustrates the inevitable tension; how to draw the balance between these values is a persistent theme in discussions of arbitration. Recall also *Graham v. Scissor–Tail, Inc.,* supra p. 463.

(3) After *McMahon*, an SEC study found that virtually all brokerage firms required customers to sign a pre-dispute arbitration agreement as a condition for opening a margin or option account; arbitration clauses were also included in over a third of all cash accounts. The SEC considered briefly—and then rejected—a staff proposal to prohibit firms from denying services to a customer who refused to sign a pre-dispute arbitration agreement. At the same time, however, similar proposals were surfacing in Congress and in a number of states. See 20 BNA Sec. Reg. & Law Rep. 1053 (1988); 20 id. 1219 (1988); 20 id. 1436 (1988) (regulation promulgated by Massachusetts Securities Division barring broker-dealers from requiring an arbitration clause as a "non-negotiable precondition" to brokerage transaction).

(4) Often a claim assumed to be "nonarbitrable" (for example, a claim brought under the Securities Act of 1933 before *McMahon*) will be joined with another where arbitrability is clear (for example, a fraud claim based on state law). Both claims are likely to arise out of the same facts. What is the best procedure to handle such disputes? Where the arbitrable and nonarbitrable claims were truly "inextricably intertwined," many courts thought that all of them ought to be decided

in one forum in the interest of efficiency. Separating arbitrable and nonarbitrable claims, it was suggested, would prevent fast and inexpensive settlement and would lead to duplicate proceedings and inconsistent results. As a consequence, arbitration of *any* of the claims was denied.

The Supreme Court ended this practice in Dean Witter Reynolds Inc. v. Byrd, 470 U.S. 213 (1985). In *Byrd,* the Court made it clear that the FAA *requires* a court to grant a motion to compel arbitration of *any* arbitrable claim. The FAA's primary purpose, to ensure judicial enforcement of private agreements to arbitrate, required that courts "rigorously enforce" such agreements even if the result is "piecemeal litigation" and "the possibly inefficient maintenance of separate proceedings in different forums."

If arbitration of the state claim is not stayed pending a trial of the non-arbitrable statutory claim, might the arbitration have a collateral estoppel effect in the later court action? The Court in *Byrd* concluded that a stay of arbitration was not necessary "to protect the federal interest in the federal-court proceeding." It left for another day the question of the award's possible collateral estoppel effect. However, references in the Court's opinion to the case of *McDonald v. City of West Branch* suggest a likely answer. See infra p. 535.

(5) "RICO," the Racketeer Influenced and Corrupt Organizations Act, makes it unlawful to use any money derived "from a pattern of racketeering activity" in the operation of an interstate enterprise. "Racketeering activity" is defined as the violation—no actual prior conviction is necessary—of certain predicate statutes: for example, those dealing with bribery and narcotics sales, but also including "mail fraud" and "fraud in the sale of securities." A "pattern" of such activity is found when at least two such violations occur within a period of ten years. The RICO statute follows the model of the antitrust laws in giving a private cause of action, including the right to attorney's fees and treble damages, to persons injured by such conduct. See 18 U.S.C. §§ 1961–1968.

As Justice O'Connor notes in *McMahon,* the scope of RICO has in recent years been dramatically extended far beyond the activities of "the archetypal, intimidating mobster" to reach ordinary business disputes involving "respected and legitimate" enterprises. It was inevitable, then, that in commercial transactions where the parties had entered into an arbitration agreement the question would arise whether a RICO claim was arbitrable.

c. Limitations on Remedies in Arbitration

WILLOUGHBY ROOFING & SUPPLY CO., INC. v. KAJIMA INTERNATIONAL, INC.

United States District Court, Northern District Alabama, 1984.
598 F.Supp. 353.

LYNNE, SENIOR DISTRICT JUDGE.

[The parties entered into a contract by which Willoughby, as subcontractor, was to construct and install a roof on a building for Kajima, the general contractor on a certain construction project. Willoughby claimed that it had prepared its bid on the roofing job in reliance on certain representations by Kajima as to the plans and specifications that would have to be followed. Following its acceptance of the bid, however, Kajima altered the plans and specifications so that the costs to Willoughby of completing the contract would have been substantially higher than anticipated. Willoughby sought to renegotiate the contract price or to submit a new bid. However, although Willoughby had gone to considerable expense in preparing to fulfill the contract under the original specifications, Kajima chose instead to cancel the contract and engage another subcontractor to do the work.

[Willoughby filed a lawsuit seeking compensatory and punitive damages for breach of contract, fraud, and breach of the duty of good faith and fair dealing. Kajima moved to stay the proceedings pending arbitration. The contract between the parties provided that "all claims, disputes, and other matters in question arising out of, or relating to, this Agreement or a Work Assignment or the breach thereof" were to be resolved by arbitration in accordance with the Construction Industry Arbitration Rules of the American Arbitration Association.]

This arbitration clause is, of course, quite broad, and it evinces an intent of the parties to vest the arbitrators with authority to decide virtually any claim that could arise in relation to the contract and its performance. * * *

Convinced that the arbitration clause did indeed cover all of the plaintiffs claims, including the claims for compensatory and punitive damages for fraud, the Court granted the stay. An arbitration panel was selected, and the plaintiffs claims were presented to that panel. Finding those claims to be meritorious, the panel awarded the plaintiff $150,000 in unspecified damages.

At this point, the defendant first objected that the arbitrators had awarded punitive damages and that to do so was beyond their authority. In order to clarify the issue, the Court on April 26, 1984, ordered that the award be resubmitted to the same arbitration panel for an explicit breakdown of the claims for which damages were provided. [The arbitrators subsequently found that Willoughby was entitled to $41,091.25 in compensatory damages; they further found that:]

KAJIMA INTERNATIONAL, INC., did make misrepresentations of material facts, that these facts were willfully made to deceive WILLOUGHBY ROOFING & SUPPLY CO., INC., that these misrepresentations were made by KAJIMA INTERNATIONAL, INC., to be relied upon by WILLOUGHBY ROOFING & SUPPLY CO., INC., and that in fact WILLOUGHBY ROOFING & SUPPLY CO., INC., did rely on these misrepresentations and that WILLOUGHBY ROOFING & SUPPLY CO., INC., suffered damages as a result of this reliance.

For these wrongful acts of KAJIMA INTERNATIONAL, INC., we find that KAJIMA INTERNATIONAL, INC., should pay punitive damages of $108,908.15.

Now unhappy with the bed it has made for itself, Kajima no longer wishes to lie in it. Consequently, Kajima now seeks an order vacating this award on two separate grounds: (1) the contract between the parties does not authorize the arbitrators to award punitive damages; and (2) even if the contract does authorize the arbitrators to make such an award, public policy prohibits them from doing so. As discussed below, however, neither of these arguments is sufficiently persuasive to displace the plenary deference traditionally owing to the decisions of arbitrators as a matter of federal policy.

The contention that the arbitration clause involved in this case is not broad enough to empower the arbitration panel to award punitive damages is one that must fail. As the defendant has candidly admitted, "it would have been difficult, if not impossible, for the parties to have drafted a *broader* arbitration provision." Moreover, the arbitration clause incorporates by reference the Construction Industry Arbitration Rules. Rule 43, of those rules provides that

> The arbitrator may grant *any remedy or relief* which is just and equitable and within the terms of the agreement of the parties (emphasis supplied).

When the extremely broad arbitration clause is read in light of the equally broad grant of remedial power in Rule 43, it is clear that the parties by their contract have authorized the arbitrators to award punitive damages. The contract purports to place no limits on the remedial authority of the arbitrators, nor should one be implied to exclude the authority to award punitive damages. The parties certainly had the power to limit the arbitrator's ability to fashion appropriate remedies [7], but they chose not to do so. As defendants have conceded, strong federal policy requires a liberal construction of arbitration agreements, not a strict one.

* * *

Only in the presence of "clear and express exclusions" could it be said that the arbitrators lacked authority under the contract to consider the plaintiff's claims for punitive damages. No such exclusions are

7. Arbitration clauses expressly withholding from arbitrators the authority to decide claims for punitive damages are certainly not uncommon.

present, and in their absence the contract is clearly broad enough to authorize the arbitrators to consider the plaintiff's claim for punitive damages and to grant such relief where it is just and equitable to do so. Therefore, the contention that the contract itself denies the arbitrators the power to award punitive damages is a contention that must fail.[12]

This brings us to the defendant's second contention. Does public policy prohibit the parties to a contract from vesting an arbitration panel with authority to consider their claims for punitive damages for fraud in the inducement or performance of the contract? The Court thinks not.

It is true, as Kajima points out, that certain state courts have held that under the law of those states arbitrators cannot award punitive damages even if the parties authorize them to do so. See, e.g., Garrity v. Lyle Stuart, Inc., 40 N.Y.2d 354, 353 N.E.2d 793, 386 N.Y.S.2d 831 (1976). Decisions such as those, however, deal only with the powers of arbitrators under state law and state public policy. Federal law and federal policy under the Federal Arbitration Act apply to the arbitration provision in the case *sub judice,* since that provision is part of a written contract evidencing a transaction in interstate commerce. Even if Alabama law and policy were deemed consistent with that of New York * * *, it would not control the issue presented here despite the stipulation contained in the contract that Alabama law would generally be deemed to govern the agreement. "Although the parties to a contract can agree that a certain state's law will govern the resolution of issues submitted to arbitration (i.e., plaintiff's entitlement to punitive damages, assuming [a certain state's substantive] law applies), federal law governs the categories of claims subject to arbitration" and the "resolution of issues concerning the arbitration provision's interpretation, construction, validity, revocability, *and enforceability.*" * * *

Southland Corp. v. Keating firmly establishes that it is the "federal substantive law" of arbitrability that governs questions such as the one presented here. Therefore, if federal policy allows enforcement of an arbitration provision vesting the arbitrators with the authority to award punitive damages, then such a provision remains enforceable despite contrary state law or policy.

* * *

This Court agrees that there is no public policy bar which prevents arbitrators from considering claims for punitive damages. The Supreme Court has emphasized that the arbitration process can be a viable method of dispute resolution only if "it serves as a vehicle for handling any and all disputes that arise under the agreement," and

---

12. Even if the original arbitration clause were not broad enough in and of itself to authorize the award of punitive damages, by voluntarily submitting the plaintiff's fraud claims to arbitration without reservation of the claim made for punitive damages and without objecting to the authority of the arbitrators to award claimed relief, Kajima in effect extended the authority of the arbitrators to include these matters. * * *

only if the arbitrators are given a great deal of flexibility in the fashioning of appropriate remedies. The remedy of punitive damages is one to which a plaintiff is traditionally entitled under Alabama law "when the fraud is malicious, oppressive or gross and the misrepresentation is made with knowledge of its falsity and with the purpose of injuring him." That is precisely what the arbitrators found in this case. Where the arbitrators are concededly vested with the authority to hear and resolve the plaintiff's claim of fraud, it would be anomalous indeed to deny them remedial power commensurate with that authority. To deny arbitrators the full range of remedial tools generally available under the law would be to hamstring arbitrators and to lessen the value and efficiency of arbitration as an alternative method of dispute resolution. This would not sit well with the strong federal policy favoring arbitration.

The defendant insists, however, that because an award of punitive damages serves not only to punish the present wrongdoer for willful or wanton misconduct, but also to deter others in society at large, the power to award them should not be wielded by anyone other than judge or jury. The defendant raises the spectre of overly partial arbiters manipulated by the party in a superior bargaining position, who may award punitive damages out of bias and prejudice. That spectre has more bark than bite, however, for the Arbitration Act expressly provides for the vacation of an arbitral award where the award was "procured by corruption, fraud or undue means," or where there was "evident partiality or corruption in the arbitrators." The mere possibility of bias or corruption no more justifies a wholesale withdrawal of the authority of arbitrators to make an award of punitive damages than it would a wholesale withdrawal of their authority to resolve disputes at all. If corruption or evident partiality in fact surfaces, naturally an award of punitive damages emanating from such circumstances should be set aside. Clearly, however, the possibility of an occasional abuse of power is no grounds for an absolute bar on the award of punitive damages by arbitrators.

Kajima also complains that to allow arbitrators to hear and decide claims for punitive damages is to displace the court and jury as an engine for imposing a social sanction designed more to punish and deter than to compensate. Of course, the argument that it is unfair to allow an arbitrator to displace a court and jury is one that has been sounded before. Not only litigants but state courts as well have questioned the ability of arbitrators to properly dispense justice. Many state courts have therefore declared contractual agreements to submit all disputes to arbitration to be totally unenforceable as a matter of public policy because they "defeat the jurisdiction of courts." But Congress has enunciated a broad and pervasive federal policy that overrides all such arguments. * * * There is no reason to believe that the Act's mandate of enforceability did not extend to agreements to arbitrate issues of punitive damages. Nor is there reason to believe that the purposes of punitive awards—punishment of the present wrongdoer and deterrence of others who might otherwise engage in similar conduct—will not be furthered by arbitral awards every bit as much as by formal judicial awards. Indeed, an arbitrator steeped in the practice of a given trade is often better equipped than a judge not only to decide what behavior so transgresses the limits of acceptable commercial practice in that trade as to warrant a punitive award, but also to determine the amount of punitive damages needed to (1) adequately deter others in the trade from engaging in similar misconduct, and (2) punish the particular defendant in accordance with the magnitude of his misdeed.

The wisdom of allowing arbitrators to consider and resolve issues of punitive damages becomes all the more plain when we consider the practical effect of a contrary result. Defendant urges that merely by agreeing to arbitration, a plaintiff has automatically forfeited his right to punitive damages because arbitrators are prohibited by public policy from awarding such damages. Thus, by entering an arbitration agreement the plaintiff has contractually waived his right to punitive damages. Yet, not only would such a mandatory result seriously undermine the value and sufficiency of the arbitral process as a method of dispute resolution, it would also constitute a total frustration of the public policies and purposes served by punitive damage awards. Merely by agreeing to arbitrate a defendant could escape the monetary sanction of punitive damages that the law would otherwise impose upon him for gross and malicious conduct. Both the policies of deterrence and of punishment would be completely thwarted in a broad range of commercial transactions involving agreements to arbitrate. Moreover, granting such automatic immunity could well encourage grossly unjustified conduct in certain cases by making it more economically feasible. Surely that would be a much more serious distortion of public policy than by vesting the authority to award such damages in an impartial and experienced arbiter.

Even if the plaintiff who has agreed to arbitration is not deemed to have automatically waived his right to be heard on the issue of punitive damages, the practical effect of a bar on the arbitrability of such issues would be unsatisfactory. In essence, where tort and contract claims are mixed and punitive damages are sought, to follow the *Garrity* rule in these circumstances would require two trials—one before the arbitrator and then "a separate judicial trial on essentially the same facts—obviously a wasteful exercise." This would undermine the chief advantages and purposes of arbitration—to relieve congestion in the courts and to achieve a quick, inexpensive and binding resolution of all disputes that arise between the parties to an agreement.

* * *

It may be, as the defendant belatedly claims, that the informalities and lack of judicial review attendant to arbitration render that method of dispute resolution less desirable than a full judicial trial when it comes to the airing of claims for punitive damages. But having chosen arbitration as the method of resolution of "all claims, disputes and other matters . . . arising out of or relating to" its agreement with

Willoughby Roofing, and having vested the arbitrators with authority to grant "any remedy or relief which is just and equitable," it may fairly be said that Kajima got what it bargained for.

* * *

Accordingly, the motion to vacate or modify the arbitrator's award will be DENIED, and the Court will enter a judgment in accordance with the arbitral award.

[The Court of Appeals affirmed "substantially on the basis of the district court's opinion," 776 F.2d 269 (11th Cir.1985).]

Notes and Questions

(1) In the absence of an arbitration clause, could a court have awarded punitive damages to Willoughby Roofing? Should an arbitrator be able to award punitive damages in circumstances where a court could *not* do so?

See Associated General Contractors v. Savin Brothers, 45 A.D.2d 136, 356 N.Y.S.2d 374 (1974), aff'd, 36 N.Y.2d 957, 373 N.Y.2d 555, 335 N.E.2d 859 (1975). Savin, a construction firm, was bound by its membership in the contractors' association (AGC) to engage in labor negotiations exclusively through the association. It was important for AGC to maintain a united front in collective bargaining; therefore, if any company withdrew its designation of AGC as sole bargaining representative the agreement allowed the arbitrator to award damages "in an amount no less than three times the daily liquidated damage amount provided for" in each construction contract to which the company was a party within the area, "together with such other and further damages as the arbitrator in his discretion may determine." Savin entered into an independent contract with the Teamsters Union in breach of its agreement with AGC, and the arbitrator applied the contract formula to award AGC $104,400 in damages. The court found the contract provision to be a "penalty" clause, intended to deter breach and not relating "in any recognizable manner" to the damages suffered by AGC. It nevertheless upheld the award, noting that "when arbitration is the means of policing collective bargaining and other labor agreements, 'there may be a positive need for power in the arbitrator to impose and enforce a penalty * * *.'"

(2) Garrity v. Lyle Stuart, Inc., 40 N.Y.2d 354, 386 N.Y.S.2d 831, 353 N.E.2d 793 (1976) held it to be against public policy for arbitrators to award punitive damages "even if agreed upon by the parties." *Garrity* involved a contract dispute in which an author sought unpaid royalties from her publisher, as well as punitive damages for "malicious withholding of royalties." The court noted that punitive damages have long been held unavailable for "mere breach of contract." It went on, however, to observe that even if a court could impose punitive damages on these facts, "it was not the province of arbitrators to do so":

> For centuries the power to punish has been a monopoly of the State, and not that of any private individual. The day is long past

since barbaric man achieved redress by private punitive measures. * * * The law does not and should not permit private persons to submit themselves to punitive sanctions of the order reserved to the State.

Can *Garrity* be distinguished from the *Savin* case, decided by the same court the preceding year? Even on identical facts, could a New York court today follow *Garrity*?

Recall Justice Blackmun's discussion in *Mitsubishi* of the function of treble damage awards in antitrust cases. Is this relevant to the problem in *Garrity*?

(3) Consider this observation in Morgan, Contract Theory and the Sources of Rights: An Approach to the Arbitrability Question, 60 So. Cal.L.Rev. 1059, 1075 (1987):

> [A]n arbitration purporting to award punitive damages * * * utilizes the breaching party's liability as a means of achieving some further (i.e., extrinsic) social good. * * * [P]unitive damages are comprehended as a distributive or regulatory creation of the state. Given that the issue necessarily arises in the context of litigation, the judicial branch is the obvious governmental vehicle for administering the distributive claim. Absent legislative conferral of this authority on some other branch, removal of the distributive power from the judiciary is as inconceivable as, say, an attempt to establish the private assessment and collection of tax.

(4) Strictures such as those in *Garrity* against arbitral "punishment" may as a practical matter turn out to be meaningless unless the arbitrator is ingenuous enough to label his award as punitive. As all first-year law students know, calculating "compensatory" damages in contract cases is hardly an exact science. In addition, arbitrators may find in particular cases that remedies other than the traditional award of damages are warranted; for example they may think it appropriate, on a theory of unjust enrichment, to require the defendant to "disgorge" the benefits he has made from breach. Cf. International Union of Operating Engineers v. Mid–Valley, Inc., 347 F.Supp. 1104 (S.D.Tex. 1972). In the absence of a reasoned opinion or a transcript, it will be difficult to say that the arbitrator has in fashioning appropriate remedies gone beyond permitted "flexibility" to forbidden "punishment."

(5) Staklinski was hired as an executive. His contract provided that should he become "permanently disabled" he would receive reduced compensation for the next three years, and then the contract would end. Several years later the company's Board determined that Staklinski had become permanently disabled; he disagreed with this finding and the dispute was submitted to arbitration. The arbitrator found in favor of Staklinski and ordered the corporation to reinstate him. The court confirmed the award: "The power of an arbitrator to order specific performance in an appropriate case has been recognized from early times. * * * Whether a court of equity could issue a specific performance decree in a case like this is beside the point." In

the Matter of the Arbitration between Staklinski v. Pyramid Electric Co., 6 N.Y.2d 159, 188 N.Y.S.2d 541, 160 N.E.2d 78 (1959). See also In the Matter of the Arbitration between Grayson–Robinson Stores, Inc. v. Iris Construction Corp., 8 N.Y.2d 133, 202 N.Y.S.2d 303, 168 N.E.2d 377 (1960) (specific performance of a contract to construct a building.).

d. Arbitral Awards and Statutory Rights: Res Judicata and Collateral Estoppel

McDONALD v. CITY OF WEST BRANCH, MICHIGAN

Supreme Court of the United States, 1984.
466 U.S. 284, 104 S.Ct. 1799, 80 L.Ed.2d 302.

JUSTICE BRENNAN delivered the opinion of the Court.

The question presented in this § 1983 action is whether a federal court may accord preclusive effect to an unappealed arbitration award in a case brought under that statute.[1] In an unpublished opinion, the Court of Appeals for the Sixth Circuit held that such awards have preclusive effect. We granted certiorari, and now reverse.

On November 26, 1976, petitioner Gary McDonald, then a West Branch, Mich., police officer, was discharged. McDonald filed a grievance pursuant to the collective-bargaining agreement then in force between West Branch and the United Steelworkers of America (the Union), contending that there was "no proper cause" for his discharge, and that, as a result, the discharge violated the collective-bargaining agreement. After the preliminary steps in the contractual grievance procedure had been exhausted, the grievance was taken to arbitration. The arbitrator ruled against McDonald, however, finding that there was just cause for his discharge.

McDonald did not appeal the arbitrator's decision. Subsequently, however, he filed this § 1983 action against the City of West Branch and certain of its officials, including its Chief of Police, Paul Longstreet. In his complaint, McDonald alleged that he was discharged for exercising his First Amendment rights of freedom of speech, freedom of association, and freedom to petition the government for redress of grievances. The case was tried to a jury which returned a verdict against Longstreet, but in favor of the remaining defendants.

On appeal, the Court of Appeals for the Sixth Circuit reversed the judgment against Longstreet. The court reasoned that the parties had agreed to settle their disputes through the arbitration process and that

---

1. Title 42 U.S.C. § 1983 provides in pertinent part:

"Every person who, under color of any statute, ordinance, regulation, custom, or usage, of any State . . . subjects, or causes to be subjected, any citizen of the United States or other person within the jurisdiction thereof to the deprivation of any rights, privileges, or immunities secured by the Constitution and laws, shall be liable to the party injured in an action at law, suit in equity, or other proper proceeding for redress."

the arbitrator had considered the reasons for McDonald's discharge. Finding that the arbitration process had not been abused, the Court of Appeals concluded that McDonald's First Amendment claims were barred by res judicata and collateral estoppel.

At the outset, we must consider whether federal courts are obligated by statute to accord res judicata or collateral-estoppel effect to the arbitrator's decision. Respondents contend that the Federal Full Faith and Credit Statute, 28 U.S.C. § 1738, requires that we give preclusive effect to the arbitration award.

Our cases establish that § 1738 obliges federal courts to give the same preclusive effect to a state-court judgment as would the courts of the State rendering the judgment. * * * [H]owever, "[a]rbitration decisions . . . are not subject to the mandate of § 1738." This conclusion follows from the plain language of § 1738 which provides in pertinent part that the "*judicial proceedings* [of any court of any State] shall have the same full faith and credit in every court within the United States and its Territories and Possessions as they have by law or usage in the courts of such State . . . from which they are taken." (Emphasis added.) Arbitration is not a "judicial proceeding" and, therefore, § 1738 does not apply to arbitration awards.

Because federal courts are not required by statute to give res judicata or collateral-estoppel effect to an unappealed arbitration award, any rule of preclusion would necessarily be judicially fashioned. We therefore consider the question whether it was appropriate for the Court of Appeals to fashion such a rule.

On two previous occasions this Court has considered the contention that an award in an arbitration proceeding brought pursuant to a collective-bargaining agreement should preclude a subsequent suit in federal court. In both instances we rejected the claim.

Alexander v. Gardner–Denver Co., 415 U.S. 36 (1974), was an action under Title VII of the Civil Rights Act of 1964 brought by an employee who had unsuccessfully claimed in an arbitration proceeding that his discharge was racially motivated. Although Alexander protested the same discharge in the Title VII action, we held that his Title VII claim was not foreclosed by the arbitral decision against him.[8] In addition, we declined to adopt a rule that would have required federal courts to defer to an arbitrator's decision on a discrimination claim when "(i) the claim was before the arbitrator; (ii) the collective-bargaining agreement prohibited the form of discrimination charged in the suit under Title VII; and (iii) the arbitrator has authority to rule on the claim and to fashion a remedy."

---

8. The Court of Appeals in *Gardner–Denver* had concluded that the Title VII suit was barred by the doctrines of election of remedies and waiver, and by "the federal policy favoring arbitration of labor disputes." In addition to holding that none of these doctrines justified a rule of preclusion, we noted that "[t]he policy reasons for rejecting the doctrines of election of remedies and waiver in the context of Title VII are equally applicable to the doctrines of res judicata and collateral estoppel."

Similarly, in *Barrentine v. Arkansas–Best Freight System, Inc.*, 450 U.S. 728 (1981), Barrentine and a fellow employee had unsuccessfully submitted wage claims to arbitration. Nevertheless, we rejected the contention that the arbitration award precluded a subsequent suit based on the same underlying facts alleging a violation of the minimum wage provisions of the Fair Labor Standards Act. Our rejection of a rule of preclusion in *Barrentine* and our rejection of a rule of deferral in *Gardner–Denver* were based in large part on our conclusion that Congress intended the statutes at issue in those cases to be judicially enforceable and that arbitration could not provide an adequate substitute for judicial proceedings in adjudicating claims under those statutes. These considerations similarly require that we find the doctrines of res judicata and collateral estoppel inapplicable in this § 1983 action.

Because § 1983 creates a cause of action, there is, of course, no question that Congress intended it to be judicially enforceable. Indeed, "[t]he very purpose of § 1983 was to interpose the federal courts between the States and the people, as guardians of the people's federal rights—to protect the people from unconstitutional action under color of state law." And, although arbitration is well suited to resolving contractual disputes, our decisions in *Barrentine* and *Gardner–Denver* compel the conclusion that it cannot provide an adequate substitute for a judicial proceeding in protecting the federal statutory and constitutional rights that § 1983 is designed to safeguard. As a result, according preclusive effect to an arbitration award in a subsequent § 1983 action would undermine that statute's efficacy in protecting federal rights. We need only briefly reiterate the considerations that support this conclusion.

First, an arbitrator's expertise "pertains primarily to the law of the shop, not the law of the land." An arbitrator may not, therefore, have the expertise required to resolve the complex legal questions that arise in § 1983 actions.[9]

Second, because an arbitrator's authority derives solely from the contract, an arbitrator may not have the authority to enforce § 1983. As we explained in *Gardner–Denver*: "The arbitrator . . . has no general authority to invoke public laws that conflict with the bargain between the parties. . . . If an arbitral decision is based 'solely upon the arbitrator's view of the requirements of enacted legislation,' rather than on an interpretation of the collective-bargaining agreement, the arbitrator has 'exceeded the scope of the submission,' and the award will not be enforced." Indeed, when the rights guaranteed by § 1983 conflict with provisions of the collective-bargaining agreement, the arbitrator must enforce the agreement.

Third, when, as is usually the case, the union has exclusive control over the "manner and extent to which an individual grievance is

---

9. Indeed, many arbitrators are not lawyers. In addition, amici AFL–CIO and the United Steelworkers of America note that "[t]he union's case in a labor arbitration is commonly prepared and presented by non-lawyers."

presented," there is an additional reason why arbitration is an inadequate substitute for judicial proceedings. The union's interests and those of the individual employee are not always identical or even compatible. As a result, the union may present the employee's grievance less vigorously, or make different strategic choices, than would the employee. Thus, were an arbitration award accorded preclusive effect, an employee's opportunity to be compensated for a constitutional deprivation might be lost merely because it was not in the union's interest to press his claim vigorously.

Finally, arbitral factfinding is generally not equivalent to judicial factfinding. As we explained in *Gardner–Denver*, "[t]he record of the arbitration proceedings is not as complete; the usual rules of evidence do not apply; and rights and procedures common to civil trials, such as discovery, compulsory process, cross-examination, and testimony under oath, are often severely limited or unavailable."

It is apparent, therefore, that in a § 1983 action, an arbitration proceeding cannot provide an adequate substitute for a judicial trial.[11] Consequently, according preclusive effect to arbitration awards in § 1983 actions would severely undermine the protection of federal rights that the statute is designed to provide. We therefore hold that in a § 1983 action, a federal court should not afford res judicata or collateral-estoppel effect to an award in an arbitration proceeding brought pursuant to the terms of a collective-bargaining agreement.[13]

The judgment of the Court of Appeals is reversed, and the case is remanded for further proceedings consistent with this opinion.

Notes and Questions

(1) The district court in *Alexander v. Gardner–Denver* (discussed in *McDonald*) had granted summary judgment to the employer; it feared that "[t]o hold that an employee has a right to an arbitration of a

---

11. In addition to diminishing the protection of federal rights, a rule of preclusion might have a detrimental effect on the arbitral process. Were such a rule adopted, employees who were aware of this rule and who believed that arbitration would not protect their § 1983 rights as effectively as an action in a court might bypass arbitration.

13. Consistent with our decisions in *Barrentine* and *Gardner–Denver*, an arbitral decision may be admitted as evidence in a § 1983 action. As in those cases:

"We adopt no standards as to the weight to be accorded an arbitral decision, since this must be determined in the court's discretion with regard to the facts and circumstances of each case. Relevant factors include the existence of provisions in the collective-bargaining agreement that conform substantially with

[the statute or constitution], the degree of procedural fairness in the arbitral forum, adequacy of the record with respect to the issue [in the judicial proceeding], and the special competence of particular arbitrators. Where an arbitral determination gives full consideration to an employee's [statutory or constitutional] rights, a court may properly accord it great weight. This is especially true where the issue is solely one of fact, specifically addressed by the parties and decided by the arbitrator on the basis of an adequate record. But courts should ever be mindful that Congress . . . thought it necessary to provide a judicial forum for the ultimate resolution of [these] claims. It is the duty of courts to assure the full availability of this forum."

grievance which is binding on an employer but is not binding on the employee—a trial balloon for the employee, but a moon shot for the employer—would sound the death knell for arbitration clauses in labor contracts." 346 F.Supp. 1012, 1019 (D.Colo.1971). This prediction has not of course been borne out. Many collective bargaining agreements now include non-discrimination clauses and often incorporate Title VII or similar state statutes; labor arbitrators regularly decide such cases and engage in interpreting this language. See generally Fletcher, Arbitration of Title VII Claims: Some Judicial Perceptions, Proceedings, 34th Annual Meeting, Nat'l Academy of Arbitrators 218 (1982). But given the holdings in *Gardner–Denver* and *McDonald* what incentive is there—if employees are able to get "a second bite of the apple"— for employers to agree to submit such disputes to arbitration? Would you advise Hopewell College to do so in its dispute with Mary Kate Sheridan, see supra p. 12?

(2) An employee of an investment firm was discharged and brought suit claiming that the firm had discriminated against him in violation of the Age Discrimination in Employment Act. The employer's attempt to invoke the arbitration clause in the employment agreement was rebuffed. The court relied on cases like *Gardner–Denver* and *McDonald:*

> Though *Alexander* involved an attempt to preclude subsequent judicial consideration of a Title VII race discrimination case previously grieved, rather than an effort to compel arbitration, this court finds *Alexander*'s analysis informative. * * * "[T]he remedy for * * * discrimination was intended to be provided by the courts."

Steck v. Smith Barney, Harris Upham & Co., Inc., 661 F.Supp. 543 (D.N.J.1987).

(3) In neither *McDonald* nor *Gardner–Denver* had the arbitration award been judicially confirmed. (The *McDonald* opinion notes that the award was "unappealed.") Would the result in either case have been different if the award *had* been confirmed?

(4) An employer who fires a worker for engaging in union activity, or other protected "concerted activities for the purpose of collective bargaining," will have committed an "unfair labor practice" in violation of the National Labor Relations Act. Such action is likely to be at the same time a violation of any collective bargaining agreement between the employer and the union. See NLRB v. City Disposal Systems, Inc., 465 U.S. 822 (1984) (individual employee's assertion of his right, grounded in collective bargaining agreement, to refuse to drive an unsafe truck was legally protected "concerted activity"). If such a dispute has been submitted to arbitration, the National Labor Relations Board may be asked to defer to the resulting award. The NLRB may even be asked to defer to *prospective* awards, and to stay its hand by declining to hear an unfair labor practice complaint where the arbitral

process has not yet begun. The analogy to the problem posed by such cases as *McDonald* and *Gardner–Denver* is clear.

The decisions in this area have followed no steady course. The NLRB now presumes that the arbitrator has adequately considered the "unfair labor practice" question if the issue under the collective bargaining agreement is "factually parallel" to it and if "the arbitrator was presented generally with the facts relevant to resolving" it. In these circumstances the Board has announced that it will defer to the arbitral award "[u]nless the award is 'palpably wrong,' i.e., unless the arbitrator's decision is not susceptible to an interpretation consistent with the Act." Olin Corp., 268 NLRB 573, 115 LRRM 1056 (1984). This deferral policy has encountered a hostile reception in some courts. The Eleventh Circuit, for example, found that *Olin* represented "an abdication of Board responsibility"; the court concluded, citing *McDonald* and *Gardner–Denver,* that the Board's standard "does not protect sufficiently an employee's rights granted by the National Labor Relations Act." Taylor v. NLRB, 786 F.2d 1516 (11th Cir.1986). See also Kanowitz, Alternative Dispute Resolution and the Public Interest: The Arbitration Experience, 38 Hastings L.J. 239, 275–86 (1987).

D. THE ARBITRATION PROCEEDING

Within broad limits * * * private parties who submit an existing dispute to arbitration may write their own ticket about the terms of submission, if they can agree to a ticket. [The authors refer to an old story about a person who, in a dream, was threatened by an ominous character and who asked, tremulously, "Wh-what are you going to do now?"—only to receive the answer, "How do I know? This is *your* dream."] The arbitration of an existing dispute is the parties' dream, and they can make it what they want it to be.

The trouble is that it takes time and money to draft elaborate private laws * * *. Only in the most exceptional circumstances can a private disputant stop to negotiate and draft a complete constitution, together with a substantive and procedural code, for the governance of his private court.[1]

Rather than draft their own "procedural code," parties to arbitration agreements commonly prefer to incorporate by reference the standard rules for the conduct of arbitration proceedings prepared by institutions like the AAA. This allows them to avoid having to reinvent the wheel through lengthy negotiation and drafting—especially at a time when there may not be much incentive for cooperation—and instead to build upon the experience of others. In the materials that follow, frequent reference will be made to the practice of the AAA and particularly to its Commercial Arbitration Rules. But it must be remembered that arbitration remains ultimately "the parties' dream." It is always necessary to consider carefully the special features of each

---

1. H. Hart & A. Sacks, The Legal Process 336 (1958).

individual transaction, with a view to adding to the pre-existing structure or adapting it in light of the parties' particular circumstances.

1. The Decision–Makers

a. Selection of Arbitrators

Selecting the arbitrators is obviously a critical aspect of the arbitration process. After all, the ability to have a dispute decided by "judges" of one's own choosing is perhaps the most distinctive characteristic of this dispute resolution mechanism. How to provide for arbitrator selection is therefore an essential question for the parties in their planning.

The parties may, of course, simply try to agree by name on the individuals who will arbitrate their dispute. The arbitrator might, for example, be named in the original agreement. Or selection of the arbitrator might be left for later agreement on an ad hoc basis after a dispute arises. The choice of the "appropriate" arbitrator may in fact often be a function of the nature of the dispute which has arisen, or of the issues which happen to be in contention. In labor arbitration, for example, the parties may prefer lawyers as arbitrators when the issue is one of arbitrability, but may well prefer economists for wage disputes in "interest" arbitration, and industrial engineers for disputes over job evaluation.[2]

However, reliance on this method of arbitrator selection carries obvious dangers. When the arbitrator is named in advance, he may have become unwilling or unable to serve by the time a dispute later arises. This may then open up a challenge to the whole process; one party may argue that his agreement to arbitration was not unconditional but dependent on the personal choice of this "known and trusted expert," and that therefore arbitration should not proceed in his absence.[3] Such an argument will rarely be found persuasive, but in any event a means must be found to select a replacement.

On the other hand, where the agreement contemplates only that the parties will select their arbitrator *after* a dispute arises, there is an obvious potential for a recalcitrant party to drag his feet. The larger the stakes in the transaction, the more likely it is that the parties will wish to retain at least a veto over the identity of the decision-maker. Consider for example the agonizingly prolonged contract dispute between the Hunt brothers of Texas and the major oil-producing companies, a complex case arising out of various interests in Libyan oil concessions and involving sixteen parties and a welter of legal issues. The arbitration extended over a period of seven years; more than *two*

2. See Retzer and Petersen, Strategies of Arbitrator Selection, 70 Lab.Arb. 1307, 1319 (1978).

3. See Uniform Commercial Code § 2–305, Comment 4; Ballas v. Mann, 3 Misc. 2d 445, 82 N.Y.S.2d 426 (Sup.Ct.1948) (was intention to arbitrate "the dominant intention, the personality of the arbitrator being an auxiliary incident rather than the essence?").

years were consumed by the process of screening arbitrators, "as arbitrators proposed by one party were rejected by one or more of the other parties." The complexity of the issues in the case made the search for the requisite "arbitrators of unusual legal qualifications and broad experience in complicated transactions" particularly difficult. The court, however, made it clear that much of the delay was due to the tactics of the Hunts and their "campaign of obstruction to impede and defeat the arbitration." [4]

Under AAA rules, as soon as a demand for arbitration is made the AAA distributes to the parties a short list of potential arbitrators. It chooses these from its extensive panel of arbitrators, trying to match the names to the nature of the dispute and the industry involved. It may, for example, suggest arbitrators who have had experience in solar heating or landscape architecture if the dispute centers on practice in those trades. The parties may in their agreement have already specified the background or qualification of their arbitrators. In maritime arbitration, for example, it is the usual practice to stipulate that the arbitrators "shall be commercial men"—a phrase not meant to exclude women, but definitely meant to exclude lawyers. Unless the parties have already ruled out the possibility, however, it is customary to have at least one attorney on the list. Indeed, lawyers play a dominant part in many AAA arbitrations. As of 1986, for example, the AAA's construction arbitration panel contained 32,000 names, of whom almost half were attorneys—more than twice as many as the next largest professional category, engineers.

The information that the parties are given about a potential arbitrator is not extensive; it usually contains summary biographical information indicating the arbitrator's profession, present and past employment, education, and areas in which he claims expertise. There is no mechanism analogous to voir dire in which the parties have the opportunity to examine potential arbitrators prior to selection—although in large cases they have an obvious incentive to do some research on their own. Under AAA procedure, each party is allowed to cross off the list any names he finds unacceptable. Each then ranks the remaining names in order of preference, and from these the AAA is supposed to appoint an arbitrator "in accordance with the designated order of mutual preference." (The British refer to this method as "knocking the brains out of the panel.") [5] In the (unusual) event that every name turns out to be objectionable to one or both of the parties, the AAA may at that point simply choose another name from its panel without submitting any further lists; barring disqualification for cause, this selection is final.

Arbitration can proceed before any number of arbitrators—it is, again, "the parties' dream." But the most common pattern is to use

4. See Hunt v. Mobil Oil Corp., 654 F.Supp. 1487 (S.D.N.Y.1987).

5. Bernstein, Nudging and Shoving All Parties to a Jurisdictional Dispute Into Arbitration: The Dubious Procedure of *National Steel,* 78 Harv. L.Rev. 784, 790–91 (1965).

either a single individual or three arbitrators. Under AAA rules, a single arbitrator is to be used unless the parties specify otherwise or unless the AAA "in its discretion" selects a larger number. In 1986, over 80% of the construction cases administered by the AAA were held before a single arbitrator. In complex cases or cases where the stakes are large it is common, however, to use three neutral arbitrators; current AAA policy is to use three arbitrators where the amount at controversy exceeds $100,000. (The ICC's rule of thumb is that only a single arbitrator is warranted in cases involving less than $1 million). With three arbitrators, of course, far more time is consumed in selection, in scheduling the hearings, and, probably, in hearing time; the fees paid to the arbitrators are also likely to be higher.

What do parties look for in selecting arbitrators? In labor cases, where a large cadre of professional arbitrators has developed, it is often observed that parties have a strong preference for only the most experienced and active arbitrators. A recent survey submitted a sample case to a selected number of union and management representatives and asked for their preferences as to whom they wanted to hear the case: 47.6% of the management representatives and 61.5% of the union representatives chose a decision-maker whose primary occupation was as a "full-time arbitrator."[6] Some union and management representatives, in responding to another survey, indicated that they would require a potential arbitrator to have a case load of at least fifty arbitrations in one year.[7] The fact that many labor arbitration opinions are published not only helps the parties in doing "research" on potential arbitrators; it also serves to focus even greater attention on the well-known "name" arbitrators whose cases appear regularly in the reports.

This leads to a classic "Catch–22." Without experience, it is difficult for an arbitrator to be chosen to hear a labor case—and difficult therefore to develop the experience and reputation enabling him to be chosen to hear future cases. In 1985, there were 3400 names on the AAA's panel of labor arbitrators; only one-third of them had any cases at all that year. (Only 10% heard more than 20 cases). The natural result of this selective demand is that there are often lengthy delays before the chosen arbitrator will have the time to hear and dispose of a given case; the most experienced arbitrators may not be available for a hearing within several months after being asked to serve. While this is not perhaps a long time in comparison with some crowded judicial dockets, it is still troubling for a supposedly "expeditious" resolution process—particularly in cases where an employee has been discharged, and the employer is facing potential liability for back pay.

The profession of "labor arbitrator" is made possible by the often substantial fees that arbitrators are regularly paid for their services in

6. See Nelson, The Selection of Arbitrators, Lab.L.J., October 1986, at 703, 711.

7. Rezler and Petersen, Strategies of Arbitrator Selection, 70 Lab.Arb. 1307, 1308 (1978).

labor cases. We have already noted the possible effects of this arrangement on the decision patterns of professional arbitrators. See supra p. 427. Commercial arbitrators, in contrast, rarely hear more than one or two cases a year; the supply of acceptable arbitrators here is therefore relatively more elastic. In addition, commercial arbitrators frequently "donate" their time as a public service. When a hearing lasts longer than one or two days, however, it is customary for the parties to pay the arbitrators a per diem fee. (The arbitrators in the Hunt–Mobil Oil arbitration each received $1500 per hearing day—understandably enough, at the high end of the usual range.) This is in addition to the administrative fee, based on the amount of the claim, which is paid to institutions like the AAA and the ICC for their services in supervising the arbitration.

Notes and Questions

(1) Another traditional pattern in arbitration is a "tripartite" board, in which each party is allowed to select one arbitrator and a third, "neutral" chairman is chosen by the other two (or in the absence of agreement, by an institution like the AAA).

What effects might this kind of panel have on the decision-making process? The AAA's Commercial Arbitration Rules provide that where there is a panel of more than one arbitrator, decision is to be by *majority vote* unless the agreement provides otherwise. Where the other two arbitrators agree on a particular result, may the neutral be led to acquiesce in what is in reality a negotiated settlement being given the prestige of an arbitral award? See supra p. 429. And where the other two arbitrators *disagree,* may the neutral be forced to trim or compromise his own views in order to obtain a majority? Consider In re Publishers' Ass'n. of N.Y. and N.Y. Typographical Union, 36 Lab. Arb. 706 (1961). The neutral arbitrator here voted with the employer to discharge a worker but wrote, in an unusually candid opinion, that this penalty had been "forced upon" him. While he would have preferred a lesser penalty such as a disciplinary suspension, his most "patient and painstaking efforts" had convinced him that "there was no possibility whatever of an award issuing which would reflect a view intermediate to the polar position of my colleagues." He therefore saw no choice other than to join in the position which was *closest* to the one he preferred!

Would it have been possible or appropriate for the neutral in *Publishers' Association* to have acted differently? To avoid placing such a burden on the neutral, would it not be better simply to stipulate that in the absence of a majority decision the final decision is to be made by the neutral alone—or even that the function of the party-appointed arbitrators is always to be merely advisory? This is in fact commonly provided in collective bargaining agreements. And in that case, is any purpose ever served by having a tripartite board at all? Can you think of any countervailing advantages to using a tripartite board with party-named representatives? See Zack, Tripartite Panels: Asset or Hindrance in Dispute Settlement?, Proceedings, 34th Annual Meeting, Nat'l Academy of Arbitrators 273, 279 (1982) (deliberations between neutral and party-appointed arbitrators can help clarify technical issues, provide assurance that the neutral fully understands the issues and background of the case, and allow discussion and review of the possible implications of the neutral's written opinion).

(2) Where the parties are unable to agree on an arbitrator and the proceeding is not being administered by an institution like the AAA, modern statutes empower a court to make the choice. See FAA, § 5.

Assume an arbitration clause provides that if the parties cannot agree on a neutral arbitrator for a tripartite panel, the choice is to be made "by drawing lots." Under § 5, can one of the parties refuse to follow this procedure and instead ask the court to appoint the neutral? See Pacific Reinsurance Management Corp. v. Ohio Reinsurance Corp., 814 F.2d 1324 (9th Cir.1987) ("the intent of Congress was to spur the arbitral process forward, rather than to let it stagnate into endless bickering over the selection process").

(3) Three members of a family were parties to a partnership agreement: Charles, Albert (Charles' son), and Isidore (Charles' brother). The agreement provided for arbitration in which Charles and Albert would jointly name one arbitrator, Isidore would name another, and the two arbitrators would select a third.

However, the drafting of this clause proved to be inept. There was a change of alignment in the partnership not originally contemplated; Isidore and Charles, complaining about Albert's lack of concern for the partnership, sought arbitration. Charles and Albert could not jointly agree on an arbitrator; Albert insisted that he be permitted to select an arbitrator independently since the interests of the other two parties were identical and adverse to his. On application to the court to name an arbitrator, what result? See Lipschutz v. Gutwirth, 304 N.Y. 58, 106 N.E.2d 8 (1952).

(4) When there is a continuing relationship between the parties, it may be expected that a number of disputes will surface on a regular basis. Some collective bargaining agreements (for example, the agreements between the major automobile manufacturers and the United Auto Workers) provide therefore for one or several "permanent umpires" charged in advance with arbitrating all future disputes. Where arbitration has been institutionalized in this manner the process of selection of ad hoc arbitrators, and challenges to their qualifications, are thus avoided. Of course, use of a permanent arbitrator may make it impossible for the parties to tailor the choice of arbitrator to the issues raised in the particular dispute. But it is a powerful advantage of the "permanent umpire" that he may be expected over time to become intimately familiar with the relationship, the industry setting, and the background of future controversies. He should also be able to build a body of consistent interpretation and "case law" that the parties

themselves can use in settling grievances short of arbitration. See F. Elkouri & E. Elkouri, How Arbitration Works 119–29 (4th ed. 1985).

b. Arbitral Impartiality

COMMONWEALTH COATINGS CORP. v. CONTINENTAL CASUALTY CO.

Supreme Court of the United States, 1968.
393 U.S. 145, 89 S.Ct. 337, 21 L.Ed.2d 301.

MR. JUSTICE BLACK delivered the opinion of the Court.

At issue in this case is the question whether elementary requirements of impartiality taken for granted in every judicial proceeding are suspended when the parties agree to resolve a dispute through arbitration.

[Having read this far, what do you think the answer is going to be?—Eds.]

The petitioner, Commonwealth Coatings Corp., a subcontractor, sued the sureties on the prime contractor's bond to recover money alleged to be due for a painting job. The contract for painting contained an agreement to arbitrate such controversies. Pursuant to this agreement petitioner appointed one arbitrator, the prime contractor appointed a second, and these two together selected the third arbitrator. This third arbitrator, the supposedly neutral member of the panel, conducted a large business in Puerto Rico, in which he served as an engineering consultant for various people in connection with building construction projects. One of his regular customers in this business was the prime contractor that petitioner sued in this case. This relationship with the prime contractor was in a sense sporadic in that the arbitrator's services were used only from time to time at irregular intervals, and there had been no dealings between them for about a year immediately preceding the arbitration. Nevertheless, the prime contractor's patronage was repeated and significant, involving fees of about $12,000 over a period of four or five years, and the relationship even went so far as to include the rendering of services on the very projects involved in this lawsuit. An arbitration was held, but the facts concerning the close business connections between the third arbitrator and the prime contractor were unknown to petitioner and were never revealed to it by this arbitrator, by the prime contractor, or by anyone else until after an award had been made. Petitioner challenged the award on this ground, among others, but the District Court refused to set aside the award. The Court of Appeals affirmed.

* * * [B]oth sides here assume that [the FAA] governs this case. Section 10 sets out the conditions upon which awards can be vacated. The two courts below held, however, that § 10 could not be construed in such a way as to justify vacating the award in this case. We disagree and reverse. Section 10 does authorize vacation of an award where it was "procured by corruption, fraud, or undue means" or "[w]here there was evident partiality * * * in the arbitrators." These provisions show a desire of Congress to provide not merely for *any* arbitration but for an impartial one. It is true that petitioner does not charge before us that the third arbitrator was actually guilty of fraud or bias in deciding this case, and we have no reason, apart from the undisclosed business relationship, to suspect him of any improper motives. But neither this arbitrator nor the prime contractor gave to petitioner even an intimation of the close financial relations that had existed between them for a period of years. We have no doubt that if a litigant could show that a foreman of a jury or a judge in a court of justice had, unknown to the litigant, any such relationship, the judgment would be subject to challenge. This is shown beyond doubt by Tumey v. State of Ohio, 273 U.S. 510 (1927), where this Court held that a conviction could not stand because a small part of the judge's income consisted of court fees collected from convicted defendants. Although in *Tumey* it appeared the amount of the judge's compensation actually depended on whether he decided for one side or the other, that is too small a distinction to allow this manifest violation of the strict morality and fairness Congress would have expected on the part of the arbitrator and the other party in this case. Nor should it be at all relevant, as the Court of Appeals apparently thought it was here, that "[t]he payments received were a very small part of [the arbitrator's] income * * *." For in *Tumey* the Court held that a decision should be set aside where there is "the slightest pecuniary interest" on the part of the judge, and specifically rejected the State's contention that the compensation involved there was "so small that it is not to be regarded as likely to influence improperly a judicial officer in the discharge of his duty * * *." Since in the case of courts this is a *constitutional* principle, we can see no basis for refusing to find the same concept in the broad statutory language that governs arbitration proceedings and provides that an award can be set aside on the basis of "evident partiality" or the use of "undue means." It is true that arbitrators cannot sever all their ties with the business world, since they are not expected to get all their income from their work deciding cases, but we should, if anything, be even more scrupulous to safeguard the impartiality of arbitrators than judges, since the former have completely free rein to decide the law as well as the facts and are not subject to appellate review. We can perceive no way in which the effectiveness of the arbitration process will be hampered by the simple requirement that arbitrators disclose to the parties any dealings that might create an impression of possible bias.

[Justice Black then referred to the AAA rules of procedure which, "while not controlling in this case," called on an arbitrator "to disclose any circumstances likely to create a presumption of bias or which he believes might disqualify him as an impartial Arbitrator."]

[B]ased on the same principle as this Arbitration Association rule is that part of the 33d Canon of Judicial Ethics which provides:

33. Social Relations

* * * [A judge] should, however, in pending or prospective litigation before him be particularly careful to avoid such action as may reasonably tend to awaken the suspicion that his social or business relations or friendships, constitute an element in influencing his judicial conduct.

This rule of arbitration and this canon of judicial ethics rest on the premise that any tribunal permitted by law to try cases and controversies not only must be unbiased but also must avoid even the appearance of bias. We cannot believe that it was the purpose of Congress to authorize litigants to submit their cases and controversies to arbitration boards that might reasonably be thought biased against one litigant and favorable to another.

Reversed.

MR. JUSTICE WHITE, with whom MR. JUSTICE MARSHALL joins, concurring.

While I am glad to join my Brother Black's opinion in this case, I desire to make these additional remarks. The Court does not decide today that arbitrators are to be held to the standards of judicial decorum of Article III judges, or indeed of any judges. It is often because they are men of affairs, not apart from but of the marketplace, that they are effective in their adjudicatory function. This does not mean the judiciary must overlook outright chicanery in giving effect to their awards; that would be an abdication of our responsibility. But it does mean that arbitrators are not automatically disqualified by a business relationship with the parties before them if both parties are informed of the relationship in advance, or if they are unaware of the facts but the relationship is trivial. I see no reason automatically to disqualify the best informed and most capable potential arbitrators.

The arbitration process functions best when an amicable and trusting atmosphere is preserved and there is voluntary compliance with the decree, without need for judicial enforcement. This end is best served by establishing an atmosphere of frankness at the outset, through disclosure by the arbitrator of any financial transactions which he has had or is negotiating with either of the parties. In many cases the arbitrator might believe the business relationship to be so insubstantial that to make a point of revealing it would suggest he is indeed easily swayed, and perhaps a partisan of that party.* But if the law requires the disclosure, no such imputation can arise. And it is far better that the relationship be disclosed at the outset, when the parties are free to reject the arbitrator or accept him with knowledge of the relationship and continuing faith in his objectivity, than to have the relationship come to light after the arbitration, when a suspicious or disgruntled party can seize on it as a pretext for invalidating the

---

* In fact, the District Court found—on the basis of the record and petitioner's admissions—that the arbitrator in this case was entirely fair and impartial. I do not read the majority opinion as questioning this finding in any way.

award. The judiciary should minimize its role in arbitration as judge of the arbitrator's impartiality. That role is best consigned to the parties, who are the architects of their own arbitration process, and are far better informed of the prevailing ethical standards and reputations within their business.

Of course, an arbitrator's business relationships may be diverse indeed, involving more or less remote commercial connections with great numbers of people. He cannot be expected to provide the parties with his complete and unexpurgated business biography. But it is enough for present purposes to hold, as the Court does, that where the arbitrator has a substantial interest in a firm which has done more than trivial business with a party, that fact must be disclosed. If arbitrators err on the side of disclosure, as they should, it will not be difficult for courts to identify those undisclosed relationships which are too insubstantial to warrant vacating an award.

MR. JUSTICE FORTAS, with whom MR. JUSTICE HARLAN and MR. JUSTICE STEWART join, dissenting.

I dissent and would affirm the judgment.

The facts in this case do not lend themselves to the Court's ruling. The Court sets aside the arbitration award despite the fact that the award is unanimous and no claim is made of actual partiality, unfairness, bias, or fraud.

* * *

Both courts below held, and petitioner concedes, that the third arbitrator was innocent of any actual partiality, or bias, or improper motive. There is no suggestion of concealment as distinguished from the innocent failure to volunteer information.

The third arbitrator is a leading and respected consulting engineer who has performed services for "most of the contractors in Puerto Rico." He was well known to petitioner's counsel and they were personal friends. Petitioner's counsel candidly admitted that if he had been told about the arbitrator's prior relationship "I don't think I would have objected because I know Mr. Capacete [the arbitrator]."

Clearly, the District Judge's conclusion, affirmed by the Court of Appeals for the First Circuit, was correct, that "the arbitrators conducted fair, impartial hearings; that they reached a proper determination of the issues before them, and that plaintiff's objections represent a 'situation where the losing party to an arbitration is now clutching at straws in an attempt to avoid the results of the arbitration to which it became a party.'"

* * *

I do not believe that it is either necessary, appropriate, or permissible to rule, as the Court does, that, regardless of the facts, innocent failure to volunteer information constitutes the "evident partiality" necessary under § 10(b) of the Arbitration Act to set aside an award. "Evident partiality" means what it says: conduct—or at least an attitude or disposition—by the arbitrator favoring one party rather than the other. This case demonstrates that to rule otherwise may be a palpable injustice, since all agree that the arbitrator was innocent of either "evident partiality" or anything approaching it.

Arbitration is essentially consensual and practical. The United States Arbitration Act is obviously designed to protect the integrity of the process with a minimum of insistence upon set formulae and rules. The Court applies to this process rules applicable to judges and not to a system characterized by dealing on faith and reputation for reliability. Such formalism is not contemplated by the Act nor is it warranted in a case where no claim is made of partiality, of unfairness, or of misconduct in any degree.

Notes and Questions

(1) Did Justice White really "join" in Justice Black's opinion? Note that the votes of Justices White and Marshall were essential to a majority in *Commonwealth Coatings*.

(2) The current version of the AAA's Commercial Arbitration Rules requires neutral arbitrators to "disclose to the AAA any circumstances likely to affect impartiality, including any bias or any financial or personal interest in the result of the arbitration or any past or present relationship with the parties or their counsel." The AAA shall then "determine whether the Arbitrator should be disqualified and shall inform the parties of its decision, which shall be conclusive." (Rule 19). A "Code of Ethics for Arbitrators in Commercial Disputes" has also been adopted by the AAA and by the American Bar Association. Canon II of this Code provides that "An Arbitrator should disclose any interest or relationship likely to affect impartiality or which might create an appearance of partiality or bias":

A. Persons who are requested to serve as arbitrators should, before accepting, disclose:

(1) Any direct or indirect financial or personal interest in the outcome of the arbitration;

(2) Any existing or past financial, business, professional, family or social relationships which are likely to affect impartiality or which might reasonably create an appearance of partiality or bias. Persons requested to serve as arbitrators should disclose any such relationships which they personally have with any party or its lawyer, or with any individual whom they have been told will be a witness. They should also disclose any such relationships involving members of their families or their current employers, partners or business associates.

E. In the event that an arbitrator is requested by all parties to withdraw, the arbitrator should do so. In the event that an arbitrator is requested to withdraw by less than all of the parties because of alleged partiality or bias, the arbitrator should withdraw unless either of the following circumstances exists:

(1) If an agreement of the parties, or arbitration rules agreed to by the parties, establishes procedures for determining challenges to arbitrators, then those procedures should be followed; or

(2) If the arbitrator, after carefully considering the matter, determines that the reason for the challenge is not substantial, and that he or she can nevertheless act and decide the case impartially and fairly, and that withdrawal would cause unfair delay or expense to another party or would be contrary to the ends of justice.

Notes to this "Canon" make clear that it is

intended to be applied realistically so that the burden of detailed disclosure does not become so great that it is impractical for persons in the business world to be arbitrators, thereby depriving parties of the services of those who might be best informed and qualified to decide particular types of cases.

(3) What use can be made of the AAA Rules and Canons in a judicial proceeding to vacate an arbitral award? Judge Posner has written that:

[E]ven if the failure to disclose was a material violation of the ethical standards applicable to arbitration proceedings, it does not follow that the arbitration award may be nullified judicially. * * * The arbitration rules and code do not have the force of law. If [a party] is to get the arbitration award set aside it must bring itself within the statute * * *.

The American Arbitration Association is in competition not only with other private arbitration services but with the courts in providing—in the case of the private services, selling—an attractive form of dispute settlement. It may set its standards as high or as low as it thinks its customers want. The [FAA] has a different purpose—to make arbitration effective by putting the coercive force of the federal courts behind arbitration decrees that affect interstate commerce or are otherwise of federal concern. * * * The standards for judicial intervention are therefore narrowly drawn to assure the basic integrity of the arbitration process without meddling in it. Section 10 is full of words like corruption and misbehavior and fraud. The standards it sets are minimum ones. * * * The fact that the AAA went beyond the statutory standards in drafting its own code of ethics does not lower the threshold for judicial intervention.

Merit Insurance Co. v. Leatherby Insurance Co., 714 F.2d 673 (7th Cir. 1983).

Do you agree?

(4) If courts held arbitrators to the same standards of isolation and purity to which they hold Article III judges, an adverse decision might invariably become the occasion for frantic research by the losing party

into possible links between his adversary and the arbitrator. The obvious dangers to the arbitral process have led courts to be unreceptive to such attempts.

In their reluctance to set aside awards on these grounds courts have also been sensitive to the need for decision-makers with extensive professional experience and knowledge, and to what Judge Posner has called the necessary "tradeoff between impartiality and expertise." *Merit Insurance Co.*, 714 F.2d at 679. A good example is presented by International Produce, Inc. v. A/S Rosshavet, 638 F.2d 548 (2d Cir. 1981). This was a maritime arbitration in which the neutral arbitrator was the Vice–President of a management firm retained by owners of various commercial vessels. After the hearings had begun, this arbitrator's firm became involved in an unrelated arbitration involving another vessel. It happened that the law firms representing the parties in the second arbitration were the same firms that were handling the *International Produce* arbitration; in this second proceeding the arbitrator appeared as a non-party witness, prepared in his testimony by one of the law firms and cross-examined by the other. Although requested to withdraw, the arbitrator refused to do so, and his award was successfully challenged in district court. The Second Circuit held that the award should not have been vacated:

> It is not unusual that those who are selected as arbitrators in maritime arbitrations have had numerous prior dealings with one or more of the parties or their counsel. * * * Arbitrator Klosty aptly analogized New York's maritime-arbitration community to a busy harbor, where the wakes of the members often cross.

> The most sought-after arbitrators are those who are prominent and experienced members of the specific business community in which the dispute to be arbitrated arose. Since they are chosen precisely because of their involvement in that community, some degree of overlapping representation and interest inevitably results. Those chosen as arbitrators in important shipping arbitrations have typically participated in a great number of prior maritime disputes, not only as arbitrators but also as parties and witnesses. They have therefore almost inevitably come into contact with a significant proportion of the relatively few lawyers who make up the New York admiralty bar. Under these circumstances, a decision on our part to vacate arbitration awards whenever a mere appearance of bias can be made out would seriously disrupt the salutary process of settling maritime disputes through arbitration.

Of course, the alleged conflict of interest in *International Produce* was immediately known to both of the parties in the case as soon as it arose. Would the matter be different—should a higher standard be imposed—if one party is claiming that the arbitrator failed before the hearing to disclose facts about his relationship with the other?

(5) Are party-appointed representatives on tripartite boards held to the same standards of fairness, impartiality, and disclosure as other arbitrators? The "Code of Ethics for Arbitrators in Commercial Disputes" provides that party-appointed arbitrators "should observe all of the obligations of Canon I ["An Arbitrator Should Uphold the Integrity and Fairness of the Arbitration Process"]. They "may be predisposed toward the party who appointed them." But "in all other respects [they] are obligated to act in good faith and with integrity and fairness. For example, non-neutral arbitrators should not engage in delaying tactics or harassment of any party or witness and should not knowingly make untrue or misleading statements to the other arbitrators."

With respect to Canon II concerning *disclosure,* the Code provides that non-neutral party-appointed arbitrators "need not include as detailed information as is expected from persons appointed as neutral arbitrators"; in addition, they "are not obligated to withdraw if requested to do so by the party who did not appoint them."

(6) Assuming that proper disclosure is made, can a party appoint its own attorney as "its" arbitrator on a tripartite board? Can it appoint a member of its Board of Directors? See In the Matter of the Arbitration between the Astoria Medical Group v. Health Ins. Plan of Greater N.Y., 11 N.Y.2d 128, 227 N.Y.S.2d 401, 182 N.E.2d 85 (1962) (yes; "[t]he right to appoint one's own arbitrator * * * becomes a valued right, which parties will bargain for and litigate over, only if it involves a choice of one believed to be sympathetic to his position or favorably disposed to him."). Does it follow, then, that an individual party can itself sit as "its" own arbitrator? See Edmund E. Garrison, Inc. v. International Union of Operating Engineers, 283 F.Supp. 771 (S.D.N.Y.1968) (no).

(7) Cf. W.L. Craig, W. Park, & J. Paulsson, International Chamber of Commerce Arbitration § 13.03 at 39 (Oceana, 1984):

Irrespective of one's right in principle to insist that all arbitrators be independent, the advisability of a challenge remains a question of tactics more than one of philosophy. After years of observing international arbitration in practice, the authors have concluded it is best to challenge as infrequently as possible, perhaps on the maxim "better the devil you know than the one you don't." At least for the claimant, little purpose is served by causing one's adversary to have to replace its nominee; the proceedings are delayed, and the replacement nominee may be no more independent than his predecessor. * * * An arbitrator who shows himself to be the mere agent of a party is probably not worth challenging. His weight within the tribunal will be discounted and the chairman is likely to lend a more attentive ear to his other co-arbitrator.

(8) A collective bargaining agreement provided that all disputes between the union and an employer association would be referred to a "permanent umpire." The union and the association, in a joint letter,

appointed a particular arbitrator "for the duration [of the collective bargaining agreement] unless terminated sooner by either party." Eight years later the union purported to terminate the employment of the umpire, who at that point was being paid an annual salary of $68,000. The union took the position that the words "either party" referred to the two parties to the collective bargaining agreement. The employer association claimed that the union lacked the authority unilaterally to dismiss the umpire; on its reading of the letter, "either party" meant the umpire on one hand, and *both* union and association on the other. Should this dispute be submitted to the permanent umpire for decision? See Pitta v. Hotel Association of New York City, Inc., 806 F.2d 419 (2d Cir.1986).

(9) On occasion a losing party, claiming that the arbitrator did not decide fairly or that he proceeded in violation of the rules, will bring a suit directly against the arbitrator or the administering institution. Such claims are usually rebuffed with an invocation of "arbitral immunity." Just as with judges, it is thought that "the independence necessary for principled and fearless decision-making can best be preserved by protecting these persons from bias or intimidation caused by the fear of a lawsuit arising out of the exercise of official functions within their jurisdiction." Corey v. New York Stock Exchange, 691 F.2d 1205 (6th Cir.1982). This "federal policy" dictates that the only remedy for a disgruntled party is under § 10 and § 11 of FAA and not by means of collateral attacks on the award. A similar interest in protecting arbitrators also means that when a court *does* hear a motion under § 10 or § 11, it is unlikely to permit depositions or examination of the arbitrators themselves aimed at developing a factual basis for impeaching the award.

Compare, however, Baar v. Tigerman, 140 Cal.App.3d 979, 189 Cal. Rptr. 834 (1983). Under AAA rules, an arbitrator has 30 days after the closing of hearings to render his decision. In *Baar* the arbitrator (after four years of intermittent hearings) did not meet that deadline. When an award had not been rendered after seven months, one of the parties filed a written objection which under the state arbitration statute deprived the arbitrator of any further authority. This party then brought a suit against the arbitrator and the AAA, and the court held that a cause of action had been stated for "breach of contract and negligence." The cases granting "arbitral immunity" were distinguished on the grounds that they protected arbitrators "acting in a quasi-judicial capacity" and involved "alleged misconduct in arriving at a decision"; *Baar*, by contrast, involved a simple "failure to make an award."

Who is acting as an "arbitrator" for purposes of "arbitral immunity"? Should immunity be extended to an architect, employed and paid by the owner of a construction project and charged with interpreting the contract documents and deciding whether the contractor has substantially performed? See Lundgren v. Freeman, 307 F.2d 104, 116–19 (9th Cir.1962)(granting immunity when architect was acting as "quasi-arbitrator"). What about an accountant who is hired by both parties to a contract for the sale of stock to determine the earnings of the company? See Wasyl, Inc. v. First Boston Corp., 813 F.2d 1579 (9th Cir. 1987) (claim of breach of contract and gross negligence by defendant in appraisal of value of partnership interest; immunity granted). Cf. Arenson v. Casson Beckman Rutley & Co., [1975] 3 All E.R. 901, [1975] 3 W.L.R. 815 (H.L.) ("It would be absurd if the situation were that, when an expert is asked by one customer to value a picture, he is liable in damages if he is shown to have done so negligently, but that if two customers had jointly asked him to value the same picture he would have been immune from suit") (Lord Kilbrandon).

2. Conduct of the Proceeding

a. Introduction

In any discussion of arbitration it is almost mandatory to mention the supposed "informality" of the process: "The essence of arbitration is its freedom from the formality of ordinary judicial procedure." [1] However, there is not merely one "form of procedure" for arbitration in the United States, but an almost infinite variety:

> At one extreme, we have what is practically courtroom procedure, with carefully drawn submissions, formal procedures, emphasis upon technicalities, formal opening and closing statements, arguments as to the admissibility and relevance of evidence, qualifications of witnesses, and the burden of proof, and briefs, rebuttal briefs, and sur-rebuttal briefs. At the other extreme, we have an atmosphere which is barely distinguishable from a mediation proceeding; the issue is vague and ill-defined, everybody talks at the same time, says irrelevant things, no standards of evidence appear, and the arbitrator seems to be working chiefly at the task of securing agreement between the disputants. Between the extremes are innumerable shadings and variations.[2]

The personality and the professional background of the arbitrator, the attitudes and the relationship of the parties, the issues in contention—all will influence the way the arbitration proceeds. Nevertheless, as we will see, there are some common threads.

In addition, "even in the most informal of proceedings certain minimum requirements of 'due process' must be met if the award is to be legally binding." [3] State and federal statutes governing arbitration mandate certain elements supposed to be essential to a fair hearing. Under the Uniform Arbitration Act, "[t]he parties are entitled to be heard, to present evidence material to the controversy and to cross-

1. Canuso v. City of Philadelphia, 326 Pa. 302, 192 A. 133 (1937).

2. Stein, The Selection of Arbitrators, N.Y.U. Eighth Annual Conference on Labor 291, 293 (1955).

3. R. Smith, L. Merrifield & D. Rothschild, Collective Bargaining and Labor Arbitration 212 (1970).

examine witnesses appearing at the hearing." § 5(c). The parties also have the right to be represented by an attorney, and any waiver of that right prior to the hearing is ineffective. § 6.

Attorneys can play a useful role in arbitration. In framing and focusing the issues, and in eliciting and marshalling the evidence, the attorney can help create a more coherent and rational process. However, the use of attorneys—along with the adversarial proceedings that seem to be envisaged by the arbitration statutes—may be responsible for some of the vociferous complaints about the growing "legalization" of the arbitration process. These complaints seem to be heard most loudly in the self-contained enclave of labor arbitration. One observer, for example, has written:

> In the past two decades, a change in orientation of labor arbitrators and a rise in the use of attorneys as advocates have accelerated the introduction into labor arbitration of procedures that approximate those of the courts. * * *

[The former president of the National Academy of Arbitrators has written that]

> * * * The ratio of hard fought, legalistic arbitration presentations to problem-solving presentations is increasing. I now have more long, drawn-out cases in which employers and unions present prehearing briefs, spend endless hours haggling over the language of the submitted issue, have stenographic records made of the hearings and insist upon briefs, reply briefs, and sometimes, reply briefs to the reply briefs. * * *

> Legalism adds to the complexity of arbitration, and correspondingly to the confusion of an employee. The impersonality that legalism brings to the process undermines its credibility. Employees who have been assisted in their grievances by union representatives who may have known them for years may be represented at the arbitration by attorneys whom they have seen for the first time on the day of the arbitration. When these attorneys, competent though they may be, neglect to raise questions that the grievants feel are important, which they feel would have been asked by union representatives, the grievants feel cheated.[4]

In this debate, however, as in most others, where one ends up may well depend upon one's starting point. The author of the preceding excerpt is a "Professor of Human Resource Development" in a College of Business. A lawyer, in contrast, is far more likely to be using a judicial yardstick when he evaluates arbitration. He may be struck most forcibly by the way in which the process *falls short* of the "judicial solemnity"[5] and the "due process" model with which he is most comfortable. The sections that follow explore some of the ways in which the typical arbitration will differ from litigation. An attorney

---

4. Raffaele, Lawyers in Labor Arbitration, 37 Arb.J. No. 3 (Sept. 1982).

5. See, e.g., Bayer & Abrahams, The Trouble with Arbitration, 11 Litigation 30 (Winter 1985).

who is unfamiliar with the process may at first find it difficult to adapt himself to the different quality of advocacy expected in arbitration, and must struggle to adjust his behavior to the different style and atmosphere of an arbitration proceeding. He needs to bear in mind, for example, that commercial arbitrators "are not generally amused by forensic brilliance" [6] developed by lawyers for courtroom use. Arbitrators, it has been said, are likely to be "unimpressed by arguments resting upon the abstract 'rights' of the parties. The arbitrator will chiefly want to know whether the parties conducted themselves honorably and fairly and made a genuine effort to settle their differences by negotiation." [7]

b. Evidence

The classic illustration of the relative "informality" of the arbitration process is the usual absence of the rules of evidence, which play such a dominant role in any courtroom. Under the AAA's Commercial Arbitration Rules, "[t]he Arbitrator shall be the judge of the relevancy and materiality of the evidence offered and conformity to legal rules of evidence shall not be necessary." (Rule 31).

An arbitrator is in fact more likely to get into trouble by following the rules of evidence than by ignoring them—and far more likely to get into trouble by excluding evidence than by admitting it. Section 10(c) of the FAA allows a court to vacate an award where the arbitrator was "guilty of misconduct" "in refusing to hear evidence pertinent and material to the controversy." There are many cases in which an arbitrator's disregard of testimony in reliance on rules of evidence has caused his award to be vacated, on the ground that a party has been denied a "fair hearing." See, e.g., Harvey Alum. v. United Steelworkers of America, 263 F.Supp. 488 (C.D.Cal.1967). Perhaps as a consequence, the common tendency of arbitrators seems to be to admit most proffered evidence and to consider it "for whatever it may be worth." "I am prepared to listen to just about anything a party wants me to hear." [8]

A good example is provided by one lawyer's account of his service on an arbitration panel. In this construction case a contractor who had built a building for a private school submitted a substantial claim for "extras," work done but supposedly not covered by the contract price:

> In his opening statement to the panel, the lawyer for the school asserted that even without the extras, the contractor had made a profit. He then gave the arbitrators an affidavit from the school's controller. It stated that the school, which enjoyed an excellent reputation in the community, would have to raise each student's tuition at least $1,300 a year just to pay the interest on the amount

6. Houston, Textile Transactions, in A. Widiss (ed.), Arbitration 145, 172–74 (1979).

7. L. Fuller & M. Eisenberg, Basic Contract Law 434 (3d ed. 1972).

8. McDermott, An Exercise in Dialectic: Should Arbitration Behave As Does Litigation?, Proceedings, 33rd Annual Meeting, Nat'l Academy of Arbitrators 1, 14 (1981).

sought by the contractor. The affidavit also stated that the school had granted scholarships to at least 28 students, who might have to withdraw if the contractor obtained the award he was seeking.

[Over an objection by the contractor's lawyer that the affidavit was "incompetent, irrelevant, hearsay, prejudicial, and not probative on any issue in dispute," the panel (which also included an architect and an engineer) received it in evidence. The arbitration lasted for weeks, with copious, and confusing, evidence offered on each of the contractor's claims:]

> Among the few facts which retained their persuasive power throughout the arbitration were the points the school lawyer had made at the outset. Almost every day, in private conversations over lunch or over an early evening drink, or during any one of the several recesses taken during the day, one or more of the arbitrators mentioned that the contractor had already made a profit and that granting the claim would injure the school and hurt innocent scholarship students.

The ultimate decision was in favor of the school.[9]

This lowering of barriers to the admission of evidence in arbitration is often the subject of serious criticism—particularly on the part of lawyers, who are likely to find it "chaotic," "sloppy," and worse. Is such criticism well-founded? Or may it rest at least in part on a misunderstanding of the premises of arbitration? The opportunity to present evidence that is not particularly reliable or even particularly relevant by the usual standards of the courtroom may nevertheless provide arbitrators with an insight into the "total situation" of the parties not afforded by a narrower scope of inquiry. And when the parties are engaged in a continuing relationship, such an opportunity can permit a useful "ventilation" of a grievance; as in mediation, when the parties are given a sense that they have had a full opportunity to "have their say" on points that are personally important to them, the process is legitimated and their confidence in it increased: "This is therapy evidence."[10] Nor is it even true that generosity in admitting evidence will necessarily prolong the hearings. Laying a proper "foundation" for evidence and qualifying witnesses, making a series of witnesses personally available for the purposes of cross-examination, and resolving the inevitable wrangles over admissibility, all may consume at least as much if not more time than does the present practice.

Notes and Questions

(1) In none of the statutes governing arbitration is there any mention of improperly *admitting* evidence as a form of arbitral "mis-

9. Roth, When to Ignore the Rules of Evidence in Arbitration, 9 Litigation 20 (Winter 1983).

10. Jones, Evidentiary Concepts in Labor Arbitration: Some Modern Variations on Ancient Legal Themes, 13 U.C.L.A. L.Rev. 1241, 1254 (1966).

conduct." Can an award ever be vacated on such grounds? See In the Matter of the Arbitration between Norma Brill v. Muller Brothers, Inc., 40 Misc.2d 683, 243 N.Y.S.2d 905 (1962), in which the arbitrator received in evidence a detective agency report consisting of a "dime-novel series of stories about the petitioner and her behavior, said to be gathered from her former neighbors" and "detailing specific acts of alleged avarice, malice and chicanery." The trial court, calling this "hearsay on hearsay" and "thoroughly unfair evidence," "inflammatory and prejudicial to the highest degree," vacated the award. Higher courts, however, reversed, 17 App.Div. 804, 232 N.Y.S.2d 806 (1962), aff'd, 13 N.Y.2d 776, 242 N.Y.S.2d 69, 192 N.E.2d 34 (1963).

(2) In the course of an arbitration between a brokerage firm and one of its customers, the customer—an attorney—revealed that the firm had made him a settlement offer of $135,000. The arbitrators sustained the firm's objection to this evidence, but later awarded the customer $145,000. The firm moved to vacate the award under § 10(a) of the FAA. The court, however, found that the customer's disclosure had not denied the firm a "fundamentally fair hearing" and denied the motion: "A district court is not free to impose court procedures on the unstructured and informal nature of an arbitration proceeding." The court nevertheless condemned the customer's tactics as "gamesmanship, pure and simple," and warned that "[t]he future of alternative dispute resolution is surely bleak if interested contestants in search of solutions or compromise become hobbled by their adversarial instincts and seek to replace substance and clarity with irrelevancy or distortion." Ouziel v. Shearson Lehman Brothers, Inc., No. CV 86–1822 (RJD) (E.D.N.Y., Apr. 11, 1988.)

See also the discussion concerning the inadmissibility of settlement negotiations at supra p. 181.

(3) Should the arbitrator be expected to make a decision based solely on the evidence received at the hearing? After all, one of the premises of arbitration is that the arbitrator may himself be an "expert," chosen to bring to the process his own knowledge and familiarity with the subject matter. It seems clear that an arbitrator, unlike a judge, is free to draw on this background. In one commercial dispute, for example, the arbitrators awarded the buyer money damages for non-delivery even though no evidence as to the market price of the goods had been introduced. Judge Learned Hand dismissed the seller's argument that this constituted arbitral "misconduct," remarking that if the arbitrators "were of the trade, they were justified in resorting to their personal acquaintance with its prices." When the parties have chosen arbitration, he added, "they must be content with its informalities; they may not hedge it about with those procedural limitations which it is precisely its purpose to avoid." American Almond Prods. Co. v. Consolidated Pecan Sales Co., 144 F.2d 448, 450–51 (2d Cir.1944). See also In the Matter of the Arbitration between Oinoussian Steamship Corp. of Panama v. Sabre Shipping Corp., 224 F.Supp. 807 (S.D. N.Y.1963) (arbitrators allegedly relied on trade custom not mentioned

at hearing; "it would be carrying coals to Newcastle to require presentation of evidence to experts in the field").

However, the arbitrator's relative freedom in supplementing the evidence introduced by the parties is hardly a license to make his own independent investigation into the facts of the dispute. Where the quality of goods is in dispute, an arbitrator who gives samples of the goods to his own salesmen for the purpose of obtaining an opinion as to "merchantability" is inviting a court to vacate his award for "misconduct.". See Stefano Berizzi Co. v. Krausz, 239 N.Y. 315, 146 N.E. 436 (1925) (Cardozo, J.) ("The plaintiff, knowing nothing of the evidence, had no opportunity to rebut or even to explain it."). So is the arbitrator who in attempting to fix the rental value of real estate asks the opinion of real estate brokers as to the value of similar property. See 290 Park Ave. v. Fergus Motors, 275 App.Div. 565, 90 N.Y.S.2d 613 (1949).

Under the AAA's Commercial Arbitration Rules, "[a]ll evidence shall be taken in the presence of all of the arbitrators and all of the parties, except where any of the parties is absent in default or has waived the right to be present." (Rule 31). If an arbitrator "deems it necessary to make an inspection or investigation in connection with the arbitration," he must notify the AAA of his intention to do so, and the AAA in turn notifies the parties: "Any party who so desires may be present at such inspection or investigation. In the event that one or both parties are not present at the inspection or investigation, the Arbitrator shall make a verbal or written report to the parties and afford them an opportunity to comment." (Rule 33).

c. Discovery

Another illustration of the relative informality of arbitration is the sharply limited availability of discovery, both "pre-trial" and at the hearing itself.

A starting point is a common statutory provision such as § 7 of the Uniform Arbitration Act:

(a) The arbitrators may issue subpoenas for the attendance of witnesses and for the production of books, records, documents and other evidence, and shall have the power to administer oaths.

* * *

(b) On application of a party and for use as evidence, the arbitrators may permit a deposition to be taken, in the manner and upon the terms designated by the arbitrators, of a witness who cannot be subpoenaed or is unable to attend the hearing.

See also § 7 of the FAA.

Issuance or enforcement of a subpoena is, however, rarely necessary; an informal request for information by the arbitrator at a hearing usually suffices. At least where it is a *party* who has been requested to produce evidence, he will be reluctant to antagonize the arbitrator by refusing; in addition, he will be aware that should he decline to produce the information, the arbitrator is likely to draw the inference that it would have been unfavorable to him. "[U]sually an informal indication that such an inference will or may be drawn is sufficient to extract the document." [11]

The provisions of § 7 leave it to the discretion of the arbitrator to decide what materials he feels he needs to resolve the dispute; a party has no "right," for example, to the issuance of a subpoena. It is of course conceivable that an arbitrator's refusal to order the production of evidence could evoke a successful challenge to the award. In one maritime case, the arbitrators had refused to order the shipowner to produce the ship's logs during the proceeding; a court indicated that this could constitute a violation of § 10(c) of the FAA where the charterer of the ship could "show prejudice as a result." The court noted that the ship's logs are "perhaps the most important items of documentary evidence in any maritime controversy," and failure to supply them before the hearings end could prejudice the ability of a party "not only in cross examination of witnesses, but in the preparation of its own case." [12] Such judicial action is, however, extremely rare.

True "discovery" in the litigation sense—for example, interrogatories and depositions taken before "trial" for the purposes of "trial" preparation—is even more limited. Provisions such as § 7 of the Uniform Arbitration Act assume, of course, that the arbitrators have already been named. Even where the arbitration panel is in place, the power of arbitrators to order pre-hearing discovery—at least in the absence of an agreement between the parties—is doubtful. An arbitrator's authority to order the production of documents in advance of the hearing has been upheld, see Stanton v. Paine Webber Jackson & Curtis, Inc., 685 F.Supp. 1241 (S.D.Fla.1988). In other jurisdictions even this authority has been denied, see North American Foreign Trading Corp. v. Rosen, 58 A.D.2d 527, 395 N.Y.S.2d 194 (1977) (arbitration panel "exceed[ed] its authority by directing pre-arbitration disclosure"). In any event the full range of discovery provided by the Federal Rules of Civil Procedure will not be available: While the Rules apply to motions made under the FAA (for example, to compel arbitration or to confirm an award), it is clear that they do not apply to *the conduct of the actual proceedings* by the arbitrators. There are, however, some state statutes that do envisage more extensive arbitral discovery. For example, the Texas version of the Uniform Arbitration Act adds to § 7 that the arbitrators "may authorize a deposition of an adverse witness for discovery or evidentiary purposes, such depositions to be taken in the manner provided by law for depositions in a civil action pending in a district court." Tex.Civ.Stat. art. 230B. See also

11. Lowenfeld, The *Mitsubishi* Case: Another View, 2 Arb.Int'l 178, 184 (1986).

12. In the Matter of the Arbitration between Chevron Transport Corp. v. Astro Vencedor Compania Naviera, S.A. 300 F.Supp. 179 (S.D.N.Y.1969).

Cal.Code Civ.Pro. §§ 1283.05, 1283.1 ("right to take depositions and to obtain discovery" in arbitration of personal injury claims).

The general unavailability of pre-hearing discovery in arbitration often leads parties to an arbitrable dispute to seek discovery ordered and supervised by a *court*. A fairly liberal attitude towards allowing discovery is exemplified by Bigge Crane & Rigging Co. v. Docutel Corp., 371 F.Supp. 240 (E.D.N.Y.1973). In *Bigge*, a subcontractor brought suit against a general contractor for payments due under a construction contract. The plaintiff, asserting that it had been given "no explanation" of the reasons it had not been paid for the work performed, then sought to take depositions of the defendant's employees and to obtain inspection of job records, contracts, and other documents. The defendant moved for a stay of the action under § 3 of the FAA and for an order compelling arbitration. The court granted the motion and stayed the trial pending completion of arbitration—"without prejudice," however, "to the rights of [the parties] to utilize the pretrial discovery procedures of the Federal Rules of Civil Procedure in a manner which does not delay the course of the arbitration":

> In this case there will have been considerable delay by the time the elaborate proceedings of the American Arbitration Association for the selection of arbitrators have been completed; and the arbitrators, selected for this particular case, may be under some pressure to complete their task promptly. On the other hand, discovery proceedings in the court action can go forward while the selection of arbitrators and scheduling of a hearing is under way.

> * * *

> Arbitration is not a separate proceeding independent of the courts, as was sometimes thought. The courts are brigaded with the arbitral tribunal in proceedings to compel arbitration or stay judicial trials, proceedings to enforce or quash subpoenas issued by arbitrators and proceedings to enforce or set aside arbitral awards. * * * [T]he court believes that it should exercise discretion to permit discovery in this case because (1) discovery is particularly necessary in a case where the claim is for payment for work done and virtually completed, and the nature of any defense is unknown; (2) the amounts involved are so substantial that any expense in taking depositions is relatively small; [and] (3) the action has proceeded to such a point that the taking of depositions can probably be accomplished without delaying the arbitration.

Most cases, however, are considerably more restrictive than *Bigge*. There is a tendency to require that pre-arbitration discovery be "necessary" to a party to allow him to "present a proper case to the arbitrators," or even that "extraordinary circumstances" be present, before a court may order it. See In re the Application of Moock, 99 A.D.2d 1003, 473 N.Y.S.2d 793 (1984); International Components Corp. v. Klaiber, 54 A.D.2d 550, 387 N.Y.S.2d 253 (1976) ("absolutely necessary"). Cf. Ferro Union Corp. v. SS Ionic Coast, 43 F.R.D. 11 (S.D.Tex.

1967) (foreign flag vessel with foreign crew was about to leave American port; defendant moved for § 3 "stay" but in view of "exceptional situation" court ordered immediate discovery to allow gathering of facts which might otherwise be lost). See generally Note, Relaxing the Standard for Court–Ordered Discovery in Aid of Commercial Arbitration, 50 Fordham L.Rev. 1448 (1982).

Notes and Questions

(1) Reluctance to make pre-hearing discovery widely available in arbitration may reflect the concern that this would be inconsistent with the goal of rapid and inexpensive dispute resolution. Looming over the debate is likely to be the specter of the "abuse" of the discovery process—"unfocused, unthoughtful, often massive, and always expensive"—which many observers blame for the delay and excessive cost characterizing complex federal litigation. See Lundquist, In Search of Discovery Reform, 66 A.B.A.J. 1071 (1980). The fear is expressed that the use of pre-hearing discovery would add one further layer of complexity and "legalism" to a process which in the eyes of some observers has already come too much to resemble formal adjudication. In addition, there is a concern that judicial supervision and administration of the discovery process might interfere with the functions of the arbitrators chosen by the parties, and "preshape" the issues presented to them for decision. The point is also frequently made that by choosing arbitration, the parties have voluntarily accepted the risk that pre-hearing discovery and the other "procedural niceties which are normally associated with a formal trial" would not be available to them. Burton v. Bush, 614 F.2d 389, 390 (4th Cir.1980).

Nevertheless, procedure in arbitration is flexible enough so that some of the same advantages offered by "pre-trial" discovery can be worked into the process. For example, the AAA's Commercial Arbitration Rules make provision for an off-the-record pre-hearing conference to be held with the AAA administrator, at the parties' request or at the AAA's discretion. Such pre-hearing conferences are quite common in more complex cases. They provide an opportunity for the plaintiff's claim to be outlined in greater detail and for the issues to be refined, as well as for information to be exchanged and uncontested facts to be stipulated. In addition, while a trial is likely to proceed more or less continuously once it has begun, an arbitration proceeding may readily be adjourned or continued at the arbitrator's discretion, to allow a party to study and respond to information revealed as a result of arbitrator-issued subpoenas. "If [the arbitrators] wish to allow the questioner further opportunity to investigate after receiving the answers they will do so. What more is there to an examination before trial?" Motor Vehicle Accident Indemnification Corp. v. McCabe, 19 A.D.2d 349, 243 N.Y.S.2d 495 (1963).

(2) At an arbitration hearing the arbitrator orders the plaintiff to produce certain documents; the plaintiff refuses to comply, asserting

that this material consists of the confidential communication of information to his attorney and is thus exempt from subpoena on the basis of the attorney-client privilege. The arbitrator then announces that following his usual practice, he will conclude that the evidence if produced would have been unfavorable to the plaintiff; his award is in favor of the defendant. On the plaintiff's motion to vacate the award, what result?

The California Evidence Code makes the testimonial privileges applicable in all "proceedings," a term defined to include arbitration and any other hearing "in which, pursuant to law, testimony can be compelled to be given." Cal. Evidence Code §§ 901, 910. Section 913 further provides that if a privilege is exercised not to testify or disclose information, "the trier of fact may not draw any inference therefrom as to the credibility of the witness or as to any matter at issue in the proceeding."

(3) A party to a collective bargaining agreement frequently needs information to help him decide whether to carry a grievance to arbitration in the first place. For example, a collective bargaining agreement may state a general policy against the subcontracting of work, and provide that where equipment is moved to another plant, employees who are laid off as a result may transfer to the new location. In such a case, when machinery is moved out of the plant, the union will need to know where it has gone and what it is being used for. See NLRB v. Acme Industrial Co., 385 U.S. 432 (1967). To obtain such information in advance of arbitration, the Union may appeal to the National Labor Relations Board. In *Acme*, the Board found that the employer's refusal to furnish information about the removed equipment was in violation of the statutory duty to "bargain in good faith" because the information was "necessary in order to enable the Union to evaluate intelligently the grievances filed." The employer was therefore ordered to furnish the information to the union prior to any arbitration hearing. The Supreme Court held that this order should be enforced; Justice Stewart wrote that:

> Far from intruding upon the preserve of the arbitrator, the Board's action was in aid of the arbitral process. Arbitration can function properly only if the grievance procedures leading to it can sift out unmeritorious claims. For if all claims originally initiated as grievances had to be processed through to arbitration, the system would be woefully overburdened. Yet, that is precisely what the respondent's restrictive view would require. It would force the union to take a grievance all the way through to arbitration without providing the opportunity to evaluate the merits of the claim. The expense of arbitration might be placed upon the union only for it to learn that the machines had been relegated to the junk heap.

Invoking the Board's enforcement machinery can, however, be a slow and cumbersome process. See Jones, Blind Man's Buff and the *Now-*

Problems of Apocrypha, Inc. and Local 711—Discovery Procedures in Collective Bargaining Disputes, 116 U.Pa.L.Rev. 571 (1968).

3. The Courts and the Arbitration Proceeding

a. "Waiver" of the Right to Arbitration

DE SAPIO v. KOHLMEYER

Court of Appeals of New York, 1974.
35 N.Y.2d 402, 362 N.Y.S.2d 843, 321 N.E.2d 770.

RABIN, J. The plaintiff-respondent James De Sapio was employed as a block trader by defendant-appellant Kohlmeyer from November, 1970 until April, 1971, at which time he was discharged. In January, 1972, plaintiff sought employment with another firm which, like Kohlmeyer, was a member of both the New York and American Stock Exchanges. In so applying, plaintiff authorized an investigation of his employment history. As part of the investigation, a representative of the defendant Fidelifacts interviewed a partner of Kohlmeyer. Subsequently, plaintiff instituted this action alleging that the Kohlmeyer partner published defamatory remarks to the investigator regarding the facts underlying plaintiff's discharge. The complaint further alleges that Fidelifacts republished the defamation in its report to plaintiff's prospective employer.

As part of its answer, Kohlmeyer pleaded as an affirmative defense that it had arbitration agreements with the plaintiff providing that any controversy between them arising out of plaintiff's employment or the termination of his employment "shall be settled by arbitration." Following its answer, Kohlmeyer obtained a deposition of plaintiff and then moved to stay the action on the basis of the agreements to arbitrate. Special Term denied the stay on the ground that the instant action for defamation could not be said to arise out of either plaintiff's employment or its termination. The Appellate Division affirmed.

* * *

In this court, the plaintiff-respondent defends the correctness of Special Term's denial of the motion for a stay on two grounds: (1) Kohlmeyer waived any right to move for a stay; and (2) the arbitration agreements do not apply to this action because they were no longer effective and because this controversy did not arise out of plaintiff's employment or its termination. We agree with the waiver argument advanced by plaintiff-respondent and consequently do not reach the other issues raised. The defendant Kohlmeyer waived any right to stay the action by its affirmative use of the judicial proceedings.

While the party who commences an action may generally be assumed to have waived any right it may have had to submit the issues to arbitration, this assumption, of course, does not apply to a defendant. Nevertheless a defendant's right to compel arbitration, and the concomitant right to stay an action, does not remain absolute regardless of the degree of his participation in the action. In Matter of Zimmerman [236 N.Y. 15, 139 N.E. 764 (1923)], we held that the right of a defendant to compel arbitration was not absolute down to the time of trial and could be forfeited prior to trial. The defendant in *Zimmerman* waived his right to compel arbitration and stay the action when he set up a counterclaim, gave notice of trial, and procured an order for the taking of a deposition in preparation for trial. On the other hand, interposing an answer of itself does not work to waive a defendant's right to a stay.

The crucial question, of course, is what degree of participation by the defendant in the action will create a waiver of a right to stay the action. In the absence of unreasonable delay, so long as the defendant's actions are consistent with an assertion of the right to arbitrate, there is no waiver. However, where the defendant's participation in the lawsuit manifests an affirmative acceptance of the judicial forum, with whatever advantages it may offer in the particular case, his actions are then inconsistent with a later claim that only the arbitral forum is satisfactory. Thus, entering a stipulation to extend the time to answer is a purely defensive action and is not inconsistent with a later attempt to force arbitration. In contrast, contesting the merits through the judicial process is an affirmative acceptance of the judicial forum and waives any right to a later stay of the action. Board of Educ. v. Mancuso Bros., 25 Misc.2d 122, [204 N.Y.S.2d 410 (1960)] (motion for summary judgment).

In the present case, plaintiff urges that two actions of the defendant Kohlmeyer constitute a waiver of any right to stay the action: (1) interposing a cross claim demanding apportionment of any liability; and (2) procuring a deposition of plaintiff. We agree that each of these actions is a sufficiently affirmative use of the judicial process so as to be inconsistent with a later motion to stay. The defendant Fidelifacts is not a party to any arbitration agreement with the other litigants, and Kohlmeyer would not be able to obtain apportionment of liability in arbitration. Similarly, Kohlmeyer's utilization of judicial discovery procedures is also an affirmative acceptance of the judicial forum. The availability of disclosure devices is a significant differentiating factor between judicial and arbitral proceedings. "It is contemplated that disclosure devices will be sparingly used in arbitration proceedings. If the parties wish the procedures available for their protection in a court of law, they ought not to provide for the arbitration of the dispute."

* * *

In light of these differences between arbitral and judicial proceedings with regard to the availability of discovery, the defendant's procurement of a pretrial deposition of plaintiff in the judicial action constitutes an election between the forums available for resolving the dispute, and therefore a waiver of any right to stay the action. The courtroom may not be used as a convenient vestibule to the arbitration hall so as to allow a party to create his own unique structure combining litigation and arbitration.

Accordingly, the order of the Appellate Division should be affirmed and the question certified answered in the affirmative.

Notes and Questions

(1) The *De Sapio* case is typical in assuming that it is for the court rather than an arbitrator to decide the threshold question whether a party's "participation in the lawsuit" constitutes a "waiver" of the right to arbitration. See supra p. 480.

(2) Cases like *De Sapio* seem to counsel that a decision whether or not to pursue arbitration under an arbitration clause should be made at the earliest possible moment. In contrast, many *federal* cases seem to be considerably slower in finding "waiver" where a party has vacillated and participated in litigation before moving to compel arbitration. Given the "strong federal policy favoring enforcement of arbitration agreements between knowledgeable business people," a finding of waiver is not favored in federal court; the party asserting it bears a heavy burden of proof. Knorr Brake Corp. v. Harbil, Inc., 556 F.Supp. 489 (N.D.Ill.1983).

Federal courts therefore tend to ask whether one of the parties will have been "prejudiced" if his adversary is permitted to take part in litigation and then later demand arbitration. In one case, a customer brought suit against a brokerage firm; the firm asserted a counterclaim, moved for summary judgment, and engaged in discovery. At least 35 depositions were noticed by both sides, and the district court considered at least eight discovery motions, four of which were made by the defendant. "The parties participated in four status conferences, five hearings on pending motions, and two pretrial conferences"; a number of trial dates were set and cancelled. Then, more than four years after the complaint was filed, the defendant moved to compel arbitration. Considering "the extent of the moving party's trial-oriented activity," and the "substantial time and effort" expended by the plaintiff in repeatedly arguing motions and preparing for trial, the court found that the defendant's right to arbitration had been waived. Fraser v. Merrill Lynch Pierce, Fenner & Smith, Inc., 817 F.2d 250 (4th Cir.1987).

Without such a finding of "prejudice," the fact that a party has delayed in calling for arbitration will not be enough to cause a waiver of his right to arbitrate. (In many cases delay in demanding arbitration will simply reflect the fact that negotiations over a settlement of the dispute are being carried on.) Nor will the mere fact that he has filed pleadings in the lawsuit. So, for example, a party has been allowed to seek arbitration thirteen months after the filing of a complaint, even though he had filed an answer and a demand for a jury trial, answered interrogatories, and permitted the taking of depositions. J & S Construction Co., Inc. v. Travelers Indemnity Co., 520 F.2d 809 (1st Cir.1975). See also Maxum Foundations, Inc. v. Salus Corp., 779 F.2d 974 (4th Cir.1985) (defendant asserted counterclaim and filed third-party complaint, attended depositions noticed by the plaintiff, and issued its own interrogatories and requests for document production).

Whether a party has suffered enough "prejudice" to warrant a finding of waiver is obviously an inquiry heavily dependent on the facts of the particular case; the large number of variables makes prediction of results problematical. In many cases courts seem to predicate a finding of waiver on the benefits obtained by a party from using judicial discovery mechanisms not available in arbitration. See, e.g., Miller Brewing Co. v. Fort Worth Distributing Co., Inc., 781 F.2d 494, 498 (5th Cir.1986) (defendant's claim of waiver upheld; defendant's "position would be prejudiced and compromised in arbitration by [plaintiff's] use of pre-trial discovery going to the merits"). In other cases, the benefits of pre-trial discovery obtained by the party seeking arbitration seems to play a smaller role. A court may even note that the party resisting arbitration and claiming waiver will *himself* derive advantages from the discovery that has already taken place. See *Knorr Brake*, supra (plaintiff's claim of "waiver" rejected; plaintiff's "participation in discovery will be as valuable to them in arbitration as in a trial"; in addition, plaintiff's efforts to dismiss the defendant's counterclaim "will certainly be of value in resolving the arbitrable issues").

(3) Where at an early stage in the litigation the defendant has put the plaintiff on notice that he intends to seek arbitration, a finding of waiver is particularly unlikely, even where the defendant later actively participates in the lawsuit. See Tenneco Resins, Inc. v. Davy Intern., AG, 770 F.2d 416 (5th Cir.1985) (defendant's answer to the complaint raised the defense of an arbitration clause; defendant later served interrogatories and requests for production of documents; held, no waiver). A court is likely to reason that where the plaintiff had been given adequate notice, he was able to seek a protective order from the court limiting or prohibiting any further discovery and so minimizing further expense; he could at least "forestall" discovery until the question of arbitrability is resolved. See Shinto Shipping Co., Ltd. v. Fibrex & Shipping Co., Inc., 572 F.2d 1328 (9th Cir.1978) (party "should have sought the protective orders rather than scheming to void the entire arbitration process"; claim of waiver rejected).

(4) Is the *De Sapio* case consistent with the federal cases discussed in the preceding notes? Is a separate state standard of waiver permissible in cases falling within the ambit of the FAA?

(5) A finding of waiver is more readily made where it is the *plaintiff* in a lawsuit who later seeks to compel arbitration of the dispute. See, e.g., Christensen v. Dewor Developments, 33 Cal.3d 778, 191 Cal.Rptr. 8, 661 P.2d 1088 (1983) (plaintiff filed complaint in order to "have some feel for what the Defendants' position would be at arbitration"). The court in *De Sapio* goes so far as to suggest that a plaintiff "may generally be assumed" to have waived any right to arbitration. See also Note, Contractual Agreements to Arbitrate Disputes: Waiver of the Right to Compel Arbitration, 52 So.Cal.L.Rev.

1513 (1979), which advocates that a plaintiff who files suit over an arbitrable issue should be "deemed" to have waived any right to arbitration. Are there any virtues in such a mechanical rule? What of the case where a plaintiff files a complaint and then, the same day, changes his mind and makes a formal demand for arbitration? See Cavac Compania Anonima Venezolana De Administracion y Comercio v. Board for Validation of German Bonds in the U.S., 189 F.Supp. 205 (S.D.N.Y.1960).

(6) The AAA's Commercial Arbitration Rules provide that "[n]o judicial proceedings by a party relating to the subject matter of the arbitration shall be deemed a waiver of the party's right to arbitrate." (Rule 47(a)). What is the legal effect of this Rule? If the arbitration in *De Sapio* took place under AAA auspices, would Rule 47(a) change the result in that case? Would it change the result in *Fraser v. Merrill Lynch Pierce, Fenner & Smith,* supra note (2)?

One court, in refusing to give effect to the AAA Rule, thought that "[t]he parties are precluded from contracting to exclude the court from jurisdiction over this issue." United Nuclear Corp. v. General Atomic Co., 93 N.M. 105, 597 P.2d 290 (1979). Another common approach is to avoid the issue through creative re-interpretation. It has been suggested, for example, that Rule 47(a) is intended to apply only to provisional remedies such as attachment and injunctions in aid of arbitration, and is not meant to allow a party to "switch course" after seeking a judicial resolution of a dispute. Seidman & Seidman v. Wolfson, 50 Cal.App.3d 826, 123 Cal.Rptr. 873 (1975).

(7) A finding that the right to arbitration has been waived is often a value-laden judgment, comprehensible only as a response to other, unarticulated policies. An extreme example of this point is Davis v. Blue Cross of Northern California, 25 Cal.3d 418, 158 Cal.Rptr. 828, 600 P.2d 1060, (1979). A number of insureds alleged in a class action that Blue Cross had refused to pay for hospital expenses to which they were entitled. Shortly after the filing of the complaint Blue Cross moved to submit the disputes to a "medical arbitration panel" as required by the policies. The trial court found that the arbitration clause had been "buried in an obscure provision" of the agreements and that Blue Cross, in rejecting claims, had failed to bring the arbitration procedure to its insureds' attention. The Supreme Court of California agreed with the trial court that Blue Cross had "breached its duty of good faith and fair dealing" to its insureds "by failing timely or adequately to apprise them of the availability" of arbitration and that "as a consequence, Blue Cross waived any right subsequently to compel its insureds to resort to arbitration."

Is this a case of "waiver"? How have the plaintiffs been prejudiced by Blue Cross's failure to inform them of the availability of arbitration? In the course of its opinion, the Supreme Court also noted that:

> Under hospitalization policies, in which disputes over benefits may frequently involve a simple disagreement between the insured's

physician and the insurer's medical consultant as to the reasonableness of fees or the necessity for certain medical procedures, the existence of an arbitral process will often enable the insured to obtain an impartial review of the insurer's decision without the need to incur the significant expense of legal counsel; as a consequence, the reduced cost of the process may make it practicable for the insured to secure a binding resolution of disputes over smaller claims than would otherwise be financially feasible.

How does the court's finding of "waiver" respond to this rhetoric about the advantages of the arbitration process?

b. Interim Measures

TERADYNE, INC. v. MOSTEK CORP.
United States Court of Appeals, First Circuit, 1986.
797 F.2d 43.

[Mostek manufactured and marketed semiconductor components for use in computers and telecommunications equipment. Virtually all of Mostek's supply of laser systems and memory testers, which were essential to its manufacturing operations, were provided by Teradyne. Mostek always bought from Teradyne pursuant to the terms of a Quantity Purchase Agreement (QPA), which provided that Mostek would get price discounts on Teradyne equipment if it ordered certain minimum quantities, and that Mosek would be liable for cancellation and rescheduling charges if it cancelled an order.

[In early 1985 a dispute arose between the parties over cancellation charges claimed by Teradyne. At that time the 1984 QPA had expired; Mostek had held off entering into a QPA for 1985 because it was experiencing financial difficulties. As consideration for waiving the claimed charges, Teradyne demanded that Mostek place an order for twenty memory testers; Teradyne also supposedly "insisted" that before it would fill earlier orders placed by Mostek at the quoted prices, Mostek had to enter into a new QPA for 1985. In March 1985, Mostek did agree to enter into a QPA for 1985 and to place an order for twenty memory testers.

[Later that year, Mostek cancelled its orders; it refused to pay the cancellation charges demanded by Teradyne, assessed at 70% of the original purchase price. In September Teradyne requested arbitration, claiming approximately $3,500,000 for cancellation charges, goods and services invoiced, and incidental and consequential damages. In October Mostek's parent company announced that Mostek would cease operations; in November, substantially all of Mostek's assets were sold for approximately $71 million in cash. The proceeds of the sale were deposited in a separate bank account in Mostek's name and dedicated to the payment of the claims of its creditors. Teradyne then brought an action seeking an injunction ordering Mostek to set aside sufficient funds to satisfy a judgment pending the outcome of arbitration. The district court enjoined Mostek from disposing of or encumbering $4,000,000 of its assets and directed it to set that amount aside in an interest-bearing account to satisfy any arbitration award obtained by Teradyne.

[The First Circuit first held that the district court's "interlocutory order which has the attributes of both an attachment and an injunction" should be treated as a preliminary injunction, and was therefore appealable.

[The court then addressed Mostek's contention "that the policy of the Arbitration Act precludes the grant of preliminary injunctive relief in an arbitrable dispute."]

The Arbitration Act does not address this issue specifically and it has not previously been ruled upon by this circuit. Other circuits, however, have examined the issue in some detail. The Second, Fourth and Seventh Circuits all take the view that a court can, and should, grant a preliminary injunction in an arbitrable dispute whenever an injunction is necessary to preserve the status quo pending arbitration.

* * *

The Fourth Circuit's examination of this issue, in Merrill Lynch, Pierce, Fenner & Smith, Inc. v. Bradley, 756 F.2d 1048 (4th Cir.1985), focused on the effect of § 3 of the Arbitration Act on the court's power to issue preliminary injunctive relief. * * * Merrill Lynch sued Bradley, a former account executive, for damages for alleged breach of contract, and sought injunctive relief to prevent Bradley from using its records and soliciting its clients. The district court granted Merrill Lynch a preliminary injunction * * * and ordered expedited arbitration, both parties having agreed that the dispute was arbitrable. Bradley appealed, claiming that the injunction was an abuse of discretion because § 3 of the Arbitration Act precluded a court from considering the merits of an arbitrable dispute. The Fourth Circuit rejected this argument, holding that nothing in § 3 abrogated the equitable power of district courts to enter preliminary injunctions to preserve the status quo pending arbitration. The court also stated that it thought its decision would further rather than frustrate the policies underlying the Arbitration Act by ensuring that the dispute resolution would be a meaningful process.

* * *

Running counter to the approach taken by the Second, Fourth and Seventh Circuits is that taken by the Eighth Circuit in Merrill Lynch, Pierce, Fenner & Smith, Inc. v. Hovey, 726 F.2d 1286 (8th Cir.1984) * * *. Hovey involved a petition by Merrill Lynch for an injunction against five former employees to prevent them from using Merrill Lynch's records and from soliciting Merrill Lynch clients. The employees counterclaimed, seeking to compel arbitration pursuant to New York Stock Exchange rules regulating dispute resolution procedures. The district court granted Merrill Lynch a preliminary injunction and refused to submit the dispute to arbitration. The employees appealed, claiming that the dispute was arbitrable. The Eighth Circuit held that the dispute was arbitrable and that issuing a preliminary injunction was, therefore, precluded by § 3 of the Arbitration Act. The court took the view that granting preliminary injunctive relief in an arbitrable dispute ran counter to the "unmistakably clear congressional purpose that the arbitration procedure, when selected by the parties to a contract, be speedy and not subject to delay and obstruction in the courts." (quoting *Prima Paint Corp.*) [supra p. 455].

* * *

[W]e are persuaded that the approach taken by the Second, Fourth and Seventh Circuits should be followed. We hold, therefore, that a district court can grant injunctive relief in an arbitrable dispute pending arbitration, provided the prerequisites for injunctive relief are satisfied. * * * We believe that the congressional desire to enforce arbitration agreements would frequently be frustrated if the courts were precluded from issuing preliminary injunctive relief to preserve the status quo pending arbitration and, ipso facto, the meaningfulness of the arbitration process. Accordingly, we hold that it was not error for the district court to issue the preliminary injunction before ruling on the arbitrability of this dispute. We next consider whether Teradyne established the prerequisites for such relief.

[The court then turned to the question whether the criteria for preliminary injunctive relief were satisfied. In the First Circuit, a court must find: "that plaintiff will suffer irreparable injury if the injunction is not granted"; "that such injury outweighs any harm which granting injunctive relief would inflict on the defendant"; and "that plaintiff has exhibited a likelihood of success on the merits."]

The district court here clearly articulated its reasons for finding that Teradyne had satisfied the prerequisites for injunctive relief. It held that Mostek's freedom to dispose of its assets created a substantial risk of irreparable harm to Teradyne, given that Mostek was in the process of winding down after selling the bulk of its assets, that it had failed to provide adequate assurances to alleviate Teradyne's concerns, and that it could at any time make itself judgment proof. Further, the court found that the affidavits submitted to it showed a likelihood that Teradyne would succeed on its contractual claims, and that the balance of hardships was in Teradyne's favor. The court dismissed Mostek's claims that the injunction would create a ripple effect whereby the creditors would rush to court seeking similar relief, noting that the injunction would have no precedential effect on other disputed claims, and that Mostek could pay undisputed claims and thereby avoid any possible ripple effect on them.

* * *

Although Mostek realized assets far exceeding Teradyne's claims when the sale of its assets occurred, the record shows that those assets were being used to pay off creditors' claims and wind down expenses in what Mostek itself described as an "orderly liquidation process." Further, the amount Mostek received for its assets was stated to be subject to a number of unspecified offsets and debits and no assurances were given that Mostek would be able to pay a Teradyne judgment.

* * * Moreover, Mostek has done nothing to alleviate the court's concern that it will prove unable to satisfy a judgment in favor of Teradyne; the number of its creditors and of claims outstanding remain unspecified and no concrete assurances have been given by Mostek that it will have liquid assets sufficient to satisfy a judgment against it. Under these circumstances, we affirm the district court's conclusion that the possible hardship to Teradyne of having a $3–4 million judgment prove worthless, outweighed the inchoate hardship to Mostek of having $4 million of its assets tied up in an interest bearing account pending judgment.

[The court then turned to the trial court's conclusion that Teradyne had a "reasonable likelihood of success on the merits." Mostek had argued that the 1985 QPA and the order for the twenty memory testers were "void for duress"; it asserted "that Teradyne took advantage of Mostek's weak financial condition and used its position, as Mostek's only source of supply, to force Mostek to sign the QPA and to place the new order."]

Mostek's allegations of undue pressure exerted on it by Teradyne are rebutted to some extent by Teradyne's account of the facts which indicates that Mostek entered the 1985 QPA voluntarily in order to obtain discounts on its 1984 orders and that it ordered the twenty memory testers of its own accord. But, even if the facts were as Mostek alleges, it is not clear that it has made out a prima facie case of economic duress.

It is well established that not all economic pressure constitutes duress. * * * [Under Massachusetts law,] "[m]erely taking advantage of another's financial difficulty is not duress," * * * the person alleging financial difficulty must allege that it was "contributed to or caused by the one accused of coercion," and the assertion of duress "must be proved by evidence that the duress resulted from defendant's wrongful and oppressive conduct and not by plaintiff's necessities." There is no indication here that Teradyne caused or contributed to Mostek's financial difficulties. Indeed, Mostek itself concedes that its difficulties came about as a result of a downturn in the semiconductor industry. Accordingly, we see no abuse of discretion in the trial court's conclusion that Teradyne had shown a likelihood of success on the merits.

Affirmed.

Notes and Questions

(1) Will the arbitrator be bound by the views of the First Circuit as to the "merits" of the controversy? Is he likely to be influenced by them? Might this "threaten the independence of the arbitrator's

ultimate determination"? Cf. The Guinness–Harp Corp. v. Jos. Schlitz Brewing Co., 613 F.2d 468, 471 n. 1 (2d Cir.1980).

(2) Under the New York arbitration statute a court, whether or not an arbitration proceeding is pending,

> may entertain an application for an order of attachment or for a preliminary injunction in connection with an arbitrable controversy, but only upon the ground that the award to which the applicant may be entitled may be rendered ineffectual without such provisional relief.

N.Y.C.P.L.R. § 7502(c) (effective 1986). An attachment granted under this section becomes void if it is not followed within 60 days by the institution of arbitration proceedings or a motion to compel arbitration. See also § 8 of the FAA.

(3) Rule 34 of the AAA's Commercial Arbitration Rules provides:

> The arbitrator may issue such orders as may be deemed necessary to safeguard the property which is the subject matter of the arbitration without prejudice to the rights of the parties or to the final determination of the dispute.

Provisional relief granted by an arbitrator will not, of course, always be an adequate substitute for the sort of judicial order approved in *Teradyne*. (Why not?) Nevertheless such relief, if backed by the courts, can often be an effective way of preserving the status quo pending a final decision. See, e.g., Sperry Intern. Trade, Inc. v. Government of Israel, 532 F.Supp. 901 (S.D.N.Y.1982), in which arbitrators required the parties to place the proceeds of a letter of credit in a joint escrow account, pending a later decision on the merits of the underlying claim. The district court temporarily enjoined one of the parties from taking any action to collect the proceeds and confirmed the arbitrators' order within two weeks. It rejected the argument that the order was not "final" within the meaning of § 10(d) of the FAA.

(4) Under the New York Convention, each contracting state is required to "recognize" written agreements to arbitrate controversies; the courts of each nation, when seized of an arbitrable matter, "shall, at the request of one of the parties, refer the parties to arbitration * * *." (Article II(3)). Curiously enough, it has been held that this language prohibits a court from issuing an order of attachment in a case falling within the Convention. The New York Court of Appeals, in denying such an order, wrote:

> It is open to dispute whether attachment is even necessary in the arbitration context. Arbitration, as part of the contracting process, is subject to the same implicit assumptions of good faith and honesty that permeate the entire relationship. Voluntary compliance with arbitral awards may be as high as 85%. Moreover, parties are free to include security clauses (e.g., performance bonds or creating escrow accounts) in their agreements to arbitrate.

* * *

The essence of arbitration is resolving disputes without the interference of the judicial process and its strictures. When international trade is involved, this essence is enhanced by the desire to avoid unfamiliar foreign law.

Cooper v. Ateliers De la Motobecane, S.A., 57 N.Y.2d 408, 456 N.Y.S.2d 728, 442 N.E.2d 1239 (1982).

Is this convincing? Does the language of the New York Convention require this result? Might it not be argued—given the complexity, delays, and risks inherent in international commercial disputes—that judicial intervention is *particularly* appropriate to insure that an arbitration award will ultimately be meaningful? It has been said that the United States "stands alone" among all the signatories to the New York Convention in having case-law to the effect that pre-arbitration attachment is incompatible with the treaty. W.L. Craig, W. Park & J. Paulsson, International Chamber of Commerce Arbitration § 27.04 at 47 (1986); see also Becker, Attachments in Aid of International Arbitration—the American Position, 1 Arb. Int'l 1 (1985).

(5) The Norris–La Guardia Act, 29 U.S.C. § 101, broadly prohibits federal courts from issuing injunctions in labor disputes. The Supreme Court has nevertheless held that where a union has agreed to settle certain disputes through arbitration, a strike over such a dispute may be enjoined prior to arbitration. In Boys Markets, Inc. v. Retail Clerks Union, 398 U.S. 235 (1970), the Supreme Court pointed out that

> the very purpose of arbitration procedures is to provide a mechanism for the expeditious settlement of industrial disputes without resort to strikes, lockouts, or other self-help measures. This basic purpose is obviously largely undercut if there is no immediate, effective remedy for those very tactics that arbitration is designed to obviate.

See also Local Lodge No. 1266 v. Panoramic Corp., 668 F.2d 276 (7th Cir.1981) (preliminary injunction issued to restrain *employer* from selling corporate assets, pending a decision by an arbitrator on the union's claim that the sale would violate the collective bargaining agreement; "status quo injunction" is "necessary to prevent arbitration from being rendered a meaningless ritual").

c. Multi–party Situations

Many disputes that may be amenable to settlement by arbitration are considerably more complex than the simple two-party disputes we have been considering throughout most of this chapter. In a number of common fact patterns, several related players have an interest in resolving a controversy which has arisen out of a single transaction:

(i) The Owner of a new building will have entered into separate contracts with the General Contractor (who is responsible for construction) and with an Architect (who acts as the Owner's representative in designing and overseeing the project). Owner may make a claim against Contractor for alleged defects in construction; Contractor may answer that any defects are attributable to Architect's failings in specifying materials or in inspecting the work. Should Contractor's defense be upheld, Owner may wish to assert a claim against Architect for negligence. Another common scenario is a claim by Contractor against Owner. Contractor may claim that he was unable to comply with the plans and specifications for the project because they called for the use of materials that were unobtainable; this, he asserts, caused him delay and economic loss. Should Contractor's claim be upheld, Owner's position will be that he is entitled to indemnification from Architect for anything he owes to Contractor.[1]

(ii) An owner of a ship suitable for transporting cargo will typically concern himself only with building, financing, and maintaining the vessel, and will enter into a long-term lease of the ship to a Charterer. Charterer may himself be only a middleman speculating on increases in shipping rates; he may then "subcharter" the vessel to someone actually interested in carrying cargo for particular voyages. During the course of one such voyage, the ship may suffer structural damage. Shipowner will seek compensation from Charterer; Charterer in turn will claim that the Sub-charterer is responsible for the damage and will seek indemnity from him.[2]

(iii) The Egyptian Government purchased wheat from four American suppliers; it then chartered a vessel from a Shipper to carry the cargo from Texas to Egypt. During loading, it was discovered that the wheat contained insects; Shipper had to delay loading to fumigate the cargo, and claimed damages for the delay from the Government. The Government naturally took the position that it could not be held liable: "the flour must have been contaminated either before loading, in which case the Suppliers would be liable, or after loading, in which case [the Shipper] would be liable."[3]

In these cases, the party "in the middle"—for example, Owner in case (i) or Charterer in case (ii)—has an obvious interest in a single proceeding to resolve the interrelated disputes. The Owner who must first assert a claim against Contractor, and only later seek to hold Architect responsible, is faced with more than just the duplication of time and expense inherent in separate proceedings. There is in addition the real possibility of inconsistent results in the two forums. Owner may be unable to overcome Contractor's defense based on deficiencies in the project specifications; yet he may also fail, in a later proceeding, to carry the burden of showing that Architect was negligent in preparing the specifications. In such a case Owner would much

1. See, e.g., Consolidated Pacific Engineering, Inc. v. Greater Anchorage Area Borough, 563 P.2d 252 (Alaska 1977); Litton Bionetics, Inc. v. Glen Construction Co., Inc., 292 Md. 34, 437 A.2d 208 (1981).

2. See Miller, Consolidated Arbitrations in New York Maritime Disputes, 14 Int'l Bus. Lawyer 58 (1986).

3. In the Matter of the Arbitration between the Egyptian Co. for Maritime Transport and Hamlet Shipping Co., Inc., 1982 A.M.C. 874 (S.D.N.Y.1981).

prefer to sit back and let Contractor and Architect "fight out" between themselves the causes of the construction defects.

Suppose, now, that the agreement between Owner and Contractor contains a clause providing for the arbitration of all disputes; however, the agreement between Owner and Architect contains no arbitration clause. In such a case there will in all probability be no way to insure that all the claims are heard at the same time in a single proceeding. Certainly a party who has never agreed to arbitrate a dispute cannot be coerced into the process. By contrast, one powerful advantage of litigation is that a court with jurisdiction over all the interested parties can bring them all into the action. In a lawsuit against Contractor, Owner would be able to join a claim "in the alternative" against Architect (see Fed.R.Civ.P. 20(a)); if he is a defendant, Owner can "implead" Architect as a "third-party defendant." (See Fed.R.Civ.P. 14(a)). And if there are pending separate "actions involving a common question of law or fact," a court "may order a joint hearing or trial of any or all of the matters in issue in the actions" or may "order all the actions consolidated." (Fed.R.Civ.P. 42(a)).

What if *both* contracts (between Owner and Contractor, and between Owner and Architect) contain provisions for the arbitration of future disputes? Can the various arbitration proceedings be "consolidated"?

The long-standing policy of the AAA is that it will not consolidate separate arbitration proceedings unless all the parties consent or unless all the agreements explicitly provide for consolidation. The AAA has little incentive to force consolidation upon unwilling parties—and may, in fact, fear that doing so will impair the enforceability of the resulting award. So parties in the Owner's position will often resort to seeking a court order for the consolidation of the separate arbitrations. Once a court order has been issued, the AAA is off the hook and is then willing to administer the consolidated arbitrations.

The willingness of courts to order consolidated arbitration varies greatly. Some courts will do so even over the objections of one of the parties, "as an incident of the jurisdiction statutorily conferred on a court generally to enforce arbitration agreements."[4] It will then be stressed that "interests of efficiency, economy, and avoidance of circuity" support a consolidated hearing before the same panel of arbitrators. In other jurisdictions, however, lack of "privity" between, say, Architect and Contractor is seen as a barrier to ordering consolidated arbitrations. It may even be suggested that where the agreement provides for arbitration under AAA auspices, the parties presumably contracted on the understanding that consolidation, in accordance with AAA practice, would not be ordered without their consent.[5]

---

4. Litton Bionetics, 437 A.2d at 217.

5. See, e.g., Pueblo of Laguna v. Cillessen & Son, Inc., 101 N.M. 341, 682 P.2d 197 (1984).

Even if a court is willing to order that the Owner–Contractor and the Owner–Architect arbitrations be heard together, further questions are still likely to arise. One obvious concern is whether it is possible to dovetail the provisions of two arbitration agreements that differ in important respects. For example, where one agreement calls for arbitration in Texas and the other in California, courts have tended to deny consolidation—as they have when the agreements call for administration by two different institutions. Another thorny recurring problem has been that of selection of the arbitrators. Assume, for example, that both the Owner–Contractor and the Owner–Architect agreements call for a "tripartite" arbitration panel. Who then is to hear a consolidated arbitration?

In one case, a general contractor sought to consolidate arbitration proceedings with a number of his subcontractors arising out of a delay in construction. Apparently each of the subcontractors was blaming the others for the delay; according to the general, the work of all the subs was "interrelated and interdependent" so that it was difficult to apportion responsibility among them. The arbitration agreements between the general and the subs were identical and called for tripartite arbitration. The trial court ordered a consolidated arbitration in which the general would name one arbitrator and the subs *collectively* would name another. This was reversed on appeal: The obvious objection to this method is that it denied each subcontractor his contractual "right" to name "his own" arbitrator.[6]

Some courts, trying to find a solution to this problem, have straightforwardly proceeded to restructure the arbitration panel. In a number of consolidated arbitrations involving three parties, a court has taken it upon itself to direct a *five*-member panel. Under this method each party retains his right to name an arbitrator; then, presumably to insure an odd number of arbitrators, those selected choose *two* neutrals. See Compania Espanola De Petroleos, S.A. v. Nereus Shipping, S.A., 527 F.2d 966 (2d Cir.1975) ("New situations require new remedies"). This solution of course is not without its own weaknesses. Consider, for example, case (iii) at the beginning of this section: How large would the arbitration panel have to be if this approach is used there? Another problem is illustrated by the *Nereus* case, which involved a consolidated arbitration among a Shipowner, a Charterer, and the guarantor of the Charterer's obligations (with whom the Shipowner had a separate contract). Is a five-member panel in such circumstances entirely fair to the Shipowner?

A party "in the middle," who would like to consolidate related arbitrations, is often well advised to offer to waive his own right to select an arbitrator. If he does so any objections to consolidation by other parties, based on their own right to name their own arbitrators, are immediately mooted. And a court is then able to enforce the

6. See Atlas Plastering, Inc. v. Superior Court, County of Alameda, 72 Cal.App.3d 63, 140 Cal.Rptr. 59 (1977).

arbitration agreement in its original form without feeling obliged to rewrite it.[7]

Notes and Questions

(1) Under Rule 81(a)(3) of the Federal Rules of Civil Procedure, the federal rules apply "in proceedings under" the FAA "to the extent that matters of procedure are not provided for" in that statute. When a federal court is asked to compel arbitration, does this Rule give it the same power to order consolidation of related arbitrations involving a "common question of law or fact" as it would have to consolidate "actions" under Rule 42(a)? Or does the Rule simply mean that a court can consolidate two *judicial* proceedings to compel *two separate* arbitrations, or to enforce two separate awards, where there are common issues going to arbitrability or enforcement? See Robinson v. Warner, 370 F.Supp. 828 (D.R.I. 1974) (relying on Rule 81 to order consolidation of arbitration proceedings); cf. The Ore & Chemical Corp. v. Stinnes Interoil, Inc., 606 F.Supp. 1510 (S.D.N.Y.1985) (§ 4 of the FAA precludes use of the Federal Rules to alter terms of arbitration agreement).

(2) The standard-form Owner–Contractor construction agreement, prepared by the American Institute of Architects, provides:

4.5.5. No arbitration arising out of or relating to the Contract Documents shall include, by consolidation or joinder or in any other manner, the Architect, the Architect's employees or consultants, except by written consent containing specific reference to the Agreement and signed by the Architect, Owner, Contractor and any other person or entity sought to be joined. No arbitration shall include, by consolidation or joinder or in any other manner, parties other than the Owner, Contractor, a separate contractor [with whom the Owner has entered into a separate agreement related to the project] and other persons substantially involved in a common question of fact or law whose presence is required if complete relief is to be accorded in arbitration. No person or entity other than the Owner, Contractor or a separate contractor * * * shall be included as an original third party or additional third party to an arbitration whose interest or responsibility is insubstantial.

AIA Document A201, General Conditions of the Contract for Construction (1987 edition).*

A similar provision appears in the standard-form construction contract prepared and jointly adopted by the National Society of Professional Engineers and the American Consulting Engineers Coun-

---

7. See, e.g., Sociedad Anonima De Navegacion Petrolera v. Cia. de Petroleos de Chile S.A., 634 F.Supp. 805, 809 n. 4 (S.D.N.Y.1986).

* Copyright 1987 The American Institute of Architects. AIA copyrighted material has been reproduced with the permission of The American Institute of Architects. Further reproduction is prohibited.

cil. What might be the reasons for this hostility to consolidation on the part of these professionals?

Owner, who may expect to be "in the middle" in future controversies, will naturally resist the inclusion of such provisions. In what other ways might he attempt at the contract negotiation stage to ensure the later consolidation of related arbitration proceedings? If Owner does not have the assurance that he will be able to settle all related disputes at the same time through consolidated arbitration, he might in some cases simply prefer to avoid arbitration completely. Some Owner–Contractor agreements in fact contain an "escape clause," freeing the Owner from any obligation to submit disputes with the Contractor to arbitration if the Owner, "in order to fully protect its interests, desires in good faith to bring in or make a party to any [dispute] * * * the Architect, or any other third party who has not agreed to participate in and be bound by the same arbitration proceeding."

See generally Stipanowich, Arbitration and the Multiparty Dispute: The Search for Workable Solutions, 72 Iowa L.Rev. 473 (1987).

(3) Assume that Owner is a party to an arbitration agreement with Contractor, but not with Architect. When Contractor demands arbitration, Owner responds that for the sake of "efficiency," a court should refuse to compel arbitration so that the entire dispute can be resolved in one judicial proceeding. Such an argument has occasionally succeeded in some state courts. See, e.g., Prestressed Concrete, Inc. v. Adolfson & Peterson, Inc., 240 N.W.2d 551 (Minn.1976) ("Where arbitration would increase rather than decrease delay, complexity, and costs, it should not receive favored treatment").

This was the fact pattern presented to the Supreme Court in Moses H. Cone Memorial Hospital v. Mercury Construction Co., 460 U.S. 1 (1983). Owner had filed a state court action against Contractor— seeking a declaratory judgment that their dispute was not arbitrable— and also against Architect, claiming indemnity for any liability to Contractor. Contractor then brought an action in *federal* court against Owner, under § 4 of the FAA, to compel arbitration. Owner, having taken the care in his own action to join a defendant who was not subject to an arbitration agreement, was then in a position to argue that Contractor's action should be stayed, so that the entire dispute could be disposed of in the parallel *state* action. Otherwise, he asserted, there would have to be "piecemeal litigation." The Supreme Court held that it was an abuse of discretion for the district court to grant a stay of the federal action, which at the time was "running well ahead of the state suit." To the Court, Owner's argument was misconceived: If the dispute between Owner and Contractor were in fact arbitrable, then "piecemeal litigation" was inevitable no matter *which* court, state or federal, decided the question of arbitrability. For "the relevant federal law *requires* piecemeal resolution when necessary to give effect to an arbitration agreement."

Recall also the analogous problem of closely "intertwined" *claims,* some arbitrable and some non-arbitrable, which the Supreme Court resolved in *Dean Witter Reynolds Inc. v. Byrd,* supra p. 527.

(4) The California Arbitration Act permits a court to order consolidation of separate arbitrations when "[t]he disputes arise from the same transactions or series of related transactions" and "[t]here is common issue or issues of law or fact creating the possibility of conflicting rulings by more than one arbitrator or panel of arbitrators." Cal.Code Civ.Pro. § 1281.3. However, a court may *stay* arbitration, or *refuse* enforcement of an arbitration agreement, if one of the parties is also a party to pending *litigation* with a third party "arising out of the same transaction," and if there is a "possibility of conflicting rulings on a common issue of law or fact." Cal.Code Civ.Pro. § 1281.2(c).

Where a transaction is in interstate commerce, would such a refusal or stay of arbitration pursuant to the statute violate federal law? See Board of Trustees of Leland Stanford Univ. v. Volt Information Sciences, Inc., 195 Cal.App.3d 349, 240 Cal.Rptr. 558 (1987) (no; parties "chose to be governed by California law, thus incorporating the California rules of civil procedure").

(5) The result of the Supreme Court's decision in *Moses Cone* was that arbitrability would be decided in federal court, even though a state court proceeding raising the same question was pending. What might be the advantages to the plaintiff of a federal court determination of arbitrability? Note that under § 6 of the FAA, the plaintiff's request for an order compelling arbitration would be treated as a motion; the Act envisages "an expeditious and summary hearing, with only restricted inquiry into factual issues." The federal district court could therefore have resolved the matter "in very short order." 460 U.S. at 22 & n. 26. Are the summary procedures envisaged by §§ 3 and 4 of the Act available in state as well as federal courts? See *Southland v. Keating,* supra p. 437.

(6) The district court's order in *Moses Cone* staying the federal suit was held to be immediately appealable as a "final decision," since such a stay pending resolution of the state court action effectively meant that there would be no further litigation in federal court. Orders granting or denying motions to compel arbitration, made under § 4 of the FAA in an independent proceeding, have also been held to be immediately appealable. Assume, however, that in a pending lawsuit a district court is asked under § 3 of the FAA to stay the action in favor of arbitration. Is the court's order granting or denying such a motion immediately appealable? Or can the propriety of the order be tested only after the full trial (if a stay is denied) or the arbitration proceeding (if the stay is granted) has run its course? For all the complexities of this subject, see C. Wright, A. Miller, & E. Cooper, Federal Practice and Procedure §§ 3914, 3923 (1977 and 1988 Supp.). After the Supreme Court's decision in Gulfstream Aerospace Corp. v. Mayacamas Corp., 108 S.Ct. 1133 (1988), it seems clear at least that orders granting a stay

of an ongoing action under § 3 are no longer appealable. See Commonwealth Ins. Co. v. Underwriters, Inc., 846 F.2d 196 (3d Cir.1988) ("The statutory policy is that of rapid and unobstructed enforcement of arbitration agreements"); see also Zosky v. Boyer, 856 F.2d 554 (3d Cir. 1988) ("We do not decide whether an order denying a motion for arbitration is distinguishable for purposes of appealability from an order staying proceedings or compelling arbitration").

(7) Even if the overall dispute must be settled in "piecemeal" fashion, it should at least be possible for any lawsuit between Owner and Architect to be stayed until the conclusion of the Owner–Contractor arbitration. See Hikers Industries, Inc. v. William Stuart Industries (Far East) Ltd., 640 F.Supp. 175 (S.D.N.Y.1986). In *Hikers* the exclusive licensee of a trademark brought suit against both his licensor and a retailer to whom the licensor had sold goods allegedly in violation of the license. The licensee had an arbitration agreement only with the licensor; however, the court held that "sound judicial administration" dictated that the suit be stayed as to the *retailer* also. The court noted that since the licensee's claims against the retailer were "derivative" of his claims against the licensor, the arbitrator's decision would be "helpful" and would "provide the court with insight into the issues of law and fact." (Note that a stay would also prevent the licensee from taking advantage of federal discovery in order to aid it in arbitration with the licensor.) The stay was to be lifted, however, if the licensor-licensee arbitration was not completed within six months.

Does this procedure tend to avoid duplication of effort and inconsistent results? In the suit against the retailer, what would be the effect of an arbitrator's decision that the licensor's sales were not in violation of the license agreement?

Where two arbitration proceedings are pending which cannot for some reason be consolidated, may a court under the FAA order that one proceeding be stayed until the other is concluded?

(8) Arbitration clauses are often included by franchisors, brokerage firms, health insurers and others in contracts of "adhesion." See p. 463 supra. Such contracts may give rise to a large number of claims presenting common questions; the repercussions of the defendant's actions may be widespread, but the monetary harm to individual claimants may be so insignificant that the expense even of arbitration proceedings would not be warranted. And a victory in arbitration for one particularly determined claimant would not necessarily lead to any recovery for any others, or alter the defendant's behavior.

Presumably, the defendant's motion to compel arbitration may no longer be denied simply on the ground that a class action would be a more suitable means of resolving the problem. But could the notion of "consolidation" be expanded to permit these similar cases to be heard together in a "class arbitration"? Would this be feasible and desirable? See Note, Classwide Arbitration: Efficient Adjudication or Procedural

Quagmire, 67 Va. L.Rev. 787 (1981). Cf. *Southland Corp. v. Keating,* at
supra p. 437.

E. VARIATIONS ON A THEME

1. "Compulsory" "Arbitration"

THOMAS v. UNION CARBIDE AGRICULTURAL PRODUCTS CO.

Supreme Court of the United States, 1985.
473 U.S. 568, 105 S.Ct. 3325, 87 L.Ed.2d 409.

[Pesticide manufacturers are required to register their products
with the Environmental Protection Agency (EPA), and must submit
research and test data to the EPA concerning the product's health,
safety, and environmental effects. The development of a potential
commercial pesticide may require the expenditure of millions of dollars
annually over a period of several years. Frequently, after one product
has been registered, *another* applicant may wish to register the same or
a similar product. Can the EPA consider, in support of this second
application, data already in its files that had been submitted by the
previous registrant? By avoiding some duplication of test data, this
would presumably result in lower costs and increased competition.
(Such later registrations are colloquially known as "me too" or "follow
on" registrations.)

[The Federal Insecticide, Fungicide, and Rodenticide Act (FIFRA)
allows the EPA to consider such data (after a 10–year period of
exclusive use), but "only if the applicant has made an offer to compensate the original data submitter." "In effect, the provision instituted a
mandatory data-licensing scheme." See Ruckelshaus v. Monsanto Co.,
467 U.S. 986, 992 (1984). If the original data submitter and the second
applicant fail to agree on the terms of compensation, then either may
ask for binding arbitration. The proceedings are before private arbitrators named by the parties or by the Federal Mediation and Conciliation
Service, and are governed by the rules of the AAA. The arbitration
award is "final and conclusive," with no judicial review "except for
fraud, misrepresentation, or other misconduct by one of the parties to
the arbitration or the arbitrator." If the original data submitter fails
to participate in an arbitration proceeding, he forfeits any right to
compensation for the use of his data; if a "follow-on" applicant fails to
participate, his application is denied.

[A number of large firms engaged in the development and marketing of pesticides challenged this arbitration scheme, claiming that
Article III of the Constitution bars Congress from requiring arbitration
of disputes concerning compensation "without also affording substantial review by tenured judges of the arbitrator's decision." A unanimous Supreme Court upheld the FIFRA arbitration scheme.

[In an earlier case, the Court had suggested that Congress could not establish Article I "legislative courts" to adjudicate "private rights" disputes. Such disputes, involving "the liability of one individual to another under the law as defined," "lie at the core of the historically recognized judicial power." Northern Pipeline Construction Co. v. Marathan Pipe Line Co., 458 U.S. 50 (1982). Justice O'Connor, writing for the Court, found that the situation in *Thomas* was different:]

[T]he right created by FIFRA is not a purely "private" right, but bears many of the characteristics of a "public" right. Use of a registrant's data to support a follow-on registration serves a public purpose as an integral part of a program safeguarding the public health. Congress has the power, under Article I, to authorize an agency administering a complex regulatory scheme to allocate costs and benefits among voluntary participants in the program without providing an Article III adjudication. It also has the power to condition issuance of registrations or licenses on compliance with agency procedures. Article III is not so inflexible that it bars Congress from shifting the task of data valuation from the agency to the interested parties.

   * * * Congress, without implicating Article III, could have authorized EPA to charge follow-on registrants fees to cover the cost of data and could have directly subsidized FIFRA data submitters for their contributions of needed data. Instead, it selected a framework that collapses these two steps into one, and permits the parties to fix the amount of compensation, with binding arbitration to resolve intractable disputes. Removing the task of valuation from agency personnel to civilian arbitrators, selected by agreement of the parties or appointed on a case-by-case basis by an independent federal agency, surely does not diminish the likelihood of impartial decisionmaking, free from political influence.

* * *

The danger of Congress or the Executive encroaching on the Article III judicial powers is at a minimum when no unwilling defendant is subjected to judicial enforcement power as a result of the agency "adjudication." See, e.g., L. Jaffe, Judicial Control of Administrative Action 385 (1965) (historically judicial review of agency decisionmaking has been required only when it results in the use of judicial process to enforce an obligation upon an unwilling defendant).

We need not decide in this case whether a private party could initiate an action in court to enforce a FIFRA arbitration. But cf. 29 CFR pt. 1440, App. § 37(c) (1984) (under rules of American Arbitration Association, parties to arbitration are deemed to consent to entry of judgment). FIFRA contains no provision explicitly authorizing a party to invoke judicial process to compel arbitration or enforce an award. In any event, under FIFRA, the only potential object of judicial enforcement power is the follow-on registrant who explicitly consents to have his rights determined by arbitration.

* * *

Our holding is limited to the proposition that Congress, acting for a valid legislative purpose pursuant to its constitutional powers under Article I, may create a seemingly "private" right that is so closely integrated into a public regulatory scheme as to be a matter appropriate for agency resolution with limited involvement by the Article III judiciary. To hold otherwise would be to erect a rigid and formalistic restraint on the ability of Congress to adopt innovative measures such as negotiation and arbitration with respect to rights created by a regulatory scheme.

[Justice Brennan, joined by Justices Marshall and Blackmun, wrote in concurrence:]

Congress has decided that effectuation of the public policies of FIFRA demands not only a requirement of compensation from follow-on registrants in return for mandatory access to data but also an administrative process—mandatory negotiation followed by binding arbitration—to ensure that unresolved compensation disputes do not delay public distribution of needed products. ∗ ∗ ∗ Although a compensation dispute under FIFRA ultimately involves a determination of the duty owed one private party by another, at its heart the dispute involves the exercise of authority by a federal government arbitrator in the course of administration of FIFRA's comprehensive regulatory scheme. As such it partakes of the character of a standard agency adjudication.

Notes and Questions

(1) In one FIFRA case arbitrators awarded Stauffer (the original registrant) one-half of its direct testing cost for a chemical, plus a royalty on all sales of the product by PPG (the second applicant) between 1983 and 1992. PPG asked the court to vacate this award; it argued that the arbitrators were limited to compensating Stauffer for the actual cost of producing the test data and could not make an award based on the value to PPG of earlier market entry. The court granted Stauffer's motion to dismiss, concluding that "Congress intentionally left to the arbitrators the choice of what formula to use in determining compensation." PPG Industries, Inc. v. Stauffer Chemical Co., 637 F.Supp. 85 (D.D.C.1986).

FIFRA originally provided that in the absence of an agreement between the parties as to compensation, the figure was to be determined by the EPA. However, the court noted that "[t]he EPA found this task to be beyond its means":

Congress concluded that the EPA lacked the requisite expertise in determining compensation, and Congress and the EPA agreed that a determination of compensation did not require "active government involvement." Consequently, Congress removed all suggestion of a standard from the statute and replaced EPA with binding arbitration as the mechanism for determining what compensation was proper. It seems quite reasonable to this Court that Congress intentionally obliterated all suggestion of a standard in view of the fact that not even the EPA could identify a formula which would adequately compensate a data submitter in every case. Congress determined to leave the matter to arbitrators who had more expertise and could evaluate each case individually.

The court also rejected the argument that such "standardless delegation" to private arbitrators was an unconstitutional delegation of legislative authority:

> [T]he concern with delegation to private parties has to do with the private party's interest in the industry being regulated. See, e.g., [A.L.A. Schechter Poultry Corp. v. United States, 295 U.S. 495 (1935)] (holding unconstitutional a statute delegating power to institute penal provisions to a body comprised of members of the industry involved). The private parties involved here are not members of the pesticide industry, but rather disinterested arbitrators appointed by the FMCS, which adopted the roster of the American Arbitration Association.

Is it important in FIFRA cases to develop a body of "common law" concerning the measure of compensation, in order to provide guidance for the future conduct of registrants and later applicants? Will a series of arbitration awards be likely to provide such standards and criteria of decision? How is the "expertise" of the individual arbitrators likely to aid in resolving the disagreement in *PPG* as to the choice of the appropriate standard of compensation? See Harter, Points on a Continuum: Dispute Resolution Procedures and the Administrative Process, in Administrative Conference of the United States, Sourcebook: Federal Agency Use of Alternative Means of Dispute Resolution 309 (1987).

(2) The Commodity Futures Trading Commission (CFTC) is an independent agency established by Congress. The CFTC requires members of commodity exchanges like the Chicago Board of Trade (CBOT) to submit disputes with customers to arbitration if their customers request it; at CFTC insistence, this requirement is incorporated into the rules of the exchanges. Geldermann, a member of the CBOT, refused to arbitrate a customer-initiated claim, and brought suit challenging the arbitration requirement. The court held that "by virtue of its continued membership in the CBOT," Geldermann had "consented to arbitration, and thus waived any right he may have possessed to a full trial before an Article III court." The court also rejected Geldermann's claim that the mandatory arbitration scheme violated its right to a jury trial: Since "Geldermann is not entitled to an Article III forum, the Seventh Amendment is not implicated." That Geldermann "had no choice but to accept the CBOT's rules" if it were to continue in business was irrelevant. Geldermann, Inc. v. CFTC, 836 F.2d 310 (7th Cir.1987).

The statute creating the CFTC also provides an alternative "reparations procedure" by which the agency itself may hear complaints brought by aggrieved customers of commodity brokers. (In addition, courts have found in the statute an implied private cause of action for investors). In one such CFTC proceeding, the broker asserted a counterclaim for the balance owed by the investor on his account—a "traditional" state-law action for debt. The investor invoked Article III to challenge the CFTC's authority to hear the counterclaim, but the Supreme Court rejected this challenge: "[I]t seems self-evident that just as Congress may encourage parties to settle a dispute out of court or resort to arbitration without impermissible incursions on the separation of powers, Congress may make available a quasi-judicial mechanism through which willing parties may, at their option, elect to resolve their differences." CFTC v. Schor, 478 U.S. 833 (1986).

Is arbitration under FIFRA similarly limited to "willing parties"? Consider the Court's characterization in *Thomas* of the pesticide registration scheme as "voluntary," and its reliance on the fact that the follow-on registrant "explicitly consents to have his rights determined by arbitration."

(3) In some jurisdictions individuals may not take certain cases to trial without having first submitted the dispute to some form of "arbitration." Since the right to a later trial *de novo* is preserved, this compulsory arbitration serves more as a "screening device," discouraging marginal claims and giving plaintiffs a preliminary inexpensive view of how their claim looks to a disinterested third party. See the discussion of medical malpractice arbitration at supra p. 429; see also the discussion of court-administered arbitration at infra p. 628.

Mandatory Arbitration in Public Employment

A number of statutes require the arbitration of "interest" disputes between a state or local government, and a union representing its employees, concerning the terms of a new collective bargaining agreement. Fairly typical examples of the growing number of such statutes are Rhode Island's Fire Fighter's Arbitration Act and Policemen's Arbitration Act.[1] In recognition of "the necessity to provide some alternative method of settling disputes where employees must, as a matter of public policy, be denied the usual right to strike," the legislation requires that where a city and a union cannot reach agreement, "any and all unresolved issues" shall be submitted to arbitration. The arbitration panel is to be tripartite—one arbitrator being named by each of the parties and the third, in the absence of agreement, by the chief justice of the state supreme court. The legislation attempts to enumerate the "factors" which the panel must take into account— including the "interest and welfare of the public," the "community's ability to pay," and a comparison of wage rates and employment conditions with prevailing local conditions "of skilled employees of the building trades and industry" and with police or fire departments in cities of comparable size.

1. R.I.Stat. § 28–9.1–10; R.I.Stat. § 28–9.2–10.

It is obvious that "interest" disputes in public sector employment are intimately connected to the political process. Many public services, such as police protection and education, raise questions that are "politically, socially, or ideologically sensitive." [2] A number of such sensitive issues have in fact been held to be "non-bargainable"—despite their obvious impact on the working conditions of public employees—and thus outside the permissible scope of "interest" arbitration. Such "non-negotiable matters of governmental policy" might in public education include questions of curriculum or of class size; in police services, questions of the manpower level of the force or a civilian review board for police discipline. See, e.g., San Jose Peace Officer's Ass'n v. City of San Jose, 78 Cal.App.3d 935, 144 Cal.Rptr. 638 (1978) (police policy governing when officer is allowed to fire weapon; "The forum of the bargaining table with its postures, strategies, trade-offs, modifications and compromises is no place for the 'delicate balancing of different interests: the protection of society from criminals, the protection of police officers' safety, and the preservation of all human life, if possible.' ").

In a more general sense, however, the resolution of *all* disputes over the terms of public employment—even disputes over nuts and bolts issues like wages—is inescapably "political." To resolve a wage dispute by applying the "factors" set out in the Rhode Island legislation requires an accommodation of the competing interests of employees, taxpayers, and the users of public services. The arbitrator will inevitably be led to determine priorities among various public programs, the level of public services, or the need and feasibility of increased public revenue. Such exercises of judgment are necessarily political compromises. It has been suggested in fact that "interest" arbitration of public-sector disputes may be inconsistent with the democratic premise that governmental priorities are to be fixed by elected representatives, responsible to all the competing interest groups and responsive to the play of political forces. Resolving public sector "interest" disputes, it is asserted, is not an exercise in neutral, "objective" adjudication but rather one in "legislative" policymaking:

> The size of the budget, the taxes to be levied, the purposes for which tax money is to be used, the kinds and levels of governmental services to be enjoyed, and the level of indebtedness are issues that should be decided by officials who are politically responsible to those who pay the taxes and seek the services. The notion that we can or should insulate public employee bargaining from the political process either by arbitration or with some magic formula is a delusion of reality and a denigration of democratic government.[4]

It should not be surprising, then, that the constitutionality of compulsory interest arbitration in the public sector has repeatedly been

---

2. H. Wellington & R. Winter, The Unions and the Cities 23 (1971).

4. Summers, Public Sector Bargaining: Problems of Governmental Decisionmaking, 44 U.Cinn. L.Rev. 669, 672 (1975). See also Grodin, Political Aspects of Public Sector Interest Arbitration, 64 Cal. L.Rev. 678 (1976).

challenged. Successful challenges have been rare.[5] Nevertheless, it is clear that there are real tensions here with the values traditionally underlying the arbitration process. It seems hard to justify compulsory "interest" arbitration on the usual rationale that the process is merely an extension of the parties' own bargaining, an application of "self-government" in the workplace. In the final analysis, how does compulsory "interest" arbitration in public-sector employment differ from decisions made directly by a governmental agency? Compare Rhode Island's compulsory arbitration statutes with the Nebraska scheme, which entrusts the settlement of public-sector "interest" disputes to a state "Commission of Industrial Relations" consisting of five "judges" named for six-year terms by the Governor with the advice and consent of the legislature.[6]

Some years ago the Rhode Island Supreme Court rebuffed a constitutional attack on that state's compulsory arbitration statutes by the simple device of characterizing the arbitrators as "public officers" rather than as mere "private persons": The arbitration panel *must* be considered "an administrative or governmental agency," reasoned the court; after all, the arbitrators had been granted "a portion of the sovereign and legislative power of the government"![7] But such a semantic tour de force obviously does not resolve the problem. If the arbitrators are appointed on an ad hoc basis, with no continuing legislative or administrative oversight, there may be no real accountability to the electorate; these are "hit and run" decision-makers.[8] If, in contrast, the arbitrators are *not* to be private decision-makers and are instead made politically responsible, may not the neutrality of the entire process be called into question? Does the arbitrator not then become merely "an agent of government involved primarily in implementing public policy"?[9] Is it implicit in the very notion of an "impartial" or "neutral" arbitrator that the decision-maker is *not* to be responsive to political intervention, or to be held accountable for his decision by any constituency? Or might the personal "accountability" of private arbitrators be affected in any event by the well-known need of those in the profession to maintain their acceptability for future employment?

Notes and Questions

(1) Is the same judicial deference traditionally accorded arbitral awards appropriate in the case of compulsory "interest" arbitration in the public sector? In many states with such statutes, the arbitration

---

5. See, e.g., Salt Lake City v. International Association of Firefighters, 563 P.2d 786 (Utah 1977) ("power conferred on the panel of arbitrators is not consonant with the concept of representative democracy").

6. Neb.Rev.Stat. § 48–801 ff.

7. City of Warwick v. Warwick Regular Firemen's Ass'n, 106 R.I. 109, 256 A.2d 206 (1969).

8. Dearborn Fire Fighters Union v. City of Dearborn, 394 Mich. 229, 231 N.W.2d 226, 243 (1975) (Kavanagh, C.J., concurring).

9. Grodin, supra n. 4, 64 Cal. L.Rev. at 693–94.

panel is in fact treated for purposes of review much like an administrative agency. A record of the proceedings and a written decision are required, and courts may examine the result to see whether it is "supported by substantial credible evidence present in the record." See Division 540, Amalgamated Transit Union v. Mercer County Improvement Authority, 76 N.J. 245, 386 A.2d 1290 (1978).

Is it primarily the fact that "interest" rather than grievance arbitration is involved that may call for more extensive judicial review? See, e.g., Craver, The Judicial Enforcement of Public Sector Interest Arbitration, 21 B.C.L.Rev. 557, 572 (1980) (deference to arbitral determinations gives rise to the "possibility of catastrophic consequences resulting from an entirely intemperate award"). Or is it the fact that the arbitration is not based on the consent of the parties? Or are there still other reasons?

New York law imposes arbitration as the means of settling the labor disputes of private non-profit hospitals. Either hospital or union may request arbitration of any employee *grievance* arising out of the collective bargaining agreement. In addition, *"interest"* arbitration to fix the terms of a new agreement may be invoked on the motion of the State Industrial Commissioner. The New York Court of Appeals has held that "due process limitations affecting compulsory arbitration" requires the scope of review of all such awards to be broader than under the state's general arbitration statute. To comply with constitutional requirements, a grievance award could only be sustained if a reviewing court found that it was supported by "substantial evidence." In addition, the court held that "interest" awards must be scrutinized to determine whether the arbitrators acted in an "arbitrary or capricious manner" and whether their "indirect exercise of the police power [is] justified by the public interest":

> [T]he device for arbitration is a substitute for a determination of the dispute by an administrative or regulatory agency. As a substitute device, however, its objective may not be accomplished under lower constitutional standards than would be required of an administrative or regulatory agency.

Mount St. Mary's Hospital of Niagara Falls v. Catherwood, 26 N.Y.2d 493, 311 N.Y.S.2d 863, 260 N.E.2d 508 (1970).

(2) A study of a national sample of police contracts concluded, not unexpectedly, that "police salaries will be higher in states where arbitration is available than in states where it is not." As far as actual *use* of arbitration is concerned, however, there was "little or no difference between negotiated and arbitrated salaries." Feuille & Delaney, Collective Bargaining, Interest Arbitration, and Police Salaries, 39 Ind. & Lab. Rel. Rev. 228 (1986).

2. Final–Offer Arbitration

For almost 100 years professional baseball players were bound to their teams for life by the sport's infamous "reserve clause." In consequence, most players had little choice but to accept the salary their team was willing to pay them. In recent years, however, collective bargaining between the clubs and the players' union has replaced the old "reserve clause" with a system that considerably enhances player mobility between teams. At the same time, it has introduced a novel form of "interest" arbitration to fix salaries where player and team cannot agree.

At the present time baseball players who have been in the Major Leagues for at least six years can choose to become "free agents," and can have their salaries determined through negotiation in the free market with other teams which might be interested in them.[10] Players with fewer than six years in the Majors are still not free to look elsewhere, but are tied to their original team unless they are traded or released. However, those with at least *three* years service do have the right to submit the question of their salary to binding arbitration.

Salary disputes are submitted to arbitration in January. The collective bargaining agreement specifies a number of criteria which the "interest" arbitrator must consider in determining salaries for the coming season—for example, the player's contribution to the team (including his "overall performance, special qualities of leadership, and public appeal") and "comparative baseball salaries" (which may include salaries paid to free agents). He is instructed *not* to consider salary offers made by either party prior to arbitration, salaries in other sports or occupations, or the financial situation of player or team. The hearing is to be private and informal. Unless extended by the arbitrator, each party is limited to one hour for an initial presentation and one-half hour for rebuttal, and there is to be no written opinion by the arbitrator.

The most distinctive feature of this arbitration scheme is the limits it places on the discretion of the arbitrator. The arbitrator is not free to choose whatever salary figure he thinks is appropriate. Instead, the player and the club each submits to him a "final offer" on salary for the coming season (these "final offers" need not be the figures offered during prior negotiations). The arbitrator may then award "only one or the other of the two figures submitted."

What is the rationale behind this final-offer arbitration? As we have seen, in conventional arbitration it is often assumed that arbitrators will have a tendency to compromise and "split the difference" between the parties in an effort to maintain their future acceptability.

---

10. At least in theory. In a recent grievance arbitration, an arbitrator found that the owners of baseball teams had been acting in concert to restrain salaries by refraining from bidding competitively on "free agents." See New York Times, September 22, 1987, p. 1.

Being aware of this, the parties at the bargaining stage are likely to hold back concessions that they would otherwise be willing to make, to avoid giving the game away. "If the parties view conventional arbitration as a procedure for securing compromise, bargaining tactics dictate that each party preserve a position *from* which the arbitrator can move to a compromise." [11] Indeed, the party which stakes out the *most extreme* initial position may hope to gain the most from an eventual arbitral compromise, and this is often said to have a "chilling effect" on good-faith bargaining.[12] On the other hand, the constraints imposed by "final-offer arbitration" should have the opposite effect on the parties' negotiating behavior. Where the arbitrator is prevented from compromising, each party may fear that if its offer is perceived as extreme or "unreasonable," the arbitrator will choose the offer of the *other* party. Fear of such disagreeable consequences impels each party to adjust his bargaining position to make it more "reasonable"—and thus more likely to be chosen—than his opponent's. There is thus set up a movement of each party towards the other, narrowing the difference between them and at best making any arbitration award unnecessary. Ideally, "final-offer arbitration" operates as a "doomsday weapon that invariably induces negotiated settlement." [13]

To some extent this dynamic can be observed in major league baseball. In 1987, 108 players (of the 160 who were eligible) demanded salary arbitration; in most cases, however, the salary dispute was settled without a hearing and in fact only 26 players ultimately had their salaries determined by an arbitrator. Salaries for players in arbitration, including those settling before the hearing, rose an average of 72% each year in the decade between 1976 and 1986, and team owners tend to believe that the arbitration process is largely responsible for this dramatic escalation. For more information about salary arbitration in baseball, see generally J. Dworkin, Owners Versus Players: Baseball and Collective Bargaining (1981).

Final-offer arbitration is also frequently used to resolve "interest" disputes in public-sector employment. In baseball, however, arbitrators determine only the player's *salary* for one season; all of the other terms of employment are contained in the "Uniform Player's Contract" that is made part of the collective bargaining agreement. In contrast, public-sector "interest" arbitrators are frequently charged with determining a wide range of bargainable issues, all going to make up the terms of employment in the new agreement.

In some states, the statutory scheme calls for each party to present to the arbitrators a "package" including a position on *all* the bargainable issues not yet agreed on. The arbitrators must then choose what they consider to be the most reasonable of the two "packages." In other states, in contrast, the arbitrators are allowed to consider each

---

11. Chelius & Dworkin, An Economic Analysis of Final–Offer Arbitration as a Conflict Resolution Device, 24 J. Conflict Res. 293, 294 (1980).

12. See Feuille, Final Offer Arbitration and the Chilling Effect, 14 Ind.Rel. 302 (1975).

13. Id. at 307.

issue separately and to choose between the positions of the parties on an issue-by-issue basis. This variation enables them to develop their own compromise "package" by balancing the parties' positions on the various issues. See, e.g., Mich.Comp.Laws § 423.238 (arbitration panel shall adopt "last offer of settlement" "as to each economic issue").

Notes and Questions

(1) How might the strategy and bargaining behavior of the parties differ depending on whether the final-offer arbitration is to be on an "issue-by-issue" or "package" basis?

(2) It should be obvious that all forms of final-offer arbitration have the greatest impact on the party who is the more risk-averse. In determining their final offers, both parties are faced with a trade-off. They must weigh the loss involved in making a particular concession (say, a reduction in salary demands) against the greater probability of having their offer chosen by the arbitrator should an award become necessary. The more risk-averse party will be likely to move further in adjusting his demand downwards, in the direction of "reasonableness," in order to reduce the chances of an unfavorable result. This is particularly likely where arbitration is on a "package" basis. There is some evidence that unions nominally "win" public-sector "interest" arbitrations more frequently than public employers, and this would seem to support the proposition that the unions are more likely than the employer to be risk-averse. See Farber, An Analysis of Final–Offer Arbitration, 24 J. Conflict Res. 683 (1980); Bloom, Collective Bargaining, Compulsory Arbitration, and Salary Settlements in the Public Sector, 2 J. Labor Research 369 (1981).

See also H. Raiffa, The Art and Science of Negotiation 118 (1982):

> [I]t seems that the proportion of cases going to final-offer arbitration is smaller than the proportion going to conventional arbitration. This is often cited as an advantage of final-offer arbitration. Of course, the logic is marred a bit because conventional arbitration preceded by a round of Russian roulette would still do better.

(3) The concern is often expressed that final-offer arbitration on a "package" basis may lead to results that are unworkable or inequitable. Consider, for example, the dilemma of the arbitrator in an "interest" dispute between a city and a firefighter's union. The union submits a proposal on salary and benefits which the arbitrators find preferable to the city's. However, the union has also included a "zinger," in the form of a demand for mandatory manning levels at certain fire stations—an unusual proposal which the arbitrators find objectionable. (Perhaps union negotiators slipped in this demand hoping that it would be carried along by the force of their "irresistible" economic package; perhaps they were forced to include it for reasons of internal union politics.) In such circumstances, arbitrators often express frustration at being limited to choosing one package or the other. See generally J.

Stern, C. Rehmus, J. Lowenberg, H. Kasper & B. Dennis, Final Offer Arbitration: The Effects on Public Safety Employee Bargaining (1975).

Is it a sufficient answer to such concerns to say that the *whole point* of final-offer arbitration is to discourage actual arbitration, and that "if the case reaches the arbitrator, the parties both deserve whatever they get"? Zack, Final Offer Selection—Panacea or Pandora's Box, 19 N.Y.L.F. 567, 585 (1974). Consider the following proposal for an alternative system of final-offer arbitration by "package": Each side is to submit *three* different final offers. The arbitrator chooses one of the six packages presented to him but does not reveal his choice to the parties; instead, he merely announces *which side* has made the better offer. The *losing party* is then allowed to choose one of the three packages submitted by the winning party, and this becomes the final award. See Donn, Games Final–Offer Arbitrators Might Play, 16 Ind. Rel. 306, 312 (1977). What might be the advantages of such a system?

3. "Med–Arb"

There are many different styles of arbitration. One arbitrator may see himself chiefly as a passive adjudicator, presiding over the confrontation of adversaries. At the other extreme may be found the arbitrator who intervenes actively, in an effort to help the parties reach their own mutually agreeable settlement without the need for an imposed award.

Combining the roles of mediator and adjudicator poses a unique challenge to an arbitrator's skill: "When you sit there with the parties, separately or together—listening, persuading, cajoling, looking dour or relieved—your responsibility is a heavy one. Every lift of your eyebrow can be interpreted as a signal to the parties as to how you might eventually decide an issue if agreement is not reached." [14] This style of arbitration is seen most frequently in public-sector "interest" disputes. In fact, one survey estimates that arbitrators with experience in such disputes first attempt to mediate in at least 30 to 40 percent of their cases.[15]

Frequently, the statutory procedure for the settlement of public-sector disputes encourages and even institutionalizes "med-arb." For example, Michigan's form of final-offer arbitration permits the parties to revise their offers as the hearing progresses; in addition the arbitrators, after hearing evidence, may remand the dispute to the parties for further negotiations before the ultimate "final" offers must be submitted. In the course of the hearing, the arbitrator may indicate that on a particular issue he is "leaning towards" the position of one party. It

---

14. Bairstow, The Canadian Experience, Proceedings, 34th Annual Meeting, Nat'l Academy of Arbitrators 93 (1982).

15. J. Stern, C. Rehmus, J. Lowenberg, H. Kasper & B. Dennis, Final–Offer Arbitration: The Effects on Public Safety Employee Bargaining 140 (1975).

does not require much imagination to see how this may influence the settlement process, and may force an adjustment in the position taken by the *other* party. In addition, use in public-sector "interest" disputes of a tripartite panel may also encourage resort to mediation techniques. In the executive session following the hearing, the neutral arbitrator has the opportunity to consult with his "partisan" colleagues. He may be expected to make efforts to reduce the area of disagreement between them, and can certainly draw on them in order to put together a coherent package reflecting the parties' true priorities.

The New Jersey statute is even more explicit, expressly mandating that in the "interest" disputes of police and firefighters, the arbitrators "may mediate or assist the parties in reaching a mutually agreeable settlement." [16] Arbitrators under this statute are often quite outspoken in inducing settlement by advising parties of the unacceptability of their positions. This is what has often been termed "mediation with a club." One arbitrator explained that "I beat up on the parties. I believe that scaring them helps them to settle their own dispute." [17]

FULLER, COLLECTIVE BARGAINING AND THE ARBITRATOR

Proceedings, Fifteenth Annual Meeting, National Academy of Arbitrators 8, 29–33, 37–48 (1962).

There remains the difficult problem of mediation by the arbitrator, where instead of issuing an award, he undertakes to persuade the parties to reach a settlement, perhaps reinforcing his persuasiveness with "the gentle threat" of a decision. Again, there is waiting a too-easy answer: "Judges do it." Of course, judges sometimes mediate or at least bring pressure on the parties for a voluntary settlement. Sometimes this is done usefully and sometimes in ways that involve an abuse of office. In any event the judiciary has evolved no uniform code with respect to this problem that the arbitrator can take over ready-made. Judicial practice varies over a wide range. If the arbitrator were to pattern his conduct after the worst practices of the bench, arbitration would be in a sad way.

Analysis of the problem as it confronts the arbitrator should begin with a recognition that mediation or conciliation—the terms being largely interchangeable—has an important role to play in the settlement of labor disputes. There is much to justify a system whereby it is a prerequisite to arbitration that an attempt first be made by a skilled mediator to bring about a voluntary settlement. This requirement has at times been imposed in a variety of contexts. Under such systems the mediator is, I believe, invariably someone other than the arbitrator. This is as it should be.

---

16. N.J.Stat. § 34: 13A–16f(3).

17. Weitzman & Stochaj, Attitudes of Arbitrators toward Final–Offer Arbitration in New Jersey, 35 Arb. J. 25, 30 (1980).

Mediation and arbitration have distinct purposes and hence distinct moralities. The morality of mediation lies in optimum settlement, a settlement in which each party gives up what he values less, in return for what he values more. The morality of arbitration lies in a decision according to the law of the contract. The procedures appropriate for mediation are those most likely to uncover that pattern of adjustment which will most nearly meet the interests of both parties. The procedures appropriate for arbitration are those which most securely guarantee each of the parties a meaningful chance to present arguments and proofs for a decision in his favor. Thus, private consultations with the parties, generally wholly improper on the part of an arbitrator, are an indispensable tool of mediation.

Not only are the appropriate procedures different in the two cases, but the facts sought by those procedures are different. There is no way to define "the essential facts" of a situation except by reference to some objective. Since the objective of reaching an optimum settlement is different from that of rendering an award according to the contract, the facts relevant in the two cases are different, or, when they seem the same, are viewed in different aspects. If a person who has mediated unsuccessfully attempts to assume the role of arbitrator, he must endeavor to view the facts of the case in a completely new light, as if he had previously known nothing about them. This is a difficult thing to do. It will be hard for him to listen to proofs and arguments with an open mind. If he fails in this attempt, the integrity of adjudication is impaired.

These are the considerations that seem to me to apply where the arbitrator attempts to mediate before hearing the case at all. This practice is quite uncommon, and would largely be confined to situations where a huge backlog of grievances seemed to demand drastic measures toward an Augean clean-up. I want now to pass to consideration of the case where the arbitrator postpones his mediative efforts until after the proofs are in and the arguments have been heard. * * *

One might ask of mediation first undertaken after the hearing is over, what is the point of it? If the parties do not like the award, they are at liberty to change it. If there is some settlement that will effect a more apt adjustment of their interests, their power to contract for that settlement is the same after, as it is before, the award is rendered. One answer would be to say that if the arbitrator undertakes mediation after the hearing but before the award, he can use "the gentle threat" of a decision to induce settlement, keeping it uncertain as to just what the decision will be. Indeed, if he has a sufficiently Machiavellian instinct, he may darkly hint that the decision will contain unpleasant surprises for both parties. Conduct of this sort would, however, be most unusual. Unless the role thus assumed were played with consummate skill, the procedure would be likely to explode in the arbitrator's face.

There is, however, a more convincing argument for mediative efforts after the hearing and before the award. This lies in the peculiar fact—itself a striking tribute to the moral force of the whole institution of adjudication—that an award tends to resist change by agreement. Once rendered it seems to have a kind of moral inertia that puts a heavy onus on the party who proposes any modification by mutual consent. Hence if there exists the possibility of a voluntary settlement that will suit both parties better than the award, the last chance to obtain it may occur after the hearing and before the award is rendered. This may in fact be an especially propitious moment for a settlement. Before the hearing it is quite usual for each of the parties to underestimate grossly the strength of his adversary's case. The hearing not uncommonly "softens up" both parties for settlement.

What, then, are the objections to an arbitrator's undertaking mediative efforts after the hearing and before rendering the award, this being often so advantageous a time for settlement? Again, the objection lies essentially in the confusion of role that results. In seeking a settlement the arbitrator turned mediator quite properly learns things that should have no bearing on his decision as an arbitrator. For example, suppose a discharge case in which the arbitrator is virtually certain that he will decide for reinstatement, though he is striving to keep his mind open until he has a chance to reflect on the case in the quiet of his study. In the course of exploring the possibilities of a settlement he learns that, contrary to the position taken by the union at the hearing, respectable elements in the union would like to see the discharge upheld. Though they concede that the employee was probably innocent of the charges made by the company, they regard him as an ambitious troublemaker the union would be well rid of. If the arbitrator fails to mediate a settlement, can he block this information out when he comes to render his award?

It is important that an arbitrator not only respect the limits of his office in fact, but that he also appear to respect them. The parties to an arbitration expect of the arbitrator that he will decide the dispute, not according to what pleases the parties, but by what accords with the contract. Yet as a mediator he must explore the parties' interests and seek to find out what would please them. He cannot be a good mediator unless he does. But if he has then to surrender his role as mediator to resume that of adjudicator, can his award ever be fully free from the suspicion that it was influenced by a desire to please one or both of the parties?

Finally, in practice the settlement mediated after the hearing will seldom be free from some taint of being "rigged." Indeed, when an agreement is reached under the express or implied threat of an award, the distinction between agreement and award is lost; the "rigged award" blends into the coerced settlement, and it may at a given time be uncertain which will emerge from the discussions. During these discussions it is most unusual for all affected to know at all times just what is going on.

These, then, are the arguments against the arbitrator's undertaking the task of mediation. They can all be summed up in the phrase, "confusion of role." Why, then, should any arbitrator be tempted to depart from his proper role as adjudicator? In what follows I shall try to analyze the considerations that sometimes press him toward a departure from a purely judicial role.

* * *

[Fuller then discusses "polycentric" (that is, "many-centered") problems—the type of problem exemplified by the testator who in her will left a varied collection of paintings to two museums "in equal shares." See supra p. 28.]

[P]robably the nearest counterpart to Mrs. Timken's will is the following case: Union and management agree that the internal wage structure of the plant is out of balance—some jobs are paid too little in comparison with others, some too much. A kind of wage fund (say, equal to a general increase of five cents an hour) is set up. Out of this fund are to be allotted, in varying amounts, increases for the various jobs that will bring them into better balance. In case the parties cannot agree, the matter shall go to arbitration. Precisely because the task is polycentric, it is extremely unlikely that the parties will be able to agree on most of the jobs, leaving for arbitration only a few on which agreement proved impossible. Since in the allotment every job is pitted against every other, any tentative agreements reached as to particular jobs will have to lapse if the parties fail in the end to reach an agreement on the reorganization of the wage structure as a whole. In short, the arbitrator will usually have to start from scratch and do the whole job himself.

Confronted with such a task the arbitrator intent on preserving judicial proprieties faces a quandary much like that of a judge forced to carry out Mrs. Timken's "equal" division through adjudicative procedures. * * *

What modifications of his role will enable the arbitrator to discharge this task satisfactorily? The obvious expedient is a resort to mediation. After securing a general education in the problems involved in reordering the wage scale, the arbitrator might propose to each side in turn a tentative solution, inviting comments and criticisms. Through successive modifications a reasonably acceptable reordering of rates might be achieved, which would then be incorporated in an award. Here the dangers involved in the mediative role are probably at a minimum, precisely because the need for that role seems so obvious. Those dangers are not, however, absent. There is always the possibility that mediative efforts may meet shipwreck. Prolonged involvement in an attempt to work out a settlement agreeable to both parties obscures the arbitrator's function as a judge and makes it difficult to reassume that role. Furthermore, a considerable taint of the "rigged" award will in any event almost always attach to the final solution. The very fact that this solution must involve a compromise of interests within the union itself makes this virtually certain.

* * *

There is one general consideration that may incline the arbitrator to resolve any doubts presented by particular cases in favor of assuming a mediative role. This lies in a conviction—to be sure, not expressed in the terms I am about to employ—that all labor arbitrations involve to some extent polycentric elements. The relations within a plant form a seamless web; pluck it here, and a complex pattern of adjustments may run through the whole structure. A case involving a single individual, say a reclassification case, may set a precedent with implications unknown to the arbitrator, who cannot see how his decision may cut into a whole body of practice that is unknown to him. The arbitrator can never be sure what aspects of the case post-hearing consultations may bring to his attention that he would otherwise have missed.

That there is much truth in this observation would be foolish to deny. The integrity of the adjudicative process can never be maintained without some loss, without running some calculated risk. Any adjudicator—whether he be called judge, hearing officer, arbitrator, or umpire—who depends upon proofs and arguments adduced before him in open court, with each party confronting the other, is certain to make occasional mistakes he would not make if he could abandon the restraints of his role. The question is, how vital is that role for the maintenance of the government—in this case a system of industrial self-government—of which he is a part?

In facing that question as it arises in his practice, the arbitrator ought to divest himself, insofar as human nature permits, of any motive that might be called personal. It has been said that surgeons who have perfected some highly specialized operation tend strongly to favor a diagnosis of the patient's condition that will enable them to display their special skills. Can the arbitrator be sure he is immune from a similar desire to demonstrate virtuosity in his calling? It is well known in arbitrational circles that combining the roles of arbitrator and mediator is a tricky business. The amateur who tries it is almost certain to get in trouble. The veteran, on the other hand, takes an understandable pride in his ability to play this difficult dual role. He would be less than human if he did not seek out occasions for a display of his special talents, even to the point of discerning a need for them in situations demanding nothing more than a patient, conscientious judge, about to put a sensible meaning on the words of the contract.

* * *

Sometimes judgment on the issues here under discussion is influenced by a kind of slogan to the effect that an agreed settlement is always better than an imposed one. As applied to disputes before they have gone to arbitration, this slogan has some merit. When the case is in the hands of the arbitrator, however, I can see little merit in it, except in the special cases I have tried previously to analyze. After all, successful industrial self-government requires not only the capacity to reach and abide by agreements, but also the willingness to accept and conform to disliked awards. It is well that neither propensity be lost through disuse. Furthermore, there is something slightly morbid about the thought that an agreement coerced by the threat of decision is somehow more wholesome than an outright decision. It suggests a little the father who wants his children to obey him, but who, in order to still doubts that he may be too domineering, not only demands that they obey but insists that they do so with a smile. After having had his day in court, a man may with dignity bend his will to a judgment of which he disapproves. That dignity is lost if he is compelled to pretend that he agreed to it.

Notes and Questions

(1) One arbitrator has noted that,

[y]ou have to recognize the danger is there even by the mere overture to the arbitrator to step outside and "Let's have a look at this." It could be nothing more than one side broadly indicating, "Yes, we are ready to compromise this," and the other side saying, "Under no circumstances. We think we have a solid case." Back we go into the room, and you have to decide. It is conceivable that that conversation is going to influence the arbitrator. * * * I just don't think you can say even in the most cautious way that there won't be some prejudice.

Panel Discussion (Valtin), Proceedings, 33rd Annual Meeting, National Academy of Arbitrators 232 (1981).

Is it fair to suggest, then, that the "med-arb" process may often serve as an invitation to the parties to be candid—an invitation which only the more inexperienced or ingenuous of the two is likely to accept?

(2) Recall the survey of litigators that found that a majority preferred judges in pre-trial conferences to "actively offer suggestions and observations for the settlement of the case." See Chapter II, supra p. 169. Does this discussion affect your view of Fuller's criticisms with respect to arbitrators who depart from the proper "judicial role"?

(3) Some schemes of "med-arb" provide for the different functions of mediation and arbitration to be performed by different individuals. If mediation fails, the dispute is then entrusted to a separate arbitrator who has the power to make a binding award. See Iowa Code §§ 20.20–20.22; Goldberg, The Mediation of Grievances Under a Collective Bargaining Contract: An Alternative to Arbitration, 77 Nw.U.L.Rev. 270 (1982).

In some cases, however, the mediator is charged also with making a *recommendation* to the ultimate decision-maker as to how the dispute should be resolved. This is true, for example, under California's mandatory mediation scheme, where the mediator may make a recommendation to the court as to child custody and visitation matters. See supra p. 291. How might the possibility of such a recommendation by the mediator affect the mediation process? See J. Folberg & A. Taylor, Mediation 277–78 (1984):

> The consensus among mediators appears to confirm that the trust and candor required in mediation are unlikely to exist if the participants know the mediator may be formulating an opinion or recommendation that will be communicated to a judge or tribunal. The recommendation of the mediator, particularly in a child custody and visitation case, would generally be given such great weight that the mediator, in effect, would be switching roles from decision facilitator to decision maker. The confusion and suspicion created by this crossover role taint the validity, effectiveness, and integrity of the mediation process.

> The participants may, in some circumstances, agree or contract for the mediator to decide the matter if they are unable to do so or to testify as to a recommendation. Using the informal, consensual process of mediation with no evidentiary or procedural rules as the basis for an imposed decision does, however, create a considerable risk that the more clever or sophisticated participant may distort or manipulate the mediation in order to influence the mediator's opinion.

4. Non–Binding Arbitration

AMF INCORPORATED v. BRUNSWICK CORPORATION

United States District Court, Eastern District New York, 1985.
621 F.Supp. 456.

WEINSTEIN, CH. J.:

In this case of first impression, AMF Incorporated seeks to compel Brunswick Corporation to comply with their agreement to obtain a non-binding advisory opinion in a dispute over the propriety of advertising claims. For reasons indicated below, the agreement to utilize an alternative dispute resolution mechanism must be enforced.

AMF and Brunswick compete nationally in the manufacture of electronic and automatic machinery used for bowling centers. In earlier litigation before this court, AMF alleged that Brunswick had advertised certain automatic scoring devices in a false and deceptive manner. Brunswick responded with counterclaims regarding advertisements for AMF's pinspotter, bowling pins and automatic scorer. In 1983 the parties ended the litigation with a settlement agreement filed with the court. Any future dispute involving an advertised claim of "data based comparative superiority" of any bowling product would be submitted to an advisory third party, the National Advertising Division ("NAD") of the Council of Better Business Bureaus, to determine whether there was experimental support for the claim.

Paragraph 9 of the agreement reads as follows:

* * *

Should either party make a claim to data based comparative superiority, the other may request that substantiation for the same be delivered to the agreed upon advisory third party, subject to the provisions of this agreement, whereupon the party who has made the claim shall promptly comply.

Both parties agree to submit any controversy which they may have with respect to data based comparative superiority of any of their products over that of the other to such advisory third party for the rendition of an advisory opinion. Such opinion shall not be binding upon the parties, but shall be advisory only. . . .

NAD was created in 1971 by the American Advertising Federation, American Association of Advertising Agencies, Association of National Advertisers, and the Council of Better Business Bureaus "to help sustain high standards of truth and accuracy in national advertising." It monitors television, radio, and print advertising, and responds to complaints from individual consumers, consumer groups, local Better Business Bureaus, competitors, professional and trade associations, and state and federal agencies. If NAD finds that the advertising claims are unsupported, and the advertiser refuses to modify or discontinue the advertising, the organization will complain to the appropriate governmental authority. Voluntary compliance with NAD's decisions has been universal. Reportedly no advertiser who has participated in the complete process of a NAD investigation and NARB appeal has declined to abide by the decision.

In March and April 1985, Brunswick advertised its product, Armor Plate 3000, in a trade periodical called *Bowler's Journal*. Armor Plate is a synthetic laminated material used to make bowling lanes. It competes with the wood lanes produced by AMF. "The wood lane. A relic of the past," claims the advertisement, under a sketch of a horse and buggy. It goes on to detail the advantages of Armor Plate; and, as indicated in the footnote to the advertisement, strongly suggests that research supports the claim of durability as compared to wood lanes.

By replacing your worn out wood lanes with Armor Plate 3000, Brunswick's high tech laminated surface, what you're doing is saving money. Up to $500.00 per lane per year in lost revenue and upkeep.

That's because today's high technology has helped make Armor Plate 3000 so tough and good looking that it seems to last forever.*

---

* Continuing independent research projects that Armor Plate 3000 will now last over twenty years before the possible need arises to replace a small lane area much like replacing a broken board in a wood lane.

AMF, disputing the content of the advertisement, sought from Brunswick the underlying research data referred to in the footnote. Brunswick replied that having undertaken the expenses of research it would not make the results available to AMF. Thereupon AMF informed Brunswick that it was invoking Paragraph 9 of the settlement agreement and requested that Brunswick provide substantiation to an independent third party. Brunswick responded that its advertisement did not fall within the terms of the agreement. AMF now brings this action to compel Brunswick to submit its data to the NAD for nonbinding arbitration.

* * *

A. *Arbitration*

1. The Act

AMF characterizes the settlement agreement as one subject to the Federal Arbitration Act. The Act provides for enforcement of agreements to "settle" disputes arising after the agreement was entered into.

* * *

Brunswick argues that the parties did not contemplate the kind of arbitration envisaged by the Act because the opinion of the third party is not binding on AMF and Brunswick and the agreement cannot settle the controversy. Arbitration, Brunswick argues, must present an alternative to litigation; that is, it must provide "a final settlement of the controversy between the parties."

* * *

The Federal Arbitration Act, adopted in 1925, made agreements to arbitrate enforceable without defining what they were. * * * At no time have the courts insisted on a rigid or formalistic approach to a definition of arbitration.

Case law following the passage of the Act reflects unequivocal support of agreements to have third parties decide disputes—the essence of arbitration. No magic words such as "arbitrate" or "binding arbitration" or "final dispute resolution" are needed to obtain the benefits of the Act.

* * *

Arbitration is a creature of contract, a device of the parties rather than the judicial process. If the parties have agreed to submit a dispute for a decision by a third party, they have agreed to arbitration. The arbitrator's decision need not be binding in the same sense that a judicial decision needs to be to satisfy the constitutional requirement of a justiciable case or controversy.

2. Application of the Act to the Facts

Under the circumstances of this case, the agreement should be characterized as one to arbitrate. Obviously there is a controversy between the parties—is there data supporting Brunswick's claim of superiority. Submission of this dispute will at least "settle" that issue, even though the parties may want to continue related disputes in another forum.

It is highly likely that if Brunswick's claims are found by NAD to be supported that will be the end of AMF's challenge to the advertisement. Should the claims not be found to be supported, it is probable that Brunswick will change its advertising copy. Viewed in the light of reasonable commercial expectations the dispute will be settled by this arbitration. That it may not end all controversy between the parties for all times is no reason not to enforce the agreement.

The mechanism agreed to by the parties does provide an effective alternative to litigation, even though it would not employ an adversary process. That the arbitrator will examine documents in camera and ex parte does not prevent recognition of the procedure as arbitration since the parties have agreed to this special practice in this unique type of dispute. Courts are fully familiar with the practice since prosecutorial and business secrets often require protection by ex parte and in camera proceedings during the course of a litigation.

In a confidential-submission scheme, such as the one agreed to here, adversarial hearings cannot take place. But this fact does not militate against application of the Act. Rather it supports arbitration since the special arbitrator may be more capable of deciding the issue than is a court which relies so heavily on the adversary process. Moreover, the particular arbitrator chosen by these parties is more capable than the courts of finding the faint line that separates data supported claims from puffery in the sometimes mendacious atmosphere of advertising copy.

B. *Contract to Employ an Alternative Dispute–Resolution Mechanism*

1. Consent Agreements as Enforceable Contracts

Whether or not the agreement be deemed one to arbitrate, it is an enforceable contract to utilize a confidential advisory process in a matter of serious concern to the parties.

* * *

The settlement agreement evinces a clear intent by both parties to require confidential submission to the NAD of disputes concerning advertised data-based claims of superiority. This settlement facilitated the termination of AMF's lawsuit and Brunswick's counterclaim. Both parties bargained for and benefited from the stipulation.

2. Equity Jurisdiction

Untenable is the defendant's argument that there is an adequate remedy at law so that equity is without jurisdiction. Specific performance is available as a remedy where the remedy at law is not appropriate if such equitable relief will not force a "vain order."

* * *

The alternative dispute resolution (ADR) procedure agreed upon in the settlement is designed to reduce the acrimony associated with protracted litigation and to improve the chances of resolving future advertising disputes. This form of ADR is designed to keep disputes of this kind out of court.

The value of this settlement agreement lies largely in the particular experience and skill of the NAD as a resolver of disputes. In the fourteen years since its formation, the NAD has developed its own process of reviewing complaints of deceptiveness, coupling relative informality and confidentiality with safeguards to ensure procedural fairness. As the NAD puts it: "Speed, informality and modest cost are three chief benefits of [this] self-regulatory system." To these advantages of the special ADR system designed by the parties is added the unique ability of the NAD to decide what is fair in advertising. A judge might make this inquiry, but ultimately it would have to defer to the very expertise that NAD offers without resort to the courts.

General public policy favors support of alternatives to litigation when these alternatives serve the interests of the parties and of judicial administration. Here AMF and Brunswick agreed in June 1983 that a special ADR mechanism would serve them better than litigation. Such decisions are encouraged by no less an observer than the Chief Justice of the United States. In his words, ADR devices are often superior to litigation "in terms of cost, time, and human wear and tear." Remarks of Warren E. Burger, Chief Justice of the United States, at the Twin Cities Advisory Council of the American Arbitration Association, St. Paul, Minn., August 21, 1985.

* * *

A remedy at law would be inadequate since it could only approximate the skilled, speedy and inexpensive efforts available by way of specific performance. A law suit would deny AMF the practical specialized experience that the parties agreed to have available for an examination of data-based comparative advertising. A court decision and an NAD decision would have different effects on the parties' reputations within the bowling products industry. In short, a remedy at law falls short of providing many of the advantages of specific performance.

* * *

AMF's petition to compel the submission of data pursuant to Paragraph 9 of the settlement agreement of June 30, 1983 is enforceable under the Federal Arbitration Act and pursuant to this court's equity jurisdiction.

Notes and Questions

(1) As we have seen throughout this chapter, the term "arbitration" is most often used to refer to processes which like adjudication result in a final and binding "decision." It is possible to conceive of "nonbinding" arbitration as being closer to other dispute resolution mechanisms which use a neutral's opinion, not as the final stage of the process, but merely as a device to nudge the parties into settlement. The hope here, as expressed by the court in *Brunswick,* is that the

prediction of a neutral expert will cause the parties to reassess their own partisan estimates of the likely outcome of adjudication. Or perhaps the neutral's report may enable negotiators (such as attorneys, or union or management representatives in collective bargaining) to withdraw gracefully and without loss of face from hardened positions, or "sell" a compromise settlement to reluctant clients or constituents. Through these means the parties may be induced to resolve a dispute themselves without resort to an imposed third-party solution.

Questioning whether this process should really be called "arbitration" at all may amount to little more than a semantic quibble— although, as the *Brunswick* case indicates, the question can have real legal significance.

For a discussion of similar dispute resolution mechanisms, see the material on the mini-trial, court-administered arbitration, and the summary jury trial in Chapter V, infra p. 612.

(2) An insured was injured in an automobile accident and made a claim under the uninsured motorist provision of his policy. The policy contained an arbitration clause, which provided that if the damages awarded by the arbitrators exceeded the statutory minimum coverage for uninsured motorists ($25,000), then either party might demand a trial de novo. The arbitrators awarded the insured $45,000. The court held that the insurer had no right to a new trial; the trial de novo provision "contravenes public policies favoring arbitration and judicial economy" and was thus "void as against public policy." Schmidt v. Midwest Family Mutual Ins. Co., 413 N.W.2d 178 (Minn.App.1987).

What precisely is the nature of the "public policy" argument here? Are you convinced?

(3) Another similar device, employed frequently in public-sector employment disputes, is that of the neutral "fact-finder." Under some statutes, "interest" disputes not settled by mediation are submitted to a "fact-finder," who after hearing evidence from the parties makes a recommendation for the resolution of all the issues in dispute. See, e.g., 43 Pa.Stat. §§ 1101.801, 1101.802; 150E Mass.Gen.Laws § 9. The term "fact-finder" may be chosen to lend an air of precision and inevitability to the process. But the fact-finder, in issuing his recommendations, is still likely to make the same sorts of value judgments and show the same concern for the acceptability of his conclusions to the parties as is typical of the "interest" arbitrator.

A unique feature of the fact-finding process is that the recommendations of the fact-finder are usually made public. The goal is for the resulting public scrutiny and pressure of "public opinion" to make it more difficult for the parties to reject the fact-finder's recommendations. See, e.g., Ore.Rev.Stat. § 243.722(3), (4) (fact-finder's recommendations shall be "publicized" unless parties agree to accept them or agree to submit the dispute to final and binding arbitration). In all but the most exceptional cases, however, there is room for considerable skepticism as to the extent of any public awareness of or concern for the reports of public-sector fact-finders.

Fact-finding is in some states the final prescribed stage in the resolution of public-sector "interest" disputes. In other states, both mediation and then fact-finding are imposed as preliminary steps before mandatory arbitration. Under some statutory schemes fact-finding is to precede final-offer arbitration. See, e.g., N.J.Stat. § 34:13A–16 (police and fire departments). Iowa's version of final-offer arbitration adds further flexibility to the process: The arbitrators are allowed to choose not only one of the parties' last offers, but also—as a third option—the recommendation of the fact-finder on each "impasse item." 3A Iowa Code §§ 20.21, 20.22. As might be expected this recommendation usually turns out to be a compromise, an intermediate position between the positions taken by the parties. And in those cases where an award proves necessary, the arbitrators tend overwhelmingly to choose the recommendation of the fact-finder. Even where this option is not given to the arbitrator, the fact-finder's recommendation will often simply be incorporated into the final offer of one of the parties; the arbitration may then become a "show cause" hearing as to why this offer should not be accepted. "For those disputes that are not going to get resolved at the bargaining table, fact-finding is where the concrete for the foundation of an arbitration award is first poured." Holden, Final Offer Arbitration in Massachusetts, 31 Arb.J. 26, 28–29 (1976).

What might be the advantages and disadvantages of combining fact-finding and arbitration in this way? Might this two-step process tend to dilute the supposed benefits of final-offer arbitration? See generally Bierman, Factfinding: Finding the Public Interest, 9 Rutgers–Camden L.J. 667 (1978).

5. "Rent a Judge"

A California statute provides that "upon the agreement of the parties," a court may "refer" a pending action to any person or persons whom the parties themselves may choose. The court may also "refer" an action where the parties had previously entered into a written contract calling for a referee to hear controversies that might arise in the future. Referees may be asked:

> to try any or all of the issues in an action or proceeding, whether of fact or of law, and to report a statement of decision thereon; [or] to ascertain a fact necessary to enable the court to determine an action or proceeding.

Cal.Code Civ.Pro. §§ 638, 640.

After hearing the case, the referees are to report their decision to the court within twenty days after the close of testimony; judgment must then be entered on the referees' decision "in the same manner as if the action had been tried by the court." Cal.Code Civ.Pro. §§ 643, 644.

CHRISTENSEN, PRIVATE JUSTICE: CALIFORNIA'S
GENERAL REFERENCE PROCEDURE

1982 American Bar Foundation Research J. 79, 81–82, 103.

The statute says nothing at all about the qualifications of referees. Presumably, the parties might agree to have a case referred to almost anyone—to another lawyer, perhaps, or even to a layman. But parties using this statutory procedure are seeking judicial determination of their causes, and so references are made to retired judges selected by the parties. The reasons are obvious. A retired judge who would be acceptable to both parties would almost surely possess acknowledged judicial skills and, in many instances, expertise in the particular kind of case at issue, thus ensuring a trial that is both expeditious and fair.

The statute is also silent about the time and place of trials by referees. As a consequence, the parties and the referee are free to select the times and places that will be most convenient. This has obvious advantages with respect to such things as securing the presence of witnesses, and it means that trials can be scheduled at times that will be most advantageous to counsel. Moreover, because the procedure is most often used by parties who want to get to trial promptly, both sides know that when they do go to trial both parties will be ready, thus avoiding the continuances and postponements that are often so frustrating in the course of regular trials in courts.

Trials by referees are conducted as proper judicial trials, following the traditional rules of procedure and evidence. Transcripts are made of the proceedings, and the judgment of the referee becomes the judgment of the court. It is thus enforceable and appealable, as any other judgment would be. One lawyer who uses the reference procedure suggests that parties might agree to submit disputes to retired judges for decision independently, without any court order, but that they use the statutory procedure to preserve their rights of enforcement and appeal. Unlike trials in courts, however, trials by referees are conducted privately, without the presence of either the public or the press. Again, there appears to be no statutory requirement that this be so.

In theory, almost any kind of case might be referred to a referee for trial. The consensual portion of the statute imposes no restrictions. In practice, however, the procedure has been used primarily in technical and complex business litigation involving substantial amounts of money. The case in which the procedure was first used, for instance, was a complicated dispute between a medical billing company and two attorneys who had acquired interests in the company. Other examples have been a suit by major oil companies against a California governmental agency over air pollution control standards, a contract dispute between a nationally known television entertainer and his broadcasting company employer, and an action between a giant motor vehicle manufacturer and one of its suppliers over the quality of parts supplied.

The compensation of a retired judge appointed to try a case as a referee is also the subject of agreement between the parties, and the cost is borne equally by the parties.

* * *

One judge had, while on the bench, handled a great many asbestosis cases brought by employees of a large industry in the area, achieving some success both in trying the cases and in effecting settlements. Upon retirement, he began to take asbestosis cases on a reference basis, and at present he is working virtually full time on them. Clearly, he is being sought for private trials because of his expertise. [Another] judge has, since retirement, put together a group of three or four other retired judges, whom he offers to the courts to handle large, complex cases requiring specialized knowledge. The group operates almost like a law firm; the courts may simply call in for a judge to whom they may refer a case requiring a particular expertise.

Notes and Questions

(1) The California scheme appears to be the most often-used, and is certainly the most highly-publicized, in the country. However, comparable procedures exist in some other states. In some cases the "referee" is *required* to be a retired judge. Under the Texas statute, for example, a "special judge" must be a retired or former district judge with at least four years service, who has "developed substantial experience in his area of specialty" and who each year completes five days of continuing legal education courses. Here too, however, the parties are free to select their own "special judge" and to agree with him on the fee that he is to be paid. See Tex.Civ.Stat. art. 200d.

(2) How does the California or Texas reference procedure differ from arbitration? Are there reasons why parties might prefer to utilize the reference procedure rather than to submit an existing dispute to arbitration?

Consider the following provisions of the Texas statute:

Sec. 5. Rules and statutes relating to procedure and evidence in district court apply to a trial under this Act.

Sec. 6. (a) A special judge shall conduct the trial in the same manner as a court trying an issue without a jury.

(b) While serving as a special judge, the judge has the powers of a district court judge except that he may not hold a person in contempt of court unless the person is a witness before him.

Sec. 11. The special judge's verdict must comply with the requirements for a verdict by the court. The verdict stands as a verdict of the district court. * * *

Section 13. The right to appeal is preserved. * * *

(3) The following excerpts from a student-written note raise a number of objections to the California reference procedure. In light of everything that you have read in this chapter on arbitration, how do you assess these criticisms?

While the comparatively affluent can realize the cost and time savings of hiring a referee, other litigants may not. Those appearing pro se, for example, or who are represented by Legal Aid or by attorneys appearing pro bono or on a contingency fee basis, may be able to afford little or no out-of-pocket expenditure prior to entry of a judgment and hence will be unable to hire a referee. The use of referees paid by the parties, then, in effect creates two classes of litigants: wealthy litigants, who can afford the price of a referee, and poorer litigants, who cannot. The former group obtains all of the advantages of reference, while the latter must endure all the systemic disadvantages that led wealthy litigants to seek reference in the first place.

Such a system of reference is clearly unfair to the poorer litigant and may even run against the best interests of society. It would allow, in the extreme case, an utterly frivolous suit to obtain a speedy trial solely because the litigants were wealthy, while forcing a suit involving issues important to society and vital to the parties to languish for a considerable time awaiting trial. Even if the suits are similar, the bias against the poor is still striking. If, for example, the poor litigant is in court because he needs to protect a valuable property interest affected by the dispute, his interest is kept in jeopardy for a longer period of time than that of a similarly situated litigant using the referee system. The state's action in according the wealthy the privilege of using a faster form of procedure gives them an additional property right, the right to be more secure in their ownership.

* * *

A due process problem may arise when referees are privately paid, particularly if overloading in the regular court system has driven some parties to a reference procedure they otherwise might not have chosen. As early as 1215, Magna Charta declared that it was wrong for the government to sell justice or to delay or deny it to anyone. In a private reference system, the state does not sell justice, but it does sanction the payment of private adjudicators to act in its place. The ultimate product purchased by these payments is a judgment that is entered on the court rolls and enforced by state authority. To whom the payments ultimately go is not nearly so important as the fact that they are made, with the sanction of the state, in order to obtain a state-monopolized enforceable order.

* * *

The secrecy available to those using the California reference system presents another troubling constitutional problem concerning the public's basic first amendment right to scrutinize the workings of governmental institutions.

* * *

Functionally a referee's court is identical to a trial court and should not be entitled to any immunity from public scrutiny because it is privately funded. In fact, the one distinction between the two types of trial bodies, the differing accountability of the adjudicators, illustrates the need for even greater public supervision of referee trials. Judges are broadly accountable to the general public and open trials compel conscientious attendance to their public responsibility. Private referees, however, are accountable only to the more limited group of persons for whom they decide cases. Their decisions may have widespread public impact—as, for example, in California where a case in which the state Air Resources Board was a defendant was tried before a referee—and they are enforced by the public to the same extent as those of state court judges. Yet they can be made in secret. If the argument in favor of a first amendment right of access to supervise governmental functions has any force, it is even more compelling in matters in which the public is affected and governmental authority is exercised by those who, but for public scrutiny, would have no other accountability.

Note, The California Rent–A–Judge Experiment: Constitutional and Policy Considerations of Pay–As–You–Go Courts, 94 Harv.L.Rev. 1592, 1601–02, 1607, 1608–10 (1981).

Chapter V

FORMAL SETTLEMENT PROCESSES: REALITY–TESTING BEFORE THIRD PARTIES

Experimentation has led to many variations in the traditional ADR processes of negotiation, mediation, and arbitration. Perhaps the most significant variation, which could now well be viewed as a distinctive process of its own, is a formal or structured settlement process involving nonbinding reality-testing before third parties. It has long been recognized that opposing parties and their attorneys often have very different perceptions of the merits of their cases. Self-deception is a very human quality, and the divisiveness of legal disputes promotes blindness to the strengths of the other side. Parties can sometimes only be persuaded of the unreality of their views by testing them before third parties whose judgment they have reason to trust. A trial certainly serves this purpose, but it may not be necessary to reach that point if reality-testing can come earlier. This is the premise on which a variety of techniques providing "trial runs" of a case before third parties are based.

Nonbinding trial runs involve attorney time and other expenses (as well as court time if the judge is involved in the process), and therefore are not likely to be efficient unless they lead to settlement short of trial. Thus trial runs should be part of a structured settlement process that will encourage parties to reach an agreement based on the information they receive from the proceeding. There are a variety of ways to do this. The third party could render a formal, non-binding, decision, or simply share her reactions to the case with the parties and their attorneys. Then the third party could preside over settlement discussions, or leave it to the parties to carry out their own discussions. The third party(s) could be drawn from a number of different groups, including ordinary jurors, lawyers, judges, or experts. On the other hand, the audience might not be third parties, but rather the parties themselves, or, in the case of corporate parties, persons with decision-making authority who were not personally involved in the dispute. Each of these variations, and many others, has its own advantages and disadvantages in providing the kind of reality-testing or prediction of likely judgment that will aid in settlement. The following materials will explore the principal trial-run mechanisms that have been developed in recent years in light of their propensity to accomplish a fair and successful settlement.

A. EXTRAJUDICIAL SETTLEMENT PROCESSES

As reflected in negotiation, mediation, and arbitration, extrajudicial means of structured settlement have advantages that make them popular. They can be initiated by the parties themselves without the necessity or burden of court oversight, and they allow the flexible private ordering process to take place. Extrajudicial processes have particularly been favored by corporations and business entities which can afford to pay for a private procedure, which want to avoid the delay and rigidity of the courts, and which may seek confidentiality that litigation cannot offer.

1. The Mini–Trial

Words sometimes catch the imagination and take on a life of their own, and so it is with the "mini-trial." This term was attached by a New York Times story to a formal settlement device created in 1977 in connection with a corporate dispute. It is not strictly speaking a trial at all, but a process that combines elements of adjudication with other processes such as negotiation and mediation. It refers to a proceeding, usually presided over by a neutral advisor, in which each side presents its case in shortened form to the Chief Executive Officers of the parties as a prelude to settlement negotiations between them. The term is sometimes used indiscriminately to refer to any form of shortened or summarized trial (rather than using the more specific titles, such as "summary jury trial" or "court-annexed arbitration"). Of course, certain features of the mini-trial format can be used in other processes, including those that are judicially-supervised, and thus in certain cases it may be appropriate to use the term to describe those features.

OLSON,
AN ALTERNATIVE FOR LARGE CASE DISPUTE RESOLUTION
6 Litigation 22 (Winter 1980).

[The author served as one of the counsel in the 1977 *TRW* case for which the mini-trial was devised.]

In the case for which the mini-trial was developed, the plaintiff, Telecredit, Inc., of Los Angeles, held several patents on computerized charge-authorization and credit-verification devices. The defendant, TRW, Inc., was a manufacturer of those devices. In response to Telecredit's contention that its patents were infringed by TRW's devices, TRW alleged that Telecredit's patents were invalid and unenforceable. Telecredit sought not only substantial damages for past infringement, but also an injunction restraining future infringement. The injunction would have destroyed one of TRW's major product lines.

When the mini-trial concept was developed, the parties had already obtained expert opinions to support their positions and had slugged their way through extensive, tedious, and costly discovery. While the case was somewhat simplified by earlier discovery, TRW's exposure was not materially lessened, and the parties were as far apart on the merits as they were when suit was filed. The parties had spent hundreds of thousands of dollars on discovery, and more remained before the case would be brought even to the threshold of a lengthy trial.

The procedure eventually developed called for a six-week schedule of expedited but limited discovery, the exchange of position papers and exhibits, and a two-day mini-trial. At the mini-trial each side could present through two, top-management representatives its "best case" on the issues of infringement, validity, and enforceability. Management on each side could then independently assess the theories, strengths, and weaknesses of the respective positions. Opposing management could next meet without counsel and try to resolve the dispute from the new perspectives obtained at the mini-trial.

There was also a mutually selected "neutral advisor" for the mini-trial. The advisor—in this case a lawyer and former Court of Claims judge with widely recognized expertise in patent law—was there strictly to *moderate* the proceedings; he was not authorized to impose, or even to "jaw-bone," to reach a compromise of the dispute. Rather, in the event management did not resolve the dispute in their initial discussions after the mini-trial, the advisor was to submit a written and nonbinding opinion discussing the relative strengths and weaknesses of the parties' positions and predicting the likely outcome of courtroom trial. Thereafter, management was to meet again to try to resolve the dispute with the added spur of the advisor's opinion. We believed that the party against whom the advisor opined would be willing to make significant concessions. More generally, we thought that the conclusions of the advisor would cause the parties to be more realistic in their evaluations and demands as they discussed disposition of the case immediately after the mini-trial. On a practical level the advisor's opinion, although nonbinding, would be coercive because the persons involved would have to explain to auditors and corporate superiors why they ignored the advisor.

The procedure included these other significant aspects:

- The parties postponed all pending discovery in the case, except discovery viewed as absolutely necessary to prepare for the mini-trial, with no waiver of the right to take further discovery if the case was not settled. Partial depositions, for example, could be taken without prejudicing the right to take a full deposition of the same person at a later time.

- By mutual agreement, any discovery disputes that arose during the six weeks of expedited, limited discovery could be submitted to the advisor for his "advice."

- The parties would initially share the fees and expenses of the advisor—with assessment against the eventual losing party in the event that a settlement could not be reached and a trial was conducted.

- The parties stipulated about basic source material to be submitted to the advisor before the mini-trial.

- The parties exchanged in advance and submitted to the advisor all exhibits to be used at the mini-trial and short briefs in the form of "introductory statements."

- The advisor could submit written questions to the parties' technical experts before the mini-trial.

- The rules of evidence would not apply during the mini-trial.

- There would be unlimited scope for the material offered during each party's presentation at the mini-trial. The advisor could ask clarifying questions, but was explicitly told he could not preside like a judge or arbitrator or limit the parties' presentations.

- There was insulation of the mini-trial procedure and its results from the court. Resort to the court on any aspect of the mini-trial was forbidden. The written submissions prepared specifically for the mini-trial and the oral statements made during the mini-trial were inadmissible at trial for any purpose, including impeachment. However, evidence that was otherwise admissible was not rendered inadmissible by use at the mini-trial.

- The advisor was disqualified as a trial witness, consultant, or expert for either party, and his advisory opinion could not be used for any purpose in any dispute between the parties.

The presentations were made primarily by attorneys, with significant participation by the parties' experts, each a noted computer authority. Telecredit also presented a former employee of one of its licensees, and TRW used one of its scientists to present a technical aspect of its case.

The mini-trial's question and answer sessions were particularly useful in defining and narrowing each side's contentions. Where difficulties arose, the advisor aided the discussion with his questions. Occasionally, the advisor's comments indicated where he felt serious problems existed for each side. This participation by a neutral observer was particularly helpful in bringing home to the participants the strengths and weaknesses of their cases.

Immediately after the mini-trial ended, top management for each side met privately without lawyers. Within one-half hour, they reached in principle an agreement that became the basis for resolving the dispute. Although the details took several weeks to tie up, the drain on both corporations' treasuries was plugged, and a case that had threatened to occupy the time and energy of a federal court for months was terminated without an additional day of court time.

*   *   *

Many business disputes are overly litigated and not settled because the corporate manager has given up and left the matter to his lawyers. He has reported to his board of directors that the dispute is now in the courts. The mini-trial was specifically designed to bring the problem back to the corporate managers. It established a structure for rational communication outside the courts.

In the typical settlement negotiation involving businessmen, there is seldom a thorough exploration of the merits of the dispute. Rather, to the extent the merits are discussed at all (usually only at the first few meetings), the negotiations consist of simplistic overstatements of each side's position, followed by, "Well, we won't convince each other of the merits of our position; let's talk about the numbers." Anticipating such shallow treatment of the merits by the other side is a good reason for a litigant to reserve his best arguments for future use—perhaps at a point in the case when discovery by the other side on the issue will not be available. When significant points are made, they are usually ignored rather than tested.

*   *   *

The mini-trial returns the dispute to the businessmen, educates them, and then allows them to use their developed skills—assessing risk and negotiating—to resolve the dispute. Once again, the corporate managers' egos and judgments are on the line. Both can contribute significantly to the ultimate resolution.

GREEN,
GROWTH OF THE MINI–TRIAL
9 Litigation No. 1, 12, 17–20 (Fall 1982).

[The author, a professor of law at Boston University, has worked extensively with mini-trials and is the author of the Mini-Trial Handbook, published by the Center for Public Resources.]

The typical mini-trial contains only one of the two features of a trial: after a short period of pretrial preparation, the lawyers (and their experts, if desired) make informal, abbreviated, and confidential presentations of each side's best case. The mini-trial drops the second main feature of a trial: no third party pronounces judgment. The most distinctive characteristic of the mini-trial is that the lawyers present their cases not to a judge, an arbitrator, a jury, or any other third party with the power to make a binding decision, but rather to the principals themselves.

In the classic mini-trial with corporations involved, the principals are business executives with settlement authority. The lawyers design their presentations to give the parties a clear and balanced conception of the strengths and weaknesses of the positions on both sides. In other words, the principals receive a crash course on the subject of the dispute conducted in an informal setting but through the adversary process. The purpose of the presentation phase is to exchange information. The principals enter confidential settlement negotiations immediately afterwards.

In the classic format, mini-trials have been presided over by a jointly selected "neutral adviser." The adviser moderates the proceedings, poses questions, and highlights crucial facts and issues. But during the presentation phase, he does not preside like a judge, an arbitrator, or even a mediator. If the principals do not reach settlement quickly after the information exchange, they may ask the neutral adviser to give a nonbinding opinion about how a judge or a jury would decide the case and why. With these views in hand, the parties then resume direct negotiations.

The mini-trial is not arbitration, a close relation with which it is often confused. Unlike the mini-trial, arbitration is characterized by a final, binding result (often a compromise) announced by a third party after formal and complete presentation by trial lawyers for each side, with little or no participation by the clients.

* * *

The mini-trial seems best suited to cases with mixed questions of law and fact. Thus, for example, the mini-trial has been successfully used in cases of products liability, patent infringement, government contracts, and employee grievances. The mini-trial might also be used to resolve an antitrust case where the sticking point to settlement is the scope and definition of the relevant market, or an unfair-competition case where the propriety of business practices is at issue. But a case that turns solely on issues of law will be better resolved by summary judgment. Where a case turns on the credibility of witnesses, the mini-trial will probably not be effective. Where the factual disputes are technical ones and promise a battle of the experts at trial, you should consider putting on a mini-trial.

You should at least consider a mini-trial in every case. The proposed amendments to Fed.R.Civ.P. 16 governing pretrial conferences expressly include consideration of extra-judicial procedures to resolve the dispute. The Advisory Committee Notes expressly mention the mini-trial as an example of such a procedure. But lawyers sensitive to the needs of their clients for quicker and cheaper alternates to litigation should consider the possibilities of a mini-trial without waiting for the pretrial conference.

Trial lawyers often ask how to suggest a mini-trial without showing weakness. The question contains a false assumption. An invitation to a dialogue on the merits amounts to a testing by the other side in front of an eminent neutral adviser and the principals. Such a test demonstrates strength, not weakness.

The best way to begin a mini-trial is the direct way. Outside counsel, house counsel, or even management should never hesitate to call on the other side and suggest a mini-trial. In disputes between corporations, the driving force for a mini-trial often will be the businessman responsible for the case or the general counsel. But mini-trials have been suggested by outside counsel as well, and the trend may be in that direction.

Much momentum toward settlement follows the negotiations on the procedures of a mini-trial. Thus it may be wiser not to approach the other side with a detailed mini-trial procedure, but simply to offer to participate in good faith in some such process. Joint design of the mini-trial procedure increases the chances of success.

Notes and Questions

(1) The mini-trial is peculiarly the result of concerns by corporate officers that business litigation has become too costly and cumbersome. A principal philosophical thrust is, as indicated by Olson, that it "returns the dispute to the businessmen." But why isn't traditional negotiation sufficient? Why the need for a formalized procedure? The answer in part may be that when business deals go sour, the persons involved are too close to the dispute to be able to settle it among themselves. Traditionally they have turned to lawyers, partly to bail them out and partly to shift the blame if litigation turns out badly. Lawyers, in turn, have relied on the adversary litigation process, because it is what they know and what they can do. The mini-trial attempts to reduce the influence of both the lawyers and the business personnel who were involved in the arrangements that gave rise to the dispute, by presenting the case to the Chief Executive Officers or their delegees. It worked in the *TRW* case where substantial stakes were involved, litigation had proven costly, positions had hardened, and there was room for compromise. Is it less likely to be effective if a company's integrity is on the line, major public policy issues dominate, there are unresolved legal issues, or the credibility of contradictory witnesses from each company is central?

(2) What is lost when a case that might have taken weeks or months to try is squeezed into a two-day mini-trial? Although witnesses may be presented in a mini-trial (unlike a summary jury trial, see infra, pp. 656–57), lengthy examination and cross-examination is not possible. The virtues and vices of summarization of evidence is considered again in connection with summary jury trial and court-annexed arbitration, infra pp. 660–65.

(3) Is a contract clause requiring the parties to submit any dispute to a mini-trial legally enforceable? This may depend on the specificity of the language and the context of the dispute. The usual remedy for breach of contract is damages, but how could a dollar figure be placed on a failure to engage in a mini-trial? Is a mini-trial clause therefore specifically enforceable because damages are inadequate? Would ad-

ministering such specific enforcement cause the same kinds of difficulties that has led courts to refuse specific enforcement of contracts for personal services? Professor Green argues that "it may be possible to specifically enforce a mini-trial clause by setting forth the procedures to be followed at the mini-trial in detail," making the court's job of supervising performance easier. Green, Growth of the Mini-Trial, *supra* at 18. Recall *AMF, Inc. v. Brunswick Corp., supra* p. 601, in which a court specifically enforced an agreement for "nonbinding arbitration," both under the Federal Arbitration Act and the court's general equity jurisdiction.

(4) One of the attractions of the mini-trial is its confidentiality. It is a form of settlement negotiation and therefore enjoys the protections of Federal Rule of Evidence 408. (See supra pp. 181, 343.) Those protections should apply to all parts of a mini-trial, including the information-exchange, neutral advisor's opinion or comments, negotiations, and any settlement. But since Rule 408 only prohibits admissibility, rather than discovery, further privilege is necessary. Cases involving mediator privilege may be relevant (see supra pp. 350–68).

A contract clause that statements, documents, results, or other information arising in a mini-trial will not be admissible in a later trial or proceeding is standard. But while a court may be willing to specifically enforce a non-disclosure clause against the parties, can third-parties be prevented from using discovery devices to obtain the information? Green suggests incorporating the mini-trial agreement in a court order, thus entitling it to the protection of Rule 26(c)(7) for "trade secret or other confidential research, development, or commercial information." But he notes that courts have allowed subsequent litigators access even to previously sealed court records, and that the government may have special powers to discover evidence, as under anti-trust statutes.

(5) The reputation or prestige of the neutral advisor is often considered to be critical to the success of the mini-trial. The Center for Public Resources (CPR) has a list of persons who have agreed to serve as neutral advisors that includes such legal luminaries as Griffin Bell, Archibald Cox, Lloyd Cutler, Marvin Frankel, and Elliot Richardson.

(6) Detailed mini-trial procedures have been drawn up by various organizations. See, *e.g.,* E. Green, The CPR Legal Program Mini-Trial Handbook, in Corporate Dispute Management (1985), which sets out procedures for a six week schedule, with two weeks for discovery and a 2½ day trial. Plaintiff's case-in-chief is presented on the first afternoon; defendant's rebuttal and plaintiff's response on the second morning; defendant's case-in-chief on the second afternoon; and plaintiff's rebuttal and defendant's response on the third morning. Negotiations without the advisor are held on the third afternoon. Some mini-trials have provided for shortened depositions, *e.g.,* half a day for an expert witness. Although unusual, a mini-trial without a neutral advisor is also possible.

2. Joint Defense Agreements for Loss Allocation

Today multiple-party suits, and particularly multiple-defendant suits, are the rule rather than the exception. For example, in a product liability case, the plaintiff may sue both the retailer who sold him the product and the manufacturer. The designer of the product may be added as well, either by the plaintiff or the manufacturer. If the product involves component parts, the manufacturers of those parts may be additional parties, as may be the suppliers of the materials used by the prime manufacturer. "In the absence of a sharing agreement each of the defendants has an incentive to attempt to escape liability by proving that if there was any defect in the product, it was caused by the acts or omission of another party. When the multi-party defendants have completed their discovery, the plaintiff's case frequently has been significantly strengthened." [1]

The solution of defense strategists to this disadvantageous position has been an agreement between defendants and potential defendants that they will make a common front against the plaintiff and leave the allocation of their respective liability to non-binding ADR procedures (with an ultimate right to sue) after the initial suit is over. Such an agreement gives co-defendants the confidence to join a common defense, perhaps accepting the same lawyers and waiving the opportunity to file cross-claims, knowing that their rights against other defendants are not lost. The ADR procedures indicate cooperativeness among the parties and a willingness to reality-test their respective liabilities while still preserving their rights ultimately to seek a court remedy.

The following procedures were devised for joint defendant loss allocation in toxic tort cases:

CENTER FOR PUBLIC RESOURCES, MODEL ADR PROCEDURES: RULES FOR LOSS ALLOCATION IN TOXIC TORT CASES

(1987).

1. PURPOSE

Lawsuits are brought at times, usually by groups of individuals, against suppliers of chemicals or other products, alleging adverse health effects, personal injuries or other damages resulting from exposure to such products in the workplace or elsewhere ("toxic tort" suits). Defendants in such lawsuits may consider it advisable to enter into coordinated defense or shared counsel arrangements. A judgment

1. Jones, The Utility of Pre–Trial Sharing Arrangements Among Multi–Party Defendants, 2 Alts. to the High Cost of Lit. No. 12, 7, 8 (Dec. 1984). See also Gray, Dispute Resolution Clauses: Some Thoughts on Ends & Means, 2 Alts. to the High Cost of Lit. No. 8, 12 (Aug. 1984).

against defendants, or a settlement entered into by a group of defendants, may well leave open the basis for allocating such judgment or settlement among the defendants, particularly in cases of coordinated defense. Initially, the parties may attempt to arrive at an allocation agreement by negotiations among themselves. Should they not be prepared to engage in such negotiations, or should such negotiations fail to result in an agreement among all parties, a private Alternative Dispute Resolution (ADR) procedure may well result in a mutually acceptable resolution. These Rules provide for such a procedure, culminating in a mini-trial, unless agreement is reached at an earlier juncture. The procedure is non-binding, unless the parties otherwise agree.

These Rules implement a memorandum entitled "An ADR Procedure for Loss Allocation In a Joint Defense Agreement," by Edward A. Dauer, Deputy Dean of Yale Law School, and Professor J.D. Nyhart of the Massachusetts Institute of Technology, in the December 1984 issue of "*Alternatives* to the High Cost of Litigation," published by the Center for Public Resources (CPR).

2. INITIATION OF PROCEDURE

The procedure is initiated when two or more defendants in a toxic tort suit shall have entered into an ADR Agreement to use the procedure herein and incorporating these Rules to attempt to allocate among themselves the judgment or settlement in such suit before pursuing legal avenues; and when such defendants (herein referred to as the parties) file a request for a loss allocation ADR with the Center for Public Resources (CPR). The request will include:

(a) The names and addresses of the parties and of their counsel for the ADR; and

(b) A brief description of the nature of the liability to be allocated, including copies of any underlying verdict, decision, order and/ or settlement.

(c) A copy of the ADR Agreement among the parties.

(d) If the parties have agreed to be bound by the Settlement Counsel's opinion pursuant to #7(g) hereof, a statement to that effect.

By agreeing to participate in the ADR, each party agrees that it will not commence contribution or indemnity litigation or other legal action against any other party to the ADR before the ADR is concluded. The ADR shall be deemed concluded upon the receipt by all parties of the Settlement Counsel's opinion pursuant to # 7(g), or upon execution and delivery by all parties of a settlement agreement.

3. SETTLEMENT COUNSEL

(a) Selection

Within seven working days of receipt of the request for ADR, CPR will forward to the parties a list of the names of not less than five members of the bar whom CPR proposes as Settlement Counsel, stating their per diem fees. Each party may strike from the list the names of any persons who are unacceptable to it, and will return the list within five working days of receipt to CPR, which will designate the Settlement Counsel from the panel members acceptable to all parties. If no person named on the list is acceptable to all parties, CPR will submit a second list of not less than five names under the same procedure. If a mutually acceptable Settlement Counsel is not selected after submission of two panels, CPR will designate a Settlement Counsel not previously rejected by a party. Failure of a party to return a list within the stipulated time limit shall be deemed a waiver by that party of its right to strike nominees from such list.

(b) Functions

The Settlement Counsel shall be the joint counsel of the parties, representing their common interest in arriving at an equitable loss allocation in an efficient manner. He shall not represent any party individually, and each party may have separate counsel. The Settlement Counsel shall have the functions set forth herein. He shall manage the ADR and attempt to bring about a settlement among the parties. The parties shall cooperate with the Settlement Counsel and shall comply promptly with any reasonable requests for information he may make.

4. PRELIMINARY CONFERENCE

Within 30 days of his designation, the Settlement Counsel, on not less than seven days' notice to the parties, will hold a preliminary conference to be attended by representatives of the parties at a place and time he determines. At this conference the Settlement Counsel will:

(a) Confirm the amount of the settlement or judgment to be allocated and any stipulation with regard thereto of the parties;

(b) Receive the advice of the parties as to the questions of fact, science and law that they perceive;

(c) Discuss the possibility of settlement among the parties at that point in time;

(d) Discuss the need for a neutral Science Adviser and the identity of such an adviser.

5. SCIENCE ADVISER

If at least one half of the parties represented at the preliminary conference recommend the appointment of a neutral Science Adviser, the Settlement Counsel shall promptly appoint a Science Adviser, giving consideration to the parties' proposals as to whom to appoint. The Science Adviser, who shall be the representative of the Settlement Counsel, shall consult on the scientific issues in the ADR with the parties' technical staff and with whomever else he chooses. The Settlement Counsel and the Science Adviser shall hold a meeting of the parties' science or technical representatives within 45 days of the Science Adviser's appointment, at a place and time determined by the Settlement Counsel and on at least seven days' notice to the parties. At such meeting, the Science Adviser shall orally express his views on the scientific issues, e.g. what is and is not "known," what is agreed and what is contended. For purposes of this paragraph, "one half" of the parties shall be any party or group of parties which acknowledge that they are likely to be responsible for at least one half of the total amount to be allocated in the ADR. In the absence of any such acknowledgment, "one half" shall be based on the number of parties to the ADR, considering a parent corporation and any subsidiary as one.

6. FURTHER CONFERENCE

If a Science Adviser is appointed, and a meeting of the parties' technical representatives is held, as contemplated by #5, the Settlement Counsel at his discretion may hold a further meeting of the parties at a place and time he determines, within ten days of the aforesaid meeting, on not less than seven days' notice to the parties. The purpose of such meeting, in which the Science Adviser shall participate, shall be to further explore the possibility of the parties' reaching agreement.

7. MINI–TRIAL PROCEEDINGS

(a) Outline of Mini–Trial

The mini-trial shall consist of (i) an "information exchange" in which each party shall orally present its position on loss allocation to the Settlement Counsel and senior management representatives of all parties, provided that parties with similar positions may make joint presentations, and in which the Science Adviser (if there be one) orally states his views on the scientific issues in the ADR; (ii) negotiations among the management representatives following the information exchange to arrive at a settlement agreement; (iii) if no settlement agreement is reached, the issuance by the Settlement Counsel of an allocation opinion.

(b) Notice

Promptly following the preliminary conference pursuant to #4, the Settlement Counsel, by written notice to all parties, shall call a mini-trial to be held at a place and time specified in such notice, to commence not less than sixty days, and not more than ninety days, from the date of the preliminary conference; provided that if a further conference is held pursuant to #6, the mini-trial shall commence not less than thirty days, and not more than sixty days, from the date of such further conference.

(c) Appointment of Management Representatives

Each party will appoint a Management Representative, who will participate in the information exchange, and who will have authority to agree to loss allocation or other form of settlement on behalf of his company.

(d) Preparation for the Information Exchange

Subject to these Rules, counsel for the parties shall attempt to agree among themselves promptly following the preliminary conference on rules governing discovery; submission of memoranda and documents; the length, sequence and nature of presentations at the information exchange; the use of expert or fact witnesses; and any other relevant procedural matters. Discovery will be limited to a minimum in scope and time, and as a rule affidavits will be used in lieu of depositions. Any issues as to which counsel do not agree will be submitted to the Settlement Counsel for his determination, which shall be final and binding.

(e) The Information Exchange

The Settlement Counsel shall preside at the information exchange. Formal rules of evidence and procedure will not apply. Each party will present its direct case and rebuttal, in the order and subject to the time limits previously established. All reasonable efforts shall be made to limit the time required for presentations. When numerous parties participate, they will be urged to form groups having similar interests, and to make joint presentations. Presentations may be made by counsel and other representatives. Presentations may be interrupted only by the Settlement Counsel. Each party may ask clarifying questions of counsel and witnesses for any other party during question and answer periods, the scheduling of which shall be determined in advance by agreement or by the Settlement Counsel.

(f) Negotiations

At the close of the information exchange, the Management Representatives will meet without the Settlement Counsel or the Science Adviser to endeavor to settle upon a mutually acceptable allocation. If they have not succeeded within two hours of commencement of their meeting, the Settlement Counsel will join them and endeavor to facilitate settlement, calling upon the Science Adviser as the Settlement Counsel deems appropriate.

(g)   Allocation by the Settlement Counsel

If the parties have not reached agreement within 30 days of the close of the information exchange, the Settlement Counsel will promptly issue an opinion allocating the share of each party. Such opinion will be limited to the mathematical allocation. Such opinion will not be binding upon the parties, unless they otherwise agreed in their ADR Agreement or another instrument; provided that in any subsequent litigation for contribution or indemnification, parties which rejected the Settlement Counsel's allocation and which receive a judgment less favorable than that recommended by the Settlement Counsel shall pay the costs (including counsel fees) of the other parties to that litigation, sharing equally such costs.

8. CONFIDENTIALITY

The parties agree that the proceedings hereunder are confidential settlement negotiations. All aspects of such proceedings are privileged, confidential, inadmissible as evidence and not discoverable in any other proceeding to the maximum extent allowed by law, including but not limited to all statements, submissions, and written materials of or on behalf of the parties, the Settlement Counsel, and the Science Adviser. No transcript or stenographic record will be made of any proceeding. All documents obtained during discovery will be returned to the originating party after the close of proceedings.

9. COSTS

All expenses of the ADR, including the fees of the Settlement Counsel and the Science Adviser and CPR's fee for its services initially will be borne equally by the parties and will be payable monthly upon receipt of bills therefor. Once the parties have arrived at a loss allocation agreement, all such expenses shall be re-allocated retroactively and prospectively in the liability ratio established by such agreement; provided that if no such agreement is reached within 30 days of the close of the information exchange, and the Settlement Counsel issues an allocation opinion, as contemplated by # 7(g), such expenses shall be re-allocated in accordance with such opinion, whether or not all parties accept the opinion. The parties will attempt to agree at the outset of the ADR upon the designation of a Treasurer for the ADR. Failing such agreement, the Settlement Counsel may appoint a Treasurer from among the parties.

10. CONSENT OF PARTIES

Parties requesting loss allocation pursuant to these Rules will be bound by these Rules, unless and to the extent the parties unanimously otherwise agree in writing. The parties shall make good faith efforts to resolve promptly among themselves any issues arising among them as to interpretation or implementation of these Rules. Failing such resolution, any party may refer any such issue to the Settlement Counsel in writing, with copy to all other parties. The Settlement Counsel's determination thereof shall be final and binding on all parties.

By participating in the ADR, each party agrees to waive any claim it may otherwise have against the Settlement Counsel, arising out of the ADR, except for claims of gross negligence or willful misconduct; and the parties jointly and severally agree to hold the Settlement Counsel harmless against any claims asserted against him, arising out of the ADR, except for a claim resulting in a judgment of gross negligence or willful misconduct.

11. CONFLICTS OF INTEREST

Any person invited to serve as Settlement Counsel or Science Adviser shall be informed of the identities of all parties to the ADR and shall be requested to disclose any conflict of interest he perceives to exist by virtue of past relationship with a party or otherwise, which could reasonably be deemed by any of the parties to affect his impartiality. If such person discloses such a situation, he shall not serve, unless all parties agree to the person's serving upon being informed of the circumstances. In addition, if any party demonstrates to the satisfaction of CPR or a majority of the other parties that any such person has a conflict of interests which may affect his impartiality, such person shall not serve.

Notes and Questions

(1) The "Settlement Counsel" is expected to represent the defendants' "common interest in arriving at an equitable loss allocation in an efficient manner." He has broader powers than a mini-trial neutral advisor, although he may also perform that role if a mini-trial is held. How close is his role to that of the activist mediator under Feinberg's procedures (supra p. 320) or of the special master in McGovern's example (supra p. 331)? What is the role of the "Science Adviser"?

(2) Should those co-defendants who have a good defense to liability or who are likely to be apportioned a small percentage of causation enter an agreement not to assert their rights in the principal trial? Aren't they just aiding the "bad guy" defendants? Are such agreements in the public interest? Could they be challenged by plaintiffs?

3. Industry–Wide Claims Settlement Facility

The Asbestos Claims Facility, created in 1984 by an agreement (referred to as the "Wellington Agreement," in recognition of the drafting role performed by Dean Harry Wellington of Yale Law School) between various insurers and manufacturers of asbestos, provides another approach to use of ADR procedures for non-binding reality testing before third parties. The Facility was established to encourage the settlement of all asbestos-related claims against all members. It provides a central place to file claims in an attempt to avoid the filing of suits across the country, and seeks to give claimants a fair evaluation of their claims and offers of settlement without the discovery and legal costs associated with litigation. It also provides a forum for manufacturers and insurers to avoid costly litigation in determining responsibility for liability claims.

MARCUS & SHERMAN,
THE ASBESTOS CLAIMS AGREEMENT
Complex Litigation 834 (1985).

The Facility is governed by a Board of Directors containing equal representation from producer and insurer members. The Facility provides services for the resolution of two kinds of claims: (1) claims against producers by individuals suffering from asbestos-related conditions, and (2) claims by producers against insurance carriers.

Claims by individuals, including both those who have suits pending and those who do not, can be filed directly with the Facility. It will provide claims adjusters who obtain information from the claimants as to such matters as their medical impairment and its connection with asbestos. Following procedures set out in a special Claims Manual, the adjusters will make a determination of liability and, if favorable to the claimant, an offer of compensation based in part on data from cases previously tried or settled. If an individual claimant rejects the offer he may pursue relief in court. Claimants may be represented by an attorney, although the simplified procedure allows for resolution without attorneys. The Facility hires an attorney experienced in asbestos litigation to provide services, to the extent they are needed, for all defendants involved in any individual claim. The goal of the procedure is to provide more compensation at less cost because expenses for discovery, trial preparation, and attorneys can be reduced.

The second type of claim—by producers against insurers—is also to be resolved without judicial proceedings. Most of the issues which have arisen as to the respective liability of producers and insurance carriers are specifically reserved for ADR. The Facility maintains an "Alternative Dispute Resolution Branch" to perform this function. Negotiation is required with the assistance of a Panel of Neutrals. If it is not successful, a trial is held before a Trial Judge (selected from a panel of Trial Judges approved by the initial subscribers). A tight trial schedule is followed, allowing only three days for each case in chief and a seventh day for rebuttal.

One further aspect of the Agreement has important implications for the industry-wide settlement of mass tort claims. In subscribing, producers agree to a "producer-allocation formula" whereby each will be liable for a share of every successful claim against any of the producers. Each producer's share will be based on the percentage of liability that has been awarded by trial or settlement in all prior terminated asbestos litigation. Thus, rather than market share liability, the Agreement opts for "litigation experience share liability." There is a similar "insurer allocation formula" which binds each insurer subscriber to a predetermined share of successful claims. Producer and insurer formulae bind the subscribers not only with respect to claims settled through the facility, but also to settlements and judgments resulting from litigation. The Agreement thus represents advance resolution of the issues of contribution and indemnity.

Obviously this plan could only work if enough claimants bring their cases to the Facility, or if enough producers and insurers become subscribers. A relatively small number of attorneys represent a large number of asbestos claimants, and their role in establishing the Facility has considerably improved the likelihood that it will have cases. Another potential stumbling block arises from the fact that the Wellington Agreement has not been signed by all producers and insurers. Claimants could be deterred from filing with the Facility if they cannot be assured of resolving their claims against all defendants in one extrajudicial proceeding. All three groups—producers, insurers, and claimants—must feel that there are advantages from the accelerated and less formal procedures, and if that feeling changes the grand scheme could come tumbling down.

B. COURT–ADMINISTERED SETTLEMENT PROCESSES

The settlement conference, in which the judge reasons with and "jawbones" the parties in hopes of achieving a settlement, has become a fixture in many courts (see *supra* p. 167). But in the last decade interest has grown in developing procedures that would offer the parties greater accuracy in assessing the strengths and weaknesses of their cases. This has resulted in the marrying of court-supervised settlement discussions with ADR procedures for non-binding third-party evaluation of cases.

1. Court–Annexed Arbitration

Some thirty-five years ago, Pennsylvania adopted a court-supervised system of mandatory, non-binding arbitration of certain cases. In the past decade court-annexed arbitration has been adopted by local rule in a number of federal district courts and an increasing number of state courts. Typically court-annexed arbitration procedures require that parties in cases in which the claim for damages is less than a specified amount (for example, $100,000) go through a non-binding proceeding before an arbitration panel, usually made up of lawyers. Evidence is presented in summarized form, and the entire proceeding takes less than half a day. Either party can refuse to accept the arbitrators' judgment and demand a trial *de novo*. The following materials describe one such program in Pittsburgh:

ADLER, HENSLER, & NELSON, SIMPLE JUSTICE: HOW LITIGANTS FARE IN THE PITTSBURGH COURT ARBITRATION PROGRAM

vii-ix, 9–14, 87–94 (1983).

[The authors conducted their study under the auspices of The Institute for Civil Justice.]

In jurisdictions that have established compulsory court arbitration programs, litigants who file civil damage suits within a specified monetary limit are not permitted to take their cases to trial unless they have previously attempted, but failed, to arbitrate the dispute. The court administers the arbitration process. Arbitrators are attorneys or retired judges who serve voluntarily and are paid small honoraria. Informal hearings, with relaxed rules of evidence, are conducted outside of a regular courtroom. After a hearing is concluded, the arbitrators deliberate for a short time and return a judgment, which is communicated to the litigants within the next few days. If the parties accept the arbitrators' verdict, it is entered as a judgment of the court and is legally enforceable. Either party may reject the arbitrators' decision and request that the court schedule a trial, at which point the case returns to the regular trial calendar. But often there is some cost associated with appealing the arbitrators' verdict. If a trial is held, the case is heard *de novo*—without reference to the arbitration hearing or its outcome.

Among various court reforms attempted nationwide, compulsory court arbitration is particularly attractive to policymakers. It promises not only simple, fast, and inexpensive adjudication to litigants, but also a means of reducing judicial workloads and controlling public expenditures for the civil justice system. Since 1952, when Pennsylvania established the first such program, more than 100 trial courts around the nation have adopted some form of court-administered arbitration. But there are many unresolved questions about the utility and appropriateness of these programs. Does arbitration resolve disputes faster and cheaper without greatly increasing public expenditures? What kinds of disputes can be resolved through arbitration? Who wins and who loses in arbitration? Are litigants who are ordered to take their cases to arbitration, rather than to trial, satisfied with the process, or do they perceive it as a second-class form of justice?

* * *

As a site for this study, the Institute selected the Pittsburgh (Allegheny County) Court of Common Pleas. Established in 1959, the Pittsburgh arbitration program is one of the oldest in the country. It has acquired a reputation as one of the most efficient of such programs, processing a large proportion of the court's civil caseload quickly and inexpensively. Although state law authorizes arbitration for cases up to $20,000, until recently the jurisdictional limit of the Pittsburgh program was $10,000 [changed to $20,000 in 1983]. In 1982, the program was responsible for about 64 percent of all civil case dispositions in the Pittsburgh court (Allegheny County Court of Common Pleas, 1982). The average time between case filing and arbitration hearing was three months. Previous studies of the program indicated that the per case costs to operate the program were less than one-tenth the costs of processing cases through the regular trial division.

* * *

At the beginning of each court day, the parties whose cases have been scheduled for hearing assemble in the Arbitration center, a room that once served as a courtroom but that has since been remodeled to produce a large waiting room surrounded by six smaller hearing rooms. Panels of three arbitrators each assemble in each of these hearing rooms. Arbitration cases are called and assigned numbers in the daily queue of cases awaiting hearing. The panels then begin hearing the first set of cases. As soon as a panel completes hearing and deliberating on a case, a new case is sent in to that hearing room, in the order of the assigned numbers. Because the length of time required for hearings varies, this system results in a more or less random assignment of arbitrators to cases. * * *

The parties themselves play no role in choosing the arbitrators, nor do they have a formal opportunity to object to their assignment. This "rough and ready" procedure for random assignment contrasts sharply with the more elaborate and often time-consuming procedures for randomly assigning arbitrators that many jurisdictions use to guard against arbitrator bias.

The Pennsylvania Supreme Court rules require that arbitrators be "active" members of the bar and that the chairman of each panel have a minimum of three years of experience in practice. * * *

Some counties use a computer to randomize arbitrator assignment, but in Pittsburgh the arbitration director uses a manual, less standardized procedure to choose panel members. Wherever possible he seeks a balance between plaintiff and defense attorneys. The chairman is seen as the linchpin; and if there is a solid, experienced person in this spot, the other two members may be an attorney only a few months out of law school and an unknown quantity summoned for the first time.

* * *

Arbitrators are not expected to do any advance preparation for hearings. Their task is simply to listen to both sides present their case and then to make an on-the-spot decision on the dispute. Hearings generally last 30–45 minutes. After each hearing, the arbitrators deliberate briefly and record their decision. Each panel sits for several hours, hearing cases in order, until all of the scheduled cases have been heard. Arbitrators are paid $100 a day, and they generally hear four or five cases during the time they sit. * * *

The arbitrators' decision is transmitted by mail that day to the parties. Any party wishing to appeal the award must request a trial de novo within 30 days and accompany the appeal with a payment reimbursing the court for the cost of arbitrating his suit.

* * *

The court recruits volunteer arbitrators with apparent ease. The list of arbitrators currently numbers around 2500, more than half of the total number of attorneys practicing in Pittsburgh. Anyone admitted to the bar in Allegheny County may volunteer to serve as an arbitrator by filling in a form indicating the nature of his practice and areas of expertise, defining the extent of his availability as either "ready" or "infrequent," and by appearing briefly for an interview with a judge. The task of recruiting arbitrators is made easier by the ready availability of young, newly trained lawyers for whom a $100 honorarium apparently represents an acceptable fee for four to five hours of work.

* * *

Attorneys who practice in arbitration say that arbitrators are "after a kind of rough, basic, fairness." Reflecting this view, one arbitrator commented:

> Occasionally I've been on a board and heard a case where the equities were clearly all on one side, but not necessarily the law. Then we might say "Let's be *fair* here! If anyone wants to appeal, the judge can be *legal*."

Another arbitrator put it this way:

> If you are looking to do justice, you must sometimes bend the rules a little for these people. Public perceptions of justice are much more important than adherence to legal niceties.

* * *

Our study of the Pittsburgh program demonstrates that court-administered arbitration *can* produce extraordinarily rapid disposition of civil claims, without great expense to the taxpayers.

To produce speedy disposition, the court must exert tight control over the scheduling of arbitration hearings. The Allegheny Court of Common Pleas has achieved this control by centralizing program administration. When the responsibility for scheduling arbitration hearings is in the hands of individual attorney-arbitrators, the court must either accept the fact that the attorneys will tend to continue cases in order to accommodate their own and their colleagues' schedules, or it must allocate staff time to "riding herd" on the arbitrators. When the full responsibility for scheduling cases is in the court's hands, the court can set the pace at which arbitration hearings will be held.

Setting a fast pace for arbitration hearings depends on having an adequate supply of arbitrators available, using a simple arbitrator assignment policy, and making efficient use of the arbitrators' time while they are volunteering to serve.

* * *

Finally, speedy disposition of arbitration cases without substantial increases in court expenditures requires that the responsibility for valuing cases to determine their eligibility for arbitration be assigned, initially, to litigants and their attorneys. Court assessment of case value requires additional expenditure of court resources; where judges are required to value cases, as in the California program, this constitutes a further drain on the courts' scarcest and most expensive resource and is likely to delay the scheduling of cases for arbitration hearings.

When the responsibility for valuing a case is placed in the parties' hands, compulsory arbitration, despite its name, becomes a voluntary program. The cases that arrive at the arbitration hearing rooms have been "self-selected" by the plaintiffs as appropriate for such a program. Plaintiffs' attorneys who believe their cases are not susceptible to arbitration or who, for other reasons, choose to *avoid* expeditious resolution are free, in the short run, to declare that their cases are worth more than the jurisdictional limit of the program and not eligible to be filed in arbitration. Our analysis of caseload statistics for the Pittsburgh arbitration program strongly suggests that many personal injury cases that are worth less then $10,000 are initially filed by plaintiffs' attorneys in the regular trial division. Such cases are heard in arbitration only if they remain active for over a year and eventually are scheduled for pretrial settlement hearings with a judge. At that time, if the parties fail to arrive at a settlement, the judge will order the case "down" to arbitration. The judge's authority to order the case to arbitration is the basis for calling the program "compulsory."

By not allocating resources for assessing the value of *all* cases at an early stage of the pretrial process, the court gives up the opportunity to expedite all "arbitration-eligible" disputes. In a sense, the court says to the plaintiffs in such suits,

> If you want a quick resolution of a dispute over a modest amount, we will provide it. If not, we will let you adopt your own schedule for settling the dispute up until the point when judicial resources are available for dealing with it. But we will not let you spend the most expensive of court resources, trial time, on such a dispute unless you first attempt to resolve it through arbitration.

* * *

Court-administered arbitration programs do not do away with the need for legal representation. Our study of the California program indicated that it would be difficult, if not impossible, for the average individual to bring a case in arbitration without legal assistance. In Pittsburgh, a substantial proportion of litigants *do* appear at arbitration hearings without benefit of counsel, but a *pro se* litigant is evidently at a considerable disadvantage against a represented opponent.

The *pro se* litigant's disadvantageous position is probably an inevitable result of the adversarial approach to resolving disputes. Success in the adversarial process depends on having a particular set of social skills—articulateness, assertiveness, etc.—that characterize most litigators but are not necessarily shared by others. Further, even when the adversarial procedure is greatly simplified (by comparison with trial) previous experience with and knowledge about the procedure is useful. Attorneys who routinely litigate in the Pittsburgh arbitration program know its formal and informal rules; they understand what kinds of evidence may be submitted, and they know what sorts of arguments are likely to persuade arbitrators. *Pro se* litigants are at a disadvantage on both points.

It is not clear what can or should be done to improve the *pro se* litigant's position. Prohibiting representation on both sides (an approach adopted by 11 out of 52 small claims programs nationwide) does not necessarily equalize the parties' positions, if one party, although not a lawyer, represents an institution that litigates frequently. The Allegheny Court of Common Pleas could improve the instructions it provides to litigants on how to prepare for and present a case in arbitration. It could provide additional training materials for arbitrators and systematize the arbitrators' approach to a hearing involving *pro se* litigants; it could also socialize arbitrators to accept *pro se* litigation as appropriate when the litigant chooses to adopt it. Despite such efforts, however, *pro se* litigants will probably continue to suffer a disadvantage when they try to take on the American legal system without a lawyer.

Among arbitrators and some institutional litigators in Pittsburgh we found a tendency to discount the possibility that the program may on some occasions deliver unjust or incorrect outcomes by noting that the litigant can always appeal an unsatisfactory award. Over time, this can become an excuse for not attempting to improve imperfect procedures. For example, the belief that an appeal is readily available to the litigant may lead arbitrators to be less deliberate in their consideration of a case than they should be, or it may lead program administrators to be less careful in their selection of arbitrators than they should be.

* * *

How Individual Litigants Evaluate Arbitration

We found little evidence that individual litigants have in their minds a paradigm of judge and jury trial against which they measure the arbitration process and find it wanting. Instead, most individual litigants whom we interviewed had a very simple model of what constitutes a fair hearing of a dispute. Satisfaction with the arbitration program depended on perceived fairness, measured by this "fair hearing" standard, and on the objective outcome of the case.

The Trial Paradigm

Both the lay public and serious legal scholars share a model of the American adversarial system that includes a black-robed judge, conducting a public trial before a jury, in a formal courtroom environment. The private, informal arbitration procedure, conducted by three ordinary attorneys in business suits, sitting without a jury around a table in a small hearing room, clearly does not fit this model. But our interviews suggest that most individual litigants whose cases are brought to arbitration do not miss the formal attributes of the traditional adversarial process.

The Missing Judge and Jury

Only six out of the 66 individual litigants interviewed said they would have preferred to have a judge hear their case; another three wanted a jury, and two would have been happier with either a judge or jury. But the majority of litigants were pleased by the provision of three adjudicators to hear their case, with 25 percent of respondents volunteering to the interviewer that "three heads are better than one." Many individual litigants seemed to regard the three-member panel more as a kind of professional mini-jury than as a judge-substitute. Several respondents expressed a preference for attorneys, rather than a judge, to hear their case, on the grounds that the former had more contact with "ordinary people" and a greater understanding of their concerns.

* * *

Privacy

About 70 percent of respondents favored holding hearings in private, and some were particularly relieved to find that their disputes would not be heard in open court. Privacy was strongly desired and, by many, seen almost as a right. These litigants did not perceive their cases, brought for decision to a public dispute resolution process, as in any sense public business, nor did they express any desire for a public, open hearing as affording a guarantee of fair process.

* * *

The Fair Hearing Paradigm

In place of the trial paradigm, most litigants used a very simple standard for evaluating arbitration: They wanted an opportunity to have their case heard and decided by an impartial third party. When this requirement was met, they reported that the arbitration process had been "fair." When asked why they had come to this conclusion, they were unlikely to offer elaborate rationales. "They heard us both out, listened the same to both sides," or "We got an equal chance to tell our stories," were typical responses.

Hypothetical questions from the interviewers, implying that suits elsewhere are frequently resolved by attorneys and adjudicators without the appearance of the parties, seemed puzzling to many respondents, who assumed that the only fair way to decide their case was the process that they had experienced. A few attorneys made comparative comments about arbitration, noting that some of their clients' cases would have received shorter shrift and rougher justice in other jurisdictions. But individual litigants themselves made no reference to such alternatives, taking it for granted that they had a right to appear in person, to be heard fully, and to be treated even-handedly. Where this right had been recognized, essentially nothing more was demanded. Even the identity and qualifications of the arbitrators were unimportant, so long as neutrality was assured.

More than 80 percent of the individual litigants whom we interviewed found their hearings "fair" according to this simple standard.

* * *

Arbitrator Bias

No respondents expressed any wish to choose their own adjudicators, and no questions were raised about any possible predispositions in the arbitrators provided by the court. * * *

Except for those respondents who felt that the arbitrators were uninterested in or biased against them, most individual litigants appeared to have given little thought or attention to the qualifications of the arbitrators who heard their case. A few were complimentary in passing, remarking that the panel had been "congenial," "courteous," or "concerned," but to most their arbitrators appear to have been shadowy figures exciting little interest or curiosity.

* * *

All but two respondents knew that their arbitrators were attorneys, yet many seemed to believe that they were full-time court appointees rather than occasional volunteers. All accepted their arbitrators without question as a "given" feature of the process, showing no curiosity about either their identity or qualifications. Some respondents could not even remember what their arbitrators had looked like.

* * *

An Acceptable Form of Justice

Critics of court arbitration have worried that it may deliver "second-class" justice to citizens with small claims and modest resources for litigation. Their standard of "first-class" justice includes the full panoply of judge-and-jury trial and due process safeguards that are provided by our traditional adversarial process. Our interviews indicate that litigants whose cases were heard in the Pittsburgh arbitration program share neither the critics' concern that the quality of justice is denigrated by arbitration, nor their standards for evaluating quality.

Individual litigants who bring cases to arbitration in Pittsburgh have very simple requirements: They want a speedy, inexpensive procedure that provides a full hearing of their dispute before an impartial third party, and an opportunity to challenge if the outcome proves unacceptable. They are generally indifferent to the qualifications of the third-party adjudicators as long as they are neutral, and to the setting in which the hearing is held. But they appreciate the informality and privacy of the arbitration process. Most of those we interviewed found that their requirements were met.

Institutional litigants who depend upon the arbitration program for routine resolution of large numbers of civil suits also have rather simple requirements. They too want a speedy, inexpensive procedure, but they are less sensitive than individual litigants to the qualitative aspects of the hearing process. They judge arbitration primarily on the basis of the outcomes it delivers. They attribute unfavorable outcomes to the judgment of the arbitrators, not to the lack of opportunity for discovery or for cross-examining witnesses, or to the absence of other attributes of the trial process. Most institutional litigants whom we interviewed find that arbitration awards are generally within a predictable, acceptable range. They deal with the occasional unsatisfactory award through the appeals process, which they view as an essential "fail-safe" feature of the arbitration program.

Our interview data suggest that arbitration's informal procedures may lead some litigants to infer that they were treated unfairly. A "rough and ready" procedure for assigning arbitrators to cases, administered in a flexible fashion so as to accommodate parties and attorneys' schedules, may in some circumstances lead litigants to believe that their case has been matched with arbitrators who are predisposed in favor of one of the disputants. The use of volunteer attorneys as adjudicators may give rise to speculations about the influence of personal motivations on the decisionmaking process that might not occur to the litigant if the adjudicator were a black-robed judge. Allowing the arbitrators broad discretion in determining the pace of the hearing may lead litigants to wonder whether they have been granted a proper opportunity to present their cases.

* * *

Our interviews suggest further that the average citizen's notion of "fairness" does not incorporate the judicial robes, formal procedures, or the various components of due process that are the hallmark of trial. But his notion of fairness is not simply cheap, quick dispute resolution. Rather, the average individual seems to believe that a "fair" dispute resolution procedure is one that provides an opportunity for a hearing of the facts of the case before a neutral third-party adjudicator. Our data suggest that ability to appeal the arbitration award contributes to individuals' perceptions that the process is fair. We find no evidence in our interview data that the typical individual litigant envisions a model of "first-class" justice against which the arbitration process is judged and found wanting. Rather, individual litigants appear to believe that it is appropriate to tailor dispute resolution procedures to the nature of the disputes and, perhaps, that it is acceptable to invest smaller amounts of resources on resolving simple disputes than might be required to dispose of more complicated cases.

Attorneys who make frequent use of the arbitration program clearly assess acceptability on different grounds. They are more likely to measure the arbitration process against trial court procedures and arbitrators against judges, and they sometimes find the program wanting on both grounds. Institutional litigants, however, compare the court arbitration program to other mechanisms for disposing of civil claims with which they are familiar: for insurance companies, intercompany arbitration; for banks, institutional collection procedures. But the predictability of outcomes is probably the institutional litigants' most important criterion for assessing the arbitration program. An institutional litigant judging that an award is outside the expected range is likely to appeal. The availability of a quick and inexpensive appeal process may therefore be an essential aspect of arbitration's acceptability to these litigants.

Notes and Questions

(1) Court-administered arbitration in one form or another is now being used in a number of state court systems other than Pennsylvania and, by local rule, in a number of federal district courts. See Ebener & Betancourt, Court–Annexed Arbitration: The National Picture (Rand Corp.1985) (16 states and 11 federal district courts as of February, 1985). The general outlines of the various programs are similar, but there is considerable experimentation with differing procedures.

(2) The court-annexed arbitration programs used in federal courts derive from similar pilot programs established in 1985 in ten federal district courts. See, *e.g.*, Rule 300–9, U.S.Dist.Ct., W.D.Tex. (May 6, 1985), which provides that cases meeting the established criteria will be referred for arbitration within 20 days after the filing of the last pleading. The clerk will forthwith furnish the parties a list of five arbitrators, each will be entitled to strike one, and the clerk will constitute a three-person panel. The hearing will take place within 40 days of the selection of the panel (with authority in the arbitrators to grant a continuance of up to 100 days). The hearing will normally take about three hours.

(3) What sorts of cases should be channelled into court-administered arbitration? The existing programs are generally limited to claims for money damages, and the principal criterion has been the amount of money claimed. The federal district court programs based on local rules sweep more broadly than the Pennsylvania plan, and often divert cases involving under $100,000 into compulsory arbitration (the Northern District of California proposed a raise to $150,000 in 1988). Legislation was introduced in 1986 to require arbitration in all federal courts of civil actions based on a negotiable instrument or contract, or for personal injury or property damage, with not more than $100,000 in controversy; this legislation, however, was not enacted.

In deciding which cases are suitable for court-supervised arbitration, should the amount of damages claimed be the deciding factor?

Under the federal court programs, there are also subject-matter limitations: In some programs only actions based on a negotiable instrument or contract or for personal injury or property damage are sent to compulsory arbitration (*e.g.,* Rule 300–9(c) (W.D.Tex.)); others include all civil actions but explicitly exclude social security and prisoners' civil rights cases (*e.g.,* Local Civil Rule 8 § 3(A) (E.D.Pa.); Local Arbitration Rule § 3(A) (E.D.N.Y.)). In addition, courts are sometimes given discretion to exempt cases that are otherwise arbitrable where a party has shown good cause for relief by demonstrating "the existence of significant and complex questions of law or fact" in the action (*e.g.,* Rule 300–9(d)(3) (W.D.Tex.)). The Department of Justice has recommended that district court arbitration rules exempt any case "in which the objectives of arbitration would not appear to be realized, because the case involves complex or novel legal issues, or because legal issues predominate over factual issues * * *." 28 C.F.R. § 50.20(b)(5) (statement of policy).

(4) How should the arbitrators be chosen? The usual procedure is random selection, as in Pennsylvania. Would a better system be to specially select arbitrators for balance (*e.g.,* as between plaintiff's and defendant's lawyers), type of legal speciality, or age and experience? Would you want arbitrators who specialize in that area of the law or those who are non-specialists and who might bring a broader perspective to the evaluation? Should the attorneys have a role in the selection? It is common in federal programs to allow each side to strike one name from a list of five arbitrators furnished by the court. Rule 300–9(e)(1) (W.D.Tex.). Consider Hensler, What We Know and Don't Know About Court–Administered Arbitration, 69 Judicature 270, 278 (1986): "If the attorneys have some say in the selection, they may be more inclined to accept the award, but providing for attorney participation may require a cumbersome and time-consuming process. If the court is in charge of assigning the arbitrators, the process may be expedited but litigant and attorney satisfaction may decrease." Should there be a requirement that arbitrators have practiced a certain number of years?

(5) Unlike the summary jury trial (see *infra* p. 652), court-annexed arbitration is generally expected to take place early in the litigation, without an opportunity for full discovery. It is viewed as a quick and inexpensive alternative to litigation; Judge Harry Edwards has referred to it as a "poor man's mini-trial." Edwards, Alternate Dispute Resolution: Panacea or Anathema?, 99 Harv. L.Rev. 668, 673 (1986). Can a case be properly arbitrated without full discovery? Note that parties are encouraged to "decide what discovery is crucial to the hearing and conduct that discovery in advance of arbitration." Handbook of Alternative Dispute Resolution 50 (State Bar of Texas 1987). Is this feasible?

(6) Do arbitrators have subpoena and other supervisory powers? In programs like Pittsburgh's, they are selected immediately before the arbitration and thus would have no occasion to exert such powers. In federal programs, they are usually assigned in advance and could enter

orders governing such matters as a continuance and discovery.   Under the Mandatory Arbitration Program of the D.C. Superior Court, arbitrators have the authority to issue subpoenas, rule on evidence, decide discovery disputes, compel the production of documents, enter judgment by default or consent, and stay execution of such judgments if the parties agree to schedule payments.   "Mandatory Arbitration Program Proposed in D.C. Court," Legal Times 11 (Sept. 8, 1986).   Does this make arbitrators too much like judges to permit them to be an effective third party?

(7) What rules of evidence apply in court-annexed arbitration? Rule 300–9(f)(3) (W.D.Tex.) is typical: "In receiving evidence, the arbitrators shall be guided by the Federal Rules of Evidence, but they shall not thereby be precluded from receiving evidence which they consider to be relevant and trustworthy and which is not privileged."   Are there therefore any constraints on what the arbitrators will hear?

(8) A variation of court-annexed arbitration is the "moderated settlement conference."   An early version, adopted in the U.S. District Court for N.D. California, was called the "Early Neutral Evaluation" project.   See Brazil, Kahn, Newman & Gold, 69 Judicature 279 (1986). The moderated settlement conference, as implemented in Harris County (Houston), Texas, involves a hearing before three volunteer lawyers and is very similar to court-annexed arbitration.   The hearing is governed by a strict schedule, as follows:

Panel Introductory statement	5 minutes
Plaintiff's presentation	10–30 minutes
Defendant's presentation	10–30 minutes
Panel questions/answers	10–30 minutes
Plaintiff's summation	5 minutes
Defendant's summation	5 minutes
Panel deliberates	15–30 minutes
Panel issues an opinion	5–10 minutes

O'Brien & Kovach, Moderated Settlement Conference, 51 Tex.B.J. 38 (1988).

(9) Court-annexed arbitrators need not necessarily be lawyers, and some programs have used such experts as architects, engineers, accountants, and doctors.   When would a mixed panel of lawyers and other experts be useful?   Under many programs, lawyers serve as arbitrators without pay.   It may be more difficult to get other experts to do the same.

(10) Are multiple arbitrators necessary for effective arbitration, or is one enough?   Consider Hensler, supra at 277: "If only one arbitrator is required to hear each case, it will be easier to administer the program and easier to meet the demand for volunteer arbitrators.   But attorneys may be more inclined to question the decision of a single arbitrator, leading to a higher rate of appeal.   If three or five arbitrators are required, the task of administering the program will be

greater, and the per case costs for arbitrator fees may be more, but practitioners may be more inclined to accept the arbitration outcome."

(11) The success rate of court-annexed arbitration programs has been good. In most programs perhaps only 2% or 3% of the cases originally diverted to court-supervised arbitration later go on to a full-scale trial. This trial rate is often substantially lower than the rate at which comparable cases would have gone to trial in the absence of any arbitration program, and it has in fact been estimated that court-administered programs may reduce the actual number of trials by as much as one-third or even one-half. See Levin, Court–Annexed Arbitration, 16 J.Law Reform 537, 542–43 (1983).

Various explanations can be given for the program's success. To begin with, court-supervised scheduling and the elastic supply of arbitrators tend to reduce delays before the hearing. As a result attorneys may be forced to take a "hard look" at the value of their cases long before they would otherwise reach the courthouse steps; the order to arbitrate may thus stimulate earlier settlements. When a case does proceed to arbitration, the necessity to file for a trial *de novo* favors allowing the entry of judgment to stand. Even where the losing party rejects the result, the arbitration award must still be reckoned with. It may still serve as a settlement technique—used by the attorneys as a negotiating tool with their own clients to encourage them to settle, and as a basis for settlement discussions with the other side—and may tend to reduce even further the likelihood of a trial. See Lind & Shapard, Evaluation of Court–Annexed Arbitration in Three Federal District Courts 8–10, 83–88 (Federal Judicial Center 1983).

(12) Confidentiality of the proceedings and arbitral awards are guaranteed by court-annexed arbitration rules. This contrasts with certain medical malpractice statutes that require claims to be heard by a "review panel" as a prerequisite to a court remedy (see *supra* p. 430). Under some of these statutes, the panel's award may be admitted in evidence in later judicial proceedings. See La.R.S. § 40:1299.47(H) (report of the "expert opinion" of panel is "admissible," but is not "conclusive."); Md.Code § 3–2A–06(d) (award is "presumed to be correct," and the burden of proof is shifted to the party rejecting it). The contention that the right to a jury trial is unduly burdened by medical malpractice arbitration provisions admitting the panel decision into evidence has been rejected. See Lacy v. Green, 428 A.2d 1171 (Del. Super.1981) ("the jury is still the ultimate trier of fact"); Beatty v. Akron City Hospital, 67 Ohio St.2d 483, 424 N.E.2d 586 (1981) ("no different from any other expert testimony received at trial").

(13) Is an arbitrator capable of judging credibility when he only hears a summary of a witness' evidence? This issue will be explored more fully *infra* pp. 660–65. Under some medical malpractice arbitration statutes, review panels are prevented from deciding matters like credibility which do not "require expert opinion." There is also often a provision for court review to ensure that the statute has been complied

with and that the award is supported by "substantial evidence." 18 Del.Code § 6811; see Ohio Rev.Code § 2711.21 (judicial review to ensure that panel's findings of fact are not "clearly erroneous"). But however limited, once admitted into evidence the impact of the medical review panel's "expert" determination is likely to be great, and, although the evidence is not entirely clear, the *de novo* trial rate following panel determinations appears to be low. See Sakayan, Arbitration and Screening Panels: Recent Experience and Trends, 17 The Forum 682 (1982).

(14) In a diversity case, a federal court is required to apply the state arbitration requirements. See Woods v. Holy Cross Hospital, 591 F.2d 1164 (5th Cir.1979) (upholding dismissal of suit where there was no prior hearing before a malpractice review panel as required by a state law requiring that the chairman of the three-member review panel be a state judge and that the findings be admissible in evidence at trial). However, a federal court is not required to apply a state statute that would "impinge upon the broad procedural powers of the federal district courts to control and further techniques for settlement." Seck v. Hamrang, 657 F.Supp. 1074 (S.D.N.Y.1987). See generally Alexander, State Medical Malpractice Screening Panels in Federal Diversity Actions, 21 Ariz. L.Rev. 959 (1979).

(15) A California statute creates a mandatory scheme for the resolution of fee disputes between attorneys and clients. At the client's request, a lawyer must submit any such dispute to arbitration under rules promulgated by the local bar association. This is intended to "alleviate the disparity in bargaining power" between attorney and client and provide the client (for whom arbitration is voluntary) with "an effective inexpensive remedy * * * which does not necessitate the hiring of a second attorney." Manatt, Phelps, Rothenberg & Tunney v. Lawrence, 151 Cal.App.3d 1165, 1174, 199 Cal.Rptr. 246, 252 (1984). The arbitration is to be non-binding unless the parties agree otherwise; if a party demands a trial *de novo* but does not obtain a result more favorable than in arbitration, he may have to pay the other side's costs and attorneys' fees at trial. Cal.Bus. & Prof.Code §§ 6200–6204.

(16) A creative use of arbitration in conjunction with structured negotiation was developed by Judge Robert Parker (U.S.Dist.Ct., E.D. Tex.) for use in asbestos cases. Plaintiff and defendant may agree to a process in which there is a 60–day evaluation period, followed by a 40-day period for negotiation. If the case is not settled, arbitration by neutral arbitrators selected by mutual consent will take place within 90 days, with 20 days more for making objections. There is a right to a *de novo* trial with the provision that plaintiffs must waive punitive damages and defendants must waive the state-of-the-art defense (*i.e.,* that the asbestos was used in the safest way then known). See Arthurs, Texas Judge Rides Herd on Asbestos Suits, Legal Times, May 19, 1986, 1; Two–Step Plan Set up for Texas Asbestos Cases, 5 Alt. to Higher Lit. Costs 33 (Mar. 1987). After the program had been in effect for 14

months, 316 judgments, a smaller number than expected, had been entered, leading the U.S. Magistrate monitoring the program to comment that it "probably needs to be fine-tuned rather than scuttled." Asbestos Settlement Program Short of Goal, The Texas Lawyer (May 9, 1988).

Sanctions For Failure to Participate in Arbitration

Court-annexed arbitration is a nonbinding settlement device that leaves intact the right to a *de novo* trial. What if a party refuses to come, or attends but refuses to participate? New England Merchants National Bank v. Hughes, 556 F.Supp. 712 (E.D.Pa.1983), denied a right to trial *de novo* to a defendant who offered no excuse for failing to appear at the arbitration hearing, thus resulting in a final judgment for the plaintiff in the amount of $31,000 that the arbitrators had awarded. The court observed that under those circumstances "the goals of the arbitration program and the authority of this Court would be seriously undermined" if the defendant were allowed to demand a trial. Under the rules of one federal court, "appropriate sanctions" may be imposed, "including, but not limited to, the striking of any demand for a trial *de novo*" against a party who "fails to participate in the arbitration process in a meaningful manner." Rule 300–9(f)(2) (W.D.Tex.).

The propriety of sanctioning parties for refusing to participate in court-annexed arbitration raises questions of both interpretation of the particular rule involved and its constitutionality. Consider the following cases:

GILLING v. EASTERN AIRLINES, INC.

United States District Court, District of New Jersey, 1988.
680 F.Supp. 169.

SAROKIN, DISTRICT JUDGE.

I. *Introduction*

In order for the compulsory arbitration program to function properly, it is essential that the parties participate in a meaningful manner. This is particularly so in a case such as this in which one of the parties is a substantial corporation and the other party is one or more individuals. The purposes of the arbitration program are to provide the parties with a quick and inexpensive means of resolving their dispute while, at the same time, reducing the court's caseload.

These purposes are thwarted when a party to the arbitration enters into it with the intention from the outset of rejecting its outcome and demanding a trial de novo. Rather than reducing the cost and promoting efficiency in the system, such an attitude increases the costs and reduces the efficiency. Furthermore, such conduct can serve to discourage the poorer litigant and diminish his or her resolve to proceed to final judgment. Explicit in this court's arbitration program is the need for the parties to participate in good faith. Failure to do so warrants appropriate sanctions by the court.

Here, defendants move for trial de novo after the entry of an adverse arbitration award. The court grants the motion, but imposes sanctions on defendants for failure to participate in the arbitration meaningfully.

II. *Background*

Plaintiffs were passengers aboard a flight of defendant Eastern Air Lines from Miami to Martinique on November 27, 1983. They allege that they were wrongfully ejected from their flight during a stopover in St. Croix after two incidents on board involving knives. Their complaint states claims for breach of contract, negligence, false imprisonment, battery, assault, slander, invasion of privacy, infliction of emotional distress and conversion.

The court referred the matter to compulsory arbitration, as General Rule 47 requires. The arbitrator heard the case on May 20, 1987. The defendants did not attend the arbitration; their appearance was through counsel. Although the parties dispute the extent of defense counsel's presentation at the arbitration, they agree that she presented summaries of the defendants' position and read at least a few passages from deposition testimony and answers to interrogatories. The arbitrator found for each of the plaintiffs.

Within the thirty days allotted by General Rule 47(G)(1), defendants moved for a trial de novo. Plaintiffs opposed the motion, contending that defendants' failure to participate meaningfully in the arbitration as General Rule 47(E)(3) requires deprived them of their right to demand a trial de novo. As the court was unable to evaluate the meaningfulness of the defendants' participation in the arbitration, the court remanded the case to the arbitrator for a factual finding on that question.

On November 12, 1987, the arbitrator made the requested factual findings. Letter of Daniel E. Isles, Esq., Arbitrator (November 12, 1987). He found as a fact that defendants' attorney did not participate in the arbitration proceeding in a meaningful manner:

> I find as a fact that she merely "went through the motions." I find as a fact that the foregoing was a predetermined position taken by her office, even though that position remains obscure to me. I find as a fact that her "participation" in the arbitration proceeding rendered it a sham . . . .
>
> I was . . . flabbergasted when [defendants' counsel] arrived with no witnesses. She stated . . . that all Eastern personnel were on assignment, and that she would render fact summaries and position summaries. While she may have read a few interrogatories and answers [sic] a few lines from one or more deposition transcripts, ninety five percent (95%) of her participation was in fact stating position summaries on behalf of Eastern, and stating

fact summaries as to what Eastern's personnel may have said in their own depositions . . . .

I recall another event that occurred at the arbitration proceeding which further buttresses my within findings of fact. At the end of the hearing I asked [defendants' counsel] as to whether she wanted damage awards broken down into compensatory damages and punitive damages, if I should determine to make such damage awards. Her reply to me as best I can paraphrase it now was "Do what you want, or, we don't care what you do, we won't pay it anyway."

After the arbitrator filed his fact findings with the court, the defendants renewed their motion for a trial de novo. Defendants couple their request for a de novo trial with a request that the court vacate the arbitrator's findings.

III. *Discussion*

General Rule 47(E)(3) provides that

the arbitration hearing may proceed in the absence of any party who, after notice, fails to be present. In the event that a party fails to participate in the arbitration process in a meaningful manner, as determined by the arbitrator, the Court may impose appropriate sanctions, including, but not limited to, the striking of any demand for a trial de novo filed by that party.

Defendants ask the court to vacate the arbitrator's finding that they did not participate in the arbitration in a meaningful manner. After examining General Rule 47, the court is unable to discover any standard of review of an arbitrator's findings. The rule simply authorizes the court to devise a sanction "in the event that a party fails to participate in the arbitration process in a meaningful manner, *as determined by the arbitrator.*" The rule thus appears to place the determination of meaningfulness entirely in the hands and discretion of the arbitrator, without being subject to district court review.

However, even if the court does have the authority to disturb an arbitrator's finding of no meaningful participation, it declines to do so in this case. The arbitrator had ample opportunity to observe the conduct of counsel at the arbitration. He had the opportunity to measure the earnestness of the defendants' presentation against the gravity of the plaintiffs' allegations and the defendants' potentially sizeable exposure to liability. Although the defendants are correct that General Rule 47 did not require them to present live testimony, the arbitrator was certainly entitled to factor their decision not to call witnesses into his overall assessment of the meaningfulness of their participation. The arbitrator, examining the totality of the defendants' participation at the arbitration, concluded that the reading of brief position summaries and deposition and interrogatory excerpts did not amount to meaningful participation in the context of this case. The court concludes that this finding was supported by substantial evidence and was not clearly erroneous.

Defendants argue that the enforcement of General Rule 47(E)(3) against them would deprive them of their constitutional right to a jury trial and conflict with the Federal Rules of Civil Procedure. The court notes that compulsory pre-trial arbitration procedures like the one at issue in this case have withstood constitutional attack. *See Kimbrough v. Holiday Inn,* 478 F.Supp. 566 (E.D.Pa.1979); *New England Merchants v. Hughes,* 556 F.Supp. 712 (E.D.Pa.1983); *Rhea v. Massey–Ferguson,* 767 F.2d 266 (6th Cir.1985). In the *New England Merchants* case, the court approved the denial of a demand for trial de novo by a party who refused to participate in arbitration at all.

The court, however, need not reach the defendants' constitutional claim, for the rule does not require the court to deny the application for trial de novo. Rather, it allows the court to choose an "appropriate sanction," only one of which is the rather draconian striking of a demand for trial de novo. While such an extreme sanction may be appropriate where a party absolutely refuses to participate in or even attend arbitration, the court declines to deprive defendants of their day in court because of their limited performance at arbitration, without in any way condoning it.

General Rule 47(E)(3) allows the court to devise an "appropriate sanction." In this case, where the defendants demonstrated such contempt for the arbitration proceeding, it is only fair that they should have to pay for it. The court therefore orders that defendants reimburse plaintiffs for all costs and fees which they incurred in preparing for and participating in the arbitration, as well as costs and fees incurred in opposing defendants' demand for a trial de novo.

The court has determined to impose this more limited sanction, although denial of the trial de novo would have been warranted, because of the lack of clear guidelines as to what participation is "meaningful." However, counsel should be on notice that a trial de novo will not be automatically permitted in those cases in which the party seeking it views the arbitration proceeding merely as a meaningless interlude in the judicial process.

LYONS v. WICKHORST

Supreme Court of California, 1986.
42 Cal.3d 911, 231 Cal.Rptr. 738, 727 P.2d 1019.

Bird, Chief Justice.

Does a trial court exceed its authority when it dismisses a plaintiff's action with prejudice because no evidence was presented at a court-ordered arbitration?

In June of 1980, appellant Edward Lyons filed a lawsuit against respondent Erwin Wickhorst seeking actual, compensatory, and punitive damages for unlawful arrest and false imprisonment. Since appellant did not seek damages in excess of $25,000, the trial court ordered mandatory arbitration pursuant to Code of Civil Procedure section 1141.11.

The first arbitration hearing was set for November of 1982. Immediately prior to the arbitration, appellant informed the arbitrator and counsel for respondent that he did not intend to present any evidence in support of his case. In response, respondent made no attempt to refute appellant's claims. Thus, no evidence was introduced at the first hearing.

The superior court appointed a new arbitrator and set a new hearing for June of 1983. During this second attempt at arbitration, appellant once again declined to present evidence. Respondents did not attend the hearing after informing the arbitrator that attendance would be futile in light of appellant's refusal to proceed.

Although no evidence was presented during either of the two hearings, the arbitrator entered an award in favor of respondents. On the same day that the award was entered, appellant requested a trial de novo pursuant to section 1141.20. Upon motion by respondent, the court dismissed the action stating that appellant's refusal to offer any evidence at the court-ordered arbitration hearings "border[ed] on contempt," and was a "continuing and willful rejection of the whole arbitration program."

Appellant challenges the authority of the trial court to dismiss his action for failure to participate in the mandatory arbitration procedures.

In dismissing appellant's action, the trial court relied in part on section 581 and the "Rules of Court Ordered Arbitration." Section 581 authorizes dismissal by the court in any of the following situations: (1) neither party appears at the trial following 30 days notice of time and place; (2) a demurrer is sustained without leave to amend; (3) the plaintiff abandons the case prior to final submission, or (4) either party fails to appear and the other party requests dismissal. None of these scenarios occurred in the present case.

Similarly, neither the judicial arbitration statutes (§§ 1141.10–1141.32) nor the rules of judicial arbitration (Cal.Rules of Court, rules 1600–1617) permit the courts to dismiss an action because of a plaintiff's failure to present evidence at a judicially mandated arbitration proceeding. A separate provision—section 128.5—authorizes a trial court to order a party to a judicial arbitration proceeding to pay "any reasonable expenses, including attorney's fees" which the opposing party incurs "as a result of *bad-faith actions*" or frivolous or delaying tactics in such a proceeding. Thus, the trial court's dismissal of appellant's action was not expressly authorized by statute.

In the absence of express statutory authority, a trial court may, under certain circumstances, invoke its limited, inherent discretionary power to dismiss claims with prejudice. However, this power has in the past been confined to two types of situations: (1) the plaintiff has failed to prosecute diligently; or (2) the complaint has been shown to be "fictitious or a sham" such that the plaintiff has no valid cause of action.

The discretion to dismiss an action for lack of prosecution has recently been recodified in section 583.410. Section 583.410 permits the court to dismiss an action for lack of prosecution provided that one of several enumerated conditions has occurred. Generally, the court may not dismiss unless "(1) [s]ervice has not been made within two years after the action is commenced . . . (2) [t]he action is not brought to trial within . . . [t]hree years after [it] is commenced . . . [or] (3) [a] new trial is granted and the action is not again brought to trial . . . within two years. . . ." (§ 583.420.) * * * No such delay occurred in the present case. Similarly, no claims were made by respondents that appellant's complaint did not allege a sufficient basis upon which to plead a valid cause of action. Nor did the trial court state on the record that its order of dismissal was entered for this reason.

[The Court drew an analogy to Fed.R.Civ.Pro. 41(b), which has been interpreted as only allowing dismissal for failure to comply with a court order if the pattern of conduct was severe and deliberate and if less severe alternatives are not available.]

Likewise, this court must examine the circumstances under which appellant's motion for a trial de novo was dismissed. The dismissal of appellant's complaint was both without notice and without an opportunity to be heard. At the time of appellant's motion, neither the judicial arbitration statutes, nor the rules of judicial arbitration provided standards to guide the exercise of the court's discretion in granting or denying the motion.

Hebert v. Harn (1982) 133 Cal.App.3d 465, 184 Cal.Rptr. 83 was the first appellate opinion to address the question of the appropriate sanction for a party's nonparticipation in the judicial arbitration process. In *Hebert,* the defendant failed to participate in a mandated arbitration proceeding, and the arbitrator issued an award in favor of the plaintiff. The trial court denied the defendant's timely request for a trial de novo, relying on a local rule of court which required a party who had failed to participate in an arbitration proceeding to demonstrate good cause for its nonparticipation as a prerequisite for obtaining a trial de novo. On appeal, the *Hebert* court concluded that the governing statutes did not authorize denial of a de novo trial under these circumstances and invalidated the local rule.

The court in *Hebert* noted that unlike the legislation establishing prerequisites to appealing a small claims court judgment, the judicial arbitration provisions did not authorize the dismissal of timely motions for a trial de novo even where the moving party had failed to participate in the proceeding. The omission of similar requirements in the arbitration statute was held to demonstrate a legislative intent that access to the court for a new trial be procedurally unfettered. In addition, the court suggested that the local rule of court might have been intended to improve the administration of the judicial arbitration scheme, and, therefore, expressly invited the Legislature to consider amending the statute. * * *

[T]he 1984 amendment to section 128.5 addressed the precise problem that is presented here. The Legislature chose not to provide for dismissal as a sanction if a party refuses to participate. Rather, it authorized a court to impose additional costs and attorney fees on the errant party or his attorney.

The Legislature squarely considered the problem of nonparticipation in judicial arbitration proceedings and decided to put teeth into the "mandatory" nature of the process by authorizing the assessment of expenses, including attorney's fees, against a nonparticipating party.

An immediate and unconditional dismissal entered at the first suggestion of noncooperation is too drastic a remedy in light of the fact that arbitration was not intended to supplant traditional trial proceedings, but to expedite the resolution of small civil claims.

Mosk, Broussard and Grodin, JJ., concur.

Bird, Chief Justice, concurring.

In order to secure a majority for today's decision, I have omitted from my opinion any discussion of the implications of the trial court's actions on the constitutional jury trial guarantee. I write separately to express my concern regarding this issue.

* * *

[T]he compulsory arbitration proceeding cannot operate as a substitute for the constitutional guarantee of a jury trial. The current scheme does not embody any of the features of the jury system deemed essential to the political viability of our legal system. Thus, the analogy implicitly accepted by the trial court here between a judicially mandated arbitration proceeding and a court proceeding does not support the drastic foreclosure of rights that an unconditional dismissal represents.

The judicial arbitration statute was enacted as an alternative to the traditional method of dispute resolution with the hope that it might help offset a seemingly ever increasing judicial workload. In responding to the demand for improving the efficient resolution of small civil claims, the Legislature made clear that the procedures employed should be simple, economical, and expedient. The arbitration scheme, however, was not intended entirely to supplant traditional trial proceedings.

As with other court-annexed arbitration systems, the scheme in this state provides for a hearing that is considerably less formal than a trial in a court of law. The arbitrator's powers are expressly limited to nine listed functions. The most important are: (1) to permit testimony to be offered by deposition; (2) to permit evidence to be offered and introduced as provided in the rules; (3) to rule on the admissibility and relevancy of evidence offered; (4) to decide the law and facts of the case and to make an award accordingly; and (5) to award costs, not to exceed the statutory cost of the suit.

All disputes regarding procedural, evidentiary, or discovery matters beyond the scope of these powers must be brought to the attention of the supervising court. In addition, the rules of evidence governing civil actions apply only partially to judicial arbitration. The Evidence Code is relaxed in several areas permitting the introduction of certain forms of written testimony and documentary evidence not admissible in court.

Under the present scheme, *any* person may serve as an arbitrator if selected by the parties. Legal training is not a prerequisite because arbitrators need not conform their decisions to judicial precedent. Furthermore, the arbitrator is not required to make findings of fact or conclusions of law, and no official record of the proceeding need be kept.

These characteristics of the compulsory arbitration scheme provide more than adequate proof that the system was *not* intended to be a substitute for a judicial determination on the merits in small civil cases. Arbitrators have limited powers and are free to disregard legal precedent. Procedural safeguards required in court proceedings are relaxed considerably in arbitration proceedings.

More significantly, the Legislature unconditionally provided for a trial de novo on demand following arbitration. The Legislature recognized the constitutional problems that could arise if the arbitration hearing were to be construed as a substitute for a judicially supervised trial.

The right to trial by an impartial jury is one of the oldest guarantees in the Constitution. It plays a fundamental role in maintaining our intricate system of governmental checks and balances by safeguarding our citizens against arbitrary or excessive governmental action, reinforcing personal commitment to society through concrete participation in an important governmental function, and permitting the infusion of the common sense judgment of laymen into an often rigid judicial process. Dedication to these concepts demands that the jury system remain a vital part of the American judicial system.

In searching for instant solutions to increasingly complex social and economic problems, various modifications of the legal process have been suggested. The court-annexed arbitration scheme is one of the results of efforts in recent years to streamline court procedures, relieve congestion of court calendars, and reduce expenditures.

Although complexity, congestion, delay, and expense are legitimate concerns, these factors have never justified the sacrifice of fundamental rights. Efforts to expedite and efficiently administer the legal process are commendable. However, our interest in economy and speed must be tempered by the recognition that certain fundamental institutions are so essential to our system of justice that we cannot change them drastically without dramatically altering the foundation of the rule of law and the basic shape of our governmental structure.

* * *

Penalizing a litigant by dismissing his action for failure to present evidence at a compulsory arbitration proceeding places too high a premium on achieving the goals of expediency and efficiency. An involuntary dismissal may clear the dockets of troublesome cases, but it demonstrates a strikingly indifferent attitude toward the fundamental constitutional right to a trial by jury.

The state's interest in providing a forum for the quick resolution of relatively small civil claims cannot overcome appellant's right to a jury trial. * * *

REYNOSO, JUSTICE, concurring.

I agree with the majority that dismissal here was too drastic a penalty for appellant's refusal to present evidence at the arbitration proceedings. * * *

On the other hand, since it is clear that the judicial arbitration program was intended by the Legislature to be mandatory, the trial courts should actively support it by taking appropriate measures to encourage or require good-faith participation by litigants. As the majority points out, Code of Civil Procedure section 128.5, empowering trial courts to require payment of reasonable expenses incurred as a result of bad-faith actions or tactics, is made expressly applicable to judicial arbitration proceedings. Section 128.5 provides a means of avoiding the danger that a party will refuse to participate in the judicial arbitration process as a strategic tactic, attempting to assure that the trial court judgment will be more favorable to it than the "default" arbitration award, thus permitting the party to avoid the award-of-costs penalty provided by section 1141.21. If a trial court concludes that a nonparticipating party has pursued such a tactic, it may appropriately award the costs that would have been recoverable under section 1141.21 as an element of the monetary sanctions authorized by section 128.5.

* * *

LUCAS and PANELLI, JJ., concur.

GRODIN, JUSTICE, concurring.

Unlike the Chief Justice I believe that the Legislature may constitutionally authorize a trial court to dismiss an action if a plaintiff intentionally refuses to participate in a legislatively-established, mandatory judicial arbitration process. Indeed, as a policy matter, it may well be that dismissal is the most appropriate sanction for such conduct.

I have joined the lead opinion, however, because as I read the relevant statutes, the Legislature has to date declined to authorize the denial of a trial de novo and the dismissal of the plaintiff's action as a sanction for such conduct.

Notes and Questions

(1) The trial judge in *Gilling* did not determine whether denial of a trial *de novo* violated the defendant's right to jury trial because he approved the lesser sanction of imposition of costs and fees. Likewise the majority in *Lyons* avoided the constitutional issue by finding that the California statutes and rules do not authorize denial of a trial *de novo*. Do you agree with Chief Justice Byrd's argument that the efficiency interests served by court-annexed arbitration are insufficient to override the right to jury trial under these circumstances? Is the relevant question whether court-annexed arbitration is an adequate substitute for jury trial, or whether a party who chooses not to participate in that valid process thereby waives the right to jury trial?

(2) As a policy matter, should an appeal from court-annexed arbitration be treated differently from an appeal from a small claims court, which, under California statutes, may be denied for failure to participate in the proceeding?

(3) Court-annexed arbitration rules often impose sanctions against a party who rejects the arbitral award and seeks a *de novo* trial in order "to serve as a brake or deterrent on the taking of frivolous and wholly unjustified appeals." Application of Smith, 381 Pa. 223, 233, 112 A.2d 625, 630, appeal dismissed, 350 U.S. 858 (1955). Sometimes the penalty is small. Rule 300–9 (U.S.Dist.Ct., W.D.Tex.) requires the party seeking a trial to pay the expenses of the arbitration process (generally $75 each for three arbitrators, or $225), and in Pennsylvania, any party who wishes a trial must reimburse the state for all fees paid to the arbitrators. Some programs impose stiffer sanctions but make them dependent on the outcome of the appeal. In one Michigan program a party who rejects a unanimous valuation of the panel must compensate his opponent for the costs at trial—including attorney's fees—if he does not improve his position by at least 10% over the figure proposed by the arbitrators. Shuart, Smith & Planet, Settling Cases in Detroit: An Examination of Wayne County's "Mediation" Program, 8 Just.Sys.J. 307 (1983). See also Cal.Civ.Pro.Code § 1141.21 (party who does not obtain more favorable result than in arbitration must pay arbitrators' fees to county and the other party's court costs and expert witness fees).

Similarly, medical malpractice statutes sometimes impose financial sanctions on the party demanding a trial *de novo*. In Massachusetts, a plaintiff who has lost before the arbitration panel may pursue his claim through "the usual judicial process" only by posting a $2000 bond, payable to the defendant for his expert witness and attorneys' fees in case the plaintiff does not ultimately prevail. Mass.Gen.Laws ch. 231 § 60B.

Do these sanctions for requesting a trial abridge the right to jury trial?

2. Summary Jury Trial

The summary jury trial is a shortened trial, usually lasting less than a day, in which the lawyers summarize their cases before a jury empanelled under usual procedures. A judge or magistrate presides. The jury verdict is advisory and non-binding—although the jurors are not usually told this explicitly. It was developed by Judge Thomas Lambros, of the U.S. District Court for the Northern District of Ohio, and is now in use in a number of federal and state courts.

Judge Lambros conceived of the device in 1980 while trying two personal injury suits that he believed should have settled: "The reason that they didn't was that counsel and their clients felt that they could obtain a better resolution from a jury than from their pretrial settlement negotiations. It occurred to me that if only the parties could gaze into a crystal ball and be able to predict, with a reasonable amount of certainty, what a jury *would* do in their respective cases, the parties and counsel would be more willing to reach a settlement rather than going through the expense and aggravation of a full jury trial." [1]

LAMBROS,
SUMMARY JURY TRIAL—AN ALTERNATIVE METHOD OF RESOLVING DISPUTES
69 Judicature 286, 286–290 (1986).

The decision to use summary jury trial rarely turns on the substantive legal aspects of a case, but rather depends upon the dynamics of the controversy. Summary jury trial has been used in a wide range of cases from relatively simple negligence and contract actions to complex mass tort and antitrust cases. Many lawyers and some judges might shy away from assigning a complex case to summary jury trial; it is, however, the complex case that is most suitable for this alternative method of dispute resolution.

Obviously, if a case is only expected to require a day or two to try, there is little advantage in conducting a summary jury trial—the litigants and the court might as well simply try the case. While there may be some grounds to suggest that a highly technical case is difficult for a jury to resolve, those factors apply as much to a standard trial as they do to the summary jury process. At least in the summary jury process, the jurors will have the entire fact situation presented to them in a period of time during which they can focus their full attention on

---

1. Lambros, The Summary Jury Trial,
103 F.R.D. 461, 463 (1984).

the case, rather than spread out over weeks or months when key facts can be forgotten. This advantage has been borne out in actual summary jury trial situations where complex antitrust cases have been effectively presented (and resolved) through the summary jury trial process. Thus, the court should generally assume that the longer the trial, the greater the potential value of the summary jury proceeding.

The psychological effect of "courtroom combat" is important with regard to litigants who are either too stubborn to see their opponent's point of view, or who feel that settlement would be an admission of weakness and would prefer to have their "day in court." Any trial, however long or short, exacts some sacrifice or penalty from the litigants in the form of financial costs and emotional stress. Some litigants have the ability to handle that stress, others do not. The summary jury trial provides a forum in which the litigant can get a taste of the trial ahead and thereby more logically evaluate his or her position.

*   *   *

Final pre-trial conference

The decision whether a case should be sent to summary jury trial is normally made at the final pre-trial conference. After the assignment decision is made, the judge determines whether the housekeeping details of a summary jury trial can be disposed of during that pre-trial conference, or whether the case requires one additional pre-trial conference to ready it for summary jury trial.

Certain matters must be addressed at the conference preceding the summary jury trial. The judge should determine that discovery has been substantially completed. All motions relating to the merits of the case should be resolved so that parties understand exactly how they will have to present their case at trial, and can shape their summary jury trial presentation to parallel most closely the presentation they expect to make at the time of trial.

The judge should also take time at the pre-trial conference to set the limits for evidentiary presentation at the summary jury trial. The judge should hear objections to the use of certain evidence and consider motions *in limine.* In general, the conference should be used by the judge to elicit problem areas concerning the materials that may be presented or opinions that may be expressed. The judge should not hesitate to make rulings on motions and to inform counsel as to what lines of summarization will be permitted and what areas will be excluded. As a result of such conferencing, the actual presentations by counsel during the summary jury trial are likely to flow without interruption.

Additionally, the judge and counsel should engage in a dialogue on summary jury trial technique. For those attorneys who are new to the procedure, it is worthwhile for the judge to explain the process in some detail and to review examples of techniques that attorneys have previously used effectively. It may be useful to distribute a written explanation of the process as a means of introducing the attorneys and their clients to summary jury trial.

The conference before the summary jury trial also provides an opportunity for intensive, traditional settlement negotiations. The imminence of the summary jury trial brings to bear on the parties the same type of concerns experienced just prior to civil jury trial. The judge should remind the parties that their settlement positions will be unalterably affected by the advisory jury's verdict, because their demands will thereafter always be contrasted to the ultimate evaluation of the jury.

Final preparation

The day of the summary jury trial begins with the arrival of prospective jurors at the jury commissioner's office. If another judge is commencing a jury trial on the same day, the jurors who are called for that proceeding but not actually empanelled may be used in the summary jury trial. To expedite selection of the summary jury, the jury commissioner provides the prospective jurors with a questionnaire.

* * *

While the potential jurors are completing their questionnaires, the presiding judicial officer meets with counsel. This meeting gives the court and the parties an opportunity to review the case in an environment that is very similar to that existing just prior to a regular civil jury trial. The same factors that often cause settlement of cases immediately prior to a regular trial will often produce a settlement prior to the summary jury trial proceeding.

In order for the meeting to be of benefit, it is important for counsel to have their cases in a state of complete trial readiness. Each party should be required to file a trial memorandum, proposed voir dire questions, and proposed jury instructions. If an extensive presentation is anticipated, the court may also require the parties to submit exhibit lists and lists of witnesses whose testimony will be summarized during the proceeding. During this meeting, counsel are required to present all procedural and evidentiary questions which foreseeably will arise during the course of the summary jury trial. Resolution of these questions during this meeting minimizes the need for objections during the actual summary jury trial and thus contributes to the flowing character of the proceeding.

* * *

Summary jury trial format

The format of a summary jury trial is very similar to that of a traditional civil jury trial. A judge or magistrate presides over the court, which is formally brought to order. Attendance of the parties with complete settlement authority is required.

It is best if the judge who will try the case conducts the summary jury trial because, through presiding over the summary jury trial, the judge will obtain a thorough understanding of the issues presented by the case and the strengths and weaknesses of each parties' position. The judge's participation in the summary jury trial will also facilitate an open and frank discussion of the evidence during post-summary jury trial settlement negotiations.   Because the jury remains the ultimate trier of fact, the outcome of a subsequent trial probably will not be affected by the participation of the judge who presided over the summary jury trial.   Indeed, the quality of the actual jury trial may be improved because the judge will have become intimately acquainted with the legal issues posed by the case.

As an alternative, the judge may decide to assign a summary jury trial to a magistrate, thereby freeing the judge to conduct traditional trials.   This procedure can also be very effective, but it is important that the judge and the magistrate communicate in detail about the case prior to the time that the magistrate assumes responsibility for the proceeding.   The magistrate should have a thorough understanding of the issues posed by the case and the parties' settlement positions.   If a magistrate conducts the summary jury trial, it is recommended that he or she participate with the judge in the post-summary jury trial settlement negotiations.

The judge opens the summary jury trial with a few introductory remarks in which he or she introduces the trial participants and explains briefly what the case is about.   The judge then explains the summary jury trial procedure to the jury.   The judge normally states that the lawyers have reviewed all of the relevant materials and interviewed all of the witnesses and now have been asked to condense all of the evidence and present it to the jury in a narrative form.   They are also told that the attorneys will be permitted to summarize both the evidence and legal arguments in support of their respective positions.

The prospective jurors are advised that at the conclusion of the case they will be instructed on the applicable law and the use of the verdict form.   They are further advised they are expected to consider the case just as seriously as they would if the case was presented to them in the conventional manner and that their verdict must be a true verdict based on the evidence.   They are further told that the proceeding will be completed in a single day and that their verdict will aid and assist the parties in resolving their dispute.   Nothing more is said about the non-binding nature of the summary jury trial; nothing more need be said.   Although the jurors are not misled to believe that the proceeding is equivalent to a binding jury trial, the non-binding character of the proceeding is not emphasized.   By adopting this balance the judge may candidly explain the procedure without minimizing the jurors' responsibilities.

Following the judge's introduction of the case to the prospective jurors, the judge conducts a brief voir dire generally posing questions to the jury collectively. This process is expedited through the use of the completed juror profile forms. The judge may make additional inquiries of the jury based on voir dire questions proposed by the attorneys. Counsel are normally permitted to exercise challenges for cause as well as peremptory challenges, although the number of challenges should be limited, and counsel should be encouraged to accept the jurors as they find them, since prolonged voir dire will defeat the goal of conducting the summary jury trial efficiently.

Jury selection is followed by the presentations of counsel. Although the goal of expedited presentation is always kept in mind, the length and format of the proceeding may be adjusted to accommodate the particular needs of the case. Counsel are usually given one hour each for the presentations. This period is usually broken down so that plaintiff devotes approximately 45 minutes to its case in chief, followed by defendant being given a similar period for its main presentation. A 15 minute period may then be given to the parties for their respective rebuttal and surrebuttal. The total time of the proceeding may be extended if the case involves particularly complex issues or more than two parties. It is recommended that each side give the jury a three-to-five minute overview of its case before the formal presentations. This will give the jury a "fix" on the whole case, obviating the need to wait a full hour before learning about the defense.

Fair presentations

As with all other aspects of the summary jury trial process, form should not be allowed to overcome substance. The judge must be especially sensitive to a commonsense notion of fairness. This concept must necessarily extend beyond technical questions of whether the summary by counsel of the evidence is accurate, to such questions as whether the jury is being given a fairly accurate sense of the weight of the evidence. For example, if plaintiff can support a crucial fact in its case only through the rather questionable testimony of one witness, while defendant can present five independent witnesses to confirm the opposite, counsel for plaintiff should not be able to speak of that fact as proof beyond refutation.

Lawyers should also be reminded by the court of Disciplinary Rule 7–106 regarding trial conduct, in particular that portion of the disciplinary rule that forbids a lawyer from asserting personal knowledge of the facts in issue or personal opinions as to the justness of a cause or the credibility of a witness. It is true that the effectiveness of the trial attorney as an advocate will have a marked effect upon the results of the summary jury proceeding; this is no less true, however, at the time of trial and is a factor that each party should be weighing in evaluating the settlement value of the case.

In making their presentations to the jury, counsel are limited to representations based on evidence that would be admissible at trial. Although counsel are permitted to mingle representations of fact with legal arguments, considerations of responsibility and restraint must be observed. Counsel may only make factual representations supportable by reference to discovery materials. These materials include depositions, stipulations, signed statements of witnesses, and answers to interrogatories or requests for admissions. Additionally, an attorney may make representations based on the assurance that he or she has personally spoken with a witness and is repeating what that witness stated. Discovery materials may be read aloud but not at undue length. Counsel may submit these materials in full to the jury for their consideration during deliberations. Each juror is provided a note pad and is permitted to take notes.

Physical evidence, including documents, may be exhibited during a presentation and submitted for the jury's examination during deliberations. These exhibits may be marked for identification, but are returned to the appropriate party at the end of the proceeding.

By virtue of the nature of the summary jury trial, objections during the proceeding are not encouraged. However, in the event counsel overstep the bounds of propriety as to a material aspect of the case, an objection will be received and, if well taken, will be sustained and the jury instructed appropriately.

Jury deliberations

At the conclusion of the summary jury trial presentations, the jury is given an abbreviated charge dealing primarily with the applicable substantive law and, to a lesser extent, with such boilerplate concepts as burden of proof and credibility. The jury is normally given a verdict form containing specific interrogatories, a general inquiry as to liability, and an inquiry as to the plaintiff's damages. The jurors are encouraged to return a unanimous verdict and are given ample time to reach such a consensus. However, if, after diligent efforts, they are unable to return a unanimous verdict, each juror should be given a verdict form and should be instructed to return a separate verdict. These separate views will be of value to the lawyers in exploring settlement.

Once the jury has been excused to deliberate, the court may engage the parties in settlement negotiations. These negotiations have a special sense of urgency in that they are conducted in the shadow of an imminent verdict. The negotiations are informed by the perspectives gained through observation of the summary jury trial.

When the jurors complete their deliberations, the court receives their unanimous verdict or individual verdicts. At this time, the judge, the attorneys, the parties, and the jurors engage in a dialogue unique to summary jury trial. The judge may ask the jurors a broad variety of questions ranging from the general reason for the decision to their perceptions of each party's presentation. Counsel may also inquire of the jurors both as to their perspectives on the merits of the case and their responses to the style of the attorneys' presentations. This dialogue affords an opportunity to gain an in-depth understanding of the strengths and weaknesses of the parties' respective positions. The dialogue may serve as a springboard for meaningful settlement negotiations.

A flexible procedure

Summary jury trial is designed to accommodate the needs and styles of its various users. Judges and lawyers should not hesitate to modify the procedure as they may see fit to meet the demands of cases before them. The following alternatives are presented only by way of example:

• The judge may permit certain key witnesses to testify in an abbreviated form, especially when a case turns upon the credibility of a witness's testimony on one or two key facts.

• The summary jury trial might be converted into a "summary bench trial," conducted in front of a judge, other than the one assigned to the case, who serves as an independent sounding board for the positions of the party.

• The parties may agree to conduct the summary jury trial at a very early stage of the proceedings, especially when most of the facts are not in dispute and the only real issue hindering settlement is jury perception of the amount of damages to be awarded. To facilitate such an early summary jury trial, the parties should adopt an accelerated and condensed discovery format with a view to preparing the case for summary jury trial within 60 to 90 days after the commencement of the action. Naturally, this will require voluntary document production and cooperation among counsel in initially taking only adversarial witness interviews rather than full-scale depositions.

• A videotape presentation may effectively summarize a litigant's position as well as provide the jury with a view of the actual witnesses and evidence involved in the case. In a case before Judge Lee R. West of the United States District Court for the Western District of Oklahoma, an attorney prepared a videotape for viewing by a summary jury in lieu of a live presentation. The film provided an overview of all aspects of the plaintiff's case in a personal injury action. It included an animated reconstruction of the accident scene, pictures showing the plaintiff's injuries and their effect on his everyday life, and pictures of each of the plaintiff's lay and expert witnesses with summarizations of their probable testimony dubbed in by the plaintiff's attorney.

• Agreement to a binding result, or a binding result within a certain range; *i.e.,* establishing a high-low range within which the case shall settle.

*   *   *

Post-summary trial conference

In some cases settlement is achieved during or immediately after the summary jury trial. Usually, however, several days to a month are required for the parties to assess and evaluate the summary jury trial verdict. In such cases post-summary jury trial conferencing between the judge and the attorneys should proceed on a continuing basis up to the time of trial. Such discussions will assure that settlement remains a top priority item and will prevent the experiences of the summary jury trial from growing stale. It is important that trial not be scheduled so closely upon the heels of the summary jury trial proceeding so as to cut short this process of assessment and negotiation.

At the post-summary jury trial conference, the subjective evaluations of the attorneys are no longer the primary focus of the discussions. Rather, the court should focus the parties upon the reality of the summary jury trial verdict and the perception of the cases indicated by the advisory jurors. It need hardly be said that the court can very effectively focus the parties' attention upon the fact that another jury would render a verdict similar to that of the advisory jury if the case were to go to trial.

If a settlement is not achieved during the post-summary jury trial conference, the case is programed for a civil jury trial. The jury trial is normally scheduled to occur approximately one month after the summary jury trial but may be continued if meaningful settlement negotiations are ongoing.

Notes and Questions

(1) Advocates of summary jury trials claim that they effect a high settlement rate. See Cook, A Quest for Justice: Effective and Efficient Alternative Dispute Resolution Processes, 1983 Detroit College of L.Rev. 1129, 1133 (use by federal judges in Michigan, Pennsylvania, Oklahoma, Massachusetts, and Ohio resulted in a 94% settlement rate after the summary trial). Federal judges continue to report a higher settlement rate of cases after summary jury trial than in other cases. Summary Jury Trials Gain Favor, Nat.L.J. 1 (June 10, 1985).

(2) Critics, however, have asked whether the cases that settle after summary jury trials would not have settled anyway. Applying an economic model to an admittedly "crude" set of statistics, Judge Richard A. Posner of the U.S. Court of Appeals for the Seventh Circuit, concluded that summary jury trials did not result in a decrease in the number of trials nor an increase in judicial efficiency. Posner, The Summary Jury Trial and Other Methods of Alternate Dispute Resolution: Some Cautionary Observations, 53 U.Chi.L.Rev. 366, 377–85 (1986). He also found the technique "lavish" because a judge must devote a full day to settling one case.

(3) Critics have also questioned summary jury trial verdicts as an accurate indication of what a jury in a full trial would do. Judge Posner argues: "The jury's principal function is to determine the credibility of witnesses, yet there are no witnesses in the summary jury trial. The credibility assessed is that of the lawyers. A jury may react quite differently when confronted with the actual witnesses." Posner,

supra at 374. Furthermore, he fears that lawyers may hold back some
of their best evidence or arguments in an effort to surprise the opponent at the real trial. A number of lawyer critics have claimed that
summary jury trial results are distorted, citing examples of cases in
which the verdict at a full trial, after failure to settle, was quite
different from that of the summary jury trial. Summary Jury Trials
Assailed as Inaccurate and Ineffective, 4 BNA Civil Trial Manual 96,
97–8 (Mar. 23, 1988).

(4) Consistent with the emphasis on confidentiality in settlement
negotiations, the summary jury trial is closed to the public. This was
challenged by a number of newspapers that had been excluded from a
summary jury trial involving the design of a nuclear power plant; the
papers brought suit claiming that they had been denied their First
Amendment right of access to the "trial." The district court denied the
claim and in addition issued a gag order restraining communications
between the jurors and the press and public, and sealing the transcript
and the list of jurors; the court continued these orders in effect after
the parties had reached a settlement. The Sixth Circuit affirmed,
holding that the newspapers' claim of a public "right to know" had no
validity with respect to summary jury trials: "At every turn the
summary jury trial is designed to facilitate pretrial settlement of the
litigation, much like a settlement conference," and "[s]ettlement techniques have historically been closed to the press and public." In
addition,

> where a party has a legitimate interest in confidentiality, public
> access would be detrimental to the effectiveness of the summary
> jury trial in facilitating settlement [and thus] would have signifi-
> cant adverse effects on the utility of the procedure as a settlement
> device. Therefore, allowing access would undermine the substan-
> tial governmental interest in promoting settlements *   *   *.

Judge Edwards concurred in holding that "the negotiations which led
to the settlement of this case could properly be conducted in camera,"
but did not agree that the record could appropriately remain sealed
after settlement. Cincinnati Gas & Electric Co. v. General Elec. Co.,
117 F.R.D. 597 (S.D. Ohio 1987), aff'd 854 F.2d 900 (6th Cir.1988).

The Summarization Technique

The summary jury trial, like other structured settlement devices,
achieves its economy from a shortened trial-run that depends entirely,
or heavily, upon summarization of testimony. The lack of live testimony raises serious questions as to the ability of the jurors to make the
same kind of judgment that is made in a full trial. The following
excerpt criticizes the absence of traditional adversarial techniques such
as cross-examination, raising a question whether it is suited to getting
at the truth:

BRUNET,
QUESTIONING THE QUALITY OF ALTERNATE DISPUTE
RESOLUTION
62 Tulane L.Rev. 1, 39–40 (1987).

There is some question, however, whether attorney evidence summaries constitute an adequate reality surrogate to a full trial. There is no way to recreate the reality of a given situation. Most direct evidence presented to a judicial trial is one step removed from the actual event and can be only an imperfect perception. The attorney summations of evidence used in a summary jury trial add an additional layer of distance from the actual events that are the object of fact finding.

Moreover, attorney witness summations cannot resolve factual questions of veracity and credibility. Any lawyer who has ever tried a case knows that the trier of fact has expertise in discerning witness credibility and veracity. A full trial achieves careful consideration of issues of witness believability. These advantages of trial are absent from summary jury trial. Attorney witness summaries simply are incomparable to actual consideration of witness demeanor. As Judge Posner has stated, "We do not need a jury of laymen to decide which of two lawyers is more credible." Litigious clients, who are skilled at evaluating the strengths and weaknesses of their own and an opponent's case, are unlikely to settle cases involving demeanor or veracity issues. Lawyers, under an affirmative duty to provide clients with clear appraisals of settlement offers, should help to identify and explain to clients the unreliability problem of summary jury trial proof taking. In effect, suits involving substantial issues of veracity such as intent or conspiracy are inappropriate for summary jury trial. Permitting summary jury trial of such issues institutionalizes inaccuracy and harms dispute resolution quality.

It must be remembered that use of summarization in a summary jury trial does not mean that the witnesses have not been examined and cross-examined. Depositions will normally have been taken of witnesses, with full opportunity for both sides to get at the truth. Contradictory evidence is also fully available and can be brought out by the attorneys in a summarization. The distinction from a trial is that the jurors themselves will not get to observe the witnesses' testimony, but will have to rely on the attorneys' summarizations.

Summarization, of course, lacks the immediacy of live testimony. There are, however, techniques available to give it more life. Summarization also arguably has certain advantages. By focusing on the essential meaning of testimony, rather than quibbling over language and nuances as often occurs in examination and cross-examination, it may offer an opportunity for jurors to reach the crux of the dispute with greater facility and understanding. We use summarization in various legal contexts without qualms over a fact-finders' ability to make judgments as to its accuracy. The question is ultimately whether it carries sufficient indicia of accuracy to justify its use in nonbinding settlement processes.

SHERMAN,
RESHAPING THE LAWYER'S SKILLS FOR COURT–SUPERVISED ADR
51 Tex.B.J. 47, 48–9 (1988).

The art of summarization is the centerpiece of court-supervised ADR proceedings. It is already familiar to attorneys who, in letters, memoranda, and briefs, are constantly called on to boil down information, synthesize it, and present it in a shortened form. A good deal of what is required in ADR involves summarization of testimony by witnesses (in the form of depositions, statements, answers to interrogatories, and other discovery). Perhaps the closest analogues to this skill in litigation are found in closing argument to the jury, appellate argument, presentations to administrative agencies, or by "written narrative statements."

Closing argument to a jury involves summarization of the evidence in the context of the legal issues and is often about the same length as ADR presentations. However, several differences should be noted. In closing argument, counsel are limited to comment on evidence in the record, while counsel may raise any matter in an ADR proceeding that would be admissible at trial. "Representations of facts must be supportable by reference to discovery materials, including depositions, stipulations, documents, and formal admissions, or by a professional representation that counsel has spoken with the witness and is repeating that which the witness stated." [1]

There are also greater limitations on counsel's statement of the law in a closing argument. Counsel may not purport to state what the law is and may at most indicate what he believes the court will instruct. In contrast, under "court-annexed arbitration" and "moderated settlement conference" (but not "summary jury trial"), there are no instructions on the law, and counsel are entitled to argue the law as they understand it.

In both closing argument and ADR, counsel are strongly discouraged from interrupting an opponent with an objection. In ADR, each side is entitled to present its "best shot," and even if opposing counsel misstates the evidence or the law, correction should be made during the opposing party's presentation rather than by interrupting. When one side has completed its presentation and thus does not have an opportunity to respond, the judge or presiding arbitrator would seem to have

1. Lambros, The Summary Jury Trial and Other Alternative Methods of Dispute Resolution, 103 F.R.D. 461, 471 (1984).

the authority to allow a brief response if it is claimed to be necessary to correct serious misstatements.

An ADR presentation also has similarities to appellate argument. The appellate lawyer, especially when dealing with sufficiency of the evidence, must summarize the evidence and relate it to the law in much the same manner as does the ADR presenter. Good appellate lawyers learn that long quotes from the record are generally to be avoided and that a few key words or sentences from testimony, combined with summarization, are often more effective.

An ADR presentation also has similarities to the submission of witnesses' testimony in writing that is required in various administrative agency hearings. That practice has been justified as a more efficient way to present evidence to the hearing officer, especially when the information is technical. "The question and answer method is a strained device for obtaining information in an orderly fashion," [2] and written summarizations of testimony "save substantial amounts of actual hearing time." [3] Some federal courts have also adopted the practice of requiring direct testimony of witnesses to be presented in the form of "written narrative statements." Although this has been criticized as "trial by affidavit," the practice has been upheld on appeal.[4]

A genuine concern with the ADR summarization method is that there is no opportunity for cross-examination which may be necessary to assess credibility when there is disputed testimony. Cross-examination, however, may take place on deposition. It is up to counsel to convey through his summarization the effect of the cross-examination of the witness on deposition and any discrepancies and flaws in the witness' total testimony. The ADR decision-maker, however, will not have the opportunity to observe the witness and assess his credibility, and, in certain cases, that can be a significant loss. For this reason, allowing brief appearances of witnesses or showing portions of a videotaped deposition, as is done in some "court-annexed arbitration" proceedings, seems desirable, and courts should be open to allowing such developments.[5]

Counsel in ADR should strive to provide some change of pace and animation to provide relief from what would otherwise simply be a long speech. The counsel's role in court-supervised ADR might be described as "the counsel as TV anchor." Counsel has to weave together evi-

2. McElhaney, An Introduction to Direct Examination, 2 Litigation 37 (1976).

3. Horne, Presenting Direct Testimony in Writing, 3 Litigation 30, 31 (1977).

4. See Chapman v. Pacific Tel. & Tel. Co., 613 F.2d 193, 197–98 (9th Cir.1979); Solomon, Techniques for Shortening Trials, 65 F.R.D. 485, 489–90 (1974).

5. Regarding the "summary jury trial," compare Lambros, supra, at 471 ("No testimony is taken from sworn witnesses. Counsel simply summarize the anticipated testimony of trial witnesses and are free to present exhibits to the jury.") with Model Stipulated Order for Conditional Summary Trial, U.S.Dist.Ct., D.Mass., issued by Judge Robert Keeton (counsel may present evidence in narrative form, question and answer form, or argument on the facts and law).

dence from a variety of sources to present a coherent picture. Neither counsel nor Ted Koppel could hold their audience's attention if all they did was summarize. The counsel, however, has the more difficult job because ADR discourages the use of live witnesses. The full ramifications of use of videotaped depositions have not been explored in the context of ADR, but it would seem that, if counsel can agree in advance on edited versions, it should be permitted.

It is counsel's task in ADR to make the dry words of a deposition or other discovery come to life and leave an impression upon the audience. Instead of simply reading excerpts from depositions, counsel may read the questions and have co-counsel read the answers. A refinement that has been allowed in ADR is having co-counsel answer questions with a summarization that relies on various sources for the answer. Thus counsel might ask what problems were encountered in using the defendant's product, and his co-counsel would discuss eight problems, drawing on all the available testimony from a number of persons and sources. This technique poses a risk that the summarization will not be an accurate synthesis of the evidence. But that is a risk inherent in any summarization, and the professionalism of the attorneys and the threat of being shown to have misstated are deterrents to such conduct.

Visual aids (such as lists of summarized points, graphs, illustrations, or photographs displayed on charts or overhead projectors) are useful devices for ADR. Unlike closing argument to the jury in which visual aids used must already be in evidence, the visual aids in ADR are being presented for the first time. It would seem advisable to allow for examination of an opponent's visual aids in advance so that any objection can be made, hopefully resulting in a correction satisfactory to both sides.

Another technique for making a presentation more understandable is to pass out to each juror, arbitrator, or moderator a spiral notebook with the essential documents to which counsel wants to refer. Counsel then need only cite the document or page number for the listeners to be able to refer to it.

Court-annexed ADR procedures are still in flux as courts assess the results of different kinds of processes. There are a number of troubling questions still to be resolved concerning such matters as the amount of discovery permitted before ADR, the use of live or videotaped testimony, the availability of court sanctions for lack of good faith compliance, and the standard of fair representation as to expected testimony.

Notes and Questions

(1) Should an attorney be allowed to refer to facts or testimony not contained in formal discovery such as a deposition? Note that Judge Lambros would permit "a professional representation that counsel has spoken with the witness and is repeating that which the witness stated." What problems do you see with this?

(2) Traditional deposition practice by lawyers is not to examine one's own witnesses at deposition unless there is reason to believe they will be unavailable. Would a lawyer be at a disadvantage in a summary jury trial if he had not rehabilitated his witness after an opposing attorney's direct examination on deposition? Should the prospect of a summary jury trial alter the lawyer's approach to depositions? Could fuller depositions serve the interests of settlement in other ways as well?

Judicial Power to Require Participation in Summary Jury Trial

STRANDELL v. JACKSON COUNTY
United States Court of Appeals, Seventh Circuit, 1987.
838 F.2d 884.

Before WOOD and RIPPLE, CIRCUIT JUDGES, and GORDON, SENIOR DISTRICT JUDGE.

RIPPLE, CIRCUIT JUDGE.

* * *

Mr. Tobin represents the parents of Michael Strandell in a civil rights action against Jackson County, Illinois. The case involves the arrest, strip search, imprisonment, and suicidal death of Michael Strandell. In anticipation of a pretrial conference on September 3, 1986, the plaintiffs filed a written report concerning settlement prospects. The plaintiffs reported that they were requesting $500,000, but that the defendants refused to discuss the issue. At the pretrial conference, the district court suggested that the parties consent to a summary jury trial. * * *

Mr. Tobin informed the district court that the plaintiffs would not consent to a summary jury trial, and filed a motion to advance the case for trial. The district court ordered that discovery be closed on January 15, 1987, and set the case for trial.

During discovery, the plaintiffs had obtained statements from 21 witnesses. The plaintiffs learned the identity of many of these witnesses from information provided by the defendants. After discovery closed, the defendants filed a motion to compel production of the witnesses' statements. The plaintiffs responded that these statements constituted privileged work-product; they argued that the defendants could have obtained the information contained in them through ordinary discovery. The district court denied the motion to compel production; it concluded that the defendants had failed to establish "substantial need" and "undue hardship," as required by Rule 26(b)(3) of the Federal Rules of Civil Procedure.

On March 23, 1987, the district court again discussed settlement prospects with counsel. The court expressed its view that a trial could not be accommodated easily on its crowded docket and again suggested that the parties consent to a summary jury trial. On March 26, 1987, Mr. Tobin advised the district court that he would not be willing to submit his client's case to a summary jury trial, but that he was ready to proceed to trial immediately. He claimed that a summary jury trial would require disclosure of the privileged statements. The district court rejected this argument, and ordered the parties to participate in a summary jury trial.

On March 31, 1987, the parties and counsel appeared, as ordered, for selection of a jury for the summary jury trial. Mr. Tobin again objected to the district court's order compelling the summary jury trial. The district court denied this motion. Mr. Tobin then respectfully declined to proceed with the selection of the jury. The district court informed Mr. Tobin that it did not have time available to try this case, nor would it have time for a trial "in the foreseeable months ahead." The court then held Mr. Tobin in criminal contempt for refusing to proceed with the summary jury trial.

* * *

The district court filed a memorandum opinion setting forth its reasons for ordering a summary jury trial. The district court noted that trial in this case was expected to last five to six weeks, and that the parties were "poles apart in terms of settlement." It further noted that summary jury trials had been used with great success in such situations.

* * *

The court then determined that Rule 16 of the Federal Rules of Civil Procedure permits a mandatory summary jury trial.

* * *

We begin by noting that we are presented with a narrow question: Whether a trial judge may *require* a litigant to participate in a summary jury trial to promote settlement of the case. We are *not* asked to determine the manner in which summary jury trials may be used with the consent of the parties. Nor are we asked to express a view on the effectiveness of this technique in settlement negotiations.

A.

In turning to the narrow question before us—the legality of *compelled* participation in a summary jury trial—we must also acknowledge, at the very onset, that a district court no doubt has substantial inherent power to control and to manage its docket. That power must, of course, be exercised in a manner that is in harmony with the Federal Rules of Civil Procedure. * * *

In this case, the district court quite properly acknowledged, at least as a theoretical matter, this limitation on its power to devise a new method to encourage settlement. Consequently, the court turned to

Rule 16 of the Federal Rules of Civil Procedure in search of authority for the use of a mandatory summary jury trial. In the district court's view, two subsections of Rule 16(c) authorized such a procedure. As amended in 1983, those subsections read:

> The participants at any conference under this rule may consider and take action with respect to
>
> · · ·
>
> (7) the possibility of settlement or the use of extrajudicial procedures to resolve the dispute;
>
> · · ·
>
> (11) such other matters as may aid in the disposition of the action.

Fed.R.Civ.P. 16(c)(7), (11).

Here, we must respectfully disagree with the district court. We do not believe that these provisions can be read as authorizing a *mandatory* summary jury trial. In our view, while the pretrial conference of Rule 16 was intended to foster settlement through the use of extrajudicial procedures, it was not intended to require that an unwilling litigant be sidetracked from the normal course of litigation. The drafters of Rule 16 certainly intended to provide, in the pretrial conference, "a neutral forum" for discussing the matter of settlement. Fed.R.Civ.P. 16 advisory committee's note. However, it is also clear that they did not foresee that the conference would be used "to impose settlement negotiations on unwilling litigants. . . ." *Id.; see also* 6 C. Wright, A. Miller & M. Kane, *Federal Practice and Procedure* § 1525 (Supp.1987) ("As the Advisory Committee Note indicates, this new subdivision does not force unwilling parties into settlement negotiations."). While the drafters intended that the trial judge "*explor[e]* the use of procedures other than litigation to resolve the dispute,"—including "*urging* the litigants to employ adjudicatory techniques outside the courthouse,"—they clearly did not intend to *require* the parties to take part in such activities. Fed.R.Civ.P. 16 advisory committee's note (emphasis supplied). As the Second Circuit, commenting on the 1983 version of Rule 16, wrote: "Rule 16 . . . was not designed as a means for clubbing the parties—or one of them—into an involuntary compromise." *Kothe v. Smith,* 771 F.2d 667, 669 (2d Cir.1985).

* * *

Our decision is consistent with two decisions issued by this court prior to the 1983 amendments to Rule 16. In *J.F. Edwards Constr. Co. v. Anderson Safeway Guard Rail Corp.,* 542 F.2d 1318 (7th Cir.1976), the court ruled that a district court could not use Rule 16 to compel parties to stipulate facts to which they could not voluntarily agree. One year later, in *Identiseal Corp. v. Positive Identification Sys.,* 560 F.2d 298 (7th Cir.1977), this court reiterated that Rule 16 was noncoercive when it determined that district courts lacked the power to order that a party undertake further discovery. The court said:

> The limit of the court's power was to compel plaintiff to consider the possibility of conducting discovery, and there is no evidence in

the record that plaintiff's attorney rejected the district court's preferred method of litigating the action without giving it serious consideration.

Id. at 302. Although *J.F. Edwards* and *Identiseal* antedate the amendments to Rule 16, nothing in the amended rule or in the Advisory Committee Notes suggests that the amendments were intended to make the rule coercive.

The use of a mandatory summary jury trial as a pretrial settlement device would also affect seriously the well-established rules concerning discovery and work-product privilege. *See* Fed.R.Civ.P. 26(b)(3); *see also Hickman v. Taylor*, 329 U.S. 495, 67 S.Ct. 385, 91 L.Ed. 451 (1947). These rules reflect a carefully-crafted balance between the needs for pretrial disclosure and party confidentiality. Yet, a compelled summary jury trial could easily upset that balance by requiring disclosure of information obtainable, if at all, through the mandated discovery process. We do not believe it is reasonable to assume that the Supreme Court and the Congress would undertake, in such an oblique fashion, such a radical alteration of the considered judgments contained in Rule 26 and in the case law. If such radical surgery is to be performed, we can expect that the national rule-making process outlined in the Rules Enabling Act will undertake it in quite an explicit fashion.[5]

B.

The district court, in explaining its decision to compel the use of the summary jury trial, noted that the Southern District of Illinois faces crushing caseloads. The court suggested that handling that caseload, including compliance with the Speedy Trial Act, required resort to such devices as compulsory summary jury trials. We certainly cannot take issue with the district court's conclusion that its caseload places great stress on its capacity to fulfill its responsibilities. However, a crowded docket does not permit the court to avoid the adjudication of cases properly within its congressionally-mandated jurisdiction. As this court said in *Taylor v. Oxford*, 575 F.2d 152 (7th Cir.1978): "Innovative experiments may be admirable, and considering the heavy case loads in the district courts, understandable, but experiments must stay within the limitations of the statute."

Judgment of contempt vacated.

---

5. Legislation has been offered in Congress that would allow district courts to convene mandatory summary jury trials. *See* H.R. 473, 100th Cong., 1st Sess., 133 Cong.Rec.H. 157 (daily ed. Jan. 7, 1987) ("Alternative Dispute Resolution Promotion Act of 1987"); S. 2038, 99th Cong., 2d Sess., 132 Cong.Rec.S. 848 (daily ed. Feb. 3, 1986) ("Alternative Dispute Resolution Promotion Act of 1986").

ARABIAN AMERICAN OIL CO. V. SCARFONE

United States District Court, Middle District of Florida, 1988.
119 F.R.D. 448.

KOVACHEVICH, DISTRICT JUDGE.

This cause is before the Court on Defendants', Robert Work and Jerry Konidaris, motions to excuse participation in summary trial. Mr. Work's motion was filed March 22, 1988, alleging that there is no possibility of settlement in the case, that even if settlement were possible the settlement must occur between Plaintiff and Defendant Scarfone, and that he desires to avoid the expenditure of time and money that participation in the summary trial would require.

* * *

Konidaris joins the motion of Defendant Work, adding the factor that he is an individual with limited financial resources who lives and works in Greece and that it would be "absolutely meaningless and highly expensive for KONIDARIS to have to attend a Summary Jury Trial through himself or through his counsel."

* * *

Rule 16(a)(1) and (5) and (c)(11) has been cited as a basis for the utilization of summary trial procedures. That rule gives the court the power to direct parties to appear before it for various purposes, including expediting the disposition of the action; facilitating the settlement of the case; and taking action in regard to matters which may aid in the disposition of the action. Rule 16 calls these procedures conferences, but what is in a name. The obvious purpose and aim of Rule 16 is to allow courts the discretion and processes necessary for intelligent and effective case management and disposition. Whatever name the judge may give to these proceedings their purposes are the same and are sanctioned by Rule 16.

Statistically, the Middle District of Florida has the worst record in the nation for protracted trials; an accumulation of lengthy, untried causes, literally awaiting decades for trial disposition are delayed because of their extraordinary projected trial time. This Court has effectively utilized summary trials since 1985; without it, opportunity for resolution is delayed, and, justice is denied. The parties herein have had ample notice of this procedure; in fact, the January 1988 summary trial setting would have been held, but for courtroom space limitations. Defendants, for the first time, now raise objections on the eve of the April 12 and 13 summary trial; this constitutes a two-day investment on a *real* trial projected by the parties to consume 210 courtroom hours, or, seven courtroom weeks. Litigants are entitled to their day in court, but not, to somebody else's day.

Under Article Three of the U.S. Constitution, definite work is assigned to, or expected of, the trial court; that is our duty. The inherent jurisdiction of the trial court to determine, set, and use management policies should not be abrogated; it is in the best position to identify, separate, process, and complete *all* of the cases for which it is held responsible, accountable, and exists to perform. Without the authority to perform the task, the ultimate mission of the courts of the United States—to promptly administer justice in all matters properly before the court—is adversely affected.

The summary trial represents one alternative dispute resolution process which courts are employing in an effort to secure to civil litigants just, speedy, and inexpensive determination of their claims (Rule 1, Fed.R.Civ.P.) of which litigants may be otherwise deprived because of the overwhelming and overburdening caseloads which befall many district courts. The summary trial does not abolish any substantive rights of the parties; they are still entitled to a binding trial, if the summary proceedings do not lead to ultimate settlement of the cause of action.

Even if the summary procedures do not culminate in settlement of the case, the value of the summary trial in crystalizing the issues and the proof is immeasurable to the later binding trial, to which all parties come more fully prepared and rehearsed in their roles and the trial procedure. All attorneys and parties must be treated equally. Many attorneys come to trial prepared; *others do not.* After the jury is sworn in an involved case, it is an embarrassing professional exercise before the court and jury to see lawyers floundering in their presentations due to inadequate preparation, whether it be the facts from witnesses, or the law in proposed jury instructions and verdict interrogatories. The reality is that too many will *not* get ready until the day of a trial; a summary trial *forces* that day and that preparation!

This Court finds the summary trial to be a legitimate device to be used to implement the policy of this Court to provide litigants with the most expeditious and just case resolution. The Court does not find the *Strandell* case from the Seventh Circuit persuasive or binding precedent to this Court.

* * * Any contention that individual defendants should be excused from participation based on reasons, such as inability to appear for financial reasons, should be addressed by the magistrate before whom the summary trial is scheduled.

Notes and Questions

(1) District courts in other circuits have also disagreed with *Strandell,* see Williams v. Hall, 120 F.R.D. 43 (E.D.Ky.1988), and thus resolution of federal court's power to compel participation in a summary jury trial seems destined for ultimate decision by the Supreme Court.

(2) Is a required participation in a summary jury trial akin to the coercion to settle found improper in *Kothe* (after the parties failed to settle on respective settlement offers of $20,000 and $50,000, the judge sanctioned the defendant, stating he was "determined to get the attention of the carrier")?

(3) Does the judge in *Arabian American Oil* answer the *Standell* objection that a compelled summary jury trial affects discovery and work-product privileges? Is an attorney entitled not to disclose his best case until trial? Is the federal court practice of requiring parties to identify their witnesses and to indicate the substance of their expected testimony an invasion of the work-product privilege?

(4) Is inability to participate in a summary jury trial for financial reasons a valid justification? Note that *American Arabian Oil* left this issue to the magistrate. What criteria should he use?

(5) Was *Strandell* a less appropriate case for a summary jury trial than *American Arabian Oil*? Would a proper pretrial conference have weeded it out from summary jury trial requirements?

3. Appellate ADR

Appellate courts have recently turned to ADR in an attempt to require parties to engage in meaningful settlement negotiations pending appeal. Appellate cases seem particularly well suited to ADR since there are few imponderables; the facts, the record, and the judgment are all known, and the range of possible outcomes is narrowed. But parties and lawyers who have gone through a trial (or other court proceeding) are sometimes so emotionally committed to their position, and so angry about the tactics of the other side, that settlement is difficult. For this reason, mandatory ADR helps each side to save face and provides a structure for reaching agreement.

An example of an appellate ADR program is that adopted by the U.S. Court of Appeals for the D.C. Circuit in 1987 for mandatory mediation of cases on a random basis. Relying on experience from five circuit courts of appeals and a number of state appellate courts, the program cited the following four critical factors: (a) the primary goal must be achieving settlements, rather than refining cases, (b) the mediators should be specially trained in mediation techniques, (c) attorneys and parties must attend at least the first conference, and (d) the conference must be scheduled soon after an appeal is filed.[1]

Under the D.C. Circuit procedures, the mediator schedules the initial meeting within 45 days of assignment. Counsel prepare, within 15 days, position papers of not more than 10 pages, outlining their views on key facts and legal issues. These papers are not given to opposing counsel unless the mediator requests it. The mediator may also require production of key documents.

---

1. "Appellate Mediation," 1 BNA ADR Rep. 75 (June 11, 1987). See also Evans & Ramage, Alternative Dispute Resolution Procedures at the Appellate Level, I The Appellate Advocate No. 2, 3 (Texas State Bar Appellate Practice and Advocacy Section, Winter, 1988) (procedures of First Court of Appeals for referring cases, after screening and conferral with counsel, to an ADR process, especially a "moderated settlement conference" with three attorneys).

The initial meeting must be attended by counsel or other person with authority to settle the case. Parties are encouraged, but not required, to attend. All proceedings and statements made are privileged and are not subject to disclosure. If the mediator makes any suggestion as to the advisability of a change in a party's position, counsel are required to transmit these suggestions to their client. They must advise their clients that the mediator is an experienced attorney selected by the court to act as an impartial volunteer to help reach agreement and avoid further expense and uncertainty.

Any agreement reached will be reduced to writing. If no agreement is reached, the mediator notifies the Circuit Executive and the case is returned to the clerk's office for normal processing. If more time is needed, a joint stipulation can be submitted to hold the appeal in abeyance to allow the parties to continue settlement negotiations.

Chapter VI

ADMINISTRATIVE AND LEGISLATIVE PROCESSES

Dispute resolution for lawyers typically includes the four primary processes (litigation, negotiation, mediation, and arbitration) and the many variations designed to meet specialized needs and constituencies (e.g., med-arb, mini-trial, summary jury trial). Lawyers use each process regularly—by itself, simultaneously with others, in series, or in some other complementary manner. Some client problems, however, take lawyers in a different direction—toward the executive or legislative rather than the judicial branch of government.

Legal work in the administrative and legislative processes has a distinctive quality that sets it apart from the bulk of legal work in other processes: It is not exclusively, or even primarily, the province of the lawyer.

> The representation of private interests before the federal government entails a broad set of tasks, not all of which are performed by the same representatives. These include offering formal advocacy before Congress, federal agencies, or courts, maintaining contacts with other interest groups or with government officials, monitoring proposed changes in rules and regulations, and mobilizing public support. Few of these activities are, as a matter of licensing, the exclusive province of lawyers.[1]

Chapter VI provides an introductory understanding of the administrative and legislative processes. The discussion of each begins with a description of the process as a dispute resolving system—an alternative, prelude or complement to litigation—and then reviews some applications of recent ADR techniques within that process. These materials are not intended to be a substitute for taking separate courses in Administrative Law and Legislation, nor are they planned as a review of the typical undergraduate Political Science course. Our intent is to introduce students to the forms and limits of two additional processes that can be useful to the practicing lawyer and to stimulate further inquiry in directions not ordinarily taught in law school.

A. THE ADMINISTRATIVE PROCESS

1. The Process

Our nation's founders designed a system to separate the major functions of government into three distinct branches because they

---

1. Nelson & Heinz, Lawyers and the Structure of Influence in Washington, 22 Law & Soc'y Rev. 701, 716 (1988).

feared the corrupted use of the combined power that all could generate if used together. James Madison referred to these dangers in *The Federalist,* No. 47: "The accumulation of all powers, legislative, executive and judiciary, in the same hands, whether of one, a few, or many, and whether hereditary, self-appointed, or elective, may justly be pronounced the very definition of tyranny."

Lawyers have often expressed similar fears about overreaching power concentrated in an administrative process which combines within one governmental structure the separate functions of rulemaking, investigation, prosecution, and adjudication. Indeed, the history of administrative law and procedure can be largely seen both as a description of the frictions caused by the same organization performing these four different functions, and as an evaluation of the methods designed to avoid those frictions by clarifying and separating the tasks.

The administrative process grew from a recognition that the judicial system was not suitable for handling certain types of disputes. In fact, the administrative process could be considered the first alternative dispute resolution process. Beginning almost a century ago, governments faced steadily increasing demands for organized conflict resolution systems that did not rely on the traditional court route. The need was especially acute in such areas as securities transactions, banking and insurance activities, interstate transportation (particularly railroads), child labor, and health. In each area, the disputes were closely related to important public objectives; the number of disputes was high and the need for rapid results great; the parties were involved in a continuing activity which they did not want to defer or cancel while waiting for resolution; and the parties were willing to telescope the process and summarize the needed evidence through informal procedures. The result has been the establishment of and tremendous growth in the administrative process.

At the heart of the administrative process is the notion that (1) under general statutory guidelines adopted by the legislature, (2) an agency will establish clearly defined and more detailed regulations for acceptable behavior in its area of authority (rulemaking), (3) will monitor compliance with those laws and regulations (investigation), and (4) when necessary will enforce the rules by prosecuting violators in accordance with the law (prosecution), (5) in administrative proceedings presided over by "judges" selected and supervised by either the agency itself or a separate administrative agency (adjudication).

Much like an arbitrator under a contract, an agency's activities cannot be separated from the statute which created it, articulated its objectives, established the positions, and authorized its functions. Still, the statute may not tell the true story about how the agency operates. Recall the Veterans Administration's pension and disability benefits program discussed in the *Walters* case, supra p. 55. The *Walters* Court interpreted the congressional act as trying to create an efficient and "nonadversarial" system for determining benefit amounts so that the veterans themselves would receive the pension money, not their lawyers. The process apparently operated well enough for typical cases. But the agency's ability to handle large numbers of cases fairly and efficiently came under severe strain when it was presented with complex cases raising serious issues of liability and causation. In such circumstances financial constraints on the agency and the burdens imposed by mass processing weakened the intended functional separation—in practice the "executive" and prosecutorial aspects of the agency's operations tended to overwhelm the adjudicative function.

There is no single generic administrative agency. Agencies exist in a great variety of structural forms at every level of government—from huge international hierarchical bureaucracies, like the United States Department of Defense or the United Nations Educational, Scientific and Cultural Organization (UNESCO), to small more egalitarian commissions, like state agencies for the arts and many local city planning offices. Each agency may be headed either by a single director or secretary (the Secretary of State), or a multi-member council or commission (the National Labor Relations Board); either appointed by higher authority and consented to by one legislative house (Director of the Office of Management and Budget) or elected (a state attorney general). Its organizational structure may be fixed and formal (the U.S. Department of Agriculture), or more flexible and informal (the Office of the Governor in most states), depending usually on size and function; its mandate may be broad and sweeping (state departments of social services) or narrow and clearly circumscribed (state commissions for the blind).

Congress, state legislatures, and the lawyers who practice before government agencies have fortunately brought significant uniformity to the operation of the administrative process in recent decades. The Federal Administrative Procedure Act (APA),[2] adopted in 1946, recognized the benefits of uniform operating procedures across vastly different subject areas and sizes of functional constituencies. It has served as both a model and a catalyst for state statutes with similar objectives. Other legislation has provided additional guidelines for agency action—defining limits for access to agency information (the Freedom of Information Act [3]), establishing open meetings requirements (the Sunshine Act [4]), and setting a date on which the agency is abolished ("sunset" laws adopted in many states [5]). Taken as a whole, these rules operate for agency action much like the Rules of Civil Procedure do for the courts and, as such, are tools the lawyer must use effectively. In the words of an experienced public interest lawyer:

> [A]dministrative law is a system of dispute resolution under the aegis of the Administrative Procedure Act. The APA contains no preferences between liberals and conservatives, and neither

2. Federal Administrative Procedure Act, 5 U.S.C. § 553.

3. 5 U.S.C. § 552(a).

4. 5 U.S.C. § 552(b).

5. See, e.g., Tex.Government Code Ann. § 325 (Vernon 1988).

determines outcomes of specific cases nor establishes substantive standards. It simply provides guidelines for determining how administrative agencies shall make their decisions and under what circumstances the courts may overturn them.[6]

Lawyers seem to dominate administrative activity, both internally and in outside agency practice, although they are less involved in governmental policymaking than in activities related to the more traditional legal field of litigation, rule drafting and interpretation, and legal counseling. This concentration is understandable given the influence of legal education and the fact that the lawyer who represents private interests is primarily interested in the impact that an agency's action (or inaction) has on a client's business or dispute. Lawyers "predominate in fields in which the primary institutional actors are the courts or regulatory agencies."[7]

A recent study of Washington agencies in the agriculture, energy, health, and labor policy areas found clear patterns in the distribution of lawyers practicing before agencies on behalf of clients. They were "overrepresented" among specialists in foreign trade, commodities trading, and food safety (agriculture), in the nuclear, oil, and coal subfields (energy), in regulation of food and drugs, health care providers, and health professions, and in health care payment and insurance (health), and in labor relations, employment standards, private pensions, and occupational safety (labor). The lawyer is first and foremost an advocate in regular private practice, and she serves in this role in governmental areas as well. It is not surprising then that lawyers are not primarily involved with the policymaking aspects of government, nor are they usually serving in a mediating capacity among various private interests that are vying for public favor:

> Washington lawyers, like corporate lawyers generally, appear to be predominately organized around and responsive to client interests. They hold social and political values that are similar to those of their clients; they typically have regular and enduring client relationships; and, when there are sharp conflicts between competing groups, they communicate with their own clients rather than with the lawyers representing the other side.[8]

Case Study: The Texas Water Commission

Recent activity at the Texas Water Commission provides a good example of the administrative process at work—and the lawyer's role in its successful operation.

6. Morrison, The Administrative Procedure Act: A Living And Responsive Law, 72 Va.L.Rev. 253 (1986).

7. Nelson & Heinz, supra note 1, at 722. See also Marcotte, The Rewards of Government Service, A.B.A.J., Aug. 1, 1988, p. 66.

8. Nelson & Heinz, supra note 1, at 755–56.

Until 1985 the Texas Water Commission was one of three parttime appointive commissions within the Texas Department of Water Resources. The Governor appointed all three commissioners to staggered terms of six years. The Commission's only duties were to hear evidence on water use requests and grant or deny the permits. It had no staff of its own, nor did it have rulemaking or enforcement powers. In 1985, however, the Texas legislature restructured the Commission, giving it rulemaking and enforcement authority (in addition to its permit responsibilities) in areas of water quality, water rights, waste water discharge, supervision of municipal water districts, coastal oil and hazardous spill prevention and control, hazardous waste control, and other matters relating to water.[9] (The 1985 legislation also subjected the Commission to the Texas Sunset Act, terminating its existence on September 1, 1997, unless previously reauthorized by separate legislative act.[10])

The Commission presently sets state water policy under general legislative guidelines, establishes rules governing water quality and use, grants permits for operations consistent with those rules, investigates compliance, and enforces its own rules. The Commission staff includes a separate Office of Hearing Examiners composed of attorneys who take evidence and public comment on permit applications, petitions to alter water rates, and enforcement proceedings, and who, after reviewing this record, make recommendations to the Commissioners. The Commission also includes an Office of Public Interest headed by an advocate appointed by the Commission, who represents the "public interest" on matters of environmental quality and consumer protection.

As examples of agency action: In early 1987, the Commission adopted "tough new waste water discharge standards for tributaries in the Colorado River watershed" in western Texas in order to maintain good water quality levels.[11] In late 1986, it granted a waste water discharge permit for a county utility district northwest of Fort Worth, even after its own hearing examiner recommended denial based on repeated prior violations by the same operator and a finding that the extra discharge from the new plant would degrade the quality of the Clear Fork of the Trinity River. In September 1987, the Commission approved a transfer of an operating permit for a six-acre hazardous waste processing and storage site in north-central Texas after taking substantial testimony and evidence both in favor of and in opposition to continued use of the site. During the 1985–87 period, the Commission also levied heavy fines on several cities for municipal waste water violations, including $165,000 on Austin and $500,000 on Houston. In the case of Houston, enforcement actions were being taken against almost half of the 51 plants in that city because of non-compliance with Commission standards that had extended over many years. Commission staff proposed a fine of $1.4 million, but in response to an offer by

9. Tex.Water Code Ann. § 5.013.

10. Id. at § 5.014.

11. Collier, Water Lawyer's Advantage Is Unfair, Critics Say, Austin American–Statesman, June 5, 1988, p. 1.

Houston to make an immediate and substantial investment (roughly $30 million) to improve existing facilities, the Commission's final order reduced the fine to $500,000.

Lawyers play an important role in Water Commission activities. Texas governors have often appointed lawyers as commissioners—in 1988 the three-member Commission included two lawyers, with the third, a former police chief, sheriff, and county commissioner. (Other commissioners in the past have had technical expertise in fields related to water, such as engineering or geology.) The staff includes an executive director and a public interest advocate (both are currently lawyers), a General Counsel who advises the commissioners on state and federal water law, and a Legal Division that prepares and revises agency rules and provides legal advice concerning permit applications, hearings, enforcement actions, and administrative lawsuits involving the agency.

In addition, most parties who want their views heard on matters considered by the Water Commission are represented by lawyers. The procedures are technically complicated—knowing when, how, and where to take action is important to the success of a desired project. Many Austin law firms, therefore, have specialists who handle mainly Water Commission business. (Similar specialization exists for agency activities in most other state capitols and, in even more pronounced form, for federal agency work in Washington). The same lawyers and their office staff work regularly with the same agency officials and their office personnel—over many years, for many different clients, and on many different projects. A specializing lawyer will often build a good working relationship with Commission staff to give his client's projects and interests the best chance to succeed. And the best way for a newly graduated lawyer to establish himself as a competent practitioner in Texas water law (or federal food and drug regulation for that matter) is to work for several years in the legal division of the Texas Water Commission (or the Food and Drug Administration), or be hired as an associate in a law firm that has partners specializing in such practice.

This of course raises ethical issues for both the legal profession and the political world. Whenever long-term public/private working relationships play such a significant role in a regulatory process, there are obvious questions of favored treatment for those who have the "best" relationship. Moreover, the nature of an agency's activities encourages both a fulltime commitment by outside lawyers and the development of special expertise by agency personnel within. One feeds off the other. For instance, Austin lawyer Lee Biggart began his career as the governor's legislative aide, was appointed to the Texas Water Commission in 1981, was Chairman from 1982–1984, left the Commission in 1986, and is now recognized as the most influential lawyer practicing before the Commission—someone who counts two of the three existing commissioners plus the executive director among his close friends. Biggart expanded his role in water law matters when former Executive

Director Soward resigned from the Water Commission in December 1987 to become Biggart's law partner.[12]

Movement from outside the agency to inside, and then outside again, creates a "revolving door" problem that is decried at all levels of government. For example, the executive director of Common Cause of Texas referred to the charges against Biggart of improper insider favoritism as "a classic example of the revolving door, showing all the problems of regulators leaving public service and immediately representing the regulated. It violates the most basic principles of conflict of interest." [13] One commissioner, commenting on the same situation, stated that even major law firms "feel like they or their clients need to hire Lee Biggart as counsel in order to ensure that their client gets adequate representation before the commission. To me that gives at least the appearance that the process is not fair." A lobbyist for the Sierra Club's Lone Star Chapter said that commission regulars "recognize the fact you don't always win or lose a case on the technical or legal merits. A lot depends on who the players are and who you know. If Lee Biggart is on your side, your side has a leg up." [14]

This symbiotic relationship between public agency work and private legal practice is even more common at the federal level. The need for experienced lawyers handling legal matters inside the agency and representing interested parties outside rises with increasing technical complexity of the subject matter and a larger agency workload. Movement back and forth is natural under these conditions; abuse occurs when public decisions are made, or appear to be made, not on the merits of the case but on the relationships of the parties or their lawyers. For instance, what caused increased public attention to focus on Biggart was his letter to a potential client, Unisys Corporation, in which he stated:

> "Our ties with the commissioners, executive office and staff of the Texas Water Commission will provide Unisys effective assistance and counsel in these efforts. We will also be able to 'open doors' in the commission which would not otherwise be open to Unisys as a matter of course, to enable Unisys to have opportunities to show the commission that Unisys can and will meet its needs." [15]

The underlying premise of this appeal is that relationships count for a great deal in public agency work—to get a fair hearing before the Commission, you would do well to have a friend of the Commission as your personal advocate. What may be the most disconcerting part of this story is that many insiders viewed Biggart's chief fault as having put his appeal in a letter; they asserted that lawyers doing business before public agencies make such appeals verbally all the time.

The role of the Biggart firm in the conduct of the Texas Water Commission was first raised publicly by an investigative article in the

12. Id.   14. Id.
13. Id.   15. Id.

Austin newspaper. Does the account above, based on that article, indicate any wrongdoing by the Biggart firm? Does it indicate an inappropriate role by a lawyer in the administrative process? Is the Texas Water Commission fairly typical of administrative agencies, at least at the state level, in its amenability to influence by former insiders? Is this in part a consequence of the rapid expansion of its authority into new areas? Is the reliance on former insiders simply a legitimate response to its need to rely on attorneys with expertise? It is not a simple task to distinguish between an attorney's legitimate trading on his expertise and a more sinister form of influence peddling.

Limits to Administrative Action

The administrative process has significant economic and social effects on individuals, families, and businesses. The process must therefore conform to certain standards, which serve as limits to administrative action. What are those standards? Do they incorporate concepts such as due process or judicial review which are so much a part of the court's procedures? Is there a tradeoff between quality in resolving disputes and the efficiency and relationship priorities that are so important to the administrative process?

DeLONG, NEW WINE FOR A NEW BOTTLE: JUDICIAL REVIEW IN THE REGULATORY STATE
72 Va.L.Rev. 399, 405–06, 411–13, 417–18 (1986).

American political thought is largely premised on the candidly cynical belief that no one can be trusted absolutely and that anyone (especially a powerful government official) who even *asks* to be regarded as absolutely trustworthy is almost certainly up to no good. A logical implication of this belief is the principle that every part of government, including the agencies, must be restrained by an effective countervailing power. Of course, this does not mean that the public should never trust the government, since that attitude would lead only to the more subtle tyranny of ineffectiveness and chaos. In the administrative setting the principle simply means that the potential for control must always exist.

[The author then articulates six reasons for controlling agency action: our cultural demand for due process and equal protection in government decision-making; the need to promote competent performance in agencies that are often immune to customer dissatisfaction and product competition; the tendency of agencies to overreach their limited scopes of authority; the importance of balancing error tolerance in setting regulatory standards; the need to coordinate among the numerous agencies and programs providing services to the public; and the necessity for sound handling of public expenditures and the regulation of the economy.]

The principal control mechanisms in our system of government are words in law books. This elementary truth makes courts the primary institutions for agency control, because courts are the official interpreters of the sacred constitutional and statutory texts. Even Congress cannot authoritatively establish the meaning of previously enacted legislation, except by passing a new law. The recurring arguments over the amount of deference due an agency determination do not affect this basic division of power because courts ultimately determine the deference due.

In addition to interpreting the statutes that govern administrative agencies, the courts have the authority to conduct substantive review of agency actions, authority derived either from the APA and statutes modeled on it, or from specific congressional injunctions requiring courts to review agency actions for the substantiality of the evidence and for arbitrariness. Moreover, the courts and Congress have diluted the standing doctrine to the point that anyone with some ingenuity and a strong interest in an agency decision can find a way to challenge the decision in court.

The prominence of judicial review in this structure makes the court system the logical focal point for anyone concerned with control of agency action, especially for people who write for and read law journals. It also creates an intellectual trap. Lawyers and judges may concentrate on the role of courts while ignoring the reviewing functions of other institutions, and they may emphasize the power of legal language while neglecting the importance of institutional dynamics and internal incentive structures. Such legal ethnocentrism distorts analysis, because mechanisms other than judicial review play important roles in controlling agency behavior.

The most important alternative form of control is an agency's internal gyroscope. That officials and agencies cannot be completely trusted does not mean that they can never be trusted, and to a large extent the administrative system rests on the assumption that officials act in good faith and that external control mechanisms are backup rather than primary systems. Another major source of control—though historically more potential than actual—is the Executive Office of the President and particularly the Office of Management and Budget. The OMB's influence over the agencies' budgets is an important limitation on agency power. Moreover, the OMB clears the agencies' statements and legislative proposals, and in recent years it has assumed responsibility for reviewing and coordinating agency regulations.

The President's power to fire top agency officials can be another instrument of control, but this authority barely scratches the working levels of an agency and remains largely a negative power. The President can fire top officials for letting their subordinates do things the President does not want done, but it is difficult for the President to force the agency to respect his policy preferences if the permanent staff does not willingly cooperate.

Other nonjudicial institutions also exercise some control over agencies. The General Accounting Office (formally a congressional institution) polices the actual flow of dollars to agencies and engages in some policy analysis of administrative regulations. The Office of Personnel Management controls personnel matters, often enforcing the laws that protect the public from the dangers of undue governmental efficiency and productivity. The Department of Justice coordinates agencies' legal positions. Congress also exercises much informal control over the agencies, in addition to its formal oversight hearings and budget reviews.

No examination of the role of courts is complete without consideration of the effects of the gravitational pulls exercised by these other institutions. More subtly, thorough analysis of judicial review requires an examination of the interactions between the courts and these other controlling institutions. The central issues are how the courts can help or inhibit the other institutions (and vice versa) and how courts can use the other institutions to improve their own methods of agency review.

* * *

The traditional approach to judicial review [of administrative action] consists of three steps, in ascending order of intensity and difficulty. First, the court determines if the proceeding was procedurally correct in that interested parties received the opportunities to participate guaranteed by the Constitution and relevant statutes. Second, the court decides whether the agency properly interpreted its statutory mandate. Third, the court ascertains whether the agency action was substantively within the zone of reasonableness. Depending on the applicable legal doctrine, this final step is essentially a determination of whether the agency evidence was sufficient or the agency action arbitrary.

The courts are most comfortable when assessing the procedural regularity of agency action. They are less eager to interpret the agency's statutory authority, given the extraordinary complexity of some regulatory schemes, but interpretation is a familiar judicial task covered by known rules of decision. The judiciary typically prefers not to reverse an agency on the last of the three tests, largely because the standards are so amorphous and because the chances of illegitimate encroachment on agency expertise and discretion loom so large. If necessary, courts will undertake a substantive review, but judges will try to focus on the strength of the logical link between the agency's data and conclusions rather than on the abstract wisdom of the agency's policy.

Although this is a reasonable approach to review, the courts might profitably consider expanding their purview to include an evaluation of the roles and functioning of other mechanisms of control. A court's role under this conception would be to ensure that somebody somewhere in the system performed adequate quality control and to recognize that the somebody need not necessarily be a court. This alternative orientation suggests three possible areas of judicial inquiry—control exercised by the agency's internal processes, by other organs of the executive branch, and by Congress.

Notes and Questions

(1) Many elected executives and legislators have shown increasing interest in building institutional control of the administrative rulemaking power. As DeLong indicated, the Office of Management and Budget has steadily expanded its efforts to bring this rulemaking discretion under the President's policy control. The following was written by two former officials of the Office of Management and Budget:

> Since the earliest days of the Republic, presidents have taken the steps they deemed necessary to maintain some control over the activities of the executive branch—to ensure that officials' statements and actions followed presidential policies and were consistent with each other. For example, President Jefferson reported approvingly that President Washington had routinely reviewed the correspondence prepared by his cabinet officials before it was mailed, a practice that Jefferson resumed. With the growth of the executive branch, later presidents took more formal steps to maintain their influence over the executive bureaucracy. In 1921, the Bureau of the Budget was created to consolidate all executive branch budget submissions. Shortly thereafter, agency positions on proposed legislation were also routed through the Bureau of the Budget.

> In the 1970's, growing dissatisfaction with government regulation led to formal presidential oversight of executive branch rulemaking. This oversight function was eventually entrusted to the Office of Management and Budget (OMB) within the Executive Office of the President. The same rationale applied: the president wanted to ensure that regulations were consistent with each other and with administration policies and priorities. Modest initial efforts begun during the Nixon administration have been strengthened and expanded by each president who followed.

> President Reagan's regulatory review program evolved from these earlier efforts and extended them in two crucial respects. First, the initial programs directed agencies to assess the social costs and benefits of their rules; the Reagan program directs agencies to *decide* regulatory questions according to the assessments of costs and benefits. It directs that, insofar as statutory law permits, agencies may take regulatory action only if the expected benefits to society outweigh the expected costs, and agencies must set their regulatory priorities to maximize the net aggregate benefits to society. Second, the initial programs required White House review of selected rulemaking proposals and were vague about the prerogatives of agencies to issue rules over the

objections of the president's staff; the Reagan program requires
White House review of virtually all rules, and requires agencies to
reconsider rules in light of White House objections, while making it
clear that agencies retain their statutory discretion and obligations.

DeMuth and Ginsburg, White House Review of Agency Rulemaking, 99
Harv.L.Rev. 1075, 1075–76 (1986).

(2) One obvious means of control over governmental action is the
electoral process. Every two or four years the public has an opportunity at the polls to change the direction of public policy. Statutory
interpretation in the administrative area appears to have important
political overtones. Should administrative action conform to the ideological persuasion of those who drafted the statute, or should it be
flexible enough to respond to the wishes of subsequent administrations?

To take a specific example, the Reagan Administration's Department of Transportation in 1981 rescinded a 1977 DOT standard which
required passive restraints (airbags or automatic seatbelts) in all cars
by 1982. In Motor Vehicle Manufacturers Assoc. v. State Farm Mutual
Automobile Ins. Co., 463 U.S. 29 (1983), the Supreme Court held that
the rescission was arbitrary and capricious because the DOT had failed
to find that the standard would not help motor vehicle safety. Justice
Rehnquist, dissenting, refers directly to the political questions involved:

> The agency's changed view of the standard seems to be related to
> the election of a new President of a different political party. It is
> readily apparent that the responsible members of one administra-
> tion may consider public resistance and uncertainties to be more
> important than do their counterparts in a previous administration.
> A change in administration brought about by the people casting
> their votes is a perfectly reasonable basis for an executive agency's
> reappraisal of the costs and benefits of its programs and regula-
> tions. As long as the agency remains within the bounds estab-
> lished by Congress, it is entitled to reassess administrative records
> and evaluate priorities in light of the philosophy of the administra-
> tion.

Id. at 59.

How does Rehnquist's reference to the democratic election process
differ from the "public interest" concerns raised by Professor Fiss
(supra p. 38)? When does a legitimate requirement of adherence to
statutory guidelines (and to the administrative regulations that interpret them) become an inflexible obstacle to democratic change?

(3) The administrative process affects what many consider to be
essentially private conduct. We expect private parties who take actions that touch on the public interest to conform to statutory and
agency guidelines: telephone or electric utilities to charge only at rates
approved by the state public utility commission; developers and contractors to build houses or shopping centers which meet the zoning,
waste water discharge, and other requirements for the particular building site; and airline companies and pilots to comply with flight schedul-

ing, personnel safety, and equipment rules established by the Federal Aviation Administration.

But agency action also creates a broader "ripple" effect in the private sector. Two or more private groups can be counted upon to be on opposite sides of any important issue before a public agency: Private neighborhood groups, environmental advocates, and business developers are usually pitted against one another when new public facilities (such as airports, homes for the mentally ill, sewage disposal plants, or a new dam) are built, or existing facilities have reached capacity, or expanding population and economic activity are increasing the demand for public services beyond original forecasts. To a greater or lesser degree, depending on the activity, the public agency may become more of a *mediator* among the various private interests than an *enforcer* of the public interest. Because so much money and other benefits are usually at stake, this clash of private groups frequently becomes an all-out effort to "capture" the agency. Recent actions before the Texas Water Commission, see supra p. 678, reflect this drive by private interests to use lawyers as tools for such influence.

Administrative Adjudication

Adjudication is the administrative function which most closely follows judicial procedure. The APA, in sections 554 through 557, provides a format for adjudicative hearings which conforms in many respects to the court model: an impartial administrative law judge, receiving evidence during a hearing that is usually open to the public, with parties having the right to be represented by counsel, with prescribed procedures for the complaint, briefs, and discovery, and with findings and a decision to be based on the evidence in the record. But there are differences, which stem from the reasons that prompted the legislature to place the adjudicative proceeding in an administrative rather than judicial setting. And those differences raise questions whether the parties are receiving fair treatment and a just result.

For example, the operations of elementary and secondary schools are usually governed by general state laws, leaving to local school boards and superintendents broad discretion to adopt procedures to handle specific disputes. Serious disturbances had occurred in an Ohio high school in 1971, and the school administrators, interpreting their authority under Ohio law, suspended many students for ten days without giving the students either notice of the charges against them or an opportunity to be heard. A class action suit was filed, claiming that the Ohio statute permitting such action was unconstitutional. The Supreme Court, in Goss v. Lopez, 419 U.S. 565 (1975), held that the Due Process Clause requires that an administrative process protect a student's right to an education, and that the procedures used in Ohio in that instance were inadequate to protect that right. The Court tried to address the difficult questions of what standards should be applied and how to balance the countervailing interests:

Disciplinarians, although proceeding in utmost good faith, frequently act on the reports and advice of others; and the controlling facts and the nature of the conduct under challenge are often disputed. The risk of error is not at all trivial, and it should be guarded against if that may be done without prohibitive cost or interference with the educational process.

The difficulty is that our schools are vast and complex. Some modicum of discipline and order is essential if the educational function is to be performed. Events calling for discipline are frequent occurrences and sometimes require immediate, effective action. Suspension is considered not only to be a necessary tool to maintain order but a valuable educational device. The prospect of imposing elaborate hearing requirements in every suspension case is viewed with great concern, and many school authorities may well prefer the untrammeled power to act unilaterally, unhampered by rules about notice and hearing. But it would be a strange disciplinary system in an educational institution if no communication was sought by the disciplinarian with the student in an effort to inform him of his dereliction and to let him tell his side of the story in order to make sure that an injustice is not done. * * *

We do not believe that school authorities must be totally free from notice and hearing requirements if their schools are to operate with acceptable efficiency. Students facing temporary suspension have interests qualifying for protection of the Due Process Clause, and due process requires, in connection with a suspension of 10 days or less, that the student be given oral or written notice of the charges against him and, if he denies them, an explanation of the evidence the authorities have and an opportunity to present his side of the story. The Clause requires at least these rudimentary precautions against unfair or mistaken findings of misconduct and arbitrary exclusion from school.

There need be no delay between the time "notice" is given and the time of the hearing. In the great majority of cases the disciplinarian may informally discuss the alleged misconduct with the student minutes after it has occurred. We hold only that, in being given an opportunity to explain his version of the facts at this discussion, the student first be told what he is accused of doing and what the basis of the accusation is. Lower courts which have addressed the question of the nature of the procedures required in short suspension cases have reached the same conclusion. Since the hearing may occur almost immediately following the misconduct, it follows that as a general rule notice and hearing should precede removal of the student from school. We agree with the District Court, however, that there are recurring situations in which prior notice and hearing cannot be insisted upon. Students whose presence poses a continuing danger to persons or property or an ongoing threat of disrupting the academic process may be immediately removed from school. In such cases, the necessary notice and rudimentary hearing should follow as soon as practicable, as the District Court indicated.

* * *

We stop short of construing the Due Process Clause to require, countrywide, that hearings in connection with short suspensions must afford the student the opportunity to secure counsel, to confront and cross-examine witnesses supporting the charge, or to call his own witnesses to verify his version of the incident. Brief disciplinary suspensions are almost countless. To impose in each such case even truncated trial-type procedures might well overwhelm administrative facilities in many places and by diverting resources, cost more than it would save in educational effectiveness. Moreover, further formalizing the suspension process and escalating its formality and adversary nature may not only make it too costly as a regular disciplinary tool but also destroy its effectiveness as part of the teaching process.

On the other hand, requiring effective notice and informal hearing permitting the student to give his version of the events will provide a meaningful hedge against erroneous action. At least the disciplinarian will be alerted to the existence of disputes about facts and arguments about cause and effect. He may then determine himself to summon the accuser, permit cross-examination, and allow the student to present his own witnesses. In more difficult cases, he may permit counsel. In any event, his discretion will be more informed and we think the risk of error substantially reduced.[16]

Notes and Questions

(1) The Court points to greater informality and efficiency, and less adversariness, as important reasons to support an administrative process for handling enforcement proceedings. The Court's discussion of the VA procedure in *Walters,* supra pp. 56–57, seems to rest on similar values. But each of these reasons also appears to increase the potential for an unjust resolution of the dispute. How does the Court balance these countervailing forces? It seems to rely on formal hearing procedures and the right to counsel—hallmarks of the judicial system—to provide control over an administrator's power to adjudicate disputes. Similar "legal" control mechanisms are found in the procedures and deadlines of the APA. Yet, the Court permits many short cuts to accommodate the function for which the "administrative" adjudication was established. Is this "second-class justice" for those who are unfortunate enough to have disputes in these areas—an "injustice" that is

---

16. Goss v. Lopez, 419 U.S. 565, 580–84 (1975).

politically acceptable only because of our inability or unwillingness to fund a judicial system adequate to handle all disputes?

(2) One factor that appears to argue more for administrative than judicial handling of these disputes is the importance of continuing the program activity. In *Goss,* the Court does not question the need to keep the school open for students, even those accused of wrongdoing. It would be difficult, if not impossible, for school employees to provide formal adjudicative hearings to parties in all possible disputes over school rules while continuing the regular educational program. Is this factor also present in the imposition of fines by the Texas Water Commission for waste-water disposal permit violations (see supra p. 677)? In other areas where administrative adjudication is the norm?

2. Application of ADR Techniques

As the benefits of recent innovations in negotiation, mediation, and arbitration have become better known, many government officials have tried to apply these new techniques to administrative activities. Proponents of ADR seem to share important objectives—to improve accessibility, acceptability, efficiency, and fairness in the system, bringing more people, including those most directly affected, into the decision-making process. Many agency administrators have successfully adopted changes in operational procedures during the past five years, building a sizable collaborative effort into the administrative process. The most notable examples are in the rulemaking function, where administrators have woven negotiation and mediation techniques into what was otherwise a rather formal and adversarial regulatory pattern established by the APA.[17] William French Smith, Attorney General of the United States from 1981 to 1985, explains the early efforts to improve the quality of administrative rulemaking:

SMITH, ALTERNATIVE MEANS OF DISPUTE RESOLUTION: PRACTICES AND POSSIBILITIES IN THE FEDERAL GOVERNMENT

1984 Mo. J. Dispute Res.
9, 11–15.

Perhaps the most promising alternative to traditional adversarial rulemaking now being explored in a number of federal agencies is "negotiated rulemaking." This procedure contemplates an informal process of bargaining among parties affected by a proposed regulation. The process is intended to culminate in an agreement that becomes the basis for an agency rule. The procedure, still in its infancy, usually takes one of two forms.

In one approach, the government agency merely acts as overseer of the negotiations. The agency begins the process by publishing a

17. See 5 U.S.C. § 553.

description of a proposed rule topic in the Federal Register and a general invitation to participate in negotiations. The agency selects a manageable number of representatives from those responding to participate in the bargaining sessions. Agency officials are not present at these sessions. The negotiators develop a proposed rule through the process of compromise, which the agency then publishes along with a statement of basis and purpose drafted by the negotiators. Thereafter, the agency receives public comments, evaluates the negotiated proposal, and promulgates a final rule.

In the second form of negotiated rulemaking, the agency actually participates in the negotiations. After a number of private representatives are selected as negotiators, the agency presents them with its interpretation of the statute involved. Negotiations then begin, and because the agency is one of the negotiators, it must agree to all bargains. If the negotiators cannot agree, the notice and comment process begins under the current system. If the parties reach an agreement, the agency publishes the bargain as a proposed rule and accepts public comment.

In either form, negotiated rulemaking offers a number of potential advantages over traditional adversarial rulemaking. For example, negotiation may yield better rules. While the adversary system encourages parties to take extreme positions, negotiation yields a pragmatic search for intermediate solutions. In negotiation, one party is more likely to discover and to consider economic, political, and other constraints on another party. In sum, the parties are more likely to address all aspects of a problem in attempting to formulate a workable solution.

Another possible advantage is that negotiated rulemaking may increase the acceptability of the rule promulgated by the agency. As one commentator has noted:

> The adversary process usually declares winners and losers and designates a "right" answer. Thus, adversaries may see each other and the agency as enemies and grow alienated from the result. Negotiation, by contrast, fosters detente among participants and has few clear-cut losers. All suggest solutions and ultimately believe they have at least partly consented to the compromise rule.[18]

While negotiated rulemaking may offer these and other advantages, there are a number of practical and legal constraints to its use. Not all issues lend themselves to negotiations. This is the case with most all-or-nothing issues, such as whether to require airbags in automobiles. Broad issues that do not directly affect a narrowly concentrated group of persons or entities are also unlikely to be capable of resolution in negotiated rulemaking.

18. Note, Rethinking Regulation: Negotiation as an Alternative to Traditional Rulemaking, 94 Harv.L.Rev. 1871, 1877 (1981).

It may also be difficult to select the appropriate representatives for the negotiations. The proposed rule will affect large numbers of people in many cases, but effective negotiations will be possible only if the number of negotiators is kept to a manageable size. Thus, negotiated rulemaking typically will require that groups or persons with a common viewpoint be represented by a single negotiator. The practical considerations aside, it may be legally imperative that this representative be an appropriate spokesperson for the affected groups, so as to satisfy the Administrative Procedure Act, which requires that informal rulemaking reflect fair consideration of all affected interests, and due process, which mandates that valid interests not be arbitrarily excluded.

* * *

To the extent these rules interfere with negotiated rulemaking, exemptions should be considered. Exemptions would guarantee negotiations the privacy and flexibility needed for success, without sacrificing the concerns these rules were designed to protect. The negotiation process itself will supply virtually the same safeguards that public meetings provide and, in any event, the product of negotiation will be published as a notice of proposed rulemaking so that others will have an opportunity to examine any agreements, and participate in the rulemaking process before the rule becomes final.

POU, FEDERAL AGENCY USE OF "ADR": THE EXPERIENCE TO DATE

Admin. Conf. of the U.S., Sourcebook: Federal Agency Use of Alternative
Means of Dispute Resolution.
101, 102–04 (1987).

It is worth noting initially that agencies frequently are not well situated to terminate controversies without full judicial or administrative airing of all sides. Disputes involving the government often are more complex, and have far greater impact and precedential value, than most individual consumer, employment or negligence cases. Where the meaning of civil rights law or the validity of a complicated environmental regulatory scheme is at issue, the interest in satisfying all parties and avoiding lengthy, expensive controversies may be outweighed by a need for authoritative opinions definitively explicating legal responsibilities, for open processes to develop social policies, and for executive flexibility. Agency officials' efforts to reduce formalization are complicated by a variety of factors that seldom trouble private parties; many are apprehensive over ADR because of these uncertainties, as well as others like the following:

(1) *Finality often cannot be assured.* Proposed regulations, orders, and settlements often are subjected routinely to multiple layers of intra-agency and inter-agency review, public comment and judicial

second-guessing, a situation that can only discourage other parties from negotiating with federal officers whose agreements' finality cannot always be assured. Means must be found to ensure that top decisionmakers are involved in, or apprised of, sensitive negotiations, and to streamline agency and OMB review of negotiated rules and orders.

(2) *Public officials may feel less able to assess their interest and strike bargains* in some cases than would individuals or corporations, since public duties are often more nebulous and susceptible to second-guessing by Congress or the press. * * * More mundane, but in some ways more worrisome, is the result of a recent minitrial leading to a settlement by the Army Corps of Engineers of a large construction dispute, where subsequent criticism by regional personnel spurred an investigation by the agency's inspector general. The inspector general's report (not publicly available) reportedly was favorable to the process, but such investigations, unless infrequent, would almost certainly chill all parties' interest in experimenting with ADR methods in place of seeking the "insulation" of a "regular" decision.

(3) *Public access and other procedures imposed by statutes* like the Freedom of Information Act, Federal Advisory Committee Act, and Administrative Procedure Act create duties that can inhibit an atmosphere conducive to negotiation.

(4) *Procedural restrictions are often mandated by court decision.* To cite but one example, limits on *ex parte* contacts in all formal proceedings and even some informal rulemakings would require changes in judicial doctrine or statute for use of informal alternatives.

(5) *The General Accounting Office has prohibited use of outside arbitrators to determine liability* of the United States, though permitting it where only the amount was subject to arbitration. This prohibition has been frequently criticized, and the Administrative Conference has called on Congress to act in many cases to authorize arbitration of various claims. Representatives of Justice and GAO have also suggested that, in some instances, delegation of a governmental decision to a private arbitrator may raise constitutional questions.

(6) *Budget limits, and procurement procedures* imposed by the Federal Acquisition Regulation and the Competition in Contracting Act, affect acquisition of the services of private mediators and arbitrators. While this has positive aspects—including encouraging development of in-house expertise, enhancing inter-agency cooperation (e.g., with FMCS or CRS), and ensuring quality work in a field with some "experts" of dubious credentials—it may delay, complicate, and even prevent agency action in some instances where ADR would help.

(7) *The unclear extent of an agency official's authority to bind his or her successors* in a settlement adds uncertainty.

* * *

(9) *The role of judicial review often presents fundamental problems.* A prime tenet of ADR is that an initial investment of time and money to resolve a dispute consensually is likely to avoid the cost, delay, and

other troubles associated with litigation. Many agencies' negotiated rules and other settlements, however, will be subject to some judicial review—for example, where (1) a court must approve a settlement, (2) a party changes its mind or cannot control its constituents, or (3) an affected party not participating directly in the negotiations questions the agency's jurisdiction, alleges inadequate representation in the negotiating process, or otherwise challenges the legality of the settlement. Should the standard of review be relaxed in light of consensus? If so, how does one decide whether representation has been adequate and when a consensus has been reached? Can the agency record, which the courts use as a basis for review, be curtailed in light of the need for fast, confidential negotiations? To what degree should a mediator's confidentiality be protected? The implications of these questions are just beginning to be worked out.

It should be clear that ADR techniques are hardly cure-alls and their costs can be substantial. Still, they present government agencies with clear opportunities to resolve disputes more quickly and satisfactorily, reduce rancor in their dealings with some regulated parties, and stand as counterweights to a perilous trend toward procedural complexity.

Notes and Questions

(1) The progress that ADR techniques have made in the federal government during the past decade can be tracked by the successive recommendations published by the Administrative Conference of the United States (ACUS)—in 1982, 1985, 1986, 1987, and 1988 (1 C.F.R. §§ 305.82–4, 85–5, 86–3, 86–8, 87–11, and 88–5). The first two recommendations (1982 and 1985) focus exclusively on negotiated rulemaking. In 1986, ACUS provided guidelines for agency use of a broad range of techniques, including voluntary and mandatory arbitration, settlement methods using mediation, mini-trials and negotiation, and other private sector dispute mechanisms. Recommendation 86–3 (1 C.F.R. § 305.86–3) contains these general intent sections:

> 1. Administrative agencies, where not inconsistent with statutory authority, should adopt the alternative methods discussed in this recommendation for resolving a broad range of issues. These include many matters that arise as a part of formal or informal adjudication, in rulemaking, in issuing or revoking permits, and in settling disputes, including litigation brought by or against the government. Until more experience has been developed with respect to their use in the administrative process, the procedures should generally be offered as a voluntary, alternative means to resolve the controversy.

> 2. Congress and the courts should not inhibit agency uses of the ADR techniques mentioned herein by requiring formality where it is inappropriate.

Then ACUS recommendation 87–11 (Alternatives for Resolving Government Contract Disputes) stated:

> Most knowledgeable government officials, contractors and attorneys agree that government contract appeals have become too onerous, too expensive and too time-consuming. * * *
>
> Several ADR methods are particularly appropriate to resolving many government contract claims, and a few agencies have begun to experiment successfully with them. The Conference urges all major contracting agencies and persons who deal with them, to explore seriously the potential uses for ADR and to begin creating an atmosphere in which these methods can be readily employed.

The recommendation continues by describing how to find neutrals, defining special methods of mediation, mini-trial, and settlement as they would apply to contract disputes; outlining the need for documentation and oversight; and providing some guides for training and outreach. Recommendation 88–5 (Agency Use of Settlement Judges) sets out procedures for appointing a settlement judge, conducting the negotiations, ensuring confidentiality, and reporting the results to the presiding judge (who must not serve as the settlement judge). ACUS is presently reviewing whether to develop a roster of neutrals for use by government agencies and, if so, what qualifications are appropriate and how should the roster be made available to both outside practitioners and government agencies (see supra p. 278, for a discussion of mediator credentials).

(2) Congress is presently considering legislation to define, encourage, and delimit the use of negotiation and mediation in the administrative rulemaking process. Several Senate subcommittees conducted hearings in late Spring 1988 on S. 1504 (introduced by Senators Grassley of Iowa and Levin of Michigan), which provides guidelines for the use of negotiated rulemaking procedures. These guidelines require an agency to determine first that a negotiated rule making committee is in the public interest. The elements of "public interest" are (1) a need for the rule, (2) "a limited number of identifiable interests that will be significantly affected," (3) "a reasonable likelihood that the rule can be developed by a negotiated rule making committee composed of persons who can adequately represent the interests identified," (4) a reasonable likelihood that the "committee will reach a consensus on the proposed rule within a fixed period of time," (5) no unreasonable delay caused by this procedure, (6) no unreasonable increase in agency expense, and (7) the consensus will be used as "the basis for the rule proposed by the agency for notice and comment." The agency can use a "convenor" to help identify the interests affected, who would represent each interest, and what issues are of concern.

According to the bill, after notice and time for comment, the agency may establish the committee and proceed toward consensus. The committee may appoint an impartial mediator to chair the meetings and assist in the deliberating. The mediator is chosen by committee consensus, although the agency has certain rights to nominate the first two potential mediators. The agency has the authority to terminate the committee at any time if it determines that the committee "is not making sufficient progress toward reaching a consensus," or if no further need exists. Finally, the bill requires ACUS to maintain "a roster of individuals who are qualified to act as convenors or mediators in negotiated rule making proceedings," but agencies would not be required to use names from this list exclusively.

(3) Rulemaking is not the only administrative function to which the "new technology" of negotiation and mediation is being applied; enforcement is another. Consent decrees and settlement agreements are two methods by which the government concludes litigation short of trial. Both methods can serve the public interest by maintaining community standards of safety, health, and welfare through early voluntary compliance rather than a lengthy court process. Yet, consent decrees present unique problems for public agencies: An agency may be forced to respond to a court's order to do certain political acts, such as devising regulations or requesting appropriations, which have been assigned by the Constitution to the discretion of the political branches, or its discretion to change regulations at some future date may be foreclosed unless a court agrees.

A 1986 memorandum by the Attorney General set out guidelines for agency action regarding consent decrees and settlement agreements. After discussing limits to agency use of consent decrees, the memorandum continued:

> Settlement agreements—similar in form to consent decrees, but not entered as an order of the court—remain a perfectly permissible device for the parties and should be strongly encouraged. [This memorandum], however, places some restrictions on the substantive provisions which may properly be included in settlement agreements. For example, Section II.B.1 [of this memorandum] allows a department or agency to agree in a settlement document to revise, amend, or promulgate new regulations, but only so long as the department or agency is not precluded from changing those regulations pursuant to the APA. Similarly, under Section II.B.2. the Secretary or agency administrator may agree to exercise his discretion in a particular manner, but may not divest himself entirely of the power to exercise that discretion as necessary in the future. The guidelines further provide that in certain circumstances where the agreement constrains agency discretion, a settlement agreement should specify that the only sanction for the government's failure to comply with a provision of a settlement agreement shall be the revival of the suit. Revival of the suit as the sole remedy removes the danger of a judicial order awarding damages or providing specific relief for breach of an undertaking in a settlement agreement.

Memorandum of Attorney General Meese, U.S. Dept. of Justice, March 13, 1986.

It is often suggested that the strength of ADR is in its flexibility and informality. Has the Attorney General's memorandum placed any substantial barriers in the way of federal attorneys or administrators who want to use ADR in resolving disputes? Does a settlement agreement concluded by an agency last year bind that agency's discretion this year? What if an intervening election places a new political party and administration in control? Should administrators be able to include provisions in a consent decree or settlement agreement providing relief which, if the case were fully litigated, the court could not otherwise order?

(4) There are few compensating rewards (in internal promotion, favorable recognition, or higher salary) for the administrator who wants to use new ADR techniques, and the political price the agency must pay can sometimes be high. Public reaction to proposed consent decrees or other settlements is frequently loud and critical, even though the administrators may believe they are properly balancing two competing public interests: the strict enforcement of important safety and health regulations versus early assured correction of currently dangerous but arguably lawful activity.

For example, the Federal Trade Commission and General Motors reached an agreement in 1983 by which certain consumer complaints against the company would be submitted to arbitration under Better Business Bureau auspices. See supra p. 432. Upon publishing the proposed settlement, the FTC received substantial mail from consumers, consumer advocacy groups, and others, much of it strongly critical of the proposal. FTC Commissioner Douglas, in a separate opinion, stated the case for the Commission approving this settlement:

* * * Virtually by definition, a negotiated settlement cannot fulfill all of the demands of either party. Also to be considered is the innovative nature of the agreement: The Commission, in lieu of pursuing protracted and risky litigation, has embarked upon what it believes to be a highly promising but admittedly somewhat novel means of effectuating prompt consumer redress. * * *

The critics of the settlement would apparently prefer the Commission had taken this case to court in an attempt to make all injured consumers in this matter whole once again. What they have failed to point out is that this is much easier said than done. Due to the way that Congress has delegated authority to the Commission to enforce the consumer protection laws, the Commission would have had to file *two successive* suits against GM and win each (as well as all of the inevitable appeals) before any money could be reimbursed to consumers.

* * *

Only if the Commission could prove that GM had acted dishonestly and fraudulently with respect to each component, and only after GM had exhausted all appeals, would consumers be eligible for redress. A reasonable estimate of the length of time involved would be eight to ten years; that is, as late as 1993. How many injured consumers might be expected to be around and to possess sufficient evidence to collect that redress in ten years? Many consumers suffered losses on the order of $400 as early as 1976 and few would have had the foresight to retain the records necessary to document their claims. How many of those people would feel that justice had been served by a payment of $400 in *1993* dollars— assuming that the courts found them to be entitled to anything at all? * * *

Clearly, if we were to pursue such a course, the only sure winners would be the army of lawyers who would be employed to litigate this matter for the next eight to ten years.

In the Matter of General Motors, 102 F.T.C. 1741, 1746–48 (1983).

As another example, the U.S. Department of Justice and several manufacturers of all-terrain vehicles (ATVs) signed a consent decree in 1987, concluding litigation in which the Government had accused the ATV industry of selling a product that was causing substantial injury to consumers. At the federal district court hearing on the question of whether to accept the consent decree, members of Congress, state attorneys general, and representatives of consumer and medical groups complained bitterly that the proposed consent decree was inadequate in dealing with safety and fairness problems and that its approval would result in more serious injuries and deaths. Government and industry representatives, clearly in a defensive posture, claimed that, although imperfect, the proposed settlement would improve safety conditions immediately, require an industry commitment to a constructive safety education program, and be better for the public than a long and expensive lawsuit with an uncertain outcome. After asking for and receiving more information from the parties, the federal judge approved the settlement on April 28, 1988, as fair, reasonable, and in the public interest.

(5) Technical and scientific complexities in many areas of regulation often make it difficult to determine violations or the degree of compliance, much less prove them in court. Allocating liability for cleaning up a toxic waste site that has been forty years in the building may require substantial investigation and careful analysis of complex historical data, much of it hotly disputed by the interested parties. The government and other innocent parties may want the desired action sooner rather than later.

The EPA has encouraged the use of negotiation and mediation techniques to resolve liability and allocation problems among the interested parties in Superfund site cleanup operations. See 1 C.F.R. § 305.84–4, Negotiated Cleanup of Hazardous Waste Sites Under CERCLA [Comprehensive Environmental Response, Compensation and Liability Act, or Superfund]. A steering committee process has become a principal method to structure the parties' actions. A steering committee is chosen by and represents the entire group of potentially responsible parties [PRPs] involved with a particular cleanup site.

The principal function of the steering committee is to negotiate a tentative settlement agreement with the agencies on behalf of the PRPs. Upon completion of the negotiations, the committee submits a tentative settlement to all PRPs for approval. The committee also deals with allocating settlement costs among the PRPs. Ancillary functions consist of serving as a conduit for information between the agencies and the PRPs, and gathering and sometimes generating technical and factual information about the site. The steering committee also plays a role in carrying out a settlement once one has been achieved. Carrying out the settlement may involve only the collection of money, or, in the case of a PRP-conducted remedial investigation or cleanup, it may require oversight of the investigation or the cleanup process itself.

* * *

Steering committees emerged as a practical response to agencies's needs to administer certain aspects of CERCLA. The law permits EPA to clean up hazardous waste sites and seek reimbursement from responsible parties of expenditures from the Superfund. CERCLA also authorizes EPA, in appropriate cases, to order responsible parties to undertake cleanups themselves. State agencies have similar obligations and duties under both CERCLA and analogous state laws. Obviously, both tasks—reimbursement and agency-ordered private action—require negotiations. Unless the agencies can achieve most of their cleanups and reimbursements through out-of-court settlements, they will be faced with a daunting and unmanageable litigation docket. However, in situations with multiple PRPs the agencies are beset with the practical problem of deciding with whom they should negotiate. Clearly, if the agencies were to negotiate separately with each individual PRP, the large number of parties involved would prevent the agencies from carrying out negotiations. Indeed, such negotiations might be even more daunting than litigation. On the other hand, if the agencies were to attempt to negotiate with only some of the PRPs on an individual basis, ignoring the remainder, questions would arise over the criteria the agencies used in choosing the "victims." Those criteria would be difficult to construct and even more difficult to apply. The procedure the EPA advanced to solve the problem was to negotiate with none of the PRPs individually, but instead to negotiate with steering committees which, while limited in size, would speak for all or most PRPs.

Moorman, The Superfund Steering Committee: A Primer, The Environmental Forum 13–14 (February 1986).

The biggest task of the steering committee is to develop a consensus among all parties on the questions of liability for and allocation of the cost of cleanup. Can you list the negotiation and mediation techniques which the agency or the PRPs might use to serve these objectives?

(6) The interaction between a steering committee and the EPA (or other government agency enforcing the law) presents an interesting dilemma for traditional regulatory theory:

> One oddity of the steering committees is that they derive their strength not from the PRP companies, but rather from the agencies. Only to the extent the agencies give the committees respect, do they have respect. If an agency takes actions that undermine or hinder a committee, the committee will become ineffective or even collapse.

> * * * Thus, the odd reality is that the agencies must foster their adversaries, the committees, and must aid them in accomplishing their tasks. Failure to foster the committee's work only impedes settlements. Tough, adversarial tactics by an agency against a committee simply cause the committee to stall.

> * * *

> CERCLA settlements depend on the steering committee. The lynch pin of the agencies' settlement program is the effectiveness of the committees. Indeed, to the extent that the success of CERCLA depends on achieving settlements, then the success of CERCLA depends on the effectiveness of the committees.

> Agency officials complain that PRPs do not undertake enough volunteer settlements. They make these complaints, however, with apparent forgetfulness that the steering committees must arrange for the cleanups. Cleanup is a complicated task that requires a great deal of cooperation from the agencies. Without incentives for doing the cleanups themselves and without much encouragement and cooperation, the committees quickly conclude that the path of least resistance is to forego direct cleanup and to arrange a reimbursement settlement instead. If the agencies want more PRP cleanups, they must do more to help the committees accomplish this aim.

Moorman, id. at 19–20.

Why should the EPA—or the public—prefer the responsible parties to participate directly in the cleanup, rather than merely to reimburse the Superfund for cleanup services done by others? What is the EPA's primary goal? How should the EPA interact with steering committees?

(7) By order dated April 15, 1987, the United States Claims Court implemented two ADR techniques as new operating procedures: the settlement judge and the mini-trial procedure. According to the order, both techniques are "voluntary and flexible, and should be employed early in the litigation process in order to minimize discovery." The parties must agree jointly to use the procedures, which are probably most appropriate "where the parties anticipate a lengthy discovery period followed by a protracted trial. These requirements typically will

be met where the amount in controversy is greater than $100,000 and trial is expected to last more than one week." Notice to Counsel, General Order No. 13, U.S. Claims Court (April 15, 1987), reprinted in Administrative Conference of the U.S., Sourcebook: Federal Agency Use of Alternative Means of Dispute Resolution 732 (1987).

––––––––––

ADR and the Freedom of Information Act

An area of increasing litigation in recent years is requests for access to information held by a public agency (usually the FBI or the CIA) under provisions of the Freedom of Information Act. New case filings in federal district court have been averaging over 500 per year, with only about 2% reaching trial. The vast majority are either settled (usually before the pre-trial conference) or terminated on motion for summary judgment.[1]

Scott Armstrong, co-author of *The Brethren* and Executive Director of the National Security Archive, cites two examples of problems faced by those who request information through FOIA procedures.

> Last month, my friend and former colleague from the Washington Post, Chuck Babcock, called me with the happy news that the CIA had granted him 3,200 pages of material on Richard Helms' involvement in the ITT/Chile case, cleared for release only 8 years, 5 months, and 6 days after he requested a small portion of very specific documents relating to that case.
>
> Since the agency is demanding fees from Mr. Babcock which he is considering but has not yet decided to appeal on behalf of the Washington Post, he does not yet know what earth-shaking stories might be still awaiting after 8 years, 5 months, and 6 days.
>
> Examples like this are myriad. Ourselves, at the National Security Archive, thought we had circumvented many of the problems of procedural processing within the State Department by identifying materials using the subject matter tags that the Department itself uses to identify them.
>
> After they turned down our initial request, we appealed indicating again that these materials could not be better identified, were retrievable by computer. They turned down our appeal and we took the Department to court.
>
> Now 1 year after filing the requests, the negotiations are beginning to bear some fruit, and I understand the Department is now willing to process the request as originally filed.
>
> If we are lucky, we will have our materials in another 15 to 20 months. Although my counsel insists that I am not at liberty to discuss the details of the negotiations, I should note that these

––––––––––

1. Grunewald, Administrative Mechanisms for Resolving Freedom of Information Act Disputes 8–17 (Final Report to Admin.Conf. of U.S., 1986).

negotiations have been particularly time consuming primarily because of the Department of State's intransigence and the failure of the Department of Justice simply to say that it will not defend such a blatant abuse of FOIA discretion.[2]

In December 1986, the Administrative Conference of the U.S. published a study of FOIA appeals which proposed two possible reforms: a new administrative tribunal to hear and decide FOIA cases (with limited judicial review), and an FOIA ombudsman to receive and investigate complaints and issue non-binding reports. Congress has begun hearings on the two proposals. As might be expected, the tribunal has drawn the most heated criticism. Critics agree on the basic reasons for opposition—as stated in the words of Professor Grunewald:

> There was virtual unanimity in the view that judicial enforcement has been critical in the development of Federal access policy. The courts are seen as having molded, in the face of agency resistance, a vague and far-reaching statute into a generally manageable set of substantive and procedural rules for access. Equally important, the courts are unquestionably perceived as a force of independence in the disposition of FOIA cases.[3]

Allan Adler, Legislative Counsel for the American Civil Liberties Union, stated in the same congressional hearings that

> I think it is fair to say the ACLU remains skeptical of the wisdom and viability of establishing an administrative tribunal as an alternative to de novo judicial review. * * *
>
> I think the reason that Congress decided correctly that the Federal courts should play the primary role in FOIA dispute resolution was the recognition that regardless of what the particular administration's policies of the moment were, there would be an institutional resistance by the executive branch that would require a coequal branch of the Government standing on its own solid constitutional footing to be able to enforce the law according to the dictates of Congress.[4]

Judge Posner expressed frustration in handling FOIA disputes in Savage v. Central Intelligence Agency, 826 F.2d 561 (7th Cir.1987), an appeal by a prison inmate from an administrative denial of a waiver of duplicating fees:

> We cannot forbear to express concern about the waste of judicial resources that is involved in allowing a person to obtain two levels of federal judicial review of an agency's denial of a claim for $39.20. Of course, every person—even the humblest—even a prison inmate—should have a remedy of some kind against the arbitrary denial of his legal rights. But surely there is a better

---

2. Hearings before House Subcom. on Gov't Operations, FOIA: Alternative Dispute Resolution Proposals, Statement of S. Armstrong, p. 163–64 (Dec. 2, 1987).

3. Id., Statement by M. Grunewald, p. 5 (Dec. 1, 1987).

4. Id., Statement of A. Adler, pp. 75–76 (Dec. 1, 1987).

way—having due regard for the rise in federal judicial caseloads, the limited capacity of the federal judiciary, and the costs imposed on litigants whose equally weighty or weightier concerns are pushed farther back in the queue—to provide such a remedy in a $39.20 case than by giving the claimant the full run of the Article III courts. Could not claims for waiver of duplicating fees under the Freedom of Information Act, which usually are tiny, be subjected (if below some dollar threshold) to informal but binding arbitration, without judicial review, given that many labor disputes—technically "minor disputes" but often involving substantial stakes—are subject to compulsory arbitration under the Railway Labor Act with virtually no judicial review? Or to final resolution by an informal appellate board within the agency requested to waive? * * *

As we have done previously in suggesting the Congress consider the establishment of a small-claims procedure, arbitral or administrative, for claims under the Federal Tort Claims Act, so we now suggest that Congress consider the establishment of such a procedure for fee-waiver requests under the Freedom of Information Act. These requests do not have the kind of symbolic resonance that requires the Article III judiciary to be empowered to review the denial of them. * * * No rational system of government burdens its highest courts with a class of litigation dominated by petty cases typically brought for their nuisance value by persons on whose hands time hangs heavy. Not even the cause of prisoner's rights is helped by a flood of trivial suits that distracts judicial attention from the occasional meritorious one.

There has been general support for the proposal to create an information access ombudsman. The ombudsman concept is of course premised on the recognition of the need for "new protections against bureaucratic bungling and abuses of power."[5] In the early 1980's, Australia, New Zealand, and Canada adopted ombudsman offices specifically for access to information disputes. The ombudsman office proposed by the ACUS study is very similar in its basic outline. Experience in the three Commonwealth countries has shown that informal conciliation procedures used by the ombudsman (or "information minister") are the most effective means of resolving disputes. Some experts have suggested that the effectiveness of an FOIA ombudsman office would be severely limited if it is attached to the Department of Justice, as originally designed in the ACUS study. Ombudsman offices within state and local governments and foreign nations have traditionally been supervised by the legislature, giving them an independence from the executive and a visibility essential to success in resolving citizen disputes with government bureaucracy.

5. D. Rowat, The Ombudsman Plan: The Worldwide Spread of An Idea v (Rev. 2d ed. 1985).

B. THE LEGISLATIVE PROCESS

Congress and state legislatures now share a prominent role in shaping the legal norms with which the lawyer works, but this was not always the case. Before 1900 the Anglo–American common law process—the judicial system—was the primary source for the standards used to resolve private disputes. But since the turn of the century, Congress and the legislatures have been increasingly called upon to create complex legal structures for both private and public conduct. Some examples include, in private law, antitrust legislation, securities regulations, labor-management relations, landlord-tenant laws, the Uniform Commercial Code, and occupational safety and health laws; in public law, the income tax code, clean air/water pollution control regulation, nuclear/toxic waste management, fair housing codes, and equal employment opportunity laws. The lawyer usually takes these laws as she finds them, interpreting them in the light most favorable to her client's interests. But in some cases it is impossible to develop an interpretation that is both consistent with precedent and satisfactory for the client's interests. The lawyer will then look elsewhere to alter the legal norms that apply.

It is natural for lawyers to use the litigation process regularly to try to change these norms or their interpretation. Success in litigation—having the court reinterpret the law or hold it unconstitutional—has major benefits for the lawyer and her client: The change attaches to the client's existing dispute, it takes effect for others immediately (unless the decree establishes a different timetable), and the lawyer's reputation gets a credible boost among her peers.

Another method of changing legal norms, however, is through the legislative process—the subject of this section. Lawyers have generally regarded the legislature as a "non-legal" forum, and the legislative process as dominated by "politics," thereby presenting an unfriendly environment for someone trained in legal analysis and experienced in the judicial system. The following materials are intended to change that image: The legislative process can be a productive and accessible process for the lawyer in helping her clients.

1. The Process

For lawyers, there is a close relationship between the administrative and legislative processes. The following excerpt is from a letter sent by a large Washington law firm to prospective clients; it describes the relationship more graphically than any descriptive paragraph could:

> Cadwalader [Cadwalader, Wickersham & Taft] has five partners and one counsel in its Washington office who have held senior positions in the Treasury or the Internal Revenue Service. Consequently, we have an extraordinarily effective legislative tax prac-

tice. We have direct access to members of congressional writing committees and members of their staffs, as well as direct access to senior officials in the Treasury and at the Internal Revenue Service. Moreover, since Cadwalader is a transaction-oriented firm, we bring a competency in technical areas of tax law which no pure lobbyist can possess.

* * *

Cadwalader provides more than pure access to important members of the tax-writing committees—we have such access to many members, but access alone is not our stock in trade. Rather, our principal value is that whether we are dealing with members of Congress, key staff personnel or officials at the Treasury Department or the IRS, we are working with individuals who know us from prior experience (often when we were with government), and with whom we share a bond of trust.[1]

There is little question in the minds of the lawyers who wrote that letter that experience in the administrative process serves the private lawyer well in the legislative, and vice versa. The writers also assumed that public officials in the two branches, although separated by constitutional mission and physical location, work closely together in the regular course of government business. And for special subject matters (such as tax law), these public officials and the private lawyers who handle client interests in that area have a close working relationship on issues of mutual concern. Although some private lawyers specialize in only one process, most choose to represent clients in one or more related subject matter fields in both the administrative and legislative forums. Thus, the first section of Chapter VI, on the administrative process, serves as an introduction to the second section.

The heart of the legislative process is most often described as the creation of laws by Congress or a state legislature: the introduction of a bill by a member of either the House of Representatives or the Senate; assignment by leadership to the appropriate committee covering that subject matter; subcommittee and committee hearings and mark-up; the report of the approved draft to the full house for debate, amendment, and passage; similar consideration in the other house, from subcommittee hearings through floor action; joint discussion in conference committee to work out differences, if any, in the versions passed by the two houses; and transmission of the final bill to the executive for signature or veto. This is the "textbook" process by which Congress or a legislature takes formal action to establish or change legal norms:

> [K]eep in mind that the manner in which our governments make law is itself governed by law. The legitimacy of government—its composition, selection, and procedures—occupies a large part of the federal and state constitutions and, in the case of local governments, is grounded in statutes and charters. Laws govern

1. Washington Post, May 27, 1988, pp. 1, A14.

even lawmaking by the people themselves. Some of these laws define the legitimacy of lawmaking institutions, for example, the number of their members, their qualifications, their election, the length of their term in office. Others define the prerequisites of lawmaking procedure; for instance, the central concept of enactment by a majority of a legal quorum, or sometimes a larger number; passage of the same text by two separate houses; the assent of an independent executive or reenactment after consideration of his objections. What is not fixed in constitutions and statutes is often spelled out in the rules of the lawmaking body itself. Bribery, the classic threat to the integrity of government, is universally outlawed by statute or constitution. The Court has spoken of the *"due"* functioning of the legislative process under the speech and debate clause.

Two things are striking about this body of rules for the lawmaking process. One is that over the years its successive authors have measured the process, explicitly or implicitly, by the standard of its legitimacy—the basic constitutional standard of democratic accountability or, if you will, of a republican form of government. That is not a universal practice in the world. The architects of our system have identified what from time to time they have perceived as prerequisites of legitimate lawmaking and as threats to its achievement, they have debated alternative solutions both in institutional and in procedural forms, and they have known how to state these solutions with considerable precision and detail. The second striking thing is that these rules of the lawmaking process, with some exceptions, are followed as a matter of course, unquestioningly, not with a constant weighing of possible sanctions for their violation. We would not say this with equal confidence about daily practice in the processes of criminal and administrative law. In short, due process in lawmaking in many, if not all, respects is a very concrete, well understood set of institutional procedures.[2]

The "textbook" description, however, provides only the foundation for the lawyer's understanding of the impact and potential of the legislative process. Although attention is usually focused on how a bill *becomes* a law, the lawyer's client often wants to *stop* a bill from being passed. The lawyer's efforts then are focused on fortifying the resistance points in the process. Lobbyists generally agree that it is many times easier to "kill" a bill than to pass one.

In addition to the formal ways of taking action, the legislative process includes a host of informal mechanisms for influencing public and private conduct. Of this list, the public hearing is probably the most important. For example, the 1986 congressional hearings on the Iranian arms-for-hostages scandal, featuring White House staff mem-

2. Linde, Due Process of Lawmaking, 55 Neb.L.Rev. 197, 240–41 (1976).

bers (most notably, Marine Colonel Oliver North) and private defense contractors, helped shape American foreign policy in the Middle East and Central America, altered the domestic political power balance, and struck a note of fear in many administrative offices with respect to the taking of initiatives.

Moreover, the press and electronic media give congressional and state legislative hearings a visibility that can be frightening to those public officials or private business executives who are used to operating in relative secrecy. Hearings, therefore, provide a forum for legislative oversight of administrative rulemaking and for more informal supervision of public and private conduct. See, for example, the discussion of the House subcommittee hearings on FOIA procedures, supra p. 699. There is probably no way to measure the effect that the need to defend one's conduct before a congressional committee has on the plans and actions of public administrators or private parties, but logic suggests that the influence can be substantial.

Lawyers and Lawmaking

Lawyers play as prominent a role in the legislative as they do in the administrative process. They usually make up the largest single occupational group among legislators—in the mid-1980's, 60% of the U.S. Senate and 40% of the House of Representatives were lawyers (the percentages are somewhat lower in state legislatures). They also serve as legislative and administrative aides to legislators, committee staff members, legislative research and drafting assistants, and lobbyists for private interests. In short, lawyers form a large part of the personnel pool for the legislative process, and the "revolving door" factor (see supra p. 676) adds a dynamic quality to this talent pool.

As the Cadwalader letter suggested, for example, outside law firms are competing seriously for clients who want substantive expertise and lobbying access, especially in the tax law field. Congress has been spending more time recently on tax legislation—passing nine major bills during the period 1975–87—and this expanded legislative activity has increased the demand for legal talent both inside and outside government. The effect in the tax law field is undoubtedly replicated in most other areas in which government is a primary actor.

HAAS, CHANGING PARTNERS
National Journal 1684–88 (June 25, 1988).

The Internal Revenue Service (IRS), relying on its interpretation of the 1986 Tax Reform Act and prior law, announced in January 1987 that under some circumstances, it could tax all deferred compensation, such as vacation time, earned by employees of states, localities and tax-exempt organizations.

Affected interests moved quickly. Representatives of cities, municipal officials, labor unions, hospitals and other institutions met, formed two coalitions and began pursuing legislative changes last year to block the agency's plans.

* * *

* * * [F]ormer congressional and Treasury Department staff members who played key roles in drafting the 1986 tax bill now work as lobbyists for clients who are seeking to change the new law or are trying to hold on to benefits they have won under the statute.

* * *

Whether such former aides are necessarily more effective lobbyists than others is open to question. Certainly, former government colleagues return their telephone calls faster than those of other lobbyists, if only because their names on pink phone slips are familiar. Drop-in visits by former aides are also perhaps more easily accommodated.

But, particularly if former aides are relying on the merits of arguments rather than the pure muscle of campaign dollars, they don't have much edge over others. Current staff assistants are still beholden to their bosses—the Members—and Members remain tied to back-home concerns. Thus, it's the former aides who learned about those concerns while working for Congress who can tap them for effective lobbying.

* * *

Realistically, then, no aide leaves Capitol Hill with a monopoly on knowledge or authorship of a particular provision. If aides return as lobbyists seeking changes in provisions that they helped write, they will have to convince others who participated in the drafting that the provisions weren't done right the first time. And if the ex-staff members' arguments are made on behalf of clients, they will be taken with the same grain of salt as those of any other lobbyists.

Still, on some technical issues that aren't politically charged, tax-writing staffs enjoy enormous power. Aides may be told to implement a policy and then be left largely alone, with wide leeway on how to do it. The more sweeping a tax bill is (and the 1986 Tax Reform Act was the most sweeping in decades), the more latitude is given to aides.

Disagreements arise later about what aides actually tried to do. A former aide, lobbying for a clarification of the intent of a pension-related provision enacted in 1986, said that among the several aides asked, no consensus had formed. In such a case, a former aide's own memory of the 1986 drafting sessions could give him or her a step up over other lobbyists working for tax changes.

In fact, current aides sometimes call their former colleagues who are now lobbyists, asking them to recall how a drafting decision was made in 1986 and what was intended. Because many decisions were made in late-night sessions, with paper to record the decisions in short supply, often the best guide to decision making is the memory of aides.

At that point, former aides who now lobby raise the issue of perception: Should these key individuals, who held such important tax-writing posts, come back to lobby for legislative changes? Can the public trust the remaining staff members, with whom the lobbyists once worked, not to sneak language into law that benefits ex-staff members' clients?

*   *   *

At the very least, consistency [in lobbying rules] might help. The House doesn't restrict former staff members from lobbying Capitol Hill. Because employees of the Joint Taxation Committee are on the House payroll, its ex-staff members aren't restricted either. In the Senate, the one-year rule bars former committee aides from lobbying that committee's members and staff; an ex-tax aide to any Senator may not lobby the Senator or the Senator's personal staff.

Notes and Questions

(1) What makes the lobbying activity of a former legislative aide improper would appear to be the existence of undue influence, based on personal relationships the former aide established while on the public payroll. Does the Senate's one-year prohibition against lobbying the former aide's committee or Senator's staff address this reason? On Oct. 21, 1988, Congress approved a more uniform lobbying restriction package for both executive and legislative officials. The Post-Employment Restrictions Act of 1988 prohibits members of Congress, their top aides, and committee staffers from lobbying certain individuals and agencies for one year after leaving office.

(2) Clients may ask former legislative aides to lobby against provisions which they not only helped write into current law but which they continue to support personally. This obviously raises a problem of credibility: A former aide who had a reputation for being strongly against a particular tax deduction while serving on the staff of the Joint Taxation Committee may well have difficulty convincing his former colleagues with arguments to the contrary. Does it raise any ethical issues?

LINDE, DUE PROCESS OF LAWMAKING

55 Neb.L.Rev. 197, 220–23 (1976).

[T]he test [for due process of law in legislation] depends on attributing a purpose to the lawmakers; but laws are often an accommodation of several unrelated purposes. Commonly, a law will push toward a goal only within the limits of objectives that may or may not be apparent in retrospect. Legislative declarations and legislative history cannot be relied on to reflect the actual balance of considerations that shaped the law, and often no such records are available. Although proponents might have wished for more and opponents for less, all that is certain about the law as a means to an end is that a majority could be found to undertake what the law in fact undertakes, no more, no less. That much is its immediate goal.

*   *   *

Many of our laws simply reflect old notions of right and wrong, or sympathy toward the equity of some particular claim to legislative consideration, without intending to achieve any pragmatic aim. Such a law may be unconstitutional if it pursues a goal that the Constitution forbids, but not because the values it reflects are merely sentimental, or parochial, or old-fashioned, or foolish, rather than goal-oriented.

Even a law originally enacted to serve one pragmatic end, such as health or safety, will remain on the books as long as other vested interests that have grown up around the law retain legislative sympathy. Building codes once written to assure safe standards of materials and construction survive technological changes because they protect existing sources of materials and employment. * * * Delay in changing old laws for such reasons may stand in the way of progress, but it cannot be called an irrational means toward the ends served by legislative inaction. So far as I know, neither does the due process clause deny our political process such policy choices as, for instance, to sacrifice economic efficiency in order to preserve the livelihood of bricklayers, or independent druggists, or dairy farmers. In any event, the ostensible issue of rational means turns once again into an issue of the legitimacy of ends.

Finally, judicial review of rationality is irretrievably ambivalent about time—whether to match past facts to past purposes, or present facts to past purposes, or present facts to present purposes—because it is ambivalent about its premise, whether it means to review the one-time reasonableness of lawmakers or the continuing reasonableness of laws.

* * *

What, then, does the formula demand of lawmakers? * * * It looks something like this: A rational policy must be one that is designed to move events toward some goal. At a minimum, therefore, it requires three elements: some knowledge of present conditions; the identification of a preferred future, or a goal; and a belief that the proposed action will contribute to achieving the desired goal, a belief that is sometimes called the instrumental hypothesis. Of these elements, the decision on the goal is plainly a value judgment; knowledge of the present situation and the instrumental hypothesis each involve judgments about facts, about cause and effect.

The choice of action, however, involves elements beyond these three. If you know where you are and where you wish to go, there remains the choice between getting there quickly by car or more cheaply on foot. This is again a choice between different values, even when we assign some common denominator to the values of time, of your need for exercise and fear of being mugged, and of exposing yourself to polluted air when walking and your qualms about adding to pollution by driving. If rationality requires you to compute these elements, you are likely to stay where you are, and so is a legislature. Finally, there is the political element. If another member of the family wants to use the car, is an argument worth the strain on other goals that you seek in your relationship? When a policy is to be made, not by one decisionmaker, but collectively over a period of time, by an assembly of equals with different views of both ends and means, the ranking and accommodation of competing priorities become the most decisive element of all.

STEWART, FORWARD: LAWYERS AND THE LEGISLATIVE PROCESS
10 Harv. J. on Legislation 151, 152–58 (1973).

A statute does not spring full blown from the legislature, but the lawyer often acts as if it had. In contrast to judge-made law, where the origins and development of a rule elicit close attention, statutory law is typically taken as a "given," with scant professional concern for the social, economic, and political soil out of which the statute grew or the parliamentary procedures and strategic compromises which shaped its content. The lawyer's concern is generally fixed on the statute's implementation by administrators and courts, and any quarrying he may undertake in the legislative history is usually limited to a search for quotations that can be used as ammunition in the battle of statutory interpretation.

The lawyer's lack of concern with the legislative process and the interplay of that process with the substance of legislation is reflected in the legal literature. Although there are a number of periodic surveys of legislative output, normally limited to a particular jurisdiction or subject matter, they usually contain only brief summaries of the substantive changes that have been accomplished in the law. Here, as elsewhere in the literature, the processes that produced the statute are generally ignored; to the extent that such processes are considered at all, it is usually from a judicial perspective, most commonly in the context of statutory interpretation or judicial control of legislative procedure. While there are exceptions in the legal literature to this indictment, the general record of professional concern with this subject is meagre, particularly in comparison to the quantity and quality of legal scholarship that has been devoted to lawmaking by appellate courts or administrative agencies.

This lack of expressed interest on the part of lawyers in the legislative process is surprising when we consider not only the importance of statutory law today, but also the fact that lawyers have long been major participants in that process. In recent years well over half of all United States Senators and Representatives have been lawyers, and while the percentage in state legislatures is lower, it is still considerable. Moreover, lawyers are prominent in a variety of legislative roles other than that of legislator. In Congress lawyers man technical facilities, such as the legislative drafting service, and serve as professional staff for committees, the leadership, or individual congressmen. In addition, they play important roles in the legislative process as lobbyists or counsel for both governmental and private clients.

In light of this manifold involvement in the legislative process, the bar has been surprisingly reticent both about its activities and its professional responsibilities in this area. Even at the level of biographical accounts of the lawyer's role in the legislative process, there is little to be found.

There is also little published on the extent of the bar's professional responsibilities in the legislative arena. At one level, there are important unresolved issues concerning the ethical limits of legislative advocacy. Is it proper for a lawyer to engage in the "manufacture" of legislative history, and, if so, what are the proper limits of the practice? May a lawyer-lobbyist devote himself to advancing his clients' interests with the same whole-hearted zeal he may assume in the context of adversary litigation, or must he also take account of larger and potentially conflicting obligations to the public interest, however defined? Charles Horsky attempted to raise some of these issues,[14] but elsewhere in the legal literature such questions are normally passed over, if they are recognized at all. The Canons of Ethics and the new Code of Professional Responsibility provide little illumination on such questions.

In addition there are larger issues of the profession's responsibilities as a body. First, there is the question of expanding the provision of legal representation to various interests affected by the legislative process. Are interest groups which can afford to hire lawyer-lobbyists significantly advantaged in the legislative struggle compared to those that cannot? If so, is the bar under an obligation, similar to that it has accepted in criminal proceedings and has begun to recognize in civil proceedings in courts and before administrative agencies, to provide such representation to all? How should any such obligation be discharged? Second, does the bar have an obligation to improve the quality of statutory law from the perspective of society as a whole? The efforts of the American Law Institute, the American Bar Association, and other law-reform agencies in drafting and advocating legislation appear to presuppose such an obligation, although such efforts have sometimes been attacked as covert promotions of clients' interests. Third, there is the related matter of the bar's responsibility in improving the legislature as an institution. While the bar investigates and proposes reforms of almost every conceivable aspect of the workings of courts and agencies, there is scarcely any organized professional study of or concern with the functioning and possible improvement of the legislature.

14. C. Horsky, The Washington Lawyer 34–58 (1952). See also J. Goulden, The Superlawyers (1972); Inside Washington Law: The Roles and Responsibilities of the Washington Lawyer, 38 Geo.Wash.L.Rev. 527 (1970).

The bar's responsibilities in these areas are rooted in the on-going and substantial involvement in the legislative process of lawyers acting in various professional capacities. This involvement implies a correlative duty to ensure that the process is equitable and yields sound results from the viewpoint of society as a whole. Moreover, lawyers have a responsibility to the sound working of the legal order as a whole, and it is myopic to suppose this goal can be achieved by focusing on the functioning of courts or agencies alone and in isolation, when all parts of the legal order, including the legislature, act in dynamic interdependence.

Why has the bar failed substantially to examine the legislative process and its involvement and responsibilities in that process? Half a century ago an explanation might have been found in the mystique of the common law as proclaimed by Langdell, Carter, and others who saw judge-made law as the fittest evolution of social standards, tailored interstitially to the conditions of the times. Landis tellingly satirized the reverence which the law schools and the profession had for the common law as against legislation:

> . . . . For the common law [lawyers] have untold respect; it is of their making. Its "perfection of human reason," as Lord Coke stated the case, makes the lawyer proud of his heritage, and the layman fearful to intrude. Contrast with this the statute, appearing merely as the voice of a majority, and seemingly only as durable as that majority. It simply states its commands and pleads no reasons for its cause. No precedents patently restrain the legislature; it does what it pleases. And what it pleases, means to the true common law lawyer, what the butcher, the baker and the candlestick maker pleases—a laying on of profane hands upon the law. What respect can attach to this process? What principles underlie these sporadic and vacillating commands? [24]

Deflating analyses by the legal realists of judge-made law and recognition of the growing importance of statute law have since undermined the exaggerated pretensions of the common law. Yet allegiance to judge-made rules as the archetype of law lingers on, reflecting the continued emphasis on judicial decisions in legal education and the fact that most lawyers are predominantly concerned in their day-to-day work as litigators or counsellors with influencing or predicting court decisions. Only a comparatively small proportion of the total profession is involved in the legislative process on a regular basis. From the perspective of most practicing lawyers there is thus a good deal of common sense appeal in John Chipman Gray's notion that statutes are only "sources of law" and that operative significance is given to law only in the decisions of courts.

24. Landis, The Study of Legislation in Law Schools, An Imaginary Inaugural Lecture, 39 Harv.Graduates' Mag. 433 (1931).

However, lawyers may often neglect valuable opportunities to advance clients' interests through the legislative process, in large part because they have not been trained to be effective participants in it. If so, the law schools must bear a considerable measure of responsibility, for they have largely neglected the training of lawyers in legislative roles.

This neglect may account in part for the attitude that lobbying is a somewhat disreputable activity for a lawyer, or that the legislative process does not call upon the distinctive intellectual skills of the profession. This latter attitude is illustrated by an exchange occurring some years ago between two senators, both lawyers. Senator Reed, who had but recently joined the Senate from law practice, had engaged the veteran Senator Norris over a question of law:

Senator Reed: "How long has the gentleman been in Congress?"

Senator Norris: "Twenty-nine years."

Senator Reed: "It is too much to expect a senator to remain a lawyer after all that time."

Such attitudes may explain in part why the legal literature contains so little about the legislative process and lawyers' involvement in it, but the difficulties of the subject are also a factor. Contrast, for example, the analysis of a statute with that of a court decision. A judicial opinion will contain within itself the controlling facts, the pertinent background, the surrounding state of the law, and the reasoning behind the result. A statute, on the other hand, contains little or nothing about the problem it was designed to solve or the pertinent facts. The complex process by which the particular provisions in question came to be law remain hidden behind the general words of the enacting clause. These facts can be ascertained, if at all, only by protracted labor in the legislative history. Many of the most important aspects of a statute's history, including the private initiatives for its enactment, the reactions of antagonistic interest groups, and the compromise negotiations which occurred, rarely appear in any printed record. These difficulties are obviously multiplied when we pass from the enactment of a particular statute to a consideration of the legislative process as a whole.

Notes and Questions

(1) A common task for lawyers is to pull together from existing sources (committee reports, statements on the floor, amendments offered and passed—or defeated) a legislative history for statutes that may be ambiguous on their face. Given Linde's view of the rationality of legislative purposes, is the lawyer's work in shaping legislative history a matter of legal analysis or creative reasoning?

(2) Linde mentions the important value judgments that are a natural part of the legislative process. This policy-making function is the operational step that separates the legislative from the judicial

process. In their study of the influence of Washington lawyers (see supra p. 676), Nelson and Heinz found that lawyers did not play a substantial role in developing policy:

> * * * The visibility of such lawyers as Dean Acheson, Abe Fortas, and Clark Clifford has fostered an image of the Washington lawyer as a generalist power broker who combines legal expertise with political connections and thus plays a central role in policy making. This image is not an accurate depiction now, and we doubt that it ever was. Although a handful of Washington lawyers are power brokers, for the most part they are legal technicians. Their monopoly of litigation and their specialization in the arcane procedures of particular regulatory agencies give them an important—but not the central—position in the market for Washington representation.
>
> * * *
>
> The dramatic growth in Washington law practice is evidence of the strength of demand for such legal expertise, but our data make it clear that this demand is limited to a relatively narrow range of issues and functions. Lawyers are especially expert in the manipulation of formal rules, both substantive and procedural. Their competitive advantage, compared to other representatives, increases with the level of formality of the decision-making process. If this is so, the importance of the role of lawyers in policy representation is likely to be greater if policy is made through formal procedures and the application of formal rules than if it results from more informal, less rule-bound processes.
>
> * * * Most of the policy decisions made in Washington are not dictated by preexisting rules, nor do they even depend upon the interpretation of such rules. Rather, they are explicit choices among available policy options with no pretense of determining the winners and losers according to established legal rights; the decisions are instead asserted to be based on a values preference or on a judgment about the course that is likely to be wise or advantageous. Nor are most of these decisions made through the formal procedures in which lawyers have a special claim to expertise. The formalities of procedural due process are much less the rule than are telephone calls, personal visits to members of Congress and other public officials, give-and-take negotiations with allies and adversaries, and close monitoring of the trade press. In these latter activities, lawyers have no special advantage. Nonlawyer representatives who are experienced in the ways of the federal government will probably be at least equally skilled in these procedures. Moreover, although many lawyers have considerable substantive expertise in the area of their specialization, they certainly have no monopoly (and probably no comparative advantage) with respect to such substantive knowledge. In the policy areas that we studied, knowledge of medicine, agronomy, international trade, geological engineering, or labor relations will often be useful

to the representative, and we found many persons with such education backgrounds in our sample of representatives. Despite the claims of legal education, lawyers seem unlikely to match the substantive authority of representatives who have spent their entire careers working in health care or in atomic energy. The increasing dominance of representation by organizational insiders may even in part reflect a demand or need for increased substantive expertise as regulatory issues become more specific and complex.

Nelson & Heinz, Lawyers and the Structure of Influence in Washington, 22 Law & Soc'y Rev. 701, 756–58 (1988).

(3) The need to make value choices creates the sometimes divisive forces of self-interest and factionalism that appear to mark all legislative activity. These forces are not new to modern legislatures; in 1787 James Madison discussed their impact on the new republic in The Federalist, No. 10:

> No man is allowed to be a judge in his own cause, because his interest would certainly bias his judgment, and, not improbably, corrupt his integrity. With equal, nay with greater reason, a body of men are unfit to be both judges and parties at the same time; yet what are many of the most important acts of legislation but so many judicial determinations, not indeed concerning the rights of single persons, but concerning the rights of large bodies of citizens: And what are the different classes of legislators but advocates and parties to the causes which they determine? Is a law proposed concerning private debts? It is a question to which the creditors are parties on one side and the debtors on the other. Justice ought to hold the balance between them. Yet the parties are, and must be, themselves the judges; and the most numerous party, or in other words, the most powerful faction must be expected to prevail. Shall domestic manufacturers be encouraged, and in what degree, by restrictions on foreign manufacturers? are questions which would be differently decided by the landed and the manufacturing classes, and probably by neither with a sole regard to justice and the public good. The apportionment of taxes on the various descriptions of property is an act which seems to require the most exact impartiality; yet there is, perhaps, no legislative act in which greater opportunity and temptation are given to a predominant party to trample on the rules of justice. Every shilling with which they overburden the inferior number is a shilling saved to their own pockets.

> It is in vain to say that enlightened statesmen will be able to adjust these clashing interests and render them all subservient to the public good. Enlightened statesmen will not always be at the helm. Nor, in many cases, can such an adjustment be made at all without taking into view indirect and remote considerations, which will rarely prevail over the immediate interest which one party

may find in disregarding the rights of another or the good of the whole.

The inference to which we are brought is that the *causes* of faction cannot be removed and that relief is only to be sought in the means of controlling its *effects*.

(4) It has been fifteen years since Stewart wrote his article. Law schools and lawyers are necessarily paying more attention to legislation. Statutory considerations now pervade almost every law school course: landlord-tenant laws in Property, the Uniform Commercial Code in Contracts and Sales, the Family Code in Domestic Relations, and so on. Paradoxically, there is little attention paid to the *process* by which statutes are made—for example, to the role of legislative leadership, the committee and budgeting structure, public hearings, administrative oversight, constituent relations, and the activities of lobbyists.

(5) Stewart raises many ethical issues for the lawyer and the legal profession: The education of new lawyers in the lawmaking process would appear to be a requirement not only because of the prevalence and importance of statutes, but also because of the need to help lawyers provide "valuable opportunities to advance client's interests through the legislative process." Moreover, the fact that so many lawyers are employed in the legislative process—as legislators, committee and agency staff, and lobbyists—is further evidence of the need for more educational effort. In addition, Stewart suggests that there may be a duty for lawyers to help assure equal access to the legislative process by individuals or groups that otherwise could not afford it. If there is such a duty, it is perhaps shared with other groups in society as well as the government. Could lawyers satisfy this duty by providing public-interest lobbyists in much the same way lawyers now provide Public Defenders, legal aid services, and court-appointed attorneys to represent indigents in criminal and civil matters?

2. Applications of ADR Techniques

Many obstacles exist to expanded use of ADR methods in the legislative process. A legislator may at times equate her public role with that of an impartial mediator in the policymaking process, when in fact she will usually play an independent role as a party to the controversy (albeit representing the public). The legislator or her staff may not be sensitive to the need for credible impartiality in a mediating role, and in some cases they will simply not know about the more systematic dispute resolution methods discussed in the preceding chapters. Moreover, demands on the legislator's time are intense, and her staff is typically very busy just keeping pace with legislative and constituent business. Finally, legislators are most familiar with traditional "logrolling," which is the vote-trading process primarily used for resolving issues in the legislative arena. Successful legislators quickly learn to count: To pass a bill or take other action, you need the votes of only 50% plus one. "Logrolling" typically does not include attempts to build a consensus beyond that majority.

Despite these obstacles, many members of Congress and state legislatures are seeing the advantages of using ADR methods in carrying out their functions, and as ADR knowledge becomes more widespread among the public, citizens and their lobbyists are asking legislators to act in ways that make use of the recent advances in negotiation and mediation theory and technique. Legislators are beginning to look more for consensus—a solution which all interested parties will accept, although not necessarily prefer. Conflict resolution theory suggests the following steps for building that consensus on public issues:

• Identify the interested parties—those whose agreement is necessary to go ahead, and those whose opposition could delay or destroy the program.

• Define and understand the problem as viewed from the multiple perspectives of the different interested parties.

• Shape the forum or "table" which the parties will accept and use to structure their discussion of the problem.

• Build consensus on a definition of the problem and its major contributing causes.

• Outline the goal—what should the situation look like when the problem is eliminated or the new policy implemented.

• List the interests that the parties have in common, and try to expand them consistent with their basic needs, values, and interests.

• Develop a single-text draft solution from the full discussion, and have the group improve this draft as a joint project.

• Encourage each party to make a realistic assessment of the final draft solution in light of his alternative to reaching agreement.

A major issue in this collaborative process is the inherent conflict between elected representatives and private interests. Legislators are selected by general election to represent all the residents of a jurisdiction to determine the policy, norms, and direction of the community. They are responsible for the results, and the public holds them accountable at the next election. On the other hand, many private interests—business groups, trade associations, neighborhood and civic organizations, environmental interests, etc.—continue to express concern about the lack of citizen input into governmental decisions. One proposal to bridge the gap between the two groups is to use focus groups and a facilitated decision-making process to develop solutions to public problems. These issues are highlighted in the following example of local governmental action in Arapahoe County, Colorado.

KUNDE & RUDD, CITIZENS AT THE TABLE: REPRESENTING THE ALREADY REPRESENTED IN ARAPAHOE COUNTY *

Perhaps no problem is more vexing and full of contradictions for the organizer of a negotiation than working on how to represent "citizens" or "the public" at a table where formal representatives of official governing bodies whose jurisdiction includes those citizens also sit. Not only is there the uncomfortable question of how can people not formally chosen by an official process (such as election or appointment according to constitutional authority) be equated to those who are, but there is the question as to which "citizens" or members of the "the public" will receive recognition while others do not. * * *

A series of disputes in the Southeast Corridor [of metropolitan Denver] developed over the past decade as the Denver Tech Center, one of the nation's earliest and most impressive research parks located and expanded at the junction of I–25 south and the I–225 by-pass south of the city. An incredible commercial real estate boom coupled with liberal state laws for the formation of special districts enabled the development of an extensive area of "tax plums" which attracted aggressive annexation interests in nearby cities. The problem was complicated by state laws in Colorado which in essence provide "contract zoning" for land brought into a municipality under annexation agreements. * * * The contract zoning feature encouraged developers to seek "competitive annexation bids" to guarantee certainty of the most favorable zoning features. * * * Very much left out of these intricate bidding wars were the increasing numbers of homeowners who came to live in the area, who sometimes found that some city had annexed the entire area surrounding them and left their subdivision without a commercial or industrial tax base to support the more expensive urban services that would surely come with increasing population density.

A group of homeowners became increasingly angry at the result of the annexation battles, and banded together to seek incorporation of a new city called Centennial, covering much of the unincorporated area left in the corridor. Their incorporation petition was resisted by competing municipalities and the county government, but was most directly fought by developers who would be included in the incorporation. The developers were concerned because the incorporation would usurp their ability to bargain for favorable development conditions among competing governments. They were especially concerned because an incorporation would not provide the same ironclad zoning protection that an annexation contract would provide.

* Unpublished preliminary report on the Arapahoe County mediation, March 1988, on file with the Conflict Clinic, Inc. James Kunde is an associate of the Kettering Foundation and was principally responsible for developing the NIS program; Jill Rudd was a graduate assistant working with the team on the Arapahoe County project.

718 ADMINISTRATIVE & LEGISLATIVE PROCESSESCh. 6

The developers' legal representatives were able to stop the incorporation in court. However, it was stopped on a correctable technicality that a second effort by the homeowners might easily overcome, and it had cost the developers upwards of $200,000 in legal fees to fight it the first time.

Shortly after the incorporation court case was decided, an ad hoc group of homeowners, developers and public officials got together and began talking about seeking some sort of mediation service to help the parties come together and seek out less expensive ways to solve problems in the area. One of the members of the group had heard about the Negotiated Investment Strategy that had been developed by the Kettering Foundation as an intergovernmental problem-solving tool. Basically the NIS is a process that uses the structure and techniques of formal mediation for exploring problem-solving and joint action by governments even though a formal dispute might not exist.

* * * On the basis of the request from the ad hoc group [the mediator] put together a team of people under a contract with the Conflict Clinic to explore how a mediated process similar to NIS could work with the problems of the Southeast Corridor. * * *

As interviews and discussions got under way with the principals involved in the Southeast Corridor disputes, a structure of five logical negotiating teams emerged. These were the city of Aurora, the city of Greenwood Village, Arapahoe County, concerned developers, and "homeowners." As discussions developed a number of other entities such as Cherrycreek School District and Castlewood Fire District became "observers." * * *

As the process reached the stage of establishing a steering committee, negotiating teams and ground rules, the issue of how to represent the homeowners became the most important and difficult to work through. Both the "developers" and "homeowners" teams differed from the teams representing formal governing bodies. While the nature of the discussions was established from the beginning to be exploratory and non-binding from a legal standpoint, it was clear that there would be public scrutiny of the process, and that representation at the table would almost certainly be challenged.

The representation of developers at the table was quickly resolved by two ad hoc meetings with a majority of larger developers active in the area. * * *

While the process for establishing a "developers" team was important for some of the same representation questions that were involved in establishing a homeowners team, it was more straightforward. The universe of potential parties was infinitely smaller. There were less than two dozen major developers active in the area. While the representation question later broadened to include consideration of businesses which were not "developers," it was still a more manageable universe because there was an active chamber of commerce structure, and there was a good degree of communication among most members of what could logically be called a "business community." The same was not true of the homeowners.

There are two fundamental conditions which may create a demand by citizens for direct representation at a negotiating table when formal governmental representatives are also present. First, there are times when a governmental body is clearly a corporate party acting on behalf of its interests that are at odds with the interests of a group of citizens. A governmental body seeking to decide a neighborhood zoning issue or the site for a waste disposal plant are good examples of this kind of circumstance. The citizen group at odds with the governing body is clearly defined. The group is defined by its specific interest, for example, an affected neighborhood. In this instance the affected group may elect representatives or the issue may be so narrow that anyone concerned can be seated and participate.

The second condition is present when the limits of representative action are at issue. In this instance the standard is "public permission."

* * *

In the circumstance of the Southeast Corridor dispute, virtually all of the "homeowners" involved were citizens of Arapahoe County, which had formal status at the table. Arapahoe County has a typical county governing structure with a three person elected Board of County Commissioners, a set of separately elected officials such as a Sheriff and an auditor and numerous official public commissions, including a Planning Commission that works with a staff hired by the County Manager. Arapahoe County is a large county geographically, containing 385,221 citizens, 12 political subdivisions, and 820 square miles. Like many such units of government that include both incorporated cities and unincorporated areas, some services are provided throughout the county, and others are provided only to unincorporated areas. Because of the size and the complexity of the county it is difficult for citizens to feel as close to county officials as they might feel to officials of a smaller governmental corporation. In fact, lack of identity and lack of representation on major issues were the two biggest concerns named by homeowners in pre-negotiation interviews and in problem statements at the table.

The homeowner representation issue in Arapahoe County had elements of both causes for representation demands. In some instances the homeowners were aggrieved parties to a specific action proposed (for example, annexations), and in other instances there was a general concern that governance of the entire unincorporated area had become a conversation between "them"—the professional governmental officials of the various political subdivisions and special districts.

* * *

One advantage of bringing individuals together for direct representation in negotiations is that the process permits the individual participants to test and legitimize their conflicting values and attitudes.

More important, the negotiation process provides the opportunity for creation of a "shared belief" or "vision," which can only be created through group discussion. * * * Creation of a shared belief or vision as a result of the negotiation process creates a synergistic effect, and provides the force for movement and change.

* * *

The process facilitated by the team from the Conflict Clinic involved four major steps. The first step was the formation of the official steering committee which met and mapped out the ground rules. The Steering Committee was comprised of one member from each of the five teams: * * * The Steering Committee met on July 29, 1987, and developed the official ground rules. All members agreed upon the ground rules and agreed to go forward with the process.

Step two of the process was preparation for and participation in a session to jointly define the problems to be addressed. This step was completed on August 23, resulting in the statement distributed back to all the parties for further study and review with constituents not at the table.

Step three of the process called for each team to develop a proposed solution to the problems and present it at a joint session. During the joint session on September 23, a "single text" process was used to combine the proposals, sort out agreements and decide upon further work.

The fourth and final step of the process was to convert the preliminary agreements into specific language, and to agree upon an ongoing system for working on unresolved issues.

The teams developed goals, options and outcomes, in the hope that an agreement could also be reached on an organization or governance structure to proceed with implementation of the agreements. The analysis of structure led to the conclusion that the best results in terms of outcomes were most likely to be delivered by structural options that would be most difficult to agree upon and implement. This led the members of the drafting committee to suggest the creation of a body called "an Interim Advisory Group," which could proceed with efforts to implement the current agreements, pursue further discussions to develop other agreements and consider how the long term governance structure questions might be handled.

* * *

At the fourth and final joint session, January 13, 1988, it became clear to all of the parties that the heart of the agreement was the development of the Interim Advisory Group and the potential of the group to advise the County Commissioners on how to address the needs of the unincorporated area of Arapahoe County. The decision was made, therefore, that the County, citizens, and business and commercial interests would be the signatories to an agreement that outlined the goals and procedures of the Interim Advisory Group. The two municipalities were not as likely to be affected directly by the work of the

Interim Advisory Group. Moreover, in order to make the agreement legally and politically acceptable to the municipalities, it would have been necessary to substantially modify ideas that were very important to the other three parties.

Notes and Questions

(1) The Negotiated Investment Strategy is a strategy specifically designed to help urban communities handle serious conflicts over issues of public and private investment planning, social equality and neighborhood cohesion, and patterns of future growth. From 1977 through 1980 the Kettering Foundation funded NIS experiments in three metropolitan areas in the midwest: Columbus, Gary, and St. Paul. A roundtable conference report in 1981, evaluating these efforts, cited a number of achievements: written agreements for specific, coordinated public/private investment, expedited implementation of projects, improved working relationships both within the local community and among public officials at all levels, and the development of a new process for resolving public planning and policy differences. See Kettering Foundation, Mediation and New Federalism: Proceedings of a Roundtable on the Negotiated Investment Strategy, July 8, 1981.

(2) During the spring and summer of 1988, Arapahoe County made some progress in handling its differences. What had triggered the move to incorporate the new town of Centennial (and the resulting lawsuits) was a feeling by residents of the unincorporated areas that their homes and futures were at the mercy of a political system that excluded them. This alienation has apparently dissipated. The earlier fervent drive to annex land has slowed considerably, and recent annexations have been neither harmful nor unexpected—the homeowners in the unincorporated neighborhoods have been included in the decision-making process.

A Priority Board (the new name for the Interim Advisory Board) was appointed with county, commercial, and homeowner representatives, and the county commissioners and their staff appear to be looking to the board members—and through them to the public—for guidance on major county issues. The board initially selected two issues for special work: recreational parks and economic health. An outside facilitator held focus groups to develop educational booklets dealing with these issues, and in May the board sponsored a town meeting on parks. The county has begun distributing a local newsletter to encourage a sense of "community" where none existed before, and has hired a community liaison person to help develop a partnership between county residents and county government. The focus during the fall of 1988 has been on how to link these efforts to inform and include the public in the choices facing the county with the need for county officers to make specific decisions—to build and maintain a park, purchase land for airport expansion, or prepare certain roads for commercial growth.

(3) Negotiation and mediation techniques help elected leaders tap citizen participation without delegating their responsibility for the ultimate decision. For example, Congress and the President were virtually powerless to improve an admittedly unworkable immigration program, despite the almost fulltime efforts over eight years of two respected legislators and the universal recognition that a crisis was rapidly approaching. Reform legislation was passed in 1986 only after the many outside "special interests" (Hispanic groups, AFL–CIO, agricultural production and worker organizations, public interest groups, and certain members of Congress whose constituents were particularly affected) met together and agreed upon a compromise package.

(4) The 1988 effort to amend the Federal Housing Act provides another example of the use of consensus—building techniques. As reported in the Congressional Quarterly, June 18, 1988, at p. 1682:

> Key members of Congress, civil rights lawyers and officials of the National Association of Realtors, who have been at odds over the legislation [new fair-housing provisions] for nine years, say they believe they have resolved the major sticking point, and they hope the House can act on a bill before the end of June.

* * *

> Because time is short in the 100th Congress, the measure must be negotiated in advance. There is no time for a protracted floor fight.

> The House Judiciary Committee April 27 [1988] approved a bill (HR 1158) that would strengthen the 1968 housing law by giving the Department of Housing and Urban Development (HUD) the authority to levy fines and issue injunctions against individuals who discriminate in the sale or rental of housing.

> Currently HUD can only offer mediation of disputes. Enforcement of the anti-bias laws depends on private lawsuits or the Justice Department, which can sue when officials believe they see a pattern or practice of housing discrimination.

> Both sides in the fight agree that the 1968 law needs to be changed, but they have disagreed over the best way to give HUD more authority.

> HR 1158 would set up a new system of administrative-law judges who would hear cases of alleged housing discrimination. Proponents said this procedure would provide a fast and effective method of resolving disputes.

> But the Realtors and the Reagan administration contended that the process was constitutionally flawed because it could subject a defendant to fines without benefit of a jury trial, as required under the Seventh Amendment of the Constitution.

> Although HR 1158 came out of the Judiciary Committee by a 26–9 vote, the contentious debate made clear to chief sponsors Don Edwards, D–Calif., and Hamilton Fish Jr., R–N.Y., and to civil

rights lobbyists that they needed to keep talking with the Realtors about possible compromises.

The talks bore fruit the week of June 13, according to participants, when both sides came up with the general outlines of an agreement.

Under the compromise, the administrative-law-judge procedure in HR 1158 would remain intact. But any party to the dispute could elect to have a trial in federal court. In those instances, HUD would represent the interests of the plaintiff.

John Blount, vice president for congressional affairs for the Realtors, who participated in many of the negotiations, said his organization was pleased with the deal. In an interview June 16 from Chicago, the Realtors' national headquarters, Blount said the Realtors believed the election procedure solved the Seventh Amendment problem, because an individual could choose a jury trial.

Blount specifically praised Fish, in whose office most of the talks took place, and civil rights lawyers, who he said showed a willingness to compromise.

Civil rights lobbyists declined to comment publicly on the negotiations, saying that more work had to be done. But participants said they believed the deal was a workable one, in large part because a new enforcement mechanism—even if it meant going to federal court—could serve as an incentive to resolve disputes through conciliation.

A critical time in the discussions, participants said, was the evening of June 14, when civil rights lawyers had a long conference call to Chicago with Realtor representatives. The following day, officials from the organization flew to Washington for a face-to-face meeting with the civil rights lawyers, Fish and Edwards to discuss the details of the proposal.

(5) Different groups and individuals, both inside and outside government, have always presented a challenge to the efficiency of legislative and executive decisionmaking. As Kunde and Rudd point out, we elect political leaders to make the policy decisions which shape our communities and determine directions for the future. Yet, we all (including the elected officials) belong to an overlapping array of special interest groups that can delay, and in some cases veto, the most determined efforts of a legislator, the legislature, or an executive. And we expect, and for the most part applaud, the possible "inefficiencies" of this system. However, the application of ADR techniques tries to bring together all the various players who are interested in a particular problem—legislative, executive, and private—to build a consensus on possible solutions in an efficient way. The net effect may be to create an informal working relationship that is intended to bridge the natural divisiveness created by our checks-and-balances system.

———

Members of Congress and state legislatures are turning more frequently to ADR techniques to improve policy design and implementation. The following brief case studies exemplify the use of (or the failure to use) these principles: first, to handle a difficult legislative issue, then to provide effective oversight of executive rulemaking, and finally to design a complex solution to a chronic private sector problem.

1) State Funding of Education.

In January 1987, Texas legislators found themselves in an untenable position (although probably typical for legislators in most states): on the one hand, growing demands for more state aid to help local school funding and for a more equitable allocation formula within the state, and on the other, a decreasing tax revenue caused by a drastic drop in world oil prices and a stagnant economy. Moreover, as with most legislatures, Texas faced a relatively short session filled with many difficult and politically sensitive issues. Legislative leadership sought a workable formula to balance school funding with other increased money needs of the state, with the political agenda of their members, and with the citizen outcry for good services at low tax cost.

The Chairman of the Texas Senate's Education Committee proposed a two-day workshop for a small group of top public education policymakers in the state. The participants would be five members each from the Senate and House of Representatives, two members of the state Board of Education, the Commissioner of Education, and representatives of the Governor, Lt. Governor, and the Speaker of the House. The aim was to assess the interests and needs of the major stakeholders in the public education system, move toward a consensus on goals, resources available, and priorities, and identify specific next steps and a timetable for implementation.

The plan as it stood was not particularly novel, but the Committee Chairman added a new twist. The workshop agenda would be coordinated and facilitated by an outside third party with experience in public policy disputes.

The workshop was held as planned, and the group, with its outside facilitator, worked through definitions of the problem and the causes, developing a rough outline of an acceptable solution. The Senate and House leadership then successfully moved the 1987 Texas legislature to agreement on the volatile education funding issue without rancor or delay. In the words of the executive assistant to the Senate Education Committee Chairman:

> * * * The consensus building that [the facilitator] did was not significantly challenged during the entire legislative session.
> * * *
>
> The leadership of the Legislature can exhibit a great deal of control over the agenda IF the major players have confidence in a deal. The consensus building mechanism worked well enough that the major issues were largely settled in the minds of the leadership.

It was very hard to undermine that solidarity even though the policies that we were defending had high price tags and our fiscal distress was very deep.[1]

2) Congress and Executive Secrecy Oaths.

Accurate and timely information can be a powerful asset in any process; in the political process, it is an essential ingredient to success. Many disagreements between the legislative and executive branches are founded on acquisition or disclosure of information. The federal government is especially prone to these arguments because of the sensitive nature of foreign policy and intelligence activities, major tasks for the federal executive.

On April 12, 1982, President Reagan signed Executive Order 12,359, establishing substantive and procedural requirements for classified documents. Following this Order the President directed all people with authorized access to classified information to sign a nondisclosure agreement as a condition of access.[2]

In 1983, Standard Form 189 was drafted to comply with the presidential directive.

> SF 189 is a life-long nondisclosure agreement that federal employees are required to sign as a precondition for being granted access to classified information. If an employee refuses to sign SF 189, then he or she is denied access to classified information, which can result in job loss or reassignment. Of the almost two and a half million federal employees who are cleared for access to classified information, more than 1.7 million have already been compelled to sign SF 189.[3]

SF 189 raised two problems: it placed a "chilling factor" on federal employee conversation with members of Congress and their staffs, and it broadened the definition of classified to include "classifiable" information—a document that meets all the requirements for classification "but which as a result of negligence, time constraints, error, lack of opportunity or oversight, has not been marked as classified information." [4] The Director of the Information Security Oversight Office in the General Services Administration later clarified this definition by limiting "classifiable" to only those documents "in the process of being classified."

This executive policy escalated into a serious political conflict when several federal administrators refused to give reports to members of Congress unless those members signed SF 189. The federal employees union had already filed a lawsuit to enjoin the Administration from

---

1. Excerpt from a letter from Douglas Brookman to James H. Laue, February 1, 1988, in the files of the Conflict Clinic, Inc., George Mason University, Fairfax, Virginia.

2. National Security Decision Directive Number 84, Para. 1(a).

3. Amici Curiae Brief, page 4, National Federation of Federal Employees v. U.S., Civil Action No. 87–2284 OG, U.S.Dist.Ct. for the District of Columbia (1987).

4. 52 Fed.Reg. 28,802 (Aug. 3, 1987); 52 Fed.Reg. 29,793 (Aug. 11, 1987).

requiring SF 189 as a condition for employment, and the slap at congressional access to information brought a bipartisan group of legislators into the court as *amici curiae.*

To gain the attention of the executive branch, Senator Charles Grassley, one of the *amici* and a member of the Senate Armed Services Committee, placed a hold on Senate confirmation of all general officers of the U.S. Army until the controversy over SF 189 could be ironed out. Senator Grassley convened two meetings of congressional and executive representatives interested in this issue with the objective of working out a solution to the problem. The ranking member of the Armed Services Committee, Senator John Warner, attended the meetings in the role of a "neutral mediator" in hopes of lifting the hold on officer confirmations; he was not considered a principal in the SF 189 controversy. In fall 1987, at the conclusion of the second meeting, participants appeared to be in agreement, and therefore, in response to Senator Warner's request, Senator Grassley agreed to release his hold on the confirmations. Within three weeks Senate confirmation of Army general officers was back on track, but the "agreement" on SF 189 had fallen apart. The Senate adopted a rider on a critical appropriations bill in late November prohibiting the executive from using SF 189 for fiscal year 1988, and the President signed the bill into law on December 22, 1987.

The new year failed to thaw the freeze in the relationship due to the events of the previous fall. In February 1988, seven members of Congress and the federal employees union filed suit against Central Intelligence Agency Director William Webster, the overseer of the executive's nondisclosure program, claiming that the administration was refusing to comply with the new appropriations law. On May 27, the federal district court held that the restrictive clause barring the administration from enforcing SF 189 was an unconstitutional intrusion on the President's power to protect government secrets, and the plaintiffs, of course, appealed. Meanwhile, the interested members of Congress were drafting permanent legislation to prevent the implementation of SF 189 and planning a series of public hearings on that legislation.

On July 28, 1988, a federal district judge declared unconstitutional the inclusion in SF 189 of the term "classifiable" as currently defined. The heart of the case, according to the judge, was a "constitutionally inherent conflict between the obligation of the executive to safeguard national security information and the rights of citizens to speak freely and be guided by reasonably clear and narrow statutory proscriptions on the free speech right." [5] The court decision required the GSA to notify all federal employees of a reasonable and workable definition of "classifiable" within 60 days.

5. Washington Post, Aug. 2, 1988, p. A19.

Following the decision, Mark Roth, chief counsel for the American Federation of Government Employees, predicted that the issue would breed further litigation: "In the real world the federal employee is not going to know what's expected of him." Senator Grassley commented that "this decision legitimizes a chilling effect. If we were concerned before about the flow of information to Congress, we should be even more concerned now." On August 3, the GSA's Information Security Oversight Office announced that it would abandon the term "classifiable," a decision it said it had reached some time before the judge's decision was made public.[6]

3) Farm Debtors and Creditors.

In response to the farm crisis of the mid-1980's Iowans were calling for government action. Yet, an obvious solution had not appeared, nor did it seem likely that the usual legislative research and public hearing process would develop a viable option that could win majority support on the floors of both houses. The Lt. Governor was contacted by an Iowa resident from a rural area, a retired Farmers Home Administration official who had mediated several farmer-creditor disputes on a volunteer basis. This constituent convinced the Lt. Governor that mediation of such disputes works in many cases, but that individual volunteers—scattered throughout the state and working alone—could not stem the flood of foreclosures. Lt. Governor Anderson then took the unusual step of asking an outside facilitator to help pull together the members of a planning group. The group was composed of legislative leaders and representatives from the Governor, the Secretary of Agriculture, the Cooperative Extension Service, the Iowa Banker's Association, several farm advocate organizations, state religious leaders, and various creditor interests. The objective was to fashion a consensus for a process that would help individual farmers, their bankers, and other creditors to work through options for renegotiation of debt repayment schedules—or to identify other acceptable (although perhaps not preferred) alternatives. The group was to build on the state's experience with county mediation programs during the Depression of the 1930's.

With the help of the facilitator, the participants designed a mediation process intended to produce creative options for individual farmers and creditors, and constructed a private nonprofit corporation to operate it (see *supra* p. 327, note (7), for a discussion of the mediation service itself). All major stakeholders in the state's farm crisis, because they participated in shaping the solution, were committed to seeing it work. The non-profit service began operations immediately, using start-up grant monies from a private agri-business corporation. Members of the key legislative committees had contributed to the development of the plan, and they drafted and helped pass the legislation needed to support the agreed-upon process. The legislation required a mediation option

6. Id.; Washington Post, Aug. 3, 1988, p. A15.

as part of the court's foreclosure process, and appropriated state funds to operate the mediation service statewide.[7]

Notes and Questions

(1) The design of a consensus-building process for public issues involves identifying the appropriate parties for the task and structuring a forum and agenda that will support constructive interaction. For the three case studies, how did the "convening" public officials differ in their approaches to identifying interested parties and structuring interaction? Did these differences affect the outcomes?

(2) Senator Grassley wanted to play a "mediating" role, but he was not impartial on the issues presented in the SF 189 controversy. Did this prevent him from serving as an effective mediator? Would "convenor" be a more appropriate term for his role? What steps might he have taken to establish a more effective process for resolving the dispute?

(3) At the outset, lawyers often assume that the application of ADR techniques to the legislative process is merely "business as usual" for the political branch of government. The three case studies, however, show the use of several nontraditional methods which appear to have changed the processes by which legislators (and others) dealt with each other on important issues. Because the legislative process is naturally flexible and informal, it should be receptive to innovation, but there may be obstacles. What effect might such factors as the importance of personal working relationships, the attention of the media, or the demands of the "next election" have on the acceptability of new techniques of negotiation and mediation?

7. Wall St.J., May 5, 1987, p. 20.

FURTHER REFERENCES

In addition to the principal selections throughout this book, there are other sources that may be useful to the reader for reference. These books and articles are listed by chapter.

Chapter I

Books:

R. Abel (ed.), The Politics of Informal Justice: The American Experience (2 vols. 1982).

J. Auberbach, Unequal Justice (1976).

M. Frankel, Partisan Justice (1980).

S. Goldberg, E. Green and F. Sander, Dispute Resolution (1985).

J. Lieberman, The Litigious Society (1981).

J. Marks, E. Johnson and P. Szanton, Dispute Resolution in America: Processes in Evolution (1984).

L. Riskin and J. Westbrook, Dispute Resolution and Lawyers (1987).

W. Ury, J. Brett, and S. Goldberg, Getting Disputes Resolved: Designing Systems to Cut the Cost of Conflict (1988).

Articles:

Brunet, Questioning the Quality of Alternate Dispute Resolution, 62 Tulane L.Rev. 1 (1987).

Bush, Dispute Resolution Alternatives and the Goals of Civil Justice: Jurisdictional Principles for Process Choice, 1984 Wis.L. Rev. 893.

Delgado, Dunn, Brown, Lee, & Hubbert, Fairness and Formality: Minimizing the Risk of Prejudice in Alternative Dispute Resolution, 1985 Wis.L.Rev. 1359.

Edwards, Alternative Dispute Resolution: Panacea or Anathema?, 99 Harv.L.Rev. 668 (1986).

Galanter, Why the "Haves" Come Out Ahead: Speculations on the Limits of Legal Change, 9 Law & Soc'y Rev. 95 (1974).

———, Reading the Landscape of Disputes: What We Know And Don't Know (And Think We Know) About Our Allegedly Contentious and Litigious Society, 31 U.C.L.A. L.Rev. 4 (1983).

———, Justice in Many Rooms: Courts, Private Ordering, and Indigenous Law, 19 J. Pluralism & Unofficial L. 1 (1981).

Sander, Varieties of Dispute Processing, 70 F.R.D. 111 (1976).

Special Issue on Dispute Processing and Civil Litigation, 15 Law & Soc'y Rev. 401 (1980–81).

Symposium on Dispute Resolution, 88 Yale L.J. 905 (1979).

Symposium on Informal Dispute Resolution, 13 Law & Social Inquiry 113 (1988).

Chapter II

Books:

R. Axelrod, The Evolution of Cooperation (1984).

M. Bazerman and R. Lewicki, Negotiating in Organizations (1983).

W. Brazil, Effective Approaches to Settlement: A Handbook for Lawyers and Judges (1988).

_____, Settling Civil Suits (1985).

J. Carter, Negotiation: The Alternative to Hostility (1984).

Center for the Study of Foreign Affairs, International Negotiation (1984).

D. Druckman (ed.), Negotiations: Social–Psychological Perspectives (1977).

J. Dunlop, Dispute Resolution, Negotiation and Consensus Building (1984).

H. Edwards and J. White, The Lawyer as a Negotiator (1977).

R. Fisher and S. Brown, Getting Together: Building A Relationship That Gets to Yes (1988).

_____ and W. Ury, Getting to Yes: Negotiating Agreement Without Giving In (1981).

C. Karrass, Give and Take (1974).

_____, The Negotiating Game (1970).

L. Kriesberg, Social Conflicts (1973, 1982).

D. Lax and J. Sebenius, The Manager As Negotiator: Bargaining for Cooperation and Competitive Gain (1986).

R. Lewicki and J. Litterer, Negotiation (1985).

T. Milburn and K. Watman, On the Nature of Threat (1981).

G. Nierenberg, Fundamentals of Negotiating (1973).

D. Pruitt, Negotiation Behavior (1981).

_____ and J. Rubin, Social Conflict: Escalation, Stalemate, and Settlement (1986).

H. Raiffa, The Art & Science of Negotiation (1982).

J. Rubin and B. Brown, The Social Psychology of Bargaining and Negotiation (1975).

T. Schelling, The Strategy of Conflict (1960, 1980).

J. Sebenius, Negotiating the Law of the Sea (1984).

G. Williams, Legal Negotiation and Settlement (1982).

W. Zartman, The Practical Negotiator (1982).

Articles:

Eisenberg, Private Ordering Through Negotiation: Dispute Settlement and Rulemaking, 89 Harv.L.Rev. 637 (1976).

Fisher, Negotiating Power: Getting and Using Influence, 27 Am. Behavioral Scientist 149 (Nov.–Dec. 1983).

Guernsey, Truthfulness in Negotiation, 17 U.Rich.L.Rev. 99 (1982).

Gulliver, Negotiations as a Mode of Dispute Settlement: A General Model, 7 Law & Soc'y Rev. 667 (1973).

Harter, Negotiating Regulations: A Cure for Malaise, 71 Geo.L.J. 1 (1982).

Murray, Understanding Competing Theories of Negotiation, 2 Negotiation J. 179 (1986).

Nader, Disputing Without Force of Law, 88 Yale L.J. 900 (1979).

Steele, Deceptive Negotiating and High–Toned Morality, 39 Vand. L.Rev. 1387, 1403 (1986).

Symposium on Litigation Management, 53 U.Chi.L.Rev. 306 (1986).

White, Machiavelli and the Bar: Ethical Limitations on Lying in Negotiation, 1980 Am.Bar Fdtn.Research J. 976.

Whitman, Dispute Resolution, Bargaining, and the Selection of Cases for Trial: A Study of the Generation of Biased and Unbiased Data, 17 J. of Legal Studies 313 (1988).

Chapter III

Books:

L. Bacow and M. Wheeler, Environmental Dispute Resolution (1984).

G. Bingham, Resolving Environmental Disputes (1986).

J. Bossey (ed.), Disputes and Settlements: Law and Human Relations in the West (1986).

S. Carpenter and W. Kennedy, Managing Public Disputes: A Practical Guide to Handling Conflict and Reaching Agreements (1988).

W. Felstiner and L. Williams, Community Mediation in Dorchester, Massachusetts (1980).

J. Folberg and A. Taylor, Mediation: A Comprehensive Guide to Resolving Conflict Without Litigation (1984).

J. Henry and J. Lieberman, The Manager's Guide to Resolving Legal Disputes (1986).

H. Irving and M. Benjamin, Family Mediation: Theory and Practice of Dispute Resolution (1987).

S. Keltner, Mediation: Toward a Civilized System of Dispute Resolution (1988).

F. Knebel and G. Clay, Before You Sue (1988).

W. Maggiolo, Techniques of Mediation (1986).

C. Moore, The Mediation Process: Practical Strategies for Resolving Conflict (1986).

N. Rogers and R. Salem, A Student's Guide to Mediation and the Law (1987).

A. Talbot, Environmental Mediation (1981).

Articles:

Chaykin, The Liabilities and Immunities of Mediators: A Hostile Environment for Model Legislation, 2 J. on Dispute Resolution 1 (1986).

Cooley, Arbitration vs. Mediation: Explaining the Differences, 69 Judicature 263 (1986).

Fuller, Mediation—It's Forms and Functions, 44 S.Cal.L.Rev. 305 (1971).

Lemmon (ed.), Dimensions and Practice of Divorce Mediation, 1 Mediation Quarterly (Sept. 1983).

Moore (ed.), Practical Strategies for the Phases of Mediation, 16 Mediation Quarterly 1 (1987).

Paquin, Protecting the Interests of Children in Divorce Mediation, 26 J.Fam.L. 279 (1987–88).

Pearson and Vanderkooi, The Decision to Mediate: Profiles of Individuals Who Accept and Reject the Opportunity to Mediate Contested Child Custody and Visitation Issues, 6 J. of Divorce 17 (1982).

Phillips and Piazza, The Role of Mediation in Public International Disputes, 34 Hastings L.J. 1231 (1983).

Riskin, Mediation and Lawyers, 43 Ohio St.L.J. 29 (1982).

———, Toward New Standards for the Neutral Lawyer in Mediation, 26 Ariz.L.Rev. 329 (1984).

Saposneck (ed.), Applying Family Therapy Perspectives to Mediation, 14 Mediation Quarterly (1986–1987).

Singer, Nonjudicial Dispute Resolution Mechanisms: The Effects on Justice for the Poor, 13 Clearinghouse Rev. 569 (1979).

Welton, Pruitt and McGillicuddy, The Role of Caucusing in Community Mediation, 32 J. of Conflict Resolution 181 (1988).

Chapter IV

Books:

R. Coulson, Business Arbitration: What You Need to Know (1982).

W. Craig, W. Park and J. Paulsson, International Chamber of Commerce Arbitration (1984).

R. David, Arbitration in International Trade (1985).

M. Domke, Commercial Arbitration (rev. ed. 1984).

F. Elkouri and E. Elkouri, How Arbitration Works (4th ed. 1985) (labor arbitration).

G. Goldberg, A Lawyer's Guide to Commercial Arbitration (1977).

P. Hays, Labor Arbitration: A Dissenting View (1966).

L. Kanowitz, Alternative Dispute Resolution (1986).

S. Lazarus et al., Resolving Business Disputes: The Potential of Commercial Arbitration (1965).

A. Redfern and M. Hunter, Law and Practice of International Commercial Arbitration (1986).

J. Stern, C. Rehmus, J. Lowenberg, H. Kasper and B. Dennis, Final–Offer Arbitration: The Effects on Public Safety Employee Bargaining (1975).

A. Widiss (ed.), Arbitration: Commercial Disputes, Insurance, and Tort Claims (1979).

A. Zack (ed.), Arbitration in Practice (1984) (labor arbitration).

Articles:

Bonn, The Predictability of Nonlegalistic Adjudication, 6 Law and Soc'y Rev. 563 (1972).

Bruff, Public Programs, Private Deciders: The Constitutionality of Arbitration in Federal Programs, 67 Tex.L.Rev. (Feb.1989).

Craver, The Judicial Enforcement of Public Sector Interest Arbitration, 21 B.C.L.Rev. 557 (1980).

Getman, Labor Arbitration and Dispute Resolution, 88 Yale L.J. 916 (1979).

Hirshman, The Second Arbitration Trilogy: The Federalization of Arbitration Law, 71 Va.L.Rev. 1305 (1985).

Kaden, Judges and Arbitrators: Observations on the Scope of Judicial Review, 80 Colum.L.Rev. 267 (1980).

Kanowitz, Alternative Dispute Resolution and the Public Interest: The Arbitration Experience, 38 Hastings L.J. 239 (1987).

Kerr, International Arbitration vs. Litigation, (1980) J. Business Law 164.

Mentschikoff, Commercial Arbitration, 61 Colum.L.Rev. 846 (1961).

_____, The Significance of Arbitration—A Preliminary Inquiry, 17 Law & Contemp. Probs. 698 (1952).

Morgan, Contract Theory and the Sources of Rights: An Approach to the Arbitrability Question, 60 S.Cal.L.Rev. 1059 (1987).

Stipanowich, Rethinking American Arbitration, 63 Ind.L.J. 425 (1988).

Chapter V

Books:

Court–Annexed Arbitration, Report of Subcommittee on Alternative Means of Dispute Resolution, Committee on Corp. Counsel, ABA (1984).

Center for Public Resources, ADR and the Courts: A Manual for Judges and Lawyers (1987).

P. Ebener and D. Betancourt, Court–Annexed Arbitration: The National Picture (The Rand Corp. 1985).

D. Provine, Settlement Strategies for Federal District Judges (Federal Judicial Center, 1986).

B. Steen, Arbitration/Big Case: ABC's of Dispute Resolution, The Multi–Door Courthouse Project: Examining the Arbitration Door (1985).

Articles:

Alternatives to the High Cost of Litigation, Special Issue on Judicial ADR (1985).

Levin, Court–Annexed Arbitration, 16 J. of Law Reform 537 (1983).

Nejelski and Zeldin, Court–Annexed Arbitration in the Federal Courts: The Philadelphia Society, 42 Md.L.Rev. 787 (1983).

Newton and Swenson, Adjudication by Privately Compensated Judges in Texas, 36 Baylor L.Rev. 813 (1984).

Provine, Managing Negotiated Justice: Settlement Procedures in the Courts, 12 Just.Sys.J. 91 (1987).

Posner, The Summary Jury Trial and Other Methods of ADR: Some Cautionary Observations, 53 U.Chi.L.Rev. 366 (1986).

Chapter VI

Books:

Administrative Conference of the United States, Sourcebook: Federal Agency Use of Alternative Dispute Resolution (Office of the Chairman 1987).

L. Bacon and M. Wheeler, Environmental Dispute Resolution ch. 11 (1984) (negotiated rulemaking).

G. Bingham, Resolving Environmental Disputes (1986).

H. Eulau and J. Sprague, Lawyers in Politics (1964).

N. Huelsberg and W. Lincoln (eds.), Successful Negotiating in Local Government (1985).

G. Meeks, Jr., Managing Environmental and Public Policy Conflicts: A Legislator's Guide (National Conference of State Legislators, 1985).

R. Richman, O. White, Jr. and M. Wilkinson, Intergovernmental Mediation: Negotiations in Local Government Disputes (1986).

L. Susskind and J. Cruikshank, Breaking the Impasse: Consensual Approaches to Resolving Public Disputes (1987).

S. Zagoria, The Ombudsman: How Good Governments Handle Citizen Grievances (1988).

Articles:

Forester, Planning in the Face of Conflict: Mediated Negotiation in Local Land Use Permitting Processes (Lincoln Institute for Land Policy, 1986).

Heinz, The Power of Lawyers, 17 Ga.L.Rev. 891 (1983).

Herman, Mediation in a Regional Setting: Facilitating Dispute Resolution and Decision Making (National Association of Regional Councils, 1987).

Laumann, Heinz, Nelson, and Salisbury, Washington Lawyers and Others: The Structure of Washington Representation, 37 Stan. L.Rev. 465 (1985).

Nelson and Heinz, Lawyers and the Structure of Influence in Washington, 22 Law & Soc'y Rev. 701 (1988).

APPENDIX A

FEDERAL RULES OF CIVIL PROCEDURE

Rule 11.

SIGNING OF PLEADINGS, MOTIONS, AND OTHER PAPERS; SANCTIONS

Every pleading, motion, and other paper of a party represented by an attorney shall be signed by at least one attorney of record in the attorney's individual name, whose address shall be stated. A party who is not represented by an attorney shall sign the party's pleading, motion, or other paper and state the party's address. Except when otherwise specifically provided by rule or statute, pleadings need not be verified or accompanied by affidavit. The rule in equity that the averments of an answer under oath must be overcome by the testimony of two witnesses or of one witness sustained by corroborating circumstances is abolished. The signature of an attorney or party constitutes a certificate by the signer that the signer has read the pleading, motion, or other paper; that to the best of the signer's knowledge, information, and belief formed after reasonable inquiry it is well grounded in fact and is warranted by existing law or a good faith argument for the extension, modification, or reversal of existing law, and that it is not interposed for any improper purpose, such as to harass or to cause unnecessary delay or needless increase in the cost of litigation. If a pleading, motion, or other paper is not signed, it shall be stricken unless it is signed promptly after the omission is called to the attention of the pleader or movant. If a pleading, motion, or other paper is signed in violation of this rule, the court, upon motion or upon its own initiative, shall impose upon the person who signed it, a represented party, or both, an appropriate sanction, which may include an order to pay to the other party or parties the amount of the reasonable expenses incurred because of the filing of the pleading, motion, or other paper, including a reasonable attorney's fee.

As amended 1983, 1987.

Rule 16.

PRETRIAL CONFERENCES; SCHEDULING; MANAGEMENT

(a) **Pretrial Conferences; Objectives.** In any action, the court may in its discretion direct the attorneys for the parties and any

736

unrepresented parties to appear before it for a conference or conferences before trial for such purposes as

(1) expediting the disposition of the action;

(2) establishing early and continuing control so that the case will not be protracted because of lack of management;

(3) discouraging wasteful pretrial activities;

(4) improving the quality of the trial through more thorough preparation, and;

(5) facilitating the settlement of the case.

(b) Scheduling and Planning. Except in categories of actions exempted by district court rule as inappropriate, the judge, or a magistrate when authorized by district court rule, shall, after consulting with the attorneys for the parties and any unrepresented parties, by a scheduling conference, telephone, mail, or other suitable means, enter a scheduling order that limits the time

(1) to join other parties and to amend the pleadings;

(2) to file and hear motions; and

(3) to complete discovery.

The scheduling order also may include

(4) the date or dates for conferences before trial, a final pretrial conference, and trial; and

(5) any other matters appropriate in the circumstances of the case.

The order shall issue as soon as practicable but in no event more than 120 days after filing of the complaint. A schedule shall not be modified except by leave of the judge or a magistrate when authorized by district court rule upon a showing of good cause.

(c) Subjects to Be Discussed at Pretrial Conferences. The participants at any conference under this rule may consider and take action with respect to

(1) the formulation and simplification of the issues, including the elimination of frivolous claims or defenses;

(2) the necessity or desirability of amendments to the pleadings;

(3) the possibility of obtaining admissions of fact and of documents which will avoid unnecessary proof, stipulations regarding the authenticity of documents, and advance rulings from the court on the admissibility of evidence;

(4) the avoidance of unnecessary proof and of cumulative evidence;

(5) the identification of witnesses and documents, the need and schedule for filing and exchanging pretrial briefs, and the date or dates for further conferences and for trial;

(6) the advisability of referring matters to a magistrate or master;

(7) the possibility of settlement or the use of extrajudicial procedures to resolve the dispute;

(8) the form and substance of the pretrial order;

(9) the disposition of pending motions;

(10) the need for adopting special procedures for managing potentially difficult or protracted actions that may involve complex issues, multiple parties, difficult legal questions, or unusual proof problems; and

(11) such other matters as may aid in the disposition of the action.

At least one of the attorneys for each party participating in any conference before trial shall have authority to enter into stipulations and to make admissions regarding all matters that the participants may reasonably anticipate may be discussed.

(d) Final Pretrial Conference. Any final pretrial conference shall be held as close to the time of trial as reasonable under the circumstances. The participants at any such conference shall formulate a plan for trial, including a program for facilitating the admission of evidence. The conference shall be attended by at least one of the attorneys who will conduct the trial for each of the parties and by any unrepresented parties.

(e) Pretrial Orders. After any conference held pursuant to this rule, an order shall be entered reciting the action taken. This order shall control the subsequent course of the action unless modified by a subsequent order. The order following a final pretrial conference shall be modified only to prevent manifest injustice.

(f) Sanctions. If a party or party's attorney fails to obey a scheduling or pretrial order, or if no appearance is made on behalf of a party at a scheduling or pretrial conference, or if a party or party's attorney is substantially unprepared to participate in the conference, or if a party or party's attorney fails to participate in good faith, the judge, upon motion or the judge's own initiative, may make such orders with regard thereto as are just, and among others any of the orders provided in Rule 37(b)(2)(B), (C), (D).* In lieu of or in addition to any other sanction, the judge shall require the party or the attorney representing the party or both to pay the reasonable expenses incurred because of any noncompliance with this rule, including attorney's fees, unless the

* ["(B) An order refusing to allow the disobedient party to support or oppose designated claims or defenses, or prohibiting that party from introducing designated matters in evidence; (C) An order striking out pleadings or parts thereof, or staying further proceedings until the order is obeyed, or dismissing the action or proceed-ing or any part thereof, or rendering a judgment by default against the disobedient party; (D) In lieu of any of the foregoing orders or in addition thereto, an order treating as a contempt of court the failure to obey any orders except an order to submit to a physical or mental examination." Rule 37(b)(2).]

judge finds that the noncompliance was substantially justified or that other circumstances make an award of expenses unjust.

As amended 1983, 1987.

Rule 68.

OFFER OF JUDGMENT

At any time more than 10 days before the trial begins, a party defending against a claim may serve upon the adverse party an offer to allow judgment to be taken against the defending party for the money or property or to the effect specified in the offer, with costs then accrued.   If within 10 days after the service of the offer the adverse party serves written notice that the offer is accepted, either party may then file the offer and notice of acceptance together with proof of service thereof and thereupon the clerk shall enter judgment.   An offer not accepted shall be deemed withdrawn and evidence thereof is not admissible except in a proceeding to determine costs.   If the judgment finally obtained by the offeree is not more favorable than the offer, the offeree must pay the costs incurred after the making of the offer.   The fact that an offer is made but not accepted does not preclude a subsequent offer.   When the liability of one party to another has been determined by verdict or order or judgment, but the amount or extent of the liability remains to be determined by further proceedings, the party adjudged liable may make an offer of judgment, which shall have the same effect as an offer made before trial if it is served within a reasonable time not less than 10 days prior to the commencement of hearings to determine the amount or extent of liability.

As amended 1948, 1966, 1987.

APPENDIX B

FEDERAL RULES OF CRIMINAL PROCEDURE

Rule 11.

PLEAS

(e) Plea Agreement Procedure.

(1) In General. The attorney for the government and the attorney for the defendant or the defendant when acting pro se may engage in discussions with a view toward reaching an agreement that, upon the entering of a plea of guilty or nolo contendere to a charged offense or to a lesser or related offense, the attorney for the government will do any of the following:

(A) move for dismissal of other charges; or

(B) make a recommendation, or agree not to oppose the defendant's request, for a particular sentence, with the understanding that such recommendation or request shall not be binding upon the court; or

(C) agree that a specific sentence is the appropriate disposition of the case.

The court shall not participate in any such discussions.

(2) Notice of Such Agreement. If a plea agreement has been reached by the parties, the court shall, on the record, require the disclosure of the agreement in open court, or on a showing of good cause, in camera, at the time the plea is offered. If the agreement is of the type specified in subdivision (e)(1)(A) or (C), the court may accept or reject the agreement, or may defer its decision as to the acceptance or rejection until there has been an opportunity to consider the presentence report. If the agreement is of the type specified in subdivision (e)(1)(B), the court shall advise the defendant that if the court does not accept the recommendation or request the defendant nevertheless has no right to withdraw his plea.

(3) Acceptance of a Plea Agreement. If the court accepts the plea agreement, the court shall inform the defendant that it will embody in the judgment and sentence the disposition provided for in the plea agreement.

(4) Rejection of a Plea Agreement. If the court rejects the plea agreement, the court shall, on the record, inform the parties of this fact, advise the defendant personally in open court or, on a showing of good cause, in camera, that the court is not bound by the plea agreement, afford the defendant the opportunity to then withdraw his plea, and advise the defendant that if he persists in his guilty plea or plea of nolo contendere the disposition of the case may be less favorable to the defendant than that contemplated by the plea agreement.

(5) Time of Plea Agreement Procedure. Except for good cause shown, notification to the court of the existence of a plea agreement shall be given at the arraignment or at such other time, prior to trial, as may be fixed by the court.

(6) Inadmissibility of Pleas, Plea Discussions, and Related Statements. Except as otherwise provided in this paragraph, evidence of the following is not, in any civil or criminal proceeding, admissible against the defendant who made the plea or was a participant in the plea discussions:

(A) a plea of guilty which was later withdrawn;

(B) a plea of nolo contendere;

(C) any statement made in the course of any proceedings under this rule regarding either of the foregoing pleas; or

(D) any statement made in the course of plea discussions with an attorney for the government which do not result in a plea of guilty or which result in a plea of guilty later withdrawn.

However, such a statement is admissible (i) in any proceeding wherein another statement made in the course of the same plea or plea discussions has been introduced and the statement ought in fairness be considered contemporaneously with it, or (ii) in a criminal proceeding for perjury or false statement if the statement was made by the defendant under oath, on the record, and in the presence of counsel.

APPENDIX C

FEDERAL RULES OF EVIDENCE

Rule 408.

COMPROMISE AND OFFERS TO COMPROMISE

Evidence of (1) furnishing or offering or promising to furnish, or (2) accepting or offering or promising to accept, a valuable consideration in compromising or attempting to compromise a claim which was disputed as to either validity or amount, is not admissible to prove liability for or invalidity of the claim or its amount. Evidence of conduct or statements made in compromise negotiations is likewise not admissible. This rule does not require the exclusion of any evidence otherwise discoverable merely because it is presented in the course of compromise negotiations. This rule also does not require exclusion when the evidence is offered for another purpose, such as proving bias or prejudice of a witness, negativing a contention of undue delay, or proving an effort to obstruct a criminal investigation or prosecution.

Rule 409.

PAYMENT OF MEDICAL AND SIMILAR EXPENSES

Evidence of furnishing or offering or promising to pay medical, hospital, or similar expenses occasioned by an injury is not admissible to prove liability for the injury.

Rule 410.

INADMISSIBILITY OF PLEAS, PLEA DISCUSSIONS, AND RELATED STATEMENTS

Except as otherwise provided in this rule, evidence of the following is not, in any civil or criminal proceeding, admissible against the defendant who made the plea or was a participant in the plea discussions:

(1) a plea of guilty which was later withdrawn;

(2) a plea of nolo contendere;

(3) any statement made in the course of any proceedings under Rule 11 of the Federal Rules of Criminal Procedure or comparable state procedure regarding either of the foregoing pleas; or

(4) any statement made in the course of plea discussions with an attorney for the prosecuting authority which do not result in a plea of guilty or which result in a plea of guilty later withdrawn.

However, such a statement is admissible (i) in any proceeding wherein another statement made in the course of the same plea or plea discussions has been introduced and the statement ought in fairness be considered contemporaneously with it, or (ii) in a criminal proceeding for perjury or false statement if the statement was made by the defendant under oath, on the record and in the presence of counsel.

As amended 1975, 1980.

APPENDIX D

AMERICAN BAR ASSOCIATION MODEL CODE OF PROFESSIONAL RESPONSIBILITY

DISCIPLINARY RULES

DR 1–102 Misconduct.

(A) A lawyer shall not:

(1) Violate a Disciplinary Rule.

(2) Circumvent a Disciplinary Rule through actions of another.

(3) Engage in illegal conduct involving moral turpitude.

(4) Engage in conduct involving dishonesty, fraud, deceit, or misrepresentation.

(5) Engage in conduct that is prejudicial to the administration of justice.

(6) Engage in any other conduct that adversely reflects on his fitness to practice law.

DR 4–101 Preservation of Confidences and Secrets of a Client.

* * *

(B) Except when permitted under DR 4–101(C), a lawyer shall not knowingly:

(1) Reveal a confidence or secret of his client.

(2) Use a confidence or secret of his client to the disadvantage of the client.

(3) Use a confidence or secret of his client for the advantage of himself or of a third person, unless the client consents after full disclosure.

(C) A lawyer may reveal:

(1) Confidences or secrets with the consent of the client or clients affected, but only after a full disclosure to them.

(2) Confidences or secrets when permitted under Disciplinary Rules or required by law or court order.

(3) The intention of his client to commit a crime and the information necessary to prevent the crime.

(4) Confidences or secrets necessary to establish or collect his fee or to defend himself or his employees or associates against an accusation of wrongful conduct.

744

DR 6–101 Failing to Act Competently.

(A) A lawyer shall not:

    (1) Handle a legal matter which he knows or should know that he is not competent to handle, without associating with him a lawyer who is competent to handle it.

    (2) Handle a legal matter without preparation adequate in the circumstances.

    (3) Neglect a legal matter entrusted to him.

DR 7–102 Representing a Client Within the Bounds of the Law.

(A) In his representation of a client, a lawyer shall not:

    (1) File a suit, assert a position, conduct a defense, delay a trial, or take other action on behalf of his client when he knows or when it is obvious that such action would serve merely to harass or maliciously injure another.

    (2) Knowingly advance a claim or defense that is unwarranted under existing law, except that he may advance such claim or defense if it can be supported by good faith argument for an extension, modification, or reversal of existing law.

    (3) Conceal or knowingly fail to disclose that which he is required by law to reveal.

    (4) Knowingly use perjured testimony or false evidence.

    (5) Knowingly make a false statement of law or fact.

    (6) Participate in the creation or preservation of evidence when he knows or it is obvious that the evidence is false.

    (7) Counsel or assist his client in conduct that the lawyer knows to be illegal or fraudulent.

    (8) Knowingly engage in other illegal conduct or conduct contrary to a Disciplinary Rule.

(B) A lawyer who receives information clearly establishing that:

    (1) His client has, in the course of the representation, perpetrated a fraud upon a person or tribunal shall promptly call upon his client to rectify the same, and if his client refuses or is unable to do so, he shall reveal the fraud to the affected person or tribunal, except when the information is protected as a privileged communication.

    (2) A person other than his client has perpetrated a fraud upon a tribunal shall promptly reveal the fraud to the tribunal.

As amended in 1974.

DR 7–105 Threatening Criminal Prosecution.

(A) A lawyer shall not present, participate in presenting, or threaten to present criminal charges solely to obtain an advantage in a civil matter.

APPENDIX D

DR 9–101   Avoiding Even the Appearance of Impropriety.

* * *

(C) A lawyer shall not state or imply that he is able to influence improperly or upon irrelevant grounds any tribunal, legislative body, or public official.

AMERICAN BAR ASSOCIATION MODEL RULES OF PROFESSIONAL CONDUCT

RULE 1.1 Competence

A lawyer shall provide competent representation to a client. Competent representation requires the legal knowledge, skill, thoroughness and preparation reasonably necessary for the representation.

RULE 1.2 Scope of Representation

(a) A lawyer shall abide by a client's decisions concerning the objectives of representation, subject to paragraphs (c), (d) and (e), and shall consult with the client as to the means by which they are to be pursued. A lawyer shall abide by a client's decision whether to accept an offer of settlement of a matter. In a criminal case, the lawyer shall abide by the client's decision, after consultation with the lawyer, as to a plea to be entered, whether to waive jury trial and whether the client will testify.

(b) A lawyer's representation of a client, including representation by appointment, does not constitute an endorsement of the client's political, economic, social or moral views or activities.

(c) A lawyer may limit the objectives of the representation if the client consents after consultation.

(d) A lawyer shall not counsel a client to engage, or assist a client, in conduct that the lawyer knows is criminal or fraudulent, but a lawyer may discuss the legal consequences of any proposed course of conduct with a client and may counsel or assist a client to make a good faith effort to determine the validity, scope, meaning or application of the law.

(e) When a lawyer knows that a client expects assistance not permitted by the rules of professional conduct or other law, the lawyer shall consult with the client regarding the relevant limitations on the lawyer's conduct.

RULE 1.6 Confidentiality of Information

(a) A lawyer shall not reveal information relating to representation of a client unless the client consents after consultation, except for disclosures that are impliedly authorized in order to carry out the representation, and except as stated in paragraph (b).

(b) A lawyer may reveal such information to the extent the lawyer reasonably believes necessary:

(1) to prevent the client from committing a criminal act that the lawyer believes is likely to result in imminent death or substantial bodily harm; or

(2) to establish a claim or defense on behalf of the lawyer in a controversy between the lawyer and the client, to establish a defense to a criminal charge or civil claim against the lawyer based upon conduct in which the client was involved, or to respond to allegations in any proceeding concerning the lawyer's representation of the client.

RULE 2.2 Intermediary

(a) A lawyer may act as intermediary between clients if:

(1) the lawyer consults with each client concerning the implications of the common representation, including the advantages and risks involved, and the effect on the attorney-client privileges, and obtains each client's consent to the common representation;

(2) the lawyer reasonably believes that the matter can be resolved on terms compatible with the clients' best interests, that each client will be able to make adequately informed decisions in the matter and that there is little risk of material prejudice to the interest of any of the clients if the contemplated resolution is unsuccessful; and

(3) the lawyer reasonably believes that the common representation can be undertaken impartially and without improper effect on other responsibilities the lawyer has to any of the clients.

(b) While acting as intermediary, the lawyer shall consult with each client concerning the decision to be made and the considerations relevant in making them, so that each client can make adequately informed decisions.

(c) A lawyer shall withdraw as intermediary if any of the clients so request, or if any of the conditions stated in paragraph (a) is no longer satisfied. Upon withdrawal, the lawyer shall not continue to represent any of the clients in the matter that was the subject of the intermediation.

RULE 3.3 Candor Toward the Tribunal

(a) A lawyer shall not knowingly:

(1) make a false statement of material fact or law to a tribunal;

(2) fail to disclose a material fact to a tribunal when disclosure is necessary to avoid assisting a criminal or fraudulent act by the client;

(3) fail to disclose to the tribunal legal authority in the controlling jurisdiction known to the lawyer to be directly adverse

to the position of the client and not disclosed by opposing counsel; or

(4) offer evidence that the lawyer knows to be false. If a lawyer has offered material evidence and comes to know of its falsity, the lawyer shall take reasonable remedial measures.

(b) The duties stated in paragraph (a) continue to the conclusion of the proceeding, and apply even if compliance requires disclosure of information otherwise protected by rule 1.6.

(c) A lawyer may refuse to offer evidence that the lawyer reasonably believes is false.

(d) In an ex parte proceeding, a lawyer shall inform the tribunal of all material facts known to the lawyer which will enable the tribunal to make an informed decision, whether or not the facts are adverse.

RULE 4.1 Truthfulness in Statements to Others

In the course of representing a client a lawyer shall not knowingly:

(a) make a false statement of material fact or law to a third person; or

(b) fail to disclose a material fact to a third person when disclosure is necessary to avoid assisting a criminal or fraudulent act by a client, unless disclosure is prohibited by rule 1.6.

RULE 4.4 Respect for Rights of Third Persons

In representing a client, a lawyer shall not use means that have no substantial purpose other than to embarrass, delay, or burden a third person, or use methods of obtaining evidence that violate the legal rights of such a person.

RULE 8.4 Misconduct

It is professional misconduct for a lawyer to:

(a) violate or attempt to violate the rules of professional conduct, knowingly assist or induce another to do so, or do so through the acts of another;

(b) commit a criminal act that reflects adversely on the lawyer's honesty, trustworthiness or fitness as a lawyer in other respects;

(c) engage in conduct involving dishonesty, fraud, deceit or misrepresentation;

(d) engage in conduct that is prejudicial to the administration of justice;

(e) state or imply an ability to influence improperly a government agency or official; or

(f) knowingly assist a judge or judicial officer in conduct that is a violation of applicable rules of judicial conduct or other law.

APPENDIX E

THE UNITED STATES ARBITRATION ACT

9 U.S.C. § 1 (1925)

CHAPTER 1. GENERAL PROVISIONS

§ 1. "Maritime Transactions," and "Commerce" Defined; Exceptions to Operation of Title

"Maritime transactions," as herein defined, means charter parties, bills of lading of water carriers, agreements relating to wharfage, supplies furnished vessels or repairs of vessels, collisions, or any other matters in foreign commerce which, if the subject of controversy, would be embraced within admiralty jurisdiction; "commerce," as herein defined, means commerce among the several States or with foreign nations, or in any Territory of the United States or in the District of Columbia, or between any such Territory and another, or between any such Territory and any State or foreign nation, or between the District of Columbia and any State or Territory or foreign nation, but nothing herein contained shall apply to contracts of employment of seamen, railroad employees, or any other class of workers engaged in foreign or interstate commerce.

§ 2. Validity, Irrevocability, and Enforcement of Agreements to Arbitrate

A written provision in any maritime transaction or a contract evidencing a transaction involving commerce to settle by arbitration a controversy thereafter arising out of such contract or transaction, or the refusal to perform the whole or any part thereof, or an agreement in writing to submit to arbitration an existing controversy arising out of such a contract, transaction, or refusal, shall be valid, irrevocable, and enforceable, save upon such grounds as exist at law or in equity for the revocation of any contract.

§ 3. Stay of Proceedings Where Issue Therein Referable to Arbitration

If any suit or proceeding be brought in any of the courts of the United States upon any issue referable to arbitration under an agreement in writing for such arbitration, the court in which such suit is pending, upon being satisfied that the issue involved in such suit or proceeding is referable to arbitration under such an agreement, shall on application of one of the parties stay the trial of the action until such arbitration has been had in accordance with the terms of the agreement, providing the applicant for the stay is not in default in proceeding with such arbitration.

§ 4. Failure to Arbitrate Under Agreement; Petition to United States Court Having Jurisdiction for Order to Compel Arbitration; Notice and Service Thereof; Hearing and Determination

A party aggrieved by the alleged failure, neglect, or refusal of another to arbitrate under a written agreement for arbitration may petition any United States district court which, save for such agreement, would have jurisdiction under Title 28, in a civil action or in admiralty of the subject matter of a suit arising out of the controversy between the parties, for an order directing that such arbitration proceed in the manner provided for in such agreement. Five days' notice in writing of such application shall be served upon the party in default. Service thereof shall be made in the manner provided by the Federal Rules of Civil Procedure. The court shall hear the parties, and upon being satisfied that the making of the agreement for arbitration or the failure to comply therewith is not in issue, the court shall make an order directing the parties to proceed to arbitration in accordance with the terms of the agreement. The hearing and proceedings, under such agreement, shall be within the district in which the petition for an order directing such arbitration is filed. If the making of the arbitration agreement or the failure, neglect, or refusal to perform the same be in issue, the court shall proceed summarily to the trial thereof. If no jury trial be demanded by the party alleged to be in default, or in the matter in dispute is within admiralty jurisdiction, the court shall hear and determine such issue. Where such an issue is raised, the party alleged to be in default may, except in cases of admiralty, on or before the return day of the notice of application, demand a jury trial of such issue, and upon such demand the court shall make an order referring the issue or issues to a jury in the manner provided by the Federal Rules of Civil Procedure, or may specially call a jury for that purpose. If the jury find that no agreement in writing for arbitration was made or that there is no default in proceeding thereunder, the proceeding shall be dismissed. If the jury find that an agreement for arbitration was made in writing and that there is a default in proceeding thereunder, the court shall make an order summarily directing the parties to proceed with the arbitration in accordance with the terms thereof.

§ 5. Appointment of Arbitrators or Umpire

If in the agreement provision be made for a method of naming or appointing an arbitrator or arbitrators or an umpire, such method shall be followed; but if no method be provided therein, or if a method be provided and any party thereto shall fail to avail himself of such method, or if for any other reason there shall be a lapse in the naming of an arbitrator or arbitrators or umpire, or in filling a vacancy, then upon the application of either party to the controversy the court shall designate and appoint an arbitrator or arbitrators or umpire, as the case may require, who shall act under the said agreement with the same force and effect as if he or they had been specifically named therein; and unless otherwise provided in the agreement the arbitration shall be by a single arbitrator.

§ 6. Application Heard as Motion

Any application to the court hereunder shall be made and heard in the manner provided by law for making and hearing of motions, except as otherwise herein expressly provided.

§ 7. Witnesses Before Arbitrators; Fees; Compelling Attendance

The arbitrators selected either as prescribed in this title or otherwise, or a majority of them, may summon in writing any person to attend before them or any of them as a witness and in a proper case to bring with him or them any book, record, document, or paper which may be deemed material as evidence in the case. The fees for such attendance shall be the same as the fees of witnesses before masters of the United States Courts. Said summons shall issue in the name of the arbitrator or arbitrators, or a majority of them, and shall be signed by the arbitrators, or a majority of them, and shall be directed to the said person and shall be served in all the same manner as subpoenas to appear and testify before the court; if any person or persons so summoned to testify shall refuse or neglect to obey said summons, upon petition the United States court in and for the district in which such arbitrators or a majority of them, are sitting may compel the attendance of such person or persons before said arbitrator or arbitrators, or punish said person or persons for contempt in the same manner provided on February 12, 1925, for securing the attendance of witnesses or their punishment for neglect or refusal to attend in the courts of the United States.

§ 8. Proceedings Begun by Libel in Admiralty and Seizure of Vessel or Property

If the basis of jurisdiction be a cause of action otherwise justiciable in admiralty, then, notwithstanding anything herein to the contrary, the party claiming to be aggrieved may begin his proceeding hereunder by libel and seizure of the vessel or other property of the other party according to the usual course of admiralty proceedings, and the court shall then have jurisdiction to direct the parties to proceed with the arbitration and shall retain jurisdiction to enter its decree upon the award.

§ 9. Award of Arbitrators; Confirmation; Jurisdiction; Procedure

If the parties in their agreement have agreed that a judgment of the court shall be entered upon the award made pursuant to the arbitration, and shall specify the court, then at any time within one year after the award is made any party to the arbitration may apply to the court so specified for an order confirming the award, and thereupon the court must grant such an order unless the award is vacated, modified, or corrected as prescribed in sections 10 and 11 of this title. If no court is specified in the agreement of the parties, then such application may be made to the United States court in and for the district within which such award was made. Notice of the application shall be served upon the adverse party, and thereupon the court shall have jurisdiction of such party as though he had appeared generally in the proceeding. If the adverse party is a resident of the district within which the award was made, such service shall be made upon the adverse party or his attorney as prescribed by law for service of notice of motion in an action in the same court.

§ 10. Same; Vacation; Grounds; Rehearing

In either of the following cases the United States court in and for the district wherein the award was made may make an order vacating the award upon the application of any party to the arbitration—

(a) Where the award was procured by corruption, fraud, or undue means.

(b) Where there was evident partiality or corruption in the arbitrators, or either of them.

(c) Where the arbitrators were guilty of misconduct in refusing to postpone the hearing, upon sufficient cause shown, or in refusing to hear evidence pertinent and material to the controversy; or of any other misbehavior by which the rights of any party have been prejudiced.

(d) Where the arbitrators exceeded their powers, or so imperfectly executed them that a mutual, final, and definite award upon the subject matter submitted was not made.

(e) Where an award is vacated and the time within which the agreement required the award to be made has not expired the court may, in its discretion, direct a rehearing by the arbitrators.

§ 11. Same; Modification or Correction; Grounds; Order

In either of the following cases the United States court in and for the district wherein the award was made may make an order modifying or correcting the award upon the application of any party to the arbitration—

(a) Where there was an evident material miscalculation of figures or an evident material mistake in the description of any person, thing, or property referred to in the award.

(b) Where the arbitrators have awarded upon a matter not submitted to them, unless it is a matter not affecting the merits of the decision upon the matter submitted.

(c) Where the award is imperfect in matter of form not affecting the merits of the controversy.

The order may modify and correct the award, so as to effect the intent thereof and promote justice between the parties.

§ 12. Notice of Motions to Vacate or Modify; Service; Stay of Proceedings

Notice of a motion to vacate, modify, or correct an award must be served upon the adverse party or his attorney within three months after the award is filed or delivered. If the adverse party is a resident of the district within which the award was made, such service shall be made upon the adverse party or his attorney as prescribed by law for service of notice of motion in an action in the same court. If the adverse party shall be a nonresident then the notice of the application shall be served by the marshal of any district within which the adverse party may be found in like manner as other process of the court. For the purposes of the motion any judge who might make an order to stay the proceedings in an action brought in the same court may make an order, to be served with the notice of motion, staying the proceedings of the adverse party to enforce the award.

§ 13. Papers Filed with Order on Motions; Judgment; Docketing; Force and Effect; Enforcement

The party moving for an order confirming, modifying, or correcting an award shall, at the time such order is filed with the clerk for the entry of judgment thereon, also file the following papers with the clerk:

(a) The agreement: the selection or appointment, if any, of an additional arbitrator or umpire; and each written extension of the time, if any, within which to make the award.

(b) The award.

(c) Each notice, affidavit, or other paper used upon an application to confirm, modify, or correct the award, and a copy of each order of the court upon such an application.

The judgment shall be docketed as if it was rendered in an action.

The judgment so entered shall have the same force and effect, in all respects, as, and be subject to all the provisions of law relating to, a judgment in an action; and it may be enforced as if it had been rendered in an action in the court in which it is entered.

* * *

CHAPTER 2. CONVENTION ON THE RECOGNITION AND ENFORCEMENT OF FOREIGN ARBITRAL AWARDS

§ 201. Enforcement of Convention

The Convention on the Recognition and Enforcement of Foreign Arbitral Awards of June 10, 1958, shall be enforced in United States courts in accordance with this chapter.

§ 202. Agreement or Award Falling Under the Convention

An arbitration agreement or arbitral award arising out of a legal relationship, whether contractual or not, which is considered as commercial, including a transaction, contract, or agreement described in section 2 of this title, falls under the Convention. An agreement or award arising out of such relationship which is entirely between citizens of the United States shall be deemed not to fall under the Convention unless that relationship involves property located abroad, envisages performance or enforcement abroad, or has some other reasonable relation with one or more foreign states. For the purpose of this section a corporation is a citizen of the United States if it is incorporated or has its principal place of business in the United States.

§ 203. Jurisdiction; Amount in Controversy

An action or proceeding falling under the Convention shall be deemed to arise under the laws and treaties of the United States. The district courts of the United States (including the courts enumerated in section 460 of title 28) shall have original jurisdiction over such an action or proceeding, regardless of the amount in controversy.

§ 204. Venue

An action or proceeding over which the district courts have jurisdiction pursuant to section 203 of this title may be brought in any such court in which save for the arbitration agreement an action or proceeding with respect to the controversy between the parties could be brought, or in such court for the district and division which embraces the place designated in the agreement as the place of arbitration if such place is within the United States.

§ 205. Removal of Cases From State Courts

Where the subject matter of an action or proceeding pending in a State court relates to an arbitration agreement or award falling under the Convention, the defendant or the defendants may, at any time before the trial thereof, remove such action or proceeding to the district court of the United States for the district and division embracing the place where the action or proceeding is pending. * * *

§ 206. Order to Compel Arbitration; Appointment of Arbitrators

A court having jurisdiction under this chapter may direct that arbitration be held in accordance with the agreement at any place therein provided for, whether that place is within or without the United States. Such court may also appoint arbitrators in accordance with the provisions of the agreement.

§ 207. Award of Arbitrators; Confirmation; Jurisdiction; Proceeding

Within three years after an arbitral award falling under the Convention is made, any party to the arbitration may apply to any court having jurisdiction under this chapter for an order confirming the award as against any other party to the arbitration. The court shall confirm the award unless it finds one of the grounds for refusal or deferral of recognition or enforcement of the award specified in the said Convention.

§ 208. Chapter 1; Residual Applications

Chapter 1 applies to actions and proceedings brought under this chapter to the extent that chapter is not in conflict with this chapter or the Convention as ratified by the United States.

INDEX

†